MW01350635

PROGRAMMING AND
PROBABILITY MODELS
IN OPERATIONS RESEARCH

PROGRAMMING AND PROBABILITY MODELS IN OPERATIONS RESEARCH

DONALD P. GAVER
United States Naval Postgraduate School

GERALD L. THOMPSON
Carnegie–Mellon University

BROOKS/COLE PUBLISHING COMPANY
Monterey, California
A Division of Wadsworth Publishing Company, Inc.

ISBN: 0–8185–0057–3
L.C. Catalog Card No: 72–90938
Printed in the United States of America

1 2 3 4 5 6 7 8 9 10—77 76 75 74 73

PREFACE

The purpose of this book is to describe many types of mathematical models that have become familiar and useful in the field of Operations Research (we make no distinction between alternative names such as Management Science or Systems Analysis). In brief, operations research involves the construction of explicit models for situations in which individuals interact with physical, economic, or biological systems. The ultimate goal is to use the models to understand and improve the interaction. The language of the models is mathematical, and the use of the digital computer is often important.

Our book is a text suitable for undergraduate and graduate students who have studied calculus. Explanation of other basic mathematics required for most operations research modeling tasks is included. Specifically, the book contains a development of linear algebra and probability theory. Many of the examples and exercises originated in our own consulting experiences. An asterisk at the beginning of a section or exercise signifies that the material immediately following is difficult or optional and may be skipped.

The book was written and has been used in classes at the Graduate School of Industrial Administration, Carnegie–Mellon University. We are indebted to many students and colleagues who have helped us make improvements in the presentation; our special thanks go to Dr. V. Srinivasan, University of Rochester, for his contributions. Topics from the book have been presented in the Operations Research Departments of The University of California, Berkeley, and the United States Naval Postgraduate School. Although the book was written for classroom use, we believe that it is suitable for self-study, since most topics are developed step by step.

Among friends and colleagues who have made helpful comments are R. Hook and M. Mazumdar of Westinghouse Research Laboratories and M. De Groot of Carnegie–Mellon University. We thank the reviewers of our manuscript: Curtis Eaves, Stanford University; C. R. Glassey, The University of California, Berkeley; Robert L. Graves, University of Chicago; and Kenneth R. Rebman, California State University, Hayward. We are indebted to our editors Ginny Decker and, especially, Phyllis London. Jack Thornton of Brooks/Cole has been a wise and helpful friend. Most of all, we thank our wives, Fran and Dorothea, for their patience and encouragement.

Donald P. Gaver
Gerald L. Thompson

CONTENTS

INTRODUCTION

SYSTEMS AND MODELS

The past few decades have seen the widespread application of quantitative methods to the solution of systems problems. Rather than define *system* here, we will simply note that the following are examples of systems: the production-warehouse-distribution facilities of a large company; the transportation network and traffic control arrangements in a large city; the complex arrangement of men, machines, computers, and other equipment scattered around the world during a manned space flight. Systems problems arise whenever an organization has more than two men or two machines; they are of crucial importance when fairly large numbers of men and machines are grouped in an organization.

The essential characteristics of a system include the following:

(a) It has many components involving men, machines, and natural forces or outcomes.

(b) It was created to achieve certain goals or objectives that may or may not be consistent. (For example, an assignment might be to create a noise-less, mass-transportation system that offers maximum user convenience without polluting the atmosphere.)

(c) It contains numerous subsystems that interact with each other in complex ways. Each subsystem has its own subgoals, which may agree with or differ from the overall system goals to varying degrees.

(d) It has control of some but usually not all of the relevant variables necessary to achieve its goals. The remaining variables are controlled by chance, by natural laws, or sometimes by other competing systems.

(e) It is dynamic—that is, constantly changing. Its goals, systems components, resources, and obligations vary with time.

The usual problem posed by a system is how to set the control variables to make the system achieve or come close to its goals in the best possible manner. We will call this the *problem of management*. The application of mathematics and other quantitative methods to the solution of management problems has been called *management science* or *operations research*. This book is devoted to the study of a number of mathematical methods that have been found useful in these areas.

The first step in applying mathematics to management is to define a *mathematical model*—that is, an abstract representation of the "real-world" systems. The model can be stated in terms of mathematical equations, flow diagrams, computer programs, and so on. Inputs to the model are the data collected from the real world and the actual decisions made by managers. Outputs from the model are predictions as to how the real-world system would behave if, in fact, the model's decisions were implemented. The worth of these predictions depends on comparison of the actual outcomes with the predictions. A mathematical model will tend to be valuable if it fits reality closely. If the fit is poor, modifications should be made in the model; possibly, new data gathered, new predictions made, and new outcomes observed—a cycle that may require repetition. This type of a feedback or self-improvement process is typical of applied science in general and management science in particular.

Experience over many years has produced a number of useful model types. The major purpose of this book is to describe some of these. Model types are classified in terms of their formal structure rather than in terms of a particular application.

Chapters 1 through 6 are devoted to mathematical programming models, linear and nonlinear. Within the general linear programming model, there are many specific model types, such as transportation and assignment models, goal programming models, and network and flow models. These specific model types may be applied in many different contexts, such as scheduling, production, manpower, and investment problems. For nonlinear programming, the model types include convex, quadratic, and piecewise linear models.

Chapters 7 through 12 cover probability models and applications. Among the model types covered here are Markov chain models, queuing models, inventory models, birth-and-death processes, and decision theory and analysis. These find applications in repair-facility design, communications and computing, marketing and finance, and traffic and transportation.

In Chapter 13, we introduce the reader to a variety of different models that combine both probability and programming aspects. Among the models covered are game theory, chance-constrained programming, Markov decision theory, and programming with recourse.

STAGES OF AN OPERATIONS RESEARCH STUDY

It should not be assumed that the work of applying operations research techniques to practical problems can be divided so that the functional-area specialist formulates the model, a mathematician provides its solution, and a practical manager implements it. Instead, a much more complicated, interactive process that involves "successive approximations" to the problem is needed. We will outline this procedure in a series of steps (which, again, need not be distinct).

1. *Problem identification.* An operations research problem usually is stated in a fuzzy, imprecise way at first. A company executive may merely express the feeling that personnel selection, or perhaps project scheduling in a certain manufacturing area, could be improved. The operations researcher and those responsible for the particular area under study (for example, lower-level managers) must formulate specific questions and agree on objectives.

2. *Information and data collection.* If an existing system is to be improved, something should be known about how and why it is presently operating. This includes

consideration of constraints imposed by law, politics, and other intangible factors such as tradition and personalities. If historical data on costs, demands for service, personnel availability, and so on are available, they should be studied and interpreted—if possible, in cooperation with those responsible for the area. Sometimes, this process of information gathering and analysis is enough to stimulate valuable changes in the way a system performs.

3. *Model selection and construction.* The operations research approach is typified by explicit model building—the basis of the model coming from the insight provided by step 2 and from general experience. Usually, models are constructed in mathematical language, which requires that explicit assumptions be made about the relationships of variables. To be useful, a model must have a solution technique that provides a constructive method (often a computer program) for finding the solution. The solution technique and perhaps even the way the model is represented in the computer program become part of the model. Some models demand the creation of mathematical theories for their solution; these theories may be minor variants of known theories, or they may be entirely new theories. Finally, the elusive quality of "mathematical taste" may cause some models and methods to be preferred over others.

4. *Calculation of solutions to the model.* Practical considerations of computational feasibility may influence both the model development and the choice of solution techniques. For example, for small scheduling problems or problems with special structure, integer-programming models may be useful. For medium and large problems in many industrial situations, only techniques such as simulation and heuristic programming are of practical value. Hence, part of the process of setting up a model and devising solution techniques is the constant evaluation of the computational demands made by models and methods. As computers become larger and more efficient, the sizes of the problems they can handle will increase; but practical problems will continue to place unlimited demands on computers.

5. *Model validation and use.* A model's performance predictions must be tested to see how closely they approach reality. Serious discrepancies indicate that the model must be refined, modified, or replaced.

6. *Model implementation.* Many operations research studies result in models that are mathematically beautiful, computationally feasible, but never used because they have ignored the psychological and organizational problems of the people who must implement them. Such results can be bitterly disappointing to an operations researcher, who may feel that his effort has been wasted. The conclusion should be that the implementation process must become part of the model. The most successful operations researcher will also participate in the actual implementation of his mathematical model. Implementation problems may be very mundane; for example, they may include the design of easy-to-use report forms or the use of color-coded parts tags.

Most of this book is devoted to elaboration of step 3, model selection and construction. However, the other steps in the application of operations research techniques are equally important, and we urge the reader to keep them in mind so that he has a balanced point of view toward operations research application techniques.

PROGRAMMING AND PROBABILITY MODELS IN OPERATIONS RESEARCH

CHAPTER 1

DISTRIBUTION PROBLEMS AND THE TRANSPORTATION METHOD*

1.1 INTRODUCTION

Many decision problems involve the assignment of elements of one set of objects to elements of another set subject to certain rules. Usually there is a criterion function that evaluates the worth of one particular assignment relative to another, and the mathematical problem is to choose an assignment that optimizes the value of the criterion function. We shall call such problems *distribution problems* and illustrate them with some simple examples.

EXAMPLE 1.1.1. A certain family with three children, Jane, Jim, and Joe, is vacationing in a cabin. There are three jobs to be done daily: sweeping the floor,

---

* The study of this chapter may be delayed, if desired, until linear programming has been covered in Chapter 4. However, the transportation model is an intuitively appealing and elementary branch of linear programming that can be covered independently.

If studied first, Chapter 1 can be used to build up the reader's intuition about the general case of linear programming.

A definite attempt has been made to write this chapter in an elementary and self-contained way so that readers can cover the material without assistance. We have had encouraging results in assigning the chapter as self-study material that is covered entirely outside of class.

washing the dishes, and making the beds. Each child must do one of these jobs and all must be done. Their parents permit the children to charge prices for each job depending on how onerous each child finds each job. The price table (prices are in cents) is shown in Figure 1.1.1.

	Sweep Floor	Wash Dishes	Make Beds	Required No. of Jobs
Jane	15¢	5	20	1
Jim	11	15	8	1
Joe	7	20	12	1
No. of Jobs to be done	1	1	1	

FIGURE 1.1.1

The parents want to assign one job to each child so that all the jobs are done and so that the total cost of doing all of them is minimized. The solution in this case is obvious—let each child do the job for which his price is lowest: Jane, wash dishes, Jim, make beds; and Joe, sweep floor. The total cost of this assignment is $5 + 8 + 7 = 20$¢ per day. We shall indicate this solution by setting the chosen costs in Figure 1.1.1 in **bold-faced type**. The result is shown in Figure 1.1.2. (The 1 marked above each of the circles will be explained later.) It is obvious that the assignment of jobs

15	⑤ ¹	20
11	15	⑧ ¹
⑦ ¹	20	12

FIGURE 1.1.2

to children shown is the least costly since each child is assigned to that job for which he charges least.

EXAMPLE 1.1.2. Suppose that the prices the children charge are as shown in Figure 1.1.3. Now it is impossible to assign to each child his lowest price job since both Jane and Jim charge their lowest price for washing dishes, and only one of them

	Sweep Floor	Wash Dishes	Make Beds	
Jane	9	8	20	1
Jim	12	7	10	1
Joe	8	12	10	1
	1	1	1	

FIGURE 1.1.3

can be assigned to that job. Suppose that we proceed by first assigning Jane to dishwashing and then make the smallest cost assignments thereafter. The result is in Figure 1.1.4. The cost of this assignment is $8 + 8 + 10 = 26¢$.

9	(8) ^1	20
12	7	(10) ^1
(8) ^1	12	10

FIGURE 1.1.4

If we first assign Jim to dishwashing, we obtain the result of Figure 1.1.5, which has the same total cost: $9 + 7 + 10 = 26¢$. It is not immediately obvious that these two assignments are optimal—that is, that they have the lowest total cost and that there are no other optimal solutions—but you can convince yourself that this is the case by trying other possible assignments. Later we will develop general methods that will show that both of the solutions in Figures 1.1.4 and 1.1.5 are optimal for the problem of Figure 1.1.3.

(9) ^1	8	20
12	(7) ^1	10
8	12	(10) ^1

FIGURE 1.1.5

EXAMPLE 1.1.3. In problems of this sort, it is not necessary that each person be assigned exactly one job or that the number of jobs be equal to the number of persons. Suppose that the children are assigned two more jobs: getting firewood and buying groceries. Suppose also that the boys are required to do two jobs each while Jane must do only one job; finally, assume that Jane must not be required to do either of the two new jobs. The new problem is shown in Figure 1.1.6.

	Sweep Floor	Wash Dishes	Make Beds	Get Wood	Buy Food	Required No. of Jobs
Jane	9	8	20	100	100	1
Jim	12	7	10	11	6	2
Joe	8	12	10	9	7	2
No. Times Done	1	1	1	1	1	

FIGURE 1.1.6

Note that we assigned the price 100¢ for Jane doing either of the new jobs (getting wood or buying food)—such a high price that she will never be assigned to either of these jobs in any minimum-cost (optimal) solution. It is easy to extend the solution of either Figure 1.1.4 or 1.1.5 to a solution of Figure 1.1.6. For instance, the extension of the solution of Figure 1.1.4 is given in Figure 1.1.7. The cost of this

9	(8) 1	20	100	100	1
12	7	(10) 1	11	(6) 1	2
(8) 1	12	10	(9) 1	7	2
1	1	1	1	1	

FIGURE 1.1.7

assignment is $8 + 10 + 6 + 8 + 9 = 41$¢. In Exercise 17 of Exercise Set 1.3, you will be asked to show that this solution is optimal. Note that the numbers above each bold-faced entry in a given row add up to the total number of jobs to be assigned to the person corresponding to that row.

EXAMPLE 1.1.4. To extend the previous example still further, suppose that some of the jobs have to be done more than once a day. Specifically, suppose that the floor must be swept twice, the dishes washed three times, and wood obtained four times. Also assume that Jane must do three jobs and each of the boys must do four. The problem now becomes that of Figure 1.1.8. Notice that the total number of jobs to be done is 11, which is also the total number of jobs to be assigned to the children.

	Sweep Floor	Wash Dishes	Make Beds	Get Wood	Buy Food	Required No. of Jobs
Jane	9	8	20	100	100	3
Jim	12	7	10	11	6	4
Joe	8	12	10	9	7	4
No. Times Done	2	3	1	4	1	

FIGURE 1.1.8

You may try to find various trial-and-error solutions to this problem. One such solution is shown in Figure 1.1.9. The numbers above the bold-faced entries

9	⑧ ³	20	100	100
12	7	10	⑪ ⁴	6
⑧ ²	12	⑩ ¹	9	⑦ ¹

FIGURE 1.1.9

indicate the number of times the person corresponding to the row is to do the job corresponding to the column. Thus, Jane is to wash dishes three times; Jim is to get wood four times; and Joe is to sweep the floor twice, make beds once, and buy food once. The total cost is given by

$$3 \cdot 8 + 4 \cdot 11 + 2 \cdot 8 + 1 \cdot 10 + 1 \cdot 7 = 101¢$$

because Jane washes dishes three times and receives 8¢ each time, Jim gets wood four times and receives 11¢ each time and so on.

It is not clear whether the solution in Figure 1.1.9 is the lowest-cost solution. In fact, it is not, and in Exercise 18 of Exercises 1.3 you will be asked to find a solution costing only 92¢, which is the optimal solution. It should now be clear to you that it is desirable to have mathematical methods for solving such problems, since the time it takes to find a solution by trial and error is considerable, and there is usually no way of knowing whether such a trial solution is optimal.

Let us consider an entirely different situation that leads to the same kind of a problem. The next example is the classical distribution problem, the so-called *transportation problem*, the context in which these kinds of problems were first formulated.

EXAMPLE 1.1.5. A manufacturer of a certain good owns three warehouses and supplies three markets. Each warehouse contains known quantities of the good and each market has known demands. In addition, the unit shipping costs from each warehouse to each market are known. These data are best exhibited in the table of Figure 1.1.10:

	Market 1	Market 2	Market 3	
Warehouse 1	3 $/Ton	2 $/Ton	3 $/Ton	50 T
Warehouse 2	10 $/Ton	5 $/Ton	8 $/Ton	70 T } Supplies
Warehouse 3	1 $/Ton	3 $/Ton	10 $/Ton	20 T
	50 T	60 T	30 T	140

Demands

FIGURE 1.1.10

Note that the total supplies in the warehouse add up to 140 tons, which is equal to the sum of the demands at the markets. How shall the manufacturer ship his goods to the markets from the warehouses so that the total transportation cost will be a minimum?

We will consider the solution of this problem in detail in the next section.

Many other examples of distribution problems in various contexts can be given, and a number of them are presented in the exercises. It is important in formulating these problems that you be sure to include the dimensions of each of the quantities involved (such as $/ton) as we have done in Figure 1.1.10.

All of the distribution problems that we will consider here have a common format: the problem can always be stated as a *matrix* (that is, a rectangular array) *of numbers plus rim conditions.* The combination of a matrix and rim conditions will also be called a *tableau,* and all of the calculations necessary to solve the problem can be made by constructing a series of such tableaux.

The tableau of an $m \times n$ transportation problem is illustrated in Figure 1.1.11. In that figure the matrix has *m rows* and *n columns.* The entries of the matrix

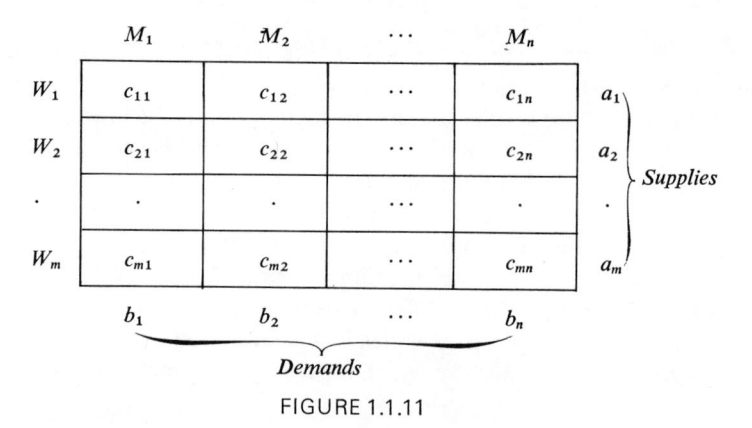

	M_1	M_2	$\cdots$	M_n	
W_1	c_{11}	c_{12}	$\cdots$	c_{1n}	a_1
W_2	c_{21}	c_{22}	$\cdots$	c_{2n}	a_2 } Supplies
.	.	.	$\cdots$	.	.
W_m	c_{m1}	c_{m2}	$\cdots$	c_{mn}	a_m
	b_1	b_2	$\cdots$	b_n	

Demands

FIGURE 1.1.11

are called *cells*. The cell in the ith row and jth column has associated with it a number c_{ij} that gives the unit cost of utilizing that cell in a solution. The numbers $a_1, \ldots, a_m$ and $b_1, \ldots, b_n$ are called the *rim conditions*. We can typically think of the a_i's as the amount stored in W_i and the b_j's as the amount demanded at M_j. Of course, exact interpretations of these numbers will vary from context to context. For instance, in the camp example above (Examples 1.1.1 to 1.1.4), the a_i's were the numbers of jobs each person was to have, and the b_j's were the numbers of each kind of job that had to be done.

EXERCISES 1.1

Set up the following problems as transportation problems. Save your work for use in later exercises.

1. A certain company has warehouses in Philadelphia, Pittsburgh, and Wilkes-Barre. It has stored 200, 150, and 125 units of its goods in each of these places, respectively. It has received demands for 175 units at Oil City, 185 units at Harrisburg, 50 units at Chambersberg, and 65 units at Clearfield. The distances between these cities are:

	Oil City	Harrisburg	Chambersburg	Clearfield
Philadelphia	220	80	100	160
Pittsburgh	60	150	100	75
Wilkes-Barre	160	80	110	105

Transportation costs are 10¢ per mile. Set up the problem.

2. A company has four machines, M_1, M_2, M_3, and M_4, which are serviced by four maintenance crews, A, B, C, and D. M_1 must be serviced three times a month, M_2 four times, M_3 once, and M_4 two times a month. The times it takes each of the crews to service each of the machines are given in the following table:

	A	B	C	D
M_1	2	6	100	3
M_2	100	4	2	1
M_3	1	2	2	1
M_4	3	2	4	2

If A, B, C, and D are to be assigned 2, 3, 3, and 2 of these jobs respectively, how shall the assignment be made in order to minimize the total time?

3. A car rental agency serves five cities. Normally, cities 1 and 2 have a surplus of cars, whereas 3, 4, and 5 have a deficiency. In a certain week city 1 has a surplus of 60 cars, city 2 has a surplus of 40 cars, and cities 3, 4, and 5 have needs for 10, 50, and 40 cars, respectively. The table of distances between the various cities is as follows:

		Cities			
	1	2	3	4	5
1	0	150	50	40	70
2	150	0	30	90	25
Cities 3	50	30	0	60	40
4	40	90	60	0	20
5	70	25	40	20	0

The company employs drivers to take cars from surplus to deficit cities. How should the company send its cars to meet the demands so that the total mileage driven for this purpose is minimized?

4. At a party there are six boys and six girls. Jim would like to dance with either Jean, Nancy, or Ann; Joe would like to dance with Betty, Joan, Dolores, or Ann; Robert will dance with Joan, Nancy, or Ann; Donald will dance with Betty, Jean, Nancy, or Dolores; Albert will dance with Betty or Dolores; and John would like to dance with Joan. Is there a way of assigning partners so that each boy gets to dance with a girl of his choice?

5. Make up a distribution problem from some real-life situation in your experience.

6. There are two vacancies on each of three committees. Adams and Smith are to be assigned to two vacancies each, and Brown and Jones to one vacancy each. In order to decide how the assignments are to be made, each man is asked to list the committees in order of his preference, with 1 for the most desirable, 2 for the next most desirable, and 3 for the least desirable. Their ratings are as follows:

	Committee No.		
	1	*2*	*3*
Adams	1	2	3
Brown	3	2	1
Jones	2	1	3
Smith	1	3	2

(a) Set up the problem of assigning men to committees as a transportation problem. Discuss the significance of the minimum-cost solution.

(b) Suppose that Adams says that committees 1 and 2 are equally attractive to him and assigns them both the number 1. Set up the corresponding problem.

(c) Continuing with (b), suppose that Brown says that committees 2 and 3 are equally attractive and assigns them both the number 1. Set up the resulting problem.

7. (a) In Exercise 6, suppose that three numbers a, b, and c with $0 < a < b < c$ are assigned for first, second, and third choices. Set up the resulting problem.

(b) In Exercise 6, suppose that Adams uses the numbers 1, 4, and 7 to record his first, second, and third choices, while the others continue to use the numbers 1, 2, and 3. Set up the resulting problem.

(c) Duplicate lines of the problem matrix to show how to prevent Adams from getting two assignments to the same committee.

8. A local dairy has received a contract to supply milk to six different schools, each school requiring approximately the same quantity of milk each day. The dairy has two large and two small trucks and wants to assign two of the schools to each large truck and one to each small truck. Because of other demands, the additional mileage required for each truck to service each school varies as shown in the following table:

		Schools					
		1	*2*	*3*	*4*	*5*	*6*
	L_1	4	2	6	8	0	5
Trucks	L_2	3	4	10	7	2	12
	S_1	0	10	9	6	3	7
	S_2	1	6	5	5	6	8

Here L_1 and L_2 stand for the large trucks and S_1 and S_2 stand for the small trucks. Set up the transportation problem that will determine the assignment of trucks to schools. The object is to minimize the total additional miles that must be traveled in order to service the six schools.

9. A company has three factories and serves six markets. The price for its good varies from market to market as does the demand. The following table gives the necessary information:

	M_1	M_2	M_3	M_4	M_5	M_6
Price	63	64	61	62	60	63
Quantity Demanded	51	42	58	53	49	47
Shipping Cost from A	10	12	9	14	8	12
Shipping Cost from B	8	9	13	11	10	14
Shipping Cost from C	12	7	10	13	15	10

Suppose that the unit costs of making the good in each of the factories are:

$$42 \text{ in factory } A,$$
$$39 \text{ in factory } B,$$
$$40 \text{ in factory } C.$$

(a) Compute the *negative* of the net profit obtained by fulfilling one unit of the demand at each market from each of the factories, and enter these numbers in a 3×6 table.

(b) Suppose the capacity of factory A is 180, of B is 145, and of C is 110. Add the rim conditions to the transportation matrix you found in (a).

(c) Show that the optimal solution to the problem maximizes net profit by "minimizing negative profit."

(d) Find a feasible shipping plan.

10. In a certain high school there are six periods each day $(P_1, \ldots, P_6)$. One section of senior English must be taught during each period. There are four teachers to teach these classes. Teachers A and B are to take one section each, and Teachers C and D are to take two sections each. The teachers have been asked to rate each period in terms of teaching preference, and their ratings are given in the table below:

Ratings by Period

Teacher	P_1	P_2	P_3	P_4	P_5	P_6
A	1	2	3	4	5	6
B	3	1	5	4	6	2
C	2	1	3	5	4	6
D	6	5	4	1	2	3

Set up the distribution problem that will assign teachers to sections so that the resulting total score will be minimized. (*Note*: 1 is the highest rating and 6 the lowest for each teacher.)

11. Suppose that periods 1, 2, and 3 are in the morning and periods 4, 5, and 6 are in the afternoon. Also suppose that teacher D can teach at most one afternoon class. Show that the following transportation problem will have a solution that assigns him to at most one afternoon class.

	P_1	P_2	P_3	P_4	P_5	P_6	
A	100	1	2	3	4	5	6	1
B	100	3	1	5	4	6	2	1
C	100	2	1	3	5	4	6	2
D $\big\{$	0	6	5	4	100	100	100	2
	0	100	100	100	1	2	3	1
	1	1	1	1	1	1	1	

12. Consider an $m \times n$ transportation problem. Show in general that it is possible to constrain the sum of some or all variables in a single row or column by defining a new transportation problem with one more row and column and suitable cost and rim entries. (*Hint:* Exercise 11 provides a specific example.)

13. An international airline serves city A on one side of the Atlantic and cities B, C, and D on the other side. Normally, cities A and C have a surplus of planes and cities B and D a deficit. The costs of transporting empty planes from city to city are shown in the following table:

	B	D
A	100	175
B	0	30
C	40	50

Suppose that A has 20 surplus planes, C has a surplus of 10, and B and D need 15 planes each. Set up the corresponding problem. (The reason for listing B as both a surplus and a deficit city will be clear in the next exercise.)

14. Suppose that we permit city B of Exercise 13 to demand b planes, which will be *transshipped* to other cities. Modify the problem so that B has supply of b planes and demand of $b + 15$ planes.
(a) Solve the problem for $b = 20$, 15, 10, 5, 4.
(b) Show that in each solution the number of planes shipped from B to B may be interpreted as planes not *transshipped*.
(c) From your experience in part (a), what value of b will allow the lowest-cost solution and also leave no planes at B that have not been transshipped?

15. Rework 14 given an additional storage cost of five units for routing a plane through B. What now is the optimal value of b?

16. For the problem in Exercise 6, show that the data in the tableau below will prevent an

	Committee No.			
	1	*2*	*3*	
Adams	1 / 100	100 / 2	3 / 100	1 / 1
Brown	3	2	1	1
Jones	2	1	3	1
Smith	1 / 100	100 / 3	2 / 100	1 / 1
	2	2	2	

optimal solution that assigns Adams and Smith to the same committee more than once. Criticize this problem formation.

1.2   INITIAL BASES AND FEASIBLE SOLUTIONS

We have seen many interpretations of distribution problems in the examples and exercises of the previous section. In order to talk about distribution problems in general, we will adopt the model interpretation of Example 1.1.5 and the general tableau of Figure 1.1.11. Thus we consider a distribution problem in which there are m warehouses, $W_1, \ldots, W_m$, and n markets, $M_1, \ldots, M_n$. Also, c_{ij} is the cost of shipping one unit of the good from W_i to M_j; a_i is the amount stored in W_i; and b_j is the amount demanded in M_j.

The mathematical problem is to decide on the amounts, labeled w_{ij}, to be shipped from W_i to M_j for each i and j. Thus there are mn variables, $w_{11}, w_{12}, \ldots, w_{21}, w_{22}, \ldots, w_{mn}$, whose values must be determined. Since it is undesirable to ship goods from a market back to a warehouse, we will impose the condition

$$(1.2.1) \qquad w_{ij} \geq 0 \qquad \text{(Nonnegativity)}$$

on each of these mn variables.

In order to state the other conditions that the variables must satisfy, we must first briefly review the use of the summation notation for subscripted variables. The symbol

$$\sum_{j=1}^{n} w_{ij}$$

means the sum of all the w's with i held fixed and j running from 1 to n—that is,

$$\sum_{j=1}^{n} w_{ij} = w_{i1} + w_{i2} + \cdots + w_{in}.$$

For instance, if $i = 3$ and $n = 4$,

$$\sum_{j=1}^{4} w_{3j} = w_{31} + w_{32} + w_{33} + w_{34}.$$

Sometimes we want to sum over both subscripts i and j; thus

$$\sum_{i=1}^{m} \sum_{j=1}^{n} w_{ij} = w_{11} + w_{12} + \cdots + w_{21} + w_{22} + \cdots + w_{mn}.$$

We will frequently make use of the following rather obvious algebraic identity:

$$(1.2.2) \qquad \sum_{i=1}^{m} \left[\sum_{j=1}^{n} w_{ij} \right] = \sum_{j=1}^{n} \left[\sum_{i=1}^{m} w_{ij} \right].$$

In Exercise 21, you will be asked to prove this identity.

Let us now interpret the sum of all the w_{ij} over the subscript j. It is obvious that $\sum_{j=1}^{n} w_{ij}$ equals the total amount shipped from W_i to all the markets, since w_{i1} is the amount shipped from W_i to M_1, w_{i2} is the amount shipped from W_i to M_2, and so on. Because it is physically impossible to ship more from W_i than the total amount a_i stored there, we have the obvious requirement that

$$(1.2.3) \qquad \sum_{j=1}^{n} w_{ij} \leq a_i.$$

We will insist (initially) on a stronger condition—namely, that all the goods stored in W_i are shipped out; that is,

$$(1.2.4) \qquad \sum_{j=1}^{n} w_{ij} = a_i.$$

Later we will show how to relax (1.2.4) to (1.2.3).

In the same manner we can see that $\sum_{i=1}^{m} w_{ij}$ equals the total amount received at M_j from all the warehouses since w_{1j} is the amount shipped from W_1 to M_j, w_{2j} is the amount shipped from W_2 to M_j, and so on. The point of the distribution problem is to meet the demand b_j at market M_j, so we have another obvious restriction:

$$(1.2.5) \qquad\qquad \sum_{i=1}^{m} w_{ij} \geq b_j.$$

Again we will insist (initially) on a stronger condition,

$$(1.2.6) \qquad\qquad \sum_{i=1}^{m} w_{ij} = b_j,$$

and will show later how it can be relaxed.

In order to have (1.2.4) and (1.2.6) hold, a straightforward use of (1.2.2) shows that we must also require that

$$(1.2.7) \qquad \sum_{i=1}^{m} a_i = \sum_{j=1}^{n} b_j \qquad \text{(Equality of rim requirements)}.$$

DEFINITION 1.2.1. By a *feasible solution* to the transportation problem in Figure 1.1.11, we shall mean any set of values w_{ij}, for $i = 1, \ldots, m$ and $j = 1, \ldots, n$, that satisfies (1.2.1), (1.2.4), and (1.2.6).

Given a feasible solution, it is easy to compute the cost of carrying out the shipping instructions that it provides. Such a feasible solution says to ship w_{ij} units from W_i to M_j. Since c_{ij} is the unit cost of shipping on this route, the cost of the shipment is clearly $c_{ij} w_{ij}$. If we sum over all subscripts i and j, the cost of the feasible shipping schedule is

$$(1.2.8) \qquad\qquad \sum_{i=1}^{m} \sum_{j=1}^{n} w_{ij} c_{ij}.$$

Our objective is to find a feasible solution that minimizes (1.2.8). We will show that this can always be done if (1.2.7) is satisfied. In Section 1.4 we will show how to modify the problem when (1.2.7) is not satisfied.

Figure 1.2.1 summarizes the transportation problem.

> *The Transportation Problem*
> Find quantities w_{ij} satisfying
> $$\min \sum_{i=1}^{m} \sum_{j=1}^{n} w_{ij} c_{ij}$$
> subject to the conditions:
> $$\sum_{j=1}^{n} w_{ij} = a_i$$
> $$\sum_{i=1}^{m} w_{ij} = b_j$$
> $$w_{ij} \geq 0$$

FIGURE 1.2.1

In the simple examples and exercises of Section 1.1 it was easy to find feasible solutions by inspection in most cases. But for m and n large (say 100 or more) it is not at all easy. Thus it is necessary to develop more general methods that will work on distribution problems of any size. Shortly we will describe three such methods. But first we must develop some elementary notation from the theory of graphs that will be used in describing feasible solutions and in representing them on the cost matrix.

By a *graph* we mean a set of nodes and arcs connecting some pairs of nodes. For instance, the diagrams in Figure 1.2.2 are graphs. If two nodes are connected by an arc, they will be said to be *neighboring*. Thus, in both diagrams of Figure 1.2.2, nodes a and b are neighboring, but a and c are not.

Here, we will consider graphs (S) in which the nodes are some or all of the cells of the matrix of Figure 1.1.11. Let N be the set of the mn cells in the cost matrix of that figure. By a *line* we mean any row or column of the matrix. Clearly there are $m + n$ lines in the matrix.

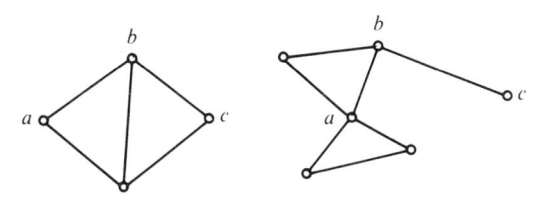

FIGURE 1.2.2

DEFINITION 1.2.2. Let $S \subset N$ be an arbitrary subset of N. We will make S into a graph by defining *neighboring* as follows: two nodes (i_1, j_1) and (i_2, j_2) of S are said to be *neighboring* if

(a) they lie on the same line and
(b) no node of S lies between them.

An *arc* is a line segment connecting two neighboring nodes of S. (Note that each arc lies on a line.) Finally, a *graph* of N consists of a subset S of N and the arcs that connect the neighboring nodes of S.

EXAMPLE 1.2.1. Suppose $m = 2$ and $n = 3$; consider the graph for which $S = N = \{(1, 1), (1, 2), (1, 3), (2, 1), (2, 2), (2, 3)\}$. It is shown in Figure 1.2.3. We have not shown the c_{ij} entries because we wish to emphasize the graph itself. Note that no arc is drawn between $(1, 1)$ and $(1, 3)$ since they are not neighboring—the node $(1, 2)$ lies between them on the same line.

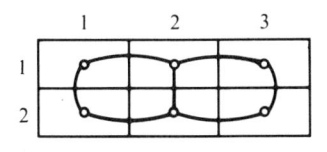

FIGURE 1.2.3

EXAMPLE 1.2.2. Suppose that $m = 3$ and $n = 4$; consider the graph for which

$$S = \{(1, 1), (1, 3), (2, 2), (2, 4), (3, 2), (3, 3)\}.$$

Its diagram is shown in Figure 1.2.4. Note that the arcs between $(1, 3)$ and $(3, 3)$ and $(2, 2)$ and $(2, 4)$ appear to cross at the $(2, 3)$ node. But $(2, 3)$ is not part of the graph so the crossing is irrelevant as far as the graph is concerned.

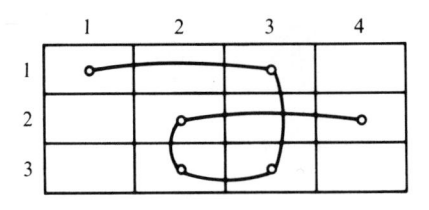

FIGURE 1.2.4

DEFINITION 1.2.3. Let S be a graph of N. The degree of a node in S is the number of different arcs entering that node. A *cycle* of S is a graph C of S such that

(a) every node of C has degree 2, and
(b) the two arcs to each node of C lie on *different* lines.

EXAMPLE 1.2.1 (continued). The graph of Figure 1.2.3 has three cycles, namely

$$C_1 = \{(1, 1), (1, 2), (2, 1), (2, 2)\},$$
$$C_2 = \{(1, 1), (1, 3), (2, 1), (2, 3)\},$$
$$C_3 = \{(1, 2), (1, 3), (2, 2), (2, 3)\}.$$

The cycles are pictured in Figure 1.2.5.

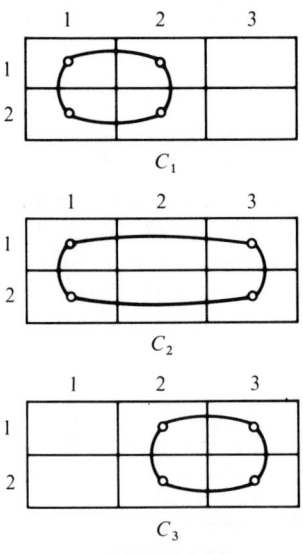

C_1

C_2

C_3

FIGURE 1.2.5

EXAMPLE 1.2.3. Let $m = 3$ and $n = 4$, and let

$$S = \{(1, 1), (1, 3), (2, 2), (2, 4), (3, 2), (3, 3), (3, 4)\},$$

which is the same as the graph of Figure 1.2.4 with the additional point $(3, 4)$. Now let

$$C = \{(2, 2), (2, 4), (3, 2), (3, 4)\}.$$

In Figure 1.2.6, the graph of S is shown with light lines and that of C with heavy lines. (The heavy link from $(3, 2)$ to $(3, 4)$ exists only in C, not in S.) Clearly C is a cycle

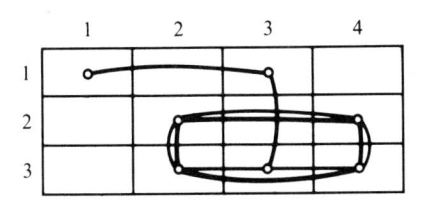

FIGURE 1.2.6

of S according to Definition 1.2.3, since each node has degree 2, and the two arcs to each node lie one on a horizontal line and the other on a vertical line.

We come now to a definition that will be important in the definition of basic solutions to distribution problems.

DEFINITION 1.2.4. A graph B of N is a *basis* for N if and only if

(a) B consists of exactly $m + n - 1$ nodes;
(b) B has no cycles.

EXAMPLE 1.2.4. Consider the case $m = 3$ and $n = 4$; the graph of Figure 1.2.4 is a basis for N, whereas the graph of Figure 1.2.6 is not because it contains a cycle. None of the graphs of Figures 1.2.3 and 1.2.5 are bases since they do not have the correct number of nodes and since they also contain cycles. The graph of Figure 1.2.7 contains the correct number of nodes, but it also contains a cycle, namely, $\{(1, 1), (1, 3), (3, 1), (3, 3)\}$, and hence is not a basis. Finally the graph of Figure 1.2.8 is a basis.

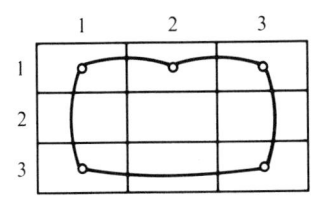

FIGURE 1.2.7

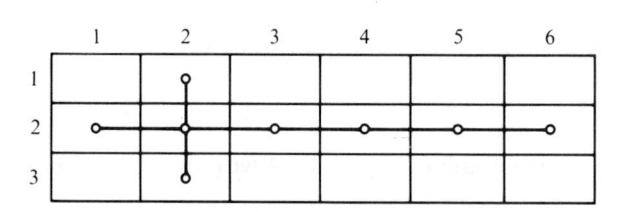

FIGURE 1.2.8

We will next demonstrate three methods for simultaneously finding a *basis* and an *initial feasible solution*—that is, a set of w_{ij}'s satisfying (1.2.1), (1.2.4), and (1.2.6)—for any transportation problem, regardless of size. Any one of these methods can be used as a starting point for the transportation algorithm (to be described in the next section), but the one we will describe last (the VAM method) is usually considered superior for hand computations because it generally requires fewer pivots.

I. The *minimum-entry method* for obtaining an initial basis and feasible solution involves these steps.

(1) Pick the smallest entry in the cost matrix.

(2) Ship the maximum amount possible by that route so that either a warehouse is emptied or a market demand fulfilled.

(3) Delete the line (row or column) corresponding to the used-up warehouse or the fully supplied market demand; in case both of these happen simultaneously (the degenerate case) cross out *either* the row *or* the column unless there is exactly one row remaining, in which case cross out the column, mark the minimum entry (for example, circle it), and write above the entry the amount shipped. Reduce the demands and supplies in the lines containing the minimum entry.

(4) If all lines are crossed out, stop; otherwise, return to (1).

We will use the problem of Figure 1.1.10 to illustrate the minimum-entry method. The smallest entry is the 1 in the lower left-hand corner. That cost is associated with warehouse 3 and market 1. We call this *cell* (3, 1). Since warehouse 3 has 20 tons of supply and market 1 needs 50 tons, we can ship the whole 20 tons from warehouse 3 to market 1; thus, $w_{31} = 20$. We indicate this on the cost matrix of Figure 1.2.9. Note that we crossed out the third row since the supply in W_3 was less

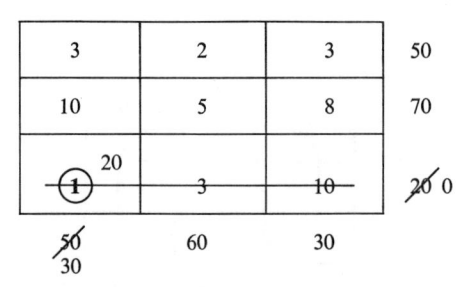

FIGURE 1.2.9

than the demand in M_1. We have thus completed steps 1 through 3 of the algorithm. Since not all lines are crossed out, we return to step 1 and repeat the process. The smallest entry in the remaining matrix is the 2 in the (1, 2) cell. Warehouse 1 has 50 tons to supply and M_2 needs 60 tons. Hence we choose $w_{12} = 50$, reduce the amount in W_1 to 0, reduce the demand at market 2 to 10, and cross out the first row, completing steps (1)–(3) for the second time. The result is shown in Figure 1.2.10. The only part

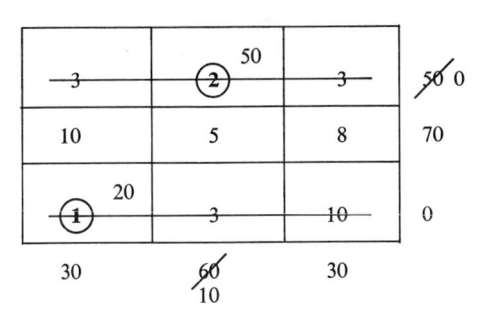

FIGURE 1.2.10

of the matrix that remains is the second row. You may verify that the algorithm requires three more steps in which we successively mark the 5 entry, then the 8 entry, and then the 10 entry in the second row. The completed basis and basic solution are drawn on the matrix of Figure 1.2.11. The cells (nodes) of the basis correspond to the bold-faced entries, and the links of the basis are shown on the matrix.

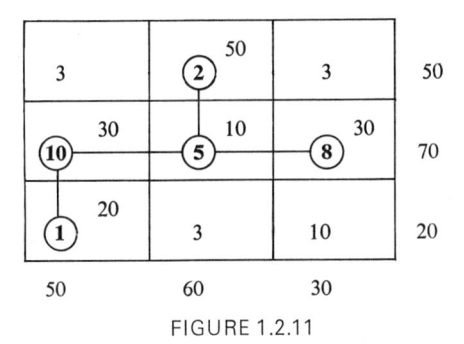

FIGURE 1.2.11

The rim conditions have been restored to their original values in the figure so that it is easy to check that we have a solution.

Since $m = n = 3$ we have $m + n - 1 = 5$. Therefore, the five bold-faced cells in Figure 1.2.11 form a basis since their graph has no cycles. From the matrix we can read off an initial feasible shipping schedule as follows.

$$
\begin{array}{lll}
w_{11} = 0 & w_{12} = 50 & w_{13} = 0 \\
w_{21} = 30 & w_{22} = 10 & w_{23} = 30 \\
w_{31} = 20 & w_{32} = 0 & w_{33} = 0
\end{array}
$$

It is easy to check that these are nonnegative numbers whose sums satisfy the rim conditions, hence form a feasible solution. The cost of this shipping schedule is

$$\sum_{i,j} w_{ij} c_{ij} = 50 \cdot 2 + 30 \cdot 10 + 10 \cdot 5 + 30 \cdot 8 + 20 \cdot 1 = \$710.$$

However, we shall see later that this is not the lowest-cost schedule.

EXAMPLE 1.2.5. This example illustrates the instruction (3) reference above to the degenerate case in which supplies and demands are used up simultaneously. Consider the following tableau.

1	2	50
4	3	40
50	40	

By the minimum-entry method, we ship 50 units by the (1, 1) cell as our first choice. We can then cross out either the row or the column—suppose we cross out the row. The minimum entry remaining is the 3 in cell (2, 2). Again, the warehouse is emptied and the market fully supplied. However, if we now cross out the *row* we will have eliminated *all* remaining cells and our solution, while feasible, is not basic since it has two rather than three cells in it. We obtain the solution shown here—a feasible

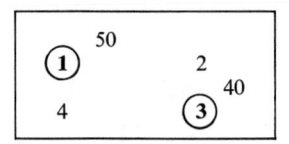

solution with two cells. However, if we refer to the instructions in part (3) of the minimum-entry method, we see that we should cross out the column containing 3 instead of the row so that we obtain the following:

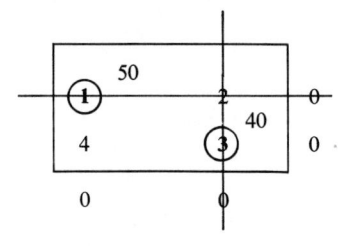

We see that we still have a 1 × 1 transportation problem with zero rim conditions, which is easy to solve by shipping 0 by the (2, 1) cell. We now have a basic feasible solution as is required.

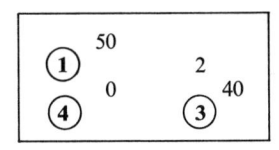

The idea of a basic solution is needed later for the proofs of the theorems and also for ease in writing computer programs.

Because we will find the degenerate case occurring fairly often in small problems with integer data, we must make the definition of the degenerate case more explicit.

DEFINITION 1.2.5. A transportation problem is said to be *degenerate* if there exist proper subsets $I \subset \{1, \ldots, m\}$ and $J \subset \{1, \ldots, n\}$ such that

(1.2.9)
$$\sum_{i \in I} a_i = \sum_{j \in J} b_j.$$

The problem is *nondegenerate* if (1.2.9) is false for all proper subsets I and J.

Clearly the examples in Figures 1.1.3 and 1.1.6 as well as the one in Example 1.2.5 are degenerate, since it is easy in each case to choose subsets I and J for which (1.2.9) holds.

II. The *northwest-corner rule* for obtaining an initial basis and feasible solution follows these steps.

(1) Choose the entry in the northwest (upper left-hand) corner of the matrix.

(2) Ship the maximum amount possible by this route so that either the warehouse is emptied or the market demand is satisfied.

(3) Delete the line corresponding to the used-up warehouse or fully supplied market; in case both of these happen simultaneously (the degenerate case) cross out either the row or the column unless there is exactly one row left, in which case cross out the column. Designate the cost used and mark above the entry the amount shipped. Reduce the supplies and demands in the lines containing the cost used.

(4) If all lines are crossed out, stop; otherwise, return to (1).

Note that, except for instruction (1), the method is virtually identical to that of the minimum-entry method.

We illustrate the northwest-corner rule with the problem of Figure 1.1.10. The first northwest-corner entry is the 3 in the (1, 1) position. Note that W_1 has 50 tons and M_1 has 50 tons, so we can completely fulfill the demand of M_1 by emptying warehouse 1. This is an example of degeneracy, since by choosing $I = \{1\}$ and $J = \{1\}$, we have

$$\sum_{i \in I} a_i = 50 = \sum_{j \in J} b_j.$$

However, the degeneracy will not bother us in constructing the initial basis. By instruction II(3), we can strike out *either* the first row or the first column. Suppose we choose to strike out the first row. Then we have the matrix of Figure 1.2.12. In the

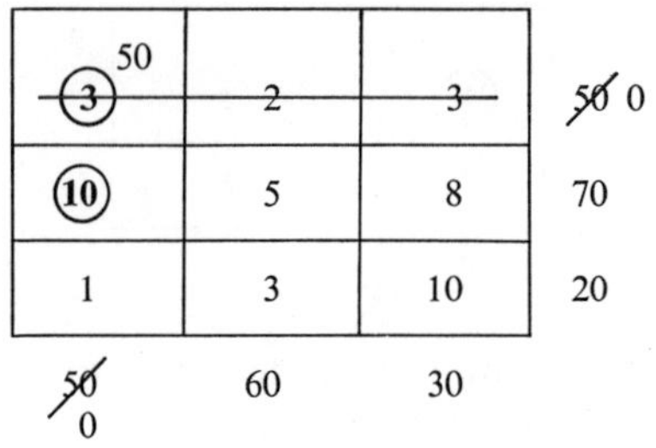

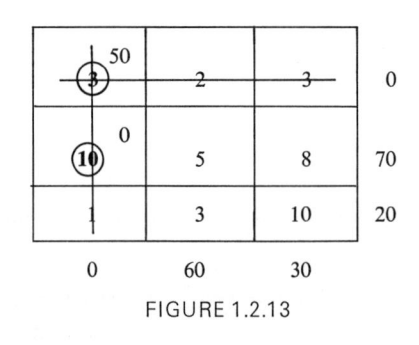

FIGURE 1.2.12

remaining matrix the northwest-corner entry is 10. This entry connects market M_1 with W_2. Since M_1's demands are fully satisfied, we include this cell in the basis but ship 0 by that route. We thus cross out the first column, as in Figure 1.2.13. Now the northwest-corner entry is 5. We use this route to ship 60 to the second market, leaving a residue of 10 tons in W_2. The matrix becomes that shown in Figure 1.2.14.

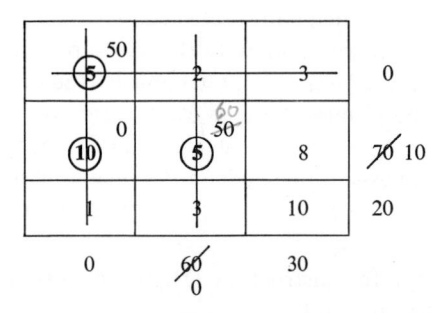

FIGURE 1.2.13

FIGURE 1.2.14

Two more steps are needed to complete the northwest-corner rule. The basis and shipping schedule obtained are indicated in Figure 1.2.15. Note that the rim requirements have been omitted but that they can be deduced from the feasible schedule shown by merely summing the shipments in each row and column. The bold-faced entries form a graph with five nodes and no cycles, hence they are a basis. The cost of the initial solution in Figure 1.2.15 is

$$50 \cdot 3 + 10 \cdot 0 + 60 \cdot 5 + 10 \cdot 8 + 20 \cdot 10 = \$730,$$

which is higher than before.

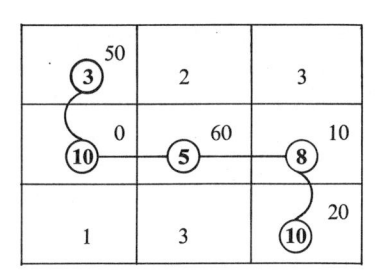

FIGURE 1.2.15

Note that the northwest-corner rule is simply a systematic way of constructing an initial basis, whereas the minimum-entry method tries to achieve a low total cost by choosing the smallest available cost at each step. The next method is more successful in that it looks "two steps ahead" in developing a criterion for the choice of the next basis cell.

III. The VAM (Vogel Advanced Start Method) for obtaining an initial basic solution proceeds as follows.

(1) Compute the difference of the two smallest entries in each row and each column and mark this difference opposite each row and column. (In case there is just one entry in a row or a column, mark that entry.)

(2) Choose the largest difference so marked and utilize the smallest entry in that row or column to empty a warehouse or completely fulfill a market demand.

(3) Delete the line (row or column) corresponding to the used-up warehouse or fully supplied market; in case both of these happen simultaneously (the degenerate case) cross out either the row or the column unless there is exactly one row remaining, in which case cross out the column. Circle or otherwise designate the cost used and mark above the circle the amount shipped by that route. Reduce the supplies and demands in the lines containing the cost used.

(4) If all lines are crossed out, stop; otherwise, return to 1.

Note that instructions (3) and (4) are the same as in the other two methods.

We illustrate the method with the example of Figure 1.1.10. The row and column differences (of the smallest and next smallest entries) are included in Figure 1.2.16. Note that the maximum difference is the 5 in the third column. Hence we ship as much as possible using the minimum entry, which is $c_{13} = 3$, in the third column.

	2	1	5	
1	3	2	3	50
3	10	5	8	70
2	1	3	10	20
	50	60	30	

FIGURE 1.2.16

The rationale behind this choice is clear; if we don't ship via the smallest entry in the third column, at a cost of 3 $/ton, then we will have to use the next higher cost, which is 8 (or perhaps even the cost of 10 eventually); the amount of the difference between the smallest and next smallest cost is a measure of the "regret" we have for not making use of the smallest cost in that column. We now carry out steps (3) and (4), at the same time recomputing the row differences; since a column was struck out on the previous step, the remaining column differences in columns 1 and 2 will be the same. The result is shown in Figure 1.2.17. Now the maximum difference occurs

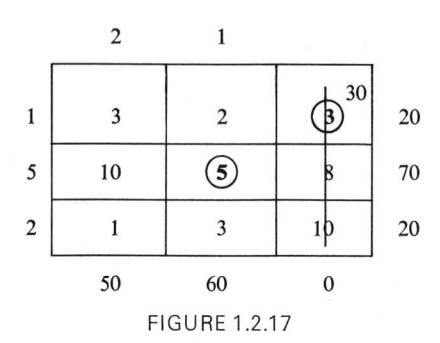

FIGURE 1.2.17

in the second row, so we ship as much as possible using the minimum-cost entry, namely $c_{22} = 5$. It turns out that we can ship 60 to M_2 from W_2 and completely satisfy its demand. The result is in Figure 1.2.18. Since only the first column remains,

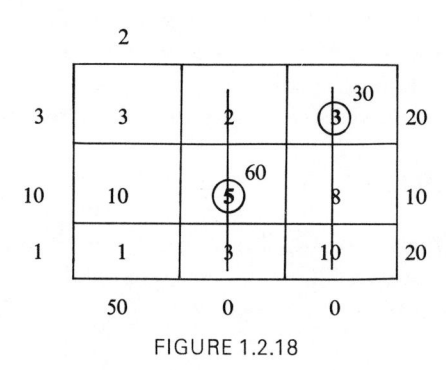

FIGURE 1.2.18

we list it as instructed in III(1). The next step is to bring in the 10 entry, followed by the 3 entry and the 1 entry. The final basic solution is displayed in Figure 1.2.19. You can verify that it is a basis. Its cost is

$$20 \cdot 3 + 30 \cdot 3 + 10 \cdot 10 + 60 \cdot 5 + 20 \cdot 1 = \$570,$$

which is much lower than either of the two previous costs. We shall see, however, that this is still not the lowest-cost feasible shipping schedule.

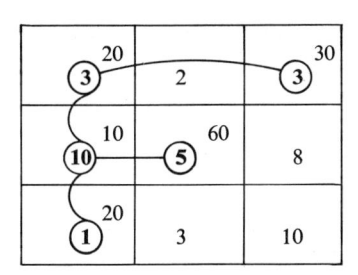

FIGURE 1.2.19

THEOREM 1.2.1. For any transportation problem stated as in Figure 1.2.1 that satisfies condition (1.2.7), there is always an initial feasible basic solution.

Proof: A proof based on method I—the minimum-entry method—is outlined in Exercise 22 of Exercise Set 1.2.

EXERCISES 1.2

1–14. Use each of the three rules given in this section to find starting bases for the first 14 exercises of Section 1.1.

*15. Prove that a basis has at least one entry in each row and each column—that is, at least one on each line.

*16. If $m + n > 2$ prove that, in a basis, there are at least two nodes that have power 1.

*17. Prove that any graph having $m + n$ nodes in a matrix contains a cycle, provided $mn > m + n$.

*18. A graph is said to be *connected* if it is possible to go from every node to every other node along arcs of the graph. Show that any subgraph that is connected and has $m + n - 2$ elements does not have an entry on at least one line.

19. For $m = n = 3$, write out in detail the conditions given in equations (1.2.1), (1.2.3), (1.2.5), (1.2.7), and (1.2.9).

20. Prove the identity (1.2.2) for $m = n = 2$.

21. Prove identity (1.2.2) for the general case by showing that the two sides of the identity are just two different ways of adding up all the entries in a matrix.

*22. Prove Theorem 1.2.1 by carrying out the following steps:
(a) Use the minimum-entry method to show that the theorem is true when $m = n = 1$.
(b) Assume that the theorem is true when $m + n \leq k - 1$; this is the *induction hypothesis*. Suppose that we have a problem with $m + n = k$.
  (i) If the minimum entry has unequal rim conditions, show that the minimum-entry method will create a problem with $m + n = k - 1$, for which the theorem is true.
  (ii) If the minimum entry has equal rim conditions, then show that if m and n are both > 1, either the row or the column can be struck out, whereas if $m = 1$ and $n > 1$, we *must* cross out a column, and if $m > 1$ and $n = 1$, we *must* cross out a row. If $m = n = 1$, then a column is crossed out.

---

* Here and elsewhere, problems marked with asterisks are of above average difficulty, usually involving proofs. They may be skipped without loss of essential information.

23. Consider the problem whose initial tableau is shown.

8	3	7	100
5	4	9	180
1	6	4	90

140	110	120

Show that the VAM start is not optimal.

1.3   THE TRANSPORTATION ALGORITHM

In the preceding section three different methods were described for finding initial basic solutions. In the particular example considered, the lowest-cost solution found was obtained by the VAM method, but we did not know whether or not it was the optimum solution. The next two theorems will tell us a method for recognizing an optimum solution.

THEOREM 1.3.1. Let $x_1, \ldots, x_m$ and $y_1, \ldots, y_n$ be arbitrary constants; then every solution to the $m \times n$ transportation problem with costs c_{ij} and given rim conditions is a solution to the transportation problem with costs $c_{ij} - x_i - y_j$ and the same rim conditions, and conversely. Moreover, a solution is optimal in one problem if and only if it is optimal in the other.

Proof: Let w_{ij} be a feasible solution to the problem with costs matrix c_{ij}, and let x_i and y_j be arbitrary numbers. Consider the following calculation:

$$\sum_i \sum_j w_{ij}(c_{ij} - x_i - y_j) = \sum_i \sum_j w_{ij} c_{ij} - \sum_i \left(\sum_j w_{ij}\right) x_i - \sum_j \left(\sum_i w_{ij}\right) y_j,$$

$$= \sum_i \sum_j w_{ij} c_{ij} - \left(\sum_i a_i x_i + \sum_j b_j y_j\right),$$

$$= \sum_i \sum_j w_{ij} c_{ij} - K,$$

where $K = \sum_i a_i x_i + \sum_j b_j y_j$ is a constant since the a_i's, b_j's, x_i's, and y_j's are all constants. In the calculation above we used (1.2.4) and (1.2.6) in going from the second to the third step; these equations are satisfied for any basic feasible solution. Now subtracting a constant from an objective function does not alter the minimization problem (although it does alter the final value of the objective function). Hence, every feasible solution to the problem with costs c_{ij} is a solution to the problem with costs $c_{ij} - x_i - y_j$, and conversely. It is obvious that any feasible solution w_{ij} that minimizes $\sum_i \sum_j w_{ij} c_{ij}$ also minimizes the same quantity with K subtracted. Hence optimal solutions for one problem are optimal in the other, and conversely.

Using Theorem 1.3.1, we can add or subtract entries to rows and columns of the cost matrix without changing the set of optimal solutions. We will prove that it is possible to do this in such a way that the cells of a feasible basis all have zero costs. You will find it easy to do this by trial and error methods right now, as will be shown in examples. Later on an algorithm will be supplied. Once this has been done, you will be able to use the next theorem to recognize an optimum solution.

THEOREM 1.3.2. Let c_{ij} be the costs of a transportation problem with a basic feasible solution, w.

(a) If there exist numbers x_i and y_j such that the costs $c_{ij} - x_i - y_j$ are 0 in the basis cells and are nonnegative in the other cells, then w is an optimum solution —that is, a feasible solution that has minimum cost.

(b) If there exist numbers x_i and y_j such that the costs $c_{ij} - x_i - y_j$ are 0 in the basis cells and there is at least one negative cost in some nonbasis cell, and if the problem is nondegenerate, then w is not optimal—that is, there exists another feasible basic solution w' that has lower cost than w.

(c) If the problem is degenerate and the assumptions of (b) hold, then there may or may not be a lower-cost solution.

We shall not prove this theorem until much later when we have the duality theorem for the transportation problem. However, you can use it from the start to recognize when feasible solutions are optimal.

To illustrate Theorems 1.3.1 and 1.3.2, we return to the initial feasible solution given by the VAM method (Figure 1.2.19). Observe that the values of x_i and y_j marked in Figure 1.3.1, when subtracted from their respective lines, will alter the matrix entries so that the basis cells have zero costs. (The x_i's and y_j's were determined by trial and error. An algorithm for determining them is given in Section 1.4.)

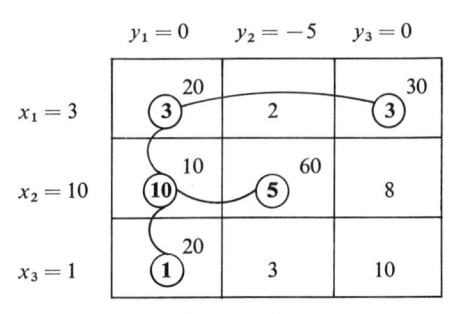

FIGURE 1.3.1

The rim conditions are not marked in the figure since they can be deduced by adding their w_{ij} values across rows and columns. After subtracting the x's and y's from the cost entries in the corresponding rows and columns, the equivalent problem shown in Figure 1.3.2 is obtained. By Theorem 1.3.1, we know that the problems in Figures 1.3.1 and 1.3.2 are equivalent. Also note that in Figure 1.3.2 the costs in the basis cells are 0. But the solution shown there is not optimal, since by Theorem 1.3.2, a solution can be optimal only if every cell has nonnegative entries, and the entry in the second row, third column, is -2. Next, we will discuss a method for improving on this feasible solution.

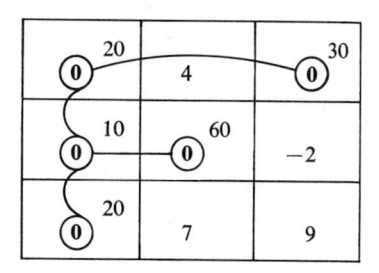

FIGURE 1.3.2

The *transportation algorithm* is a method for introducing a new cell into a feasible basic solution and removing an old cell from that solution in such a way that another basic solution is obtained whose cost is no greater. And, if the original problem is nondegenerate (see Definition 1.2.5), after a finite number of such steps the transportation method will determine an optimum solution. The flow diagram of the method is shown in Figure 1.3.3.

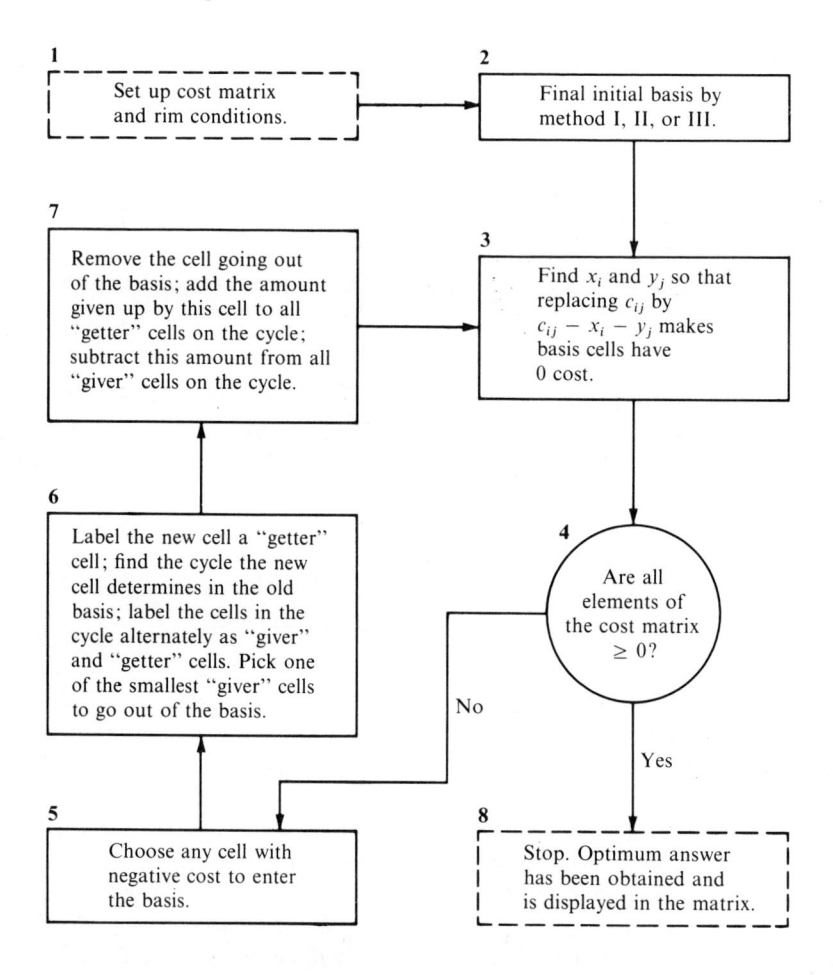

FIGURE 1.3.3. Flow diagram for the transportation method

Using such a flow diagram is very easy. The boxes (numbered 1 and 8) with dashed outlines indicate the beginning and end of the computation. The boxes with solid lines indicate specific instructions that must be carried out. And an instruction enclosed in an oval or circle (such as 4) indicates a question, the answer to which will determine the box to use in the next step.

Let us use the flow diagram to solve the problem in Figure 1.3.2. We have already completed the steps in boxes 1, 2, and 3 of Figure 1.3.3. Going now to box 4, we see that not all cells have nonnegative costs since there is a -2 entry in the second row, third column. Hence we select this cell to bring into the basis and determine the (unique) cycle that the new cell will make when it is added to the set of basis elements. The result is shown in Figure 1.3.4. Starting with the $(2, 3)$ cell as a "getter" cell,

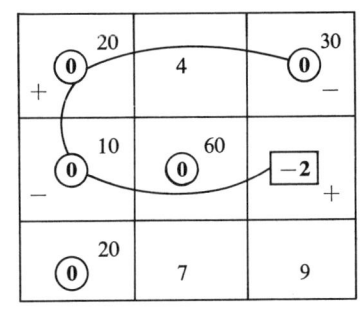

FIGURE 1.3.4

we go to the $(2, 1)$ cell, which is a "giver," then to the $(1, 1)$ cell, which is a "getter," and then to the $(1, 3)$ cell, which is a "giver" cell. (For convenience, a " $+$ " can be used to designate getter cells and a " $-$ " to designate giver cells.)

The $(2, 1)$ cell can give 10, and the $(1, 3)$ cell can give 30. The least of these two is 10, so we select the $(2, 1)$ cell to go out of the basis. This completes the instructions in box 6 of Figure 1.3.3. To take out the $(2, 1)$ cell, as instructed in box 7, we go around the cycle again, giving 10 to the getter cells and taking away 10 from the giver cells. The reason for doing this is, of course, to keep the rim conditions satisfied. The result is shown in Figure 1.3.5. We have now completed the instructions in box 7 and thus we return to box 3. We must change the -2 entry to 0, and it is easy to see that this can be accomplished by adding 2 to the second row. This puts 2 in the basis cell at $(2, 2)$, and to correct for this we subtract 2 from the second column. The result

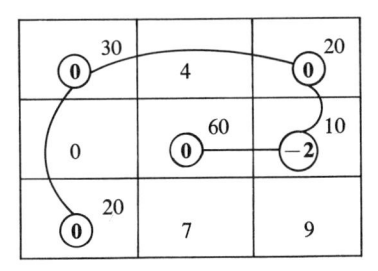

FIGURE 1.3.5

is shown in Figure 1.3.6. Reference to Theorem 1.3.2(a) shows that the solution given in Figure 1.3.6 is optimum. The cost of this optimum schedule is $570 - 2 \cdot 10 = \$550$, since the cost of the schedule in Figure 1.3.4 was 570, and we shipped 10 units at a cost of -2 each. The total cost may also be computed directly from the costs given in Figure 1.3.1. The short method of computing the cost, which was used above, is recorded in the next theorem.

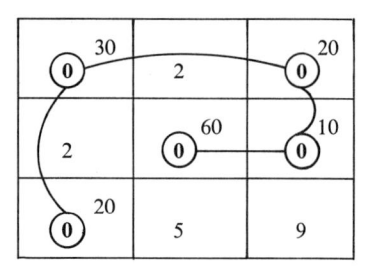

FIGURE 1.3.6

THEOREM 1.3.3. Suppose that the cost of a given feasible basic solution is C and that x's and y's have been subtracted from rows and columns of the cost matrix so that the basis cells have cost 0; suppose also that a cell with negative cost $-k$ is to be added to the basis and that w units are to be shipped by this route; then the cost of the new basic solution is $C - wk$.

The proof of the theorem follows immediately from the fact that only the routes indicated by the basis cells are used in the basic feasible solution.

It is obvious that the cost of the optimum solution to a transportation problem is unique. But it may happen that there is more than one basic feasible solution that will produce this optimum. The following theorem tells when there are alternate optima.

THEOREM 1.3.4. *Alternate Optima.* Let c_{ij} be the costs of a nondegenerate transportation problem corresponding to a basic feasible optimum solution—that is, such that the costs in the basis cells are 0 and the costs in the nonbasis cells are nonnegative; then the optimum solution is unique if and only if the costs in the nonbasis cells are all *positive*. Otherwise, there is an alternate optimum solution.

EXAMPLE 1.3.1. This example illustrates Theorem 1.3.4 and the method of its proof.

Since all the nonbasis costs are positive in Figure 1.3.6, we see that the optimum solution shown there is unique.

Let us arbitrarily alter the tableau of Figure 1.3.6 by changing the cost to zero in the (3, 2) position, as shown in Figure 1.3.7. We enclose the cost in that cell in a rectangle in order to indicate that it is to be brought into the basis, as shown. We label the new cell a getter cell and go around the cycle it determines, alternately marking the cells as giver and getter just as instructed in box 6 of Figure 1.3.3. Cell

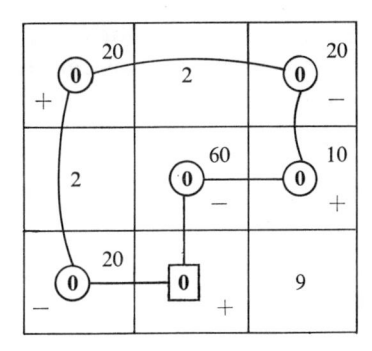

FIGURE 1.3.7

(3, 2) is a getter, (3, 1) is a giver cell that can give 20, (1, 1) is a getter cell, (1, 3) a giver cell that can give 20, (2, 3) a getter cell, and (2, 2) a giver cell that can give 60. The smallest amount that can be given is 20, which can be given by both (3, 1) and (1, 3). Hence either of these can be chosen to leave the basis. Suppose we select (1, 3) to leave the basis and give 20 to the giver cells and take away 20 from the getter cells. The result is shown in Figure 1.3.8. Note that none of the costs needs to be changed.

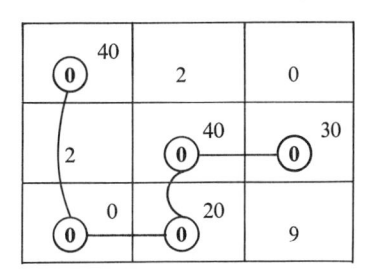

FIGURE 1.3.8

If we instead select (3, 1) to leave the basis, the final cost matrix and basis are as shown in Figure 1.3.9.

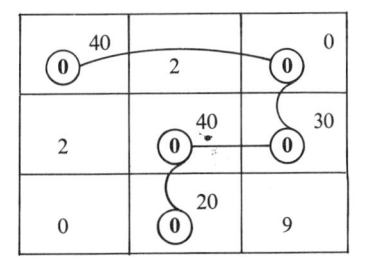

FIGURE 1.3.9

There is no other way to introduce 0 cells into the basis without reconstructing an optimal solution already seen. Hence in the present example there are exactly three different basic optimal strategies (by different we mean that they have different bases).

DEFINITION 1.3.1. Let w_{ij} and w'_{ij} for $i = 1, \ldots, m$ and $j = 1, \ldots, n$ be two optimum solutions to a transportation problem. Then a *convex combination* of these two solutions will mean the solution

$$w''_{ij} = aw_{ij} + (1 - a)w'_{ij},$$

where a is any number satisfying $0 \leq a \leq 1$.

THEOREM 1.3.5. Let w_{ij} and w'_{ij} be optimum feasible solutions to a transportation problem; then any convex combination is also optimum and feasible.

We will prove this theorem later.

EXAMPLE 1.3.1 (continued). Let us illustrate Theorem 1.3.5. The solution shown in Figure 1.3.10 is optimal (although not basic) for the problem in Figure 1.3.7.

⓪ 30	2	⓪ 10
2	⓪ 50	⓪ 20
⓪ 10	⓪ 10	9

FIGURE 1.3.10

This solution can be presented as one half times the solution in Figure 1.3.7 plus one half of the solution in either Figure 1.3.8 or Figure 1.3.9.

The transportation algorithm described above finds only basic solutions. Sometimes there are managerial reasons for finding alternate optima and nonbasic solutions. For instance, the nonbasic solution in Figure 1.3.10 makes use of more routes than the basic solutions do. It has the advantage of "spreading the business" and thus reducing the dependence of the company on just a few transportation facilities.

EXERCISES 1.3

1. Use the transportation method (Figure 1.3.3), to solve the problem in the text that uses the minimum-cost starting solution shown in Figure 1.2.11.

2. Work the same problem starting with the basis in Figure 1.2.15.

3–16. Use the transportation method to solve each of the first 14 problems given in Exercise Set 1.1.

17. Show that the solution indicated in Figure 1.1.7 is optimal for that problem.

18. Show that the optimal solution to the problem of Figure 1.1.8 costs 92¢.

19. Solve the following transportation problem:

2	7	4	5
3	3	1	8
5	4	7	7
1	6	2	14

7	9	18

20. The following problem is discussed in detail in Chapter II of *Management Models* by Charnes and Cooper.* It has several alternate optima. Work the problem and find all

2	1	2	3	3	5
2	2	2	1	−1	5
3	3	2	1	2	6

2	2	4	4	4

alternate optima. The −1 cost in cell (2, 5) can be interpreted as a subsidy for using that route.

1.4   FINDING THE x's AND y's AND CYCLES

In box 3 of Figure 1.3.3, we are instructed to find x's and y's so that the basis cells have zero costs. And in box 6 we are instructed to find the unique cycle determined by the new cell coming into the basis. Although we found both of these problems easy to do by trial and error for small examples, we have not yet proved that it can be done for arbitrarily large examples, nor have we given constructive methods for solving these two problems. This section will fill in these gaps. However, if you are not interested at the moment in these two questions, you may skip over the present section without loss of continuity.

A flow diagram of an algorithm for finding the x's and y's is shown in Figure 1.4.1. You will find it easy to carry out the process described there. To illustrate the computation, we work a simple example.

EXAMPLE 1.4.1. We use the VAM start on the 3×3 problem shown in Figure 1.2.19. Since the last row has a unique basis element in it, we cross it out and mark it with 1 as shown in Figure 1.4.2. Observe that the remaining 2×3 tableau is that of a transportation problem and that the remaining basis cells form a basis for the reduced problem. Carry out the rest of the algorithm in the upper loop of Figure 1.4.1 (boxes 2, 3, 4, and 5) by marking and crossing out the following lines: column 3 mark with 2, column 2 mark with 3, row 1 mark with 4, and row 2 mark with 5. Since k now equals $5 = 3 + 3 - 1$, we go to box 6 of Figure 1.4.1. Thus we enter the lower loop of the flow diagram (boxes, 6, 7, and 8). Carrying out the instruction in box 6, we restore the second row, obtaining the result in Figure 1.4.3. The

---

* From A. Charnes and W. W. Cooper, *Management Models and Industrial Applications of Linear Programming*, Vol. I. Copyright © 1961 by John Wiley & Sons, Inc. Reprinted by permission.

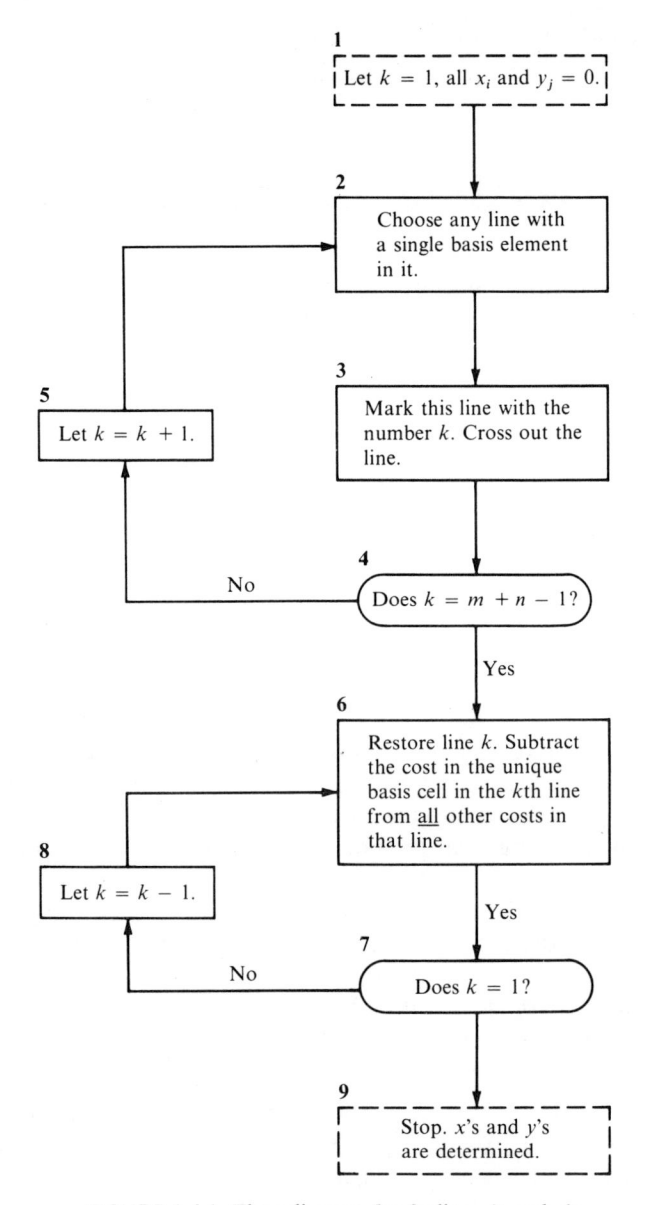

FIGURE 1.4.1. Flow diagram for finding x's and y's

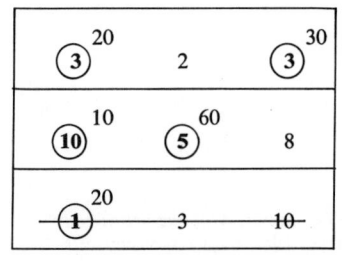

FIGURE 1.4.2

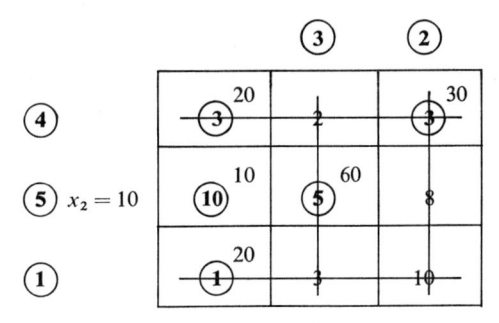

FIGURE 1.4.3

unique basis element is the 10 entry. Then, following the instruction in box 6, we subtract 10 from the second row. We then restore the first row (corresponding to the fact that $k = 4$ and we have numbered the first row 4) and subtract the unique basis entry in the first row, namely 3, from the first row. Then restore column 2, and subtract the unique basis entry, -5, from the second column (note that we had subtracted 10 from row 2, which makes the $(2, 2)$ entry equal to -5). This is equivalent to adding 5 to the second column. Next we restore column 3 and note that its basis element has zero cost; and finally restore row 3 and subtract 1 from row 3. The final result is shown in Figure 1.4.4. Note that it is exactly the same as the solution for the x's and y's shown in Figure 1.3.1. And, of course, the solution for the x's and y's indicates that the optimal shipment is not yet found because the $(2, 3)$ cell will have a negative cost at the end of the computation. Note that the process of Figure 1.4.1 always

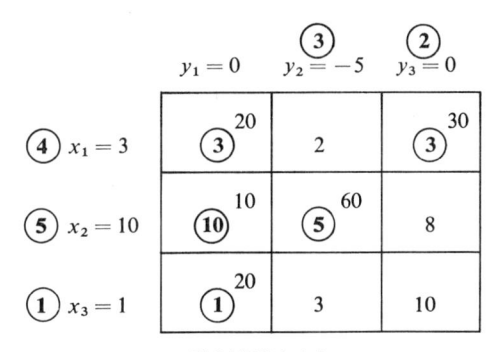

FIGURE 1.4.4

leaves one line not crossed out. In our example it was column 1. The x or y value corresponding to this line is set to zero, as shown in Figure 1.4.4 where $y_1 = 0$.

With a little practice, you will find this algorithm very easy to apply.

We must next prove that the computational process shown in Figure 1.4.1 is indeed an algorithm—that is, that it will always locate a solution for the x_i's and y_j's. The proof that it works is contained in the proof of the following theorem.

THEOREM 1.4.1. Let c_{ij} be the costs of any $m \times n$ transportation problem. Let B be a basis for it, and consider the following $m + n - 1$ simultaneous equations:

(1.4.1) $$c_{ij} - x_i - y_j = 0 \quad \text{for} \quad (i, j) \text{ in } B.$$

(a) There is at least one solution x_i^o, y_j^o to these equations for $i = 1, \ldots, m$ and $j = 1, \ldots, n$.

(b) Every other solution x_i, y_j to these equations is of the form

(1.4.2) $$x_i = x_i^o + \delta \quad \text{and} \quad y_j = y_j^o - \delta,$$

for some constant δ.

(c) Every set of x_i and y_j of the form given in (1.4.2) for an arbitrary constant δ is a solution to (1.4.1).

(d) There are infinitely many (in fact, a one parameter family of) solutions to (1.4.1).

Proof: In order to prove (a), we must show that the computational process shown in Figure 1.4.1 gives a constructive way of finding the x's and y's that always works—that is, one that is an algorithm. Strictly speaking, the proof should be by mathematical induction. We will not give a complete formal proof here, but instead will sketch the important justifications needed.

First, we need to show that we can always make the choice indicated in box 2 of Figure 1.4.1. Suppose, on the contrary, that we had a transportation problem with basis B such that every line had at least two basis cells in it. Since each cell appears in both a row and a column, it will be counted twice, once for its row and once for its column. Since there are $m + n$ lines and each one has at least two cells in it, there are at least $\frac{1}{2}[2(m + n)] = m + n$ cells in the basis B. But we know that B has exactly $m + n - 1$ cells, which is a contradiction. Hence there is at least one line with a unique basis cell.

We now go to box 3 of Figure 1.4.1 and cross out the line. The remaining matrix has $m + n - 1$ lines and $m + n - 2$ basis cells. Hence by the argument of the previous paragraph there is at least one line with a unique basis cell in it. Therefore, the upper loop (boxes 2, 3, 4, and 5) of the computational process of Figure 1.4.1 can always be carried out.

We now go to the lower loop indicated by boxes 6, 7, and 8 of the figure. Each time the process comes to box 6 there is a unique basis element in the line so that there is a unique number to be subtracted from the corresponding line. Hence the lower loop can be carried out.

When we have terminated the computational process of Figure 1.4.1, we will have determined one solution to equations (1.4.1), which proves part (a) of the theorem.

To prove part (b), we assume that x_i, y_j for $i = 1, \ldots, m$ and $j = 1, \ldots, n$ is another solution for (1.10). We compare it with the solution x_i^o, y_j^o given by the process of Figure 1.4.1. We repeat again the computation in the lower loop. Suppose that $(1, 1)$ is the last cell marked in the upper loop of Figure 1.4.1. Then we have

$$c_{11} = x_1 + y_1 = x_1^o + y_1^o.$$

Choose $\delta = x_1 - x_1^o$. It follows that

$$y_1 = x_1^o + y_1^o - x_1 = y_1^o - (x_1 - x_1^o) = y_1 - \delta.$$

Now the next to the last line crossed out has to correspond to a basis entry in either row 1 or column 1—suppose that it is the cell $(1, j)$ for $j > 1$. Then we have

$$c_{1j} = x_1 + y_j = x_1^o + y_j^o,$$

which implies that

$$y_j = y_j^o - (x_1 - x_1^o) = y_j^o - \delta.$$

By continuing this argument, you can show that (1.4.2) holds for all basis cells, thereby completing the proof of (b).

The proof of (c) follows by simple substitution of (1.4.2) into (1.4.1) and the assumption that x_i^o and y_j^o are solutions.

Part (d) follows from parts (b) and (c), which show that x_i, y_j are solutions to (1.4.1) if and only if they have the form (1.4.2).

The flow diagram of the algorithm for finding the unique cycle determined in the basis when a new cell is added to it is shown in Figure 1.4.5. In Exercise 19, an outline of the proof that the method constitutes an algorithm for finding the cycle is given.

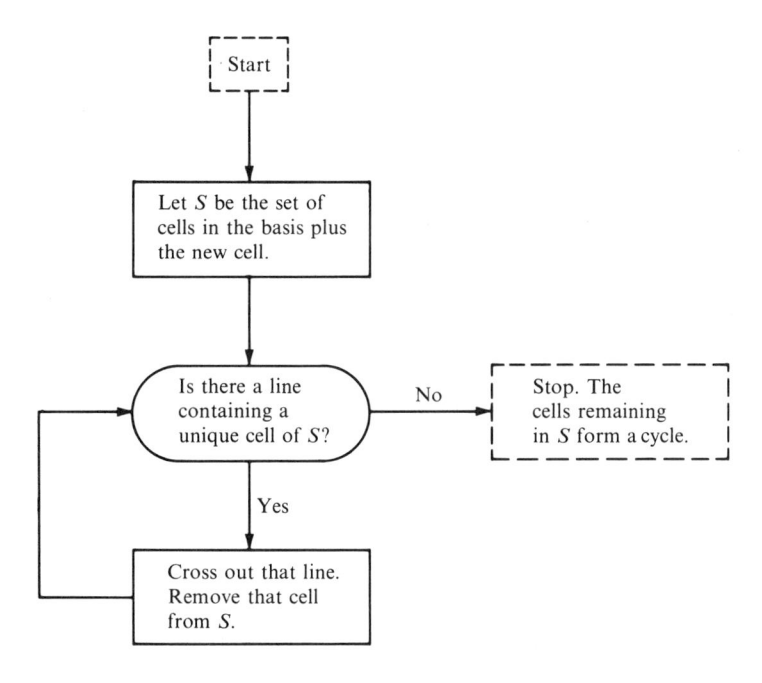

FIGURE 1.4.5

EXAMPLE 1.4.2. Consider the problem in Figure 1.4.6, where we have marked the basis cells $B_1, \ldots, B_7$ and have indicated the new cell, namely, $(4, 3)$, with a box. Following the steps of the flow diagram of Figure 1.4.5, we consecutively cross the second row and the second column. It is then obvious that the cycle is $(4, 3)$, B_7, B_1, B_3, B_6, B_5, and $(4, 3)$ again.

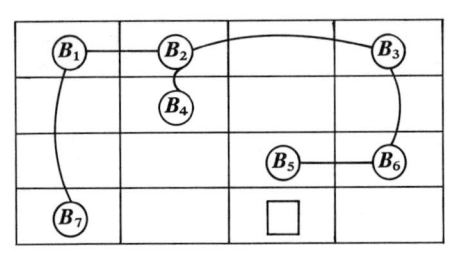

FIGURE 1.4.6

EXERCISES 1.4

1–14. Rework Exercises 1–14 of Section 1.1, using the algorithms of the present section to find the x's, y's, and cycles.

15. Do the same for Exercise 17 of Section 1.3.

16. In Figure 1.4.6, find the cycle when the new cell is at each of the following locations.
(a) $(2, 1)$ (b) $(2, 3)$ (c) $(3, 1)$
(d) $(3, 2)$ (e) $(4, 2)$ (f) $(4, 4)$

17. Write a flow diagram for marking giver and getter cells on a cycle found by the method of Figure 1.4.5.

18. Prove that a cycle has either 0 or 2 elements on a line. Use this fact to show that the number of elements in a cycle is even.

19. Consider the flow diagram of Figure 1.4.5. Let Y be the cell added to the basis set.
(a) Show that Y will not be crossed out by the algorithm.
(b) Show that the cells remaining at the end of the algorithm will have power ≥ 2.
(c) Assume that Y has power 3 or more after the algorithm is finished. Show that this leads to a contradiction.
(d) Show that there is a contradiction if any other remaining cell has power greater than or equal to 3.

*20. In Theorem 1.4.1 suppose there are two optimal shipping patterns with bases B and B', where $B \neq B'$. Prove that the corresponding x and y solutions are different—that is, not related by equations (1.4.2)—only if the problem is degenerate.

1.5   VARIANTS OF THE TRANSPORTATION PROBLEM; THE ASSIGNMENT PROBLEM; DEGENERACY

In the present section we will discuss how to handle cases in which the equality of rim requirements, defined in (1.2.7), does not hold. Then we will discuss degeneracy, particularly in the context of optimal-assignment problems that exhibit considerable degeneracy.

If equation (1.2.7) does not hold, then the sum of the supplies will be either greater than or less than the sum of the demands. These two cases will be discussed separately.

Suppose that the sum of the supplies exceeds the sum of the demands; that is,

$$(1.5.1) \qquad \sum_{i=1}^{m} a_i > \sum_{j=1}^{n} b_j \qquad \text{(Supplies exceed demands).}$$

This is, in fact, usually the case in a well-managed inventory situation. Obviously, one would expect to be able to reduce total shipping cost for this case, since lower-cost routes can usually be used more heavily. The next example illustrates this case.

EXAMPLE 1.5.1. Consider the problem of Figure 1.1.10 in which we assume that each warehouse has 10 more units than are shown. We must decide on the best shipping pattern. To do this, we invent a *fictitious market* whose demand is 30 to take up the excess inventory. When a warehouse is instructed to ship to that fictitious market, what it does instead is to "ship to itself"—that is, retain the merchandise. What should the transportation cost of such "self-shipment" be? One way of deciding this is to say that such a transportation cost is equal to storage cost plus spoilage cost (if any). These costs may be very small compared to other transportation costs, in which case they may be replaced by 0. Suppose we assume they are very small for the problem of Figure 1.1.10. Then, by increasing the amounts at each warehouse by 10 units, we get the problem of Figure 1.5.1. Here the fictitious market is M_4,

			M_4	
③ 20	② 10	③ 30	0	60
10	⑤ 50	8	⓪ 30	80
① 30	3	10	0	30
50	60	30	30	

FIGURE 1.5.1

which accounts for the self-shipping activities. In the figure, the VAM start for the problem is shown. It is easy to show that the cost of the indicated shipping schedule is \$450, which is \$100 less than the previous cost of \$550. If we determine the correct x's and y's in order to change the costs in the basis cells to 0, we obtain the tableau of Figure 1.5.2, where the indicated shipping schedule is actually the (unique) optimum. Note that warehouse 2 keeps 30 units, while warehouses 1 and 3 ship out all of

⓪ 20	⓪ 10	⓪ 30	3
4	⓪ 50	2	⓪ 30
⓪ 30	3	9	5

FIGURE 1.5.2

their inventory. That this is a good thing to do is obvious by observing that the smallest shipping cost from warehouse 2 is \$5, which is greater than either of the two lowest costs from each of the other two warehouses.

Suppose now that the sum of the supplies is less than the sum of the demands —that is,

$$(1.5.2) \qquad \sum_{i=1}^{m} a_i < \sum_{j=1}^{n} b_j \qquad \text{(Demands exceed supplies).}$$

We now have a rationing problem, since we must allocate scarce goods among competing markets, and some demands will be left unfulfilled.

EXAMPLE 1.5.2. We consider the problem of Figure 1.1.10, but increase each of the market demands by 10. To see how to allocate the available supplies, we create a *fictitious warehouse* that can supply the excess demand. We must decide on the shipping costs from this fictitious warehouse. Various rationale for doing this are possible; for instance, we could use stock-out costs, the estimated loss in sales, the cost of expediting shipments from some other source, and so on. For the present example, we shall simply assume that these costs are negligible and use 0 as the shipping cost, obtaining the problem of Figure 1.5.3. Here W_4 is the fictitious warehouse.

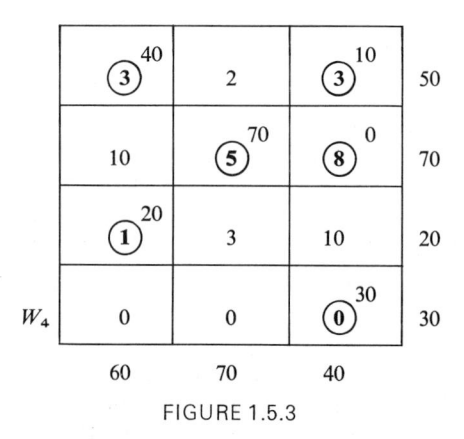

FIGURE 1.5.3

Also indicated on the figure is a VAM start solution, which is optimal and has total cost of $520. Here market 3 is not supplied 30 units. There is an alternate optimum in which market 1 is not supplied 30 units. And there are a number of convex combinations of these solutions in which both markets are not supplied part of their demands. You will be asked to find these in Exercise 5.

Sometimes transportation problems are such that there is no route defined between certain warehouses and certain markets. This might be true if, for instance, there were a mountain, a lake, or an impassable desert between them. Such a route can be eliminated from active consideration by simply putting a very high cost on it relative to the other route costs. Then such a route will be avoided in any optimal solution. (Recall that we did this in Example 1.2.3.)

Similarly, if one wishes to force the use of a certain route, it can be assigned a very low cost or even a negative cost so that it will always be used in optimal solutions. Negative costs can be interpreted as *subsidy payments* for the use of the route.

An important class of transportation problems are the so-called optimal-assignment problems, defined as follows.

DEFINITION 1.5.1. An *optimal-assignment problem* is a transportation problem in which $m = n$, $a_i = 1$ for $i = 1, \ldots, n$, and $b_j = 1$ for $j = 1, \ldots, n$. For this problem i indexes a set of n persons and j indexes a set of n jobs; c_{ij} is interpreted as the negative of the value of person i in job j; the problem is to assign people to jobs so that each person has one job and each job is assigned one person such that the total value is maximized—that is, so that the negative value is minimized.

Examples 1.1.1 and 1.1.2 are assignment problems.

Optimal-assignment problems can be solved by the transportation method, but there is one difficulty: assignment problems are notoriously degenerate. To see this, refer to Definition 1.2.5 and note that, since $a_i = 1$ and $b_j = 1$, we have

$$\sum_{i \in I} a_i = \sum_{i \in J} b_j$$

for *any* two subsets I and J having the *same* number of elements. As we mentioned earlier, the transportation algorithm is not guaranteed to work for degenerate problems. Actually, it almost always does work without any difficulty, except in the following situation. The transportation method may *cycle*; that is, it may go through a series of steps bringing new cells into the basis at zero levels and taking old cells out until, after a number of such steps, you arrive at the same shipping pattern that had been constructed earlier! This whole process could then be repeated again and again without improving the shipping costs and without ever reaching an optimum solution.

The next theorem will show that for every degenerate transportation problem there is an equivalent nondegenerate problem, the solution of which can be used to derive a solution for the original degenerate problem. In order to establish an equivalent nondegenerate problem for Figure 1.2.1, we assume that the original problem can be scaled so that the a_i's and b_j's are integers. Such scaling can always be done without a loss of generality. Now let ε be a nonnegative number less than 1, and consider the derived transportation problem of Figure 1.5.4. The differences between the problems of Figures 1.2.1 and 1.5.4 are the following: Figure 1.5.4 has one more

$$\text{Min} \sum_{i=1}^{m} \sum_{j=1}^{n+1} w_{ij} c_{ij} \qquad (c_{i,\,n+1} = 0, \text{ all } i)$$

Subject to:

$$\sum_{j=1}^{n+1} w_{ij} = a_i + \frac{\varepsilon}{m+1} \qquad i = 1, \ldots, m$$

$$\sum_{i=1}^{m} w_{ij} = b_j \qquad j = 1, \ldots, n$$

$$\sum_{i=1}^{m} w_{i,\,n+1} = \frac{m\varepsilon}{m+1} = b_{n+1}$$

$$w_{ij} \geq 0$$

FIGURE 1.5.4

column (the $n + 1$ column), all of whose costs are 0; the demand for the last column is $m\varepsilon/(m + 1)$; and each of the a_i's is modified to be $\varepsilon/(m + 1)$ larger than before.

THEOREM 1.5.1. If the a_i's and b_j's are positive integers, then the problem of Figure 1.5.4 is not degenerate; if we set $\varepsilon = 0$ in an optimum solution for the first n columns of Figure 1.5.4, we get an optimum solution for Figure 1.2.1.

Proof: The assumption that the a_i's and b_j's are positive involves no loss of generality since warehouses with 0 supply or markets with 0 demand can clearly be omitted from the problem. Now observe that for any proper subsets $I \subset \{1, \ldots, m\}$ and $J \subset \{1, \ldots, n + 1\}$ we have

$$(1.5.3) \qquad \sum_{i \in I} \left(a_i + \frac{\varepsilon}{m + 1} \right) \neq \sum_{j \in J} b_j,$$

since the right-hand side of (1.5.3) is always either an integer or an integer plus $m\varepsilon/(m + 1)$ and the left-hand side is always an integer plus $k\varepsilon/(m + 1)$, where $k < m$. Therefore, since $0 < \varepsilon < 1$, no two partial sums of the a_i's and b_j's can be equal and the problem is not degenerate.

Suppose now that we have an optimal solution to the problem of Figure 1.5.4. (In the next section we will show that the transportation method will always provide one.) Since the optimality criterion depends on only the costs in the matrix and does not depend on the rim conditions, by setting $\varepsilon = 0$, we obtain a feasible (but not necessarily basic since it may not have enough basis cells) least-cost solution for the problem of Figure 1.2.1.

Actually, the transportation method works well on most degenerate problems. The following rule will make it work with probability 1 on any such problem: whenever a new cell can profitably be introduced into the basis, choose at random among all those that are eligible to come into the basis.

EXAMPLE 1.5.3. Consider the assignment problem in Figure 1.1.3. Using the method outlined in the proof of Theorem 1.5.1, we set up the matrix in Figure 1.5.5.

9	8	20	0	$1 + \varepsilon/4$
12	7	10	0	$1 + \varepsilon/4$
8	12	10	0	$1 + \varepsilon/4$
1	1	1	$3\varepsilon/4$	

FIGURE 1.5.5

Let us apply the VAM start to the problem. Since there is a zero in every row, we can begin by choosing one of the rows having the largest minimum entry. Since rows 1 and 3 have 8 as the largest (positive) minimum entry we can choose either. Let us choose row 3, which means that we make cell $(3, 4)$ the first basis cell, and choose

$w_{34} = 3\varepsilon/4$. We thus cross out the last column, and all the rest of the basis cells will be in the first three columns. At the completion of the VAM start we arrive at the matrix of Figure 1.5.6. If we now set $\varepsilon = 0$, we make $w_{13} = 0$, $w_{23} = 0$, and $w_{33} = 1$.

$\textcircled{9}$ ^{1} 8	8	$\textcircled{20}$ $\varepsilon/4$	0
12	$\textcircled{7}$ ^{1}	$\textcircled{10}$ $\varepsilon/4$	0
8	12	$\textcircled{10}$ $1 - \varepsilon/2$	$\textcircled{0}$ $3\varepsilon/4$

FIGURE 1.5.6

The resulting solution displayed in the first three columns of Figure 1.5.6 is a least-cost solution to the original problem (see Exercise 6).

It should be noted that the starting choice above for the first basis cell in the fictitious market column can be carried out for any degenerate transportation problem so that the resulting solution will be optimum and basic. The results of Theorem 1.5.1 can thus be correspondingly sharpened.

EXERCISES 1.5

1. In Figure 1.1.1, suppose that the dishes have to be washed three times a day. Who should do the work?

2. In Figure 1.5.1, suppose that W_1 and W_3 have storage costs of a dollars per unit and that W_2 has cost of $2a$ dollars per unit.   How big does a have to be before the solution indicated in that figure is no longer optimal?

3. In Figure 1.5.3, suppose M_1 and M_3 have costs $2a$ and M_2 has cost a of not meeting demands. How big does a have to be before the indicated solution changes?

*4. Show that every transportation problem can be considered as an optimal-assignment problem by changing constraints of the form

$$w_{11} + w_{12} + \cdots + w_{1n} = a$$

into a conjunction of constraints of the form

$$w_{11}^{(1)} + w_{12}^{(1)} + \cdots + w_{1n}^{(1)} = 1,$$
$$w_{11}^{(2)} + w_{12}^{(2)} + \cdots + w_{1n}^{(2)} = 1,$$
$$\cdots$$
$$w_{11}^{(a)} + w_{12}^{(a)} + \cdots + w_{1n}^{(a)} = 1.$$

What does this mean in terms of the size of the resulting tableau?

5. (a) In the example in Figure 1.5.3, find an alternate optimum in which market 1 is not supplied with 30 units.

   (b) By taking a convex combination of the two solutions to this problem, find a (nonbasic) solution to the problem in which each of the two markets is not supplied with 10 units.

6. Find the optimal solution to the problem given in the first three columns of Figure 1.5.6. Show that the displayed solution, though not optimal, has least cost.

7. Show that the problem in Exercise 23 of Section 1.2 has an alternative solution.

1.6   DUALITY IN THE TRANSPORTATION PROBLEM

In the present section we shall derive a problem, called the *dual* problem, that shares the same coefficients as the transportation problem and hence is very closely related to it. To keep names straight we shall call the original problem the *primal* problem. We shall show that one of these problems has a solution if and only if the other one does and that the solution of one problem can be interpreted in the context of the other problem. In Chapter 4 we will see the same kind of connection between the general linear programming problem and its dual problem.

The pair of dual problems for the transportation problem of Figure 1.1.11 are defined as follows:

THE MINIMIZING PROBLEM	THE MAXIMIZING PROBLEM
(1.6.1) $\text{Min} \sum_i \sum_j w_{ij} c_{ij}$	(1.6.5) $\text{Max} \sum_i a_i x_i + \sum_j b_j y_j$
Subject to:	Subject to:
(1.6.2) $\sum_j w_{ij} = a_i$	
(1.6.3) $\sum_i w_{ij} = b_j$	
(1.6.4) $w_{ij} \geq 0$	(1.6.6) $x_i + y_j \leq c_{ij}$

Note that expressions (1.6.1) through (1.6.4) are exactly the transportation problem as stated in Figure 1.2.1. Also (1.6.6) is the same as (1.4.1). Only the objective function, (1.6.5), of the maximizing problem is new.

Two other observations are in order. First note that for equation (1.6.6) to make sense, it is necessary that the units of the x_i's and y_j's be the same as the units of the c_{ij}'s. For the classical transportation problem (Figure 1.1.11) this means that, since the units of c_{ij} are \$/ton (the shipping cost), the units of x_i are also \$/ton (at warehouse i) and the units of y_j are \$/ton (at market j). Later we will give a more detailed interpretation of these quantities.

Before we can prove Theorem 1.6.1, which gives the connection between the two problems, we must prove two lemmas.

LEMMA 1.6.1. Let x_i, y_j, w_{ij} be feasible solutions for the maximizing and minimizing problems. Then

(1.6.7)
$$\sum_i a_i x_i + \sum_j b_j y_j \leq \sum_i \sum_j w_{ij} c_{ij}.$$

In other words,

(a) given any feasible x_i and y_j's, the expression

$$\sum_i a_i x_i + \sum_j b_j y_j$$

provides a *lower bound* for the solution value of the minimizing problem;
    (b) given any feasible w_{ij}'s, the expression

$$\sum_i \sum_j w_{ij} c_{ij}$$

provides an *upper bound* for the solution value of the maximizing problem.

    Proof: If we multiply (1.6.2) by x_i and sum over i, we get

(1.6.8) $$\sum_i \sum_j w_{ij} x_i = \sum_i a_i x_i.$$

Similarly, multiplying (1.6.3) by y_j and summing over j gives

(1.6.9) $$\sum_i \sum_j w_{ij} y_j = \sum_j b_j y_j.$$

Since (1.6.4) requires w_{ij} to be nonnegative, if we multiply (1.6.6) by it, the sense of the inequality will be preserved. Summing over i and j, we obtain

(1.6.10) $$\sum_i \sum_j w_{ij} x_i + \sum_i \sum_j w_{ij} y_j \leq \sum_i \sum_j w_{ij} c_{ij}.$$

If we now add (1.6.8) and (1.6.9) and use (1.6.10), we obtain

(1.6.11) $$\sum_i \sum_j w_{ij}(x_i + y_j) = \sum_i a_i x_i + \sum_j b_j y_j \leq \sum_i \sum_j w_{ij} c_{ij},$$

which proves (1.6.7).

    Statements (a) and (b) of Lemma 1.6.1 are simply verbal interpretations of (1.6.7).

    LEMMA 1.6.2. For a nondegenerate transportation problem with positive rim conditions, every feasible basic optimal solution has positive w_{ij} for every (i,j) cell in the basis.

    Proof: As in the proof of Theorem 1.4.1, there is at least one cell in the basis that is unique in a line. It can't have $w_{ij} = 0$, because of the positivity of the rim requirements. Cross it out and consider the new transportation problem having one less line. It also must have positive rim requirements, since they are of the form

$$\pm \left[\sum_{j \in J} b_j - \sum_{i \in I} a_i \right],$$

and no such sum can be 0 because of the nondegeneracy assumption. Hence we can repeat the reasoning given above and prove step by step that each $w_{ij} > 0$. This completes the proof.

    The next theorem gives the connection between the solutions to the maximizing and minimizing problems stated above.

    THEOREM 1.6.1. Let c_{ij} be any $m \times n$ transportation problem having positive rim conditions a_i and b_j. Consider the minimizing and maximizing problems defined by expressions (1.6.1) through (1.6.6).

(a) The minimizing problem has a feasible solution with components $w_{ij}{}^o$ satisfying (1.6.2), (1.6.3), and (1.6.4) and such that

$$\sum_{i,j} w_{ij}{}^o c_{ij} = \text{Min} \sum_{i,j} w_{ij} c_{ij}$$

if and only if the maximum problem has a feasible solution with components $x_i{}^o$ and $y_j{}^o$ satisfying (1.6.6) and such that

$$\sum_i a_i x_i{}^o + \sum_j b_j y_j{}^o = \text{Max}\left[\sum_i a_i x_i + \sum_j b_j y_j\right].$$

(b) The equality

$$\sum_{i,j} w_{ij}{}^o c_{ij} = \sum_i a_i x_i{}^o + \sum_j b_j y_j{}^o$$

holds for feasible $w_{ij}{}^o$, $x_i{}^o$, $y_j{}^o$ if and only if $w_{ij}{}^o$ and $x_i{}^o$, $y_j{}^o$ are optimal solutions to their respective problems.

Proof: To prove (a), assume that the transportation problem is nondegenerate and that the a_i's and b_j's are positive integers. By Theorem 1.5.1 this involves no loss of generality.

Now let w'_{ij} be an optimum solution to the minimizing problem. We must show that we can construct from it a basic feasible optimal solution. Consider the set S of the cells (i,j) of the matrix for which $w'_{ij} > 0$. The same kind of argument used in the proof of Lemma 1.6.2 shows that the fact that the problem is nondegenerate implies that S has at least $m + n - 1$ positive members. We must select a subset B of S that is a basis—that is, one that has exactly $m + n - 1$ members and does not contain a cycle. In order to do this we use the following algorithm.

(i) If any line of the matrix has a single element of S, adjoin that cell to B and cross out the line after removing from the rim requirements the amount shipped by that cell.

(ii) If the hypothesis of (i) does not hold, choose any element of S and construct any cycle in S that the element determines; then remove the cell from S that has the smallest shipment by alternately giving to and getting from each cell on the cycle the amount that cell shipped; now go back to see if (i) holds; if not, repeat (ii). Since we either remove an element from S each time or else add an element to B, the algorithm will end up with a set of cells in B. The number of such cells will be $m + n - 1$ (see Exercise 19) and will form a basis. Now let $w_{ij}{}^o$ be the corresponding basic solution that also will be optimal since its value is the same as that of w'_{ij}.

We now use the algorithm of Section 1.4 to find the corresponding $x_i{}^o$'s and $y_j{}^o$'s. Since $w_{ij}{}^o$ is an optimum solution, we must have that

$$c_{ij} = x_i{}^o - y_j{}^o \geq 0,$$

for (i,j) not in B (or else we could use the transportation algorithm to find a lower-cost shipping schedule by introducing one of the cells for which this inequality is violated, which contradicts optimality of $w_{ij}{}^o$). By Lemma 1.6.2, every w_{ij} is positive, hence introducing such a cell would lower the cost.

We now observe that

(1.6.12) $$w_{ij}{}^o(c_{ij} - x_i{}^o - y_j{}^o) = 0$$

for *all* i and j, since (1) $w_{ij}^o = 0$ for (i,j) not in B, and (2) $c_{ij} - x_i^o - y_j^o = 0$ for (i,j) in B. Summing (1.6.12) over all i and j gives

$$(1.6.13) \qquad \sum_{i,j} w_{ij}^o\, c_{ij} = \sum_i a_i x_i^o + \sum_j b_j x_j^o,$$

which implies that the maximum problem is solved by x_i^o and y_j^o. This follows from Lemma 1.6.1, since the left-hand side of (1.6.13) gives an upper bound for the maximum problem, and (1.6.13) shows that the lower bound is actually taken on.

In a similar manner, if we start with x_i^o and y_j^o as optimum solutions to the maximizing problem, we can construct an optimum solution w_{ij}^o to the minimizing problem. A sketch of the proof of this is given in Exercise 20.

The proof of (b) is asked for in Exercise 21. Using Theorem 1.6.1, it is now possible to give a proof of Theorem 1.3.2. See Exercise 22 for a sketch of the proof—you are asked there to fill in details.

Our next task is to find an economic interpretation of the dual variables x_i and y_j. We know from Theorem 1.4.1 that there are infinitely many solutions for these variables. In fact, if x_i^o and y_j^o are any solutions to the maximizing problem, then every other solution is of the form $x_i = x_i^o + \delta$ and $y_j = y_j^o - \delta$. There are two special solutions among all of these that we wish to single out, namely:

(I) Choose δ so that all the x_i are nonpositive and at least one x_i is equal to 0.

(II) Choose δ so that all the y_j are nonpositive and at least one y_j is equal to 0.

Because δ is completely arbitrary, it is obvious that each of these conditions can be attained (but not, of course, simultaneously).

THEOREM 1.6.2. The interpretations of the values of the dual variables are the following.

(i) Let $\sum a_i \geq \sum b_j$. Let x_i, y_j be the dual solutions satisfying (I) above; then x_i can be interpreted as the rate of savings (or imputed value) per unit of additional quantity of the good at the ith warehouse. It is further possible to determine the range of increase of supply in the ith warehouse over which this savings rate can be maintained.

(ii) Assume $\sum a_i \leq \sum b_j$. Let x_i, y_j be the dual solutions satisfying (II) above; then the y_j can be interpreted as the rate of savings (or imputed value) per unit of additional good at the jth market. It is further possible to determine the range of increase of supply at the jth market over which this savings rate can be maintained.

The details of proof of this theorem are not given here; they are suggested in Exercise 23. Many more related results are given in the papers by Srinivisan and Thompson listed at the end of the chapter. However, we shall illustrate the theorem and its proof with the problem of Figure 1.1.10 in Example 1.6.1.

EXAMPLE 1.6.1. The solution to the example of Figure 1.1.10 together with the values of the x's and y's satisfying (I) above are shown in Figure 1.6.1. In

	8	5	8	5	
$x_1 = -5$	(3) 30	2	(3) 20	(0) a	$50 + a$
$x_2 = 0$	10	(5) 60	(8) 10	0	70
$x_3 = -7$	(1) 20	3	10	0	20
	50	60	30	a	

FIGURE 1.6.1

that figure, an extra column has been added so that we can consider the possibility of increasing the amount in the first warehouse. Note that $x_1 = -5$, so we should be able to *save* \$5 for every additional ton at the first warehouse, at least over a certain range. Let a be the additional amount to be stored at W_1. We have added a fictitious market with demand a so that supplies equal demands. Note that a basis cell shipping a units has been placed in the $(1, 4)$ cell and that 5 is subtracted from column 4 to put zero cost in that cell. Now there is a cost of -5 in the $(2, 4)$ cell, and the matrix of Figure 1.6.2 is obtained, and on it the cycle determined by the $(2, 4)$ cell is marked.

(0) 30	2	(0) 20	(0) a
2	(0) 60	(0) 10	−5
(0) 20	5	9	2

FIGURE 1.6.2

Marking cell $(2, 4)$ as a getter cell, cell $(2, 3)$ as a giver that can give 10, cell $(1, 3)$ as a getter cell, and cell $(1, 4)$ as a giver cell that can give a, we see that for a any number between 0 and 10 we can save 5 \$/ton for each additional ton at warehouse 1. For instance, for $a = 8$ we have the solution in Figure 1.6.3, which costs \$510, a figure \$40 less than the solution in Figure 1.3.6.

(0) 30	2	(0) 28	5
2	(0) 60	(0) 2	(0) 8
(0) 20	5	9	7

FIGURE 1.6.3

In Exercise 1, you are asked to carry out the same analysis for warehouse 3 and its dual price. And in Exercises 2 and 3, you are asked to carry out the analysis for the dual variables at the various markets.

Our final task is to state a theorem on the existence of solutions to transportation problems.

THEOREM 1.6.3. Every transportation problem having costs c_{ij} with nonnegative rim conditions a_i and b_j has a solution that can be found in a finite number of steps by the transportation algorithm.

Proof: By Theorem 1.5.1, the problem is equivalent to a nondegenerate problem. By the methods of Sections 1.3 and 1.4, we can find initial basic feasible solutions to the maximizing and minimizing problems. By Lemma 1.6.2, $w_{ij} > 0$ for every cell (i, j) in the basis B. Hence at every step of the transportation algorithm, the value of the objective function of the minimizing problem is decreased by a finite amount, which is guaranteed to be greater than some fixed amount (namely, the smallest absolute difference of $\sum_{i \in I} a_i - \sum_{j \in J} b_j$, for $I \subset \{1, \ldots, m\}$ and $J \subset \{1, \ldots, n\}$). By Lemma 1.6.1, the minimum problem is bounded below. Hence in a finite number of steps, the minimum will be achieved by the transportation algorithm.

EXERCISES 1.6

1. Show that the dual price for warehouse W_3 has the interpretation claimed for it in Theorem 1.6.2, part (i). Find the range over which shipments can be varied and still have the interpretation hold.

2. In Example 1.6.1, find the dual variables associated with the markets that satisfy condition (II). Show that M_1 and M_3 have equal dual variables.

3. Show that the dual variables found in Exercise 2 have the interpretations claimed for them in Theorem 1.6.2, part (ii). Find the range over which these interpretations hold.

4–17. For each of the first 14 exercises following Section 1.1, find the values of and give interpretations for the dual variables.

18. For the classical transportation problem in Figure 1.1.11, discuss how the solution of the dual problem can be used in determining the best location for a new warehouse.

*19. Show that the algorithm given in the proof of Theorem 1.6.1 terminates with a basis set consisting of $m + n - 1$ cells.

*20. Let x_i^o and y_j^o be optimum solutions to the maximizing problem; consider the set S for which $c_{ij} = x_i^o + y_j^o$. Develop an algorithm for finding a feasible w_{ij} that satisfies rim requirements and such that $w_{ij} = 0$ if (i, j) is not in S. Use this to prove part (b) of Theorem 1.6.1.

*21. Show that if the equality in Theorem 1.6.1(b) holds, then the corresponding w_{ij}^o, x_i^o, y_j^o, if feasible, are also optimal. (*Hint:* Use Lemma 1.6.1.) Use equation (1.6.13) to show that the converse is also true.

*22. (a) Show that Theorem 1.3.2(a) follows immediately from Theorem 1.6.1(b).
    (b) Use the transportation algorithm for introducing new cells into the basis to prove Theorem 1.3.2(b).

(c) Show that the following solution is a least-cost solution that is not optimal for the problem displayed.

(*Hint*: Pivot once using the transportation method.)

(d) Show that (c) is an example of the phenomenon mentioned in Theorem 1.3.2(c).

*23. Use the work displayed in Example 1.6.1 and the work you did in Exercises 1–3 above to construct a proof of Theorem 1.6.2.

1.7   APPLICATIONS—MODEL TYPES

Although the transportation model was originally derived to solve the problem of finding a lowest-cost shipping pattern from warehouses to markets, we have seen in the preceding examples and exercises that there are numerous other applications of the model to seemingly unrelated topics. In the present section we will discuss several other important applications. In each case we will write down a formulation of the general problem in terms of equations (or ask you to write down such a formulation). The general formulation we will call a *model type*.* The importance of model types is the following: whenever a problem is derived, in whatever context, whose equations correspond (or can be made to correspond) exactly or approximately to one of the model types, then the special solution technique developed for the model type may be used to solve the original problem.

We begin by restating the equations of the transportation problem and its dual, as given in (1.6.1)–(1.6.6).

THE MINIMIZING PROBLEM

(1.7.1) $\text{Min} \sum\limits_{i=1}^{m} \sum\limits_{j=1}^{n} w_{ij} c_{ij}$

(1.7.2) $\sum\limits_{j=1}^{n} w_{ij} = a_i$

(1.7.3) $\sum\limits_{i=1}^{m} w_{ij} = b_j$

(1.7.4) $w_{ij} \geq 0$

THE MAXIMIZING PROBLEM

(1.7.5) $\text{Max} \sum\limits_{i=1}^{m} a_i x_i + \sum\limits_{j=1}^{n} b_j y_j$

(1.7.6) $x_i + y_j \leq c_{ij}$

* This term is due to Abraham Charnes and William W. Cooper in *Management Models and Industrial Applications of Linear Programming*, 2 Volumes; see Chapter 1 and Chapter 14. Other uses of model types (without using that term) occur in *Linear Programming and Extensions* by George Dantzig. We shall see many other explicit or implicit uses of the idea of model types later on in this book. The idea is of fundamental and general importance in scientific applications.

In addition to these equations and inequalities we have the following two assumptions:

Assumption 1.

$$\sum_{i=1}^{m} a_i = \sum_{j=1}^{n} b_j$$

Assumption 2. The problem is not degenerate.

These assumptions are needed so that our computing procedure will be guaranteed to work.

Model Type 1. The *classical transportation model* is defined by expressions (1.7.1)–(1.7.5) and Assumptions 1 and 2. The problem stated in these expressions always has a solution, and the transportation algorithm will find that solution in a finite number of steps.

As we know from the work in the preceding two sections, problems that do not satisfy Assumptions 1 and 2 may be transformed into equivalent problems which do satisfy these hypotheses.

Model Type 2. The *assignment model* is obtained from the classical transportation model by assuming $m = n$ and $a_i = b_j = 1$, for $i, j = 1, \ldots, m$. In Exercise 1, you will be asked to show how this model may be extended to include the case where $m \neq n$. Note that this problem is always degenerate so that the procedures outlined in Section 1.5 are especially needed for it.

Model Type 3. The *profit-maximization transportation model.* In Exercise 9 of Section 1.1, we worked a problem in which the objective was to maximize total profits in a warehouse-market situation. For each market j, we were given a demand b_j and a selling price s_j; for each warehouse i, we were given a supply a_i and a variable unit operating cost v_i; and for each warehouse-market pair i, j, we were given the unit shipping cost d_{ij}. The problem was then to solve a transportation problem with supplies a_i, demands b_j, and costs

$$(1.7.7) \qquad\qquad c_{ij} = -s_j + v_i + d_{ij},$$

where the interpretation of c_{ij} is the negative of the profit per unit of supplying market j from warehouse i.

In many applications, the profit-maximization model is more appropriate than the classical transportation model, which tries to minimize shipping·costs. If Assumption 1 holds, we know by Theorem 1.3.1 that the two objectives are the same. However, if $\sum a_i < \sum b_j$ or if $\sum a_i > \sum b_j$, then profit maximization can lead to different behavior than cost minimization. Exercises 2–4 go into this phenomenon, as well as into the connection between the variable costs and prices and the dual variables.

Model Type 4. The (zero change cost) *production scheduling* (or smoothing) *model.* We start by working an example. Suppose that a manufacturer wishes to schedule production of a factory during June, July, and August when there is less production time than usual because of vacations. He pays his workers $1.40 per hour regular time and $2.10 per hour overtime. If he produces in a given month and stores the product for sale the next month, he must pay an inventory storage of 20¢ per unit.

Suppose that he has available 600 hours regular time and 300 hours overtime in June, and 400 hours regular time and 200 hours overtime in both July and August. Finally, assume he estimates demands of 500, 600, and 600 units for the three months and that each unit produced takes one hour of worker time. We can set up the following transportation problem to minimize production cost:

	June	July	August	
June Reg.	1.4	1.6	1.8	600
June Over	2.1	2.3	2.5	300
July Reg.	100	1.4	1.6	400
July Over	100	2.1	2.3	200
Aug. Reg.	100	100	1.4	400
Aug. Over	100	100	2.1	200
	500	600	600	

The reason for the entries of 100 is to prevent the model specifying production in later months from being used in an earlier month. In Exercise 5, you will be asked to show that the optimal solution is as follows:

June: Use all 600 units of regular time, saving 100 units for use in July. Do not use overtime.

July: Use 400 units of regular time and 100 units of overtime.

Aug.: Use all 400 units of regular time and all the 200 units of overtime.

The general model would use the transportation tableau given in Figure 1.7.1.

	Period 1	Period 2	$\cdots$	Period n	
R_1	c	$c + s$	$\cdots$	$c + (n-1)s$	e_1
O_1	v	$v + s$		$v + (n-1)s$	f_1
R_2		c	$\cdots$	$c + (n-2)s$	e_2
O_2		v		$v + (n-2)s$	f_2
$\vdots$	$\cdot$	$\cdot$	$\cdots$	$\cdot$	$\vdots$
R_n			$\cdots$	c	e_n
O_n				v	f_n
	d_1	d_2	$\cdots$	d_n	

FIGURE 1.7.1

The interpretations of the symbols in Figure 1.7.1 are as follows. The demand in period i is d_i; the amount of regular time in period i is e_i and the amount of overtime in period i is f_i; c is the regular-time wage rate; v is the overtime wage rate; and s is the unit storage cost. The crossed out cells in the matrix are not to be used in the solution.

Model Type 5. The *caterer model.* The caterer problem is that of a caterer who needs to have clean napkins for each day over a period of days. Some of the clean napkins may be purchased new, and some may be dirty napkins from previous days that have been washed by a laundry service. The cost of new napkins is 20¢ each, the cost of a fast one-day laundry service is 15¢ per napkin, and the cost of a slow two-day laundry service is 8¢ per napkin. Suppose the caterer needs to have 40, 70, and 60 clean napkins for the next three days. How many shall he buy new and how many shall he have laundered by each of the services?

In order to solve this problem, we set up the transportation problem given in the matrix:

	Day 1	*Day 2*	*Day 3*	
Napkins bought	.2	.2	.2	170
Dirty napkins first day	100	.15	.08	40
Dirty napkins second day	100	100	.15	70
	40	70	60	

The 100 entries prevent dirty napkins from being used until after they have been washed. The only possibly puzzling entry in this matrix is the 170 as the rim condition of the first row. This is equal to the sum of all the demands for napkins. Obviously not all napkins will be bought new, but since the sum of the row rim conditions is greater than the sum of the column conditions, it is necessary to add a fictitious column that will take up the slack.

In Exercise 8 you will be asked to show that the solution to the problem above is: buy 40 new napkins for day 1 and 70 new napkins for day 2; wash all 40 dirty napkins from the first day by the slow laundry service for use on day 3, and wash 20 of the dirty napkins from day 2 by the fast laundry service for use on day 3.

Obviously this problem can be extended to more classes of laundry service, more days, and completely different types of services. Actually, the first application of the caterer problem was for the repair of airplane engines by either a fast floating maintenance ship, or a slow land-based facility.

Model Type 6. The *transshipment model.* We have already seen an example of transshipment in Exercise 14 of Section 1.1. Let us work a more general situation. Consider a warehouse-market problem in which there are two warehouses, *A* and *B*, and three markets, 1, 2, and 3. Suppose the distances between pairs are given by the numbers in Figure 1.7.2. Such distance tables are frequently used in maps. Now

	B	1	2	3
A	3	10	8	9
	B	14	7	13
		1	5	2
			2	3

FIGURE 1.7.2

suppose warehouses A and B have supplies of 350 and 500 units, and markets 1, 2, and 3 have demands of 200, 350, and 275. The corresponding transportation problem and its optimal solution costing 7425 units are given below:

	1	2	3	
A	⑩ ²⁰⁰	8	⑨ ¹⁵⁰	350
B	14	⑦ ³⁵⁰	⑬ ¹²⁵	500
	200	350	275	

Suppose now we introduce the possibility that warehouse can ship to warehouse or market to market or even market to warehouse—that is, we permit transshipment. In order to do this we define a new transportation problem in which warehouses and markets occur in both rows and column. The new problem is shown in Figure 1.7.3. We have filled in the distance entries using the data from Figure 1.7.2. Note also that we have put in 0's on the diagonal of the matrix indicating that the distance from a warehouse to a warehouse or a market to a market is zero.

	A	B	1	2	3	
A	0	3	10	8	9	350
B	3	0	14	7	13	500
1	10	14	0	5	2	0
2	8	7	5	0	3	0
3	9	13	2	3	0	0
	0	0	200	350	275	

FIGURE 1.7.3

This problem is equivalent to the previous one since the rim conditions do not yet permit transshipment. If we knew how much each warehouse or market should transship, we could just add that amount to both row and column. The problem is that we don't know. However, we know that the maximum amount that could possibly be transshipped is not greater than either the sum of the supplies or the sum of the demands. In this case, the sum of the supplies is 850 and the sum of the demands is 825. Any convenient number larger than both can be used—let us use 1000. Suppose we add this number to all rim conditions. Then if there is an advantage for a given market to transship, it can do so; otherwise the unused transshipment amount will appear on the main diagonal, which has zero costs and hence does not affect the total transportation cost. The new problem, together with its solution, appears in Figure 1.7.4.

	A	B	1	2	3	
A	1000 (0)	3	200 (10)	8	150 (9)	1350
B	3	1000 (0)	14	475 (7)	13	1500
1	10	14	1000 (0)	5	2	1000
2	8	7	5	875 (0)	125 (3)	1000
3	9	1	2	3	1000 (0)	1000
	1000	1000	1200	1350	1275	

FIGURE 1.7.4

The total cost of this optimal solution is 7050, which is 375 units less than the cost of the previous solution. In order to see how this saving is accomplished, we look down the diagonal of the cost matrix. Note that the only transshipment point is market 2, which transships 125 units to market 3. It gets those 125 units from warehouse B. The cost of shipping from warehouse B to market 3 directly is 13 units. But by shipping first to market 2, at a cost of 7, and then to market 3 at a cost of 3, the indirect shipping cost is 10. This saves 3 per unit, and since we're shipping 125 units, the total saving is 375. Note also that the 1000 figure we added for possible transshipments could have been any other figure greater than or equal to 125 without changing the solution. Obviously it is better to have this figure be large so that you will not prevent in advance any transshipment that might be useful.

The general transshipment model is given in Figure 1.7.5. Note that each market and each warehouse is listed in both the row and the column. The quantity s

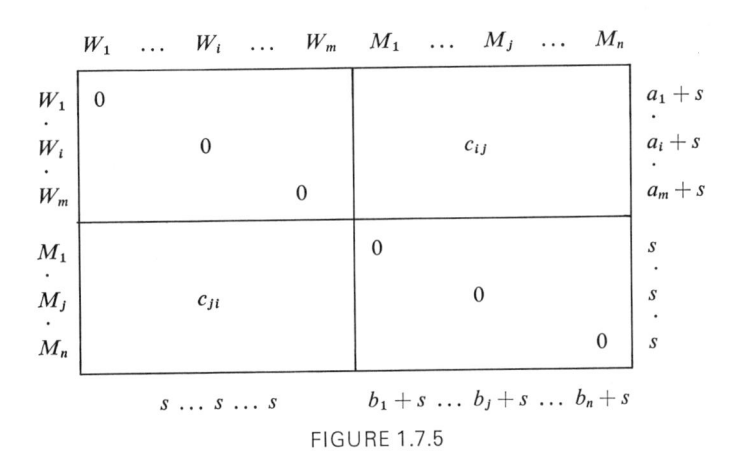

FIGURE 1.7.5

is the maximum transshipment amount, which was chosen to be 1000 in the example above. In general, s should be chosen to be a number greater than the larger of the total demands and total supplies in order to be safe. The cost matrix is given by c'_{ij}.

In order to see what its entries are, let us denote by c_{ij} the distance between W_i and M_j, by d_{ij} the distance between M_i and M_j, and by e_{ij} the distance between W_i and W_j. Then we have

(1.7.8)
$$c'_{ij} = \begin{cases} e_{ij} & \text{if } 1 \le i, j \le m \\ c_{ij} & \text{if } 1 \le i \le m, \, m+1 \le n \le m+n \\ c_{ji} & \text{if } m+1 \le i \le m+n, \, 1 \le j \le n \\ d_{ij} & \text{if } m+1 \le i, j \le m+n \end{cases}$$

and, of course, we always have

(1.7.9)
$$c'_{ii} = 0 \quad \text{for} \quad i = 1, \ldots, m+n.$$

Actually, because we assume symmetry of distances, we also have

(1.7.10)
$$c'_{ij} = c'_{ji} \qquad \text{for all } i, j.$$

Because of this symmetry condition, we can write the equations of the transshipment model as follows:

(1.7.11)
$$\sum_{\substack{i<j \\ 1 \le i,j \le m+n}} c'_{ij}(w_{ij} + w_{ji})$$

Subject to:

(1.7.12)
$$\sum_{j=1}^{m+n} (w_{ij} - w_{ji}) = a_i$$

(1.7.13)
$$\sum_{i=1}^{m+n} (w_{ij} - w_{ji}) = -b_j$$

(1.7.14)
$$w_{ij} \ge 0$$

In Exercise 11, you will be asked to derive these equations for $m = 2$ and $n = 3$.

There is one more observation that is in order. In constraints (1.7.12) and (1.7.13), the variables w_{ij} and w_{ji} always occur in the form $w_{ij} - w_{ji}$. This implies (although we won't see the reason until later) that at most one of them can be positive. That is, we have the additional result that

(1.7.15)
$$w_{ij} w_{ji} = 0$$

in any basic optimal feasible solution. Intuitively this is clear, since if it pays to ship from point i to point j then it must not simultaneously pay to ship in the reverse direction. For if we did so then we would, in effect, be shipping goods around a circle, which is obviously of no value whatsoever.

EXERCISES 1.7

1. Suppose you had an assignment problem with $m \ne n$. Discuss how the assignment algorithm could be used by first adding dummy rows or columns.

2. (a) Solve the following problem:

9	11	40
12	10	30
22	34	

(b) Solve the following problem:

11	13	40
16	14	30
22	34	

(c) Assume that the problem in (a) is a cost-minimization problem, and assume that the problem in (b) is derived from (a) because of a variable cost of 2 at warehouse 1 and a variable cost of 4 at warehouse 2. Use these examples to show that cost minimization does not necessarily lead to profit maximization, and conversely.

3. Calculate and interpret the dual solutions to the problems in parts (a) and (b) of Exercise 2.

4. Use Exercises 2 and 3 to show the following: if the differences in dual variables between a pair of factories or warehouses is less than the differences in the corresponding variable costs, then cost minimization and profit maximization lead to different solutions.

5. Show that the optimal solution to the zero change cost production scheduling (or smoothing) model is as stated in the text.

6. Extend the production smoothing model of Figure 1.7.1 to the case in which there are k classes of labor types instead of two classes.

7. Extend the production smoothing model of Figure 1.7.1 to the case in which the storage charge for two months is not necessarily twice that for one month. Include the case of perishable goods that spoil and become worthless after a certain number of months.

8. (a) Solve the caterer problem in the text, and show that the answer given there is correct.
(b) Set up and solve the caterer problem with the same numerical data but for four days in which the demands are for 80, 50, 100, and 40 napkins.

9. Extend the caterer problem to the case where there are k classes of laundry service. Set up the corresponding transportation matrix.

10. Consider the transshipment example in Figure 1.7.3. Suppose there is a $1 charge for each unit transshipped through a point. Show how to include this possibility in the transportation matrix, and solve the problem given there with this new requirement.

11. Derive equations (1.7.8)–(1.7.14) for the case in which $m = 2$ and $n = 3$. In particular, explain where equations (1.7.12) and (1.7.13) come from.

12. Suppose we consider a transshipment problem among points in a city that has one-way streets so that the distance from point x to point y may be different from the distance from point y to point x. Discuss how to extend the transshipment model to include this possibility. What differences will this cause in expressions (1.7.8)–(1.7.15)?

SUGGESTED READING

Charnes, A., and Cooper, W. W. *Management Models and Industrial Applications of Linear Programming.* 2 Vols. New York: John Wiley, 1961.

Dantzig, G. B. *Linear Programming and Extensions.* Princeton, N.J.: Princeton University Press, 1963.

Ford, L. R., and Fulkerson, D. R. *Flows in Networks.* Princeton, N.J.: Princeton University Press, 1963.

Simmonard, M. *Linear Programming.* Englewood Cliffs, N.J.: Prentice-Hall, 1966.

Srinivasan, V. and Thompson, G. L. An operator theory of parametric programming for the transportation problem. Parts I and II. *Naval Research Logistics Quarterly*, 1972, **19**, 205–252.

CHAPTER 2

LINEAR ALGEBRA

2.1 VECTORS AND MATRICES

A *matrix* is a rectangular array of numbers written in the form

$$A = \begin{bmatrix} a_{11} & a_{12} & \cdots & a_{1n} \\ a_{21} & a_{22} & \cdots & a_{2n} \\ \cdot & \cdot & \cdots & \cdot \\ a_{m1} & a_{m2} & \cdots & a_{mn} \end{bmatrix}.$$

Here the letters a_{ij} stand for real numbers for $i = 1, \ldots, m$ and $j = 1, \ldots, n$, and m and n are positive integers. The entry a_{ij} is called the i, jth *component of A*. Observe that the matrix A has m *rows* and n *columns*. For this reason it is called an $m \times n$ matrix. If $m = 1$, the matrix is an n-component *row vector*; and if $n = 1$, the matrix is an m-component *column vector*.

Examples of matrices are the following:

$$[1, \ -1, \ 0] \qquad \begin{bmatrix} 2 \\ 4 \\ 6 \end{bmatrix} \qquad \begin{bmatrix} 0 & 1 & 0 \\ 0 & 0 & 0 \\ 1 & 0 & 0 \end{bmatrix}$$

$$\begin{bmatrix} 1 & -2 \\ 3 & -4 \\ 5 & -6 \end{bmatrix} \qquad \begin{bmatrix} -2 & 5 & 6 & 8 & -7 \\ 10 & 0 & 1 & -3 & -9 \end{bmatrix}$$

The shape of a matrix is determined by the number of rows and columns it has. The first example above is a 1×3 matrix, which is also a three-component row vector; the second example is a 3×1 matrix, which is also a three-component column vector; the third example is a 3×3 square matrix; the fourth example is a 3×2 matrix; and the fifth example is a 2×5 matrix. Sometimes, as in the first example, commas are added for clarity.

DEFINITION 2.1.1. Two matrices A and B of the same *shape*—that is, having the same number of rows and columns—are said to be *equal* if $a_{ij} = b_{ij}$, for $i = 1, \ldots, m$ and $j = 1, \ldots, n$.

Note that two matrices *not* of the same shape are *never* equal.

There are many reasons for using matrices. One reason is that frequently it is possible to classify numbers in two different ways; and then the result of such a classification can be summarized in a matrix with one attribute being specified by the row and the other by the column. This use will be illustrated in Example 2.1.3, which is an accounting application. Another reason is that, using matrices, it is possible to carry out arithmetic operations on *sets* of numbers just as easily (in principle) as on single numbers. The way this is done is illustrated in the next definition.

DEFINITION 2.1.2. Let A and B be two $m \times n$ matrices with components a_{ij} and b_{ij}, respectively. Let k be a number.

(a) The *numerical* or *scalar* multiple, kA, of A is the matrix whose components are ka_{ij}, for $i = 1, \ldots, m$ and $j = 1, \ldots, n$.

(b) The sum $A + B$ of the two matrices A and B is the matrix whose entries are $a_{ij} + b_{ij}$, for $i = 1, \ldots, m$ and $j = 1, \ldots, n$.

The following are examples of these two arithmetic operations on matrices:

(a) $\qquad -3\begin{bmatrix} -2 & 5 & 6 & 0 \\ 10 & 0 & 1 & -1 \end{bmatrix} = \begin{bmatrix} 6 & -15 & -18 & 0 \\ -30 & 0 & -3 & 3 \end{bmatrix}$

(b) $\qquad \begin{bmatrix} 1 & 0 \\ 0 & 4 \\ -5 & -6 \end{bmatrix} + \begin{bmatrix} 0 & 2 \\ 3 & 0 \\ 10 & 12 \end{bmatrix} = \begin{bmatrix} 1 & 2 \\ 3 & 4 \\ 5 & 6 \end{bmatrix}$

Note that it is very easy to remember how to do these two operations, since they simply act *componentwise* on the matrices involved. Note also that we never add together two matrices that are not of the same shape.

There is a special $m \times n$ matrix O, all of whose entries are 0's. It is called the *zero matrix*. Examples of zero matrices are as follows:

$$O_{1 \times 3} = [0 \quad 0 \quad 0] \qquad O_{3 \times 2} = \begin{bmatrix} 0 & 0 \\ 0 & 0 \\ 0 & 0 \end{bmatrix} \qquad O_{4 \times 4} = \begin{bmatrix} 0 & 0 & 0 & 0 \\ 0 & 0 & 0 & 0 \\ 0 & 0 & 0 & 0 \\ 0 & 0 & 0 & 0 \end{bmatrix}$$

Usually we do not indicate the shape of O but it can be determined from the context.

When $k = -1$, the matrix kA is usually denoted by $-A = (-1)A$ and is called the *negative* of A. Since the elements of $-A$ are $(-1)a_{ij} = -a_{ij}$, we see that $A - A = A + (-A) = O$, since $a_{ij} - a_{ij} = 0$ for every i and j. (Note that the O in the equation $A - A = O$ has the same number of rows and columns as A.)

There are a number of elementary results that can be derived for carrying out the operations on matrices described above. These are embodied in the following theorem.

THEOREM 2.1.1. Let A, B, and C be matrices having m rows and n columns; let O be the $m \times n$ zero matrix; and let h and k be numbers. Then the addition and scalar multiplication operators defined above satisfy the following identities (laws):

A0. If A and B are matrices and k a number, then $A + B$ and kA are matrices. (Closure law)

A1. $A + B = B + A$ (Commutative law of addition)

A2. $A + (B + C) = (A + B) + C$ (Associative law of addition)

A3. $A + O = A$ (Additive identity law)

A4. $A - A = O$ (Additive inverse law)

S1. $h(kA) = (hk)A$ (Mixed associative law)

S2. $1A = A$ (Unity law)

S3. $h(A + B) = hA + hB$ (Distributive law for a number over matrices)

S4. $(h + k)A = hA + kA$ (Distributive law for numbers over a matrix)

(*Note:* A1–A4 are the addition laws; S1–S4 are the scalar multiplication laws.)

Proofs: We will prove only some of these results, leaving the others for exercises. You will see that they are all easy consequences of the corresponding laws for numbers.

Proof of A1. The i,jth element of $A + B$ is $a_{ij} + b_{ij}$. By the usual rules for ordinary numbers, we have $a_{ij} + b_{ij} = b_{ij} + a_{ij}$, and the latter is the i,jth element of $B + A$. Hence, by Definition 2.1.1, $A + B = B + A$.

Proof of A2. The i,jth element of $A + (B + C)$ is $a_{ij} + (b_{ij} + c_{ij})$, which by elementary rules for numbers is equal to $(a_{ij} + b_{ij}) + c_{ij}$, the i,jth element of $(A + B) + C$. Hence by Definition 2.1.1, A2 holds.

Because of rule A2 we can write triple sums as $A + B + C$, without indicating parentheses. What the rule establishes is that the sum is uniquely defined, however the parentheses are inserted. The same rule can be proved for sums of four, five, six, . . . vectors.

The proof of rule A3 is Exercise 5 and rule A4 has already been proved.

Proof of S1. The i,jth element of the matrix $h(kA)$ is $h(ka_{ij})$ which, by elementary rules for numbers, is equal to $(hk)a_{ij}$ which is the i,jth element of $(hk)A$. Hence, by Definition 2.1.1, rule S1 holds.

The proofs of rules S2, S3, and S4 are asked for in Exercises 8–10.

EXAMPLE 2.1.1. One of the most common reasons for wanting to multiply matrices by numbers and add them together is the process of taking *averages*. For instance, suppose that a town has two stores and that the prices they charge for bread, chicken, eggs, and milk are given in the following two vectors:

$$
\begin{array}{cccc}
& Bread & Chicken & Eggs & Milk \\
Store\ 1 & [21\ \text{¢/loaf} & 31\ \text{¢/lb.} & 63\ \text{¢/doz.} & 23\ \text{¢/qt.}] = X \\
Store\ 2 & [22 & 29 & 65 & 25\ ] = Y
\end{array}
$$

We can compute the average prices for these quantities in two different ways: the first, by adding $\frac{1}{2}X$ to $\frac{1}{2}Y$, and the second, by computing $\frac{1}{2}(X + Y)$. By rule S4, the result is the same by either process. It is easy to see that this is

$$
\frac{1}{2} X + \frac{1}{2} Y = \frac{1}{2}(X + Y) = [21.5 \quad 30 \quad 64 \quad 24].
$$

EXAMPLE 2.1.2. As another instance in which an average score is of interest consider the following situation. Suppose that two tests, A and B, are administered to each of the seniors in high school and college in each of the 50 states of the United States. The average scores for all the students in state j might be summarized in a matrix S_j as follows:

$$
\begin{array}{ccc}
& Test\ A & Test\ B \\
High\ School & \begin{bmatrix} 71 & 82 \\ College & 75 & 89 \end{bmatrix} = S_j
\end{array}
$$

Now suppose that we want the overall average for all states in the United States. We can again obtain this result in two different ways, as follows:

$$
\frac{1}{50} (S_1 + S_2 + \cdots + S_{50}) = \frac{1}{50} S_1 + \frac{1}{50} S_2 + \cdots + \frac{1}{50} S_{50}.
$$

EXAMPLE 2.1.3. A small firm has made the following transactions during the month:

Cash sales	$600
Charge sales	900
Collections on bills rendered	650
Payments on bills received	150

Suppose it wants to record these purchases in some bookkeeping system and has set up the following accounts: cash, accounts receivable, and sales.

The most common (hand) method of bookkeeping is the so-called double-entry system in which each number is recorded *twice*, once as a debit and once as a credit. Let us show that we can doubly classify each number by recording it once in matrix with the row being the account that is to be credited and the column being the account that is to be debited. We thus achieve the same effect as the double-entry system. The required matrix is:

$$Account\ Debited$$

		Cash	Accounts Rec.	Accounts Pay.	Sales
	Cash			150	
Account	Accts. Rec.	650			
Credited	Accts. Pay.				
	Sales	600	900		

You should convince yourself that the numbers are entered in the proper place. For instance, the $600 of cash sales must obviously be debited to cash and credited to sales and hence must appear in the (4, 1) entry of the matrix. And the $900 of charge sales will increase accounts receivable and hence must be debited there, and credited to sales. The other entries should be justified similarly. Suppose now that we want to know the amount of cash received during the month. It is obviously the sum of the entries in the first column, which is $1250. Similarly, the amount of cash disbursed is the sum of the entries in the first row, or $150. The net cash remaining is then $1250 − 150 = $1100. It is possible to extend the bookkeeping system outlined here to a full-fledged system that does all the conventional accounting operations using matrix operations.

EXAMPLE 2.1.4. In many cases it is convenient to interpret the sum and scalar multiplication of vectors geometrically. Let us consider the case of two-component row vectors. A vector $x = (a, b)$ can be considered the coordinates of a point in the plane. To see this, select two intersecting lines as axes in the plane and label them x_1 and x_2. Then to plot the point $x = (a, b)$, we start at the origin, which is the intersection of the two axis lines, and move a units along the first axis (to the right if $a > 0$ and to the left if $a < 0$). Then we move a distance b along a line parallel to the second axis (up if $b > 0$ and down if $b < 0$). The point determined is the one whose coordinates in the plane are (a, b), as shown in Figure 2.1.1.

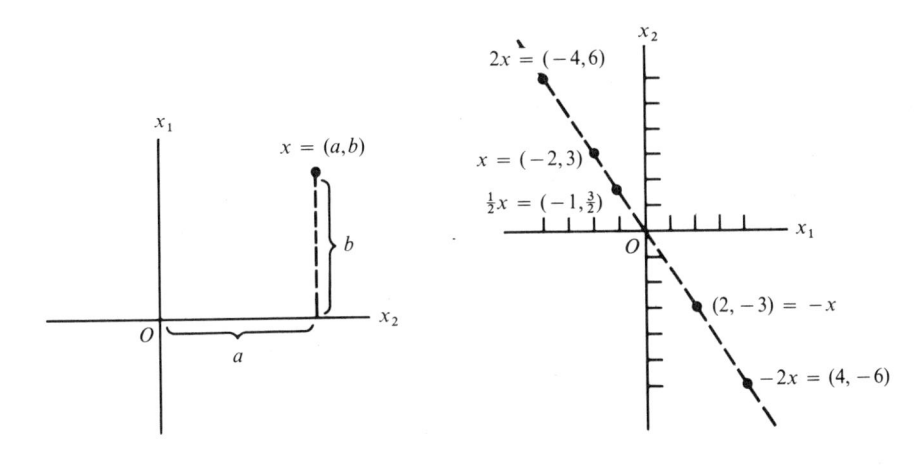

FIGURE 2.1.1   FIGURE 2.1.2

The idea of multiplying a vector by a scalar can also be characterized geometrically. In Figure 2.1.2 we have shown the point $x = (-2, 3)$ and also the points $2x, \frac{1}{2}x, -x$, and $-2x$. Note that all these points lie on a straight line through the origin. (Later we will call this line a subspace.)

The sum of two vectors, $x = (a, b)$ and $y = (c, d)$, can be given the geometric interpretation shown in Figure 2.1.3. For obvious geometric reasons, vector addition is sometimes said to be carried out by "completing the parallelogram."

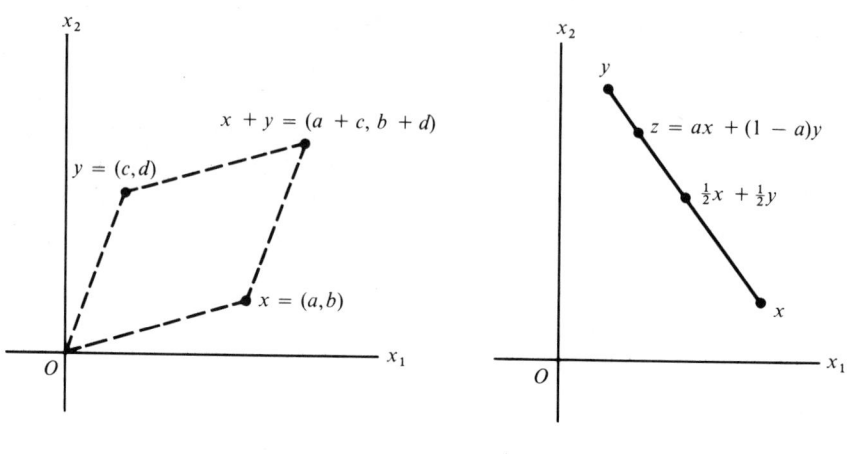

FIGURE 2.1.3   FIGURE 2.1.4

As we have seen above, the average of two vectors is frequently of interest. In Figure 2.1.4 we have plotted two points x and y and their average, $\frac{1}{2}x + \frac{1}{2}y$. Note that the average vector is located at the midpoint of the line segment between x and y. More generally, the vector $z = ax + (1 - a)y$, with $0 \le a \le 1$, will be a point on the line segment between x and y. A typical such point is shown in Figure 2.1.4.

EXERCISES 2.1

1. Consider the following vectors and matrices:

$$A = \begin{bmatrix} 1 & 0 \\ 0 & 1 \end{bmatrix} \qquad B = \begin{bmatrix} 2 & 4 \\ 4 & 3 \end{bmatrix} \qquad C = \begin{bmatrix} 0 & 1 \\ 1 & 0 \end{bmatrix} \qquad u = [1 \quad -1]$$

$$v = [-3 \quad 2 \quad -5] \qquad w = [0 \quad 1 \quad 0] \qquad x = [-1 \quad -1 \quad -1] \qquad z = [3 \quad -4].$$

Compute the following quantities, when possible:

(a) $5A$ (b) $2A + B - 4C = ?$ (c) $u + v$ (d) $-u + 7z$

(e) $3v - 2w + 5x$ (f) $A + w$ (g) $hu + kz$ (h) $hA - kC$

2. Perform the following operations:

(a)
$$2\begin{bmatrix} -1 & 2 \\ 0 & 6 \\ -1 & 0 \end{bmatrix} - 5\begin{bmatrix} -1 & 0 \\ 0 & 2 \\ 5 & 4 \end{bmatrix} = ?$$

(b)
$$-2\begin{bmatrix} 1 & -2 & 3 \\ -4 & 5 & -6 \end{bmatrix} + 4\begin{bmatrix} 2 & -1 & 0 \\ 0 & -2 & 1 \end{bmatrix} = ?$$

(c)
$$\begin{bmatrix} 1 & 0 & 1 \\ 0 & 1 & 0 \end{bmatrix} + \begin{bmatrix} 3 & -3 \\ 0 & 1 \\ 5 & -6 \end{bmatrix} = ?$$

(d) $a[1 \quad 0 \quad 0] + b[0 \quad 1 \quad 0] + c[0 \quad 0 \quad 1] = ?$

(e)
$$a\begin{bmatrix} 1 \\ 0 \\ 0 \end{bmatrix} + b\begin{bmatrix} 0 \\ 1 \\ 0 \end{bmatrix} + c\begin{bmatrix} 0 \\ 0 \\ 1 \end{bmatrix} = ?$$

3. Prove that $OA = O_{m \times n}$, if A is an $m \times n$ matrix.

4. If O is an $m \times n$ zero matrix, prove that $aO = 0$ for any number a.

5. Prove rule A3.

6. Consider the equation
$$\begin{bmatrix} x_1 \\ x_2 \\ x_3 \end{bmatrix} + \begin{bmatrix} -2 \\ 3 \\ 1 \end{bmatrix} = \begin{bmatrix} 5 \\ -1 \\ 0 \end{bmatrix}$$
Solve for x_1, x_2, and x_3.

7. Consider the equation
$$\frac{1}{2}\begin{bmatrix} x_1 \\ x_2 \\ x_3 \end{bmatrix} - 3\begin{bmatrix} 12 \\ -2 \\ 1 \end{bmatrix} = \begin{bmatrix} 7 \\ 15 \\ 9 \end{bmatrix}$$
Solve for x_1, x_2, and x_3.

8. Prove rule S2.

9. Prove rule S3.

10. Prove rule S4.

11. In how many ways can parentheses be inserted in the triple sum $A + B + C$? Discuss these in light of rule A2.

12. In how many ways can parentheses be inserted in the quadruple sum $A + B + C + D$? Use rule A2 to show that they are all equal.

13. Construct a set of axes on a sheet of paper. On these, plot the vectors
$a = [3, 1]$, $b = [2, 6]$, $c = [-2, 4]$, and $d = [-2, -1]$.
Now compute and plot the following vectors.

(a) $-2a$ 　　　　(b) $\frac{1}{2}(a + c)$ 　　　　(c) $\frac{1}{3}b + \frac{2}{3}d$

(d) $\frac{1}{3}(a + b + c)$ 　　　　(e) $2a - b + 3d$.

14. Suppose that a data file contains the age, height, weight, and salary of each person in the file. Answer the following questions concerning the vectors having these four components.
(a) Does it make sense to multiply one of these vectors by 2?
(b) Does it make sense to average two or more of these vectors?
(c) Does it make sense to multiply one of the vectors by -1?
(d) What kinds of operations would be meaningful in terms of personnel studies?

15. Let $x = (x_1, \ldots, x_n)$. Define $x \geq 0$ to mean that $x_i \geq 0$ for every i. Define $x \leq 0$ analogously. Now prove that if $x \geq 0$, then $-x \leq 0$.

16. If x and y are n-component row vectors, define $x \geq y$ to mean $x - y \geq 0$ (see Exercise 15). Now prove that if $x \geq y$ and $y \geq z$, then $x \geq z$.

17. If $\{x^{(1)}, \ldots, x^{(k)}\}$ is a set of k n-dimensional vectors show how to find a vector y such that $y \geq x^{(i)}$, for $i = 1, \ldots, k$. Also show how to find a vector z such that $z \leq x^{(i)}$, for $i = 1, \ldots, k$.

18. Consider the following vectors:

$$x = [-2,\ 0,\ 2], \quad y = [-5,\ -1,\ 0], \quad z = [1,\ 1,\ 1], \quad w = [2,\ 3,\ 4].$$

Referring to Exercises 15–17, show the following:
(a) $x \geq y$
(b) $w \geq x$
(c) There is or is not a relationship between x and z.
(d) There is a vector b greater than each of the four vectors given (see Exercise 17).
(e) There is a vector c less than each of the four vectors.

2.2   ABSTRACT VECTOR SPACES

In the preceding section we defined row and column vectors as one-row and one-column matrices. In this section, we will take a somewhat more abstract point of view and regard a vector as any member of a set having certain properties that are just like those displayed in Theorem 2.1.1.

DEFINITION 2.2.1. Let V be any nonempty set of objects that have the following properties (called axioms):

A0.   If x and y are vectors in V and k is a number, then addition and scalar multiplication (that is, multiplication by numbers) of vectors are defined, and $x + y$ and kx are vectors in V.   (Closure law)

A1. $x + y = y + x$ (Commutative law of addition)

A2. $x + (y + z) = (x + y) + z$ (Associative law of addition)

A3. There exists an element O in V such that $x + O = x$ for all x in V.   (Additive identity law)

A4. There exists for each x in V an element $-x$ such that $x - x = O$.   (Additive inverse law)

S1. If h and k are scalars, then $h(kx) = (hk)x$.   (Mixed associative law)

S2. $1x = x$ for all x (Unity law)

S3. If h is a scalar, then $h(x + y) = hx + hy$.   (Distributive law for a number over vectors)

S4. If h and k are scalars, then $(h + k)x = hx + kx$.   (Distributive law for numbers over a vector)

(*Note:* A1–A4 are addition laws; S1–S4 are scalar multiplication laws.) Then V is called a *vector space* and the elements of V are called *vectors*.

Let R_m be the set of all m-component row vectors. By the definitions of the preceding section, if x and y are two m-component row vectors and k is a scalar, then $x + y$ and kx are m-component row vectors so that axiom A0 is satisfied. By Theorem 2.1.1 the other eight axioms are also satisfied, so R_m is a vector space. In the same way, C_n, the set of all n-component column vectors, is also a vector space over the real numbers.

We shall be concerned almost exclusively with these two vector spaces in this part of the book. However, we will first demonstrate with Example 2.2.1 that many more sets of objects can be vector spaces besides R_m and C_n.

EXAMPLE 2.2.1. Let P_2 be the set of all polynomials of degree at most 1. Such a polynomial can be written $a_0 + a_1 t = p(t)$ where t is the variable. If $q(t) = b_0 + b_1 t$, then clearly $p(t) + q(t) = (a_0 + b_0) + (a_1 + b_1)t$, which again is at most a first degree polynomial. Also, $kp(t) = k(a_0 + a_1 t) = ka_0 + ka_1 t$, again a first degree polynomial. Hence axiom A0 is satisfied. The O polynomial is clearly $O = 0 + 0t$, the additive inverse of $p(t)$ is $-p(t) = -a_0 - a_1 t$, and both of these are at most first degree polynomials. The detailed proof that the rest of the axioms are satisfied for P_2 is left as Exercise 1. Note that, geometrically, we can interpret P_2 as the set of all nonvertical straight lines in the plane, which is quite a different vector space than the set of all points in the plane (R_2).

In exactly the same way P_n, the set of all polynomials of degree at most $n - 1$, is a vector space. You should try to visualize the geometric interpretation of this vector space in the plane.

The only operations on vectors that we can perform in an abstract vector space are (a) the addition of two vectors and (b) the scalar multiplication of a vector by a number. Addition was initially defined for two vectors, but axiom A2 permits us to define it for the sum of three or more vectors (see Exercises 11–12 of Section 2.1).

We now want to study sums of scalar multiples of vectors. In this book we will define three kinds of such sums as follows.

DEFINITION 2.2.2. Let $S = \{x^{(1)}, \ldots, x^{(r)}\}$ be a nonempty set of vectors in a vector space, and let $k_1, \ldots, k_r$ be scalars (numbers).

(a) By a *linear combination* of the vectors in S, we mean the sum

$$(2.2.1) \qquad \sum_{i=1}^{r} k_i x^{(i)} = k_1 x^{(1)} + \cdots + k_r x^{(r)}.$$

(b) By a *weighted combination* of the vectors in S, we mean a linear combination in which the scalars k_i satisfy

$$(2.2.2) \qquad \sum_{i=1}^{r} k_i = k_1 + \cdots + k_r = 1.$$

(c) By a *convex combination* of the vectors in S, we mean a weighted combination in which the scalars satisfy, in addition to the conditions in (2.2.2), the r inequality conditions

$$(2.2.3) \qquad k_i \geq 0 \qquad \text{for } i = 1, \ldots, r.$$

In other words, a convex combination is a nonnegative weighted combination of vectors.

Note that in (2.2.1) it is assumed that *every* vector $x^{(i)}$ in S occurs in the linear combination. In the present section we shall study only linear combinations of vectors and reserve the study of the weighted and convex combinations for later sections.

You should note that a familiar example of taking a convex combination is the process of averaging vectors, as illustrated in Examples 2.1.1 and 2.1.2.

DEFINITION 2.2.3. Let $S = \{x^{(1)}, \ldots, x^{(r)}\}$ be a nonempty set of vectors. Then vector y is said to be a *linear combination of the vectors in S* if and only if there exist numbers $k_1, \ldots, k_r$ such that

$$(2.2.4) \qquad\qquad y = \sum_{i=1}^{r} k_i x^{(i)}.$$

LEMMA 2.2.1. Let $S = \{x^{(1)}, \ldots, x^{(r)}\}$ be any nonempty set of vectors in V; then

(a) O (the zero vector in V) is a linear combination of vectors in S; and
(b) if y is a linear combination of vectors in S, then so is $-y$.

Proof: (a) Take $k_i = 0$, for $i = 1, \ldots, r$, and observe that

$$\sum_{i=1}^{r} k_i x^{(i)} = 0x^{(1)} + \cdots + 0x^{(r)} = O + \cdots + O = O,$$

which proves that O is a linear combination.

(b) if $y = \sum_{i=1}^{r} k_i x^{(i)}$ is a linear combination, then clearly

$$-y = -1\left(\sum_{i=1}^{r} k_i x^{(i)} \right) = \sum_{i=1}^{r} -k_i x^{(i)}$$

is also a linear combination.

EXAMPLE 2.2.2. In Example 2.1.4 we saw that the set of all scalar multiples of a single nonzero vector could be interpreted geometrically as a line through the origin (see Figure 2.1.2). In the same manner the set of all linear combinations of the vectors [1, 1, 0] and [0, 0, 1] can be represented as a plane through the origin in three-space (see Figure 2.2.1). In general, the set of all linear combinations of a finite set of m-component vectors can always be interpreted as a plane through the origin in m-space. This interpretation will be dealt with more thoroughly in Section 2.7.

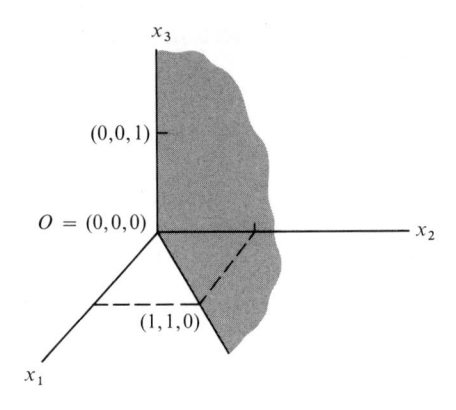

FIGURE 2.2.1

DEFINITION 2.2.4. Let V' be any nonempty subset of V. Then V' is a *subspace of V* if and only if the following two conditions hold:

(a) If x and y are in V', then $x + y$ is also in V';

(b) If x is in V' and k is a number, then kx is also in V'.

Note that these conditions are the same as the closure law (axiom A0) in Definition 2.2.1.

THEOREM 2.2.1. A subspace V' of V is a vector space with the same definitions of addition and scalar multiplication.

Proof: Axiom A0 (the closure law) of Definition 2.2.1 is true by virtue of the conditions of Definition 2.2.4. Axioms A1, A2, S1, S2, S3, and S4 all hold since V' is a subset of V. We need only show that O and $-x$ belong to V'. But let x be any vector in V'; observe that $0x = O$ belongs to V'. Also, $(-1)x = -x$ belongs to V', so V' is a vector space.

DEFINITION 2.2.5. Let $S = \{x^{(1)}, \ldots, x^{(r)}\}$ be a nonempty subset of V. Let V' be the set of all linear combinations of vectors in S; then V' is the *subspace spanned* by the vectors in S.

To justify this definition, we must prove that V' is a subspace.

THEOREM 2.2.2. The set V' of vectors spanned by $S = \{x^{(1)}, \ldots, x^{(r)}\}$ is a subspace.

Proof: We need only prove that (a) and (b) of Definition 2.2.4 hold. If $x = \sum k_i x^{(i)}$ and $y = \sum h_i x^{(i)}$ then, using A1, A2, S3, and S4, we have

$$x + y = \sum k_i x^{(i)} + \sum h_i x^{(i)} = \sum (k_i + h_i)x^{(i)}$$

so that $x + y$ is a linear combination of vectors in S. Also, using S1 and S3,

$$kx = k \left(\sum k_i x^{(i)} \right) = \sum k(k_i x^{(i)}) = \sum (kk_i)x^{(i)},$$

which is a linear combination of vectors in S.

EXAMPLE 2.2.3. The set of all vectors spanned by the vectors [1, 0, 0] and [0, 1, 0] is the same as the set of all vectors in R_3 that have the last component zero. This is, of course, a plane in three-space, which is frequently called a "coordinate plane."

If S is any nonempty subset of V, we have seen that O can always be represented in at least *one* way as a linear combination of vectors in S. We now consider the case in which O can be represented in *only* one way as a linear combination of vectors in S.

DEFINITION 2.2.6. Let $S = \{x^{(1)}, \ldots, x^{(r)}\}$ be any nonempty set of vectors in V; then the vectors in S are said to be *linearly independent* if O is represented *uniquely* as a linear combination of the vectors in S.

An equivalent definition is: the vectors $x^{(1)}, \ldots, x^{(r)}$ in S are linearly independent if a relation of the form

(2.2.5) $$\sum_{i=1}^{r} k_i x^{(i)} = O$$

implies $k_i = 0$, for $i = 1, \ldots, r$.

THEOREM 2.2.3. If the vectors $x^{(1)}, \ldots, x^{(r)}$ in S are linearly independent, then every vector in V', the subspace they span, is represented *uniquely* as a linear combination of vectors in S.

Proof: Suppose there is a vector x in V' such that $x = \sum h_i x^{(i)}$ and $x = \sum k_i x^{(i)}$. Subtracting,

$$x - x = \sum h_i x^{(i)} - \sum k_i x^{(i)} = \sum (h_i - k_i)x^{(i)} = O.$$

Since the vectors in S are linearly independent, we have

$$h_i - k_i = 0 \quad \text{or} \quad h_i = k_i \quad \text{for} \quad i = 1, \ldots, r,$$

which proves that the two representations of x are identical.

DEFINITION 2.2.7. Let $V' \subset V$ be a subspace of V, and let $B = \{b^{(1)}, \ldots, b^{(r)}\}$ be a finite subset of V' that

(a) spans V', and
(b) is linearly independent.

Then the vectors in B are said to be a *basis for V'*. The *dimension of V'* is the number of elements in the basis.

If B is a basis for V', then by Theorem 2.2.3, every vector y in V' can be represented uniquely as a linear combination of vectors in B. For this reason we frequently call the numbers k_i in the expression $y = \sum k_i b^{(i)}$ the *coordinates of y relative to the basis B*. Thus in a sense we can describe V' by using B. For this reason bases are important.

In Section 2.6 we will show that every basis for a subspace V' has the *same* number of elements. Hence the dimension of V' is a unique number and does not depend on the basis used to describe it.

Since V is a subspace of itself, it is possible for it to have a basis. If it does have a basis, it is called a *finite dimensional vector space*. In this book we shall study only finite dimensional vector spaces.

EXAMPLE 2.2.4. Consider the set R_3 of all three component row vectors. The *natural basis* for R_3 consists of the vectors

$$\{[1,\ 0,\ 0],\ [0,\ 1,\ 0],\ [0,\ 0,\ 1]\}.$$

Let us prove that they are linearly independent. If

$$k_1[1,\ 0,\ 0] + k_2[0,\ 1,\ 0] + k_3[0,\ 0,\ 1] = [k_1,\ k_2,\ k_3] = [0,\ 0,\ 0],$$

then clearly $k_1 = k_2 = k_3 = 0$, so they are linearly independent. Similarly, if $[a,\ b,\ c]$ is *any* vector in R_3, then

$$[a,\ b,\ c] = a[1,\ 0,\ 0] + b[0,\ 1,\ 0] + c[0,\ 0,\ 1]$$

so that the vectors span R_3. Hence, they are a basis for it.

Similarly, in R_m the set of m distinct vectors having all components equal to zero except for exactly one component that is equal to 1 is the natural basis for R_m. The natural basis for C_n is defined similarly. In Section 2.5 we shall present an algorithm for finding a basis for any finite subset of vectors in R_m or C_n.

EXERCISES 2.2

1. Show that the O element whose existence is assumed in axiom A3 is unique. (*Hint:* Assume there are two such elements and show that they are equal.)

2. Show that the additive inverse, $-x$, of axiom A4 is unique.

3. Show that P_2, the set of all polynomials of degree at most 1, satisfies axioms A1–A4 and S1–S4.

4. Show that the set of all polynomials of degree *exactly* 1 is not a vector space.

5. Show that a polynomial of degree at most 1 has a graph that is a nonvertical straight line in the plane. Hence give a geometric description of the set P_2.

6. Give a geometric description of the set P_3 of all polynomials of degree at most 2. (*Hint:* Follow the method given in Exercises 3 and 4.)

7. Consider the vectors

$$x^{(1)} = \begin{bmatrix} 3 \\ 0 \\ -2 \end{bmatrix}, \qquad x^{(2)} = \begin{bmatrix} -1 \\ 1 \\ -1 \end{bmatrix}, \qquad x^{(3)} = \begin{bmatrix} 3 \\ 0 \\ 4 \end{bmatrix}, \qquad x^{(4)} = \begin{bmatrix} 1 \\ -2 \\ 3 \end{bmatrix}.$$

(a) Find the vector that is the linear combination of these vectors with weights $k_1 = 2$, $k_2 = -1$, $k_3 = 5$, and $k_4 = 6$.

(b) Divide the k's in (a) by a suitable number so that the linear combination becomes a weighted combination.

(c) Is the result in (b) a convex combination of the vectors?

8. Prove that if $z = \sum k_i y^{(i)}$ is a linear combination of vectors and if, for each i, $y^{(i)} = \sum h_{ij} x^{(j)}$ is a linear combination of vectors, then z is a linear combination of the vectors $x^{(j)}$.

9. Is a weighted combination of weighted combinations of vectors also a weighted combination of vectors? (*Hint:* Rework Exercise 8 with $\sum k_i = 1$ and $\sum h_{ij} = 1$.)

10. Is a convex combination of convex combinations of vectors also a convex combination of vectors? (*Hint:* Rework Exercise 9 with $k_i \geq 0$ and $h_{ij} \geq 0$.)

11. Sketch in three-space the planes that are the set of all linear combinations of the following sets of vectors:

(a) [0, 1, 1], [1, 0, 1],

(b) [-1, 0, 0], [0, -1, -1],

(c) [1, 1, 1], [0, 1, 1].

12. Which of the following subsets of C_3, defined by putting constraints on the components of a typical vector

$$X = \begin{bmatrix} x_1 \\ x_2 \\ x_3 \end{bmatrix},$$

are subspaces of C_3?

(a) The set of all vectors such that $x_1 = 0$.

(b) The set of all vectors such that $x_3 = 1$.

(c) The set of all vectors such that $3x_1 - 2x_2 - x_4 = 0$.

(d) The set of all vectors such that $x_2 = 1 - x_3 + 4x_2$.

(e) The set of all vectors such that $x_1{}^2 = x_2$.

(f) The set of all vectors such that $\sqrt{x_1{}^2} = 0$.

(g) The set of all vectors such that $\sqrt{x_1{}^2} = 1$.

13. Which of the following sets of vectors are linearly independent and which are linearly dependent?

(a) $\begin{bmatrix} 1 \\ 0 \\ 0 \end{bmatrix}, \begin{bmatrix} 0 \\ 1 \\ 0 \end{bmatrix}, \begin{bmatrix} 5 \\ 4 \\ 0 \end{bmatrix}.$

(b) $\begin{bmatrix} 2 \\ -3 \end{bmatrix}, \begin{bmatrix} -5 \\ 7 \end{bmatrix}, \begin{bmatrix} 1 \\ 9 \end{bmatrix}.$

(c) $\begin{bmatrix} 3 \\ 2 \\ 1 \end{bmatrix}, \begin{bmatrix} 5 \\ 0 \\ -4 \end{bmatrix}, \begin{bmatrix} 11 \\ 4 \\ -2 \end{bmatrix}.$

(d) [5, 2, 7], [15, 6, 21].

(e) [4, 0, 5], [0, 1, -6], [3, 0, 4].

14. Let $x^{(1)}$, $x^{(2)}$, and $x^{(3)}$ be three linearly independent vectors in C_3. If we use them as a basis for the space, show that their coordinates relative to this basis are

$$\begin{bmatrix} 1 \\ 0 \\ 0 \end{bmatrix}, \quad \begin{bmatrix} 0 \\ 1 \\ 0 \end{bmatrix}, \quad \begin{bmatrix} 0 \\ 0 \\ 1 \end{bmatrix}.$$

(*Hint:* Observe that $x^{(1)} = 1x^{(1)} + 0x^{(2)} + 0x^{(3)}$.)

15. Let A_1, A_2, A_3 be vectors in C_3, and let A be the matrix with these vectors as columns. If b is any other vector in C_3, show that, in order to find whether b is a linear combination of the columns of A, we must solve the equation $A_1 x_1 + A_2 x_2 + A_3 x_3 = b$, where the x_i's are unknowns (variables).

16. Determine whether the vector

$$\begin{bmatrix} 1 \\ 2 \\ -2 \end{bmatrix}$$

is a linear combination of the following sets of vectors:

(a) $$\begin{bmatrix} 1 \\ 0 \\ 0 \end{bmatrix}, \quad \begin{bmatrix} 0 \\ 1 \\ 0 \end{bmatrix}, \quad \begin{bmatrix} 0 \\ 0 \\ 1 \end{bmatrix}.$$

(b) $$\begin{bmatrix} 1 \\ 2 \\ 0 \end{bmatrix}, \quad \begin{bmatrix} -2 \\ 1 \\ 0 \end{bmatrix}.$$

(c) $$\begin{bmatrix} -1 \\ 0 \\ -4 \end{bmatrix}, \quad \begin{bmatrix} 3 \\ 4 \\ 0 \end{bmatrix}.$$

(d) $$\begin{bmatrix} 1 \\ 0 \\ -5 \end{bmatrix}, \quad \begin{bmatrix} 3 \\ -5 \\ -3 \end{bmatrix}, \quad \begin{bmatrix} -2 \\ 4 \\ 3 \end{bmatrix}.$$

17. If V' is a subspace of a vector space V and V'' is a subspace of V', show that V'' is a subspace of V.

18. Show that the intersection of two subspaces of a vector space V is a vector space.

19. Let V' be spanned by the vectors $x^{(1)}, \ldots, x^{(k)}$ and let V'' be spanned by the vectors $x^{(1)}, \ldots, x^{(k)}, z$. Show that $V'' = V'$ if and only if z is a linear combination of $x^{(1)}, \ldots, x^{(k)}$.

2.3   MULTIPLICATION OF VECTORS AND MATRICES

So far we have considered only the addition and scalar multiplication of vectors and matrices. There are instances in which we will want to multiply two vectors together, as the following example shows.

EXAMPLE 2.3.1. A man goes to a supermarket and buys 6 lemons, 12 eggs, and 3 pounds of chicken. If the prices are 4¢ per lemon, 6¢ per egg, and 40¢ per pound of chicken, what is his bill? Let us reformulate his purchases in terms of vectors: his purchases (demands) are given by the row vector $d = [6, \ 12, \ 3]$, and the prices by the column vector $p = \begin{bmatrix} 4 \\ 6 \\ 40 \end{bmatrix}$. We want to calculate the product dp. The way the cashier figures it is

$$dp = [6, \ 12, \ 3] \begin{bmatrix} 4 \\ 6 \\ 40 \end{bmatrix} = 6 \cdot 4 + 12 \cdot 6 + 3 \cdot 40 = 24 + 72 + 120 = 216,$$

or \$2.16. She performs this multiplication with a cash register that does "cumulative multiplications."

A flow diagram of cumulative multiplication, which we shall take as our definition of vector multiplication, is given in Figure 2.3.1 for the case of multiplying a k-component row vector w by a k-component column vector x.

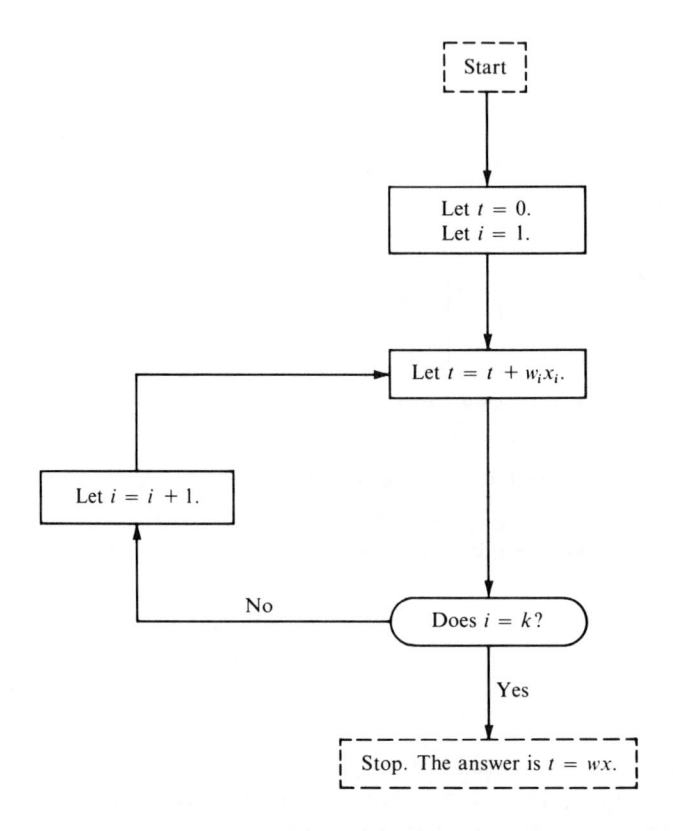

FIGURE 2.3.1

DEFINITION 2.3.1. Let w be a row vector and x a column vector, each having k components. Then the product, wx, is defined by

$$(2.3.1) \qquad wx = [w_1, \ldots, w_k]\begin{bmatrix} x_1 \\ \vdots \\ x_k \end{bmatrix} = w_1 x_1 + \cdots + w_k x_k = \sum_{i=1}^{k} w_i x_i.$$

The process of carrying out this computation is given by the flow diagram in Figure 2.3.1.

Note that the result of the multiplication of a row vector times a column vector is a *number*. Note also that we can carry out the multiplication *only* when the two vectors have the *same* number of components.

Some examples of vector multiplication are:

$$[1, \ -2, \ 3]\begin{bmatrix} 1 \\ 1 \\ 1 \end{bmatrix} = 1 \cdot 1 - 2 \cdot 1 + 3 \cdot 1 = 1 - 2 + 3 = 2,$$

and

$$[1, \ 0, \ 0]\begin{bmatrix} 0 \\ -5 \\ 6 \end{bmatrix} = 1 \cdot 0 + 0 \cdot (-5) + 0 \cdot 6 = 0 + 0 + 0 = 0.$$

The second example shows that the product of two nonzero vectors can equal 0. Another such example is

$$[2, \ -1]\begin{bmatrix} 1 \\ 2 \end{bmatrix} = 2 \cdot 1 - 1 \cdot 2 = 2 - 2 = 0.$$

We next show how to define the product of matrices that are more general than row vectors times column vectors.

DEFINITION 2.3.2. Let A be an $m \times k$ matrix and let B be a $k \times n$ matrix; then the product matrix $C = AB$ is defined to be the $m \times n$ matrix whose components are

$$c_{ij} = [a_{i1}, \ \ldots, \ a_{ik}]\begin{bmatrix} b_{1j} \\ \vdots \\ b_{kj} \end{bmatrix} = a_{i1}b_{1j} + \cdots + a_{ik}b_{kj}.$$

In other words, the i, jth entry of C is the product of the ith row of A times the jth column of B.

There are several things to note about the definition. First, the multiplication of A times B is defined *only* if the number of columns of A is equal to the number of rows of B. Second, the number of rows of A and C are the same, and the number of columns of B and C are the same. The following equation indicates this clearly:

$$(2.3.2) \qquad\qquad A_{m \times k} B_{k \times n} = C_{m \times n}.$$

Finally, note that the product of A and B is obtained by repeated application of the definition of a row vector times a column vector given in Definition 2.3.1.

Some examples of matrix multiplication are as follows.

$$[1 \quad -1 \quad 0]\begin{bmatrix} 6 & -2 \\ -3 & 5 \\ 2 & -2 \end{bmatrix} = [9 \quad -7]$$

$$\begin{bmatrix} 6 & -2 \\ -3 & 5 \\ 2 & -2 \end{bmatrix}\begin{bmatrix} 2 \\ 1 \end{bmatrix} = \begin{bmatrix} 10 \\ -1 \\ 2 \end{bmatrix}$$

$$\begin{bmatrix} 1 & -2 & 3 \\ 1 & -1 & 0 \end{bmatrix}\begin{bmatrix} 6 & -2 \\ -3 & 5 \\ 2 & -2 \end{bmatrix} = \begin{bmatrix} 18 & -18 \\ 9 & -7 \end{bmatrix}$$

$$\begin{bmatrix} 6 & -2 \\ -3 & 5 \\ 2 & -2 \end{bmatrix}\begin{bmatrix} 1 & -2 & 3 \\ 1 & -1 & 0 \end{bmatrix} = \begin{bmatrix} 4 & -10 & 18 \\ 2 & 1 & -9 \\ 0 & -2 & 6 \end{bmatrix}$$

You should be sure to note that the product, AB, is defined in that order. It may or may not be possible to define the other product, BA. And even when it is possible, the result may be quite different. Thus, if

$$A = \begin{bmatrix} 1 & 0 \\ 1 & 0 \end{bmatrix} \quad \text{and} \quad B = \begin{bmatrix} 0 & 0 \\ 1 & 1 \end{bmatrix},$$

then

$$AB = \begin{bmatrix} 1 & 0 \\ 1 & 0 \end{bmatrix}\begin{bmatrix} 0 & 0 \\ 1 & 1 \end{bmatrix} = \begin{bmatrix} 0 & 0 \\ 0 & 0 \end{bmatrix},$$

whereas

$$BA = \begin{bmatrix} 0 & 0 \\ 1 & 1 \end{bmatrix}\begin{bmatrix} 1 & 0 \\ 1 & 0 \end{bmatrix} = \begin{bmatrix} 0 & 0 \\ 2 & 0 \end{bmatrix}.$$

It is clear the $AB \neq BA$.

The multiplication of matrices satisfies some rules that are contained in the following theorem.

THEOREM 2.3.1. Let A, B, and C be matrices of suitable shapes, and let k be a number. Then when the products listed below are defined on either side of the equation, they will be defined on the other side of the equation and they will be equal:

M1. $A(BC) = (AB)C$ (Associative law of multiplication)
M2. $A(kB) = k(AB) = (kA)B$ (Mixed associative law for multiplication)
M3. $A(B + C) = AB + AC$ (Left-hand distributive law)
M4. $(A + B)C = AC + BC$ (Right-hand distributive law)

The proofs of these rules are straightforward and are outlined in Exercises 4–7.

DEFINITION 2.3.3. Let A be an $m \times n$ matrix with components a_{ij}. Then the *transpose of A*, denoted by A', is the $n \times m$ matrix obtained by interchanging rows and columns of A; that is,

$$(2.3.3) \qquad\qquad a'_{ij} = a_{ji}.$$

For instance, the transpose of

$$A = \begin{bmatrix} 6 & -2 \\ -3 & 5 \\ 2 & -2 \end{bmatrix} \quad \text{is the matrix} \quad A' = \begin{bmatrix} 6 & -3 & 2 \\ -2 & 5 & -2 \end{bmatrix}.$$

The transpose of the matrix

$$\begin{bmatrix} 1 & 2 \\ 3 & 4 \end{bmatrix} \quad \text{is the matrix} \quad \begin{bmatrix} 1 & 3 \\ 2 & 4 \end{bmatrix}.$$

THEOREM 2.3.2. The transpose operation satisfies the following identities:

$$(A')' = A,$$
$$(AB)' = B'A',$$
$$(A + B)' = A' + B'.$$

The proofs of these results are outlined in Exercises 9–11.

The final topic of this section will be that of *partitioned matrices*. To explain this concept, let us define a guillotine cut in a matrix. A *guillotine cut* in a matrix is a partition of the rows or columns into two nonempty disjoint sets. It can be represented by a line drawn between two rows or two columns. For instance, the matrix

$$A = \left[\begin{array}{cc|ccc} 1 & 0 & 0 & 0 & 0 \\ 0 & 1 & 0 & 0 & 0 \\ \hline 1 & 2 & 4 & -6 & 0 \\ 3 & -1 & -1 & 0 & 5 \end{array} \right]$$

has two guillotine cuts indicated by the lines. Note that we can write A as

$$A = \begin{bmatrix} A_{11} & A_{12} \\ A_{21} & A_{22} \end{bmatrix},$$

where the A_{ij}'s are the matrices into which A is divided by the cuts. Consider now the partitioned matrix

$$B = \left[\begin{array}{cc|cc} 5 & 4 & 1 & 1 \\ 3 & -1 & -1 & -1 \\ \hline -3 & 4 & 0 & 0 \\ 0 & -1 & 0 & 0 \\ -1 & 0 & 0 & 1 \end{array} \right].$$

Note that B can be written as

$$B = \begin{bmatrix} B_{11} & B_{12} \\ B_{21} & B_{22} \end{bmatrix},$$

with the B_{ij}'s defined by the partitions. Suppose now that we want to multiply A times B. Since A has five columns and B has five rows, this is possible. Moreover since the partition of the columns of A agrees with the partition of the rows of B, we can carry out the multiplication in "block form," as follows:

$$AB = \begin{bmatrix} A_{11} & A_{12} \\ A_{21} & A_{22} \end{bmatrix} \begin{bmatrix} B_{11} & B_{12} \\ B_{21} & B_{22} \end{bmatrix} = \begin{bmatrix} A_{11}B_{11} + A_{12}B_{21} & A_{11}B_{12} + A_{12}B_{22} \\ A_{21}B_{11} + A_{22}B_{21} & A_{21}B_{12} + A_{22}B_{22} \end{bmatrix}.$$

If we carry out this multiplication we find the result to be:

$$AB = \left[\begin{array}{cc|cc} 5 & 4 & 1 & 1 \\ 3 & -1 & -1 & -1 \\ \hline -1 & 24 & -1 & -1 \\ 10 & 9 & 4 & 9 \end{array} \right].$$

Note that the rows in the product matrix are partitioned like the rows of A and that the columns are partitioned like the columns of B. Block multiplication is particularly useful when some of the blocks, such as A_{12} above, are zero matrices. We will find other uses for partitioned matrices in the creation of tableaus for computations—for example, in the simplex method of linear programming to be discussed in the next two chapters.

EXERCISES 2.3

1. Consider the following vectors:

$$x = [5, \; -4, \; 7] \qquad y = [2, \; -4, \; 0] \qquad z = [1, \; -2] \qquad t = \begin{bmatrix} 3 \\ -3 \end{bmatrix}$$

$$w = \begin{bmatrix} 2 \\ 0 \\ -2 \end{bmatrix} \qquad v = \begin{bmatrix} 1 \\ -1 \\ 0 \end{bmatrix} \qquad e = [1, 1, 1] \qquad f = \begin{bmatrix} 1 \\ 1 \\ 1 \end{bmatrix}$$

When possible compute the following quantities:

   (a) xf (b) ew (c) $(x + y)(w + v)$

   (d) $\dfrac{1}{2}(x + y)f$ (e) $e(5w - 4v)$ (f) zt

                          (g) $\dfrac{1}{2}(x + z)f$

2. For Exercise 2 give interpretations for the answers found in parts (a), (b), (d), and (e) of Exercise 1.

3. Consider the following matrices:

$$A = \begin{bmatrix} 1 & 0 & 0 \\ 0 & 0 & 1 \\ 0 & 1 & 0 \end{bmatrix} \qquad B = \begin{bmatrix} -2 & 3 & 0 \\ 4 & 0 & -5 \\ 0 & 6 & 2 \end{bmatrix} \qquad C = \begin{bmatrix} 1 & -1 \\ 1 & -2 \\ 1 & -3 \end{bmatrix}$$

$$D = \begin{bmatrix} -3 & 2 & -1 & 1 \\ 6 & -5 & 0 & 1 \end{bmatrix} \qquad G = \begin{bmatrix} 0 & 1 \\ -5 & -1 \end{bmatrix} \qquad H = \begin{bmatrix} 0 & 0 \\ -1 & 1 \end{bmatrix}$$

Perform the following operations when possible, utilizing when necessary the vectors e and f of Exercise 1.

(a) AB (b) CA (c) ABC
(d) Bf (interpret the answer)   (e) eB (interpret the answer)
(f) DG (g) DGH (h) Show that $GH \neq HG$
(i) DC (j) eC (interpret answer)
(k) $(A + B)C$

4. Assume that $A_{m \times k}$, $B_{k \times h}$, and $C_{h \times n}$ are three matrices with dimensions as indicated. Write out expressions for the i, jth entry of both sides of the equation

$$A(BC) = (AB)C$$

by using summation notation. Use the fact that the order of summations can be interchanged to show that the expressions are equal.

5. Prove rule M2 of Theorem 2.3.1 by writing out a summation expression for the left-hand side.

6. By writing out the summation expression for the left-hand expression of M3, show that it can be changed into the expression for the right-hand side.

7. Prove M4 by a technique similar to that used in Exercise 6.

8. Find the transposed matrices of the matrices A, B, C, D, G, and H of Exercise 3.

9. Prove that $(AB)' = B'A'$ by carrying out the following steps:
   (a) Write an expression for the i, jth term of AB.
   (b) Show that this is the j, ith term of $(AB)'$.
   (c) Write an expression for the j, ith term of $B'A'$.
   (d) Show that the expressions in (b) and (c) are the same.

10. Prove that $(A + B)' = A' + B'$ by carrying out steps analogous to those in Exercise 8.

11. Show that $(A')' = A$.

12. If A is $m \times n$, show that $O_{k \times m} A = O_{k \times n}$ and $AO_{n \times h} = O_{m \times h}$.

13. If A has a zero row show that AB does also.

14. If A has two equal rows show that AB does also.

15. If $x \neq O$ is such that $xA = O$, show that $xC = O$, where $C = AB$.

16. If $y \neq O$ satisfies $By = O$, show that $Cy = O$ where $C = AB$.

17. Use Exercise 15 to show that the maximum number of linearly independent rows of AB is at most as many as the maximum number of linearly independent rows of A.

18. Use Exercise 16 to show that the maximum number of linearly independent columns of AB is at most as many as the maximum number of linearly independent columns of B.

19. A square matrix A is said to be *symmetric* if $A = A'$. Which of the following matrices is symmetric?

(a) $\begin{bmatrix} 0 & 1 & 0 & 0 \\ 1 & 0 & 5 & -1 \\ 0 & 5 & 1 & 0 \\ 0 & -1 & 0 & 10 \end{bmatrix}$ (b) $\begin{bmatrix} 0 & 1 & 0 \\ 0 & 0 & 1 \\ 1 & 0 & 0 \end{bmatrix}$

(c) $\begin{bmatrix} 1 & 0 & 1 \\ 0 & -1 & 2 \\ 1 & -2 & 3 \end{bmatrix}$ (d) $\begin{bmatrix} 0 & 1 & 2 & 3 \\ 1 & 1 & 4 & 5 \\ 2 & 4 & 2 & 6 \\ 3 & 5 & 6 & 3 \end{bmatrix}$

20. If A is *any* square matrix, show that $B = \frac{1}{2}(A + A')$ is a symmetric matrix.

21. A square matrix A is said to be *skew-symmetric* if $A = -A'$. Which of the following matrices are skew-symmetric?

(a) $\begin{bmatrix} 0 & -1 & 2 \\ 1 & 0 & -3 \\ -2 & 3 & 0 \end{bmatrix}$

(b) $\begin{bmatrix} 0 & 1 & 2 & 3 \\ -1 & 0 & 1 & 2 \\ -2 & -1 & 0 & 1 \\ -3 & -2 & -1 & 0 \end{bmatrix}$

(c) $\begin{bmatrix} 1 & 1 & 0 \\ 1 & 1 & 1 \\ 0 & 1 & 1 \end{bmatrix}$

(d) $\begin{bmatrix} 0 & 1 & 0 \\ -1 & 0 & -1 \\ 0 & 1 & 0 \end{bmatrix}$

22. Show that a square matrix A is skew-symmetric only if $a_{ii} = 0$ for all i.

23. If A is any square matrix, show that $C = \frac{1}{2}(A - A')$ is skew-symmetric.

24. If A is any square matrix and B and C are as defined in Exercises 20 and 23, show that $A = B + C$. Hence conclude that any square matrix can be written as the sum of a symmetric and a skew-symmetric matrix.

25. Square the matrices in Exercise 21(a), (b), and (d), and show that they are symmetric.

26. Prove that the square of a skew-symmetric matrix is symmetric.

27. Use block operations to carry out the matrix product BA for the partitioned matrices on page 75. Display the product of each block used in the calculation.

28. Perform the following matrix multiplications using block operations. Partition each matrix first to simplify calculations.

(a) $\begin{bmatrix} 5 & 0 & 1 & 0 \\ 1 & 0 & 0 & 1 \\ 0 & 1 & 6 & -7 \\ 1 & 0 & -7 & 6 \end{bmatrix}^2$

(b) $\begin{bmatrix} 1 & 0 & 7 & 6 \\ 0 & 1 & -2 & 3 \\ 0 & 0 & 4 & -5 \\ 0 & 0 & -7 & 8 \end{bmatrix} \begin{bmatrix} 12 & -2 & 5 & -4 \\ -4 & 11 & -3 & -2 \\ 1 & 0 & 0 & 0 \\ 0 & 1 & 0 & 0 \end{bmatrix}$

2.4 SQUARE MATRICES

Square matrices are important for many applications in later parts of this book. Hence we devote the present section to their discussion. All matrices in this section will be assumed to be square.

The *main diagonal* of a square matrix A consists of the entries a_{ii}—that is, it starts at the upper left-hand corner and proceeds downward to the lower right-hand corner. For instance, the $n \times n$ *identity matrix*, $I_{n \times n}$, has 1's on the main diagonal and 0's elsewhere. Examples of the 2×2, 3×3, and 4×4 identity matrices are:

$$\begin{bmatrix} 1 & 0 \\ 0 & 1 \end{bmatrix} \quad \begin{bmatrix} 1 & 0 & 0 \\ 0 & 1 & 0 \\ 0 & 0 & 1 \end{bmatrix} \quad \begin{bmatrix} 1 & 0 & 0 & 0 \\ 0 & 1 & 0 & 0 \\ 0 & 0 & 1 & 0 \\ 0 & 0 & 0 & 1 \end{bmatrix}.$$

As observed in the exercises of the previous section, the identity and zero matrices satisfy special multiplication identities. Namely,

$$IA = AI = A$$

and

$$OA = AO = O$$

for any (square matrix) A.

We will be particularly interested in matrices A and B such that $AB = I$. Consider the matrices

$$A = \begin{bmatrix} 2 & 5 \\ 1 & 3 \end{bmatrix} \quad \text{and} \quad B = \begin{bmatrix} 3 & -5 \\ -1 & 2 \end{bmatrix}.$$

By direct multiplication we can show that

$$AB = \begin{bmatrix} 2 & 5 \\ 1 & 3 \end{bmatrix} \begin{bmatrix} 3 & -5 \\ -1 & 2 \end{bmatrix} = \begin{bmatrix} 1 & 0 \\ 0 & 1 \end{bmatrix};$$

$$BA = \begin{bmatrix} 3 & -5 \\ -1 & 2 \end{bmatrix} \begin{bmatrix} 2 & 5 \\ 1 & 3 \end{bmatrix} = \begin{bmatrix} 1 & 0 \\ 0 & 1 \end{bmatrix}.$$

DEFINITION 2.4.1. If A is a square matrix and B is such that $BA = AB = I$, then B is called the *inverse* of A and denoted by A^{-1}. A matrix A that possesses an inverse is said to be *nonsingular*. If A has no inverse, it is *singular*.

It can be shown, although we will not do so here, that if B is such that $AB = I$, then $BA = I$ also.

To justify this definition, we must prove that A^{-1}, if it exists, is unique.

THEOREM 2.4.1. If $AB = BA = I$ and if $AC = CA = I$, then $B = C = A^{-1}$.

Proof: Start with $AB=I$. Multiply on the left by C to get

(2.4.1) $$CAB = C(AB) = (CA)B = IB = B.$$

Next start with $CA = I$; multiply on the right by B to get

(2.4.2) $$CAB = (CA)B = C(AB) = CI = C.$$

From (2.4.1) and (2.4.2) we can see that $CAB = C = B$, as was to be shown.

THEOREM 2.4.2. If A and B are nonsingular matrices, then so is AB; moreover, $(AB)^{-1} = B^{-1}A^{-1}$.

Proof: By direct computation we have

$$(AB)(B^{-1}A^{-1}) = (AB)(B^{-1})A^{-1} = A(BB^{-1})A^{-1} = AA^{-1} = I,$$

and

$$(B^{-1}A^{-1})(AB) = B^{-1}(A^{-1}A)B = B^{-1}B = I.$$

So by Definition 2.4.1, AB is nonsingular and $(AB)^{-1} = B^{-1}A^{-1}$.

COROLLARY. The product of any number of nonsingular matrices is nonsingular; the inverse of the product is the product of inverses in reverse order.

Since $II = I$ it is obvious that the identity matrix I is nonsingular and that $I^{-1} = I$—that is, I is its own inverse. In order to have other examples of nonsingular matrices, we define permutation matrices.

DEFINITION 2.4.2. A *permutation matrix* is a square matrix having only 0 and 1 entries and such that in each row and each column there is exactly one 1 entry.

Clearly, the $n \times n$ identity matrix I is also a permutation matrix for every n. Other examples are:

$$\begin{bmatrix} 0 & 1 & 0 \\ 0 & 0 & 1 \\ 1 & 0 & 0 \end{bmatrix} \quad \begin{bmatrix} 1 & 0 & 0 & 0 \\ 0 & 0 & 1 & 0 \\ 0 & 0 & 0 & 1 \\ 0 & 1 & 0 & 0 \end{bmatrix} \quad \begin{bmatrix} 0 & 1 & 0 & 0 \\ 1 & 0 & 0 & 0 \\ 0 & 0 & 0 & 1 \\ 0 & 0 & 1 & 0 \end{bmatrix}.$$

The reason for the name *permutation matrix* is that when a vector is multiplied by one of these matrices, its components are interchanged, or permuted. (See Exercises 4 and 5.) Permutation matrices have several other important properties and are useful in many applications.

THEOREM 2.4.3. If P is a permutation matrix, then $P^{-1} = P'$.

Proof: Consider the ith row of P. Suppose the unique nonzero entry is $p_{ik} = 1$; then $p_{ki}' = 1$. Consider the product $C = PP'$. Since $p_{ij} = 0$ for $j \neq k$, and $p_{kj}' = 0$ for $j \neq i$, we see that $c_{ii} = 1$ and $c_{ij} = 0$ for $j \neq i$. Hence $C = I$, and therefore $P' = P^{-1}$, as was to be shown.

Another important nonsingular matrix is a *pivot matrix*, which we will introduce with an example.

EXAMPLE 2.4.1. Let a be a three-component column vector such that $a_2 \neq 0$. Consider the matrix Q that is obtained from the 3×3 identity matrix when the second column of $I_{3 \times 3}$ is replaced by a:

$$Q = \begin{bmatrix} 1 & a_1 & 0 \\ 0 & a_2 & 0 \\ 0 & a_3 & 1 \end{bmatrix}.$$

It is easy to find the inverse of Q, which is

$$Q^{-1} = P = \begin{bmatrix} 1 & -a_1/a_2 & 0 \\ 0 & 1/a_2 & 0 \\ 0 & -a_3/a_2 & 1 \end{bmatrix}.$$

To check, let us compute

$$QP = \begin{bmatrix} 1 & a_1 & 0 \\ 0 & a_2 & 0 \\ 0 & a_3 & 1 \end{bmatrix} \begin{bmatrix} 1 & -a_1/a_2 & 0 \\ 0 & 1/a_2 & 0 \\ 0 & -a_3/a_2 & 1 \end{bmatrix} = \begin{bmatrix} 1 & 0 & 0 \\ 0 & 1 & 0 \\ 0 & 0 & 1 \end{bmatrix}.$$

You should also check that $PQ = I$. The pivot matrix formed from A is the matrix $P = Q^{-1}$.

DEFINITION 2.4.3. Let a be a nonzero n-component column vector such that $a_i \neq 0$. Then $P(a, i)$, the ith *pivot matrix formed from* a, is the matrix obtained by replacing the ith column of $I_{n \times n}$ by the vector

$$
\begin{bmatrix}
-a_1/a_i \\
\vdots \\
-a_{i-1}/a_i \\
1/a_i \\
-a_{i+1}/a_i \\
\vdots \\
-a_n/a_i
\end{bmatrix}.
$$

Note that the ith pivot matrix can be formed if and only if $a_i \neq 0$.

THEOREM 2.4.4. If a is an n-component column vector with $a_i \neq 0$, then the ith pivot matrix $P(a, i)$ formed from a is nonsingular, and its inverse is obtained by replacing the ith column of I by a.

The proof of this theorem is Exercise 10. Note that Example 2.4.1 illustrates the theorem when $n = 3$.

EXAMPLE 2.4.2. Consider the five vectors A, B, C, X, and Y shown in Figure 2.4.1. Initially, A, B, and C are the basis vectors, so they have coordinates consisting of all zeros except for one 1 as shown. In this basis system the coordinates of

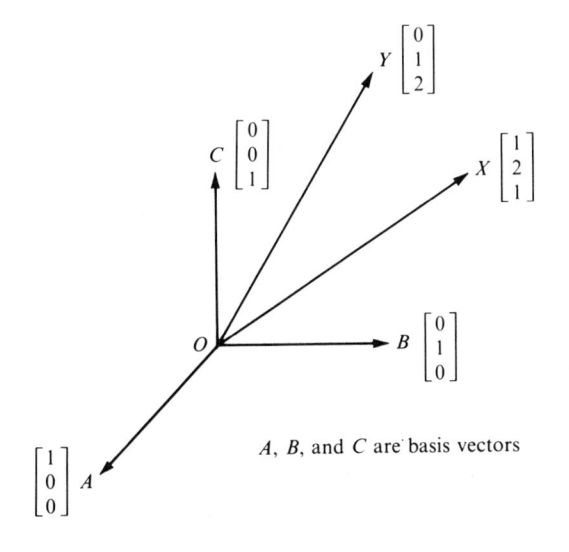

FIGURE 2.4.1

X and Y are as shown. Because the coordinates are as shown, we know that the following linear relationships hold:

$$X = A + 2B + C \quad \text{and} \quad Y = B + 2C.$$

Suppose now that we wanted to introduce X into the basis and take B out of the basis. One way to do this is to solve these two linear relations for B and Y in terms of A, X, and C. This gives

$$B = -\frac{1}{2}A + \frac{1}{2}X - \frac{1}{2}C \quad \text{and} \quad Y = -\frac{1}{2}A + \frac{1}{2}X + \frac{3}{2}C.$$

In other words the coordinates of B and Y relative to the basis consisting of A, X, and C are

$$B = \begin{bmatrix} -\frac{1}{2} \\ \frac{1}{2} \\ -\frac{1}{2} \end{bmatrix} \quad \text{and} \quad Y = \begin{bmatrix} -\frac{1}{2} \\ \frac{1}{2} \\ \frac{3}{2} \end{bmatrix}.$$

The new coordinates of all five vectors are shown in Figure 2.4.2.

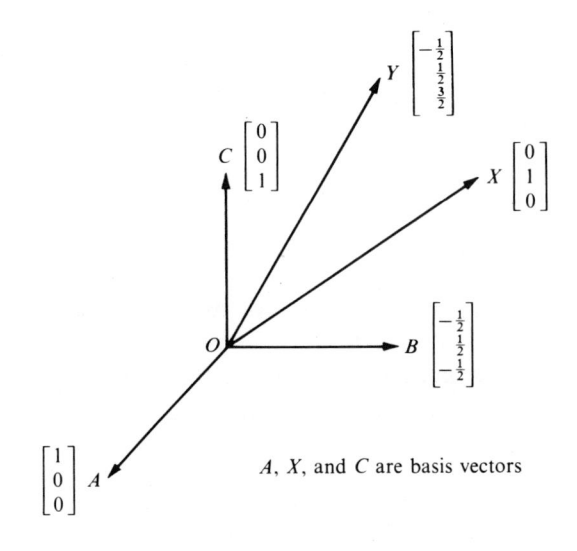

FIGURE 2.4.2

Another way to calculate the change is to compute $P(X, 2)$ as shown.

$$P(X, 2) = \begin{bmatrix} 1 & -\frac{1}{2} & 0 \\ 0 & \frac{1}{2} & 0 \\ 0 & -\frac{1}{2} & 1 \end{bmatrix}$$

We can then calculate the new coordinates of Y and B as follows:

$$B = \begin{bmatrix} 1 & -\frac{1}{2} & 0 \\ 0 & \frac{1}{2} & 0 \\ 0 & -\frac{1}{2} & 1 \end{bmatrix} \begin{bmatrix} 0 \\ 1 \\ 0 \end{bmatrix} = \begin{bmatrix} -\frac{1}{2} \\ \frac{1}{2} \\ -\frac{1}{2} \end{bmatrix},$$

$$Y = \begin{bmatrix} 1 & -\frac{1}{2} & 0 \\ 0 & \frac{1}{2} & 0 \\ 0 & -\frac{1}{2} & 1 \end{bmatrix} \begin{bmatrix} 0 \\ 1 \\ 2 \end{bmatrix} = \begin{bmatrix} -\frac{1}{2} \\ \frac{1}{2} \\ \frac{3}{2} \end{bmatrix}.$$

We shall see that in general when we multiply vectors in C_n by a pivot matrix, we are, as above, changing the basis in C_n. That is, the effect of multiplying by a pivot matrix is to put a vector into the basis and take some other vector out of the basis. We will call this process "pivoting," and we will see that the reason for pivoting is to discover linear relationships among vectors.

THEOREM 2.4.5. Let $\{X_1, \ldots, X_n\}$ be a basis for C_n and suppose that the components of vectors A and B relative to this basis are the n-component column vectors a and b. Assume that $a_i \neq 0$ and let $P(a, i)$ be the ith pivot matrix formed from a. Then the components of B relative to the basis $\{X_1, \ldots, X_{i-1}, A, X_{i+1}, \ldots, X_n\}$ can be obtained from its coordinates relative to the original basis by calculating

$$
P(a, i)b =
\begin{bmatrix}
1 & & & -a_1/a_i & & & \\
& \ddots & & \vdots & & & \\
& & 1 & -a_{i-1}/a_i & & & \\
& & & 1/a_i & & & \\
& & & -a_{i+1}/a_i & 1 & & \\
& & & \vdots & & \ddots & \\
& & & -a_n/a_i & & & 1
\end{bmatrix}
\begin{bmatrix}
b_1 \\
\vdots \\
b_{i-1} \\
b_i \\
b_{i+1} \\
\vdots \\
b_n
\end{bmatrix}.
$$

Proof: We know that $A = a_1 X_1 + \cdots + a_i X_i + \cdots + a_n X_n$, so in order to take X_i out of the basis and put A into the basis, we solve this equation for X_i and obtain

$$
X_i = \frac{1}{a_i}(-a_1 X_1 + \cdots - a_{i-1}X_{i-1} + A - a_{i+1}X_{i+1} - \cdots - a_n X_n).
$$

Substituting this into the expression for B we have

$$
B = b_1 X_1 + \cdots + b_{i-1}X_{i-1} + b_i X_i + b_{i+1}X_{i+1} + \cdots + bX,
$$

$$
= \left(b_1 - \frac{a_1 b_i}{a_i}\right)X_1 + \cdots + \left(b_{i-1} - \frac{a_{i-1}b_i}{a_i}\right)X_{i-1} + \frac{b_i}{a_i}A
$$

$$
+ \left(b_{i+1} - \frac{a_{i+1}b_i}{a_i}\right)X_{i+1} + \cdots + \left(b_n - \frac{a_n b_i}{a_i}\right)X_n.
$$

You should now check that these components are the same as those given by the product $P(a, i)b$ as given in the statement of the theorem.

As mentioned above, pivoting enables us to discover relationships among vectors that are obvious in one coordinate system but not in others. The final theorem of this section shows why this is important.

THEOREM 2.4.6. *Invariance of Linear Relations.* Let $S = \{A_1, \ldots, A_r\}$ be a set of column vectors in C_n, and let B be any nonsingular matrix. Then a linear relation of the form

(2.4.3)
$$
\sum_{i=1}^{r} k_i A_i = 0
$$

holds if and only if the linear relation

(2.4.4) $$\sum_{i=1}^{r} k_i\, BA_i = 0$$

holds.

Proof: If (2.4.3) holds, then multiplying both sides of the equation by B and using M2 gives (2.4.4). And if (2.4.4) holds, then multiplying both sides of that equation by B^{-1} (which is assumed to exist) and using M2 yields (2.4.3).

This theorem will be of fundamental importance for our future work. It says, in effect, that any linear relation discovered in one coordinate system (that is, one having any one set of basis elements) also holds in any other coordinate system (that is, one having any other set of basis elements). What we will do repeatedly in the future is employ pivoting operations to change from one basis to another. Each time we do we will discover new linear relations among the vectors. Theorem 2.4.6 tells us that, regardless of how they were discovered, these linear relationships hold in all coordinate systems.

We close this section by defining powers of a square matrix. If A is a square matrix then we can define the product A^3, which we call A^2 in analogy to the square of an ordinary number. Similarly, we define $A^3 = AAA$, and $A^n = AA \cdots A$ (n factors). A^n is called the *nth power of A*. Exercises 12–14 deal with powers of square matrices.

EXERCISES 2.4

1. Show that the following pairs of matrices are inverses.

   (a) $\begin{bmatrix} 1 & 0 & 0 \\ 0 & 2 & 0 \\ 0 & 0 & 3 \end{bmatrix}$ and $\begin{bmatrix} 1 & 0 & 0 \\ 0 & \frac{1}{2} & 0 \\ 0 & 0 & \frac{1}{3} \end{bmatrix}$

   (b) $\begin{bmatrix} 1 & 0 & 0 \\ 2 & 1 & 0 \\ 3 & 2 & 1 \end{bmatrix}$ and $\begin{bmatrix} 1 & 0 & 0 \\ -2 & 1 & 0 \\ 1 & -2 & 1 \end{bmatrix}$

   (c) $\begin{bmatrix} 1 & 3 & -2 \\ 0 & -5 & 4 \\ 2 & -3 & 3 \end{bmatrix}$ and $\begin{bmatrix} -3 & -3 & 2 \\ 8 & 7 & -4 \\ 10 & 9 & -5 \end{bmatrix}$

2. If A is a square matrix and $y \neq 0$ a vector such that $Ay = O$, then prove that A cannot have an inverse. (*Hint:* Assume the contrary and obtain a contradiction.)

3. Use the result of Exercise 2 to show that the following matrices do not have inverses.

   (a) $\begin{bmatrix} 0 & 0 \\ 1 & 2 \end{bmatrix}$

   (b) $\begin{bmatrix} 1 & -1 & 2 \\ -1 & 1 & -2 \\ 3 & -4 & 5 \end{bmatrix}$

   (c) $\begin{bmatrix} 1 & -2 & 3 \\ -4 & 5 & -6 \\ -3 & 3 & -3 \end{bmatrix}$

4. Let $x = [x_1, x_2, x_3, x_4]$ and consider the following permutation matrices.

$$P = \begin{bmatrix} 0 & 1 & 0 & 0 \\ 1 & 0 & 0 & 0 \\ 0 & 0 & 0 & 1 \\ 0 & 0 & 1 & 0 \end{bmatrix} \qquad Q = \begin{bmatrix} 0 & 1 & 0 & 0 \\ 0 & 0 & 1 & 0 \\ 0 & 0 & 0 & 1 \\ 1 & 0 & 0 & 0 \end{bmatrix} \qquad R = \begin{bmatrix} 0 & 1 & 0 & 0 \\ 0 & 0 & 1 & 0 \\ 1 & 0 & 0 & 0 \\ 0 & 0 & 0 & 1 \end{bmatrix}$$

(a) Show that xP is the vector x with the first two and last two components interchanged.

(b) Show that xQ is obtained from x by putting x_4 in place of x_1 and moving each other component one step to the right.

(c) Describe the effect of xR.

(d) Prove that any 4×4 permutation matrix will merely interchange the components of x when x is multiplied by it.

5. Let x be an n-component row vector and P an $n \times n$ permutation matrix. Prove that the vector xP is obtained from x by relisting its components in some order. (*Hint:* Use the definition of a permutation matrix.)

6. (a) If P is an $n \times n$ permutation matrix that sends x_i into x_j's spot, show that P' (its transpose) will send x_j into x_i's spot.

(b) Use the statement in (a) to prove Theorem 2.4.3, which states that P' is the inverse of P.

(c) Show that $(P')^{-1} = P$.

7. Find the inverses of the permutation matrices given in Exercise 4.

8. Consider the vectors:

$$a = \begin{bmatrix} -1 \\ 2 \\ 5 \end{bmatrix} \qquad b = \begin{bmatrix} 0 \\ 2 \\ \frac{1}{2} \\ -1 \end{bmatrix}$$

(a) Construct the pivot matrix $P(a, 2)$.

(b) Construct $P(a, 3)$.

(c) Construct $P(b, 4)$.

(d) Construct $P(b, 3)$.

(e) Is it possible to construct $P(b, 1)$?

9. Find the inverses of the pivot matrices found in Exercise 8 by using Theorem 2.4.4, and check to be sure they are correct.

10. Change the basis in Figure 2.4.1 by putting in Y and taking out C. Compute the new coordinates for all five vectors and mark them on a figure like 2.4.1.

11. Let a be an n-component vector, with $a_i \neq 0$. Construct $P(a, i)$. Then construct Q, the matrix obtained by replacing the ith column of I, the identity matrix, with a. Prove in general that $P(a, i)$ and Q are inverses.

12. Consider the following matrices:

$$A = \begin{bmatrix} 1 & 0 \\ 1 & 1 \end{bmatrix} \qquad B = \begin{bmatrix} 1 & 0 \\ 0 & 2 \end{bmatrix} \qquad C = \begin{bmatrix} 1 & -1 \\ -1 & 1 \end{bmatrix}$$

$$O = \begin{bmatrix} 0 & 0 \\ 0 & 0 \end{bmatrix} \qquad I = \begin{bmatrix} 1 & 0 \\ 0 & 1 \end{bmatrix}$$

(a) Compute the squares of each of these matrices (that is, A^2, B^2, ..., I^2).
(b) Compute the cube of each matrix.
(c) Compute the nth power of each matrix.
(d) Compute $aA^2 + bA + cI$.
(e) Compute $3A^2 - 5B^3 + I^{10}$.

13. A square matrix D is said to be a *diagonal* matrix if its only nonzero entries are on the main diagonal. (For instance, B and I in Exercise 12 are diagonal.) If D and E are diagonal matrices, prove that $DE = ED$.

14. Show how to compute the nth power of a diagonal matrix.

15. Find the inverse of the diagonal matrix

$$\begin{bmatrix} a & 0 \\ 0 & b \end{bmatrix} \quad ab \neq 0.$$

16. Describe in general the inverse of a diagonal matrix.

17. Call the product of a diagonal matrix and a permutation matrix a *modified permutation matrix*. An example is

$$\begin{bmatrix} 0 & 2 & 0 \\ 0 & 0 & 4 \\ 3 & 0 & 0 \end{bmatrix}.$$

Find its inverse.

18. Write a general description of the inverse of a modified permutation matrix.

2.5   THE SOLUTION OF SIMULTANEOUS LINEAR EQUATIONS

You are undoubtedly familiar with methods for solving sets of simultaneous linear equations from your study of high school algebra. In this section we shall take a rather different approach to the problem, based on the ideas we have already developed. Our approach will be general, will always work, and will lead into the simplex method for solving linear programming problems.

EXAMPLE 2.5.1. Consider the following simultaneous linear equations:

(2.5.1)
$$\begin{aligned} x_1 + 3x_2 - 2x_3 &= 2, \\ -5x_2 + 4x_3 &= 0, \\ 2x_1 - 3x_2 + 3x_3 &= 5. \end{aligned}$$

We note first of all that this set of equations can be written in matrix form as

(2.5.2)
$$Ax = \begin{bmatrix} 1 & 3 & -2 \\ 0 & -5 & 4 \\ 2 & -3 & 3 \end{bmatrix} \begin{bmatrix} x_1 \\ x_2 \\ x_3 \end{bmatrix} = \begin{bmatrix} 2 \\ 0 \\ 5 \end{bmatrix} = b.$$

Another very useful way to view the solution of these equations is in column vector form, as follows:

(2.5.3)
$$\begin{bmatrix} 1 \\ 0 \\ 2 \end{bmatrix} x_1 + \begin{bmatrix} 3 \\ -5 \\ -3 \end{bmatrix} x_2 + \begin{bmatrix} -2 \\ 4 \\ 3 \end{bmatrix} x_3 = \begin{bmatrix} 2 \\ 0 \\ 5 \end{bmatrix} = b.$$

In this form, it is clear what we are seeking—namely, we want to write the vector

$$b = \begin{bmatrix} 2 \\ 0 \\ 5 \end{bmatrix}$$

as a linear combination of the vectors

$$\begin{bmatrix} 1 \\ 0 \\ 2 \end{bmatrix} \quad \begin{bmatrix} 3 \\ -5 \\ -3 \end{bmatrix} \quad \begin{bmatrix} -2 \\ 4 \\ 3 \end{bmatrix}.$$

The coefficients of the linear combination are the "unknowns," variables $x_1, x_2,$ and x_3.

Let us solve the equations (2.5.1) using the method of successive elimination of variables. First let's use the first equation to eliminate x_1 from the other equations. Since x_1 does not occur in the second equation, it is unchanged; but we multiply the first equation by 2 and subtract it from the third equation in order to eliminate x_1 from the third equation. The resulting new set of equations is

(2.5.4)
$$\begin{aligned} x_1 + 3x_2 - 2x_3 &= 2, \\ -5x_2 + 4x_3 &= 0, \\ -9x_2 + 7x_3 &= 1. \end{aligned}$$

Next we use the second equation to eliminate x_2 from each of the other equations. To do this we divide the second equation by -5 to make the coefficient of x_2 equal to 1. We then multiply the resulting new second equation by -3 and add it to the first equation. Next multiply the new second equation by 9 and add it to the third equation. The new set of equations is

(2.5.5)
$$\begin{aligned} x_1 \quad + \tfrac{2}{5}x_3 &= 2, \\ x_2 - \tfrac{4}{5}x_3 &= 0, \\ -\tfrac{1}{5}x_3 &= 1. \end{aligned}$$

The last step is to multiply the third equation by -5 to make the coefficient of x_3 equal to 1. Then multiply the resulting third equation by $\tfrac{2}{5}$ and subtract it from the first equation. Finally multiply the new third equation by $\tfrac{4}{5}$ and add it to the second equation. The resulting set of equations is

(2.5.6)
$$\begin{aligned} x_1 \quad &= \quad 4, \\ x_2 \quad &= -4, \\ x_3 &= -5. \end{aligned}$$

We see that the desired values of the x_i's are displayed. You should check to see that these values satisfy the original equations (2.5.1).

We have illustrated a rather traditional method for solving linear equations in order to help you recall the technique. Note that the basic process was that of using an equation to "eliminate a variable" from the other equations. This operation (sometimes called Gauss-Jordan elimination) is the basic step of constructive linear algebra, and we shall call it *pivoting*. In the last section we saw that pivoting can be performed by multiplying by a pivot matrix and also that this process can be interpreted as one of replacing one vector in the basis by another vector. Here we will show that each time a pivot is carried out, new linear relations among the original vectors are discovered which, by Theorem 2.4.4, must hold in any other coordinate system.

EXAMPLE 2.5.1 (continued). To illustrate that a linear relation that holds for one coordinate system holds for any coordinate system, let us resolve (2.5.1) using the "detached coefficient" tableau and pivot matrices. First observe that the column vector on the right-hand side of (2.5.3) can be written in terms of the "natural basis" of C_3—that is, the vectors E_1, E_2, and E_3—as follows:

$$(2.5.7) \qquad b = \begin{bmatrix} 2 \\ 0 \\ 5 \end{bmatrix} = 2\begin{bmatrix} 1 \\ 0 \\ 0 \end{bmatrix} + 0\begin{bmatrix} 0 \\ 1 \\ 0 \end{bmatrix} + 5\begin{bmatrix} 0 \\ 0 \\ 1 \end{bmatrix} = 2E_1 + 0E_2 + 5E_3.$$

But, as observed above, what we want to do to "solve" the equations is to write the vector b on the right of (2.5.3) in terms of the vectors on the left. The initial *detached coefficient tableau* is a *labeled, partitioned matrix*, obtained as follows:

$$T^{(0)} = \begin{array}{c} \\ E_1 \\ E_2 \\ E_3 \end{array} \begin{array}{ccc} A_1 & A_2 & A_3 \\ \left[\begin{array}{ccc} 1 & 3 & -2 \\ 0 & -5 & 4 \\ 2 & -3 & 3 \end{array}\right. & \left|\begin{array}{c} 2 \\ 0 \\ 5 \end{array}\right] \end{array}.$$

Note that the coefficients of the matrix are just those in (2.5.1) and note also that we have not written the variables at all. Instead the column vectors A_1, A_2, and A_3 indicate the position of the variables. The vertical line that partitions the matrix corresponds to the equals signs in (2.5.1). The row labels indicate the initial basis for C_3, which is the natural basis. The initial linear relation expressed in (2.5.7) is indicated in the coefficients to the right of the vertical line. We call the initial tableau $T^{(0)}$.

We construct the next tableau by pivoting on the $(1, 1)$ entry of $T^{(0)}$, which is the 1 in the upper left-hand corner. The effect of the pivoting can be obtained by constructing the first pivot matrix obtained from A_1, namely

$$P_1 = P(A_1, 1) = \begin{bmatrix} 1 & 0 & 0 \\ 0 & 1 & 0 \\ -2 & 0 & 1 \end{bmatrix}.$$

Now let us calculate the new tableau $T_1 = P_1 T^{(0)}$. It is

$$P_1 T^{(0)} = T^{(1)} = \begin{array}{c} \\ A_1 \\ E_2 \\ E_3 \end{array} \begin{array}{ccc} A_1 & A_2 & A_3 \\ \left[\begin{array}{ccc} 1 & 3 & -2 \\ 0 & -5 & 4 \\ 0 & -9 & 7 \end{array}\right. & \left|\begin{array}{c} 2 \\ 0 \\ 1 \end{array}\right] \end{array}.$$

Note that A_1 is now in the basis and E_1 is out of the basis. We have relabeled the first row A_1 to indicate this change. It is also evident from the numbers in the column farthest to the right that the following linear relation holds:

$$b = \begin{bmatrix} 2 \\ 0 \\ 5 \end{bmatrix} = 2A_1 + 0E_2 + 1E_3 = 2\begin{bmatrix} 1 \\ 0 \\ 2 \end{bmatrix} + 0\begin{bmatrix} 0 \\ 1 \\ 0 \end{bmatrix} + 1\begin{bmatrix} 0 \\ 0 \\ 1 \end{bmatrix}.$$

That this is so can easily be verified by direct calculation. Thus we have the desired vector expressed in terms of A_1, E_2, and E_3.

We now would like to introduce either A_2 or A_3 into the basis. In order to make our calculation similar to those used above let us introduce A_2 into the basis by pivoting on the -5 entry at the $(2, 2)$ position of the matrix. We thus need to calculate $P_2 = P(A_2, 2)$, which is

$$P_2 = P(A_2, 2) = \begin{bmatrix} 1 & \frac{3}{5} & 0 \\ 0 & -\frac{1}{5} & 0 \\ 0 & -\frac{9}{5} & 1 \end{bmatrix}.$$

We next find $T^{(2)} = P_2 T^{(1)}$, which is

$$P_2 T^{(1)} = T^{(2)} = \begin{array}{c} \\ A_1 \\ A_2 \\ E_3 \end{array} \begin{array}{ccc} A_1 & A_2 & A_3 \\ \left[\begin{array}{ccc|c} 1 & 0 & \frac{2}{5} & 2 \\ 0 & 1 & -\frac{4}{5} & 0 \\ 0 & 0 & -\frac{1}{5} & 1 \end{array}\right] \end{array}.$$

We have discovered the new linear relation $b = 2A_1 + 0A_2 + 1E_3$. You should verify that this relation holds in the original coordinate system as well.

The last pivot is that which replaces E_3 by A_3 by pivoting on the $\frac{1}{5}$ entry in the $(3, 3)$ position of $T^{(2)}$. The pivot matrix is

$$P_3 = P(A_3, 3) = \begin{bmatrix} 1 & 0 & 2 \\ 0 & 1 & -4 \\ 0 & 0 & -5 \end{bmatrix}.$$

We now obtain the final tableau

$$P_3 T^{(2)} = T^{(3)} = \begin{array}{c} \\ A_1 \\ A_2 \\ A_3 \end{array} \begin{array}{ccc} A_1 & A_2 & A_3 \\ \left[\begin{array}{ccc|c} 1 & 0 & 0 & 4 \\ 0 & 1 & 0 & -4 \\ 0 & 0 & 1 & -5 \end{array}\right] \end{array}.$$

From this we see that $b = 4A_1 - 4A_2 - 5A_3$, which is our desired objective—b written as a linear combination of the A vectors—and which gives a solution to the simultaneous equations that agrees with that previously found.

You may have found the multiplication of the pivot matrix times the old tableau somewhat tedious. It is possible to construct the new tableau, $T^{(s)}$, directly from the old tableau, $T^{(s-1)}$, by following the flow diagram in Figure 2.5.1.

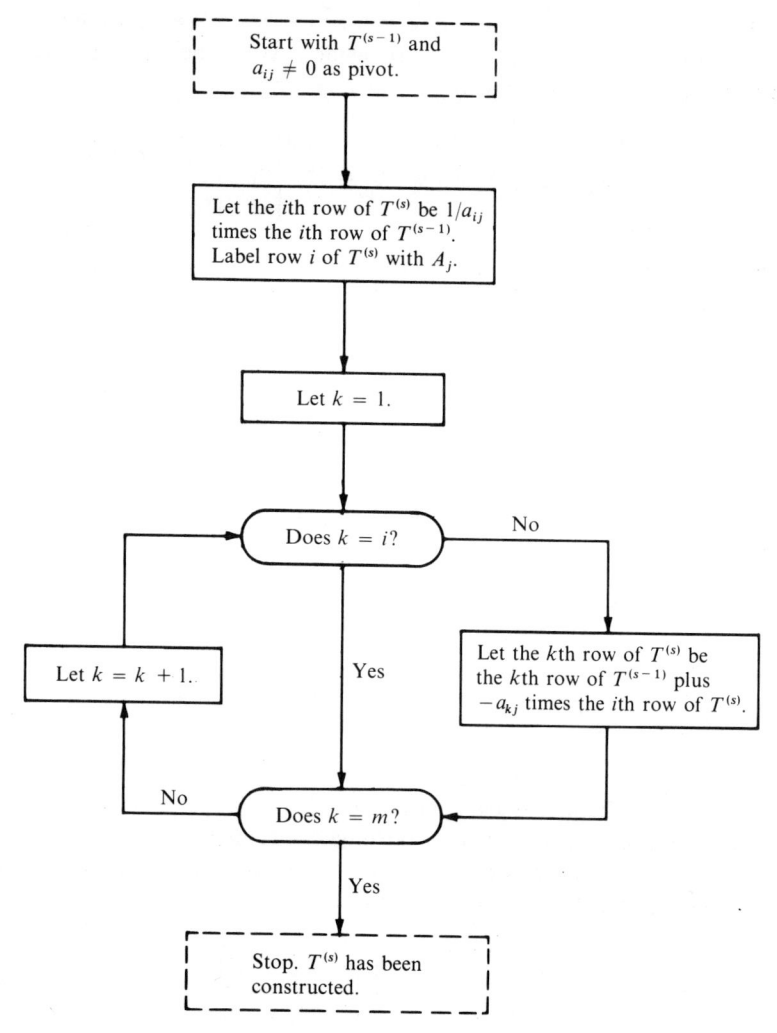

FIGURE 2.5.1. Flow diagram for constructing $T^{(s)}$ from $T^{(s-1)}$ by pivoting on $a_{ij} \neq 0$

You should try out the algorithm on the previous example and show that $T^{(1)}$ is obtained properly from $T^{(0)}$, that $T^{(2)}$ is obtained from $T^{(1)}$, and so on, by following its instructions.

EXAMPLE 2.5.1 (continued). Let us further illustrate the use of the algorithm in Figure 2.5.1 by starting with tableau $T^{(1)}$ and pivoting on the -9 entry at the $(3, 2)$ location. If we follow the steps in the flow diagram, we find that

$$
T^{(2)'} = \begin{array}{c} \\ A_1 \\ E_2 \\ A_2 \end{array}
\begin{array}{c} \overset{A_1}{} \overset{A_2}{} \overset{A_3}{} \\ \left[\begin{array}{ccc|c} 1 & 0 & \frac{1}{3} & \frac{7}{3} \\ 0 & 0 & \frac{1}{9} & -\frac{5}{9} \\ 0 & 1 & -\frac{7}{9} & -\frac{1}{9} \end{array}\right]. \end{array}
$$

Note that the basis now consists of A_1, E_2, and A_2 and that the linear relation

$$b = \frac{7}{3}A_1 - \frac{5}{9}E_2 - \frac{1}{9}A_2$$

holds. You should verify that this is so in the original coordinate system.

As a final step, we pivot on the (2, 3) entry of $T^{(2)'}$ to obtain the final tableau

$$T^{(3)'} = \begin{array}{c} \\ A_1 \\ A_3 \\ A_2 \end{array}\begin{array}{ccc} A_1 & A_2 & A_3 \\ \left[\begin{array}{ccc|c} 1 & 0 & 0 & 4 \\ 0 & 0 & 1 & -5 \\ 0 & 1 & 0 & -4 \end{array}\right] \end{array}.$$

Note that we obtain the linear relation $b = 4A_1 - 4A_2 - 5A_3$, which gives exactly the same answer as before (as it must) to the original set of equations (2.5.1)—namely, $x_1 = 4$, $x_2 = -4$, and $x_3 = -5$.

In our examples so far we have not discussed methods for choosing the next element on which to pivot, nor have we characterized how the process might terminate. A complete description of these possibilities is given in the flow diagram of Figure 2.5.2, and we will use and discuss the method described there in working the remaining examples.

EXAMPLE 2.5.2. Consider the three simultaneous equations in four unknowns shown in (2.5.8).

$$(2.5.8) \qquad \begin{array}{rcrcrcrcr} 3x_1 & + & 5x_2 & + & 6x_3 & - & x_4 & = & 3 \\ x_1 & + & 2x_2 & - & 2x_3 & & & = & -2 \\ 5x_1 & + & 8x_2 & + & 14x_3 & - & 2x_4 & = & 8 \end{array}$$

Let us use the flow diagram of Figure 2.5.2 to solve them. The initial tableau is:

$$T^{(0)} = \begin{array}{c} \\ E_1 \\ E_2 \\ E_3 \end{array}\begin{array}{cccc} A_1 & A_2 & A_3 & A_4 \\ \left[\begin{array}{cccc|c} 3 & 5 & 6 & -1 & 3 \\ 1 & 2 & -2 & 0 & -2 \\ 5 & 8 & 14 & -2 & 8 \end{array}\right] \end{array}.$$

We start out with $i = 1$ and ask if the first equation has a nonzero coefficient. Obviously it does, so we arbitrarily select one to pivot on. Let's select the bold-faced 3 in $T^{(0)}$ as the initial pivot. (Any of the three other numbers in the first row could have been chosen.) Carrying out the pivot operations indicated in Figure 2.5.1, we obtain the tableau

$$T^{(1)} = \begin{array}{c} \\ A_1 \\ E_2 \\ E_3 \end{array}\begin{array}{cccc} A_1 & A_2 & A_3 & A_4 \\ \left[\begin{array}{cccc|c} 1 & \frac{5}{3} & 2 & -\frac{1}{3} & 1 \\ 0 & \frac{1}{3} & -4 & \frac{1}{3} & -3 \\ 0 & -\frac{1}{3} & 4 & -\frac{1}{3} & 3 \end{array}\right] \end{array}.$$

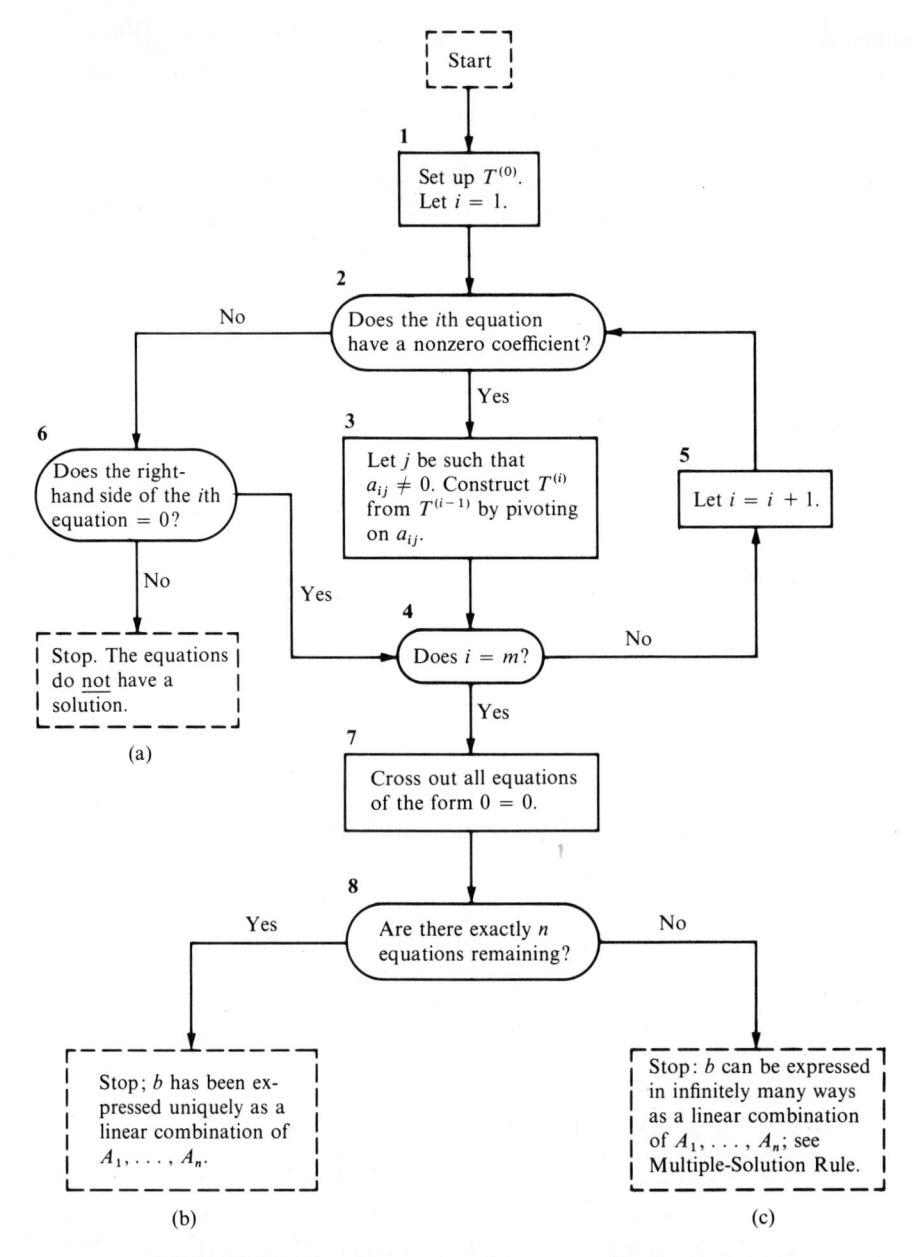

FIGURE 2.5.2. Flow diagram for solving m equations in n unknowns

We next go to the circle in the flow diagram that asks if $i = m = 3$. The answer is no so we change i from 1 to 2 and ask if the second equation in $T^{(1)}$ has a nonzero coefficient. The answer is yes and we pivot on the $\frac{1}{3}$ entry in $T^{(1)}$, obtaining

$$T^{(2)} = \begin{array}{c} \\ A_1 \\ A_2 \\ E_3 \end{array} \begin{array}{cccc} A_1 & A_2 & A_3 & A_4 \\ \left[\begin{array}{cccc} 1 & 0 & 22 & -2 \\ 0 & 1 & -12 & 1 \\ 0 & 0 & 0 & 0 \end{array}\right. & \left|\begin{array}{c} 16 \\ -9 \\ 0 \end{array}\right]. \end{array}$$

We go again to the circle in the flow diagram that asks if $i = 3$. The answer is no so we change i from 2 to 3 and ask if the third equation in $T^{(2)}$ has a nonzero coefficient. The answer is no. We then go to box 6, which asks if the right-hand side of the third equation is 0. The answer is yes so we go to box 4 and ask if $i = 3$. The answer is yes so we go to box 7. Following that instruction we cross out the third equation and go to box 8. We ask if there are 4 equations remaining; since the answer is no, we go to box (c), which says that there are infinitely many solutions. Before we explain how to obtain these solutions from $T^{(2)}$, we will make a definition.

DEFINITION 2.5.1. In any tableau, the *basic variables* are those whose labels appear on the rows of the tableau. All other variables are called *nonbasic*.

Note that the vectors corresponding to basis variables form a basis for C_m.

Clearly if we stop at box (b) of the flow diagram, every variable with an A_i label will be basic, and we will have expressed b as a linear combination of these columns. But if we stop at box (c) of the flow diagram, there will be both basic and nonbasic variables. In either case, solutions to the original equations can be obtained by following the rule stated below.

Multiple-Solution Rule

Set the nonbasic variables (if any) equal to arbitrary values (0 is a common choice for them) and solve in the final tableau for the values of the basic variables. The result is a solution to the original equations.

EXAMPLE 2.5.2 (continued). If we rewrite tableau $T^{(2)}$ in terms of variables we obtain

$$\begin{aligned} x_1 + 22x_3 - 2x_4 &= 16, \\ x_2 - 12x_3 + x_4 &= -9. \end{aligned}$$

Here x_1 and x_2 are basic variables (see Definition 2.5.1) and x_3 and x_4 are nonbasic. Solving for the basic variables, we get

(2.5.9)
$$\begin{aligned} x_1 &= 16 - 22x_3 + 2x_4, \\ x_2 &= -9 + 12x_3 - x_4. \end{aligned}$$

Following the multiple-solution rule, we see that x_3 and x_4 can take on arbitrary values in (2.5.9) so that x_1 and x_2 can be determined. Thus, if $x_3 = x_4 = 0$, we get $x_1 = 16$ and $x_2 = -9$ as solutions to (2.5.8). You should check these values by substitution. Similarly, if we let $x_3 = 1$ and $x_4 = -2$, we get $x_1 = -10$ and $x_2 = 5$, which are also solutions to (2.5.8).

EXAMPLE 2.5.3. Suppose we use the equations (2.5.8) except that we change the 8 on the right-hand side of the third equation to 11. We obtain the initial tableau

$$T^{(0)} = \begin{array}{c} \\ E_1 \\ E_2 \\ E_3 \end{array} \begin{array}{c} \begin{array}{cccc} A_1 & A_2 & A_3 & A_4 \end{array} \\ \left[\begin{array}{cccc|c} 3 & 5 & 6 & -1 & 3 \\ 1 & 2 & -2 & 0 & -2 \\ 5 & 8 & 14 & -2 & 11 \end{array} \right]. \end{array}$$

Pivoting as before on the **3** in $T^{(0)}$, we obtain

$$
\begin{array}{c}
\begin{array}{ccccc} & A_1 & A_2 & A_3 & A_4 \end{array} \\
\begin{array}{c} A_1 \\ T^{(1)} = E_2 \\ E_3 \end{array}
\left[
\begin{array}{cccc|c}
1 & \frac{5}{3} & 2 & -\frac{1}{3} & 1 \\
0 & \frac{1}{3} & -4 & \frac{1}{3} & -3 \\
0 & -\frac{1}{3} & 4 & -\frac{1}{3} & 6
\end{array}
\right].
\end{array}
$$

Pivoting on the $\frac{1}{3}$ entry, we obtain, for $i = 2$, the tableau

$$
\begin{array}{c}
\begin{array}{ccccc} & A_1 & A_2 & A_3 & A_4 \end{array} \\
\begin{array}{c} A_1 \\ T^{(2)} = A_2 \\ E_3 \end{array}
\left[
\begin{array}{cccc|c}
1 & 0 & 22 & -2 & 16 \\
0 & 1 & -12 & 1 & -9 \\
0 & 0 & 0 & 0 & 3
\end{array}
\right].
\end{array}
$$

Box 4 asks if $i = 3$, which it does not, so we set i equal to 3 and go to box 2. Now we find the last row of $T^{(2)}$ without a nonzero coefficient (to the left of the vertical line). Hence we go to box 6, where we are told to check the right-hand side of the row. We note that the right-hand entry is 3, which is nonzero, hence we go to box (a) and stop, noting that there are no solutions to the original equations. That there are no solutions will be proved in the next section, but inspection of the form of the last row of $T^{(2)}$ shows that this is so since that row corresponds to the equation

$$0x_1 + 0x_2 + 0x_3 + 0x_4 = 3,$$

which clearly does not have a solution.

The three examples (2.5.1, 2.5.2 continued, and 2.5.3) show the three ways that the algorithm in the flow diagram of Figure 2.5.2 can terminate for a given original set of simultaneous equations: (a) with exactly one solution, (b) with infinitely many solutions, or (c) with no solution. The theorems of the next section will prove that these three cases are mutually exclusive and exhaustive, but we prove here that the algorithm described in Figure 2.5.2 will terminate in a finite number of steps.

THEOREM 2.5.1. The algorithm of Figure 2.5.2 will terminate in one of the three boxes (a), (b), or (c) in at most m steps. Hence the equations $Ax = b$ have either (a) a unique solution, (b) infinitely many solutions, or (c) no solution.

Proof: Each time we go around the main loop, which consists of boxes 2, 3, 4, and 5, the value of i is increased by 1, hence we will go around this loop at most m times. If we go to box 6 and get no to the question there, we will stop in (a) in m or fewer steps. If in box 4 we get the answer yes, we leave the main loop and go to 7, then 8, and then to either (b) or (c), where we stop after exactly m circuits of the main loop.

You may have observed that the process of pivoting in order to solve simultaneous linear equations depends on the coefficients to the left of the equals signs (that is, to the left of the vertical line in a tableau) and not at all on the right-hand side. For this reason it is possible to solve, all in one tableau, several sets of simultaneous equations that have the same left-hand sides and different right-hand sides. One case in which this is desirable is in the process of finding the inverse of a matrix. For example, if A is an $n \times n$ matrix, in order to find the first column of A^{-1}, we must solve the equations

$$Ax^{(1)} = E_1,$$

where E_1 is the column vector with 1 in the first row and 0's elsewhere. Similarly, to find the second column of A^{-1}, we must solve

$$Ax^{(2)} = E_2,$$

and so on. In other words, we must solve n sets of simultaneous linear equations

$$Ax^{(1)} = E_1, Ax^{(2)} = E_2, \ldots, Ax^{(n)} = E_n.$$

This can be accomplished by starting with the tableau $(A\,|\,I)$ and pivoting, as the following example shows.

EXAMPLE 2.5.4. Find the inverse of the matrix

$$A = \begin{bmatrix} 1 & 3 & -2 \\ 0 & -5 & 4 \\ 2 & -3 & 3 \end{bmatrix}.$$

We start with the initial tableau

$$T^{(0)} = \begin{array}{c} \\ E_1 \\ E_2 \\ E_3 \end{array} \begin{bmatrix} \overset{A_1}{1} & \overset{A_2}{3} & \overset{A_3}{-2} & 1 & 0 & 0 \\ 0 & -5 & 4 & 0 & 1 & 0 \\ 2 & -3 & 3 & 0 & 0 & 1 \end{bmatrix}.$$

Note that we have the three right-hand sides in the three columns to the right of the vertical line. Pivoting on the **1**, we obtain

$$T^{(1)} = \begin{array}{c} A_1 \\ E_2 \\ E_3 \end{array} \begin{bmatrix} \overset{A_1}{1} & \overset{A_2}{3} & \overset{A_3}{-2} & 1 & 0 & 0 \\ 0 & -5 & 4 & 0 & 1 & 0 \\ 0 & -9 & 7 & -2 & 0 & 1 \end{bmatrix}.$$

Next, we pivot on the -5 entry and get

$$T^{(2)} = \begin{array}{c} A_1 \\ A_2 \\ E_3 \end{array} \begin{bmatrix} \overset{A_1}{1} & \overset{A_2}{0} & \overset{A_3}{\frac{2}{5}} & 1 & \frac{3}{5} & 0 \\ 0 & 1 & -\frac{4}{5} & 0 & -\frac{1}{5} & 0 \\ 0 & 0 & -\frac{1}{5} & -2 & -\frac{9}{5} & 1 \end{bmatrix}.$$

The last pivot is on the $-\frac{1}{5}$ entry, giving

$$T^{(3)} = \begin{array}{c} A_1 \\ A_2 \\ A_3 \end{array} \begin{bmatrix} \overset{A_1}{1} & \overset{A_2}{0} & \overset{A_3}{0} & -3 & -3 & 2 \\ 0 & 1 & 0 & 8 & 7 & -4 \\ 0 & 0 & 1 & 10 & 9 & -5 \end{bmatrix}.$$

You should check directly that the matrix on the right-hand side of the vertical line is inverse A^{-1}.

In Exercise 14, you will be asked to show that $A^{-1} = P_3 P_2 P_1$, which are the pivot matrices found in Example 2.5.1. In Exercise 15, you will be asked to find the inverse by a different sequence of pivots that requires a reordering of rows and columns before A^{-1} is written correctly. If A has no inverse, the process will stop in box (a) of Figure 2.5.2 (see Exercise 6).

EXAMPLE 2.5.5. As a final example let us discuss the solutions of the homogeneous linear equations $Ax = 0$. Since the right-hand sides are always 0, when we apply the flow diagram of Figure 2.5.2, we will always end up in either box (b) or (c). Hence in the tableau we do not need to keep the right-hand sides. As an example, consider the following equations.

$$\begin{aligned} 6x_1 + 5x_2 - 9x_3 &= 0 \\ 7x_1 + 6x_2 - 2x_3 &= 0 \\ x_1 + x_2 + 7x_3 &= 0 \end{aligned}$$

The initial tableau (omitting the right-hand sides) is

$$T^{(0)} = \begin{array}{c} \\ E_1 \\ E_2 \\ E_3 \end{array} \begin{array}{ccc} A_1 & A_2 & A_3 \\ \begin{bmatrix} 6 & 5 & -9 \\ 7 & 6 & -2 \\ 1 & 1 & 7 \end{bmatrix} \end{array}.$$

Pivoting on the **6** we get

$$T^{(1)} = \begin{array}{c} \\ A_1 \\ E_2 \\ E_3 \end{array} \begin{array}{ccc} A_1 & A_2 & A_3 \\ \begin{bmatrix} 1 & \frac{5}{6} & -\frac{3}{2} \\ 0 & \frac{1}{6} & \frac{17}{2} \\ 0 & \frac{1}{6} & \frac{17}{2} \end{bmatrix} \end{array}.$$

Pivoting on the $\frac{1}{6}$, we obtain the final tableau,

$$T^{(2)} = \begin{array}{c} \\ A_1 \\ A_2 \\ E_3 \end{array} \begin{array}{ccc} A_1 & A_2 & A_3 \\ \begin{bmatrix} 1 & 0 & -44 \\ 0 & 1 & 51 \\ 0 & 0 & 0 \end{bmatrix} \end{array}.$$

From this final tableau, which was obtained by ending in box (c) of Figure 2.5.2, we can see several different things. First of all, the linear relation $A_3 = -44A_1 + 51A_2$ is evident. Second, it is clear that vectors A_1 and A_2 are linearly independent. Because of the relation noted above, it is clear that A_1, A_2, and A_3 are linearly dependent since A_3 can be written as a linear combination of A_1 and A_2. In other words, $\{A_1, A_2\}$ is a maximal linearly independent subset of $\{A_1, A_2, A_3\}$. Third, if we solve from the final tableau for x_1 and x_2, we get

$$\begin{aligned} x_1 &= 44x_3, \\ x_2 &= -51x_3; \end{aligned}$$

that is, every solution to $Ax = 0$ is of the form

$$\begin{bmatrix} x_1 \\ x_2 \\ x_3 \end{bmatrix} = \begin{bmatrix} 44 \\ -51 \\ 1 \end{bmatrix} x_3.$$

In other words, the set of all solutions to $Ax = 0$ consists of all multiples (positive, negative, and zero) of the vector

$$\begin{bmatrix} 44 \\ -51 \\ 1 \end{bmatrix}.$$

In the next section we will prove the general theorem of which the Example 2.5.5 is a special case.

EXERCISES 2.5

1. Find all solutions to the following sets of equations.

(a)
$$\begin{aligned}
3x_1 \quad\quad - 4x_3 &= -8 \\
-x_1 + x_2 + 2x_3 &= 0 \\
-2x_1 \quad\quad + 3x_3 &= 4
\end{aligned}$$

(b)
$$\begin{aligned}
2x_1 - 5x_2 + 6x_3 \quad\quad &= 2 \\
x_1 - 3x_2 \quad\quad + 7x_4 &= -1
\end{aligned}$$

(c)
$$\begin{aligned}
2x_1 - 4x_2 + 2x_3 &= 1 \\
x_2 + 7x_3 &= 1 \\
-4x_1 + 10x_2 + 10x_3 &= 1
\end{aligned}$$

2. Assume that the matrix

$$\left[\begin{array}{cccc|c}
1 & 0 & -2 & 0 & 5 \\
0 & 1 & 1 & 7 & -2 \\
0 & 0 & 0 & 0 & 0
\end{array}\right]$$

is a final tableau after the solution process of Figure 2.5.2 has been completed. Label it properly, and write all solutions to the original set of equations.

3. Show that the following set of simultaneous equations has the tableau of Exercise 2 as its final tableau.

$$\begin{aligned}
2x_1 - 3x_2 - 7x_3 - 21x_4 &= 16 \\
5x_2 + 5x_3 + 35x_4 &= -10 \\
5x_1 - 4x_2 - 14x_3 - 28x_4 &= 33
\end{aligned}$$

4. Find another set of three simultaneous equations in four variables for which the matrix shown in Exercise 2 is the final tableau.

5. Solve the following three sets of simultaneous equations $Ax = b$ where

$$A = \begin{bmatrix} 0 & 2 & 0 & 8 \\ 2 & 1 & 0 & 0 \\ 2 & 3 & 1 & 9 \end{bmatrix} \quad \text{and} \quad b = \begin{bmatrix} 2 \\ 3 \\ 6 \end{bmatrix} \quad \text{or} \quad \begin{bmatrix} -2 \\ -1 \\ -2 \end{bmatrix} \quad \text{or} \quad \begin{bmatrix} 0 \\ 2 \\ 1 \end{bmatrix}.$$

You will need only one tableau.

6. Find the inverse of each of the following matrices (if it exists).

(a) $\begin{bmatrix} 3 & -2 \\ -4 & 3 \end{bmatrix}$
(b) $\begin{bmatrix} 0 & 1 & -6 \\ 4 & 0 & 5 \\ 3 & 0 & 4 \end{bmatrix}$

(c) $\begin{bmatrix} 1 & 0 & 1 \\ 0 & 1 & 1 \\ 1 & 1 & 0 \end{bmatrix}$ (d) $\begin{bmatrix} 1 & 4 & 6 \\ 0 & 2 & 5 \\ 0 & 0 & 3 \end{bmatrix}$ (e) $\begin{bmatrix} 1 & 0 & 1 & 0 \\ 0 & 1 & 1 & 0 \\ 1 & 1 & 0 & 0 \\ 0 & 0 & 0 & 1 \end{bmatrix}$

(f) $\begin{bmatrix} 5 & -4 & 2 \\ 0 & 3 & -4 \\ 10 & -5 & 0 \end{bmatrix}$ (g) $\begin{bmatrix} 1 & 0 & 1 & 0 \\ 0 & 1 & 0 & 1 \\ 1 & 1 & 1 & 0 \\ 1 & 1 & 1 & 1 \end{bmatrix}$

7. In using the flow diagram of Figure 2.5.2, we go down the list of equations one after the other and try to find a nonzero coefficient in the equation immediately after the one we have just considered. It is best from the numerical analysis and computer programming points of view to find the coefficient of largest absolute value in each of the equations not yet pivoted on and use that as the pivot. (We did not bother with this rule in working previous examples.) Construct a flow diagram for carrying out the same procedure as that defined in Figure 2.5.2, except specify that the next pivot chosen is to be the coefficient of largest absolute value not yet pivoted on. Discuss reasons why this is a better choice for pivot, taking into account the fact that electronic computers can carry only a finite number of decimal places for any number.

8. In order to have an inverse, what conditions must the matrix $\begin{bmatrix} a & b \\ c & d \end{bmatrix}$ satisfy?

9. Derive a formula for the inverse of the matrix in Exercise 8 when the matrix satisfies the necessary conditions.

10. Under what conditions does the inverse matrix of Exercise 8 have integer components, assuming that a, b, c, and d are integers?

11. Prove that a diagonal matrix always has an inverse if its diagonal entries are nonzero; give a formula for finding the inverse.

12. A square matrix is upper (lower) triangular if all entries below (above) the main diagonal are zeros. For instance, the matrices

$$\begin{bmatrix} 1 & 0 & 0 \\ 2 & 1 & 0 \\ 3 & 2 & 1 \end{bmatrix} \text{ and } \begin{bmatrix} 1 & -2 & 3 \\ 0 & -4 & 5 \\ 0 & 0 & 6 \end{bmatrix}$$

are lower and upper triangular, respectively.
(a) Find the inverses of these matrices.
(b) Give easy rules for constructing the inverses of 3×3 upper and lower triangular matrices.

13. For the following matrices, find the unique vector $w = (w_1, w_2, w_3)$ such that $wA = w$ and $w_1 + w_2 + w_3 = 1$.

(a) $\begin{bmatrix} 0 & 1 & 0 \\ \frac{1}{2} & 0 & \frac{1}{2} \\ \frac{1}{3} & \frac{1}{3} & \frac{1}{3} \end{bmatrix}$ (b) $\begin{bmatrix} \frac{1}{2} & \frac{1}{2} & 0 \\ 0 & \frac{1}{2} & \frac{1}{2} \\ \frac{1}{2} & \frac{1}{2} & 0 \end{bmatrix}$

(c) $\begin{bmatrix} 0 & 1 & 0 \\ 0 & \frac{1}{2} & \frac{1}{2} \\ 1 & 0 & 0 \end{bmatrix}$ (d) $\begin{bmatrix} \frac{1}{4} & \frac{1}{4} & \frac{1}{2} \\ \frac{1}{3} & \frac{1}{3} & \frac{1}{3} \\ \frac{3}{5} & \frac{1}{5} & \frac{1}{5} \end{bmatrix}$

14. Using the matrix in Example 2.5.4, show by direct calculation that $A^{-1} = P_3 P_2 P_1$.

15. Using the tableaux in Example 2.5.4, pivot on the (3,1) cell of $T^{(0)}$, then on the (2, 2) cell of $T^{(1)}$, then on the (1, 3) cell of $T^{(2)}$. Show that the final tableau is of the form $(P\,|\,B)$, where P is a permutation matrix. Show that $A^{-1} = P'B$ and explain why.

16. Using the computations in Exercise 15, show that $BA = P$.

17. Use the flow diagram of Figure 2.5.2 to show that if a square matrix A does not have an inverse, then there exist vectors $x \neq 0$ and $y \neq 0$ such that $xA = 0$ and $Ay = 0$.

18. Prove the converse of the statement in Exercise 17.

19. If A and B are square matrices with n rows and columns, show that $C = AB$ is non-singular if and only if both A and B are nonsingular. (*Hint:* Use Exercises 17 and 18.)

2.6   THEOREMS ON LINEAR EQUATIONS AND DIMENSIONS

In this section we will discuss from a theoretical point of view the solutions of m simultaneous linear equations in n variables,

$$(2.6.1) \qquad\qquad\qquad Ax = b,$$

utilizing the constructive methods developed in the previous section. We will also prove the statement made in Section 2.2 that the dimension of a finite dimensional vector space is unique.

THEOREM 2.6.1. The following three statements are equivalent concerning the solution of (2.6.1):

 (i)   The algorithm of Figure 2.5.2 terminates in box (a).
 (ii)   There exists a row vector w_0 such that $w_0 A = 0$ and $w_0 b = -1$.
 (iii)   Equations (2.6.1) have no solution.

Proof: We shall show that statement (i) implies (ii), that (ii) implies (iii), and finally that (iii) implies (i).

(*i*) *implies* (*ii*). Suppose that after k pivots the algorithm of Figure 2.5.2 terminates in box (a) at tableau $T^{(k)}$. Then in $T^{(k)}$ there is a row, say row i, such that there are all zeros to the left of the vertical line and a nonzero entry, say $d_i \neq 0$, to the right of the line. Let $P_1, P_2, \ldots, P_k$ be the sequence of pivot matrices such that $T^{(k)} = (P_k \cdots P_2 P_1)T^{(0)} = MT^{(0)}$, where we have defined $M = P_k \cdots P_1$. Now let f_i be the m-component row vector that has a 1 entry in the ith column and 0's elsewhere. Finally, define the m-component row vector

$$(2.6.2) \qquad\qquad\qquad w_0 = -\left(\frac{1}{d_i}\right)f_i M.$$

By direct computation $w_0 A = 0$, since $f_i MA = f_i(P_k \cdots P_1)A = 0$ by assumption. Also, $w_0 b = -1$, since $f_i Mb = f_i(P_k \cdots P_1)b = d_i$ by assumption.

(*ii*) *implies* (*iii*). We will prove this by showing that it is impossible to have a solution to (2.6.1) and also have the condition in (ii) hold. Suppose, in fact, that there is an x_0 such that $Ax_0 = b$ and a w_0 such that $w_0 A = 0$ and $w_0 b = -1$. From these assumptions we can calculate

$$0 = 0x = (w_0 A)x = w_0(Ax_0) = w_0 b = -1,$$

which is clearly a contradiction. Hence if (ii) holds, equations (2.6.1) cannot have a solution.

(*iii*) *implies* (*i*). We will prove the contrapositive—namely, that if the algorithm of Figure 2.5.2 does not terminate in box (a), the equations have a solution. But the latter statement is clearly true, since if the algorithm does not terminate in (a) it will terminate in either (b) or (c), and the rules of the previous section indicate how to obtain a solution from the final tableau.

THEOREM 2.6.2. If $n > m$, then either there is no solution or else there are infinitely many solutions to equations (2.6.1).

Proof: When the algorithm of Figure 2.5.2 is applied, the answer to the question in box 8, if the process ever reaches that box, is always no. Hence the algorithm must terminate in either box (a), meaning the equations have no solution, or else in box (c), meaning they have infinitely many solutions.

THEOREM 2.6.3. If $b = 0$, then equations (2.6.1) always have a solution.

Proof: The answer to the question in box 6 of Figure 2.5.2 is always yes, so the algorithm must terminate in either box (b) or (c).

COROLLARY. If $b = 0$ and $n > m$, then there are infinitely many solutions.

Proof: Apply Theorems 2.6.2 and 2.6.3.

THEOREM 2.6.4. Let A be an $m \times n$ matrix.

(i) The set of all solutions to the linear equations $Ax = 0$ is a vector subspace of C_n.

(ii) Suppose the equations $Ax = 0$ are solved by means of the algorithm in Figure 2.5.2 and that there are n_1 basic and n_2 nonbasic variables, where $n_1 + n_2 = n$. Then (a) the maximal number of linearly independent columns of A is n_1; (b) the dimension of the vector space of solutions of $Ax = 0$ is n_2; and (c) a basis for this vector space can be constructed from the n_2 columns corresponding to the nonbasic variables in the final tableau T_k.

Proof: (i) We need only show that the conditions of Definition 2.2.3 are satisfied. If x and y are such that $Ax = 0$ and $Ay = 0$, then $A(x + y) = Ax + Ay = 0 + 0 = 0$. Similarly, $A(kx) = k(Ax) = k(0) = 0$. Hence the set of all solutions is a vector subspace of C_n.

(ii) (a) The pivoting process of Figure 2.5.2 exchanges some of the natural basis vectors $E_1, \ldots, E_m$ of C_m for some of the columns of A. Suppose y is a vector that is a linear combination of a linearly independent subset S of columns of A. If all the vectors in S are already in the basis, then y itself is expressed in terms of those vectors and no others. The coefficients of this expression must be unique since the vectors in S are linearly independent. Hence y cannot be brought into the basis. That is, if y is any column of A not yet in the basis and if y is a linear combination of columns of A already in the basis, then y cannot be brought into the basis. On the other hand, if y is not a linear combination of vectors already in the basis, then it cannot be expressed as a linear combination of them and hence has a nonzero coefficient in its column that can be pivoted on. Thus such a y can be brought into the basis. Therefore, when the pivoting process of Figure 2.5.2 stops, the maximum number of linearly independent columns of A will have been put into the basis.

(ii) (b) (c). When the process of Figure 2.5.2 terminates in box (b) or (c), there will be n_1 variables that are basic and $n_2 = n - n_1$ that are nonbasic. The original set of equations will have been transformed into an equivalent set of equations in which the coefficients of the basic variables are 1 in exactly one equation and 0 in all other equations.

Let $T = T^{(k)}$ be the final tableau. In order to solve for the basic variables in terms of the nonbasic variables, we must move the nonbasic variables to the right-hand side of the equations. This can be accomplished by the following procedure: let the indices of the nonbasic variables be $j_1, j_2, \ldots, j_{n_2}$. Define n_2 vectors C_p by the following rules.

$$c_{j_p}^{(p)} = 1$$

$$c_q^{(p)} = -t_{ij_p} \qquad \text{if row } i \text{ of } T \text{ is labeled with basic variable } q$$

$$c_i^{(p)} = 0 \qquad \text{for all other rows } i$$

It is easy to see that these vectors are linearly independent since the pth vector has a 1 entry in the j_pth row and all other vectors have 0's in this row. It also follows by construction that arbitrary linear combinations of these vectors are solutions to the equations $Ax = 0$. Hence the dimension of the vector space of solutions is n_2, and we have produced a basis for this vector space.

EXAMPLE 2.6.1. To illustrate this construction process, consider the final tableau T.

$$
T = \begin{array}{c} \\ A_2 \\ A_1 \\ E_3 \end{array}
\begin{array}{cccc} A_1 & A_2 & A_3 & A_4 \end{array}
\begin{bmatrix} 0 & 1 & -2 & -6 \\ 1 & 0 & 3 & 1 \\ 0 & 0 & 0 & 0 \end{bmatrix}
$$

Clearly x_1 and x_2 are basic variables, and x_3 and x_4 are nonbasic. To construct the C vector corresponding to the nonbasic variable x_3, we note that $c_2^{(1)} = 2$ since the first row is labeled A_2. Similarly, $c_1^{(1)} = -3$. Finally, $c_3^{(1)} = 1$, and $c_4^{(1)} = 0$ since 4 is a nonbasic variable. The second vector has $c_2^{(2)} = 6$, $c_1^{(2)} = -1$, $c_3^{(2)} = 0$, and $c_4^{(2)} = 1$. Thus, the two vectors

$$
C_1 = \begin{bmatrix} -3 \\ 2 \\ 1 \\ 0 \end{bmatrix} \quad \text{and} \quad C_2 = \begin{bmatrix} -1 \\ 6 \\ 0 \\ 1 \end{bmatrix}
$$

form a basis for solutions to the equations $Ax = 0$. You should show that these vectors are linearly independent and that $TC_1 = 0$ and $TC_2 = 0$ hold. Now suppose that A was the original matrix. Then since $T = MA$, where M is a nonsingular matrix, it follows that $Tx = 0$ if and only if $Ax = 0$, so the original form of the equations is, in fact, immaterial.

THEOREM 2.6.5. If V is a vector space with a basis of n vectors $\{B_1, \ldots, B_n\}$, then any set of $n + 1$ vectors in V is linearly dependent.

Proof: Let $A_1, \ldots, A_{n+1}$ be a set of $n + 1$ vectors in V. These vectors have coordinates relative to the basis—say

$$A_k = \begin{bmatrix} a_{1k} \\ a_{2k} \\ \vdots \\ a_{nk} \end{bmatrix} \qquad \text{for } k = 1, \ldots, n + 1.$$

Let A be the corresponding $n \times (n + 1)$ matrix. If we can find a nonzero solution to the equations $Ax = 0$, then we will have shown that the columns of A, and hence the vectors $A_1, \ldots, A_{n+1}$, are linearly dependent. But, by the corollary to Theorem 2.6.3, these equations have infinitely many solutions and hence at least one nonzero solution. This completes the proof.

THEOREM 2.6.6. Let V be a vector space. If V has two bases, one with k vectors and one with h vectors, then $h = k$.

Proof: Suppose $h \geq k + 1$. Take any subset of $k + 1$ of the second basis set and use Theorem 2.6.5 to show that they are linearly dependent, which is contrary to the assumption that they are linearly independent. Hence $h \leq k$. By a symmetric argument, $k \leq h$. The two conclusions show that $h = k$.

THEOREM 2.6.7. Let V' be a k-dimensional subspace of an n-dimensional vector space V. Let $\{B_1, \ldots, B_n\}$ be a basis for V, and let $\{A_1, \ldots, A_k\}$ be a basis for V'. Then it is possible to replace k of the basis vectors for V by those for V'.

The proof is Exercise 4 of Exercises 2.6.

THEOREM 2.6.8. If x and y are two solutions to the nonhomogeneous equations $Aw = b$, then $x - y$ is a solution to the homogeneous equations $Az = 0$.

Proof: If $Ax = b$ and $Ay = b$, then $A(x - y) = Ax - Ay = b - b = 0$, as was to be shown.

This theorem establishes that, in order to find all solutions to $Ax = b$, the following procedure can be used:

(i)   Find any one particular solution to $Ax = b$.

(ii)   Find, as above, all solutions to the homogeneous equations $Ax = 0$.

(iii)   Then every solution to $Ax = b$ can be represented as the sum of the particular solution plus a solution to the homogeneous equations.

EXERCISES 2.6

1. Let x be a four-component column vector and A, the matrix

$$A = \begin{bmatrix} 2 & -1 & 8 & 8 \\ 3 & 0 & 9 & 3 \\ 4 & 2 & 8 & -8 \end{bmatrix}.$$

(a) Show that $AC_1 = 0$, where C_1 is as in Example 2.6.1.
(b) Show that $AC_2 = 0$, where C_2 is as in Example 2.6.1.
(c) Set up the initial tableau formed from A, and pivot on the -1 entry at a_{12}.
(d) Pivot on the entry in the second row and first column of the next tableau.
(e) Show that the resultant tableau is T of Example 2.6.1.
(f) Find a nonsingular matrix M such that $T = MA$. (*Hint:* It will be the product of two pivot matrices.)
(g) Show that A has at most two linearly independent rows and at most two linearly independent columns.
(h) Describe the set of all solutions to the equations $Ax = 0$.

2. Consider the following final tableau.

$$T = \begin{matrix} & A_1 & A_2 & A_3 & A_4 \\ A_3 & \begin{bmatrix} 0 & 1 & 1 & -2 \\ E_2 & 0 & 0 & 0 & 0 \\ A_1 & 1 & 5 & 0 & 0 \end{bmatrix} \end{matrix}$$

(a) Consider the equations $Tx = 0$. Find a basis for the set of all solutions to these.
(b) What is the maximal number of linearly independent rows and columns that T has?
(c) If $T = MA$ where M is nonsingular, what is the maximal number of linearly independent rows (or columns) that A can have? Prove your statement.

3. Prove that the maximal number of linearly independent rows of A is equal to the maximum number of linearly independent columns of A. (*Hint:* Consider the solutions of $Ax = 0$. Using the method of the previous section, construct a series of tableaus $T^{(0)}$, $T^{(1)}$, ..., $T^{(k)}$. Show that a pivot can be chosen in a row only if the row in question is not linearly dependent on the rows in which previous pivots were chosen.)

4. Prove Theorem 2.6.7 by following these steps:
(a) Show that the coordinates of B_1, ..., B_n are "unit vectors"—that is, vectors with one 1 entry and the rest 0 entries.
(b) Suppose that the vectors A_j are written in terms of the basis $(B_1, ..., B_n)$ and have coordinates

$$\begin{bmatrix} a_{1j} \\ \vdots \\ a_{nj} \end{bmatrix}.$$

Let A be the $n \times k$ matrix so obtained.
(c) Set up the initial tableau $(A \mid I)$ labeling the first k columns with A_1, ..., A_k and the last n columns B_1, ..., B_n.
(d) Now show that you can make a series of k pivot steps that will bring in the A vectors and remove k of the B vectors from the basis.

5. Let C_0 be any solution to $Ax = b$, and let $C_1, ..., C_{n_2}$ be a basis for the set of all solutions to $AZ = 0$. Show that x is a solution to $Ax = b$ if and only if x can be written

$$x = C_0 + \sum_{i=1}^{n_2} k_i C_i.$$

(*Hint:* Show that $x - C_0$ solves $Az = 0$.)

2.7   THE GEOMETRY OF VECTOR SPACES

In this section we will take a slightly different point of view concerning the methods we have been developing in order that we may give "geometric" interpretations to these operations. In Chapter 4 we give "economic" interpretations. You will find both of these interpretations useful in understanding the processes we are using.

Let x be the column vector of variables $x_1, \ldots, x_n$, let A be a row vector having n components, and let b be a number. Then an equation of the form $Ax = b$ is called an *open statement*. Such a statement is true for some vectors x in C_n and false for others. For instance, if we take the first equation in (2.5.1), namely

$$(2.7.1) \qquad x_1 + 3x_2 - 2x_3 = \begin{bmatrix} 1 & 3 & -2 \end{bmatrix} \begin{bmatrix} x_1 \\ x_2 \\ x_3 \end{bmatrix} = 2,$$

we see that it is true for the vectors $\begin{bmatrix} 0 \\ 0 \\ -1 \end{bmatrix}$ and $\begin{bmatrix} -1 \\ 1 \\ 0 \end{bmatrix}$ and false for the vector $\begin{bmatrix} 1 \\ 0 \\ 1 \end{bmatrix}$.

Every vector in C_3 makes the equation either true or false.

DEFINITION 2.7.1. Let $A \neq O$ be an n-component row vector and b a number; then the set of all x for which the open statement $Ax = b$ is true is called its *truth set*. The truth set of $Ax = b$ is also called a *hyperplane* in C_n.

Thus the truth set of (2.7.1) is an ordinary plane in three-space, as you will recall from elementary analytic geometry. Note that the vector O in C_n lies on the hyperplane if and only if $b = 0$. Clearly, O is not in the truth set of (2.7.1).

We can now give a geometric interpretation to the problem of finding solutions to m simultaneous linear equations in n variables, $Ax = b$. Specifically, we are trying to find the intersection of m hyperplanes in C_n. We can also say that we are trying to find the truth set of the conjunction of the m open statements that are the individual linear equations. Thus equations (2.5.1) can be written as

$$(x_1 + 3x_2 - 2x_3 = 2) \wedge (-5x_2 + 4x_3 = 0) \wedge (2x_1 - 3x_2 + 3x_3 = 5),$$

where $\wedge$ is the symbol for "and."

Using this geometric interpretation it is easy to see why three equations in three unknowns may have either no solution, a unique solution, or infinitely many solutions. Thus if two of the three planes are distinct and parallel, the three equations will have no solution. If no two are parallel and they meet at a point (such as the planes of the walls of a room), then there is a unique solution. If the three planes all contain the same line (as the pages of a book), then there are infinitely many solutions.

DEFINITION 2.7.2. A *subspace* in C_n is the intersection of a finite number of hyperplanes that go through the origin; that is, the right-hand sides of the equations of all these hyperplanes must be zero. A *flat* in C_n is the intersection of a finite number of hyperplanes.

Thus a subspace is a flat, but the converse is true if and only if every hyperplane containing the flat goes through the origin.

THEOREM 2.7.1. A subspace is the solution set of $Ax = O$, where A is an $m \times n$ matrix. Similarly, a flat is the solution set of $Ax = b$, where A is an $m \times n$ matrix and b is an m-component column vector that may or may not be O.

Proof: $Ax = O$ is simply the equation restatement of the definition of a subspace; similarly, $Ax = b$ is the equation restatement of the definition of a flat.

We have seen in the previous sections that a subspace of C_n has a basis consisting of a finite number of linearly independent vectors and that the pivoting method of Figure 2.5.2 can be used to find such a set of basis vectors. We thus have two different ways of describing a subspace: (i) as the intersection of a finite number of hyperplanes, $Ax = O$, and (ii) as the set of all linear combinations of a finite set of (basis) vectors. Thus the solution of simultaneous linear equations can be interpreted as going from the first way of describing a subspace to the second. We shall shortly see that a similar result is true for flats.

EXAMPLE 2.7.1. Consider in C_3 the subspace defined by $Ax = O$, where

$$A = \begin{bmatrix} 2 & 0 & -4 \\ -1 & 3 & 11 \\ -2 & 2 & 10 \end{bmatrix}.$$

After setting up the initial tableau and pivoting twice we find the final tableau

$$T = \begin{matrix} & A_1 & A_2 & A_3 \\ A_1 & \begin{bmatrix} 1 & 0 & -2 \\ A_2 & 0 & 1 & 3 \\ E_3 & 0 & 0 & 0 \end{bmatrix} \end{matrix}.$$

Using the methods of the previous section, we find that the truth set of $Ax = O$ consists of all multiples of the vector

$$\begin{bmatrix} 2 \\ -3 \\ 1 \end{bmatrix}.$$

Hence the solution is a line through the origin.

DEFINITION 2.7.3. Consider two flats defined by $Ax = b$ and $Cx = d$. They are said to be *parallel* if and only if the subspace (truth set) defined by $Ax = O$ equals, contains, or is contained in the subspace defined by $Cx = O$.

EXAMPLE 2.7.2. Show that the two planes in C_3 defined by

$$Ax = \quad 2x_1 + \quad x_2 - 4x_3 = \quad 7,$$
$$Cx = -4x_1 - 2x_2 + 8x_3 = -2$$

are parallel. Observe that

$$[-4, \ -2, \ 8] = -2[2, \ 1, \ -4]$$

so that $C = -2A$. Hence the truth sets of $Ax = O$ and $Cx = O$ are identical, and the planes are parallel.

A similar result holds in general as the following theorem shows.

THEOREM 2.7.2. Let $Ax = b$ and $Cx = d$ be the equations of two hyperplanes in C_n. They are *parallel* if and only if there is a number $k \neq 0$ such that $A = kC$. They are *coincident* only if it is also true that $b = kd$.

Proof: By the algorithm of Figure 2.5.2, it follows that $Ax = O$ and $Cx = O$ will define the same space if and only if $A = kC$ for some $k \neq 0$. If this is the case, then an x such that $Ax = b$ will also satisfy $Cx = d$ if and only if $b = kd$.

Our next task is to show that a flat may be described as a combination of points and that such a combination can be found by pivotal methods. We illustrate the process with an example.

EXAMPLE 2.7.3. Let us write the line defined as the intersection of the two planes whose equations are

$$
\begin{aligned}
4x_1 + x_2 - 5x_3 &= 7, \\
-3x_1 - 2x_2 &= -4,
\end{aligned}
$$

in parametric form. Setting up the initial tableau and pivoting twice, we arrive at the final tableau

$$
\begin{array}{c}
\begin{array}{ccc} A_1 & A_2 & A_3 \end{array} \\
\begin{array}{c} A_1 \\ A_2 \end{array}
\left[\begin{array}{ccc|c}
1 & 0 & -2 & 2 \\
0 & 1 & 3 & -1
\end{array}\right].
\end{array}
$$

Hence all solutions to the original set of equations can be written as

$$
\begin{bmatrix} x_1 \\ x_2 \\ x_3 \end{bmatrix} = \begin{bmatrix} 2 \\ -1 \\ 0 \end{bmatrix} + p \begin{bmatrix} 2 \\ -3 \\ 1 \end{bmatrix},
$$

where p is an arbitrary number. Note that the form of this equation is $x = A_0 + pA_1$— that is, that the line is the sum of the vector A_0 plus an arbitrary multiple of the vector A_1. The geometric picture of Figure 2.7.1 shows this.

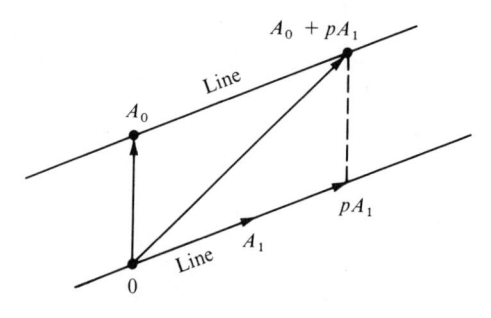

FIGURE 2.7.1

DEFINITION 2.7.4. Consider the flat in C_n defined by m equations in n unknowns, and of the form $Ax = b$. Suppose that by pivotal operations we find that the truth set of these equations is given by

(2.7.2.) $x = A_0 + p_1 A_1 + \cdots + p_k A_k,$ $AA_0 = b,$ $AA_i = 0$ for $i = 1, \ldots, k,$

where $k \le n, p_1, \ldots, p_k$ are arbitrary numbers and $A_1, \ldots, A_k$ are linearly independent. Then (2.7.2) is said to be the *parametric form* of the flat, and k is the *dimension* of the flat. A flat of dimension $n - 1$ is called a *hyperplane*, and a flat of dimension 1 is called a *line*.

You should carefully note that A_0 is a point on the flat; that is, $AA_0 = b$, *but* $A_1, \ldots, A_k$ are not points on the flat since $AA_i = 0$ for $i = 1, \ldots, k$. For a way of expressing a flat as a weighted combination of points *on* the flat, see the next section.

THEOREM 2.7.3. Two lines in C_n, written in parametric form as $D_0 + D_1 p$ and $E_0 + E_1 q$, are parallel if and only if there is a constant $t \ne 0$ such that $E_1 = t D_1$.

Proof: Suppose that the hyperplane form of the first line is $Ax = b$. Then since D_0 is a point on the line, $AD_0 = b$. But $A(D_0 + D_1 p) = b$ for all p. This implies $AD_1 = 0$, so the truth set of $Ax = 0$ consists of all multiples of D_1. Now the two lines are parallel if and only if E_1 is in that truth set. This can happen if and only if there is a $t \ne 0$ such that $E_1 = t D_1$.

Note that the lines in Examples 2.7.1 and 2.7.3 are parallel by virtue of this test.

As a final topic on parallelism, let us find the conditions under which a line is parallel to a flat—for instance, a hyperplane. The next theorem gives the answer.

THEOREM 2.7.4. A line in C_n, written in parametric form as $E_0 + E_1 p$, is parallel to or coincident with the k-dimensional flat where $0 < k \le n$ and whose equations are $Ax = b$ if and only if $AE_1 = 0$.

Proof: Since $k > 0$, the flat $Ax = b$ cannot consist of only a single point. Let $Cx = d$ be the equations of the line $E_0 + E_1 p$. Then, as before, $CE_1 = 0$. Hence the truth set of $Cx = 0$ consists of all multiples of E_1. Therefore, the given line is parallel to the flat with equations $Ax = b$ if and only if $A(pE_1) = p(AE_1) = 0$ for all p. This can happen if and only if $AE_1 = 0$.

EXAMPLE 2.7.4. Show that the line given in Example 2.7.3 is parallel to the plane whose equation is

$$x_1 - 2x_3 = \begin{bmatrix} 1 & 0 & -2 \end{bmatrix} \begin{bmatrix} x_1 \\ x_2 \\ x_3 \end{bmatrix} = 0.$$

It was found in the previous example that $E_1 = \begin{bmatrix} 2 \\ -3 \\ 1 \end{bmatrix}$. Hence

$$AE_1 = [1 \quad 0 \quad -2]\begin{bmatrix} 2 \\ -3 \\ 1 \end{bmatrix} = 2 - 2 = 0,$$

so the line and plane are parallel.

EXAMPLE 2.7.5. Find the parametric equation of a line parallel to the line of Example 2.7.3 that passes through the point $\begin{bmatrix} 1 \\ -1 \\ 1 \end{bmatrix}$. This is very easy since, using Theorem 2.7.3, the desired equation is

$$\begin{bmatrix} x_1 \\ x_2 \\ x_3 \end{bmatrix} = \begin{bmatrix} 1 \\ -1 \\ 1 \end{bmatrix} + p\begin{bmatrix} 2 \\ -3 \\ 1 \end{bmatrix}.$$

EXAMPLE 2.7.6. Find the parametric equation of a line through the point $\begin{bmatrix} -2 \\ 0 \\ 7 \end{bmatrix}$ that is parallel to the plane whose equation is

$$Ax = (5 \quad -2 \quad 0)x = 3.$$

By Theorem 2.7.4, we can choose any vector E_1 such that $AE_1 = 0$. For instance, $E_1 = \begin{bmatrix} 2 \\ 5 \\ 0 \end{bmatrix}$ will do. Hence the desired equation is

$$\begin{bmatrix} x_1 \\ x_2 \\ x_3 \end{bmatrix} = \begin{bmatrix} -2 \\ 0 \\ 7 \end{bmatrix} + p\begin{bmatrix} 2 \\ 5 \\ 0 \end{bmatrix}$$

for the line.

EXERCISES 2.7

1. Which of the following planes are parallel? Which are coincident?
   (a) $\quad 3x_1 - 9x_2 + 6x_3 = \quad 2$
   (b) $\quad -x_1 + 3x_2 - 2x_3 = \quad 0$
   (c) $\quad -x_1 \qquad + 2x_3 = \quad 5$
   (d) $-9x_1 + 27x_2 - 18x_3 = -6$
   (e) $\quad 4x_1 \qquad - 8x_3 = -20$

2. Find the equations of planes that are parallel to each of the planes of Exercise 1 that pass through the point $\begin{bmatrix} 1 \\ -2 \\ 1 \end{bmatrix}$.

3. Show that the points
   $$\begin{bmatrix} 5 \\ -2 \end{bmatrix}, \quad \begin{bmatrix} -3 \\ 1 \end{bmatrix}, \quad \text{and} \quad \begin{bmatrix} -11 \\ 4 \end{bmatrix}$$
   are collinear in C_2.

4. Find three collinear points among

$$\begin{bmatrix} 1 \\ 2 \\ -3 \end{bmatrix}, \quad \begin{bmatrix} 1 \\ 1 \\ 1 \end{bmatrix}, \quad \begin{bmatrix} 0 \\ 1 \\ 0 \end{bmatrix}, \quad \begin{bmatrix} 1 \\ 4 \\ -11 \end{bmatrix}.$$

5. Show that the lines through the points

$$\begin{bmatrix} 7 \\ 2 \end{bmatrix} \quad \text{and} \quad \begin{bmatrix} -1 \\ 1 \end{bmatrix}$$

and

$$\begin{bmatrix} 15 \\ 5 \end{bmatrix} \quad \text{and} \quad \begin{bmatrix} -1 \\ 3 \end{bmatrix}$$

are parallel.

6. Show that the lines defined by

$$3x_1 + 2x_2 \qquad = \quad 4$$
$$-x_1 \qquad + 2x_3 = -2$$

and

$$5x_1 + 2x_2 \qquad = 20$$
$$3x_1 + 2x_2 + 2x_3 = 10$$

are not parallel.

7. Find the equation of the hyperplane through the point $\begin{bmatrix} 2 \\ -1 \\ 0 \end{bmatrix}$ that is parallel to the line

through the points

$$\begin{bmatrix} 1 \\ 1 \\ 1 \end{bmatrix} \quad \text{and} \quad \begin{bmatrix} 1 \\ 2 \\ 3 \end{bmatrix}.$$

8. The three lines through the origin $\begin{bmatrix} 0 \\ 0 \\ 0 \end{bmatrix}$ and each of the points

$$\begin{bmatrix} 1 \\ 0 \\ 0 \end{bmatrix}, \quad \begin{bmatrix} 0 \\ 1 \\ 0 \end{bmatrix}, \quad \text{and} \quad \begin{bmatrix} 0 \\ 0 \\ 1 \end{bmatrix}$$

are called *coordinate* axes. Find the equations of three lines through the point $\begin{bmatrix} 2 \\ -2 \\ 1 \end{bmatrix}$

that are parallel to each of the coordinate axes.

9. Two nonparallel flats in C_n are said to be *skew* if they do not intersect. Show that the lines whose equations are

$$x = \begin{bmatrix} 4 \\ -1 \\ 0 \end{bmatrix} + k \begin{bmatrix} 1 \\ 1 \\ 1 \end{bmatrix} \quad \text{and} \quad x = \begin{bmatrix} 3 \\ 0 \\ 2 \end{bmatrix} + t \begin{bmatrix} -1 \\ 1 \\ -1 \end{bmatrix}$$

are skew.

10. Are the two lines given by

$$x = \begin{bmatrix} 3 \\ -1 \\ 2 \end{bmatrix} + k \begin{bmatrix} 1 \\ 1 \\ 1 \end{bmatrix} \quad \text{and} \quad x = \begin{bmatrix} -4 \\ 0 \\ 0 \end{bmatrix} + t \begin{bmatrix} -2 \\ -2 \\ -2 \end{bmatrix}$$

skew?

11. Prove that two nonintersecting lines in C_3 are either parallel or skew.

12. Prove that two intersecting lines in C_3 are coincident if and only if they are parallel.

13. Show that the lines defined by

$$-x_1 + x_2 + 5x_3 = -3$$

$$x_1 + x_2 + x_3 = 1$$

and

$$x_2 + 3x_3 = -5$$

$$2x_1 + x_2 - x_3 = -25$$

are parallel. Work this problem in two ways, once using Theorem 2.7.3 and once using Theorem 2.7.4.

14. Find the equation of a plane in C_3 through the three points

$$\begin{bmatrix} 1 \\ -1 \\ 2 \end{bmatrix}, \begin{bmatrix} 3 \\ 0 \\ 1 \end{bmatrix}, \begin{bmatrix} 0 \\ 1 \\ -1 \end{bmatrix}.$$

15. Prove that three points in C_3 determine a unique plane not containing the origin if and only if their coordinate vectors are linearly independent.

16. Show that three points in C_3 are coplanar with O if and only if their coordinates are linearly dependent.

17. Show that three points in C_3 are collinear if one point can be written as a weighted combination of the other two.

18. Show that the following lines intersect:

$$\begin{bmatrix} 3 \\ 0 \\ 3 \end{bmatrix} + p \begin{bmatrix} -6 \\ 2 \\ 0 \end{bmatrix}$$

and

$$\begin{bmatrix} 0 \\ -1 \\ 0 \end{bmatrix} + q \begin{bmatrix} 5 \\ -1 \\ 1 \end{bmatrix}.$$

19. Prove that the lines $D_0 + D_1 p$ and $E_0 + E_1 q$ intersect if and only if $D_0 - E_0$ can be written as a linear combination of D_1 and E_1.

2.8   SOLUTION OF GEOMETRIC PROBLEMS*

In this section we will first derive the weighted combination form of the equations for a flat. Then we will show how to go from the parametric form to the weighted combination form and vice versa. Next, we will derive a method for going from the weighted combination form to the hyperplane form of the equations for a flat. The remainder of the section is devoted to illustrating how to solve geometric problems using these various forms of the equations for flats.

THEOREM 2.8.1. If x and y are two solutions of the equations $Ax = b$, then so is $w_1 x + w_2 y$ for any two numbers w_1 and w_2 such that $w_1 + w_2 = 1$.

Proof: By assumption $Ax = b$ and $Ay = b$. Hence,

$$A(w_1 x + w_2 y) = w_1 Ax + w_2 Ay = (w_1 + w_2)b = b,$$

using the fact that $w_1 + w_2 = 1$.

DEFINITION 2.8.1. Let $B_0, B_1, \ldots, B_k$ be $k + 1$ vectors that satisfy $Ax = b$ and such that $B_1, \ldots, B_k$ are linearly independent—that is, $B_1, \ldots, B_k$ are points in the flat defined by $Ax = b$. Then the *weighted combination* form of the flat is given by

$$x = w_0 B_0 + w_1 B_1 + \cdots + w_k B_k = \sum_{i=0}^{k} w_i B_i,$$

where $w_0, w_1, \ldots, w_k$ are arbitrary numbers satisfying

$$\sum_{i=0}^{k} w_i = w_0 + w_1 + \cdots + w_k = 1.$$

EXAMPLE 2.8.1. Consider again the line of Example 2.7.3. Its parametric equation was found to be

$$\begin{bmatrix} x_1 \\ x_2 \\ x_3 \end{bmatrix} = \begin{bmatrix} 2 \\ -1 \\ 0 \end{bmatrix} + p \begin{bmatrix} 2 \\ -3 \\ 1 \end{bmatrix}.$$

Hence we can find points on the line by assuming various values of p. Specifically, we choose $p = 0$ and $p = 1$ and obtain the points $\begin{bmatrix} 2 \\ -1 \\ 0 \end{bmatrix}$ and $\begin{bmatrix} 4 \\ -4 \\ 1 \end{bmatrix}$ on the line. Using these points, we find the weighted combination form of the equations of the line to be

$$\begin{bmatrix} x_1 \\ x_2 \\ x_3 \end{bmatrix} = w_0 \begin{bmatrix} 2 \\ -1 \\ 0 \end{bmatrix} + w_1 \begin{bmatrix} 4 \\ -4 \\ 1 \end{bmatrix} = w_0 B_0 + w_1 B_1,$$

---

* This section is intended for those interested in exploring the geometry of vector spaces more fully. It may be skipped without loss of continuity.

where $w_0 + w_1 = 1$. The geometric picture for this line is given in Figure 2.8.1. You should carefully compare this picture with the one in Figure 2.7.1. Note that in Figure 2.8.1 both B_0 and B_1 are on the given line, whereas in Figure 2.7.1, A_0 is on the line while A_1 is *parallel* to the line, not *on* the line.

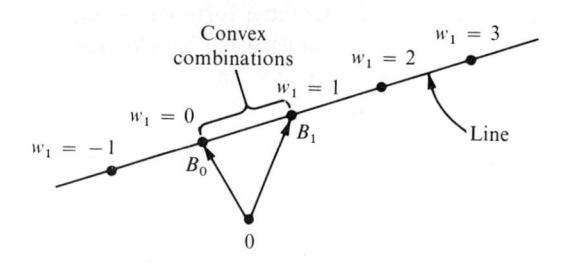

FIGURE 2.8.1

Note also that in the figure various values of w_1 are marked on the line. (Only w_1 need be marked since $w_0 = 1 - w_1$, and its value is thereby determined.) Note from the figure that the points on the line between B_0 and B_1 correspond to the values of w_1 and hence w_0 that lie between 0 and 1. These points are called convex combinations of B_0 and B_1, as defined in Section 2.2. We will study convex combinations of vectors more fully in the next chapter.

Before proving the next theorem, which states how to take the parametric form of the equations for a flat into the weighted combination form and vice versa, we will restate the definitions of the parametric and weighted combination forms.

Consider the k-dimensional flat with equations $Ax = b$.

(a) Its parametric form is given by

$$x = A_0 + p_1 A_1 + \cdots + p_k A_k,$$

where $AA_0 = b$, $AA_i = 0$, for $i = 1, \ldots, k$, and where $A_1, \ldots, A_k$ are linearly independent.

(b) Its weighted combination form is given by

$$x = w_0 B_0 + w_1 B_1 + \cdots + w_k B_k,$$

where $AB_i = b$ for $i = 0, \ldots, k$ and $w_0 + \cdots + w_k = 1$, and where $B_1, \ldots, B_k$ are linearly independent.

THEOREM 2.8.2. (a) The following transformations take the parametric form into the weighted combination form:

$$\begin{aligned}
B_0 &= A_0 \\
B_i &= A_i + A_0 \\
w_i &= p_i
\end{aligned} \Bigg\} \quad \text{for } i = 1, \ldots, k$$

$$w_0 = 1 - p_1 - p_2 - \cdots - p_k$$

(b) The following transformations take the weighted combination form into the parametric form:

$$\left.\begin{array}{l} A_0 = B_0 \\ A_i = B_i - B_0 \\ p_i = w_i \end{array}\right\} \quad \text{for } i = 1, \ldots, k$$

Proof: (a) Since $AA_0 = b$ and $A_0 = B_0$, we have $AB_0 = b$. Since $B_i = A_i + A_0$, $AA_i = 0$, $AA_0 = b$, we have

$$AB_i = A(A_i + A_0) = AA_i + AA_0 = 0 + b = b.$$

Finally, if $A_1, \ldots, A_k$ are linearly independent, so are $B_1 = A_1 + A_0, \ldots, B_k = A_k + A_0$ (see Exercise 10).

The proof of (b) is left as Exercise 11.

EXAMPLE 2.8.2. Put the line whose parametric equation is

$$\begin{bmatrix} x_1 \\ x_2 \\ x_3 \end{bmatrix} = \begin{bmatrix} 1 \\ -1 \\ 1 \end{bmatrix} + p_1 \begin{bmatrix} 2 \\ -3 \\ 1 \end{bmatrix} = A_0 + p_1 A_1$$

into weighted combination form.

Using the transformations given in Theorem 2.8.1, we must compute

$$A_0 + A_1 = \begin{bmatrix} 1 \\ -1 \\ 1 \end{bmatrix} + \begin{bmatrix} 2 \\ -3 \\ 1 \end{bmatrix} = \begin{bmatrix} 3 \\ -4 \\ 2 \end{bmatrix}$$

so that the weighted combination form is

$$\begin{bmatrix} x_1 \\ x_2 \\ x_3 \end{bmatrix} = w_0 \begin{bmatrix} 1 \\ -1 \\ 1 \end{bmatrix} + w_1 \begin{bmatrix} 3 \\ -4 \\ 2 \end{bmatrix}, \quad w_0 + w_1 = 1.$$

EXAMPLE 2.8.3. Put the plane through the three points

$$\begin{bmatrix} 2 \\ 0 \\ -3 \end{bmatrix}, \begin{bmatrix} 7 \\ -5 \\ 2 \end{bmatrix}, \begin{bmatrix} 0 \\ 2 \\ -3 \end{bmatrix}$$

into parametric form.

Its weighted combination form is

$$\begin{bmatrix} x_1 \\ x_2 \\ x_3 \end{bmatrix} = w_0 \begin{bmatrix} 2 \\ 0 \\ -3 \end{bmatrix} + w_1 \begin{bmatrix} 7 \\ -5 \\ 2 \end{bmatrix} + w_2 \begin{bmatrix} 0 \\ 2 \\ -3 \end{bmatrix}, \quad w_0 + w_1 + w_2 = 1.$$

Following the transformation equation, we next compute

$$A_1 = B_1 - B_0 = \begin{bmatrix} 7 \\ -5 \\ 2 \end{bmatrix} - \begin{bmatrix} 2 \\ 0 \\ -3 \end{bmatrix} = \begin{bmatrix} 5 \\ -5 \\ 5 \end{bmatrix};$$

$$A_2 = B_2 - B_0 = \begin{bmatrix} 0 \\ 2 \\ -3 \end{bmatrix} - \begin{bmatrix} 2 \\ 0 \\ -3 \end{bmatrix} = \begin{bmatrix} -2 \\ 2 \\ 0 \end{bmatrix}.$$

Hence, its parametric equation form is

$$\begin{bmatrix} x_1 \\ x_2 \\ x_3 \end{bmatrix} = \begin{bmatrix} 2 \\ 0 \\ -3 \end{bmatrix} + p_1 \begin{bmatrix} 5 \\ -5 \\ 5 \end{bmatrix} + p_2 \begin{bmatrix} -2 \\ 2 \\ 0 \end{bmatrix}.$$

Suppose now we wanted the equation of the plane going through the three points of Example 2.8.3. It can be found by taking the parametric form of the equation of the plane and eliminating the parameters from the equations by pivoting. We will first discuss the general problem and then solve the specific one.

Let us discuss in general the process of going from the parametric form of the equations for a flat to the hyperplane form. We have

$$x = A_0 + p_1 A_1 + \cdots + p_k A_k \quad \text{or} \quad p_1 A_1 + \cdots + p_k A_k = x - A_0.$$

Clearly these are a set of nonhomogeneous equations for the p's in terms of the x's. It is also clear that for some x's these equations will have a solution but that for other x's they will not. Thus the x's will have to satisfy certain relations in order that the equations have solutions. We illustrate how to discover these needed relations by the pivoting procedure.

EXAMPLE 2.8.4. Find the equation of the plane through the three points of Example 2.8.3. We start with the tableau

$$\begin{bmatrix} 5 & -2 & x_1 & -2 \\ -5 & 2 & x_2 & \\ 5 & 0 & x_3 + 3 \end{bmatrix}$$

whose columns are A_1, A_2, and $x - A_0$, respectively. Pivoting on the 5 in the first row we have

$$\begin{bmatrix} 1 & -\frac{2}{5} & \frac{1}{5}x_1 & -\frac{2}{5} \\ 0 & 0 & x_1 + x_2 & -2 \\ 0 & 2 & -x_1 + & x_3 + 5 \end{bmatrix}.$$

Pivoting again on the second entry in the third row we obtain the final tableau

$$\begin{bmatrix} 1 & 0 & (\frac{1}{5})x_3 + \frac{3}{5} \\ 0 & 0 & x_1 + x_2 & -2 \\ 0 & 1 & -(\frac{1}{2})x_1 & +(\frac{1}{2})x_3 + \frac{5}{2} \end{bmatrix}.$$

Because of the two zeros in the second row we see that the original equations will have a solution for the parameters if and only if the right-hand side of the second equation is zero—that is, if

$$x_1 + x_2 = 2$$

and this is the desired equation of the plane through the three points. You should verify that the original three points do in fact satisfy this equation.

EXAMPLE 2.8.5. Find the equations of two independent planes through the line of Example 2.8.2. We start with the tableau

$$\begin{bmatrix} 2 & x_1 & -1 \\ -3 & x_2 & +1 \\ 1 & x_3 & -1 \end{bmatrix}$$

and pivot on the 2 entry in the first row. The new tableau is

$$\begin{bmatrix} 1 & \frac{1}{2}x_1 & -\frac{1}{2} \\ 0 & \frac{3}{2}x_1 + x_2 & -\frac{1}{2} \\ 0 & -\frac{1}{2}x_1 & +x_3 - \frac{1}{2} \end{bmatrix}.$$

After multiplying through the second and third rows of this tableau by 2, we find that the desired equations are as follows:

$$3x_1 + 2x_2 \qquad = 1,$$
$$-x_1 \qquad + 2x_3 = 1.$$

Let us review the process we have just illustrated in Examples 2.8.4 and 2.8.5. We started with the parametric form of the equations

$$p_1 A_1 + \cdots + p_k A_k = x - A_0,$$

which we wanted to solve. Hence we set up the initial tableau

$$(A_1 \quad A_2 \quad \cdots \quad A_k \quad | \quad x - A_0),$$

and we pivoted on successive rows of the tableau, choosing nonzero entries to the left of the vertical line. When no further pivots were possible, we looked at the final tableau for rows which had all zeros to the left of the vertical line. Setting the right-hand sides of these rows equal to zero then gave the equations of the desired hyperplanes.

In Exercise 12 you will be asked to set up the initial tableau if the process is started with the weighted combination form of the flat instead of the parametric form.

In the remainder of this section we will solve some geometric problems using the methods given above.

EXAMPLE 2.8.6. Find the equation of the plane through the line of Example 2.8.2 and the point $\begin{bmatrix} 3 \\ 0 \\ -3 \end{bmatrix}$. Since

$$\begin{bmatrix} 3 \\ 0 \\ -3 \end{bmatrix} - \begin{bmatrix} 1 \\ -1 \\ 1 \end{bmatrix} = \begin{bmatrix} 2 \\ 1 \\ -4 \end{bmatrix},$$

the parametric form of the plane is

$$\begin{bmatrix} x_1 \\ x_2 \\ x_3 \end{bmatrix} = \begin{bmatrix} 1 \\ -1 \\ 1 \end{bmatrix} + p_1 \begin{bmatrix} 2 \\ -3 \\ 1 \end{bmatrix} + p_2 \begin{bmatrix} 2 \\ 1 \\ -4 \end{bmatrix};$$

hence the initial tableau is

$$\begin{bmatrix} 2 & 2 & & x_1 & -1 \\ -3 & 1 & & x_2 & +1 \\ 1 & -4 & & x_3 & -1 \end{bmatrix}.$$

Suppose we pivot on the second 2 in the first row. We get

$$\begin{bmatrix} 1 & 1 & \frac{1}{2}x_1 & -\frac{1}{2} \\ -4 & 0 & -\frac{1}{2}x_1 + x_2 & +\frac{3}{2} \\ 5 & 0 & 2x_1 & + x_3 - 3 \end{bmatrix}.$$

Pivoting next on the -4 in the second row gives

$$\begin{bmatrix} 0 & 1 & \frac{3}{8}x_1 + \frac{1}{4}x_2 & -\frac{1}{8} \\ 1 & 0 & \frac{1}{8}x_1 - \frac{1}{4}x_2 & -\frac{3}{8} \\ 0 & 0 & \frac{11}{8}x_1 + \frac{5}{4}x_2 + x_3 - \frac{9}{8} \end{bmatrix}.$$

After multiplying the last row through by 8 we have the desired equation:

$$11x_1 + 10x_2 + 8x_3 = 9.$$

You should verify that the original line and point satisfy this equation.

EXAMPLE 2.8.7. Find the point at which the line whose weighted combination equation is

$$x = w_0 \begin{bmatrix} 7 \\ 5 \\ -2 \end{bmatrix} + w_1 \begin{bmatrix} -3 \\ 2 \\ 0 \end{bmatrix}, \qquad w_0 + w_1 = 1,$$

pierces the plane whose equation is

$$-x_1 + 4x_2 + 2x_3 = 5.$$

It is easiest if we first change to the parametric form of the line, which is

$$x = \begin{bmatrix} 7 \\ 5 \\ -2 \end{bmatrix} + p_1 \begin{bmatrix} -10 \\ -3 \\ 2 \end{bmatrix}.$$

We next substitute these values of the x's into the equation of the plane and set $p_1 = p$ to obtain

$$-(7 - 10p) + 4(5 - 3p) + 2(-2 + 2p) = 5.$$

Simplifying, we have $2p = -4$, which is solved by $p = -2$. The corresponding value of x is $x = \begin{bmatrix} 27 \\ 11 \\ -6 \end{bmatrix}$. You can check that this point lies on both the line and the plane.

EXAMPLE 2.8.8. Show that the line of Example 2.8.2 is coplanar with the line whose weighted combination equation is

$$x = w_0 \begin{bmatrix} 1 \\ 2 \\ -2 \end{bmatrix} + w_1 \begin{bmatrix} -3 \\ 8 \\ -4 \end{bmatrix}, \qquad w_0 + w_1 = 1.$$

We change to parametric form

$$x = \begin{bmatrix} 1 \\ 2 \\ -2 \end{bmatrix} + p_1 \begin{bmatrix} -4 \\ 6 \\ -2 \end{bmatrix}$$

and note that the two lines are parallel and hence coplanar.

Exercise 1 asks you to find the equation of the plane that contains both the lines.

EXERCISES 2.8

1. Find the equation of the plane that contains the lines of Example 2.8.8.

2. Consider the planes whose equations are
    (i) $8x_1 - 3x_2 + 3x_3 = 4$,
    (ii) $x_1 \qquad - 3x_3 = 8$.
    Which of the following lines and points lie on these planes?

    (a) The line through the points $\begin{bmatrix} 8 \\ 20 \\ 0 \end{bmatrix}$ and $\begin{bmatrix} 11 \\ 29 \\ 1 \end{bmatrix}$.

    (b) The point $\begin{bmatrix} 2 \\ 0 \\ -4 \end{bmatrix}$.

    (c) The line through the points $\begin{bmatrix} 11 \\ 0 \\ 1 \end{bmatrix}$ and $\begin{bmatrix} 2 \\ 2 \\ -2 \end{bmatrix}$.

    (d) The line whose parametric equation is

    $$\begin{bmatrix} 5 \\ 11 \\ -1 \end{bmatrix} + p_1 \begin{bmatrix} 3 \\ 9 \\ 1 \end{bmatrix}.$$

    (e) The point $\begin{bmatrix} 3 \\ 2 \\ -1 \end{bmatrix}$.

3. Find the points where the line whose parametric equation is

    $$x = \begin{bmatrix} 2 \\ -2 \\ 1 \end{bmatrix} + p_1 \begin{bmatrix} 3 \\ 9 \\ 1 \end{bmatrix}$$

    pierces each of the planes of Exercise 2.

4. Which of the following sets of points are collinear? In each case of collinearity, find the equations of the line.

(a) $\begin{bmatrix} 7 \\ -1 \\ 2 \end{bmatrix}, \quad \begin{bmatrix} 3 \\ -4 \\ 0 \end{bmatrix}, \quad \begin{bmatrix} -1 \\ -7 \\ -2 \end{bmatrix}$

(b) $\begin{bmatrix} 0 \\ 1 \\ 1 \end{bmatrix}, \quad \begin{bmatrix} 0 \\ 1 \\ 0 \end{bmatrix}, \quad \begin{bmatrix} 3 \\ 2 \\ 1 \end{bmatrix}$

(c) $\begin{bmatrix} 1 \\ 0 \\ 1 \end{bmatrix}, \quad \begin{bmatrix} 1 \\ 1 \\ 0 \end{bmatrix}, \quad \begin{bmatrix} 1 \\ -2 \\ 3 \end{bmatrix}$

(d) $\begin{bmatrix} -1 \\ 0 \\ 1 \end{bmatrix}, \quad \begin{bmatrix} 3 \\ 2 \\ 1 \end{bmatrix}, \quad \begin{bmatrix} 7 \\ 4 \\ 1 \end{bmatrix}$

5. Which of the following sets of points are coplanar? When coplanarity is found, determine the equation of the plane.

(a) $\begin{bmatrix} 1 \\ 1 \\ -1 \end{bmatrix}, \quad \begin{bmatrix} 0 \\ 2 \\ 0 \end{bmatrix}, \quad \begin{bmatrix} 2 \\ 0 \\ -2 \end{bmatrix}, \quad \begin{bmatrix} 0 \\ -3 \\ -3 \end{bmatrix}$

(b) $\begin{bmatrix} 1 \\ 0 \\ 0 \end{bmatrix}, \quad \begin{bmatrix} 0 \\ 1 \\ 1 \end{bmatrix}, \quad \begin{bmatrix} 1 \\ 0 \\ 1 \end{bmatrix}, \quad \begin{bmatrix} 1 \\ 2 \\ 3 \end{bmatrix}$

(c) $\begin{bmatrix} -13 \\ 0 \\ 0 \end{bmatrix}, \quad \begin{bmatrix} -1 \\ 3 \\ 0 \end{bmatrix}, \quad \begin{bmatrix} 1 \\ 0 \\ -2 \end{bmatrix}, \quad \begin{bmatrix} 2 \\ -2 \\ -3 \end{bmatrix}$

6. Find the equation of the plane through the point $\begin{bmatrix} 1 \\ -1 \\ 1 \end{bmatrix}$ and each of the following lines:

(a) $\begin{bmatrix} 3 \\ 0 \\ -4 \end{bmatrix} + p_1 \begin{bmatrix} 0 \\ 1 \\ -2 \end{bmatrix}.$

(b) The line through the points $\begin{bmatrix} 1 \\ 0 \\ -1 \end{bmatrix}$ and $\begin{bmatrix} 0 \\ 2 \\ -2 \end{bmatrix}.$

(c) $w_0 \begin{bmatrix} 7 \\ -5 \\ 2 \end{bmatrix} + w_1 \begin{bmatrix} 3 \\ 3 \\ -2 \end{bmatrix}, \qquad w_0 + w_1 = 1.$

7. Which of the following lines are coplanar in pairs? For those coplanar pairs, find the equation of their plane.

(a) The line through $\begin{bmatrix} 1 \\ 1 \\ 1 \end{bmatrix}$ and $\begin{bmatrix} 4 \\ -1 \\ 3 \end{bmatrix}.$

(b) The line with equation $\begin{bmatrix} 5 \\ 0 \\ 4 \end{bmatrix} + p_1 \begin{bmatrix} 3 \\ -2 \\ 2 \end{bmatrix}$.

(c) The line through the points $\begin{bmatrix} 1 \\ 1 \\ 0 \end{bmatrix}$ and $\begin{bmatrix} 0 \\ 7 \\ 6 \end{bmatrix}$.

(d) The line through the points $\begin{bmatrix} 10 \\ 3 \\ -6 \end{bmatrix}$ and $\begin{bmatrix} 5 \\ -7 \\ -2 \end{bmatrix}$.

8. Prove that if a line whose equation is $C + pD$ does not intersect the plane whose equation is $Ax = b$, then it is parallel to it.

9. In order to solve each of the following geometric problems, which of the three forms of the equations of a flat are preferable—(i) the hyperplane form, (ii) the parametric form, or (iii) the weighted combination form?
   (a) Determine whether three points form a triangle in the plane.
   (b) Determine whether four points in space are coplanar.
   (c) Determine whether two planes are parallel.
   (d) Determine whether two lines are parallel.
   (e) Determine whether two lines are skew.
   (f) Determine whether a given point lies on a line.
   (g) Determine whether a point in a plane is inside or outside a given triangle.
   (h) Determine whether a line pierces a plane.
   (i) Determine whether a line segment pierces a plane.
   (j) Determine whether a line segment lies inside a triangle.

10. Let $b \neq 0$. Assume that $AA_0 = b$ and that $A_1, \ldots, A_k$ are linearly independent vectors such that $AA_i = 0$, for $i = 1, \ldots, k$. Show that $A_1 + A_0, \ldots, A_k + A_0$ are linearly independent by carrying out the following contrapositive argument:
    (a) Assume the contrary—that

$$\sum_{i=1}^{k} c_i(A_i + A_0) = 0, \qquad \text{and some } c_i, \text{ say } c_1 \neq 0.$$

Solve for A_1.
    (b) Using the fact that $AA_1 = 0$, show that

$$\sum_{i=1}^{k} c_i = 0.$$

(c) Use the result of (b) to show that $A_1, \ldots, A_k$ are not linearly independent, which is a contradiction.

11. Prove Part (b) of Theorem 2.8.2.

12. Suppose that we have a flat expressed in weighted combination form as

$$x = w_0 B_0 + w_1 B_1 + \cdots + w_k B_k, \qquad w_0 + w_1 + \cdots + w_k = 1.$$

Show that in order to put the equation of the flat into hyperplane form, we start with the following initial tableau:

$$[B_1 - B_0 \quad B_2 - B_0 \quad \cdots \quad B_k - B_0 \quad | \quad x - B_0].$$

Discuss the relation of this initial tableau with the initial tableau for the parametric form of the equation of the flat.

*13. Let $x = w_0 B_0 + w_1 B_1 + \cdots + w_k B_k$, where $B_1, \ldots, B_k$ are linearly independent. Show that the flat does *not* go through the origin if and only if $B_0, B_1, \ldots, B_k$ are linearly independent.

SUGGESTED READING

Birkhoff, G., and MacLane, S. *A Survey of Modern Algebra*, Third Edition. New York: Macmillan, 1965.

Hadley, G. *Linear Algebra*. Reading, Mass.: Addison-Wesley, 1961.

Johnson, R. E. *First Course in Abstract Algebra*. Englewood Cliffs, N.J.: Prentice-Hall, 1953.

Kemeny, J. G., Schleifer, A. S., Jr., Snell, J. L., and Thompson, G. L., *Finite Mathematics with Business Applications*, Second Edition. Englewood Cliffs, N.J.: Prentice-Hall, 1972.

CHAPTER 3

CONVEX SETS

3.1   INTRODUCTION

You are undoubtedly familiar with inequality statements from high school algebra. Thus, if A is a row vector with n components, x is a column vector of n variables, and b is a number, then the inequality $Ax \leq b$ is an open statement. That is, the statement is true for some vectors x in C_n and false for others. For example, if we consider the inequality

(3.1.1) $$3x_1 + 4x_2 = \begin{bmatrix} 3 & 4 \end{bmatrix} \begin{bmatrix} x_1 \\ x_2 \end{bmatrix} \leq 12,$$

we see that it is true for $x = \begin{bmatrix} 1 \\ 1 \end{bmatrix}$ and for $x = \begin{bmatrix} 0 \\ 0 \end{bmatrix}$, but that it is false for $x = \begin{bmatrix} 2 \\ 2 \end{bmatrix}$ and $x = \begin{bmatrix} 6 \\ -1 \end{bmatrix}$ and so on. The set of all vectors for which (3.1.1) is true is the shaded

---

* This chapter presents a geometric approach to convex sets, linear inequalities, and the simplex method. Chapter 4 will present an independent algebraic approach to the simplex method. Therefore, readers who are interested only in the algebraic approach to the simplex method should cover only Section 3.1; they may skip the rest of Chapter 3 without loss of continuity.

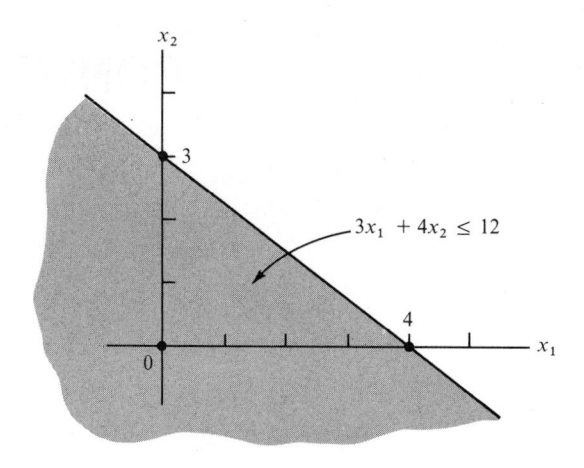

FIGURE 3.1.1

half-plane in Figure 3.1.1. Note that the half-plane consists of all the points on the line $3x_1 + 4x_2 = 12$ and all points *below* it. This is easy to see because if we start with a point on the line and decrease x_2 (holding x_1 constant), we will continue to have the inequality satisfied. But if we increase x_2 (still holding x_1 constant) we will cease to satisfy the inequality. In the same way, if we start with a point on the line and decrease x_1 while holding x_2 constant, the inequality continues to be satisfied. And it is not satisfied if we increase x_1, and so on.

DEFINITION 3.1.1. Let $A \neq 0$ be an n-component row vector and b a number; then the set of all x for which the open statement $Ax \leq b$ is true is its *truth set* and is also defined to be a *closed half-space* in C_n. The truth set of $Ax < b$ is an *open half-space* in C_n.

As an example of an open half-space, consider

$$(3.1.2) \qquad 3x_1 + 4x_2 = \begin{bmatrix} 3 & 4 \end{bmatrix} \begin{bmatrix} x_1 \\ x_2 \end{bmatrix} < 12.$$

Clearly, its truth set is the shaded area of Figure 3.1.1, but *not* including the line whose equation is $3x_1 + 4x_2 = 12$.

DEFINITION 3.1.2. Let $Ax \leq b$ or $Ax < b$ be a closed and an open half-space, respectively; for each of these the *bounding hyperplane* is the truth set of $Ax = b$.

From these definitions it is clear that the difference between a closed and an open half-space is simply that the closed half-space contains its bounding hyperplane, while the open half-space does not. In this book we shall deal principally with closed half-spaces.

Exactly the same remarks are possible for a half-space defined by a linear inequality of the form $Ax \geq b$. This can be easily seen, since multiplying $Ax \geq b$ by -1 gives the equivalent open statement $-Ax \leq -b$, which is of the form given above.

THEOREM 3.1.1. If x and y are two solutions to the linear inequality open statements $Ax \leq b$ or $Ax < b$, then so is any convex combination $z = px + (1 - p)y$, where $0 \leq p \leq 1$.

Proof: Since $0 \leq p \leq 1$, it is also true that $0 \leq 1 - p \leq 1$. Then, using elementary rules for working with inequalities, we have that $Ax \leq b$ and $Ay \leq b$ imply

$$Az = A(px + (1 - p)y) = pAx + (1 - p)Ay \leq pb + (1 - p)b = b,$$

as was to be shown. The same proof works if the $\leq$ signs are replaced by $<$.

The fact that a half-space contains convex combinations of pairs of points that belong to it means that it is convex in the sense of the following definition.

DEFINITION 3.1.3. A set C of points in C_n is said to be *convex* if, for every x and y belonging to C, the vector $z = px + (1 - p)y$ also belongs to C for all numbers p satisfying $0 \leq p \leq 1$.

THEOREM 3.1.2. The intersection of two or more convex sets is also a convex set.

Proof: Let S and T be convex sets and let $C = S \cap T$. Suppose x and y belong to C. Then both x and y belong to S; hence $z = px + (1 - p)y$ also belongs to S since it is convex. It is also true that x and y belong to T, hence so does z. Thus, z belongs to $S \cap T = C$.

Suppose now that A is an $m \times n$ matrix, x an n-component column vector, and b an m-component column vector. Then $Ax \leq b$ is the conjunction of m inequality open statements, and its truth set is the intersection of the m corresponding half-spaces. By Theorem 3.1.2, its truth set is then a convex. We thus have proved the following theorem.

THEOREM 3.1.3. The intersection of a finite number of (closed or open) half-spaces is a convex set.

DEFINITION 3.1.4. A *polyhedral convex set* is the intersection of a finite number of closed half-spaces. In other words, a polyhedral convex set is the truth set of simultaneous inequality statements $Ax \leq b$.

EXAMPLE 3.1.1. Consider the inequality statement $Ax \leq b$, where

$$A = \begin{bmatrix} 3 & 4 \\ -1 & 0 \\ 0 & -1 \end{bmatrix}, \quad x = \begin{bmatrix} x_1 \\ x_2 \end{bmatrix}, \quad \text{and} \quad b = \begin{bmatrix} 12 \\ -1 \\ -1 \end{bmatrix}.$$

The corresponding inequality statements are

$$3x_1 + 4x_2 \leq 12,$$
$$-x_1 \quad\quad \leq -1 \quad \text{or} \quad x_1 \geq 1,$$
$$-x_2 \leq -1 \quad \text{or} \quad x_2 \geq 1.$$

The first half-space was sketched in Figure 3.1.1. The second half-space is the half-plane to the right of the line $x_1 = 1$; and the third half-space is the half-plane above the line $x_2 = 1$. The intersection of these three is the triangle shaded in Figure 3.1.2.

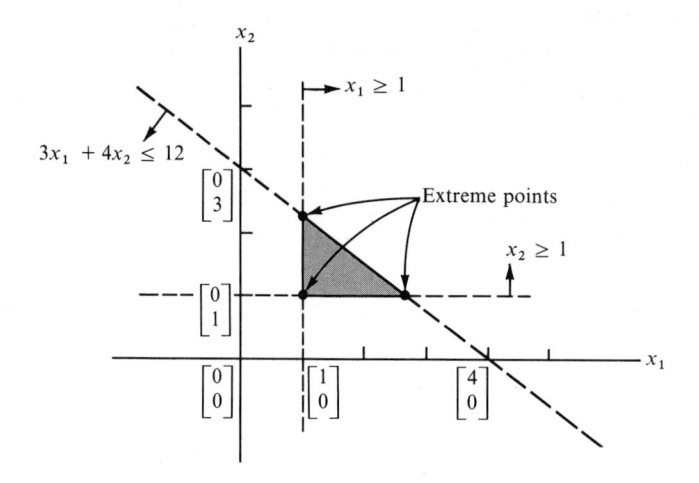

FIGURE 3.1.2

Note that the convex set includes the three corners, the three sides, and the interior of the triangle. Note also that given two points in the triangle (including boundary lines and points), all the points on the line segment between the two—that is, all the convex combinations of the two points—also belong to the triangle. This is the geometric interpretation of a convex set.

Of special importance are the corner points of the triangle, which we will call extreme points.

DEFINITION 3.1.5. Let C be a polyhedral convex set in C_n defined by the inequalities $Ax \le b$. Then a point z is an *extreme point of C* if

(a) z belongs to C—that is, $Az \le b$—and

(b) z is the unique intersection of n bounding hyperplanes of C (where n is the dimension of the space).

EXAMPLE 3.1.2. Find the extreme points of the convex set of Example 3.1.1. They are marked on Figure 3.1.2. The one in the lower left-hand corner of the triangle is obviously $\begin{bmatrix} 1 \\ 1 \end{bmatrix}$. To find the one in the lower right-hand corner of the triangle, we must solve the simultaneous equations $3x_1 + 4x_2 = 12$ and $x_2 = 1$. The solution can easily be found as $\begin{bmatrix} \frac{8}{3} \\ 1 \end{bmatrix}$. Similarly, the upper left-hand corner of the triangle is the simultaneous solution of the equations $3x_1 + 4x_2 = 12$ and $x_1 = 1$, which yields the point $\begin{bmatrix} 1 \\ \frac{9}{4} \end{bmatrix}$.

EXAMPLE 3.1.3. Find the extreme points of the convex set defined by $Ax \leq b$, where

$$A = \begin{bmatrix} 0 & -1 \\ -1 & 1 \end{bmatrix}, \qquad x = \begin{bmatrix} x_1 \\ x_2 \end{bmatrix}, \qquad b = \begin{bmatrix} 0 \\ 0 \end{bmatrix}.$$

Hence the corresponding inequalities are

$$-x_2 \leq 0 \quad \text{or} \quad x_2 \geq 0,$$
$$-x_1 + x_2 \leq 0 \quad \text{or} \quad x_2 \leq x_1.$$

The convex set is pictured in Figure 3.1.3. Note that it has exactly one extreme point, namely the origin, $\begin{bmatrix} 0 \\ 0 \end{bmatrix}$. Note also that the convex set contains any *ray*, or half-line, that starts at the origin and makes an angle between 0 and 45° with the horizontal axis. One such ray is shown dotted in the figure. Another ray, parallel to the 45° constraint, is also shown. Infinitely many other rays, or half-lines, are contained in the convex set.

A convex set that contains a ray, such as the one in Figure 3.1.3, is said to be *unbounded*. A convex set that does not contain a ray is said to be *bounded*. An example is given in Figure 3.1.2.

EXAMPLE 3.1.4. Suppose we add the inequality

$$3x_1 + 4x_2 \leq 12$$

to those of the previous example. Then the corresponding convex set becomes the triangle pictured in Figure 3.1.4, which is a bounded set. In Exercise 1, you will be asked to find its extreme points.

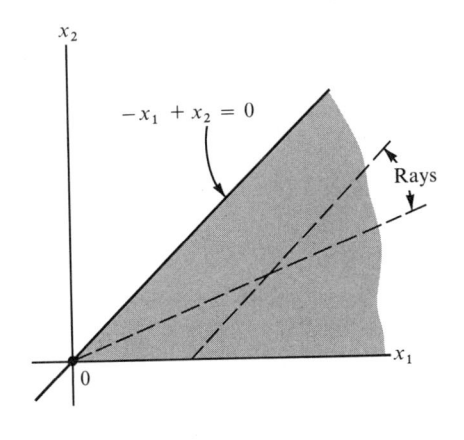

FIGURE 3.1.3

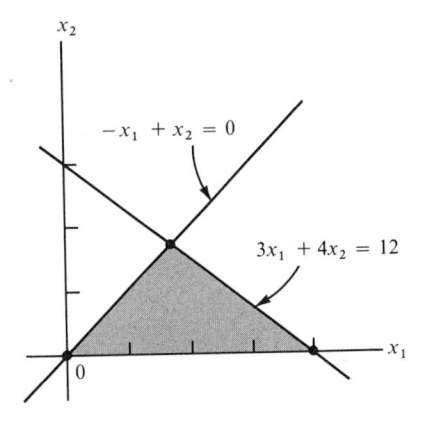

FIGURE 3.1.4

This procedure of making an unbounded set into a bounded set by the technique of adding an additional constraint has been called *regularization* by Charnes and Cooper. We shall see later that it is a very useful technique.

EXERCISES 3.1

1. Find the extreme points for the convex set in Example 3.1.4.

2. Find the extreme points and sketch the convex sets $Ax \leq b$ defined by the following sets of data. Which sets are bounded and which are unbounded?

(a) $\quad A = \begin{bmatrix} -1 & -1 \\ 1 & 0 \\ 0 & 1 \end{bmatrix}, \quad b = \begin{bmatrix} -2 \\ 2 \\ 2 \end{bmatrix}$

(b) $\quad A = \begin{bmatrix} -2 & 1 \\ 1 & -2 \end{bmatrix}, \quad b = \begin{bmatrix} -2 \\ -2 \end{bmatrix}$

(c) $\quad A = \begin{bmatrix} -1 & -1 & -1 \\ 1 & 1 & 1 \end{bmatrix}, \quad b = \begin{bmatrix} -2 \\ 4 \end{bmatrix}$

(d) $\quad A = \begin{bmatrix} 1 & 1 \\ -1 & 1 \\ 1 & -1 \\ -1 & -1 \end{bmatrix}, \quad b = \begin{bmatrix} 1 \\ 1 \\ 1 \\ 1 \end{bmatrix}$

(e) $\quad A = \begin{bmatrix} 1 & 0 & 0 \\ -1 & 0 & 0 \\ 0 & -1 & 0 \\ 0 & 0 & -1 \end{bmatrix}, \quad b = \begin{bmatrix} 5 \\ -3 \\ 0 \\ 0 \end{bmatrix}$

3. Show that the following sets of inequalities are equivalent—that is, have exactly the same truth set.

$$\text{(i)} \quad Ax \leq b$$
$$\text{(ii)} \quad Ax + y = b, \quad y \geq 0$$

4. Which of the following sets are convex? For those that are convex, which are polyhedral?

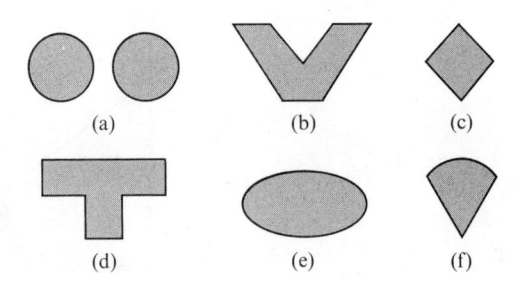

   (a)   (b)   (c)

   (d)   (e)   (f)

5. Show by examples that the union of two convex sets may or may not be convex.

6. If A and B are two sets, the *difference*, $A - B$, consists of the points *in A* that are *not in B*.
(a) Show that $(A - B) \cap \tilde{A} = \emptyset$.
(b) If A and B are convex sets, show by example that $A - B$ may or may not be convex.

7. Show that the empty set, $\emptyset$, is (vacuously) a convex set.

8. If $A, B, A - B, B - A$ are all convex sets, must $A \cup B$ be convex?

9. A man goes to a store to buy x shirts, y neckties, and z handkerchiefs. Assume shirts cost \$5, neckties \$3, and handkerchiefs \$1. Write in inequality form the following constraints on his purchases, and find all whole-number solutions to each problem, assuming that all earlier constraints continue to hold.
    (a) He must buy nonnegative amounts of each.
    (b) He must not spend more than \$21.
    (c) He must buy at least one of each.
    (d) He must buy more shirts than neckties.
    (e) He must buy not more than four handkerchiefs.
    (f) He must spend exactly \$21. (*Hint:* There is only one solution.)
    (g) He must buy not more than two shirts.

10. Is the convex combination of two whole-number solutions to one of the parts of Exercise 9 a solution in the mathematical sense? In the economic sense?

11. Show that the set of all convex combinations of the points

$$\begin{bmatrix} 0 \\ 1 \end{bmatrix} \quad \text{and} \quad \begin{bmatrix} 1 \\ 0 \end{bmatrix}$$

    consists of a line segment in the plane.

12. Show that the set of all convex combinations of the points

$$\begin{bmatrix} 1 \\ 0 \\ 0 \end{bmatrix}, \quad \begin{bmatrix} 0 \\ 1 \\ 0 \end{bmatrix}, \quad \text{and} \quad \begin{bmatrix} 0 \\ 0 \\ 1 \end{bmatrix}$$

    consists of a triangle in C_3, including interior, sides, and corners.

13. Give an interpretation for the set of all convex combinations of the four points

$$\begin{bmatrix} 1 \\ 0 \\ 0 \\ 0 \end{bmatrix}, \quad \begin{bmatrix} 0 \\ 1 \\ 0 \\ 0 \end{bmatrix}, \quad \begin{bmatrix} 0 \\ 0 \\ 1 \\ 0 \end{bmatrix}, \quad \begin{bmatrix} 0 \\ 0 \\ 0 \\ 1 \end{bmatrix}$$

    in C_4.

14. Consider the inequalities $Ax \le b$, where A is $m \times n$. The ith inequality, $A_i x \le b_i$, is said to be "tight" at the point x^o if $A_i x^o = b_i$.
    (a) Write three inequalities that determine the triangle bounded by the points

$$\begin{bmatrix} 0 \\ 0 \end{bmatrix}, \quad \begin{bmatrix} 1 \\ 0 \end{bmatrix}, \quad \begin{bmatrix} 0 \\ 1 \end{bmatrix}$$

    in C_2.
    (b) Choose a point in the interior of the triangle defined in (a). Which of the inequalities are tight?
    (c) Choose points on each of the edges of the triangle in (a). Which of the inequalities are tight?
    (d) Choose each of the extreme points of the triangle in (a). Which of the inequalities are tight at each of them?

3.2   RESTRICTED PIVOT METHODS FOR SOLVING LINEAR INEQUALITIES

In the previous sections of this chapter we have considered linear inequalities of the form

$$(3.2.1) \qquad\qquad Ax \le b.$$

We now would like to derive methods for finding solutions to these. Rather than solve this problem directly we consider the seemingly more difficult problem:

$$(3.2.2) \qquad\qquad Ax \le b, \qquad x \ge 0.$$

Note that we have added n inequalities, called *nonnegativity constraints*, on the components of x. Initially this may seem like a step in the wrong direction. However, most of the applied problems with which we shall deal will, by their very nature, have the constraints $x \ge 0$ imposed on the variables. In any case, it is possible to show that by adding variables in the proper way, problems (3.2.2) and (3.2.1) are mathematically equivalent. (See Exercise 6.)

We shall now impose a condition on the b vector; namely, we assume that

$$(3.2.3) \qquad\qquad b \ge 0.$$

In Chapter 4 we will show how to remove this assumption.

We next make an important step that will turn (3.2.2) into *equality* rather than *inequality* statements. Namely, we define an m-component column vector y of variables y_i and consider the system:

$$(3.2.4) \qquad\qquad Ax + y = b, \qquad x \ge 0 \quad \text{and} \quad y \ge 0.$$

It is easy to see that (3.2.2) and (3.2.4) are equivalent, since if we have a solution to (3.2.2), we can define

$$y = b - Ax \ge 0.$$

Conversely, a solution to (3.2.4) implies that $Ax \le b$, since $y \ge 0$.

Next we observe that an initial solution to (3.2.4) is obvious; namely,

$$(3.2.5) \qquad\qquad x = 0 \quad \text{and} \quad y = b \ge 0.$$

But this solution is not interesting. In order to find other solutions that make some components of x positive, we consider the concept of restricted pivoting.

Consider the following initial tableau for the system of equations and inequalities (3.2.4):

$$
T^{(0)} =
\begin{array}{c}
\begin{matrix} A_1 & \cdots & A_n & E_1 & \cdots & E_m \end{matrix} \\
\left[
\begin{array}{ccc|ccc|c|l}
a_{11} & \cdots & a_{1n} & 1 & \cdots & 0 & b_1 & E_1 \\
\vdots & \cdots & \vdots & \cdot & \cdots & \cdot & \cdot & \cdot \\
a_{m1} & \cdots & a_{mn} & 0 & \cdots & 1 & b_m & E_m
\end{array}
\right]
\end{array}
$$

Notice that we have partitioned $T^{(0)}$ into three parts, the part containing the A vectors, the part containing the E vectors, and the b vector. This is not necessary, but is a common convention.

In much of the linear programming literature, the y_i variables are called *slack* or *dummy variables* since they take up the slack and convert inequalities to equalities. From our point of view, they simply correspond to the natural basis vectors in C_m. We will use the name *slack variables* for the y_i's when we wish to refer to them.

We shall transform the initial tableau into later tableaux by multiplying by pivot matrices. However, we will not permit the use of every element of the tableau as a pivot. Let T be any tableau constructed in the pivoting process. The following restrictions must be observed in the selection of the next pivot element:

(R1)   Do not choose a pivot in the last column.

(R2)   Let J be the index of the column (either an A or an E column) that is to be brought into the basis. For each i such that $t_{iJ} > 0$—that is, each positive* t_{iJ}—compute the ratio b_i/t_{iJ}. Now let the pivotal row index I be chosen such that

$$\frac{b_I}{t_{IJ}} = \underset{t_{iJ} > 0}{\text{Minimum}} \frac{b_i}{t_{iJ}}.$$

We call this restriction the *minimum-ratio restriction*.

The reason for these restrictions is that, using them, the nonnegativity of the last column is preserved in the pivoting process, as the next theorem indicates.

THEOREM 3.2.1. Let T be a tableau with nonnegative last column; let P be a pivot matrix constructed from a column of T using restrictions (R1) and (R2); then PT has a nonnegative last column.

Proof: For simplicity, let us prove the theorem for $m = 3$. The proof in the general case proceeds in exactly the same way.

Let $b \geq 0$ be the last column of T, and suppose that we are bringing in the A_2 column of T and taking out E_2. Then the pivot matrix is

$$P = P(A_2, 2) = \begin{bmatrix} 1 & -a_{12}/a_{22} & 0 \\ 0 & 1/a_{22} & 0 \\ 0 & -a_{32}/a_{22} & 1 \end{bmatrix},$$

where, by the assumption that (R2) has been followed, both

$$(3.2.6) \qquad \text{either} \quad a_{12} < 0 \quad \text{or} \quad \frac{b_1}{a_{12}} \geq \frac{b_2}{a_{22}}$$

and

$$(3.2.7) \qquad \text{either} \quad a_{32} < 0 \quad \text{or} \quad \frac{b_3}{a_{32}} \geq \frac{b_2}{a_{22}}.$$

---

* If there is no positive t_{iJ}, then column J cannot be brought into the basis at this step. See Exercise 12. In the next chapter, we will see that when this happens the corresponding problem has no solution.

We must show that each component of Pb is nonnegative. We have

$$Pb = \begin{bmatrix} b_1 - \dfrac{a_{12} b_2}{a_{22}} \\[2ex] \dfrac{b_2}{a_{22}} \\[2ex] b_3 - \dfrac{a_{32} b_2}{a_{22}} \end{bmatrix}.$$

Since $b_2 \geq 0$ and $a_{22} \geq 0$, we have immediately that the second component of Pb is nonnegative. If $a_{12} = 0$, then the first component of Pb is simply b_1, which is assumed to be nonnegative. Hence, assume $a_{12} \neq 0$. We can then write the first component of Pb as

$$(3.2.8) \qquad b_1 - \frac{a_{12} b_2}{a_{22}} = a_{12} \left[\frac{b_1}{a_{12}} - \frac{b_2}{a_{22}} \right].$$

If a_{12} is negative then both factors on the right of the equals sign in (3.2.8) are also negative so that their product is positive. And if a_{12} is positive, then the second factor on the right in (3.2.8) is positive by (3.2.6), so the product of both terms on the right of (3.2.8) is still positive.

A similar analysis shows that the third component of Pb is also nonnegative. Hence $Pb \geq 0$.

Because of this theorem, any sequence of pivots chosen to satisfy restrictions (R1) and (R2) will always lead to a feasible solution for x and y in (3.2.4). In Exercise 4 you will be asked to show that violating these rules leads to infeasible x's and y's.

DEFINITION 3.2.1. A *basic solution* to the system (3.2.4) is any solution (that is, x and y vectors satisfying (3.2.4)) found from a final tableau $T^{(R)}$ by setting the nonbasic variables equal to 0 and setting the basic variables equal to the right-hand sides.

EXAMPLE 3.2.1. Find all basic solutions to

$$(3.2.9) \qquad \begin{aligned} x_1 + 2x_2 &\leq 4, \\ 3x_1 + x_2 &\leq 6. \end{aligned}$$

Following the rules given above, we introduce slack variables y_1 and y_2, obtaining the following system:

$$\begin{aligned} x_1 + 2x_2 + y_1 \qquad &= 4, \\ 3x_1 + x_2 \qquad + y_2 &= 6; \end{aligned}$$

so the initial tableau is as follows.

	A_1	A_2	E_1	E_2		
$T^{(0)} =$	1	2	1	0	4	E_1
	3	1	0	1	6	E_2

Observe that, because the E_1 and E_2 vectors form the initial basis, this tableau corresponds to $x = \begin{bmatrix} 0 \\ 0 \end{bmatrix}$ and $y = \begin{bmatrix} 4 \\ 6 \end{bmatrix}$. Thus the value of y_1 corresponds to the entry in the first column opposite the label E_1, and the value of y_2 corresponds to the entry in the first column opposite the label E_2.

Suppose now that we want to bring A_1 into the basis and take out either E_1 or E_2. In order to determine which one goes out, we compute the ratios $b_1/a_{11} = 4/1 = 4$ and $b_2/a_{21} = 6/3 = 2$. Since the minimum ratio was the second one by (R2), the second row is pivotal; that is, the pivot is the bold-faced **3** entry in $T^{(0)}$. Carrying out the pivotal process we find the second tableau to be as follows.

$$T^{(1)} = \begin{array}{cccc|c|c} A_1 & A_2 & E_1 & E_2 & & \\ 0 & \dfrac{5}{3} & 1 & -\dfrac{1}{3} & 2 & E_1 \\ 1 & \dfrac{1}{3} & 0 & \dfrac{1}{3} & 2 & A_1 \end{array}$$

Notice that we relabeled the second row A_1, since that vector came in and E_2 went out of the basis. Hence the basic solution to the original inequalities that are displayed in this tableau is

$$x = \begin{bmatrix} 2 \\ 0 \end{bmatrix} \quad \text{and} \quad y = \begin{bmatrix} 2 \\ 0 \end{bmatrix}.$$

Now suppose we wish to bring in A_2. We compute the ratios $b_1/a_{21} = 2/(\frac{5}{3}) = \frac{6}{5}$ and $b_2/a_{22} = 2/(\frac{1}{3}) = 6$. The minimum ratio is the first, so the first row is pivotal, and $\frac{5}{3}$ is the pivot. Carrying out the pivoting process we have the next tableau as follows.

$$T^{(2)} = \begin{array}{cccc|c|c} A_1 & A_2 & E_1 & E_2 & & \\ 0 & 1 & \dfrac{3}{5} & -\dfrac{1}{5} & \dfrac{6}{5} & A_2 \\ 1 & 0 & -\dfrac{1}{5} & \dfrac{2}{5} & \dfrac{8}{5} & A_1 \end{array}$$

Because of the labeling we see that

$$x = \begin{bmatrix} \frac{8}{5} \\ \frac{6}{5} \end{bmatrix} \quad \text{and} \quad y = \begin{bmatrix} 0 \\ 0 \end{bmatrix}.$$

Suppose, finally, that we bring E_2 back into the basis. The minimum ratio (in fact, the only ratio) is taken on in the second row, so we pivot on the $\frac{2}{5}$ entry and obtain:

$$T^{(3)} = \begin{array}{cc} & \begin{array}{cccc} A_1 & A_2 & E_1 & E_2 \end{array} \\ & \left[\begin{array}{cc|cc|c} \frac{1}{2} & 1 & \frac{1}{2} & 0 & 2 \\ \frac{5}{2} & 0 & -\frac{1}{2} & 1 & 4 \end{array} \right] \begin{array}{c} A_2 \\ E_2 \end{array} \end{array}$$

Again the labeling indicates that the current answer is

$$x = \begin{bmatrix} 0 \\ 2 \end{bmatrix} \quad \text{and} \quad y = \begin{bmatrix} 0 \\ 4 \end{bmatrix}.$$

In Exercise 1, you are asked to show that no matter what further pivoting is done, any subsequent tableau will be one of the four we have just generated. Figure 3.2.1 pictures the convex set defined by the inequalities (3.2.7). Note that each of the extreme points is one of the basic solutions we found in the pivoting process above. Note also that as we pivoted we moved around the boundary of the convex set in the direction indicated by the arrows.

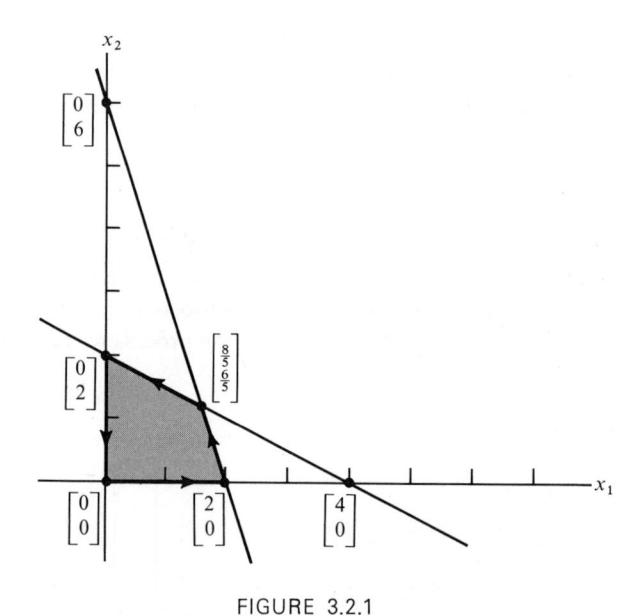

FIGURE 3.2.1

In Chapter 4 we shall show that (a) a basic solution to the inequalities (3.2.4) corresponds to an extreme point of the convex set of all solutions, and conversely; and (b) every solution to (3.2.4) is a convex combination of the extreme points.

THEOREM 3.2.2. There are a finite number of basic solutions.

Proof: Consider the space C_m of the columns of the tableaux. There are $m + n$ vectors to be considered, namely, $A_1, \ldots, A_n$ and $E_1, \ldots, E_m$. Of these, there are exactly m in the basis corresponding to each tableau. But from $m + n$ vectors, at most $\binom{m+n}{m} = \dfrac{(m+n)!}{m!\,n!}$ bases can be constructed. Hence there are at most the same number of tableaux and the same number of basic solutions to the inequalities $Ax \leq b$.

EXERCISES 3.2

1. Consider the four tableaux, $T^{(0)}$, $T^{(1)}$, $T^{(2)}$, and $T^{(3)}$, of Example 3.2.1. In each of the tableaux, exactly two of the four vectors A_1, A_2, E_1, and E_2 are in the basis. For each of the tableaux, try bringing in each of the two vectors *not* in the basis and show that one of the four tableaux will be constructed by the pivoting process (possibly with the two rows interchanged).

2. Find all basic solutions to the inequalities $Ax \leq b$, with the data given in (a) and (b) below.

   (a) $A = \begin{bmatrix} 1 & 1 \\ 2 & 1 \end{bmatrix}, \qquad b = \begin{bmatrix} 6 \\ 8 \end{bmatrix}$

   (b) $A = \begin{bmatrix} 7 & -4 \\ -5 & 3 \end{bmatrix}, \qquad b = \begin{bmatrix} 28 \\ 15 \end{bmatrix}$

   (c) Sketch the convex sets for (a) and (b) and show that the basic solutions correspond to extreme points.

3. For each of the tableaux in Exercise 2(a), show that if each of the vectors not in the basis is brought into the basis, then one of the tableaux already there will be generated again.

4. In Example 3.2.1, carry out a pivot that violates the minimum-ratio rule. Show that a point that is the intersection of bounding hyperplanes is obtained, but that the point does *not* belong to the convex set—that is, does not satisfy all the inequalities. (*Hint:* Try pivoting on the 1 entry in the A_1 column of $T^{(0)}$.)

5. An inequality is said to be *superfluous* if the convex set defined without it is the same as the convex set defined with it. Consider the convex set defined by the inequalities

$$x_1 + x_2 \leq 6,$$
$$2x_1 + x_2 \leq 8,$$
$$3x_1 + 2x_2 \geq 0,$$

   and

$$x \geq 0.$$

   Show that the third inequality is superfluous.

6. In Exercise 5, assume that x_1 is a variable that should not be constrained to be non-negative. Show that we can permit this, while keeping within the format developed, by carrying out the following steps:
   (a) Replace x_1 by carrying out the following substitution:

$$x_1 = x_1{}^+ - x_1{}^-.$$

   (b) Set up the initial tableau for the new problem with two new columns labeled $A_1{}^+$ and $A_1{}^-$ for the two new variables. Show that $A_1{}^+ = -A_1{}^-$.
   (c) Prove that $A_1{}^+$ and $A_1{}^-$ cannot both be in the basis.
   (d) Use the pivoting algorithm to find all extreme points. Use the formula in (a) to show that x_1 may be either positive or negative at the extreme points.
   (e) Show that the third inequality of Exercise 5 is no longer superfluous.
   (f) Draw the convex set for (e) and explain.

7. Consider the convex set defined by

$$x_1 - 2x_2 \leq 0,$$
$$-4x_1 + x_2 \leq 0.$$

(a) Show that it has exactly one extreme point.
(b) Show that the constraints $x_1 \geq 0$ and $x_2 \geq 0$ are superfluous.
(c) Show that the convex set is unbounded.

8. In Exercise 7, add the constraint

$$x_1 + x_2 \leq 100.$$

Set up the initial tableau and carry out the pivoting process to show that the new convex set now is bounded and has three extreme points. (Recall that this process of adding an artificial constraint is called regularization by Charnes and Cooper.) Discuss how regularization helps in the consideration of unbounded convex sets.

9. Show that the constraint

$$a_1x_1 + a_2x_2 + \cdots + a_nx_n \leq b$$

always has a solution with $x \geq 0$ if $a_i \leq 0$ for $i = 1, \ldots, n$ and $b \geq 0$. (*Hint:* Try $x = 0$.)

10. Show that a constraint of the form given in 9 is always superfluous.

11. Show that $Ax \leq b$, $x \geq 0$, always has at least one feasible solution if $b \geq 0$.

12. Consider the constraint system

$$x_1 - x_2 \leq 1,$$
$$4x_1 - 2x_2 \leq 8.$$

(a) Set up the initial tableau to solve this system subject to $x \geq 0$.
(b) Show that it is *not* possible to bring in the A_2 vector on the first step.
(c) Show that it is possible to bring in A_2 on the next step.
(d) Draw the convex set and find all extreme points.

3.3   MAXIMIZING A LINEAR FUNCTION ON A CONVEX SET

If c is an n-component row vector, d a number, and x an n-component column vector, then a *linear function* of x is an expression of the form $cx + d$. An important class of applied problems, called *linear programming* problems, involve finding the maximum of a linear function defined on a convex set. They can be written in the form:

Max cx

(3.3.1)   Subject to:

$$Ax \leq b$$
$$x \geq 0$$

We can reformulate this problem as one involving only inequalities by replacing the maximizing problem by the inequality

(3.3.2) $cx \geq z^o,$

where z^o is a parameter. We now try various values of z^o, our objective being to choose z^o as large as possible so that the inequality system

(3.3.3) $$cx \geq z^o, \qquad Ax \leq b, \quad \text{and} \quad x \geq 0$$

has a solution. To put this problem in the form used previously, we replace $cx \geq z^o$ by $-cx \leq -z^o$ so that the initial tableau is as follows.

(3.3.4)

A	I	b
$-c$	0	$-z^o$

As in the previous section, we shall assume that

(3.3.5) $$b \geq 0.$$

You may have wondered why we put a line separating the new constraint (3.3.2) from the upper part of the tableau, and also why we did not introduce a slack variable for this constraint. The reasons are that we are going to make z^o so large that (a) constraint (3.3.2) is superfluous or redundant and (b) (3.3.2) is satisfied as an equality so that the slack variable, if there were one, would be zero. Also, for reasons that will become clear later, we will not want to choose a pivot in the last row. Still other reasons for this convention will be found later.

We now want to carry out restricted pivoting on the initial tableau (3.3.4). However, in addition to the two restrictions, (R1) and (R2), that we had in the previous section, we shall add two more, namely:

(R3)   Do not choose a pivot in the last row.

(R4)   Call the entries in the last row in columns 2 through $m + n + 1$ *indicators*; then allow a column to be brought into the basis only if its indicator is *negative*.

As we shall see, the effect of restriction (R4) is to make the pivoting process move from extreme point to extreme point in such a way that the value of cx on these points either increases or stays the same. We will see in the next chapter that the indicator of a column measures the *marginal rate of change* of the objective function if that column is brought into the basis.

In order to see how the pivoting process works, we set up the initial tableau for the case $m = 3$ and $n = 2$. The initial tableau is as follows.

	A_1	A_2	E_1	E_2	E_3		
$T^{(0)} =$	a_{11}	a_{12}	1	0	0	b_1	E_1
	a_{21}	a_{22}	0	1	0	b_2	E_2
	a_{31}	a_{32}	0	0	1	b_3	E_3
	$-c_1$	$-c_2$	0	0	0	$-z_0$	

Now suppose that $-c_2 < 0$ and that we have selected a_{22} as the pivot. The pivot matrix is

$$P_1 = \begin{bmatrix} 1 & -a_{12}/a_{22} & 0 & 0 \\ 0 & 1/a_{22} & 0 & 0 \\ 0 & -a_{32}/a_{22} & 1 & 0 \\ 0 & c_2/a_{22} & 0 & 1 \end{bmatrix}.$$

We now calculate the new tableau as $T^{(1)} = P_1 T^{(0)}$, which is shown below.

	A_1	A_2	E_1	E_2	E_3	
	$a_{11} - \dfrac{a_{21}a_{12}}{a_{22}}$	0	1	$-\dfrac{a_{12}}{a_{22}}$	0	$b_1 - \dfrac{b_2 a_{12}}{a_{22}}$	E_1
$T^{(1)} =$	$\dfrac{a_{21}}{a_{22}}$	1	0	$\dfrac{1}{a_{22}}$	0	$\dfrac{b_2}{a_{22}}$	A_2
	$a_{31} - \dfrac{a_{32}a_{21}}{a_{22}}$	0	0	$-\dfrac{a_{32}}{a_{22}}$	1	$b_3 - \dfrac{b_2 a_{32}}{a_{22}}$	E_3
	$-c_1 + \dfrac{a_{21}c_2}{a_{22}}$	0	0	$\dfrac{c_2}{a_{22}}$	0	$-z^o + \dfrac{c_2 b_2}{a_{22}}$	

There are several important features to be noted about this tableau. First, note that the current value of x is

$$x = \begin{bmatrix} 0 \\ b_2/a_{22} \end{bmatrix}$$

so that $cx = c_2 b_2/a_{22}$, and hence $cx - z^o = (c_2 b_2/a_{22}) - z^o$, which is the entry in the lower right-hand corner of the tableau. Second, since we chose a negative indicator, $-c_2$, we have $c_2 > 0$, hence $cx = c_2 b_2/a_{22} \geq 0$ since each term is positive or zero. Thus in going from $T^{(0)}$ to $T^{(1)}$, the entry in the lower right-hand corner has not decreased. These two results are true in general, as the following theorem indicates.

THEOREM 3.3.1. If we start with an initial tableau (3.3.4) under assumption (3.3.5) and we pivot, using restrictions (R1)–(R4), then

(a) the entry in the lower right-hand corner of the tableau is always $cx - z^o$, where x is associated with the current tableau.

(b) at each pivot step the value of cx (hence of $cx - z^o$) either increases or stays constant.

Proof: We have indicated above the first step of the proof, and later steps are proved in a similar manner.

Suppose now that we have carried out a series of pivots, following restrictions (R1)–(R4), and have arrived at a tableau in which all the indicators (entries in the last row) are nonnegative. Since (R4) requires that we bring in vectors that have negative indicators, we see that the pivoting process cannot be carried further. We shall see in the next theorem that this means that we have discovered the maximum of the linear function cx.

THEOREM 3.3.2. If all the indicators in tableau $T^{(k)}$ are nonnegative (and we set $z^o = 0$) then the entry in the lower right-hand corner of $T^{(k)}$ gives the maximum value of cx. Moreover, if x^o is the vector associated with $T^{(k)}$, then x^o solves the maximizing problem (3.3.1).

Proof: Suppose the contrary—that x^1 is a vector that yields a greater value for cx; that is, suppose $Ax^1 + y^1 = b$, $x^1 \geq 0$, and $cx^1 > cx^o$. Define the partitioned matrices:

$$A^* = \begin{bmatrix} A \\ -c \end{bmatrix}, \quad I^* = \begin{bmatrix} I \\ 0 \end{bmatrix}, \quad \text{and} \quad b^* = \begin{bmatrix} b \\ -cx^1 \end{bmatrix}$$

Then by hypothesis, we have

$$A^*x^1 + I^*y^1 = b^*.$$

Now let M be the product of all the pivot matrices needed to obtain $T^{(k)}$ from $T^{(0)}$— that is, $M = P_k P_{k-1} \cdots P_2 P_1$. Then, multiplying the previous equation on the left by M, we have

$$(3.3.6) \qquad\qquad MA^*x^1 + MI^*y^1 = Mb^*.$$

Now MA^*, MI^*, and Mb^* are just the parts of the final tableau $T^{(k)}$. Let us look at the last row. On the left of the last row of (3.3.6), every entry is nonnegative since we found that to be true for $T^{(k)}$. But on the right, the entry is $cx^o - cx^1$, which, by assumption, is negative. Since the components of x^1 and y^1 are nonnegative, we have a sum of nonnegative numbers adding up to a negative number, which is a contradiction. Hence the theorem is true.

Note that once the problem is solved, if we set z^o equal to the optimum value of the objective function, then inequalities (3.3.3) contain the optimum solution x^o.

EXAMPLE 3.3.1. Solve the following maximizing problem:

$$\text{Max } x_1 + 2x_2$$

Subject to:

$$2x_1 + x_2 \leq 8$$
$$x_1 + x_2 \leq 6$$
$$-x_1 + x_2 \leq 4$$
$$x_1, x_2 \geq 0$$

We begin by setting up the initial tableau:

	A_1	A_2	E_1	E_2	E_3		
$T^{(0)} =$	2	1	1	0	0	8	E_1
	1	1	0	1	0	6	E_2
	-1	**1**	0	0	1	4	E_3
	-1	-2	0	0	0	0	

Notice that we set $z^o = 0$. Notice also that both columns A_1 and A_2 have negative indicators. Let us bring in A_2. The ratios are $8/1 = 8$ for the first row, $6/1 = 6$ for the second row, and $4/1 = 4$ for the third row. Hence the pivot is the **1** in the third row. Carrying out the pivoting, we get

$T^{(1)} =$	3	0	1	0	-1	4	E_1
	2	0	0	1	-1	2	E_2
	-1	1	0	0	1	4	A_2
	-3	0	0	0	2	8	

(We omitted the column labels since they are the same as for $T^{(0)}$.) The x vector associated with $T^{(1)}$ is $x = \begin{bmatrix} 0 \\ 4 \end{bmatrix}$. Since $c = [1 \quad 2]$, we see that $cx = [1 \quad 2]\begin{bmatrix} 0 \\ 4 \end{bmatrix} = 8$, which is the entry in the lower right-hand corner of $T^{(1)}$, as asserted by Theorem 3.3.1(a). There is still a negative indicator with the A_1 column; hence we bring it in. We compute the ratios $4/3$ for the first row and $2/2 = 1$ for the second row. Notice that we do not compute the ratio for the third row since the entry is negative and hence is not eligible for a pivot. The minimum ratio is taken on in the second row, so we pivot on the 2 in the second row and A_1 column. The new tableau is:

	A_1	A_2	E_1	E_2	E_3		
	0	0	1	$-\dfrac{3}{2}$	$\dfrac{1}{2}$	1	E_1
$T^{(2)} =$	1	0	0	$\dfrac{1}{2}$	$-\dfrac{1}{2}$	1	A_1
	0	1	0	$\dfrac{1}{2}$	$\dfrac{1}{2}$	5	A_2
	0	0	0	$\dfrac{3}{2}$	$\dfrac{1}{2}$	11	

Now all indicators are nonnegative, so we have arrived at the situation described in Theorem 3.3.2. Accordingly we see that $x = \begin{bmatrix} 1 \\ 5 \end{bmatrix}$ solves the original maximizing problem, and the value of the linear function is $cx = [1 \quad 2]\begin{bmatrix} 1 \\ 5 \end{bmatrix} = 11$ at its maximum.

A sketch of the convex set is shown in Figure 3.3.1. The dotted lines on the figure are those of the straight lines $cx = k$ for various values of k. For instance, the graph of $cx = 0$ goes through the origin; and $cx = 11$ goes through the point $\begin{bmatrix} 1 \\ 5 \end{bmatrix}$, which is the solution point.

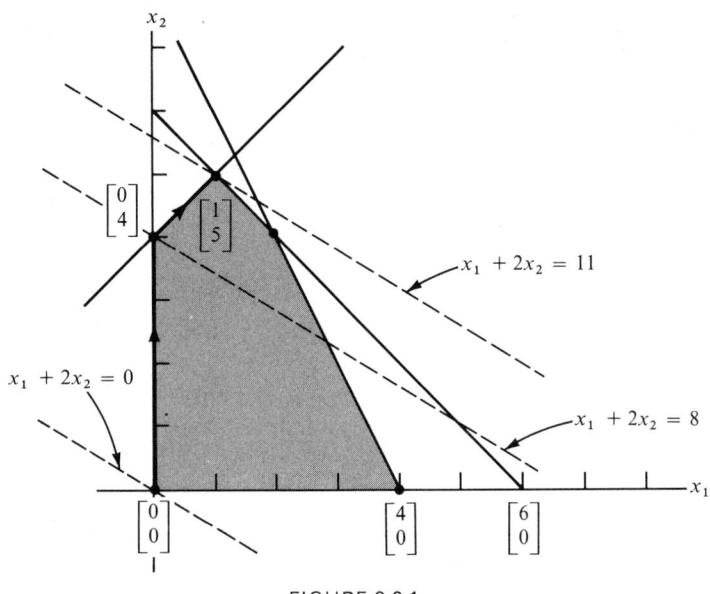

FIGURE 3.3.1

Also marked in the figure is the heavy line path traced during the pivoting process. Namely, the initial tableau is associated with the origin, $O = \begin{bmatrix} 0 \\ 0 \end{bmatrix}$, tableau $T^{(1)}$ is associated with $\begin{bmatrix} 0 \\ 4 \end{bmatrix}$, and tableau $T^{(2)}$ is associated with $\begin{bmatrix} 1 \\ 5 \end{bmatrix}$.

You may have wondered what would have happened if we had brought in the A_1 vector first. In Exercise 1 you will be asked to show that the pivoting process would have traced around the other side of the convex set in Figure 3.3.1. In this case three pivots will be needed instead of two, since it is obvious from the figure that three extreme points instead of two will be encountered in the pivoting process.

The final topic of this section will be the introduction of the so-called *dual problem* to (3.3.1). To define it, we let w be a row vector of m variables, $w_1, \ldots, w_m$, and consider the following minimizing problem.

$$\text{Min } wb$$

(3.3.7)   Subject to:

$$wA \geq c$$
$$w \geq O$$

This is the *dual problem*. To keep names straight, problem (3.3.1) is frequently called the *primal problem*. Notice that these two problems share the same data, namely,

A, b, and c. As we shall see, they share many other properties. We will show in the next chapter that the primal problem has a solution if and only if the dual problem does, and if x^o and w^o are solutions, then $cx^o = w^o b$. We shall also see that the pivoting method we have outlined will solve both problems simultaneously.

In order to see where the components of the vector w come from, consider the initial tableau (3.3.4). The initial basis consists of m m-component vectors, $E_1, \ldots, E_m$; these are the "natural" basis vectors in C_m. Each time we pivot, we go from one set of linearly independent m-component column vectors to another as a basis in C_m. Suppose we consider the coefficients of each of these column vectors as the coefficients in the original tableau of a hyperplane in C_m of the form $wE = -e$, where E is one of these basis vectors and e is the entry in the last row of the tableau. There are m of these hyperplane equations, and the coefficients form a linearly independent set. Hence these m equations will have a unique point of intersection. Call the point of intersection w. Let us refer to this as the *basis intersection point*.

THEOREM 3.3.3. Let $T^{(k)}$ be the tableau obtained by pivoting k times from an initial tableau $T^{(0)}$; and let w be the basis intersection point associated with $T^{(k)}$; then

(a) the components of w appear under the E_i vectors in the tableau $T^{(k)}$ in the last row; that is, w_i is the entry in the last row of the E_i column of the tableau $T^{(k)}$.

(b) the entry $wA_j - c_j$ appears in the last row under the column labeled A_j.

(c) the entry in the lower right-hand corner is $wb - z^o$.

Proof: All these results can be verified directly from the earlier calculations we made in going from $T^{(0)}$ to $T^{(1)}$. The proofs for later steps are similar.

THEOREM 3.3.4. If in tableau $T^{(k)}$ all indicators are positive, then w solves the minimizing problem (3.3.7).

Proof: By Theorem 3.3.3(a), when we reach tableau $T^{(k)}$, each $w_i \geq 0$—that is, each is nonnegative. By Theorem 3.3.3(b), $wA_j - c_j \geq 0$ so that $wA \geq c$. Hence w solves the constraints of (3.3.7). Because of restrictions (R1)–(R4), the x associated with each tableau is always feasible; that is, $Ax \leq b$ and $x \geq 0$. Multiplying $wA \geq c$ by $x \geq 0$, we have $wAx \geq cx$. Similarly, multiplying $Ax \leq b$ by $w \geq 0$, we have $wAx \leq wb$. Hence,

$$cx \leq wAx \leq wb;$$

that is, cx is always a lower bound to the minimizing value wb. In the same manner, if w is a feasible vector (that is, $w \geq 0$ and $wA \geq c$), then wb is an upper bound to cx, the maximizing value. However, in the tableaux we always had $cx - z^o = wb - z^o$, which implies $cx = wb$ for each w and x associated with a tableau. Hence, when all indicators are nonnegative, the maximizing problem takes on its upper bound and the minimizing problem takes on its lower bound, so we have a simultaneous solution to both maximizing and minimizing problems.

EXAMPLE 3.3.1 (continued). Let us find the w vectors and the minimum function values wb associated with each tableau in the example. They are,

with $T^{(0)}$, $w = [0,\ 0,\ 0]$, $wb = [0,\ 0,\ 0]\begin{bmatrix}8\\6\\4\end{bmatrix} = 0.$

with $T^{(1)}$, $w = [0,\ 0,\ 2]$, $wb = [0,\ 0,\ 2]\begin{bmatrix}8\\6\\4\end{bmatrix} = 8.$

with $T^{(2)}$, $w = [0,\ 3/2,\ 1/2]$, $wb = [0,\ 3/2,\ 1/2]\begin{bmatrix}8\\6\\4\end{bmatrix} = 11.$

Note that $wb = cx$ at each tableau.

It is interesting to sketch the convex set $wA \geq c$ and to follow the pivoting process on it. Since $m = 3$, the graph is three dimensional as shown in Figure 3.3.2. If we recall that $w_1 = 0$ throughout the pivoting process employed, it is possible to get a two-dimensional picture of the process, which is shown in Figure 3.3.3. Notice that in Figure 3.3.2 the planes are labeled A_1, A_2, E_1, E_2, E_3 and that the pivoting process moves from one intersection of three of these five planes to another intersection of three planes. Thus we have the geometrical interpretation of the pivoting process as moving from one intersection of hyperplanes represented by the columns of the first tableau to another. Recall that the algebraic interpretation of pivoting is that of changing from one basis to another. In the next chapter we shall give an economic interpretation of pivoting, and these three interpretations can be used to facilitate understanding of this fundamental process.

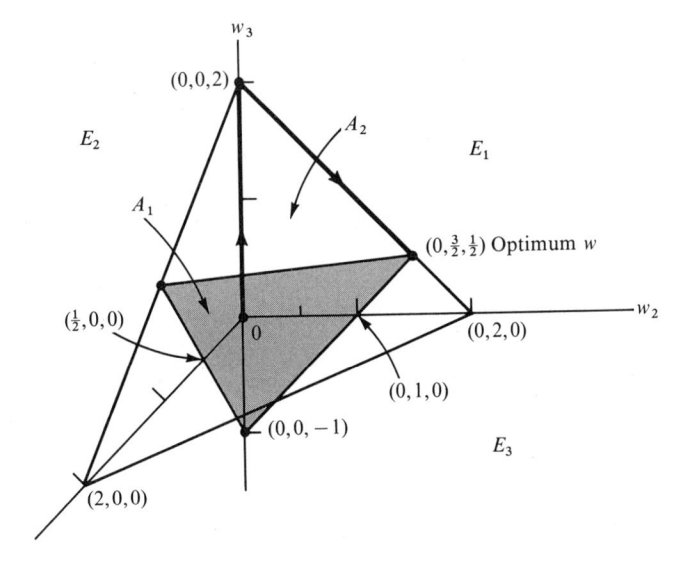

FIGURE 3.3.2

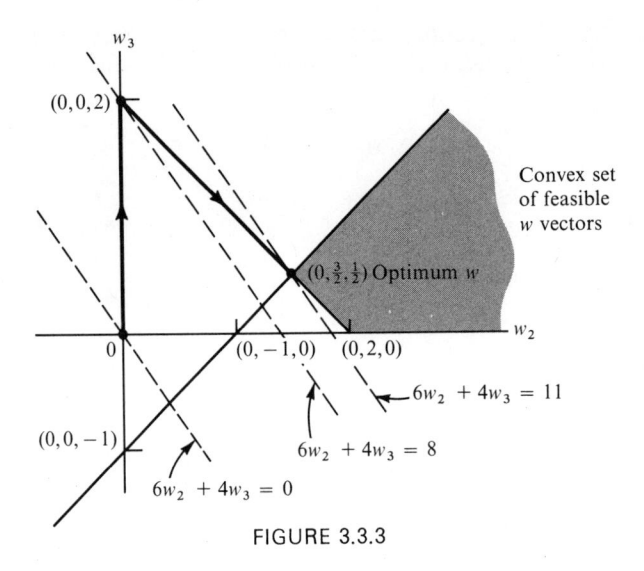

FIGURE 3.3.3

EXERCISES 3.3

1. Rework Example 3.3.1 by starting with tableau $T^{(0)}$ and bringing in vector A_1 first. Show that three pivots are needed, and show that the path traced in the pivoting process is opposite the path in the convex set shown in Figure 3.3.1.

2. In Exercise 1, consider the dual problem during the steps of the pivoting process. Trace out its path on Figure 3.3.2.

3. Solve the following problem:

$$\text{Max } x_1 + x_2$$
$$\text{Subject to:}$$
$$x_1 + 2x_2 \leq 4$$
$$3x_1 + x_2 \leq 12$$
$$x_1, x_2 \geq 0$$

4. Set up the dual problem for Exercise 3 and interpret its solution from the calculations you made there. Draw the convex sets for the direct and dual problems and mark on them the paths taken in the pivoting process. Also mark lines of the form $cx = k$ and $wb = h$ for suitable h and k so that they go through the points pivoted on.

5. Maximize the linear function $3x_1 + 2x_2$ subject to the constraints given in Exercise 2(a) of Section 3.2. Draw the convex sets and give complete geometric interpretations for both the primal and dual problems.

6. Repeat Exercise 5 with the constraints given in Exercise 2(b) of Section 3.2.

7. A plant makes two products, bobsleds and playpens. The requirements for each are:

	Wood (sq. ft.)	Labor (man-hr.)	Bolts	Rope (ft.)	Glue (pts.)	Varnish (qts.)	Plastic (ft.)
Bobsleds	20	10	20	20	1	2	0
Playpens	10	15	10	0	.5	1	20
Amounts on hand	1000	400	200	150	5	20	500

Bobsleds are sold for $18 and playpens for $12.

(a) Set up the problem of maximizing the gross revenue of the firm.

(b) Set up the dual problem.

(c) Draw the convex set of feasible vectors for the minimizing problem.

8. Frequently, linear programming problems are stated as minimizing problems as in (3.3.7). Thus the primal problem is a minimizing one. In this case, its dual problem is the maximizing problem (3.3.1). In other words, if the primal problem is minimizing then the dual problem is maximizing, and vice versa. Show that the dual of the dual problem is the original problem in either case.

9. Resolve Exercise 3 with the objective function $ax_1 + x_2$, where a is a parameter. Over what range of values will the same x^o solve the maximizing problem?

10. Consider a minimizing problem:

$$\text{Min } wc$$
$$\text{Subject to:}$$
$$wA \geq b$$
$$w \geq 0$$

Show that an equivalent maximizing problem is:

$$\text{Max } -c'x$$
$$\text{Subject to:}$$
$$(-A)'x \leq (-b)'$$
$$x \geq 0,$$

where $x = w'$.

11. Consider the minimizing problem:

$$\text{Min } 3w_1 + 2w_2$$
$$\text{Subject to:}$$
$$w_1 - w_2 \leq 1$$
$$4w_1 - 2w_2 \leq 8$$
$$w_1, w_2 \geq 0$$

Use the method in Exercise 10 to derive an equivalent maximizing problem.

SUGGESTED READING

Charnes, A., and Cooper, W. W. *Management Models and Industrial Applications of Linear Programming*, 2 Vols. New York: John Wiley, 1961.

Dantzig, G. B. *Linear Programming and Extensions.* Princeton, N.J.: Princeton University Press, 1963.

Hadley, G. *Linear Programming.* Reading, Mass.: Addison-Wesley, 1962.

Hillier, F. S., and Lieberman, G. J. *Introduction to Operations Research.* San Francisco: Holden-Day, 1967.

Simmonard, M. *Linear Programming.* Englewood Cliffs, N.J.: Prentice-Hall, 1966.

Wagner, H. M. *Principles of Operations Research with Applications to Managerial Decisions.* Englewood Cliffs, N.J.: Prentice-Hall, 1969.

CHAPTER 4

THE SIMPLEX METHOD FOR LINEAR PROGRAMMING

4.1 THE SIMPLEX METHOD FOR NONNEGATIVE RIGHT-HAND SIDES

In Chapter 3, we gave an introduction to linear programming and the simplex method, using geometric ideas. Here we shall give an algebraic introduction to this important method which can be read independently of all but the first section of Chapter 3. In Section 4.2, we will give economic interpretations to the various steps of the simplex method. Study of the unstarred sections of the present chapter is important for understanding later parts of the book.

A *linear programming problem* requires the maximization or minimization of a linear function of variables subject to linear inequality constraints. The *canonical form* of such a problem is one of the two problems shown in Figure 4.1.1. The three

THE MAXIMIZING PROBLEM	THE MINIMIZING PROBLEM
Max cx	Min wb
Subject to:	Subject to:
$Ax \leq b$	$wA \geq c$
$x \geq 0$	$w \geq 0$

FIGURE 4.1.1

matrices A, b, and c, appearing in each problem have the following dimensions: A is $m \times n$, b is $m \times 1$, and c is $1 \times n$. The column vector x has n components, hence is $n \times 1$, and the row vector w has m components and hence is $1 \times m$.

EXAMPLE 4.1.1. Consider the following maximizing problem:

Max $12x_1 + 18x_2$

Subject to:

$$2x_1 + \ x_2 \leq 4$$
$$x_1 + 2x_2 \leq 4$$
$$x_1 \qquad \geq 0$$
$$x_2 \geq 0$$

If we define the following quantities,

$$x = \begin{bmatrix} x_1 \\ x_2 \end{bmatrix}, \quad A = \begin{bmatrix} 2 & 1 \\ 1 & 2 \end{bmatrix}, \quad b = \begin{bmatrix} 4 \\ 4 \end{bmatrix}, \quad c = [12, \ 18],$$

then it is easy to see that $m = n = 2$ and that we have a maximum problem of the form stated in the left half of Figure 4.1.1.

EXAMPLE 4.1.2. Consider the following minimizing problem:

Min $4w_1 + 4w_2$

Subject to:

$$2w_1 + \ w_2 \geq 12$$
$$w_1 + 2w_2 \geq 18$$
$$w_1 \qquad \geq 0$$
$$w_2 \geq 0$$

Then, defining $w = (w_1, w_2)$ and using the same A, b, and c given in Example 4.1.1, we see that we have a minimum problem of the form stated in the right half of Figure 4.1.1.

The fact that the maximum and minimum problems of these two examples share the same data, namely the A, b, and c, means that they are *dual* linear programming problems. The original problem (either maximizing or minimizing) is called the *primal* problem, and the other one its dual problem. Clearly the dual of the dual problem is the original primal problem.

In specific applications, such as those described in the next section, the original problem of interest may be either a maximizing or a minimizing problem from which we derive the data matrices, A, b, and c. As soon as we have these, we can automatically write the dual problem. As we shall see, the solutions to the dual problem have important economic and managerial significance in relation to the originally stated problem. Also, it turns out that the simplex method will automatically solve both problems simultaneously!

In order to initiate the simplex method, the initial data A, b, and c (obtained from either type of problem) are inserted into the initial tableau of Figure 4.1.2.

$$T^{(0)} = \begin{array}{|c|c|c|} \hline A_{(m \times n)} & I_{(m \times m)} & b_{(m \times 1)} \\ \hline -c_{(1 \times n)} & O_{(1 \times m)} & O_{(1 \times 1)} \\ \hline \end{array}$$

FIGURE 4.1.2

The dimensions of each matrix in the tableau are marked in parentheses; I stands for an identity matrix and O stands for a zero matrix. The lines in the tableau are inserted for visual convenience.

The simplex method is an algorithm that, by a sequence of pivots, changes tableau $T^{(0)}$ into $T^{(1)}$, then $T^{(1)}$ into $T^{(2)}$, and so on, in such a way that (a) the entry in the lower right-hand corner increases monotonically and (b) after a finite number of steps, the solution to the original problem (and its dual problem) is displayed. (We have already discussed the method in Section 3.3, but we will give an independent algebraic discussion of it here.)

The simplex method we are going to describe in the present section requires two assumptions (both of which will be removed in later sections):

(i) The *positivity assumption*: we assume $b > 0$.

(ii) The *nondegeneracy assumption*: we assume that it is *not* possible to write b as a linear combination of fewer than m columns of A and I.

We will show how to relax the first assumption in Section 4.6 and how to relax the second in Section 4.8.

In order to interpret the simplex tableau, we restate the linear programming problems, which are dual to each other, after adding *slack variables* y (an $m \times 1$ vector of variables y_i) and z (a $1 \times n$ vector of variables z_j). The new problem statement is given in Figure 4.1.3 and is called the *equality form* of a linear programming problem.

	Max cx			Min wb
	Subject to:			Subject to:
(4.1.1)	$Ax + y = b$		(4.1.3)	$wA - z = c$
(4.1.2)	$x \geq 0, y \geq 0$		(4.1.4)	$w \geq 0, z \geq 0$

FIGURE 4.1.3

Vectors x and y that satisfy (4.1.1) and (4.1.2) are called *feasible vectors* for the maximizing problem. Similarly, vectors w and z satisfying (4.1.3) and (4.1.4) are feasible vectors for the minimizing problem.

It is easy to show that the problems stated in Figures 4.1.1 and 4.1.3 are equivalent by showing that the sets of feasible x and w vectors in each case are the same and that the slack variables do not affect the functions being optimized. The proof of this is outlined in Exercise 1.

Since we have assumed that $b \geq 0$, the following vectors will solve (4.1.1), (4.1.2), and (4.1.3) (but not necessarily (4.1.4)):

(4.1.5) $x = 0$, $y = b$, $w = 0$,   and $z = -c$.

Note that x, y, and w are nonnegative and therefore feasible. But z is nonnegative only if $-c \geq 0$, which means we already have a solution to the problem. (This happens only in the rare case when $c \leq 0$.) Note also that initially $cx = wb = 0$. What the simplex method does is to start with these initial vectors and carry out pivot steps, always keeping (4.1.1), (4.1.2), and (4.1.3), as well as $cx = wb$, satisfied. When finally (4.1.4) is also satisfied, the simplex method stops with the solutions to both the primal and dual problems displayed.

In order to keep track of the values of the variables during the pivoting process, we label the initial tableau as shown in Figure 4.1.4. At the top we have the x_j

x_1	x_2	$\cdots$	x_n		y_1	y_2	$\cdots$	y_n			
a_{11}	a_{12}	$\cdots$	a_{1n}		1	0	$\cdots$	0		b_1	$= y_1$
a_{21}	a_{22}	$\cdots$	a_{2n}		0	1	$\cdots$	0		b_2	$= y_2$
.	.	$\cdots$	.		.	.		.		.	
a_{m1}	a_{m2}	$\cdots$	a_{mn}		0	0	$\cdots$	1		b_m	$= y_m$
$-c_1$	$-c_2$	$\cdots$	$-c_n$		0	0	$\cdots$	0		0	$= cx$
$= z_1$	$= z_2$	$\cdots$	$= z_n$		$= w_1$	$= w_2$	$\cdots = w_m$			$= wb$	

Indicators

FIGURE 4.1.4

variables in the first n columns and the y variables in the next m columns. On the right we indicate that the initial values of the y variables are $y_i = b_i$, as in (4.1.5). At the bottom of the columns labeled x_j, we have $z_j = -c_j$ as initial values; at the bottom of the columns labeled y_i, we have $w_i = 0$ as initial values. (These values are also indicated in (4.1.5).) Also notice that the quantities in the last row, except for those in the rightmost column, are called *indicators*. The use of these indicators will be explained shortly. Finally, in the lower right-hand corner of the tableau, we have an entry that is marked $= cx$ on the right and also $= wb$ on the bottom. The initial value shown is 0.

As the simplex method proceeds, the labels at the top of the columns and the equalities at the bottom do not change. The equalities at the right change, but are always equal to one of the x_j or y_i variables. We call the variables at the right *basic variables*. The x_j and y_i variables that do *not* appear on the right of the tableau are *nonbasic variables*. Thus initially, variables $x_1, \ldots, x_n$ are nonbasic. Also, as the simplex computation proceeds, the entry in the lower right-hand corner of the tableau will steadily increase but will always be equal to cx and wb for the current values of x and w that are displayed in the tableau.

The flow diagram for the simplex method, valid under the positivity and nondegeneracy assumptions, is shown in Figure 4.1.5. (For those of you who have covered all of Chapter 3, note that the four restrictions given in Section 3.3 are satisfied; however, they are specifically taken care of in the flow diagram so there is no need to refer back to that section.)

Before we explain some of the reasons for the various steps, we work examples that illustrate the use of the flow diagram in Figure 4.1.5.

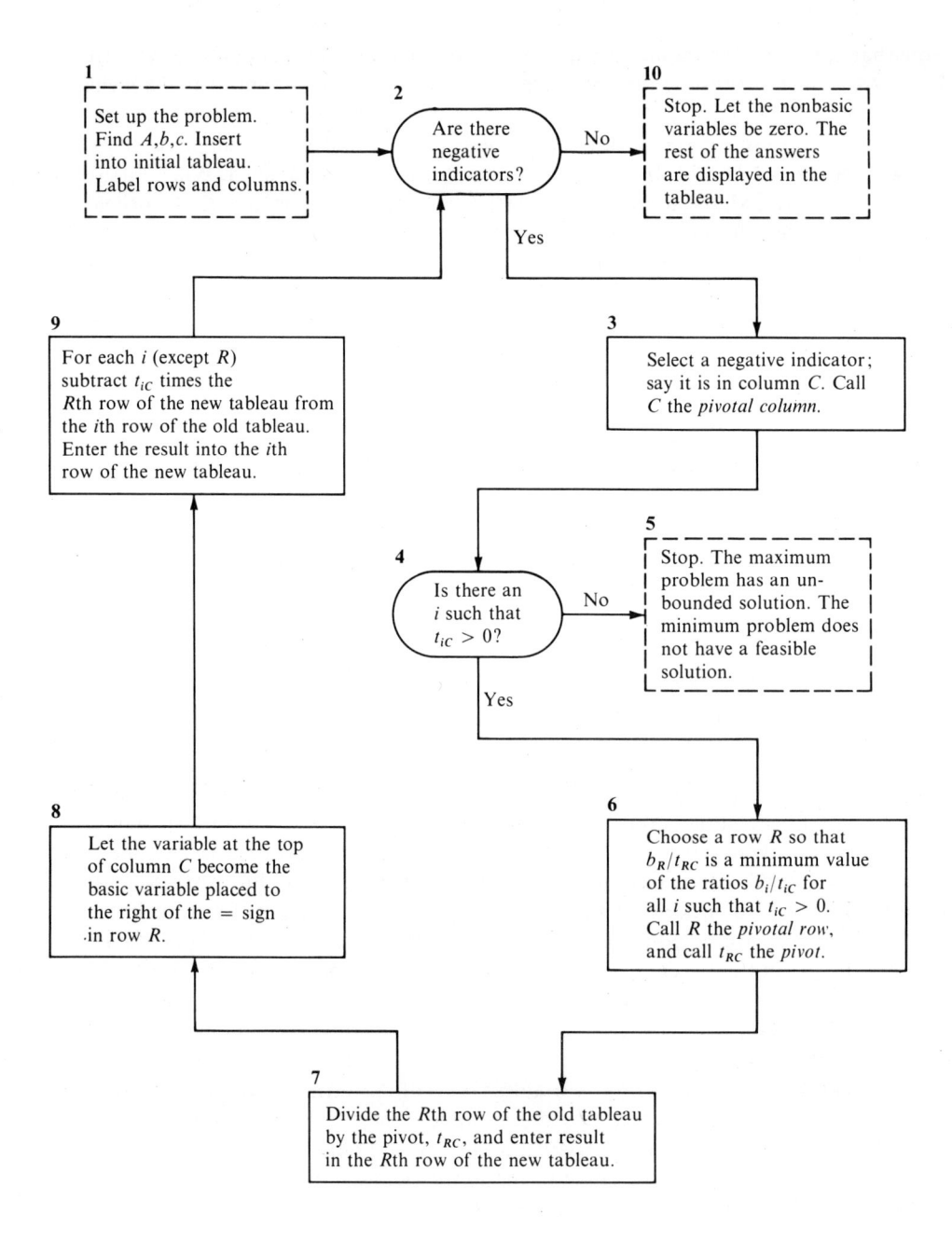

FIGURE 4.1.5. Flow diagram for the simplex method when $b \geq 0$

EXAMPLE 4.1.3. Let us take the data A, b, and c derived in Examples 4.1.1 and 4.1.2 and substitute those data into the initial tableau, Figure 4.1.2, and label it as in Figure 4.1.4. The result is:

	x_1	x_2	y_1	y_2		
$T^{(0)} =$	2	1	1	0	4	$= y_1$
	1	2	0	1	4	$= y_2$
	-12	-18	0	0	0	$= cx$
	$= z_1$	$= z_2$	$= w_1$	$= w_2$	$= wb$	

This completes the instructions given in box 1 of the flow diagram. Note that there are two negative indicators, -12 and -18, so the answer to the question in box 2 is yes and we go to box 3. Suppose we choose the most negative indicator; that is, we choose $C = 2$ for box 3 of the flow diagram. Since there are two positive entries in the second column, the answer to the question in box 4 is yes and we go to box 6. We must compute the ratios b_i/t_{iC}, for $i = 1, 2$. These ratios are $4/1 = 4$ and $4/2 = 2$, and the minimum is taken on when $R = 2$, which becomes the pivot row with $t_{22} = 2$ the pivot, shown bold-faced in the tableau. We next construct tableau $T^{(1)}$, following the instructions in boxes 7, 8, and 9 of the flow diagram. Notice that we do not repeat the labels at the top and bottom of the columns since they will be the same as those in $T^{(0)}$. Also notice that, as instructed in box 8, we replace y_2 on the right of row 2 with a new variable, x_2. Now y_1 and x_2 are basic variables, and x_1 and y_2 are nonbasic.

$T^{(1)} =$	$\frac{3}{2}$	0	1	$-\frac{1}{2}$	2	$= y_1$
	$\frac{1}{2}$	1	0	$\frac{1}{2}$	2	$= x_2$
	-3	0	0	9	36	$= cx$

Indicators

We now are back at box 2 of Figure 4.1.5. Note that there is still one negative indicator, -3, so $C = 1$. The answer to the question in box 4 is yes, so we compute the ratios: $2/(3/2) = 4/3$ and $2/(1/2) = 4$. The minimum-ratio rule gives $R = 1$ and pivot $3/2$. Carrying out the pivoting steps gives the next tableau:

	x_1	x_2	y_1	y_2		
$T^{(2)} =$	1	0	$\frac{2}{3}$	$-\frac{1}{3}$	$\frac{4}{3}$	$= x_1$
	0	1	$-\frac{1}{3}$	$\frac{2}{3}$	$\frac{4}{3}$	$= x_2$
	0	0	2	8	40	$= cx$
	$= z_1$	$= z_2$	$= w_1$	$= w_2$	$= wb$	

Indicators

We are again at box 2 of Figure 4.1.5 and we note that all indicators are now nonnegative, so we go to box 10, which says that the solution has been found and that the answers are displayed. From the bottom row we can read the w and z vectors as:

$$z^o = [0, 0] \quad \text{and} \quad w^o = [2, 8].$$

According to the rule given in box 10, the values of all nonbasic variables should be set equal to zero. Using this rule, we see from $T^{(2)}$ that the optimal x and y vectors are

$$x^o = \begin{bmatrix} \frac{4}{3} \\ \frac{4}{3} \end{bmatrix} \quad \text{and} \quad y^o = \begin{bmatrix} 0 \\ 0 \end{bmatrix}.$$

We also see that $cx^o = w^o b = 40$, and we can check this by means of the following computation:

$$cx^o = [12, 18]\begin{bmatrix} \frac{4}{3} \\ \frac{4}{3} \end{bmatrix} = 4 \cdot 4 + 6 \cdot 4 = 40 = [2, 8]\begin{bmatrix} 4 \\ 4 \end{bmatrix} = w^o b.$$

EXAMPLE 4.1.4. We next illustrate the method with a problem that terminates in box 5 of Figure 4.1.5. Consider the initial tableau:

	x_1	x_2	y_1	y_2		
$T^{(0)} =$	-1	1	1	0	2	$= y_1$
	1	-1	0	1	2	$= y_2$
	-1	-1	0	0	0	$= cx$
	$= z_1$	$= z_2$	$= w_1$	$= w_2$	$= wb$	

Since there are two equal negative indicators, we choose the first and make $C = 1$. There is only one positive entry in the column, so the answer to box 4 is yes and we go to box 6 where we must choose $R = 2$. Carrying out the pivoting process, we obtain:

	x_1	x_2	y_1	y_2		
$T^{(1)} =$	0	0	1	1	4	$= y_1$
	1	-1	0	1	2	$= x_1$
	0	-2	0	1	2	$= cx$
	$= z_1$	$= z_2$	$= w_1$	$= w_2$	$= wb$	

Indicators

Returning to box 2, we still have a negative indicator, -2, in column 2, but there are no positive entries in this column. Hence the answer to the question in box 4 of the flow diagram is no and the algorithm terminates in box 5 with the signal that the original maximizing problem has no finite solution and the minimizing problem no feasible solution. The next theorem shows why these facts are correct. You are asked to give an independent proof for this example in Exercise 2.

THEOREM 4.1.1. If, in the pivoting sequence, a tableau is found with a nonpositive column and a negative indicator, then

(a) the original maximizing problem has "unbounded" solutions; that is, there are feasible x vectors such that cx is greater than any preassigned positive number.

(b) the original minimizing problem does not have any feasible solutions.

Proof: (a) Assume first of all that the initial tableau has the property stated; that is, there is an index j such that the jth column of A, denoted by $A^{(j)}$, is nonpositive. Then we have the initial solution

$$x = 0, \qquad y = b \geq 0, \qquad c_j > 0, \quad \text{and} \quad A^{(j)} \leq 0.$$

Now observe that we can define other feasible solutions in terms of a parameter, $p \geq 0$, and a column vector, $f^{(j)}$, which has a 1 in the jth place and zeros elsewhere; namely

$$x^* = f^{(j)}p \geq 0 \quad \text{and} \quad y^* = b - A^{(j)}p \geq 0.$$

To check that these two vectors are feasible, note that

$$Ax^* + y^* = Af^{(j)}p + b - A^{(j)}p = A^{(j)}p + b - A^{(j)}p = b,$$

so x^* and y^* are feasible for all $p \geq 0$. But we also have $cx^* = cf^{(j)}p = c_j p$, which can be made arbitrarily large by making p large, since $c_j > 0$. Hence the maximum problem has an unbounded solution in this case. If, at a later stage in the computation, tableau $T^{(k)}$ has the property of the theorem, a similar analysis again shows the existence of unbounded solutions.

(b) Suppose, on the contrary, that w^* were feasible for the minimizing problem. Then $w^*A \geq c$ so that $w^*Ax \geq cx$ for all feasible x. Hence the maximizing problem would be bounded, which contradicts the fact proved in (a) that there are unbounded solutions to the maximizing problem. Hence there are no feasible w vectors.

The theorem just proved explains the terminal box 5 of the flow diagram. We must still explain why the optimum solution is obtained when we reach the terminal box 10. The next theorem provides the explanation. It is called the *duality theorem* and is the most important theorem in the theory of linear programming.

THEOREM 4.1.2. *Duality Theorem*. The maximum problem has as a solution a feasible vector x^o such that $cx^o = \max cx$ if and only if the minimum problem has a solution that is a feasible vector w^o such that $w^o b = \min wb$. Moreover, the equality $cx^o = w^o b$ holds for feasible vectors x^o and w^o if and only if they are solutions to their respective problems.

We shall prove this theorem in Section 4.8. However, note that the second statement of the theorem shows that when box 10 of the flow diagram is entered, the current solution shown in the last tableau is optimal, since that solution has a pair of feasible vectors x^o and w^o such that $cx^o = w^o b$.

EXAMPLE 4.1.5. Our final example shows that the w variables may become negative during the course of the computation. It also shows that the selection of pivotal columns may have an important effect on the number of pivots needed to solve a given problem. The initial tableau of the problem is:

$$
T^{(0)} =
\begin{array}{c}
\begin{array}{ccccc}
x_1 & x_2 & x_3 & y_1 & y_2 \\
\end{array} \\
\begin{array}{|ccc|cc|c|}
\hline
3 & 2 & 1 & 1 & 0 & 13 \\
2 & 3 & 1 & 0 & 1 & 12 \\
\hline
-6 & -6 & -4 & 0 & 0 & 0 \\
\hline
\end{array}
\end{array}
\begin{array}{c}
= y_1 \\
= y_2 \\
\\
= cx
\end{array}
$$

$$= z_1 \quad = z_2 \quad = z_3 \qquad = w_1 \quad = w_2 \qquad = wb$$

Here there are three negative indicators, and, if we use the most-negative-indicator rule, we can choose the first one and make $C = 1$. Using the ratio rule of box 6 of Figure 4.1.5, we see that $R = 1$. After pivoting, we have

$$
T^{(1)} =
\begin{array}{|ccc|cc|c|}
\hline
1 & \dfrac{2}{3} & \dfrac{1}{3} & \dfrac{1}{3} & 0 & \dfrac{13}{3} \\
0 & \dfrac{5}{3} & \dfrac{1}{3} & -\dfrac{2}{3} & 1 & \dfrac{10}{3} \\
\hline
0 & -2 & -2 & 2 & 0 & 26 \\
\hline
\end{array}
\begin{array}{c}
= x_1 \\
\\
= y_2 \\
\\
= cx
\end{array}
$$

On the next step we can choose either of the -2 indicators. We select $C = 3$ (for the other choice, see Exercise 3). The ratio rule requires $R = 2$, and pivoting provides:

$$
T^{(2)} =
\begin{array}{|ccc|cc|c|}
\hline
1 & -1 & 0 & 1 & -1 & 1 \\
0 & 5 & 1 & -2 & 3 & 10 \\
\hline
0 & 8 & 0 & -2 & 6 & 46 \\
\hline
\end{array}
\begin{array}{c}
= x_1 \\
= x_3 \\
\\
= cx
\end{array}
$$

Note that now the sole negative indicator is the -2 in column 4. Hence $C = 4$ and $R = 1$. Pivoting gives:

$$
T^{(3)} =
\begin{array}{|ccc|cc|c|}
\hline
1 & -1 & 0 & 1 & -1 & 1 \\
12 & 2 & 3 & 1 & 0 & 1 \\
\hline
2 & 6 & 0 & 0 & 4 & 48 \\
\hline
\end{array}
\begin{array}{c}
= y_1 \\
= x_3 \\
\\
= cx
\end{array}
$$

$$= z_1 \ = z_2 \ = z_3 \qquad = w_1 \ = w_2 \qquad = wb$$

Since there are no negative indicators in $T^{(3)}$, we have achieved the optimal solution

$$w^o = [0,\ 4], \qquad z = [2,\ 6,\ 0]$$

$$x^o = \begin{bmatrix} 0 \\ 0 \\ 12 \end{bmatrix}, \qquad y = \begin{bmatrix} 1 \\ 0 \end{bmatrix},$$

and the common value of the two dual programs is 48.

Observe that it is possible to go from $T^{(0)}$ to the final tableau of $T^{(3)}$ in one pivot step if the -4 indicator is chosen instead of the -6 indicator in $T^{(0)}$. Thus the most-negative-indicator rule is not always the best possible choice for pivots. Figure 4.1.6 shows the w-space. The heavy lines show the path of the pivot steps described above, and the dotted line shows the path if the -4 indicator is chosen in $T^{(0)}$.

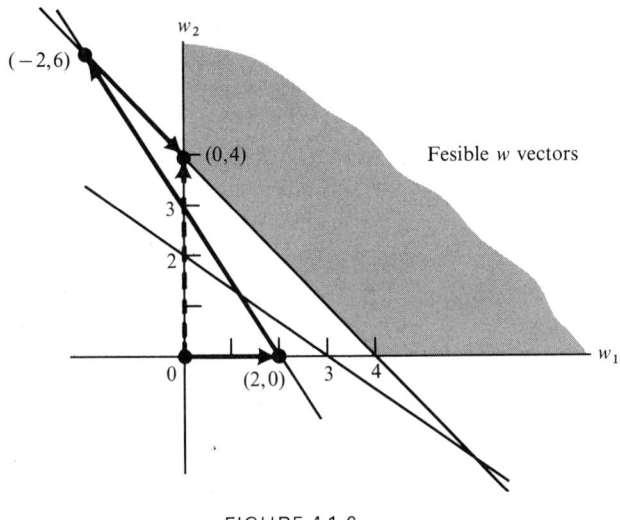

FIGURE 4.1.6

EXERCISES 4.1

1. Show that the pairs of problems stated in Figures 4.1.1 and 4.1.2 are equivalent by carrying out the following steps:
    (a) Given solutions x and w to Figure 4.1.1, show how to define vectors y and z such that all these vectors satisfy the problems in Figure 4.1.2.
    (b) Given vectors x, y, w, and z satisfying the problems in Figure 4.1.2, show that just the x and w vectors will satisfy the problems in Figure 4.1.1.

2. Draw the bounding hyperplanes of the convex sets corresponding to the problem in $T^{(0)}$ of Example 4.1.4, and show that the set of feasible w vectors is empty. Also show that the set of feasible x vectors contains a ray—that is, is unbounded.

3. In Example 4.1.5, select the first -2 indicator in $T^{(1)}$ and show that an additional pivot step is needed to find the optimum answer. Locate the new point in Figure 4.1.5.

4. Show that the following problem is degenerate.

3	2	1	1	0	12
2	3	1	0	1	12
-6	-6	-4	0	0	0

Try the simplex method on it, and show that the degeneracy does not affect it. Compare your calculations with those in Example 4.1.5.

5. Solve the following problems, whose initial tableaux are given. Show that the first problem can be solved with one pivot but that the second needs two.

(a)

7	6	1	0	1
3	4	0	1	1
−70	−90	0	0	0

(b)

7	4	1	0	1
3	6	0	1	1
−60	−90	0	0	0

6. Try the simplex method on the following problem. Explain your results.

0	5	1	0	1
−2	12	0	1	1
−5	−5	0	0	0

7. Use the most-negative-indicator rule to show that the following problem can be solved in three pivots. Also show that no divisions are necessary.

0	1	0	1	1	0	0	0	20
−1	1	−1	1	0	1	0	0	15
−1	0	−1	1	0	0	1	0	8
0	0	−1	1	0	0	0	1	15
40	−110	110	−170	0	0	0	0	0

8. A feed-mix company makes three kinds of feeds having the following compositions:

	Corn	Oats	Wheat
Mix 1	90%	10%	0%
Mix 2	70%	20%	10%
Mix 3	50%	30%	20%

Suppose that the company can sell these for a profit of \$27, \$21, and \$14 per ton; assume that the company has on hand 1800 tons of corn, 1000 tons of oats, and 600 tons of wheat. If all production can be sold and the blending process is equally expensive for each blend, how many tons of each should be produced to maximize gross revenue?

(a) Set up the problem and solve, using the simplex method.

(b) Suppose that the management of the company decides it wants to produce at least three times as much of mix 3 as of mix 2 and at least three times as much of mix 2 as of mix 1. Set up the corresponding maximizing problem but do not solve it unless you have a computer available.

(c) In (b), will the gross revenue be more or less than in (a)? (It is not necessary to solve (b) in order to answer this question.)

9. In the diet problem, we try to buy foods so that our minimum daily requirements for nutrients are satisfied at minimum cost. Suppose that we consider buying three foods, $F1$, $F2$, and $F3$, in order to obtain nutrients A, B, and C and that we have the following data:

Food	Nutrient (units/lb)			Cost ($/lb)
	A	B	C	
F1	3	1	0	20
F2	0	5	2	25
F3	0	0	4	15
Min. Daily Requirements (units/day)	9	18	16	

(a) Set up the diet problem as a minimizing linear programming problem.

(b) What are the units of the primal problem—that is, the units of w_i and z_i?

(c) What are the units of the corresponding dual problem—that is, of x_j and y_j?

(d) Solve the problem and give interpretations to the variables of the primal problem.

(e) Give interpretations to the variables of the dual problem for the optimum solution.

4.2 ECONOMIC INTERPRETATIONS OF THE SIMPLEX METHOD

As we saw in the previous section, every linear programming problem, whether maximizing or minimizing, has a corresponding dual problem. Moreover, these two problems either both have or both do not have finite solutions; and when they do have finite solutions they share a common value. In the present section we shall discuss the implications that the solutions to these two dual problems have on each other. We will see that the solution to the dual problem (a) assigns either "imputed values" or "imputed costs" to activities represented by constraints and (b) determines the effect on the objective function of relaxing the constraints.

The first step in the interpretation of the dual variables is to determine the physical dimensions or units of all the data quantities and variables, including the dual variables. We illustrate this process with two examples, one a maximizing problem and the other a minimizing problem.

EXAMPLE 4.2.1. A toy manufacturer makes fire trucks and scooters in a factory that is divided into two shops, the plastics shop and the assembly shop. Two men work in each shop for seven and a half hours each day, so there are 900 man-minutes available in each shop each day. Suppose that it takes four minutes to fabricate the parts for the fire truck in the plastics shop and two minutes to assemble it in the assembly shop. Similarly, it takes one minute to fabricate a scooter in the plastics shop and three minutes to assemble it in the assembly shop. If the manufacturer can sell his entire output and if he makes a gross profit of $2 on each fire truck and $1 on each scooter, how many of each should he produce each day?

Since this is a maximizing problem, we let x_1 be the number of trucks and x_2 the number of scooters produced. Then the problem is to maximize cx subject to $Ax \leq b$, $x \geq 0$, where

$$A = \begin{bmatrix} 4 & 1 \\ 2 & 3 \end{bmatrix}, \qquad b = \begin{bmatrix} 900 \\ 900 \end{bmatrix}, \qquad \text{and} \quad c = [2, \ 1].$$

In order to clearly display the dimensions of the known data, we display them in the *data box* (a term due to A. W. Tucker) shown in Figure 4.2.1. Here the decision vari-

$$x_1\left(\frac{\text{trucks}}{\text{day}}\right) \qquad x_2\left(\frac{\text{scooters}}{\text{day}}\right)$$

w_1	$4\ \dfrac{\text{Plas. S. min.}}{\text{truck}}$	$1\ \dfrac{\text{Plas. S. min.}}{\text{scooter}}$	$900\ \dfrac{\text{Plas. S. min.}}{\text{day}}$	
w_2	$2\ \dfrac{\text{Assem. S. min.}}{\text{truck}}$	$3\ \dfrac{\text{Assem. S. min.}}{\text{scooter}}$	$900\ \dfrac{\text{Assem. S. min.}}{\text{day}}$	

$$2\ \frac{\$}{\text{truck}} \qquad\qquad 1\ \frac{\$}{\text{scooter}}$$

FIGURE 4.2.1

ables are x_1, which is to be the number of trucks made per day, and x_2, the number of scooters made per day. Note that we can read off the constraints of the maximizing problem by multiplying the x_i's into the corresponding coefficients in each row. Similarly, we can read off the constraints of the dual minimizing problem by multiplying the w_i's into the columns. Thus, the inequality form of the two linear programming problems is the following:

$$\text{Max } 2x_1 + x_2 \qquad\qquad\qquad \text{Min } 900w_1 + 900w_2$$

Subject to: $\qquad\qquad\qquad\qquad\qquad$ Subject to:

$$
\begin{aligned}
4x_1 + 1x_2 &\le 900 \\
2x_1 + 3x_2 &\le 900 \\
x_1 &\ge 0 \\
x_2 &\ge 0
\end{aligned}
\qquad\qquad
\begin{aligned}
4w_1 + 2w_2 &\ge 2 \\
1w_1 + 3w_2 &\ge 1 \\
w_1 &\ge 0 \\
w_2 &\ge 0
\end{aligned}
$$

Now we want to see how to work with the dimensional fractions. An expression such as "4 Plas. S. min./truck" should be read as "4 plastic shop minutes per truck." Moreover, when products of dimensional quantities are indicated, the dimensions may be handled as if they were algebraic quantities. For instance, if we write the first primal equation including all dimensions, we obtain

$$\left(4\frac{\text{Plas. S. min.}}{\text{truck}}\right)\left(x_1\frac{\text{trucks}}{\text{day}}\right) + \left(1\frac{\text{Plas. S. min.}}{\text{scooter}}\right)\left(x_2\frac{\text{scooters}}{\text{day}}\right) \le 900\frac{\text{Plas. S. min.}}{\text{day}}.$$

Note that if we cancel the common term "trucks" from numerator and denominator of the first product, we obtain the dimensions "plastic shop minutes/day," which is the same as the dimensions of the right-hand side of the inequality. Similarly, if we cancel the common term "scooter" from numerator and denominator of the two terms in the second product on the left, we again obtain the dimensions of the right-hand side.

In any applied problem, when we add two terms together or compare two different terms, it must always be true that they have the same dimensions. We shall use this fact to derive the correct dimensions for the dual variables. Later we will find that the dimensions of the dual variables will help in giving their economic and managerial interpretations.

In order to find the dimensions of the dual variables let us write the first of the dual equations. We have

$$w_1\left(4\,\frac{\text{Plas. S. min.}}{\text{truck}}\right) + w_2\left(2\,\frac{\text{Assem. S. min.}}{\text{truck}}\right) \geq 2\,\frac{\$}{\text{truck}}$$

We know that each term on the left must have the same dimensions as the dimensions of the right-hand side. It follows that the dimensions of w_1 must be "$/Plas. S. min." since the denominator would then cancel with the numerator of the dimensions of the 4 coefficient, and the dimensions of the product would then be "$/truck," as they should be. In the same manner, we can deduce that dimensions of w_2 are "$/Assem. S. min."

Later we will solve the problem presented in this example and give interpretations to the solution.

In order to make easier the task of finding the dimensions of the variables, in Figure 4.2.2 we have stated the rules for determining the dimensions of the primal and dual variables.

Rules for Determining Dimensions of Variables

A. The dimension of x_j is the ratio of the dimension of b_j divided by the dimension of a_{ij} for any i.

B. The dimension of w_i is the ratio of the dimension of c_j divided by the dimension of a_{ij} for any j.

FIGURE 4.2.2

You should check for yourself that these rules give the correct dimensions for both primal and dual variables in the previous example. We apply them next to a minimizing example.

EXAMPLE 4.2.2. A mining company owns two mines, each of which produces copper, zinc, and lead. The cost of running either mine for a shift is $500, and, at most, one shift per day can be worked in each mine. Each shift that mine 1 is worked produces five tons of copper, five tons of zinc, and one ton of lead. Each shift that mine 2 is worked produces four tons of copper, six tons of zinc, and two tons of lead. It is desired to produce at least 30 tons of copper, at least 40 tons of zinc, and at least 10 tons of lead per week. How many shifts shall each mine be worked in order to meet these production quotas while minimizing the cost of operating both mines?

This is a minimizing problem. We let w_1 be the number of shifts mine 1 is worked each week and w_2, the number of shifts that mine 2 is worked each week. The basic data, together with the dimensions of all the quantities, are summarized in the data box of Figure 4.2.3. Note that we got the dimensions of the constants and

w_1 and w_2 from the problem description. But we used rule A in Figure 4.2.2 to deduce the dimensions of x_1, x_2, and x_3. For instance, the dimensions of x_2 can be found as

$$\text{dimension of } x_2 = (\text{dimension of } b_1)/(\text{dimension of } a_{12}),$$

$$= \left(\frac{\$}{\text{M1 Shift}}\right)\Big/\left(\frac{\text{T. Zinc}}{\text{M1 Shift}}\right),$$

$$= \left(\frac{\$}{\text{M1 Shift}}\right)\left(\frac{\text{M1 Shift}}{\text{T. Zinc}}\right),$$

$$= \frac{\$}{\text{T. Zinc}}.$$

In Exercise 1, you are asked to show that we would have obtained the same result if we had divided the dimensions of b_2 by the dimensions of a_{22}. The dimensions of the other x variables are determined similarly.

		$x_1\ \dfrac{\$}{\text{T. Cop.}}$	$x_2\ \dfrac{\$}{\text{T. Zinc}}$	$x_3\ \dfrac{\$}{\text{T. Lead}}$		
w_1	$\dfrac{\text{M1 Shifts}}{\text{week}}$	$5\ \dfrac{\text{T. Cop.}}{\text{M1 Shift}}$	$5\ \dfrac{\text{T. Zinc}}{\text{M1 Shift}}$	$1\ \dfrac{\text{T. Lead}}{\text{M1 Shift}}$	$500\ \dfrac{\$}{\text{M1 Shift}}$	
w_2	$\dfrac{\text{M2 Shifts}}{\text{week}}$	$4\ \dfrac{\text{T. Cop.}}{\text{M2 Shift}}$	$6\ \dfrac{\text{T. Zinc}}{\text{M2 Shift}}$	$2\ \dfrac{\text{T. Lead}}{\text{M2 Shift}}$	$500\ \dfrac{\$}{\text{M2 Shift}}$	*Costs*
		$30\ \dfrac{\text{T. Cop}}{\text{week}}$	$40\ \dfrac{\text{T. Zinc}}{\text{week}}$	$10\ \dfrac{\text{T. Lead}}{\text{week}}$		

Requirements

FIGURE 4.2.3

You will notice a basic similarity between the dual-variable dimensions of both of these examples. In the first example, the dual variables have dimensions of $/plastic shop minute or $/assembly shop minute—we shall call these *imputed values* of labor time. Note that, although the units of these dual variables are like wage rates, the imputed value of a man-minute here has nothing to do with a man's actual wage rate per minute; rather it is, so to speak, the contribution to gross revenue of his time after paying for materials but before paying for labor, overhead, and so on. This could be either more or less than his real wage rate, but the most typical case is that it is considerably more than his wage rate. The real use of the dual variables is in making managerial decisions. Thus, if we can obtain more labor in either shop, the dual variable indicates to the manager how valuable it is. He can use the dual variables to decide whether to use overtime, to subcontract, to expand his shop, and so on.

Similarly, in the second example, the dual variables have interpretations of $/ton of each of the metals. These have interpretations as *imputed costs* of producing additional quantities of each of the kinds of ore. Again, the imputed cost is a measure of the contribution of the costs of running the mines to each of the products, and these costs can also be used in making managerial decisions. For instance, if a manager finds that he can sell more copper at a stated price, he can begin with the imputed cost of producing copper, add to it other costs, such as transportation cost, overhead, and so on, and make his decision as to whether to accept the sale.

In the next section we carry out parametric analysis to show that the simplex method actually indicates in complete detail how the imputed values and imputed costs can be achieved. But first let us use the simplex method to solve Example 4.2.1, carrying out dimensional analysis on each step. We will find the results useful when we get to parametric programming.

EXAMPLE 4.2.1 (continued). We put the numbers and the dimensions from the data box of Figure 4.2.1 into the initial tableau of Figure 4.2.4. There are two negative indicators; suppose we choose the -2; the minimum-ratio rule then selects the **4**, bold-faced in the figure, as pivot. When dividing through the first row to construct the new tableau, we also divide through by the dimensions so that the dimensions of the first row of the new tableau are changed, as shown in Figure 4.2.5. Notice, in particular, that the dimensions of the entry in the last column of the first row are trucks per week, which is correct, since by the simplex rule this quantity is set equal to x_1. Notice also that when we multiply the first row of the new tableau by 2 (Assem. S. min/truck), the dimensions of the resulting row agree with those of the second row of the old tableau, so we can subtract them and form the second row of the new tableau. The same happens when we construct the third row of the new tableau.

From the second tableau it is obvious that we can still make a profit of $.50 per scooter, since the second column has a negative indicator. Going through the minimum-ratio rule, we find that the **5/2** in the second column is the new pivot. Dividing through by this pivot and its dimensions, we obtain the new, and final, tableau in Figure 4.2.6, with dimensions marked on each of the numbers.

x_1 $\dfrac{\text{trucks}}{\text{day}}$	x_2 $\dfrac{\text{scooters}}{\text{day}}$	y_1 $\dfrac{\text{Plas. S. min.}}{\text{day}}$	y_2 $\dfrac{\text{Assem. S. min.}}{\text{day}}$		
$4\ \dfrac{\text{Plas. S. min.}}{\text{truck}}$	$1\ \dfrac{\text{Plas. S. min.}}{\text{scooter}}$	1	0	$900\ \dfrac{\text{Plas. S. min.}}{\text{day}}$	$= y_1$
$2\ \dfrac{\text{Assem. S. min.}}{\text{truck}}$	$3\ \dfrac{\text{Assem. S. min.}}{\text{scooter}}$	0	1	$900\ \dfrac{\text{Assem. S. min.}}{\text{day}}$	$= y_2$
$-2\ \dfrac{\$}{\text{truck}}$	$-1\ \dfrac{\$}{\text{scooter}}$	0	0	0	$= cx$

FIGURE 4.2.4

1	$\dfrac{1}{4}\ \dfrac{\text{trucks}}{\text{scooter}}$	$\dfrac{1}{4}\ \dfrac{\text{trucks}}{\text{Plas. S. min.}}$	0	$225\ \dfrac{\text{trucks}}{\text{day}}$	$= x_1$
0	$\dfrac{5}{2}\ \dfrac{\text{Assem. S. min.}}{\text{scooter}}$	$-\dfrac{1}{2}\ \dfrac{\text{Assem. S. min.}}{\text{Plas. S. min.}}$	1	$450\ \dfrac{\text{Assem. S. min.}}{\text{day}}$	$= y_2$
0	$-\dfrac{1}{2}\ \dfrac{\$}{\text{scooter}}$	$\dfrac{1}{2}\ \dfrac{\$}{\text{Plas. S. min.}}$	0	$450\ \dfrac{\$}{\text{day}}$	$= cx$

FIGURE 4.2.5

1	0	$\dfrac{3}{10}\dfrac{\text{trucks}}{\text{Plas. S. min.}}$	$-\dfrac{1}{10}\dfrac{\text{trucks}}{\text{Assem. S. min.}}$	$180\dfrac{\text{trucks}}{\text{day}}$	$=x_1$
0	1	$-\dfrac{1}{5}\dfrac{\text{scooters}}{\text{Plas. S. min.}}$	$\dfrac{2}{5}\dfrac{\text{scooters}}{\text{Assem. S. min.}}$	$180\dfrac{\text{scooters}}{\text{day}}$	$=x_2$
0	0	$\dfrac{2}{5}\dfrac{\$}{\text{Plas. S. min.}}$	$\dfrac{1}{5}\dfrac{\$}{\text{Assem. S. min.}}$	$540\dfrac{\$}{\text{day}}$	$=cx$

$=z_1\quad =z_2\qquad\qquad =w_1\qquad\qquad\qquad =w_2$

FIGURE 4.2.6

Notice that we have found the optimum production mix to be to produce 180 trucks and 180 scooters per day for a daily profit of $540. Notice also that the dual variable $w_1{}^0$ is equal to $\$.40$ per plastic shop minute, while the dual variable $w_2{}^0$ equals $\$.20$ per assembly shop minute. We can thus conclude that if the workers in each shop get a regular-time pay of $4.00 per hour and 50% overtime, then it pays to hire them at the overtime rate of $.10 per minute, provided the other costs involved are not too large.

In Exercises 4 and 5, you are asked to carry out a similar dimensional analysis for the simplex-method solution of the mining problem given in Example 4.2.2.

EXERCISES 4.2

1. (a) Show that the dimensions of x_2 in Example 4.2.2 are $/T. Zinc by dividing the dimensions of b_2 by the dimensions of a_{22}.
   (b) Find the dimensions of x_1 in two ways: first, divide the dimensions of b_1 by the dimensions of a_{11}, and second, divide the dimensions of b_2 by the dimensions of a_{21}; show that the results are the same.

2. Using Example 4.2.1, show that the following results are true concerning the units of tableau elements:
   (a) When a pivoting step is made, only the dimensions of the pivot row change. These changes can be effected by dividing through the pivot row by the dimensions of the pivot element.
   (b) The 1's in the columns corresponding to basic variables are pure numbers—that is, have no dimensions.
   (c) During the pivoting process, the dimensions of the last row are never changed.

3. In Example 4.2.1, assume that the owner of the toy shop can subcontract labor for either shop at a rate of $.30 per minute. What should he do? (*Hint:* You do not need to solve a linear programming problem to answer this question.)

4. From Figure 4.2.3, construct the initial tableau for Example 4.3.2 and solve it. In each tableau, mark the dimensions of each of the numbers. Give interpretations to the dual variables in the final answer.

5. In Exercise 4, assume the mine owner can sell additional copper at $40 per ton, additional zinc at $65 per ton, and additional lead at $32 per ton. What should he do? (*Hint:* You do not need to solve a linear programming problem to answer this question.)

6. Set up the initial tableau for the bobsled-playpen example given in Exercise 7 of Exercises 3.3. Mark the dimensions of each entry. Do the same for each subsequent tableau. Give interpretations for the numbers in the final tableau.

7. In a maximizing problem such as Example 4.2.1, suppose that a dual variable is zero. What is the managerial significance of this result?

8. In a minimizing problem such as Example 4.2.2, suppose that a dual variable is zero. What is the managerial significance of this result?

9. Consider the transportation problem whose matrix is:

	M_1	M_2	
W_1	$3 \dfrac{\$}{\text{ton}}$	$7 \dfrac{\$}{\text{ton}}$	25 tons
W_2	$6 \dfrac{\$}{\text{ton}}$	$4 \dfrac{\$}{\text{ton}}$	20 tons
	15 tons	30 tons	

(a) State the problem as a minimizing linear programming problem, marking the dimensions of all numbers in the initial tableau.
(b) Use the simplex method to solve it.
(c) Relate the pivoting steps in the simplex method in part (b) to the corresponding steps of the transportation method given in Chapter 1.
(d) Give interpretations to the numbers in the final tableau.
(e) Discuss the connections between the dual variables found by the simplex method and those found by the transportation method.

10. Consider a minimizing problem such as

$$\text{Min } wb$$
$$\text{Subject to:}$$
$$wA \geq c$$
$$w \geq 0$$

(a) Show that it can be written as a maximizing problem by replacing A, b, and c by A', b', and c'.

$$A^* = -A', \quad b^* = -c', \quad c^* = -b'.$$

(b) Discuss the relationships between the two forms of the problem, including the dual-variable analysis.

4.3 PARAMETRIC PROGRAMMING AND POSTOPTIMAL ANALYSIS

In many practical applications of linear programming the values of the components b_i and c_j are not completely fixed but can be changed (perhaps at a cost). In this section we shall make use of the results of the previous section in order to study the effects of such changes.

EXAMPLE 4.3.1. Suppose we rework the truck-scooter example of the previous section given an increase in the number of daily man-minutes in the plastics shop from 900 to $900 + \delta$, where $\delta \geq 0$. In Exercise 1, you will be asked to show that if this change is made in the initial tableau of Figure 4.2.4 and if the corresponding series of pivots are carried out, the new final tableau, corresponding to the one appearing in Figure 4.2.6, is as shown in Figure 4.3.1. We note immediately that only the

x_1	x_2	y_1	y_2		
1	0	$\dfrac{3}{10}\ \dfrac{\text{trucks}}{\text{Plas. S. min.}}$	$-\dfrac{1}{10}\ \dfrac{\text{trucks}}{\text{Assem. S. min.}}$	$\left(180 + \dfrac{3\delta}{10}\right)\dfrac{\text{trucks}}{\text{day}}$	$= x_1$
0	1	$-\dfrac{1}{5}\ \dfrac{\text{scooters}}{\text{Plas. S. min.}}$	$\dfrac{2}{5}\ \dfrac{\text{scooters}}{\text{Assem. S. min.}}$	$\left(180 - \dfrac{\delta}{5}\right)\dfrac{\text{scooters}}{\text{day}}$	$= x_2$
0	0	$\dfrac{2}{5}\ \dfrac{\$}{\text{Plas. S. min.}}$	$\dfrac{1}{5}\ \dfrac{\$}{\text{Assem. S. min.}}$	$\left(540 + \dfrac{2\delta}{5}\right)\dfrac{\$}{\text{day}}$	$= cx$
$= z_1$	$= z_2$	$= w_1$	$= w_2$		

FIGURE 4.3.1

last column of the tableau has been changed and also that the change can easily be predicted, from the final tableau in Figure 4.2.6, as follows: in order to get the tableau of Figure 4.3.1 from Figure 4.2.6, multiply the third column (the one under y_1) by plastic shop minutes per day and add the product to the last column. Note that since δ has dimensions of plastic shop minutes per day, when we multiply these dimensions by the dimensions of the y_1 column in Figure 4.2.6, we get exactly the dimensions of the last column! Note in particular that the value of the objective function has increased from 540 to $540 + 2\delta/5 = 540 + w_1^o\delta$. This agrees with our interpretation of the dual variable w_1^o in the preceding section; namely, that the value of this dual variable is the rate at which we can change the gross profit if we increase the number of plastic shop man-minutes by a small amount.

However, the final tableau in Figure 4.3.1 also tells us exactly how the additional profit is to be achieved. For each additional amount δ of plastics shop manminutes, we make $3\delta/10$ *additional* trucks and $\delta/5$ *fewer* scooters; hence our net change in daily gross profit is

$$2\left(\frac{3\delta}{10}\right) - 1\left(\frac{\delta}{5}\right) = \frac{2}{5}\delta.$$

These interpretations are obvious from the dimensions of these quantities, since, for instance, the dimensions of the coefficient $3/10$ were trucks per plastic shop minute and the dimensions of the coefficient $-1/5$ were scooters per plastic shop minute. We can interpret these coefficients as *trade-off* numbers that tell us how to alter our optimal production plan in case we decide to increase the daily number of minutes available in the plastic shop.

The next question we would like to ask is how large can δ be if we also require that the final tableau in Figure 4.3.1 should remain optimal? Since the only changes appear in the last column, we need only check there. The coefficient $180 + (3\delta/10)$ will remain positive no matter how large δ becomes. But the term $180 - (\delta/5)$ is positive only if $\delta \leq 900$. For larger δ's the x_2 term becomes negative.

We can also observe that the analysis we carried out did not really make use of the fact that δ was constrained to be nonnegative. If we consider negative δ's, the changes will still give the tableau of Figure 4.3.1. Now, however, when we try to compute the most negative that δ can become, we see that the coefficient $180 - (\delta/5)$ remains positive, but $180 + (3\delta/10)$ puts a limitation on δ, namely $-600 \leq \delta$.

We conclude that the tableau in Figure 4.3.1 is the tableau of an optimum solution provided δ satisfies $-600 \leq \delta \leq 900$. In terms of the original coefficient, the number of daily plastic shop minutes, we see that this number can lie in the range $900 - 600 = 300$ to $900 + 900 = 1800$. If we let b_1 be the number of plastic shop minutes, we see that it must satisfy $300 \leq b_1 \leq 1800$ in order that the tableau be optimal. Notice that for the indicated range, the dual solution w^o is always the same.

We can carry out the same kind of analysis for the assembly shop minutes coefficient—it will involve the column under y_2 in Figure 4.2.6. In Exercise 2, you will be asked to show that if we let b_2 be the number of assembly shop minutes available, then, provided $450 \leq b_2 \leq 1800$, the corresponding tableau, like that in Figure 4.3.1, will remain optimal and the dual solution w^o will also remain optimal.

The analysis we have just performed is sometimes called *ranging analysis*, since it involves the determination of the ranges in which data coefficients can lie while w^o remains optimal. The same kind of analysis can be carried out in the same way for a general linear programming problem. We summarize results in a theorem.

THEOREM 4.3.1. Let x^o and w^o be optimal solutions displayed in the final tableau T^o for the problem: Maximize cx subject to $Ax \leq b$ and $x \geq 0$. Now assume the coefficient b_i is replaced by $b_i + \delta$.

(a) The new final tableau T^δ will differ from T^o only in the last column; it can be obtained from T^o by replacing the elements $t^o_{i,\,m+n+1}$ in the last column by

$$t^\delta_{i,\,m+n+1} = t^o_{i,\,m+n+1} + \delta t^o_{i,\,j+n},$$

where $t^o_{i,\,j+n}$ are the entries in the column of T^o under the variable y_j. The basic x_j and y_i variables and the value of the objective function will be correspondingly changed, but the nonbasic x_j and y_i variables are unchanged.

(b) If we choose δ in the interval $\mu^- \leq \delta \leq \mu^+$ or, equivalently, if we choose b_i in the interval between $b_i - \mu^-$ and $b_i + \mu^+$, where

$$\mu^+ = \operatorname*{Min}_{t_{i^o,\,j+n} < 0} \frac{t^o_{i,\,m+n+1}}{-t^o_{i,\,j+n}} \quad \text{and} \quad \mu^- = \operatorname*{Min}_{t_{i^o,\,j+n} > 0} \frac{t^o_{i,\,m+n+1}}{t^o_{i,\,j+n}},$$

then tableau T^δ is optimal. (In case there is no j such that $t^o_{i,\,j+n} < 0$, set $\mu^+ = \infty$.) In particular, w^o remains the optimal dual solution for all δ in this interval.

EXAMPLE 4.3.2. Let us illustrate the theorem by extending the truck-scooter example of the previous section. Suppose there are 20 men working in each shop so that there are 9000 minutes available each day; also suppose there is a shipping department employing three men who work one minute packing either a truck or a scooter for shipment. The initial tableau of the new problem, dimensions omitted, is shown in Figure 4.3.2, and the final tableau, obtained after two pivots, is shown in Figure 4.3.3.

	x_1	x_2	y_1	y_2	y_3		
Plastic Shop	4	1	1	0	0	9000	$= y_1$
Assembly Shop	2	3	0	1	0	9000	$= y_2$
Packing Shop	1	1	0	0	1	700	$= y_3$
	-2	-1	0	0	0	0	$= cx$

FIGURE 4.3.2

	x_1	x_2	y_1	y_2	y_3		
	1	0	$\frac{1}{3}$	0	$-\frac{1}{3}$	2100	$= x_1$
	0	0	$\frac{1}{3}$	1	$-\frac{10}{3}$	3000	$= y_2$
	0	1	$-\frac{1}{3}$	0	$\frac{4}{3}$	600	$= x_2$
	0	0	$\frac{1}{3}$	0	$\frac{1}{3}$	5000	$= cx$
	$= z_1$	$= z_2$	$= w_1$	$= w_2$	$=.w_3$		

FIGURE 4.3.3

Let us carry out ranging analysis for this problem. If we assume that the number of minutes in the plastic shop is changed by δ, we derive from Figure 4.3.3 that δ must satisfy the following constraints:

$$2100 + \frac{\delta}{3} \geq 0, \qquad 3000 + \frac{\delta}{3} \geq 0, \quad \text{and} \quad 600 - \frac{\delta}{3} \geq 0.$$

From the first two inequalities, we find $\delta \geq -6300$ and $\delta \geq -9000$, from which we conclude that $\mu^- = 6300$. From the last inequality, we find $\delta \leq 1800$, so $\mu^+ = 1800$. Hence the range in plastic shop minutes, b_1, is required to be $2700 \leq b_1 \leq 10,800$.

In order to find the range for the assembly shop minutes, we note first of all that $w_2{}^o = 0$, which means that we have unused assembly shop minutes in the optimal solution. Since $y_2 = 3000$, it follows that we have 3000 such unused minutes. It is clear that we could increase the number of assembly shop minutes available indefinitely without changing the optimal dual solution, since they will be surplus unused minutes with 0 imputed value. However, if we *decrease* the number of assembly shop minutes, b_2, we see that if it goes below 3000—the number of excess minutes—then the dual solution will no longer be valid. Hence the range on b_2 is $6000 \leq b_2 < \infty$.

In Exercise 4, you will be asked to show that the range of the packing shop minutes is $2250 \leq b_3 \leq 3600$.

It is obvious that we can perform the same kind of ranging analysis on the coefficients c_j with similar results. The following theorem summarizes the results.

THEOREM 4.3.2. Let x^o, w^o, and T^o be as in the statement of Theorem 4.3.1. Assume that the coefficient c_j is replaced by $c_j + \delta$.

(a) The new final tableau T^δ will differ from T^o only in the last row. If x_j is not basic, the only change needed is to replace $t^o_{m+1,j}$ by $t^o_{m+1,j} + \delta$. If x_j is basic, let i be the unique row of x_j, the jth column, that has the 1 entry. Then T^δ can be obtained from T^o by replacing the elements $t^o_{m+1,k}$ in the last row by

$$t_{m+1,k} = t^o_{m+1,k} + \delta t^o_{i,k}.$$

The basic w_i and z_j variables and the value of the objective function will be correspondingly changed, but the nonbasic w_i and z_j variables will be unchanged.

(b) If we choose δ in the interval $\mu^- \leq \delta \leq \mu^+$ or, equivalently, choose c_j in the interval between $c_j - \mu^-$ and $c_j + \mu^+$, where

$$\mu^+ = \operatorname*{Min}_{\substack{t^o_{i,k} > 0 \\ k \neq j}} \frac{t^o_{m+1,k}}{t^o_{i,k}} \quad \text{and} \quad \mu^- = \operatorname*{Min}_{\substack{t^o_{i,k} < 0 \\ k \neq j}} \frac{t^o_{m+1,k}}{-t^o_{i,k}},$$

the tableau T^δ is optimal. (In case there is no k such that $t^o_{i,k} < 0$, set $\mu^- = -\infty$.) In particular, x^o remains the optimal primal solution for all δ in this interval.

EXAMPLE 4.3.2 (continued). Let us apply this result to the optimum final tableau in Figure 4.3.3. To find the tableau T^δ if we let c_1 vary, we multiply the first row (except for the (1, 1) entry) by δ and subtract from the last row. We get two conditions on δ, namely, $\frac{1}{3} - \frac{1}{3}\delta \geq 0$ and $\frac{1}{3} + \frac{1}{3}\delta \geq 0$, from which we obtain $\mu^- = 1$ and $\mu^+ = 1$. It follows that δ must be in the interval $-1 \leq \delta \leq 1$ or, equivalently, $1 \leq c_1 \leq 3$.

Similarly, if we let c_2 vary, we find T^δ by multiplying the third row of the tableau in Figure 4.3.3 by δ (except for the (3, 2) entry) and subtract from the last row. We obtain two conditions on δ, namely, $\frac{1}{3} + \frac{1}{3}\delta \geq 0$ and $\frac{1}{3} - \frac{4}{3}\delta \geq 0$, from which we obtain $\mu^- = -1$ and $\mu^+ = \frac{1}{4}$. It follows that δ must be in the interval $-1 \leq \delta \leq \frac{1}{4}$, or, equivalently, $0 \leq c_2 \leq \frac{5}{4}$.

Other names for ranging analysis are parametric programming and postoptimal analysis. Still another name is *sensitivity analysis*, a term which emphasizes the fact that we are exploring the possible changes in the coefficients that will not affect optimality of the solutions found. In many cases, specifying the data to use in a linear programming problem is a difficult task, sometimes involving an estimating procedure. Sensitivity analysis is important since it enables us to determine the effects of errors in coefficient estimates on the resulting decisions.

A similar type of parametric programming analysis can be carried out for variations in the a_{ij} coefficients, but we shall not discuss that here.

EXERCISES 4.3

1. Change the 900 in the first row, last column of Figure 4.2.4 to $900 + \delta$, and show that the tableau in Figure 4.3.1 is obtained after two pivots.

2. In Example 4.3.1, show that the range on b_2 is $450 \leq b_2 \leq 1800$.

3. Solve the problem in Figure 4.3.2 and show that the final tableau is as shown in Figure 4.3.3.

4. In Example 4.3.2, show that the range of b_3 is $450 \leq b_3 \leq 900$.

5. In Exercise 4 of Exercises 4.2, you solved the mining problem, marking all dimensions on the numbers.
   (a) Give interpretations to the coefficients in the final tableau as trade-off numbers for changes in optimal production plans if some of the requirements or costs are changed.
   (b) Find the ranges of each of the b_i and c_j for which the final solution will remain optimal.

4.4   DERIVATION OF DUAL PROBLEMS

Many practical problems lead to linear programming problems having mixtures of equality and inequality constraints and nonnegative and unconstrained variables. In the preceding sections, we have seen how to set them up for solution by computer. In the present section we shall discuss the derivation of and interpretation of the dual problems for such primal problems.

We begin by first proving a theorem that includes three special cases, and then we state the general theorem.

THEOREM 4.4.1. The following pairs of problems are dual to each other:

(a)   Max cx Min wb
         Subject to: Subject to:
            $Ax = b$ $wA \geq c$
            $x \geq 0$ w unrestricted

(b)   Max cx Min wb
         Subject to: Subject to:
            $Ax = b$ $wA = c$
            x unrestricted w unrestricted

(c)   Max cx Min wb
         Subject to: Subject to:
            $Ax \leq b$ $wA = c$
            x unrestricted $w \geq 0$

Proof: (a) Consider the maximizing problem in (a). An equivalent problem is:

   Max cx
   Subject to:
   $$Ax \leq b$$
   $$-Ax \leq -b$$
   $$x \geq 0$$

since $Ax \leq b$ and $Ax \geq b$ are equivalent to $Ax = b$. Now assign dual variables w^+ to $Ax \leq b$ and w^- to $-Ax \leq -b$. Then by the previous rules for constructing dual problems, we have as the dual problem the following:

$$\text{Min } w^+ b - w^- b$$

Subject to:

$$w^+ A - w^- A \geq c$$
$$w^+, w^- \geq 0$$

Rewriting this problem, we have

$$\text{Min}(w^+ - w^-)b$$

Subject to:

$$(w^+ - w^-)A \geq c$$
$$w^+, w^- \geq 0$$

Notice that the variables w^+ and w^- always occur as a pair—namely, $w^+ - w^-$. Hence we can substitute

$$w = w^+ - w^-$$

and observe that, since w^+ and w^- are nonnegative variables, w is unrestricted—that is, can be positive, negative, or zero. (We have already made use of this transformation in Section 4.1.) Now the minimizing problem becomes

$$\text{Min } wb$$

Subject to:

$$wA \geq c$$
$$w \text{ unrestricted}$$

as was to be shown.

(b) In order to formulate the maximum problem in (b) with unrestricted variables, we make the substitution $x = x^+ - x^-$, where $x^+, x^- \geq 0$. Then we have

$$\text{Max } c(x^+ - x^-)$$

Subject to:

$$A(x^+ - x^-) = b$$
$$x^+, x^- \geq 0$$

Using part (a), we obtain the dual problem as

$$\text{Min } wb$$

Subject to:

$$wA \geq c$$
$$-wA \leq -c$$
$$w \text{ unrestricted}$$

But obviously the dual problem above is just

$$\text{Min } wb$$

Subject to:

$$wA = c$$

w unrestricted

as was to be shown.

The proof of part (c) is Exercise 1.

In the general case we may have some equalities and some inequalities in both the primal and dual problems. The general case is included in the following theorem, which includes Theorem 4.4.1.

THEOREM 4.4.2. The following pair of problems ((4.5.1) and (4.5.2) below) are dual to each other.

$$\text{Max } c^{(1)}x^{(1)} + c^{(2)}x^{(2)}$$

(4.4.1)   Subject to:

$$A^{(11)}x^{(1)} + A^{(12)}x^{(2)} = b^{(1)}$$
$$A^{(21)}x^{(1)} + A^{(22)}x^{(2)} \le b^{(2)}$$
$$x^{(2)} \ge 0$$

$x^{(1)}$ unrestricted

Here $A^{(11)}$ is $m_1 \times n_1$, $A^{(12)}$ is $m_1 \times n_2$, $A^{(21)}$ is $m_2 \times n_1$, and $A^{(22)}$ is $m_2 \times n_2$, and the dimensions of the other vectors are correspondingly determined.

$$\text{Min } w^{(1)}b^{(1)} + w^{(2)}b^{(2)}$$

(4.4.2)   Subject to:

$$w^{(1)}A^{(11)} + w^{(2)}A^{(21)} = c^{(1)}$$
$$w^{(1)}A^{(12)} + w^{(2)}A^{(22)} \le c^{(2)}$$
$$w^{(2)} \ge 0$$

$w^{(1)}$ unrestricted

The proof of this theorem follows the method of the previous theorem and is requested in Exercise 2.

As an aid in remembering and applying the theorem, we present the diagram of Figure 4.4.1. Notice that the various constraints and objective functions for each problem can be read off from either the rows or the columns of the diagram.

As still another way of remembering the rules for dual variables, the following two rules should be observed:

(i) The dual variable corresponding to an inequality constraint must be constrained to be nonnegative.

(ii) The dual variable corresponding to an equality constraint is unrestricted.

These rules apply to both maximizing and minimizing problems and are probably the most succinct way of remembering the duality relationships.

The main use we will have for the theorems given above will be in the proofs of basic theorems of matrix game theory and Markov chains in later chapters.

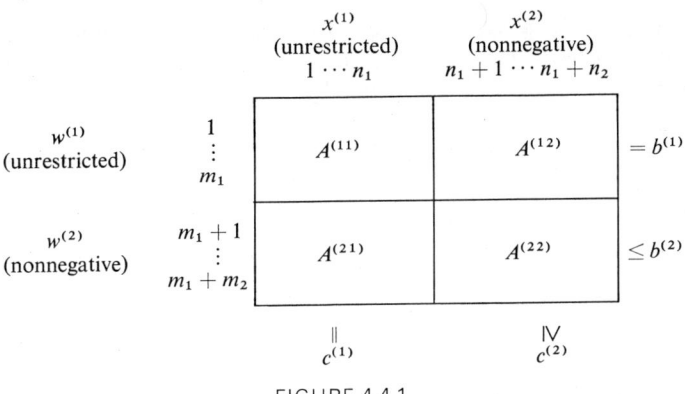

FIGURE 4.4.1

EXERCISES 4.4

1. Prove part (c) of Theorem 4.4.1.

2. Prove Theorem 4.4.2.

3. Set up the dual problem for the following:

$$\text{Max } x_1 + x_2 + x_3$$

Subject to:

$$\begin{aligned}
x_1 + x_2 \quad &= 2 \\
x_2 + x_3 &\geq 1 \\
x_1 \quad + x_3 &\leq 5 \\
x_1, x_2, x_3 &\geq 0
\end{aligned}$$

Which constraints are equalities, and which variables are unrestricted?

4. Find and interpret the dual problem for

$$\text{Max } x_1 + 2x_2$$

Subject to:

$$\begin{aligned}
x_1 + x_2 &\geq 2 \\
x_1 + x_2 &\leq 4 \\
x_1, x_2 &\geq 0
\end{aligned}$$

5. The three cases of Theorem 4.4.1 can be found in one of the four parts of the A matrix in Figure 4.4.1. Which part of the theorem corresponds to which area? What is the interpretation of the remaining area?

4.5   LINEAR PROGRAMMING PROBLEMS IN STANDARD FORM

In the canonical forms of the dual linear programming problems we have studied so far, the constraints were all inequalities and they were all $\leq$ for a maximizing problem and $\geq$ for a minimizing problem. Also, each of the variables was restricted to be nonnegative. However, when deriving a linear programming problem in an applied situation, it frequently happens that some constraints are = constraints, some inequalities go the wrong way for their type of problem, and some variables are unrestricted instead of being nonnegative.

In the present section we will show how to put any linear programming problem into standard form. Since many linear programming codes written for computers will accept constraints of any kind, it is not necessary to understand the material in this section if such a computer code is available. Therefore the present section may be regarded as optional and can be skipped if desired without loss of essential continuity.

EXAMPLE 4.5.1. Suppose that we are solving a maximizing problem with equality constraints

$$\begin{aligned} x_1 + x_2 + x_3 &= 5, \\ -x_1 + x_2 + x_3 &= 7, \\ x_1 - x_2 + x_3 &= 9, \end{aligned}$$

(4.5.1)

and we wish to transform these into "$\leq$" constraints. This may be done by (a) rewriting them as such inequalities and (b) adding one more inequality whose coefficients are the negative sums of the coefficients in the given equalities. Thus, an equivalent set of inequalities is

$$\begin{aligned} x_1 + x_2 + \ x_3 &\leq 5, \\ -x_1 + x_2 + \ x_3 &\leq 7, \\ x_1 - x_2 + \ x_3 &\leq 9, \\ -x_1 - x_2 - 3x_3 &\leq -21. \end{aligned}$$

(4.5.2)

To show that (4.5.1) and (4.5.2) are equivalent, observe that the last inequality of (4.5.2) has as its left-hand side the negative sum of the entries of the first three inequalities and that the right-hand side is the negative sum of the right-hand sides; that is,

$$-x_1 - x_2 - 3x_3 = -[(x_1 + x_2 + x_3) + (-x_1 + x_2 + x_3) + (x_1 - x_2 + x_3)],$$
$$-21 = -[5 + 7 + 9].$$

Multiplying through by -1, the last inequality in (4.5.2) thus is equivalent to

$$[(x_1 + x_2 + x_3) + (-x_1 + x_2 + x_3) + (x_1 - x_2 + x_3)] \geq 21.$$

However, adding together the first three inequalities of (4.5.2), we obtain the opposite inequality, and the two together imply the equality; that is,

$$(x_1 + x_2 + x_3) + (-x_1 + x_2 + x_3) + (x_1 - x_2 + x_3) = 21 = 5 + 7 + 9.$$

However, the only way that the first three inequalities of (4.5.2) can hold, as well as this equality, is for the first three inequalities of (4.5.2) also to hold as equalities. Hence (4.5.1) and (4.5.2) are equivalent.

THEOREM 4.5.1. Let A be an $m \times n$ matrix, b an $m \times 1$ vector, and e a $1 \times m$ vector with all components 1. Then the equations (a), $Ax = b$, and the inequalities (b), $Ax \leq b$ and $-eAx \leq -eb$, have the same truth set—that is, are equivalent.

The proof of this theorem, which imitates the proof of the equivalence of (4.5.1) and (4.5.2) in Example 1, is Exercise 5. Note that eA and eb are matrices that are sums of coefficients in columns.

An analogous equivalence holds for $\geq$ inequalities and equations, as the following theorem shows.

THEOREM 4.5.2. Let A be an $m \times n$ matrix, c a $1 \times n$ vector, and f an $n \times 1$ vector with all components 1. Then the equations (a), $wA = c$, and the inequalities (b), $wA \geq c$ and $w(-Af) \geq -cf$, have the same truth set—that is, are equivalent.

A numerical example of this kind of equivalence is given in Exercise 8.

A second statement of a linear programming problem that is not in canonical form originally is the case in which some of the variables are not nonnegative—that is, are unrestricted. As we saw in the previous chapter, the restricted pivoting techniques arrive at solutions in which all variables are nonnegative. Hence we need some technique for removing this constraint when it is not needed. The method is illustrated in the next example.

EXAMPLE 4.5.2. Consider the following system of inequalities:

$$(4.5.3) \qquad \begin{aligned} 3x_1 + 4x_2 + 5x_3 &\leq 7, \\ -x_1 + 2x_2 + 7x_3 &\leq 1, \\ x_3 &\geq 0. \end{aligned}$$

Note that x_1 and x_2 are completely unrestricted; that is, they may be positive, negative, or zero. We shall show how to reformulate the problem by adding a single new variable so that all the resulting variables are nonnegative.

Let x_4 be the new variable. Define

$$(4.5.4) \qquad \begin{aligned} x_1 &= x_1{}^+ - x_4, \\ x_2 &= x_2{}^+ - x_4, \end{aligned}$$

where $x_1{}^+$ and $x_2{}^+$ are new variables that will replace x_1 and x_2. All three of the new variables are to be nonnegative. If we substitute (4.5.4) into (4.5.3), we obtain

$$(4.5.5) \qquad \begin{aligned} 3x_1{}^+ + 4x_2{}^+ + 5x_3 - 7x_4 &\leq 7, \\ -x_1{}^+ + 2x_2{}^+ + 7x_3 - x_4 &\leq 1, \\ x_1{}^+, x_2{}^+, x_3, x_4 &\geq 0. \end{aligned}$$

We shall now show that (4.5.3) and (4.5.5) are equivalent—that is, have the same truth set.

We show first that a solution $x_1{}^+$, $x_2{}^+$, x_3, and x_4 of (4.1.5) in nonnegative numbers yields a solution to (4.5.3) with x_1 and x_2 unrestricted. To see this, let x_1 and x_2 be defined from (4.5.4) and note that they may be positive, negative, or zero, depending on the relative sizes of $x_1{}^+$, $x_2{}^+$, and x_4. By direct substitution, it follows that since $x_1{}^+$, $x_2{}^+$, x_3, and x_4 satisfy (4.5.5), the corresponding x_1, x_2, and x_3 satisfy (4.5.3).

As a specific numerical example, consider the values

$$x_1{}^+ = 7, \qquad x_2{}^+ = 0, \qquad x_3 = 1, \quad \text{and} \quad x_4 = 3,$$

which satisfy (4.5.5), and the values related by (4.1.4),

$$x_1 = 4, \quad x_2 = -3, \quad x_3 = 1,$$

which satisfy (4.5.3).

We must also show that any solution to (4.5.3) yields a solution to (4.5.5). Let x_1, x_2, and x_3 be a solution to (4.5.3). If both x_1 and x_2 are greater than or equal to zero, let $x_4 = 0$; otherwise, let $x_4 = -a$, where a is the most negative of x_1 and x_2. Then let

(4.5.6)
$$x_1^+ = x_1 + x_4,$$
$$x_2^+ = x_2 + x_4,$$

which are clearly derived from (4.5.4). It is easy to show that x_1^+, x_2^+, x_3, and x_4 are all nonnegative and satisfy (4.5.3).

As a specific numerical example, consider

$$x_1 = -2, \quad x_2 = -4, \quad x_3 = 1,$$

which solves (4.5.3), and the corresponding values,

$$x_1^+ = 2, \quad x_2^+ = 0, \quad x_3 = 1, \quad \text{and} \quad x_4 = 4,$$

derived by the above process, which satisfy (4.5.5).

THEOREM 4.5.3. Let A be an $m \times n$ matrix, x be $n \times 1$, and b be $m \times 1$. Consider the inequalities

(4.5.7)
$$Ax \leq b, \quad x_{t+1}, \ldots, x_n \geq 0,$$

and $x_1, \ldots, x_t$ unrestricted. Define a new variable, x_{n+1}, and new variables x_j^+, defined by

(4.5.8)
$$x_j = x_j^+ - x_{n+1}, \quad j = 1, \ldots, t,$$

where all the new variables are nonnegative. Let x^* be the $(n+1) \times 1$ vector with components $x_1^+, \ldots, x_t^+, x_{t+1}, \ldots, x_n, x_{n+1}$, and let $A^* = (A, A_{n+1})$ be an $m \times (n+1)$ matrix with the first n columns identical to those in A and the last column, A_{n+1}, defined as

(4.5.9)
$$a_{i, n+1} = -\sum_{j=1}^{t} a_{ij}.$$

Then the inequalities

(4.5.10)
$$A^* x^* \leq b, \quad x^* \geq 0$$

are equivalent to those in (4.5.7).

The proof of this theorem imitates that of the example above and is asked for in Exercise 9. The analogous result for $\geq$ inequalities is contained in the next theorem.

THEOREM 4.5.4. Let A be $m \times n$, w be $1 \times m$, and c be $1 \times n$. Consider the inequalities

(4.5.11)
$$wA \geq c, \quad w_{t+1}, \ldots, w_m \geq 0,$$

and $w_1, \ldots, w_t$ unrestricted. Define new nonnegative variables $w_1{}^+, \ldots, w_t{}^+$ and w_{m+1} satisfying

$$(4.5.12) \qquad w_i = w_i{}^+ - w_{m+1} \qquad \text{for } i = 1, \ldots, t.$$

Let w^* be the $1 \times (m + 1)$ vector with components $w_1{}^+, \ldots, w_t{}^+, w_{t+1}, \ldots, w_n, w_{n+1}$, and let A^* be the $(m + 1) \times n$ matrix with the first m rows identical with A and the last row defined by

$$(4.5.13) \qquad a_{m+1, j} = - \sum_{i=1}^{t} a_{ij}.$$

Then the inequalities

$$(4.5.14) \qquad w^* A^* \geq c, \qquad w^* \geq 0,$$

are equivalent to those in (4.5.11).

A numerical example of this kind of equivalence is given in Exercise 6.

The third way in which an inequality may not be in canonical form is when it is a $\geq$ inequality instead of a $\leq$ inequality. But it is easy to change the direction of an inequality sign by multiplying through by -1. Thus, the inequality $3x_1 - 4x_2 \geq -1$ is equivalent to $-3x_1 + 4x_2 \leq 1$.

We recall to you the canonical forms of dual linear programming problems. These are displayed in Figure 4.5.1.

THE MAXIMIZING PROBLEM	THE MINIMIZING PROBLEM
Max cx	Min wb
Subject to:	Subject to:
$Ax \leq b$	$wA \geq c$
$x \geq 0$	$w \geq 0$

FIGURE 4.5.1. Canonical forms of linear programming problems

The process for taking any statement of a linear programming problem having nonnegative and/or unrestricted variables and putting it into canonical form as given in Figure 4.5.1 is summarized in the flow diagram of Figure 4.5.2. (For the case of nonpositive variables see Exercise 14.) We illustrate the use of the process in the next example.

EXAMPLE 4.5.3. Put into canonical form the maximizing linear programming problem defined by:

$$\text{Max } 7x_1 - 3x_2 + x_3$$
$$\text{Subject to:}$$
$$-x_1 + x_2 + x_3 = 15$$
$$3x_2 + x_3 = 8$$
$$3x_1 - 5x_2 + 2x_3 \geq -1$$
$$x_3 \geq 0$$
$$x_1 \text{ and } x_2 \text{ are unrestricted.}$$

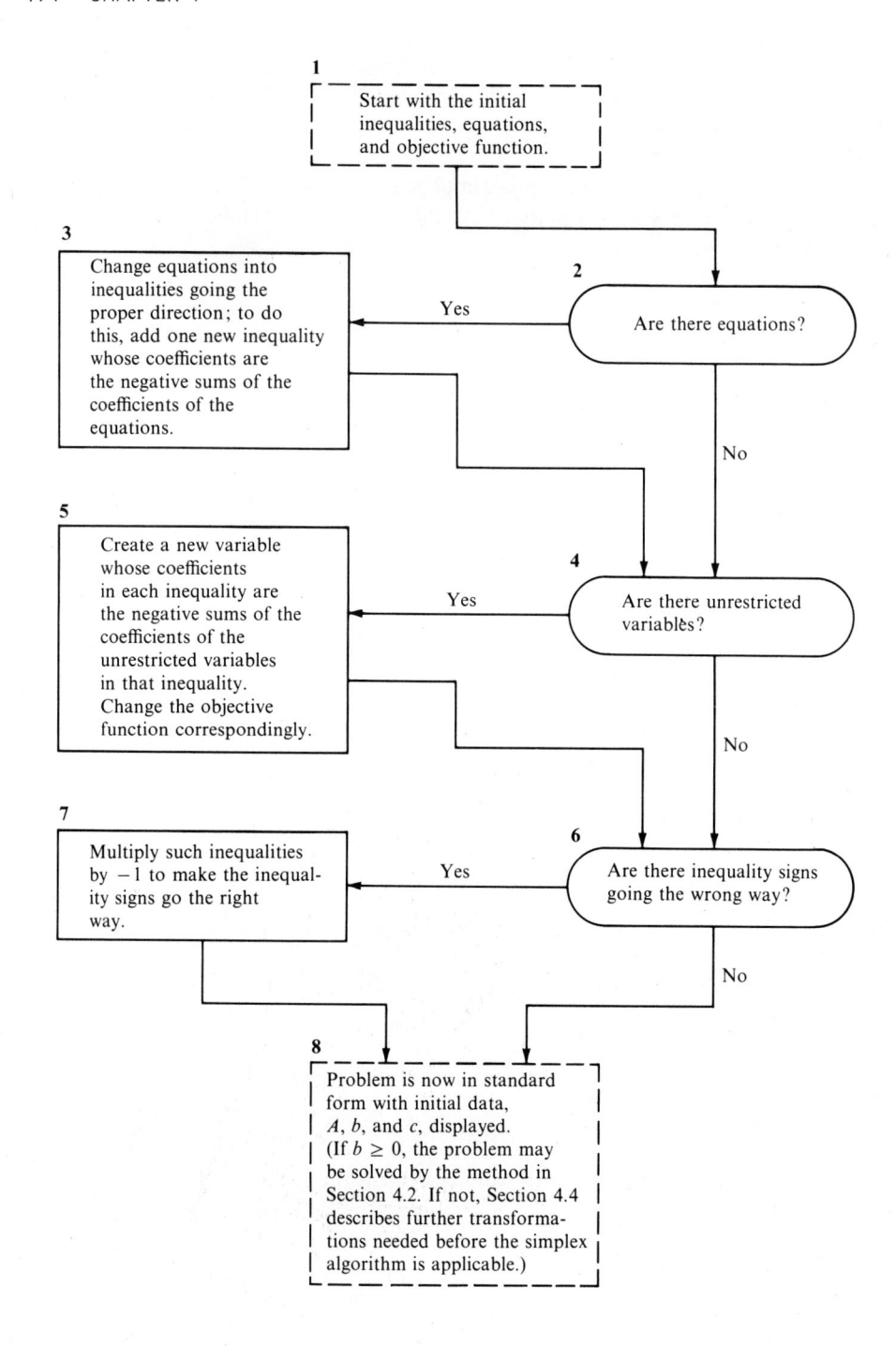

FIGURE 4.5.2. Flow diagram for putting either a maximizing or a minimizing problem into standard form

The initial data are shown, so we apply the steps of the flow diagram in Figure 4.5.2. In box 2 the answer is yes so we go to box 3 and follow the instructions for changing the two equations into $\leq$ type inequalities. The result is:

$$\text{Max } 7x_1 - 3x_2 + x_3$$

Subject to:

$$-x_1 + x_2 + x_3 \leq 15$$
$$3x_2 + x_3 \leq 8$$
$$3x_1 - 5x_2 + 2x_3 \geq -1$$
$$x_1 - 4x_2 - 2x_3 \leq -23$$
$$x_3 \geq 0$$

The new inequality has coefficients that are the negative sums of the coefficients in the two equations.

Since x_1 and x_2 are unrestricted variables, the answer to the question in box 4 of Figure 4.5.2 is yes, so we follow the instructions in box 5. The resulting problem is:

$$\text{Max } 7x_1^+ - 3x_2^+ + x_3 - 4x_4$$

Subject to:

$$-x_1^+ + x_2^+ + x_3 \leq 15$$
$$3x_2^+ + x_3 - 3x_4 \leq 8$$
$$3x_1^+ - 5x_2^+ + 2x_3 + 2x_4 \geq -1$$
$$x_1^+ - 4x_2^+ - 2x_3 + 3x_4 \leq -23$$
$$x_1^+, x_2^+, x_3, x_4 \geq 0$$

The final step is, of course, to change the third inequality into a $\leq$ type by multiplying through by -1. The resulting inequality is

$$-3x_1^+ + 5x_2^+ - 2x_3 - 2x_4 \leq 1,$$

which must now be inserted in the previous problem. The problem is now in the standard form of Figure 4.5.1. The data A, b, and c are as follows:

$$A = \begin{bmatrix} -1 & 1 & 1 & 0 \\ 0 & 3 & 1 & -3 \\ -3 & 5 & -2 & -2 \\ 1 & -4 & -2 & 3 \end{bmatrix}$$

$$b = \begin{bmatrix} 15 \\ 8 \\ 1 \\ -23 \end{bmatrix}$$

$$c = [7, \ -3, \ 1, \ -4]$$

Since b is not a nonnegative vector, the problem must be further transformed, as remarked in box 8 of Figure 4.5.2, before the simplex algorithm can be applied. These transformations will be discussed further in Section 4.6.

EXERCISES 4.5

1. Consider the equations

$$-3x_1 + 5x_2 - x_3 = 7,$$
$$2x_1 - 6x_2 - 2x_3 = 9.$$

(a) Change them into an equivalent set of three $\leq$ inequalities.
(b) Change them into an equivalent set of three $\geq$ inequalities.
(c) Discuss the relationship between your answers in (a) and (b). Show that in both cases at least one of the coefficients on the right-hand side is negative.

2. Rework Exercise 1 assuming that an objective function

$$x_1 - 2x_2 + 3x_3$$

is to be maximized and that x_1 and x_2 are unrestricted variables.

3. Show that if equations $Ax = b$, $b \neq 0$, are changed into equivalent inequalities, the resulting right-hand sides must have at least one positive and one negative coefficient.

4. Show that the procedure in the flow diagram of Figure 4.5.2 terminates with at most one new row and one new column being added to the A matrix. Show also that the b and c vectors each have at most one new component added to them.

5. Prove Theorem 4.5.1 as follows:
(a) If $Ax = b$, show that both $Ax \leq b$ and $-Ax \leq -b$ are true. From the latter, prove that $-eAx \leq -eb$.
(b) If $-eAx \leq -eb$, show that $eAx \geq eb$. From $Ax \leq b$, show that $eAx \leq eb$. Now prove $eAx = eb$. From the latter and $Ax \leq b$, show that $Ax = b$.

6. Consider the equations

$$w_1 - 7w_2 + 6w_3 = 5,$$
$$-9w_1 + 8w_2 - 3w_3 = -4,$$
$$2w_1 + 3w_2 - 5w_3 = -1.$$

(a) Change these equations into an equivalent set of four $\geq$ inequalities.
(b) Suppose that the function to be minimized is

$$w_1 + w_2 + w_3$$

and that w_1 and w_2 are unrestricted. Find an equivalent set of inequalities and an equivalent objective function.

7. Show that if the equations $wA = c$, $c \neq 0$, are changed into an equivalent set of $\geq$ inequalities, at least one of the right-hand sides must be negative.

8. Prove Theorem 4.5.2 by reasoning analogous to that given in Exercise 5.

9. Prove Theorem 4.5.3.

10. Consider the minimizing problem

$$\text{Min } w_1 - 2w_2 + 3w_3$$

Subject to:

$$5w_1 - 3w_2 - 5w_3 \geq -1$$
$$-7w_1 + 2w_2 + 4w_3 \geq 6$$
$$w_3 \geq 0$$

where w_1 and w_2 are unrestricted. State an equivalent problem with four variables in which all are nonnegative variables.

11. Prove Theorem 4.5.4.

12. Write the dual to the problem in Example 4.5.3 after it has been put into canonical form.

13. Put the following problems into canonical form:

(a)
$$\text{Max } 7x_1 + 3x_2 + 4x_3$$
Subject to:
$$12x_1 - 5x_2 + 5x_3 = 9$$
$$-x_1 - 2x_2 + 5x_3 = 11$$
$$2x_1 + 3x_2 - 7x_3 \geq -5$$
$$x_1 \qquad\qquad \geq 0$$

(b)
$$\text{Min } 5w_1 + 5w_2 + 2w_3$$
Subject to:
$$w_1 - 7w_2 + 5w_3 = 9$$
$$-w_1 + 6w_2 - 12w_3 = 10$$
$$10w_1 + 8w_2 - w_3 \leq 0$$
$$w_2 \qquad\qquad \leq 0$$

(*Hint:* First make the substitution $w_2 = -w_2{}^+$.)

14. Devise a method for putting into canonical form a problem in which some of the variables are constrained to be *nonpositive* instead of nonnegative. Extend the flow diagram of Figure 4.5.2 to take care of nonpositive variables.

15. Suppose in Exercise 13(a) that the last inequality is $x_1 \geq 5$. Show how to put the problem into canonical form.

16. Suppose in Exercise 13(b) that the last inequality is $w_2 \leq -20$. Show how to put the problem into canonical form.

4.6 EXTENSION OF THE SIMPLEX METHOD TO NONPOSITIVE RIGHT-HAND SIDES

Up to now the simplex algorithm that we have discussed has depended on the assumption that the b vector was nonnegative. Here we shall demonstrate three ways in which this assumption can be relaxed so that the simplex method can be extended to cover other cases. Standard linear programming codes make use of one of the three methods in order to handle such problems.

We shall discuss the following maximization problem:

$$\text{Max } cx$$

(4.6.1)   Subject to:

$$Ax \leq b$$
$$x \geq 0$$

This problem may be obtained as the dual of a minimizing problem. Here we assume that b is not necessarily nonnegative.

Method I (Thompson). Observe that the problem (4.6.1) is equivalent to the problem:

$$\text{Max } cx + Kx_{n+1}$$

(4.6.2)   Subject to:

$$Ax - bx_{n+1} \leq 0$$
$$x_{n+1} \leq 1$$
$$x, x_{n+1} \geq 0$$

where K is a large positive number. The reason for this is that, in order to maximize $cx + Kx_{n+1}$ for large K, the variable x_{n+1} must be made as large as possible; its upper bound is 1. And when x_{n+1} is made equal to 1, the constraints of (4.6.2) and those of (4.6.1) are the same, whereas the objective function of (4.6.2) differs by K from that of (4.6.1). Moreover, if there is no feasible solution to (4.6.2) with $x_{n+1} = 1$, then there is no feasible solution at all to (4.6.1). Note that (4.6.2) *always* has a feasible solution since $x = 0$ and $x_{n+1} = 0$ *is* feasible for it. But (4.6.1) may or may not have a feasible solution. Hence, we conclude that (4.6.1) and (4.6.2) are equivalent if and only if there is a solution to (4.6.2) with $x_{n+1} = 1$.

EXAMPLE 4.6.1. Use the first method to put the problem

$$\text{Max } x_1 + x_2 + x_3$$

Subject to:

$$x_1 + x_2 \qquad\; = 2$$
$$x_2 + x_3 \geq 1$$
$$x_1 \qquad + x_3 \leq 5$$
$$x_1, x_2, x_3 \geq 0$$

into equivalent form. We replace the first equation by a pair of inequalities thus:

$$x_1 + x_2 \leq 2,$$
$$-x_1 - x_2 \leq -2.$$

Upon adding a new variable x_4, we obtain the equivalent problem:

$$\text{Max } x_1 + x_2 + x_3 + 1000x_4$$

(4.6.3)   Subject to:

$$x_1 + x_2 \qquad\qquad - 2x_4 \leq 0$$
$$-x_1 - x_2 \qquad\quad + 2x_4 \leq 0$$
$$- x_2 - x_3 + \; x_4 \leq 0$$
$$x_1 \qquad + x_3 - 5x_4 \leq 0$$
$$x_4 \leq 1$$
$$x_1, x_2, x_3, x_4 \geq 0$$

Note that we have chosen $K = 1000$. This is sufficiently large that the most-negative-indicator rule will bring in the fourth column vector first so that x_4 will take on a positive value. The original problem now has a solution if and only if the new problem has an optimal solution with $x_4 = 1$. In Exercise 1, you will be asked to solve the new problem and relate its solution to the original one.

It should be remarked that the practical use of this method requires care, since the new problem usually is degenerate (see Section 4.8) and steps must be taken in order to prevent possible cycling in the simplex method. Cycle prevention is discussed later.

Method II (Charnes). We briefly outline this method as follows:

(a) Make all the components of b nonnegative by multiplying inequalities with negative b_i's by -1.

(b) For equality constraints add one slack variable with a $+1$ coefficient.

(c) For each wrong-way inequality, add one slack variable with -1 coefficient and one slack variable with $+1$ coefficient.

(d) Put each slack variable with a $+1$ coefficient added in steps (b) and (c) into the objective function multiplied by a coefficient $-M$, where M is a large positive number.

(e) For each right-way inequality, add one slack variable with $+1$ coefficient.

(f) The original problem has a solution only if the slack variables having $-M$ coefficients in the objective function are driven out of the basis.

EXAMPLE 4.6.2. Let us work the problem of Example 4.6.1, using the so-called " big M " method of Charnes. For the first equality, we add one slack variable, y_1, with a $+1$ coefficient, and we also add $-My_1$ to the objective function. For the second inequality, we add slack variables $y_2 - y_3$ and put the term $-My_2$ into the objective function. Finally, we add slack variable y_4 to the third right-way inequality. Thus the equivalent problem is now:

$$\text{Max } x_1 + x_2 + x_3 - My_1 - My_2$$

(4.6.4)   Subject to:

$$
\begin{aligned}
x_1 + x_2 \quad\quad + y_1 \quad\quad\quad\quad &= 2 \\
x_2 + x_3 \quad\quad + y_2 - y_3 \quad\quad &= 1 \\
x_1 \quad\quad + x_3 \quad\quad\quad\quad + y_4 &= 5 \\
x_1, x_2, x_3, y_1, y_2, y_3, y_4 &\geq 0
\end{aligned}
$$

Since the problem is maximizing, the simplex method will, if possible, drive y_1 and y_2 to 0 and will obtain nonnegative numbers for the rest of the variables. Such answers will be possible only if the original problem has a solution. If such a solution is found, note that the first restriction will then be satisfied as an equality, the second restriction as a wrong-way inequality, and the third restriction as a right-way inequality. Thus the method will have found a solution to the originally stated problem.

In Exercise 2, you will be asked to solve the problem in Example 4.6.2 by the big-M method and compare its solution with the solution given by the Method I.

Method III (Dantzig-Orden). This method is similar to—in fact, equivalent to—the big-M method (see Exercise 6). It has the advantage that a computer does not have to simultaneously handle very large numbers (the M's) and small numbers (the other coefficients). The present method has two phases, called Phase I and Phase II. The only difference between the two phases is that a different objective function is used in each phase. The initial setup is just as in the big-M method, with slack variables being added in the same way. In the Phase I computation, the objective function is just the sum of the negatives of the slack variables that are to be driven out of the basis—that is, just the slack variables that were put into the objective function with $-M$ coefficients in the big-M method. If Phase I terminates with a solution that has zero objective function value, indicating that all the undesired slack variables have been driven from the basis, then Phase II starts, using the original objective function.

In practice, it is easy to implement this method by simply adding two rows at the bottom of the tableau, one with the Phase I objective function and the other with the original objective function, and carry out all the calculations on both. As soon as Phase I is completed (if it can be), then that objective function row is discarded and Phase II takes over, using the other objective function row. If Phase I cannot be completed with the initial objective function having zero value, then the original problem does not have a solution.

EXAMPLE 4.6.3. To show how this method is implemented, we show only the initial tableau, with the two objective function rows at the bottom. We use all the slack variables as in Example 4.6.2. The initial tableau is:

	x_1	x_2	x_3	y_1	y_2	y_3	y_4	
	1	1	0	1	0	0	0	2
	0	1	1	0	1	−1	0	1
	1	0	1	0	0	0	1	5
Phase I	0	0	0	1	1	0	0	0
Phase II	−1	−1	−1	0	0	0	0	0

The first step of Phase I is to make y_1 and y_2 basic variables by pivoting twice. This yields the tableau:

	x_1	x_2	x_3	y_1	y_2	y_3	y_4		
	1	1	0	1	0	0	·0	2	$= y_1$
	0	1	1	0	1	−1	0	1	$= y_2$
	1	0	1	0	0	0	1	5	$= y_4$
Phase I	−1	−2	−1	0	0	0	0	−3	
Phase II	−1	−1	−1	0	0	0	0	0	

Note that the basic variables are y_1, y_2, and y_4 and that the initial value of the Phase I objective function is -3. Pivoting is now carried on in the normal way, using the Phase I criterion function until the objective value of zero is obtained for Phase I. In the example at hand, the first pivot makes x_2 basic and y_2 nonbasic. The second pivot makes y_3 basic and y_1 nonbasic. The tableau then obtained is:

x_1	x_2	x_3	y_1	y_2	y_3	y_4		
1	0	-1	1	-1	1	0	1	$= y_3$
1	1	0	1	0	0	0	2	$= x_2$
1	0	1	0	0	0	1	5	$= y_4$
Phase I 1	0	-1	2	0	0	0	0	
Phase II 0	0	-1	1	0	0	0	2	

Having achieved a zero value for the Phase I objective function and having made y_1 and y_2 nonbasic variables, we can cross out the Phase I objective row and also the y_1 and y_2 columns and complete the problem using the Phase II objective function. In the example at hand, this can be accomplished by making x_3 basic and y_4 nonbasic. The final tableau with the deletions mentioned above is:

x_1	x_2	x_3	y_3	y_4		
2	0	1	1	0	6	$= y_3$
1	1	0	0	0	2	$= x_2$
1	0	1	0	1	5	$= x_3$
1	0	0	0	1	7	$= cx$

The final optimal solution then is $x = (0, 2, 5)'$, and the objective value is 5. You should substitute these values back into the original problem statement to show that the problem is feasible.

EXERCISES 4.6

1. Solve the problem given in (4.6.3). Indicate the tableau in which a feasible solution to the original problem is first found.

2. Solve the problem given in (4.6.4). Relate the steps to the analogous steps in Exercise 1.

3. Complete the details of the solution to Example 3. Relate each step to the corresponding steps in Exercises 1 and 2.

4. Consider the problem:

$$\text{Max } x_1 + 2x_2$$

Subject to:

$$x_1 + x_2 \geq 2$$
$$x_1 + x_2 \leq 4$$
$$x_1, x_2 \geq 0$$

(a) Show that Method I leads to the following initial tableau:

x_1	x_2	x_2	y_1	y_2	y_3		
-1	-1	2	1	0	0	0	$= y_1$
1	1	-4	0	1	0	0	$\Rightarrow y_2$
0	0	1	0	0	1	1	$= y_3$
-1	-2	-1000	0	0	0	0	

(b) Show that Method II leads to the initial tableau:

x_1	x_2	y_1	y_2	y_3		
1	1	-1	1	0	2	$= y_4$
1	1	0	0	1	4	$= y_3$
-1	-2	0	M	0	0	

and that after pivoting to make y_2 a basic variable, it becomes:

x_1	x_2	y_1	y_2	y_3		
1	1	-1	1	0	2	$= y_2$
1	1	0	0	1	4	$= y_3$
$-1-M$	$-2-M$	M	0	0	$-2M$	

(c) Show that Method III leads to the following initial tableau after pivoting to start Phase I:

	x_1	x_2	y_1	y_2	y_3		
	1	1	-1	1	0	2	$= y_2$
	1	1	0	0	1	4	$= y_3$
Phase I	-1	-1	1	0	0	-2	
Phase II	-1	-2	0	0	0	0	

5. In Exercise 4 work each part, starting from the given initial tableau, and show that the same answer is obtained in each case. Draw a diagram of the convex set of feasible vectors and indicate the pivot procedure on the diagram.

6. Show that Methods II and III are equivalent.

7. Prove that (4.6.1) has a feasible solution if and only if (4.6.2) has a feasible solution with $x_{n+1} = 1$.

8. Consider the minimization problem:

$$\text{Min } -w_1 - w_2 + 5w_3$$

Subject to:

$$-w_1 \qquad + w_3 \geq 2$$
$$- w_2 + w_3 \geq 1$$
$$w_1, w_2, w_3 \geq 0$$

(a) Write the dual to the problem.
(b) Set up the initial tableau by each of the three methods.
(c) Select one of the methods and find the solution.
(d) Draw the convex set of feasible vectors for the maximizing problem and interpret the solution.

9. Consider the linear programming problem:

$$\text{Max } x_1 + 2x_2$$

Subject to:

$$x_1 + x_2 \leq 1/2$$
$$-x_1 - x_2 \leq -1$$
$$x_1, x_2 \geq 0$$

(a) Show directly that the problem has no feasible solution. (*Hint:* Assume that there is a feasible solution; add the constraints and obtain a contradiction.)
(b) Set up the tableau for the problem using Method I and show that there is a solution with $x_3 = 0$. Because this is optimal, prove that the original problem has no feasible solution.
(c) Use Method II to show that the problem has no solution.
(d) Use Method III to show that the problem has no solution.

10. Discuss the advantages and disadvantages of each of the three methods from the point of view of (a) theory and (b) practical computations.

4.7   APPLICATIONS—MODEL TYPES

In Section 1.7, we discussed the idea of model types for the transportation problem—that is, general models derived from applied situations. In the case of linear programming, the number of model types is enormous, and we select only a few for discussion here.

Model Type 1. The *cost-minimization model.* In this class of problems, we are faced with certain requirements that must be met, and we have available certain activities that can be used to fulfill these requirements; each activity has a unit cost for its operation, and we want to select the subset of activities and the intensity of each activity such that we fulfill the stated requirements at the lowest possible cost. For instance, in the mining example of Section 4.2, we wanted to operate the two mines in the most economical way in order to fulfill the production requirements. Other examples occur in the exercises.

To give another example, suppose we return to the production scheduling example of Section 1.7. We considered a manufacturer who wanted to plan his summer production schedule to meet demands of 500 units in June, 600 in July, and 600 in August. During that period he had a total of 1400 man-hours of regular time and 700 man-hours of overtime available. In that example, the regular and overtime amounts were allocated among the various months, but here we shall try to find the most economical allocation. We shall also assume that he has 100 units on hand at the beginning of June and that he wants to have 200 units in inventory at the beginning of September to meet a heavier fall demand. As before, each unit requires one man-hour to produce and there is a \$.20-per-unit storage charge for each month a unit is held in storage. Wage rates are \$1.40 and \$2.10 for regular and overtime, respectively.

In order to state this problem as a linear programming problem we define the following variables:

	Regular Time	Over-time	Inven-tory	Demand
June	P_1	O_1	I_1	D_1
July	P_2	O_2	I_2	D_2
August	P_3	O_3	I_3	D_3
September	—	—	I_4	—

We assume that the production in each month is available to meet the demand during that month. Also, by assumption, $I_1 = 100$ and $I_4 = 200$ and, also, $D_1 = 500$, $D_2 = 600$, and $D_3 = 600$. We can define the inventory variables in terms of the others by means of the following equations:

$$I_2 = I_1 + P_1 + O_1 - D_1,$$
$$I_3 = I_2 + P_2 + O_2 - D_2,$$
$$I_4 = I_3 + P_3 + O_3 - D_3.$$

All these equations say is that the amount carried forward into the next month's inventory is the excess of the sum of the previous inventory plus this month's regular and overtime production over demand during the month. The only other constraints are the ones mentioned earlier that restrict the total amount of regular and overtime; they are

$$P_1 + P_2 + P_3 \le 1400,$$
$$O_1 + O_2 + O_3 \le 700.$$

Using these definitions we can set up the initial tableau as in Figure 4.7.1. Note that we have charged zero for the September inventory, since that will be paid during that month, not during the period in question. In Exercise 1, you will be asked to explain each entry in the tableau of Figure 4.7.1.

P_1	P_2	P_3	O_1	O_2	O_3	I_1	I_2	I_3	I_4	
1			1			1	−1			= 500
	1			1			1	−1		= 600
		1			1			1	−1	= 600
1	1	1								≤ 1400
			1	1	1					≤ 700
						1				= 100
									1	= 200
−1.4	−1.4	−1.4	−2.1	−2.1	−2.1	−.2	−.2	−.2	0	

FIGURE 4.7.1

Although the tableau of Figure 4.7.1 is 7×10 even without slack variables, it can be solved by inspection—see Exercise 2. The optimal solution involves overtime equal to regular time in August, which may be objectionable to management. A way of handling this difficulty is suggested in Exercise 3. Finally, in Exercise 4, you are asked to derive the tableau for the n-stage production smoothing example.

Model Type 2. The *profit-maximization model.* The general problem here is to select a combination of activities, each of which makes certain demands on fixed resources, so that the total demands on each resource do not exceed given bounds and also so that the gross profit is maximized. We have seen several examples of this problem—for example, the scooter-truck example· of Section 4.2. Let us work one more example that we will carry over to the next model type.

The example we shall discuss is that of *machine loading*—that is, selecting the most profitable combination of products to manufacture with a given set of machine resources. Suppose that a manufacturer produces two products, A and B, using three types of machines, lathes, grinders, and drill presses. The fraction of an hour that each product requires per unit on each machine, as well as the monthly machine capacities, is shown in the table of Figure 4.7.2.

Product	*Lathe*	*Grinder*	*Drill Press*
A	.01	.03	.03
B	.02	.01	.015
Monthly Machine Hours Available	4000	4500	4800

FIGURE 4.7.2

If the manufacturer makes a (gross) profit of 10¢ on product A and 15¢ on product B, how many of each type should he produce each month? In Exercise 7, you will be asked to show that the optimal production pattern is to produce 80,000 units of A and 160,000 units of B for a monthly gross profit of $32,000.

The problem above assumes that the manufacturer can sell everything he produces. Suppose instead that he estimates that he can sell up to 120,000 units of A and up to 140,000 units of B. In Exercise 8, you will be asked to show that his optimal production pattern now is to produce 90,000 units of A and 140,000 units of B for a gross profit of $30,000.

Model Type 3. The *multistage investment model.* Many practical problems involve multistage decisions, either because the decisions are spread over time or because the problems involve a process that necessitates several stages of production. We shall illustrate the first possibility here and the second in the exercises.

Suppose that the manufacturer just discussed wants to expand his plant by investing money in the purchases of new lathes, grinders, and drill presses, which cost $1600, $960, and $1440 each, respectively. Assume that it takes a month to order and install each kind of machine and that each new lathe will add 160 hours per month of lathe time, each new grinder will add 240 hours per month of grinder time, and each new drill press will add 240 hours per month of drill-press time. Assume also that the manufacturer estimates that he can increase sales by 10% each month. If he has K dollars to invest in new equipment, what mix of new machinery should he buy and what is the rate at which he could expect to increase his gross profit?

In order to turn this into a linear programming problem, define the following variables:

x_1 production of A the first month
x_2 ”   ” B ”   ”   ”
x_3 ”   ” A ” second   ”
x_4 ”   ” B ”   ”   ”
y_1 number of new lathes bought
y_2 number of new grinders bought
y_3 number of new drill presses bought

The tableau of the linear programming problem appears in Figure 4.7.3. Let us

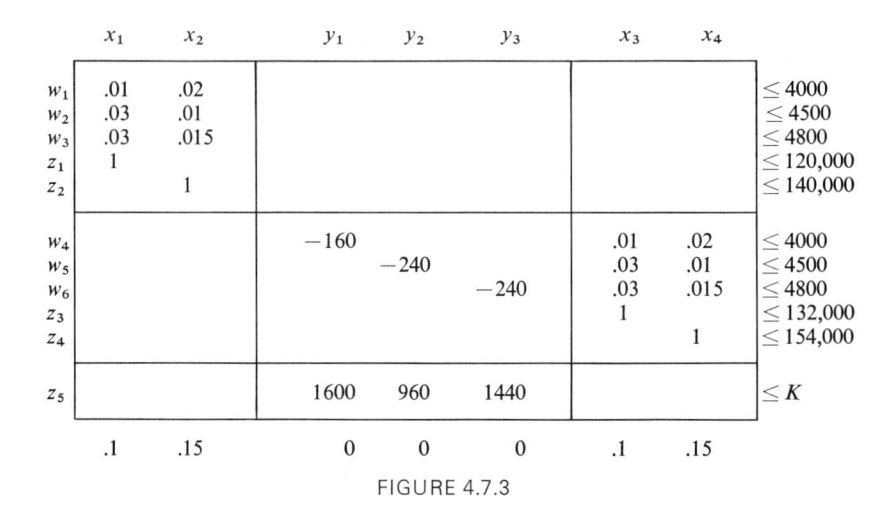

	x_1	x_2	y_1	y_2	y_3	x_3	x_4	
w_1	.01	.02						≤ 4000
w_2	.03	.01						≤ 4500
w_3	.03	.015						≤ 4800
z_1	1							$\leq 120{,}000$
z_2		1						$\leq 140{,}000$
w_4			-160			.01	.02	≤ 4000
w_5				-240		.03	.01	≤ 4500
w_6					-240	.03	.015	≤ 4800
z_3						1		$\leq 132{,}000$
z_4							1	$\leq 154{,}000$
z_5			1600	960	1440			$\leq K$
	.1	.15	0	0	0	.1	.15	

FIGURE 4.7.3

explain how the constraints of this problem were derived. The first five constraints are for the first month's production and are exactly the same as the constraints derived for the problem considered in the previous model type. The sixth constraint can be rewritten as

$$.01x_3 + .02x_4 \leq 4000 + 160y_1.$$

What this constraint says is that the production of A and B during the second month, indicated by x_3 and x_4, is constrained by the availability of lathe time. The amount of lathe time per month is 4000 hours plus 160 hours times the number of new lathes purchased. Constraints 7 and 8 are the second month's constraints on grinders and drill presses, respectively. Constraints 9 and 10 give the maximum sales of A and B during the second month, which are 10% higher than the corresponding sales during the first month. Finally, constraint 11 gives the limit on investment in new machines to be less than K, the total amount to be invested. Labels for dual variables for each constraint occur on the left of Figure 4.7.3.

This problem has been solved on a computer for various values of K. The results are tabulated in Figure 4.7.4. We have listed only the variables that change as the amount of investment changes. The dual variables w_4, w_5, and w_6 give the imputed value, measured in dollars per machine hour, of each of the new machines. The dual

| | New Machines | | | Second Month's Production | | Imputed Value of New Machines | | | | Gross Profit |
| | La. | Gr. | D.P. | | | | | | | |
K	y_1	y_2	y_3	x_3	x_4	w_4	w_5	w_6	z_5	
0	0	0	0	83,000	154,000	0	0	3.33	.556	61,400
1000	0	0	.694	88,556	,,	0	0	3.33	.556	61,956
2000	.085	0	1.295	93,357	,,	3.57	0	2.14	.357	62,436
3000	.308	0	1.741	96,929	,,	3.57	0	2.14	.357	62,793
4000	.497	.16	2.119	99,950	,,	2.5	1	1.5	.25	63,095
10000	1.434	2.035	3.99	114,950	,,	,,	,,	,,	,,	64,595
16000	2.372	3.910	5.87	129,950	,,	,,	,,	,,	,,	66,095
17000	2.5	4.167	6.125	132,000	,,	0	0	0	0	66,300

FIGURE 4.7.4

variable z_5 gives the imputed value of investment dollars, measured in dollars of gross profit per dollar of investment.

Let us explain some of the entries in Figure 4.7.4. You will be asked to explain others in Exercise 11. Note that there are four sets of dual variables. The first set is valid from $K = 0$ up to K somewhere between \$1000 and \$2000. Another set of dual variables becomes valid and holds up to K between \$3000 and \$4000. A third set of dual variables then takes over and holds up to K between \$16,000 and \$17,000. For higher values of K, the dual variables all become identically zero. One of the most important dual variables is z_5, which measures the "effectiveness" of an investment dollar. Note that initially over half of an investment dollar will be returned in a month as gross profit. Later about 36¢ will be so returned. For still larger values of K only 25¢ will be returned, and for K larger than about 17,000, the investment of a dollar in new machines will simply add overcapacity. The value of this dual variable can be used to predict the total change in gross profit over its range of validity. For instance, when $K = 4000$, there is gross profit of 63,095. By investing \$6000 more, the gross profit can be raised to 64,595, which is an additional \$1500, as can be predicted since $z_5 \cdot 6000 = (.25)6000 = 1500$. Note that if we calculate the net profit by subtracting any other per unit charges, we can obtain the "payback" period for the investment. For example, if there is an additional charge of 15¢ per unit produced, then initially the net profit will be about 41¢ per unit, so the payback period would be about two and a half months. For larger investments, the net profit is 21¢ $(= 36 - 15)$, so the payback period is a little under five months. Finally, for large investments, the net profit is 10¢ $(= 25 - 15)$, so the payback period is ten months. Managers frequently use the payback number in deciding whether or not to make a given investment.

Note, in Figure 4.7.4, that we initially buy only drill presses for small K, but as K increases we start buying some lathes and for K sufficiently large, we buy all three kinds of machines. Note also that the optimum solution indicates that we should buy fractional numbers of machines. Obviously we cannot buy .308 of a lathe, so these numbers will have to be rounded in some way to become integers. In the case of investment dollars, constraints such as the last one in the tableau of Figure 4.7.3 are frequently not "rigid," and a certain amount of leeway may be inserted to help in the rounding process.

It should be clear that we have not considered every factor in our problem statement. For instance, the present factory may have free floor space so that new machines can be easily installed. But if too many are installed, there will come a point at which new buildings will be needed to house the machinery. Also not included are the problems of hiring and training new workers and adding to the management staff as needed in the expansion. What this means is that these other factors will have to be considered outside the linear programming problem or else the model will have to be extended to include some of them. The question of what to include and what to omit from a model is a matter that requires experience.

Model Type 4. The *warehousing model.* A certain dealer owns a warehouse that can store a maximum of $C = 600$ units of a given commodity. He has on hand $I_0 = 100$ units and knows that the buying and selling prices of the commodity over the next five time periods will be as listed in Figure 4.7.5. He is permitted to sell up to the

Period	Buying Price	Selling Price
1	15	16
2	17	17
3	21	20
4	19	19
5	16	20

FIGURE 4.7.5

amount he has in his warehouse at the beginning of the period. And if he buys in a given period, delivery will be made so that it is in storage at the beginning of the next period. If we let x_j be the amount he buys in period j and y_j the amount he sells in that period, what should his optimal buying and selling strategy be?

Let us start by writing the selling constraints. In the first period he must not sell more than his initial inventory; that is,

$$y_1 \leq I_0.$$

In the second period, he has on hand $I_0 + x_1 - y_1$, since he will have received delivery on his first period purchases, x_1, and he will have delivered his first period sales, y_1. Hence the constraint on his second period selling is

$$y_2 \leq I_0 + x_1 - y_1.$$

The same kind of analysis shows that his next period constraint is

$$y_3 \leq I_0 + x_1 + x_2 - y_1 - y_2.$$

And, in general, his jth period constraint is

$$y_j \leq I_0 + \sum_{k=1}^{j-1} x_k - \sum_{k=1}^{j-1} y_k.$$

Let us rewrite this with all the variables on the left. We get

(4.7.1)
$$-\sum_{k=1}^{j-1} x_k + \sum_{k=1}^{j} y_k \leq I_0$$

as the selling constraints for $j = 1, \ldots, n$, where n is the number of periods. In our example, $n = 5$. (*Note:* When $j = 1$, the first summation in (4.7.1) is from 1 to 0—by convention such a summation is 0.)

We can derive the buying constraints similarly. For the first period we cannot buy more than the empty warehouse space we will have at the beginning of period 1. Initially the empty space is given by $C - I_0$, and additional space will be created by our first period sales. Hence,

$$x_1 \leq C - I_0 + y_1.$$

Similarly, in the second period we will have used up x_1 units of storage space, but we will have freed y_2 units, so we must have

$$x_2 \leq C - I_0 - x_1 + y_1 + y_2.$$

In general, we will have

$$x_j \leq C - I_0 - \sum_{k=1}^{j-1} x_k + \sum_{k=1}^{j} y_k.$$

Or, rewriting with all variables on the left, we have

(4.7.2)
$$\sum_{k=1}^{j} x_k - \sum_{k=1}^{j} y_k \leq C - I_0$$

as the selling constraints for $j = 1, \ldots, n$.

Suppose we let p_j be the purchase price and s_j the selling price for the commodity in period j. Then the objective function the operator wants to maximize is clearly

(4.7.3)
$$-\sum_{j=1}^{n} p_j x_j + \sum_{j=1}^{n} s_j y_j.$$

Hence we have a linear programming problem to choose x_j and y_j, for $j = 1, \ldots, n$, so as to maximize (4.7.3) subject to (4.7.1) and (4.7.2) and also, of course, $x_j, y_j \geq 0$. This is the general form of the warehousing problem.

Figure 4.7.6 shows the initial tableau for the five-period example described earlier. Notice the triangular patterns of 1's and -1's, which are characteristic of the warehouse problem.

x_1	x_2	x_3	x_4	x_5	y_1	y_2	y_3	y_4	y_5	
					1					$\leq 100 = I_0$
-1					1	1				≤ 100
-1	-1				1	1	1			≤ 100
-1	-1	-1			1	1	1	1		≤ 100
-1	-1	-1	-1		1	1	1	1	1	≤ 100
1					-1					$\leq 500 = C - I_0$
1	1				-1	-1				≤ 500
1	1	1			-1	-1	-1			≤ 500
1	1	1	1		-1	-1	-1	-1		≤ 500
1	1	1	1	1	-1	-1	-1	-1	-1	≤ 4500
-15	-17	-21	-19	-16	16	17	20	19	20	

FIGURE 4.7.6

The solution to this problem can be shown to be as follows:

Period	1	2	3	4	5
Buy	600	0	0	600	0
Sell	100	0	600	0	600

Notice that the solution has the following characteristics: (a) if the optimum solution indicates that one should buy in a given period, then buy to fill the warehouse, and (b) if the optimum solution indicates that one should sell in a given period, then sell to empty the warehouse. It can be shown in general that the solution will always have these characteristics, which permit the development of special solution techniques other than the simplex method for the warehousing problem. However, we will not go into those methods here.

The solution of the dual problem to the warehouse problem is also very interesting. By playing back and forth between the primal and dual problems and by using the theorem of the alternative, to be discussed in Section 4.8, it is possible to devise another special technique for solving the warehousing problem. This is discussed in Exercise 13.

Other variants of the warehouse model have been discussed in the literature. One of them involves the warehouse model with cash constraints (Charnes and Cooper). The other involves multicommodity warehouse problems (Rao).

Model Type 5. Goal programming models arise when the constraints of a linear programming problem are inconsistent—that is, when they have an empty set of feasible vectors. In other words, the problem has been stated so that there is no way to simultaneously satisfy all the constraints. What the goal programming model does is to permit a violation of some or all of the constraints, but at a penalty; hence the new problem is to find a solution that violates the constraints in such a way as to minimize the total penalty costs.

An example will make this clear. Suppose a man wants to buy three stocks according to the following rules: (a) he wants twice as much of stock 1 as of 2, (b) he wants as much of stock 2 as of stock 3, (c) he wants at least 100 shares of stock 3. Let x_1 be the number of shares of stock 1 purchased, x_2 the number of shares of 2, and x_3 the number of shares of 3. If the prices of the three stocks are 15, 23, and 18, and if the man has \$5000 to invest, how many shares of each stock shall he buy?

Let us first write down the constraints corresponding to the rules given above. We have

$$
\begin{aligned}
x_1 - 2x_2 \qquad\quad &= 0, \\
x_2 - \quad x_3 &= 0, \\
- \quad x_3 &\le -100, \\
15x_1 + 23x_2 + 18x_3 &\le 5000.
\end{aligned}
$$

(4.7.4)

In Exercise 14, you will be asked to show that there are no feasible solutions to expressions (4.7.4).

Suppose that our stock customer decided to relax his rules and permit the first two equations in (4.7.4) to be satisfied as inequalities but to charge the model a penalty for doing so. Specifically, he does not mind if they are $\geq$ type inequalities, but he wants to charge a penalty if they are $<$ inequalities. The new model for his rules now becomes:

$$(4.7.5) \quad \begin{aligned} x_1 - 2x_2 \qquad\qquad + x_4 - x_5 \qquad\qquad\quad &= 0, \\ x_2 - x_3 \qquad\qquad + x_6 - x_7 &= 0, \\ - x_3 \qquad\qquad\qquad\qquad &\leq -100, \\ 15x_1 + 23x_2 + 18x_3 \qquad\qquad\qquad &\leq 5000. \end{aligned}$$

In Exercise 15 you will be asked to show that this achieves his objectives.

We now add an objective function to the model. Specifically, let us charge a penalty of 100 for x_4 or x_6 being positive, since that corresponds to each of the first two equations in (4.7.4) becoming $<$ inequalities. The objective function becomes

$$(4.7.6) \quad \text{Max} \qquad\qquad - 100x_4 \; - 100x_6 .$$

We now have a linear programming problem, the initial tableau of which is shown in Figure 4.7.7. It can be shown that the solution to the linear programming problem is

x_1	x_2	x_3	x_4	x_5	x_6	x_7	
1	−2		1	−1			= 0
	1	−1			1	−1	= 0
		−1					≤ −100
15	23	18					≤ 5000
0	0	0	−100	0	−100	0	

FIGURE 4.7.7

$x_1 = 120.8$, $x_2 = 60.4$, and $x_3 = 100$. The entire \$5000 is invested. Note that the first constraint of (4.6.4) corresponding to rule (a) is satisfied but that the second constraint, corresponding to rule (b), is violated.

Suppose now we reduce the penalty for violating the first constraint to 10, while keeping the penalty for violating the second constraint at 100. Now the solution is $x_1 = 60$, $x_2 = 100$, $x_3 = 100$. Again the entire \$5000 is invested. The second constraint holds as an equality, but the first constraint is violated.

In order to state the general goal programming model, we start with a maximizing linear programming problem stated in equality form:

$$\text{Max } cx$$
$$(4.7.7) \quad \text{Subject to:}$$
$$Ax = b$$
$$x \geq 0$$

Suppose now that the equality constraints are inconsistent—that is, have no feasible solution. Now define two vectors z^+ and z^- that measure by how much the vector Ax is greater than or less than b. Define penalty (row) vectors P^+ and P^- that measure how much such violations from the "goals" represented by the b vector will be penalized. Then define the new linear programming problem

$$\text{Max } cx - P^+z^+ - P^-z^-$$

(4.7.8)   Subject to:

$$Ax - z^+ + z^- = b$$

$$x, z^+, z^- \geq 0$$

which is the "goal programming" version of (4.7.7). It should be noted immediately that mixing together in the objective function a "real" objective function, represented by cx, and a penalty objective function, represented by $-P^+z^+ - P^-z^-$, can cause severe problems, since the optimal solution may trade off real objectives versus penalty objectives. In order to minimize this effect, the coefficients of P^+ and P^- should be made much smaller or much larger in magnitude than the coefficients of c.

One final question may have occurred to you. Why should anyone write down inconsistent constraints? It might seem that if a firm knows what it is doing, it should not have conflicting objectives. But quite the opposite is true. Departments or divisions in a firm may have quite different objectives. The sales division wants to increase market share, production wants to minimize production costs, personnel wants to minimize employee turnover, advertising wants to increase market "penetration," accounting wants to keep within budgets, and so on. If the various constraints are stated by various divisions, then inconsistency is almost inevitable. The goal programming model may be one way in which one can come "as close as possible" to satisfying a number of inconsistent and incompatible objectives.

EXERCISES 4.7

1. Give an interpretation for each nonzero coefficient in each row of the tableau in Figure 4.7.1.

2. (a) By direct reasoning involving the counting of the number of hours of regular time and overtime and the number of production hours demanded, show that one optimal solution to the linear programming problem of Figure 4.7.1. is given by:

Period	1	2	3
Regular Time	400	600	400
Overtime	0	0	400

(b) Similarly, show that another solution is:

Period	1	2	3
Regular Time	0	600	800
Overtime	400	0	0

(c) Criticize both these solutions.

3. Add constraints to the production scheduling example that require that the amount of overtime in a given month be at most half the amount of regular time. Set up the new tableau and solve by inspection.

4. Set up the n-stage production scheduling model. Indicate the structure of coefficients of the initial tableau. Include constraints such as those suggested in Exercise 3.

5. Exercises 8 and 9 of Exercises 4.1 are *blending problems*. Show that blending problems, in general, are cost minimization problems.

6. State the mining problem of Section 4.2 as a maximization problem; that is, the problem is to maximize the negative sum of the costs. Interpret the dual solution and relate it to the way it was discussed in Section 4.2.

7. Set up the initial tableau and solve the machine-loading problem whose data are given in Figure 4.7.2, without constraints on the amounts that can be sold.

8. Solve the machine-loading problem when it is assumed that, at most, 120,000 units of A and 140,000 units of B can be sold.

9. (a) Interpret the dual solution to the optimal solution of Exercise 7. Show that, if new machines are to be purchased, the most desirable machine is a lathe.
   (b) Do the same for the dual solution of Exercise 8. Now show that the most desirable new machine is a drill press.
   (c) Explain the change in decisions in parts (a) and (b).

10. Explain the nonzero entries in each row of the tableau of Figure 4.7.3. Show that it characterizes the multistage investment model.

11. Consider the solutions given in Figure 4.7.4.
   (a) Show that in each row the z_5 entry together with the gross-profit entry can be used to predict an upper bound for the gross profit on the next line. When is the upper bound attained?
   (b) Show how to predict each entry in the x_3 column.
   (c) For each range in which a given dual solution is valid, indicate which constraints are "tight" and which are "slack." In other words, in the optimum solution, which machines have unused production hours and which do not?
   (d) For each range in which a given dual solution is valid, indicate how y_1, y_2, and y_3 together with w_4, w_5, and w_6 may be used to predict the net change in gross profit for a given change in K.

12. (a) Derive the equations for a warehousing model in which there is a requirement for a terminal inventory position as well as for an initial inventory.
   (b) Suppose in the warehouse five-period example there is a requirement for a terminal inventory of 300 units. Set up the initial tableau. If you are ambitious, solve it.

*13. The "complementary slackness" condition to be discussed in the next section is the following. Consider an optimal solution to a linear programming problem; for each constraint, one or both of the following must be true.
   (i) The constraint is satisfied as an equality.
   (ii) The dual variable associated with the constraint is zero.
   Use this property to devise a special method, distinct from the simplex method, for solving the warehouse example in the text. If you are ambitious, extend it to the general case.

14. Show that there are no values of x_1, x_2, and x_3 that simultaneously satisfy the constraints of (4.7.4).

15. Show that by adding slack variables x_4, x_5, x_6, and x_7 to the constraints of (4.7.4), the system (4.7.5) is obtained that always has feasible solutions. Show that the objective function (4.7.6) penalizes the first two inequalities in (4.7.5) for being $<$ inequalities.

16. In Figure 4.7.7, show that at most one of the vectors labeled x_4 and x_5 can be in the basis. Do the same for x_6 and x_7.

*17. In the general goal programming model stated in (4.7.8), consider the sum $-z_j{}^+ + z_j{}^-$.
   (a) If $-z_j{}^+ + z_j{}^- > 0$, show that $z_j{}^+ = 0$.
   (b) If $-z_j{}^+ + z_j{}^- < 0$, show that $z_j{}^- = 0$.
   (c) Show that at most one of the columns corresponding to $z_j{}^+$ and $z_j{}^-$ can be in the basis in any basic feasible solution.

4.8   THEOREMS ON THE SIMPLEX METHOD

In this section and the next we shall discuss some theorems that give additional results and further insight into the simplex method.

THEOREM 4.8.1. (a) If x^* is a vector displayed in the simplex tableau at any time during the computational process and if $b \geq 0$, then x^* is an extreme point of the convex set $Ax \leq b$, $x \geq 0$.

(b) If w^* is a vector displayed in the simplex tableau at any time during the computational process, then it is the intersection of hyperplanes of the form $wA^{(k)} = c_k$ corresponding to vectors in the basis. In the final tableau, the w displayed is an extreme point of the convex set of solutions of $wA \geq c$, $w \geq 0$.

Proof: (a) The initial basis for the simplex method consists of the vectors $E_1, \ldots, E_m$ corresponding to the intersection of the hyperplanes $w_1 = 0, \ldots, w_m = 0$, $y_1 = b_1, \ldots, y_m = b_m$. Suppose at some stage that the feasible vector x^* is displayed and the current basis consists of the vectors

$$A_{j(1)}, \ldots, A_{j(k)}, E_{j(k+1)}, \ldots, E_{j(m)}.$$

Let the pivot rows corresponding to each of these vectors be $i(1)$, $i(2)$, $\ldots$, $i(k)$, $i(k+1)$, $\ldots$, $i(m)$. Such pivot rows can be found since they correspond to the unique 1 entry in the corresponding column of the tableau. Because the pivoting process always displays the intersection of the hyperplanes corresponding to pivot rows, we see that x^* is the intersection of the bounding hyperplanes

$$A^{i(1)}x = b_{i(1)}, \ldots, A^{i(k)}x = b_{i(k)}$$

(where $A^{i(h)}$ is the hth row of A) and the hyperplanes

$$x_{i(k+1)} = 0, \ldots, x_{i(m)} = 0.$$

Since the original basis vectors were linearly independent, this point of intersection is unique. Hence, x^* is an extreme point of the convex set defined by $Ax \leq b$, $x \geq 0$.

The proof of (b) is similar.

THEOREM 4.8.2. Consider the dual problems:

Max cx	Min wb
Subject to:	Subject to:
$Ax \leq b$	$wA \geq c$
$x \geq 0$	$w \geq 0$

(a) If x^* is any *feasible* vector for the maximizing problem and if w^o is any *optimal* vector for the minimizing problem, then $cx^* \leq w^o b$; that is, a feasible vector for the maximizing problem provides a lower bound for the minimizing problem.

(b)   If x^o is any optimal vector for the maximizing problem and if w^* is any feasible vector for the minimizing problem, then $cx^o \leq w^*b$; that is, any feasible w vector provides an upper bound for the maximizing problem.

Proof: We shall prove both parts at once. Let w^* and x^* be feasible; that is,

(4.8.1) $Ax^* \leq b, \qquad x^* \geq 0,$

(4.8.2) $w^*A \geq c, \qquad w^* \geq 0.$

Multiplying the first inequality by w^* and using the fact that it is nonnegative, we obtain $w^*Ax^* \leq w^*b$. Similarly, multiplying the first inequality in (4.8.2) by x^* and using the fact that x^* is nonnegative, we obtain $cx^* \leq w^*Ax^*$. Putting these two together, we obtain

$$cx^* \leq w^*b$$

for all feasible w^* and x^*. Hence, in particular, this inequality is true when either w or x (or both) are optimal for their respective problems.

We must now consider the question of degeneracy in linear programming problems.

DEFINITION 4.8.1. A linear programming problem is *column degenerate* if b is a linear combination of fewer than m columns of A and $I_{(m \times m)}$. A linear programming problem is *row degenerate* if c is a linear combination of fewer than n of the rows of A and $I_{(n \times n)}$.

THEOREM 4.8.3. Every linear programming problem can be replaced by one that is not column degenerate and whose solutions are arbitrarily close to the original problem.

We shall not give the proof of this theorem. However, the following argument is an intuitive proof. There exists a vector b^* that is not a linear combination of fewer than m columns of A and $I_{(m \times m)}$ (this is intuitively obvious, but rather tedious to show); hence, the vector $b + kb^*$ is not a linear combination of fewer than m of these vectors. By making k very small, it is obvious that the solution of the problem with data A, b, and c and the solution of the problem with data A, $b + kb^*$, and c will be arbitrarily close.

THEOREM 4.8.4. If the linear programming problem with data A, b, and c is not column degenerate and $b \geq 0$, then the simplex method applied to it will terminate in a finite number of steps in one of the following two ways:

(a) Optimal feasible solutions x^o and w^o will be displayed.

(b) A nonpositive column will be found, indicating that the original problem has no finite solution.

Proof: Consider the flow diagram of Figure 4.1.5. Each time we go around the main loop of the diagram we bring a new column vector into the basis and take out the old one. The new column vector corresponds to a negative indicator. Since b is not a linear combination of fewer than m columns of A and I, the entries in the first m rows of the first m columns will always be positive; hence each time we bring in a new column vector, we will *increase* the current value of $cx = wb$, as indicated in the lower right-hand corner of the tableau. It is never possible to have the same basis twice since the value of $cx = wb$ is unique for a given basis. However, there are only a finite number of possible bases, namely at most $\begin{bmatrix} m+n \\ m \end{bmatrix}$ bases, so we can go around the main loop of the flow diagram at most this many times. We must therefore terminate in a finite number of steps at one of the two terminal boxes of that diagram, corresponding to the cases (a) and (b) above.

THEOREM 4.8.5. *The Duality Theorem.* Consider the dual linear programming problems with data A, b, and c. The maximum problem has a (finite) optimal solution x^o if and only if the minimum problem has a (finite) optimal solution w^o. Moreover, the equality $cx^o = w^o b$ holds for feasible x^o and w^o if and only if they are optimal for their respective problems.

Proof: By the first method in Section 4.4, we can replace the problem by one in which $b \geq 0$. By the result of Theorem 4.8.3, we can replace that problem by one which is not column degenerate. By Theorem 4.8.4, we can apply the simplex method and arrive at an optimal solution for both problems (if one exists) in a finite number of steps. At the optimum, the equality $cx^o = w^o b$ is displayed in the tableau.

Suppose, on the other hand, that x^o and w^o are feasible and such that $cx^o = w^o b$. By Theorem 4.8.2, $w^o b$ is an upper bound for the maximum problem. Since $cx^o = w^o b$, it follows that x^o is optimal since it makes the objective function take on its upper bound. A similar argument proves that w^o is optimal.

THEOREM 4.8.6. *Complementary Slackness Theorem.* Let x^o, y^o, w^o, and z^o be optimal solutions to the dual linear programming problems:

Max cx	Min wb
Subject to:	Subject to:
$Ax + y = b$	$wA - z = c$
$x, y \geq 0$	$w, z \geq 0$

Then we have

(a) $w_i^o y_i^o = 0$, for $i = 1, \ldots, m$;
(b) $z_j^o x_j^o = 0$, for $j = 1, \ldots, n$.

Remark: It is easy to state this theorem in words for either the primal or the dual problem. Note that each constraint (for either problem) has a slack variable and an associated dual variable. The complementary slackness theorem states that, at the optimum for each constraint, either its *slack variable* or its *associated dual variable* is zero (or possibly both).

Proof: At the optimum, we have

$$w^o b = w^o A x^o = c x^o.$$

Rewriting the first equality, we have

$$w^o y^o = w^o(b - Ax^o) = 0.$$

Since $w^o \geq 0$ and $y^o \geq 0$, it is possible to have $w^o y^o = 0$ if and only if $w_i^o y_i^o = 0$, for $i = 1, \ldots, m$. This completes the proof of (a). The proof of (b) is similar (see Exercise 1).

It is interesting to give interpretations of this theorem in economic terms—this is suggested in Exercise 2.

EXERCISES 4.8

1. Prove part (b) of the complementary slackness theorem.

2. For the inequalities $Ax \leq b$, interpret b_i as the ith resource. If the ith constraint is satisfied as a strict inequality—that is, if its slack variable is positive—at the optimum, we say the ith resource is in surplus. Show that the complementary slackness theorem can be stated as follows: if the ith resource is in surplus at the optimum, then the corresponding dual price is zero; and if the dual variable is positive, then the ith resource is used up completely.

3. In the minimizing problem, the constraints $wA \geq c$ can be interpreted as production requirements. Give an economic interpretation of the complementary slackness theorem in terms of production requirements being satisfied in excess and also interpret the corresponding dual variable.

4.9*   FURTHER THEOREMS ON THE SIMPLEX METHOD

We continue analyzing linear programming problems and their solutions as they appear in the simplex computational process.

THEOREM 4.9.1. *The Extended Complementary Slackness Theorem.* If $w^{(1)}$, $x^{(1)}$, $y^{(1)}$, and $z^{(1)}$ and $w^{(2)}$, $x^{(2)}$, $y^{(2)}$, and $z^{(2)}$ are two optimal solutions to the same linear programming problem, then

(a) $w_i^{(h)} y_i^{(k)} = 0$, for $h, k = 1, 2$ and $i = 1, \ldots, m$;
(b) $z_j^{(h)} x_j^{(k)} = 0$, for $h, k = 1, 2$ and $j = 1, \ldots, n$.

Proof: We shall prove (a) only; the proof of (b) is similar.

We know that $cx^{(1)} = w^{(1)}b = w^{(2)}b = cx^{(2)}$; we also know that $w^{(1)}A \geq c$ and $x^{(2)} \geq 0$, and that $Ax^{(2)} \leq b$ and $w^{(1)} \geq 0$. Multiplying these pairs of inequalities together and using the first set of equalities, we obtain

$$w^{(1)}b \geq w^{(1)}Ax^{(2)} \geq x^{(2)}c = w^{(2)}b = w^{(1)}b.$$

It follows that all the inequalities must be equalities, and in particular,

$$w^{(1)}[b - Ax^{(2)}] = w^{(1)}y^{(2)} = 0.$$

With both vectors being nonnegative, the only way this can happen is for each product $w_i^{(1)}y_i^{(2)}$ to equal zero for $i = 1, \ldots, m$. The proof for the other values of h and k is similar.

Our next theorem concerns itself with multiple solutions.

THEOREM 4.9.2. (a) There are two solutions, $w^{(1)} \neq w^{(2)}$, only if the problem is column degenerate.

(b) There are two solutions, $x^{(1)} \neq x^{(2)}$, only if the problem is row degenerate.

Proof of (a): Suppose there exist two basic solutions, $w^{(1)} \neq w^{(2)}$. Let $A^{(1)}$ and $c^{(1)}$ be the largest subset of columns of A and c such that $w^{(1)}A^{(1)} = c^{(1)}$; and let $A^{(2)}$ and $c^{(2)}$ be the largest subset of columns of A and c such that $w^{(2)}A^{(2)} = c^{(2)}$. We now have two cases:

Case 1. $A^{(1)} = A^{(2)}$ and $c^{(1)} = c^{(2)}$. Then the rows of $A^{(1)}$ must not be linearly independent or else $w^{(1)} = w^{(2)}$. Hence there is an index j which is the row label of the ith row in the final tableau for $w^{(2)}$ but not for $w^{(1)}$, so $w_i^{(1)} = 0$ and $w_i^{(2)} > 0$. By the extended theorem of the alternative, $y^{(2)} = 0$, so there is at least one zero in the first column of the final tableau for $w^{(1)}$. But that means that b can be written as a linear combination of fewer than m of the columns of A and I, and therefore the original problem is column degenerate.

Case 2. $A^{(1)} \neq A^{(2)}$ and $c^{(1)} \neq c^{(2)}$. Then there exists an index j such that

$$w^{(1)}A_j = 0 \quad \text{and} \quad w^{(2)}A_j > 0,$$

and j is a basis column in the final tableau for $w^{(1)}$. But then the extended complementary slackness theorem implies that $x_j^{(1)} = 0$, so that, also in the final tableau for $w^{(1)}$, there is a zero in the first column. As before, this implies that the original problem was column degenerate.

The proof of (b) is similar.

Exercises 1 and 2 provide counterexamples for the converses of the two statements of Theorem 4.9.2.

THEOREM 4.9.3. Consider a linear programming problem with data A, b, and c. Suppose there are k basic E vectors in the final simplex tableau. Then,

(a) there are at most $m - k$ positive x_j^o in the basic solution;
(b) there are at most $m - k$ positive w_i^o in the basic solution.

Proof of (a): Since there are k E vectors in the final solution, there must be $m - k$ A vectors in the final solution. Hence there are at most that many positive x_j^o's.

COROLLARY. If $n > m$, then there is at least one $x_j^o = 0$. If $n < m$ then at least one $w_i^o = 0$.

THEOREM 4.9.4. Given a linear programming problem with data A, b, and c, let $T^{(0)}$ be the initial tableau and $T^{(k)}$ the final tableau. Suppose the final tableau is labeled with indices $j(1), j(2), \ldots, j(m)$, which are selected from the column numbers $1, 2, \ldots, n, n + 1, \ldots, n + m$. Let R be the matrix consisting of the first m entries of $T_{j(1)}^{(0)}, T_{j(2)}^{(0)} \ldots, T_{j(m)}^{(0)}$, and let S be the matrix in the I area of $T^{(k)}$. Then R and S are inverses of each other; that is, $RS = I$.

Proof: Let $P_1, P_2, \ldots, P_k$ be the pivot matrices used in the computational process; then

$$T^{(k)} = (P_k P_{k-1} \cdots P_2 P_1)T^{(0)}.$$

Clearly S is equal to $P_k P_{k-1} \cdots P_1$, ignoring the last row and column. And also, because the final basis consists of vectors $j(1), \ldots, j(m)$, we have

$$(P_k P_{k-1} \cdots P_1)T_{j(h)}^{(0)} = E_h \qquad \text{for } h = 1, \ldots, m,$$

which proves the assertion.

Since the simplex method gives a constructive method for determining whether a linear programming problem has a solution, it is always possible to let that method determine whether a solution exists. But sometimes it is nice to know in advance that a solution exists. The following theorem gives some sufficient conditions for solutions to exist.

THEOREM 4.9.5. Either of the following conditions is sufficient for the dual linear programming problems, with data A, b, and c, to have solutions:

(a) The set of feasible vectors is nonempty and bounded for either of the dual problems.

(b) The matrix A has no zero rows or columns and both $A \geq 0$ and $b \geq 0$.

Proof: (a) A linear function on a bounded closed set takes on both its maximum and minimum values. Hence if either set of feasible vectors is nonempty and bounded, that problem has a finite optimum. By the duality theorem, the other problem also has a finite solution.

(b) If $b \geq 0$, then there is at least one feasible vector, namely $x = 0$, for the inequalities $Ax \leq b$ and $x \geq 0$. Also, the set of feasible x vectors is bounded. To see this, let A_j be the ith row of A and consider the inequalities $A^i x \leq b_i$. Since $A \geq 0$ and has no zero columns, this inequality restricts the size of all variables x_j for which $a_{ij} \neq 0$. And since A has no zero rows, every variable is restricted by at least one such inequality. Hence, by (a), both problems have solutions.

In Exercise 3, another sufficiency result is presented.

EXERCISES 4.9

1. Consider the problem with data

$$A = \begin{bmatrix} 2 & 1 & 1 \\ 1 & 2 & 1 \end{bmatrix}, \qquad b = \begin{bmatrix} 5 \\ 5 \end{bmatrix}, \qquad c = [4, \ 4, \ 2].$$

(a) Show that it is column degenerate.

(b) Show that it has a unique w solution vector.

(c) Draw the w-vector space and explain why this shows that the converse to Theorem 4.9.2(a) is false.

2. Consider the problem with data

$$A = \begin{bmatrix} 1 & 1 \\ 2 & 1 \\ 1 & 2 \end{bmatrix}, \qquad b = \begin{bmatrix} 4 \\ 4 \\ 4 \end{bmatrix}, \qquad c = [1 \ \ 1].$$

(a) Show that it is row degenerate.

(b) Show that the x solution vector is unique.

(c) Draw the x-vector space and explain why this shows that the converse to Theorem 4.8.2(b) is false.

3. If A and c are nonpositive and A has no nonzero rows or columns, show that the corresponding linear programming problem always has a solution regardless of b.

4. Show that the mining problem of Section 4.2 has multiple w solutions if we change c_3 to 8. Which case of the proof of Theorem 4.9.2 does this example fall under? Construct an example that falls under the other case.

SUGGESTED READING

Charnes, A., and Cooper, W. W. *Management Models and Industrial Applications of Linear Programming*, 2 Vols. New York: John Wiley, 1961.

Dantzig, G. B. *Linear Programming and Extensions*. Princeton, N.J.: Princeton University Press, 1963.

Hadley, G. *Linear Programming*. Reading, Mass.: Addison-Wesley, 1962.

Hillier, F. S., and Lieberman, G. J. *Introduction to Operations Research*, San Francisco: Holden-Day, 1967.

Simmonard, M. *Linear Programming*. Englewood Cliffs, N.J.: Prentice-Hall, 1966.

Wagner, H. M. *Principles of Operations Research with Applications to Managerial Decisions*. Englewood Cliffs, N.J.: Prentice-Hall, 1969.

CHAPTER 5

SPECIAL LINEAR PROGRAMMING TOPICS*

5.1 CPM, MAXIMAL FLOW, AND OTHER NETWORK MODELS

Many large linear programming models involve a network—that is, a set of nodes, some of which are connected by arcs. One example that we have already treated in great detail in Chapter 1 is the transportation model, which involves a very special (bipartite) graph. In the present section, we shall discuss other important kinds of network models.

Two applications that give rise to network models are (a) *multistage processes*, which require that a given job be completed before another can begin, and (b) *materials-flow processes* in which materials such as oil, steel, or stock certificates must flow through specific channels whose capacities are restricted. Our first example, the critical-path method (CPM), will illustrate problems of type (a) and the second example, the maximal-flow problem, will illustrate those of type (b).

---

* The topics covered in this chapter are optional, and most of the rest of the book is independent of them.

EXAMPLE 5.1.1. *The Critical-Path Method* (CPM). Most projects can be broken down into small parts which we shall call *tasks* or *jobs*. For instance, in building a house, jobs might be excavating, laying footers, building the foundation, putting up walls, framing windows, and so on. Work on some pairs of jobs can proceed simultaneously—that is, in *parallel*—while other jobs must be worked on in series. Thus, in the house-building example, it is possible to do rough plumbing and electrical work at the same time, but it is necessary to put up the walls before one can construct the roof.

An easy way to indicate the technological precedence relationships among the various jobs in a project is by means of a *project graph*. An example of a project having six jobs is shown in Figure 5.1.1. In that figure, jobs are represented by *arrows* —that is, *directed arcs*—and the time for job i is denoted by T_i. Notice in the diagram that jobs 1 and 2 can be worked on in parallel, while jobs 1 and 3 (or 1 and 4) must be done serially—that is, job 3 cannot be started until job 1 is finished.

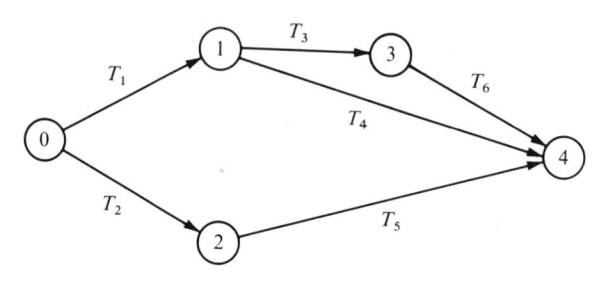

FIGURE 5.1.1

Although there are other ways to represent precedence relationships among jobs graphically (see Exercise 4), in this book we will use the method shown in Figure 5.1.1 almost exclusively.

Suppose the project is started at time 0. Then a very important question is what is the earliest time at which the project can be finished? The smallest time that can elapse from time 0 until the project is completely finished is called the project's *early completion time*. It is not hard to see that the earliest completion time of the project is equal to the longest path through the network—by length of path we mean the sum of the completion times on the path. In the example of Figure 5.1.1, there are only three paths, namely, 1–3–6, 1–4, and 2–5. Hence, given the values of the T_i's, it is an easy matter to find which sum, $T_1 + T_3 + T_6$, $T_1 + T_4$, or $T_2 + T_5$ is the largest.* However, in larger graphs there may be a large number of such paths, and this method is clearly too cumbersome.

A very simple algorithm has been developed for finding the longest path in any project graph (see Exercise 1). The method involves successively finding the maximum of finite sets of numbers, and it works very rapidly, even for large graphs.

However, rather than talk about the most common method, we should like to discuss a linear programming formulation of the longest-path problem. We do this for two reasons. First, it will show the kind of structure a typical network problem has and second, we will use the linear programming format later in discussing chance constrained programming.

---

*In a later chapter networks that involve jobs having uncertain duration are studied. In such a case the probability distribution of project completion times is of interest.

In order to state the linear programming problem corresponding to the longest-path problem, refer to Figure 5.1.1 and think of node 0 as a *source* and node 4 as a *sink*. Try to send one unit of material from the source 0 to the sink 4 by means of the longest possible path. The following maximizing problem captures this formulation: let variable x_i be associated with job t_i; since we are sending one unit from node 0 to node 4, each x_i must satisfy $0 \leq x_i \leq 1$. In fact, it will automatically turn out that each x_i is either 0 or 1 in the optimal solution, and the x_i's that are equal to 1 pick out the longest path in the network.

$$\text{Max } t_1 x_1 + t_2 x_2 + t_3 x_3 + t_4 x_4 + t_5 x_5 + t_6 x_6$$

Subject to:

$$
\begin{array}{r}
-x_1 - x_2 \qquad\qquad\qquad = -1 \\
x_1 \quad - x_3 - x_4 \qquad\qquad = 0 \\
x_2 \qquad\qquad - x_5 \qquad = 0 \\
x_3 \qquad\qquad - x_6 = 0 \\
x_4 + x_5 + x_6 = 1 \\
x_1, x_2, x_3, x_4, x_5, x_6 \geq 0
\end{array}
$$

(5.1.1)

Notice that there is a constraint for each node. The first constraint, corresponding to node 0, says that either x_1 or x_2 equals 1, meaning that one unit is shipped out of node 0, the source. Similarly, the last constraint, corresponding to node 4, says that either x_4, x_5, or x_6 is 1, meaning that one unit comes into node 4 (the sink). All the other constraints, corresponding to intermediate nodes, say that what comes in to each node must go out of the node. Notice also that in each column there are exactly two nonzero entries, one $+1$ and one -1. The minus one occurs in the constraint corresponding to the node that is at the tail of the arrow, and the plus one occurs at the constraint corresponding to the point of the arrow. The matrix of coefficients is called the *incidence matrix* of the project graph (see Exercises 17 and 18).

To summarize, the primal linear programming problem corresponding to a project graph has as many variables as there are arcs, or jobs, and as many constraints as there are nodes. Each variable occurs in exactly two constraints, once with a -1 and once with a $+1$ coefficient. The x_i's that are equal to 1 in the final optimal solution will pick out the longest path in the network (or one of the longest paths if there are more than one).

The dual problem is also interesting. Here there are as many variables as there are nodes and as many constraints as there are arcs (jobs) in the graph. The dual problem is as follows.

$$\text{Min } -w_0 \qquad\qquad + w_4$$

Subject to:

$$
\begin{array}{r}
-w_0 + w_1 \qquad\qquad\qquad \geq t_1 \\
-w_0 \qquad + w_2 \qquad\qquad \geq t_2 \\
-w_1 \qquad + w_3 \qquad \geq t_3 \\
-w_1 \qquad\qquad + w_4 \geq t_4 \\
-w_2 \qquad + w_4 \geq t_5 \\
-w_3 + w_4 \geq t_6
\end{array}
$$

(5.1.2)

Notice that the constraints are $\geq$ since the corresponding x_j's are nonnegative variables but that the w_i's are unrestricted variables because the constraints of (5.1.1) are equality constraints. However, a careful examination of the problem indicates that if we make an arbitrary choice of w_0, then the values of all the other variables are determined. The most common choice is to make $w_0 = 0$, and if this choice is made then all the other w_i's are necessarily nonnegative (see Exercise 7).

There is also a close connection between the solution of the dual problem and the method used in Exercise 1 to find the longest path in the graph. This is discussed in Exercise 5.

EXAMPLE 5.1.2. *The Shortest-Path Problem.* We saw that the critical-path problem was solved by means of a longest-path problem. Suppose we consider a graph that indicates the distances between nodes, and suppose that we are located at one node and want to get to another by means of the shortest route. It is clear that a very similar linear programming problem will suffice to solve this problem. To illustrate, consider the very simple graph in Figure 5.1.2. Here there are three nodes and three

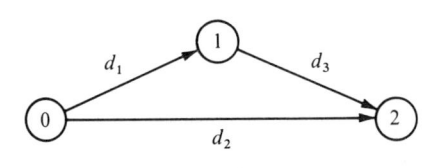

FIGURE 5.1.2

directed arcs. Suppose 0 is the source and 2 the sink; that is, suppose we want to find the shortest path from 0 to 2. Then the primal problem is a minimization problem. Let w_1, w_2, and w_3 correspond to links whose distances are d_1, d_2, and d_3. The problem is then as follows.

$$\text{Min } w_1 d_1 + w_2 d_2 + w_3 d_3$$

Subject to:

$$(5.1.3) \qquad \begin{aligned} -w_1 - w_2 \quad &= -1 \\ w_1 \qquad - w_3 &= 0 \\ w_2 - w_3 &= 1 \\ w_1, w_2, w_3 &\geq 0 \end{aligned}$$

Here again we interpret the problem as one of trying to send one unit from node 0 to node 2, but by the shortest possible path. Note that there is a constraint for each node and that the interpretation for each constraint is similar to that of the longest-path problem. The dual problem is:

$$\text{Max } -x_0 + x_3$$

Subject to:

$$(5.1.4) \qquad \begin{aligned} -x_0 + x_1 \qquad &\leq d_1 \\ -x_0 \qquad + x_2 &\leq d_2 \\ - x_1 + x_2 &\leq d_3 \end{aligned}$$

Again we have a dual variable for each node, and again they are unrestricted variables, since the constraints of the primal problem are equalities.

Notice that the matrix of coefficients is again the incidence matrix of the graph. A specific example of a shortest-path problem is given in Exercise 8.

EXAMPLE 5.1.3. *The CPM/Cost Problem.* In many projects it is possible to shorten the completion time of a job by spending more money. In general, the amount by which a given job can be shortened by spending additional money is not linearly related to the amount of money spent. We shall assume, however, that the relationship is, in fact a straight-line function, as pictured in Figure 5.1.3. Here D_j

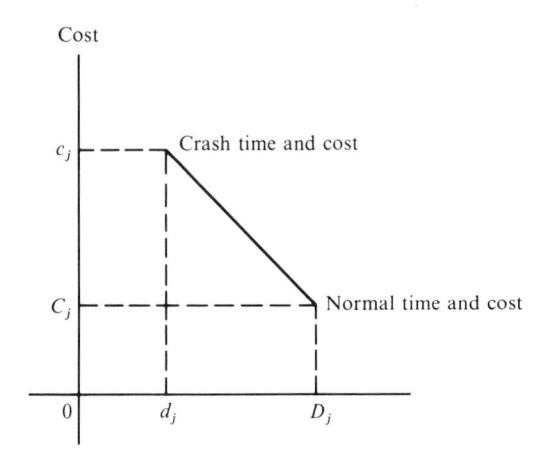

FIGURE 5.1.3

and C_j are the normal time and cost of doing the jth job, and d_j and c_j are the "crash" (shortest) time and cost of doing job j. It is assumed that for times in between d_j and D_j, the cost is linearly related, as in the figure. Suppose v_j is the fraction of normal time used on the jth job and $(1 - v_j)$ is the fraction of crash time used, where $0 \le v_j \le 1$. Then the resulting time is

$$(5.1.5) \qquad t_j = d_j(1 - v_j) + D_j v_j = d_j + (D_j - d_j)v_j$$

and the resulting cost, from Figure 5.1.3, is

$$(5.1.6) \qquad k_j = c_j(1 - v_j) + C_j v_j = c_j - (c_j - C_j)v_j.$$

We must now set up a linear programming problem that will determine the v_j's as well as the other variables indicating the resulting longest path and the dual solutions.

To do this we go to the linear programming problem in (5.1.2), set $w_0 = 0$ as suggested earlier, and make it into a maximizing problem by changing the signs of all coefficients. In order not to be confused by variable names, we replace w_i by y_i and the problem becomes:

$$\text{Max} \qquad -y_4$$
$$\text{Subject to:}$$

(5.1.7)
$$
\begin{aligned}
-y_1 & & & \le -t_1 \\
& -y_2 & & \le -t_2 \\
y_1 & & -y_3 & \le -t_3 \\
y_1 & & -y_4 & \le -t_4 \\
& y_2 & -y_4 & \le -t_5 \\
& & y_3 - y_4 & \le -t_6
\end{aligned}
$$

This problem is exactly equivalent to (5.1.2). Now we want to state some goal on the length of the longest path ($=$ the finish time of the project) and try to minimize the cost of achieving that goal. The constraint on the finish time is of the form $y_4 \le K$, where K is the target finish time. If we put expressions (5.1.5) into the right-hand sides of the constraints of (5.1.7) and if we put the negative sum of the k_j of (5.1.6) into the objective function, the resulting problem will determine the optimum v_j's that will achieve the goal finish time at minimum cost. The tableau of the resulting linear programming problem is given in Figure 5.1.4. If we interpret $c_j - C_j$ as the total

y_1	y_2	y_3	y_4	v_1	v_2	v_3	v_4	v_5	v_6	
-1				$D_1 - d_1$						$\le -d_1$
	-1				$D_2 - d_2$					$\le -d_2$
1		-1				$D_3 - d_3$				$\le -d_3$
1			-1				$D_4 - d_4$			$\le -d_4$
	1		-1					$D_5 - d_5$		$\le -d_5$
		1	-1						$D_6 - d_6$	$\le -d_6$
				1						≤ 1
					1					≤ 1
						1				≤ 1
							1			≤ 1
								1		≤ 1
									1	≤ 1
			1							$\le K$
0	0	0	0	$c_1 - C_1$	$c_2 - C_2$	$c_3 - C_3$	$c_4 - C_4$	$c_5 - C_5$	$c_6 - C_6$	

FIGURE 5.1.4

saving from using normal instead of crash time, we can interpret the resulting problem as that of maximizing crash cost savings.

As a specific example, consider the data in Figure 5.1.5. In Exercise 9, you

	Normal		*Crash*	
	Time (days)	*Cost* ($)	*Time* (days)	*Cost* ($)
t_1	20	190	9	450
t_2	12	40	8	75
t_3	2	15	1	25
t_4	25	260	19	425
t_5	37	340	21	560
t_6	18	160	7	240

FIGURE 5.1.5

will be asked to show that the early completion time for normal job times is 49 with a total cost of 1,005 and that the early completion time if all jobs are crashed is 29 with a total cost of 1,775. The linear programming problem corresponding to these data when substituted into Figure 5.1.4 is given in Figure 5.1.6.

y_1	y_2	y_3	y_4	v_1	v_2	v_3	v_4	v_5	v_6	
-1				11						≤ -9
	-1				4					≤ -8
1		-1				1				≤ -1
1			-1				6			≤ -19
	1		-1					16		≤ -21
		1	-1						11	≤ -7
				1						≤ 1
					1					≤ 1
						1				≤ 1
							1			≤ 1
								1		≤ 1
									1	≤ 1
			1							$\leq K$
0	0	0	0	260	35	10	165	220	80	

FIGURE 5.1.6

The problem in Figure 5.1.6 has been solved for several values of K ranging from 49 down to 29. The results for each of the y_j's and v_j's, together with the dual variable of the last constraint, which indicates the marginal cost of shortening the early completion time by one more day, are given in Figure 5.1.7. Notice that as we

Total Cost			$K =$								
	y_1	y_2	y_3	y_4	v_1	v_2	v_3	v_4	v_5	v_6	w_{13}
1,005	20	12	22	49	1	1	1	1	1	1	8.75
1,040	20	8	22	45	1	0	1	1	1	1	37.39
1,127	15	8	17	40	.55	0	1	1	.69	1	37.39
1,414	10	8	17	35	.09	0	1	1	.38	1	37.39
1,516	9	8	11	30	0	0	1	.3	.06	1	41.25
1,658	9	8	11	29	0	0	1	.17	0	1	48.52

FIGURE 5.1.7

decrease $K = y_4$, it becomes necessary to crash more and more jobs to achieve the desired completion time goal. But notice also that to achieve the shortest possible completion time of 29, the optimal solution involves crashing jobs 1, 2, and 5 completely, doing jobs 3 and 6 at normal time, and doing job 4 between normal and crash times. The total cost of achieving this shortest time is 1,658, which is less than 1,775, the cost of crashing all jobs. Also observe that w_{13}, the dual variable associated with the constraint $y_4 \leq K$, gives the marginal cost of shortening the project by one more day beyond the current level. This variable is clearly nondecreasing with K.

The results on this small example are fairly typical of the results to be obtained on a much larger project. A realistically sized project might involve between 500 and 10,000 jobs.

It should also be pointed out that there are other methods for solving CPM/cost problems that are faster. One is due to Ford and Fulkerson and is discussed in the reference given at the end of the chapter.

EXAMPLE 5.1.4. *The Maximal-Flow Problem.* Suppose we consider a directed graph as being a transportation-type network in which the edges represent physical devices for carrying a single homogeneous product. For instance, the edges could represent pipelines carrying oil or telephone lines carrying messages. Also, suppose there is a single source and a single sink. The problem to be solved is, if each edge has a limited capacity, how shall we arrange the flow through the network in order to maximize the total amount sent from the source to the sink?

A specific example appears in Figure 5.1.8. In the figure the various edges are

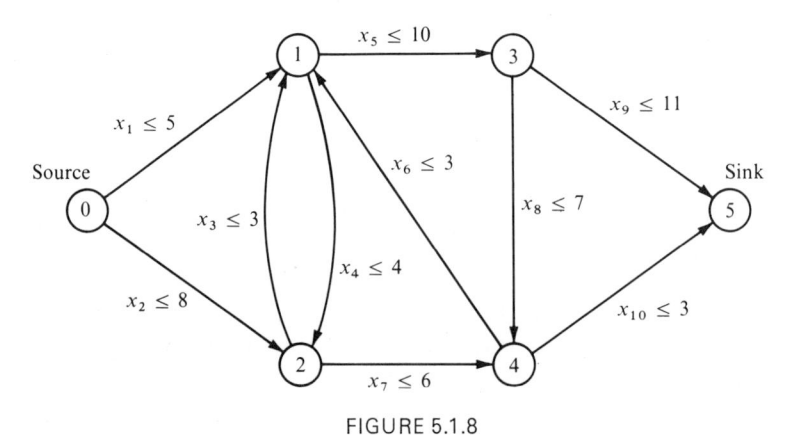

FIGURE 5.1.8

marked with a variable name, x_j, and a capacity that the variable must not exceed. From our previous experience, it is easy to see that the maximal-flow problem can be solved by solving the following linear programming problem:

$$
\begin{array}{ll}
\text{Max} & x_9 + x_{10} \\
\text{Subject to:} &
\end{array}
$$

$$
\begin{aligned}
x_1 & \leq 5 \\
x_2 & \leq 8 \\
x_3 & \leq 3 \\
x_4 & \leq 4 \\
x_5 & \leq 10 \\
x_6 & \leq 3 \\
x_7 & \leq 6 \\
x_8 & \leq 7 \\
x_9 & \leq 11 \\
x_{10} & \leq 3 \\
-x_1 \quad\; - x_3 + x_4 + x_5 - x_6 & = 0 \\
- x_2 + x_3 - x_4 \quad\quad\; + x_7 & = 0 \\
- x_5 \quad\quad + x_8 + x_9 & = 0 \\
+ x_6 - x_7 - x_8 \quad\quad + x_{10} & = 0
\end{aligned}
$$

(5.1.8)

The objective function is simply that of trying to maximize the total flow of material into the sink, node 5. The first ten constraints are simply the upper-bound constraints on edge flows, as marked in Figure 5.1.8. The last four constraints are material-flow constraints, one for each node except for the source and the sink nodes. At each such node, the corresponding constraint simply says that what flows into the node must flow out of the node.

The problem of (5.1.8) has been solved with

$$x = (5, 8, 3, 0, 10, 2, 5, 0, 10, 3)'$$

being the optimal maximizing vector. The maximal flow is 13.

The dual problem to (5.1.8) is also interesting. It can be shown—see Exercise 15—that if the arc capacities are stated to be integers, then each dual variable w_i is either 0 or 1. The optimal dual solution to (5.1.8) is, in fact,

$$w = (1, 1, 0, 0, 0, 0, 0, 0, 0, 0, 1, 1, 1, 1).$$

The last four 1's correspond to the node constraints for which the right-hand side is necessarily fixed. However the first two 1's correspond to edges x_1 and x_2 and indicate that if either capacity is increased, then the total flow can also be increased. Notice that if we remove arcs x_1 and x_2 from the graph, it would be separated into two parts with the source in one part and the sink in the other part. This is an example of a *cut*. The capacity of this cut is the sum of the capacities of the edges in the cut, which in this case is 13. Since the capacity of the cut is the same as the maximal flow, we have a specific example of the so-called min-cut, max-flow theorem of Ford and Fulkerson. This is discussed further in Exercise 15.

It should also be remarked that Ford and Fulkerson have devised a method for solving maximal-flow problems that does not involve the simplex method (see the reference at the end of the chapter).

We remark again that special techniques that are more efficient than the simplex method have been devised for solving each of the problems given above. However, if a problem is modified slightly so that it is not one of the specific kinds discussed above, then these special techniques are no longer applicable. In these cases, the simplex method will still work. In other words, the simplex method is very general, or, as is sometimes said, robust. Exercise 16 gives some simple extensions of the models described which illustrate this point.

EXERCISES 5.1

1. Consider the following longest-path algorithm:
   0. Mark node 0 (the source) with 0.
   1. Consider a node, all of whose predecessors have been marked: mark it with the maximum of the mark on a predecessor node that is connected to it by a job plus that job time; mark the arc along which the maximum occurred with an *.
   2. If the sink node has been marked, stop. Otherwise go to 1.
   (a) Using the normal-time data of Figure 5.1.5, employ the algorithm above to find the longest path in the graph of Figure 5.1.1. Show that it is 2–5 and that its length is 49.
   (b) Repeat (a), using the crash-time data of Figure 5.1.5. Show that the longest path is the same but that its length is now 29.

2. Define two dummy jobs Start and Finish. Show that the project of Figure 5.1.1 can be redrawn with jobs being represented by boxes as follows:

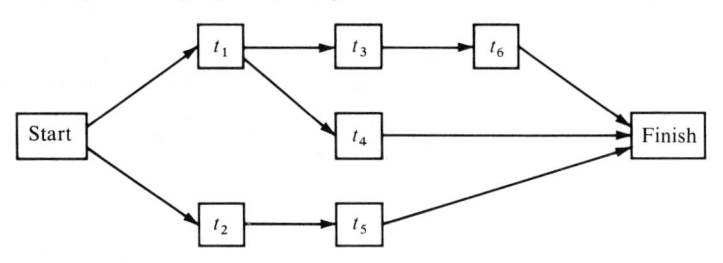

(a) Modify the algorithm of Exercise 1 so that it applies to the new project graph.
(b) Apply the new algorithm to the normal- and crash-time data, and check answers with those of Exercise 1.

3. The design of a new piece of electronic gear involves the following nine jobs, given with their job times and predecessors:

Job No.	Description	Job Time	Predecessors
1.	Block out design	4	—
2.	Design special circuits	9	1
3.	Test standard circuits	6	1
4.	Test special circuits	8	2, 3
5.	Design rack	5	2
6.	Pretest whole circuit	12	4, 3
7.	Make rack drawings	5	5, 6
8.	Make circuit drawings	11	6
9.	Deliver designs	1	7, 8

(a) Draw the arrow diagram of the project and find its early completion time.
(b) Draw the box diagram of the project and use the method of Exercise 2 to find the early completion time.
(c) Discuss the advantages and disadvantages of each method.

4. Consider the precedence diagram where boxes represent jobs:

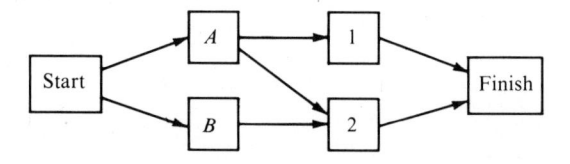

Show that, in order to draw the corresponding diagram in which arrows represent jobs, one dummy job (with 0 job time) must be added.

5. Show that the longest-path algorithm described in Exercise 1 can be used to devise an algorithm for solving the dual problem in (5.1.2).

*6. Consider a CPM problem, written with jobs as arrows, having n jobs and m nodes. Show that the corresponding linear program and its dual are of the form:

$$\text{Max } tx \qquad\qquad \text{Min } wa = -w_0 + w_m$$
$$\text{Subject to:} \qquad\qquad \text{Subject to:}$$
$$Ex = a \qquad\qquad\qquad wE \geq t$$
$$x \geq 0$$

t is an n-component row vector of job times; E is an $m \times n$ matrix having entries of 0 and ± 1 and also having exactly two nonzero entries in each column (a $+1$ and a -1); and a is an m-component column vector with -1 as its first entry, $+1$ as its last entry, and 0's elsewhere.

*7. If all job times are positive in (5.1.2), show that the choice $w_0 = 0$ implies that all $w_i \geq 0$. Do the same for the problem in Exercise 6.

*8. Consider a graph with n nodes and m edges (directed). Suppose it is desired to find the shortest path from one node to another. Set up a linear programming problem for solving the problem. Devise an algorithm similar to that in Exercise 1 for solving the problem.

9. Show that the cost for normal completion time for the data of Figure 5.1.5 is 1,005 while the cost for crash completion times is 1,775. Show that the answers given in Figure 5.1.7 solve the problem of Figure 5.1.6 for the various values of K indicated.

10. Consider the problem with project graph as follows:

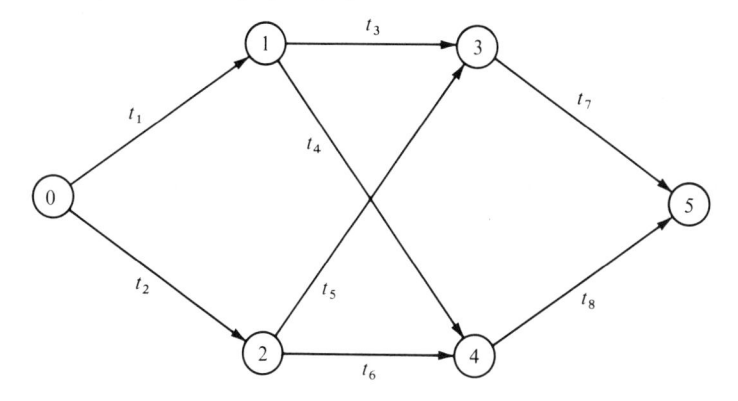

Suppose the data for normal and crash times and costs are:

	Normal		Crash	
	Time (days)	Cost ($)	Time (days)	Cost ($)
t_1	51	105	36	210
t_2	17	37	10	65
t_3	29	42	14	72
t_4	48	111	24	225
t_5	91	250	49	410
t_6	68	180	38	260
t_7	21	62	12	93
t_8	14	23	8	52

(a) Find the early completion time using the normal data.
(b) Find the early completion time using the crash data.
(c) Set up the linear programming problem for solving the CPM/cost problem. If you have computer time, solve it.

11. (a) Set up a linear programming problem for the problem in Figure 5.1.1 in which there is a constraint for each path from 0 to 4. How many constraints are there?
(b) Discuss the advantages and disadvantages of this method over the one presented in the text.

12. (a) Set up the CPM/cost problem whose data are given in Figure 5.1.5, using the path formulation of Exercise 11(a).

(b) Discuss the advantages and disadvantages of this formulation over the method presented in the text.

13. In the problem of Figure 5.1.6, make the objective function be that of minimizing y_4 subject to a constraint that sets a goal for cost savings over the crash-time cost. (This can be accomplished by interchanging the last row of the tableau and the objective function and by making necessary sign and inequality changes.) Discuss the advantages and disadvantages of this formulation over the one presented in the text.

14. (a) For the solution to the maximal-flow problem of (5.1.8), show that since $x_3 = 3$, it's upper bound, and also since it s dual variable, w_3, equals 0, there is an alternate optimal solution with a smaller value of x_3.

(b) Find the alternate optimum and interpret.

*15. (a) In (5.1.8), show that if the capacity of any arc is increased by one unit, the value of the objective function either increases by one unit or stays the same.

(b) Use (a) to show that the values of w_i, for $i = 1, \ldots, 10$, must be either 0 or 1.

(c) Use the duality theorem of linear programming to show that the solution to the dual problem *must pick out a set of arcs whose total capacity is equal to the maximal flow*. (This is the min-cut, max-flow theorem of Ford and Fulkerson.)

*16. An algorithm is said to be *robust* if it can handle slight variations in the basic model for which it was originally designed. For each of the following cases, show that the linear programming algorithm will handle the change in the model that the special algorithm cannot handle without substantial modification:

(a) The CPM problem in which there are constraints connecting several different job times.

(b) The CPM/cost problem in which there are constraints connecting several different job times.

(c) The maximal-flow problem in which there are constraints involving capacities on several different arcs.

In each case, construct a simple example and develop the corresponding linear programming tableau.

17. Show that the incidence matrix of the graph of Figure 5.1.1 is

$$\begin{bmatrix} -1 & -1 & 0 & 0 & 0 \\ 1 & 0 & -1 & -1 & 0 \\ 0 & 1 & 0 & 0 & -1 \\ 0 & 0 & 1 & 1 & 1 \end{bmatrix}$$

where the rows are identified with nodes and the columns with arcs.

18. (a) Draw an arbitrary project graph. (Note that a project graph must have a unique beginning node and a unique ending node. Also it must not have cycles.)

(b) If your graph has m nodes and n arcs, set up the $m \times n$ incidence matrix, E.

(c) Show that every column of E has exactly two nonzero entries, a $+1$ and a -1. Give the significance of the locations of these two entries.

5.2 THE REVISED SIMPLEX METHOD AND THE CONDENSED TABLEAU

In this section we shall discuss how large linear programming problems may be solved on a digital computer with the aid of properly organized calculations. In the next section we shall discuss another way to accomplish the same task.

Most computer manufacturers have software programs that will solve linear programming problems in which the maximization problem has at most 1000 constraints but arbitrarily large numbers of variables. Sometimes even the number of constraints is increased to slightly over 4000 with still an unlimited number of variables. A complete discussion of all the numerical-analysis problems encountered in solving such large problems is definitely beyond the scope of this book. However, we shall discuss the basic theoretical idea that such programs use—namely, the so-called *revised simplex method*.

The first step in the revised simplex method is the manner in which data are stored. Since the "core memory" of a computer is limited in size, it is necessary to use auxiliary memory, such as tapes or discs, to store the coefficients of the problem. Hence the coefficients of the A and c matrices are entered into auxiliary memory column by column, and they are transferred into core memory as needed during the computational process. To explain further, the access time of core memory is (for current computers) on the order of a few microseconds, whereas the access time of auxiliary memory is several milliseconds. Hence it is very costly to "call out" data from auxiliary memory, and this should be done only rarely. In the revised simplex method, the computer first calls out a few columns of the data, carries out computations on them, then calls out more columns, and so on. The timing of each of these steps is carefully balanced for efficiency. However, we shall not go into the methods used.

The second factor that enables the revised simplex method to handle large problems is that with this method the entire tableau is never updated at one time. Instead, each time we consider a column to see whether it should be brought into the basis, we first update it, using the original data that have been called in from auxiliary memory. In order to do this, we need keep in core memory only the product of the pivot matrices used in the pivoting process. To see why this is a good idea, let us compute the memory requirements—that is, the number of memory cells used—for each technique. The table in Figure 5.2.1 illustrates these requirements. Note that for

m	n	Size of Simplex Tableau $(m+1) \times (m+n+1)$	Size of Pivot Matrix $(m+1) \times (m+1)$
9	10	200	100
9	100	11,000	100
99	100	20,000	10,000
99	1000	110,000	10,000
99	10,000	1,010,000	10,000
999	1000	1,100,000	1,000,000
999	10,000	11,000,000	1,000,000
999	100,000	101,000,000	1,000,000

FIGURE 5.2.1

small "square" problems, the pivot matrix is half as big as the simplex tableau but that as the number, n, of variables increases, the size of the simplex tableau increases rapidly although the pivot matrix stays the same size.

Still another factor that is important is a practical one. In the experience of people who set up and solve large problems, data tend to be "sparse"; that is, there are very few nonzero entries—perhaps less than 1 or 2% of all entries. Also the number of pivots needed is likely to be rather small—perhaps on the order of m or $2m$. Moreover, if one follows the pivoting procedure in detail, it frequently happens that a vector will enter the basis, then leave it, then, at a later stage in the computation, enter again, and so on. At any stage of the computation, only relatively few vectors in the A area of the tableau will be in the basis. This factor also tends to reduce the memory requirements.

Before talking further about the revised simplex method, let us illustrate it with an example.

EXAMPLE 5.2.1. Consider the problem whose A, b, and $-c$ data are as in Figure 5.2.2. Notice that we have not included the identity-matrix part of the tableau since we will keep track of that separately. We keep columns A_1, A_2, A_3, and A_4 in

A_1	A_2	A_3	A_4	
1	−1	4	3	8
1	1	3	−2	6
−2	−5	−12	5	0

FIGURE 5.2.2

auxiliary memory (including the last row, which has the entries of $-c$ in it). In core memory, we keep the b column, including the last row entry, which is initially 0 but which at later steps will give the current value of the program. In core memory we store the matrix $P^{(n)}$, where $P^{(0)}$ is defined by

$$P^{(0)} = \begin{array}{c} \\ E_1 \\ E_2 \\ E_3 \end{array} \begin{array}{c} E_1\ \ E_2\ \ E_3 \\ \begin{bmatrix} 1 & 0 & 0 \\ 0 & 1 & 0 \\ 0 & 0 & 1 \end{bmatrix} \end{array},$$

which is just a 3×3 identity matrix. As the computation proceeds, the matrix $P^{(n)}$, for $n = 1, \ldots$, will be just the product of the pivot matrices used up to step $n - 1$ of the pivoting process.

On the first pivot we examine the first column of the tableau of Figure 5.2.2 and see that it has a negative indicator, so it should be brought into the basis. The ratio rule indicates that the vector E_2 should be taken out of the basis. Hence the pivot matrix is:

$$P^{(1)} = P_1 = \begin{bmatrix} 1 & -1 & 0 \\ 0 & 1 & 0 \\ 0 & 2 & 1 \end{bmatrix}$$

which gives

$$P_1 b = \begin{bmatrix} 2 \\ 6 \\ 12 \end{bmatrix};$$

so the current value of the program is 12. We now multiply the second column of the tableau of Figure 5.2.2 by $P^{(1)}$, obtaining the vector $\begin{bmatrix} -2 \\ 1 \\ -3 \end{bmatrix}$. Since it has a negative indicator, it must be brought into the basis. The pivot matrix needed to do this is

$$P_2 = \begin{bmatrix} 1 & 2 & 0 \\ 0 & 1 & 0 \\ 0 & 3 & 1 \end{bmatrix},$$

since A_1 has to leave the basis so that A_2 can come in. The pivot matrix that records the effect of these two basis changes is given by

$$P^{(2)} = P_2 P_1 = \begin{bmatrix} 1 & 1 & 0 \\ 0 & 1 & 0 \\ 0 & 5 & 1 \end{bmatrix}.$$

Notice that this is just the matrix that would be obtained if we had introduced A_2 first, since A_1 left the basis when A_2 came in. We now examine the third column A_3, and obtain

$$P^{(2)}A_3 = \begin{bmatrix} 7 \\ 3 \\ 3 \end{bmatrix},$$

which has a positive indicator, so it need not be brought into the basis. Finally, we look at A_4, obtaining

$$P^{(2)}A_4 = \begin{bmatrix} 1 \\ -2 \\ -5 \end{bmatrix},$$

and see that it has a negative indicator. When it comes in the basis, vector E_1 leaves, so the pivot matrix is

$$P_3 = \begin{bmatrix} 1 & 0 & 0 \\ 2 & 1 & 0 \\ 5 & 0 & 1 \end{bmatrix},$$

and also

$$P^{(3)} = P_3(P_2 P_1) = P_3 P^{(2)} = \begin{bmatrix} 1 & 1 & 0 \\ 2 & 3 & 0 \\ 5 & 10 & 1 \end{bmatrix}.$$

Using this pivot matrix, we go back and recheck its product with each of the columns of Figure 5.2.2 and find that all the indicators remain nonnegative, indicating that a solution has been found. To find the optimal-solution vectors, we calculate

$$P^{(3)}b = \begin{bmatrix} 14 \\ 34 \\ 110 \end{bmatrix},$$

so the value of the program is 110 and the optimal x is

$$x^o = \begin{bmatrix} 0 \\ 34 \\ 0 \\ 14 \end{bmatrix}.$$

The way that x^o was determined was to recall that A_2 and A_4 are in the final basis and that A_2 entered the basis by a pivot in the second row, whereas A_4 entered the basis by a pivot in the first row. The optimal dual solution can be read off the last row of $P^{(3)}$ in the first two columns so that

$$w^o = [5, \ 10].$$

This follows since the first two columns correspond exactly to the slack vectors in the usual simplex tableau.

There is still an additional factor that reduces the memory requirements of the revised form of the simplex method and that is the so-called *product form of the inverse*. This follows from the simple observation that in any pivot matrix there is exactly one column that is different from the identity matrix and hence only this column need be remembered since the rest of the matrix can be easily constructed. Thus, we can construct P_1 and P_2 by knowing that

$$\text{the second column of } P_1 \text{ is } \begin{bmatrix} -1 \\ 1 \\ 2 \end{bmatrix};$$

$$\text{the second column of } P_2 \text{ is } \begin{bmatrix} 2 \\ 1 \\ 3 \end{bmatrix}.$$

It is also easy to determine the product of two such pivot matrices by constructing special rules (see Exercise 3). Hence it is not necessary to remember an entire $(m + 1) \times (m + 1)$ matrix; instead, just one column vector for each pivot that has been made in the computational process must be remembered.

Another problem that arises in solving large-scale linear programming problems is one of accuracy. Current computers have six to eight places of decimal accuracy with single-precision arithmetic and twice that with double-precision arithmetic. As the solution of the problem proceeds, the numbers being used are the result of hundreds and thousands of multiplications, divisions, and additions of the original data numbers. On each such arithmetic operation, significant digits are lost, so there is a gradual "drift" away from the original data and a consequent loss of accuracy. For this reason, commercially available codes employ "reinversion of basis" techniques. Such techniques simply halt the process of computation, return to the original data and basis, and then recalculate the product of the pivot matrices necessary to go from the original basis to the current one. In this manner, the accuracy of computation results can be restored. In practice it has been found necessary to reinvert the basis at regular intervals in order to complete the solution of large-scale problems.

Another way in which the memory requirements may be reduced for a linear programming problem is by means of the so-called *condensed simplex tableau*. In this method we keep in high speed memory all the columns of the constraints, but not those of the slack variables. Hence, the condensed simplex tableau is not as effective as the revised simplex method for reducing the number of memory locations required. It is actually a very useful method for hand calculations since it reduces the tableau size considerably. An outline of the steps involved is as follows.

1. Set up the initial tableau, labeling the sides and top with either vectors or variables as desired.

2. If there are no negative indicators, the solution has been found. Stop.

3. If there is a negative indicator, pivot as usual.

4. Replace the pivot column of the tableau by the unique column of the pivot matrix that is not a natural basis vector.

5. Interchange labels of the pivot row and pivot column.

6. Go to 2.

We illustrate the computation with an example.

EXAMPLE 5.2.2. Consider the problem:

$$\text{Max } x_1 + 2x_2$$

Subject to:

$$2x_1 + x_2 \leq 8$$
$$x_1 + x_2 \leq 6$$
$$-x_1 + x_2 \leq 5$$
$$x_1, x_2, x_3 \geq 0$$

The initial tableau is:

x_1	x_2		
2	1	8	y_1
1	1	6	y_2
-1	1	4	y_3
-1	-2	0	

FIGURE 5.2.3

Notice that we have labeled the rows and columns with the variable names. Also the initial basis consists of the three slack vectors corresponding to the slack variables y_1, y_2, and y_3. The initial values of y_1, y_2 and y_3 are 8, 6, and 4, respectively. Suppose we choose to bring in the second vector, corresponding to the -2 indicator. The minimum-ratio rule indicates that the pivot row is the third row. Carrying out the pivot step, we get the tableau shown.

x_1	x_2		
3	0	4	y_1
2	0	2	y_2
-1	1	4	y_3
-3	2	8	

Following step 4 of the process listed above, we replace the second column by the required column of the pivot matrix, and then, following step 5, we interchange the labels on the pivot row and pivot column, obtaining:

x_1	y_3		
3	-1	4	y_1
2	-1	2	y_2
-1	1	4	x_2
-3	2	8	

Upon examining this tableau, we find there is still a negative indicator in the first column. Carrying out the required steps of the computation, we now have as the last tableau:

y_2	y_3		
$-3/2$	$1/2$	3	y_1
$1/2$	$-1/2$	1	x_1
$1/2$	$1/2$	5	x_2
$3/2$	$1/2$	11	

Since there are no more negative indicators, the solution is available in the tableau. Clearly the maximizing solution vector is $x^o = \begin{bmatrix} 1 \\ 5 \end{bmatrix}$, as can be read from the labels on the right. The dual solution vector can be read by finding what slack variables are *not* in the final basis, and these are exactly those slack variables listed on the top of the tableau. Hence $w^o = [0, \ 3/2, \ 1/2]$.

In Exercise 1, you will be asked to rework this problem with the usual tableau and show that no information is lost when using the condensed simplex tableau.

EXERCISES 5.2

1. Work the problem in Figure 5.2.2, using the standard simplex tableau, and compare the solution with that found by the revised simplex method.

2. Work the following problem by the revised simplex method, indicating the steps for bringing in each column vector for checking, and so on.

$$\text{Max } 6x_1 + 6x_2 + 4x_3$$

Subject to:

$$3x_1 + 4x_2 + x_3 \leq 12$$
$$2x_1 + 3x_2 + x_3 \leq 12$$
$$x_1, x_2, x_3 \geq 0$$

3. Work the Example in Figure 5.2.2, using the product form of the inverse to keep track of the current pivot matrix

4. Work the example in Exercise 2 using the condensed simplex tableau.

5. Find the product form of the inverse of each of the following matrices:

(a) $\begin{bmatrix} 4 & 0 & 8 \\ 0 & 1 & -6 \\ 2 & 0 & 4 \end{bmatrix}$
(b) $\begin{bmatrix} 4 & 0 & 5 \\ 0 & 1 & -6 \\ 3 & 0 & 4 \end{bmatrix}$

(c) $\begin{bmatrix} 1 & 0 & 1 \\ 0 & 1 & 1 \\ 1 & 1 & 0 \end{bmatrix}$

6. Use the revised form of the simplex method to solve the following linear programming problem:

$$\text{Min } 200w_1 + 160w_2$$

Subject to:

$$6w_1 + 2w_2 \geq 12$$
$$2w_1 + 2w_2 \geq 8$$
$$4w_1 + 12w_2 \geq 24$$
$$w_1, w_2 \geq 0$$

5.3 THE DECOMPOSITION METHOD FOR LINEAR PROGRAMMING

In the previous section we discussed ways in which large linear programming problems could be solved with digital computers. One common observation is that, frequently, the coefficient matrix of a linear program has a special structure that reflects the "physical situation" being modeled by the problem. Also, as a larger part of a company's operations are included in the model, the size of the corresponding linear program tends to become larger and larger. These two tendencies—larger and larger problems having special structure—have led to another way of handling such problems. Here we will discuss one of them briefly, the *decomposition method* of Dantzig and Wolfe.

Suppose that we have a linear programming problem of the form:

$$\text{Max } c^{(1)}x^{(1)} + c^{(2)}x^{(2)}$$

Subject to:

(5.3.1)
$$A^{(1)}x^{(1)} \qquad\qquad \leq b^{(1)}$$
$$A^{(2)}x^{(2)} \leq b^{(2)}$$
$$D^{(1)}x^{(1)} + D^{(2)}x^{(2)} \leq r$$
$$x^{(1)}, x^{(2)} \geq 0$$

The lowercase letters represent vectors and the uppercase letters, matrices. Dimensions must be appropriate so that the indicated matrix multiplications are well defined.

The structure indicated in (5.3.1) might occur, for instance, in modeling a firm that has two branches, indicated by the superscripts (1) and (2), and a main office that controls a resource vector, r. Each branch of the firm requires certain amounts of the resources r in order to operate; hence, they "compete" for these scarce resources. In addition, each branch has its peculiar own independent constraints. The main office has the problem of coordination—that is, the problem of allocating the proper amounts of the scarce resources so that the operation of each branch will maximize the overall profitability of the firm. One common way to carry out this coordination is to charge each branch "transfer prices" for the use of the scarce resources. As we shall see, generally just charging transfer prices will not be enough to lead to optimal behavior, but a combination of transfer prices plus resource allocations will be sufficient. The example that we discuss next specifically illustrates this point.

Let us begin by assuming that the main office has decided to charge a row vector w^* of unit transfer prices for each resource. That is, w_i^* is the unit price of resource r_i. Using these prices, we define subproblems:

$$\text{Max } c^{(k)}x^{(k)} - w^*D^{(k)}x^{(k)} = (c^{(k)} - w^*D^{(k)})x^{(k)}$$

(5.3.2)
$$\text{Subject to:}$$
$$A^{(k)}x^{(k)} \le b^{(k)}$$
$$x^{(k)} \ge 0$$

for $k = 1, 2$. To see where this problem came from, notice that when the kth branch is operating at level $x^{(k)}$, it demands $D^{(k)}x^{(k)}$ of the scarce resources and the value or transfer cost of these is $w^*D^{(k)}x^{(k)}$. Hence its net "profit" for this level of operation is its gross sales, $c^{(k)}x^{(k)}$, minus the total transfer cost of the scarce resources used. If the kth branch regards itself as a profit center, then it will optimize its behavior by maximizing its profit; that is, it will solve the problem in (5.3.2). The problem of the main office is to determine correct transfer prices so that the branch offices will, in fact, end up with behavior that is optimal for the overall corporation.

Suppose that the subproblems (5.3.2) have been solved for several choices of transfer prices w^*. For each such choice, there will be a basic optimal solution and profit, which we shall indicate by

(5.3.3)
$$x^{(k,\,i)} \quad \text{and} \quad p^{(k,\,i)},$$

for $i = 1, \ldots, t$ and $k = 1, 2$. We shall call these optimal solutions *proposals*. As we see, for each transfer price vector w^* given by the main office, a proposal is received back from each of the branch offices. We now turn to the way in which the main office can use these proposals to alter the transfer prices.

We know that each basic optimal solution $x^{(k,\,i)}$ of a subproblem is an extreme point of the convex set of feasible solutions of that subproblem. Moreover, every convex combination of such basic solutions is a *feasible* solution to the subproblem. What we shall do is to set up a *master problem* for the main office that finds the optimum convex combination of proposals for each branch office in order to maximize the overall profitability of the firm. The *master problem* is given by

$$\text{Max } \sum_{i=1}^{t} p^{(1,\,i)}\lambda_i + \sum_{i=1}^{t} p^{(2,\,i)}\mu_i$$

Subject to

(5.3.4)
$$\sum_{i=1}^{t} E^{(1,i)}\lambda_i + \sum_{i=1}^{t} E^{(2,i)}\mu_i \leq r$$

$$\sum_{i=1}^{t} \lambda_i = 1$$

$$\sum_{i=1}^{t} \mu_i = 1$$

$$\lambda_i, \mu_i \geq 0$$

Here λ_i is the weight given to proposal $x^{(1,i)}$, μ_i is the weight given to proposal $x^{(2,i)}$, and $E^{(k,i)} = D^{(k)}x^{(k,i)}$ is the demand on the scarce resources made by proposal $x^{(k,i)}$.

The dual problem to the master problem is also of interest. Let w^* be a row vector of dual variables associated with the resource constraints in (5.3.4), and let variables w_λ and w_μ be associated with the last two constraints of (5.3.4). Then the dual to the master problem is:

$$\text{Min } w^*r + w_\lambda + w_\mu$$

Subject to:

(5.3.5)
$$w^*E^{(1,i)} + w_\lambda e_\lambda \qquad \geq p^{(1,i)}$$
$$w^*E^{(2,i)} \qquad + w_\mu e_\mu \geq p^{(2,i)}$$
$$w^* \geq 0$$

w_λ and w_μ are unrestricted

Here e_λ is a row vector of all 1's with the same number of components as $p^{(1,i)}$, and e_μ is a row vector of all 1's having the same number of components as $p^{(2,i)}$. As usual, the solutions to the dual problem have very important interpretations concerning the master problem. We list several of them.

(a) At any stage in the computation the prices of the scarce resources are given by the vector w^* of the solution to the dual problem.

(b) If $w_\lambda < 0$, then the first branch is unprofitable at the current prices for scarce resources.

(c) If $w_\mu < 0$, then the second branch is unprofitable at the current prices for scarce resources.

(d) There is no need to consider a proposal from branch 1 whose profitability is not at least w_λ since it will not improve the solution to the master problem.

(e) Similarly, there is no need to add a new proposal to the master problem from branch 2 whose profitability does not exceed w_μ since it will not improve the solution to the master problem.

We now outline the steps of the decomposition algorithm.

(0) Set the resource prices $w^* = 0$. Set $w_\lambda = 0$ and $w_\mu = 0$.

(1) Solve the subproblems (5.3.2) for $k = 1, 2$. If the corresponding solutions $x^{(k,i)}$ and $p^{(k,i)}$ are more profitable than the corresponding dual prices, include these proposals in the master problem (5.3.4). If there are new proposals, go to (2). Otherwise the computation is finished; go to (3).

(2) Solve the new master problem and its dual. Find new dual prices w^*, w_λ, and w_μ. Go to (1).

(3) Use the solution to the last master problem to give allocations to the branch offices so that the resource demands of the branches on scarce resources will be properly coordinated. Use the final dual prices to calculate the transfer prices that will be charged to each of the branches.

To make the steps of the method clear, let us work an example.

EXAMPLE 5.3.1. A wood-products company has two divisions, Eastern and Western. The wood is produced at a sawmill in the northwestern part of the country and shipped in the company's own trucks to the divisions. Eastern makes x_1 bobsleds and x_2 playpens each month, using $6x_1 + 2x_2 = x_3$ units of wood. Western makes y_1 desks and y_2 tables each month, using $y_3 = 3y_1 + 5y_2$ units of wood. In a particular month, the main office has 5000 units of wood and 15000 units of truck capacity available. It assigns transfer prices w_1^* and w_2^* to the use of the wood and truck capacity, respectively. Finally, each division has a labor constraint.

The constraints of the main office involve wood and truck capacity as follows:

$$x_3 + \ y_3 \le \ 5000 \quad \text{(wood constraint)},$$
$$5x_3 + 2y_3 \le 15000 \quad \text{(truck capacity constraint)}.$$

The subproblem faced by Eastern is:

$$\text{Max } 15x_1 + 8x_2 - (w_1^* + 5w_2^*)x_3$$

Subject to:

(5.3.6)
$$
\begin{aligned}
6x_1 + 2x_2 - x_3 &\le \ \ \ 0 \quad \text{(wood constraint)} \\
3x_1 + 5x_2 \ \ \ \ \ \ &\le 4000 \quad \text{(labor constraint)} \\
x_1 \ \ \ \ \ \ \ \ \ \ \ &\ge \ \ \ 0 \\
x_2 \ &\ge \ \ \ 0
\end{aligned}
$$

Here, 15 is the gross profit on bobsleds, and 8 is the gross profit on playpens. Similarly, the subproblem faced by Western is:

$$\text{Max } 10y_1 + 11y_2 - (w_1^* + 2w_2^*)y_3$$

Subject to:

(5.3.7)
$$
\begin{aligned}
3y_1 + 5y_2 - y_3 &\le \ \ \ 0 \quad \text{(wood constraint)} \\
4y_1 + 4y_2 \ \ \ \ \ \ &\le 3000 \quad \text{(labor constraint)} \\
y_1 \ \ \ \ \ \ \ \ \ \ \ &\ge \ \ \ 0 \\
y_2 \ &\ge \ \ \ 0
\end{aligned}
$$

Ten is the gross profit on desks and 11 the gross profit on tables. Note that the transfer price on wood in each division is determined by the prices that the main office charges for each of the scarce resources, wood and truck capacity, according to the amount of each that is used by each division. Since Eastern is far from the wood-supply source, it must pay proportionately more for the use of trucking capacity.

As a first observation, notice that both problems (5.3.6) and (5.3.7) have as a feasible solution all variables set equal to zero—that is, to shut down the division.

This might be a good thing to do if one of the divisions is very much more profitable than the other.

However, each division considered by itself is profitable provided the transfer prices are sufficiently small. Let us begin by solving each of the divisional problems under the assumption that the transfer prices are zero. It is easy to show that in this case the optimal solution for Eastern is

$$x^{(1)} = \begin{bmatrix} 4000/3 \\ 0 \end{bmatrix}$$

giving profit $p_E^{(1)} = 20{,}000$. However, in order to implement this solution, $x_3 = 8000$, which is more units of wood than the main office has on hand! Also, 40,000 units of truck capacity would be required, which again is more than is on hand.

Similarly, with zero transfer prices, the optimal solution for Western is

$$y^{(1)} = \begin{bmatrix} 0 \\ 750 \end{bmatrix}$$

with profit $p_W^{(1)} = 8250$. Here $y_3 = 3750$ units of wood and 7500 units of truck capacity are needed, both of which are within the current capacity limits.

The main office must now arbitrate between these two proposals and decide what fraction of each it should accept, since obviously not all of either can be kept. Let λ_1 be the fraction of Eastern's proposal 1 that is to be accepted. Then $1 - \lambda_1$ is the fraction of the complete closing of Eastern that is accepted. Similarly, let μ_1 be the fraction of Western's proposal 1 that is to be accepted; then $1 - \mu_1$ is the fraction of the closing down of Western to be accepted. The master problem faced by the main office is clearly

$$\text{Max } 20{,}000\lambda_1 + 8250\mu_1$$

Subject to:

(5.3.8)
$$\begin{aligned}
8000\lambda_1 + 3750\mu_1 &\leq 5000 \\
40{,}000\lambda_1 + 7500\mu_1 &\leq 15{,}000 \\
\lambda_1 &\leq 1 \\
\mu_1 &\leq 1
\end{aligned}$$

The optimal solution to this problem is given by

$$\lambda_1 = .889, \qquad \mu_1 = .208, \qquad \text{profit} \qquad p_0^{(1)} = 11{,}500,$$

and the dual variables are

$$w_1^* = 2 \quad \text{and} \quad w_2^* = .1, \qquad w_\lambda = 0, \qquad w_\mu = 0.$$

Hence, the main office now charges transfer prices of \$2 on a unit of wood and 10¢ per unit of trucking capacity.

After the main office sends out its new transfer prices to the divisions, they reconsider their optimization problems. Eastern calculates that it must now pay $w_1^* + 5w_2^* = 2.5$ for each unit of wood that it asks for from the main office. Resolving (5.3.6) with this total transfer price, it returns with a new proposal,

$$x^{(2)} = \begin{bmatrix} 0 \\ 800 \end{bmatrix},$$

giving profit $p_E^{(2)} = 6400$, exclusive of the transfer cost. Similarly, Western calculates its total transfer price as $w_1^* + 2w_2^* = 2.2$ for each unit of wood. Resolving (5.3.7) with this number gives

$$y^{(2)} = \begin{bmatrix} 750 \\ 0 \end{bmatrix}$$

with profit $p_W^{(2)} = 7500$, exclusive of the transfer cost.

After the main office receives the new proposals from both divisions it must set up a new master problem that includes them, since it must decide on what fraction it should accept of each of the proposals made so far. It calculates that $x^{(2)}$ requires 1600 units of wood and 8000 units of trucking capacity, while $y^{(2)}$ requires 3750 units of wood and 7500 units of trucking capacity. Hence the second master problem is:

$$\text{Max } 20{,}000\lambda_1 + 6400\lambda_2 + 8250\mu_1 + 7500\mu_2$$

Subject to:

$$
\begin{aligned}
8000\lambda_1 + 1600\lambda_2 + 3750\mu_1 + 2250\mu_2 &\leq 5000 \\
40{,}000\lambda_1 + 8000\lambda_2 + 7500\mu_1 + 4500\mu_2 &\leq 15{,}000 \\
\lambda_1 + \lambda_2 &\leq 1 \\
\mu_1 + \mu_2 &\leq 1
\end{aligned}
$$

(5.3.9)

The solution to this problem is given by

$$\lambda_1 = .078, \qquad \lambda_2 = .922, \qquad \mu_1 = 1, \qquad \mu_2 = 0$$

and with dual prices

$$w_1^* = 0, \qquad w_2^* = .425, \qquad w_\lambda = 5587.5, \qquad w_\mu = 3000.$$

The main office now sends the new transfer prices back to the divisions and asks for new proposals.

In Exercise 1, you will be asked to complete the calculation and show that the new proposal of Eastern is the same as $x^{(2)}$, while the new proposal of Western is the same as $y^{(1)}$. Also, the value of Eastern's program is equal to w_λ and the value of Western's program is w_μ. Hence, the computation is ended.

It should be noted, however, that the main office must not only provide transfer prices, it must also give each division quotas on wood in order to obtain optimal behavior. Notice that it simply tells Western to use its first proposal, but it must give detailed instructions to Eastern to use .078 of its first proposal and .922 of its second proposal. Eastern cannot determine these fractions by solving its own subproblem, since each time it does this it always comes out with one of the previously generated proposals. It thus appears that transfer prices alone are not enough to determine optimal decentralized behavior of a multidivisional firm but that a combination of transfer prices and quotas on raw materials is enough.

Let us conclude this discussion of the decomposition method by listing its advantages and disadvantages. First of all, note that the main office can solve the coordination problem without knowing anything about the technology of the subproblems. For instance, it does not need to know anything about the labor problems of the divisions. Similarly, the divisions do not need to know anything about the main office's resource constraints. The transfer prices are all the division needs to determine optimal proposals. Second, with decomposition techniques, it is possible to solve much bigger problems than would be otherwise possible. Problems with up to 50,000 constraints have been handled in this manner.

However there are also some disadvantages. In actual calculations it has been found that the transfer-price vector tends to fluctuate rather wildly, which causes somewhat erratic computational behavior. Second, the list of proposals tends to become very long—so long that not all can be saved in core memory of a present-day computer. Hence, some kind of a rule for deciding when to drop a proposal is needed. Exactly what rules are used depend on the person who writes the program, and these are frequently held confidential. However, among the rules used are:

(a) Drop a proposal if it becomes unprofitable—that is, if it drops out of the final basis of the master program.

(b) Save the ten best proposals only.

(c) Save as many proposals as possible. When memory space becomes short, drop the least profitable ones.

Needless to say, these rules are somewhat ad hoc in nature.

Still another disadvantage is that some parts of the computation must be repeated several times. For instance, a proposal might enter the list, be dropped as unprofitable, then re-enter later when it becomes profitable again, only to be dropped again, and so on. For this reason, it is usually best to solve a problem with the original simplex method if it is small enough for the core memory. Decomposition remains useful for problems that are too large for core memory.

EXERCISES 5.3

1. In Example 5.3.1, show that, using the transfer prices from the second master problem,
   (a) Eastern's new proposal is $x^{(2)}$.
   (b) Western's new proposal is $y^{(1)}$.
   (c) The value of Eastern's program is w_λ.
   (d) The value of Western's program is w_μ.
   (e) Use the results to show that no further computations will improve the solution found in the second master problem.

2. Consider a decomposed problem in which the master constraints are

$$x_1 \quad + 2y_1 \quad \leq 6,$$
$$2x_2 \quad + y_2 \leq 8,$$

and the two divisional constraints are

$$\text{Max } 3x_1 + 2x_2$$

Subject to:

$$x_1 + x_2 \leq 5$$
$$x_1 \quad \leq 3$$
$$x_2 \leq 4$$

and

$$\text{Max } 2y_1 + 2y_2$$

Subject to:

$$2y_1 + y_2 \leq 10$$
$$y_2 \leq 6$$

Solve the problem, using the decomposition method. (*Hint:* It is necessary to solve three master problems.)

3. Formulate Example 5.3.1 as an ordinary linear program without the decomposition format and show that it is 4×4.

4. Formulate the problem in Exercise 2 as an ordinary linear programming problem and show that it is 7×4.

5. Suppose the master problem has m_u constraints and the t subproblems are $m_k \times n_k$, for $k = 1, \ldots, t$. What will the dimensions of the problem be if treated as an ordinary linear programming problem?

*6. Suppose the master problem yields a dual price, w_λ, associated with the proposals from a division and also new transfer prices. Suppose that the division sets up the problem with the new transfer prices and makes a proposal whose profitability is at most w_λ. Show that the new proposal will not improve the profitability of the master problem on the next calculation.

*7. Set up the notation for the problem of a company with d divisions and one central office. (*Hint:* You should end up with equations similar to (5.3.1)–(5.3.4).)

5.4   APPLICATIONS OF INTEGER AND MIXED – INTEGER PROGRAMMING

When a linear programming problem must be solved in such a way that all variables in the optimal solution have only integer values, we call it an *integer programming problem*. And when some but not all of the variables have this integer requirement, we call it a *mixed-integer programming problem*. In the next section we shall discuss solution techniques for these problems. However, we go into applications in the present section in order to motivate the need for such solution techniques.

In order to make the following examples clear, we shall use the notation δ or δ_i for variables that must be integer in value, and x or x_i for variables that may or may not take on integer values.

EXAMPLE 5.4.1. *Off-On Constraints.* Suppose we wish a variable to take on the value a or else to be 0. It is easy to accomplish this by means of the following conditions:

$$x = \delta a;$$
$$0 \le \delta \le 1 \text{ and } \delta \text{ an integer.}$$

It is clear that if δ satisfies the last two conditions the only possible values it can take on are 0 and 1. So if $\delta = 0$, then $x = 0$, and if $\delta = 1$, then $x = a$, as required.

EXAMPLE 5.4.2. *Off-On Intervals.* Suppose we want x either to be 0 or else to be in a fixed interval between a and b. The following inequalities accomplish these requirements.

$$\delta a \le x \le \delta b;$$
$$0 \le \delta \le 1 \text{ and } \delta \text{ integer.}$$

Again it is clear that if $\delta = 0$, then $x = 0$, and if $\delta = 1$, then x satisfies $a \le x \le b$. These are the only possible values for δ.

EXAMPLE 5.4.3. *A Discrete Valued Variable.* We can extend Example 5.4.1 to make a variable x take only one of a finite number of values $a_1, a_2, \ldots, a_n$, as follows:

$$x = a_1\delta_1 + a_2\delta_2 + \cdots + a_n\delta_n,$$

$$\sum_{i=1}^{n} \delta_i = 1, \qquad 0 \le \delta_i \le 1 \text{ and } \delta_i \text{ an integer.}$$

Again the conditions on the δ_i's require that exactly one of them should be 1 and the rest 0. And if $\delta_i = 1$, then $x = a_i$.

EXAMPLE 5.4.4. *Either-Or Constraints.* We can extend Example 5.4.2 to make a variable x lie in either one interval or another. Suppose the two intervals are (a_1, b_1) and (a_2, b_2); then consider the inequalities:

$$a_1\delta_1 + a_2\delta_2 \le x \le b_1\delta_1 + b_2\delta_2,$$

$$\delta_1 + \delta_2 = 1, \qquad 0 \le \delta_i \le 1 \text{ and } \delta_i \text{ an integer.}$$

It follows that exactly one of the δ_i's must be 1 and the other 0. If $\delta_1 = 1$, then x is restricted to (a_1, b_1), and if $\delta_2 = 0$, x is restricted to (a_2, b_2). In Exercise 5, you are asked to extend this to n intervals.

EXAMPLE 5.4.5. *Extended Either-Or Constraints.* Suppose we want a vector x to lie either in the convex set determined by the constraints $A^{(1)}x \le b^{(1)}$ or else in the convex set $A^{(2)}x \le b^{(2)}$. We can handle this in a slightly different manner than the method used in Example 5.4.4—namely,

$$A^{(1)}x \le b^{(1)} + (1 - \delta_1)M_1,$$

$$A^{(2)}x \le b^{(2)} + (1 - \delta_2)M_2,$$

$$\delta_1 + \delta_2 = 1, \qquad 0 \le \delta_i \le 1 \text{ and } \delta_i \text{ an integer.}$$

Here M_i, for $i = 1, 2$, represents a vector of very large (in absolute value) numbers so that when it is added to the right-hand sides of the corresponding constraint set, the constraints become completely ineffective. Again exactly one of the δ_i's will be 1 and the other 0, and the corresponding constraints will be effective and ineffective, respectively.

In Exercise 6, you will be asked to show that the "truth set" of either-or constraints is the union of the truth sets of the individual constraints. You will also be asked to extend Example 5.4.5 to the case of n convex sets.

EXAMPLE 5.4.6. *Implications.* Sometimes we need to express conditional relations among constraints. A simple example will illustrate the idea. Suppose that, in order for a certain variable x to be positive, it is necessary that another variable y exceed a certain threshold value. In other words, suppose we wish to express:

$$(x > 0) \Rightarrow (y \ge a).$$

This conditional statement can be reformulated as:

$$(x = 0) \quad \text{or} \quad (y \ge a).$$

It is well known from elementary logic (see any of the logic references at the end of the chapter) that a conditional statement can be expressed as an either-or statement by negating the hypothesis. The either-or statement can be expressed as

$$x \le \delta M, \qquad y \ge a\,\delta,$$
$$0 \le \delta \le 1, \; \delta \text{ integer.}$$

Again M is a very large number. In Exercise 16, you will be asked to formulate constraints corresponding to other conditional statements.

Our remaining examples will be more immediately applicable than the previous ones.

EXAMPLE 5.4.7. *The Knapsack Problem*. A hiker wishes to go on a camping trip and does not wish to carry more than 60 pounds in his pack. Unfortunately in laying out his equipment he finds its total weight to be 90 pounds. There are three objects he wants to take, so in order to decide which combination is best, he attaches a value to each. Suppose his data are:

Object	Value	Weight	Value/Weight
1	70	40	1.75
2	50	30	1.67
3	30	20	1.5

Notice that he has listed the objects in order of decreasing value-to-weight ratio.
In order to solve his problem, he must solve the following integer programming problem:

$$\text{Max } 70x_1 + 50x_2 + 30x_3$$

(5.4.1)   Subject to:

$$40x_1 + 30x_2 + 20x_3 \le k = 60$$
$$x_1, x_2, x_3 \ge 0 \text{ and integer}$$

In many versions of this problem, he will take at most one of each object, but we will not impose that restriction here.
One way of getting a feasible solution to the problem is to take as many units as possible of the most valuable item first (that is, the one with the largest value/weight ratio), then as many of the second as possible, and so on. If this is done for the given problem, the solution is: $x_1 = 1$, $x_2 = 0$, $x_3 = 1$, objective function $= 100$. Note that there is an alternative solution with the same objective value for which $x_2 = 2$ and the others are 0. Let us call the first solution discussed above the *largest-ratio solution*. Other solutions to the problem for other k values are given in Figure 5.4.1. Notice that the largest-ratio rule gives an optimum answer quite often. In Exercise 13, you will be asked to show that for continuous linear programming this method always gives the optimum solution.

k	Optimal Solution				Largest-Ratio Solution			
	x_1	x_2	x_3	Value	x_1	x_2	x_3	Value
40	1	0	0	70	1	0	0	70
50	0	1	1	80	1	0	0	70
60	1	0	1	100	1	0	1	100
	0	2	0	100				
70	1	1	0	120	1	1	0	120
80	2	0	0	140	2	0	0	140

FIGURE 5.4.1

Knapsack problems occur quite often in applications, and special methods have been developed for solving such problems having large numbers of variables. A branch-and-bound method for solving knapsack problems is discussed in Section 5.6.

EXAMPLE 5.4.8. *A Job Shop Scheduling Problem.* Consider a machine shop that has three machines and produces two goods. Each good must go on the machines in a certain order and will take a known amount of machining time. The data are given in Figure 5.4.2. In the row labeled Good 1, we see that the first good must first go

Good 1	3 (10 hr)	2 (6 hr)	1 (5 hr)
Good 2	2 (7 hr)	1 (4 hr)	3 (9 hr)

FIGURE 5.4.2

to machine 3, where it takes ten hours, then to machine 2, where it takes six hours, and finally to machine 1, where it takes five hours. Similarly, the order and times are given for Good 2. The problem is to schedule the times at which each good should be worked on by each machine in order to minimize the overall completion time of all the goods. We can formulate this as an integer programming problem. To do this let

$x_j{}^i$ = the time at which the ith good goes on the jth machine.

Also let x be the early completion time of all the jobs. Then our objective is to

(5.4.2)   Minimize x

subject to the following technological constraints:

(5.4.3)
$$x_3{}^1 \geq 0 \qquad x_2{}^2 \geq 0$$
$$x_2{}^1 \geq x_3{}^1 + 10 \qquad x_1{}^2 \geq x_2{}^2 + 7$$
$$x_1{}^1 \geq x_2{}^1 + 6 \qquad x_3{}^2 \geq x_1{}^2 + 4$$
$$x \geq x_1{}^1 + 5 \qquad x \geq x_3{}^2 + 9$$

Notice that these are derived exactly from the data of Figure 5.4.2. We also have some noninterference constraints that prevent the assignment of two different goods to the same machine at the same time. These are by their very nature either-or constraints, as follows:

$$
(x_3{}^1 + 10 \le x_3{}^2) \quad \text{or} \quad (x_3{}^2 + 9 \le x_3{}^1)
$$

$$(5.4.4) \qquad (x_2{}^1 + \ 6 \le x_2{}^2) \quad \text{or} \quad (x_2{}^2 + 7 \le x_2{}^1)$$

$$
(x_1{}^1 + \ 5 \le x_1{}^2) \quad \text{or} \quad (x_1{}^2 + 4 \le x_1{}^1)
$$

In order to state these last three constraints, it is necessary, as we have seen earlier, to add three 0–1 variables as in Example 5.4.5 and Exercise 15.

It is clear that if we had m goods on n machines, where m and n were fairly large, there would be an astronomical number of constraints. In Exercise 16, you will be asked to calculate this number. In any case, scheduling problems lead to integer programming problems that have a very large number of variables and constraints and hence are difficult to solve. Research in this area is needed to improve solution techniques.

Another example of an integer programming problem is the so-called traveling-salesman problem discussed in Exercises 17–19.

Our last two examples are of mixed-integer programming problems—that is, linear programming problems in which some but not all the variables are required to be integers.

EXAMPLE 5.4.9. *The Fixed-Charge Problem.* The operation of many kinds of facilities involves a variable cost that depends on the level at which the facility is operated and also a fixed charge that is independent of the level of operation. The graph of a typical fixed-charge cost function appears in Figure 5.4.3. Here b is the

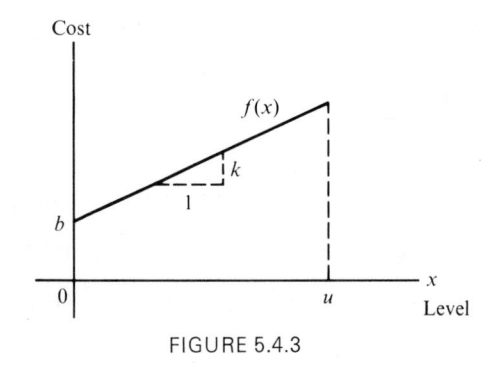

FIGURE 5.4.3

fixed charge, k is the unit variable cost, and u represents the maximum level at which the facility can be operated.

Now suppose that we consider a generator-scheduling problem in which an electric power company requires (or demands) d units of electric power and has two generating facilities that have fixed-charge cost functions like that in Figure 5.4.2. In this case the fixed charge is the so-called "spinning cost"—that is, the cost of speeding up the generator from rest to a sufficient speed that it can safely be put "on-line" and used to generate power. The company must decide which facility or facilities to turn on and at what levels to run them. Its problem may be stated as the following mixed-integer problem:

$$\text{Min } k_1 x_1 + k_2 x_2 + \delta_1 b_1 + \delta_2 b_2$$

Subject to:

(5.4.5)

$$
\begin{aligned}
x_1 + x_2 &\geq d \\
x_1 &\leq u_1 \delta_1 \\
x_2 &\leq u_2 \delta_2 \\
\delta_1 &\leq 1 \\
\delta_2 &\leq 1 \\
x_1 x_2, \delta_1, \delta_2 &\geq 0
\end{aligned}
$$

δ_1 and δ_2 must be integers

Notice that if $\delta_1 = 0$, then $x_1 = 0$ also; that is, the first generator is shut down. Also, the fixed cost of b_1 is not added to the production cost. On the other hand, if $\delta_1 = 1$, then x_1 may take on any value from 0 to u_1, and the fixed charge b_1 is added to the production cost. Similar remarks hold for the second generator.

It is easy to see how to extend this problem to the many generator case, which would be more realistic (see Exercise 20).

EXAMPLE 5.4.10. *Maximization or Minimization of a Piecewise Linear Function.* The true cost function of an electric generator is not a completely linear function over all its power ranges. Instead, it can be closely approximated by a piecewise linear function, an example of which appears in Figure 5.4.4. Notice that one can

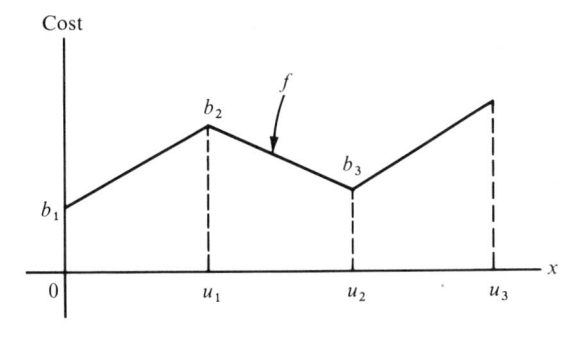

FIGURE 5.4.4

think of the corner points of the function as involving successive fixed charges b_1, b_2, and b_3. These can be computed as follows:

(5.4.6) b_1 is given, $b_2 = u_1 k_1 + b_1$, $b_3 = (u_2 - u_1)k_2 + b_2$.

Then the problem of minimizing the function shown in Figure 5.4.4 is as follows.

$$\text{Min } k_1 x_1 + k_2 x_2 + k_3 x_3 + b_1 \delta_1 + b_2 \delta_2 + b_3 \delta_3$$

Subject to:

$$0 \le x_1 \le \delta_1 u_1$$
$$\delta_2 u_1 \le x_2 \le \delta_2 u_2$$
(5.4.7)
$$\delta_3 u_2 \le x_3 \le \delta_3 u_3$$
$$\delta_1 + \delta_2 + \delta_3 = 1$$
$$\delta_1 + \delta_2 + \delta_3 \ge 0 \text{ and integer}$$

Of course, in an actual applied problem there may be other constraints as well. Notice that in this case the variables x_1, x_2, and x_3 can take on any numerical value, whereas the variables δ_1, δ_2, and δ_3 are 0–1 integer variables. In other words, this model is a mixed-integer programming problem.

The importance of the last example is that any nonlinear function of one variable may be approximated by a piecewise linear function and handled by the technique described above. Of course, this method is not without its difficulties, including the fact that mixed-integer programming methods are not, as yet, completely reliable for solving arbitrary problems. Without doubt, such methods will be improved as the result of continuing research.

EXERCISES 5.4

1. Write a set of constraints that will require a variable x to lie either in the interval $1 \le x \le 2$ or in the interval $5 \le x \le 10$.

2. Write a set of constraints that will require a variable x either to be equal to 17 or else to be in the interval $51 \le x \le 75$.

3. Write a set of constraints that will require a variable x to be equal to exactly one of the following values:

$$e^a, \quad e^{-a}, \quad \sin a, \quad \cos a, \quad a^2.$$

4. In Example 5.4.3, suppose we require $\sum_{i=1}^{n} \delta_i = k$, for k an integer and $k < n$. Describe the resulting set of possible values for x.

5. Extend Example 5.4.4 so that x is required to be in exactly one of n different intervals.

6. (a) Show in Example 5.4.5 that the truth set of the either-or constraints given there is the union of two convex sets.
   (b) Extend Example 5.4.5 to the case in which there are n convex sets, and give the corresponding geometric interpretation.

7. In Exercise 6(b), suppose that we wanted exactly two of the constraints to hold instead of exactly one constraint. Describe the set of inequalities necessary to accomplish this. Do the same for the requirement that exactly $k < n$ of the constraints should hold.

8. (a) Show graphically how to write the star of David as the union of two triangles.
   (b) Show graphically how to write the star of Bethlehem as the union of three triangles.

9. Write the constraints that require the two-component column vector x to satisfy the following.

$$\text{either} \quad \begin{array}{c} 0 \le x_1 \le 1 \\ 0 \le x_2 \le 1 \end{array} \quad \text{or} \quad \begin{array}{c} 1 \le x_1 \le 2 \\ 1 \le x_2 \le 2 \end{array}$$

Draw a picture of the resulting truth set.

10. Set up inequalities for requiring the following implications to hold:
    (a) $(x + y > 0) \Rightarrow (z = 2x + y)$
    (b) $(x > 0) \Rightarrow (y = 3x + 5)$ (draw graph)
    (c) $(x + y > 0) \Rightarrow (x - y = 5)$
    (d) $[(x > 0) \text{ or } (y > 0)] \Rightarrow (5x + 2y = 10)$

11. Verify by trial and error that the entries of Figure 5.4.1 are correct for the knapsack problem as stated.

12. Benefit/cost analysis has received much attention in governmental circles. Discuss how this method is similar to and can be set up like a knapsack problem.

*13. Suppose that we permit a knapsack problem to be solved in continuous variables and that we permit at most one of each object to be selected. Show, using the simplex method, that the corresponding linear programming problem is solved by using the largest-ratio solution and that it will involve accepting each of the most valuable objects in decreasing order, with a fractional part of the last object selected.

14. Solve the knapsack problem with the following data:

Object	Value	Weight
1	85	41
2	72	32
3	61	24
4	45	17
5	37	15

(*Hint:* First put the objects in largest ratio order.)

15. Add three 0–1 variables to Example 5.4.8 in order to state the either-or constraints (5.4.4).

16. For the job shop scheduling problem in which each of m goods must be processed on each of n machines, show that there are $(n + 1)m$ technological constraints and $n \begin{bmatrix} m \\ 2 \end{bmatrix}$ either-or constraints. How many 0–1 variables will be needed?

*17. A salesman wishes to go to each of n cities exactly once before returning home, and he wants to plan his route so that the total distance he travels is minimized. This is the so-called *traveling salesman problem*. For $i, j = 1, \ldots, n$, let d_{ij} be the distance from city i to city j; define a 0–1 variable x_{ij} to be equal to 1 if he travels on the road from city i to city j and 0 otherwise. Show that the following is an integer programming formulation of the problem:

$$\text{Min} \sum_{i,j=1}^{n} d_{ij} x_{ij}$$

Subject to:

$$\sum_{i=1}^{n} x_{ij} = 1 \quad \text{(the salesman must enter city } j)$$

$$\sum_{j=1}^{n} x_{ij} = 1 \quad \text{(the salesman must leave city } i)$$

$$u_1 = 0$$

$$u_j - u_i \geq M(x_{ij} - 1) + 1, \quad M \text{ a large number}$$

(The last constraint says that there is a renumbering of the cities, with u_i being the number of city i, which corresponds to the order in which the cities should be traveled in the optimal path.) Show that there are $n^2 + n$ variables and the same number of constraints. How many would this be for a 50-city problem? For a 100-city problem? Do you think this is a practical method for problems of this size?

18. Solve the five-city traveling salesman problem with the following table of distances:

	2	3	4	5
1	13	14	20	25
2		12	13	12
3			25	20
4				14

Trial-and-error methods will produce the solution rather quickly.

19. Set up the integer programming problem for the five-city problem of Exercise 18 and find the values of x_{ij}, u_i, for $i, j = 1, \ldots, 5$. Give interpretations.

20. Extend the generator-scheduling problem stated in (5.4.5) to the case of n generators.

21. At Thanksgiving and Christmas, turkeys are frequently offered for sale at two different prices. For instance, up to 16 pounds, they might cost 75¢ a pound, and for 16 pounds or more, 65¢ a pound.
  (a) Draw the graph of this cost function, showing that it is flat from 16 pounds to over 18 pounds.
  (b) Write inequalities that express this nonlinear cost function.
  (c) Explain why it is usually impossible to purchase a 17-pound turkey at this time; and if it were possible, it would be rational for the butcher to give you a pound "free" and call it a 16-pound turkey.

22. Trucking rates often are stated with a discount. For instance, suppose that a firm's rates for traveling between two points are 50¢ a pound for a load up to 20,000 pounds; 38¢ a pound for a load up to 100,000 pounds; 29¢ a pound for a load over 100,000 pounds.
  (a) Draw the graph of the cost function, showing that it has level parts and is piecewise linear.
  (b) Write the nonlinear function in terms of variables and inequalities.
  (c) Show that in some ranges the cost of additional pounds is zero and that it therefore frequently pays to say that a load is heavier than it actually is.

23. Extend (5.4.7) to a piecewise linear function having n pieces.

24. Suppose that in Figure 5.4.3 we have $k_1 < k_2 < k_3$.
  (a) Draw the graph of the objective function

$$f(x) = k_1 x_1 + k_2 x_2 + k_3 x_3,$$

where $x = x_1 + x_2 + x_3$ and the x_i's satisfy

$$0 \leq x_1 \leq u_1,$$
$$0 \leq x_2 \leq u_2,$$
$$0 \leq x_3 \leq u_3$$

for various values of the k's, including some cases in which some of them are negative.

(b) Show that the problem of minimizing $f(x)$ subject to the linear constraints in (a) and $x \geq d$ can be solved as an ordinary linear programming problem. Assume various values of the number d, which can be interpreted as a demand.

5.5   INTEGER PROGRAMMING METHODS

As the examples of the preceding section indicate, there are many interesting problems that can be formulated as integer programming problems. But to be useful, automatic techniques for solving such problems rapidly and reliably are needed. Unfortunately, at the present time there is no single method that can be applied to any integer programming problem with the same degree of assurance of success as one has when, for instance, the simplex method is applied to an arbitrary linear programming problem. However, there is an enormous amount of effort going into research in this area and we can expect rapid improvements in the future.

In this section we shall discuss three out of perhaps fifty or so current approaches to solving integer programming problems. We will indicate the methods generally without going into a complete description of the corresponding algorithms.

A. *Cutting-Plane Methods* (Gomory). We shall first discuss two so-called cutting-plane methods for solving integer programming problems. Both of these methods are due to Ralph Gomory. We need a preliminary definition.

DEFINITION 5.5.1. Let a be a number; by $[a]$, we shall mean the "integer part" of a; that is, $[a]$ is the largest integer less than or equal to a. Thus we can write

(5.5.1) $$a = [a] + f \qquad \text{where } 0 \leq f < 1.$$

We shall call f the *fractional part* of a.

As examples, note that $[3] = 3$, $[-0.5] = -1$, $[0.5] = 0$, and $[5.5] = 5$. Thus, $3 = 3 + 0$, $-0.5 = -1 + 0.5$, $0.5 = 0 + 0.5$, and $5.5 = 5 + 0.5$.

Now suppose we have an equality constraint of the form

(5.5.2) $$\sum_{j=1}^{n} a_j x_j = b \qquad \text{where } x_j \geq 0 \text{ and integer.}$$

Suppose we write

$$a_j = [a_j] + f_j \qquad \text{for } j = 1, \ldots, n \text{ and } b = [b] + f.$$

Then it is clear that, since $f_j \geq 0$ and $x_j \geq 0$, we have

(5.5.3) $$\sum_{j=1}^{n} [a_j] x_j \leq b.$$

Moreover, the left-hand side of (5.5.3) is an integer; hence it follows that the even stronger inequality holds:

(5.5.4) $$\sum_{j=1}^{n} [a_j] x_j \leq [b].$$

Now suppose we substitute $a_j = [a_j] + f_j$ and $b = [b] + f$ into equation (5.5.2). We obtain

(5.5.5) $$\sum [a_j]x_j + \sum f_j x_j = [b] + f$$

or, rewriting,

(5.5.6) $$\sum f_j x_j - f = [b] - \sum [a_j]x_j \geq 0,$$

where the last inequality follows from (5.5.4). Rewriting (5.5.6), we have

(5.5.7) $$\sum_{j=1}^{n} f_j x_j \geq f.$$

This inequality is called a *fractional cut*. The reason it is called a cut is that it is a derived constraint that, in general, is different from the original constraint. Hence it usually cuts away part of the original feasible set of feasible vectors. The important thing for integer programming is that, because of the way it was derived, the cut (5.5.7) will never cut away any integer point. In other words, any nonnegative integer vector x whose components satisfy (5.5.2) will also satisfy (5.5.7).

EXAMPLE 5.5.1. Consider the constraint

(5.5.8) $$2x_1 + 3x_2 = 11.$$

One way of deriving cuts from such a constraint is to divide by the coefficients of the variables and then apply (5.5.7). Suppose we divide (5.5.8) by 2, obtaining

$$x_1 + \frac{3}{2} x_2 = \frac{11}{2}.$$

From this we derive the cut

$$\frac{1}{2} x_2 \geq \frac{1}{2} \quad \text{or, equivalently,} \quad x_2 \geq 1$$

by applying (5.5.7). Also, dividing (5.5.8) by 3 to get rid of the x_2 variable, we obtain

$$\frac{2}{3} x_1 + x_2 = \frac{11}{3},$$

which gives the cut

$$\frac{2}{3} x_1 \geq \frac{2}{3} \quad \text{or, equivalently,} \quad x_1 \geq 1.$$

Figure 5.5.1 gives the original constraint set, which is the line segment from $(0, \frac{11}{3})$ to $(\frac{11}{2}, 0)$, and indicates the parts removed by these two cuts. Notice that in this case (but not in general) the two cuts are sufficient to isolate the only two points, $(1, 3)$ and $(4, 1)$, that have integer components that satisfy the original constraint (5.5.8).

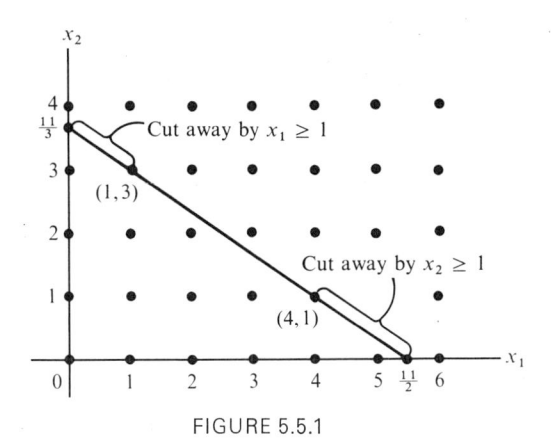

FIGURE 5.5.1

Let us briefly outline how fractional cuts are used to solve the integer programming problem:

$$\text{Max} \sum_{j=1}^{n} c_j x_j$$

(5.5.9)   Subject to:

$$\sum_{j=1}^{n} a_{ij} x_j = b_i$$

$$x_j \geq 0 \text{ and integer}$$

0. Solve the problem as an ordinary linear programming problem, ignoring the integer requirements.

1. If the solution has x_j equal to an integer for $j = 1, \ldots, n$, stop since the optimum has been obtained. If not, at least one x_j has a fractional value. Choose one and use the constraint in which it appears in the final tableau of the previous problem to derive a fractional cut.

2. Add the fractional cut to the problem and solve again as an ordinary linear programming problem. Go to 1.

Clearly, this technique will cause the tableau to grow in size since new constraints are continually being added. There are ways of dropping constraints after a time which help alleviate the problem. (See the references at the end of the chapter.) It has been proved that the method will converge in a finite number of steps, but experience with the program has shown that for some problems this finite number is huge.

As a second class of Gomory cuts, we shall derive the so-called all-integer cuts. These rest on the following lemma and theorem.

LEMMA 5.5.1. Let a, a_1, and a_2 be numbers and let x be an integer nonnegative variable. Then

(a) $[a_1 + a_2] \geq [a_1] + [a_2]$,

(b) $[ax] \geq [a]x$.

Proof: (a) Write $a_1 = [a_1] + f_1$ and $a_2 = [a_2] + f_2$; then clearly, since $0 \le f_i < 1$,

$$a_1 + a_2 \ge [a_1] + [a_2].$$

But since the right-hand side is an integer, it also follows that

$$[a_1 + a_2] \ge [a_1] + [a_2].$$

(b) Write $a = [a] + f$. Then, since $x \ge 0$ and x is an integer,

$$ax = [a]x + fx \ge [a]x.$$

Again, since the right-hand side is an integer, it also follows that

$$[ax] \ge [a]x,$$

completing the proof.

THEOREM 5.5.1. If $p > 0$ is any number and x is a nonnegative vector with integer components satisfying

(5.5.10)
$$\sum_{j=1}^{n} a_j x_j \le b,$$

then

(5.5.11)
$$\sum_{j=1}^{n} \left[\frac{a_j}{p} \right] x_j \le \left[\frac{b}{p} \right].$$

(Constraint (5.5.11) is called an *all-integer cut.*)

Proof: Since (5.5.10) is true, it remains true if we divide each side by $p > 0$; that is,

$$\sum_{j=1}^{n} \frac{a_j}{p} x_j \le \frac{b}{p}.$$

Taking the integer part of each side we get:

$$\left[\sum_{j=1}^{n} \frac{a_j}{p} x_j \right] \le \left[\frac{b}{p} \right].$$

Applying Lemma 5.5.1(a) repeatedly, we obtain

$$\sum_{j=1}^{n} \left[\frac{a_j}{p} x_j \right] \le \left[\sum_{j=1}^{n} \frac{a_j}{p} x_j \right] \le \left[\frac{b}{p} \right].$$

Now we apply Lemma 5.5.1(b) to each factor on the left-hand side and obtain (5.5.11).

EXAMPLE 5.5.2. Consider the constraint $3x + 5y \le 16$, with $x \ge 0$, $y \ge 0$, and x and y integers. The all-integer cut is given, for various p, by

$$\left[\frac{3}{p} \right] x + \left[\frac{5}{p} \right] y \le \left[\frac{16}{p} \right].$$

Many different cuts can be derived from this inequality for various values of p. We discuss here just the two cuts:

$$p = \frac{5}{2} \quad \text{which gives} \quad x + 2y \leq 6;$$

$$p = \frac{3}{2} \quad \text{which gives} \quad 2x + 3y \leq 10.$$

The original constraint set and the two cuts (shown dotted) are drawn in Figure 5.5.2. Notice that the cuts and the original constraints intersect in the three extreme integer points whose coordinates are (0, 3), (2, 2), and (5, 0). Thus in this case the integer cuts are sufficient to reduce the constraint set to its "convex hull"—that is, the smallest convex set that contains all the integer points of the original set. (In other examples this may or may not happen.) Other cuts that can be derived are discussed in Exercise 3.

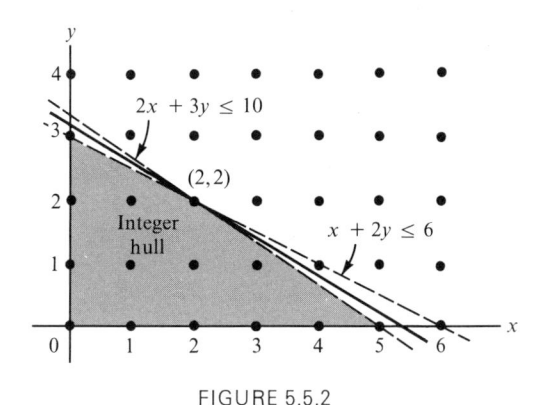

FIGURE 5.5.2

Again we shall not describe in detail how these all-integer cuts are used in the so-called all-integer integer programming algorithm. Suffice it to say that cuts are introduced as needed and used to reduce the size of the constraint set during the course of the calculation.

B. *The Additive Algorithm* (Balas). The additive algorithm was developed by E. Balas to solve minimizing problems having only 0–1 variables. In some ways it resembles the branch-and-bound method to be discussed in the next section. It is a general algorithm to be applied to any problem having only 0–1 variables, and so far it has been found to be reasonably successful for problems having up to around 150 variables. It is called the additive algorithm because it involves only additions and subtractions (no divisions or multiplications) of numbers in the original data, so there is no problem of roundoff error in the final answers, even with large problems. We shall not give a complete description of the method here; we will merely illustrate it by solving an example.

Before we do that, let us consider 0–1 problems in three variables, $x = (x_1, x_2, x_3)$. Since each x_i is either 0 or 1, it is not hard to see that there are exactly eight combinations of these values that can be taken on. Figure 5.5.3 shows the

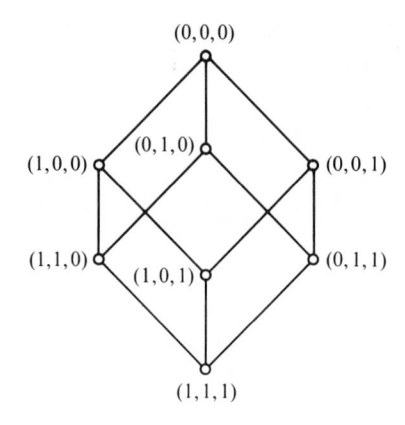

FIGURE 5.5.3

graph of these eight possibilities. Notice that the graph is drawn so that it appears to be a three-dimensional cube. This was not accidental, because for a problem with n variables, it turns out that there are $2 \cdot 2 \cdot \cdots \cdot 2 = 2^n$ possible ways in which these n variables can take on the values 0 and 1, and these 2^n points correspond to the "corners" of the hypercube in n dimensions. Since $2^{20} > 1,000,000$, it is clear that any method that is to be successful in solving a 0–1 with 20 or more variables must *not* look at every possible node in the hypercube. Even the fastest computers would soon not be able to complete such a search for even a moderate number of variables. The additive algorithm examines some of the possibilities explicitly and the rest (hopefully the largest part) of the nodes only *implicitly*. In fact, the subset of the hypercube examined in the course of applying the additive algorithm is a tree—that is, a connected graph without cycles. Let us illustrate it.

EXAMPLE 5.5.3. Suppose we must solve the problem

$$\text{Min } 12x_1 + 20x_2 + 15x_3$$

Subject to:

$$3x_1 + 8x_2 - 5x_3 \geq 3$$

(5.5.12)
$$4x_1 - 2x_2 + 7x_3 \geq 1$$
$$-8x_1 + 7x_2 - 2x_3 \geq 4$$
$$0 \leq x_j \leq 1 \qquad j = 1, 2, 3 \text{ and integer}$$

Let us define the variables d_i, $i = 1, 2, 3$, as

$$d_1 = 3 - 3x_1 - 8x_2 + 5x_3,$$
$$d_2 = 1 - 4x_1 + 2x_2 - 7x_3,$$
$$d_3 = 4 + 8x_1 - 7x_2 + 2x_3.$$

What we want to do is to make each d_i nonpositive. For any set of definite values of the x_j's, let us define the *sum of infeasibilities* to be the sum of the d_i's that are positive. Thus initially if we set $x_1 = x_2 = x_3 = 0$, we have the sum of infeasibilities as $d_1 + d_2 + d_3 = 3 + 1 + 4 = 8$. Now let us try each of the x_i's equal to 1 and calculate the sum of the infeasibilities in each case. For $x_1 = 1$, we get the infeasibility sum as $d_3 = 12$. For $x_2 = 1$, we get it to be $d_2 = 3$. And for $x_3 = 1$, we get it as $d_1 + d_3 = 8 + 6 = 14$. Let us establish a rule that requires selecting the variable that minimizes the sum of infeasibilities. Thus we choose $x_2 = 1$ first; see Figure 5.5.4. Given $x_2 = 1$, we have

$$d_1 = -5 - 3x_1 + 5x_3;$$
$$d_2 = \ \ \ 3 - 4x_1 - 7x_3;$$
$$d_3 = -3 + 8x_1 + 2x_3.$$

Now we apply the same rule. Setting $x_1 = 1$ gives an infeasibility sum of $d_3 = 5$, and setting $x_3 = 1$ gives an infeasibility sum of 0—in other words, $x_2 = x_3 = 1$ is a feasible solution. The corresponding value of the objective function is $U = 35$, which is now a feasible upper bound on the minimum value of the objective function. Since setting $x_1 = 1$ gave an infeasible solution, there is no need to investigate it further since it would involve adding still more to the objective function and would surely exceed the already attained upper bound of $U = 35$. We must still backtrack and try the second-

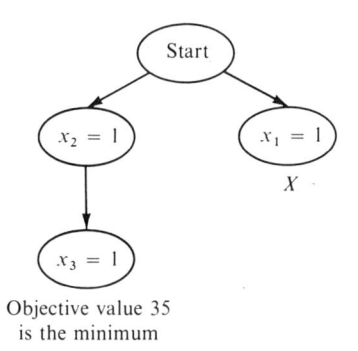

Objective value 35
is the minimum

FIGURE 5.5.4

best initial choice of a 1, namely $x_1 = 1$. This gives $d_1 = 0$, $d_2 = -3$, and $d_3 = 12$, so we must try to satisfy the last constraint. But the only variable that can help satisfy this constraint is x_2 and we have already tried that combination. Hence no further search is needed and the minimum feasible solution is $x_2 = x_3 = 1$ with objective value 35.

Clearly each step in this search process is elementary since it involves only additions and comparisons. However, the tree of possible nodes increases exponentially with the number of variables, and hence the difficulty increases accordingly. The more constraints there are, the less the search since additional constraints tend to eliminate the requirement for search down certain branches of the tree.

C. *The Stopped Simplex Method* (Thompson). The stopped simplex method is designed to solve arbitrary integer programming problems in minimizing form. It uses the ordinary simplex method as a basic subroutine to find lower bounds of individual variables. Again, the method is too detailed to describe completely, but we illustrate it with an example.

Consider the problem below.

$$\text{Min } y$$

Subject to:

$$7x + y \geq 13$$
$$-13x + 2y \geq -17$$
$$x, y \geq 0 \text{ and integer}$$

Figure 5.5.5 shows the convex set of feasible vectors (shaded) and the feasible integer

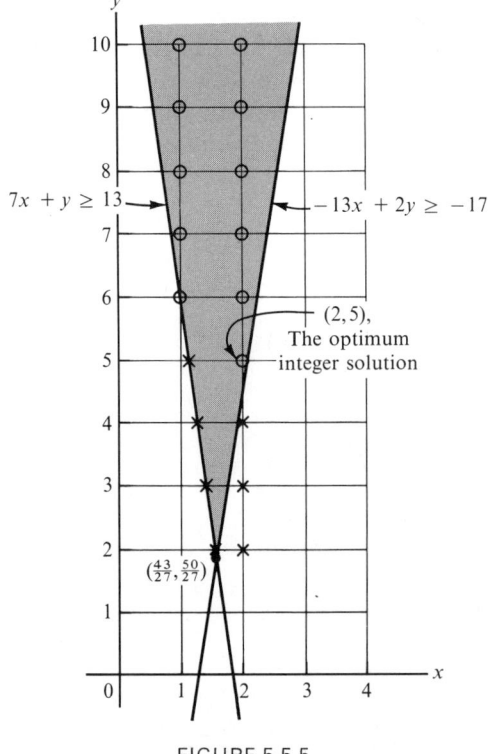

FIGURE 5.5.5

points (circled). The stopped simplex method first solves the problem as an ordinary linear programming problem and obtains the point (43/27, 50/27) as the answer. Since the coefficients of the objective function are integer, it follows that at the optimum the value of the objective function (which is just y in this case) must also be integer. Hence the stopped simplex method rounds the value of y up to its next integer value, which is 2. Then holding y fixed (or stopped) at 2, it finds the smallest value of x that is feasible, and this turns out to be the intersection of the line $y = 2$ with the constraint line $7x + y = 13$; this gives $x = 1\frac{1}{7}$. Since this is not an integer value for x, we round it up to the next possible integer value, namely, $x = 2$, and test to see if $x = 2$, $y = 2$ is feasible. It isn't, as can be seen from the Figure 5.5.5. Hence it follows that there are no feasible integer values of x when $y = 2$, since if there were—say a point $(x^*, 2)$—the coordinate x^* would have to be greater than 2. But then, by convexity, $x = 2$ would also be feasible, a contradiction. The next thing the stopped simplex method does is to increase y from 2 to 3, find the minimum value of x that is feasible, namely, $x = \frac{10}{7}$, round it up to 2 and test the point $(2, 3)$ for feasibility, which fails. Then y is increased to 4, the minimum feasible value of x is found to be $\frac{9}{7}$, and the point $(2, 4)$ is found infeasible. On the next step, y is increased to 5, the minimum value of x is found as $\frac{8}{7}$, rounded up to 2, and the point $(2, 5)$ is tested and found to be feasible and hence the optimal integer solution to the problem. Figure 5.5.5 shows the points tested and found nonintegral or integral and infeasible marked with x's.

In order to show the full power of the stopped simplex method, a larger example is needed (see Exercise 7). This method, as any successful method, only implicitly examines most of the possible candidates for the optimum integer solution. It has been found reasonably successful for problems ranging up to about 100 variables.

In this section we have outlined three of the current approaches to integer programming. Careful testing and evaluation of these methods require large amounts of computer time. Research in the area of integer programming is going on very intensively and it should be presumed that considerable advances will be made in the near future. At the present moment, results are rather sketchy, and application of integer programming methods on a large scale awaits the development of reliable codes.

EXERCISES 5.5

1. Evaluate the following:
   (a) $[-.9] = ?$
   (b) $[-101.9] = ?$
   (c) $[2,000,001.9] = ?$
   (d) $[.00001] = ?$

2. For the constraint $2x_1 + 3x_2 = 11$, derive the fractional cuts obtained when it is divided by the following numbers.
   (a) $\frac{11}{10}$
   (b) $\frac{11}{8}$
   (c) p where $\frac{11}{10} \leq p \leq \frac{11}{9}$

3. Consider the constraint whose all-integer cuts are given by

$$\left[\frac{3}{p}\right] x + \left[\frac{5}{p}\right] y \leq \left[\frac{16}{p}\right].$$

Derive the all-integer constraint obtained when p is in the following ranges.

   (a) $\frac{16}{16} < p \leq \frac{16}{15}$
   (b) $\frac{16}{15} < p \leq \frac{16}{14}$
   (c) $\frac{16}{14} < p \leq \frac{16}{13}$
   (d) $\frac{16}{13} < p \leq \frac{16}{12}$
   (e) $\frac{16}{12} < p \leq \frac{16}{11}$

4. For a constraint of the form $ax \leq b$, show that there are only a finite number of different all-integer cuts that can be derived from it.

5. Show that an infinite number of fractional cuts can be derived from a single constraint.

6. Use the additive algorithm to solve the following 0–1 problem:

$$\text{Min } 12x_1 + 20x_2 + 17x_3 + 13x_4 + 15x_5$$

Subject to:

$$3x_1 + 8x_2 - 10x_3 - 5x_4 - 5x_5 \geq 3$$
$$4x_1 - 2x_2 + 15x_3 - 2x_4 + 6x_5 \geq 1$$
$$-8x_1 + 7x_2 - 5x_3 + 14x_4 - 2x_5 \geq 4$$
$$0 \leq x_i \leq 1 \quad i = 1, \ldots, 5 \text{ and each } x_i \text{ integer}$$

7. Use the stopped simplex method to solve the following integer programming problem:

$$\text{Min } x_3$$

Subject to:

$$5x_1 + 8x_2 - 7x_3 \geq -89$$
$$-6x_1 + 5x_2 + x_3 \geq 11$$
$$3x_1 - 5x_2 + 2x_3 \geq 29$$
$$x_1, x_2, x_3 \geq 0 \text{ and integer}$$

5.6   THE BRANCH-AND-BOUND METHOD

One of the most successful methods for solving combinatorial and integer programming problems that are not too large is the so-called "branch-and-bound" method due to Eastman, Little, Murty, Sweeney, and Karel (see the references at the end of the chapter). It is an example of implicit enumeration; that is, it is a technique for enumerating either directly or implicitly all possible feasible solutions. When it can be successfully applied, most of the enumeration is implicit. We illustrate it by the solution of a knapsack problem. Then we discuss the general technique.

EXAMPLE 5.6.1. Consider the knapsack problem whose data are given in Figure 5.6.1. Notice that there are six items that can be taken on the trip. Suppose

Item	Value	Weight	Value/Weight
1	70	30	2.33
2	61	27	2.26
3	54	25	2.16
4	40	20	2.00
5	31	18	1.725
6	25	15	1.667

FIGURE 5.6.1

that the maximum weight that can be carried is 65 pounds. What combination of items yields the most total value to the camper if he will take at most one of each item?

In Figure 5.6.2 we have drawn a diagram of the computation of the branch-and-bound solution of the problem. Each circle indicates a decision, and the descrip-

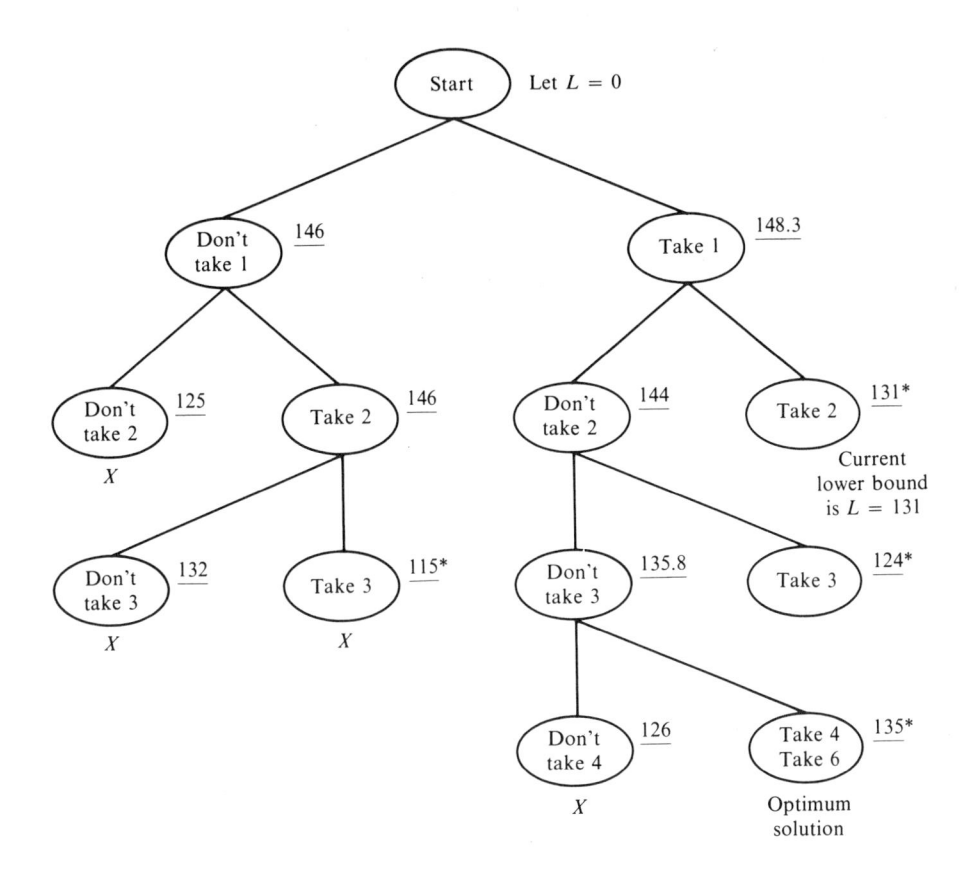

FIGURE 5.6.2

tion of the decision is given in the circle. Above and to the right of each decision is marked a number that is an upper bound to the maximum value of the objective function if all the decisions on the unique path from the node marked Start in the tree diagram to the current node are made. Let us describe how these upper-bound calculations were made for the example. For instance, consider the decision "Take 1" immediately following Start. What is an upper bound for the optimum objective-function value given that we have definitely decided to take 1? The best we can do is to also take item 2, since it has the next highest value-to-weight ratio. If we do, we will have loaded up the knapsack with $30 + 27 = 57$ pounds, leaving 8 pounds more. Now suppose we permit, *for the purposes of the upper-bound calculation only*, taking a fraction of item 3. In other words, we add $(8/25)54 = 17.3$ more units to the objective function, making $70 + 61 + 17.3 = 148.3$ in all. Although this is not a feasible solution, it gives a value to the objective function that is greater than or equal to the value that any feasible solution can possibly give, since it used the objects in the order of increasing value/weight ratio.

In order to illustrate the upper-bound calculation again, let us analyze the other decision immediately following Start—namely, the decision "Don't take 1." If we don't take 1, we could take items 2 and 3, which are the next most valuable, using up 52 of the available 65 pounds and leaving 13 unused. We again permit taking a fractional part of item 4 for the upper-bound calculation and add $(13/40)40 = 26$ to the objective function, making a total of $61 + 54 + 26 = 146$ as the upper bound for that decision.

You should check the other upper-bound numbers in the figure. You will find that sometimes, when there are only two or three items left, better lower bounds not permitting fractional decisions are used since it then becomes obvious that no further items on the list can be added. For instance, if we go down the tree from Start along the "Don't take 1, Don't take 2" branch, we see that the best that one can do is to take items 3, 4, and 5, giving a value of 125 and using up $25 + 20 + 18 = 63$ pounds. There is no point in adding a further fraction of item 6 since it cannot ever be included.

Notice also that certain endpoints in the tree are marked with an X. This indicates that the search farther down the tree can be stopped since there are no later decisions that can yield better solutions than the current feasible lower bound. Let us see how the current feasible lower bound L is calculated. At the beginning of the calculation we set $L = 0$, which is the value that can be obtained by making the decision not to take any items. Whenever we arrive at an endpoint in the tree of possible decisions that corresponds to a feasible knapsack combination, we increase the lower bound L to that feasible value if L is currently less than the feasible value; otherwise we leave L as it is. The reason that we do not need to go down a branch of the tree whose upper bound is less than or equal to the current lower bound is that there are no feasible solutions farther down that branch that can possibly be better than a feasible value already achieved. This is the *bounding* part of the branch-and-bound process. The *branching* part of the process is the obvious bifurcation of the tree each time we make a yes or no decision on taking of a given item.

The flow diagram for the general branch-and-bound calculation is given in Figure 5.6.3. Notice that it is necessary to arrange the decisions to be made in some order. In the knapsack problem above, the order was in decreasing value/weight ratio. But in other problems, some other order must be defined. The success of the method is dependent on the order in which the decisions are made, since it may result in either a fairly deep tree search or else a shallow search. The second thing that is needed for the branch-and-bound method is a way of calculating upper bounds. In the knapsack problem at hand, the method was simple. Take as many whole items in order of decreasing value/weight ratio as possible and then take a fractional part of the next one. In another problem, the upper-bound calculation would in general be quite different. A third point about the branch-and-bound method is the "search strategy," which is indicated in the first box we come to after Start in Figure 5.6.3. That is, given that we have investigated the consequences of one decision, how do we select the next decision to evaluate? There are two generally accepted techniques: one is to search all decisions at the same level (that is, at the same distance below Start) and the second is to search "in depth"—that is, go all the way down one branch until a feasible solution has been found. In most cases the search-in-depth method is the better one since obtaining a good value for L early in the computational process generally allows the elimination of large parts of the search tree, and hence the overall computation is cut down.

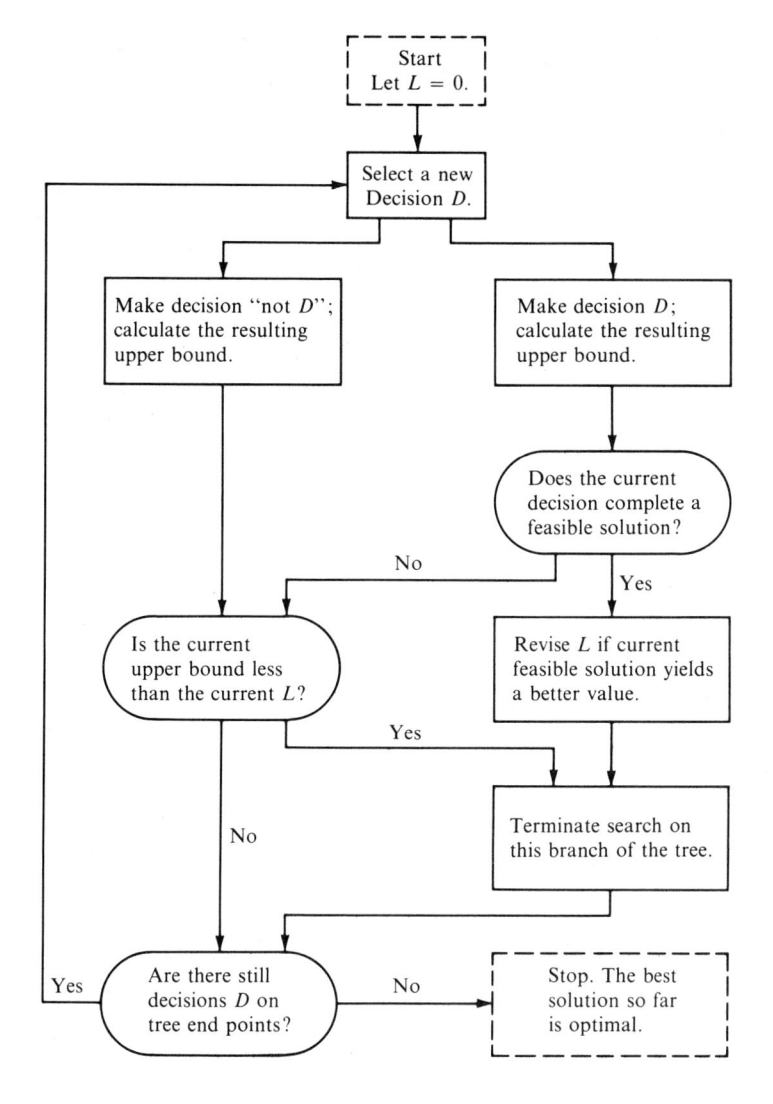

FIGURE 5.6.3. Flow diagram for solving a maximization problem using the branch-and-bound method

In the example above, there were 6 yes-no decisions. Hence the possible number of tree nodes that might have to be considered is $2^6 = 64$. Yet in Figure 5.6.2 we considered only 13 of them. This illustrates the value of implicit enumeration: it was not necessary to actually enumerate most of the possible decisions. The bounding process "cut away" most of the decision tree. It is this property that has made the branch-and-bound method useful in applications.

Among the problems to which the branch-and-bound method has successfully been applied are the job shop scheduling problem and the traveling salesman problem. Many other possibilities have been examined, and it is reasonable to predict that this method will have increasing application in the future.

EXERCISES 5.6

1. Solve Example 5.6.1 for each of the following totals for items in the knapsack.
   (a) 68 pounds
   (b) 72 pounds
   (c) 75 pounds

2. Rework Exercise 1 if more than one of each item can be taken.

3. Work the three-item knapsack problem given in Example 5.4.7 of Section 5.4.

4. Use the branch-and-bound method to find the optimum solution to the job shop scheduling problem in Example 5.4.8.

5. Use the branch-and-bound method to solve Exercise 14 of Section 5.4.

6. Use the branch-and-bound method to solve the five-city traveling salesman problem in Exercise 18 of Section 5.4.

7. Discuss how you would alter the flow diagram of Figure 5.6.3 to solve minimization problems instead of maximization problems.

8. Discuss how to use the branch-and-bound method to solve the following problems:
   (a) The fixed-charge problem of Section 5.4.
   (b) An integer programming problem with several either-or constraints.

SUGGESTED READING

Balas, E. An additive algorithm for solving linear programs with zero-one variables. *Operations Research*, 1965, **13**, 517–546.

Balinsky, M. L. Integer programming: Methods, uses, computation. *Management Science*, 1965, **12**, 253–313.

Church, A. *Introduction to Mathematical Logic*, Volume I. Princeton, N.J.: Princeton University Press, 1956.

Ford, L. R. Jr., and Fulkerson, D. R. *Flows in Networks*. Princeton, N.J.: Princeton University Press, 1962.

Gomory, R. E. An algorithm for integer solutions to linear programs. In R. L. Graves and P. Wolfe (Eds.), *Recent Advances in Mathematical Programming*. New York: McGraw-Hill, 1963.

Gomory, R. E. An all-integer integer programming algorithm. In J. F. Muth and G. L. Thompson (Eds.), *Industrial Scheduling*. Englewood Cliffs, N.J.: Prentice-Hall, 1963.

Little, J. D. C., Murty, K. G., Sweeney, D. W., and Karel, C. An algorithm for the traveling salesman problem. *Operations Research*, 1963, **11**, 972–989.

Orchard-Hays, W. *Advanced Linear-Programming Computing Techniques*. New York: McGraw-Hill, 1968.

Thompson, G. L. The stopped simplex method: I. Basic theory for mixed integer programming; integer programming. *Revue Francaise De Recherche Operationelle*, 1964, 159–182.

Thompson, G. L., Tonge, F. M., and Zionts, S. Techniques for removing nonbinding constraints and extraneous variables from linear programming problems. *Management Science*, 1966, **12**, 588–608.

CHAPTER 6

NONLINEAR PROGRAMMING PROBLEMS

6.1   UNCONSTRAINED OPTIMIZATION PROBLEMS

Many operations research problems can be solved by finding the maximum or minimum of a nonlinear function of one or more variables. We have seen ways of approximating such functions by means of linear functions and ways of solving them using linear techniques. However, very often it is better to solve them directly as nonlinear problems. In the present chapter we shall study methods for finding such solutions. The first section will treat unconstrained optimization problems, the second section, optimization problems subject to equality constraints, and the third section, optimization problems subject to inequality constraints.

In order to state the first definition, we recall the definitions of open neighborhood and open region of C_n. Let x and y be points in C_n; that is, x and y are n-component column vectors. The *distance* from x to y is

$$d(x, y) = [(x_1 - y_1)^2 + \cdots + (x_n - y_n)^2]^{1/2}.$$

By an *open neighborhood* of x, we mean the set of all y vectors N satisfying $d(x, y) < \varepsilon$ for some number $\varepsilon < 0$; that is, the open neighborhood consists of all points in the *interior* of an n-sphere with x as its center. Then, finally, an *open region* containing

x is a set of points R with x in R such that every point z in R is contained in an open neighborhood N with $N \subset R$. Obviously every open neighborhood is itself an open region.

DEFINITION 6.1.1. A function $f(x)$ for x in a subset S of C_n (the set of all n-component column vectors) has a *global maximum* at x^o in S if

$$f(x) \leq f(x^o) \qquad \text{for all } x \text{ in } S \subseteq C_n.$$

The function f has a *local maximum* at x^o if there exists an open region R containing x^o such that

$$f(x) \leq f(x^o) \qquad \text{for all } x \text{ in } R \subset S.$$

The function $f(x)$ has a local or global *minimum* at x^o if and only if the function $-f(x)$ has a similar kind of maximum at the same point.

Models for many situations arising in operations research and management science require the introduction of nonlinear functions. It is frequently reasonable to assume that these functions are differentiable, which allows us the use of calculus techniques for deriving an optimal solution. These techniques will be reviewed next.

Of course, there are many function descriptions that are not intrinsically smooth, or differentiable. Examples are discrete-valued functions described by a complicated computer program or as the set of outcomes of a series of experiments. We shall later discuss the optimization of discrete-valued nonlinear functions.

We begin with functions of a single variable.

THEOREM 6.1.1. Let $f(x)$ be a function of a single variable that has derivatives of all orders for all x in C_1. Then a necessary condition that f have a maximum or minimum at the point x^o in C_1 is that the lowest-order derivative of f that is not zero at x^o should be of even order. In formulas, we can state this as

$$f'(x^o) = 0, \qquad f''(x^o) = 0, \ldots, f^{(2k-1)}(x^o) = 0, \qquad f^{(2k)}(x^o) \neq 0, \qquad \text{for } k \geq 1.$$

Moreover, if $f^{(2k)}(x^o) < 0$, then x^o is a local maximum point, and if $f^{(2k)}(x^o) > 0$, then x^o is a local minimum point.

Proof: Using the assumptions above, we find the Taylor's series expansion in the neighborhood of x^o to be

$$f(x) - f(x^o) = \frac{f^{(2k)}(x^o)}{(2k)!}(x - x^o)^{2k} + \cdots.$$

Hence, in a very small neighborhood of x^o, the function behaves essentially the same as ax^{2k}, and the assertion is obvious for this function (see Exercise 1).

The effect of Theorem 6.1.1 is to transform the problem of finding the maximum or minimum of a function into the problem of finding points x^o such that $f'(x^o) = 0$. (More generally, if f fails to have a derivative at certain points, we will also have to find such points and test them for optimality. See Exercise 2.)

One method for finding the zero of a function that is the most reliable and easiest to program is the *binary search method,* which is stated in flow-diagram form in Figure 6.1.1. The two principal advantages of this method are that it works for any

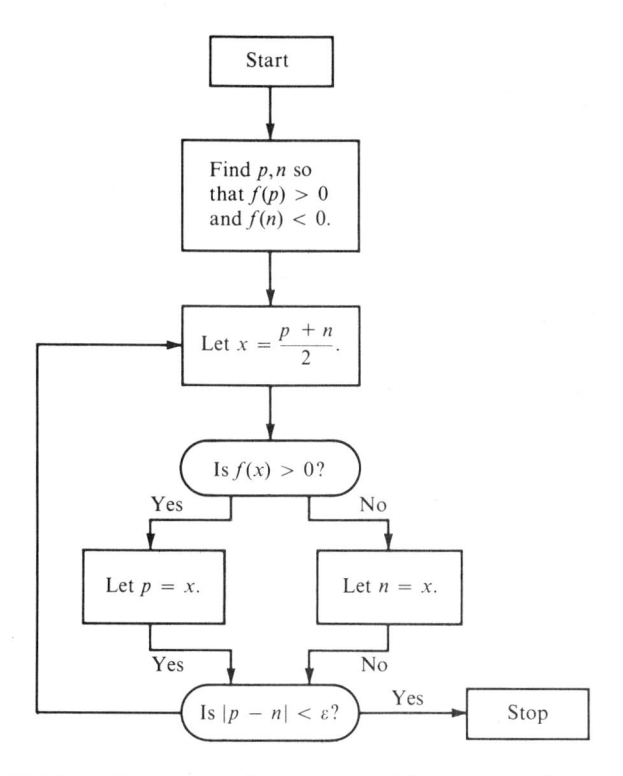

FIGURE 6.1.1. Flow diagram for binary search for the zero of $f(x)$; ε is the allowable error

function and that it converges rapidly. In fact, if we let k be the number of times the program goes around the main loop, it is easy to see that the error after k steps will be at most 2^{-k}. And since $2^{-10} \doteq .001$ and $2^{-20} \doteq .000001$, it follows that with just a few evaluations of the function we can get its zero very accurately (see Exercise 4).

EXAMPLE 6.1.1. Find a local maximum of the function

$$f(x) = x^3 - 6x^2 + 8x - 5.$$

It is easy to calculate

$$f'(x) = 3x^2 - 12x + 8,$$

and we must find a zero of the latter function. It is easy to see that $f'(0) = 8$ and $f'(1) = -1$, so we can choose $p = 0$ and $n = 1$. Suppose we choose the acceptable error to be $\varepsilon = .001$. Then Figure 6.1.2 shows the numerical computations that result from using the procedure in Figure 6.1.1. Notice that at the end of the computation we have achieved the desired degree of accuracy, with $x = .845$.

p	n	x	$f'(x)$
0	1	.5	2.75
.5	1	.75	.6875
.75	1	.875	$-.20312$
.75	.875	.8125	.23046
.8125	.875	.84375	.01074
.84375	.875	.85937	$-.09692$
.84375	.85937	.85156	$-.04327$
.84375	.85156	.84765	$-.01631$
.84375	.84765	.84570	$-.00279$
.84375	.84570	.84472	.00397
.84472	.84570	.84521	.00059

FIGURE 6.1.2

Of course, another way to find a zero of the quadratic function $3x^2 - 12x + 8$ is to use the quadratic formula. However, the use of this formula would involve a square root, which also needs to be done by either a table lookup or a computer program (see Exercise 5).

Since the second derivative is $f''(x) = 6x - 12$, it is clear that $f''(.845) < 0$ so that f has a local maximum at the argument $x = .845$, which solves the originally stated problem.

Although the binary search method is not too easy to do by hand, it is very fast using a computer and is one of the easiest methods to program. If you have a computer available, try it. It should also be observed that the binary search method works just as well for functions that are much more complicated than simple quadratic functions—even for functions defined implicitly. Examples of such are given in the exercises.

Next we shall discuss the so-called *golden section search method* for finding the maximum of a unimodal function—that is, a function that has a single maximum in a certain interval. This method does not make use of the derivative of the function and hence is applicable to the kinds of problems mentioned earlier in which the function is described as the outcome of a complicated computer program or else as the outcome of a very costly experiment. In such cases it may be either difficult or impossible to find the explicit form of the derivative of the function. It is for such problems that the golden section search method is especially valuable. A flow diagram of the method is shown in Figure 6.1.3.

The method makes use of the number

$$(6.1.1) \qquad\qquad r = \frac{\sqrt{5} - 1}{2} = .618034\ldots,$$

which has been called the golden section number, from which the method obtained its name. In order to see how this number enters the method, let us define L_k to be the *length of the interval of uncertainty* after k experiments—that is, after going around the main loop of the flow diagram in Figure 6.1.3 k times. In other words, L_k is the length of the interval in which the argument yielding the maximum of the function is known to lie after the procedure has been carried out k times. We shall see that the golden section search method has the property that $L_{k+1} = rL_k$ for each k.

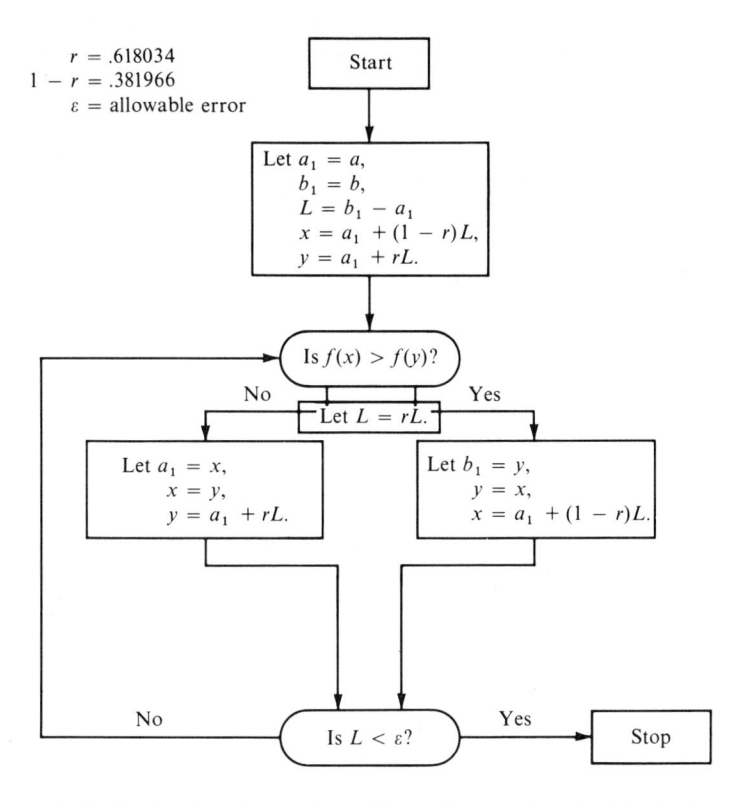

FIGURE 6.1.3. Flow diagram for golden section search method for finding the maximum of a unimodal function $f(x)$ on the interval (a, b)

In order to see how the method works, let us refer to Figures 6.1.4 and 6.1.5. In each figure it is assumed that the procedure has continued for a time and the current length of the interval is $L = b_1 - a_1$. Two intermediate points $x = a_1 + (1 - r)L$ and

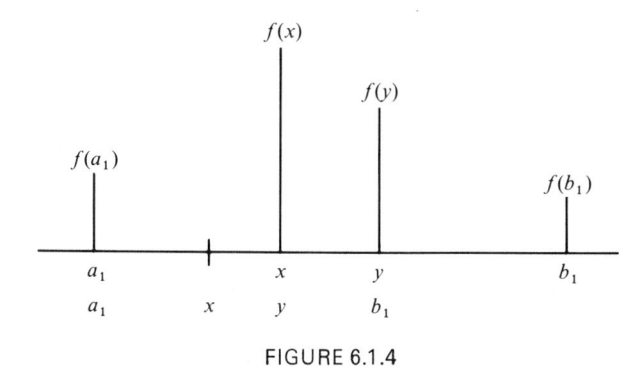

FIGURE 6.1.4

$y = a_1 + rL$ in the interval are chosen and the functional values $f(x)$ and $f(y)$ are computed. In Figure 6.1.4 it is assumed that $f(x) > f(y)$, and in Figure 6.1.5 the opposite inequality is assumed, $f(x) < f(y)$. In each figure, on the line below the interval the values of the next interval are marked. The explanation of how the new values for

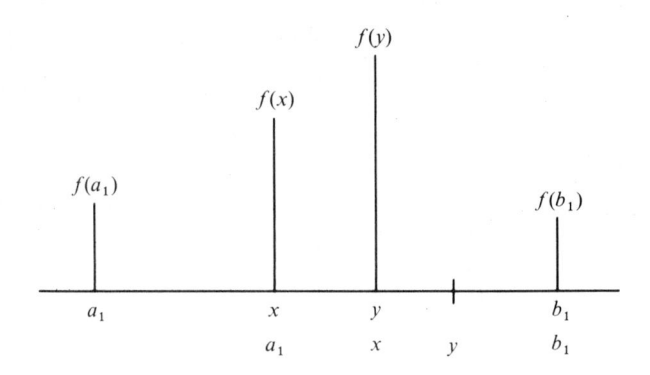

FIGURE 6.1.5

a_1, x, y, and b_1 are chosen in each case is given in the flow diagram of Figure 6.1.3. Note that in either case the length of the next interval of uncertainty is r times the old one.

EXAMPLE 6.1.2. In order to see how the method works, let us apply it to the problem of finding the maximum of the function $f(x) = x - x^2$. It is easy to see that $f'(x) = 1 - 2x$ so that the maximum is at the point $x = .5$. But applying the golden section search method results in the series of choices of a_1, x, y, and b_1 shown in Figure 6.1.6. In order to help in following the method, the values of $f(x)$ and $f(y)$

a_1	x	y	b_1	$f(x)$	$f(y)$
.00000	.38196	.61803	1.00000	.23606	.23606
.38196	.61803	.76393	1.00000	.23606	.18034
.38196	.52786	.61803	.76393	.24922	.23606
.38196	.47213	.52786	.61803	.24922	.24922
.47213	.52786	.56230	.61803	.24922	.24611
.47213	.50657	.52786	.56230	.24995	.24922
.47213	.49342	.50657	.52786	.24995	.24995
.49342	.50657	.51470	.52786	.24995	.24978
.49342	.50155	.50657	.51470	.24999	.24995
.49342	.49844	.50155	.50657	.24999	.24999
.49844	.50155	.50347	.50657	.24999	.24988
.49844	.50036	.50155	.50347	.25000	.24999
.49844	.49963	.50036	.50155	.25000	.25000
.49963	.50036	.50082	.50155	.25000	.24999
.49963	.50008	.50036	.50082	.25000	.25000

FIGURE 6.1.6

are also shown. You should follow this computation using the flow diagram of Figure 6.1.3. Notice that the computation stopped when the interval of uncertainty was about .001. Notice also that the optimum function value of .25 was approached very early in the computation, but that the extra work was necessary in order to find the value of the argument accurately.

It is interesting to compute the possible lengths of the interval of uncertainty as a function of the number of times the computation process goes around the main loop of Figure 6.1.3. It is easy to see that if $L = 1$ initially, then $L = r^k$ after k times around the main loop. Figure 6.1.7 gives the values of k and r^k for $k = 1, \ldots, 22$.

k	r^k
1	.61803
2	.38196
3	.23606
4	.14589
5	.09070
6	.05573
7	.03444
8	.02129
9	.01316
10	.00813
11	.00503
12	.00311
13	.00192
14	.00119
15	.00073
16	.00045
17	.00028
18	.00017
19	.00011
20	.00007
21	.00004
22	.00002

FIGURE 6.1.7

You may have wondered why r was chosen as it was. The explanation is given in Exercise 12.

You may also wonder how it is possible to tell when a function has a unique maximum or unique minimum point. As we shall see, a sufficient condition that f have a unique maximum is that it be a concave function. We define this concept next.

DEFINITION 6.1.2. A function $f(x)$ with x in C_n is *strictly convex* in a convex region $R \subset C_n$ if, for x, y any two points in R and t any number satisfying $0 \leq t \leq 1$,

$$(6.1.2) \qquad f(tx + (1 - t)y) < tf(x) + (1 - t)f(y).$$

The function f is merely *convex* in this region if the $<$ sign in (6.1.2) is replaced by $\leq$.

Similarly, $f(x)$ is *strictly concave* in R if, for x, y, and t as before, we have

$$(6.1.3) \qquad f(tx + (1 - t)y) > tf(x) + (1 - t)f(y).$$

And it is *concave* if the $>$ sign is replaced by $\geq$.

Intuitively speaking, a convex function is a function whose graph lies below its chord, as in Figure 6.1.8, whereas a concave function is a function whose graph always lies above its chord, as in Figure 6.1.9.

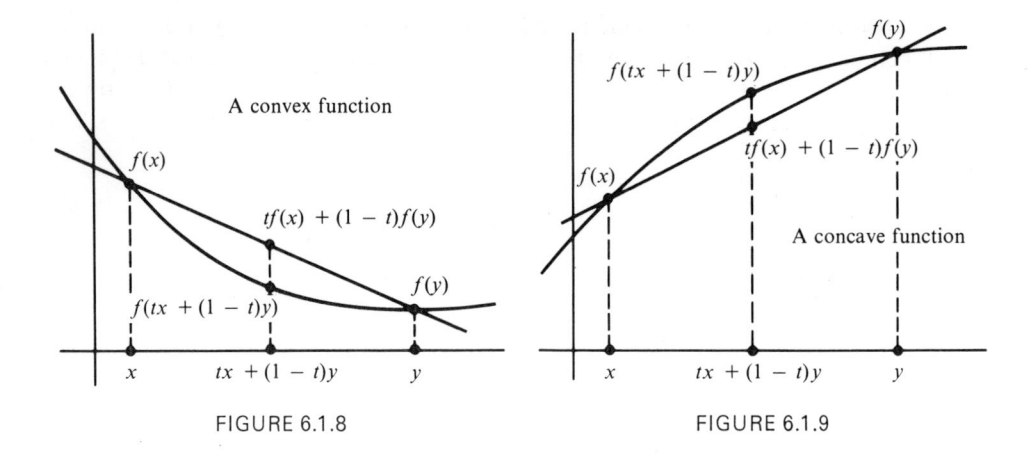

FIGURE 6.1.8

FIGURE 6.1.9

You may recall from elementary calculus that the second derivative $f''(x)$ of a function may be used to determine the regions of convexity and concavity of a function of one variable, as the following theorem indicates.

THEOREM 6.1.2. Let $f(x)$ be a function of one variable defined on an interval (a, b) and having a continuous second derivative on that interval.

(a) The function $f(x)$ is strictly convex on (a, b) if $f''(x) > 0$ for all x in (a, b); it is merely convex in the interval if $f''(x) \geq 0$.

(b) Similarly, $f(x)$ is strictly concave in (a, b) if $f''(x) < 0$ for all x in (a, b); it is concave in the same interval if $f''(x) \leq 0$.

COROLLARY. A linear function $f(x) = cx + d$ is both convex and concave on any interval.

This follows immediately from the theorem since $f''(x) = 0$ when $f(x) = cx + d$.

One of the most interesting properties of convex and concave functions is that they have unique minimum and maximum values, respectively.

THEOREM 6.1.3. Let $f(x)$ for x in C_n be defined in a convex region R of C_n.

(a) If f is a convex function on R, then it has a unique minimum value m. The set $S = \{x \mid f(x) = m\}$ is a closed convex subset of R. If f is strictly convex, then S consists of a unique point.

(b) If f is a concave function on R, then it has a unique maximum value M. The set $S = \{x \mid f(x) = M\}$ is a closed convex subset of R. If f is strictly concave, then S consists of a unique point.

EXAMPLE 6.1.3. Consider the function

$$f(x) = x^3 + x^2 - 6x.$$

It is easy to show that

$$f''(x) = 6x + 2$$

so that $f(x)$ is concave on the interval $(-\infty, 1/3)$ and convex on the interval $(1/3, \infty)$. Hence f has a unique maximum in the first interval and a unique minimum in the second interval. The graph of the function is indicated in Figure 6.1.10.

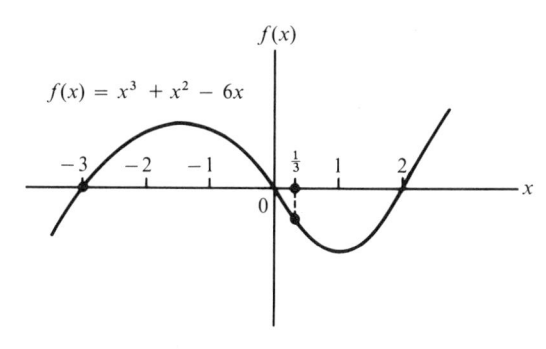

FIGURE 6.1.10

Convex and concave functions have many other properties, some of which are indicated in Exercises 16–18.

We conclude this section by discussing sufficient conditions for a function of n variables to have a maximum or minimum at a certain point x^o in C_n. The situation is considerably more complicated than that of a single variable, so we shall not be as complete as in the earlier case.

Let $f(x_1, \ldots, x_n) = f(x)$ be a function of n variables. Let us denote by f_i the partial derivative of f with respect to x_i. Also denote by f_{ij} the mixed partial of f with respect to x_i and x_j.

THEOREM 6.1.4. Let $f(x_1, x_2, x_3) = f(x)$ have continuous mixed second partial derivatives of all kinds; then sufficient conditions that $x^o = (x_1{}^o, x_2{}^o, x_3{}^o)$ should be a minimum (relative) of f are

(a) $f_1(x^o) = f_2(x^o) = f_3(x^o) = 0$;

(b) $f_{11} > 0$, $\begin{vmatrix} f_{11} & f_{12} \\ f_{21} & f_{22} \end{vmatrix} > 0$, $\begin{vmatrix} f_{11} & f_{12} & f_{13} \\ f_{21} & f_{22} & f_{23} \\ f_{31} & f_{32} & f_{33} \end{vmatrix} > 0$,

at the point x^o. Moreover, sufficient conditions that x^o should be a relative maximum at x^o are obtained by changing the first and third $>$ signs in (b) into $<$ signs.

The notation $|\ \ |$ means the determinant of the matrix. The definition of 2×2 and 3×3 determinants is as follows:

$$\begin{vmatrix} a_{11} & a_{12} \\ a_{21} & a_{22} \end{vmatrix} = a_{11}a_{22} - a_{12}a_{21};$$

$$\begin{vmatrix} a_{11} & a_{12} & a_{13} \\ a_{21} & a_{22} & a_{23} \\ a_{31} & a_{32} & a_{33} \end{vmatrix} = a_{11}a_{22}a_{33} + a_{12}a_{23}a_{31} + a_{13}a_{32}a_{21} - a_{31}a_{13}a_{22} \\ - a_{21}a_{12}a_{33} - a_{11}a_{23}a_{32}.$$

The extension of Theorem 6.1.4 to functions of n variables is straightforward but involves the determinant of $n \times n$ matrices (see the references to advanced calculus books in the suggested readings at the end of the chapter).

EXAMPLE 6.1.4. Consider the function

$$f(x_1, x_2, x_3) = (13/2)x_1{}^2 + x_2{}^2 + 5x_3{}^2 - 2x_1x_2 - 10x_1x_3 + 3x_2x_3.$$

Calculating the first partial derivatives, we have

$$f_1 = 13x_1 - 2x_2 - 10x_3;$$
$$f_2 = -2x_1 + 2x_2 + 3x_3;$$
$$f_3 = -10x_1 + 3x_2 + 10x_3.$$

Clearly the only point at which all three first partial derivatives simultaneously vanish is $x^o = (0, 0, 0)$. Calculating the second mixed partials and evaluating them at this point give:

$$f_{11} = 13 > 0, \qquad \begin{vmatrix} f_{11} & f_{12} \\ f_{21} & f_{22} \end{vmatrix} = \begin{vmatrix} 13 & -2 \\ -2 & 2 \end{vmatrix} = 22 > 0,$$

$$\begin{vmatrix} f_{11} & f_{12} & f_{13} \\ f_{21} & f_{22} & f_{23} \\ f_{31} & f_{32} & f_{33} \end{vmatrix} = \begin{vmatrix} 13 & -2 & -10 \\ -2 & 2 & 3 \\ -10 & 3 & 10 \end{vmatrix} = 23 > 0,$$

so the point $(0, 0, 0)$ is, in fact, a local minimum point of the function f.

EXERCISES 6.1

1. (a) Show that the function ax^{2k}, for $k = 1, 2, \ldots$, has a local minimum at $x = 0$ if $a > 0$ and a local maximum if $a < 0$.
   (b) Show that the function $a(x - x^o)^{2k}$, for $k = 1, 2, \ldots$, has a local minimum at $x = x^o$ if $a > 0$ and a local maximum if $a < 0$.

2. Show that ax^{2k+1}, for $k = 0, 1, 2, \ldots$, has neither a local maximum nor a local minimum at $x = 0$.

3. Show that the function $f(x) = |x|$ has a local minimum at the point $x = 0$ even though the derivative is not defined there and hence cannot be zero.

4. Construct a table of 2^k, for $k = 0, 1, \ldots, 20$. Use this to calculate how many evaluations of the function are necessary in order to get a zero of f to within a desired degree of accuracy when using the binary search technique.

5. Find the zero of the function $3x^2 - 12x + 8$ that lies between 0 and 1 using the quadratic formula. Check it with Figure 6.1.2.

6. Find the other zero of $3x^2 - 12x + 8$ by both the binary search method and also the quadratic formula. Show that it is a relative minimum.

7. Use the binary search method to find a zero of the function $f(x) = e^{x/2} - 2$. Use a table of natural logarithms to verify your answer.

8. Use the binary search method to find a zero of the function $f(x) = e^{2x} - 2x$. In this case there is no way to get the explicit form of the answer.

9. The degree of a polynomial function is the highest exponent that has a nonzero coefficient. For instance, $-x^5 + 3x^2$ is of degree 5. Show that a polynomial of odd degree has no absolute maximum or minimum.

10. Show that a polynomial of even degree has either an absolute maximum or an absolute minimum, but not both.

11. Show that the number of relative maxima and minima of an nth-degree polynomial is at most $n - 1$.

12. (a) By examining Figures 6.1.4 and 6.1.5, show that for the interval that is discarded to be of the same length regardless of whether $f(x) > f(y)$ or $f(x) < f(y)$, it is necessary to choose $x = 1 - y$ and to choose y to satisfy the ratio condition

$$\frac{y}{1} = \frac{1 - y}{y}.$$

   (b) Show that the unique positive solution to this ratio is the golden section number in (6.1.1).

13. Use the golden section method to find the unique maximum of the unimodal function $-5x^2 + 11x + 10$.

14. Show that the function in Exercise 13 is concave.

15. Show that the function $f(x) = x^3 - 6x^2 + 8x - 5$ is convex for some x and concave for other x. (*Hint:* Take the second derivative.)

16. Show that the sum of two (or more) convex functions is also a convex function. Do the same for concave functions.

17. (a) If f is a concave function and $a > 0$, show that af is also concave.
    (b) If f is a concave function and $a < 0$, show that af is convex.
    (c) Construct the analogues of (a) and (b) for convex functions.

18. Show that the convex combination of two convex functions is also convex. Do the same for concave functions.

19. Show that e^{x^2} is convex over its entire range.

20. Show that a convex function must not have "jump" discontinuities. Do the same for concave functions.

21. Show that the minimum *value* of a convex function is unique. Show that the maximum *value* of a concave function is unique.

22. If a convex function takes on its maximum value at two distinct points, then it takes it on at infinitely many points. State the analogous result for concave functions.

23. Show that the set of all x such that $f(x) = \min_y f(y) = m$ is a convex set if f is a convex function. State and prove the analogous result for concave functions.

6.2   CONSTRAINED MAXIMIZATION PROBLEMS AND LAGRANGE MULTIPLIERS

Sometimes we meet problems that involve the optimization of a nonlinear function subject to one or more linear or nonlinear equality constraints. As a first guess one might think that the obvious way to solve such a problem is to use the equality constraints to eliminate variables from the function to be maximized, thus simplifying the problem. This is a good technique when it works, but it doesn't always work since it is not easy to predict which subset of variables can successfully be eliminated to yield the correct solution point. An example will help to clarify the point.

EXAMPLE 6.2.1. On the circle whose equation is

$$x^2 + y^2 = 4,$$

find the point that is closest to the point $(1, 0)$.

Let us try to minimize the square of the distance from the point $(1, 0)$ since this will also minimize the distance. Hence our problem is as follows.

$$\text{Min } f(x, y) = (x - 1)^2 + y^2$$

Subject to:

$$x^2 + y^2 = 4$$

As a first try, let us eliminate y by using the equation $y^2 = 4 - x^2$. Then the objective function is

$$u(x) = f(x, 4 - x^2) = (x - 1)^2 + 4 - x^2 = -2x + 5.$$

We try to maximize u by setting its derivative equal to zero, but we find that $u'(x) = -2$, which is never zero! Hence elimination of y was a bad thing to do. Actually, if we had eliminated x from the objective function, we would have succeeded in solving the problem (see Exercise 1).

Now that it has been shown that difficulties may arise with the straightforward elimination approach to the problem, let us outline a systematic approach that avoids such difficulties, namely the so-called *Lagrange multiplier method*. Consider the problem shown.

(6.2.1)   Optimize $f(x, y)$

Subject to:

(6.2.2) $g(x, y) = b$ or $g(x, y) - b = 0$

In order to solve this problem we set up the *Lagrangian function*,

(6.2.3) $$L(x, y, \lambda) = f(x, y) - \lambda(g(x, y) - b),$$

where λ is the *Lagrange multiplier*, which is an added variable interpreted as a kind of penalty cost for requiring that the constraint be met; another interpretation will be given later. Now take the partial derivatives of L with respect to the three variables, obtaining

(6.2.4)
$$\begin{aligned}
L_x &= f_x - \lambda g_x, \\
L_y &= f_y - \lambda g_y, \\
L_\lambda &= g(x, y) - b = 0.
\end{aligned}$$

Notice that the third constraint in (6.2.4) is just the original constraint (6.2.2). From the first two constraints of (6.2.4), we can solve to eliminate λ provided either g_x or g_y is nonzero at the points (x, y) characterized by (6.2.4). In any case, the system (6.2.4) is a set of three equations in three unknowns and will, in general, provide at least one set of solutions for the three variables, x, y, and λ. In order to determine which set of solutions corresponds to the problem that is to be solved, it is necessary to substitute each of these solutions back into the original function to see which optimizes it.

EXAMPLE 6.2.1 (continued). Let us apply the Lagrange multiplier technique to the problem stated above. The Lagrangian function is

(6.2.5) $$L(x, y, \lambda) = (x - 1)^2 + y^2 - \lambda(x^2 + y^2 - 4).$$

Taking partial derivatives and setting them to zero yields the equations

$$L_x = 2(x - 1) - 2\lambda x = 2(x(1 - \lambda) - 1) = 0,$$
$$L_y = 2y - 2y\lambda = 2y(1 - \lambda) = 0,$$
$$L_\lambda = x^2 + y^2 - 4 = 0.$$

From the second equation we get either $\lambda = 1$ or else $y = 0$. But if $\lambda = 1$, then the first equation gives $L_x(x, y, 1) = -2 \neq 0$, so it can never be satisfied. Hence we are forced to have $y = 0$. From the third equation we have either $x = 2$ or $x = -2$; and from the first equation we get correspondingly either $\lambda = 1/2$ or $\lambda = 3/2$. Figure 6.2.1

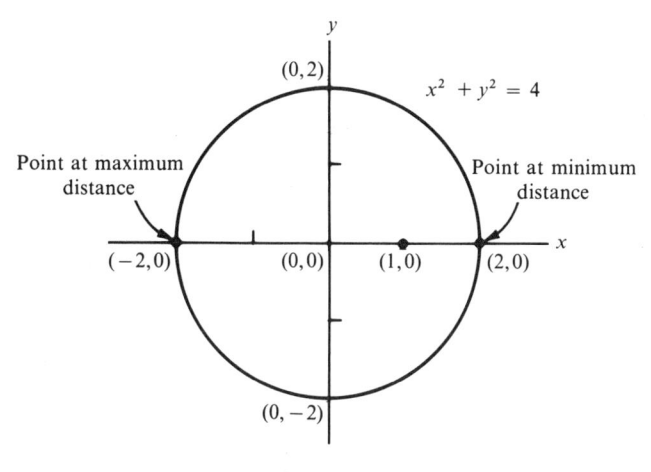

FIGURE 6.2.1

shows the circle and the point $(1, 0)$. From the figure it is obvious that the point $(2, 0)$ is the point on the circle *closest* to $(1, 0)$ and hence the point that solves the minimization problem. It is also obvious that the other point found, namely $(-2, 0)$, is the point on the circle *farthest* from $(1, 0)$ and hence the point that maximizes the distance. This emphasizes the fact that the Lagrange multiplier conditions give necessary but not sufficient conditions for the solution of the optimization problem. Further checking is necessary to see which among the points satisfying the necessary conditions gives the desired answer to the optimization problem at hand.

We state the Lagrange multiplier method as a theorem for the two-variable problem.

THEOREM 6.2.1. Let $f(x, y)$ and $g(x, y)$ have continuous first partial derivatives with respect to both variables, and assume that $g_x{}^2(x, y) + g_y{}^2(x, y) > 0$ for all (x, y) in a region R; that is, assume that at each point either $g_x \neq 0$ or $g_y \neq 0$.

(a) A necessary condition that the point (x, y) in R optimize $f(x, y)$ subject to the constraint $g(x, y) - b = 0$, where b is a number, is that there exists a number λ such that x, y, and λ solve the simultaneous equations

$$L_x = f_x(x, y) - \lambda g_x(x, y) = 0,$$
$$L_y = f_y(x, y) - \lambda g_y(x, y) = 0,$$
$$L_\lambda = g(x, y) - b = 0.$$

(b) The value of $\lambda = L_b(x, y)$ gives the instantaneous rate of change with respect to b of the optimum value of $f(x, y)$ at the optimum point.

In other words, the Lagrange multiplier λ is like a dual variable in linear programming. Its value gives the implicit value of additional resources; thus it measures the extent to which the constraint is restricting the objective function.

Proof: (a) Let $u = f(x, y)$ and suppose that $g_y \neq 0$ so that we can solve the constraint $g(x, y) = b$ for y in terms of x. From this it follows that $g_x + g_y(dy/dx) = 0$. Then we have

$$\frac{du}{dx} = f_x + f_y \frac{dy}{dx} = f_x - f_y \frac{g_x}{g_y} = 0,$$

which yields the necessary condition

$$\frac{f_x}{f_y} = \frac{g_x}{g_y},$$

and this is the same condition that is obtained by solving $L_x = 0$ and $L_y = 0$ simultaneously and eliminating λ from them.

(b) If we regard the constant b as a variable and take the partial derivative of the Lagrangian L with respect to b, we get $L_b = \lambda$. Thus λ can be interpreted as the rate of change of L with respect to b at the optimum point. But at the optimum point $L(x, y) = f(x, y)$ so that λ is also the rate of change of $f(x, y)$ with respect to small changes in the right-hand side of the constraint.

EXAMPLE 6.2.1 (continued). Let us regard the radius of the circle as b and replace the 4 in (6.2.5) by b^2. Then it is easy to calculate

$$L_b = 2\lambda b \quad \text{and} \quad \lambda = \frac{b - 1}{b}$$

so that

$$L_b = 2(b - 1).$$

Thus if, as in the original problem, $b > 1$, then increasing b increases the minimum distance from the point $(1, 0)$. But if $b < 1$, increasing b decreases the minimum distance. You should interpret these results geometrically in Figure 6.2.1. The analogous computations for the maximum point are given in Exercise 2.

Suppose now we have the more complicated problem shown below.

Optimize $f(x_1, \ldots, x_n)$

Subject to:

(6.2.6)
$$g_1(x_1, \ldots, x_n) = b_1$$
$$g_2(x_1, \ldots, x_n) = b_2$$
$$\cdots$$
$$g_m(x_1, \ldots, x_n) = b_m$$

The solution by means of Lagrange multipliers is analogous to the problem solved above. First, set up the Lagrangian function

(6.2.7)
$$L(x, \lambda) = f - \sum_{i=1}^{m} \lambda_i(g_i - b_i),$$

where the $m \lambda_i$'s are the Lagrange multipliers. As before, we take the partial derivatives of (6.2.7) with respect to each of the n variables x_j, obtaining

(6.2.8)
$$\frac{\partial L}{\partial x_j} = \frac{\partial f}{\partial x_j} - \sum_{i=1}^{m} \lambda_i \frac{\partial g_i}{\partial x_j} = 0.$$

These n equations plus the original m constraints give $m + n$ equations for determining the $m + n$ variables x_j and λ_i. Again, under suitable assumptions too complicated to state here, it is possible to solve for these variables and thus find all points that satisfy the necessary conditions for being points that optimize the function subject to the constraints. The following example will clarify the discussion.

EXAMPLE 6.2.2. Find the points on the circle $u^2 + v^2 = 4$ and the line $x + y = 8$ that are closest to each other. The graphs of these two functions are shown in Figure 6.2.2. First we set up the Lagrangian function

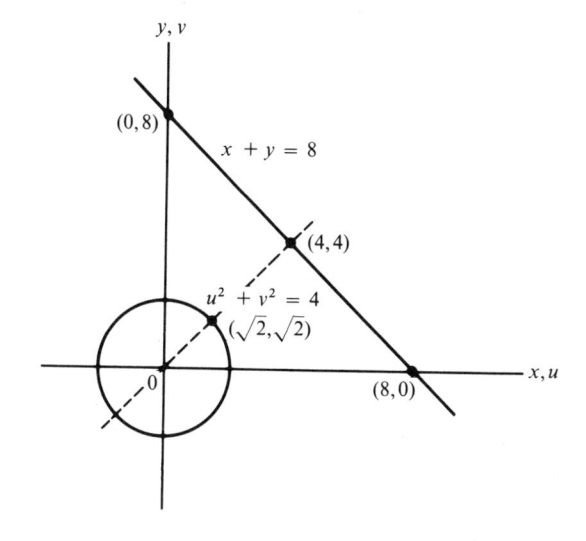

FIGURE 6.2.2

(6.2.9) $L = (u - x)^2 + (v - y)^2 - \lambda(u^2 + v^2 - 4) - \mu(x + y - 8).$

The first two terms give the square of the distance between a point (u, v) on the circle and a point (x, y) on the line (this distance is the function to be minimized). The third and fourth terms are the negatives of the Lagrange multipliers times each of the constraints. The partial derivatives are

(6.2.10) $L_x = -2(u - x) - \mu = 0,$

(6.2.11) $L_y = -2(v - y) - \mu = 0,$

(6.2.12) $L_u = 2(u - x) - 2\lambda u = 0,$

(6.2.13) $L_v = 2(v - y) - 2\lambda v = 0.$

From (6.2.10) and (6.2.11) we obtain $u - x = v - y$; substituting this relation into (6.2.12) and (6.2.13), we get $u = v$, which in turn implies $x = y$. Hence, using the original constraints, we find the two points that are closest to each other are $(4, 4)$ on the line and $(\sqrt{2}, \sqrt{2})$ on the circle. It is also easy to see that $(4, 4)$ on the line and $(-\sqrt{2}, -\sqrt{2})$ are a pair of points that are neither closest nor farthest, since we can easily find points on the line that are arbitrarily far from points on the circle. This illustrates again that the Lagrange-multiplier conditions give necessary but not sufficient conditions that a point must satisfy in order to solve an optimization problem.

EXERCISES 6.2

1. In Example 6.2.1, use the constraint $x^2 + y^2 = 4$ to eliminate x from the objective function $f(x, y) = (x - 1)^2 + y^2$, and show that ordinary differentiation techniques are sufficient to find the optimum solution.

2. In Example 6.2.1, show that at the maximum point $x = -b$, $\lambda = (1 + b)/b$ and $L_b = 2(1 + b)$ so that if b is increased, the distance of the maximum point from $(1, 0)$ always increases regardless of whether $b < 1$ or $b > 1$.

3. Find the point on the parabola $y^2 = 4x$ that is closest to the point $(1, 0)$.

4. Find the points on the parabola $y^2 = x$ that are the closest to the point $(1, 0)$.

5. Find the points on $x^2 - y^2 = 4$ (a hyperbola) that are closest to the point $(0, 1)$.

6. Find the point on the parabola of Exercise 5 that is closest to the point $(1, 1)$. (*Hint:* Set up the expression for finding the numerical values of the coordinates of the point, but do not actually carry out the computation.)

7. Find the point on the line $v = u + 4$ that is closest to some point on the parabola $y^2 = 4x$.

8. Find a point (x, y) on the hyperbola whose equation is $x^2 - y^2 = 4$ and a point (u, v) on the line whose equation is $v = 4u$ such that the distance between (x, y) and (u, v) is minimized.

6.3 OPTIMIZATION WITH INEQUALITY CONSTRAINTS

In this section we will consider the problem of maximizing or minimizing a function subject to one or more inequality constraints. In this problem it is impossible to use an inequality constraint to eliminate a variable, which is what we did, implicitly or explicitly, in the preceding section. However, as we shall see, a quite similar approach works.

First of all let us observe that a constraint of the form $g(x) \le b$ can be reformulated as an equality constraint by adding y^2 to the left-hand side thus: $g(x) + y^2 = b$. Since $y^2 \ge 0$ for any value of y, we have that every solution to the inequality gives rise to a solution to the equality and vice versa.

It might seem with the trick above that we could simply change all inequalities to equalities and apply the methods of the preceding section. We can, but it also turns out that the results we get will involve additional conditions. An example will serve to introduce some of the difficulties.

EXAMPLE 6.3.1. Find the maximum of $f(x) = x^3$ subject to the inequality constraint $x \le 10$. (The answer to this problem is obviously at $x = 10$ since x^3 is a nondecreasing function; but let's proceed as if we didn't know the answer.) We change the inequality into the equality constraint $x + y^2 = 10$. Let us set up the Lagrangian function as in the previous section:

$$(6.3.1) \qquad L(x, y, \lambda) = x^3 - \lambda(x + y^2 - 10).$$

Taking partial derivatives with respect to each of the variables, we obtain:

$$(6.3.2) \qquad \begin{aligned} L_x &= 3x^2 - \lambda = 0, \\ L_y &= -2\lambda y = 0, \\ L_\lambda &= -(x + y^2 - 10) = 0. \end{aligned}$$

As usual, the last equation simply repeats the original constraint. The first equation is familiar from the preceding section, but the second equation, namely $-2\lambda y = 0$ or $\lambda y = 0$, is new. What it says is that either $\lambda = 0$ or else $y = 0$; and if $y = 0$, it follows that $x = 10$. Hence, the second constraint says: either $\lambda = 0$ or else $x = 10$. If $\lambda = 0$, then from the first constraint in (6.3.2) we get $x = 0$ and also $f(x) = f'(x) = 0$. But if $x = 10$, we have $f(x) = 1000$, which is clearly the maximum of the function.

The constraint $\lambda y = 0$ in the example above is an example of a Kuhn-Tucker constraint. Observe that when $\lambda = 0$, we also get $f'(x) = 0$, so the first point corresponds to an "interior" optimum and the other point, $x = 10$, is an "endpoint" optimum. To tell which solves the problem at hand, it is necessary to test each. We shall see later that the Kuhn-Tucker constraints will pick out, as possible candidates for solving optimization problems, extreme points of constraint sets and also interior points at which the derivative(s) of the objective function vanish. We shall always state the optimization problem as a maximizing problem. For the minimizing case, all that is necessary is to maximize the negative of the objective function. The following theorem characterizes this result for the one-variable one-constraint case.

THEOREM 6.3.1. In order that x^o solve the problem

$$\text{Max } f(x)$$

Subject to:

$$g(x) \le b,$$

the following necessary conditions must hold.

(a) $f'(x^o) - \lambda g'(x^o) = 0$.
(b) One of the following two statements must hold:
   (i) Either $\lambda = 0$ and $g(x^o) \leq b$ (interior-point optimization);
   (ii) Or $\lambda \geq 0$ and $g(x^o) = b$ (boundary-point optimization).

Proof: Replace the constraint by $g(x) + y^2 = b$ and form the Lagrangian function

$$L(x, y, \lambda) = f(x) - \lambda(g(x) + y^2 - b).$$

Taking partial derivatives with respect to x and y, we get

$$L_x = f'(x) - \lambda g'(x) = 0,$$
$$L_y = -2\lambda y = 0.$$

(We omit the partial with respect to λ since it will simply repeat the original constraint.) The first constraint gives condition (a). From the second constraint we get $\lambda y = 0$. If $\lambda = 0$, we obtain (b)(i) as a necessary condition; and if $y = 0$, we obtain (b)(ii), except for the fact that $\lambda \geq 0$. To prove this, observe that $L_b = \lambda$. Since increasing b relaxes the constraint $g(x) \leq b$, it follows that $L_b \geq 0$ and hence $\lambda \geq 0$.

EXAMPLE 6.3.2. Find the maximum value of $f(x) = -(x - 5)^2$ subject to $x \leq 10$. We set up the Lagrangian function

$$L(x, y, \lambda) = -(x - 5)^2 - \lambda(x + y^2 - 10),$$

and take partial derivatives with respect to x and y:

$$L_x = -2(x - 5) - \lambda = 0,$$
$$L_y = -2\lambda y = 0.$$

From the second equation we get $\lambda y = 0$. If $y = 0$ we have $x = 10$ and $f(10) = -25$. And if $\lambda = 0$, we get $x = 5$ and $f(5) = 0$. Note that in the latter case, we also have $f'(5) = 0$. Since the second interior maximum is the largest, the optimum value of $f(x)$ is taken on when $x = 5$. Note that at the optimum, $\lambda = 2(x - 5) = 0$, which means that the constraint is not binding. If the constraint were $x \leq 3$, then the same kind of analysis shows that the maximum occurs when $x = 3$.

Naturally the analysis given above can be extended to more than one variable and to more than one constraint. We proceed to that case.

In the discussion that follows, we shall let x be an n-dimensional column vector and f and g_i, for $i = 1, \ldots, m$, be functions of x that have continuous first partial derivatives with respect to each of the variables x_j, for $j = 1, \ldots, n$.

(6.3.3) Max $f(x)$

Subject to the constraints:

(6.3.4) $g_i(x) \leq b_i$ for $i = 1, \ldots, m,$

where b_i is a number. As usual we add slack variables $y_i{}^2$ to the constraints (6.3.4) and form the Lagrangian

$$(6.3.5) \qquad L(x, y, \lambda) = f(x) - \sum_{i=1}^{m} \lambda_i(g_i(x) + y_i{}^2 - b_i),$$

where λ_i is the Lagrange multiplier associated with the ith constraint in (6.3.4).

Before we can state and prove the next theorem, we need the definition of what is called the constraint qualification. The need for this qualification will become evident in the proof of the theorem and in the exercises.

DEFINITION 6.3.1. Let R be the set of all vectors x that satisfy the constraints (6.3.4). Then the constraints (6.3.4) are said to satisfy the *constraint qualification* if, for every x in R, it is possible to solve the equations

$$(6.3.6) \qquad \frac{\partial L}{\partial x_j} = 0, \qquad \text{for } j = 1, \ldots, n, \quad \text{and} \quad \frac{\partial L}{\partial y_i} = 0, \qquad \text{for } i = 1, \ldots, m,$$

for nonnegative values of the Lagrange multipliers—that is, for $\lambda_i \geq 0$ and arbitrary values of the y_i's. In (6.3.6), the partial derivatives are to be evaluated at the point x in R.

THEOREM 6.3.2. If the constraints (6.3.4) satisfy the constraint qualification, then in order that the point x^o solve the maximization problem (6.3.3) subject to these constraints, the following necessary conditions must hold.

(a)   The following equations must be true:

$$(6.3.7) \qquad \frac{\partial L}{\partial x_j} = \frac{\partial f}{\partial x_j} - \sum_{i=1}^{m} \lambda_i \frac{\partial g_i}{\partial x_j} = 0 \qquad \text{for } j = 1, \ldots, n;$$

(b)   For each $i = 1, \ldots, m$, one of the following two statements must hold:

(i)   Either $\lambda_i \geq 0$ and $g_i = b_i$;
(ii) Or $\lambda_i = 0$ and $g_i \leq b_i$.

Proof: Taking the partial derivative of (6.3.5) with respect to x_j yields the necessary conditions (6.3.7). The partial of (6.3.5) with respect to y_i gives $\lambda_i y_i = 0$, from which, using the constraint qualification, we obtain the necessary conditions (b). The reason that λ_i must be ≥ 0 is the same as in Theorem 6.3.1.

An example of a problem that does not satisfy the constraint qualification is given in Exercise 6.

Theorem 6.3.2 is called the Kuhn-Tucker Theorem after the two mathematicians who first proved it. It has become the cornerstone of subsequent work on nonlinear optimization problems.

EXAMPLE 6.3.3. Find all maxima and minima of the function $f(x) = (x - 10)^2$ subject to the constraints $x \leq 20$ and $x \geq 5$. Adding the slack variables y and z and the Lagrange multipliers λ and μ, we obtain for the Lagrangian

$$(6.3.8) \qquad L(x, y, z, \lambda, \mu) = (x - 10)^2 - \lambda(x + y^2 - 20) - \mu(-x + z^2 + 5).$$

Taking partial derivatives, we have

$$L_x = 2(x - 10) - \lambda + \mu = 0,$$
(6.3.9)
$$L_y = -2\lambda y = 0,$$
$$L_z = -2\mu z = 0.$$

Thus we must solve (6.3.9) subject to all the possible ways we can solve the two Kuhn-Tucker constraints $\lambda y = 0$ and $\mu z = 0$. The first possibility is $\lambda = \mu = 0$, which makes $x = 10$ from (6.3.9) and $f(10) = 0$. This turns out to be an absolute minimum point as can be seen in Figure 6.3.1. The second possibility is $\lambda = 0$, $z = 0$ so that $x = 5$ and

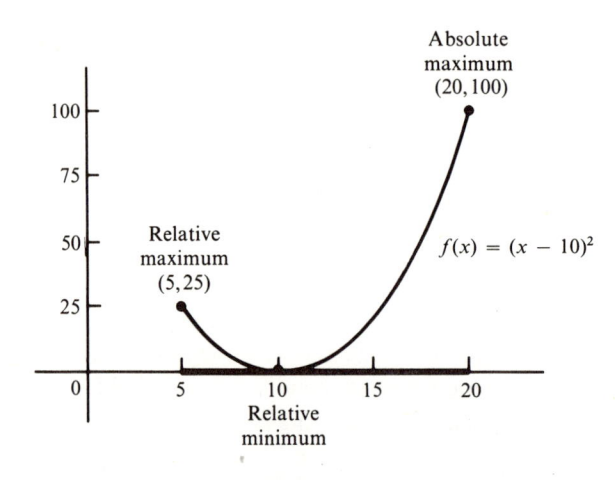

FIGURE 6.3.1

$f(5) = 25$; this is a local but not a global maximum in the interval. The third possibility is $\mu = 0$ and $y = 0$ so that $x = 20$ and $f(20) = 100$; this is the absolute maximum of the function in the interval. Finally, consider $y = z = 0$; clearly this is impossible since x cannot equal both 5 and 20.

This example clearly shows that the Kuhn-Tucker constraints pick out all the possible relative maxima and minima in the region under consideration, assuming, of course, that the constraint qualification holds.

EXAMPLE 6.3.4. Let us consider an example with nonnegativity constraints. Find the minimum of distance from the point $(8, 6)$ to the set of feasible points (x, y) determined by the constraints

$$x^2 + y^2 \le 25, \quad x \ge 0, \quad \text{and} \quad y \ge 0.$$

Clearly what we want to do is to

$$\text{Minimize } f(x) = (x - 8)^2 + (y - 6)^2$$

subject to those constraints. Introducing slack variables u, v, and w and multipliers λ, μ, and v, we write the Lagrangian function as

$$L(x, y, u, v, w, \lambda, \mu, v) = (x - 8)^2 + (y - 6)^2$$
$$- \lambda(x^2 + y^2 + u^2 - 25) - \mu(-x + v^2) - v(-y + w^2).$$

The partial derivatives with respect to x and y are

$$L_x = 2(x - 8) - 2\lambda x + \mu = 0,$$
$$L_y = 2(y - 6) - 2\lambda y + v = 0.$$

As we have seen in previous examples, the partials with respect to u, v, and w give Kuhn-Tucker constraints

$$\mu x = 0, \qquad vy = 0, \quad \text{and} \quad \lambda u = 0.$$

Since each of these products has two terms, there are in all eight different ways that the Kuhn-Tucker constraints can be satisfied! The graph of the constraint set is given in Figure 6.3.2 and will aid in sorting out the possibilities. Note that, geometrically,

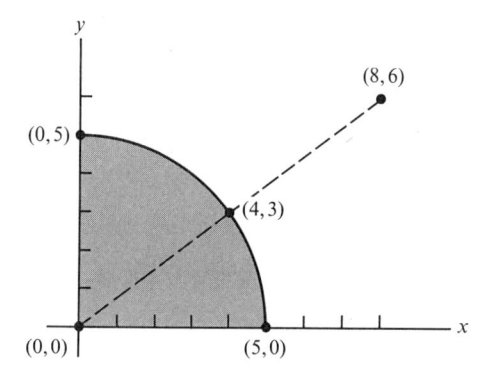

FIGURE 6.3.2

$x = 0$ means we are on the y-axis, $y = 0$ means we are on the x-axis, $u = 0$ means we are on the circle, and the various multipliers $= 0$ means that the corresponding constraints are satisfied as true inequalities. Let us first consider the case $\mu = v = u = 0$. Then from $L_x = 0$ and $L_y = 0$, we have $(1 - \lambda)x = 8$ and $(1 - \lambda)y = 6$, from which it follows that $y = 3x/4$. Solving this simultaneously with $x^2 + y^2 = 25$ gives the point $(4, 3)$ marked in Figure 6.3.2. Taking the other possible combinations of values that satisfy the Kuhn-Tucker constraints defines the other three "corner" points in the figure—namely, $(0, 0)$, $(5, 0)$, and $(0, 5)$. Of these four points, the closest is clearly $(4, 3)$, which is at distance 5 from the point $(8, 6)$, and the farthest is $(0, 0)$, which is at distance 10. The other two points $(5, 0)$ and $(0, 5)$ are at neither maximum nor minimum distance.

In Exercise 9, you will be asked to find other minimum distances to this constraint set. And in Exercise 10, you will be asked to find similar results for the constraint set with an additional constraint.

The examples above have the property that certain calculations, especially those involving the derivation of Kuhn-Tucker multipliers, are highly repetitive in nature. Let us therefore write rules for the derivation of these constraints.

Rule 1. For a constraint of the form $g(x) \le b$ whose multiplier is λ, the Kuhn-Tucker constraints are:

(6.3.10) $\lambda y = 0$ and $\lambda \ge 0$,

where y is the slack variable in the equivalent constraint $g(x) + y^2 - b = 0$.

Rule 2. For a constraint of the form $g(x) \ge b$ whose multiplier is λ, the Kuhn-Tucker constraints are:

(6.3.11) $\lambda y = 0$ and $\lambda \ge 0$,

where y is the slack variable in the equivalent constraint $-g(x) + y^2 + b = 0$. You will be asked to verify this rule in Exercise 11.

Rule 3. For a nonnegativity constraint of the form $x_j \ge 0$ with multiplier λ_j, the corresponding Kuhn-Tucker constraints are:

(6.3.12) $\lambda_j x_j = 0$ and $\lambda_j \le 0$.

In Exercise 12, you will be asked to derive this rule as a special case of Rule 2.

EXERCISES 6.3

1. Find the maximum of x^5 subject to $x \le 1$.

2. Find the minimum of $(x - 5)^5$ subject to $10 \le x$.

3. Find the maximum of e^{-x^2} subject to
   (a) $-1 \le x \le 1$;
   (b) $1 \le x \le 5$.

4. Find the maximum of $\sin x$ in the interval $-\pi/2 \le x \le 3\pi/2$.

5. Find the minimum of $\sin x$ in the same interval as in Exercise 4.

6. Show that the Kuhn-Tucker necessary conditions do not hold for the following problem:

   Max x

   Subject to:

   $$y \le (1 - x)^3$$
   $$x, y \ge 0$$

   Show that the constraint qualification does not hold for this example.

7. Find all maxima and minima of the function $f(x) = x^2(10 - x)$ in the interval $-10 \le x \le 10$.

8. Rework Exercise 7 for the interval $0 \le x \le 10$. Show that at $x = 0$, both $x = 0$ and a multiplier are zero simultaneously.

9. In Example 6.3.4 find the minimum distances from each of the following points to the constraint set.
   (a) $(-8, 6)$ (b) $(-1, -1)$ (c) $(10, 0)$

10. Consider the constraint set R defined by

    $$x^2 + y^2 \le 25, \qquad x^2 - y^2 \le 7, \qquad x \ge 0, \quad \text{and} \quad y \ge 0.$$

Find the maximum and minimum distances from each of the following points to R.
(a) (8, 6)   (b) (6, 8)   (c) (2, 0)

11. Derive Rule 2 from Rule 1 by appropriate changes. (*Hint:* Show that $L_b = -\lambda \leq 0$.)

12. Derive Rule 3 from Rule 2 by appropriate changes.

13. Find the minimum distance from (8, 4) to the constraint set defined by

$$x^2 + y^2 \leq 36, \qquad y^2 \leq 5x, \qquad x \geq 0.$$

*14. A quadratic programming problem is of the following form:

$$\text{Max} \sum_j c_j x_j - \frac{1}{2} \sum_i \sum_j q_{ij} x_i x_j$$

Subject to:

$$\sum_j a_{ij} x_j \leq b_i \qquad \text{for } i = 1, \ldots, m,$$

$$x_j \geq 0 \qquad \text{for } j = 1, \ldots, n$$

where $q_{ij} = q_{ji}$, for all i and j, and the matrix Q of these coefficients is such that the function to be maximized is concave. Define multipliers λ_i and slack variables y_i for the first constraint set and multipliers μ_j for the nonnegativity constraints.
(a) Set up the Lagrangian function.
(b) By taking the partial derivative with respect to x_j, derive the constraint

$$c_j - \sum_i q_{ij} x_i - \sum_i \lambda_i a_{ij} + \mu_j = 0 \qquad \text{for } i = 1, \ldots, m.$$

(c) Derive the Kuhn-Tucker constraints

$$\lambda_i y_i = 0, \qquad \lambda_i \geq 0 \qquad \text{for } i = 1, \ldots, m;$$

$$\mu_j x_j = 0, \qquad \mu_j \leq 0 \qquad \text{for } j = 1, \ldots, n.$$

(d) Show that, except for the constraints derived in (c), the resulting problem is an ordinary linear programming problem.

6.4 OTHER NONLINEAR PROGRAMMING METHODS

As in the case of integer programming, there is an intensive research effort being made to develop methods of solving nonlinear programming problems. It is impossible here to survey many of these, so we shall limit the discussion to just two. The first is the maximization of a separable concave function by means of piecewise linear approximations. The second is the SUMT (Sequential Unconstrained Minimization Technique) method of Fiacco and McCormick for solving nonlinear problems.

A. *Separable Concave Functions.* A function of n variables $f(x)$ is said to be separable if it can be written as

(6.4.1) $$f(x_1, \ldots, x_n) = f_1(x_1) + \cdots + f_n(x_n).$$

In other words, f can be written as a sum of n separate functions, each one of which is a function of a single variable. Suppose, in addition, that each f_j is a concave function of its argument x_j. Finally, suppose that we are trying to maximize the concave separable function f subject to linear inequality constraints; that is, the problem is as follows.

$$\text{Max } f(x)$$

(6.4.2)   Subject to:

$$Ax \le b$$

$$x \ge 0$$

We shall show that, using a piecewise linear approximation to each of the separate functions $f_j(x_j)$, we can write a linear programming problem whose solution will give an approximation to the solution of problem (6.4.2).

In Figure 6.4.1, we have drawn a concave function $f_j(x_j)$ together with a

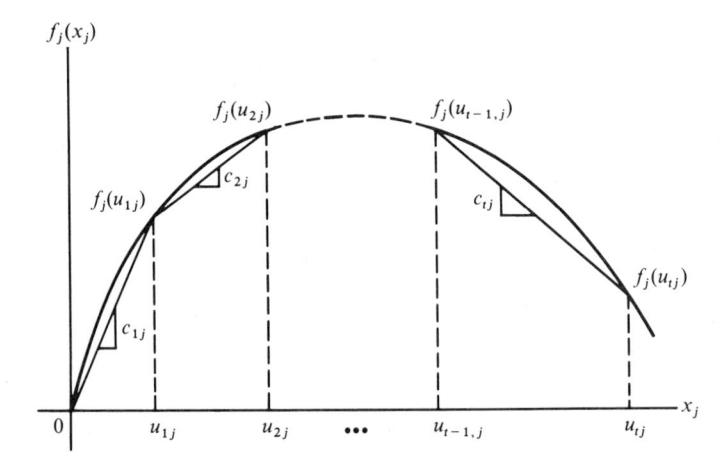

FIGURE 6.4.1

piecewise linear approximation with break points at the arguments x_j equal to u_{1j}, $u_{2j}, \ldots, u_{tj}$. The slopes of the line segments in the successive intervals are given by $c_{1j}, c_{2j}, \ldots, c_{tj}$. Notice that the piecewise linear approximation always underestimates the function f_j. Let us now define variables x_{kj} as follows:

(6.4.3) $$0 \le x_{kj} \le u_{kj} - u_{k-1,j},$$

where $u_{0,j} = 0$. From this it is clear that we can write any value x_j in the interval $0 \le x_j \le u_{tj}$ as a sum,

(6.4.4) $$x_j = x_{1j} + x_{2j} + \cdots + x_{tj},$$

since adding together all the t inequalities (6.4.3) shows that we achieve any value of x_j in that interval.

Suppose we now consider the problem of trying to maximize the concave function $f_j(x_j)$ in the interval $0 \le x_j \le b$. We define t break points,

(6.4.5) $$0 = u_{0j} < u_{1j} < u_{2j} < \cdots < u_{tj} = b,$$

and calculate the values of f_j at each point. From these we find the slopes of the piecewise linear segments as

(6.4.6) $$c_{kj} = \frac{[f_j(u_{kj}) - f_j(u_{k-1,j})]}{[u_{kj} - u_{k-1,j}]}.$$

Then, given a value of x_j, we write it as in (6.4.4) and approximate the value of $f_j(x_j)$ by

(6.4.7) $$f_j(x_j) \doteq c_{1j} x_{1j} + c_{2j} x_{2j} + \cdots + c_{tj} x_{tj}.$$

Note that in order for this approximation to work correctly, we need an additional condition on the x_{kj}'s; namely,

(6.4.8) $$\text{if } x_{kj} > 0 \quad \text{then} \quad x_{k-1,j} = u_{k-1,j}.$$

But this condition will be automatically satisfied! The reason is that the original function f_j is concave, so it follows from (6.4.5) that

$$c_{1j} > c_{2j} > \cdots > c_{tj};$$

that is, the slopes of the line segments used in the piecewise approximation are decreasing. Hence, since we are maximizing, it is optimal to use the largest values of x_{kj} fully before using any of $x_{k+1,j}$. In other words, the optimality criterion of the derived linear programming problem will automatically satisfy condition (6.4.8). This is not necessarily true for a function that is not concave, as we saw in Section 5.4. In that case, it was necessary to use an integer valued variable to force the condition to hold.

Let us now extend the analysis above for one function to the concave separable function $f(x)$ of (6.4.1). Suppose that we approximate $f_j(x_j)$ by a piecewise linear approximation having t break points, as in expressions (6.4.3) through (6.4.8). If we now want to solve the problem stated in (6.4.2), we substitute these results into those expressions and obtain the following equivalent linear programming problem that approximates the original concave problem:

$$\text{Max } f(x) \doteq \sum_{k=1}^{t} \sum_{j=1}^{n} c_{kj} x_{kj}$$

(6.4.9)   Subject to:

$$\sum_{j=1}^{n} a_{ij} \left(\sum_{k=1}^{t} x_{kj} \right) \le b_i \qquad \text{for} \qquad i = 1, \ldots, m$$

$$0 \le x_{kj} \le u_{kj} - u_{k-1,j} \qquad \begin{array}{ll} \text{for} & j = 1, \ldots, n \\ \text{and} & k = 1, \ldots, t \end{array}$$

The most important characteristic of this problem is the large number of variables: Problem (6.4.2) had n variables, whereas (6.4.9) has nt variables. And, of course, in order to get good approximations to the convex functions involved, it is desirable to have t large. One way around this difficulty is to adopt a multistage approach: first, solve a coarse approximation to the problem; then use the optimum solution to this coarse approximation to define a new refined approximation in the neighborhood of the optimum to the first problem, and so on. By this technique one can close in on the solution to the original nonlinear problem.

EXAMPLE 6.4.1. Consider the following problem.

$$\text{Max } 7\sqrt{x_1} + x_2(8 - x_2)$$

(6.4.10)   Subject to:

$$x_1 + x_2 \le 5/2$$
$$x_1, x_2 \ge 0$$

Here we have two functions, $f_1(x_1) = 7\sqrt{x_1}$ and $f_2(x_2) = x_2(8 - x_2)$, which are convex for all nonnegative arguments. The graphs of these two functions together with piecewise linear approximations with unit interval break points are shown in Figures 6.4.2 and 6.4.3. Using the procedure outlined above, we replace the two variable

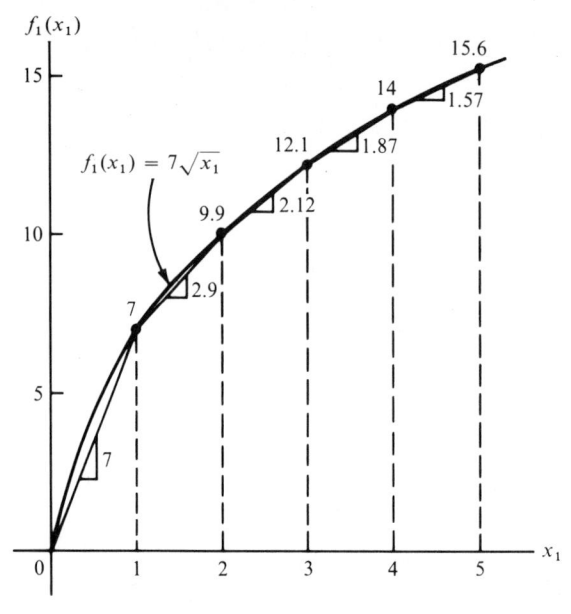

FIGURE 6.4.2

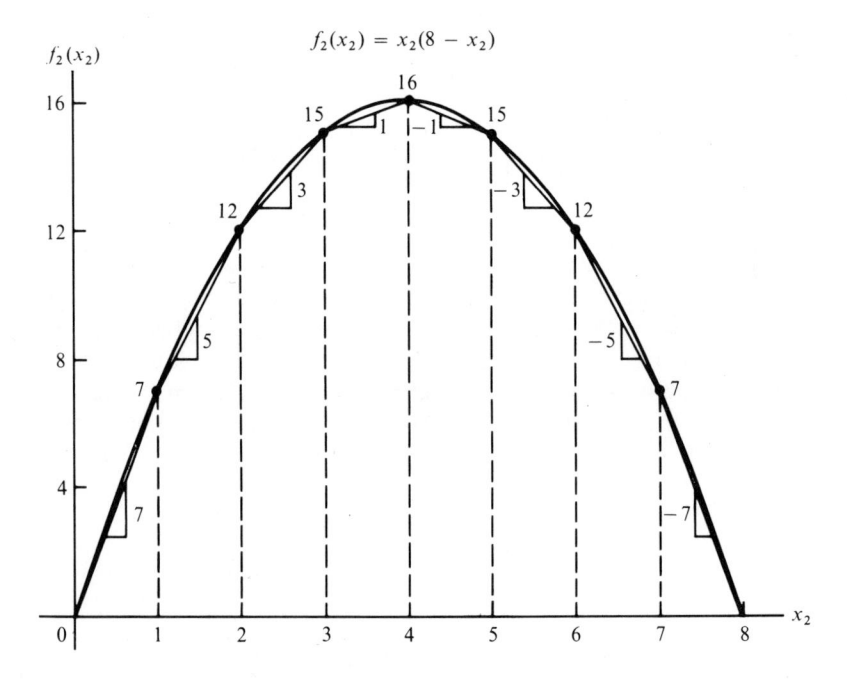

FIGURE 6.4.3

nonlinear problem given in (6.4.9) by the following ten-variable linear programming problem:

$$\text{Max } 7x_{11} + 2.9x_{21} + 2.2x_{31} + 1.87x_{41} + 1.57x_{51}$$
$$+ 7x_{12} + 5x_{22} + 3x_{32} + x_{42} - 3x_{52}$$

(6.4.11)   Subject to:

$$\sum_{j=1}^{2} \sum_{k=1}^{5} x_{kj} \leq 5/2$$

$$0 \leq x_{kj} \leq 1 \qquad \text{for} \qquad j = 1, 2; k = 1, \ldots, 5$$

The solution to this problem is obvious by inspection—namely, $x_{11} = x_{12} = x_{21} = x_{22} = x_{23} = 1$ and $x_{13} = 1/2$—since it obviously pays to take the x's with the highest coefficients first and to the maximum extent possible. Of course, the reason that the solution was so obvious was the very simple nature of the constraints. In more complicated problems, this would not be the case.

B. *The SUMT Method of Fiacco and McCormick.* As noted earlier, the letters SUMT stand for Sequential Unconstrained Minimization Technique. This technique can be applied to any constrained optimization problem. It works by first converting the constrained optimization problem into an unconstrained optimization problem by means of a technique different from anything we have so far discussed. To explain how the method works let us discuss the following problem.

$$\text{Min } f(x_1, \ldots, x_n)$$

(6.4.12)   Subject to:

$$g_i(x_1, \ldots, x_n) \geq 0 \qquad \text{for } i = 1, \ldots, m$$

The constraints are assumed to include any nonnegativity constraints that are present. What the SUMT method does is to replace the constrained minimization problem (6.4.12) by a series of parameterized unconstrained minimization problems depending on a parameter p. These problems are defined as

$$(6.4.13) \quad \text{Minimize } h(x_1, \ldots, x_n, p) = f(x_1, \ldots, x_n) - p \left[\sum_{i=1}^{m} \frac{1}{g_i(x_1, \ldots, x_n)} \right].$$

At first glance the function h defined by (6.4.13) seems very peculiar since the second summation term includes the reciprocals of the constraint functions g_i. Hence whenever the current trial point $(x_1, \ldots, x_n)$ becomes near to a boundary of the convex set of feasible vectors, the corresponding reciprocal of the constraint defining that boundary will "blow up." Hence in the search for the unconstrained minimum of (6.4.13), all boundary points that make some of the constraints in (6.4.12) hold as equalities will be avoided. However, what the method does is to vary p so that the effect of this blowup will decrease. In other words, we first solve the problem for a large p, then for a smaller p, and so on. Fiacco and McCormick have shown that the sequence of optimal solutions to this series of problems will converge to the optimal solution of (6.4.12). In practice, this method has met with considerable success, and currently it is one of the most popular methods available for solving nonlinear constrained optimization problems.

EXAMPLE 6.4.2. We will illustrate the setting up of a problem using the SUMT technique, but we will not show the steps of the numerical solution. Suppose the problem is:

$$\text{Minimize } (x_1 - 5)^2 + (x_2 - 7)^2$$

(6.4.14)   Subject to:

$$x_1^2 + x_2^2 \leq 4$$

$$x_1, x_2 \geq 0$$

You will recognize this as the problem of finding the shortest distance from the point $(5, 7)$ to the circle $x_1^2 + x_2^2 = 4$, as shown in Figure 6.4.4. The answer to the

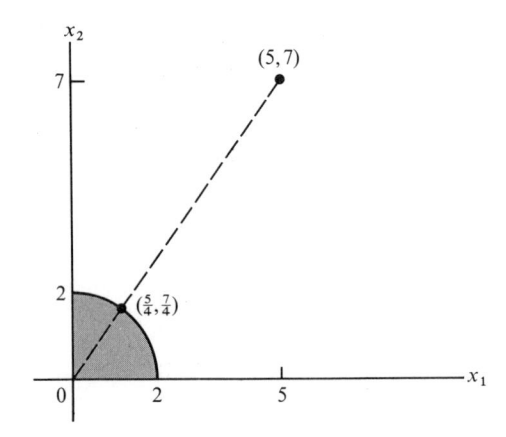

FIGURE 6.4.4

problem can easily be found by the techniques in Section 6.2 to be $(5/4, 7/4)$.

However, let us set it up for the SUMT technique. The corresponding h function of (6.4.14) is clearly

(6.4.15)

$$\text{Minimize } h(x_1, x_2, p) = (x_1 - 5)^2 + (x_2 - 7)^2 + p\left[\frac{1}{x_1} + \frac{1}{x_2} + \frac{1}{x_1^2 + x_2^2 - 4}\right].$$

This is clearly a fairly complicated function, and its derivatives are also complicated. For instance, we have

$$\frac{\partial h}{\partial x_1} = 2(x_1 - 5) + p\left[-\frac{1}{x_1^2} - \frac{2x_1}{(x_1^2 + x_2^2 - 4)^2}\right],$$

and there is a very similar expression for the partial derivative with respect to x_2. It follows that this method necessarily requires a computer for its use. We shall not go further into the details of the method, but instead we refer you to the bibliography at the end of the chapter for further details.

EXERCISES 6.4

1. Show that the method for finding the maximum of a separable concave function can be applied, with appropriate modifications, to the problem of finding the minimum of a separable convex function subject to constaints.

2. Use the piecewise approximation method to solve the following concave separable problem:

$$\text{Max } (x_1 + 2)(10 - x_1) + \left[20 - \frac{100}{x_2 + 10}\right]$$

   Subject to:

$$x_1 + x_2 \leq 6$$
$$x_1, x_2 \geq 0$$

3. Set up the problem in Example 6.4.1 for solution by the SUMT method.

4. Set up the problem in Exercise 2 for solution by the SUMT method.

SUGGESTED READING

Bracken, J., and McCormick, G. P. *Selected Applications of Nonlinear Programming.* New York: John Wiley, 1968.

Fiacco, A. V., and McCormick, G. P. *Nonlinear Programming, Sequential Unconstrainted Minimization Techniques.* New York: John Wiley, 1968.

Hadley, G. *Nonlinear and Dynamic Programming.* Reading, Mass.: Addison-Wesley, 1964.

Kuhn, H. W., and Tucker, A. W. Nonlinear Programming. In *Proceedings of the Second Berkeley Symposium on Mathematical Programming Statistics and Probability*, edited by J. Neyman, pp. 481–492. Berkeley, Calif.: University of California Press, 1950.

Mangasarian, O. L. *Nonlinear Programming.* New York: McGraw-Hill, 1969.

Wagner, H. M. *Principles of Operations Research with Applications to Managerial Decisions.* Englewood Cliffs, N.J.: Prentice-Hall, 1969.

Widder, D. V. *Advanced Calculus.* (2nd ed.) Englewood Cliffs, N.J.: Prentice-Hall, 1961.

Wilde, D. J. *Optimum Seeking Methods.* Englewood Cliffs, N.J.: Prentice-Hall, 1964.

Zangwill, W. I. *Non-Linear Programming—A Unified Approach.* Englewood Cliffs, N.J.: Prentice-Hall, 1969.

CHAPTER 7

PROBABILITY THEORY

7.1 INTRODUCTION

In probability theory, we consider a *set of outcomes* and an *experiment* that selects one of the outcomes. Exactly which outcome will be selected is not known in advance, but probability theory describes the likelihood or frequency of occurrence of each possible outcome. To do this it uses the logical design of the experiment in a manner to be specified.

EXAMPLE 7.1.1. A coin is tossed twice and a record is made of the outcome —that is, heads or tails—of each toss. The set of possible outcomes is

$$S = \{HH, HT, TH, TT\},$$

where the first symbol records the outcome of the first toss and the second symbol the outcome of the second toss. Any time the specified experiment is performed, one and only one of these four outcomes will occur.

EXAMPLE 7.1.2. A coin is tossed twice and the number of heads that turn up, regardless of whether the head occurs on the first or second toss, is recorded. Here the outcome set is

$$S' = \{2H, 1H, 0H\};$$

that is, either two, one, or zero heads will turn up.

EXAMPLE 7.1.3. A coin is tossed repeatedly until one of two things happens: (a) a head appears or (b) three successive tails appear. The outcome set here is:

$$S'' = \{H, TH, TTH, TTT\}.$$

The first outcome indicates that a head occurs on the first toss, the second outcome indicates that the first head occurs on the second toss, the third, that the first head occurs on the third toss, and the fourth outcome means that more than three tosses will be required before the first head is observed.

Once the outcome set has been defined, we are interested in subsets of outcomes.

DEFINITION 7.1.1. An *event* is a subset of an outcome space.

Typically an event is defined by a statement; that is, an event is the subset of the outcome space for which the statement is true. In other words, an *event is the truth set of an (open) statement*.

EXAMPLE 7.1.1 (continued). Consider the following events defined by the indicated statements:

Statement	Event
More heads than tails turn up.	{HH}
The last toss is a tail.	{HT, TT}
The first and last tosses are the same.	{HH, TT}

EXAMPLE 7.1.2 (continued). The following statements define the events as indicated:

Statement	Event
At least one head turns up.	{2H, 1H}
Not all tosses turn up heads.	{1H, 0H}
The first and second tosses are the same.	{2H, 0H}

EXAMPLE 7.1.3 (continued). The following statements define the indicated events:

Statement	Event
At least two throws are required.	{TH, TTH, TTT}
A head occurs.	{H, TH, TTH}
An odd number of throws is required.	{H, TTH, TTT}

You will recall that if $A, B, C, \ldots$ are subsets of a set S, then the following are events, or subsets:

(a) The set S itself is an event; every possible experimental outcome falls into S.

(b) The null or empty set, $\varnothing$, is an event; no experimental outcome occurs in $\varnothing$.

(c) If A is any event, then $\tilde{A}$ is the event " not A"; it consists of the outcomes in S that are *not* in A. $\tilde{A}$ is called the *complement* of the set A.

(d) If A and B are two events in S, then $A \cap B$ (read "A *intersection* B" or A *and* B) is the set of experimental outcomes that are in both A and B. Similarly,

$$\bigcap_{i=1}^{n} A_i = A_1 \cap A_2 \cap \cdots \cap A_n$$

is the set of experimental outcomes simultaneously in all the sets $A_1, A_2, \ldots, A_n$. If $A \cap B = \varnothing$, then the events A and B are said to be *disjoint* or *mutually exclusive*. In other words, if an experimental outcome is in A, then it cannot be in B, and conversely.

(e) If A and B are two events in S, then $A \cup B$ (read "A *union* B" or "A *or* B") is the set of experimental outcomes that are either in A or in B (or in both). Likewise,

$$\bigcup_{i=1}^{n} A_i = A_1 \cup A_2 \cup \cdots \cup A_n$$

is the set of outcomes contained in one or more of the sets $A_1, \ldots, A_n$.

In Figure 7.1.1, we have shown the Venn diagram of A and $\tilde{A}$. In Figure 7.1.2, we have shown the Venn diagram of A, B, and $A \cap B$. And in Figure 7.1.3, we have shown the Venn diagram of A, B, and $A \cup B$.

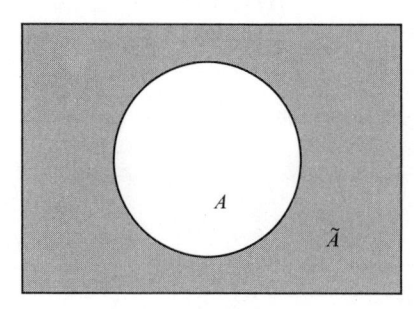

FIGURE 7.1.1

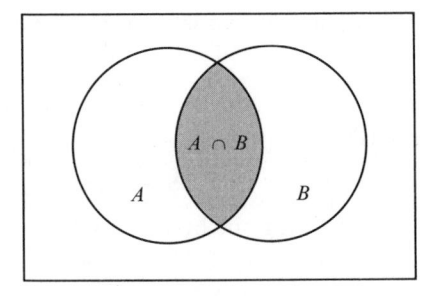

FIGURE 7.1.2

Events such as $A \cap B$ or $A \cup B$ are sometimes called *compound events*. They are usually defined by compound statements—that is, statements formed from two other statements by using the connective word "and" or the word "or." Similarly, the complementary event $\tilde{A}$ to the event A is usually defined by the negation of the statement defining A. The following examples illustrate this.

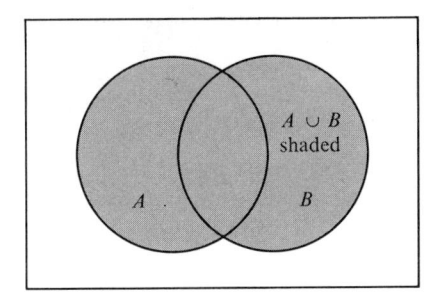

FIGURE 7.1.3

EXAMPLE 7.1.1 (continued). The following statements are made by negating or combining previously made statements. The corresponding events are also shown:

Statement	Event
There are either more heads than tails or the last toss is a tail.	{HH, HT, TT} = {HH} ∪ {HT} ∪ {TT}
It is false that the first and second tosses are the same.	{HT, TH} = {HT} ∪ {TH}

EXAMPLE 7.1.2 (continued). The same for the second example:

Statement	Event
At least one head occurs and not all tosses are heads.	{1H}
The first and second tosses are not the same.	{1H}

EXAMPLE 7.1.3 (continued). The same for the third example:

Statement	Event
At least two throws are required and an odd number is required.	{TTH, TTT}
Either a head occurs or an even number of throws is required.	{H, TH}

EXERCISES 7.1

Save your work on these exercises for use in later sections.

1. For each of the following experiments, define the outcome set:
   (a) A coin is tossed three times and the sequence of heads and tails that turn up is recorded.
   (b) A coin is tossed three times and the number of heads that turn up is recorded.
   (c) A coin is tossed until a head occurs for the first time or else a string of n tails has been observed.

2. For each of the experiments in Exercise 1, make up at least three meaningful events defined by statements.

3. For each of the events you constructed in Exercise 2, make up compound statements using the statements you constructed.

4. A deck of cards is constructed by taking just the kings and queens from an ordinary bridge deck. This deck has eight cards in it. Two cards are drawn simultaneously from the deck.
   (a) What is the set of possible outcomes?
   (b) Find the events defined by the following statements:
       A: Two queens are drawn.
       B: Two red cards are drawn.
       C: Two black kings are drawn.
   (c) Using the events in (b), define the following events verbally and by listing their elements:

$$\tilde{A}, \quad A \cap B, \quad \tilde{A} \cap C, \quad B \cup \tilde{C}$$

5. One die is rolled twice and the number turning up each time is recorded.
   (a) What is the set of outcomes of this experiment?
   (b) Find the events defined by:
       A: The numbers rolled are the same.
       B: The sum of the two numbers is greater than ten.
       C: The sum of the two numbers rolled is odd.
   (c) Define the events below both verbally and by listing their elements:

$$\tilde{B}, \quad A \cap \tilde{B}, \quad C \cup (\tilde{A} \cap B)$$

6. Two dice are rolled simultaneously and the *sum* of the numbers turning up is recorded.
   (a) What is the set of outcomes of this experiment?
   (b) What is the connection between this experiment and the one defined in Exercise 5?
   (c) Find the events defined by:
       A: The outcome is even.
       B: The outcome is less than 2.
       C: The outcome is less than 13.
       D: The outcome is a perfect square.
   (d) Define the events below both verbally and by listing their elements:

$$A \cup B, \quad \tilde{B} \cup C, \quad A \cap D, \quad A \cap \tilde{D}$$

7. Suppose you wanted to find out what the people in the United States think about a political candidate. What kind of an experiment would you perform? What are the outcomes? What are events?

7.2   PROBABILITY FOR A FINITE OUTCOME SPACE

In the present section and in the next few sections, we will assume that the outcome space of the experiment is finite. In later sections this assumption will be removed.

Let S be the set of outcomes. Sometimes we shall also say that S is the *outcome space* or *sample space*, since these terms are commonly used in the literature.

We shall use the notation "$x \in S$" to mean that "x is an element of the set S." From the previous section we saw that S could be a set of objects of almost any kind. We now consider numerical functions on S.

DEFINITION 7.2.1. A numerical function f on S is a rule that assigns a unique number $f(x)$ to each $x \in S$.

EXAMPLE 7.2.1. Let S consist of a set of people who are in a given room. Let $x \in S$. The following are numerical functions on S:

$$f(x) = \text{the amount of money in } x\text{'s pocket}$$
$$a(x) = \text{the age of } x \text{ in years}$$
$$h(x) = \text{the height of } x \text{ in inches}$$
$$m(x) = \text{the weight of } x \text{ in pounds}$$

In defining probability we need a special kind of numerical function, $w(x)$, called a weight function.

DEFINITION 7.2.2. A numerical function $w(x)$ on S is a *weight function* if it satisfies the following conditions:

(a) $w(x) > 0$,
(b) $\sum_{x \in S} w(x) = 1$.

How shall we assign the weight function? In practical cases this may be a statistical question: having repeated the experiment many times, the relative frequencies of the various outcomes are brought to bear to suggest probabilities. General experience with situations similar to the one at hand is often used. For example, if a "fair" or "untrained" coin is tossed twice, the distinguishable outcomes are

$$\text{HH, HT, TH, TT,}$$

and the notion of fairness dictates the assignment of equal weights to each outcome. That is, the weight of each outcome above is $\frac{1}{4}$. This assignment can be guided and reinforced by the following argument, based on the tree diagram of Figure 7.2.1. The leftmost node, marked Start, indicates the situation at the beginning of the experiment. "Fairness" then suggests that, in the long run, one-half of the tosses result in H and the other half in T. This puts us at the nodes labeled First toss. Subsequently, fairness again leads to the outcomes H and T for the second tosses, each with frequency $\frac{1}{2}$. Finally, then, any sequence of outcomes occurs with equal probability: first tosses lead to H one-half the time, and second tosses lead to T one-half the time; thus, the two tosses lead to HT one-quarter of the time. Of course, only "in the long run" and with perfectly balanced and independent coins will the relative frequencies approach $\frac{1}{4}$ closely. But this approach is what we expect of an ideal coin-flipping experiment, and if evidence develops—in the form of quite unequal frequencies—that this is not the case, we smell a rat and inspect the coins, flipping process, and so on, to determine the cause.

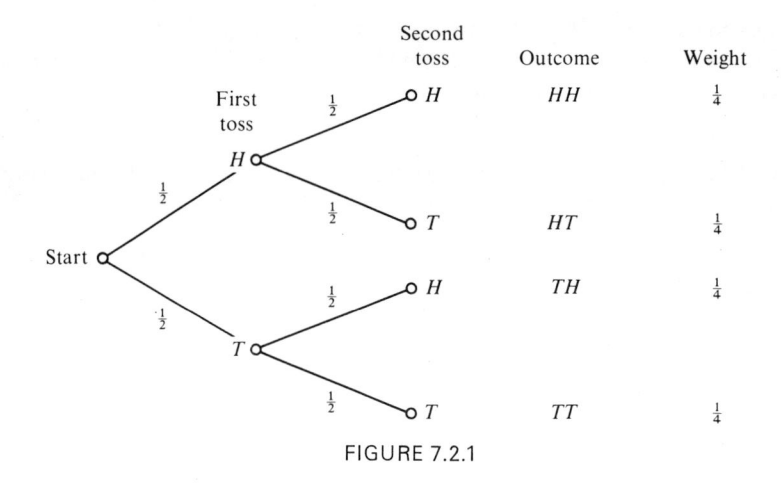

FIGURE 7.2.1

EXAMPLE 7.2.2. A coin is tossed once. If it is a balanced coin, it is equally likely that it will turn up heads or tails. Hence, it is usually sensible to assign weight $\frac{1}{2}$ to each outcome. The weight function can be described as:

Outcomes:	H	T
Weights:	$\frac{1}{2}$	$\frac{1}{2}$

If the coin were not balanced, then we might prefer to assign unequal weights to the two outcomes. However, if the coin had two heads, then the outcome space must be changed to be {H}, since by the definition, the weight function must assign a positive weight. The rationale behind this is that there is no point in including an outcome that cannot occur.

EXAMPLE 7.2.3. Let us return to Example 7.1.1 in which a coin is tossed twice. How shall we assign the weight function? Here again, it is convenient to use the "tree diagram" in Figure 7.2.1 to help. As you will recall, the node at the left, marked Start, indicates the situation at the beginning of the experiment. The tree branches to the two possibilities H or T on the first toss, and from each of these, it branches to the two possibilities H or T on the second toss. We have put weight $\frac{1}{2}$ on each of the branches of the tree. Hence, it makes sense to take the product of the weights on a path from Start to the end of the tree as the weight assigned to the path and hence to the outcome of the experiment. The weight function is defined below:

Outcomes:	HH	HT	TH	TT
Weights:	$\frac{1}{4}$	$\frac{1}{4}$	$\frac{1}{4}$	$\frac{1}{4}$

EXAMPLE 7.2.4. In Example 7.1.3 a coin is tossed until either an H or a sequence TTT appears, whichever occurs first. The outcomes can be arranged as follows:

{H, TH, TTH, TTT}

This arrangement is in order of H appearance (if at all). Again we can argue from fairness, using a tree—see Figure 7.2.2. If the coin is fair, then in the long run, one-half of all tosses should result in an immediate H and experiment termination. That is, out of N starts, close to $\frac{1}{2}N$ should reach H, and $\frac{1}{2}N$ should pass to T. Of the $\frac{1}{2}N$ that arrive

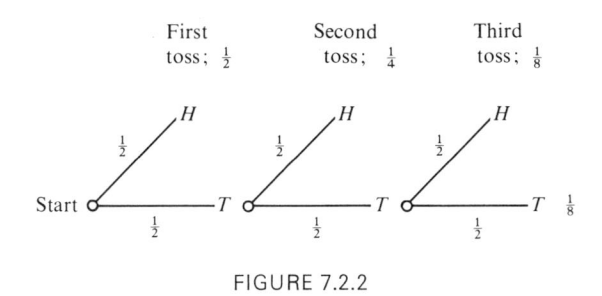

FIGURE 7.2.2

at T, $\frac{1}{2}$ of these (fairness again), or $\frac{1}{4}N$ in all, should reach H and $\frac{1}{4}N$ should reach T. Checking the diagram we see that the fraction of starts that reach H immediately should be close to

$$\frac{\frac{1}{2}N}{N} = \frac{1}{2}.$$

Similarly, the fraction of starts that result in TH is

$$\frac{(\frac{1}{2}N)(\frac{1}{2})}{N} = \frac{1}{4}.$$

Finally, the weights turn out to be

Outcomes:	H	TH	TTH	TTT
Weights:	$\frac{1}{2}$	$\frac{1}{4}$	$\frac{1}{8}$	$\frac{1}{8}$

Again, statistical evidence might be mustered to indicate that, for example, H occurred less frequently than T or, alternatively, more frequently after a T, but less frequently after an H.

EXAMPLE 7.2.5. In Example 7.1.2, the experiment performed was similar to those of Examples 7.1.1 and 7.2.3, except that only the number of heads was recorded. By looking at the listing of alternatives above, it is obvious that 1H occurs in the HT and TH outcomes. Hence the two probability weights attached to these outcomes should be added together to get the weight for 1H. Thus the weight function is:

Outcomes:	2H	1H	0H
Weights:	$\frac{1}{4}$	$\frac{1}{2}$	$\frac{1}{4}$

You should study this example carefully and satisfy yourself that this is the correct weighting. (Note that the other seemingly obvious weighting of $\frac{1}{3}$ on each alternative would not reflect the true physical situation that generates the outcomes.)

Having the weight function defined on the outcome space, we can now proceed to define the probability of an event.

DEFINITION 7.2.3. Let S be an outcome space with weight function $w(x)$ defined for each $x \in S$. Let A be an event in S (that is, a subset of S). Then the *probability of event A* is

$$P(A) = \sum_{x \in A} w(x).$$

EXAMPLE 7.2.6. We return to Examples 7.1.1 (continued) and 7.2.3. Using the definition of probability of an event given above and the weight function derived in Definition 7.2.2, we have:

Statement	Event	Probability
More heads than tails turn up.	{HH}	$\frac{1}{4}$
The last toss is a tail.	{HT, TT}	$\frac{1}{2}$
The first and last tosses are the same.	{HH, TT}	$\frac{1}{2}$

EXAMPLE 7.2.7. We return to Examples 7.1.2 (continued) and 7.2.5. Using the results there, we have:

Statement	Event	Probability
At least one head turns up.	{2H, 1H}	$\frac{3}{4}$
Not all tosses turn up heads.	{1H, 0H}	$\frac{3}{4}$
The first and second tosses are the same.	{2H, 0H}	$\frac{1}{2}$

EXAMPLE 7.2.8. We return to Examples 7.1.3 (continued) and 7.2.4. Using the results there, we have:

Statement	Event	Probability
At least two throws are required.	{TH, TTH, TTT}	$\frac{1}{2}$
A head occurs.	{H, TH, TTH}	$\frac{7}{8}$
An odd number of throws is required.	{H, TTH, TTT}	$\frac{3}{4}$

We can prove some formal results concerning the probability of events.

THEOREM 7.2.1. Let S be an outcome space and let A and B be events. Then the following results hold:

(a) $0 \le P(A) \le 1$.

(b) If $A \cap B = \varnothing$—that is, if A and B are disjoint—then

$$P(A \cup B) = P(A) + P(B).$$

(c) For any two sets A and B,
$$P(A \cup B) = P(A) + P(B) - P(A \cap B).$$

(d) $P(\tilde{A}) = 1 - P(A)$.

(e) $P(A) = 0$ if and only if $A = \varnothing$.

(f) $P(A) = 1$ if and only if $A = S$.

Proof: (a) Since $w(x) > 0$ for each $x \in A$, we have that

$$P(A) = \sum_{x \in A} w(x) \geq 0.$$

Similarly, since A is a subset of S, we see that

$$\sum_{x \in A} w(x) \leq \sum_{x \in S} w(x) = 1.$$

(b) Since $A \cup B$ consists of elements in either A or B (or both), it is obvious that

$$P(A \cup B) = \sum_{x \in A \cup B} w(x) \leq \sum_{x \in A} w(x) + \sum_{x \in B} w(x) = P(A) + P(B).$$

However, since each element of $A \cup B$ occurs once in either A or B but not in both—that is, $A \cap B = \emptyset$—every term in either summation on the right side of the inequality occurs on the left side. Hence, the inequality is an equality.

(c) Referring to the inequality above, if $A \cap B \neq \emptyset$, then each element $x \in A \cap B$ will be counted twice on the right-hand side of the inequality, once in the summation for A and once in the summation for B. To correct this, we must subtract it from the right-hand side; thus,

$$P(A \cup B) = \sum_{x \in A \cup B} w(x) = \sum_{x \in A} w(x) + \sum_{x \in B} w(x) - \sum_{x \in A \cap B} w(x),$$

$$= P(A) + P(B) - P(A \cup B).$$

An alternative proof is given in Exercise 8.

(d) Since $S = A \cup \tilde{A}$, from (b) it is clear that

$$1 = P(S) = P(A) + P(\tilde{A}).$$

Upon solving, we obtain (d).

(e) By assumption, $w(x) > 0$ for each $x \in S$; hence $P(A) = 0$ can happen only if $A = \emptyset$. For the "if" part, we observe that $S \cup \emptyset = S$ and $S \cap \emptyset = \emptyset$, so $1 = P(S) + P(\emptyset) = 1 + P(\emptyset)$, which implies that $P(\emptyset) = 0$.

(f) If $P(A) = 1$, then by (d), $P(\tilde{A}) = 0$; thus, by (e), $\tilde{A} = \emptyset$, hence $A = S$. If $A = S$, then $P(A) = P(S) = 1$.

EXAMPLE 7.2.9. Let us return to Example 7.2.4 and consider the following statements:

Statement	Event	Probability
A head occurs.	A: {H, TH, TTH}	$\frac{7}{8}$
An even number of throws is required.	B: {TH}	$\frac{1}{4}$
At most two throws are required.	C: {H, TH}	$\frac{3}{4}$

We use the previous results to calculate the following:

$$P(A \cup B) = P(A) + P(B) - P(A \cap B),$$
$$= \tfrac{7}{8} + \tfrac{1}{4} - \tfrac{1}{4} = \tfrac{7}{8};$$

$$P(A \cup C) = P(A) + P(C) - P(A \cap C),$$
$$= \tfrac{7}{8} + \tfrac{3}{4} - \tfrac{3}{4} = \tfrac{7}{8};$$

$$P(A \cup \tilde{C}) = P(A) + P(\tilde{C}) - P(A \cap \tilde{C}),$$
$$= \tfrac{7}{8} + \tfrac{1}{4} - \tfrac{1}{8} = 1.$$

We have illustrated above the process of analyzing the outcomes of an experiment, assigning weights, and obtaining the probabilities of events. Let us now try to attach an interpretation to probability statements. To a certain extent such interpretations are philosophical, but we shall not attempt to deal with these philosophical problems, nor shall we take sides in any controversy between the "frequency theory" advocates and the "Bayesians" or "neo-Bayesians." The following discussion includes a few random remarks concerning such interpretations.

Many statistical textbooks motivate and interpret the axioms and results of probability theory in terms of "frequency theory." That is, one considers a random experiment performed under given conditions and a particular event, A, that may occur as an experimental outcome. Then if the experiment is performed repeatedly—that is, N times—and if $N(A)$ represents the number of times A occurs, it is often the case that the frequency ratio,

$$\frac{N(A)}{N},$$

approximately stabilizes. That is, the frequency ratio tends to become constant as N becomes large. For instance, when a penny is flipped many times, the fraction of "heads" that appear is usually observed to approach a value near one-half. The hypothetical or theoretical value for the frequency ratio—assumed to exist—is referred to as the *probability*, $P(A)$, of event A. Of course, the particular numerical probability assigned will depend on the manner in which the experiment is performed as well as on the event itself. In principle, repeated experimentation would allow us to evaluate probabilities numerically. However, direct experimentation to evaluate probabilities, with operating personnel and equipment, is often impractical, uneconomical, or inaccurate in practice, so other approaches are sought. One approach, a sort of experimental probability theory, uses *simulation*, or *Monte Carlo*, techniques: the analysts make a model of the real situation and artificially introduce random elements. They then carry out the main part of the experimentation on a computer before checking the practical implications. Simulation techniques will be discussed in more detail later. The virtue of the theory of probability handled in a mathematical manner is that it may be used to calculate the desired probabilities—for example, by use of a neat formula—without the necessity of experimentation or simulation. The trouble with applying probability theory directly—that is, without simulation—to complex, real problems is that mathematical difficulties frequently arise. A judicious combination of mathematical theory and computer simulation or other computation is therefore often more efficient than either "pure" option. These issues will become clearer as we progress.

The "Bayesian," or "subjective probability," interpretation of probability mathematics is that probability measures one's assessment of the likelihood of an event's occurrence or of the relative likelihood of the occurrence of two or more events. This assessment is often somewhat subjective but is also subject to revision in the light of experience—that is, the results of relevant random experiments. The revision is accomplished by the application of *Bayes' formula*, a mathematical result about conditional probabilities. The application of Bayes' formula to decision theory will be described in Chapter 8.

EXERCISES 7.2

1. For Exercises 1–3 of Section 7.1, assign probability weights and determine the probability of each of the events you defined there.

2. For Exercise 4 of Section 7.1, determine the probability weight function and the probabilities of the events stated in (c).

3. For Exercise 5 of Section 7.1, determine the weight function and the probabilities of the events in (c).

4. For Exercise 6 of Section 7.1, assign the probability weight function and find the probabilities of the events in (d).

5. A die is loaded so that the probability of a face turning up is proportional to the number on it; that is, the four is twice as likely to turn up as the two. The die is rolled once.
   (a) What is the outcome space?
   (b) Determine the weight function.
   (c) What is the probability of an odd number turning up?
   (d) What is the probability that a number greater than four will turn up?
   (e) What is the probability that a prime number will turn up?

6. Two dice loaded as in Exercise 5 are rolled and the *sum* of the numbers is recorded.
   (a) What is the outcome space?
   (b) What is the weight function?
   (c) What is the probability that the sum is 11?
   (d) What is the probability that the sum is 6?

7. If $P(A) + P(B) > 1$, show that $A \cap B \neq \varnothing$.

8. Prove part (c) of Theorem 7.2.1 as follows:
   (a) Show that $A = (A \cap B) \cup (A \cap \tilde{B})$ and $(A \cap B) \cap (A \cap \tilde{B}) = \varnothing$.
   Also show $B = (B \cap A) \cup (B \cap \tilde{A})$.
   (b) From (a), show that $P(A) = P(A \cap B) + P(A \cap \tilde{B})$ and
   $P(B) = P(B \cap A) + P(B \cap \tilde{A})$.
   (c) Show that $A \cup B = (A \cap \tilde{B}) \cup (A \cap B) \cup (\tilde{A} \cap B)$ and that the intersection of each pair of terms on the right is $\varnothing$.
   (d) From (c) show that $P(A \cup B) = P(A \cap \tilde{B}) + P(A \cap B) + (\tilde{A} \cap B)$.
   (e) Prove Part (c) of Theorem 7.2.1 by using (b) and (d).

9. An outcome space has n elements and equal weights have been assigned to each of them. What is the probability of event A, given that A has j elements in it?

10. One card is drawn from an ordinary bridge deck. What is the probability that it is a face card?

11. Much experimental evidence exists to show that if a customer buys product A three times in a row he sticks with it forever. Suppose that the only competitor is product B and that if the customer ever buys B he never buys A again.
    (a) Set up the outcome space to describe a new purchaser's possible purchases. Compare to the space of Example 7.1.3.
    (b) Suppose that half of all new customers purchase A and half purchase B, but that one third of those who have purchased A once continue to buy A again and two thirds switch to B. Assign probabilities to the various experimental outcomes, as in Example 7.2.4.
    (c) Carry out the assignment above on the assumption that, on any choice opportunity, one fifth of the customers who have not permanently made up their minds purchase A and the remainder purchase B.

7.3   CONDITIONAL PROBABILITY

Suppose that we know that an event B has occurred. How does this affect the probability that A will occur? This is a common question and leads to the concept of *conditional probability*.

Let us illustrate the situation with the Venn diagram of Figure 7.3.1. Initially, the outcome, or sample space, is the whole rectangle, and events A and B are shown

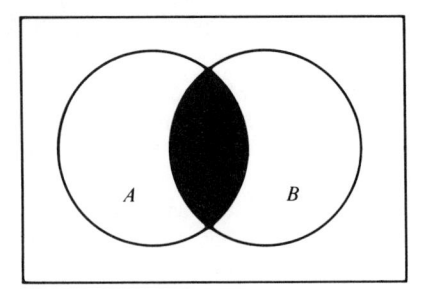

FIGURE 7.3.1

within it. If now we find out that event B has occurred, the outcome space is reduced to the subset B. Clearly the part of B for which event A occurs is the subset $A \cap B$. Since we know that the actual outcome is within B, we must assign a new weight function to the elements within B so that the sum of the new weights is 1. This can be accomplished by dividing each weight by the factor $P(B)$, because

$$\sum_{x \in B} \frac{w(x)}{P(B)} = \frac{1}{P(B)} \sum_{x \in B} w(x) = \frac{P(B)}{P(B)} = 1.$$

As remarked earlier, the part of B for which event A occurs is $A \cap B$. Hence given that B has occurred, the new probability of A, which we denote by $P(A|B)$, is given by

$$P(A|B) = \sum_{x \in A \cap B} \frac{w(x)}{P(B)} = \frac{1}{P(B)} \sum_{x \in A \cap B} w(x),$$

$$= \frac{P(A \cap B)}{P(B)}.$$

Note that for this formula to make sense, we must have $P(B) \neq 0$. We repeat the formula with this assumption:

(7.3.1) $$P(A|B) = \frac{P(A \cap B)}{P(B)} \qquad \text{provided } P(B) \neq 0.$$

The symbol $P(A|B)$ is read "the conditional probability of A given B."

EXAMPLE 7.3.1. Let us return to Example 7.1.1 in which a coin is tossed twice and the outcome of each toss is recorded. Consider the following statements:

A: Two heads turn up.   {HH}
B: The first toss turned up a head.   {HT, HH}
C: At least one of the tosses was a head.   {HH, HT, TH}

At the right we have indicated the events corresponding to the statements. We assume weights associated with fair coins. Then

$$P(A|B) = \frac{P(A \cap B)}{P(B)} = \frac{\frac{1}{4}}{\frac{1}{2}} = \frac{1}{2};$$

$$P(A|C) = \frac{P(A \cap C)}{P(B)} = \frac{\frac{1}{4}}{\frac{3}{4}} = \frac{1}{3}.$$

This result is sometimes referred to as a paradox since the two statements, "two heads turn up, given that the first toss is a head" and "two heads turn up, given that at least one of the tosses was a head," superficially seem the same. At second glance the analysis of this problem shows that statements B and C are not equivalent, and reflection reveals that B gives more information than statement C.

EXAMPLE 7.3.2. Tree diagrams are useful for looking at conditional probability in multistage experiments. The following is an example.

Two machines, A and B, produce identical parts. Machine A has probability 0.1 of producing a defective each time, whereas Machine B has probability 0.4 of producing a defective. Each machine produces one part. One of these parts is selected at random, tested, and found to be defective. What is the probability that it was produced by Machine B?

The tree diagram of this experiment is shown in Figure 7.3.2.

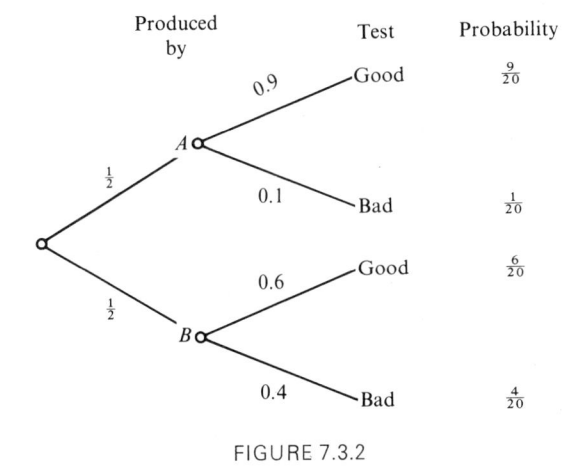

FIGURE 7.3.2

In Exercise 1, you will be asked to work this problem using the conditional probability formula given earlier in the section. But we shall work the problem here in a different way. Let us redraw the tree of Figure 7.3.2, putting the testing event first and the production event second. We obtain the tree of Figure 7.3.3. The probabilities marked in that figure are obtained by observing that the path A–Good in Figure 7.3.2 has probability $\frac{9}{20}$ and so the path Good–A must have the same probability in Figure 7.3.3. We obtain the other path probabilities in the same way. We also note from Figure 7.3.2 that the probability of the part testing Good is $\frac{9}{20} + \frac{6}{20} = \frac{15}{20} = \frac{3}{4}$. Hence the probability of Bad is $\frac{1}{4}$. The remaining four probabilities are con-

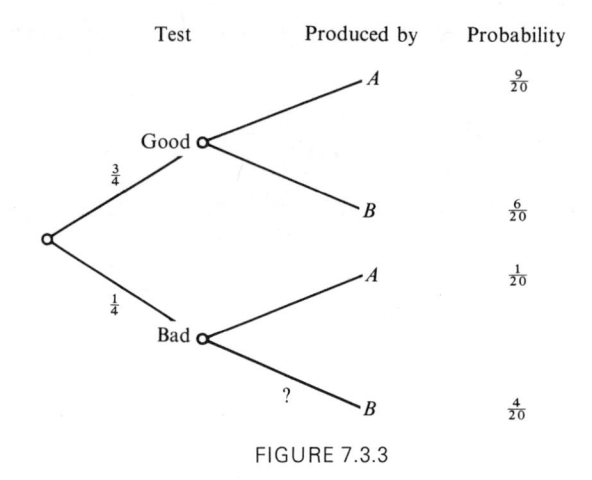

FIGURE 7.3.3

ditional probabilities, and the lower branch marked with "?" is the one we want. It is easy to calculate that probability, knowing that the product of probabilities on a path gives the path probability. Since we know the path probability and one branch probability, the other one is found by dividing thus:

$$P(\text{Made by } B \,|\, \text{it is bad}) = \frac{\frac{4}{20}}{\frac{1}{4}} = \frac{4}{5}.$$

You should observe that this is the same calculation that would be given by the conditional probability formula.

A simplification that is often reasonable in practice is that of independence, as expressed by the equality

(7.3.2) $P(A\,|\,B) = P(A).$

This means that, knowing event B has occurred, the probability of event A is left unchanged. Substituting back into (7.3.1), we have

$$P(A\,|\,B) = P(A) = \frac{P(A \cap B)}{P(B)}$$

which implies $P(A \cap B) = P(A)P(B).$

DEFINITION 7.3.1. Two events A and B are *probabilistically independent* if and only if

$$P(A \cap B) = P(A)P(B).$$

EXAMPLE 7.3.3. Suppose that we toss a coin twice. Consider

  A: The second toss is a head,
  B: The first toss is a head.

Then, it is intuitively clear that $P(A\,|\,B) = P(A)$, and this can be verified by calculation.

However, consider a different experiment in which we take the deck consisting of just the kings and queens from an ordinary bridge deck and withdraw two cards from it. Clearly the two statements

$A:$ The queen of spades is drawn,
$B:$ Both cards are red,

have positive probability. In fact, $P(A) = \frac{7}{28}$ and $P(B) = \frac{3}{14}$. However,

$$P(A \mid B) = 0,$$

so

$$P(A \cap B) = 0 \neq P(A)P(B) = \frac{3}{56};$$

thus A and B are not independent.

A final very important remark is that the independence of two statements depends very much on the way probability weights are assigned to elements in the outcome space. For some ways of assigning probability, they are independent, whereas for other ways, they are dependent.

EXERCISES 7.3

1. Work Example 7.3.2 by using formula (7.3.1).

2. If $A = \varnothing$, show that A is independent of every other statement B.

3. If neither A nor B is empty, but $A \cap B = \varnothing$, show that A and B are not independent in the probabilistic sense.

4. Consider the eight-card deck consisting of the queens and kings taken from an ordinary bridge deck. A two-card hand is drawn from it. Show that no two of the following statements are probabilistically independent.
    $A:$ The queen of spades is drawn.
    $B:$ The hand has at least one black card.
    $C:$ Two queens are drawn.
    $D:$ Two kings are drawn.
    (*Hint:* Consider A and B. If the (short) deck is well shuffled, then each card is equally likely to occur on each draw provided it has not already appeared. Thus,

    $$P(A) = P(\text{queen of spades on first draw}) + P(\text{queen of spades on second draw})$$

    $$= \frac{1}{8} + \left(\frac{7}{8}\right)\left(\frac{1}{7}\right) = \frac{1}{4},$$

    while

    $$P(\tilde{B}) = P(\text{no black card}) = P(\text{red card on first draw}) \times P(\text{red card on second draw})$$

    $$= \left(\frac{4}{8}\right)\left(\frac{3}{7}\right),$$

    so

    $$P(B) = 1 - P(\tilde{B}) = 1 - \frac{3}{14} = \frac{11}{14}.$$

Now

$$P(B|A) = 1,$$

so

$$P(B \cap A) = \frac{1}{4} \neq P(B)P(A).)$$

5. Consider the same deck as in Exercise 4, and let two cards be drawn from it. Find
   (a) the probability that both cards are kings, given that one is a king.
   (b) the probability that both cards are kings, given that one is a black king.
   (c) the probability that both cards are kings, given that one is the king of spades.

6. A die is thrown twice.
   (a) What is the probability that the sum is greater than 9, given that the first one turns up six?
   (b) What is the probability that the sum is greater than 9, given that one of them turns up six?

7. Let $A_1, A_2, \ldots, A_n$ be disjoint events ($A_i \cap A_j = \emptyset$ for any $i \neq j$), and suppose that

$$\bigcup_{i=1}^{n} A_i = A_1 \cup A_2 \cup \cdots A_n = S = \text{sample space};$$

that is, every sample outcome falls into one and only one of the A_i's.
   (a) Show that B can be expressed as

$$B = \bigcup_{i=1}^{n} (A_i \cap B).$$

   (b) Show that

$$P(B) = \sum_{i=1}^{n} P(A_i \cap B).$$

*8. Use Exercise 7 to show that

$$P(A_i|B) = \frac{P(A_i \cap B)}{\sum_{i=1}^{n} P(A_i \cap B)} = \frac{P(B|A_i)P(A_i)}{\sum_{i=1}^{n} P(A_i \cap B)}.$$

(This is Bayes' formula; it will be utilized later for decision problems.)

9. Prove that $P(A|B) = 1$ if and only if $P(\tilde{A} \cap B) = 0$ and $P(B) \neq 0$.

10. Two urns are filled with black and white balls; the first contains four white balls and one black ball, while the second contains three black and two white balls. An urn is selected at random and one ball is drawn from it and found to be black; what is the probability that it was drawn from the second urn? (Work this problem by using a tree like the one in Figure 7.3.2 and then by redrawing it as in Figure 7.3.3.)

11. Can disjoint events be independent? Can independent events be disjoint?

7.4   DISCRETE AND CONTINUOUS PROBABILITY THEORY

In the previous sections we assumed that the outcome space S was finite—that is, contained a finite number of possibilities. In the present section we shall extend the idea of probability to outcome spaces that have infinitely many outcomes. Our reasons for doing so are in part conceptual and in part for mathematical ease and convenience. Let us deal first with the conceptual.

EXAMPLE 7.4.1. A particular automatic control device is subject to occasional error. Suppose the operating time between successive errors is tabulated in days. Imagine that the first one-thousand times between successive errors is tabulated; the largest turns out to be 15 days. Although the 15-day figure may appear to be a reasonable upper bound under some conditions, it is often not truly so: on some later occasion an error may not occur for 16, 27, or 1000 or more days. There may be, in short, no reason, or sound basis, for bounding the possible number of days between errors. Thus the outcome space is the infinite set of *all* positive integers: $\{1, 2, 3, 4, \ldots\}$.

EXAMPLE 7.4.2. Consider again the error-prone control device above. Once put into continuous service, it can be considered susceptible to error at *any* time point—not just at daily intervals. Thus actual failure *possibly* occurs at $\pi = 3.14159\ldots$ days following the last error. Mathematically speaking, the entire positive real line (collection of all real numbers, including such irrationals as π, $e = 2.718\ldots$, and so on) is a suitable and convenient sample space.

Some terminology and a few more examples now follow.

DEFINITION 7.4.1. An outcome or sample space S is called *discrete* if its points can be put into one-to-one correspondence with a subset of the set of positive integers: $\{1, 2, 3, \ldots\}$.

EXAMPLE 7.4.3. The sample space of Example 7.4.1 is obviously discrete since it is itself the set of all positive integers. In this case the sample space is said to be countably infinite. If a bound exists (for example, if the wear of some vital part always causes an error every 200 days) then the sample space is finite.

EXAMPLE 7.4.4. Consider the number of vehicles on the Pennsylvania Turnpike at a fixed time t. The sample space really consists of a finite set of non-negative integers, since the length of even a miniature sports car always exceeds some minimal lower bound and the number of miles of turnpike is bounded above. Even so, the actual number of vehicles present is always far below the upper bound, and it is usually convenient to assume in such cases that the sample space is countably infinite and is the set $\{0, 1, 2, 3, \ldots\}$. Under some circumstances—when numbers become large—it turns out to be useful to approximate in such a way that, for example, the total number of cars is represented by a real number, not an integer. Such "fluid approximations" will be discussed later.

DEFINITION 7.4.2. A sample space S is *continuous* if it can be put in one-to-one correspondence with all real numbers in the interval zero to one.

We state here without proof that all real numbers in the doubly infinite open interval $(-\infty, \infty)$—that is, the set of all points

$$\{x: x \text{ is a real number}, \quad -\infty < x < \infty\}$$

—can be put into one-to-one correspondence with numbers in $(0, 1)$; for example, $y = (1 + e^x)^{-1}$ will suffice. Hence the set above is a continuous sample space. The set of numbers

$$\{x: x \text{ real}, \quad 0 \le x < \infty\}$$

is also a continuous sample space. In this case a correspondence may be established between the space above and the half-closed interval $[0, 1)$; $y = 1 - e^{-x}$ is such a correspondence.

EXAMPLE 7.4.5. A piece of string ten inches long is cut into two parts, and the length of the longest part is recorded. The sample space is the (set of all real numbers in the) interval zero to ten.

EXAMPLE 7.4.6. The duration of a telephone call may depend on how much information the two conversants wish to exchange (or on how long the baby naps, the pie requires to be baked, and so on). In any case, a sample space consisting of all nonnegative real numbers is often appropriate.

The foregoing examples indicate the sorts of situations that are likely to arise and the sample spaces, discrete or continuous, that are suggested. However, we emphasize that the choice of a sample space is often governed by the type of approach to be taken to the problem at hand. If a mathematical pencil-and-paper attack is to be made, continuous sample spaces sometimes turn out to be convenient. If, on the other hand, a computational approach is to be undertaken, then one is eventually forced to operate with discrete, finite sets. Examples should aid in guiding the selection process in practice.

DEFINITION 7.4.3. Let S represent the entire space of outcomes, and let $A, B, \ldots$ be events in (subsets of) the space S.

Recall from Section 7.2, where probability was first defined, that probability is a function, P, from the events to the real numbers in the interval $[0, 1]$. For example, $P(A) = 0.3$ means that the probability of event A is 0.3. P has the following properties:

(a) For any event, A, $0 \le P(A) \le 1$.
(b) $P(S) = 1$, and $P(\varnothing) = 0$.
(c) If $A \cap B = \varnothing$—that is, if A and B are disjoint—then

$$P(A \cup B) = P(A) + P(B);$$

otherwise,

(7.4.1) $$P(A \cup B) = P(A) + P(B) - P(A \cap B).$$

A further property is as follows:

(d) If $\{A_i, \quad i = 1, 2, \ldots\}$ is a countably infinite sequence of disjoint events, then P has the *countable additivity* property:

$$P\left(\bigcup_{i=1}^{\infty} A_i\right) = \sum_{i=1}^{\infty} P(A_i).$$

With the addition of (d), we have considerably expanded the scope of our earlier discrete probability definitions.

EXAMPLE 7.4.7.* Suppose a blindfolded child cuts the string of Example 7.4.5. Here it is perhaps reasonable to suppose that the cut location is uniformly distributed over the string length—that is, any interval of length b (with end points between the ends of the string) is equally likely to receive the cut. With this probability assignment, it follows that the probability of cutting the string at, say, $x = 5$ is zero, since we can divide the string up into equal intervals of arbitrarily small length, one of which contains $x = 5$. Since the length of the interval actually cut is less than any pre-assigned number—10^{-10}, say—the probability of a cut *at* $x = 5$ is zero. Observe that it correspondingly follows that the probability of cutting the string at a point other than $x = 5$—that is, of cutting some point in the set $\{\tilde{5}\}$—is unity. Yet $\{\tilde{5}\}$ is a proper subset of the entire sample space, S, which itself has probability unity. It is in fact possible to show that the probability of cutting the string at any one of a preassigned finite or countable set of points is zero! With a uniform distribution of probability over a continuous sample space, such "small" sets receive probability zero, while an interval receives probability proportional to its length. From interval events other events are formed by union, intersection, and so on.

DEFINITION 7.4.4. A *random variable* X is a function that assigns a numerical value to each element ω of the outcome space S.

That is, a random variable is a function, X, for which the value taken on when ω occurs is $X(\omega)$. Furthermore, a random variable is required to have the property that a probability is assigned to the set of outcomes for which X does not exceed any number x:

$$P\{\omega: X(\omega) \leq x\} = P\{X \leq x\}.$$

The function

(7.4.2) $$F_X(x) = P\{X \leq x\}$$

is called the *distribution function* of X.

EXAMPLE 7.4.8. Consider the coin flipping experiment of Example 7.1.1, and let the random variable X be the number of heads that occur. Clearly

$$\omega = \{H, H\} \quad \text{implies that} \quad X(\omega) = 2,$$

$$\omega = \{H, T\}, \text{ or } \omega = \{T, H\}, \quad \text{implies that} \quad X(\omega) = 1,$$

$$\omega = \{T, T\} \quad \text{implies that} \quad X(\omega) = 0.$$

Following the rule of Definition 7.4.3(c) leads to the distribution function below.

(7.4.3) $$F_X(x) = \begin{cases} P(\{\emptyset\}) = 0 & \text{if } x < 0 \\ P(\{T, T\}) = \dfrac{1}{4} & \text{if } 0 \leq x < 1 \\ P(\{T, T\}) + P(\{T, H\}) + P(\{H, T\}) = \dfrac{3}{4} & \text{if } 1 \leq x < 2 \\ P(\{T, T\}) + P(\{T, H\}) + P(\{H, T\}) + P(\{H, H\}) = 1 & \text{if } 2 \leq x \end{cases}$$

A graph of this distribution function appears as below.

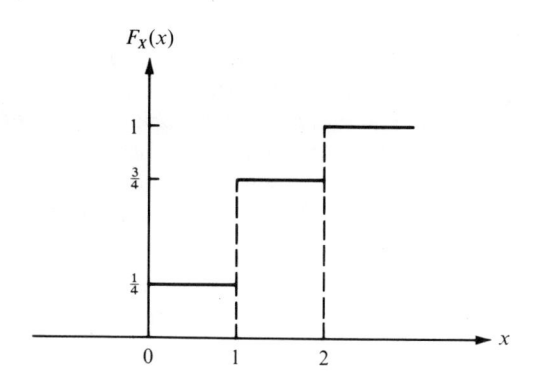

EXAMPLE 7.4.9. Consider the string-cutting experiment of Example 7.4.5. Let the random variable of interest be the distance, L, of the cut from the left-hand end of the string. Clearly $L \leq x$ if and only if the string is cut within a distance x from the left end. Hence,

$$(7.4.4) \qquad F_L(x) = P\{L \leq x\} = \begin{cases} 0 & x \leq 0 \\ \dfrac{x}{10} & 0 \leq x \leq 10 \\ 1 & x \geq 10 \end{cases}$$

This function defines a *rectangular* or *uniform* distribution. The reason for this terminology is as follows. For our string example, we can write

$$(7.4.5) \qquad F(x) = P\{L \leq x\} = \int_0^x \frac{1}{10}\, dt = \frac{x}{10}, \qquad 0 \leq x \leq 10$$

and can thus assign probability to various events by integration. Therefore,

$$P\{L > x\} = \int_x^{10} \frac{1}{10}\, dt,$$

$$P\{4 < L \leq 6\} = \int_4^6 \frac{1}{10}\, dt = \frac{2}{10},$$

and so on.

DEFINITION 7.4.5. If a distribution function may be written in the form

$$(7.4.6) \qquad P\{X \leq x\} = F(x) = \int_0^x f(t)\, dt$$

where

$$f(x) \geq 0$$

and

$$\int_{-\infty}^{\infty} f(x)\, dx = 1,$$

then f is called the *density function* (or *probability density function*) associated with F.

In the last example (Example 7.4.9),

$$(7.4.7) \qquad f(x) = \frac{dF}{dx} = \begin{cases} 0 & x \le 0 \\ \dfrac{1}{10} & 0 \le x \le 10 \\ 0 & 10 \le x \end{cases}$$

and has the shape shown in the diagram. Thus the terminology is explained.

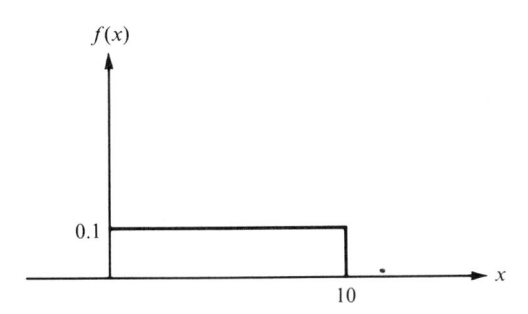

To illustrate the density function assignment of probabilities, return to Example 7.4.6. It has been empirically observed that the durations of local telephone calls are often well described by the *exponential distribution*. If D is the duration of such a call, then

$$(7.4.8) \qquad F_D(x) = P\{D \le x\} = \begin{cases} 0 & x \le 0 \\ 1 - e^{-cx} & x \ge 0,\ c > 0 \end{cases}$$

Since we can write

$$(7.4.9) \qquad F_D(x) = \int_0^x e^{-cx} c\, dx,$$

the distribution has density

$$(7.4.10) \qquad f_D(x) = e^{-cx} c \qquad x \ge 0,\ c > 0.$$

Notice that c can be any positive number—10, for example. In this case, the *density function $f_D(x)$* is greater than unity (equal to 10) at $x = 0$. We wish to emphasize that while a distribution function is never greater than unity, a density function may be arbitrarily large at certain points. The only restriction is, of course, that its integral not exceed unity.

EXERCISES 7.4

1. (a) Prove that
$$P(a < X \le b) = F_X(b) - F_X(a)$$

by observing that the event $\{X \le b\}$ is the union of the events $\{X \le a\}$ and $\{a < X \le b\}$ and by using the fundamental properties of probability (7.4.1).

   (b) If F has density f,
$$P\{X > a\} = \int_a^\infty f(x)\, dx$$

2. Let T be the time until an error occurs in the control device of Example 7.4.1. Suppose T has distribution $F_T(x)$. Use this distribution to express the probability of the following events.
   (a) $T > 100$
   (b) $50 < T < 100$
   (c) $T > 100$, conditional upon $T > 50$ $\left(Hint: P(T > 100 | T > 50) = \dfrac{P(T > 100)}{P(T > 50)} \right)$.

3. The time, X, required to complete a certain project has a density function of the following form:
   $$f_x(x) = kx(1 - x) \qquad 0 \leq x \leq 1,$$
   $$= 0 \qquad\qquad \text{otherwise.}$$
   (a) Determine k.
   (b) What is the probability that the project is completed before $x = \frac{1}{4}$? Before $x = \frac{3}{4}$?

4. A single fair die is tossed; outcomes are 1, 2, 3, 4, 5, or 6, with equal probabilities. Consider the random variable that takes on the values
   $$Y = 0 \qquad \text{if a 4 or 6 occurs,}$$
   $$= \text{face value of die otherwise.}$$
   (a) Sketch, or otherwise describe, the distribution function of Y.
   (b) What is the probability that $Y = 0$? That Y is positive and divisible by 2?

7.5 PROPERTIES OF DISTRIBUTIONS AND RANDOM VARIABLES

The examples in the last section illustrated the types of distribution functions likely to arise in probability-modeling studies. We summarize the basic properties possessed by all distribution functions.

(1) $F_X(x)$ is *nondecreasing*; that is,

if $x_2 > x_1$, then $F_X(x_2) \geq F_X(x_1)$.

(7.5.1)

(2) $\lim\limits_{x \to -\infty} F_X(x) = F_X(-\infty) = 0$.

(3) $\lim\limits_{x \to +\infty} F_X(x) = F_X(+\infty) = 1$.

You may verify these properties in general from Definition 7.4.3 and check that each of the examples has these properties.

The random variable of Example 7.4.8 takes on one of a finite number of values. More generally, a random variable that takes on one of a countable set of possible values is called *discrete*. The graph of its distribution function resembles that of Example 7.4.8 and has the form of a step function. If, on the other hand, our random variable takes on any real number (or perhaps any real numbers in an interval —see Example 7.4.9) then its distribution may have a density; in this case the random variable is said to be *continuous*, or *continuously distributed*. It is possible also to encounter distributions that are mixtures of the discrete and continuous. An example is as follows.

EXAMPLE 7.5.1. The owner of a service station notices that individual gasoline purchasers either buy no high-test gasoline, buy ten gallons of high test, or have their tank filled with high test. The others buy low-test gasoline. Letting X denote the amount of high-test gas purchased by an arbitrary arriving customer, this owner has found (from years of observation) that

$$P\{X = 0\} = 0.5, \qquad P\{X = 10\} = 0.1,$$

and that the remaining 40% of the arriving customers have their tanks filled, in which case X is reasonably assumed to be continuously distributed. It follows that X has a distribution function of the form shown:

$$(7.5.2) \qquad F_X(x) = \begin{cases} 0 & x < 0 \\ 0.5 + 0.4 \int_0^x f(t)\, dt & 0 \le x < 10 \\ 0.6 + 0.4 \int_0^x f(t)\, dt & 10 \le x \end{cases}$$

Here, f is the density describing the demand of those who have their tanks filled. The graph of such a distribution appears as below. In general, X can be considered as

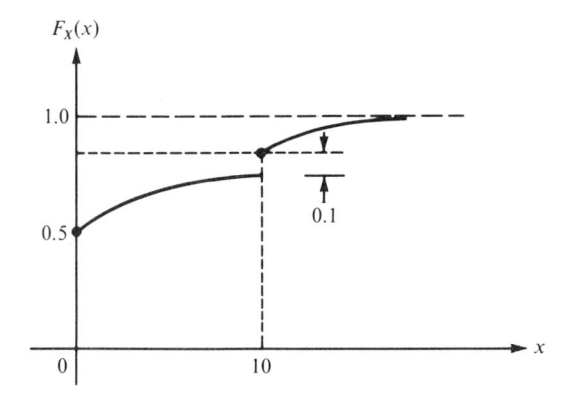

taking on either a discrete value, x_i, or a continuous value. Let p_D be the probability that X is discrete and $p_C = 1 - p_D$ be the probability that it is continuous. In Example 7.5.1, for instance,

$$p_D = 0.5 + 0.1 = 0.6,$$

and

$$P\{X = 0 \mid X \text{ discrete}\} = \frac{5}{6},$$

$$P\{X = 10 \mid X \text{ discrete}\} = \frac{1}{6}.$$

Thus, the general expression for $F_X(x)$ is

$$P\{X \le x\} = p_D \sum_{x_i \le x} P\{X = x_i | X \text{ discrete}\} + p_C \int_{-\infty}^{x} f_X(t)\, dt,$$

where f_X is any (appropriate) density function.

It is easy to see how knowledge of the distribution function of a random variable allows one to calculate the probabilities of many different events.

EXAMPLE 7.5.2. Suppose we wish to know the probability that $X > 10$. Clearly this event, which we write as $\{X > 10\}$, is the complement of the event $\{X \le 10\}$. By one of the fundamental properties of a probability (which one?),

(7.5.3) $$P\{X \le 10\} + P\{X > 10\} = 1.$$

But since

(7.5.4) $$P\{X \le 10\} = F_X(10),$$

we have

(7.5.5) $$P\{X > 10\} = 1 - F_X(10).$$

Likewise, if $a < b$, then

(7.5.6) $$P\{a < X \le b\} = F_X(b) - F_X(a),$$

and so forth.

Similarly, the distribution function of a function of a random variable is obtainable directly. We give several examples.

EXAMPLE 7.5.3. Consider the linear function

(7.5.7) $$Y = aX + b.$$

Then

(7.5.8) $$F_Y(y) = P\{Y \le y\} = P\{aX + b \le y\}.$$

Now if the constant a is positive, then the events

(7.5.9) $$\{aX + b \le y\} \quad \text{and} \quad \left\{X \le \frac{y - b}{a}\right\}$$

are equivalent, so

(7.5.10) $$F_Y(y) = F_X\left(\frac{y - b}{a}\right).$$

If a is negative, then the events

(7.5.11) $$\{aX + b \le y\} \quad \text{and} \quad \left\{X \ge \frac{y - b}{a}\right\}$$

are equivalent, and thus

(7.5.12) $$F_Y(y) = 1 - F_X\left(\frac{y - b}{a}\right).$$

EXAMPLE 7.5.4. Consider the quadratic function

$$Y = X^2.$$

Then it is clear that the events

(7.5.13) $\qquad \{Y \le y\} \quad \text{and} \quad \{-\sqrt{y} \le X \le \sqrt{y}\}$

are equivalent. Suppose that F_X has density f; then

(7.5.14)
$$P\{Y \le y\} = \int_{-\sqrt{y}}^{\sqrt{y}} f(t)dt = \int_{-\infty}^{\sqrt{y}} f(t)dt - \int_{-\infty}^{-\sqrt{y}} f(t)dt,$$
$$= F_X(\sqrt{y}) - F_X(-\sqrt{y}).$$

The distribution function of a random variable provides a great deal of information about how the latter will behave. Frequently, in fact, a short summary of this information is sufficient for practical use. Such a summary is provided by the mathematical expectation of a random variable, a concept that is closely related to the ordinary average used to summarize data.

DEFINITION 7.5.1. The *mathematical expectation* of the random variable X is

(7.5.15) $$E[X] = \sum_i x_i P\{X = x_i\}$$

if it is discrete, and

(7.5.16) $$E[X] = \int_{-\infty}^{\infty} x f_X(x)\, dx$$

if it is continuously distributed. If X has a mixed distribution, then the expectation is written as

$$E[X] = \int_{-\infty}^{\infty} x\, dF_X(x);$$

this means—see (7.5.2) for an example—that

(7.5.17) $$E[X] = p_D \left[\sum_i x_i P\{X = x_i \mid X \text{ discrete}\} \right] + p_C \left[\int_{-\infty}^{\infty} x f_X(x)\, dx \right],$$

where $p_D, p_C \ge 0$ and $p_D + p_C = 1$.

EXAMPLE 7.5.5. Consider the gasoline-purchase model of Example 7.5.1. The discrete outcomes are

$$x_1 = 0, \quad \text{and} \quad x_2 = 10$$

with

$$P\{X = x_1\} = 0.5$$

and

$$P\{X = x_2\} = 0.1,$$

so

$$p_D = 0.6.$$

Hence

$$P\{X = x_1 \,|\, X \text{ discrete}\} = \frac{5}{6}$$

and

$$P\{X = x_2 \,|\, X \text{ discrete}\} = \frac{1}{6}.$$

Let us suppose that

$$f_X(x) = \frac{1}{12} \qquad 0 \le x \le 12,$$

$$= 0 \qquad \text{otherwise.}$$

Then

$$E[X] = 0 \times 0.5 + 10 \times 0.1 + 0.4 \int_0^{12} x\frac{1}{12}\,dx,$$

$$= 1 + 0.4 \times 6 = 3.4.$$

For mathematical reasons we require in addition that in order for a random variable to possess a (finite) expectation, the series

$$(7.5.18) \qquad \sum_i |x_i| P\{X = x_i\}$$

must be finite in the discrete (countable) case, whereas in the continuous case, the integral

$$(7.5.19) \qquad \int_{-\infty}^{\infty} |x| f_X(x)\,dx$$

must be finite. Recall that $|x|$ is the *absolute value* of x: $|x| = x$ if $x > 0$, and $|x| = -x$ if $x < 0$. Various interesting random variables that occur in mathematical models may possess no finite expectation.

Very frequently one speaks simply of "the expectation of X" or the "mean of X" instead of "the mathematical expectation of X."

EXAMPLE 7.5.6. Consider the experiment of flipping a coin, and let

$$P\{H\} = P\{T\} = \frac{1}{2}.$$

If X is a random variable such that

$$X(H) = \$1, \qquad X(T) = -\$1,$$

then the mathematical expectation of X is

$$E[X] = 1 \cdot P\{H\} - 1P\{T\} = \frac{1}{2} - \frac{1}{2} = 0.$$

Let us reflect on such a coin-tossing experiment in order to give an intuitive understanding of the mathematical expectation. If a coin is tossed N times, and if N_H is the number of times heads occur, then we expect that $P\{H\}$ is *approximately* equal to N_H/N as N becomes large (always supposing that the coin doesn't wear out, roll away, and is flipped fairly). Let X represent a gambler's gain if he wagers \$1 on heads at each toss. Over the long run (N large) he wins about $\$1 \cdot N_H$ and loses about $\$1(N - N_H)$. His average winnings per toss are thus

$$\frac{\$1N_H - \$1(N - N_H)}{N} = \$1\frac{N_H}{N} - \$1\left(1 - \frac{N_H}{N}\right).$$

In a very large number of tosses, the average gain per toss is thus close to

$$\$1P\{H\} - \$1[1 - P\{H\}],$$

which equals zero if $P\{H\} = \frac{1}{2}$. You should now be able to see directly that if the coin is unfair—that is, if $P\{H\} = p$ and $P\{T\} = q$, $p \neq q$ but $p + q = 1$, then the average (expected) gain per toss is $\$1(p - q)$.

It may be said that the expectation of X *locates* the distribution of X. Thus if $E[X] = 17$, say, we need merely subtract 17 from X to obtain the new random variable

$$X' = X - 17,$$

which has expectation zero but whose distribution is otherwise unchanged. The figure below illustrates the situation. Of course, subtraction of *any* number from X

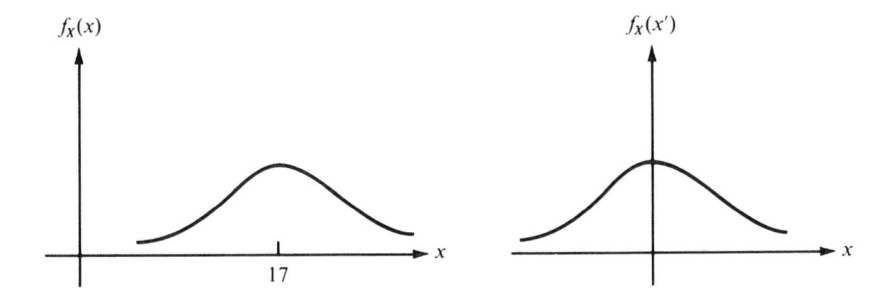

Density shifted to zero mean

merely shifts the distribution around without changing its shape, but the point is that such a shift *can* be made to zero expectation, or mean, and often is. Another point is that it is frequently convenient to allow the expectation or mean to be a *parameter* in an analytical expression (formula) for a distribution.

EXAMPLE 7.5.7. Suppose X has a uniform distribution with density as follows.

(7.5.20)
$$f_X(x) = \begin{cases} \dfrac{1}{h} & a \leq x \leq a + h \\ 0 & \text{elsewhere} \end{cases}$$

Then

$$E[X] = \int_{-\infty}^{\infty} x f_X(x)\, dx,$$

(7.5.21)

$$= \int_a^{a+h} x\, \frac{1}{h}\, dx = \frac{x^2}{2h}\bigg|_a^{a+h} = a + \frac{h}{2}.$$

Clearly the density is centered or located at $a + h/2$, as a diagram shows. Half of the

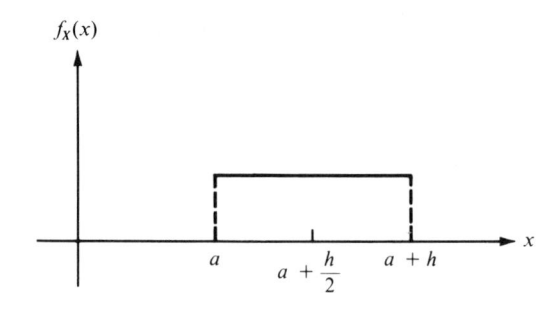

probability is between a and $a + h/2$, while the other half is between $a + h/2$ and $a + h$. If the mean is subtracted from X, the density is now symmetrically situated around zero (the origin). The probability of deviations from zero (the mean) is governed entirely by the parameter h: if h is small, the probability of large deviations from the mean is correspondingly small; the opposite is true for large h. The new density—that is, the density with mean zero—has the form

(7.5.22)
$$f_{X'}(x) = \frac{1}{h} \qquad \text{for} \quad -\frac{h}{2} \le x \le \frac{h}{2},$$

$$= 0 \qquad \text{otherwise.}$$

Still other convenient summaries of the properties of a distribution are furnished by the expectations of certain functions of the basic random variable.

THEOREM 7.5.1. The mathematical expectation of $g(X)$, where g is a (nearly) arbitrary function, is

(7.5.23)
$$E[g(X)] = \sum_i g(x_i) P\{X = x_i\},$$

if X is discrete, and by

(7.5.24)
$$E[g(X)] = \int_{-\infty}^{\infty} g(x) f_X(x)\, dx,$$

if X is continuous. If X has a mixed distribution, then

$$E[g(X)] = \int_{-\infty}^{\infty} g(x)\, dF_X(x),$$

$$= p_D \left[\sum_i g(x_i) P\{X = x_i | X \text{ discrete}\} \right] + p_C \left[\int g(x) f_X(x)\, dx \right].$$

In particular, if c is a constant, $E[cX] = cE[X]$.

Proof: Deal with the discrete case in which X assumes finitely many distinct values $x_1, x_2, \ldots, x_n$. Assume moreover that g is such that the values $y_i = g(x_i)$ are distinct; this then means that a unique inverse exists: if $g(x) = y_i$, then $x = x_i = g^{-1}(y_i)$. By Definition 7.5.1,

$$E[g(X)] = E[Y] = \sum_i y_i P\{Y = y_i\},$$

$$= \sum_i y_i P\{g(X) = y_i\},$$

(7.5.25)

$$= \sum_i g(x_i) P\{X = g^{-1}(y_i)\},$$

$$= \sum_i g(x_i) P\{X = x_i\},$$

which is (7.5.23). The generality of this proof may be increased, but the result is the same.

From a computational point of view, (7.5.23) and (7.5.24) are of value because they show that one need not first find the distribution of $Y = g(X)$, given that of X, and then sum or integrate as in (7.5.25). One need merely evaluate the sum directly. The interpretation of the expectation above is again that it represents an average where the number of items averaged is very great.

EXAMPLE 7.5.8. The construction of a round building begins by laying out a circle on the ground. Because of errors involved in establishing the radius, the radius is a random variable. It is, of course, established once and held fixed while the circle is made, but if the process were carried out again, a different radius would result. Let $f_R(x)$ denote the density function of R, the radius. Then if H is the building height, its volume is

(7.5.26)
$$V = \pi H R^2.$$

The expected volume is given by

(7.5.27)
$$E[V] = \int_{-\infty}^{\infty} \pi H x^2 f_R(x)\, dx.$$

A particular example is the following. Let

(7.5.28)
$$f_R(x) = \frac{1}{h} \qquad a - \frac{h}{2} \le x \le a + \frac{h}{2},$$

$$= 0 \qquad \text{otherwise.}$$

Then

$$E[V] = \pi H \int_{a-h/2}^{a+h/2} x^2 \frac{1}{h}\, dx = \frac{\pi H}{h} \frac{x^3}{3} \bigg|_{a-h/2}^{a+h/2},$$

(7.5.29)
$$= \frac{\pi H}{3h} \left[\left(a + \frac{h}{2} \right)^3 - \left(a - \frac{h}{2} \right)^3 \right],$$

$$= \pi H a^2 + \frac{\pi H h^2}{12}.$$

An important fact to notice is that we cannot exactly calculate $E[V] = \pi H E[R^2]$ by *first* taking the expectation of R and *then* squaring:

$$(7.5.30) \qquad\qquad E[R^2] \neq (E[R])^2.$$

You will notice that the true $E[V]$, obtained in (7.5.29), is somewhat larger than the result of simply substituting $a = E[R]$ into the volume formula. If, however, the density function does not "spread" extensively about its mean—which is the case if h is small—then clearly the second term (involving h^2) contributes relatively little, and for simplicity it may sometimes be omitted. A little reflection indicates that the parameters in many physical situations differ from occasion to occasion in a random manner, perhaps owing to manufacturing or material variations, daily weather, and so on. It is only common sense to ignore certain fluctuations when they are negligible compared to others or, perhaps, compared to the mean.

In order to obtain a convenient measure of the "spread" or "dispersion" of a random variable about its mean, we introduce the following definition.

DEFINITION 7.5.2. The *variance* of the random variable X is the expectation of the quantity $(X - E[X])^2$. We denote the variance of X by $\text{Var}[X]$ or often by σ_X^2. The *standard deviation* of X is $\sqrt{\text{Var}[X]} = \sigma_X$.

Obviously if the distribution is concentrated tightly around $E[X]$, then $X - E[X]$ and hence $(X - E[X])^2$ is small; the limiting situation occurs when all X values are equal, in which case they must all equal $E[X]$ and the expectation above is zero. If on the other hand the values of X are widely dispersed, then the expectation above—the variance—becomes large.

THEOREM 7.5.2. The variance may be written as

$$(7.5.31) \qquad\qquad \text{Var}[X] = E[X^2] - (E[X])^2.$$

If c is any constant, then

$$(7.5.32) \qquad\qquad \text{Var}[cX] = c^2 \, \text{Var}[X].$$

The variance of a constant equals zero.

Proof: By Definition 7.5.2,

$$\text{Var}[X] = E[(X - E[X])^2].$$

In terms of discrete probabilities, then,

$$\text{Var}[X] = \sum_i (x_i - E[X])^2 P\{X = x_i\},$$

$$= \sum_i (x_i^2 - 2x_i E[X] + (E[X])^2) P\{X = x_i\},$$

$$(7.5.33) \qquad = \sum_i x_i^2 P\{X = x_i\} - 2E[X] \sum_i x_i P\{X = x_i\} + (E[X])^2 \sum_i P\{X = x_i\},$$

$$= E[X^2] - 2(E[X])^2 + (E[X])^2,$$

$$= E[X^2] - (E[X])^2.$$

Likewise,

$$\text{Var}[cX] = E[(cX - E[cX])^2],$$

$$= \sum_i (cx_i - cE[X])^2 P\{X = x_i\},$$

(7.5.34)

$$= \sum_i c^2(x_i - E[X])^2 P\{X = x_i\},$$

$$= c^2 \, \text{Var}[X].$$

You will be asked to show that the variance of a constant is zero and to carry out the proofs when X is continuously distributed.

EXAMPLE 7.5.9. Suppose X has a distribution characterized as follows:

(7.5.35)

$$X = \begin{cases} +a & \text{with probability } \dfrac{1}{2} \\[2ex] -a & \text{with probability } \dfrac{1}{2} \end{cases}$$

Its distribution is discrete and appears as follows:

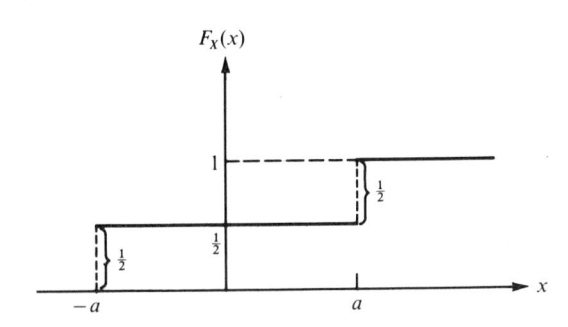

Now clearly the expectation of X is zero (you should verify this). To compute the variance we form

$$(X - E[X])^2 = (+a - 0)^2 \quad \text{with probability } \frac{1}{2},$$

(7.5.36)

$$= (-a - 0)^2 \quad \text{with probability } \frac{1}{2}.$$

Consequently,

(7.5.37) $\qquad \sigma_X^2 = E[(X - E[X])^2] = (+a - 0)^2 \dfrac{1}{2} + (-a - 0)^2 \dfrac{1}{2} = a^2.$

Let us consider random variables having distributions of the form given above, but with different values of a. Notice that the larger a is made, the greater is the dispersion of X from its mean: if $a = 100$, then the value of X is either 100 or -100, and if $a = 1$, X is either 1 or -1. Correspondingly, the variances are 10,000 and 1, respectively, reflecting the different dispersions. The standard deviations, 100 and 1, respectively, also measure the dispersion.

EXAMPLE 7.5.10. The random variable Y has the uniform distribution given by the density:

(7.5.38)
$$f_Y(y) = \begin{cases} \dfrac{1}{h} & a \le y \le a + h \\[2mm] 0 & \text{otherwise} \end{cases}$$

The mean of Y is $a + h/2$. Consequently, the variance of Y is

(7.5.39)
$$\sigma_Y^2 = E\left[\left(Y - a - \frac{h}{2}\right)^2\right] = \int_a^{a+h} \left(y - a - \frac{h}{2}\right)^2 \frac{1}{h}\, dy,$$

$$= \int_{-h/2}^{h/2} z^2 \frac{dz}{h} = \frac{h^2}{12}.$$

Again it is clear that if h is large, then Y takes on values far away from its mean and σ_Y^2 becomes large, whereas if h is small, Y concentrates near the mean.

We shall now state and prove a simple, but theoretically useful, theorem.

THEOREM 7.5.3. *Chebyshev's Inequality.* Suppose X has mean, or expectation, m and variance σ^2. Then for any $z > 0$,

(7.5.40)
$$P\{|X - m| > z\} \le \frac{\sigma^2}{z^2}.$$

Proof: Consider the expression for the variance

$$E[(X - m)^2] = \int_{-\infty}^{\infty} (x - m)^2\, dF(x) = \sigma^2.$$

Let us split the region of integration into two parts:

(7.5.41) $A = \{x: |x - m| > z\}$ and $A' = \{x: |x - m| \le z\}.$

Writing this out,

$$\sigma^2 = \int_A (x - m)^2\, dF(x) + \int_{A'} (x - m)^2\, dF(x),$$

$$\ge \int_A (x - m)^2\, dF(x).$$

In other words, we integrate first over all x such that x is in the set A, and next over x in A'. Since the latter integral is nonnegative, omitting its contribution implies the inequality. However, if x is in the set A, then $|x - m| > z$, and thus $(x - m)^2 > z^2$; therefore,

(7.5.42)
$$\sigma^2 \ge \int_A z^2\, dF(x) = z^2 P\{|X - m| > z\},$$

which completes the proof.

This theorem legitimizes our intuitive discussion of mean and variance. In words, it says that a small variance (or standard deviation) makes small the probability that a random variable differs by more than any fixed number, z, from its mean. More simply, a small variance insures that most of the probability is concentrated near the mean. The concentration becomes greater as the variance decreases. Usually, the probability bound furnished by the inequality (7.5.40) is not very tight.

EXAMPLE 7.5.11. If X is a uniformly distributed random variable with mean zero, its range is from $-h/2$ to $h/2$ (see Example 7.5.10). Then $\text{Var}[X] = h^2/12$, and hence Chebyshev's inequality states that

$$(7.5.43) \qquad P\{|X| > z\} \leq \frac{h^2}{12z^2}.$$

Suppose that $z = h/2$; then (7.5.39) states that

$$P\left\{|X| > \frac{h}{2}\right\} \leq \frac{1}{3},$$

whereas in fact the probability is zero (the density is zero below $-h/2$ and above $h/2$). You may be interested in applying the inequality when $z = h/4$ and checking your results against the true probability.

It is an important fact that the *average* of a large number of independent random observations often tends to be quite close to a constant. Chebyshev's inequality allows us to demonstrate this tendency.

THEOREM 7.5.4. *The Weak Law of Large Numbers.* Suppose X_1, X_2, ..., X_n are independently and identically distributed random variables, each with the same mean and variance, m and σ^2, respectively. Then given any number $\varepsilon > 0$, no matter how small, the probability that

$$(7.5.44) \qquad \overline{X} = \frac{X_1 + X_2 + \cdots + X_n}{n}$$

deviates from $E[X] = m$ by more than ε tends to zero as $n \to \infty$. Formally,

$$(7.5.45) \quad \lim_{n \to \infty} P\{(\overline{X} - m > \varepsilon) \cup (X - m < -\varepsilon)\} = \lim_{n \to \infty} P\{|\overline{X} - m| > \varepsilon\} = 0.$$

Proof: Observe

$$(7.5.46) \qquad E[\overline{X}] = \frac{1}{n}(E[X_1] + E[X_2] + \cdots + E[X_n]) = \frac{nm}{n} = m$$

and

$$\text{Var}[\overline{X}] = \frac{1}{n^2}(\text{Var}[X_1] + \text{Var}[X_2] + \cdots + \text{Var}[X_n]),$$

$$(7.5.47)$$

$$= \frac{n}{n^2}\sigma^2 = \frac{\sigma^2}{n}.$$

Now simply apply (7.5.40), putting $z = \varepsilon > 0$:

$$(7.5.48) \qquad P\{|\overline{X} - m| > \varepsilon\} \leq \frac{\sigma^2}{n\varepsilon^2}.$$

Apparently no matter how small ε is made, the right-hand side of (7.5.48) tends to zero with increasing n, and hence so does the probability on the left-hand side.

EXERCISES 7.5

1. Suppose X has the density function

$$f(x) = \frac{K}{x^6} \qquad \text{for } x \geq 1,$$
$$= 0 \qquad \text{for } x < 1.$$

   (a) Determine the constant K.
   (b) Find the expected value and variance of X.
   (c) Find the expected value of X^2 and X^3. (*Hint:* Use Theorem 7.5.1, expression (7.5.24). It is *not* necessary to find the density of $Y = X^2$.)
   (d) Find the distribution function of X^2 and from it, $E[X^2]$. Compare to the result of (c).

2. John must travel fifteen miles to work each morning. His rate of travel depends on the weather: on a clear day he drives at 50 m.p.h., whereas on a rainy day, his speed is reduced to 30 m.p.h. The probability that weather will be clear on a day is 0.8, and the probability of rain is 0.2.
   (a) Find the probability distribution of John's travel time.
   (b) What is John's expected travel time?
   (c) What are the variance and standard deviation of John's travel time?

3. A fair, six-sided die is tossed. Let X represent the number on the face that turns up (X values are 1, 2, 3, 4, 5, or 6).
   (a) Find the mean and variance of X.
   (b) Suppose that the die is tossed twice and that X_1 represents the number that turns up on the first toss, while X_2 represents the number that turns up on the second toss. Find the mean and variance of $X_1 + X_2$. What is the answer if the die is tossed n times, where n is arbitrary?

4. Let the random variable Y be given by

$$Y = a + bX,$$

   where X has expectation m_X and variance $\sigma_X{}^2$. Show that the expected value of Y is

$$m_Y = a + bm_X$$

   and that the variance is

$$\sigma_Y{}^2 = b^2 \sigma_X{}^2.$$

5. The annual income, I (in units of \$100,000), of a randomly selected citizen of the little town of Lynx Chapel has the following distribution:

$$F(x) = \begin{cases} 0 & x \leq 0 \\ 1 - \dfrac{1}{(1+x)^3} & x \geq 0. \end{cases}$$

   (a) Compute the mean annual income of a Lynx Chapelite.
   (b) The *median* of a continuous, always increasing distribution $F(x)$ is that number, x_{med}, having the following property:

$$F(x_{\text{med}}) = 0.5.$$

   What is the median annual income in Lynx Chapel?

6. The telephone company in Rippeyville charges for calls in the following way: \$0.10 for the first three minutes, or any part thereof; \$0.04 per minute for the part of any call exceeding three minutes. If D is the duration of a call, measured in minutes,
   (a) show that the total cost per call is as follows:

$$C = \begin{cases} 0.10 & \text{for } 0 \leq D \leq 3 \\ 0.10 + 0.04(D - 3) & \text{for } D \geq 3 \end{cases}$$

(b) Supposing that D has the exponential distribution with density

$$f_D(x) = \frac{e^{-x/3}}{3} \qquad x \geq 0,$$

$$= 0 \qquad x < 0,$$

find the expected cost per call, $E[C]$.

*7. A visitor to Las Vegas decides to play one of two slot machines and wishes to select Machine 1 or Machine 2, depending on which has the largest probability of payoff. He considers experimenting first to determine the probability, and the following strategies suggest themselves.

  (i) Play Machine 1 and Machine 2 once each. If he wins on Machine 1 and loses on Machine 2, he plays Machine 1 thereafter. If he wins on Machine 2 and loses on Machine 1, he plays Machine 2. If he loses on both or wins on both, he flips a fair coin $[P(H) = P(T)]$ and selects Machine 1 if a head turns up and Machine 2 otherwise.

  (ii) He flips a fair coin initially and plays Machine 1 if a head turns up and Machine 2 if a tail turns up.

Suppose that our gambler intends to play only four times, including any time spent in experimenting for information. Assume that Machine 1 has a probability $p_1 = 0.8$ of payoff, while Machine 2 pays off with probability $p_2 = 0.5$.

(a) Develop a tree analysis for strategies (i) and (ii).

(b) Which strategy gives the highest expected payoff? (You may wish to read the following chapter before attempting this problem.)

8. A city planner wishes to estimate the total number of square miles a city will occupy in twenty years' time. Suppose the city expands in a circular fashion and that the distribution function of its radius, R, is $F_R(x)$:

$$F_R(x) = \begin{cases} 0 & x \leq 5 \\ k(x - 5) & 5 \leq x \leq 15 \\ 1 & 15 \leq x \end{cases}$$

(a) Determine the constant k in order that F_R has a density. (*Hint:* If k is too small, there will be a jump in the distribution at $x = 15$. What happens if k is too big? Draw a picture.)

(b) The area of the city is

$$A = \pi R^2;$$

use the result of (a) to find the density function for A.

(c) What is $E[A]$?

9. Experience has shown that the monthly employment cost of a certain company depends on the number of shifts: one, two, or three. The dependence is

$$C = 4 + 0.5S + 0.3S^3,$$

where C represents monthly cost and S is the number of shifts. If the probability distribution of S is given by

$$P\{S = 1\} = 0.3,$$
$$P\{S = 2\} = 0.5,$$
$$P\{S = 3\} = 0.2,$$

find and graph the probability distribution of C. What is the probability that $C > 8$? What are the mean and variance of the monthly cost?

7.6   SOME USEFUL DISTRIBUTIONS, DISCRETE AND CONTINUOUS

A few simple probability distributions (the uniform and exponential) were introduced in the previous section. The purpose was to illustrate general properties of distributions by means of simple examples. In this section a number of additional distributions will be listed and briefly described. These will, in turn, provide the building blocks from which other, possibly more complex distributions can be derived in order to model situations arising in practice. It will also turn out that various of the distributions listed below may themselves be derived from fundamental probability arguments. Such derivations will appear from time to time in later sections.

Discrete Distributions

A. The discrete *uniform* distribution may be presented as follows: for N a positive integer,

(7.6.1)
$$P\{X = n\} = p_n = \begin{cases} \dfrac{1}{N} & \text{if } n = 1, 2, 3, \ldots, N \\ 0 & \text{otherwise} \end{cases}$$

Then

$$F_X(x) = \sum_{n \le x} p_n = \begin{cases} 0 & x < 1 \\ \dfrac{1}{N} & 1 \le x < 2 \\ \cdots & \cdots \\ \dfrac{k}{N} & k \le x < k + 1 \\ 1 & N \le x \end{cases}$$

Clearly the distribution above can begin at any point, and the separation between the individual, equally probable, possible values of X can be chosen at will. For example, if a numerical procedure is used to generate one-digit "random numbers," then the distribution of one such number denoted by R is

$$P\{R = r\} = \begin{cases} \dfrac{1}{10} & \text{if } r = 0.0, 0.1, 0.2, 0.3, \ldots, 0.9 \\ 0 & \text{otherwise} \end{cases}$$

B. The *binomial distribution* is given by the expression

(7.6.2)
$$P\{X = n\} = \binom{N}{n} p^n (1 - p)^{N-n},$$

where

$$\binom{N}{n} = \frac{N!}{(N - n)!n!} = \frac{N(N - 1)(N - 2) \cdots (N - n + 1)}{n(n - 1)(n - 2) \cdots 1}, \qquad 0 \le n \le N.$$

In the expression above, N and n are positive integers, with $n = 0, 1, 2, \ldots, N$. The parameter p is a real number: $0 \le p \le 1$.

The binomial describes the following chance situation. Suppose N individual experiments or trials are conducted, each having only two possible outcomes, which we may as well call success and failure (or heads and tails, win and lose, male and female, and so on). Then if the probability of success, p, is the same on each trial, but if the outcome of a trial—whether it be success or failure—has no influence on the outcome of any other so that trial outcomes are independent, it may be shown that the *total number of successes*, X, in the N trials has the binomial distribution.

We have already seen a specific example of the binomial distribution in the coin-tossing experiment of Example 7.4.8. One may show that the expected value of a binomial random variable is

(7.6.3)
$$E[X] = Np;$$
$$\mathrm{Var}[X] = Np(1 - p).$$

C. The *geometric distribution* is described by

(7.6.4)
$$P\{X = n\} = (1 - p)^{n-1}p \qquad n = 1, 2, 3, \ldots$$

and $0 \le p \le 1$. The geometric distribution, like the binomial, often refers to a sequence of independent trials, each having two outcomes. (These are called *Bernoulli trials* after a famous Swiss mathematician, James Bernoulli (1654–1705), one of the first probabilists.) Let us suppose that we perform such trials, for example, by flipping a coin, until the *first* success occurs. If p is the probability of a success on any trial, then the trial number, X, of the first success is a random variable, that is, $X = 1$ with probability p, $X = 2$ with probability $(1 - p)p$, and so on. If one trial is performed every Δ minutes, then ΔX represents the time to the first success; for this reason the geometric distribution is often called a *waiting-time* distribution.

The expected value of a geometrically distributed random variable is found to be

$$E(X) = \sum_{n=1}^{\infty} n(1 - p)^{n-1}p = \frac{1}{p};$$

$$\mathrm{Var}[X] = \frac{1 - p}{p^2}.$$

D. The *Poisson distribution* is given by the

(7.6.5)
$$P\{X = n\} = e^{-a}\frac{a^n}{n!}, \qquad n = 0, 1, 2, 3, \ldots; a > 0.$$

For the Poisson, $E[X] = \mathrm{Var}[X] = a$.

The Poisson distribution, as will be seen later, plays a central role in many probability models. It may be related to the sequence of Bernoulli-trial situations that also give meaning to the binomial and geometric distributions. Briefly, the Poisson is, like the binomial, a *counting* distribution. Thus the binomial is the distribution of the number of successes in N Bernoulli trials. If the number, N, of Bernoulli trials is allowed to become very large ($N \to \infty$) but the success probability is small ($p \to 0$) in such a way that $Np = a$, then it may be shown that the expression (7.6.2) giving the binomial distribution tends to the Poisson expression (7.6.5).

As an illustration of the connection between binomial and Poisson in a modeling situation, consider the next example.

EXAMPLE 7.6.1. Demand for computer time at a particular computing center may be modeled as follows. Consider a one-hour period, from 9:00 A.M. until 10:00 A.M. Users are apt to arrive independently at any time during this period; on the average, ten come in per hour. Let us, therefore, split up the hour into, say, one-minute intervals and model the arrival process as a sequence of Bernoulli trials, one occurring at each one-minute interval. There will be $N = 60$ such trials. Now in order that the expected number of arrivals per hour be some fixed number, denoted by a, we suppose that the probability of a success—here an arrival—is p, so chosen that $a = Np$. Furthermore, we assume that at most *one* arrival occurs during each one-minute time interval. With this model, the number of arrivals per hour has the binomial distribution (7.6.2); in particular, $N = 60$ and $p = \frac{1}{6}$. Now of course the division into one-minute intervals is arbitrary, and in fact a finer division (one second intervals, perhaps) may be expected to give an even better model. For one thing, the chance that two or more arrivals occur in the same interval decreases rapidly as interval size decreases. Consequently, we proceed to decrease the interval size indefinitely, allowing it to approach zero while the number of intervals correspondingly approaches infinity. At the same time the probability of success per interval must be made smaller in order to match the average number of arrivals per hour. Specifically, if the basic time interval were one second long, then there are now $N = 3600$ Bernoulli trials, and $p = \frac{1}{360}$ in order that $Np = a = 10$ arrivals per hour. The fact is that with even a *moderately* large N and small p (even for $N = 60$ and $p = \frac{1}{6}$) the Poisson expression (7.6.5) provides a very good approximation to the binomial distribution (7.6.2). We shall see more of the Poisson when we discuss the theory of queues (waiting lines) and inventories in later chapters.

Continuous Distributions

A. The continuous *uniform* or rectangular distribution has already been introduced in Example 7.4.9. Its density is of the form

(7.6.6)
$$f_X(x) = \begin{cases} \dfrac{1}{h} & \text{for } a \le x \le a + h, h > 0 \\ 0 & \text{elsewhere} \end{cases}$$

Its expected value is

(7.6.7)
$$E[X] = \int_a^{a+h} x\,\frac{dx}{h} = a + \frac{h}{2}$$

and

$$\text{Var}[X] = \frac{h^2}{12}.$$

B. The *normal* (or *Gaussian*) distribution has a density of the form

(7.6.8)
$$f_X(x) = \frac{1}{\sqrt{2\pi}\sigma} e^{-\frac{1}{2}\left(\frac{x-m}{\sigma}\right)^2},$$

where the parameter m can be any real number and σ is any positive number. The distribution function is representable (by making a change of variables) as follows:

$$(7.6.9) \qquad F_X(x) = \int_{-\infty}^{x} \frac{1}{\sqrt{2\pi}\sigma} e^{-\frac{1}{2}\left(\frac{t-m}{\sigma}\right)^2} dt = \int_{-\infty}^{\frac{x-m}{\sigma}} \frac{e^{-\frac{1}{2}z^2}}{\sqrt{2\pi}} dz,$$

and is widely tabulated (see references at the end of this chapter).

The normal distribution is of importance in a great many applications of statistics and probability. It tends to appear whenever *sums* of roughly independent and identically distributed random quantities are at issue. Thus certain measurement errors—for example, of geographic lengths—tend to be normally distributed. So, too, do the heights of individuals of the same age and so on. More specifically, recall that the binomial distribution (7.6.2) describes the distribution of the sum of the number of successes in N independent trials. It turns out that the normal distribution well approximates the binomial as N becomes large, in the sense that if the parameters m and σ^2 in the normal are taken to be

$$(7.6.10) \qquad \begin{aligned} m &= Np, \\ \sigma^2 &= Np(1-p), \end{aligned}$$

then if X is the number of binomial successes in N trials,

$$(7.6.11) \qquad P\{X \le x\} \approx \frac{1}{\sqrt{2\pi}} \int_{-\infty}^{\frac{x-m}{\sigma}} e^{-\frac{1}{2}z^2} dz.$$

We use the symbol $\approx$ to mean "is approximately equal to." Likewise, if in the Poisson distribution the parameter a becomes large (10 or greater), then if X is the number of events (arrivals) in the Poisson, putting

$$(7.6.12) \qquad \begin{aligned} m &= a, \\ \sigma^2 &= a \end{aligned}$$

gives

$$(7.6.13) \qquad P\{X \le x\} \approx \frac{1}{\sqrt{2\pi}} \int_{-\infty}^{\frac{x-m}{\sigma}} e^{-\frac{1}{2}z^2} dz.$$

THEOREM 7.6.1. Let $X_1, X_2, \ldots, X_n$ be independently and identically distributed random variables such that

$$E[X_i] = M \quad \text{and} \quad \text{Var}[X_i] = \tau^2;$$

M and τ are both finite.

$$S_n = X_1 + X_2 + \cdots + X_n.$$

Then,

$$(7.6.14) \qquad \lim_{n \to \infty} P\left\{ \frac{S_n - nM}{\tau\sqrt{n}} \le x \right\} = \frac{1}{\sqrt{2\pi}} \int_{-\infty}^{x} e^{-\frac{1}{2}z^2} dz.$$

In other words, as n becomes large, the distribution of the sum S_n approaches the normal form with mean $m = nM$ and variance $\sigma^2 = n\tau^2$. This is a simple form of the famous Central Limit Theorem. Very often the normal approximation is very satisfactory for moderately large n, especially if x is restricted to be less than or equal to 2 or 3 in magnitude.

It may be shown that the normal density has a symmetric bell shape, with

$$E[X] = m$$

(7.6.15)   and

$$\text{Var}[X] = \sigma^2.$$

Needless to say, not every symmetric bell-shaped density is normal.

C. The *gamma* or *Erlang* distribution has the density

(7.6.16)
$$f_X(x) = \begin{cases} e^{-\alpha x} \dfrac{(\alpha x)^{\beta - 1}}{\Gamma(\beta)} \alpha & x \geq 0 \\ 0 & x < 0 \end{cases}$$

where α and β are both real and positive. Here $\Gamma(\beta)$ is the gamma function, a generalization of the factorial; $\Gamma(\beta) = (\beta - 1)!$ when β is an integer. Notice that when $\beta = 1$, the gamma density is the *exponential* density introduced in Example 7.4.6.*

The gamma density is frequently invoked in probability modeling studies. The density (7.6.16) may appear as shown below:

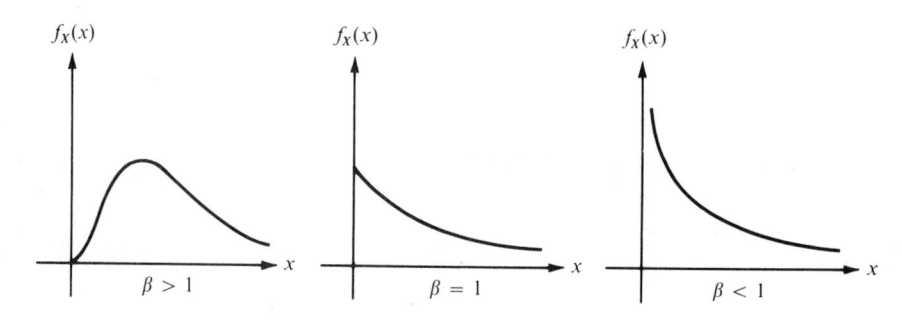

FIGURE 7.6.1

If one tabulates the times, say, to complete certain manufacturing or repair activities, the density is likely to resemble one of these gamma forms. It may be shown that the *sum* of N independent random variables, each having the exponential density $e^{-\alpha x}\alpha$, is itself gamma distributed with parameters $\beta = N$ and α. The mean and variance of the gamma are

$$E[X] = \frac{\beta}{\alpha}$$

(7.6.17)   and

$$\text{Var}[X] = \frac{\beta}{\alpha^2}.$$

---

* In general (for noninteger β), the gamma function is defined by the integral

$$\Gamma(\beta) = \int_0^\infty e^{-y} y^{\beta - 1} \, dy \qquad \text{for } \beta > 0.$$

Again, for integer β,

$$\int_0^x e^{-y} \frac{y^{\beta - 1} \, dy}{(\beta - 1)!} = \left[1 - \left(1 + x + \frac{x^2}{2!} + \frac{x^3}{3!} + \cdots + \frac{x^{\beta - 1}}{(\beta - 1)!} \right) e^{-x} \right].$$

Note that when $\beta = 1$, the expression above gives the mean and variance of the exponential distribution as

$$E[X] = \frac{1}{\alpha}, \qquad \text{Var}[X] = \frac{1}{\alpha^2}.$$

D. The *Weibull* distribution is given by

(7.6.18)
$$F_X(x) = \begin{cases} 1 - e^{-(ax)^b} & x \geq 0 \\ 0 & x < 0 \end{cases}$$

where a and b are positive constants. Its density is

(7.6.19)
$$f_X(x) = ab(ax)^{b-1} e^{-(ax)^b},$$

for $x \geq 0$, and zero otherwise.

The Weibull distribution has found wide application for the description of the *time to failure* of electronic devices (radars, computers, and so on). Suppose that such a device is initially in good operating condition; then if X represents the number of hours until failure occurs, X is often reasonably taken to be Weibull distributed. We notice that if $b = 1$, the Weibull is again of *exponential* form.

E. The *beta* distribution has a density of the form

(7.6.20)
$$f_X(x) = \begin{cases} kx^{p-1}(1-x)^{q-1} & 0 \leq x \leq 1 \\ 0 & \text{otherwise} \end{cases}$$

where p and q are both positive real numbers, and the constant k is selected so that the beta density integrates to unity:

(7.6.21)
$$k = \frac{\Gamma(p+q)}{\Gamma(p)\Gamma(q)}.$$

The beta distribution has mean and variance equal to

(7.6.22)
$$E[X] = \frac{p}{p+q},$$

$$\text{Var}[X] = \frac{pq}{(p+q)^2(p+q+1)}.$$

Many of the distributions above are of direct use in modeling studies for reasons suggested here and for other reasons to appear later.

We briefly mention methods of *fitting* one of the distributions above when data are available (by this we mean using the data to estimate the parameters of the chosen distribution). Two methods are of wide use and suggest themselves for initial consideration. They are the *method of moments* and the method of *maximum likelihood*. Of these two, the method of moments is frequently the easiest, whereas maximum likelihood is best when large quantities of data are available—for precise statements of results, a book on mathematical statistics should be consulted. For many distributions the two methods essentially or exactly agree. Imagine, then, that a sample of n observations is available from one of our distributions: denote these observations on the random variable X, by $x_1, x_2, \ldots, x_n$. The method of moments proceeds by computing the *sample moments* or averages:

$$(7.6.23) \qquad m_1 = \frac{x_1 + x_2 + \cdots + x_n}{n} = \frac{1}{n} \sum_{i=1}^{n} x_i$$

$$(7.6.24) \qquad m_2 = \frac{x_1^2 + x_2^2 + \cdots + x_n^2}{n},$$

$$(7.6.25) \qquad m_3 = \frac{x_1^3 + x_2^3 + \cdots + x_n^3}{n},$$

$$\cdots$$

One then equates the sample moments to the corresponding expectations of X, X^2, X^3, and so on, in the theoretical distribution of model and solves for the unknown parameters. For illustration see the next example.

EXAMPLE 7.6.2. Suppose the time, X, to repair a computer is gamma distributed with parameters α and β (see C above). If n actual repair times are observed, we compute m_1 and m_2 as shown above and set down the following equations (see (7.6.17)):

$$(7.6.26) \qquad m_1 = \frac{\beta}{\alpha},$$

$$(7.6.27) \qquad m_2 - m_1^2 = \frac{\beta}{\alpha^2}.$$

In the second of the equations above, $m_2 - m_1^2$ is set equal to the sample variance:

$$(7.6.28) \qquad s^2 = \frac{1}{n} \sum_{i=1}^{n} (x_i - m_1)^2.$$

Let $\bar{\alpha}$ and $\bar{\beta}$ denote the solutions of these equations:

$$(7.6.29) \qquad \bar{\alpha} = \frac{m_1}{s^2}$$

and

$$(7.6.30) \qquad \bar{\beta} = \frac{m_1^2}{s^2}.$$

We then use $\bar{\alpha}$ and $\bar{\beta}$ as our estimates of the unknown parameters.

To carry out the maximum-likelihood method, the *likelihood function L* is formed

$$(7.6.31) \qquad L = f(x_1 | \theta) f(x_2 | \theta) \cdots f(x_n | \theta);$$

here θ represents the unknown parameters. The likelihood function is proportional to the probability of actually observing the values $x_1, \ldots, x_n$. Thereafter, L is maximized by choice of θ; the numbers obtained, denoted by $\hat{\theta}$, are then the maximum likelihood estimates sought.

EXAMPLE 7.6.3. A piece of electronic equipment (for example, the computer just mentioned) fails at an exponentially distributed random time following last repair.

The exponential density is specified in terms of the unknown parameter θ:

(7.6.32)
$$f_X(x, \theta) = e^{-x/\theta} \frac{1}{\theta} \qquad x \geq 0, \theta > 0,$$

$$= 0 \qquad x < 0.$$

It can be shown that θ is the expected value of the time to failure. Suppose n such times to failure have been observed: $x_1, x_2, \ldots, x_n$. The likelihood function can be written as

(7.6.33)
$$L = e^{-x_1/\theta} \frac{1}{\theta} \cdots e^{-x_n/\theta} \frac{1}{\theta}.$$

The maximum-likelihood approach is to choose θ so as to maximize L. Now it is usually easiest, and equivalent, to maximize the (natural) logarithm of the likelihood in order to determine θ. Thus we differentiate:

(7.6.34)
$$\frac{d}{d\theta} \log L = \frac{d}{d\theta} \left[-\sum_{i=1}^{n} \frac{x_i}{\theta} + n \log \theta \right],$$

$$= \frac{\sum_{i=1}^{n} x_i}{\theta^2} - \frac{n}{\theta},$$

and set the result equal to zero and solve to find the estimate

(7.6.35)
$$\hat{\theta} = \frac{1}{n} \sum_{i=1}^{n} x_i = \bar{x},$$

the sample mean. As seems plausible, the sample mean is used to estimate the population mean, or expectation, θ. This is the same result as that which would be obtained by means of the method of moments. It is of interest to notice that if the exponential is expressed in terms of the parameter, $\lambda = 1/\theta$, the estimate is

(7.6.36)
$$\hat{\lambda} = \frac{1}{\bar{x}}$$

In general, it turns out to be true that the maximum likelihood possesses the *invariance property*, by which is meant the following. Suppose θ is an unknown parameter and g is a continuous monotonic (either increasing or decreasing) function of θ. Then the maximum likelihood estimate of $g(\theta)$ is simply $g(\hat{\theta})$, $\hat{\theta}$ being the maximum likelihood estimate of θ. In other words,

(7.6.37)
$$\hat{g}(\theta) = g(\hat{\theta}).$$

Unfortunately, it is not always possible to solve explicitly the equations obtained by setting the differentiated log-likelihood function equal to zero. For an example, we refer to the situation of Example 7.6.2. Here the likelihood function is

$$L(\alpha, \beta) = e^{-\alpha x_1} \frac{(\alpha x_1)^{\beta - 1}}{\Gamma(\beta)} e^{-\alpha x_2} \frac{(\alpha x_2)^{\beta - 1}}{\Gamma(\beta)} \cdots e^{-\alpha x_n} \frac{(\alpha x_n)^{\beta - 1}}{\Gamma(\beta)}.$$

Then

$$\log L = -\alpha \sum_{i=1}^{n} x_i + (\beta - 1) \sum_{i=1}^{n} \log x_i + (\beta - 1)n \log \alpha - n \log \Gamma(\beta),$$

and the equations to be solved are

$$(7.6.38) \qquad \frac{\partial \log L}{\partial \alpha} = 0 \quad \text{or} \quad \sum_{i=1}^{n} x_i = \frac{(\beta - 1)n}{\partial \alpha}$$

and

$$(7.6.39) \qquad \frac{\partial \log L}{\partial \beta} = 0 \quad \text{or} \quad \sum_{i=1}^{n} \log x_i + n \log \alpha = n \frac{d}{d\beta} \log \Gamma(\beta).$$

Now these equations must be solved simultaneously in order to find the maximum likelihood estimates $\hat{\alpha}$ and $\hat{\beta}$, a task that must be carried out numerically. In this particular case, tables have been prepared to facilitate obtaining the estimates.

Note that neither the maximum likelihood estimate nor the moment estimate will ordinarily equal the quantity being estimated. Since the estimates are constructed from observations, they have probability distributions. It is valuable to know the form of this *sampling distribution*, and fortunately it can be shown that under broad regularity conditions, the maximum likelihood estimate has approximately the normal distribution as the number of observations utilized becomes large. In case several unknown parameters are involved, the distribution becomes a multivariate, or joint, normal; for discussion of this idea, see the next section. In any case, for a single unknown parameter θ, it may be shown that as the sample size $n \to \infty$, the maximum likelihood estimate $\hat{\theta}$ has the normal distribution with mean θ and variance given by

$$(7.6.40) \qquad \sigma_{\hat{\theta}}^2 \approx \frac{1}{n} \frac{1}{\int_{-\infty}^{\infty} \left(\frac{\partial \log f(x, \theta)}{\partial \theta}\right)^2 f(x, \theta) \, dx},$$

where $f(x, \theta)$ is the density function associated with the observations. Finally, the maximum likelihood estimate is *efficient*: it usually tends to have at least as small a variance as does any other estimate when the sample size, n, becomes large.

EXAMPLE 7.6.3 (continued). Here $f(x, \theta)$ is the exponential given by (7.6.32). Thus, according to the discussion above, the maximum likelihood estimate is approximately normally distributed as n, the sample size, becomes large. To compute the variance, observe that

$$\ln f(x, \theta) = -\frac{x}{\theta} - \ln \theta.$$

Differentiation gives

$$(7.6.41) \qquad \frac{\partial \ln f}{\partial \theta} = \frac{x}{\theta^2} - \frac{1}{\theta}.$$

Squaring and integrating give the denominator of (7.6.40):

$$\frac{1}{\theta^2} \int_0^\infty \left(\frac{x}{\theta} - 1\right)^2 e^{-x/\theta} \frac{1}{\theta} \, dx = \frac{1}{\theta^2};$$

you may change variables ($z = x/\theta$) and verify this. Thus

$$(7.6.42) \qquad \sigma_{\hat{\theta}}^2 \approx \frac{\theta^2}{n}.$$

In fact in this case the expression above is exactly correct for every n value, since $n\hat{\theta}$ is the sum of n exponentially distributed random variables and hence is a gamma-distributed random variable with mean $n\theta$ and variance $n\theta^2$.

You should not conclude that the method of moments and that of maximum likelihood are the only methods of parameter estimation. Such is far from true. For example, it is sometimes useful to estimate by means of *order statistics*: one takes a sample of n observations, $x_1, x_2, \ldots, x_n$, and then arranges them in increasing order:

$$x_{(1)}(= \text{smallest of } x_1, \ldots, x_n), \qquad x_{(2)}(= \text{second smallest}), \ldots,$$

$$x_{(n)}(= \text{largest of } x_1, \ldots, x_n).$$

Intuitively one sees that, for example, the *range*,

$$R_n = x_{(n)} - x_{(1)},$$

measures the spread or dispersion of the underlying distribution (as does the standard deviation), while the *median*, or middle value $x_{(n+1)/2}$ when n is odd, measures the location of the distribution. Oftentimes it is easier to compute such statistics than it is to make the moment or maximum likelihood estimates. While estimates based on order statistics are perhaps inefficient in large samples, they are quite good enough when samples are small and quick answers are desired. You should refer to textbooks on mathematical statistics for further, and deeper, discussion of the problems of estimating model parameters, discriminating between alternative models, and so on.

EXERCISES 7.6

1. Show that the mathematical expectation of a random variable X is $E[X] = (N+1)/2$ if X has the discrete uniform distribution. In particular, the expected value of a one-digit random number is 0.45.

2. A certain complex system has three vital components, each of which survives a mission (a moonshot, perhaps) with probability p. Each component fails independently. Use the binomial distribution to calculate the probability that the mission is successful if
    (a) all components must survive in order that the mission succeed.
    (b) at least two components must survive to ensure success.

3. It has been stated that the Poisson distribution well approximates the binomial when N is large and p is small. Carry out the following steps, which tend to verify this statement.
    (a) Show, from (7.6.2), that for a binomial random variable

    $$P\{X = 0\} = (1 - p)^N.$$

    Then substitute $p = a/N$, and let $N \to \infty$. Compare to the probability of zero as given by the Poisson.

    (*Hint:* $\lim_{N \to \infty} \left(1 + \dfrac{x}{N}\right)^N = e^x$.)

    (b) Let $Np = a = 10$ and $N = 60$. Calculate numerically $P\{X = 0\}$, $P\{X = 1\}$, $P\{X = 2\}$, using the binomial formula (7.6.2). Then apply the Poisson formula (7.6.5) with $a = 10$ to calculate the same probabilities.

4. A group of n experts is brought together to solve a certain complex technical problem. Supposing that each man works independently and has an equal probability p of solving the problem in a given time, what is the probability that the problem remains unsolved at the end of the allotted time? Criticize the model proposed.
    (a) Suppose that $p = 0.5$ and $n = 4$; what is the probability of achieving a solution?
    (b) Suppose that two of the four men have a probability of 0.75 of achieving a solution and that the other two have a probability of 0.25. The average probability of the group is thus 0.5. Is the group's probability the same as in (a)? Explain.

5. The cost of producing N special transistors to order is of the form

    $$C = a + bN + cN^2,$$

    where a, b, and c are all positive. If N has the Poisson distribution

    $$P\{N = n\} = e^{-m} \frac{m^n}{n!} \qquad n = 0, 1, 2, \ldots,$$

    show that

    $$E[C] = a + bm + c[m^2 + m].$$

    (*Hint:* Let $(N - m)^2 = N^2 - 2Nm + m^2$ and take expectations to find $E[N]^2$.)

6. A construction firm makes ten bids a year on jobs. Each bid is independently accepted with probability 0.2. The company breaks even if it can land three or more jobs, and pays an extra dividend if it does six or more jobs.
    (a) Calculate the probability of breaking even.
    (b) Calculate the probability of breaking even without an extra dividend.
    (c) What is the probability that the company pays an extra dividend on three consecutive years?

7. An investor must decide whether to buy a particular common stock. Currently the stock is selling for $10 a share. He estimates that six months later it will sell for $$S$ a share, where S is normally distributed with mean $15, and standard deviation $6. (He has estimated these parameters by observing the past performance of other similar securities.) If the investor buys the stock,
    (a) what is the probability that he will lose money?
    (b) what is the probability that he will at least double his money?

8. A particular repair activity requires a random time, T, for completion. T is distributed according to a gamma distribution with mean 50 (minutes) and variance 500 (minutes²).
    (a) Find the parameters β and α (β is often called the *shape* parameter and α the *scale* parameter).
    (b) Calculate the probability that $T < 25$ minutes and that $T > 75$ minutes. Use the formula in the footnote of this section.
    (c) Use the mean and variance above and apply the normal distribution to approximate the probabilities above.
    (d) Apply the normal approximation to the gamma with mean 50 and variance 1250. Compare to the exact result. (You must repeat steps (a) and (b) above.)
    Compare the adequacies of the normal approximations found in (c) and (d).

7.7   JOINT AND CONDITIONAL DISTRIBUTIONS

In previous sections, emphasis was placed on the description of a single random variable and its distribution function. It is also possible and often desirable to study the joint or simultaneous behavior of two or more random variables. Some examples follow.

EXAMPLE 7.7.1. An experiment consists of tossing a coin three times. Let X represent the number of heads that occur and Y the number of tails. Apparently X and Y are random variables, since for each possible outcome of the experiment—for example, for the sample point {HTH}—there corresponds a value for X (in the example given, 2) and for Y (here, 1). Clearly, too, X and Y are *dependent*: given the value of X, Y is perfectly determined, since, in this case, $X + Y = 3$. Such a strong degree of dependence is rare. Usually with measurements of related quantities X and Y and with X observed, the distribution of the corresponding related Y is merely more tightly concentrated around some central value (dependent on X) than was true before knowledge of X was available. In the example above, the concentration is so great that Y is determined once X is given.

EXAMPLE 7.7.2. The heights and weights of a large group of executives in their thirties (precisely, a random sample of the thirtyish executive employees of a company) are recorded. The density functions of their weights appear below. Next, the

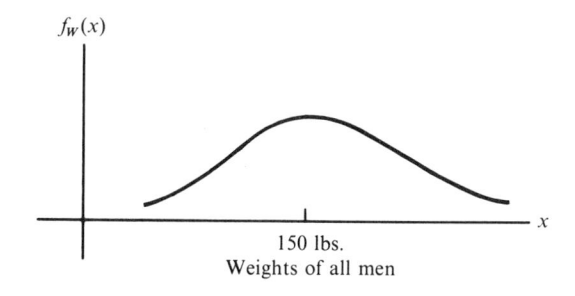

150 lbs.
Weights of all men

density function of the weights of those executives between 5 feet and 5 feet 6 inches tall was constructed, and then the density function of those of height between 6 feet and 6 feet 6 inches was recorded. The results appeared as follows. These figures are

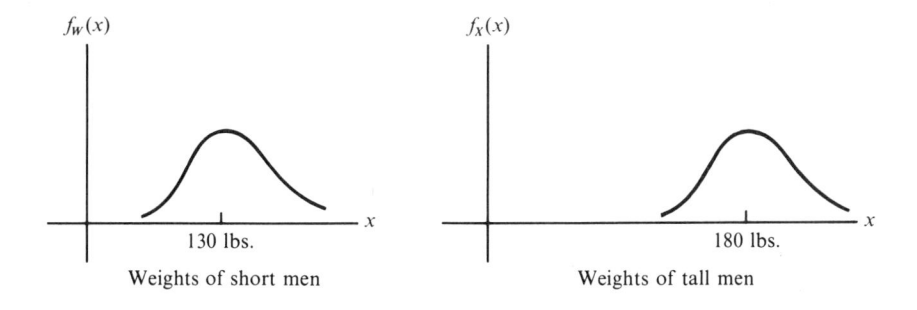

Weights of short men   Weights of tall men

intended to illustrate the dependence between height and weight: as a person becomes taller he is also likely to become heavier; this fact is reflected in the locations of the densities given. Furthermore, the variation around the mean is seen to be smaller for the densities segregated with respect to height—the *conditional densities*—than it is for the original density representing all men together. It thus appears that knowledge of a man's height allows more accurate prediction of his weight than does knowledge of his membership in a particular broad group.

DEFINITION 7.7.1. The random variables X and Y are said to have the *joint distribution* $F(x, y)$ if the probability of the event

$$(7.7.1) \qquad (X \le x) \cap (Y \le y)$$

can be expressed in terms of $F(x, y)$. Consider the following cases:

(i) *F discrete*. Then the distribution is given by

$$(7.7.2) \qquad P\{X = i, Y = j\} = p_{ij},$$

for $p_{ij} \ge 0$, and

$$(7.7.3) \qquad \sum_i \sum_j p_{ij} = 1.$$

For any x and y,

$$(7.7.4) \qquad F(x, y) = \sum_{i \le x} \sum_{j \le y} p_{ij}.$$

(ii) *F continuous*. The distribution is expressed in terms of the joint density, $f_{X,Y}(x, y)$:

$$(7.7.5) \quad P\{(X \le x) \cap (Y \le y)\} = P\{X \le x, Y \le y\} = \int_{-\infty}^{x} \int_{-\infty}^{y} f_{X,Y}(x', y')\, dx'\, dy',$$

for $f \ge 0$, $\iint f\, dx'\, dy' = 1$.

(iii) *F discrete in one variable, continuous in the other*. For example, F may be given by

$$(7.7.6) \qquad P(X = i, Y \le y) = \int_{-\infty}^{y} f_{X,Y}(i, y')\, dy'.$$

The cases above are illustrative only and do not represent all possible combinations. For example, one of the random variables may have a mixed distribution, possibly taking on certain values with positive probability and being described by a density otherwise. See Example 7.5.1 for an illustration.

The joint distribution has the following properties:

(a) $F(\infty, y) = \lim_{x \to \infty} F(x, y)$ and $F(x, \infty) = \lim_{y \to \infty} F(x, y)$

are both ordinary, one-variable (sometimes called univariate) distribution functions. They are, respectively, the distributions of Y and X alone and are called the *marginal distributions* of F. Also,

$$\lim_{y \to \infty} F(\infty, y) = \lim_{x \to \infty} F(x, \infty) = 1.$$

$(7.7.7)$ (b) $F(-\infty, y) = F(x, -\infty) = 0.$

(c) F is nondecreasing in x and y: if $x_2 > x_1$ and $y_2 > y_1$, then

$$F(x_2, y) \ge F(x_1, y) \qquad \text{for any } y$$

$(7.7.8)$ and

$$F(x, y_2) \ge F(x, y_1) \qquad \text{for any } x.$$

(d)   The event $(x_1 < X \le x_2)$ and $(y_1 < Y \le y_2)$ is represented by a rectangle in the x-y plane:

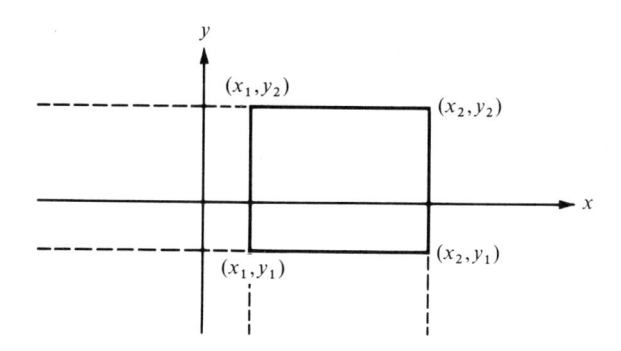

The probability of this event may be expressed as follows (obtain the probabilities of falling in the quadrants southwest of (x_2, y_2), (x_2, y_1), (x_1, y_2), and (x_1, y_1) and from these, the probability of falling in the rectangle):

$$P\{X \le x_2, Y \le y_2\} - P\{X \le x_2, Y \le y_1\} - P\{X \le x_1, Y \le y_2\} + P\{X \le x_1, Y \le y_1\}$$

(7.7.9)
$$= F(x_2, y_2) - F(x_2, y_1)$$
$$- F(x_1, y_2) + F(x_1, y_1).$$

Thus it follows that the expression above must be nonnegative for any choice of $x_1 < x_2, y_1 < y_2$. The fact (c) that F is nondecreasing in each variable separately does not guarantee (d). By the construction of our models, however, the consistency requirement above will automatically be satisfied.

A very important joint distributional situation is the following.

DEFINITION 7.7.2. Two random variables are said to be *independent* under any of the following conditions:

(i) Their joint distribution is expressed as a product:

(7.7.10)
$$F_{X,Y}(x, y) = F_X(x)F_Y(y)$$

(ii) They are continuous random variables (have densities), and the joint density is a product:

(7.7.11)
$$f_{X,Y}(x, y) = f_X(x)f_Y(y)$$

(iii) They are discrete random variables such that

$$P\{X = i\} = p_X(i) \quad \text{and} \quad P\{Y = j\} = p_Y(j),$$

for all i and j; then

(7.7.12)
$$P\{X = i, Y = j\} = p_X(i)p_Y(j).$$

(iv) One random variable (X) is discrete and the other (Y) has a density. Then,

(7.7.13)
$$P\{X = i, Y \le y\} = p_X(i) \int_{-\infty}^{y} f(y')\, dy'.$$

Although the cases above are not exhaustive, they indicate explicitly the requirements for independence. The definition above carries over directly to sets of more than two random variables.

EXAMPLE 7.7.3. An experiment consists of tossing a pair of dice. Let X equal the number on the top face for one die (1, 2, 3, 4, 5, 6), and Y, the number on the top face for the other. Reasoning that the dice have no influence on one another, we *assume* that X and Y are independent in the sense used above. Thus, the probability of the event

$$(X \le 3) \cap (Y \le 4)$$

is easily calculated to be $F_X(3) \cdot F_Y(4)$. Consequently, if the dice are fair (equal probability for all faces), this probability equals 1/3.

EXAMPLE 7.7.4. An airplane is powered by two engines. The engines are, independently, subject to failure. Their times to failure, measured from flight takeoff, are T_1 and T_2, both having the same continuous distribution function, $G(x)$, with density $g(x)$. Suppose the airplane can fly as long as at least one engine operates. We are interested in the probability that the plane will complete a mission or trip of duration t. Now the plane *fails* to make the trip in the event that

(7.7.14) $(T_1 < t) \cap (T_2 < t).$

Assuming T_1 and T_2 to be independent,

$$P\{(T_1 < t) \cap (T_2 < t)\} = P\{T_1 < t\}P\{T_2 < t\},$$
(7.7.15)
$$= G(t)G(t).$$

Thus the probability that the plane *succeeds* in making the trip is the probability of the complement of the event (7.7.14), and hence

(7.7.16) $P\{\text{success}\} = 1 - G^2(t).$

There is another useful way of viewing this situation. Notice that the plane fails if the *maximum* of the two times T_1 and T_2 is less than t. The new random variable

(7.7.17) $T = \max(T_1, T_2)$

then becomes of interest, and since the event $T \le t$ occurs if and only if $T_1 \le t$ and $T_2 \le t$, we have for the distribution of the *maximum, T, of two independently and identically distributed random variables*

(7.7.18) $F_T(t) = G^2(t).$

Obviously if we are dealing with n such random variables, the distribution is $G^n(t)$.

Discussion of the maximum of two or more random variables immediately suggests discussion of the minimum. This we do by means of another example.

EXAMPLE 7.7.5. A power generation system consists of a turbine and a generator. If either fails, the system becomes inoperative until repair takes place. Suppose that both are put into operation at the same time, that X represents the time to failure for the turbine, and Y the time to failure for the generator. The distributions of X and Y are $F(x)$ and $G(y)$ respectively. Finally, we assume X and Y are independent.

The turbine-generator system survives for a time t if and only if each component survives. Putting this another way,

(7.7.19) $\min(X, Y) > t$ if and only if $(X > t) \cap (Y > t).$

Therefore, utilizing the assumption of independence, we have

$$P\{\min(X, Y) > t\} = P\{X > t\}P\{Y > t\},$$
$$= [1 - F(t)][1 - G(t)].$$

(7.7.20)

If we let $H(t)$ denote the distribution of the minimum, it then follows that

(7.7.21) $$P\{\min(X, Y) > t\} = 1 - H(t) = [1 - F(t)][1 - G(t)],$$

or

(7.7.22) $$H(t) = 1 - [1 - F(t)][1 - G(t)].$$

If both F and G have densities—f and g respectively—then the density, h, of H is, by differentiation of (7.7.22),

(7.7.23) $$h(t) = f(t)[1 - G(t)] + g(t)[1 - F(t)].$$

An especially interesting distribution for which to compute the minimum is the exponential (see Section 7.6).

EXAMPLE 7.7.6. A computer facility involves n failure-prone subsystems. All have the same *exponential* distribution of time to failure. If one subsystem fails, the entire computer facility goes down. Assume that the distribution function of time to failure for one subsystem is, for positive a,

(7.7.24) $$F(x) = 1 - e^{-ax} \qquad t \geq 0,$$
$$= 0 \qquad\qquad t < 0.$$

Then, following the argument of the previous example, the distribution of system time to failure is, for $t > 0$,

$$H(t) = 1 - [1 - F(t)]^n,$$
$$= 1 - e^{-nat};$$

(7.7.25)

so *system* time to failure is exponentially distributed if *subsystem* times to failure are exponential and independent. Notice that the expected time to system failure is $1/n$th of the expected time for the components. Thus a complex system having many components or subsystems can often be expected to fail more frequently than a smaller system made up of the same, or possibly similar, components. However, no blanket statements can be made because design and usage considerations may bring about a reversal of this seemingly obvious comparison.

In Section 7.5, expectations of single random variables were treated, and the results illustrated. It is of interest to extend these ideas to consider expectations of certain combinations of random variables. The variables may or may not be independent.

DEFINITION 7.7.3. Suppose $g(x, y)$ is a function of two variables. Then the mathematical expectation of $g(X, Y)$, X and Y being jointly distributed random variables, is

(7.7.26) $$E[g(X, Y)] = \sum_i \sum_j g(x_i, y_j)P\{X = x_i, Y = y_j\},$$

if X and Y are discrete and take on values x_1, x_2, x_3 and $y_1, y_2, y_3, \ldots$, respectively. If X and Y are continuous, then

$$(7.7.27) \qquad E[g(X, Y)] = \int_{-\infty}^{\infty} \int_{-\infty}^{\infty} g(x, y) f_{X,Y}(x, y)\, dx\, dy.$$

The mixed-case definition is obvious and is left for you to work out. In an exactly analogous way we may define the expectation of three or more random variables. Thus, for example,

$$E[g(X, Y, Z)] = \int_{-\infty}^{\infty} \int_{-\infty}^{\infty} \int_{-\infty}^{\infty} g(x, y, z) f(x, y, z)\, dx\, dy\, dz,$$

when f is the joint density of the three variables. Again the expectation represents an average; equivalently, the various possible values of $g(x, y)$ are weighted by their probabilities, and the result is totaled.

Certain particular functions of X and Y are of special interest and have considerable use.

THEOREM 7.7.1. Let X and Y be two random variables with joint distribution $F_{X,Y}(x, y)$. Then the expectation of their sum

$$(7.7.28) \qquad Z = X + Y$$

equals the *sum* of the expectations of X and Y, whether or not the latter are independent:

$$(7.7.29) \qquad E[Z] = E[X + Y] = E[X] + E[Y].$$

Proof: We carry out the proof for the case in which X and Y have the joint density $f_{X,Y}(x, y)$. Then

$$(7.7.30) \qquad E[X + Y] = \int_{-\infty}^{\infty} \int_{-\infty}^{\infty} (x + y) f_{X,Y}(x, y)\, dx\, dy,$$

$$(7.7.31) \qquad = \int_{-\infty}^{\infty} \int_{-\infty}^{\infty} x f_{X,Y}(x, y)\, dx\, dy + \int_{-\infty}^{\infty} \int_{-\infty}^{\infty} y f(x, y)\, dx\, dy.$$

Now

$$(7.7.32) \qquad \int_{-\infty}^{\infty} f_{X,Y}(x, y)\, dy = f_X(x)$$

and

$$(7.7.33) \qquad \int_{-\infty}^{\infty} f_{X,Y}(x, y)\, dx = f_Y(y),$$

where the results are the marginal densities of X and Y respectively. Consequently, if we first integrate the leftmost integral on the right side of (7.7.31) with respect to y and the rightmost with respect to x, there results

$$(7.7.34) \qquad E[X + Y] = \int_{-\infty}^{\infty} x f_X(x)\, dx + \int_{-\infty}^{\infty} y f_Y(y)\, dy,$$

$$= E[X] + E[Y].$$

The proof goes through in exactly the same way for three or more variables. To carry it out for discrete random variables merely involves replacing the densities by probabilities and summing instead of integrating. In Exercise 4, you will be asked to show that if $Z = aX + bY$, then

$$(7.7.35) \qquad E[Z] = aE[X] + bE[Y].$$

THEOREM 7.7.2. Let X and Y be two *independent* random variables. Then the expectation of their *product* is the product of their expectations:

$$(7.7.36) \qquad E[XY] = E[X]E[Y].$$

Proof: Again assume that X and Y have densities

$$(7.7.37) \qquad E[XY] = \int_{-\infty}^{\infty} \int_{-\infty}^{\infty} xy f_{X,Y}(x, y)\, dx\, dy.$$

By the assumption of independence (see Definition 7.7.2 (ii), (1.7.11)),

$$(7.7.38) \qquad f_{X,Y}(x, y) = f_X(x) f_Y(y).$$

Therefore factorization is possible:

$$
(7.7.39) \qquad
\begin{aligned}
E[XY] &= \int_{-\infty}^{\infty} \int_{-\infty}^{\infty} xy f_X(x) f_Y(y)\, dx\, dy, \\
&= \int_{-\infty}^{\infty} x f_X(x)\, dx \int_{-\infty}^{\infty} y f_Y(y)\, dy, \\
&= E[X]E[Y].
\end{aligned}
$$

Again the proof goes through in general and for more than two independent variables. In somewhat more generality, imagine that we have two functions $g(x)$ and $h(y)$ that in no way depend on one another. Then

$$(7.7.40) \qquad E[g(X)h(Y)] = E[g(X)]E[h(Y)],$$

provided X and Y are independent.

If X and Y are *not* independent, then the expectation of XY is a useful quantity in its own right.

DEFINITION 7.7.4. If X and Y have the joint distribution $F_{X,Y}(x, y)$, then their *covariance* is

$$
(7.7.41) \qquad
\begin{aligned}
\text{Cov}(X, Y) &= E\{(X - E[X])(Y - E[Y])\}, \\
&= E\{XY - YE[X] - XE[Y] + E[X]E[Y]\}, \\
&= E[XY] - E[X]E[Y],
\end{aligned}
$$

where the last form follows from the fact that $E[X]$ and $E[Y]$ are constants and may be moved through the expectation; for example,

$$E\{XE[Y]\} = E[Y]E\{X\}.$$

The *correlation* between X and Y is

$$(7.7.42) \qquad \text{corr}(X, Y) = \frac{\text{Cov}(X, Y)}{\sqrt{\text{Var}[X]\text{Var}[Y]}}.$$

THEOREM 7.7.3. If X and Y are two random variables with joint distribution F, then

$$\text{Var}[X + Y] = \text{Var}[X] + \text{Var}[Y] + 2\,\text{Cov}[X, Y].$$

Proof: If X and Y have densities, then

$$\text{Var}[X + Y] = \iint (x + y - (E[X] + E[Y])^2 f_{X, Y}(x, y)\, dx\, dy,$$

$$= \iint [(x - E[X])^2 + (y - E[Y])^2 + 2(x - E[X])(y - E[Y])]$$

$$\times f_{X, Y}(x, y)\, dx\, dy,$$

$$= \iint (x - E[X])^2 f_{X, Y}(x, y)\, dx\, dy + \iint (y - E[Y])^2 f_{X, Y}(x, y)\, dx\, dy$$

$$+ 2 \iint (x - E[X])(y - E[Y]) f_{X, Y}(x, y)\, dx\, dy.$$

Now follow the lead of (7.7.32) and (7.7.33) to represent the first two right-hand integrals in terms of marginal densities:

$$\text{Var}[X + Y] = \int (x - E[X])^2 f_X(x)\, dx + \int (y - E[Y])^2 f_Y(y)\, dy$$

$$+ \iint (x - E[X])(y - E[Y]) f_{X, Y}(x, y)\, dx\, dy,$$

$$= \text{Var}[X] + \text{Var}[Y] + 2\,\text{Cov}[X, Y],$$

where the covariance term appears by virtue of Definition 7.7.4.

Observe that if the random variables are independent, then the covariance is zero. However, it is *not* true that a zero covariance implies independence.

EXAMPLE 7.7.7. Consider the following discrete distribution.

$$P[X = 0, Y = 1] = P[X = 0, Y = -1]$$
$$(7.7.43) \qquad = P[X = 1, Y = 0] = P[X = -1, Y = 0] = \frac{1}{4}.$$

Clearly,

$$(7.7.44) \qquad P[X = 0] = P[X = 0, Y = 1] + P[X = 0, Y = -1] = \frac{1}{2}$$

and

$$(7.7.45) \quad P[X = 1] = P[X = 1, Y = 0] = \frac{1}{4} = P[X = -1] = P[X = -1, Y = 0].$$

Consequently, $E[X] = 0$, and likewise $E[Y] = 0$. Also, $E[XY] = 0$. But by the rules of conditional probability (or even by inspection),

(7.7.46) $$P[X = 0 \mid Y = 0] = \frac{P[X = 0,\, Y = 0]}{P[Y = 0]} = 0,$$

whereas

(7.7.47) $$P[X = 0 \mid Y = 1] = \frac{P[X = 0,\, Y = 1]}{P[Y = 1]} = \frac{\frac{1}{4}}{\frac{1}{4}} = 1.$$

It is thus clear that information about Y changes the distribution of X and so X and Y are statistically dependent, even though their covariance and correlation are zero.

Let us now examine a simple model that shows the meaning and potential usefulness of the covariance.

EXAMPLE 7.7.8. The annual yield, X, of an agricultural product (wheat, say) depends on weather conditions and so may be represented as a random variable. The price, Y, of wheat depends on its abundance—that is, on yield—but also on general economic conditions. We represent this as follows:

(7.7.48) $$Y = a + bX + e,$$

where a and b are constants and X and e are independently distributed random variables. Thus price, Y, is represented as a linear combination of two random quantities. Now the constants, a and b, can be expressed in terms of expectations of X, Y, and e. According to Theorem 7.7.1 and Exercise 4, we can take expectations in (7.7.48) to show that

(7.7.49) $$E[Y] = a + bE[X] + E[e].$$

Now subtract this expression from (7.7.48), multiply the result by $X - E[X]$, and take expectations:

(7.7.50) $$E\{(Y - E[y])(X - E[X])\} = E[b\{X - E[X]\}^2] + E[(e - E[e])(X - E[X])].$$

By Definition 7.7.4, the left-hand side is $\mathrm{Cov}(X,\, Y)$, while the right-hand side involves the variance of X and the covariance of X and e:

(7.7.51) $$\mathrm{Cov}(X,\, Y) = b\,\mathrm{Var}[X] + \mathrm{Cov}(e,\, X).$$

We have assumed e and X to be independent, so

(7.7.52) $$b = \frac{\mathrm{Cov}(X,\, Y)}{\mathrm{Var}[X]}.$$

Since b is the coefficient of the linear term (part proportional to X) in (7.7.48), it appears that the covariance of X and Y tends to measure the degree of *linear* dependence between yield, X, and price, Y.

The representation (7.7.48) of wheat price vs. crop yield recalls the weight-height example (Example 7.7.2); there X plays the role of height, and Y, that of weight. A great many other models have the same general structure. Without information concerning X, the variability of Y about its mean is measured by

(7.7.53) $$\mathrm{Var}[Y] = b^2\,\mathrm{Var}[X] + \mathrm{Var}[e],$$

whereas if we *know* X to be, say, x, then the only uncertainty is furnished by e, and $\text{Var}[y] = \text{Var}[e]$, which may be much smaller than (7.7.52) if the linear dependence on X is strong. Plainly, information concerning the value of a variable (like X) that may effect the outcome of a future event is worth having. The reduction of variance by recognizing such dependence (linear, in this case) is from

$$\text{Var}[Y] = b^2 \, \text{Var}[X] + \text{Var}[e],$$

(7.7.54)
$$= \frac{\text{Cov}^2(X, Y)}{\text{Var}[X]} + \text{Var}[e],$$

when the effect of X on Y is ignored, to

(7.7.55)
$$\text{Var}[Y] = \text{Var}[e],$$

where X is known to be equal to x.

The model of Example 7.7.8 shows how the distribution of one random variable, Y, depends on the value assumed by another, X. This idea leads to the next definition.

DEFINITION 7.7.5. The *conditional distribution* of the random variable Y, given X, is defined as follows.

(a) Suppose Y and X are discrete, taking on the values $y_1, y_2, y_3, \ldots$ and $x_1, x_2, x_3, \ldots$, respectively. Their joint distribution is given by

(7.7.56)
$$P\{Y = y_j, X = x_i\} = p_{ij} \qquad (i, j = 1, 2, 3, \ldots).$$

Then the conditional probability distribution of Y, given $X = x_i$, is given by the ratio of the joint probability distribution of Y and X to the marginal probability distribution of X:

(7.7.57)
$$p_{j|i} = \frac{p_{ij}}{\sum_j p_{ij}} = \frac{p_{ij}}{p_i} \qquad \left(p_i = \sum_j p_{ij} > 0 \right).$$

This means that the conditional distribution function of Y given X is expressible as

(7.7.58)
$$F_{Y|X}(y; x_i) = \sum_{y_j \leq y} \frac{P\{Y = y_j, X = x_i\}}{P\{X = x_i\}},$$
$$= \sum_{y_j \leq y} p_{j|i} = \sum_{y_j \leq y} \frac{p_{ij}}{p_i}.$$

(b) Suppose Y and X have the joint probability density function $f_{X,Y}(x, y)$. Then the conditional density of Y, given that $x = x'$, is

(7.7.59)
$$f_{Y|X}(y; x') = \frac{f_{X,Y}(x', y)}{f_X(x')}, \qquad \left(f_X(x') = \int_{-\infty}^{\infty} f_{X,Y}(x', y) \, dy > 0 \right).$$

The cases (a) and (b) are illustrative without being exhaustive. For example, either Y or X can have mixed distributions (see Example 7.5.1). Thus Y may be continuous and X discrete (or vice versa).

(c) Suppose Y and X are distributed in such a manner that

(7.7.60) $$P\{Y \le y, X = x_i\} = \int_{-\infty}^{y} f_{X,Y}(x_i, y') \, dy'.$$

Then the conditional density of Y, given $X = x_i$ $(i = 1, 2, 3, \ldots)$, is

(7.7.61) $$f_{Y|X}(Y; x_i) = \frac{f_{X,Y}(x_i, y)}{f_X(x_i)},$$

where

(7.7.62) $$f_X(x_i) = \int_{-\infty}^{\infty} f_{X,Y}(x_i, y) \, dy.$$

As you will see subsequently, it is very often the *conditional distribution* that is fundamental when formulating models. Before we elaborate upon this point, we supply some illustrations.

EXAMPLE 7.7.9. Consider the discrete joint distribution of Example 7.7.7. It is easy to find the conditional distribution of Y, given X. If $X = 1$,

(7.7.63) $$P\{Y = 1 \,|\, X = 1\} = \frac{P\{X = 1, Y = 1\}}{P\{X = 1\}},$$
$$= 0;$$

(7.7.64) $$P\{Y = 0 \,|\, X = 1\} = \frac{P\{X = 1, Y = 0\}}{P\{X = 1\}},$$
$$= \frac{\frac{1}{4}}{\frac{1}{4}} = 1;$$

(7.7.65) $$P\{Y = -1 \,|\, X = 1\} = \frac{P\{X = 1, Y = -1\}}{P\{X = 1\}},$$
$$= \frac{0}{\frac{1}{4}} = 0.$$

If, on the other hand, $X = 0$,

(7.7.66) $$P\{Y = 1 \,|\, X = 0\} = \frac{\frac{1}{4}}{\frac{1}{2}} = \frac{1}{2},$$

(7.7.67) $$P\{Y = 0 \,|\, X = 0\} = 0,$$

(7.7.68) $$P\{Y = -1 \,|\, X = 0\} = \frac{\frac{1}{4}}{\frac{1}{2}} = \frac{1}{2}.$$

Thus the probability that Y is less than or equal to zero is unity if it is known that $X = 1$, and $\frac{1}{2}$ if $X = 0$. If nothing is known about the value of X, the calculation above must be made by use of the marginal distribution of Y alone, and the probability that Y is less than or equal to zero is assessed at $\frac{3}{4}$.

EXAMPLE 7.7.10. Let the joint density of X and Y be given by the *bivariate normal density*,

$$(7.7.69) \quad f_{X,Y}(x, y) = \frac{1}{2\pi\sigma_1\sigma_2\sqrt{1-\rho^2}} \, e^{-\frac{1}{2(1-\rho^2)}[(x/\sigma_1)^2 - 2\rho(x/\sigma_1)(y/\sigma_2) + (y/\sigma_2)^2]} \, ;$$

here σ_1 and σ_2 (both positive) are the standard deviations of X and Y, and ρ ($-1 < \rho < 1$) is the correlation of X and Y (see (7.7.42)); the expected values of X and Y are zero. It may be shown that the marginal density of X is

$$(7.7.70) \qquad\qquad f_X(x) = \frac{1}{\sqrt{2\pi\sigma_1^2}} \, e^{-\frac{1}{2}(x/\sigma_1)^2}.$$

This is accomplished by "integrating out" the y value for fixed x. You will be guided through the steps in Exercise 11. Having found (7.7.70), we can now write down an expression for the conditional density. To simplify the expression, put $u = x/\sigma_1$ and $v = y/\sigma_2$.

$$(7.7.71) \quad f_{Y|X}(y; x) = \frac{f_{X,Y}(x, y)}{f_X(x)} = \frac{1}{\sqrt{2\pi}\sqrt{1-\rho^2}} \, e^{-\frac{1}{2(1-\rho^2)}[u^2 - 2\rho uv + v^2]} e^{\frac{1}{2}u^2}.$$

After the exponent is placed over a common denominator,

$$(7.7.72) \qquad f_{Y|X}(y; x) = \frac{1}{\sqrt{2\pi}\sqrt{1-\rho^2}} \, e^{-\frac{1}{2(1-\rho^2)}[v^2 - 2\rho uv + \rho^2 u^2]}.$$

But now notice that the exponent is a perfect square:

$$v^2 - 2\rho uv + \rho^2 u^2 = (v - \rho u)^2,$$

so, returning to x and y, we have

$$(7.7.73)$$
$$f_{Y|X}(y; x) = \frac{1}{\sqrt{2\pi}\,\sigma_2\sqrt{1-\rho^2}} \, e^{-\frac{1}{2(1-\rho^2)}[y/\sigma_2 - \rho(x/\sigma_1)]^2},$$

$$= \frac{1}{\sqrt{2\pi}\,\sigma_2\sqrt{1-\rho^2}} \, e^{-\frac{1}{2}[(y - \rho(\sigma_2/\sigma_1)x)/\sigma_2\sqrt{1-\rho^2}]^2}.$$

If you now refer to the definition of the normal distribution in Section 7.6, expressions (7.6.8) and (7.6.9), you will see that the formula above, (7.7.73), represents the density of a normally distributed random variable with mean $\rho(\sigma_2/\sigma_1)x$ and variance $\sigma_2^2(1 - \rho^2)$. This density is the conditional density of Y, given that $X = x$. Putting all of this another way, we can represent Y as

$$Y = \rho\frac{\sigma_2}{\sigma_1}x + e$$

if it is known that $X = x$ (conditional on X equaling x). Here e is normally distributed, with mean zero and standard deviation $\sigma_2\sqrt{1-\rho^2}$. If the value of X is *not* known, then the unconditional mean of Y is zero and the standard deviation is σ_2. It can be seen that information concerning X reduces the amount of variation around the mean of Y, the variation being measured by the respective standard deviations.

The next example shows how a joint distribution of the type described in Definition 7.1(iii) may be derived using familiar single-variable distributions as components.

EXAMPLE 7.7.11. In the course of manufacturing certain devices, defective elements may be included. Suppose the time to failure for such a defective element has distribution $G(t)$ with density $g(t)$; $G(t) = g(t) = 0$ for $t \le 0$. The device fails as soon as one of its component elements fails. Consequently, if n such defective elements are present, the time to failure for the device is the *minimum* of the times to failure (assumed independent) of the n defective elements. The minimum has distribution $H(t) = 1 - \{1 - G(t)\}^n$ (see Example 7.7.4). Now the actual number, N, of defective elements included in a device is a random variable, N; N is independent of the failure times of the individual defective elements. Consequently the joint probability of the device's time to failure (minimum, denoted by M) and the number of defective elements is

$$(7.7.74) \qquad P\{M > t, N = n\} = P\{M > t \mid N = n\}P\{N = n\},$$

$$(7.7.75) \qquad = \{1 - G(t)\}^n P\{N = n\}.$$

The first line of this statement is, in reality, merely the fundamental definition of conditional probability slightly rearranged. Recall that if A and B are events, then

$$(7.7.76) \quad \text{or} \qquad P(A \mid B) = \frac{P(A \cap B)}{P(B)}$$

$$P(A \cap B) = P(A \mid B)P(B).$$

Then let A denote the event that $\{M > t\}$, and let B be the event that $\{N = n\}$; thus, $A \cap B$ is the event that $\{M > t\}$ and $\{N = n\}$, and (7.7.74) is seen to be the result. Now let N have the Poisson distribution:

$$(7.7.77) \qquad P\{N = n\} = e^{-a}\frac{a^n}{n!} \qquad a > 0; n = 0, 1, 2, 3, \ldots.$$

Thus

$$(7.7.78) \qquad P\{M > t, N = n\} = [1 - G(t)]^n e^{-a}\frac{a^n}{n!},$$

and hence the marginal distribution of M can be obtained from

$$P\{M > t\} = \sum_{n=0}^{\infty} [1 - G(t)]^n e^{-a}\frac{a^n}{n!} = e^{-aG(t)}$$

by subtraction from unity.

Suppose that the device has been observed for a time t and has not failed (the defective elements described above are assumed to be the only source of failure). We ask for the probability distribution of the initial number of defectives, *given* this additional information. Again the rules of conditional probability (7.7.76) may be applied, this time to show that

$$P\{N = n \mid M > t\} = \frac{P\{M > t, N = n\}}{P\{M > t\}},$$

(7.7.79)

$$= \frac{[1 - G(t)]^n e^{-a}(a^n/n!)}{e^{-aG(t)}} = e^{-a[1 - G(t)]} \frac{\{a[1 - G(t)]\}^n}{n!}.$$

In other words, the *revised* probability distribution of n, *given* the information that no failure has occurred within time t, is Poisson with mean $a[1 - G(t)]$. Since $G(t)$ increases with t, clearly the mean above is smaller than the initial mean, a, as seems right and proper: the longer the device survives, the greater is the evidence that it received a small number of defective elements initially.

Finally, differentiation of (7.7.75) with respect to t and a sign change shows that the joint distribution function of M and N can be expressed in terms of a density when $t > 0$ and $n > 0$:

(7.7.80) $$f_{M,N}(t; n) = n[1 - G(t)]^{n-1} g(t) \, P\{N = n\};$$

see Definition 7.7.1(iii).

The last example indicates the manner in which conditional probabilities can be used to derive new joint and marginal distributions—in other words, to supply new models. Also hinted at in Example 7.7.11 is the use of conditional probabilities to update and revise original probability estimates. We shall continue with this train of thought in a later section. But first, several useful properties of conditional distributions will be noted. For one thing, it is necessary to show that the definitions we have given are truly those of distribution functions, the properties of which are summarized in Section 7.5.

THEOREM 7.7.4. The expressions (7.7.57), (7.7.59), and (7.7.61) represent distribution functions.

Proof: The function $p_{j|i}$ of (7.7.57), $f_{Y|X}(y; x')$ of (7.7.59), and $f_{Y|X}(Y; x_i)$ are nonnegative, since they are ratios of probabilities or density functions, which themselves must be nonnegative. In addition, they sum or integrate to unity; for instance, from (7.7.57),

(7.7.81) $$\sum_j p_{j|i} = \sum_j \left(\frac{p_{ij}}{p_i}\right) = \frac{1}{p_i} \sum_j p_{ji} = \frac{p_i}{p_i} = 1.$$

It follows that the conditional distribution is nondecreasing. Take $b > a$. Then

$$F_{Y|X}(b; x_i) = \sum_{y_j \le b} p_{j|i} = \sum_{y_j \le b} \frac{p_{ij}}{p_i},$$

(7.7.82)

$$= \frac{1}{p_i} \sum_{y_j \le b} p_{ij} \ge \frac{1}{p_i} \sum_{y_j \le a} p_{ij}$$

by the property (c) of the joint distribution; see (7.7.8). Also, (7.7.81) shows that $F_{Y|X}(\infty; x_i) = 1$. Since the same verification procedure applies in the other cases, the details are omitted here.

Having the conditional distribution (or density) of, say, the random variable Y, given the value of X, is equivalent to possessing additional information about Y. Thus it may, for example, be of interest to know the expected value of Y when X takes a particular value; this is the *conditional expectation* of Y, given X. Unless Y and X are independent, we can anticipate that the conditional expectation will depend on the particular value or range of values that X assumes. See the height-weight illustration of Example 7.7.2.

DEFINITION 7.7.6. The *conditional expectation* of Y, given that $X = x$, is defined as follows.

(i) For X and Y discrete, assuming values $x_1, x_2, x_3, \ldots$ and $y_1, y_2, y_3, \ldots$, and with conditional probability distribution

$$P\{Y = y_j \,|\, X = x_i\} = p_{j|i},$$

the conditional expectation of Y, given $X = x_i$, is

(7.7.83)
$$E[Y \,|\, X = x_i] = \sum_j y_j \, p_{j|i}.$$

(ii) For X and Y jointly and continuously distributed, with conditional density $f_{Y|X}(y; x)$, the conditional expectation of Y, given $X = x'$, is

(7.7.84)
$$E[Y \,|\, X = x'] = \int_{-\infty}^{\infty} y f_{Y|X}(y; x') \, dy.$$

There are a variety of other cases that may be considered—for example, those in which one variable is discrete and the other continuous—but the definitions are analogous and will be omitted.

EXAMPLE 7.7.12. Refer to the defective element problem of Example 7.7.11. In that problem, we specified the conditional distribution of system time to failure, given that the number of defectives $N = n$. The conditional distribution was

(7.7.85)
$$H(t) = 1 - [1 - G(t)]^n.$$

Differentiation establishes that the density is

(7.7.86)
$$h(t) = n[1 - G(t)]^{n-1} g(t),$$

g being the density of G. Finally, the conditional expectation of the time to failure, M, given n, is

(7.7.87)
$$E[M \,|\, N = n] = \int_0^{\infty} t n[1 - G(t)]^{n-1} g(t) \, dt.$$

In case we have an exponential distribution

$$G(t) = \begin{cases} 1 - e^{-at} & a > 0, t \geq 0 \\ 0 & t < 0 \end{cases}$$

then

$$H(t) = 1 - e^{-nat}$$

and

(7.7.88) $$E[M \mid N = n] = \frac{1}{na} \qquad n = 0, 1, 2, \ldots.$$

Notice that when $n = 0$, the conditional expectation of time to failure is infinite. This stands to reason, since, according to our assumptions, if no defective elements are introduced, the system will never fail. A random variable that may assume the value infinity with nonzero probability is often referred to as being "defective" or "dishonest." The occurrence of such dishonest random variables is quite commonplace in many models.

The following simple theorem points out the fact that the unconditional expectation, $E[Y]$, can be found by removing the condition on X in the conditional expectation.

THEOREM 7.7.5. The unconditional expectation can be expressed as follows.

(i) In the discrete case,

(7.7.89) $$E[Y] = \sum_i \left(\sum_j y_j \, p_{j \mid i} \right) p_i = \sum_i E[Y \mid X = x_i] p_i.$$

(ii) In the continuous case,

(7.7.90) $$E[Y] = \int_{-\infty}^{\infty} \left(\int_{-\infty}^{\infty} y f_{Y \mid X}(y; x) \, dy \right) f_X(x) \, dx = \int_{-\infty}^{\infty} E[Y \mid X = x] f_X(x) \, dx.$$

Other cases are analogous. If the conditional expectation is written in the shortened form, $E[Y \mid X]$, and viewed as a function of the random variable X, then the formulas (7.7.90) and (7.7.91) may be written as

$$E[Y] = E\{E[Y \mid X]\}.$$

EXERCISES 7.7

1. Suppose the distribution of the time to failure of an aircraft engine is Weibull:

$$F(x) = 1 - e^{-x^2} \qquad (x \text{ in five-hour units})$$

   (a) What is the probability that a two-engine plane survives a two-hour flight?
   (b) An airline flies only two-engine planes and makes 100 two-hour flights per year. What is the expected number of failures (crashes) that will occur per year? What is the probability of no crash in a year?

2. Suppose the distribution in the previous question were changed to

$$F(x) = 1 - e^{-x} \qquad (x \text{ in five-hour units}).$$

   Answer the questions (a) and (b) of Exercise 1.

3. If $X_1, X_2, \ldots, X_n$ are independent random variables with distributions $G_1, G_2, \ldots, G_n$, show that the distribution of

$$\max(X_1, X_2, X_3, \ldots, X_n) \text{ is the product } G_1 G_2 G_3 \ldots G_n.$$

Show that if all distributions are the same, and all have density g, then the density function of the maximum is

$$g_{\max}(t) = nG^{n-1}(t)g(t).$$

4. Following the proof of Theorem 7.7.1, show that

$$E[aX + bY] = aE[X] + bE[Y].$$

$$(\textit{Hint: } \int_{-\infty}^{\infty} axf(x)\, dx = a \int_{-\infty}^{\infty} xf(x)\, dx.)$$

5. Let W be the weight of a randomly chosen member of a certain population, and let H be his height. Suppose that

$$W = \alpha H + \beta H^2 + e,$$

where α and β are constants, and H and e are independently distributed. Determine α and β in terms of moments; that is, $E[W]$, $E[H]$, $\text{Var}[H]$, $E[WH]$, and so on. Assume $E[e] = 0$. Suppose you had a table of individual weights and heights. How could you use this to estimate α and β? (*Hint:* $\text{Ave}(x_1, x_2, \ldots, x_n)$ estimates $E[X]$.)

6. Show that $\text{Var}[a + bX] = b^2 \text{Var}[X]$ if a and b are constants. (*Hint:* Compute the expectation of the square of $(a + bX) - (a + bE[X])$.)

7. Show that $\text{Var}[X + Y] = \text{Var}[X] + \text{Var}[Y]$ if X and Y are independent. (*Hint:* Compute the expectation of the square of $(X - E[X]) + (Y - E[y])$.)

8. Show that, in general,

$$\text{Var}[aX + bY] = a^2 \text{Var}[X] + b^2 \text{Var}[Y] + 2ab \text{Cov}[X, Y],$$

where a and b are constants.

9. A skiing enthusiast goes each Sunday to a particular ski area where he must pay for the use of the ski tow. He has two options: the first, to pay each time he goes and the second, to buy a season ticket.
   (a) Suppose there are 20 Sundays during the skiing season and that the occurrence of good skiing conditions on any Sunday is an independent event of probability p. If daily use of the tow costs $\$d$ and a season ticket costs $\$S$, which option allows skiing at the smallest expected cost?
   (b) If $p = 0.4$, $d = \$6$, and $S = \$42$, find the best option for the skier on an expected value basis. What is the probability that, if he buys a season ticket, he would have done better to pay each time?

10. The joint probability density of X and Y can be expressed as follows:

$$f_{X,Y}(x, y) = \begin{cases} k & \text{if } x^2 + y^2 \le 1 \\ 0 & \text{if } x^2 + y^2 > 1 \end{cases}$$

k is a positive constant.
   (a) Show that this density is nonzero only on a disc centered at the origin (disc = set of points inside and on a circle).
   (b) Find the value of k.
   (c) Find the conditional density of Y, given $X = x$.

(d) What is the expected value of Y, given $x = 1/2$?

(e) Are X and Y correlated? Are they statistically independent?

11. Refer to Example 7.7.9. We wish to show that the marginal density of X is given by (7.7.70). To simplify writing, put $u = x/\sigma_1$ and $r = y/\sigma_2$.

(a) Consider the exponent $Q = u^2 - 2\rho ur + r^2$. Show that this may be expressed as

$$Q = r^2 - 2\rho ur + \rho^2 u^2 + u^2(1 - \rho^2),$$
$$= (r - 2\rho u)^2 + u^2(1 - \rho^2).$$

(b) For fixed u, integrate on r from $-\infty$ to ∞:

$$\frac{1}{2\pi(1 - \rho^2)} \int_{-\infty}^{\infty} e^{-\frac{1}{2(1-\rho^2)}(r - \rho u)^2}\, dr\, e^{-\frac{1}{2}u^2};$$

change variables

$$\frac{r - \rho u}{\sqrt{1 - \rho^2}} = z$$

to obtain

$$\frac{1}{\sqrt{2\pi}} \int_{-\infty}^{\infty} e^{-\frac{1}{2}z^2} = 1.$$

12. Refer to the situation of Example 7.7.11. Suppose the device in question has K elements and that each one is defective with probability p, independently of other elements. Observe that the actual number, N, of defective elements has the binomial distribution.

(a) Show that the joint probability of device time to failure and number of defective elements is

$$P\{M > t,\, N = n\} = [1 - G(t)]^n \binom{K}{n} p^n (1 - p)^{K - n}$$

(b) Show that

$$P\{M > t\} = \sum_{n = 0}^{\infty} \binom{K}{n} p^n (1 - p)^{K - n}[1 - G(t)]^n,$$
$$= [1 - pG(t)]^K.$$

(*Hint:* By the binomial theorem,

$$\sum_{n = 0}^{K} \binom{K}{n} a^n b^{K - n} = (a + b)^K;$$

put $a = p[1 - G(t)]$ and $b = 1 - p$.)

13. A building project involves two stages that can go on simultaneously. One requires a random time X, the other the random time Y. Suppose both subprojects or stages are started simultaneously. Then a *project graph* may be drawn:

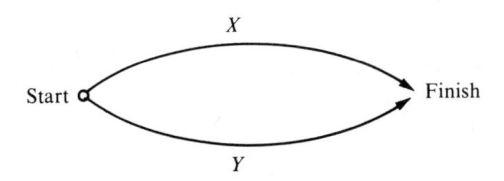

The project is completed when both stages are completed.

(a) Suppose X and Y are independent, with distributions $F_X(x)$ and $F_Y(y)$. What is the distribution of the time from project start to finish?

(b) Suppose X has the uniform density

$$f_X(x) = \frac{1}{10} \qquad 0 \le x \le 10,$$

$$= 0 \qquad \text{otherwise,}$$

and that Y is also uniform:

$$f_Y(y) = \frac{1}{15} \qquad 0 \le x \le 15,$$

$$= 0 \qquad \text{otherwise.}$$

Find the distribution of the time from project start to completion.

(c) Find the probability that Y is less than X, using the assumptions of (b).

(d) Find the expected project completion time.

*14. Refer to the previous problem, but suppose that the two stages must take place in sequence. Then the project graph appears as follows:

(a) Find the expected project duration.

(b) Find the variance of the project duration.

(c) Use the uniform distributions of Exercise 13(b) to give numerical results for (a) and (b) above. (You may wish to read the next section before attempting this problem.)

(d) Suppose a project has many (50, say) stages that take place in sequence. Each stage has duration X_1 with uniform distribution $f_X(x)$ above. How would you use the normal distribution to approximate the distribution of time to project completion? (*Hint:* Use Theorem 7.6.1.)

7.8 THE DISTRIBUTION OF SUMS OF RANDOM VARIABLES

Expressions have been given for the expectations and variances of functions of two (or more) jointly distributed random variables. It is natural to be concerned about the entire distribution of such functions. In the material that follows, the distributions of several such functions that are likely to arise in practice will be developed.

THEOREM 7.8.1. Let X and Y be two jointly distributed random variables, and let Z be their sum:

$$(7.8.1) \qquad Z = X + Y.$$

Consider these cases.

(a) *X and Y discrete.* In general, X takes on values $x_1, x_2, x_3, \ldots,$ and Y takes on $y_1, y_2, y_3, \ldots.$ Then Z takes on the values $z_k = x_i + y_j$ $(i, j, k = 0, 1, 2, \ldots).$ In particular, suppose $x_i = i,$ $y_j = j;$ then Z takes on integer values $0, 1, 2, \ldots.$ Then

$$(7.8.2) \quad P\{z = k\} = p_{0,k} + p_{1,k-1} + p_{2,k-2} + \cdots + p_{k,0} = \sum_{i+j=k} p_{ij} = \sum_i p_{i,k-1}$$

where p_{ij} is the joint probability that $X = i$ and $Y = j$. If X and Y are statistically independent, then

$$(7.8.3) \qquad P\{Z = k\} = \sum_{i+j=k} p_X(i)p_Y(j) = \sum_{i=0}^{k} p_X(i)p_Y(k - i).$$

(b) X and Y *have the joint density* $f_{X,Y}(x, y)$. Then

$$P\{Z \le z\} = \iint\limits_{x+y\le z} f_{X,Y}(x, y)\, dx\, dy,$$

$$(7.8.4)$$

$$= \int_{-\infty}^{\infty} dx \int_{-\infty}^{z-x} f_{X,Y}(x, y)\, dy.$$

If X and Y are statistically independent, then

$$P\{Z \le z\} = \int_{-\infty}^{\infty} dx \int_{-\infty}^{z-x} f_X(x)f_Y(y)\, dx\, dy,$$

$$(7.8.5) \qquad = \int_{-\infty}^{\infty} f_X(x)\, dx \int_{-\infty}^{z-x} f_Y(y)\, dy,$$

$$= \int_{-\infty}^{\infty} F_Y(z - x)f_X(x)\, dx,$$

where F_Y is the distribution function of Y. Furthermore, the density of Z is obtained by differentiation and is

$$(7.8.6) \qquad f_Z(z) = \int_{-\infty}^{\infty} f_Y(z - x)f_X(x)\, dx.$$

Proof: For (a), simply note that these events are equivalent:

$$(7.8.7) \quad (Z = k) = [(X = 0) \cap (Y = k)] \cup [(X = 1) \cap (Y = k - 1)]$$
$$\cup [(X = 2) \cap Y = k - 2] \cup \cdots \cup [(X = k) \cap (Y = 0)].$$

The various events on the right are mutually exclusive (disjoint) and exhaustive, so the sum of their probabilities gives the probability of the event on the left. So far as (b) is concerned, observe that

$$(7.8.8) \qquad (Z \le z) = (X + Y \le z),$$

and the probability of the right-hand event is obtained by integrating the joint density over that part of the x, y plane such that $x + y \le z$. The remaining transformations are standard manipulations of double integrals.

There is considerable similarity between the formulas for $P\{Z = k\}$ and $f_Z(z)$ when X and Y are independent.

DEFINITION 7.8.1. A sum of the form $\sum_i p_X(i)p_Y(k - i)$ and an integral of the form $\int_{-\infty}^{\infty} f_X(x)f_Y(z - x)\, dx$ is called a *convolution*. It will be convenient to denote the convolution operation by an asterisk:

$$(7.8.9) \qquad p_X * p_Y(k) = \sum_i p_X(i)p_Y(k - i)$$

and

(7.8.10) $$f_X * f_Y(z) = \int_{-\infty}^{\infty} f_X(x)f_Y(z - x)\, dx.$$

Notice that if the distribution or density of the sum of three independent random variables is desired, the convolution operation is merely applied again. For example, let

(7.8.11) $$Z = X + Y + U.$$

Then, since

(7.8.12) $$P\{X + Y = k\} = p_X * p_Y(k),$$

$$P\{Z = n\} = \sum_k p_X * p_Y(k)p_U(n - k) = p_X * p_Y * p_U(n).$$

An exactly similar result holds for the density case. We point out that if X has a density and Y is discrete, then $X + Y$ has a density; this is intuitively clear and may be proved in general.

EXAMPLE 7.8.1. Suppose X and Y are independent and both have the Poisson distribution. It follows that $X + Y$ has the Poisson distribution, so it is said that the Poisson is *reproductive*. To see this, look at the convolution:

$$P\{X + Y = k\} = \sum_{i+j=k} e^{-a}\frac{a^i}{i!}\, e^{-b}\frac{b^j}{j!},$$

(7.8.13) $$= \sum_{i=0}^{k} e^{-a}\frac{a^i}{i!}\, e^{-b}\frac{b^{k-i}}{(k-i)!},$$

$$= \frac{e^{-(a+b)}}{k!} \sum_{i=0}^{k} \frac{k!}{i!(k-i)!}\, a^i b^{k-i}.$$

Recall (or look up or derive by induction) the binomial formula:

(7.8.14) $$(a + b)^k = a^k + \frac{k}{1} a^{k-1}b + \cdots + \frac{k!}{i!(k-i)!} a^i b^{k-i} + \cdots + b^k.$$

Hence the sum above is $(a + b)^k$, and

(7.8.15) $$P\{X + Y = k\} = e^{-(a+b)} \frac{(a+b)^k}{k!} \qquad k = 0, 1, 2, \ldots .$$

EXAMPLE 7.8.2. Suppose the time to complete a certain project is the sum of two independent random variables X and Y. Suppose that their density functions are exponential:

(7.8.16) $$f_X(x) = e^{-ax}a \qquad \text{for } x \geq 0,$$
$$= 0 \qquad \text{otherwise}$$

and

(7.8.17) $$f_Y(x) = e^{-by}b \qquad \text{for } y \geq 0,$$
$$= 0 \qquad \text{otherwise.}$$

Assume $a \neq b$. Then $Z = X + Y$ has the density given by the convolution of f_X and f_Y:

$$(7.8.18) \qquad f_Z(z) = \int_{-\infty}^{\infty} f_Y(z-x) f_X(x) \, dx.$$

Notice that the limits on the integral above can be replaced as follows:

$$(7.8.19) \qquad f_Z(z) = \int_0^z f_Y(z-x) f_X(x) \, dx.$$

The lower limit is zero because the density of X is zero for $x < 0$; see (7.8.16). Likewise, the density of Y is zero for $y < 0$ or, equivalently, for $z - x < 0$ or for $x > z$ in the convolution (7.8.18). Now

$$f_Z(z) = \int_0^z e^{-b(z-x)} b \, e^{-ax} a \, dx,$$

$$= e^{-bz} ab \int_0^z e^{-(a-b)x} \, dx,$$

$$(7.8.20) \qquad = e^{-bz} \frac{ab}{a-b} [1 - e^{-(a-b)z}],$$

$$= \frac{ab}{a-b} [e^{-bz} - e^{-az}].$$

It is of interest that the maximum value of the density occurs at the z value,

$$(7.8.21) \qquad z_{max} = \frac{1}{a-b} \log\left(\frac{a}{b}\right),$$

which is always positive. Indeed the density (7.8.20) closely resembles the leftmost gamma density of Figure 7.6.1. It can actually be shown that if $a = b$, the present density becomes a gamma density with $\beta = 2$; see Section 7.6 and Exercise 1 of this section.

EXERCISES 7.8

1. Suppose X and Y are independently and exponentially distributed with density

$$f(x) = e^{-ax} a \qquad x \geq 0,$$
$$= 0 \qquad \text{otherwise.}$$

(a) Convolve to find their sum density:

$$f_Z(z) = \int_0^z e^{-a(z-x)} a e^{-ax} a \, dx,$$

$$= e^{-az} \left(\frac{az}{1}\right) a.$$

(b) Show that the density of n identically and exponentially distributed random variables has the gamma density with $\beta = n$. (See Section 7.6.)

2. Let the number N of defects in a single lot of K transistors be binomially distributed:

$$P\{N = n\} = \binom{K}{n}p^n(1 - p)^{K-n} \qquad n = 0, 1, \ldots, K.$$

(a) Show that the total number of defects in two lots, each of size K, is binomially distributed:

$$P\{N_1 + N_2 = n\} = \binom{2K}{n}p^n(1 - p)^{2K-n} \qquad n = 0, 1, \ldots, 2K.$$

(*Hint:* Obvious from the discussion following (7.6.2).)

(b) The following is an analytical proof.

$$P\{N_1 + N_2 = n\} = \sum_{j=0}^{n} p_{N_1}(n - j)p_{N_2}(j)$$

$$= \sum_{j=0}^{n} \binom{K}{n-j}p^{n-j}(1 - p)^{K-n+j}\binom{K}{j}p^j(1 - p)^{K-j}$$

(*)
$$= C(n)p^n(1 - p)^{2K-n},$$

where the unknown function of n required is

$$C(n) = \sum_{j=0}^{n} \binom{K}{n-j}\binom{K}{j}.$$

Verify that $C(n) = \binom{2K}{n}$ allows the expression (*) to sum to unity.

*(c) Another approach is to let $p_n(k)$ be the probability of exactly n defects among k transistors. Consider the addition of one transistor to the lot. Argue that the probability of n failures among $k + 1$ satisfies the equation

$$p_n(k + 1) = p_{n-1}(k)p + p_n(k)(1 - p),$$

$$= p\left[\binom{k}{n}p^{n-2}(1 - p)^{k-n}\right] + \left[\binom{k}{n-1}p^n(1 - p)^{k+1-n}\right](1 - p),$$

$$= p^n(1 - p)^{k+1-n}\left[\binom{k}{n} + \binom{k}{n-1}\right],$$

$$= \binom{k+1}{n}p^n(1 - p)^{k+1-n}.$$

Continue, by induction, to $2K$.

3. Suppose X is uniformly distributed over $-\frac{1}{2}$ to $\frac{1}{2}$:

$$f(x) = 1 \qquad \text{for} \quad -\frac{1}{2} \leq x \leq \frac{1}{2},$$

$$= 0 \qquad \text{otherwise.}$$

Suppose an independent Y has the same density. Show that their sum has the triangular density

$$f_Z(z) = 1 - z \qquad \text{for} \quad 0 \leq z \leq 1,$$

$$= 1 + z \qquad \text{for} \quad -1 \leq z \leq 0,$$

$$= 0 \qquad \text{otherwise.}$$

(*Hint:* The integrand of $f_Z(z) = \int_{-\infty}^{\infty} f(z-x)f(x)\,dx$ is nonzero (equals unity) if and only if $-\frac{1}{2} \le z - x \le \frac{1}{2}$. Consequently the integral is actually over the range

$$\max\left(z - \frac{1}{2}, \frac{1}{2}\right) \le x \le \min\left(z + \frac{1}{2}, \frac{1}{2}\right).)$$

4. Suppose X is uniformly distributed over $(-A, A)$ and Y is uniformly distributed over $(-B, B)$, where A and B are positive but $A > B$. Show that their sum Z has a trapezoidal density of the form

$$f_Z(z) = \begin{cases} 2BK & \text{for} \quad |z| \le A - B \\ K(A + B - |z|) & \text{for} \quad A - B \le |z| \le A + B \end{cases}$$

and $K^{-1} = 4AB$. Use the hint associated with Exercise 3.

7.9   BAYES' FORMULA AND PROBABILITY REVISION

A variety of situations in which uncertainty plays a role may be viewed as involving the elements listed below. These elements will be presented in terms of the simplest discrete setup, but later they will be used in more complex situations—for example, situations involving continuous random variables.

1. A collection of events or outcomes $A_1, A_2, \ldots$ exists, one and only one of which may occur at the occasion of a trial or experiment. That is,

$$A_i \cap A_j = 0 \qquad i \ne j$$

(7.9.1)   and

$$\bigcup_i A_i = S.$$

S is the set of possible outcomes—that is, the sample space.

2. A probability distribution over the set of events $\{A_i\}$ exists but is *unknown*. Specifically, it may be supposed that

(7.9.2) $p_i(k) = P\{A_i|k\}$

represents the probability of the event A_i, *given* that probability distribution k is actually in force. You will recognize that $p_i(k)$ is a conditional probability distribution analogous to those discussed in the previous section. The number of possible probability distributions may be small (as few as two) or large (k may represent one or more real numbers). It is descriptive and convenient to call the particular (unknown) probability distribution that is in force the *state of nature*. For short, the kth state of nature will frequently be denoted by S_k. It will be assumed that only one such distribution or state of nature actually governs the occurrences of the events A_i. Furthermore, the operative state of nature is unknown.

3. There is a probability distribution over the various possible states of nature, $\{S_k\}$. This is denoted by $\{\pi_k\}$ and is called the *prior probability distribution*. That is, π_3 gives the probability that the state of nature labeled S_3 actually is in effect.

Now since $p_i(k)$ is the conditional probability of event A_i, given S_k, and since π_k is the probability of the kth state of nature, the probability of the joint event $A_i \cap S_k$ is, by the rules of conditional probability,

$$(7.9.3) \qquad P\{A_i \cap S_k\} = p_i(k)\pi(k).$$

Since one and only one state of nature is in effect,

$$S_k \cap S_l = 0 \qquad \text{for } k \neq l,$$

and thus

$$(7.9.4) \qquad (A_i \cap S_k) \cap (A_i \cap S_l) = 0.$$

Also

$$(7.9.5) \qquad \bigcup_k (A_i \cap S_k) = A_i.$$

In short, it follows that the unconditional probability of event A_i is

$$(7.9.6) \qquad P\{A_i\} = \sum_k P\{A_i \cap S_k\} = \sum_k p_i(k)\pi_k.$$

If one knew only the various possible states of nature $[p_i(k)]$ and their probabilities (π_k), then (7.9.6) expresses all of the probabilistic information concerning A_i that is available. It is, however, sometimes possible to make an observation on the unknown state of nature and, in the light of this, to revise our prior probability distribution. Finally, this revised prior distribution—termed the *posterior distribution*—may itself be used to find an improved estimate of the probability of A_i on a future occasion. The formal, mathematical way in which this procedure is carried out is via *Bayes' formula*, a simple expression involving conditional probabilities, which will now be derived.

THEOREM 7.9.1. *Bayes' Formula.* The probability that the state of nature S_k is in force, given the information that outcome A_i has occurred, is given by

$$(7.9.7) \qquad \pi_k(i) = P\{S_k \,|\, A_i\} = \frac{P\{A_i \,|\, S_k\}P\{S_k\}}{P\{A_i\}},$$

$$= \frac{p_i(k)\pi_k}{\sum_k p_i(k)\pi_k}.$$

The probability distribution $\{\pi_k(i)\}$ over the various states of nature is called the *posterior probability distribution*. We think of $\{\pi_k(i)\}$ as being a new version of $\{\pi_k\}$, revised in the light of the information that A_i has occurred. An elementary flow chart describes the process.

Proof: Recall that

$$(7.9.8) \qquad P\{S_k \cap A_i\} = P\{S_k \,|\, A_i\}P\{A_i\} = P\{A_i \,|\, S_k\}P\{S_k\}$$

according to the definition of conditional probabilities (see Section 7.3). Hence division of the two rightmost expressions of (7.9.8) by $P\{A_i\}$ gives the first line of (7.9.7). But then (7.9.6) provides an expression for $P\{A_i\}$, and the proof is completed. It is tacitly assumed throughout that $P\{A_i\} > 0$.

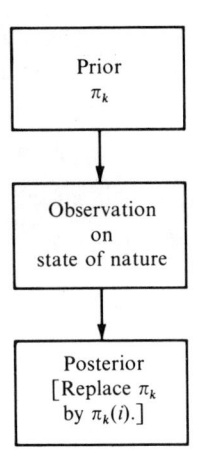

FIGURE 7.9.1

Analogous reasoning supplies a version of Bayes' formula (7.9.7) for densities and for mixed situations. See Definition 7.7.5.

Several examples now illustrate the use of Bayes' formula. You may also wish to review Example 7.3.2.

EXAMPLE 7.9.1. Three billiard balls are placed into each of two identical hats, H_1 and H_2. Two balls in H_1 are black and one is white, while one of those in H_2 is black and the other two are white. Player 2 is told this fact. Player 1 now flips a fair penny and, without revealing the result, offers a hat to Player 2 according to this rule: H_1 is offered if heads turns up, H_2 is offered if tails results. Player 2 then draws one ball and looks at it. He is now asked to guess which hat has been offered to him. It offers some guidance to calculate the probability that the hat offered is actually H_1 or H_2, depending on which ball is initially observed.

Let us apply Bayes' formula. The two outcomes for the first draw can be labeled

$$A_1: \quad \text{Black,}$$
$$A_2: \quad \text{White.}$$

Now if the states of nature are S_1, meaning that H_1 was offered to Player 2 and hence, the first draw was from H_1, and S_2, meaning that the initial draw was from H_2, then

$$P\{A_1 \mid S_1\} \equiv P\{\text{Black} \mid H_1\} = \frac{2}{3},$$

$$P\{A_2 \mid S_1\} \equiv P\{\text{White} \mid H_1\} = \frac{1}{3},$$

while

$$P\{A_1 \mid S_2\} \equiv P\{\text{Black} \mid H_2\} = \frac{1}{3},$$

$$P\{A_2 \,|\, S_2\} \equiv P\{\text{White} \,|\, H_2\} = \frac{2}{3}.$$

Since the prior probabilities are

$$\pi_1 = P\{H_1\} = \pi_2 = P\{H_2\} = \frac{1}{2},$$

(7.9.9) $$P\{S_1 \,|\, A_1\} = P\{H_1 \,|\, \text{Black}\} = \frac{P\{A_1 \,|\, S_1\}P\{S_1\}}{P\{A_1 \,|\, S_1\}P\{S_1\} + P\{A_1 \,|\, S_2\}P\{S_2\}},$$

(7.9.10) $$= \frac{(\frac{2}{3})(\frac{1}{2})}{(\frac{2}{3})(\frac{1}{2}) + (\frac{1}{3})(\frac{1}{2})} = \frac{2}{3}.$$

Consequently

$$P\{S_2 \,|\, A_1\} = P\{H_2 \,|\, \text{Black}\} = 1 - P\{H_1 \,|\, B\} = \frac{1}{3}.$$

Before the first ball was drawn, Player 2 would have been forced to estimate the probability of the two states of nature as equal—that is, to use π_1 for the probability that H_1 was offered. The knowledge gained from observing that the first ball drawn was black increases the probability that H_1 was indeed offered. Since H_1 contains more black balls than does H_2, the revision is intuitively appropriate.

EXAMPLE 7.9.2. A graduate school has many applicants from Siwash College. It has found that there are in general two types of student who apply: those of Type 1, who have a probability of 0.90 of completing the graduate course, and those of Type 2, whose probability is 0.40. Retrospectively, it has appeared that both types of students appear in approximately equal numbers and that a student's type cannot be determined from his record at Siwash. As a consequence, the chance that a random student completes the graduate program is $(0.90)(0.5) + (0.40)(0.5) = 0.65$.

Suppose now that a test becomes available with the following characteristics. A student of Type 1 passes with probability 0.95, while one of Type 2 passes with probability 0.25. If the graduate school habitually admits only those students who pass such a test, let us ask about the probability that an admitted student will actually be successful.

There are several sets of outcomes that are of interest. First, let A_1 be the event that a student passes the test, and let A_2 be the event that he fails. Let T_1 denote that the student is a Type 1, and T_2, that he is a Type 2. Consequently, according to what was said earlier, the states of nature are given by the conditional probabilities

(7.9.11) $$\begin{aligned} S_1: p_1 = P\{A_1 \,|\, T_1\} = 0.95, \\ S_2: p_2 = P\{A_1 \,|\, T_2\} = 0.25. \end{aligned}$$

The prior probabilities of the two types are equal:

(7.9.12) $$\pi_1 = P\{T_1\} = 0.5 = P\{T_2\} = \pi_2.$$

An interesting question now is the following. Supposing that a student passes the test, what is the probability that he is a Type 1? Notice that this amounts to *revising* π_1 in the light of the test evidence. By Bayes' formula,

$$\pi_1(A_1) = \frac{P\{A_1 \mid T_1\}P\{T_1\}}{P\{A_1 \mid T_1\}P\{T_1\} + P\{A_1 \mid T_2\}P\{T_2\}},$$

(7.9.13)

$$= \frac{(0.95)(0.5)}{(0.95)(0.5) + (0.25)(0.5)} = \frac{0.95}{1.20} = 0.79.$$

Next, the probability that a student who passes the test is of Type 2 is just

(7.9.14) $$\pi_2(A_1) = 1 - \pi_1(A_1) = 0.21.$$

Now if the graduate school admits only those students who pass the test, what fraction will be successful? Denoting by C the event that the course is completed successfully,

(7.9.15) $P\{\text{Successful} \mid \text{Pass Test}\} = \begin{cases} P\{C \mid T_1\}\pi_1(A_1) + P\{C \mid T_2\}\pi_2(A_1) \\[6pt] (0.90)\pi_1(A_1) + (0.40)\pi_2(A_1) \\[6pt] (0.90)\left(\dfrac{0.95}{1.20}\right) + (0.40)\left(\dfrac{0.25}{1.20}\right) = 0.80 \end{cases}$

A formal derivation of (7.9.15) is given in the Exercises. Observe that without the test, the chance that a student from Siwash will be successful is 0.65, whereas 80% of those passing the test successfully complete the graduate course. Administration of the test would seem to be useful for both the graduate school and the prospective students.

EXAMPLE 7.9.3. A machine can be in one of two states of adjustment, good (G) or bad (B). If it is in state G, then its time to failure $T\,(T > 0)$ is governed by the exponential distribution

(7.9.16) $$P\{T > t \mid G\} = e^{-gt} \qquad g > 0, t \geq 0,$$

while if it is in state B, then

(7.9.17) $$P\{T > t \mid B\} = e^{-bt} \qquad b > 0, t \geq 0.$$

Let π_g be the prior probability that an adjustment is good, and π_b be the corresponding probability that it is bad. Suppose the machine is adjusted and then put into operation. It operates without failure for time x. What is the probability that it continues to operate thereafter for an additional time t?

First, apply Bayes' formula to discover the posterior probability that adjustment state G (or B) is in effect. We have

$$P\{G \mid T > x\} = \frac{P\{T > x \mid G\}P\{G\}}{P\{T > x \mid G\}P\{G\} + P\{T > x \mid B\}P\{B\}}$$

(7.9.18)

$$= \frac{e^{-gx}\pi_g}{e^{-gx}\pi_g + e^{-bx}\pi_b}.$$

Likewise,

(7.9.19) $$P\{B \mid T > x\} = \frac{e^{-bx}\pi_b}{e^{-gx}\pi_g + e^{-bx}\pi_b}.$$

Now given that the machine is in state G at x, it survives to $t + x$ with probability

(7.9.20) $$P\{T > t + x \mid (T > x) \cap G\} = \frac{e^{-g(t+x)}}{e^{-gx}} = e^{-gt}.$$

In words, the probability given above is that of the event that the machine does not fail in a total time $t + x$, given that it survives an initial time x *and* that the initial adjustment was good (machine in state B). If the machine is initially in the state B, then the corresponding probability is e^{-bt}. Notice that (7.9.20) may be interpreted to mean that the machine's probability of surviving an additional time t after having already attained "adjustment age" x is independent of x. This "memoryless" property of the exponential (and of the exponential alone) will be exploited later when we deal with queues and other time-dependent stochastic phenomena. Now we calculate

$$P\{(T > t + x) \cap G \mid T > x\} = \frac{P\{(T > t + x) \cap G \cap (T > x)\}}{P\{T > x\}},$$

(7.9.21)
$$= \frac{P\{(T > t + x) \cap G \cap (T > x)\}}{P\{G \cap (T > x)\}} \cdot \frac{P\{G \cap (T > x)\}}{P\{T > x\}},$$

$$= P\{(T > t + x) \mid (T > x) \cap G\} P\{G \mid T > x\}.$$

An analogous formula holds when B is the initial state. Substituting from (7.9.20) and (7.9.18), the result is

(7.9.22) $$P\{(T > t + x) \cap G \mid T > x\} = e^{-gt} \frac{e^{-gx} \pi_g}{e^{-gx} \pi_g + e^{-bx} \pi_b};$$

likewise,

(7.9.23) $$P\{(T > t + x) \cap B \mid T > x\} = e^{-bt} \frac{e^{-bx} \pi_b}{e^{-gx} \pi_g + e^{-bx} \pi_b}.$$

Finally, since G and B are disjoint and exhaustive—the machine must be in one state or the other—we have the event

$$(T > t + x) = [(T > t + x) \cap B] \cup [(T > t + x) \cap G],$$

and hence the probabilities (7.9.22) and (7.9.23) are added to obtain

(7.9.24) $$P\{T > t + x \mid T > x\} = \frac{\pi_g e^{-g(t+x)} + \pi_b e^{-b(t+x)}}{\pi_g e^{-gx} + \pi_b e^{-bx}}.$$

Given that $T > x$, it is reasonable to define the new random variable $T_x = T - x$; this is the time to machine failure, measured from the time x. That is,

$$P\{T_x > t \mid T > x\} = P\{T > t + x \mid T > x\}.$$

From this, the distribution function and density of T_x can be derived directly (see Exercise 7).

The previous examples all dealt with situations in which it was assumed that there was only a small finite set of states of nature. Frequently this assumption is unwarranted and inconvenient. In such cases, it may be more reasonable to describe the probabilities of the many possible states of nature by a density function.

EXAMPLE 7.9.4. The manufacture of a semiconductor device (transistor) is completed by baking n devices together in an oven. The probability, p, that these devices will operate successfully thereafter depends on the oven temperature, which is under poor control. Hence p is represented as a random variable, the same for all devices in a batch of n but varying between batches according to the *prior probability density* $\pi_p(x)$. The graph of this density appears below:

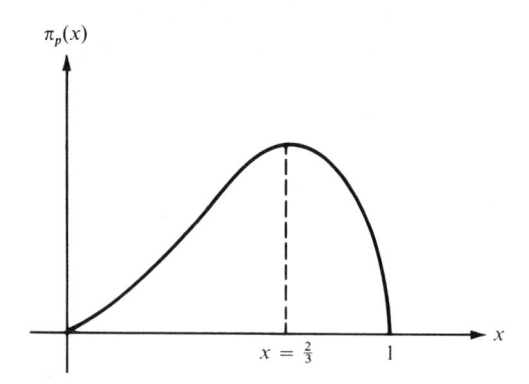

It has the analytical expression

$$(7.9.25) \qquad \pi_p(x) = 12x^2(1 - x).$$

Thus when a batch is completed, each device in it is considered to have the same success probability p, which is unknown but subject to density (7.9.25). In other words, the state of nature is determined by the unknown probability p, where p is any number from zero to one.

Imagine now that one transistor from a batch is put into operation in a simple control circuit. Let O denote the event that the circuit operates successfully; we assume for simplicity that other parts in the circuit are failure-free. Then, given that $p = x$,

$$(7.9.26) \qquad P\{O \mid p = x\} = x \qquad 0 \le x \le 1.$$

Having no further information, we compute the unconditional probability of successful operation:

$$P\{O\} = \int_0^1 P\{O \mid p = x\}\pi_p(x)\,dx,$$

$$(7.9.27)$$

$$= \int_0^1 x \cdot 12x^2(1 - x)\,dx = 12 \int_0^1 x^3\,dx - 12 \int_0^1 x^4\,dx = \frac{3}{5}.$$

But now suppose that experience with another device in the same batch is available. This device had previously been installed in the same sort of control circuit and had proved successful there. To help keep matters straight, let O_1 denote the event that this *first* device operated successfully and O_2, the event that the *second* device does so. Now,

$$P\{O_1 \mid p = x\} = x,$$

and, in the light of experience, Bayes' formula may be applied to alter the prior density $\pi_p(x)$. Use (7.9.9) to see that

(7.9.28)

$$\pi_p(x; O_1) = \frac{P\{O_1 | p = x\}\pi_p(x)}{\int_0^1 P\{O_1 | p = x\}\pi_p(x)\, dx},$$

$$= \frac{x \cdot 12x^2(1 - x)}{\int_0^1 x \cdot 12x^2(1 - x)\, dx} = 20x^3(1 - x).$$

It can now be seen that the posterior, $\pi_p(x; O_1)$, is, in view of the successful outcome for another member of the same batch, shifted towards higher probability of success. For example, the maximum (modal) value of the posterior density $\pi_p(x; O_1)$ is at $x = \frac{3}{4}$, whereas that of the prior $\pi_p(x)$ is at $x = \frac{2}{3}$. According to our revised estimate of batch-success probability, it is now possible to recalculate the probability that the second device is a success—that is, to find that

(7.9.29)

$$P\{O_2 | O_1\} = \int_0^1 P\{O_2 | p = x\}\pi_p(x; O_1)\, dx,$$

$$= \int_0^1 x \cdot 20x^3(1 - x)\, dx = \frac{2}{3}.$$

It stands to reason that this probability is higher than that found before observational evidence became available; compare (7.9.29) to (7.9.27). Thus, if information concerning the success or failure of other devices from the same batch becomes available, then the prior can be revised accordingly.

In our discussion we have alluded to the possibility of updating or revising a prior, then treating this revised probability distribution as a new prior, revising it, and so on. Let us now show that this procedure is valid. In other words, let us show that if the outcomes at, say, trials 1 and 2 are $A_i^{(1)}$ and $A_j^{(2)}$, then we may either

(a) revise the prior probabilities $\{\pi_k\}$ at the end of trial 1 to obtain the posterior distribution $\{\pi_k(A_i^{(1)})\}$, and subsequently revise this latter distribution, treated as a prior, to obtain $\{\pi_k(A_i^{(1)}, A_j^{(2)})\}$, or
(b) wait until trial 2 is over and revise all at once.

The results are the same, and the sequential revision process (a) is usually the most convenient one to adopt. The demonstration is as follows. Using Bayes' theorem and supposing that trial 2 is completed, if we follow procedure (b) we obtain (the trial outcomes are conditionally independent for given k),

(7.9.30)

$$\pi_k(A_i^{(1)}, A_j^{(2)}) = \frac{p_i(k)p_j(k)\pi_k}{\sum_k p_i(k)p_j(k)\pi_k}.$$

But by rearranging probabilities slightly, we have that

(7.9.31)

$$\pi_k(A_i^{(1)}, A_j^{(2)}) = p_j(k)\frac{p_i(k)\pi_k}{\sum_k p_i(k)\pi_k}\frac{\sum_k p_i(k)\pi_k}{\sum_k p_i(k)p_j(k)\pi_k},$$

$$= p_j(k)\pi_k(i) \cdot C,$$

where C is a constant that does not depend on k. Observe that the product $p_j(k)\pi_k(i)$ represents the numerator of Bayes' formula when the posterior of the first trial, $\pi_k(i)$, and the probability of the outcome of the second trial, given the state of nature, are brought together. C is the appropriate normalizing factor, needed to make

$$(7.9.32) \qquad\qquad \sum_k p_j(k)\pi_k(i) = 1.$$

Consequently,

$$(7.9.33) \qquad\qquad \pi_k(A_i^{(1)}, A_j^{(2)}) = \frac{p_j(k)\pi_k(i)}{\sum_k p_j(k)\pi_k(i)},$$

which proves that procedures (a) and (b) are equivalent. Of course, this proof goes through by induction to any number of trials. The density-function case is no different.

EXERCISES 7.9

1. A single six-sided die is thrown. Suppose that the probability that any face turns up is $\frac{1}{6}$. Find
    (a) the probability that a six turns up, given that an even number occurs.
    (b) the probability of a one or a three, given that an odd number occurs.

2. A 52-card bridge deck is shuffled, and a single card is dealt.
    (a) Given that the card is red, what is the probability that it is an honor (A, K, Q, or J)?
    (b) Given that the card is black, what is the probability that the next card is red?

3. Consider the following variation of the hat game of Example 7.9.1: There are four black and two white balls in H_1, and two black and four white balls in H_2.
    (a) Player 2 draws one ball. Calculate the posterior probabilities that he is drawing from H_1, given that the ball is black or white, for the two sets of priors $\pi_1 = \pi_2 = \frac{1}{2}$, and $\pi_1 = \frac{2}{3}$, $\pi_2 = \frac{1}{3}$.
    (b) Same as (a), but Player 2 draws two balls.

4. Consider Example 7.9.1.
    (a) Find the posterior probability that H_1 was offered to Player 2 if $\pi_1 = \frac{1}{4}$. If $\pi_1 = \frac{3}{4}$.
    (b) Suppose Player 2 receives $1 for each black ball in the hat offered if he guesses the number of black balls correctly. Otherwise, he receives nothing. Find his expected gain if he simply guesses without observing a ball. Compare this to his expected gain if he observes a ball before guessing. Assume that he chooses the alternative that makes his expected gain the largest.
        (*Hint:* The meaning of the word "guess" may vary. An uneducated guess might be equivalent to flipping a fair coin—heads for H_1, tails for H_2. However, assuming the prior is known to Player 2, an educated guess means that one of the hats is selected in the light of that prior plus other information available. How much better does the educated guesser do?)

5. (a) In Example 7.9.1, suppose two balls are drawn from the hat offered to Player 2. Find the probability that the remaining ball is white, given that the first ball is black and the second white. Use equally likely priors: $\pi_1 = \frac{1}{2} = \pi_2$.
    (b) Answer (a) if the first ball selected is white and the second black.

6. Refer to Example 7.9.2. Suppose the prior probabilities for students of Types 1 and 2 are $\pi_1 = 0.20$ and $\pi_2 = 0.80$. Compute the probability that a student who passes the test is of Type 1. What is the probability that a student who passes the test actually completes the graduate course?

7. Refer to the distribution of T_x, Example 7.9.3, (7.9.24).
   (a) Find the distribution function of T_x.
   (b) Find the density of T_x.
   (c) Compute $E[T_x]$ and $\text{Var}[T_x]$. What values do these numbers approach as x becomes large $(x \to \infty)$? Why? Remember that $g < b$.
   (d) Suppose $\pi_g = 0.7$, $\pi_b = 0.3$, $g = 0.25$ (days^{-1}), and $b = 1$ (days^{-1}). Find the numerical value of $E[T_x]$ for $x = 0.5$, 1, and 1.5. What value will $E[T_x]$ approach as x becomes indefinitely large?

8. The setup of Example 7.9.3 also describes the following manufacturing situation. When they are manufactured, machines (for example, television sets) are either good or bad. If good, they survive without failure to time t with probability e^{-gt}; if bad, this proba- bility is e^{-bt}, $g < b$. Let π_g be the probability that a newly manufactured set is good, and π_b, the probability that it is bad.

   Now suppose that a test period of length x is to be established. Any set sur- viving the test period is sold and is guaranteed against failure for a time t thereafter. Sets failing during test are discarded.
   (a) What is the probability that a good set survives the test period and fails during the guarantee period?
   (b) Make the same calculation for a bad set.
   (c) What is the conditional probability that a set survives the guarantee period, given that it survives the test period?
   (d) Suppose $n = 10,000$ sets are made in a year. Let $\pi_g = 0.8$, $\pi_b = 0.2$. Let $b = 2$ (years^{-1}), and $g = 0.5$ (years^{-1}). If the guarantee period is $t = 1$ (year), find the expected number of sets on which the guarantee payment is made if $x = 0.25$ (years). If $x = 0.75$ (years).
   (e) For each of the test periods above, find the expected number of good sets that are rejected during test. Find the expected number of bad sets that survive the test.

*7.10   TRANSFORM METHODS

The use of certain *transforms* of probability distributions often simplifies calculations. Also, while the transforms themselves are basically tools, they often have interesting and significant interpretations in their own right. This section provides a brief and elementary introduction and summary of the use of transforms of various kinds in applied probability studies. Transform methods will not be used extensively throughout the remainder of the text.

We start with the simplest type of transform, the generating function.

DEFINITION 7.10.1. Let p_j, $j = 0, 1, 2, \ldots$, represent a discrete probability distribution. Let X be a random variable with

(7.10.1) $$P\{X = j\} = p_j.$$

Then the *generating function* of the distribution p_j, or the random variable X—both terms are used—is the expectation

(7.10.2) $$E[z^X] = \sum_{j=0}^{\infty} z^j p_j = G(z),$$

where $G(z)$ is a function defined at least for all z in the interval $0 \le z \le 1$.

Before going on to describe the important properties and uses of the generating function, we will define another transform that is analogous.

DEFINITION 7.10.2. Let $f(x)$ be a probability density function that is zero for $x < 0$ (for example, a uniform or exponential density). Let X be a random variable with distribution given by this density. Then the expectation

$$(7.10.3) \qquad E[e^{-sX}] = \int_0^\infty e^{-sx}f(x)\,dx = \hat{f}(s)$$

is called the *Laplace transform* of the density f or of the random variable X. Here the transform variable s is any real number in the semiclosed interval $[0, \infty)$. Actually, the defining integral will sometimes converge when s is negative.

Notice that both the generating function and Laplace transform have been defined only for random variables that are zero below a certain point, usually taken to be zero. Mathematically speaking, these transforms may not converge (the sum (7.10.2) or integral (7.10.3) may become infinite) if negative j or x values are allowed and if the corresponding probability distribution $\{p_j\}$ or density f does not become sufficiently small.

We may define still another transform that does not suffer from such difficulties and that is often used.

DEFINITION 7.10.3. Let X be an arbitrary random variable that may assume both positive and negative values. The expectation

$$(7.10.4) \qquad E[e^{i\theta X}] = \varphi(\theta),$$

defined for θ any real number, is called the *characteristic function* of X (or of the distribution function of X). Here i is the imaginary number $i = \sqrt{-1}$. Some of you will recognize the characteristic function as the Fourier transform of the distribution of X; in case X has a density $f(x)$—for example, if f is the normal density—then

$$\varphi(\theta) = \int_{-\infty}^\infty e^{i\theta x}f(x)\,dx.$$

Since all of the transforms above have quite similar basic properties, we will detail these now with special reference to the generating function. Proofs will be given only when it is especially easy to do so; otherwise, you should consult a more advanced text.

THEOREM 7.10.1. *Transform Properties.* These are customarily designated by catchy, one-word terms. The three types of transforms mentioned share these properties.

1. *Unicity* or *Uniqueness.* By this is meant that to each probability distribution there corresponds one and only one transform and that to each transform there corresponds one and only one probability distribution. Putting this another way,

suppose that $g(z)$ and $h(z)$ are generating functions of the distributions $\{p_j\}$ and $\{q_j\}$, respectively. Then if the distributions are the same—that is, if $p_j = q_j$ for all j—it follows that $g(z) = h(z)$ for all z. Considering it the other way about, if $g(z) = h(z)$ for all z, then $p_j = q_j$ for all j. Entirely similar properties hold true for the other transform types.

The practical import of this property is that once a transform is found, the distribution is given *in principle*. Practically speaking, of course, the distribution must be recovered from the transform by "inversion" of the latter. This is often a difficult task that must be performed numerically or approximately.

2. *Convolutions.* Suppose X and Y are two independent random variables; take them to be discrete. Then for any z, z^X and z^Y are also independent random variables, and hence

(7.10.5) $$E[z^{X+Y}] = E[z^X z^Y] = E[z^X]E[z^Y]$$

or

(7.10.6) $$G_{X+Y}(z) = G_X(z)G_Y(z).$$

Thus the generating function of a *sum* of any number (by induction) of independent random variables is the *product* of their generating functions. If

(7.10.7) $$P\{X = i\} = P_X(i) \quad \text{and} \quad P\{Y = j\} = P_Y(j),$$

then the probability distribution of the sum is given by the *convolution*:

(7.10.8) $$P\{X + Y = k\} = \sum_{j=0}^{k} P_X(k - j)P_Y(j) = P_X * P_Y(k).$$

It follows from (7.10.6) above that

$$G_{X+Y}(z) = \sum_{k=0}^{\infty} z^k P_Y * P_Y(k),$$

(7.10.9) $$= \left(\sum_{i=0}^{\infty} z^i P_X(i) \right) \left(\sum_{j=0}^{\infty} z^j P_Y(j) \right),$$

$$= G_X(z) \, G_Y(z).$$

It follows similarly that the Laplace transform and characteristic function of a sum are the product of the transforms of the summands.

3. *Moment Generation.* One of the most useful properties of the transforms is their moment-generating capability. By this we mean the following (illustrated here in terms of the Laplace transforms; others behave analogously): differentiate $\hat{f}(s)$ with respect to s inside the integral sign:

$$\frac{d}{ds}\hat{f}(s) = \frac{d}{ds}\int_0^\infty e^{-sx}f(x)\,dx,$$

(7.10.10)

$$= \int_0^\infty \frac{d}{ds}(e^{-sx})f(x)\,dx = -\int_0^\infty xe^{-sx}f(x)\,dx.$$

Now set $s = 0$ and change the sign to obtain

(7.10.11) $$-\frac{d}{ds}\hat{f}(s)\Big|_{s=0} = \int_0^\infty xf(x)\,dx = E[X].$$

Similarly,

(7.10.12) $$\frac{d^2}{ds^2}\hat{f}(s)\Big|_{s=0} = \int_0^\infty x^2f(x)\,dx = E[X^2],$$

and so on. The formal differentiation is justified by the fact that moments actually exist (are finite). If enough moments exist, the Taylor series expansion

(7.10.13) $$\hat{f}(s) = 1 + \frac{s}{1!}E[X] + \frac{s^2}{2!}E[X^2] + \frac{s^3}{3!}E[X^3] + \cdots$$

may be justified.

Again, analogous properties hold for the generating function and characteristic function. You should note, however, that for the generating function we have

(7.10.14) $$\frac{d}{dz}G(z)\Big|_{z=1} = E[X]$$

and

(7.10.15) $$\frac{d^2}{dz^2}G(z)\Big|_{z=1} = E[X^2 - X] = E[X^2] - E[X],$$

and so on.

4. *Change of Origin and Scale.* Again consider a random variable X and its Laplace transform $\hat{f}(s)$. Let us define a new random variable by linear transformation:

(7.10.16) $$X' = aX + b.$$

Then its Laplace transform is

(7.10.17) $$E[e^{-sX'}] = E[e^{-s(aX+b)}] = e^{-sb}E[e^{-asX}],$$
$$= e^{-sb}\hat{f}(as).$$

Unfortunately, nothing quite so simple holds true for the transforms of other random variable transformations.

5. *Continuity.* Let $\{F_n(x),\ n = 1, 2, \ldots\}$ be a sequence of distribution functions that converge to a limit as $n \to \infty$. Here n may be any parameter, and the idea is that for sufficiently many fixed x values (a dense set will do) the sequence of numbers $F_1(x), F_2(x), F_3(x), \ldots$ approaches the limit $F(x)$. To be definite, suppose that F_n has density f_n and that F has a density f to which f_n tends. *Then* the Laplace transform of f_n tends to that of f,

(7.10.18) $$\hat{f}_n(s) = \int_0^\infty e^{-sx}f_n(x)\,dx \to \hat{f}(s) = \int_0^\infty e^{-sx}f(x)\,dx,$$

as $n \to \infty$. The same property is enjoyed by the generating and characteristic functions. More importantly, if $\hat{f}_n(s)$ is the transform of a distribution F_n and if $\hat{f}_n \to \hat{f}$ where $\hat{f}$

is the transform of a distribution function F, then it may be concluded that the underlying distribution $F_n \to F$. This last property is important because it is often easy to derive the transform of a distribution F_n, and afterwards it is easier to show that $\hat{f}_n \to \hat{f}$ than to show directly that $F_n \to F$.

The transforms of some familiar distributions are derived below.

THEOREM 7.10.2.

(a) The generating function of the *binomial distribution*,

$$p_j = \binom{n}{j} p^j q^{n-j}, \qquad (p + q = 1; j = 0, 1, 2, \ldots, n),$$

is

(7.10.19) $$G(z) = (pz + q)^n.$$

(b) The generating function of the *Poisson distribution*,

$$p_j = e^{-a} \frac{a^j}{j!} \qquad j = 0, 1, q, \ldots,$$

is

(7.10.20) $$G(z) = e^{-a(1-z)}.$$

(c) The generating function of the discrete uniform distribution over $(0, 1]$,

$$p_j = \frac{1}{n} \qquad j = \frac{1}{n}, \frac{2}{n}, \frac{3}{n}, \ldots, \frac{n}{n} = 1,$$

$$= 0 \qquad \text{elsewhere}$$

is

(7.10.21) $$G(z) = \frac{1}{n} \frac{(1-z)z^{1/n}}{1 - z^{1/n}}.$$

(d) The Laplace transform of the uniform distribution with density

$$f(x) = e^{-\lambda x}\lambda \qquad x \geq 0,$$
$$= 0 \qquad x < 0$$

is

(7.10.22) $$\hat{f}(s) = \frac{\lambda}{\lambda + s}.$$

(e) The Laplace transform of the exponential distribution with density

$$f(x) = e^{-\lambda x}\lambda \qquad x \geq 0,$$
$$= 0 \qquad x < 0$$

is

(7.10.23) $$\hat{f}(s) = \frac{\lambda}{\lambda + s}.$$

(f) The Laplace transform of the gamma distribution with density

$$f(x) = e^{-\lambda x} \frac{(\lambda x)^{k-1} \lambda}{\Gamma(k)}, \qquad x \geq 0,$$

$$= 0 \qquad\qquad x < 0$$

is

(7.10.24)
$$\hat{f}(s) = \left(\frac{\lambda}{\lambda + s}\right)^k.$$

(g) The characteristic function of the *normal* distribution with density

$$f(x) = \frac{1}{\sqrt{2\pi}\,\sigma}\, e^{-\frac{1}{2}\left(\frac{x-m}{\sigma}\right)^2} \qquad -\infty < x < \infty$$

is

(7.10.25)
$$\varphi(\theta) = e^{[im\theta - (\sigma^2\theta^2/2)]}.$$

Proof: From Definition 7.10.1:

(a) $G(z) = \sum_{j=0}^{n} z^j p_j = \sum_{j=0}^{n} z^j \binom{n}{j} p^j q^{n-j} = \sum_{j=0}^{n} \binom{n}{j} (pz)^j q^{n-j} = (pz + q)^n.$

(b) $G(z) = \sum_{j=0}^{\infty} z^j p_j = \sum_{j=0}^{\infty} z^j e^{-a} \frac{a^j}{j!} = e^{-a} \sum_{j=0}^{\infty} \frac{(az)^j}{j!} = e^{-a} e^{az}.$

(c) $G(z) = \sum_{j=1/n}^{1} z^j p_j = \frac{1}{n} \sum_{k=1}^{n} z^{k/n} = \frac{1}{n} \frac{(z^{1/n} - z^{(n+1)/n})}{1 - z^{1/n}}.$

(d) $\hat{f}(s) = \int_0^\infty e^{-sx} f(x)\, dx = \int_0^1 e^{-sx}\, dx = \frac{1}{s}(1 - e^{-s}).$

(e) $\hat{f}(s) = \int_0^\infty e^{-sx} e^{-\lambda x} \lambda\, dx = \frac{\lambda}{\lambda + s}$ (change variable of integration to $y = (\lambda + s)x$; also for (f) below).

(f) $\hat{f}(s) = \int_0^\infty e^{-sx} e^{-\lambda x} \frac{(\lambda x)^{k-1}}{\Gamma(k)} \lambda\, dx = \left(\int_0^\infty e^{-y} y^{k-1}\, dy \right) \left(\frac{\lambda}{\lambda + s} \right)^k \frac{1}{\Gamma(k)}$

$$= \left(\frac{\lambda}{\lambda + s} \right)^k$$

(g) $\varphi(\theta) = \int_{-\infty}^{\infty} e^{i\theta x} \frac{e^{-\frac{1}{2}\left(\frac{x-m}{\sigma}\right)^2}}{\sqrt{2\pi}\,\sigma}\, dx.$

Put $y = \dfrac{x - m}{\sigma}$:

$$\varphi(\theta) = \int_{-\infty}^{\infty} e^{i\theta(\sigma y + m)} \frac{e^{-\frac{1}{2} y^2}\, dy}{\sqrt{2\pi}}$$

$$= e^{i\theta m} \int_{-\infty}^{\infty} \frac{e^{-\frac{1}{2} y^2}}{\sqrt{2\pi}} e^{i\theta\sigma y}\, dy = e^{i\theta m} \int_{-\infty}^{\infty} e^{-\frac{1}{2}(y - i\theta\sigma)^2} \frac{dy}{\sqrt{2\pi}} e^{\frac{(i\theta\sigma)^2}{2}}$$

$$= e^{i\theta m - \frac{\theta^2\sigma^2}{2}},$$

since it may be shown that

$$\int_{-\infty}^{\infty} e^{-\frac{1}{2}(y-i\theta\sigma)^2} \frac{dy}{\sqrt{2\pi}} = 1$$

in spite of the imaginary term $i\theta\sigma$.

We now turn to some motivational examples.

EXAMPLE 7.10.1. An organization considers spending $1,000,000 immediately in order to purchase a certain invention. The invention is expected to turn into a marketable product in T years, where T is a discrete random variable having distribution given by $\{p_j, j = 1, 2, 3, \ldots\}$. At the time the product is marketed, the estimate of its market value is $3,000,000. Should the invention be purchased?

Given the length of time, T, that elapses until the invention is marketable, then it is common to examine the *present worth* of the eventual market value, V, which is

$$(7.10.26) \qquad W(T) = V d^T,$$

where $0 < d < 1$ is a discount rate. A possible value is $d = 0.95$, where time is measured in years. Considering T to be random, the expected present worth is

$$(7.10.27) \qquad E[W(T)] = V \sum_{i=1}^{\infty} d^i p_i,$$

which is recognizable as V multiplied by the *generating function* of the random variable T, evaluated at $z = d$.

One possible means for deciding whether to purchase the invention is to compare the value of the expectation (7.10.27) with the purchase price:

$$(7.10.28) \qquad \begin{array}{l} \text{Purchase if } E[W(T)] > \$1,000,000, \\ \text{Do Not Purchase if } E[W(T)] < \$1,000,000. \end{array}$$

As an extension of the last problem consider the following example.

EXAMPLE 7.10.2. An initial expenditure of $\$I$ gives rise to returns at random time intervals. That is, if the initial expenditure is at $t = 0$, the first return is V_1 at T_1, the second is V_2 at $T_1 + T_2$, the nth is V_n at $T_1 + T_2 + \cdots + T_n$. The present value of the income stream, given $T_1, T_2, \ldots$, is equal to

$$(7.10.29)$$

$$W(T_1, T_2, \ldots, T_n, \ldots) = V_1 z^{T_1} + V_2 z^{T_1+T_2} + \cdots + V_n z^{T_1+T_2+\cdots+T_n} + \cdots,$$

where z is the discount rate. Now suppose the V's all have the same distribution, as do the T's—of course, the distribution of V need not equal that of T. Furthermore, the V sequence and the T sequence are independent. The expected present value is then (putting $v = E[V]$) equal to

$$E[W] = v[g_T(z) + g_T{}^2(z) + g_T{}^3(z) + \cdots],$$

(7.10.30)

$$= v \frac{g_T(z)}{1 - g_T(z)}.$$

Here we have used the convolution property of the generating function to pass from (7.10.29) to (7.10.30).

It is sometimes convenient to let T be a continuous random variable in problems of the type given above. Then e^{-sT} is the continuous-time version of (7.10.26); s is a continuous-time discount rate analogous to the d of (7.10.26). Taking expectations then leads to the Laplace transform, $E[e^{-sT}]$. The choice between this latter formulation and the discrete-time formulation is often a matter of taste.

EXAMPLE 7.10.3. Suppose that a particular electronic computer runs constantly except when failures occur. The failures appear at random instants: the time of the first failure is $t_1 = T_1$, the time of the second is $t_2 = T_1 + T_2$, the time of the nth, $t_n = T_1 + T_2 + \cdots + T_n$. Here $\{T_i, i = 1, 2, \ldots\}$ is a sequence of independently and identically distributed random variables having distribution $F(x)$ and density function $f(x)$. Let us ask for the probability that exactly n ($n = 0, 1, 2, \ldots$) failures occur in a fixed time of duration t. Initially the computer is in perfect repair, so the time until the first failure has distribution F, and so on. Let the random variable denoting the number of failures in time t be $N(t)$. Now it is clear that

$$N(t) = 0 \quad \text{if } T_1 > t,$$
(7.10.31)
$$N(t) = 1 \quad \text{if } T_1 < t \text{ but } T_1 + T_2 > t,$$

$$\cdots,$$

$$N(t) = n \quad \text{if } T_1 + T_2 + \cdots + T_n < t \text{ but } T_1 + T_2 + \cdots + T_{n+1} > t.$$

In other words, the events on the left occur if and only if those on the right do. Thus the probabilities are equal:

$$P\{N(t) = 0\} = P\{T_1 > t\} = 1 - P\{T_1 < t\} = 1 - F(t),$$

$$P\{N(t) = 1\} = F(t) - F*F(t) = F(t) - F^{2}*(t),$$
(7.10.32)

$$\cdots,$$

$$P\{N(t) = n\} = F^{n}*(t) - F^{(n+1)}*(t),$$

where $F^{n}*(t)$ and $F^{(n+1)}*(t)$ are the n-fold and $(n+1)$-fold convolutions, respectively. Written in terms of the density function we have

(7.10.33) $$P\{N(t) = n\} = \int_0^t f^{n}*(x)\, dx - \int_0^t f^{(n+1)}*(x)\, dx.$$

Simplification results if we introduce the Laplace transform. Let us multiply both sides of (7.10.23) by e^{-st} and integrate:

(7.10.34)

$$\int_0^\infty e^{-st} P\{N(t) = n\}\, dt = \int_0^\infty e^{-st}\, dt \int_0^t f^{n*}(x)\, dx - \int_0^\infty e^{-st}\, dt \int_0^t f^{(n+1)*}(x)\, dx.$$

Notice that we are in effect transforming with respect to the parameter, t, in a probability distribution on the left-hand side. To bring the right-hand side into familiar form, integrate by parts:

$$(7.10.35) \qquad \int_0^\infty e^{-st}\, dt \int_0^t f^{n*}(x)\, dx = -\frac{1}{s} e^{-st} \int_0^t f^{n*}(x)\, dx \Bigg|_0^\infty + \frac{1}{s} \int_0^\infty e^{-st} f^{n*}(t)\, dt,$$

$$= \frac{1}{s} [\hat{f}(s)]^n.$$

This follows because if $s > 0$, the first term on the right-hand side vanishes since the exponential dwindles to zero while the integral increases to one:

$$\lim_{t \to \infty} -\frac{1}{s} e^{-st} \int_0^t f^{n*}(x)\, dx = 0,$$

and

$$\lim_{t \to 0} -\frac{1}{s} e^{-st} \int_0^t f^{n*}(x)\, dx = 0.$$

The latter limit holds true because $F(0) = 0$—we are dealing with positive random variables. The convolution property delivers the final, simple form on the second line of (7.10.35). Thus it follows that if s is multiplied into both sides of (7.10.27), we have

$$(7.10.36) \qquad \int_0^\infty P\{N(t) = n\} e^{-st} s\, dt = [\hat{f}(s)]^n - [\hat{f}(s)]^{n+1} = [1 - \hat{f}(s)][\hat{f}(s)]^n.$$

Again the transformed probability is noticeably simpler than the original. We can even give a useful *probability interpretation* to (7.10.36). Imagine that programs brought to the computer under study vary in running time in accordance with an exponential density with mean s^{-1}. Then, with probability

$$P\{N(t) = n\},$$

there are n computer breakdowns during a running time of length t. We are interested in the number of breakdowns during a random running time, R, with density

$$(7.10.37) \qquad\qquad f_R(t) = e^{-st} s \qquad s > 0.$$

Consequently, we are led to integrate to remove the condition that $R = t$:

$$(7.10.38) \qquad P\{N(R) = n\} = \int_0^\infty e^{-st} s P\{N(t) = n\}\, dt = [1 - \hat{f}(s)][\hat{f}(s)]^n.$$

As a consequence, $N(R)$ has the *geometric distribution*, regardless of the distribution of the times to failure. Of course the mean number of failures depends on $\hat{f}(s)$, the Laplace transform of the time-to-failure density. But the simple answer to this seemingly complex problem is a pleasant surprise.

EXAMPLE 7.10.4. In order to illustrate the continuity property referred to in Theorem 7.10.1, consider the discrete uniform distribution: (c) of Theorem 7.10.2. It seems intuitively clear that if the number of possible values, n, becomes large, this distribution approaches (becomes indistinguishable from) the continuous uniform distribution of (d). To demonstrate this, first convert the generating function into the Laplace transform by the substitution $z = e^{-s}$. Although the generating function of a continuous random variable is not defined, the Laplace transform of a discrete random variable is obtained by the change mentioned. We find from (c), then, that

$$(7.10.39) \qquad \hat{f}_n(s) = G_n(e^{-s}) = \frac{1}{n} \frac{(1 - e^{-s})e^{-s/n}}{1 - e^{-s/n}}.$$

Now when $n \to \infty$, the term $e^{-s/n} \to 1$ for any $s > 0$. Application of L'Hospital's rule shows that

$$\frac{1/n}{1 - e^{-s/n}} \to \frac{1}{s},$$

and hence

$$(7.10.40) \qquad \hat{f}_n(s) \to \hat{f}(s) = \frac{(1 - e^{-s})}{s},$$

which is the transform of the continuous uniform distribution over $(0, 1)$ (see (d) of Theorem 7.10.2). Hence by the continuity property, the discrete uniform distribution approaches the continuous distribution as the discretization, $1/n$, becomes small.

EXAMPLE 7.10.5. Suppose arrivals at a computer facility are modeled as follows. A one-hour period is split into n intervals of length $1/n$, and during each such interval an arrival occurs, with probability p, independently of all previous arrivals. It follows that the number of arrivals during the one-hour period, A, has the binomial distribution

$$(7.10.41) \qquad P\{A = j\} = \binom{n}{j} p^j q^{n-j}.$$

In particular, the expected number of arrivals during the one hour period is

$$(7.10.42) \qquad E[A] = np.$$

Suppose we wish to represent a situation in which the expected number of arrivals is given (perhaps analysis of past history suggests the value): $E[A] = a$. Hence, $np = a$. Clearly our model becomes more plausible if n becomes large since the intervals then become smaller and we are the more ready to accept the assumption that at most one arrival occurs during an interval. To explore the implication of letting $n \to \infty$, consider the generating function of the binomial (Theorem 7.10.2(a)), but recollect that we have $p = a/n$. Then

$$G_n(z) = (pz + 1 - p)^n = \left[1 - \frac{a}{n}(1 - z) \right]^n.$$

Now letting $n \to \infty$, we find that

$$(7.10.43) \qquad\qquad G_n(z) \to G(z) = e^{-a(1-z)},$$

and reference to (b) of Theorem 7.10.2 reveals that the limit, $G(z)$, is the generating function of the Poisson distribution. Again it follows from the continuity property that the number of arrivals, A, has a Poisson distribution under the conditions mentioned.

EXERCISES 7.10

1. Suppose a machine's time to failure, T, has an exponential distribution with density $e^{-\lambda x}\lambda (x \geq 0)$. Use the moment-generating property of the Laplace transform to find $E[T]$ and $Var[T]$.

2. Find the mean and variance of the binomial and Poisson distributions by making use of the moment-operating properties of the generating function.

3. An interesting new distribution (the Pascal, or negative binomial) may be generated by randomizing the parameter of a Poisson distribution by means of a gamma distribution. That is, if A is the number of events (arrivals, for example) during a one-hour period, and A is Poisson with mean a, then suppose a is selected at random each hour from distribution F_a. We have conditionally

$$P\{A = n \,|\, a = x\} = e^{-x}\frac{x^n}{n!},$$

and unconditionally

$$P\{A = n\} = \int_0^\infty e^{-x}\frac{x^n}{n!}f_a(x)\,dx,$$

f_a being the density of a.

(a) Show that the generating function of A is

$$G_A(z) = \sum_{n=0}^\infty z^n P\{A = n\} = \int_0^\infty e^{-x[1-z]}f_a(x)\,dx,$$

$$= \hat{f}(1 - z).$$

$$\left(Hint:\ \sum_{n=0}^\infty z^n \int_0^\infty e^{-x}\frac{x^n}{n!}f_a(x)\,dx = \int_0^\infty \left(\sum_{n=0}^\infty z^n e^{-x}\frac{x^n}{n!}\right)f_a(x)\,dx.\right)$$

(b) Let f_a be the gamma density of Theorem 7.10.2, part (f). Show that

$$G_A(z) = \left(\frac{\lambda}{\lambda + 1 - z}\right)^k.$$

This is the generating function of the negative binomial distribution.

(c) By differentiation of $G_A(z)$, find $E[A]$ and $Var[A]$. Show that

$$P\{A = 0\} = \left(\frac{\lambda}{\lambda + 1}\right)^k.$$

4. Using Exercise 3 again, if $k=1$, show that A has the geometric distribution. (*Hint:* Expand $\dfrac{\lambda}{\lambda+1-z}$ as a geometric series in z and use (7.10.2).)

5. An uninterrupted time duration Q is allocated to a certain computation. Suppose the computation duration, X, has the exponential density with parameter λ.

(a) Given that the computation terminates before Q (conditional on $X \leq Q$), show that the density of X is

$$f_X(x) = \frac{e^{-\lambda x}\lambda}{1-e^{-\lambda Q}} \qquad 0 \leq x \leq Q,$$

$$= 0 \qquad\qquad \text{otherwise.}$$

(b) Show that the Laplace transform is

$$\hat{f}_X(s) = \left(\frac{\lambda}{\lambda+s}\right)\frac{1-e^{-(\lambda+s)Q}}{(1-e^{-\lambda Q})}.$$

(c) Use the continuity property of the transform to show that if $\lambda \to 0$, the transform above tends to $(1-e^{-sQ})/sQ$. Therefore, the truncated X tends to become uniformly distributed over $(0, Q)$ as $\lambda \to 0$. Notice that this can be shown directly by letting $\lambda \to 0$ in the density formula of (a).

6. The purpose of this exercise is to show by example that if a sequence of probability distributions $\{F_n\}$ tends to a bonafide probability-distribution limit, F, there is no guarantee whatever that the corresponding expectations of the F_n distributions approach that of F.

(a) Consider the mixed Poisson:

$$P_j(n) = P\{A_n=j\} = (1-e^{-n})e^{-a}\frac{a^j}{j!} + (e^{-n})e^{-a_n}\frac{a_n{}^j}{j!},$$

where $1-e^{-n}$ may be thought of as the probability of selecting the Poisson distribution of parameter a, and e^{-n} as the probability of selecting the Poisson with parameter $a_n > 0$. Show that for every $n > 0$, $p_j(n)$ represents a probability distribution.

(b) Show that the expected value of A_n is

$$E[A_n] = a(1-e^{-n}) + a_n e^{-n}.$$

(c) Observe that if $n \to \infty$, $p_j(n) \to e^{-a}(a^j/j!)$. (*Hint:* $e^{-a_n}(a_n{}^j/j!) \leq 1$.) Therefore, the mean of the limiting distribution, which is Poisson, is

$$E[A_\infty] = a.$$

(d) Pick $a_n = be^n$, and observe that

$$\lim_{n \to \infty} E[A_n] = a+b \neq E[A_\infty].$$

SUGGESTED READING

Barr, D. R., and Zehna, P. W. *Probability*. Monterey, Calif.: Brooks/Cole, 1971. (Introductory)

Cramer, H. *Mathematical Methods of Statistics*. Princeton, N.J.: Princeton University Press, 1946. (Advanced)

Feller, W. *An Introduction to Probability Theory and Its Applications.* 2 Vols. New York: John Wiley, 1957 and 1966. (Introductory to Advanced)

Hoel, P. G., Port, S. C., and Stone, C. J. *Introduction to Probability Theory* and *Introduction to Statistical Theory.* Boston: Houghton Mifflin, 1971. (Introductory)

Lindgren, B. *Statistical Theory.* New York: MacMillan, 1962. (Introductory)

Mood, A., and Graybill, F. *Introduction to the Theory of Statistics.* New York: McGraw-Hill, 1963. (Introductory)

Parzen, E. *Modern Probability Theory and Its Applications.* New York: John Wiley, 1960. (Introductory)

Schmitt, S. A. *Measuring Uncertainty, an Elementary Introduction to Bayesian Statistics.* Reading, Mass.: Addison-Wesley, 1969. (Introductory)

CHAPTER 8

DECISION MODELS

8.1   INTRODUCTION

The previous chapter outlined many of the facts about probability theory that are useful for describing situations in which chance plays a role. It is very often convenient to act as if random phenomena govern interesting outcomes; we shall develop more complex and inclusive probability models for such phenomena in later chapters.

Still another characteristic aspect of a great many real problems is the opportunity to make a decision that influences in part the outcomes of interest. For example, the weekly demand for a certain product may apparently vary in a random fashion. Yet the opportunity may exist to carry an inventory of the product in anticipation of demand. The decision concerning the level of inventory to be carried will depend upon the cost of storing the product, the penalty associated with running short, and the probabilities of various demand levels, among other things.

In this chapter we will describe the factors that influence the making of a decision. We will then apply mathematical methods to some rather simple problems and develop decision rules for maximizing or minimizing stated objective functions. The solutions to such simple decision problems often furnish insights that are useful when realistic, large-scale situations come under study.

8.2   A PERISHABLE-GOODS INVENTORY MODEL

Many manufacturers and suppliers anticipate demands for their commodities to vary in an unpredictable way from period to period. Thus, daily demands for bread at a bakery or for afternoon newspapers fluctuate randomly. So does the seasonal demand for a new line of style goods—for example, women's wear or automobile or appliance models. Typically, the manufacturer must produce and stock his product in advance of the period's demand. No matter what level is so stocked, it is extremely unlikely that realized demand will precisely equal it: either there will be a shortage, or "stockout" as it is often called, with demand exceeding supply and sales lost (and possibly customers alienated) or there will be a quantity left over. We shall assume for the present that excess products spoil and have zero value. We also assume that the demand of one period is not affected by the stockouts of previous periods.

Assume now that there is random demand, D_n, in period n for the product, where $n = 1, 2, \ldots$. The manufacturer must decide on the amounts I_n ($I_n \geq 0$) to stock at the beginning of each period in order to meet the demand D_n. Under the assumptions outlined above, the number S_n of units sold in period n is given by

$$(8.2.1) \qquad S_n = \begin{cases} D_n & \text{if } D_n < I_n \\ I_n & \text{if } D_n \geq I_n \end{cases}$$
$$= \min(D_n, I_n).$$

In order to make the decision as to the inventory levels I_n, the manufacturer must know something about his costs and the selling price for the goods. For this model, let p_n be the selling price in the nth period, and let $C_n(x)$ be the cost of producing x units in the nth period; both p_n and $C_n(x)$ are known in advance. Then the manufacturer's net profit in the nth period is

$$(8.2.2) \qquad N_n = p_n S_n - C_n(I_n).$$

EXAMPLE 8.2.1. A daily newspaper sells for 7¢ per copy and costs the printer 2¢ per copy to print. The publisher estimates that the demand each period is approximately exponentially distributed according to the following formula:

$$(8.2.3) \qquad P[D \leq x] = (1 - e^{-x/1000}) = F_D(x) \qquad (x \geq 0)$$

with density

$$f_D(x) = e^{-x/1000} \frac{1}{1000}.$$

The graph of the demand distribution function is given in Figure 8.2.1.

The publisher must decide on the number, I_n, to print each day. His net profit per period is, from (8.2.2),

$$N = (.07)S -- (.02)I,$$

where the subscript n has been dropped because price, cost, and demand distribution are unchanged from period to period. The publisher's question is how to determine I, the number of papers to be published. Obviously, if too many copies are printed, some will be left over and money will be lost. On the other hand, if too few copies are available, sales will be lost. Some compromise must be sought.

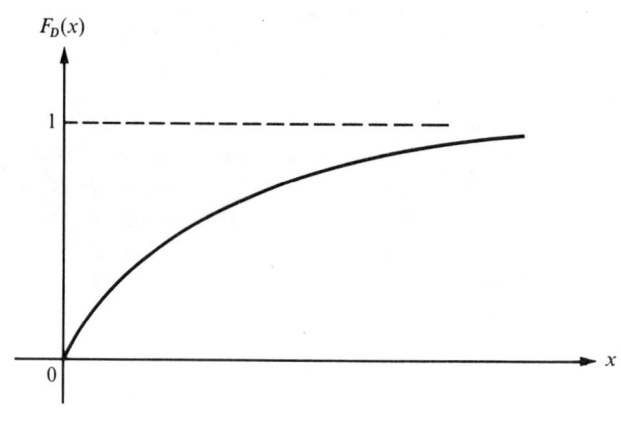

FIGURE 8.2.1

EXAMPLE 8.2.2. A grocer has observed that he never sells more than five loaves of a certain brand of bread in any one day. His records indicate that the probabilities of selling various numbers of loaves are as shown in Figure 8.2.2. If he

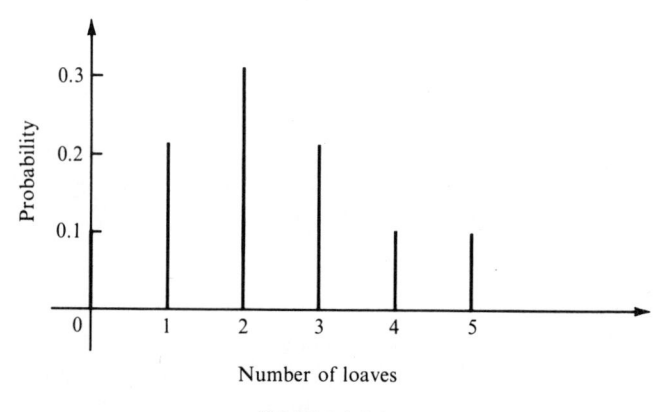

FIGURE 8.2.2

buys a loaf of bread for 12¢ and sells it for 22¢, how many should he buy, assuming that unsold loaves spoil overnight and are worthless? A compromise is required: stocking too little bread tends to lose sales, while stocking too much brings about loss from spoilage.

DEFINITION 8.2.1. An *inventory policy* is a decision rule establishing the level I_n for each period; that is, it is a sequence of values for I_n.

In the two simple examples given above, the distribution, prices, and costs do not change over time, so a decision can be made on a single day and repeated for all other days. Of course, there might be cyclical variation such that the demand for newspapers is higher on Wednesday than on Monday, or the demand for bread is higher on Saturday than on other days of the week. In such cases, the decisions would be different for different kinds of days, and one would have to establish an appropriate rule for each day of the week.

One example of an inventory policy is to stock the mean, or expected value, of demand for the day. That is,

$$(8.2.4) \qquad\qquad I_n = E(D_n).$$

Although such a policy might seem plausible, there are often better choices, as will be seen. A manufacturer will choose a policy that satisfies certain criteria that he deems important. He might, for instance, wish to maximize average net profit per period over $k(k \leq \infty)$ periods. Or he might wish to keep the average number of stockouts below a certain small number. At the same time, he will usually set an upper limit on the values of I_n so that the total amount he has to commit to this activity is limited. The requirements must be translated into specific questions about a proposed policy; in turn, these questions are translated into prescriptions for obtaining policies with desired operating characteristics.

In the discussion that follows, we will illustrate the development of certain policies exhibiting required properties or operating characteristics. Calculation of the latter will be facilitated by rather simplified assumptions concerning the probabilistic properties of the random demand. In later chapters, more realistic models that are less simple mathematically will be introduced.

We shall begin by introducing a simple, plausible policy, the form of which may be determined by making a near-minimum of assumptions about the probabilistic nature of demand.

EXAMPLE 8.2.1 (continued). The newspaper distributor wishes to set the level, I, so as to maximize his *expected net profit* per period. We proceed by determining expected net profit as a function of I. Then we select that value of I maximizing the expected net profit.

Using the representations (8.2.1), for sales as a function of demand, and (8.2.2), for profit as a function of sales, we can express the one-period profit as a function of that period's demand:

$$(8.2.5) \qquad\qquad N(D) = \begin{cases} pD - cI & \text{if } D < I \\ pI - cI & \text{if } D \geq I \end{cases}$$

In other words, the profit is a random variable that is a function of the random variable D. If we put this in terms of earlier terminology, $N = g(D)$ (see Theorem 7.5.1):

$$(8.2.6) \qquad\qquad g(x) = \begin{cases} px - cI & \text{if } x < I \\ pI - cI & \text{if } x \geq I \end{cases}$$

To find the expected profit, apply (7.5.24):

$$E[N(D)] = \int_0^\infty g(x) f_D(x)\, dx,$$

$$(8.2.7) \qquad\qquad = p\left[\int_0^I x f_D(x)\, dx + \int_I^\infty I f_D(x)\, dx \right] - cI,$$

$$= p \int_0^I x f_D(x)\, dx + pI[1 - F_D(I)] - cI.$$

Now the last expression may be maximized with respect to I. Differentiate (8.2.7) with respect to I and set the result equal to zero. Remembering that the derivative of an integral with respect to its upper limit is just the integrand

$$\frac{d}{dI} \int_0^I g(x)\,dx = g(I)$$

and that the derivative of a continuous distribution is the density, we obtain

(8.2.8) $$\frac{dE[N(D)]}{dI} = pIf_D(I) + p[1 - F_D(I)] - pIf_D(I) - c = 0.$$

After cancellation, one finds the equation

$$p[1 - F_D(I)] = c,$$

or

(8.2.9) $$F_D(I) = 1 - \frac{c}{p}.$$

Since the distribution function $F_D(I)$ is always positive, the equation above has a solution if, and only if, $p > c$. This value of I, denoted by $\bar{I}$, is the optimum inventory level. However, to complete the demonstration it must be shown that $\bar{I}$ represents a maximum. A second differentiation gives

$$\frac{d^2E[N(D)]}{dI^2} = \frac{d}{dI}\{p[1 - F_D(I)] - c\} = -pf_D(I) < 0,$$

and since f_D, being a density, is always nonnegative, it follows that the solution of (8.2.9) is indeed the optimum inventory, *provided* $p > c$. If $p < c$, then it can be seen intuitively that the newspaper business is unprofitable, and I should be zero.

The solution of (8.2.9) may be represented graphically, as shown in Figure 8.2.3. To summarize, the optimum inventory level $\bar{I}$ satisfies

(8.2.10) $$F_D(\bar{I}) = 1 - \frac{c}{p} \qquad \text{if } p > c,$$

$$= 0 \qquad \text{if } p < c,$$

where the net profit function is given by (8.2.5).

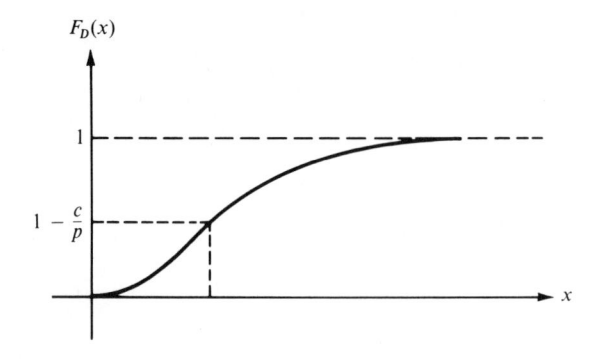

FIGURE 8.2.3

Ordinarily $p > c$ and the numerical value of $\bar{I}$, given implicitly by (8.2.7), must be determined graphically or numerically. Figure 8.2.3 indicates how a graphical solution may be obtained. If a table of the demand distribution is available, the optimal solution may also be found. Less frequently, the distribution may be explicitly inverted. Consider our Example 8.2.1, which uses the exponential demand distribution.

EXAMPLE 8.2.3. Suppose demand is exponential,

$$(8.2.11) \qquad \begin{aligned} F(x) &= 1 - e^{-x/m} & \text{if } x \geq 0, \\ &= 0 & \text{if } x < 0, \end{aligned}$$

$m = E[D]$ being the expected number of newspapers demanded during any period. Then, following (8.2.8) or (8.2.10),

$$(8.2.12) \qquad 1 - e^{-\bar{I}/m} = 1 - \frac{c}{p}.$$

so

$$e^{-\bar{I}/m} = \frac{c}{p},$$

and taking logarithms, we find

$$(8.2.13) \qquad \bar{I} = m \log_e\left(\frac{p}{c}\right) \qquad \text{for } p > c.$$

Now this inventory level may be substituted back into the cost function (8.2.7) to obtain the lowest possible inventory cost. First, however, let us rearrange the expression (8.2.7) to make it more convenient. Since (8.2.8) is the derivative of (8.2.7), we obviously can integrate to obtain

$$\begin{aligned} E[N|I] &= \int_0^I \frac{dE[N|I']}{dI'}\, dI', \\ (8.2.14) \qquad &= \int_0^I \{p[1 - F(I')] - c\}\, dI', \\ &= p \int_0^I [1 - F(I')]\, dI' - cI. \end{aligned}$$

Substituting our exponential demand distribution into (2.2.14), we find that

$$(8.2.15) \qquad E[N|I] = p \int_0^I e^{-I'/m}\, dI' - cI = pm[1 - e^{-I/m}] - cI.$$

Finally, we can substitute in our expression for $\bar{I}$, the optimal inventory level, to find the value of the optimal policy, which turns out to be

$$(8.2.16) \qquad E[N|\bar{I}] = pm\left[1 - \frac{c}{p}\right] - cm \log\left(\frac{p}{c}\right) = m\left\{p - c\left[1 + \log\left(\frac{p}{c}\right)\right]\right\}.$$

If a nonoptimal inventory level is suggested, we can substitute it into (8.2.15) and compare to (8.2.16) in order to find the advantage of $\bar{I}$. This is of interest because in practice one will never know the value of the mean or expected demand, m, precisely (nor can one be sure that the exponential distribution is appropriate). Likewise, the price and cost figures may be inaccurate. If we want to study the effect of such realistic imprecisions, we are aided by having an explicit expression such as (8.2.16). The next example indicates how a sensitivity study of the kind described may proceed.

EXAMPLE 8.2.4. At a particular shop the price of Christmas trees is \$5.00 and the unit cost is \$2.00. Demand is (approximately) exponentially distributed. The best estimate available for the expected number of trees to be demanded is

$$E[D] = m = 100,$$

but there is a possibility that the expectation may be 10% higher—that is, 110. We seek to determine how much profit will be lost, on the average, if the inventory stocked is based on the estimated mean demand of 100 if, in fact, mean demand turns out to be 110. The magnitude of the answer would indicate, for example, how much it might be worth spending to improve the quality of the demand estimation in use.

The calculation proceeds as follows. If mean demand is actually 110, then the optimal inventory level is

$$\bar{I}_{110} = 110 \log\left(\frac{5}{2}\right),$$

(8.2.17)
$$= (110)(0.916),$$

$$= 100.76,$$

and, from (8.2.16), the resulting maximum expected profit is

$$E[N\,|\,\bar{I}_{110}] = 110\{5 - 2[1 + 0.916]\} = \$128.48.$$

Now if it is believed that the mean demand is 100, then one would stock

(8.2.18)
$$\bar{I}_{100} = 100 \log\left(\frac{5}{2}\right),$$

$$= 91.6.$$

(Actually, both $\bar{I}_{110}$ and $\bar{I}_{100}$ should be rounded off to integer values.) However, to discover the profit resulting from following the policy $\bar{I}_{100}$ when $m = 110$, we must utilize the *actual* profit function, expression (8.2.15) with $m = 110$. Substituting, we find

$$E[N\,|\,\bar{I}_{100}] = 5 \times 110 \times [1 - e^{-I100/110}] - 2 \times \bar{I}_{100},$$

(8.2.19)
$$= 550[1 - e^{-0.83}] - 183.2,$$

$$= 550 \times 0.564 - 183.2,$$

$$= \$127.00.$$

It is plain to see that a 10% error in the mean demand reduces the expected profit hardly at all; hence one would not wish to spend much to improve the estimate in this case. Although such insensitivity is rather common, it does not always occur, and sensitivity analyses are worth making. In the following sections, we shall discuss in a systematic way some of the approaches that may be taken when model inputs are not known with certainty.

EXAMPLE 8.2.5. Consider the generalization of Example 8.2.1 that results if we admit the presence of a fixed ordering cost, m, in the event that any replenishment stock is required. That is, imagine that a quantity $J \geq 0$ of the stocked commodity is on hand at the beginning of a period. Such might be true for, say, an agricultural product, not all of which spoils by the end of the previous period. We then contemplate ordering up to the amount I. The expected total profit becomes

(8.2.20)

$$E[N(D)] = T_1(I) = p \int_0^I x f_D(x)\, dx + pI \int_I^\infty f_D(x)\, dx - c(I - J) - m \qquad \text{if} \quad I > J.$$

If no order is placed, expected profit is

(8.2.21) $$E[N(D)] = T_2(J) = p \int_0^J x f_D(x)\, dx + pJ \int_J^\infty f_D(x)\, dx \qquad \text{if} \quad I = J.$$

It is convenient to consider the function

(8.2.22) $$U(z) = p \int_0^z x f_D(x)\, dx + pz \int_z^\infty f_D(x)\, dx - cz.$$

It is easy to show that $d^2 U/dz^2 \leq 0$, so the graph of $U(z)$ is *concave*—see Figure 8.2.4 below. Now, as we have shown earlier, there is a value of I, here called $\bar{I}$ (traditionally,

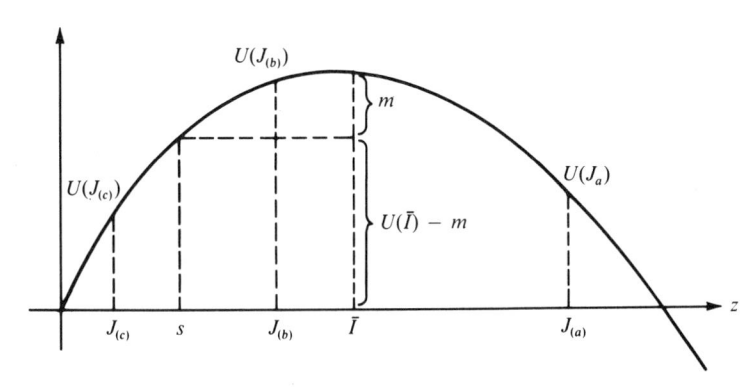

FIGURE 8.2.4

however, denoted by S), that maximizes $U(z)$. Let s denote the *smallest* z value for which

(8.2.23) $$U(s) = U(\bar{I}) - m.$$

Such a value exists by virtue of the concavity of $U(I)$; the graphical illustration of Figure 8.2.4 is helpful. It turns out that the ordering policy depends on the initial stock level, J. Consider these possible cases.

(i) $J > \bar{I}$. The point $J_{(a)}$ is a typical such J value. Then it is plain from the graph that, for any $z = I > J$,

(8.2.24) $$U(I) - m < U(J)$$

or, what is equivalent,

(8.2.25)

$$p \int_0^I x f_D(x) \, dx + pI \int_I^\infty f_D(x) \, dx - cI - m < p \int_0^J x f_D(x) \, dx + pJ \int_J^\infty f_D(x) \, dx - cJ,$$

which in turn may be rearranged to show that

$$p \int_0^I x f_D(x) \, dx + pI \int_I^\infty f_D(x) \, dx - c(I - J) - m < p \int_0^J x f_D(x) \, dx + pJ \int_J^\infty f_D(x) \, dx$$

or

(8.2.26) $T_1(I) < T_2(J),$

which proves that no new order should be placed. This comes as no surprise, for the initial inventory J is already in excess of the optimal, and one should not order even if the ordering cost m is zero.

Suppose next that

(ii) $s \leq J \leq \bar{I}$. To be definite, the point $J_{(b)}$ in Figure 8.2.4 might represent the initial stock available. Now if an order is placed, it should obviously be for an amount equal to $\bar{I} - J$, bringing stock to the level $\bar{I}$. But from the graph

(8.2.27) $U(\bar{I}) - m < U(J),$

and hence it follows as in (i) above that

(8.2.28) $T_1(I) \leq T_2(J),$

for all I $(J < I \leq \bar{I})$. Again no order is justified.

Finally, suppose that

(iii) $0 < J < s$. The point $J_{(c)}$ illustrates this situation. By choice of s (see (8.2.23)) and by concavity, it follows that

$$U(J) \leq U(\bar{I}) - m.$$

Equivalently,

$$(8.2.29) \quad p \int_0^J x f_D(x) \, dx + pJ \int_J^\infty f_D(x) \, dx - cJ \leq p \int_0^I x f_D(x) \, dx$$
$$+ p\bar{I} \int_I^\infty f_D(x) \, dx - c\bar{I} - m,$$

and so

$$(8.2.30) \quad p \int_0^J x f_D(x) \, dx + pJ \int_J^\infty f_D(x) \, dx \leq p \int_0^I x f_D(x) \, dx$$
$$+ p\bar{I} \int_I^\infty f_D(x) \, dx - c(\bar{I} - j) - m$$

or

(8.2.31) $T_1(\bar{I}) \geq T_2(J)$

and an order up to the level $\bar{I}$ is justified.

The optimal rule may be summarized as follows: if initial stock $J < s$, order up to the level $\bar{I}$, while if $J \geq s$, do not order. Such a rule, or a variation thereof, is often used in practice. A physical version, termed the "two-bin rule," operates by placing $\bar{I} - s$ units of stock in one container (first bin) and the remainder in another (second bin). Demands are satisfied from the first bin as long as it contains stock, but when the contents of the second bin must be used, an order is placed for replenishment.

EXERCISES 8.2

1. Find the numerical values of optimal inventory level $\bar{I}$ and expected net profit $E[N|\bar{I}]$ for the newspaper problem of Example 8.2.1.

2. Using the numbers of Example 8.2.4, with mean demand $m = 100$, find the expected profit resulting from the policy of stocking the mean demand—that is, $I = 100$. Explain why the policy $\bar{I}$ is superior.

3. If the optimal policy $\bar{I}$ is followed, what is the probability that inventory will be insufficient during a period—that is, that a stockout condition will occur? (*Hint:* The answer is independent of the particular distribution function assumed.) Suppose we are interested in the stockout performance over ten independent periods. What are the distribution and variance of the number of stockouts?

4. Find the optimum inventory level for the Christmas tree problem of Example 8.2.4 if it is decided to limit the number of trees stocked to 80. What is the stockout probability if $I = 150$? What is the total cost?

5. In the newspaper problem of Example 8.2.1, suppose it is believed that demand is normally distributed with mean and standard deviation 1000.
   (a) Ignoring the fact that an actual demand distribution cannot assign probability to negative demands (as the normal distribution does), use the normal distribution above to compute the "optimum" inventory level, $\bar{I}_N$. (*Hint:* Use the normal probability tables.)
   (b) If, in fact, the exponential distribution with mean 1000 (and, automatically, standard deviation 1000) governs demand, find the expected total profit resulting from stocking $\bar{I}_N$.

6. The following is a list of 20 days' simulated demands for newspapers (see Example 8.2.1). The list was developed by drawing 20 random numbers from an exponential distribution with mean 1000:

20 Simulated Demands

First Ten: 327, 693, 3109, 3712, 881, 1454, 891, 2703, 2121, 1025
Second Ten: 825, 1545, 181, 158, 1177, 3354, 1606, 67, 471, 5050

   (a) Use the average of the first ten random numbers to estimate the mean demand m.
   (b) Compute the estimated optimal inventory level, $\bar{I}$, based on the estimate of m obtained in (a). Use the exponential demand distribution.
   (c) How much profit would be lost per period, on the average, by using the estimated mean of (b) rather than the actual mean 1000?
   (d) Compare the result of using the estimate (b) with the actual mean of 1000, when the basis for comparison is behavior of the policy, $\bar{I}$, on the second ten days (each of the second ten numbers represents a daily demand).

7. According to (8.2.8), the optimal inventory policy $\bar{I}$ satisfies

$$F(\bar{I}) = 1 - \frac{c}{p} \qquad \text{for } p > c.$$

Suppose we have no basis for knowledge of the distributional form. Given a number of past demands, as in Exercise 6 above, we may estimate $F(x)$ by first arranging the demands in increasing order and computing the fraction $\leq x$. For example, let x be 900; then since out of the first ten demands, 327, 693, 881, and 891 are the only ones ≤ 900, our estimate is $F(900) \approx 0.4$. Proceeding in this way, we may estimate as follows:

x	Estimated $F(x)$
327	0.1
693	0.2
881	0.3

$$\cdots$$

(a) Using the procedure above, employ the estimated F and (8.2.8) to obtain an estimated optimal inventory level, $\bar{I}$.

(b) What is the expected net profit resulting from the use of level (a)? Compare the result of Exercise 6(c), and discuss.

(c) Carry out the procedure above, using both the first and second ten random numbers.

(d) Discuss the difficulties with this "distribution-free" procedure in the event that $c/p = 0.01$ and a history of 20 demands is available.

8. Consider the model of Example 8.2.1 as applied to some commodity that is not entirely perishable. That is, an amount $J > 0$ is available at the beginning of the period before a new order is placed. The quantity J is viewed as being left from the previous period.

(a) Show that if $J < \bar{I}$, the optimum policy is to order the difference, $\bar{I} - J$, whereas if $J > \bar{I}$, the optimum policy is to order nothing. (*Hint:* Notice that $E[N(D)]$ is concave; that is,

$$\frac{d^2 E[N(D)]}{dI^2} < 0$$

(sketch a graph) and, if $J > \bar{I}$,

$$\frac{dE[N(D)]}{dI} < 0,$$

so addition to inventory reduces profit. What cost component brings this about?)

(b) Supposing that the demand is exponential as in Example 8.2.3, that $m = 100$, $p = \$5.00$ and $c = \$2.00$. Tabulate and graph the expected profit if $J = 50$; 100; 150.

9. Consider the following variation on the model of Example 8.2.1. If goods are left over at the end of the day (or time interval), one may sell them at a reduced, or salvage, price of $\$5$ per unit. Of course, $s < p$.

(a) Show that the net one-period profit may be expressed as

$$N(D) = \begin{cases} pD + s(I - D) - cI & \text{if } D < I \\ pI & \text{if } D \geq I \end{cases}$$

(b) Write down the expected profit:

$$E[N(D)] = \int_0^I pxf_D(x)\, dx + \int_0^I s(I - x)f_D(x)\, dx + \int_I^\infty pIf_D(x)\, dx - cI.$$

(c) Differentiate $E[N(D)]$ with respect to I to show that the optimum stock level, $\bar{I}$, satisfies

$$F_D(\bar{I}) = \frac{p - c}{p - s} \qquad \text{if } \frac{p - c}{p - s} < 1.$$

What happens to the optimal inventory level if salvage price approaches selling price?

8.3 DECISIONS UNDER UNCERTAINTY: COMPONENTS OF THE PROBLEM

The previous inventory examples illustrated the use of probability models as an aid in decision making. Notice, however, that the discussion tacitly assumed complete knowledge of the probability distribution of demand during the period of interest. This assumption of complete knowledge extended as well to prices and costs. In practice, the decision maker's knowledge of such components is incomplete, being based in part on general experience with analogous or similar situations and possibly also on observations such as those of previous actual demands. Thus, parameter values and distributional forms will not be known precisely, but must be estimated. The manner of estimation should reflect not only relevant data, but judgment as well, a fact that should if possible be introduced into the analysis. Such analysis is the topic of the remaining sections of this chapter.

In order to deal with the "fuzzy-parameter" problem alluded to above, a tempting procedure is simply to compute reasonable estimates using available data and then add a leavening of subjective judgment. The estimates are then used as if they were the true values, and the decision rule is derived accordingly, using methods like those of the last section. Exercises 6 and 7 of Exercises 8.2 have illustrated the application of such methods. These procedures may work rather well under many circumstances, but ideally the estimate should be tailored to fit the particular use for which it is intended. Although we shall deal with this tailored-to-order objective, it should be pointed out that our sample problems are simple and intended as illustrations only.

Let us now turn to a discussion of the elements of a decision problem. In the next section we shall review various approaches to the selection of decisions, using the framework to be given. The following simple example will illustrate the concepts to be introduced.

EXAMPLE 8.3.1. The XYZ Corporation has the opportunity of purchasing the rights to a particular invention. Company management believes that one of two outcomes is possible if the invention is purchased:

(8.3.1) A_1: Invention a success; XYZ gains \$5 million.

     A_2: Invention a failure; XYZ "gains" $-$\$4 million.

We are assuming that the gain is net—that is, includes the purchase price of the invention. Furthermore, there are two possible states of nature, S_1 and S_2. If S_1 prevails, then the probabilities of success (A_1) and failure (A_2) are, respectively,

(8.3.2) $P\{A_1|S_1\} = p_1(1) = 0.9$ and $P\{A_2|S_1\} = p_2(1) = 0.1,$

whereas if S_2 prevails, the corresponding probabilities are

(8.3.3) $P\{A_1|S_2\} = p_1(2) = 0.3$ and $P\{A_2|S_2\} = p_2(2) = 0.7.$

The reason for the two quite different states of nature may be traced back to an essential but delicate process required in manufacturing the product. If this process can be set up and run in the XYZ plant, state of nature S_1 prevails; if not, S_2 is in force.

Without further investigation, the **XYZ** engineering manager believes that the chances are 40% that the key manufacturing operation can be made successful— that is, that S_1 will hold true—and 60% that it cannot, or that S_2 will be in force. Thus the company's prior probabilities for S_1 and S_2 are

$$\pi_1 = 0.4 \quad \text{and} \quad \pi_2 = 0.6.$$

Consequently, letting G denote the gain if the company buys the invention, then the expected value of G is, given no further information,

(8.3.4)
$$\begin{aligned}
E[G] &= E[G|S_1]\pi_1 + E[G|S_2]\pi_2, \\
&= [5p_1(1) - 4p_2(1)]\pi_1 + [5p_1(2) - 4p_2(2)]\pi_2, \\
&= [(5)(0.9) - (4)(0.1)](0.4) + [(5)(0.3) - (4)(0.7)](0.6), \\
&= \$0.86 \text{ million.}
\end{aligned}$$

Now one of the options open to **XYZ** is to set up a pilot version of the crucial manufacturing operation in advance. If it is successful, then this indicates that the actual manufacture will progress without hitch, but if the pilot operation does not work, there is evidence to the contrary. To make this formal, let $A_1{}^*$ be the event that the pilot version is successful, and $A_2{}^*$, the event that it is not. The following probabilities are defined: if S_1 prevails, then the probability of pilot plant success ($A_1{}^*$) and failure ($A_2{}^*$) are, respectively,

(8.3.5)
$$\begin{aligned}
P\{A_1{}^*|S_1\} = p_1{}^*(1) = 0.85 \quad &\text{and} \quad P\{A_2{}^*|S_1\} = p_2{}^*(1) = 0.15; \\
p_1{}^*(2) = 0.20 \quad &\text{and} \quad p_2{}^*(2) = 0.80.
\end{aligned}$$

It follows directly that the unconditional probabilities of pilot plant success and failure are

(8.3.6)
$$\begin{aligned}
P\{A_1{}^*\} &= p_1{}^*(1)\pi_1 + p_1{}^*(2)\pi_2 = 0.46, \\
P\{A_2{}^*\} &= 0.54.
\end{aligned}$$

Now if the pilot plant is constructed and used to test the manufacturing process, we can revise the prior probabilities in accordance with the outcomes. Bayes' formula (see (7.8.7)) provides that

(8.3.7)
$$\begin{aligned}
P\{S_1|A_1{}^*\} = \pi_1(1) &= \frac{P\{A_1{}^*|S_1\}P\{S_1\}}{P\{A_1{}^*\}} = \frac{(0.85)(0.4)}{(0.85)(0.4) + (0.80)(0.6)} = 0.74, \\
P\{S_2|A_1{}^*\} = \pi_2(1) &= 0.26 = 1 - \pi_1(1), \\
P\{S_1|A_2{}^*\} = \pi_1(2) &= 0.11, \\
P\{S_2|A_2{}^*\} = \pi_2(2) &= 0.89.
\end{aligned}$$

It is now natural to utilize these revised probabilities to calculate the expected gain. Imagine that the pilot plant has been constructed and the process tried. Then exactly one of the following two alternatives must occur:

1. A pilot plant is a success, so event $A_1{}^*$ occurs. Hence we use the revised probabilities $\pi_1(1) = 0.74$ and $\pi_2(1) = 0.26$ instead of $\pi_1 = 0.4$, $\pi_2 = 0.6$ to estimate the expected gain from the purchase of the invention. Recalculation of (8.3.4) gives, under these circumstances,

(8.3.8)
$$\begin{aligned}
E[G|A_1{}^*] &= E[G|S_1]\pi_1(1) + E[G|S_2]\pi_2(1), \\
&= \$2.70 \text{ million.}
\end{aligned}$$

2. A pilot plant fails, so event A_2^* occurs. We then use the probabilities $\pi_1(2) = 0.11$ and $\pi_2(2) = 0.89$ in place of the prior probabilities. It follows that

$$E[G|A_2^*] = E[G|S_1]\pi_1(2) + E[G|S_2]\pi_2(1),$$
$$= -\$0.71 \text{ million}.$$

Clearly the pilot plant experiment provides quite valuable information concerning the prospects for the invention. Needless to say, this information is bought at a price —that of constructing and running the pilot operation.

A systematic way of depicting and analyzing such a complex decision situation will be described subsequently. First, however, we review the components of the general decision situation that our example typifies.

Components of a Decision Problem

A. A *decision maker*, with *objectives*. In the example above, the XYZ Corporation, or its chief executive, was the decision maker. The objective was the desire to make a profit for the corporation. This statement of the problem oversimplifies many real situations in which a decision-making body consists of many individuals whose objectives may differ and require reconciliation. For example, the desire to make a profit may be diminished somewhat by fear of losing a large sum of money.

B. A set of possible *actions*. In Example 8.3.1, attention was focused on three possible initial actions: don't buy the invention; buy without pilot testing; and pilot test first. If the pilot-test option is selected, a further action choice will be necessary as well; namely, whether to buy or not buy, depending on the outcome of the pilot test. Thus, the term "action" can mean an *action sequence*; for example, test, then don't buy. Problems involving such a sequence of actions are often called *sequential decision problems*.

Of course, if the invention is *not* bought by XYZ, then the money that would otherwise have gone into this purchase would be available for other uses, necessitating a decision between further alternatives. One such alternative is of course to wait for further information, but if such action is taken, XYZ risks losing an opportunity to another, more aggressive (or reckless) company.

C. A set of possible *outcomes*. The two outcomes that confronted XYZ were invention success and invention failure: one, and only one, of these would eventually occur. When the decision maker chooses his action, it is not yet known which outcome will actually occur thereafter; if the outcome were known, the choice of an action would be trivial. As the example points out however, it is a decision maker's option to purchase additional information. Thus, he may be confronted with intermediate outcomes (test successful, test unsuccessful) that can be brought to bear on later decisions.

D. A *payoff table* (or matrix or function). This defines a function, which in a simple form is

$G(x, a) =$ the gain from taking action a when the outcome is x.

The function must be defined for every (x, a) (outcome, action) pair. For the sequential problem of our example, and for other similar problems, there will typically be a gain (or loss) at each stage, and these gains must be summed or otherwise combined to establish the total worth of the project. Sometimes it is more natural or convenient to assess an action in terms of a *loss* rather than in terms of a payoff or gain. Examples formulated in terms of losses will be given later.

The effect of uncertainty in the decision-making process manifests itself through the outcomes, which are assumed to occur according to probability distributions and through the subsequent payoff. In other words, the actual outcome is the result of a random process. In Example 8.3.1 we considered only two possible outcomes: success and failure. The occurrence of these was governed by an unknown probability distribution. Another problem element is as follows.

E. The *state of nature* that prevails. In Example 8.3.1 we imagined that the probability distributions governing invention success or failure were the following:

$$\text{favorable:} \quad p_1(1) = 0.9, \; p_2(1) = 0.1,$$

and

$$\text{unfavorable:} \; p_1(2) = 0.3, \; p_2(2) = 0.7.$$

We did not know which was actually in force, although the prior distribution provided some information and use of the test option would give more. A more general formulation of this problem would simply specify that the state of nature is given by an unknown probability p, which can be any number in the range zero to unity. Then,

$$P\{\text{Success}\} = P\{A_1 \,|\, S\} = p,$$

S being the unknown state of nature.

In the inventory Example 8.2.2, the possible states of nature were the exponential distributions for demand

$$P\{D \le x\} = \begin{cases} 1 - e^{-x/m} & x \ge 0; \; m > 0 \\ 0 & x < 0 \end{cases}$$

In this case, the state of nature was specified when m, the mean demand, was given. The latter can be estimated from previous demands and the result can be used, say, to up-date or revise a prior probability distribution for m just as the prior success probabilities could be revised in the light of test experience in Example 8.3.1.

In any event, the actual outcome following an action is a random variable. Consequently it is useful to introduce the next component.

F. The *expected payoff table* (or matrix or function). Let X denote the random outcome following action a. Then $G(X, a)$ is the corresponding gain. Before any action is taken it is useful to examine the expected value of G, $E[G(X, a)]$, where the expectation is taken with respect to the unknown state of nature. Thus, consider Example 8.3.1, for the moment disregarding the test option and considering just B (buy) and $\mathcal{B}$ (don't buy). Then,

$$G(A_1, B) = \$5, \qquad G(A_2, B) = -\$4,$$
$$G(A_1, \mathcal{B}) = 0 = G(A_2, \mathcal{B}).$$

Under the favorable state of nature (S_1), the expected gain from buying is

$$E[G(X, B)] = \$5p_1(1) - \$4p_2(1) = \$5p_1(1) - 4(1 - p_1(1)),$$

and the expected gain from not buying is

$$E[G(X, \bar{B})] = 0.$$

Clearly, an expected payoff table, which depends on the unknown state of nature, may now be constructed. Having reached the point described, the remaining task is to specify the action to be taken.

G. A *decision*, or *strategy*, d, designates the action to be taken. Clearly a desirable decision is one that tends to maximize the payoff. Thus one decision might be to buy in Example 8.3.1; just how appropriate this is would depend on the unknown state of nature. A (statistical) *decision function* utilizes observational information concerning the state of nature to select an action. In other words, if observations are available from the prevailing unknown probability distribution (state of nature), they provide information about it. The statistical decision function then prescribes an action appropriate to the revealed state of nature.

In the next section the problem of Example 8.3.1 will be analyzed and a decision function that maximizes expected gain for XYZ will be derived.

We remark that while the objective of maximum *expected* gain is often reasonable, it is *not* the only sensible measure. For example, XYZ may not wish to take the risk of losing a large sum of money, and so may want to make the probability of this happening small. In general, the utility of an additional sum of money (gain or loss) depends on present fortune, future obligations, frame of mind, company policy, and so on and is not always proportional to the sum itself. One may, for example, attach higher utility to a situation in which there is a 10% chance of winning $1000 and a 90% chance of nothing than to a 50% chance of winning $200 with an equivalent chance of no return. Yet both opportunities offer the same expected gain. The former is riskier and hence more attractive to some. On the other hand, even a risk-wary individual must decide in favor of such a situation if only $1000 will be of help.

The brief discussion above describes some of the issues that arise in the modern treatment of utility theory. We shall not go further into this topic, but instead suggest that you refer to the references at the end of this chapter.

8.4 DECISION-TREE STUDY OF A SEQUENTIAL DECISION PROBLEM

In the previous section, the elements of a decision problem were introduced by means of a simplified investment problem. We now proceed to analyze this problem in terms of a graphical device, first introduced in Chapter 7, called a *decision tree*.

EXAMPLE 8.4.1. Refer to the problem of Example 8.3.1. In order to organize an attack, put down a starting point (a *node*) and from it draw three lines. These represent the three possible decisions that are initially available: buy, don't buy, or test.

Selection of one of these options starts a sequence of events, some of which may be influenced by the decision maker, while others are governed by chance or possibly by the actions of a competitor. Since the initial selection is at the option of the decision maker, we denote the initial node as a D (decision) node.

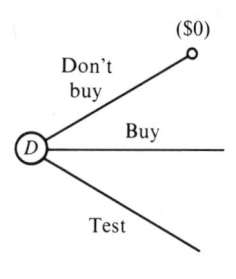

FIGURE 8.4.1

Now both the don't buy and the buy decisions have immediate and simple consequences. The net gain from the don't buy decision is zero, and this branch of the budding tree thus terminates. If the buy option is selected, a chance event now occurs: either the invention is a success (A_1 occurs) or a failure (A_2 occurs). Thus, we denote this node by C (chance), and depict the outcomes as shown in Figure 8.4.2. The two

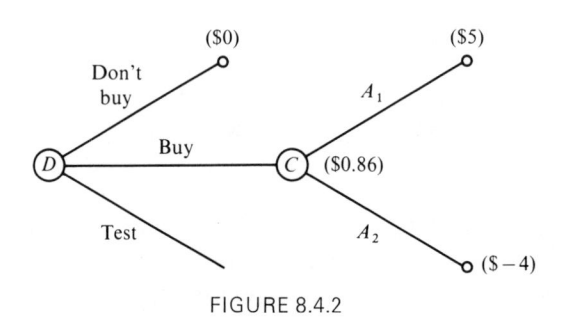

FIGURE 8.4.2

branches from C represent the two possible outcomes; the corresponding payoffs are placed at their terminating points. Thus one possibility for **XYZ** is the sequence (buy, A_1) and another is (buy, A_2). Notice that these are the *only* two paths that involve the buy option. The tree diagram is so constructed that each such sequence of events—each tree branch—is one possible decision-chance-decision alternative, and furthermore, each such alternative is represented by a branch of the tree. To evaluate the expected gain resulting from adopting the buy option, we need merely compute the expectation (8.3.4). Putting this another way, we compute

$$P\{A_1\} = P\{A_1 \mid S_1\}P\{S_1\} + P\{A_1 \mid S_2\}P\{S_2\},$$
$$= p_1(1)\pi_1 + p_1(2)\pi_2,$$
$$= (0.9)(0.4) + (0.3)(0.6) = 0.54,$$

and consequently

$$P\{A_2\} = 1 - P\{A_1\} = 0.46.$$

Then

$$E[G] = 5P\{A_1\} - 4P\{A_2\} = \$0.86.$$

We can thus simplify the tree by placing the expected payoff $0.86 at the end of the buy branch, as in Figure 8.4.2.

The branch that begins with the test option is more interesting. The possibilities are as shown in Figure 8.4.3. Consider the possible result of choosing the test option. The first node is C (chance), yielding, for example, A_1^* (test successful). If the test is successful, then our posterior probability calculation (8.3.6) shows that the state of nature S_1 prevails with probability 0.74, while S_2 prevails with probability

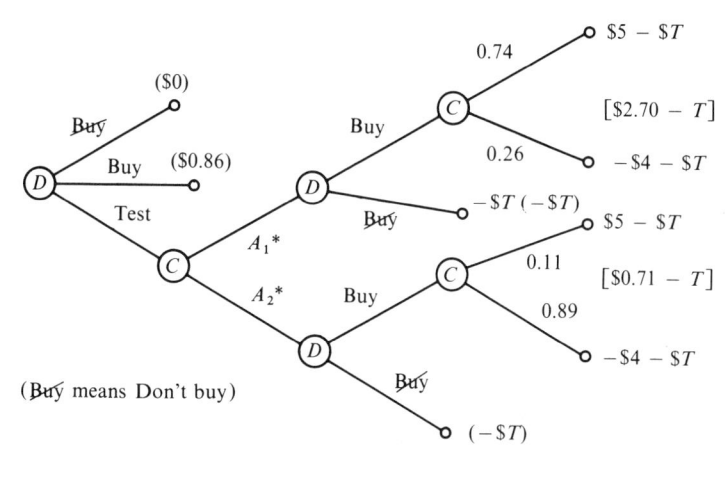

FIGURE 8.4.3

0.26. Hence, as (8.3.8) shows, the expected gain that results from the sequence (test successful, buy) is $2.70 - T$, where T represents the cost of the test, while the expected gain from (test successful, ~~buy~~) is $\$ - T$. Clearly, it is preferable to buy following the outcome test successful. If, on the other hand, the test is unsuccessful (A_2^* occurs) then a similar analysis shows that if we buy, the expected gain is $-\$0.71 - T$. Since this is less than $-\$T$, the best policy to follow is ~~buy~~ in the event that the test has been made and is unsuccessful.

To summarize the situation at this point, we may say that if the decision maker finds himself at the second decision node after having followed the test option, his optimal strategy thereafter is

    (i) buy if A_1^* occurred; expected gain = $\$2.70 - T$;
    (ii) don't buy (~~buy~~) if A_2^* occurred; expected gain = $\$ - T$.

Now suppose the decision maker wishes to evaluate the test option. The previous calculations show that (formally)

$$E[G|A_1^*, \text{follow optimal policy}] = \$2.70 - T$$

and

$$E[G|A_2^*, \text{follow optimal policy}] = \$ - T.$$

Now let us multiply by the probabilities of A_1^* and A_2^* and add. Then if the pilot plant test is conducted initially,

$$E[G\,|\,\text{test, follow optimal policy}] = E[G\,|\,A_1^*, \text{follow optimal policy}]P\{A_1^*\}$$
$$+ E[G\,|\,A_2^*, \text{follow optimal policy}]P\{A_2^*\}.$$

Now refer to (8.3.5) to obtain the probabilities of A_1^* and A_2^*; the result is

$$E[G\,|\,\text{test, follow optimal policy}] = (2.70 - T)(0.46) + (-T)(0.54) = \$1.24 - T.$$

We now see easily that the complex tree of Figure 8.4.3 may be replaced by (collapsed into) the tree shown in Figure 8.4.4. The interpretation is obvious. It is clearly better to buy immediately than to not buy. It is better to test first than to buy, if

$$\$1.24 - T > \$0.86$$

or if

$$\$T < \$0.38 \text{ million.}$$

Thus the *value of information* obtained by testing is, in this case, worth \$0.38 million.

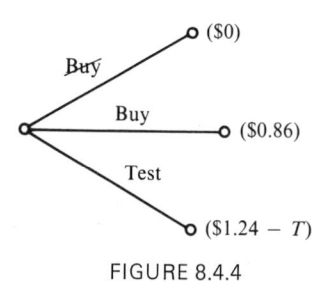

FIGURE 8.4.4

Notice that this is the value of information obtained from the test when the latter is used optimally thereafter. If the decision maker does not follow an optimal policy for some reason (that is, if he does not buy following a successful test outcome and buys otherwise) then the test is worthless.

EXERCISES 8.4

1. A speculator owns an acre of land well located near a town. Because of the way the town is developing, he can sell the property for \$10,000 in 1976, but for only \$8,000 for certain if he waits until 1977. He is determined to sell no later than 1977. Therefore, if he is to accept one of the sure offers he must do so on January 1, 1976 (\$10,000) or on January 1, 1977 (\$8,000).

    An additional factor is the possibility that the Beta company may wish to buy the land. This event has probability p. The speculator's prior probability density for p is the uniform density

$$f_p(x) = 1 \quad 0 \leq x \leq 1,$$
$$= 0 \quad \text{otherwise.}$$

Beta will pay \$20,000 if it buys. Beta's offer (if any) occurs either during 1976 or during 1977.

(a) Suppose that each year represents a binomial trial as far as Beta's buying goes. If Beta does *not* buy during 1976, compute the posterior density for p. (*Hint:* The probability of not buying $= 1 - p$.)

(b) Apply the result of (a) to compute the probability that Beta will buy in 1977, given that it did not buy in 1976.

(c) Assuming that the speculator aims to maximize expected profit, describe a decision-tree analysis to find his optimum strategy.

2. An organization is engaged in searching for a new product to market, and an attempt is made to find an appropriate budget for a one-year search. Judgment states that a product yielding approximately $\$X$ may be the outcome of the present research effort. However, the research process is risky, and may, as the other possible alternative, yield nothing. As a first model, suppose that by spending $\$r$ the company buys a probability $p(r)$ of succeeding and loses (gains nothing) with probability $1 - p(r)$; $p(r)$ increases with r. It follows that the expected net profit associated with this aspect of the company operations is, given investment of r,

$$P(r) = -r + Xp(r).$$

If X is large enough and $p(r) > 0$, this function will possess a maximum value for some positive r. There is no guarantee that by spending indefinitely —that is, by letting $r \to \infty$— $p(r)$ may be made to approach unity.

(a) Let

$$p(r) = 1 - e^{-r/m}$$

so

$$P(r) = -r + X(1 - e^{-r/m}).$$

Differentiate to obtain

$$\frac{dP(r)}{dr} = -1 + \frac{X}{m} e^{-r/m},$$

and show that

$$\text{optimum investment} \equiv \bar{r} = m \log\left(\frac{X}{M}\right).$$

(b) Show that net profit from optimum investment

$$= P(\bar{r}) = -m \log \frac{X}{M} + X - m,$$

$$= m\left[\frac{X}{m} - 1 - \log \frac{X}{m}\right].$$

(c) Show that if $X/m > 1$ the expected net profit resulting from following the optimum investment plan above is > 0.

3. An unmanned rocket is being launched and you are in charge of the launching. A certain electronic component may be either functioning or not functioning at the time of launching. On your control board there is a warning light that is not completely reliable. If the electronic component is not functioning, the warning light goes on with probability $\frac{1}{2}$; if the component is functioning, the warning light goes on with probability $\frac{1}{4}$. At the time of launching you note whether or not the warning light is on and then decide whether or not to launch the rocket. Suppose the table of losses is as follows (in millions of dollars):

	Component Functioning	Component Not Functioning
Launch	0	5
Do Not Launch	2	0

(a) Suppose the prior probability that the component is not functioning is $p = \frac{2}{8}$. If the warning light does not go on, should you launch the rocket?

(b) Suppose the warning light does go on. For what prior probabilities p that the component is not functioning will you decide to launch the rocket?

4. Each day you must decide whether to accept or reject a certain project (investment, bet, finished good, ...). If you accept and it turns out to be successful (or you win the bet or the good is not defective), you collect 10¢, but if it fails (or you lose the bet or the good is defective) you lose 20¢. If you do not accept the project, then you lose 5¢.

Suppose that the underlying process determining the success or failure of each project can be described as a Bernoulli process with stable (unchanging over time) parameter p.

What you would like to know is whether the given day's opportunity will be a success if accepted. Since the process is random, the best you can hope to know is the true underlying probabilistic process governing the outcome. In the present instance, this amounts to knowing the parameter p of the Bernoulli process.

(a) Write the gain table, showing gain for each possible action-outcome pair.

(b) Suppose that the prior distribution over the parameter p is

$$f(p) = \begin{cases} .5 & \text{that } p = 0.3 \text{ (state } s_1\text{)} \\ .5 & \text{that } p = 0.7 \text{ (state } s_2\text{)} \end{cases}$$

That is, there are only two possible states of nature as far as you are concerned; either the parameter p is 0.3 or else it is 0.7, and the former possibility is considered as likely as the latter.

(c) Write the expected gain table, showing expected gain for each action-state pair. (Note the difference between this table and the one constructed in (a).)

(d) For each possible action, compute the expected gain.

(e) What action do you recommend? Why?

(f) To get some more information, you accept the projects on two successive days. On day 1, the project is successful but on day 2, the project fails. Now, in the light of this information, redo (b) and (c).

(g) Suppose you have the opportunity to bet on three successive days and that on each day the success probability is an unknown value of p, with the prior given by (b) above. Construct a decision-tree analysis to derive the optimal policy.

5. This is a continuation of Exercise 4. Suppose a continuous prior distribution over the parameter p with limits of 0.2 and 0.8. Then

$$f(p) = \begin{cases} \dfrac{5}{3} & \text{if } 0.2 \leq p \leq 0.8 \\ 0 & \text{elsewhere} \end{cases}$$

(a) We are now back to the original situation, except that the prior distribution of the parameter p has changed. For each possible action, compute the expected gain. What is the optimal policy?

(b) Two successive acceptances result in one success followed by a failure. What is the posterior density of the parameter p?

(c) In the light of (b), compute the expected gain from each action (a_1 and a_2) given the two observations. What is the optimal action now?

(d) Suppose the two acceptances of part (b) had resulted in two successes. Find the posterior distribution of the parameter p (using the original prior $f(p) = \frac{5}{3}$, $0.2 \leq p \leq 0.8$).

8.5 SEQUENTIAL DECISIONS

A simple example involving a sequence of decisions in time—a sequential decision problem—was introduced in Section 8.3. It was then analyzed by means of the decision-tree device. The present section is devoted to a description of certain other sequential decision problems. Our examples here are not all formulated in terms of a discrete number of outcomes as was true for the earlier problems. Here we shall admit the possibility of any real number as an outcome. As a consequence, calculus can be used and some simple, nearly explicit, formulas occur. These examples illustrate the useful backwards induction method known as *dynamic programming*.

EXAMPLE 8.5.1. Put yourself in the place of a man who is moving from one city to another at the end of n weeks, and who wishes to sell his present house. He has observed that prices offered for property apparently fluctuate randomly, and he wishes to sell for as high a price as possible. If he sells too early, he may feel considerable regret if he misses a higher price later. Of course, if he waits too long, he may have to settle for something below a previous best offer. What is his best selling policy?

We will assume that a known probability distribution, $F(x)$, of weekly price offers is in effect, so the best offer when there are n weeks remaining until moving day is X_n; X_0 is thus the last price offered, X_1, the next-to-last, and so on. The prices X_0, X_1, X_2, ... are assumed to be independent random variables, each distributed according to $F(x)$. Now clearly the optimum policy takes the form of a lower bound, p_n, on the acceptable price such that, on the nth week from the deadline,

(8.5.1)   (i) if $X_n \geq p_n$, the house is sold for X_n, while
                (ii) if $X_n < p_n$, the seller waits.

Let R_m denote the maximum expected price received by the seller if he uses his optimum policy when m opportunities to sell (weeks) remain. Our procedure for finding p_n and R_m is then the classical ploy of *working backwards*.

Imagine that one week remains before moving day, and suppose the house is not yet sold. Obviously, the only thing to do is to sell at the best price offered, X_0. Consequently, the maximum expected price is just the expected price:

(8.5.2) $$R_0 = \int_0^\infty xf(x)\,dx = E[X_0] = E[X],$$

where f is the density function of weekly price. Observe that the minimum acceptable price, p_0, is zero, as seems appropriate, because, although it makes sense to hold out for a high price early in the game when many weeks remain, at the end one must settle for whatever is offered. Next consider the situation in which two weeks remain. Now *given* the best offer, X_1, on the next-to-last week, the seller

(8.5.3) $\qquad$ (i) accepts if $X_1 \geq p_1$,
$\qquad\qquad\qquad$ (ii) waits if $X_1 < p_1$.

A moment's reflection shows that if $X_1 > R_0$, the seller should accept. By doing so he receives a greater return—and hence greater expected return—than he does by waiting, since if he waits he receives only R_0. Hence, $p_1 = R_0$. The seller's expected sale price from following the strategy above is obtained by averaging over the possible values of X_1:

$$R_1 = \int_{p_1}^{\infty} xf(x)\, dx + R_0 \int_0^{p_1} f(x)\, dx,$$

(8.5.4)
$$= \int_{R_0}^{\infty} xf(x)\, dx + R_0 F(R_0),$$

$$= R_0 + \int_{R_0}^{\infty} (x - R_0)f(x)\, dx.$$

Thus one may proceed to calculate the maximum expected revenue if three periods remain, since by the same argument as above, $p_2 = R_1$ and hence

$$R_2 = \int_{p_2}^{\infty} xf(x)\, dx + R_1 \int_0^{p_2} f(x)\, dx,$$

(8.5.5)
$$= R_1 + \int_{R_1}^{\infty} xf(x)\, dx\, F(R_1),$$

$$= R_1 + \int_{R_1}^{\infty} (x - R_1)f(x)\, dx.$$

By an inductive argument then, one sees that the optimum strategy is given by

(8.5.6) $\qquad\qquad\qquad p_{n+1} = R_n$

and the maximum expected payoff by

(8.5.7) $\qquad\qquad R_n = R_{n-1} + \int_{R_{n-1}}^{\infty} (x - R_{n-1})f(x)\, dx.$

Plainly R_n, and hence p_n, increases as n increases. Thus, the more weeks (opportunities) that remain, the higher should be the acceptable selling price, as makes intuitive sense. Some explicit examples utilizing this model are given in the exercises.

EXAMPLE 8.5.2. A businessman is confronted with two investment opportunities. One is in Risky Commodities (RC), and the other is in Safe and Sure Soaps (SSS). If he invests in SSS, he receives a definite, unchanging return of $\$s$ for each period (month). If he invests in RC, he has an unknown probability, r, of a gain of $\$g$ per month; otherwise, he receives nothing. Furthermore, gains during successive periods are independent. The businessman wishes to select the investment opportunity that maximizes his expected return over T time periods (trials)—for example, over a one-year period. We will assume—somewhat unrealistically—that he can switch back and forth from RC to SSS without cost.

The issue here is that if $rg > s$ the businessman's expected gain is greatest from investment in RC, and otherwise he is better off with SSS. In order to find out which case he is confronted with, however, he must experiment with (try) RC to gain information about r.

We assume that initial information about the unknown value of r is summarized by the prior density $\pi(x)$. Thus if no other information is available, the businessman's best estimate for the probability of success of RC is

$$(8.5.8) \qquad E_0[r] = \int_0^1 x\pi(x)\, dx;$$

the subscript 0 denotes that no actual experience is at hand. If, on the other hand, the businessman has invested in RC n times and has met with success k times, this information allows him to calculate a posterior density for r, which we write as

$$(8.5.9) \qquad \pi(x; k, n) = Cx^k(1 - x)^{n-k}\pi(x),$$

C being a normalizing constant:

$$(8.5.10) \qquad C^{-1} = \int_0^1 x^k(1 - x)^{n-k}\pi(x)\, dx.$$

See Chapter 7, Example 7.8.4 for a similar setup. If the businessman has tried RC n times, then the expected value of r is

$$(8.5.11) \qquad E_{k,n}[r] = \int_0^1 x\pi(x; k, n)\, dx.$$

Again we must work backwards in order to develop the optimum strategy. Let $\varphi_{k,n}(t)$ be the expected return obtained from using an optimum policy when t time periods remain ($t \leq T$) and RC has been tried n times with k successes. Suppose that $t = 1$—that is, one period remains. Then one compares the expected gain from RC, $gE_{k,n}[r]$, with s, the gain from adopting SSS, and selects the larger:

$$(8.5.12) \qquad \varphi_{k,n}(1) = \max\left(g \int_0^1 Cx^{k+1}(1 - x)^{n-k}\pi(x)\, dx,\, s\right).$$

Next, step back one period and contemplate the possibilities, supposing one has tried RC n times, obtaining k successes. The possibilities are three:

    (i) Try RC and obtain a success—that is, \$$g$ gain.
    (ii) Try RC and obtain a failure—that is, no gain.
    (iii) Accept a certain gain of \$$s$ from SSS.

Observe that if RC is tried, then more information is procured at the same time. If case (i) occurs, information state (k, n) goes to $(k + 1, n + 1)$, whereas in case (ii), the information goes to $(k, n + 1)$. The corresponding posteriors are thus $\pi(x; k + 1, n + 1)$ and $\pi(x; k, n + 1)$. The expected return from an investment in RC at this stage is now seen to be, *given* that $r = x$, equal to

$$(8.5.13) \qquad x[g + \varphi_{k+1,n+1}(1)] + (1 - x)[0 + \varphi_{k,n+1}(1)].$$

In words, this is the (conditional) probability of success times the immediate gain, g, plus the expected gain in the last period, plus the probability of failure times the subsequent expected gain in the last period. It follows that the unconditional expected gain is obtained by taking expectations, using the posterior or density $\pi(x; k, n)$:

$$\int_0^1 x[g + \varphi_{k+1, n+1}(1)]\pi(x; k, n) \, dx + \int_0^1 (1 - x)\varphi_{k, n+1}(1)\pi(x; k, n) \, dx$$

(8.5.14)
$$= [g + \varphi_{k+1, n+1}(1)]E_{k, n}[r] + \varphi_{k, n+1}(1)\{1 - E_{k, n}[r]\}.$$

The alternative is to invest in SSS for this period, obtaining a gain of \$s, and then to act optimally during the final period. Thus, choosing the best of these alternatives we find

$$(8.5.15) \quad \varphi_{k, n}(2) = \max \begin{cases} \{g + \varphi_{k+1, n+1}(1)\}E_{k, n}[r] + \varphi_{k, n+1}(1)\{1 - E_{k, n}[r]\} \\ s + \varphi_{k, n}(1) \end{cases}$$

Further iterations can be conducted in the same manner. We see that in general

$$(8.5.16) \quad \varphi_{k, n}(t + 1) = \max \begin{cases} \{g + \varphi_{k+1, n+1}(t)\}E_{k, n}[r] + \varphi_{k, n+1}(t)\{1 - E_{k, n}[r]\} \\ s + \varphi_{k, n}(t) \end{cases}$$

Now the simple strategy of "play the winner" turns out to be optimum for this problem. By this is meant that, if the businessman has just played RC at stage t and won—that is, realized a gain of \$g—he should play RC again at stage $t + 1$. If he plays RC and *loses*, he may or may not switch to SSS, depending upon the state of his (posterior) information about r and the number of plays remaining. *However*, if it is ever advantageous for the businessman to utilize SSS, it is optimal to stay with the SSS thereafter. It may further be shown that for any given prior (assigning positive probabilities to all r values between zero and one), the businessman will not invest in RC at all if the number of investment opportunities, T, is small, but that if more time —a larger T—is available, he will start by investing in RC.

We remark that the "play the winner" strategy is *not* in general optimal when *both* investments are probabilistic—that is, if SSS pays \$s with probability q, and q is unknown but has a prior density. This type of problem is referred to picturesquely as the "two-armed bandit" problem since it is reminiscent of the problem of choosing between, say, two slot machines when there is a limited time to play. Many variations of this problem are possible, and a few of these have been treated mathematically. However, it seems quite possible to investigate numerically a variety of problems akin to the one described by making use of the appropriate backward-induction dynamic-programming relation analogous to (8.5.16). The following example illustrates the first few steps in such a process.

EXAMPLE 8.5.3. In the RC-SSS investment decision, suppose that

$$\pi(x) = 1 \qquad 0 \le x \le 1,$$
$$= 0 \qquad \text{otherwise,}$$

and that

$$g = \$2.5 \quad \text{and} \quad s = \$1.$$

Then

$$gE_0[r] = \$2.5 \int_0^1 x \, dx = \$1.25 > s = \$1;$$

thus, if no further information is available, it is optimum to invest in RC. Suppose now that RC is tried, as recommended. Consider the two possibilities:

(i) **RC** fails. Then the posterior density becomes

$$\pi(x; 0, 1) = 2(1 - x) \qquad 0 \le x \le 1.$$

(ii) **RC** succeeds. Then

$$\pi(x; 1, 1) = 2x \qquad 0 \le x \le 1.$$

Imagine now that the next stage is the last one. We are in a position to evaluate the next and last trial: if (i) occurs—RC fails—then our expectation for the last trial is

$$\varphi_{0,1}(1) = \max\left\{ g \int_0^1 x\pi(x; 0, 1)\, dx, s \right\},$$

$$= \max\left\{ (2.5) \int_0^1 x \cdot 2(1 - x)\, dx, 1 \right\},$$

$$= \max\left\{ \frac{5}{2} \cdot \frac{1}{3}, 1 \right\} = 1.$$

Hence it is better to switch to SSS at this point. If on the other hand (ii) occurs and RC succeeds, then

$$\varphi_{1,1}(1) = \max\left\{ g \int_0^1 x\pi(x; 1, 1)\, dx, s \right\},$$

$$= \max\left\{ (2.5) \int_0^1 x\, 2x\, dx, 1 \right\},$$

$$= \max\left\{ \left(\frac{5}{2}\right)\left(\frac{2}{3}\right), 1 \right\} = \frac{5}{3},$$

and it is advisable to end up with RC.

It is instructive to represent the decision alternatives for the simplified two-armed bandit problem by a decision tree. Figure 8.5.1 shows a two-stage decision tree

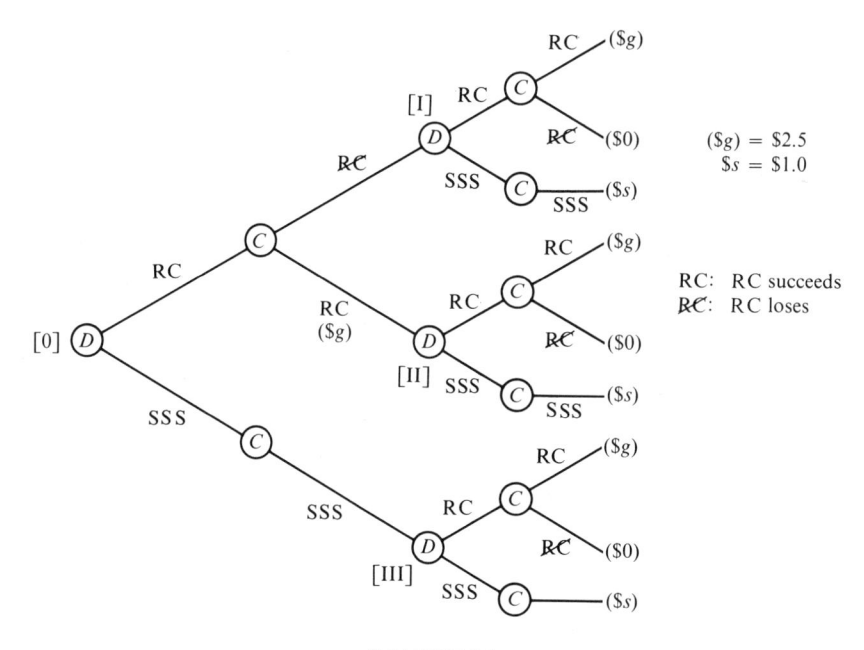

FIGURE 8.5.1

using the prior and the payoffs above. Consider the three second-stage decision nodes labeled [I], [II], and [III]. Looking ahead from each in turn, we have the expected rewards from following an optimal policy thereafter:

$$\text{From [I] (Use SSS): } \varphi_{0,1}(1) = \$1$$

$$\text{From [II] (Use RC): } \varphi_{1,1}(1) = \$1.67$$

$$\text{From [III] (Use RC): } \varphi_{0,0}(1) = \$1.25$$

Now step back to the initial decision opportunity, [0]. If at this stage

(a) RC is used, then the optimal expected payoff is seen to be

$$\int_0^1 x[2.5 + \varphi_{1,1}(1)] \, dx + \int_0^1 (1-x)[0 + \varphi_{0,1}(1)] \, dx = \frac{1}{2}[2.5 + 1.67] + \frac{1}{2}[1] = \$2.59,$$

whereas if

(b) SSS is used, then the optimal expected payoff turns out to be

$$\$1 + \$1.25 = \$2.25.$$

It thus turns out that it is best to start with RC and if RC loses, switch to SSS; however, if RC wins, continue with RC at the second opportunity. Of course, more lengthy sequences of possibilities may be handled in just this fashion, but the trees soon become quite involved, and computer assistance will be welcome.

EXAMPLE 8.5.4. In industries concerned with natural gas transmission, electric power, highway construction, and so on, demand for the industry's product increases more or less steadily through the years. To meet new demand, additional units of productive capacity (plants) are required at intervals. We shall describe a simple model in terms of which the optimal new plant size, and hence new capacity introduction intervals, may be determined.

The conflicting issues in this situation are the following. First, if x represents the productive capacity of a plant (x may be in units of barrels per year), then the cost of building a plant of capacity x is often of the form

$$(8.5.17) \qquad\qquad C(x) = ax^b \qquad (0 < b < 1, a > 0).$$

That is, b may be equal to $\frac{1}{2}$, for example. This represents an *economy of scale*: if two plants are contemplated, one of capacity $x = 1$ and the other of capacity $x = 4$, the second costs only twice as much as the first to build, although it is four times as large. Hence it is advantageous to build a new plant (or new plant addition) that is somewhat larger than necessary to meet present demand and allow for growing demand to make use of the unused capacity. The size of capacity additions is limited by the discounted value of money: if a dollar must be spent t years in the future, then e^{-rt} may be used to represent its present value; here r represents a discount rate and is related to the interest rate. Viewed from the present moment, then, it will be desirable to postpone expenditures for the new plant in order to pay for it with discounted dollars. On the other hand, it is desirable to build as large a plant as possible at present, in order to benefit from economies of scale.

We shall suppose first that demand for our product over a time of length t is a known linear function of time:

$$(8.5.18) \qquad x = \delta t \qquad \delta > 0,$$

where t is measured from some instant at which demand and supply (capacity) are equal and a new addition is required. At some time τ later, the decision maker will be in precisely the same position for the first time again. Because of the linear growth (8.5.18) and the time-independent cost function (8.5.17), the decisions to be made at $0, \tau, 2\tau, \ldots$ will be the same—that is, to build a plant of capacity $\bar{x}$. In order to determine $\bar{x}$, let

$C(x) =$ sum of all discounted future costs looking forward from any decision point of the form $0, \tau, 2\tau, \ldots,$ provided a plant of size x is built at each such moment.

Now viewing the future from the first decision point, $t = 0$, we see that $C(x)$ is the sum of the costs of building the presently needed plant, plus the discounted cost of the future additions needed at $\tau, 2\tau, 3\tau, \ldots$. We can express this as follows:

$$C(x) = ax^b + e^{-r\tau}ax^b + e^{-r(2\tau)}ax^b + e^{-r(3\tau)}ax^b + \cdots,$$
$$= ax^b + e^{-r\tau}C(x),$$
$$(8.5.19) \qquad = \frac{ax^b}{1 - e^{-r\tau}},$$
$$= \frac{a(\delta\tau)^b}{1 - e^{-r\tau}},$$

where we have used the fact that

$$x = \delta\tau.$$

Now we may differentiate (8.5.19) with respect to τ and equate the derivative to zero to find the optimum decision interval and hence, using (8.5.18), the optimum capacity, $\bar{x}$. The result is the equation

$$(8.5.20) \qquad b = \frac{r\bar{\tau}}{e^{+r\bar{\tau}} - 1}$$

for the optimum $\tau, \bar{\tau}$, which unfortunately cannot be solved explicitly. Of course a graphical or numerical solution may easily be carried out. Plainly, though, the solution of (8.5.20) is of the form

$$(8.5.21) \qquad r\bar{\tau} = f(b),$$

where $f(b)$ depends only on the economy-of-scale parameter b. Thus (8.5.20) need be solved only once for each value of b. It follows from (8.5.18) and (8.5.21) that

$$\bar{\tau} = \frac{1}{r} f(b)$$

and

$$\bar{x} = \delta\bar{\tau} = \frac{\delta}{r} f(b).$$

As the discount rate, r, increases, the optimum installation interval, $\bar{\tau}$, becomes shorter, and the optimum new plant size, $\bar{x}$, declines. This is an intuitively appealing result.

EXAMPLE 8.5.4 (continued). Suppose that the previous model is altered in such a way as to make demand increase *probabilistically*. Specifically, imagine that demand increases of size $h > 0$ occur according to a Poisson process of rate λ. (You may, at this point, wish to refer to our later discussion of the Poisson process.) Thus the total expected increased demand in a time interval of duration t is $h\lambda t$, and in order to bring this into conformity with the previous model, we must put $\delta = h\lambda$.

Now contemplate the addition of a capacity x at time intervals such that demand has grown by an amount x. Clearly such times are now of random duration. Supposing that $x = nh$, then a decision interval, τ, is the time until the occurrence of the nth event in a Poisson process with parameter $\lambda = \delta/h$. It may be shown that τ has the gamma distribution, with density

(8.5.22)
$$f_\tau(y) = e^{-\lambda y}\frac{(\lambda y)^{n-1}}{(n-1)!}\lambda \qquad \text{if } y \geq 0,$$
$$= 0 \qquad\qquad \text{otherwise.}$$

Now let

$\bar{C}(x) =$ expected value of the sum of all discounted future costs looking forward from any decision point, provided that a plant of capacity x is built at each such point.

We argue that

(8.5.23)
$$\bar{C}(x) = ax^b + E[e^{-r\tau}]\bar{C}(x),$$

whereas now

(8.5.24)
$$E[e^{-r\tau}] = \int_0^\infty e^{-ry}e^{-\lambda y}\frac{(\lambda y)^{n-1}}{(n-1)!}\lambda\, dy = \left(\frac{\lambda}{\lambda+r}\right)^n.$$

The reason is that $\bar{C}(x)$ is the sum of the initial plant cost plus the expected discounted cost of all future plants. By the properties of the Poisson process, the time to the first addition following the present has the same distribution as the time from the first to the second, and so on—namely, (8.5.22). Moreover, these times are independent. Consequently (8.5.23) follows.

We then have that

(8.5.25)
$$\bar{C}(x) = \frac{ax^b}{1 - E[e^{-r\tau}]} = \frac{ax^b}{1 - \left(\dfrac{\lambda}{\lambda+r}\right)^n},$$

$$= \frac{ax^b}{1 - \left(1 + \dfrac{r}{\lambda}\right)^{-n}} = \frac{ax^b}{1 - \left(1 + \dfrac{rh}{\delta}\right)^{-x/h}},$$

where we have used the fact that

$$n = \frac{x}{h}$$

and

$$\lambda = \frac{\delta}{h}.$$

Notice that if we let $n \to \infty$ or $h \to 0$,

$$(8.5.26) \qquad \bar{C}(x) = \frac{ax^b}{1 - e^{-rx/\delta}},$$

which is equivalent to the deterministic case (8.5.19). The reason for this equivalence is that we are letting demand become effectively deterministic: as n increases, the Poisson rate λ is made extremely rapid with the demand increases, h, correspondingly small.

It may be shown that

$$1 - \left(1 + \frac{y}{n}\right)^{-n} < 1 - e^{-y}$$

(see Exercise 6), and so it follows that the expected discounted cost, $\bar{C}(x)$, in the case of probabilistic demand always exceeds the corresponding cost, $C(x)$, in the case of deterministic demand. This is to be expected, since some penalty must be paid for demand unpredictability. The interesting question relates to the way in which the optimal investment size $\bar{x}$ depends on demand variability. But this question is easily answered if we rewrite (8.5.25) as follows:

$$(8.5.27) \qquad \bar{C}(x) = \frac{ax^b}{1 - e^{-(\theta/\delta)x}},$$

where now

$$\theta = \frac{\delta}{h} \log_e \left(1 + \frac{rh}{\delta}\right).$$

It may be shown mathematically that $\theta < r$ if h is positive. (See Exercise 8.) Now refer to the expression (8.5.19) for the deterministic growth model, and replace τ by $\bar{x}/\delta$. We obtain for the deterministic case

$$(8.5.28) \qquad C(x) = \frac{ax^b}{1 - e^{-(r/\delta)x}}.$$

and it is apparent by comparing (8.5.28) and (8.5.29) that θ is playing the role of an effective discount rate. If $\bar{C}(x)$ is optimized by choice of x (differentiate (8.5.27) with respect to x, set the derivative equal to zero, and solve the transcendental equation), we find that we must solve

$$(8.5.29) \qquad b = \frac{(\theta/\delta)x}{e^{(\theta/\delta)x} - 1}.$$

The solution of 2.5.29 is of the form

$$(8.5.30) \qquad \frac{\theta}{\delta} \bar{x} = f(b),$$

or

$$\bar{x} = \frac{\delta}{\theta} f(b).$$

Since $\theta < r$, we conclude that the *optimum capacity addition is larger in the case of stochastic demand increase than for the corresponding case of deterministic demand increase.* Here "corresponding" means that *expected* demand increase per unit time in the stochastic case is δ, which equals the certain demand increase in the deterministic case.

EXERCISES 8.5

1. Suppose that the selling price distribution for an asset (house) has the uniform density (prices in thousand-dollar units)

$$f(x) = \begin{cases} 0 & \text{if} \quad x < 20 \\ \dfrac{1}{10} & \text{if } 20 \le x < 30 \\ 0 & \text{if } 30 \le x \end{cases}$$

(a) Using the results of Example 8.5.1, calculate the maximum expected revenue from the sale if the seller has three opportunities to sell; that is, he is allowed to choose one of three consecutive prices from the density above.

(b) What is the probability that a seller following the optimum policy will sell on his first opportunity?

(c) The seller has the option of listing his house with an agent who guarantees him the following price density:

$$f(x) = \begin{cases} 0 & \text{if} \quad x < 15 \\ \dfrac{1}{30} & \text{if } 15 \le x < 45 \\ 0 & \text{if } 45 \le x \end{cases}$$

What is the most that he should pay the agent for the listing (payment is a flat fee)?

2. In the house-selling example (Example 8.5.1), suppose the weekly prices come from different distributions: the price, X_m when m weeks remain, has density $f_m(x)$. Derive the optimum policy—that is, the sequences $\{R_n\}$ and $\{p_n\}$.

3. Refer again to the problem of Example 8.5.1. Suppose five weeks remain until moving day, so we must determine p_0, p_1, p_2, p_3, and p_4. Find the optimum strategy if
(a) the *distribution of* offers X are uniformly distributed:

$$f(x) = \frac{1}{20} \quad \text{for } 0 \le x \le 20,$$
$$= 0 \quad \text{otherwise};$$

(b) the offers are exponentially distributed:

$$f(x) = e^{-x/10}\frac{1}{10} \quad x \ge 0,$$
$$= 0 \quad x < 0.$$

(c) Find the expected price received in cases (a) and (b).

(d) Suppose that the seller *thinks* that offers are uniformly distributed (according to (a)), but they are *actually* exponential (according to (b)). How much will he lose? (What is his expected loss?)

4. With reference to Example 8.5.1 and Exercise 2 above, suppose the distribution of X_n, the nth best offer from the terminal week, is given by $F_n(x)$; that is, it depends on n.
(a) Show how to compute the optimum strategy for selling.
(b) Let the density of demand on the nth week from the end be

$$f_n(x) = \frac{1}{(n+1)} \quad 0 \le x \le n+1,$$
$$= 0 \quad \text{otherwise.}$$

Exhibit the p_n and R_n sequence for $n = 0, 1, 2, 3, 4$.

(c) Let the density of demand on the nth week from the start be

$$f_n(x) = \frac{1}{(n+1)} \qquad 0 \le x \le \frac{1}{n+1},$$

$$= 0 \qquad \text{otherwise.}$$

Compute the p_n and R_n sequence for $n = 0, 1, 2, 3, 4$. Contrast the results of (b) and (c).

5. Consider the setup of Example 8.5.3. Imagine that there are three decision opportunities (stages), and complete the decision tree to discover the optimum strategy for investment at each stage.

6. Refer to Example 8.5.4 (continued). In order to show that $\bar{C}(x) < C(x)$—that is, that the expected total discounted cost in the case of stochastic demand charges exceeds that for deterministic demand charge—we use *Jensen's inequality*: if τ is any random variable, and $g(\tau)$ is a convex (to the origin) function of τ, then

(∗) $$E[g(\tau)] \ge g(E[\tau]).$$

By a convex function we mean one whose graph always lies above any tangent line; see the graph below.

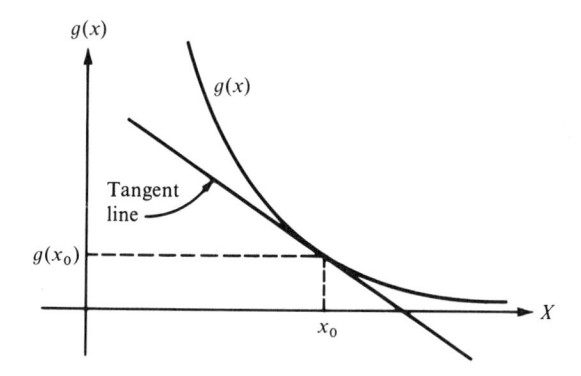

To prove (∗), observe that if

$$x_0 = E[\tau],$$

then the line described by

$$\frac{y - g(x_0)}{x - x_0} = s,$$

where s is the slope of $g(x)$ at x_0, always lies below $g(x)$. That is, by convexity,

$$y = g(x) > g(x_0) + s(x - x_0)$$

for all x. Now put $x_0 = E[\tau]$, substitute τ for x, and take expectations:

$$E[g(\tau)] > g(E[\tau]) + 0,$$

since $E(\tau - E[\tau]) = 0$.

Suppose $g(x) = e^{-rx}$ and the probability density is gamma:

$$f(x) = e^{-ax} \frac{(ax)^{n-1} a}{(n-1)!} \qquad n(\text{integer}) \ge 1.$$

Show that

$$\left(\frac{a}{a+r}\right)^{n} > e^{-rn/a}.$$

7. Suppose the cost of building a plant of size x is $\sqrt{x}$ (or $x^{1/2}$), that the interest rate parameter is $r = 0.10$, and that the growth rate $\delta = 1$.
   (a) Find the optimal new plant size, $\bar{x}$, and the optimal replacement interval, τ.
   (b) What is the total discounted cost that results from following the policy of (a)?
   (c) Suppose accumulated demand is stochastic with $\delta = 1$ and $h = \frac{1}{25}$. Find the optimal new capacity investment size, $\bar{x}$.
   (d) Compare the answer to (c) to situations in which $h = \frac{1}{10}$ and $h = \frac{1}{16}$.

8. Prove that

$$\frac{1}{h} \log_{e} (1 + bh) < b.$$

$\left(Hint: \dfrac{1}{h} \log_{e} (1 + bh) = \dfrac{1}{h} \displaystyle\int_{0}^{bh} \dfrac{dy}{1+y} < \dfrac{1}{h} \displaystyle\int_{0}^{bh} 1 \cdot dy.\right)$

9. A company is considering the purchase of an idea, the exploitation of which would constitute a new branch of its business. Because the idea is new, some time will be required to translate its acquisition into a net profit stream: a plant must be built and selling procedures developed. Thus if the idea is purchased at $t = 0$, suppose that the net profit stream becomes positive at $t = T(T > 0)$; T is a random variable whose distribution is known but the form of whose distribution can be influenced by spending money: if expenditure is at a rapid rate, T will tend to be short, whereas if expenditures are leisurely, selling and profits will be postponed.

   Let yearly profit rate be

$$R = \begin{cases} -\$B & \text{for } 0 \leq t \leq T \\ +\$A & \text{for } \quad t \geq T \end{cases}$$

   Let the distribution of T be exponential with density function $e^{-mt}m(t \geq 0)$. Recall that $E[T] = m^{-1}$. Suppose initially that an annual cost of $\$C$ is required to sustain rate m; that is,

$$m = aC \qquad a > 0.$$

   (a) If profits are discounted continuously at rate $r(r > 0)$, find the expected value of the discounted net profit stream obtainable from purchasing the idea. (*Hint:* Use the fact that the Laplace transform of the exponential density is $E[e^{-sT}] = \dfrac{m}{m+s}$; see Chapter 7, Section 7.10 for Laplace transforms.)
   (b) Show that if $B = 0$, then the expected value of (a) above increases with C, provided that the parameter $Aa/r > 1$.
   (c) If the *exposure* associated with the purchase of the idea is defined as the maximum accumulation of expense prior to the beginning of profit making, find the distribution function of the exposure and its expectation. (*Hint:* Relate exposure to T.)
   (d) Suppose that essentially the same idea becomes available to a competitor; let the competitor's time to exploit be T' with exponential distribution having parameter m'. If $T' < T$, the competitor takes the entire market and our company realizes no profit; but if $T < T'$, the tables are turned. Compute the expected value of the discounted net profit stream under those conditions. Also find the probability that the competitor beats out our company. Given that our company is beaten out, find the expected loss. Assume T and T' are independent.

SUGGESTED READING

Bellman, R. *Dynamic Programming*. Princeton, N.J.: Princeton University Press, 1957.

Bellman, R., and Dreyfus, S. *Applied Dynamic Programming*. Princeton, N.J.: Princeton University Press, 1962.

Borch, K. H. *The Economics of Uncertainty*. Princeton, N.J.: Princeton University Press, 1968.

Chernoff, H., and Moses, L. *Elementary Decision Theory*. New York: John Wiley, 1959.

DeGroot, M. *Optimal Statistical Decisions*. New York: McGraw-Hill, 1970.

Hadley, G. *Nonlinear and Dynamic Programming*. Reading, Mass.: Addison-Wesley, 1964.

Howard, R. *Dynamic Programming and Markov Processes*. Cambridge, Mass.: M.I.T. Press, 1961.

Karlin, S. Stochastic models and optimal policy for selling an asset. In *Studies in Applied Probability and Management Science*, edited by K. Arrow, S. Karlin, and H. Scarf, Stanford, Calif.: Stanford University Press, 1962.

Manne, A. S. Capacity expansion and probabilistic growth. *Econometrics*, 1961, **29**, (4), 632–649.

Pratt, J., Raiffa, H., and Schlaifer, R. *Introduction to Statistical Decision Theory*. New York: McGraw-Hill, 1965.

Raiffa, H. *Decision Analysis*. Reading, Mass.: Addison-Wesley, 1968.

Simon, H. A. *Models of Man*. New York: John Wiley, 1957.

CHAPTER 9

MARKOV CHAINS

9.1 INTRODUCTION

By and large, the probability models introduced in earlier chapters involved independent random variables. For instance, in the perishable-goods inventory model of the previous chapter, we at least implicitly assumed that the demand during the particular time period (day) under discussion bore no relation to the actual demand that occurred on the previous day. And yet there are many circumstances for which such an assumption represents an oversimplification.

EXAMPLE 9.1.1. The daily sequence of high quotations for a given common stock on the New York Stock Exchange is not adequately represented as, say, a sequence of independent and identically distributed realizations of a random variable. Price levels seem, approximately, to be generated by a mechanism like the following:

$$(9.1.1) \qquad X_{t+1} = X_t + S_t,$$

where X_t represents the price (high) on day t, and S_t is a random addition (algebraic—that is, plus or minus) to the day's price. Here the successive S_t values may perhaps be thought of as coming independently from the same distribution. Of course the generated X_t values do not have this property: the price level tomorrow is likely to be close to the price today.

Other such examples come to mind, and some will be discussed subsequently. To describe them generally, we give the following definition.

DEFINITION 9.1.1. A *stochastic process* (or *random* process) is a collection or family of random variables, $\{X_t\}$. In the example above, the time sequence of stock prices, beginning at some arbitrary initial time $t = 0$, is a stochastic process:

$$(9.1.2) \qquad X_0, X_1, X_2, \ldots, X_t, \ldots.$$

Any particular sequence of values assumed by the random variables, say the sequence

$$(9.1.3) \qquad X_0 = 3, X_1 = 14, X_2 = 11, \ldots, X_t = 1, \ldots,$$

is called a *realization* of the stochastic process $\{X_t\}$ or, frequently, a *time series*. The model of (9.1.3) would allow us to artificially generate such a realization: merely make an independent random draw from the distribution of S_t at each time or step; then, given $X_0 = i_0$, add the value obtained, $S_0 = s_0$, to x_0 to obtain x_1, the realized value of X_1. Continue by drawing another value of S_t—for example, s_1—adding, and so on. Since $\{X_t\}$ is a sequence of random variables, necessarily there must be a probability distribution assigned to the sequence. Thus, if $X_t = i_t$ is always discrete, then we must have defined

$$(9.1.4) \qquad P\{X_0 = i_0, X_1 = i_1, X_2 = i_2, \ldots, X_t = i_t, \ldots\}$$

for all value sequences $\{i_t\}$ that may be assumed by $\{X_t\}$. Notice that the subscript t refers to a time point in the first example. This will be true in almost all of our examples, and so we shall usually refer to the "time, t." A stochastic process is a mathematical construction that represents a physical, biological, or economic process that occurs in time and that is profitable to think of as being governed in part by probability laws. We shall often refer to "the state of the process (or system) at time t" as being the value assumed by X_t; it will be denoted by x_t. Thus the state of the system at $t = 2$ in the realization (9.1.3) is 11. X_t itself is often called the *state variable* of the process.

It is the purpose of this chapter to study a very important and convenient type of stochastic process, the Markov chain.

DEFINITION 9.1.2. A stochastic process $\{X_t, t = 0, 1, 2, \ldots\}$ possesses the *Markov property*, or is a *Markov chain*, if, for every time t and every sequence of possible state values $a, b, c, d, \ldots$,

$$(9.1.5)$$
$$P\{X_{t+1} = a \mid X_t = b, X_{t-1} = c, X_{t-2} = d, X_{t-3} = e, \ldots\} = P\{X_{t+1} = a \mid X_t = b\}.$$

In words, the process $\{X_t\}$ is Markov if the probability that the process is in state a at time X_{t+1}, given that it was in states b at t, c at $t - 1$, and so on really depends only on the state assumed at t—namely, b. It may be said that the evolution of the process, given the present (that is, that $X_t = b$) is independent of previous states assumed.

EXAMPLE 9.1.2. Refer to the previous stock-price-fluctuation model. Suppose that the sequence of S_t values is generated by flipping a fair coin: if H results, $S_t = \$1$, whereas if T results, then $S_t = -\$1$. Thus,

$$(9.1.6) \qquad X_t = X_{t-1} + \begin{cases} 1 & \text{with probability } \dfrac{1}{2} \\ -1 & \text{with probability } \dfrac{1}{2} \end{cases}$$

Quite clearly, if we are given that X_{t-1} equals, say, 3, then $X_t = 4$ with probability $\frac{1}{2}$, $X_t = 2$ with probability $\frac{1}{2}$, and no previous history before time $t-1$ bears any relevance to the value of X_t or, for that matter, to the values of X_{t+1}, X_{t+2}, and so on.

Conditional probabilities like those to the right of the equality sign in (9.1.5) are of basic importance in what follows. We call

$$(9.1.7) \qquad P\{X_{t+1} = j \mid X_t = i\} = p_{ij}(t)$$

the *one-step transition probability* in effect at time t, and

$$(9.1.8) \qquad P\{X_{t+n} = j \mid X_t = i\} = p_{ij}^{(n)}(t) \qquad (n = 1, 2, 3, \ldots),$$

the *n-step transition probability* at time t. The latter specifies the probability that the chain will be in state j at n time units after the time t, at which moment it was in state i. If these functions do not depend on the time, t—that is, if

$$(9.1.9) \qquad p_{ij}^{(n)}(t) = p_{ij}^{(n)} \qquad (n = 1, 2, \ldots)$$

for all t, then we speak of a Markov chain having *stationary transition probabilities*. Most of the useful mathematical theory refers to this case, but models involving time-dependent transition probabilities can be profitably devised and conveniently manipulated numerically, with the aid of a high-speed computer. However, we shall concentrate on Markov chains with stationary transition probabilities.

EXAMPLE 9.1.3. Refer to the setup of Example 9.1.2. Then suppose $X_4 = 7$. We see that the one-step transition probabilities are

$$P\{X_5 = 8 \mid X_4 = 7\} = p_{78}(4) = \frac{1}{2}$$

and

$$(9.1.10) \qquad P\{X_5 = 6 \mid X_4 = 7\} = p_{76}(4) = \frac{1}{2},$$

while

$$P\{X_5 = j \mid X_4 = 7\} = p_{7j}(4) = 0 \qquad j \neq 6, 8.$$

Consequently, the Markov chain is one of stationary transition probabilities. If, on the other hand, we flipped a coin having probabilities

$$(9.1.11) \qquad P\{H \text{ at time } t\} = p_t = \frac{1}{2} e^{-t},$$

$$P\{T \text{ at time } t\} = q_t = 1 - p_t,$$

then a Markov chain is generated with nonstationary transition probabilities. Indeed, the situation above would generate prices in a (fictional) falling market.

Although there is no restriction placed on the set of values assumed by X_t, the state space, we shall now consider only a finite set or space of alternatives.

DEFINITION 9.1.3. A *finite Markov chain* is a stochastic process having the Markov property and possessing only a finite set of states; this state space will be denoted by

$$S = \{x_1, x_2, \ldots, x_r\}.$$

Since there are exactly r distinct states, we can label them by the integers 1, 2, 3, ..., r. This is convenient and will usually be done. Sometimes consideration of states 0, 1, 2, ..., $r - 1$, r is more natural; for example, the state 0 may refer to being out of money. Such changes will be made without comment where desirable.

The one-step transition probabilities are arrayed in the *one-step transition matrix*:

(9.1.12)
$$P(t) = \begin{bmatrix} p_{11}(t) & p_{12}(t) & \cdots & p_{1r}(t) \\ p_{21}(t) & p_{22}(t) & \cdots & p_{2r}(t) \\ \cdot & \cdot & \cdots & \cdot \\ p_{r1}(t) & p_{r2}(t) & \cdots & p_{rr}(t) \end{bmatrix}$$

In the case of chains with stationary transition probabilities, which is our primary concern, the dependence on t is missing.

Clearly the elements of P are nonnegative and not greater than unity. Also

$$\sum_{j=1}^{r} p_{ij} = 1.$$

Matrices of this kind are called *stochastic*.

In order to start our Markov chain we define an initial probability (row) vector,

(9.1.13)
$$\pi_0 = [p_1^{(0)}, \; p_2^{(0)}, \; \ldots, \; p_n^{(0)}],$$

the components of which give the initial probabilities of being in each state:

(9.1.14)
$$P\{X_0 = j\} = p_j^{(0)}.$$

Similarly, the probability of being in each state at time t can be expressed as the vector

(9.1.15)
$$\pi_t = [p_1^{(t)}, \; p_2^{(t)}, \; \ldots, \; p_r^{(t)}];$$

that is,

(9.1.16)
$$P\{X(t) = j\} = p_j^{(t)}.$$

EXAMPLE 9.1.4. Again refer to the stock-price example. Suppose that if the stock price reaches a low of 0, it rebounds or is "reflected" the next time to state 1, and if it hits r, it automatically falls back to $r - 1$. Then, using the coin-flip model of (9.1.10), the one-step transitions are summarized by the matrix

$$\begin{array}{c}\begin{array}{ccccccc} & 0 & 1 & 2 & \cdots & r\end{array}\\ \boldsymbol{P} = \begin{array}{c}0\\1\\2\\3\\ \vdots \\ r\end{array}\begin{bmatrix} 0 & 1 & 0 & \cdots & 0\\ \frac{1}{2} & 0 & \frac{1}{2} & \cdots & 0\\ 0 & \frac{1}{2} & 0 & \cdots & 0\\ 0 & 0 & \frac{1}{2} & \cdots & 0\\ \cdot & \cdot & & \cdots & \cdot\\ 0 & 0 & 0 & 1 & 0\end{bmatrix}\end{array}.$$

(9.1.17)

Here we have an $r + 1$-state Markov chain with stationary transitions when the initial vector π_0 is specified.

EXAMPLE 9.1.5. Imagine that an urn contains two balls. The balls are colored either black or white and are otherwise identical. Suppose that once every minute a ball is withdrawn at random, examined, and treated as follows:

(a) if the ball drawn is black, it is painted white and replaced;

(b) if the ball drawn is white, we flip a fair coin and if the head occurs, we paint the ball black and replace, whereas if a tail occurs, we replace as is.

A tree diagram helps organize matters:

$$\text{B} \longrightarrow \text{W} \quad \boldsymbol{P}\{\text{Ball replaced W} \mid \text{Ball drawn B}\} = 1$$

$$\text{H}; \frac{1}{2} \rightarrow \text{W} \quad \boldsymbol{P}\{\text{Ball replaced B} \mid \text{Ball drawn W}\} = \frac{1}{2}$$

$$\text{W}$$

$$\text{T}; \frac{1}{2} \rightarrow \text{B} \quad \boldsymbol{P}\{\text{Ball replaced W} \mid \text{Ball drawn W}\} = \frac{1}{2}$$

Our aim is to describe the contents of the urn after this process has been repeated t times. Let X_t denote the number of black balls in the urn at t. Thus,

$$S = \{0, 1, 2\},$$

corresponding to the actual states {WW}, {WB}, and {BB}. Notice now that X_t is a Markov chain since the composition of the urn at time $t - 1$ determines the chance of drawing a black ball, and the rules (a) and (b) govern the color of the ball replaced and hence the composition at t. Specifically, considering the events in question and using the rules of conditional probability,

$$\boldsymbol{P}\{X_t = 0 \mid X_{t-1} = 0\}$$
$$= \boldsymbol{P}\{\text{Ball replaced W} \mid \text{Ball drawn B}\}\boldsymbol{P}\{\text{Ball drawn B} \mid X_{t-1} = 0\}$$
$$+ \boldsymbol{P}\{\text{Ball replaced W} \mid \text{Ball drawn W}\}\boldsymbol{P}\{\text{Ball drawn W} \mid X_{t-1} = 0\}$$
$$= (1)(0) + \left(\frac{1}{2}\right)(1) = \frac{1}{2}.$$

Likewise,

$$\boldsymbol{P}\{X_t = 1 \mid X_{t-1} = 0\}$$
$$= \boldsymbol{P}\{\text{Ball replaced B} \mid \text{Ball drawn B}\}\boldsymbol{P}\{\text{Ball drawn B} \mid X_{t-1} = 0\}$$
$$+ \boldsymbol{P}\{\text{Ball replaced B} \mid \text{Ball drawn W}\}\boldsymbol{P}\{\text{Ball drawn W} \mid X_{t-1} = 0\}$$
$$= \left(\frac{1}{2}\right)(0) + \left(\frac{1}{2}\right)(1) = \frac{1}{2}.$$

Clearly, the remaining conditional probability—that is, that $X_t = 2$—is zero. Next,

$$P\{X_t = 0 \mid X_{t-1} = 1\} = P\{\text{Ball replaced W} \mid \text{Ball drawn B}\}P\{\text{Ball drawn B} \mid X_{t-1} = 1\} = \frac{1}{2},$$

because if W is drawn, there will remain one B regardless. Then it may be verified that

$$P\{X_t = 1 \mid X_{t-1} = 1\} = \frac{1}{4},$$

while

$$P\{X_t = 2 \mid X_{t-1} = 1\} = \frac{1}{4}.$$

Finally,

$$P\{X_t = 0 \mid X_{t-1} = 2\} = 0,$$
$$P\{X_t = 1 \mid X_{t-1} = 2\} = 1,$$

so of course the remaining probability is zero. The transition matrix is thus

(9.1.18)
$$\boldsymbol{P} = \begin{array}{c} \\ 0 \\ 1 \\ 2 \end{array} \begin{array}{ccc} 0 & 1 & 2 \\ \left[\begin{array}{ccc} \frac{1}{2} & \frac{1}{2} & 0 \\ \frac{1}{2} & \frac{1}{4} & \frac{1}{4} \\ 0 & 1 & 0 \end{array}\right] \end{array}.$$

Now suppose that the initial states of the chain have distribution specified by $p_i^{(0)}$. Then the joint probability

(9.1.19) $$P\{X_0 = i, X_1 = j\} = P\{X_1 = j \mid X_0 = i\}P\{X_0 = i\} = p_i^{(0)}p_{ij},$$

so the probability of being in state j at $t = 1$ is

(9.1.20)
$$P\{X_1 = j\} = p_j^{(1)} = \sum_{j=1}^{r} p_i^{(0)}p_{ij}.$$

Notice that $p_j^{(1)}$ is the jth entry in the row matrix π_1 obtained by postmultiplying π_0 by the one-step transition matrix $\boldsymbol{P}$:

(9.1.21) $$[p_1^{(0)}, p_2^{(0)}, \ldots, p_r^{(0)}] \begin{bmatrix} p_{11} & p_{12} & \cdots & p_{1r} \\ p_{21} & p_{22} & \cdots & p_{2r} \\ \cdot & \cdot & \cdots & \cdot \\ p_{r1} & p_{r2} & \cdots & p_{rr} \end{bmatrix} = [p_1^{(1)}, p_2^{(1)}, \ldots, p_r^{(1)}]$$

or

(9.1.22)
$$\pi_0 \boldsymbol{P} = \pi_1.$$

It might be guessed that this procedure may be repeated: the new row vector π_1, when postmultiplied by $\boldsymbol{P}$, yields π_2, and so on. That this is indeed true is shown in the next theorem.

THEOREM 9.1.1. Let $\boldsymbol{P}$ be the transition matrix of a finite Markov chain with initial vector π_0. Then

(9.1.23)
$$\text{(a)} \quad \pi_t = \pi_{t-1}\boldsymbol{P},$$
$$\text{(b)} \quad \pi_t = \pi_0 \boldsymbol{P}^t,$$

where P^t represents the product of the matrix P by itself t times. This is equivalent to the statement that

$$(9.1.24) \qquad P\{X_t = j \mid X_0 = i\} = p_{ij}^{(t)}$$

is the element in the ith row and jth column of the t-step transition matrix P.

Proof: By the Markov property (9.1.5),

$$(9.1.25)$$
$$P\{X_t = j \mid X_{t-1} = i, X_{t-2} = i_2, X_{t-3} = i_3, \ldots, X_0 = i_0\} = P\{X_t = j \mid X_{t-1} = i\},$$

where $i, i_2, i_3, \ldots, i_0$ is any sequence of state values. Furthermore, by the usual conditional probability rules,

$$(9.1.26) \quad P\{X_t = j\}$$
$$= \sum_{i, i_2, i_3, \ldots, i_0} P\{X_t = j \mid X_{t-1} = i, X_{t-2} = i_2, \ldots\} P\{X_{t-1} = i, X_{t-2} = i_2, X_{t-3} = i_3, \ldots\}$$
$$= \sum_{i, i_2, i_3, \ldots, i_0} P\{X_t = j \mid X_{t-1} = i\} P\{X_{t-1} = i, X_{t-2} = i_2, \ldots, X_0 = i_0\},$$

this last expression coming from (9.1.25)—that is, the Markov property. Adding over all state values $i_2, i_3, \ldots, i_0$, the result is

$$(9.1.27) \qquad P\{X_t = j\} = \sum_i P\{X_t = j \mid X_{t-1} = i\} P\{X_{t-1} = i\},$$

or

$$(9.1.28) \qquad p_j^{(t)} = \sum_{i=1} p_{ij} p_i^{(t-1)}.$$

But the left-hand term is the element in the jth column of the row vector π_t, and the right-hand side represents the corresponding element in the row vector $\pi_{t-1} P$, which proves (a). We have already shown that $\pi_0 P = \pi_1$, and so

$$(9.1.29) \qquad \pi_2 = \pi_1 P = (\pi_0 P)P = \pi_0 P^2.$$

By induction, (b) follows.

EXAMPLE 9.1.6. Let us compute the composition of the urn of the previous example after the drawing-painting process has been repeated several times. After two time units—two successive occasions on which the urn is sampled and the sample transformed and replaced—the transition probabilities are given by

$$(9.1.30) \qquad P^2 = \begin{bmatrix} \frac{1}{2} & \frac{1}{2} & 0 \\ \frac{1}{2} & \frac{1}{4} & \frac{1}{4} \\ 0 & 1 & 0 \end{bmatrix} \begin{bmatrix} \frac{1}{2} & \frac{1}{2} & 0 \\ \frac{1}{2} & \frac{1}{4} & \frac{1}{4} \\ 0 & 1 & 0 \end{bmatrix} = \begin{bmatrix} \frac{1}{2} & \frac{3}{8} & \frac{1}{8} \\ \frac{3}{8} & \frac{9}{16} & \frac{1}{16} \\ \frac{1}{2} & \frac{1}{4} & \frac{1}{4} \end{bmatrix}.$$

After the process has been repeated three times,

$$(9.1.31) \qquad P^3 = \begin{bmatrix} \frac{1}{2} & \frac{3}{8} & \frac{1}{8} \\ \frac{3}{8} & \frac{9}{16} & \frac{1}{16} \\ \frac{1}{2} & \frac{1}{4} & \frac{1}{4} \end{bmatrix} \begin{bmatrix} \frac{1}{2} & \frac{1}{2} & 0 \\ \frac{1}{2} & \frac{1}{4} & \frac{1}{4} \\ 0 & 1 & 0 \end{bmatrix} = \begin{bmatrix} \frac{7}{16} & \frac{15}{32} & \frac{3}{32} \\ \frac{15}{32} & \frac{25}{64} & \frac{9}{64} \\ \frac{3}{8} & \frac{9}{16} & \frac{1}{16} \end{bmatrix}.$$

It turns out that if P^t is computed successively for $t = 4, 5, 6, \ldots$, the entries approach limits as $t \to \infty$, and the limiting matrix is

$$(9.1.32) \qquad \lim_{t \to \infty} P^t = \begin{bmatrix} \frac{4}{9} & \frac{4}{9} & \frac{1}{9} \\ \frac{4}{9} & \frac{4}{9} & \frac{1}{9} \\ \frac{4}{9} & \frac{4}{9} & \frac{1}{9} \end{bmatrix} = P^\infty.$$

That is, all rows become the same. The interpretation of this is that, for the particular Markov chain in question, the probability of being in state j at time t approaches a certain definite value, p_j $(0 < p_j < 1)$, as t becomes large and that this long-run probability is independent of the initial state—that is, where the chain started. You are invited to experiment with higher powers of P than those exhibited in order to gauge the rapidity of approach to the limiting values presented.

In the last example it became clear after two steps that every state can be reached from every other state—that is, that $p_{ij}^{(t)} > 0$ for some t and all states i and j. In matrix terms, $P^t > 0$ where $t = 2$, meaning that all elements of the matrix are greater than zero as soon as $t = 2$. It is easy to see that all entries are then strictly positive for all $t > 2$.

DEFINITION 9.1.4. A transition matrix with the property that $P^t > 0$ for some $t = 1, 2, \ldots$ is said to be *regular*.

Regular transition matrices have interesting properties, among them being the property of (9.1.32); such chains will be studied in Section 9.3. We shall concern ourselves next with absorbing Markov chains, which have quite different characteristics.

DEFINITION 9.1.5. An *absorbing state* in a Markov chain is a state that, once entered, cannot be left and is occupied thereafter. That is, if i is an absorbing state, then for all $n > 0$,

$$(9.1.33) \quad P\{X_{t+n} = i, X_{t+n-1} = i, X_{t+n-2} = i, \ldots, X_t = i \mid X_{t-1} = i\} = 1.$$

In terms of the transition matrix, i is absorbing if and only if P has $p_{ii} = 1$, so that the main diagonal entry associated with row (column) i is unity.

EXAMPLE 9.1.7. Jim has two pennies, and Joe has one. They match pennies until one player gets all the pennies, and then they stop. It is intuitively clear, and may be proved formally, that this kind of game does actually come to a stop after a finite number of plays. It is easy to see that if X_t represents the number of pennies that Jim has, then

$$(9.1.34) \qquad \pi_0 = [0, 1, 0, 0],$$

and the one-step transition matrix is (you should convince yourself that $\{X_t\}$ is indeed a Markov chain)

(9.1.35)
$$P = \begin{matrix} & \begin{matrix} 0 & 1 & 2 & 3 \end{matrix} \\ \begin{matrix} 0 \\ 1 \\ 2 \\ 3 \end{matrix} & \begin{bmatrix} 1 & 0 & 0 & 0 \\ \frac{1}{2} & 0 & \frac{1}{2} & 0 \\ 0 & \frac{1}{2} & 0 & \frac{1}{2} \\ 0 & 0 & 0 & 1 \end{bmatrix} \end{matrix}.$$

Notice that there are two absorbing states, 0 and 3. Also, for every other state, there is a positive probability of reaching an absorbing state.

Chains of this type will be studied in detail in the next section.

EXAMPLE 9.1.8. Modify the previous example so that the game is charitable: whenever either player captures all the pennies, he gives one back on the next step and the game continues. The transition matrix now is

(9.1.36)
$$P = \begin{bmatrix} 0 & 1 & 0 & 0 \\ \frac{1}{2} & 0 & \frac{1}{2} & 0 \\ 0 & \frac{1}{2} & 0 & \frac{1}{2} \\ 0 & 0 & 1 & 0 \end{bmatrix}.$$

In this case, there are no absorbing states. We now ask, is this chain regular? The answer to this question may be easily seen to be no, as the following argument establishes. Suppose our chain starts out in an even-numbered state—that is, 0 or 2. Then on the next trial it must move to an odd state, since entries in the transition matrix that represent transitions to even states are zero.

(9.1.37)

(Here the asterisk denotes other probabilities, some positive.) Similarly, if one starts in an odd state, the next move must be to an even state. Thus if the chain starts in an even state at $t = 0$, it will be in an even state at $t = 2, 4, 6, \ldots$ and in an odd state at $t = 1, 3, 5, \ldots$. Consequently, there is no power of the matrix P, or equivalently no value of t, such that $P^t > 0$. Hence the chain cannot be regular. Since it is possible to return to any state in a minimum of two steps having started from that state, this chain is said to be *periodic of period 2*.

In order to conclude this section we will introduce the notion of a *fixed vector*. First observe that because the row sums of P are all unity, if we define f to be the r-component column vector with all components equal to 1, we have

(9.1.38) $$Pf = f.$$

That is, f is a fixed vector on the right of P. Our next theorem shows that P always has at least one fixed vector on the left as well.

THEOREM 9.1.2. There exists at least one probability vector w with $w \geq 0$ and $wf = 1$ such that

(9.1.39) $$wP = w.$$

Proof: We want to solve the following system of equations and inequalities where I represents the identity matrix (entries δ_{ij}, where $\delta_{ii} = 1$, $\delta_{ij} = 0$, $i \neq j$):

$$w(I - P) = 0, \quad wf = 1, \quad w \geq 0.$$

To this end, consider the following linear programming problem:

Min δ

Subject to:

(9.1.40)
$$\begin{aligned} w(I - P) + \delta e &\geq 0 \\ wf &= 1 \\ w &\geq 0 \end{aligned}$$

(Here e and f are row and column vectors with all components equal to 1.) At first glance this problem would not seem to lead to the desired result because the condition $w(I - P) + \delta e \geq 0$ does not seem as strong as the condition $w(I - P) = 0$. But we shall show that there is a solution having $\delta = 0$ and all except the last constraints satisfied as equalities.

Using the rules for the construction of the dual problem we obtain the dual to (9.1.40) as follows:

Max K

Subject to:

(9.1.41)
$$\begin{aligned} (I - P)x + Kf &\leq 0 \\ ex &= 1 \\ x &\geq 0 \end{aligned}$$

Note that the variables δ and K in these two dual problems are unconstrained since they correspond to equality constraints. Note also that both problems (9.1.40) and (9.1.41) have feasible solutions obtained by selecting any pair of probability vectors w and x and then adjusting δ and K suitably for feasibility in each problem. Hence the dual problems both have optimal solutions.

Suppose, then, that w, x, δ, and K are optimal solutions. By the duality theorem we know that $\delta = K$. Now consider the probability vector

$$(9.1.42) \qquad\qquad x^* = \frac{1}{r} f.$$

Clearly x^* is feasible by (9.1.38); thus, $\delta = K \geq 0$ at the optimum. In Exercise 11, you will be asked to show that necessarily $K \leq 0$ in all feasible solutions. Hence $\delta = K = 0$ at the optimum, and, in fact, the vector x^* is optimal for the maximizing problem. Because $x^* > 0$—that is, every component of x^* is positive—the theorem of the alternative implies that the constraints $w(I - P) \geq 0$ in (9.1.40) must be satisfied as equality constraints. It follows that the optimal solution w to the minimizing linear programming problem is the desired fixed vector on the left of P. This completes the proof of the theorem. Alternative proofs are provided in the references at the end of the chapter. The interpretation of the fixed vector is important and is given in a later section.

EXERCISES 9.1

1. The *transition diagram* of a Markov chain is a graph having a vertex for each state and an arc between each pair of states for which there is positive one-step transition probability. For instance, the transition matrix and diagram for Example 9.1.5 are as follows.

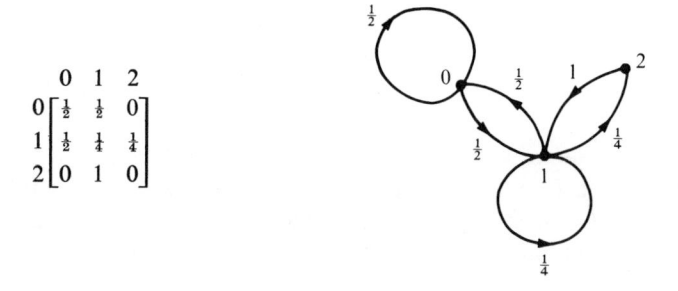

$$\begin{array}{c c c c} & 0 & 1 & 2 \\ 0 & \left[\tfrac{1}{2}\right. & \tfrac{1}{2} & 0 \\ 1 & \tfrac{1}{2} & \tfrac{1}{4} & \tfrac{1}{4} \\ 2 & 0 & 1 & \left.0\right] \end{array}$$

Draw the transition diagrams of the following Markov chains:

(a) $\begin{bmatrix} 0 & 1 & 0 \\ 1 & 0 & 0 \\ \tfrac{1}{3} & \tfrac{1}{3} & \tfrac{1}{3} \end{bmatrix}$

(b) $\begin{bmatrix} 0 & 1 \\ 1 & 0 \end{bmatrix}$

(c) $\begin{bmatrix} 0 & a & 1-a \\ b & 0 & 1-b \\ c & 1-c & 0 \end{bmatrix}$

(d) $\begin{bmatrix} 1 & 0 & 0 \\ 1 & 0 & 0 \\ 1 & 0 & 0 \end{bmatrix}$

2. Find the transition matrices of the Markov chains with the following transition diagrams.

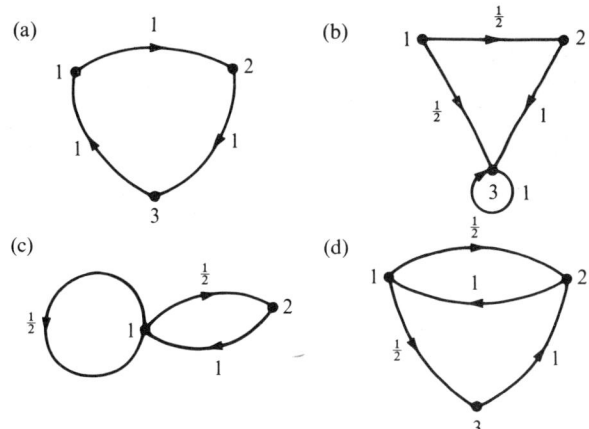

3. Change the rules for Example 9.1.5 as follows: if we draw a black ball, one-third of the time we put it back as is, and two-thirds of the time we paint it white before returning it. The rules for the white ball are unchanged. Set up the transition matrix of the new Markov chain.

4. A man is playing three slot machines. If he wins on one machine, he plays it again, but if he loses, he switches to one of the two others at random (with equal probabilities). Suppose the machines pay off with probabilities $\frac{1}{2}$, $\frac{1}{3}$, and $\frac{1}{4}$. Set up the matrix of transition probabilities.

5. Redo Exercise 4 if the three machines pay off with nonnegative probabilities a, b, and c.

6. A rat is put into a room in a maze as shown in the following diagram. During each time

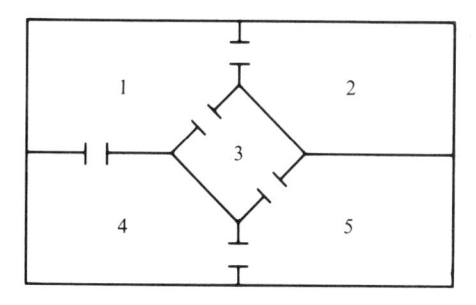

period, he selects one of the doors in the room he is in and leaves. Let the rooms be states, and set up the matrix of transition probabilities. Is the matrix regular?

7. In Exercise 6, suppose that initially the rat is put into room 1 and that food is put into room 5. The rat stays in the room having food whenever he reaches it. Set up the problem as a Markov chain. Is it an absorbing chain?

8. A man buys a stock at 10 and decides he will sell if the price drops to 8 or goes up to 14. Assume that each day the price of the stock either goes up by \$1, goes down by \$1, or stays the same. Let a be the probability it will go up and b the probability it will go down, where $0 < a + b < 1$. If $a > b$, we say that we are in an "up market," and if $a < b$, we say that we are in a "down market." Using the prices of the stock as states, set up the problem as an absorbing Markov chain.

9. Redo Example 9.1.7 with the rule that if Jim wins all three pennies, he returns one to Joe and the game continues, but if Joe wins all the pennies, the game ends. How do you think the game will end?

10. Set up a matching-pennies game as in Example 9.1.7, but let the total initial fortune of the two players be n pennies. This game is sometimes called a ruin game or a random walk.

*11. Let $x \geq 0$ be any nonnegative n-component column probability vector and let P be any $n \times n$ transition matrix of a Markov chain.
   (a) Let $M = \max_i x_i$; that is, let M be equal to the maximum component of x. Show that $x \leq Mf$, where f is the column vector of ones.
   (b) Use $P \geq 0$, $Pf = f$, to show that $Px \leq Mf$.
   (c) If $x_k = M = \max_i x_i$, and if $(Px)_k$ is the kth component of Px, show that $(Px)_k \leq M = x_k$.
   (d) Use (c) to show that $Px > x$ is always false.
   (e) Use (d) to show that the inequality $(I - P)x + Kf \leq 0$ can be true only if $K \leq 0$.

12. Consider the urn problem of Example 9.1.5. Find the fixed probability vector, w. (*Hint:* Use (9.1.39) and (9.1.18).) Compare w with the rows of (9.1.32). Speculate on the relation between P^t, as $t \to \infty$, and w.

13. There are two brands of cars on the market: The Ajax (A) and the Bomb (B). If a driver currently owns an A, the probability that he purchases an A as a replacement is p_A, while the probability that he purchases a B is $1 - p_A$. If, on the other hand, he owns a B, his next car is a B with probability p_B and an A with probability $1 - p_B$. Decisions are made only on the basis of the car currently being driven and are independent of the more remote past (for example, the car before last). Let $A_n = 1$ if a driver owns an A after he has owned exactly n cars (he is currently driving the nth); otherwise, $A_n = 0$.
   (a) Show that $\{A_n\}$ is a Markov chain.
   (b) Set up the transition matrix in terms of p_A and p_B.
   (c) Suppose $p_A = 0.5$ and $p_B = 0.8$. Imagine that a driver's first car is type A. What is the probability that his third car is type A? What is the probability that his first three cars are all A's?
   (d) Criticize the model above. (*Hint:* Is it likely that all drivers have the same probabilities p_A and p_B? What difference does this make?)

14. Write down the fixed probability vector for the Markov chain of the previous exercise.

15. Generalize the model of Exercise 13 to include memory of the car presently driven and its immediate predecessor. That is, introduce transition probabilities $r_{AA}, \ldots, r_{BB}$ as follows:

Car Before Last	Present Car	Probability of A Next
A	A	r_{AA}
A	B	r_{AB}
B	A	r_{BA}
B	B	r_{BB}

   (a) Show that if we let X_n assume states

$$1: AA = \text{Present Car } A, \text{ Car Before Last } A,$$
$$2: AB = \text{Present Car } B, \text{ Car Before Last } A,$$
$$3: BA = \text{Present Car } A, \text{ Car Before Last } B,$$
$$4: BB = \text{Present Car } B, \text{ Car Before Last } B,$$

then $\{X_n\}$ is a Markov chain.

(b) Suppose P is the one-step transition matrix of the Markov chain of (a) above. How would you calculate the probability that a driver's fourth car is type A? In answering this question, assume that an A is initially selected with probability 0.5, and then the one-step model of Exercise 13 is used to determine the second type purchased.

9.2 ABSORBING MARKOV CHAINS

We shall concentrate first on a special kind of Markov chains called absorbing Markov chains. Later we will find that results from absorbing chains can be applied to other kinds of chains.

DEFINITION 9.2.1. An *absorbing Markov chain* is a chain with transition matrix P having the following properties:

(a) There is at least one absorbing state.

(b) From every state it is possible to go to an absorbing state (in one or more steps).

The nonabsorbing states are said to be *transient states*.

By the *canonical form* for the transition matrix of an absorbing Markov chain, we shall mean the matrix written with the absorbing states listed first and the transient states last. Suppose there are s absorbing states. Then the canonical form for P is as follows:

(9.2.1)

$$P = \begin{array}{c} \\ s\ \{ \\ \\ r-s\ \{ \end{array} \begin{array}{c} \overbrace{s}^{\textit{Absorbing}} \quad \overbrace{r-s}^{\textit{Transient}} \\ \left[\begin{array}{c|c} I & O \\ \hline R & Q \end{array} \right] \end{array}$$

EXAMPLE 9.2.1. Let us put the absorbing chain of Example 9.1.7 into canonical form. The absorbing states are 0 and 3, so they are listed first; then states 1 and 2 are listed. We have

$$P = \begin{array}{c} \\ 0 \\ 3 \\ 1 \\ 2 \end{array} \begin{array}{cccc} 0 & 3 & 1 & 2 \end{array} \\ \left[\begin{array}{cc|cc} 1 & 0 & 0 & 0 \\ 0 & 1 & 0 & 0 \\ \hline \frac{1}{2} & 0 & 0 & \frac{1}{2} \\ 0 & \frac{1}{2} & \frac{1}{2} & 0 \end{array} \right].$$

From this canonical form we observe that the matrices Q and R of (9.2.1) are:

$$Q = \begin{bmatrix} 0 & \frac{1}{2} \\ \frac{1}{2} & 0 \end{bmatrix} \qquad R = \begin{bmatrix} \frac{1}{2} & 0 \\ 0 & \frac{1}{2} \end{bmatrix}.$$

These matrices will be important in later analysis of absorbing chains.

THEOREM 9.2.1. The probability that an absorbing Markov chain, having started in a transient state, is still in some transient state after n steps tends to 0 as n tends to infinity.

Proof: For each transient state s_j there is a least positive integer n_j such that the chain can move to an absorbing state in n_j steps. Let N be the largest of the n_j's. (N is a definite positive number since there are r states.) Then no matter which transient state the chain is started in, it can reach an absorbing state in N or fewer steps. Thus there is a number $p < 1$ such that the probability of being in a transient state N steps after starting in a transient state is at most p. But then the probability of being in a transient state after $2N$ steps is at most p^2, the probability of being in a transient state after $3N$ steps is at most p^3, and so on. Since $p < 1$, the probability of being in a transient state after n steps tends to 0 as n tends to infinity. In fact, our argument proves that the probability of being in a transient state after n steps tends to zero at a *geometric rate*:

$$q_{ij}^{(n)} \leq p^{(n-1)/N} \qquad \text{for } n \geq 2N.$$

COROLLARY. The matrix Q^n tends to the zero matrix as n tends to infinity.

Proof: Because of the canonical form (9.2.1), it is easy to see that

$$P^n = \begin{bmatrix} I & O \\ * & Q^n \end{bmatrix},$$

where the $*$ entry in the lower left-hand corner is a complicated expression involving Q and R. By Theorem 9.1.1, the entries of P^n give the probabilities of being in each of the states after n steps have elapsed, conditional on starting in a specified state. Thus Q^n gives the probability of being in each of the transient states (j) n steps after having started in each of these states (i). Since the Theorem 9.2.1 showed that these probabilities must tend to 0, we see that each entry in the matrix Q^n tends to 0; that is, Q^n tends to the $(r - s) \times (r - s)$ zero matrix, as was to be shown.

EXAMPLE 9.2.1 (continued). It is obvious that

$$Q^n = \begin{bmatrix} \dfrac{1}{2^n} & 0 \\ 0 & \dfrac{1}{2^n} \end{bmatrix} \text{ if } n \text{ is even} \quad \text{and} \quad Q^n = \begin{bmatrix} 0 & \dfrac{1}{2^n} \\ \dfrac{1}{2^n} & 0 \end{bmatrix} \text{ if } n \text{ is odd;}$$

from this it follows that $Q^n \to 0$ for this example.

DEFINITION 9.2.2. The *fundamental matrix* of an absorbing Markov chain is the matrix:

(9.2.2) $$N = (I - Q)^{-1} = I + Q + Q^2 + \cdots + Q^k + \cdots.$$

The *discounted fundamental matrix* for discount factor λ ($0 \leq \lambda \leq 1$) is the matrix:

(9.2.3) $$N = (I - \lambda Q)^{-1} = I + \lambda Q + \lambda^2 Q^2 + \cdots + \lambda^k Q^k + \cdots.$$

For these definitions to make sense, we must prove that the matrix $I - \lambda Q$ has an inverse for $\lambda \leq 1$, that the series on the right of (9.2.2) and (9.2.3) converge, and that the stated equalities are correct. We establish these facts in the next theorem.

THEOREM 9.2.2. For any number $0 \leq \lambda \leq 1$, the matrix $(I - \lambda Q)$ is nonsingular, and formula (9.2.3) holds. When $\lambda = 1$, (9.2.3) becomes (9.2.2).

Proof: The following identity can be established by multiplying out the right-hand side:

$$(9.2.4) \qquad I - \lambda^{n+1} Q^{n+1} = (I - \lambda Q)(I + \lambda Q + \lambda^2 Q^2 + \cdots + \lambda^n Q^n).$$

For large n, the left-hand side of (9.2.4) is a nonsingular matrix since it becomes arbitrarily close to the identity matrix. Hence, the right-hand side is also a nonsingular matrix. By Exercise 19 of Exercise set 2.5, both matrices on the right-hand side of (9.2.4) must be nonsingular. Multiplying through that equation by $(I - \lambda Q)^{-1}$, we have

$$(I - \lambda Q)^{-1}(I - \lambda^{n+1} Q^{n+1}) = I + \lambda Q + \lambda^2 Q^2 + \cdots + \lambda^n Q^n.$$

Now the left-hand side of this equality has a limit, namely $(I - \lambda Q)^{-1}$, so the right-hand side also has a limit, which is the same. Hence (9.2.3) holds.

EXAMPLE 9.2.1 (continued). The fundamental matrix for the absorbing chain is

$$(I - Q)^{-1} = \begin{bmatrix} 1 & -\frac{1}{2} \\ -\frac{1}{2} & 1 \end{bmatrix}^{-1} = \begin{bmatrix} \frac{4}{3} & \frac{2}{3} \\ \frac{2}{3} & \frac{4}{3} \end{bmatrix}.$$

Later we shall give interpretations for each of these numbers.

So far we have only made use of the square matrix Q. We now turn to the $(r - s) \times s$ matrix R. The entries of this matrix give the probabilities of moving during each time period from the transient to the absorbing states.

THEOREM 9.2.3. (a) The entries of matrix $Q^n R$ are the probabilities of reaching each of the absorbing states at step $n + 1$, given that the process starts in a transient state.

(b) The matrix $\pi_0 Q^n R$ gives the probability of absorption in each absorbing state at step $n + 1$, given that the initial vector was π_0.

Proof: As remarked in the proof of the above Corollary, the entries of Q^n give the probabilities of being in each of the transient states at time n, given that the process started in each of the transient states. The entries of matrix R give the conditional probabilities that the process moves to an absorbing state, given that it is in one of the transient states. Consider the entries of $Q^n R$. A typical one is

$$(9.2.5) \qquad a_{ik} = \sum_{j=1}^{r-s} q_{ij}^{(n)} r_{jk}.$$

The product $q_{ij}^{(n)} r_{jk}$ is the probability that the chain reaches transient state j on step n and then ends up at absorbing state k on step $n + 1$, *given* that it initially was in transient state i. Clearly the event that the last transient visit is to j cannot occur simultaneously with a last visit to $j' \neq j$. We are dealing with mutually exclusive events, and hence the sum above is the unconditional probability of moving from i to k in exactly $n + 1$ steps. Thus the entries of $Q^n R$ have the interpretation stated in (a) of the theorem.

Part (b) follows from the interpretation of π_0.

EXAMPLE 9.2.1 (continued). It is easy to calculate matrices such as the following:

$$QR = \begin{bmatrix} 0 & \frac{1}{2} \\ \frac{1}{2} & 0 \end{bmatrix} \begin{bmatrix} \frac{1}{2} & 0 \\ 0 & \frac{1}{2} \end{bmatrix} = \begin{bmatrix} 0 & \frac{1}{4} \\ \frac{1}{4} & 0 \end{bmatrix}.$$

$$Q^2 R = \begin{bmatrix} \frac{1}{4} & 0 \\ 0 & \frac{1}{4} \end{bmatrix} \begin{bmatrix} \frac{1}{2} & 0 \\ 0 & \frac{1}{2} \end{bmatrix} = \begin{bmatrix} \frac{1}{8} & 0 \\ 0 & \frac{1}{8} \end{bmatrix}.$$

$$Q^3 R = \begin{bmatrix} 0 & \frac{1}{8} \\ \frac{1}{8} & 0 \end{bmatrix} \begin{bmatrix} \frac{1}{2} & 0 \\ 0 & \frac{1}{2} \end{bmatrix} = \begin{bmatrix} 0 & \frac{1}{16} \\ \frac{1}{16} & 0 \end{bmatrix}.$$

Let us interpret the last matrix. The states involved are marked below:

$$\begin{array}{c} \quad\quad 0 \quad\; 3 \\ \begin{matrix} 1 \\ 2 \end{matrix} \begin{bmatrix} 0 & \frac{1}{16} \\ \frac{1}{16} & 0 \end{bmatrix}. \end{array}$$

Hence if Jim initially has one penny, there is probability $\frac{1}{16}$ that he will win all the pennies in exactly four matches of the pennies, and probability 0 that he will lose all his money in exactly four matches.

THEOREM 9.2.4. (a) The entries of the matrix

(9.2.6) $$NR = R + QR + Q^2 R + \cdots + Q^n R + \cdots$$

give the absorption probabilities of moving from each of the transient states to each of the absorbing states in *any number* of steps.

(b) The entries of $\pi_0 NR$ are the absorption probabilities, given the starting vector π_0.

Proof: (a) follows by adding up the terms $Q^n R$, for $n = 0, 1, \ldots$, given by Theorem 9.2.3(a); (b) follows similarly.

EXAMPLE 9.2.1 (continued). For the matching pennies example,

$$NR = \begin{bmatrix} \frac{4}{3} & \frac{2}{3} \\ \frac{2}{3} & \frac{4}{3} \end{bmatrix} \begin{bmatrix} \frac{1}{2} & 0 \\ 0 & \frac{1}{2} \end{bmatrix} = \begin{bmatrix} \frac{2}{3} & \frac{1}{3} \\ \frac{1}{3} & \frac{2}{3} \end{bmatrix}.$$

If we mark the states we have

$$\begin{array}{c} \quad\quad 0 \quad\; 3 \\ \begin{matrix} 1 \\ 2 \end{matrix} \begin{bmatrix} \frac{2}{3} & \frac{1}{3} \\ \frac{1}{3} & \frac{2}{3} \end{bmatrix}. \end{array}$$

Hence, if Jim has one penny initially, his chances of ruin—that is, of ending in state 0—are $\frac{2}{3}$, and his chances of ruining Joe are $\frac{1}{3}$. But if he starts with initial fortune of two pennies, these probabilities are reversed.

THEOREM 9.2.5. The entries of the fundamental matrix N give the mean number of times before absorption that the process is in each transient state, given that it started in each of the transient states.

Proof: Let n_{ij} be the mean or expected number of times the process is in transient state s_j, given that it started in transient state s_i. If we take into account the original state, then the n_{ij} must satisfy

(9.2.7)
$$n_{ij} = d_{ij} + \sum_k p_{ik} n_{kj},$$

where the summation is over the transient states and the quantity d_{ij} is 1 if $i = j$ and 0 otherwise, since we must count the fact that we started in a transient state. Written in matrix form, the equation is

(9.2.8)
$$N = I + QN$$

or

$$(I - Q)N = I \text{ and } N = (I - Q)^{-1},$$

as was to be shown.

COROLLARY. Let f be the $r \times 1$ vector whose components are all 1's. Then the entries of Nf give the mean number of steps before absorption, given that the process starts in each of the transient states.

Proof: The vector f merely sums the entries of N so that its interpretation is obvious.

EXAMPLE 9.2.1 (continued). We had

$$N = \begin{matrix} & 0 & 3 \\ 1 \\ 2 \end{matrix} \begin{bmatrix} \frac{4}{3} & \frac{2}{3} \\ \frac{2}{3} & \frac{4}{3} \end{bmatrix}.$$

Hence if Jim starts with one penny, it will take about $\frac{4}{3}$ steps for him to lose it or $\frac{2}{3}$ steps for him to win (if he wins). Similarly,

$$Nf = \begin{bmatrix} \frac{4}{3} & \frac{2}{3} \\ \frac{2}{3} & \frac{4}{3} \end{bmatrix} \begin{bmatrix} 1 \\ 1 \end{bmatrix} = \begin{matrix} 1 \\ 2 \end{matrix} \begin{bmatrix} 2 \\ 2 \end{bmatrix},$$

so the expected number of matches before one or the other of the players is ruined is 2.

We have not yet given an interpretation for the discounted fundamental matrix N_λ. To do this we need a new definition.

DEFINITION 9.2.3. Let F be an $r \times 1$ column matrix; the ith entry, F_i, is the *payoff* when the process is absorbed in absorbing state i. Similarly, let $F^{(k)}$ be a series of payoff vectors for $k = 1, 2, \ldots, n, \ldots$, where $F_i^{(k)}$ gives the payoff if the process is absorbed in absorbing state i at time k. Vectors F and $F^{(k)}$ are called *absorption payoff vectors*.

EXAMPLE 9.2.2. Jim and Joe found a quarter when walking down the street. They agree to play the matching pennies game of Example 9.2.1 and the quarter goes to the winner of that game. Here the absorption payoff vector for Jim is

$$F = \begin{matrix} 0 \\ 3 \end{matrix} \begin{bmatrix} 0 \\ 25 \end{bmatrix},$$

since we are denoting the states by Jim's fortune.

THEOREM 9.2.6. (a) If there is a discount factor $\lambda \leq 1$ and an absorption payoff vector F, then the entries of $N_\lambda RF$ give the expected discounted return from the Markov chain, given we started in each of the transient states.

(b) If there is a discount factor λ and absorption payoff vectors $F^{(k)}$, then, provided the following infinite series of matrices converges, the entries u_i of the vector

$$(9.2.9) \qquad U = RF^{(0)} + \lambda QRF^{(1)} + \lambda^2 Q^2 RF^{(2)} + \cdots + \lambda^n Q^n RF^{(n)} + \cdots$$

give the expected payoffs from the Markov chain, given that it was started in each of the transient states.

Proofs: Exercises 6 and 7.

EXAMPLE 9.2.2 (continued). Suppose we take $\lambda = 1$; then

$$N_1 RF = \begin{bmatrix} \frac{4}{3} & \frac{2}{3} \\ \frac{2}{3} & \frac{4}{3} \end{bmatrix} \begin{bmatrix} \frac{1}{2} & 0 \\ 0 & \frac{1}{2} \end{bmatrix} \begin{bmatrix} 0 \\ 25 \end{bmatrix},$$

$$= \begin{bmatrix} \frac{2}{3} & \frac{1}{3} \\ \frac{1}{3} & \frac{2}{3} \end{bmatrix} \begin{bmatrix} 0 \\ 25 \end{bmatrix},$$

$$= \begin{bmatrix} \frac{25}{3} \\ \frac{50}{3} \end{bmatrix}.$$

Hence Jim's expectation is $8\frac{1}{3}¢$ if he starts playing the game with one penny, and it rises to $16\frac{2}{3}¢$ if he starts the game with two pennies.

EXAMPLE 9.2.3. A building contractor has committed himself to finish a building in 40 weeks. For each week required in excess of 40, he is penalized $100. He knows that he can't finish before week 40 and that he is certain to finish by week 45. From weeks 40 to 45, he figures that his chances of finishing each week start at 0.5 and go up by 0.1 each week. Using weeks as states, the transition matrix is as follows.

	1	0	0	0	0	0	0	0	0	0	0	0
End 40	1	0	0	0	0	0	0	0	0	0	0	0
End 41	0	1	0	0	0	0	0	0	0	0	0	0
End 42	0	0	1	0	0	0	0	0	0	0	0	0
End 43	0	0	0	1	0	0	0	0	0	0	0	0
End 44	0	0	0	0	1	0	0	0	0	0	0	0
End 45	0	0	0	0	0	1	0	0	0	0	0	0
40	.5	0	0	0	0	0	0	.5	0	0	0	0
41	0	.6	0	0	0	0	0	0	.4	0	0	0
42	0	0	.7	0	0	0	0	0	0	.3	0	0
43	0	0	0	.8	0	0	0	0	0	0	.2	0
44	0	0	0	0	.9	0	0	.0	0	0	0	.1
45	0	0	0	0	0	1	0	0	0	0	0	0

The absorption payoff vector is as follows.

$$F = \begin{bmatrix} 0 \\ -100 \\ -200 \\ -300 \\ -400 \\ -500 \end{bmatrix}$$

Let us work the problem with $\lambda = 1$. The $I - Q$ matrix is:

$$I - Q = \begin{bmatrix} 1 & -.5 & 0 & 0 & 0 & 0 \\ 0 & 1 & -.4 & 0 & 0 & 0 \\ 0 & 0 & 1 & -.3 & 0 & 0 \\ 0 & 0 & 0 & 1 & -.2 & 0 \\ 0 & 0 & 0 & 0 & 1 & -.1 \\ 0 & 0 & 0 & 0 & 0 & 1 \end{bmatrix}.$$

From this we have (see Exercise 4)

$$N = (I - Q)^{-1} = \begin{bmatrix} 1 & .5 & .2 & .06 & .012 & .0012 \\ 0 & 1 & .4 & .12 & .024 & .0024 \\ 0 & 0 & 1 & .3 & .06 & .006 \\ 0 & 0 & 0 & 1 & .2 & .02 \\ 0 & 0 & 0 & 0 & 1 & .1 \\ 0 & 0 & 0 & 0 & 0 & 1 \end{bmatrix}.$$

Upon calculating NRF we have

$$NRF = \begin{matrix} 40 \\ 41 \\ 42 \\ 43 \\ 44 \\ 45 \end{matrix} \begin{bmatrix} -77.32 \\ -154.64 \\ -236.6 \\ -322.0 \\ -410.0 \\ -500.0 \end{bmatrix}.$$

These give the expected payoffs, given that the process is in each of the transient states. They can be interpreted as the contractor's expected loss, given he is in each of the states.

     It is worth mentioning at this point that computer programs can be written rather easily for evaluating the various matrix quantities, such as N, NR, and U, that have been derived. This greatly eases numerical computations.

     You will notice that the matrix techniques that have been used are especially convenient when the Markov transition probabilities are given as numbers. In some problems it is instructive and useful to consider the entries as *parameters* and find explicit simple solutions in terms of these parameters. The parameters can then be given numerical values at will, if desired. Although such parametric analysis can be carried out in terms of the matrices, an alternative approach will now be described. The description will be in terms of a simple Markov chain that allows transition to neighboring states only.

DEFINITION 9.2.4. A *random walk* is a Markov chain whose one-step transitions are as follows:

(9.2.10)
$$p_{ij} = \begin{cases} p_i & \text{if } j = i+1 \\ r_i & \text{if } j = i \\ q_i & \text{if } j = i-1 \end{cases}$$

where $p_i + r_i + q_i = 1$ and $p_i, r_i, q_i \geq 0$; otherwise $p_{ij} = 0$. A *spatially homogeneous random walk* is a random walk for which p_i, r_i, and q_i are independent of i.

EXAMPLE 9.2.4. The cash balance of a particular lending institution fluctuates up and down in \$1000 units each week. If the balance is i at week n it reaches $i+1$ the next week with probability p_i, remains the same with probability r_i, and falls by one unit with probability q_i. If the balance reaches zero, the company is without cash, or (temporarily) *ruined*, whereas if it reaches I, it never goes higher: any gain beyond that point is invested in interest-bearing securities. We thus have the boundary conditions $p_0 = 0$, $r_0 = 1$, $q_0 = 0$, meaning that zero is an absorbing state, while $p_I = 0$ and $r_I + q_I = 1$. The state I is absorbing if $r_I = 1$, whereas if $q_I > 0$, and hence $r_I < 1$, the state I is *reflecting*. This means that if the stochastic process reaches I it goes no higher, but eventually jumps back to $I - 1$ and perhaps to lower states.

We shall now show how to calculate the probability of ruin for the company. Suppose the chain is initially in state i, and let ρ_i be the probability that state 0 is reached before state I. If the initial state is i, then experience in the next time period reveals *either* a gain of one unit with probability ρ_i, from which the probability of ruin is ρ_{i+1}, *or* no change with probability r_i, from which state ruin follows with probability ρ_i, *or* a decline to $i - 1$ with probability q_i, and subsequent ruin with probability ρ_{i-1}. Addition of the probabilities of these mutually exclusive events furnishes a *difference equation* for ρ_i:

(9.2.11) $\rho_i = p_i \rho_{i+1} + r_i \rho_i + q_i \rho_{i-1}$ $i = 1, 2, \ldots, I - 1$

subject to the boundary conditions $\rho_0 = 1$, $\rho_I = 0$. Now since $r_i = 1 - p_i - q_i$, the equation above may be rewritten as follows:

$$p_i(\rho_{i+1} - \rho_i) = q_i(\rho_i - \rho_{i-1}).$$

Therefore

$$\rho_1 - \rho_0 = (\rho_1 - \rho_0),$$

$$\rho_2 - \rho_1 = \frac{q_1}{p_1}(\rho_1 - \rho_0),$$

(9.2.12)

$$\rho_3 - \rho_2 = \frac{q_2}{p_2}(\rho_2 - \rho_1) = \frac{q_1 q_2}{p_1 p_2}(\rho_1 - \rho_0),$$

$$\cdots$$

$$\rho_i - \rho_{i-1} = \frac{q_{i-1}}{p_{i-1}}(\rho_{i-1} - \rho_{i-2}) = \frac{q_1 q_2 \cdots q_{i-1}}{p_1 p_2 \cdots p_{i-1}}(\rho_1 - \rho_2).$$

Next add the left-hand sides above and take note of the cancellations:

(9.2.13)
$$\rho_i - \rho_0 = \sum_{j=0}^{i-1} \pi_j (\rho_1 - \rho_0)$$

where

$$\pi_j = \frac{q_1 q_2 \cdots q_j}{p_1 p_2 \cdots p_j} \qquad j = 1, 2, \ldots, I$$

and

(9.2.14)
$$\pi_0 = 1.$$

Now introduce the boundary conditions and observe that

(9.2.15)
$$\rho_I - \rho_0 = -1 = \sum_{j=0}^{I-1} \pi_j (\rho_1 - \rho_0) = \sum_{j=0}^{I-1} \pi_j (\rho_1 - 1).$$

Thus

(9.2.16)
$$1 - \rho_1 = \left[\sum_{j=0}^{I-1} \pi_j \right]^{-1},$$

and finally

(9.2.17)
$$1 - \rho_i = \frac{\sum_{j=0}^{i-1} \pi_j}{\sum_{j=0}^{I-1} \pi_j},$$

which determines ρ_i in terms of the one-step transition probabilities p_i and q_i.

In Exercise 13, you will be asked to consider a special case of this result.

EXERCISES 9.2

1. Put the transition matrix of Exercise 7 of the previous section in canonical form. Find and interpret the quantities N, NR, and Nf.

2. Do the same for Exercise 8 of the previous section with $a = b = 1/4$.

3. Assume Q is an upper triangular matrix; that is, it has all zero entries on and below the main diagonal.
   (a) Show that Q^2 has zeros on the diagonal above the main diagonal.
   (b) Show $Q^r = 0$.
   (c) Show that $N = I + Q + Q^2 + \cdots + Q^{r-1}$.

4. Use Exercise 4 to calculate N for Example 9.2.3.

5. Prove Theorem 9.2.6 (a).

6. Prove Theorem 9.2.6 (b).

7. A man buys a store that yields profits of $1000 (low) or $2000 (high) each month. He may sell his store at any time but he has decided to sell with probability 0.2 during a high-profit month and probability 0.5 during a low-profit month. If he does not sell and the profits are high, there is probability 1/2 that they will be high the following month, and if profits are low, there is probability 3/4 they will be low the following month.
   (a) Set up the process as a Markov chain. (*Hint:* There are two transient states and two absorbing states.)
   (b) Compute N and NR and interpret.

8. Let P be the transition matrix of an absorbing Markov chain. Suppose that when the process is in transient state i, a reward G_i is obtained. Let G be the column vector of rewards.
   (a) Show that the expected reward before being absorbed is given by $NG = G + QG + Q^2G + \cdots$.
   (b) Show that the expected discounted reward before selling is given by $N_\lambda G = G + \lambda QG + \lambda^2 Q^2 G + \cdots$, where λ is the discount factor.
   (c) Apply this to obtain the value of owning the store in Exercise 7. Assume $\lambda = 0.1$.

9. In Exercise 8, suppose we also obtain the reward F when the process is absorbed as in Theorem 9.2.6.
   (a) Show that the total expected reward is given by $NG + NRF = N(G + RF)$.
   (b) Show that the total expected discounted reward is given by

$$N_\lambda(G + RF).$$

   (c) Apply this to Exercise 8 if the selling price of the store is $10,000 in a low-profit month and $20,000 in a high-profit month. Assume $\lambda = 0.1$.

10. A certain stock has a highly erratic behavior concerning its dividend payments, and dividends are frequently skipped. However, if the dividend is skipped one year it is certain to be paid the next year; and if the dividend is paid in a given year, there is only one chance out of four that it will be paid the following year. When paid, the dividends are $1 per share.
    (a) A particular owner of the stock has probability $\frac{1}{4}$ of selling the stock in a year in which a dividend is not paid and probability $\frac{2}{3}$ of selling it in a year in which the dividend is paid. Set up a three-state Markov chain to represent his actions.
    (b) Compute N and NR and interpret.
    (c) Calculate the expected, discounted reward before being absorbed as $N_\lambda G$, where $\lambda = 0.1$.
    (d) If the price of the stock is $20 in a year in which the dividend is not paid and $35 in a year in which the dividend is paid, calculate the total expected discounted reward from $N_\lambda(G + RF)$, using $\lambda = 0.1$.

11. Prove the following identities.
    (a) $NQ = N - I$
    (b) $QN = N - I$
    (c) $NQ = QN$
    (d) $R + QNR = NR$.

12. Assume (for computational convenience) that married couples have only three fertile years during which they can have children, that they have at most one child in a given year, and that there is no infant mortality. Consider such couples to be in a state described by a pair (y, n), where $y = 0, 1, 2, 3$ gives the year (with 0, 1, 2 representing the fertile years and 3 representing the first and all subsequent infertile years) and n represents the number of children they have. The possible states are then $(0, 0)$, $(1, 0)$, $(2, 0)$, $(3, 0)$, $(1, 1)$, $(2, 1)$, $(3, 1)$, $(2, 2)$, $(3, 2)$, and $(3, 3)$.
    (a) Regard the states with $y = 3$ to be absorbing states and set up a Markov chain to describe the child-bearing behavior. Show that it is an absorbing Markov chain. Put x's for nonzero transition probabilities.
    (b) Identify the Q and R matrices.
    (c) Give interpretations for the entries of the fundamental matrix $N = (I - Q)^{-1}$.
    (d) Give interpretations for Nf.
    (e) Give interpretations for NR.

(f) Suppose you considered 10,000 marriages. If you have the numerical entries in the transition matrix, how can you predict the distribution of numbers of children that will eventually be produced by these couples?

(g) How would infant mortality affect the analysis?

13. Consider the ruin problem of Example 9.2.4.

(a) Show that when $p_i = p$ and $q_i = q$, the probability of ruin is given by

$$\rho_i = 1 - \frac{1 - (q/p)^i}{1 - (q/p)^I}.$$

(b) What is the form of ρ_i when $p = q$? (*Hint:* Either start from scratch by modifying (9.2.12) or apply L'Hospital's rule to the result of (a).)

(c) Find the probability that the random walk reaches the value I before it reaches 0. Show that the walk is absorbed in one boundary or the other eventually (assuming that I is absorbing).

14. Again consider Example 9.2.4. Let z_i denote the expected time (number of steps) until the random walk reaches state 0.

(a) Show that z_i satisfies the difference equation

$$z_i = 1 + p_i z_{i+1} + r_i z_i + q_i z_{i-1} \qquad i = 1, 2, \ldots, I - 1.$$

(b) Use the boundary conditions $z_0 = 0$ and $r_I > 0$ and solve for z_i.

9.3 REGULAR MARKOV CHAINS

We turn now to the class of regular Markov chains. We shall find that some interesting questions concerning regular chains can be answered using the theory of absorbing chains just developed.

DEFINITION 9.3.1. A Markov chain with transition matrix P is said to be a *regular Markov chain* if there exists a positive integer N such that

(9.3.1) $$P^N > 0;$$

that is, all entries of P^N are positive.

EXAMPLE 9.3.1. Consider the following transition matrix:

$$P = \begin{bmatrix} 0 & 1 & 0 \\ 0 & 0 & 1 \\ \frac{2}{3} & \frac{1}{3} & 0 \end{bmatrix}$$

To see if it is a regular chain, it is sufficient just to determine which entries in P^k are positive, not their values. Hence we consider the matrix

$$P = \begin{bmatrix} 0 & X & 0 \\ 0 & 0 & X \\ X & X & 0 \end{bmatrix},$$

where the X stands for a positive entry. Then we have

$$P^2 = \begin{bmatrix} 0 & 0 & X \\ X & X & 0 \\ 0 & X & X \end{bmatrix},$$

$$P^4 = \begin{bmatrix} 0 & X & X \\ X & X & X \\ X & X & X \end{bmatrix},$$

$$P^5 = \begin{bmatrix} X & X & X \\ X & X & X \\ X & X & X \end{bmatrix},$$

so that $P^5 > 0$ and P is regular.

It can be shown that if $P^{r^2 - 2r + 2}$ is not positive, then no higher power is either. The proof is too detailed to give here. But the result shows that not all powers of P need to be considered in order to determine whether it is regular.

We know from Theorem 9.1.2 that P has at least one fixed vector on the left. The next two theorems show that the fixed vector for a regular chain is unique and provides further characterizations of the chain.

THEOREM 9.3.1. Let $P > 0$ be a transition matrix and x an arbitrary r-component column vector. Then $P^n x \to k_x f$, where f is the r-component column vector with all 1's, and k_x is a constant that depends on x.

Proof: Let m_0 and M_0 be the minimum and maximum components of x. Let d be the minimum entry in P. By Exercise 6 of this section, we have $\frac{1}{2} \ge d > 0$. Let m_1 and M_1 be the minimum and maximum components of Px. Then clearly

$$(9.3.2) \qquad M_1 \le dm_0 + (1 - d)M_0,$$

since the components of the vector Px are an average of the components of x, and the largest average is obtained by weighting the smallest component the least and the largest component the most. By the same reasoning,

$$(9.3.3) \qquad m_1 \ge (1 - d)m_0 + dM_0.$$

(For a formal demonstration see Exercise 20.)

The two inequalities (9.3.2) and (9.3.3) imply

$$(9.3.4) \qquad M_1 - m_1 \le (1 - 2d)(M_0 - m_0).$$

By repeating this analysis, if m_n and M_n are the minimum and maximum entries of $P^n x$, we have

$$(9.3.5) \qquad M_n - m_n \le (1 - 2d)^n (M_0 - m_0).$$

Now since $0 < d \le \frac{1}{2}$, we have $0 \le 1 - 2d < 1$, and we see that $M_n - m_n \to 0$ as $n \to \infty$. Hence the components of $P^n x$ converge to the same number k_x. In other words, $P^n x \to k_x f$, as was to be shown.

THEOREM 9.3.2. Let P be a regular transition matrix and w an arbitrary fixed vector on the left (whose existence is ensured by Theorem 9.1.2). Then

(a) $w > 0$;

(b)   if f_j is the r-component column vector with 1 in the jth row and zeros elsewhere, then $P^n f_j \to w_j$;

(c)   let $W = fw$; then $P^n \to W$;

(d)   if u is any row probability vector, then $uP^n \to w$;

(e)   the fixed vector w is unique;

(f) $WP = PW = W$.

Proof: We prove this theorem for $P > 0$. The extension to arbitrary regular P's is given in Exercise 5.

(a) From Theorem 9.1.2, we have $w \geq 0$. By hypothesis, $P > 0$, hence $w = wP > 0$.

(b) Let f_i be a column vector with 1 in the ith place and 0's elsewhere. Then by Theorem 9.3.1, we have $P^n f_i \to k_i f$. Hence $w_i = wf_i = (wP^n)f_i = w(P^n f_i) \to w(k_i f) = k_i(wf) = k_i$ so that $k_i = w_i$.

(c) By (b) we know that $P^n f_i \to w_i f$. But $P^n f_i$ is the ith column of P^n and $w_i f$ is a constant column vector all of whose components are w_i. The matrix $W = fw$ is the matrix formed from these columns. Hence $P^n \to W$. In other words, $p_{ij}^{(n)} \to w_j$ for any initial state i. Hence w_j is the *long-run* probability that the chain will be observed in state j.

(d) Let u be any probability vector. Then $uP^n \to uW = (uf)w = w$.

(e) Suppose w' were another fixed vector. Then $w'P^n = w' \to w'$. But $w'P^n \to w$ by (d). Hence $w' = w$.

The proof of (f) is Exercise 2.

EXAMPLE 9.3.1 (continued). Let us find the unique fixed vector of

$$P = \begin{bmatrix} 0 & 1 & 0 \\ 0 & 0 & 1 \\ \frac{2}{3} & \frac{1}{3} & 0 \end{bmatrix}.$$

Let $w = [w_1, w_2, w_3]$. The equations $wP = w$, or $w(P - I) = 0$, together with $wf = 1$ give

(a) $-w_1 \qquad\quad + \frac{2}{3}w_3 = 0,$

(b) $\quad w_1 - w_2 + \frac{1}{3}w_3 = 0,$

(c) $\qquad\quad w_2 - w_3 = 0,$

(d) $\quad w_1 + w_2 + w_3 = 1.$

We have four equations in three unknowns. It is easy to show that the solution is

$$w = [2/8, \ 3/8, \ 3/8].$$

Let us take powers of P, using an electronic computer. Some of them are as follows.

$$P^5 = \begin{bmatrix} .222 & .111 & .667 \\ .444 & .444 & .111 \\ .074 & .481 & .444 \end{bmatrix}$$

$$P^{10} = \begin{bmatrix} .148 & .395 & .457 \\ .305 & .300 & .395 \\ .263 & .436 & .300 \end{bmatrix}$$

$$P^{15} = \begin{bmatrix} .242 & .411 & .346 \\ .230 & .358 & .412 \\ .275 & .368 & .358 \end{bmatrix}$$

$$P^{20} = \begin{bmatrix} .263 & .376 & .361 \\ .241 & .383 & .376 \\ .251 & .366 & .383 \end{bmatrix}$$

$$P^{25} = \begin{bmatrix} .252 & .370 & .377 \\ .252 & .378 & .370 \\ .247 & .375 & .378 \end{bmatrix}$$

Observe that although the convergence is slow, agreement with the fixed matrix W, which is

$$W = \begin{bmatrix} .250 & .375 & .375 \\ .250 & .375 & .375 \\ .250 & .375 & .375 \end{bmatrix},$$

is quite good for P^{25}.

Intuitively, as has been stated, the fixed vector of a regular chain represents the long-run behavior of the chain. That is, w_j is the probability that the Markov chain is in state j after some time has elapsed. Alternatively, if $wP = w$, then w_j represents the fraction of time the process is in state j in the long run. The next theorem states this "law of large numbers" more precisely.

THEOREM 9.3.3. *Law of Large Numbers for Markov Chains.* Let P be the transition matrix of a regular chain with starting vector π_0 and fixed vector w. Let $v_j^{(n)}$ be a function giving the fraction of time the process is in state j. Then

(9.3.6) $$E(v_j^{(n)}) \to w_j,$$

and for any $\varepsilon > 0$,

(9.3.7) $$P[|v_j^{(n)} - w_j| > \varepsilon] \to 0.$$

Proof: Omitted.

Notice that this result is true regardless of the starting vector π_0.

The last question we shall pose for regular Markov chains is the "first-passage" time problem. Its solution will depend on the corresponding results for absorbing chains.

DEFINITION 9.3.2. Let P be the transition matrix of a regular Markov chain. If the process is in state s_i, the *first-passage time* m_{ij} is the expected number of steps until the process reaches state s_j for the first time after the initial position. The matrix $M = \|m_{ij}\|$ is the *first-passage matrix*.

THEOREM 9.3.4. (a) For $i \neq j$, the first-passage time is finite and can be found by the following procedure: let Q be the $(r-1) \times (r-1)$ submatrix of P obtained by crossing out the jth row and jth column of P; then the numbers m_{ij} for $i \neq j$ are given by the vector $Nf = (I - Q)^{-1}f$.

(b) Let M_{dg} have the same diagonal entries as M, and zeros elsewhere. Then the first-passage matrix M satisfies (9.3.1):

$$(9.3.8) \qquad M = P(M - M_{dg}) + E,$$

where E is an $r \times r$ matrix of all 1's.

(c) Let w be the unique fixed vector on the left of P; then $m_{jj} = 1/w_j$.

Proof: (a) Let us make state j into an absorbing state. Then the first-passage times are just the mean number of steps to absorption, which are finite by the results of the previous section. The procedure outlined above calculates, for each state $i \neq j$, the first-passage times m_{ij}.

(b) Now let x_i and x_j be any two states. If we are in state x_i, then it follows that

$$(9.3.9) \qquad m_{ij} = \sum_{k \neq j} p_{ik}(m_{kj} + 1) + p_{ij},$$

since we can either go to x_j in one step or else go to an intermediate step x_k and then eventually to x_j. From this equation, we obtain

$$(9.3.10) \qquad \begin{aligned} m_{ij} &= \sum_{k \neq j} p_{ik} m_{kj} + 1, \\ &= \sum_{k} p_{ik} m_{kj} - p_{ij} m_{jj} + 1. \end{aligned}$$

Writing the latter equation in matrix form gives

$$(9.3.11) \qquad M = P(M - M_{dg}) + E,$$

as desired.

(c) Let w be the fixed vector on the left of P. Multiplying (9.3.11) by w gives

$$(9.3.12) \qquad \begin{aligned} wM &= wP(M - M_{dg}) + wE, \\ &= w(M - M_{dg}) + e, \\ &= wM - wM_{dg} + e, \end{aligned}$$

where e is the row vector of all 1's. From this it follows that

$$wM_{dg} = e,$$

and it then follows that

$$(9.3.13) \qquad m_{jj} = \frac{1}{w_j},$$

as was to be shown.

EXAMPLE 9.3.2. Consider again the transition matrix

$$P = \begin{bmatrix} 0 & 1 & 0 \\ 0 & 0 & 1 \\ \frac{2}{3} & \frac{1}{3} & 0 \end{bmatrix}.$$

We know that the fixed vector is $w = [2/8,\ 3/8,\ 3/8]$ so that the diagonal elements of M are 4, 8/3, and 8/3, respectively. To find the other elements in the first column of M, cross out the first row and first column of P to obtain

$$Q = \begin{bmatrix} 0 & 1 \\ \frac{1}{3} & 0 \end{bmatrix}$$

so that

$$Nf = (I - Q)^{-1}f = \begin{bmatrix} 1 & -1 \\ -\frac{1}{3} & 1 \end{bmatrix}^{-1} \begin{bmatrix} 1 \\ 1 \end{bmatrix} = \begin{bmatrix} \frac{3}{2} & \frac{3}{2} \\ \frac{1}{2} & \frac{3}{2} \end{bmatrix} \begin{bmatrix} 1 \\ 1 \end{bmatrix} = \begin{bmatrix} 3 \\ 2 \end{bmatrix}.$$

These entries will appear in the first column of M. Carrying out the rest of the calculations, we find the first-passage matrix to be

$$M = \begin{bmatrix} 4 & 1 & 2 \\ 3 & \frac{8}{3} & 1 \\ 2 & \frac{5}{3} & \frac{8}{3} \end{bmatrix}.$$

From this we find that the mean number of steps to go from state x_3 to state x_1 is 2, from x_2 to x_3 is 3, and so on.

EXAMPLE 9.3.3. A man believes that a certain stock price varies between 8 and 14 according to the following transition matrix.

$$P = \begin{array}{c} \\ 14 \\ 13 \\ 12 \\ 11 \\ 10 \\ 9 \\ 8 \end{array}\begin{array}{c} \begin{matrix} 14 & 13 & 12 & 11 & 10 & 9 & 8 \end{matrix} \\ \begin{bmatrix} \frac{1}{2} & \frac{1}{2} & 0 & 0 & 0 & 0 & 0 \\ \frac{1}{4} & \frac{1}{2} & \frac{1}{4} & 0 & 0 & 0 & 0 \\ 0 & \frac{1}{4} & \frac{1}{2} & \frac{1}{4} & 0 & 0 & 0 \\ 0 & 0 & \frac{1}{4} & \frac{1}{2} & \frac{1}{4} & 0 & 0 \\ 0 & 0 & 0 & \frac{1}{4} & \frac{1}{2} & \frac{1}{4} & 0 \\ 0 & 0 & 0 & 0 & \frac{1}{4} & \frac{1}{2} & \frac{1}{2} \\ 0 & 0 & 0 & 0 & 0 & \frac{1}{2} & \frac{1}{2} \end{bmatrix} \end{array}$$

Suppose he purchases the stock at one of these prices and waits until it reaches 14 to sell it. How long will he have to wait, on the average, before selling, for each initial purchase price?

To answer this question, we clearly need the first column of the first-passage matrix. To calculate this, cross out the first row and the first column of P to obtain Q as:

$$(I - Q)^{-1} = \begin{bmatrix} \frac{1}{2} & -\frac{1}{4} & 0 & 0 & 0 & 0 & 0 \\ -\frac{1}{4} & \frac{1}{2} & -\frac{1}{4} & 0 & 0 & 0 & 0 \\ 0 & -\frac{1}{4} & \frac{1}{2} & -\frac{1}{4} & 0 & 0 & 0 \\ 0 & 0 & -\frac{1}{4} & \frac{1}{2} & -\frac{1}{4} & 0 & 0 \\ 0 & 0 & 0 & -\frac{1}{4} & \frac{1}{2} & -\frac{1}{4} & 0 \\ 0 & 0 & 0 & 0 & -\frac{1}{4} & \frac{1}{2} & -\frac{1}{4} \\ 0 & 0 & 0 & 0 & 0 & -\frac{1}{2} & \frac{1}{2} \end{bmatrix}^{-1},$$

$$= \begin{bmatrix} 4 & 4 & 4 & 4 & 4 & 2 \\ 4 & 8 & 8 & 8 & 8 & 4 \\ 4 & 8 & 12 & 12 & 12 & 6 \\ 4 & 8 & 12 & 16 & 16 & 8 \\ 4 & 8 & 12 & 16 & 20 & 10 \\ 4 & 8 & 12 & 16 & 20 & 12 \end{bmatrix}.$$

Hence the first column of M, except for the first entry, is as follows.

$$M_1 = \begin{array}{c} \\ \end{array} \begin{array}{c} 14 \\ \begin{array}{r} 14 \\ 13 \\ 12 \\ 11 \\ 10 \\ 9 \\ 8 \end{array} \left[\begin{array}{c} * \\ 22 \\ 40 \\ 54 \\ 64 \\ 70 \\ 72 \end{array} \right] \end{array}$$

Thus, if the man buys the stock at price 10, he must wait, on the average, 64 days before the stock reaches 14; and if he buys it at 8, he must wait 72 days, and so on.

You will recognize that the stock-variation process of this example is precisely the spatially homogeneous random walk of Definition 9.3.3. You are invited to treat the problem parametrically (in terms of p_i, q_i, and r_i) by the methods outlined in Example 9.2.4 and Exercise 14 of Section 9.2.

It is also possible to obtain a parametric representation for the long-run probabilities w_j $(j = 1, 2, \ldots, r)$. This process is especially simple when a random walk is under consideration.

EXAMPLE 9.3.4. Consider a random walk such as that in Example 9.2.4, but modified so that $p_0 > 0$ and $q_0 > 0$. That is, ruin is not permanent when it occurs. We also insist that p_i and q_i are positive for intermediate states. Consequently there are no absorbing states. Now it is easy to see by simple probability arguments that

$$(9.3.14) \quad p_{ij}^{(n+1)} = p_{i,j-1}^{(n)} p_{j-1} + p_{ij}^{(n)} r_j + p_{k,j+1}^{(n)} q_{j+1} \quad j = 1, 2, \ldots, I-1.$$

Since the chain is clearly regular, we may invoke Theorem 9.3.2, part (b): take the limit on both sides of (9.3.14) as $n \to \infty$, and the result is

$$(9.3.15) \qquad w_j = w_{j-1} p_{j-1} + w_j r_j + w_{j+1} q_{j+1}.$$

On the boundaries we have

$$(9.3.16) \qquad w_0 = w_0 r_0 + w_1 q_1 \qquad r_0 = 1 - p_0,$$

and

$$(9.3.17) \qquad w_I = w_{I-1} p_{I-1} + w_I r_I \qquad r_I = 1 - q_I.$$

Now solve recursively, beginning with (9.3.16):

$$(9.3.18) \qquad w_1 = \frac{p_0}{q_1} w_0;$$

put $j = 1$ in (9.3.15) and solve to find

$$(9.3.19) \qquad w_2 = w_1 \frac{p_1}{q_2} = w_0 \frac{p_0 p_1}{q_1 q_2}.$$

By induction we see that

$$(9.3.20) \qquad w_{j+1} q_{j+1} = w_j p_j$$

and hence

$$(9.3.21) \qquad w_j = w_0 \left(\frac{p_0\, p_1 \cdots p_{j-1}}{q_1 q_2 \cdots q_j} \right),$$

for $j = 1, 2, \ldots, I$. Finally w_0 is determined from the condition that

$$\sum_{j=0}^{I} w_j = 1.$$

That is,

$$(9.3.22) \qquad w_0 \left[1 + \frac{p_0}{q_1} + \frac{p_0\, p_1}{q_1 q_2} + \cdots + \frac{p_0\, p_1 \cdots p_{I-1}}{q_1 q_2 \cdots q_I} \right] = 1.$$

Equations of the form above—especially (9.3.15)—will appear later, in the chapter on queuing models. An intuitive interpretation of (9.3.20) appears there also.

EXERCISES 9.3

1. In the ball-painting example in Section 9.1, we obtain the regular transition matrix

$$\begin{bmatrix} \frac{1}{2} & \frac{1}{2} & 0 \\ \frac{1}{2} & \frac{1}{4} & \frac{1}{4} \\ 0 & 1 & 0 \end{bmatrix}.$$

   Show that the fixed vector is $[\frac{4}{9}, \frac{4}{9}, \frac{1}{9}]$. Give interpretations.

2. In Examples 9.1.4 and 9.1.8, we obtain the transition matrix

$$\begin{bmatrix} 0 & 1 & 0 & 0 \\ \frac{1}{2} & 0 & \frac{1}{2} & 0 \\ 0 & \frac{1}{2} & 0 & \frac{1}{2} \\ 0 & 0 & 1 & 0 \end{bmatrix}.$$

   Although this transition matrix is not regular, show that it has a unique fixed vector. We will discuss the interpretation of this fixed vector in Section 9.5.

3. Find the unique fixed vector for the ball-painting experiment in Exercise 3 of Section 9.1. Give interpretations for its elements.

4. Consider again the slot-machine example of Exercise 4 of Section 9.1. What is the long-run fraction of times the man will play each slot machine?

5. Alter the rat-maze example of Exercise 6 of Section 9.1 so that there is a door between rooms 2 and 5. Set up the transition matrix and show that it is regular. Find the fixed vector. In the long run, what fraction of the time will the rat spend in each room? Show that it is proportional to the number of doors leading into the room.

6. If P is the transition matrix of a positive Markov chain ($P > 0$) and d is its smallest element, show that $d \leq \frac{1}{2}$. Give examples in which the limit is taken on.

7. Let P be the transition matrix of a regular Markov chain, let w be its fixed vector on the left, and let $W = fw$. Show that $WP = PW = W$.

8. In Example 9.3.4, show that the fixed vector is

$$w = [\tfrac{1}{2}, \tfrac{1}{6}, \tfrac{1}{6}, \tfrac{1}{6}, \tfrac{1}{6}, \tfrac{1}{6}, \tfrac{1}{12}].$$

   Hence show that the first entry in the first column of M_1, the first passage matrix, is 12.

9. Find the fixed vectors of the following Markov chains:

(a) $\begin{bmatrix} 0 & 1 \\ \frac{2}{3} & \frac{1}{3} \end{bmatrix}$

(b) $\begin{bmatrix} a & b \\ c & d \end{bmatrix}$ $a, b, c, d > 0$

(c) $\begin{bmatrix} 0 & \frac{1}{2} & \frac{1}{2} \\ 1 & 0 & 0 \\ \frac{2}{3} & \frac{1}{3} & 0 \end{bmatrix}$

10. Theorem 9.3.1 asserted that P^n approaches W was proved only when P was positive. Show that it holds for any regular chain by filling in the details of the following argument. Because P is assumed regular, there exists $N > 0$ such that $P^N > 0$. This proof, which is similar to that for Theorem 9.3.1, shows that the differences $M_{nN} - m_{nN}$ tend to zero as n tends to infinity. Show that the differences $M_n - m_n$ can never increase. Hence if the differences every Nth time tend to 0, so must the entire sequence.

11. In the Land of Oz the weather is a Markov process. They never have two nice days in a row. After a nice day there is equal probability that there will be rain or snow the next day. If there is either rain or snow, half the time the weather is exactly the same the next day, and the rest of the time there is equal probability of each of the other two kinds of weather.
    (a) Set up the Markov chain. (*Hint:* There are three states: Rain, Nice, Snow.)
    (b) Show that the chain is regular.
    (c) Find the fixed vector on the left and interpret.
    (d) Find the first-passage matrix.

12. A factory has two machines, only one of which is used at any given time. The machine in use breaks down with probability p any given day. The factory has a single repairman who takes two days to repair a broken machine. Let states be the pair (a, b), where a is the number of machines in operating condition at the end of the day and b is 1 if a day's work has been put in on a machine not yet repaired and 0 otherwise. Show that the transition matrix is

$$
\begin{array}{c}
 & \begin{array}{cccc} (2, 0) & (1, 0) & (1, 1) & (0, 1) \end{array} \\
\begin{array}{c} (2, 0) \\ (1, 0) \\ (1, 1) \\ (0, 1) \end{array} &
\begin{bmatrix}
q & p & 0 & 0 \\
0 & 0 & q & p \\
q & p & 0 & 0 \\
0 & 1 & 0 & 0
\end{bmatrix},
\end{array}
$$

where $q = 1 - p$. Prove that the chain is regular and find the fixed vector.

13. In Exercise 12, assume that $p = 0.5$ and that both machines are in working order. What is the mean length of time before both are broken?

14. Rework Exercise 12 with $p = 0.25$.

15. When a regular Markov chain has run for a long time, the relative probabilities of being in each state are given by the components of the fixed vector w. Hence we can think of starting the chain with w as the starting probability vector. Interpret the vector

$$t = w(M - M_{dg})$$

as being the mean number of times between successive appearances of the chain in the same state with w as the starting vector. The components of the vector t are called the *expected first-passage times in equilibrium*, or the *expected recurrence times*.

16. Show that the first-passage times in equilibrium for Exercise 13 are given by [6, 1, 3, 4].

17. Show that the first passage times in equilibrium for Exercise 14 are given by

$$[1.44, \ 2.88, \ 3.55, \ 17.88].$$

18. Discuss the differences between the answers found in Exercises 16 and 17.

19. Find the first-passage times in equilibrium for the Land of Oz example of Exercise 11. Give interpretations.

20. Refer to the proof of Theorem 9.3.1; a formal argument for the validity of (9.3.2) and (9.3.3) is now outlined. Consider vector Px and let M_1 occur for row k:

$$M_1 = \sum_{j=1}^{r} p_{kj} x_j.$$

Furthermore, let $x_l = \min_j x_j = m_0$.
(a) Show that

$$
\begin{aligned}
M_1 &= p_{k1}x_1 + p_{k2}x_2 + \cdots + p_{kl}x_l + \cdots + p_{kr}x_r, \\
&= p_{k1}x_1 + p_{k2}x_2 + \cdots + p_{kl}m_0 + \cdots + p_{kr}x_r, \\
&\leq p_{kl}m_0 + (1 - p_{kl})M_0.
\end{aligned}
$$

(b) Since $d = \min_{i,j} p_{ij}$, then there is an ε, $\varepsilon \geq 0$, such that $p_{kl} = d + \varepsilon (0 \leq d + \varepsilon \leq 1)$. Hence

$$
\begin{aligned}
M_1 &\leq (d + \varepsilon)m_0 + (1 - d - \varepsilon)M_0, \\
&\leq dm_0 + \varepsilon M_0 + (1 - d)M_0 - \varepsilon M_0 = dm_0 + (1 - d)M_0.
\end{aligned}
$$

(c) Carry out the proof for m_1 as well.

21. A man owns a stock whose price is a random walk with transition matrix given in Example 9.3.4. Imagine that he has held the stock for a long time and must sell it to send his child to college.
(a) What is the probability that he receives \$14 when he sells?
(b) Find the expected price that he receives for the stock. (*Hint:* Compute the long-run probability vector w.)

9.4   APPLICATIONS OF MARKOV CHAINS

In this section we shall discuss two applications of Markov-chain analysis. The first concerns charge accounts in a department store, and the second, finite queuing theory.

EXAMPLE 9.4.1. Many years ago department stores initiated a policy of letting customers charge their purchases rather than pay immediately. This led to a large increase in department store sales, but it also led to financial problems, since the stores found it was necessary to tie up large sums of money in accounts receivable. In addition, there was the related problem of setting up reserves for bad debts, since some of the accounts would inevitably not be paid. Department store accounts are typically small, and it is reasonable to assume that the payment behavior of each account is independent of every other account. Hence this is a case in which probabalistic analysis is reasonable. We shall discuss a Markov-chain analysis of the problem.

First, we must define states. When an account is opened, it is in state 0. If it is not paid that month, it moves to state 1. If it is not paid during the next month, it moves to state 2, and so on. But now suppose that new purchases and charges are made, and at the same time, partial payments are received. How shall we classify the account? The method frequently used is to classify the account according to the oldest unpaid dollar. To describe this, assume a customer has charges of $110; of this amount, $30 was charged three months ago, $50 one month ago, and the other $30 is a current charge. The account is then classified as being three months old. Unless payments are received during the month, it will move ahead to the four-month-old category. If partial payments of less than $30 are received, it will still move to the four-month category. But if payments between $30 and $80 are received, it becomes a two-month-old account. If payments from $80 to $110 are received, it moves to the one-month-old category. Finally, if the full $110 is received, the account moves to the paid-up state and stays there.

Let us consider a store that has eight states, six of which are indicated by 0, 1, 2, 3, 4, and 5, representing the age of the account, and two of which are p, for paid-up, and b, for bad debt. Thus the store will automatically write the account off as a bad debt if it is unpaid for more than six months. (The store may, in fact, turn the account over to a collection agency.) When the account reaches state p or b, we assume it stays there, because we will not extend further credit to bad debtors, and we treat a previously paid-up account initiating new charges as a new account. Thus p and b are absorbing states, and the rest of the states are transient. From its records, the store estimates that the probabilities of moving between pairs of states are:

$$
P = \begin{array}{c c} & \begin{array}{cccccccc} p & b & 0 & 1 & 2 & 3 & 4 & 5 \end{array} \\
\begin{array}{c} p \\ b \\ 0 \\ 1 \\ 2 \\ 3 \\ 4 \\ 5 \end{array} &
\left[\begin{array}{cc|cccccc}
1 & 0 & 0 & 0 & 0 & 0 & 0 & 0 \\
0 & 1 & 0 & 0 & 0 & 0 & 0 & 0 \\
\hline
.21 & 0 & .67 & .12 & 0 & 0 & 0 & 0 \\
.13 & 0 & .19 & .44 & .24 & 0 & 0 & 0 \\
.13 & 0 & .08 & .20 & .36 & .23 & 0 & 0 \\
.10 & 0 & .01 & .04 & .17 & .29 & .39 & 0 \\
.14 & 0 & .02 & 0 & .09 & .20 & .41 & .14 \\
.09 & .18 & .01 & .02 & .01 & .10 & .12 & .47
\end{array} \right]
\end{array}.
$$

A computer gives the fundamental matrix, correct to three decimal places, as:

$$
N = \begin{array}{c} \\ 0 \\ 1 \\ 2 \\ 3 \\ 4 \\ 5 \end{array}
\begin{array}{c} \begin{array}{cccccc} 0 & 1 & 2 & 3 & 4 & 5 \end{array} \\
\left[\begin{array}{cccccc}
3.698 & .958 & .424 & .177 & .123 & .033 \\
1.837 & 2.634 & 1.166 & .486 & .339 & .090 \\
1.358 & 1.220 & 2.385 & .994 & .694 & .183 \\
.896 & .772 & 1.126 & 2.282 & 1.594 & .421 \\
.756 & .579 & .881 & 1.102 & 2.561 & .676 \\
.505 & .417 & .509 & .720 & .909 & 2.127
\end{array} \right]
\end{array}
$$

The expected times to absorption and the absorption probabilities are:

$$
Nf = \begin{matrix} 0 \\ 1 \\ 2 \\ 3 \\ 4 \\ 5 \end{matrix}\begin{bmatrix} 5.413 \\ 6.551 \\ 6.835 \\ 7.091 \\ 6.556 \\ 5.187 \end{bmatrix}, \qquad
NR = \begin{matrix} 0 \\ 1 \\ 2 \\ 3 \\ 4 \\ 5 \end{matrix}\begin{matrix} p & b \\ \begin{bmatrix} .99413 & .00587 \\ .98386 & .01614 \\ .96699 & .03301 \\ .92422 & .07578 \\ .87824 & .12176 \\ .61717 & .38283 \end{bmatrix} \end{matrix},
$$

The interpretation of the expected times to absorption, the components of Nf, are obvious. They are the expected number of months before the account is settled in one way or another. Notice that these times are remarkably constant regardless of which transient state the account is in. Similarly, the entries of NR give the probabilities of absorption in each of the absorbing states. Notice that the probability of a new account becoming a bad debt is initially very small but that it increases rapidly as the account becomes older.

In the department store case, we are not just interested in one account, but rather in the aggregate behavior of many accounts, say 10,000 of them. For this reason we introduce the idea of a repetitive Markov chain.

DEFINITION 9.4.1. Let P be the transition matrix of an absorbing Markov chain. Let Q be the subtransition matrix of P involving only the transient states (see (9.2.1)). Suppose that initially there is a distribution vector $z^{(0)}$ of individuals in each transient state; that is, there are $z_i^{(0)}$ individuals in state i at time 0. During each time period, a vector c of new individuals is introduced into the process and the progress of these individuals is followed. Hence if we let $z^{(n)}$ be the number of individuals in each state at time n, we have

(9.4.1) $$z^{(n+1)} = z^{(n)}Q + c.$$

The resulting process is a *repetitive Markov chain*.

In a repetitive Markov chain, we are interested in the long-run behavior of the distribution $z^{(n)}$. We might also be interested in the steady-state distribution of individuals in each transition state. In the department store example, this means the number of accounts in each age category. We might also be interested in the expected discounted value of the accounts receivable. In order to make such expected value calculations, suppose that there is an interest rate, r, from which we can derive a discount rate $\lambda = 1/(1 + r)$. We also need the approximate number of dollars, d_i, that each account in age category i has charged to it. The following theorem gives the answers to those questions.

THEOREM 9.4.1. Let P be the transition matrix of a repetitive Markov chain, and let Q be its nonabsorbing part. Let c be the new-accounts vector, let $z^{(n)}$ be the vector of individuals in each state at time n, and let λ be the discount rate. Then consider the following.

(a) In the long run, the expected number of individuals in state i approaches a_i, the ith coordinate of the vector $a = cN$, regardless of the initial distribution $z^{(0)}$.

(b) Let d_i be the average number of dollars in the accounts in state i, and let C be the vector with components $C_i = c_i d_i$. Then the expected long-run distribution of charges in each age category is given by the vector CN.

(c) Using the notation of part (b), the expected monthly receipts and bad debts are given by the components of the vector CNR.

(d) Suppose that steady state has been reached and there are CN accounts in each age category. The expected present value of these accounts and the value of the eventual bad debts are given by the components of the vector $CNN_\lambda R$, where N_λ is the discounted fundamental matrix.

Proof: (a) Applying (9.4.1) repeatedly, we obtain $z^{(1)} = z^{(0)}Q + c$, $z^{(2)} = z^{(1)}Q + c = z^{(0)}Q^2 + c(I + Q)$, and so on, and eventually,

$$z^{(n+1)} = z^{(0)}Q^{n+1} + c(I + Q + Q^2 + \cdots + Q^n).$$

Since $Q^{n+1} \to 0$, we see that $z^{(n+1)} \to cN$, as was to be shown.

(b) Since the components of $a = cN$ give the long-run distribution of accounts in each age category, multiplying each account by its average charges gives the expected distribution of charges in each category.

(c) Since cN gives the expected number of *accounts* in each age category in the long run, cNR gives the expected number of accounts ending up in the paid-up or bad-debt states. Multiplying the accounts in each category by the number of dollars in each account gives the vector CNR for the number of dollars ending up in each age category.

(d) If x is *any* distribution of accounts (perhaps weighted by dollars in each account), then $xN_\lambda R$ describes the long-run discounted payoff behavior of the individuals in the Markov chain. Since, under steady-state conditions, the accounts will build up to CN dollars in each age category, the present value of the accounts receivable is clearly $CNN_\lambda R$.

Let us apply this theorem to the department store example. Let

$$c = [10,000 \quad 0 \quad 0 \quad 0 \quad 0 \quad 0];$$

that is, suppose we introduce 10,000 new accounts each month (some of which may be old accounts that previously ended up in the paid-up state). The vector of the long-run number of accounts in each age category is then

$$cN = [36,980 \quad 9,580 \quad 4,240 \quad 1,770 \quad 1,230 \quad 330].$$

Suppose we make the simple assumption that each account has \$100 in charges; that is, $d_i = 100$ for $i = 0, \ldots, 5$. Then the accounts-receivable vector is

$$CN = [3,698,000 \quad 958,000 \quad 424,000 \quad 177,000 \quad 123,000 \quad 33,000],$$

where the components are now the numbers of dollars in each age category. The expected collections and bad debts are given by

$$CNR = [994,130 \quad 5,870]$$

each month. Finally, if we use a discount factor of 0.98, the expected discounted fundamental matrix is

$$
N_\lambda = \begin{array}{c} \\ 0 \\ 1 \\ 2 \\ 3 \\ 4 \\ 5 \end{array}
\begin{array}{cccccc}
0 & 1 & 2 & 3 & 4 & 5 \\
\begin{bmatrix} 3.466 & .851 & .359 & .143 & .096 & .024 \\
1.617 & 2.486 & 1.040 & .417 & .281 & .071 \\
1.168 & 1.085 & 2.255 & .896 & .603 & .153 \\
.740 & .659 & .999 & 2.160 & 1.453 & .370 \\
.623 & .484 & .771 & .992 & 2.427 & .617 \\
.413 & .351 & .435 & .643 & .816 & 2.061 \end{bmatrix}
\end{array}.
$$

From this we can get the present value of the accounts-receivable vector above as

$$ CNN_\lambda R = [4,862,300 \quad 77,834], $$

where the first number gives the discounted value of collections and the second number, the discounted value of bad debts. These two figures might be useful if the department store were going out of business and wanted to sell its accounts receivable or if it were going to set up a reserve for bad debts.

The model above of a department store's credit problems is not perfect, but it at least provides a start on an analytical model that can be used for decision making and simulation.

EXAMPLE 9.4.2. Our second example is an application of regular Markov-chain theory to the study of finite queuing situations. Such problems arise when customers arrive at a service center and demand service of some kind. We assume that (for this problem) there is only one server. If the server is not busy, the customer is given service in the next time period. But if the server is busy the customer joins a queue *unless* the queue is too long, in which case he is turned away. For such problems we shall speak of *a system*, meaning the server plus the waiting space. If one individual is in the system then he must be undergoing service, whereas if three are in the system, then one is in service and the other two are in a *queue* (waiting line) in the waiting room.

Examples of such situations are people waiting at a post-office window, taxis at a hack stand, people waiting in line to check their hats, people in a queue at a bank, and so on. In the following chapter, we shall study models for many more such situations. The present example serves to briefly introduce methods for the analysis of congested systems.

To make the model fit real situations, we imagine that time is broken up into small intervals, the exact length of which depends on the specific application. We assume that in this small interval *at most* one customer can arrive; let us denote the probability of arrival by p. We assume that customer arrivals are statistically independent. We also assume that if a customer is being served, there is a fixed probability r that he finishes his service in any one interval, regardless of the number of previous time units of service.

One other convention is needed. We assume that arrivals and departures occur at the end of the small time interval, so if the line is empty and there is a new arrival, he cannot be given service until the next time period. And if the line is full and there is a departure, a new arrival can't fill the empty spot in the queue until the next interval.

Set $\bar{p} = 1 - p$ and $\bar{r} = 1 - r$. Using this notation, we can now deduce the transition matrix. We take as states the number of persons present in the system. Let n be the maximum number of people permitted in the system. That is, one individual is being served and $n - 1$ are waiting under maximum congestion conditions. Then, if the system currently contains n members, the person being served will finish service and depart with probability r (there cannot be a simultaneous arrival), and the waiting space will remain full (that is, the person in service will not leave) with probability $\bar{r}$. Similarly, if there are no people in the system during a given time interval, there is the probability p that there will be one arrival and the probability $\bar{p}$ that there will be no arrival and the waiting room will remain empty. Now suppose there are i people in the system, where $0 < i < n$. We move to state $i - 1$ with probability $\bar{p}r$, the product of the probabilities that there is no new arrival and that service is completed for the person in service. Similarly, we move from i to $i + 1$ with probability $p\bar{r}$, since this is the product of the probability that there is a new arrival and the probability that the person in service does not finish his service. Hence, if we are at state i, there is probability $1 - \bar{p}r - p\bar{r}$ that we will stay in this state. We now can write the matrix of transition probabilities:

$$
P = \begin{array}{c} \\ 0 \\ 1 \\ 2 \\ \cdot \\ n-1 \\ n \end{array}
\begin{array}{c}
\begin{array}{cccccc} 0 & 1 & 2 & 3 & \cdots & n-1 \quad n \end{array} \\
\left[\begin{array}{cccccc}
\bar{p} & p & 0 & 0 & \cdots & 0 \quad\quad 0 \\
\bar{p}r & 1 - \bar{p}r - p\bar{r} & p\bar{r} & 0 & \cdots & 0 \quad\quad 0 \\
0 & \bar{p}r & 1 - \bar{p}r - p\bar{r} & p\bar{r} & \cdots & 0 \quad\quad 0 \\
\cdot & \cdot & \cdot & \cdot & \cdots & \cdot \quad\quad \cdot \\
0 & 0 & 0 & 0 & \cdots & 1 - \bar{p}r - p\bar{r} \quad p\bar{r} \\
0 & 0 & 0 & 0 & \cdots & r \quad\quad \bar{r}
\end{array} \right]
\end{array}
$$

Let us work out the transition matrix when $n = 5$, $p = 0.1$, and $r = 0.5$. We have

$$
P = \begin{array}{c} \\ 0 \\ 1 \\ 2 \\ 3 \\ 4 \end{array}
\begin{array}{c}
\begin{array}{ccccc} 0 & 1 & 2 & 3 & 4 \end{array} \\
\left[\begin{array}{ccccc}
.9 & .1 & 0 & 0 & 0 \\
.45 & .5 & .05 & 0 & 0 \\
0 & .45 & .5 & .05 & 0 \\
0 & 0 & .45 & .5 & .05 \\
0 & 0 & 0 & .5 & .5
\end{array} \right]
\end{array}
$$

The fixed vector for this chain may be shown to be

$$
\begin{array}{ccccc} 0 & 1 & 2 & 3 & 4 \end{array}
$$
$$
w = [.8000 \quad .1788 \quad .0198 \quad .0022 \quad .0002].
$$

As usual these are the long-run probabilities of the process being in each of the states. Two of these are of major interest. The first component, w_0, gives the long-run fraction of times the queue is empty and hence the server idle. In the present case, we see that the server is idle $\frac{4}{5}$ of the time. The last component, w_4, gives the fraction of time that the waiting room is full and hence the fraction of time that a new customer will be turned away if he arrives.

In the table below we list the fixed vectors for other values of p and r with $n = 5$. Notice that in the third column we have listed the value of $\rho = p/r$; ρ is called the *traffic intensity coefficient*. From the table it is clear that when ρ is less than 1, the

p	r	ρ	w_0	w_1	w_2	w_3	w_4
.1	.5	.2	.80000	.1788	.0198	.0022	.0002
.2	.5	.4	.6015	.3008	.0752	.0188	.0038
.3	.5	.6	.4117	.3529	.1512	.0648	.0194
.4	.5	.8	.2468	.3291	.2194	.1462	.0585
.5	.5	1.0	.125	.250	.250	.250	.125
.6	.5	1.2	.0518	.1554	.2332	.3497	.2098
.7	.5	1.4	.0167	.0781	.1822	.4252	.2977
.8	.5	1.6	.0037	.0295	.1179	.4716	.3773
.9	.5	1.8	.0003	.0061	.0549	.4940	.446

server is idle a fairly large part of the time and there is little chance that a customer will be turned away. On the other hand when ρ is greater than 1, the server is busy most of the time and there is a substantial chance of losing business.

Actually it is possible to work out a formula for the fixed vector of the chain. In Exercise 6, you will be asked to verify that the fixed vector is given by

$$(9.4.2) \qquad w = \frac{r - p}{r\bar{r} - p\bar{p}s^n} \quad (\bar{r}, s, s^2, s^3, \ldots, s^{n-1}, \bar{p}s^n),$$

where $s = p\bar{r}/r\bar{p}$. From this we find that the probability that the server will be idle is

$$(9.4.3) \qquad w_0 = \frac{(r - p)\bar{r}}{r\bar{r} - p\bar{p}s^n}.$$

If $\rho < 1$ and n is sufficiently large, then s^n is very small so that $w_0 \approx 1 - \rho$ (see Exercise 7). Similarly, the probability of a customer being turned away is

$$(9.4.4) \qquad w_n = \frac{(r - p)\bar{p}s^n}{r\bar{r} - p\bar{p}s^n}.$$

Again if $\rho > 1$ and n is very large, we can make approximations and show that $w_n \approx 1 - 1/\rho$ (see Exercise 8).

In Exercise 9, the formula for the expected length of the queue is worked out, and then an approximate formula is derived.

EXERCISES 9.4

The first five exercises refer to the following problem: A certain fictitious graduate school has a Ph.D. program that admits about 15 students a year. To get his degree, a student must pass his qualifying examinations at the end of the second year and then write a thesis. If he doesn't finish his thesis by the end of seven years, he is dropped from the rolls of the school. The Dean of the school estimates that the probabilities of students dropping out (D), graduating (G), or passing on to the next year's work are as given by the following matrix:

$$
\begin{array}{c}
\begin{array}{ccccccccccc}
D & G & 0 & 1 & 2 & 3 & 4 & 5 & 6 & 7
\end{array}\\
\begin{array}{c}
0\\1\\2\\3\\4\\5\\6\\7
\end{array}
\left[\begin{array}{cccccccccc}
.09 & 0 & 0 & .91 & 0 & 0 & 0 & 0 & 0 & 0\\
.12 & 0 & 0 & 0 & .88 & 0 & 0 & 0 & 0 & 0\\
.21 & 0 & 0 & 0 & 0 & .79 & 0 & 0 & 0 & 0\\
.04 & .09 & 0 & 0 & 0 & 0 & .87 & 0 & 0 & 0\\
.03 & .26 & 0 & 0 & 0 & 0 & 0 & .71 & 0 & 0\\
.02 & .36 & 0 & 0 & 0 & 0 & 0 & 0 & .62 & 0\\
.02 & .50 & 0 & 0 & 0 & 0 & 0 & 0 & 0 & .48\\
.35 & .65 & 0 & 0 & 0 & 0 & 0 & 0 & 0 & 0
\end{array}\right]
\end{array}
$$

1. Set up the problem as an absorbing Markov chain with two absorbing states. Find Q and R.

2. Show that Q is upper triangular. Find directly $Q^2, Q^3, \ldots, Q^7$. Show that $Q^8 = 0$. Prove that $N = I + Q + \cdots + Q^7$, and find N.

3. Compute Nf and NR and give interpretations of each.

4. What is the probability that an entering student will graduate? What is the mean time it takes him to finish one way or the other?

5. Suppose the nonzero entries in the third row are changed from .21 and .79 to .11 and .89. How do your answers change?

6. For the queuing example, show that the formula in (9.4.2) is the fixed vector of P. (*Hint:* Do not try to derive the formula unless you are ambitious.)

7. In (9.4.3) assume that $\rho < 1$ and n is very large. Show that s^n is very small so that the denominator of the formula is approximately $r\bar{r}$. From this show that w_0 is approximately equal to $1 - \rho$.

8. In (9.4.4) assume that $\rho > 1$ and n is very large. Show that we can then neglect $r\bar{r}$ in comparison with $p\bar{p}s^n$ in the denominator. Show that then w_n is approximately equal to $1 - 1/\rho$.

9. From w show that the expected length of the queue is given by

$$
m = w_0 \cdot 0 + w_1 \cdot 1 + w_2 \cdot 2 + \cdots + w_n \cdot n,
$$

$$
= \frac{r - p}{r\bar{r} - p\bar{p}s^n}(s + 2s^2 + 3s^3 + \cdots + (n - 1)s^n + n\bar{p}s^n).
$$

Show that if ρ is considerably less than 1, the expected queue length can be underestimated by the infinite series

$$
m \approx \frac{(r - p)}{r\bar{r}}(s + 2s^2 + 3s^3 + \cdots).
$$

By summing this series, show that

$$
m \approx \frac{r - p}{r\bar{r}} \frac{s}{(1 - s)^2} = \bar{p}\frac{\rho}{1 - \rho}.
$$

9.5 CLASSIFICATION OF STATES

Different states in a Markov chain play different roles. This is particularly clear in the case of an absorbing Markov chain in which the behavior of the process when in an absorbing state is quite different from its behavior when in a nonabsorbing state. In this section we shall consider more complicated chains. We shall present an algorithm for partitioning the set of states of any Markov chain into mutually disjoint and exhaustive subsets. We shall further classify each of these subsets as being either *ergodic* or *transient*.

In order to have a convenient language in which to discuss the problem, we shall talk about a state x_i being able to "communicate with" or "send a message to" state x_j. The definition of this concept is given next.

DEFINITION 9.5.1. Let $S = \{x_1, x_2, \ldots, x_r\}$ be the set of states of a (finite) Markov chain and let $P = \|p_{ij}\|$ be the transition matrix of the chain. Then we shall say that state x_i can *communicate* with state x_j according to the following conditions:

    (a) x_i can always communicate with x_i (itself) in 0 steps.

    (b) x_i can communicate with x_j (in that direction) in one step if $p_{ij} > 0$.

    (c) x_i can communicate with x_j (in that direction) if there is a sequence $x_i = x_{i(1)}, x_{i(2)}, \ldots, x_{i(k)} = x_j$ such that one-step communication is possible between each successive pair. We shall denote such a communication by the symbol $x_i \to x_j$.

    (d) x_i and x_j have *two-way communication* if x_i can communicate with x_j and x_j can communicate with x_i. We shall denote two-way communication by $x_i \leftrightarrow x_j$.

EXAMPLE 9.5.1. Consider the Markov chain whose transition matrix is as shown in Figure 9.5.1. Let us find the communication possibilities among the states

$$
\begin{array}{c}
\begin{array}{cccc} 1 & 2 & 3 & 4 \end{array} \\
\begin{array}{c} 1 \\ 2 \\ 3 \\ 4 \end{array}
\left[
\begin{array}{cccc}
0 & 0 & 0 & 1 \\
\frac{1}{2} & 0 & \frac{1}{2} & 0 \\
0 & 0 & 1 & 0 \\
1 & 0 & 0 & 0
\end{array}
\right]
\end{array}
$$

FIGURE 9.5.1

of the chain. First of all, we have $x_i \leftrightarrow x_i$, for $i = 1, 2, 3, 4$, by part (a) of the definition. We also see that state 1 can communicate in one step with state 4 and vice versa; that is, $x_1 \leftrightarrow x_4$. We also see that $x_2 \to x_1$ in one step, and, since $x_1 \to x_4$, we also have $x_2 \to x_4$ and that $x_2 \to x_3$ in one step. As far as x_3 goes, we see that it can communicate only with itself.

DEFINITION 9.5.2. By a *communication class* of a Markov chain we shall mean a nonempty subset E_k of states of the chain with the following two properties:

    (a) Every state x_i in E_k has two-way communication with every other state x_j in E_k.

    (b) E_k is the largest possible subset of states having property (a).

EXAMPLE 9.5.1 (continued). Let us find the communication classes of the chain in Figure 9.5.1. Since x_3 is an absorbing state, it has two-way communication only with itself and thus is in a communication class by itself. States x_1 and x_4 have two-way communication only with each other, so they form a class. Finally, the remaining state, x_2, has two-way communication with itself, but only one-way communication with the other states. Thus the three communication classes are: $\{x_1, x_4\}$, $\{x_2\}$, and $\{x_3\}$.

Notice that in the example above, every state is in one and only one communication class. This is generally true, as is indicated by the following theorem.

THEOREM 9.5.1. Consider a Markov chain with states S and communication classes $E_1, \ldots, E_t$. Then the communication classes partition S; that is, every state in S is in one and only one E_k.

Proof: Let us first show that every state is in at least one communication class. By Definition 9.5.1(a), any state x_i has two-way communication with itself, so if we consider the largest subset of S that has two-way communication with x_i, by Definition 9.5.2 that subset will be one of the communication classes $E_1, \ldots, E_t$. Suppose now that x_i belongs to two communication classes, E_h and E_k. The set E_h cannot be properly contained in E_k because of the maximality property of Definition 9.5.2(b); similarly, E_h cannot be properly contained in E_k. Hence either (i) $E_h = E_k$ and we are finished or (ii) there is a state x_u in $E_h - E_k$ and there is a state x_v in $E_k - E_h$. Suppose (ii) is true. Then clearly x_u and x_v are in different equivalence classes. But because x_i belongs to both E_h and E_k, it belongs to $E_h \cap E_k$, and we have that x_i has two-way communication with x_u and also with x_v. That is, $x_u \leftrightarrow x_i \leftrightarrow x_v$, so that $x_u \leftrightarrow x_v$. Hence x_u and x_v belong to the same communication class, which is a contradiction.

Sometimes it is possible for all the members of one class to communicate with all the members of another class. We define this next.

DEFINITION 9.5.3. Communication class E_h can *communicate* with class E_k, denoted by $E_h \to E_k$, if some member of E_h can communicate with some member of E_k.

THEOREM 9.5.2. (a) If some member of E_h can communicate with some member of E_k, then every member of E_h can communicate with every member of E_k.

(b) Let E_h and E_k be two distinct classes. Then if $E_h \to E_k$, it is false that $E_k \to E_h$; in other words, at most one-way communication is possible between pairs of communication classes.

Proof: (a) Suppose x_i in E_h can communicate with x_j in E_k. Let x_u be any member of E_h, and let x_v be any member of E_k. We have

$$x_u \leftrightarrow x_i \to x_j \leftrightarrow x_v,$$

so we conclude that $x_u \to x_v$, as was to be shown.

(b) If $E_h \neq E_k$ and both $E_h \to E_k$ and $E_k \to E_h$, then by part (a) every member of E_k has two-way communication with every member of E_h, which contradicts the definition of a communication class.

EXAMPLE 9.5.1 (continued). Consider the three classes for the Markov chain of Figure 9.5.1, namely, $\{x_1, x_4\}$, $\{x_2\}$, and $\{x_3\}$. It is not hard to see that the communication possibilities between pairs of these classes are

$$\{x_2\} \to \{x_3\} \quad \text{and} \quad \{x_2\} \to \{x_1, x_4\}.$$

The easiest way to depict these relationships is in the graph of Figure 9.5.2.

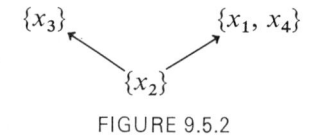

FIGURE 9.5.2

The idea of the graph of the communication classes turns out to be useful, so we define it here.

DEFINITION 9.5.4. By the *graph* of the communication classes of a Markov chain, we shall mean a set of nodes, one for each equivalence class, and a set of directed arcs between some pairs of classes. The rule for directed arcs is as follows: there is a directed arc between two distinct classes E_h and E_k if (a) $E_h \to E_k$ and (b) there is no other distinct class E_j such that $E_h \to E_j \to E_k$.

The remainder of this section will be devoted to devising an algorithm for finding the equivalence classes. In order to do this we will need the idea of a send-to and receive-from list.

DEFINITION 9.5.5. Let k be a state in a Markov chain. The *send-to* list, T_k, of state k consists of all states to which k can communicate (in one or more steps). The *receive-from* list, F_k, consists of the set of all states that can communicate with state k (in one or more steps).

THEOREM 9.5.3. If k is a state in a Markov chain, the communication class of k, E_k, is the intersection of T_k and F_k; that is, $E_k = T_k \cap F_k$.

Proof: This is almost obvious from the definition of E_k. The details of the proof are asked for in Exercise 8.

The flow diagram of Figure 9.5.3 provides a method for construction of the send-to lists T_k for each k. Let us see how it works. In box 1 of the diagram, we first put state k into the set T_k for each k. In other words, initially T_k consists of just the state with which k can communicate in 0 steps, namely itself. We then move to box 2 of the flow diagram and see that we set $k = 1$ and that we also set up a "flagging" variable $F = 0$. Moving to box 3, we next add to T_k all the states to which i can communicate in one step, and we also "raise the flag" by putting $F = 1$ whenever a new

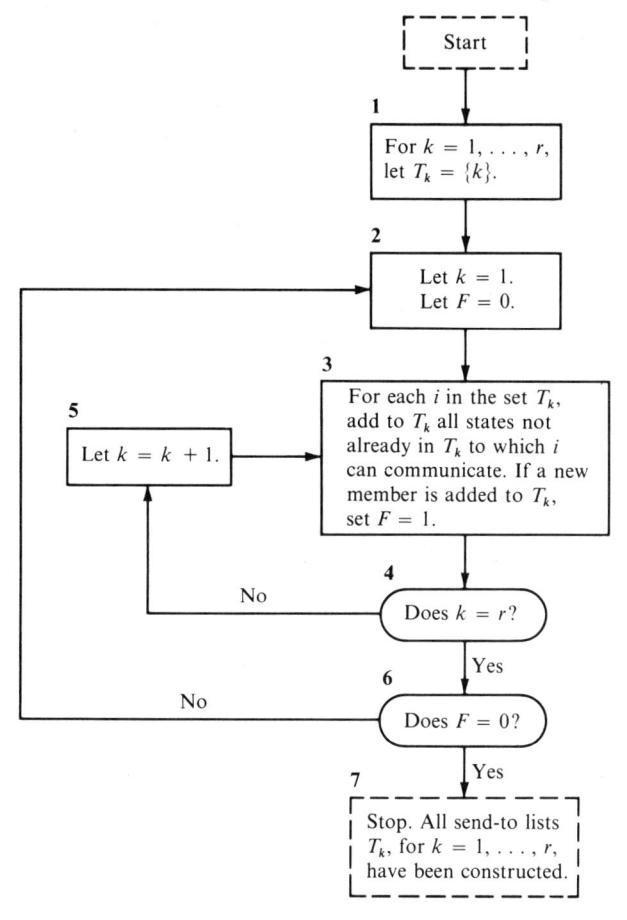

FIGURE 9.5.3

state is added to the send-to list T_k. Boxes 4 and 5 require that we go through this procedure for $k = 1, \ldots, r$. When this is finished, we go to box 6, which asks whether $F = 0$; that is, it asks whether the "flag has been raised" because, for some $k = 1, \ldots, r$, a new state was added to T_k. If $F \neq 0$, we go back to box 2 and go through the whole procedure again. But if $F = 0$, meaning that we have gone through the complete list of send-to lists without adding a new member to any one of them, then the computational process is stopped since no further additions can now be made to any list.

In Exercise 1, you will be asked to carry out this algorithm for the Markov chain in Figure 9.5.1.

After the send-to lists are completed, it is easy to find the receive-from lists. The flow diagram for this is shown in Figure 9.5.4. Notice that essentially all we have to do is to go through each send-to list T_k, and for each i belonging to T_k, we put k in F_i if it is not already there. Notice in particular that this will put k in F_k for every k. Notice that only one pass through each T_k is required to construct all the send-to lists F_k for each k.

In Exercise 1, you will be asked to find the send-to lists F_k and also the communication classes for the chain in Figure 9.5.1.

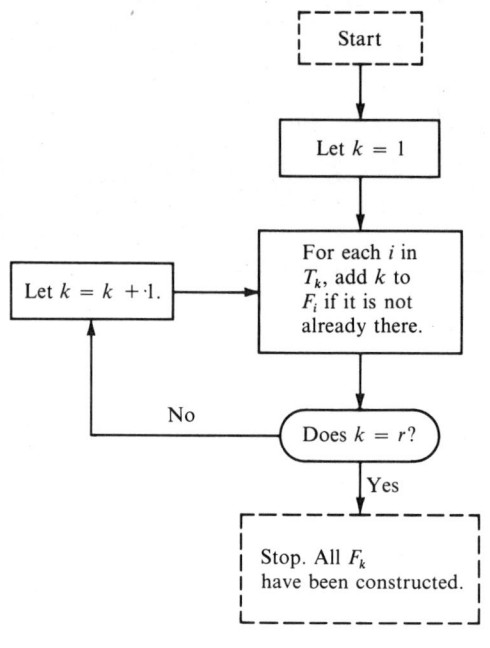

FIGURE 9.5.4

EXAMPLE 9.5.2. Let us apply the procedures above to another example. Consider the Markov chain whose transition matrix appears in Figure 9.5.5. Applying

$$
\begin{array}{c}
\;\; 1 \;\; 2 \;\; 3 \;\; 4 \;\; 5 \;\; 6 \\
\begin{array}{c} 1 \\ 2 \\ 3 \\ 4 \\ 5 \\ 6 \end{array}
\begin{bmatrix}
0 & 0 & 0 & \frac{1}{2} & \frac{1}{2} & 0 \\
0 & 1 & 0 & 0 & 0 & 0 \\
\frac{1}{3} & \frac{1}{3} & \frac{1}{3} & 0 & 0 & 0 \\
\frac{1}{4} & 0 & 0 & 0 & \frac{3}{4} & 0 \\
\frac{2}{3} & 0 & 0 & \frac{1}{3} & 0 & 0 \\
0 & 0 & \frac{1}{2} & 0 & 0 & \frac{1}{2}
\end{bmatrix}
\end{array}
$$

FIGURE 9.5.5

the flow diagrams of Figure 9.5.3 and 9.5.4, we find the send-to and receive-from lists as shown in Figure 9.5.6. Notice that dotted lines in the send-to-list column indicate the states added each time the process went down the main loop of the flow diagram

	Send-To Lists			Receive-From Lists	Communication Classes
1	1,	4, 5		1, 3, 4, 5, 6	{1, 4, 5}
2	2,			2, 3, 6	{2}
3	3,	1, 2,	4, 5	3, 6	{3}
4	4,	1, 5		4, 1, 3, 5, 6	{1, 4, 5}
5	5,	1, 4		5, 1, 3, 4, 5, 6	{1, 4, 5}
6	6,	3,	1, 2, 4, 5	6	{6}

FIGURE 9.5.6

in Figure 9.5.3, except for the last time when no new members were added to any list. The receive-from lists were constructed in one pass down the send-to lists. Finally, the communication classes were constructed by simply finding the common members on the send-to and receive-from lists of each state. The graph of the communication classes appears in Figure 9.5.7.

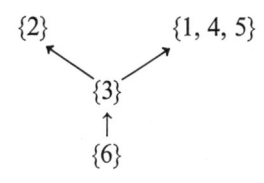

FIGURE 9.5.7

It is reasonably obvious that if the states of a Markov chain are reordered so that members of the same communication class are listed next to each other, the transition matrix will take on a special form. It is even better if the communication classes are listed from the top of the graph down. The next definitions capture this idea.

DEFINITION 9.5.6. Let E_1, E_2, ..., E_t be the equivalence classes of the Markov chain with transition matrix P. By the canonical form of P we shall mean the matrix obtained by reordering of the states, causing a corresponding reordering of rows and columns of P, such that

(i) members of a given equivalence class are listed next to each other in any order;

(ii) no equivalence class E_k is listed until all equivalence classes E_j such that $E_k \rightarrow E_j$ have already been listed.

EXAMPLE 9.5.2 (continued). Let us reorder the states so that the matrix of Figure 9.5.5 appears in canonical form. One such ordering, satisfying the conditions of Definition 9.5.6, is to list the states in the order 2, 1, 4, 5, 3, and 6, giving the matrix shown in Figure 9.5.8. The dotted lines have been put in the matrix to indicate the various equivalence classes.

	2	1	4	5	3	6
2	1	0	0	0	0	0
1	0	0	$\frac{1}{2}$	$\frac{1}{2}$	0	0
4	0	$\frac{1}{4}$	0	$\frac{3}{4}$	0	0
5	0	$\frac{2}{3}$	$\frac{1}{3}$	0	0	0
3	$\frac{1}{3}$	$\frac{1}{3}$	0	0	$\frac{1}{3}$	0
6	0	0	0	0	$\frac{1}{2}$	$\frac{1}{2}$

FIGURE 9.5.8

There are several things to notice about the canonical form in Figure 9.5.8. First of all, there are several other forms possible: for instance, we could have listed equivalence class {2} after rather than before class {1, 4, 5}; also, we could have listed the members of {1, 4, 5} in other ways such as {4, 1, 5} or {5, 1, 4}. In Exercise 5, you will be asked to find the other possible canonical forms. Second, the matrix in Figure 9.5.8 is *lower block triangular*; that is, on the main diagonal of the matrix there are nonzero square matrices called blocks; all entries above these blocks are zero, but below these blocks the entries may or may not be zero.

As a final result let us use the graph of equivalence classes to classify all states as either ergodic or transient.

DEFINITION 9.5.7. Let $E_1, \ldots, E_t$ be the equivalence classes of a Markov chain and let G be their graph.

(i) The maximal equivalence classes in G—that is, the classes on the top of G that cannot send to other states—are called *ergodic classes*. Members of ergodic classes are called *ergodic states*. If an ergodic class contains a single state, it is called an *absorbing class* and its state an *absorbing state*.

(ii) All other equivalence classes are called *transient classes*, and states in them are *transient states*.

In Exercises 6 and 7, you will be asked to characterize absorbing and regular Markov chains in light of this definition.

EXERCISES 9.5

1. (a) Find the send-to lists for the matrix in Figure 9.5.1.
   (b) Find the receive-from lists for that matrix.
   (c) Find the equivalence classes.
   (d) Draw the graph of the communication classes.

2. Identify the ergodic and transient equivalence classes and states for the Markov chain in Exercise 1.

3. Put the matrix of Figure 9.5.1 into canonical form. How many canonical forms does it have?

4. For the canonical form of Exercise 3, compute P^2, P^3, P^4. Guess at the limiting form of P^n as n becomes large.

5. How many canonical forms are there for the Markov chain of Figure 9.5.8?

6. Show that a Markov chain is absorbing if and only if every ergodic state is an absorbing state.

7. Show that a Markov chain is regular only if there is only one ergodic class. Show by example that the converse is not true.

8. Prove Theorem 9.5.3.

9. Put the following matrix in canonical form:

$$\begin{bmatrix} 0 & 0 & 0 & 0 & \frac{1}{2} & 0 & \frac{1}{2} & 0 \\ 0 & \frac{1}{2} & 0 & \frac{1}{2} & 0 & 0 & 0 & 0 \\ 0 & 0 & 1 & 0 & 0 & 0 & 0 & 0 \\ 0 & 0 & 0 & \frac{1}{2} & 0 & \frac{1}{2} & 0 & 0 \\ 0 & 0 & \frac{1}{4} & 0 & \frac{1}{4} & 0 & 0 & \frac{1}{2} \\ 0 & \frac{1}{3} & \frac{1}{3} & 0 & 0 & \frac{1}{3} & 0 & 0 \\ 0 & 0 & 0 & 0 & 0 & 0 & 0 & 1 \\ 1 & 0 & 0 & 0 & 0 & 0 & 0 & 0 \end{bmatrix}$$

10. If $P = \begin{bmatrix} A & 0 \\ 0 & B \end{bmatrix}$, where A and B are square and nonsingular, show that

$$P^{-1} = \begin{bmatrix} A^{-1} & 0 \\ 0 & B^{-1} \end{bmatrix}.$$

11. If $P = \begin{bmatrix} A & 0 \\ B & C \end{bmatrix}$, where A and C are square and nonsingular, show that

$$P^{-1} = \begin{bmatrix} A^{-1} & 0 \\ -C^{-1}BA^{-1} & C^{-1} \end{bmatrix}.$$

12. (a) Show that the example in Exercise 9 is an absorbing Markov chain.
(b) Use the canonical form and determine $I - Q$.
(c) Use the result of Exercise 11 to determine $(I - Q)^{-1}$.

13. For the matrix in Exercise 11,
(a) show that

$$P^2 = \begin{bmatrix} A^2 & 0 \\ BA + CB & C^2 \end{bmatrix};$$

(b) show that

$$P^3 = \begin{bmatrix} A^3 & 0 \\ BA^2 + 2CBA + C^2B & C^3 \end{bmatrix};$$

(c) show that

$$P^n = \begin{bmatrix} A^n & 0 \\ D^n & C^n \end{bmatrix},$$

where

$$D^n = \sum_{k=0}^{n} \binom{n}{k} C^k BA^{n-k}.$$

14. Use the result of Exercise 13 to show that if $A^n \to 0$ and $C^n \to 0$, then $P^n \to 0$.

SUGGESTED READING

Cyert, R. M., Davidson, H. J., and Thompson, G. L. Estimation of the allowance for doubtful accounts by Markov chains. *Management Science*, 1962, **8**, 287–303.

Feller, W. *An Introduction to Probability Theory and Its Applications*, Vol. 1 (2nd Edition). New York: John Wiley, 1957.

Kemeny, J. G., and Snell, J. L. *Finite Markov Chains*. Princeton, N.J.: Van Nostrand, 1960.

CHAPTER 10

SIMPLE WAITING-LINE MODELS

10.1 INTRODUCTION

In many operational situations a fixed number of *facilities* must perform some service for members of an arriving population of *customers*. Familiar examples of such facilities are bank windows, barber shops, gas stations, and cafeterias. Perhaps of more serious interest to us are telephone and data-transmission lines, automatic computers, production-line stations, highway crossing or merge points, and port facilities for berthing and unloading ships. An essential feature associated with all of these systems is that of *queuing*, or waiting in line. This occurs because processing capabilities or rates are limited, while customer arrivals often occur in an irregular, bunchy, or random fashion, thus causing temporary overloads. In spite of our first impressions, a little reflection shows that it is usually insufficient to design a service facility in such a way that service rate merely equals arrival rate on the average. It is the timing of the individual arrivals, as well as the average rate, that determines the length of the queues that form. As a consequence it is normally necessary to design service facilities with a certain amount of built-in overcapacity. That is, the average service rate of a facility must exceed the arrival rate. This overcapacity must be available to take care of occasional surges of demand. It is interesting to reflect that, when on occasion no waiting lines exist, the service facilities themselves are idle and can be considered to be waiting for customers. As we shall see, it is dangerous to eliminate all such facility idleness, since demand surges then dissipate slowly, and delays and congestion experienced by new customers rise very rapidly.

In this chapter we shall discuss a variety of simple waiting-line models. Our purpose will be to illustrate the important features of waiting-line phenomena and show how analyses may be carried out. In a later chapter methods of computer simulation will be presented for dealing with queuing or waiting-line problems.

10.2   MODEL COMPONENTS AND FIGURES OF MERIT

The general features of waiting-line systems have been described above. In this section we discuss in more detail the components of such systems. In addition, certain useful measures of system merit, or system effectiveness, will be enumerated. In later sections these measures will be evaluated in terms of such system components as arrival and service rates. Such measures of system effectiveness guide the decision maker in choosing between various system configurations.

A. Arrivals

An arrival is an event that indicates a need for service. Picturesquely, we speak of the actual item that arrives as a "customer." Customers may, but need not, be human beings: the individuals arriving at shops or gas stations are customers in the usual sense, but the same term is applied to failed machines that demand repair or airplanes that require a runway. The stream of customers that demand service at a particular facility will be called the *arrival pattern* or process. Typically such a stream must be thought of as random or stochastic, for the exact instants at which customers appear tend to vary haphazardly and unpredictably. Certainly when one considers the breakdowns of machinery in a factory, the requests for computer time, or the manner in which telephone calls appear at a switchboard, the random element is seen to be important. But even if attempts are made to schedule arrivals, as in doctor's offices, unforeseen events, such as emergencies, tend to occur and upset tight schedules.

To be specific about describing an arrival process, suppose t measures the elapsed time, for example, from the moment a factory begins operations in the morning. Then $A(t)$ might represent the number of machine breakdowns that have occurred in time t. If we choose, of course, $A(t)$ could stand for the number of orders received by time t or for some other process of arrivals. A graph of $A(t)$ on a particular day might appear as in Figure 10.2.1. Suppose $t_1 = 1.5$ hours, $t_2 = 2.3$ hours, and $t_3 = 5.7$ hours. Then if $t = 6.5$, $A(t) = 3$: there have been three machine breakdowns (arrivals) in the first 6.5 hours of factory operation on the day in question. Of course we cannot anticipate that on another day the failures will occur at the *same* times again. Rather, we only suppose that the probabilistic properties of the arrivals remain approximately the same so that the times, $t_1, t_2, t_3, \ldots$, have a specifiable (joint) probability distribution. Although many types of probability models are used to describe arrivals, the most generally useful of these will now be defined.

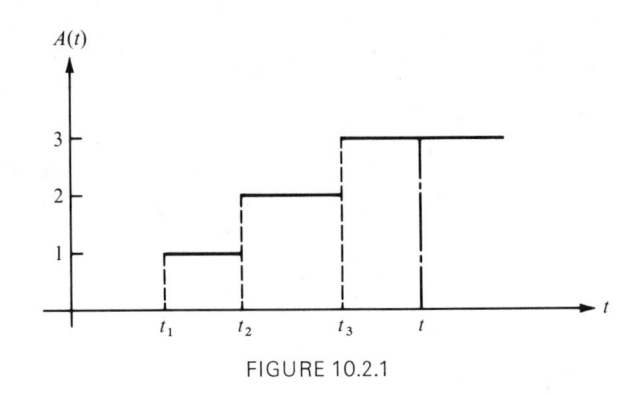

FIGURE 10.2.1

Suppose we wish to represent an arrival pattern that is "random" in the sense that a new arrival event may occur at any instant, regardless of how long or short a time has elapsed since the last such event. Furthermore, arrivals are isolated—groups of customers do not arrive simultaneously. Then the appropriate probability model is the *Poisson process*, which we now describe more formally. Let $A(t)$ denote the number of arrivals in a time of duration t. Suppose that $A(t) = n$ ($n = 0, 1, 2, \ldots$); that is, that there have been n arrivals up to time t. Then if

(i) the probability of a new arrival in the following short time interval $(t, t + h)$ is essentially λh (λ is a positive constant, called the *arrival rate*; h is any number less than λ^{-1}),

(ii) the probability of no new arrival in $(t, t + h)$ is essentially $1 - \lambda h$, and

(iii) the probability of more than one arrival in $(t, t + h)$ is negligible,

the arrivals are said to occur according to a Poisson process; in brief, we have *Poisson arrivals*. It is essential to notice that when a Poisson process governs arrivals, the probability of a new arrival in any short time interval is independent of all that has happened previously. Specifically there is no "memory" of the number of arrivals that have occurred before t, nor of the time that has elapsed since the last arrival before t. Figuratively speaking, our Poisson process evolves as if in each of the successive short time intervals, $(0, h)$, $(h, 2h)$, $(2h, 3h)$, $\ldots$, $(t - h, t)$, a biased coin is spun. If heads occur with probability λh and tails with probability $1 - \lambda h$, the instants at which heads occur will, when plotted, resemble the graph of Figure 10.2.1 and the resemblance will improve as h, the interval duration, becomes smaller. Clearly there are about t/h short time intervals, during each of which an arrival (the event heads) occurs with probability λh. Therefore the *expected* number of arrivals in time t is seen to be $(t/h)(\lambda h) = \lambda t$, since we are essentially dealing with a binomial random variable and may apply (7.6.3). Thus the expected number of arrivals per unit time is λ, which justifies the name "arrival rate." You should compare the Poisson stochastic process to the Markov chains of the last chapter. According to our description, a Poisson process is a Markov process in "continuous time"; that is, one in which the time, t, is a real number and not just an integer as before.

DEFINITION 10.2.1. Let $A(t)$ denote the number of events (arrivals) that occur in a time period of duration t. Then $A(t)$ is a *Poisson process* if the following conditional probability statements hold true: as h approaches zero,

(10.2.1) $$P\{A(t + h) = n \,|\, A(t) = n\} = 1 - \lambda h + o(h),$$

and

(10.2.2) $$P\{A(t + h) = n + 1 \mid A(t) = n\} = \lambda h + o(h),$$

while

(10.2.3) $$P\{A(t + h) > n + 1 \mid A(t) = n\} = o(h),$$

for $n = 0, 1, 2, \ldots$.

The remainder term, denoted by $o(h)$, represents a quantity that is negligible compared to h as h tends to zero. Mathematically speaking, a quantity $R(h)$ is said to be $o(h)$ (read "small oh of h") if

$$\lim_{h \to 0} \frac{R(h)}{h} = 0.$$

For instance, h^2 is $o(h)$ as h approaches zero.

Since the arrival rate, λ, is constant, we are dealing here with a *stationary*, or *time-homogeneous*, Poisson process. It is also possible, and often realistic, to allow λ to depend on time—that is, to be considered a nonstationary process. For example, the arrival rate of jobs at a computer center may be greater during some times of day than during others.

Before going on to discuss variations on the Poisson-arrivals theme, we state the following important results. Proofs will be given later.

THEOREM 10.2.1. If $A(t)$, the number of arrivals in a fixed time t, is governed by a Poisson process, then the probability distribution of $A(t)$ is given by the familiar *Poisson distribution*:

(10.2.4) $$P_n(t) = P\{A(t) = n\} = e^{-\lambda t} \frac{(\lambda t)^n}{n!} \qquad (n = 0, 1, 2, \ldots).$$

Moreover, let T represent the random time from a fixed (or randomly determined) instant of time until the next arrival. Then

(10.2.5) $$P\{T > t\} = e^{-\lambda t};$$

that is, T has the *exponential distribution*. A very important property of the Poisson process is that the random times between any two successive arrivals are independently distributed with exponential distribution given by (10.2.5). It is also true that the random time period that extends from any fixed instant until the next Poisson arrival is exponentially distributed. Our coin-tossing model helps to explain this fact.

Although the assumption of stationary Poisson arrivals is often appropriate, this is not invariably true. For example, if a single repairman is responsible for only two machines, then if both are "down" simultaneously (one being repaired and the other waiting for repair), no more arrivals will occur until the one on repair is returned to service. Thus arrival rate in this case depends on past happenings, in contrast to the Poisson assumptions. Also, if a long waiting line exists at the moment of a prospective arrival, the latter may "balk"—that is, take his business elsewhere. Similarly, if preferential service at a computer facility is given to customers submitting short jobs, individuals with long jobs may be induced to submit their work during off-peak periods. Parenthetically, we remark that sharp peaking of demand during a particular time of day leads to inefficient usage of such fixed facilities as elevators, roads, school rooms, and large computers. If inducements can be offered that will reduce the demand during such periods, both customers and facility operators may profit. Needless to say, regularly scheduled arrivals determined by appointments, as in a doctor's office, are not well approximated by a Poisson process. Nevertheless, the Poisson process is often a good approximation to actual streams of arriving customers, and it has the great advantage of being mathematically tractable. We shall discuss the treatment of other, quite different, arrival processes by computer simulation at a later stage.

EXAMPLE 10.2.1.* To further explain the "small oh" notion, consider the following illustrative examples. First, if $R(h) = h^b$, where $b > 1$, then

$$(10.2.6) \qquad \frac{R(h)}{h} = \frac{h^b}{h} = h^{b-1},$$

which tends to zero with h. Second, consider the probability of n Poisson events over an interval of length h:

$$(10.2.7) \qquad e^{-\lambda h} \frac{(\lambda h)^n}{n!} = P\{A(h) = n \,|\, A(0) = 0\}.$$

Then if $n = 0$,

$$(10.2.8) \qquad P\{A(h) = 0 \,|\, A(0) = 0\} = e^{-\lambda h} = 1 - \lambda h + R(h).$$

By the Taylor's series expansion for the exponential, the remainder after the first two terms, $R(h)$, is of order of magnitude $(\lambda h)^2/2$ and hence is $o(h)$. If $n = 1$,

$$(10.2.9) \qquad \begin{aligned} P\{A(h) = 1 \,|\, A(0) = 0\} &= e^{-\lambda h} \frac{\lambda h}{1!} = \lambda h[1 - \lambda h + R(h)], \\ &= \lambda h - (\lambda h)^2 + \lambda h(Rh). \end{aligned}$$

Here the remainder is of magnitude $-(\lambda h)^2 + \lambda h R(h)$. Now divide by h and observe that the remainder goes to zero since $R(h)$ is of order of magnitude $(\lambda h)^2/2$.

EXAMPLE 10.2.2. A certain structure experiences shocks at random instants. The magnitude of the nth shock is the random variable S_n, and successive shock magnitudes are independently and identically distributed with distribution function F; $F(x) = 0$, for $x \le 0$. Of concern is the distribution of the *maximum* shock received during time t.

A conditional probability argument is as follows. Let $S(t)$ denote the maximum shock experienced within time t. If the number of shocks, $N(t)$, is given to be n, then

$$(10.2.10) \qquad \begin{aligned} P\{S(t) \le x \,|\, N(t) = n\} &= P\{S_1 \le x\}P\{S_2 \le x\} \cdots P\{S_n \le x\}, \\ &= [F(x)]^n \end{aligned}$$

by the independence assumption. Now by conditional probabilities,

$$(10.2.11) \qquad P\{S(t) \le x\} = \sum_{n=0}^{\infty} P\{S(t) \le x \mid N(t) = n\}P\{N(t) = n\}.$$

If $N(t)$ is a Poisson process, then (10.2.11) becomes

$$(10.2.12) \qquad \begin{aligned} P\{S(t) \le x\} &= \sum_{n=0}^{\infty} [F(x)]^n e^{-\lambda t} \frac{(\lambda t)^n}{n!}, \\ &= e^{-\lambda t[1 - F(x)]}. \end{aligned}$$

Expression (10.2.12) gives the distribution function of $S(t)$ for any given t. Notice that if x approaches zero through positive values, the distribution function approaches $e^{-\lambda t}$. It is of interest that the distribution of $S(t)$ is *mixed*: there is a positive probability, equal to $e^{-\lambda t}$, of no shocks and hence of a zero maximum shock magnitude, while if F has a density there is a probability density for $S(t)$ given by

$$(10.2.13) \qquad \sum_{n=1}^{\infty} \frac{e^{-\lambda t}}{n!} (\lambda t)^n n F^{n-1} f(x),$$

for $x > 0$. Finally, suppose that we define a new λ, the arrival rate of shocks of magnitude greater than x, denoted by λ_x. Clearly we should write

$$(10.2.14) \qquad \lambda_x = \lambda P\{S > x\} = \lambda[1 - F(x)].$$

Then λ_x is the arrival rate in a Poisson process of shocks of magnitude greater than x, and expression (10.2.12) is the probability of no Poisson events of magnitude greater than x. This new interpretation makes it easy to write down directly the answers to similar problems.

B. Service

The servicing facility, or *server*, for short, may be described as the element of the service system that actually satisfies the demand of the arriving customer. Barbers, bank tellers, telephone lines and operators, typists, machine tools—even factories or sewage disposal plants—all may be considered servers in proper context. Notice that a server need not be a human being or a machine but may be combinations of these elements. A common feature of all servers is that even the fastest can only perform at a certain maximum rate and hence may be overloaded if demand becomes heavy.

The physical arrangement of the individual servers in a system varies. In the simplest systems, of course, there is only one server, as shown in Figure 10.2.2. Even

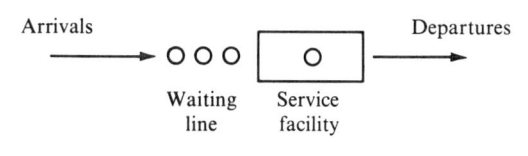

FIGURE 10.2.2

for such systems, however, complications may arise. For example, customers of different types may be segregated into individual waiting lines. For example, think of a stoplight-controlled intersection in which two (or more) lines of traffic alternate in their use of the crossing (service facility).

If essentially the same service is to be furnished to all arrivals, but one facility cannot handle the load, parallel configurations are introduced. In such cases various waiting-line arrangements may occur. For example, arriving customers may perhaps pick a line at random and stay in it. In this case, we are really dealing with several independent single-server systems. Sometimes, however, it is possible for a new arrival to pick the shortest of several lines. Alternatively, a single queue may be established, with the customer at the head of the line entering the first individual server to become vacant. Such a system is shown in Figure 10.2.3. Examples of parallel service facilities

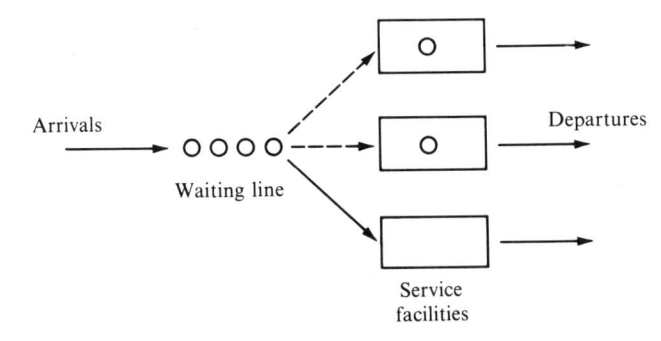

FIGURE 10.2.3

are toll booths before bridges and tunnels, barber chairs, groups of identical machines in factories, and teams of repairmen.

By way of contrast to the parallel arrangement, we have the series, or tandem, configuration. In job shop or assembly line operations it is common to find that jobs must be performed in some more or less definite sequence by a succession of servers, as shown in Figure 10.2.4.

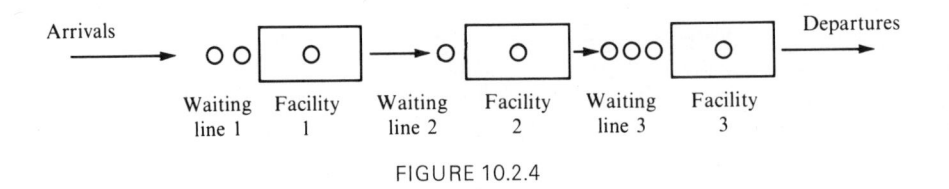

FIGURE 10.2.4

Still another possible arrangement is the cyclic system, an example of which is depicted in Figure 10.2.5. An airplane that flies from city to city, eventually returning to its place of origin, may be regarded as a customer in a cyclic system. Obviously delay at one airport (facility) tends to influence the arrival time at the next. A repairman who patrols a group of machines, making repairs where needed, plays a similar role. Notice that it may sometimes be reasonable to identify the same system element (for example, the repairman) as the server in one problem and the customer in another,

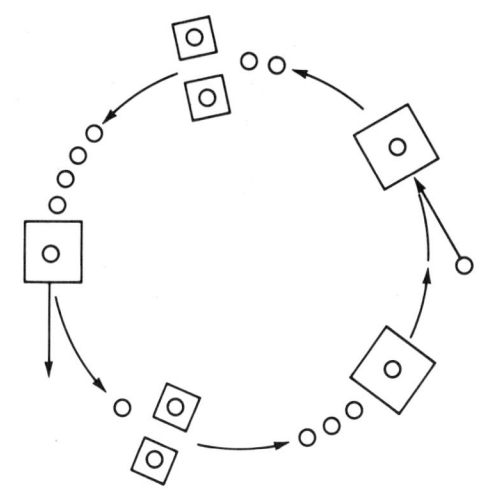

FIGURE 10.2.5

depending on circumstances. It may be worth remarking that the customers in most cyclic systems are not entirely contained in that system, but must enter and leave at some time and place, very likely to be replaced by others. This feature often need not complicate the analysis, so long as the number of customers remains the same.

Many variations and combinations of these basic setups occur. Complex job shops, maintenance activities, and computer systems typically involve a number of operations, some in parallel and some in series. In some systems, notably those involving computing and data processing, various operations involving the same customer (program) are going on simultaneously; that is, they are overlapped. However, overlapped operation is not always a physical possibility. For example, certain manufactured items must be assembled sequentially.

Having examined several of the many possible server configurations, we must now bring the duration of service into the picture. As was true of the arrival stream, it is typical to find that the *service times*—that is, the lengths of time required for an individual facility to complete the service of single customers—exhibit considerable variation and may usually be regarded as random variables. Thus the lengths of telephone conversations, the computing times required by programs submitted to a central system, and the repair times of equipment all exhibit considerable apparent random variability; hence it is natural to attempt to represent such service times in terms of a random process. We shall describe several service time processes, but the simplest, and, surprisingly, one of the most appropriate in practice, is defined below.

DEFINITION 10.2.2. *Exponential Service Times.* Let S be the service time of an arbitrary customer at a particular servicing facility. If S may be assumed to be exponentially distributed—that is, if for $\mu > 0$,

$$(10.2.15) \qquad P\{S \le x\} = 1 - e^{-\mu x} \qquad x \ge 0,$$
$$= 0 \qquad x < 0$$

—we speak of a system with *exponential service times* having service rate μ.

The most important property of exponential service times is precisely the "memoryless" property already mentioned in connection with Poisson arrivals: no matter how long an exponential service time has lasted, the *conditional* probability that the service terminates in the next short time interval is essentially μh (actually, $\mu h + o(h)$). Thus if the time, beginning with service initiation, is split into intervals $(o, h], (h, 2h], \ldots, (10h, 11h], \ldots,$ the chance that a service *that has lasted until* $11h$ terminates in $(11h, 12h]$ is μh. The same will be true of a service that has lasted to $100h$ and so on. Again, as was true of Poisson arrivals, we may imagine a biased coin being tossed in the successive h intervals to determine a particular service time. In a later chapter we show that if the service process possesses the memoryless property, then individual service times are exponential. Moreover, our coin-toss explanation shows also that successive service times are statistically independent. Finally, we point out that if a single server has exponential service time with rate μ and if it is kept constantly busy, for example, because of an enormous backlog of work, then the *output* of the server is a Poisson process of rate μ.

EXAMPLE 10.2.3. Suppose n $(n = 1, 2, \ldots)$ customers are queued up at a single server, and one customer is beginning service. Provided no other customers arrive in the meantime, the total time for which the server will be busy is

$$(10.2.16) \qquad T = S_1 + S_2 + \cdots + S_{n+1},$$

the sum of the independent service times of the $n + 1$ customers. The expected value of T is

$$E[T] = E[S_1] + \cdots + E[S_{n+1}] = (n + 1)E[S],$$

$$(10.2.17) \qquad\qquad = \frac{n + 1}{\mu},$$

if the service times are exponential with rate μ. The time T has the gamma distribution.

EXAMPLE 10.2.4. Imagine that cars approach an intersection according to a Poisson process with rate λ. If the light is red in their direction (say, north-south), they wait until it turns green and then the queue of waiting cars dissipates. Take as time origin the moment at which the last car in queue departs. A *vehicle-controlled* light operates as follows. There is a detector so arranged that if a car approaches the intersection from the north-south direction within time T of the last car's departure, the light remains green for an additional time T following the arrival time of the new car. Otherwise the light switches to red if a gap of duration $> T$ between successive cars elapses. Let N denote the number of cars that pass through the intersection in the north-south direction, following queue dissipation and until the light next changes. Apparently N also equals the number of green extensions—that is, the number of times cars consecutively arrive within time T. The probability that a car arrives before time T following queue dissipation is, by the Poisson assumption

$$(10.2.18) \qquad P\{X_1 \leq T\} = \int_0^T e^{-\lambda t} \lambda \, dt = 1 - e^{-\lambda T},$$

where X_1 is the random time between queue dissipation and first arrival thereafter. Alternatively, (10.2.18) is the probability of at least one Poisson arrival in T, easily read off from the Poisson expression (10.2.4). Now following X_1 ($X_1 < T$), an extension of T is created. If X_2, the time interval between first and second arrivals, is less than T, another extension occurs, and so on. Because of the fact that $X_1, X_2, X_3, \ldots$ are independently distributed, the probability of n or more extensions is

$$\begin{aligned} P\{N \geq n\} &= P\{X_1 \leq T, X_2 \leq T, \ldots, X_n \leq T\}, \\ &= (1 - e^{-\lambda T})^n. \end{aligned}$$
(10.2.19)

The probability of exactly n extensions is

$$\begin{aligned} P\{N = n\} &= P\{N \geq n\} - P\{N \geq n + 1\}, \\ &= (1 - e^{-\lambda T})^n - (1 - e^{-\lambda T})^{n+1} = (1 - e^{-\lambda T})^n e^{-\lambda T}. \end{aligned}$$
(10.2.20)

Consequently N has the geometric distribution. It follows that

$$E[N] = e^{\lambda T}.$$
(10.2.21)

Thus, as the arrival rate increases, the green extension time increases quite rapidly. Expression (10.2.21) implies that large queues will tend to build up in the east-west direction if λT becomes large.

EXAMPLE 10.2.5. A customer arrives at a queuing facility to find one customer in service and no queue. What is the probability that the arriving customer must wait for at least r (say, 3) times his service time? Assume that both service times are exponentially distributed with parameter μ.

The solution utilizes the memoryless property of the exponential. The waiting time W of the arrival is the unexpended service time. By the memoryless property,

$$P\{W > x\} = e^{-\mu x}.$$

Conditionally allow the arrival's service time to be $S = x$. Then

$$P\{W > rS \mid S = x\} = P\{W > rx\} = e^{-\mu rx}.$$

The condition on S is removed by multiplying by the density function of S and integrating:

$$P\{W > rS\} = \int_0^\infty P\{W > rx\} e^{-\mu x} \, \mu \, dx,$$

$$= \int_0^\infty e^{-\mu rx} e^{-\mu x} \mu \, dx = \frac{1}{1 + r}.$$

C. Scheduling, or Queue Discipline

In addition to the arrival and service components of a waiting-line system, one must consider the important feature of customer scheduling, or queue discipline. Perhaps the most familiar of scheduling rules is the "first-come, first-served" doctrine (sometimes called first-in, first-out, or FIFO), in which customers are served in order of arrival. That this rule is not always wise is easily seen: some jobs are invariably more important or urgent than others and should be served first. Alternatively, an extra service time or cost is involved when changeover from one customer type to another is made. In the latter case it may be desirable to consolidate strings of similar jobs into production runs, somewhat independently of arrival order. Changeover penalties are thus reduced.

A common scheduling procedure is that of assigning *priorities* to customers in various classes. A priority rule dictates the order in which the waiting customers will be served. Priorities can be based on the intrinsic importance of the job, as judged by the scheduler. Priority rules may also be established with the purpose of minimizing waiting time per customer, in which case the "shortest-in, first-out" rule, which allots highest priority to the job with the shortest service time, tends to be appropriate. In the establishment of priorities, or other scheduling rules, one must not forget possible behavioral factors and consequences. If people are directly involved there will undoubtedly be an attempt to "beat the game"—that is, to adjust in order to obtain what seems to be more favorable service. For example, imposition of a "shortest-in, first-out" rule at a computer center may induce customers to submit shorter programs in hopes of reducing waiting plus service (turnaround) time. However, carried to extremes, such strategy may be fruitless since the customer may simply be unable to profit by further decreases in *computer* response time: the *individual's* response time will dominate the situation. Of overriding priority are, finally, those demands associated with server breakdown, since these usually interrupt, or pre-empt, any on-going service.

Still another class of scheduling questions relates to the management of the service facilities themselves, as contrasted to queue or customer scheduling. In supermarkets and banks, it is common to close down servers (checkout lines or teller's windows) if business slackens. Then, when load builds up again, the servers are brought back into action. Naturally, the cost of keeping facilities open must be balanced against that of waiting, of lost business, or of some other measure of annoyance.

EXERCISES 10.2

1. Suppose orders appear at a warehouse location according to a Poisson process. The arrival rate, λ, equals 4 (orders per hour).
   (a) If orders begin to appear at 8:00 A.M., find the expected number and variance of the total number of orders that have accumulated by 10:00 A.M., 12:00 noon, and 4:00 P.M.
   (b) Find and graph the probability of exactly n orders in the two-, four-, and eight-hour periods above. Let n run from 0 to 30.

2. (a) Show that if a Poisson distribution has mean a, the probability can be written recursively; if

$$p_n = e^{-a} \frac{a^n}{n!},$$

then

$$p_n = \frac{a}{n} p_{n-1} \qquad n \geq 1.$$

   (b) Show that if $a < 1$, the probability $p_n < p_{n-1}$, for $n = 1, 2, 3, \ldots$.

(c) Show that if $a > 1$ is not an integer, then p_n is maximized for $n^* =$ largest n value less than a. (*Hint:* By the recursion above, p_n increases as long as $n < a$ and decreases for $n > a$.) If $a > 1$ is an integer, show that $p_{n^*} = p_{n^*+1}$, increasing for $n < n^*$ and decreasing for $n > n^* + 1$. Thus the Poisson has one maximum (or mode).

(d) Draw a graph of p_n for $a = 2$ and for $a = 2.5$.

3. Suppose a repairman is assigned to service a bank of machines in a shop. Assuming that failures occur according to a Poisson process with an expected number of ten failures per eight-hour day and that repair times are negligible, find

(a) the probability that no failures occur during a day.

(b) the expected time until the first failure. (*Hint:* The probability density of time to first failure, $f_1(t)$, is obtained by arguing that the first failure occurs in $(t, t + dt)$ if (i) no failure occurs in $(0, t)$ and then (ii) a failure occurs in $(t, t + dt)$. Thus

$$f_1(t)\, dt = (e^{-\lambda t})(\lambda\, dt).$$

The expected time to first failure is

$$\int_0^\infty t f_1(t)\, dt.$$

Alternatively, use the fact, stated in Theorem 10.2.1, that times between successive arrivals have distribution given by (10.2.5).)

(c) the expected time until the third failure. (*Hint:* Same as above, but

$$f_3(t)\, dt = e^{-\lambda t}\frac{(\lambda t)^2}{2!}\lambda\, dt.)$$

(d) the probability that exactly four failures occur within one hour after the fifth failure.

4. Management of the shop of Exercise 3 above believes that the repairman can service a shop of twice the size (that is, twice the number of similar machines). Show that the failures in the new shop occur according to a Poisson process with failure rate equal to 2.5 failures per hour. (*Hint:* One machine fails with rate λ. Therefore the probability that, if two machines fail independently, neither fails in $(t, t + dt)$ is $(1 - \lambda\, dt)^2 = 1 - 2\lambda\, dt + o(dt)$, provided both are initially up. The probability that both fail is $(\lambda\, dt)^2 = o(dt)$, and the probability that exactly one fails is $2(1 - \lambda\, dt)\lambda\, dt = 2\lambda\, dt + o(dt).)$

5. Suppose orders occur according to a Poisson process of rate λ, and suppose that order sizes are independent and come from the distribution $F(x)$. Let $N(t)$ denote the number of orders in time t.

(a) If $N(t) = n$ $(n = 0, 1, 2, 3, \ldots)$, show that the probability that the smallest order size exceeding x is $[1 - F(x)]^n$.

(b) Remove the condition that $N(t) = n$ to show that the *unconditional* smallest order received in time t is such that

$$P\{X_{\min}(t) > x\} = e^{-\lambda t F(x)}.$$

6. The number of mistakes per page of a certain test has the Poisson distribution with mean 0.3. Find the expected number of pages, out of 200, that have no mistakes. Find the expected number of pages having at least three mistakes.

7. The process of discovering a fault in a piece of electronic equipment is essentially one of testing each of many components one after another until the defective one is found. Suppose one component can be tested per time unit h (for example, per minute) and that the probability that any component is defective is p $(0 < p < 1)$. Let D be the time to discover the defective component.

(a) Show that the probability that discovery time exceeds t is $P\{D > t\} = (1 - p)^{[t/h]}$, where $[x]$ denotes the largest integer contained in x.

(b) Suppose $p = \mu h$. Show that if h, the length of the time unit, tends to zero, then $P\{D > t\} = e^{-\mu t}$, so the discovery time is exponentially distributed. (*Hint:* Use the fact that $[1 + (a/n)]^n \to e^a$ as $n \to \infty$.)

8. The time, T, required to calibrate and adjust (service) a particular control system is an exponentially distributed random variable. Suppose that the service rate of the calibration-adjustment process is one system per hour.

(a) What is the probability that a service time exceeds one hour?

(b) What is the probability that a repair takes at least 13 hours, given that its duration exceeds 12 hours?

9. Two workmen are assigned to perform the calibration and adjustment service of Exercise 8. They work independently, forming a two-server parallel service system (see Figure 10.2.3). The service rate of the first is μ_1, and that of the second is μ_2. Suppose that they simultaneously begin the first task in the morning.

(a) Show that the probability that the workman with service rate μ_1 finishes first is $\mu_1/(\mu_1 + \mu_2)$. (*Hint:* Use conditional probabilities to see that the fraction above equals $\int_0^\infty e^{-\mu_2 x} e^{-\mu_1 x} \mu_1 \, dx$. *Alternative hint:* $P\{$Workman No. 1's time $<$ Workman No. 2's time$\} = \int_0^\infty P\{$Workman No. 1 time $< x\}$. $P\{x <$ Workman No. 2 time $\leq x + dx\} = \int_0^\infty (1 - e^{-\mu_1 x}) e^{-\mu_2 x} \mu_2 \, dx$.)

(b) Suppose both workmen are engaged in the calibration procedure. Show that the probability that neither one finishes during $(t, t + h)$ is, to terms of order h (that is, neglecting terms proportional to h^2 or higher), $1 - (\mu_1 + \mu_2)h$; that the probability that exactly one finishes is $(\mu_1 + \mu_2) \, h$; and that the probability that both finish is negligible compared to h. Thus argue that if two servers with the same service rate μ operate simultaneously, the service rate is 2μ.

10. A single servicing facility has exponential service times with service rate μ. Let Poisson arrivals occur at the facility with rate λ.

(a) Show that the expected number of arrivals during a single service time is λ/μ. (*Hint:* The expected number of arrivals during a single service time of length x is λx. Use conditional expectations.)

(b) Show that the probability that there are no arrivals during an arbitrary service time is $\mu/(\lambda + \mu)$. (*Hint:* The probability that there are no arrivals during a service time of length x is $e^{-\lambda x}$. Use conditional expectations.)

11. The arrival rate of programs at a computer center is one job per minute. Each morning, preventive maintenance is carried out and the computer is down while this goes on. The time required is exponentially distributed with mean 15 minutes. Since there are occasions on which a considerable backlog builds up during this preventive maintenance period and since this contributes to later delays, it has become a policy that only 25 jobs will be accepted while preventive maintenance is in process; all jobs after the first 25 that arrive during maintenance are carried out externally at extra cost. (*Hint:* Let M be maintenance time; $m = E[M] = 15$ minutes, and the probability density of M is $f_M(x) = e^{-x/m}(1/m)$.) Given that $M = x$, the number of jobs, N, arriving during maintenance has distribution

$$P\{N = k \mid M = x\} = e^{-x} \frac{x^k}{k!}.$$

Removal of the condition on M gives the distribution of the number of arrivals during an arbitrary maintenance time:

$$P\{N(M) = k\} = \int_0^\infty e^{-x} \frac{x^k}{k!} e^{-x/m} \frac{dx}{m} = \int_0^\infty e^{-x[1 + (1/m)]} \frac{x^k}{k!} \frac{dx}{m}.$$

Substitute $y = x[1 + (1/m)]$ to get

$$P\{N(M) = k\} = \int_0^\infty e^{-y} \left[\frac{y}{1 + (1/m)}\right]^k \frac{1}{k!} \frac{dy}{[1 + (1/m)]^m} = \left(\frac{m}{1 + m}\right)^k \frac{1}{1 + m}.$$

Then

$$E[N(M)] = \sum_{k=0}^\infty k \left(\frac{m}{1 + m}\right)^k \frac{1}{1 + m} = m.$$

(a) What is the probability that programs must be run externally on any given day?

(b) What is the expected backlog of jobs waiting when preventive maintenance is finished?

12. The transmission of a message to control a space craft requires a time T. In the course of the transmission, atmospheric noise may occur; when it does, the message is garbled and must be entirely retransmitted. Assume that noise bursts appear in accordance with a Poisson process having arrival rate λ.

(a) Find the expected number of retransmissions required, and the expected time to transmit the message without noise-induced error. (*Hint:* The probability of no burst during a message is $e^{-\lambda T}$; the probability of at least one burst $= 1 - e^{-\lambda T}$; apply the geometric distribution.)

(b) Carry out the solution to part (a), assuming that the message transmission times are exponentially distributed with expectation m. (*Hint:* The conditional probability of no burst during a message is as above; the unconditional probability is

$$\int_0^\infty e^{-\lambda t} \cdot e^{-t/m} \frac{1}{m} \, dt = \frac{1}{1 + \lambda m}).$$

(c) Suppose a list of n (100, for example) independently and exponentially distributed messages is available, and suppose that these messages are transmitted one after the other with no regard to error. What is the expected number of messages transmitted without error? Describe the difference between this situation and that of (b).

13. A number of large new systems are being designed and marketed by a computer manufacturer. Each machine is sold subject to the following agreement: if any repair time in excess of one hour occurs during a warranty period of one month (30 days), the manufacturer is liable for a penalty of $1000; if no such event occurs, there is no penalty.

(a) Supposing that system failures occur at Poisson rate $\lambda = 0.1$ (failures per day) and that repair times are always two hours in duration, find the probability that the manufacturer must pay the penalty for any particular machine. Consider the warranty period to last for 30 days of actual running time; that is, do not count the repair time. (*Hint:* A failure at the end of the 30-day period does not violate the contract, so long as one hour or less of it is within the 30-day period.)

(b) Same as (a), but assume that repair times are independently and exponentially distributed with expected duration of two hours. (*Caution:* This problem is harder than other problems in this section. Use conditional probabilities.)

14. A service process possesses the *memory property* if the conditional probability that service time, S, exceeds $t + h$, given that it exceeds t, does not depend on t; that is,

$$P\{S > t + h \mid S > t\} = 1 - \mu h + o(h)$$

for h small. Putting

$$\bar{F}(t) = P\{S > t\},$$

show that

$$F(t + h) = F(t)[1 - \mu h] + o(h),$$

and, letting $h \to 0$, derive and solve a differential equation to show that

$$\bar{F}(t) = e^{-\mu t}.$$

Hence S has the exponential distribution.

(a) Suppose the service rate, μ, depends on the elapsed time, t, since service commenced. Using the same definition, show that

$$\bar{F}(t + h) = \bar{F}(t)[1 - \mu(t)h] + o(h)$$

and, letting $h \to 0$, that

$$\bar{F}(t) = e^{-\int_0^t \mu(t')dt'}$$

(b) Consider the model of (a): show that the conditional probability of repair completion in the time interval $(t, t + h]$, *given* that repair was initiated at 0 and lasted for time t, is essentially (for small h)

$$\mu(t)h = \frac{(d\bar{F}/dt)h}{\bar{F}} = \left(\frac{d}{dt} \log \bar{F}\right)h.$$

If $\mu(t)$ referred to the failure rate of an item, t being elapsed time since installation (age), $\mu(t)$ would often be called the *hazard* function.

15. The first five jobs to enter a job shop on a day have the following processing (service) times: 1.3, 0.7, 4.1, 2.9, 3.1 (hours).

(a) Suppose the jobs are processed in strict arrival order (1.3 first, 0.7 second, ...)—that is, according to FIFO. Find the delay time (waiting plus processing time) for each job. Find the waiting time alone for each job. Find the average delay time per job for the first five jobs.

(b) Let the jobs be processed according to the "shortest-in, first-out" (SIFO) rule. Repeat the calculations of part (a) above.

(c) Suppose the cost of unit delay time for the five customers is $10, $5, $15, $12, $20. Establish a processing order by computing for each job the index

$$\frac{\text{processing time}}{\text{cost per unit delay time}},$$

and process the jobs in accordance with the size of this index, the one with smallest index first, and so on. Compute the total cost of delay. Compare to the total cost of delay if (1) FIFO and (2) SIFO rules are used.

16. An entrepreneur must decide on just one investment to make during a fixed period of time of duration T. He believes that opportunities are of two varieties: those of value L and those worth H, where $L < H$ (L and H are net profits). Furthermore, opportunities appear at random—that is, in accordance with a Poisson process of rate λ. Each time an opportunity appears, it is worth L with independent probability p and H with probability $q = 1 - p$. If no opportunity appears, the profit is zero.

Suppose the following decision rule is adopted: establish a time τ, $0 \leq \tau \leq T$, and invest only in an H if one appears before τ. If the time τ terminates before an H occurs, invest in any opportunity—H or L—that turns up. Notice that he may be disappointed and receive no opportunity.

(a) Show that if the rule above is adopted, the expected gain achieved is

$$G(\tau) = H(1 - e^{-\lambda q \tau}) + (pL + qH)e^{-\lambda q \tau}(1 - e^{-\lambda(T - \tau)}).$$

(*Hint*: H opportunities appear at Poisson rate λq; this is related to the model of Example 10.2.2.)

(b) Choose τ so as to maximize $G(\tau)$. Show that the optimum τ, $\bar{\tau}$, is

$$\bar{\tau} = \max\left\{ T - \frac{1}{\lambda} \log\left[\frac{\left(1 + \dfrac{pL}{qH}\right)p}{1 - \left(1 + \dfrac{pL}{qH}\right)q} \right], 0 \right\}.$$

(c) Supposing that the entrepreneur follows the optimal decision rule described, what is the probability that his profit is zero? How should he modify $\bar{\tau}$ so as to increase his probability of *some* profit?

10.3   BIRTH-AND-DEATH-PROCESS MODELS

In following sections, a number of models for simple queuing situations will be presented. For the majority of these, the assumptions of Poisson, or Poisson-like, arrivals and of exponential service times will be made. Such assumptions, which are frequently, but not always, reasonable approximations in real situations, make it possible to derive useful formulas quite easily. Once the procedure is grasped, you will find it possible to construct models for the nonstandard situations that are always arising in practice.

To proceed, let $N(t)$ denote the number of customers present in a service system at time t. The random function $N(t)$ occupies successively the various possible state values 0, 1, 2, ... Because customers both arrive and depart, $N(t)$ does not merely increase, as did the Poisson process, but may fluctuate from zero to higher values and back. If we think of the customers in the system as a population, then the arrival process $A(t)$—that is, the Poisson process—governs the number of *births*; likewise, the service times govern the *deaths*, because, when a departure occurs, a member of the population of customers present in the system "dies." Thus the number of customers in the system—that is those waiting and being served—at each time t is the net effect of previous births and deaths, and the function $N(t)$ is therefore termed a *birth-and-death process*. We want to alter our definition of the simple Poisson pure birth process accordingly.

DEFINITION 10.3.1. A *birth-and-death process* is a Markov process in continuous time that assumes states 0, 1, 2, ... The number of states may be finite or infinite. If

(10.3.1) $$P_{ij}(t) = P\{N(t + t') = j \mid N(t') = i\}$$

are the transition probabilities of $N(t)$ (assumed stationary in time—that is, independent of t'), then

(10.3.2)
- (a) $P_{j,j+1}(h) = \lambda_j h + o(h)$ (upward transition),
- (b) $P_{j,j-1}(h) = \mu_j h + o(h)$ (downward transition),
- (c) $P_{jj}(h) = 1 - (\lambda_j + \mu_j)h + o(h)$ (fixed transition),

and transitions to non-neighboring states have negligible ($o(h)$) probabilities. λ_j and μ_j are nonnegative numbers for each j. A diagram helps to depict the possible transitions:

$$j \rightleftarrows \begin{array}{l} j+1 \quad (\lambda_j h) \\ j \qquad (1-(\lambda j + \mu_j)h) \\ j-1 \quad (\mu_j h) \end{array}$$

Thus a b-and-d process has the characteristics of Markov chains, as described in the previous chapter. The b-and-d process is, in fact, a Markov chain "in continuous time," meaning that the time variable t is allowed to take on any real number value and is not restricted to the integers.

EXAMPLE 10.3.1. *Single Server System; Poisson Arrivals and Exponential Service.* Consider a single server confronted by Poisson arrivals of rate λ and exponential service of rate μ. Let $N(t)$ denote the number of customers in the system, both those waiting and the one being served. Of course $N(t)$ may equal zero, in which case the server is idle—awaiting customers. The first step will be to set down the *transition rates*, λ_j and μ_j, described in Definition 10.3.1. To do so, suppose that $N(t) = j$, where j is either 0 or 1 or 2 .... If $j = 0$, then in the next short time interval of length h, namely in $(t, t + h)$, the only possibility is that an arrival may occur. According to our postulates for the Poisson process, such an event occurs with probability $\lambda h + o(h)$. Thus $\lambda_0 = \lambda$. Next, imagine that $N(t) = j$—to be specific, say 3. In the next period, $(t, t + h)$, one of the following events may occur.

(i) An arrival takes place, but no service is completed, which happens with probability

$$[\lambda h + o(h)][1 - \mu h + o(h)] = \lambda h + o(h),$$

since arrivals and services are independent and $\lambda \mu h^2 = o(h)$ and $ho(h) = o(h)$.

(ii) A service is completed, but there is no arrival. This event happens with probability

$$[\mu h + o(h)][1 - \lambda h + o(h)] = \mu h + o(h)$$

for the same reasons as those given for (i).

(iii) No change occurs; that is, there is no arrival and no service completion. The probability of this is

$$[1 - \lambda h + o(h)][1 - \mu h + o(h)] = 1 - (\lambda + \mu)h + o(h).$$

(iv) More than one arrival occurs, or more than one service is completed, or both. The probability of this possibility is clearly obtained by subtracting the sum of the probabilities of the mutually exclusive events of (i), (ii), and (iii) from unity; the result is $o(h)$. We will thus characterize the single-server system by a birth-and-death process with $\lambda_j = \lambda$ and $\mu_j = \mu$.

To illustrate the modeling of slightly more complex setups, consider the next example.

EXAMPLE 10.3.2. *Two-Server System*; *Poisson Arrivals and Independently and Exponentially Distributed Service*. Suppose an extra service facility is added to the system of the previous example, so that the two servers reduce a single waiting line when one exists. Notice that this situation is different from one in which each arriving customer must immediately select one server and stay in that line. Here, each customer is placed in a common line, and when a server discharges a customer, the customer at the head of the (common) line takes his place. Suppose first, then, that $N(t)$, the number of customers in the system at t, is zero. Then, just as was true in the last example, the probability of a jump from zero to one in $(t, t + h)$ equals $\lambda h + o(h)$ by Poisson process properties; hence $\lambda_0 = \lambda$. Now if $j = 1$, then only one customer is in service, and it is easy to see that the probability of a jump to two present in $(t, t + h)$ is $[\lambda h + o(h)][1 - \mu h + o(h)] = \lambda h + o(h)$, so $\lambda_1 = \lambda$, while the probability of a jump down from one to zero is $[1 - \lambda h + o(h)][\mu h + o(h)] = \mu h + o(h)$. Hence $\mu_1 = \mu$. The probability of remaining in place is $1 - (\lambda + \mu)h + o(h)$ when $N(t) = 1$. Finally consider the possibilities when $j \geq 2$. In this case, *both* servers are busy at time t. The servers act independently, and so the chance that an arrival occurs *and* neither server completes a customer's service in $(t, t + h)$ equals

$$[\lambda h + o(h)][1 - \mu h + o(h)]^2 = \lambda h + o(h);$$

thus, $\lambda_j = \lambda$, for $j = 1, 2, \ldots$. On the other hand, the probability that a service is completed but no arrival takes place is

$$2[\mu h + o(h)][1 - \mu h + o(h)][1 - \lambda h + o(h)] = 2\mu h + o(h),$$

and thus $\mu_j = 2\mu$, for $j = 2, 3, \ldots$. The probability of no change in $N(t)$ is

$$1 - (\lambda + 2\mu)h + o(h),$$

and all other changes have probability of order $o(h)$. Hence $N(t)$ is a birth-and-death process with transition rates

$$\begin{aligned} \lambda_j &= \lambda && \text{for } j = 0, 1, 2, 3, \ldots, \\ (10.3.3) \quad \mu_j &= \mu && \text{for } j = 1, \\ \mu_j &= 2\mu && \text{for } j = 2, 3, \ldots. \end{aligned}$$

To explain these further, we may think of N as changing only at the times $h, 2h, 3h, \ldots$, where h is small. Then if $N(t'h) = j$, where $t'h = t$, someone (perhaps Tyche, the goddess of chance) tosses a coin that comes up heads, signifying an arrival in $(t'h, t'h + h)$, with probability λh and tails (no arrival) with probability $1 - \lambda h$. Likewise, if $N = j \geq 2$, someone independently flips two coins—one for each server. With probability μh, heads appears on a single one of these coins, signifying customer service completion and departure from the server represented. Since the coins act independently, we can calculate the probability of zero, one, or two departures in the short time interval $(t'h, t'h + h) = (t, t + h)$ by the binomial theorem: the probability of no departures is $(1 - \mu h)^2$, the probability of one is $2\mu h(1 - \mu h)$, and the probability of two is $(\mu h)^2$. Finally, we can combine these with the arrival probabilities to obtain the probabilities above; the latter govern the evolution of N. Plainly, a time path or history for N can be generated by splitting time up into short intervals of length h and then flipping a three-sided coin with the probabilities given above to see what transpires at each time. Anyone who does this will soon see that the probability of no change—$1 - \lambda h$ or $1 - (\lambda + \mu)h$ or $1 - (\lambda + 2\mu)h$—is the largest, so consequently most of the time the state doesn't change. If $N(t) \geq 2$, the probability of an up-jump (transition to $N(t) + 1$) is λh, and the probability of a down-jump is $2\mu h$.

You should now have no trouble showing that if c servers are available, where c is any positive integer, then the only necessary modification of the example above is to change the discharge rate to

$$(10.3.4) \qquad \begin{aligned} \mu_j &= j\mu \qquad \text{for } j = 1, 2, \ldots, c - 1, \\ \mu_j &= c\mu \qquad \text{for } j = c, c + 1, c + 2, \ldots. \end{aligned}$$

These expressions are intuitively appealing, since they state that the rate of departures is proportional to the number of servicing facilities actually working.

We give one more example at this point to illustrate the way in which the transition rates λ_j and μ_j may be derived. Then we shall show how these may be easily used to find the long-run or limiting probability distribution of the number of customers in a system.

EXAMPLE 10.3.3. *Finite Arrival Source, or Repairman, Problem.* Suppose that m $(m \geq 1)$ machines are in use for continuous production, but that they are susceptible to random failure at rate λ. (Examples of such machines are looms, stills, and certain computers.) This means that if a machine is operating at time t, then the chance that it will break down between t and $t + h$ is, for small h, essentially λh, which is independent of time that the machine has been operating. Once the machine fails, it is inoperative until repair is completed. Observe that since there are a *finite* number of machines, the chance of some machine failing depends on the number down for repair at the moment. If all m machines are operative, then the probability of a failure in $(t, t + h)$ is essentially $1 - (1 - \lambda h)^m = m\lambda h + o(h)$. If j $(0 \leq j \leq m)$ machines are inoperative, then $m - j$ are operative and hence failure-prone, so the corresponding probability of exactly one failure in $(t, t + h)$ is:

$$(m - j)\lambda h(1 - \lambda h)^{m - j - 1} = (m - j)\lambda h + o(h).$$

Letting $N(t)$ represent the number of inoperative machines at time t, then if $N(t) = j$, the expression above shows that the probability of an additional failure, or "birth," is specified by

$$\lambda_j = (m - j)\lambda \qquad 0 \leq j \leq m;$$

arrivals are plainly not Poisson since the arrival rate depends on the number of machines awaiting repair. Concerning repair service, it will be assumed that there are r repairmen $(0 < r \leq m)$ and that each repair requires an independently and exponentially distributed time characterized by repair rate μ. Hence, if $N(t) = j$, then it can be seen that the overall service rate, describing the probability of a repair completion, or "death," is given by

$$(10.3.5) \qquad \begin{aligned} \mu_j &= j\mu \qquad 0 \leq j \leq r, \\ &= r\mu \qquad r \leq j \leq m. \end{aligned}$$

Setting down the transition rates λ_j and μ_j for a birth-and-death-process model is analogous to deriving the one-step transition probability matrix for a Markov chain. The transition rates determine the evolution of the b-and-d model just as the one-step transition probabilities do for its Markov chain. Consequently we can expect that for certain of our models—those that are analogous to *regular* Markov chains—there will be a long-run probability that the state variable $N(t)$ takes on any given value. This value is independent of the initial state of the system and depends only on the transition rates themselves. As we shall now see, it is very easy to derive the form of the stationary or long-run probabilities.

Letting $N(t)$ be the state variable for our b-and-d-model, we denote the transition probabilities by

$$(10.3.6) \qquad P\{N(t) = j \,|\, N(0) = i\} = P_{ij}(t).$$

Now *if* a long-run or stationary probability distribution exists, we denote it by $\{p_j, j = 0, 1, 2, \ldots\}$ and

$$(10.3.7) \qquad p_j = \lim_{t \to \infty} P_{ij}(t);$$

we know that such distributions exist for regular Markov chains, and recalling that a b-and-d process is Markov, we anticipate the occurrence of such distributions here as well.

THEOREM 10.3.1. If a b-and-d process has a stationary or long-run distribution $\{p_j\}$, then $\{p_j\}$ may be found by solving the *balance equations*

$$(10.3.8) \qquad \lambda_j p_j = \mu_{j+1} p_{j+1} \qquad j = 0, 1, 2, \ldots .$$

The solution is

$$(10.3.9) \qquad p_j = p_0 \frac{\lambda_0 \lambda_1 \lambda_2 \cdots \lambda_{j-1}}{\mu_1 \mu_2 \mu_3 \cdots \mu_j} = p_0 \prod_{i=1}^{j} \frac{\lambda_{i-1}}{\mu_i},$$

where the probability p_0 is found from the fact that

$$\sum_{j=0}^{\infty} p_j = 1,$$

so consequently from (10.3.9),

$$(10.3.10) \qquad p_0 \left[1 + \frac{\lambda_0}{\mu_1} + \frac{\lambda_0 \lambda_1}{\mu_1 \mu_2} + \frac{\lambda_0 \lambda_1 \lambda_2}{\mu_1 \mu_2 \mu_3} + \cdots \right] = 1.$$

Intuitive verifications of the facts given above, in particular of (10.3.8), will now be given. A more formal treatment using differential equations appears in the next section. Two arguments suggest the balance equations. The most heuristic appears first.

(a) Interpret p_j as the long-run or steady-state proportion of the time that the b-and-d process is in state j. For such a steady-state situation to exist, the rate at which transitions occur *out of* any state to the next higher state (that is, from j to $j + 1$) must equal the rate of transition *into* that state from the next higher one (from $j + 1$

to j). Consider a long period of time, T. Then $p_j T$ is the length of time spent in state j, and, since λ_j is the transition rate from j to $j + 1$, $\lambda_j p_j T$ is the (expected) number of transitions from j to $j + 1$ that occur in T. Likewise, $\mu_{j+1} p_{j+1} T$ is the number of transitions from $j + 1$ to j in T. Unless these two numbers are equal for *every* pair of states, no steady state can exist, and the equations of balance express this requirement. The next argument stems from the Markov character of the b-and-d process.

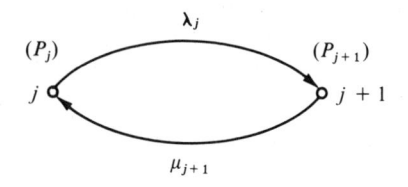

FIGURE 10.3.1. Balance-equation transitions

(b) Partition the time axis into intervals of equal length h; that is, consider times to be of the form nh. Then the one-step transition probabilities appropriate to such a partition are essentially

$$(10.3.11) \qquad P_{ij}(h) = \begin{cases} 1 - (\lambda_i + \mu_i)h & \text{if } j = i \\ \lambda_i h & \text{if } j = i + 1 \\ \mu_i h & \text{if } j = i - 1 \end{cases}$$

where we have neglected terms of order $o(h)$. We let P represent the matrix whose entries are $P_{ij}(h)$. Now if a long-run or stationary distribution exists, we have, letting the row vector $p = [p_0, p_1, \ldots]$, the fact that p must be a fixed vector

$$(10.3.12) \qquad pP = p,$$

at least if the number of states is finite (see the last chapter). In detail we have, using (10.3.11),

$$(10.3.13)$$

$$[p_0, p_1, p_2, \ldots] \begin{bmatrix} 1 - \lambda_0 h & \lambda_0 h & 0 & 0 & \cdots & 0 \\ \mu_1 h & 1 - (\lambda_1 + \mu_1)h & \lambda_1 h & 0 & \cdots & 0 \\ 0 & \mu_2 h & 1 - (\lambda_2 + \mu_2)h & \lambda_2 h & \cdots & \\ 0 & 0 & \mu_3 h & \cdots & \cdots & \end{bmatrix}$$

$$= [p_0, p_1, p_2, \ldots].$$

Row into column vector multiplication then supplies the following equations:

$$(1 - \lambda_0 h)p_0 + \mu_1 h p_1 = p_0,$$
$$\lambda_0 h p_0 + [1 - (\lambda_1 + \mu_1)h]p_1 + \mu_2 h p_2 = p_1,$$
$$\lambda_1 h p_1 + [1 - (\lambda_2 + \mu_2)h]p_2 + \mu_3 h p_3 = p_2,$$

$$(10.3.14)$$

$$\cdots,$$

$$\lambda_{j-1} h p_{j-1} + [1 - (\lambda_j + \mu_j)h]p_j + \mu_{j+1} h p_{j+1} = p_j,$$

$$\cdots.$$

Now if the right-hand term is cancelled against the same term on the left-hand side and the result is divided through by h and transposed, we find:

$$\mu_1 p_1 = \lambda_0 p_0,$$
$$\lambda_0 p_0 + \mu_2 p_2 = (\lambda_1 + \mu_1)p_1,$$
$$\lambda_1 p_1 + \mu_3 p_3 = (\lambda_2 + \mu_2)p_2,$$

(10.3.15)

$$\cdots,$$
$$\lambda_{j-1} p_{j-1} + \mu_{j+1} p_{j+1} = (\lambda_j + \mu_j)p_j,$$

$$\cdots.$$

Simplify by substituting first from the topmost equation into the second. That is, simply replace $\lambda_0 p_0$ on the far left of the second equation by $\mu_1 p_1$. The result is

(10.3.16)
$$\mu_2 p_2 = \lambda_1 p_1,$$

and we have established the balance equations for $j = 0$ and 1. Use of (10.3.16) in connection with the third equation supplies the balance equation for $j = 3$, and the general case follows similarly.

It is easy to solve the balance equations by successive substitution. Since

$$p_1 = \frac{\lambda_0}{\mu_1} p_0$$

and

$$p_2 = \frac{\lambda_1}{\mu_2} p_1,$$

we obtain

$$p_2 = \frac{\lambda_1}{\mu_2} \frac{\lambda_0}{\mu_1} p_0,$$

and so on. The requirement that $\{p_j\}$ be a probability necessitates the normalization condition and hence determines p_0. It is intuitively clear that a long-run probability distribution like $\{p_j\}$ cannot exist if our process can be absorbed at some state value.

EXAMPLE 10.3.4. Let $N(t)$ represent the number of individuals waiting and in the process of being served at time t. Let $N(0) = i > 0$, and suppose the server stops admitting any more customers when N first reaches zero. If c is the maximum value that N is allowed to assume (for example, the queuing space is limited), then

(10.3.17)
$$\begin{aligned} \lambda_j &= \lambda > 0 \quad &&\text{for } j = 1, 2, \ldots, c-1, \\ &= 0 \quad &&\text{for } j = c; \end{aligned}$$

also

$$\lambda_0 = 0.$$

The last condition prevents the arrival of more customers when the system becomes empty, and thus zero is an absorbing state. There is no long-run distribution as given by the solution of (10.3.15).

If there are an infinite number of possible states, a possibility that we admit, then it is important that normalization actually yield a finite number. For example, consider the single-server problem of Example 10.3.1. From (10.3.9), we know that

$$(10.3.18) \qquad p_j = p_0 \left(\frac{\lambda}{\mu}\right)^j$$

if a stationary distribution exists. But

$$1 = p_0 \left[1 + \frac{\lambda}{\mu} + \left(\frac{\lambda}{\mu}\right)^2 + \left(\frac{\lambda}{\mu}\right)^3 + \cdots \right],$$

and the infinite geometric series

$$1 + \frac{\lambda}{\mu} + \left(\frac{\lambda}{\mu}\right)^2 + \cdots = \frac{1}{1 - \frac{\lambda}{\mu}} \qquad \text{if } \frac{\lambda}{\mu} < 1,$$

$$= \infty \qquad \text{otherwise.}$$

Consequently,

$$p_0 = 1 - \frac{\lambda}{\mu} \qquad \text{if } \frac{\lambda}{\mu} < 1.$$

If the arrival rate λ exceeds the service rate μ, it is intuitively evident that $N(t)$ will wander off towards infinity, and this is what is being implied by the fact that p_0 is, formally speaking, equal to zero. Generally we can say that if the ratio of λ_j to μ_j is not too large and if λ_j and μ_j do not increase too rapidly, then the stochastic process $N(t)$ behaves itself, and a long-run distribution will occur. For more precise information, you should consult the references at the end of the chapter.

The balance equations will now be applied to explore the long-run behavior of the previously presented examples.

EXAMPLE 10.3.1 (continued). For the single-server system with Poisson arrivals and exponential service times, the birth-and-death process has constant rates:

$$(10.3.19) \qquad \begin{aligned} \lambda_j &= \lambda & j &= 0, 1, 2, \ldots, \\ \mu_j &= 0 & j &= 0, \\ &= \mu & j &= 1, 2, 3, \ldots. \end{aligned}$$

Thus, if the long-run distribution exists, it must be of the form

$$p_j = p_0 \left(\frac{\lambda}{\mu}\right)^j.$$

The latter can be normalized if the *traffic intensity parameter* $\rho = (\lambda/\mu) < 1$; otherwise there is no stationary distribution. When $\rho < 1$, we see from (10.3.18) that

$$(10.3.20) \qquad p_j = (1 - \rho)\rho^j \qquad j = 0, 1, 2, \ldots,$$

so the long-run number of customers in the system has the *geometric distribution*. It easily follows that the expected number of customers present is

$$(10.3.21) \qquad E[N] = \sum_{j=0}^{\infty} j(1 - \rho)\rho^j = \frac{\rho}{1 - \rho}.$$

Notice that as λ gets closer and closer to μ, and thus as ρ approaches unity, $E[N]$ approaches infinity.

EXAMPLE 10.3.2 (continued). For the two-server problem, (10.3.3) shows that the transition rates are

$$
\begin{aligned}
\lambda_j &= \lambda && \text{for } j = 0, 1, 2, \ldots, \\
\mu_j &= j\mu && \text{for } j = 0, 1, \\
\mu_j &= 2\mu && \text{for } j = 2, 3, 4, \ldots.
\end{aligned}
$$

(10.3.22)

The balance equations become

$$
\begin{aligned}
\lambda p_0 &= \mu p_1, \\
\lambda p_1 &= 2\mu p_2, \\
\lambda p_j &= 2\mu p_{j+1} && \text{for } j = 2, 3, \ldots,
\end{aligned}
$$

(10.3.23)

$$\ldots .$$

Solving these recursively we find that

$$p_1 = \frac{\lambda}{\mu} p_0,$$

$$p_2 = \frac{1}{2} \left(\frac{\lambda}{\mu}\right)^2 p_0,$$

$$p_3 = \frac{1}{4} \left(\frac{\lambda}{\mu}\right)^3 p_0,$$

$$\ldots,$$

and the general form is

$$p_j = p_0 \frac{(\lambda/\mu)^j}{j} \qquad \text{for } j = 1,$$

(10.3.24)

$$= 2p_0 \left(\frac{\lambda}{2\mu}\right)^j \qquad \text{for } j = 2, 3, \ldots.$$

To normalize, we put

(10.3.25) $\quad p_0 + p_1 + p_2 + \cdots = 1 = p_0 \left[1 + \frac{\lambda}{\mu} + 2\left(\frac{\lambda}{2\mu}\right)^2 + 2\left(\frac{\lambda}{2\mu}\right)^3 + \cdots\right].$

After the first two terms in the last sum, we have a geometric series

$$2\left(\frac{\lambda}{2\mu}\right)^2 + 2\left(\frac{\lambda}{2\mu}\right)^3 + \cdots,$$

which sums to

$$\frac{2(\lambda/2\mu)^2}{1 - (\lambda/2\mu)} = \frac{2\rho^2}{1 - \rho}.$$

For this case the service rate is 2μ so that the traffic intensity parameter is $\rho = \lambda/2\mu$. Finally one may show that

(10.3.26)
$$p_0 = \frac{1 - \rho}{1 + \rho} \quad \text{if } \rho = \frac{\lambda}{2\mu} < 1$$

and that

$$E[N] = \sum_{j=0}^{\infty} jp_j,$$

$$= p_0 \left[\frac{\lambda}{\mu} + 2 \sum_{j=2}^{\infty} j \left(\frac{\lambda}{2\mu} \right)^j \right],$$

(10.3.27)

$$= \left(\frac{1 - \rho}{1 + \rho} \right) \left[2\rho + \frac{2\rho^2(2 - \rho)}{(1 - \rho)^2} \right],$$

$$= \frac{2\rho}{(1 + \rho)(1 - \rho)}.$$

You will note that the distributions $\{p_j\}$ and the expected number of customers in the system both depend only on a suitably defined traffic intensity parameter ρ. For example, it is interesting to compare the expectations $E[N]$ for the one- and two-server systems:

$$\text{Single Server: } E[N] = \frac{\rho}{1 - \rho};$$

(10.3.28)

$$\text{Two Server: } E[N] = \frac{2}{1 + \rho} \frac{\rho}{1 - \rho}.$$
$$\text{(one line)}$$

It is of interest to compare service systems that have the same gross arrival rates and service rates. For instance, we compare a single-server system having arrival rate λ and service rate 2μ with a two-server system having arrival rate λ and each server having rate μ. For a given value of

$$\rho = \frac{\text{arrival rate}}{\text{service rate}},$$

the expected system occupancy, $E[N]$, is higher for the two-server system than for the single server, but the difference becomes relatively smaller as ρ approaches unity. The reason for this similarity for relatively large ρ is that in this case both servers are nearly always busy, and the output rate is effectively 2μ for the two-server system with just one line. Suppose, by way of contrast, however, that an arriving customer chooses randomly—that is, as if by the flip of a coin—between two servers. Then the arrival process at each server is an independent Poisson process with parameter $\lambda/2$. The expected number of customers awaiting and receiving service at *each* server equals

(10.3.29)
$$\frac{\lambda/2\mu}{1 - (\lambda/2\mu)} = \frac{\rho}{1 - \rho}.$$

Hence

(10.3.30)   Two Server: $E[N] = 2\,\dfrac{\rho}{1-\rho}$.
(two lines)

For large ρ there are nearly twice as many customers delayed at any given time if the servers are chosen independently than there are in the case of a one-line, two-server configuration. Unfortunately, the interesting situation in which an arriving customer may select the shortest line is difficult to analyze mathematically and cannot be discussed at this stage. Also, line-switching (jockeying) is not permitted.

Finally, we discuss the idea of *waiting time*, or *total delay* time. If p_j represents the long-run fraction of a time, T, during which j customers are in the system, then during this time, approximately equal to $p_j T$, j customers are delayed or detained by the system. Hence the total number of, say, customer-hours (or other relevant time units) of delay accumulated during time T is

(10.3.31) $1 \cdot p_1 T + 2 \cdot p_2 T + 3 \cdot p_3 T + \cdots = T \sum_{j=0}^{\infty} j p_j$.

Consequently the total number of customer-hours of delay per unit time is just $E[N]$. But for a process whose parameters do not change in time, it is at least intuitively clear that in the long run each arriving customer will experience the same expected delay, $E[D]$. Consequently, if customers arrive with rate λ, then over the long time period T, about λT customers arrive, each encountering the expected delay $E[D]$. The total number of customer-hours delayed is, thus, approximately equal to $\lambda T E[D]$, according to this admittedly heuristic argument. The conclusion is that

(10.3.32) $E[N] = \lambda E[D]$,

and so an individual arriving customer's expected delay becomes

(10.3.33) $E[D] = \dfrac{1}{\lambda} E[N]$.

This last argument may be made mathematically rigorous, and further discussion of the waiting and delay times of individual customers will be given in later sections. There it will be shown, for example, that a customer arriving at a single-server queuing system with Poisson arrivals and exponential service experiences (long-run) total delay, D, having probability density

(10.3.34)
$$f_D(t) = e^{-(\mu - \lambda)t}(\mu - \lambda) \qquad t \geq 0,$$
$$ = 0 \qquad\qquad\quad t < 0,$$

provided $\mu > \lambda$. This last density allows the estimation of the probability that delay will exceed any value. It also permits one to evaluate the expectations of nonlinear functions that may be of interest. We give a greatly over-simplified example to illustrate the use of (10.3.34).

EXAMPLE 10.3.5. The present price of a given security is expected to rise (in response to some favorable news) and then fall back to its present level, p_0. Let the price at time t be

(10.3.35) $p(t) = p_0 + e^{-t}(1 - e^{-t}) = p_0 + e^{-t} - e^{-2t}$.

This function has the following appearance:

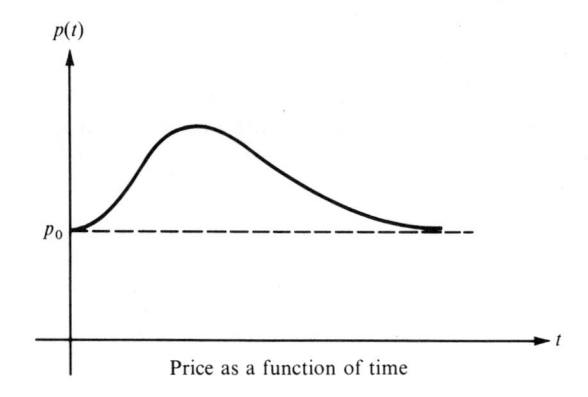

Price as a function of time

Consider an investment officer or advisor who watches the price of the security; shares of the security are owned by an organization. Consequently if advice is given to sell at $t = 0$, the transaction will actually be approved at $t = D$, where D is some random delay. The delay is caused, perhaps, by the necessity of getting the approval of some busy executive, who will be modeled as a single-server queue. Then we may utilize (10.3.34) to obtain the expected selling price when approval is received:

$$E[p(D)] = \int_0^\infty (p_0 + e^{-t} - e^{-2t}) f_D(t) \, dt,$$

$$= p_0 + \int_0^\infty e^{-t} e^{-(\mu-\lambda)t} (\mu - \lambda) \, dt - \int_0^\infty e^{-2t} e^{-(\mu-\lambda)t} (\mu - \lambda) \, dt,$$

(10.3.36)

$$= p_0 + \frac{\mu - \lambda}{\mu - \lambda + 1} - \frac{\mu - \lambda}{\mu - \lambda + 2},$$

$$= p_0 + (\mu - \lambda) \left[\frac{1}{(\mu - \lambda + 1)(\mu - \lambda + 2)} \right].$$

If it is known that the delay will be distributed in accordance with (10.3.34), then it is possible to compute the probability that approval occurs before the stock price reaches its peak value. Letting t_0 denote the value maximizing $p(t)$, we need

(10.3.37)
$$P\{D < t_0\} = 1 - e^{-(\mu-\lambda)t_0}.$$

Determination of t_0 is left to you.

EXERCISES 10.3

1. Show that $h^2 = o(h)$ as $h \to 0$ and that if $f(h) = o(h)$, then $h^2 f(h)$ is $o(h)$ as $h \to 0$.

2. Refer to (10.3.21). Show that

(a) $S(\rho) = \sum_{j=0}^\infty j\rho^j = \rho + 2\rho^2 + 3\rho^3 + \cdots,$

$$= \frac{\rho}{(1 - \rho)^2},$$

if $\rho < 1$.

(*Hint:* $S(\rho) - \rho S(\rho) = \rho + \rho^2 + \rho^3 + \cdots$. Now sum the geometric series.)

(b) Derive the expression for $E[N]$ in (10.3.21).

(c) Derive an expression for the variance of N.

3. Tabulate the expected number of customers in the single-server system of Example 10.3.1 as ρ takes on the values 0.1, 0.25, 0.5, 0.75, 0.9, and 0.95. Discuss the sensitivity of an estimate of $E[N]$ to errors in determination of ρ. For example, is a 5% error in ρ as important at $\rho = 0.25$ as at $\rho = 0.95$?

4. Compare $E[N]$, the expected number of customers in the system, in the single-server and two-server queue. Show that as ρ approaches unity, the ratio of the expectations approaches unity. Explain why. (*Hint:* As ρ approaches unity, both servers are nearly always busy, and departures occur at rate 2μ.)

5. Consider a three-parallel-server queuing system.
   (a) Argue that if the probability of an arrival in $(t, t + h)$ is $\lambda h + o(h)$ and the probability of a departure from each server is independently $\mu h + o(h)$, then the probability of three departures and one arrival in $(t, t + h)$ is $o(h)$. (*Hint:* Each departure represents a success in an independent trial; so does an arrival. Multiply the probabilities (independence).)
   (b) Suppose the probability of an arrival is $\lambda h = 4h + o(h)$ as long as the servers are not all occupied but drops to $2h + o(h)$ (customers become discouraged and go elsewhere) when a queue forms to await service. If the individual server's rate is $\mu = 2$, write down the balance equation for the system.
   (c) Solve the balance equation of (b).

6. A mechanic in a certain maintenance facility tends to work rapidly if his backlog is large, and slowly otherwise.
   (a) If his arrival rate is three jobs per minute, and if he works at rate $2j$, where j is the number of jobs that he currently has (one being worked on, $j - 1$ awaiting service), set up the balance equations.
   (b) Solve the balance equations by the method of successive substitution. Determine p_0, using the fact that
   $$\sum_{n=0}^{\infty} \frac{a^n}{n!} = e^a.$$
   (c) Out of a period of eight hours (480 minutes), estimate the average fraction of idle time that the mechanic has at his disposal. Assume that long-run probabilities may be used to represent the fraction of time in each state.

7. Suppose the mechanic in the last problem is replaced by a machine that has service rate $\mu = 4.5$ regardless of backlog.
   (a) Compare the long-run expected backlogs (backlog = queue length) for the two systems.
   (b) Compare the idleness probabilities for man and machine under the two systems of Exercises 6 and 7.

8. Consider Example 10.3.3 concerning repairmen problems.
   (a) Find the long-run probabilities $\{p_j\}$ in terms of p_0.
   (b) Find the expected number of machines awaiting and undergoing repair, $E[N]$, when $m = r$.

9. Use the formula
   $$E[D] = \frac{1}{\lambda} E[N]$$
   to compare the total delay of a customer approaching the two-server, one-line service system with the delay of a customer coming to the two-server, random-choice-of-server system.

10. A library has r duplicate volumes of an important reference book. Suppose that requests for the book occur in a Poisson manner with rate λ and that when a book is taken out, it is held for an exponentially distributed time of mean duration μ^{-1}.

(a) If $\lambda =$ ten requests per day, $\mu^{-1} = 0.25$ days, requesters queue up for the books when they are out, and service is first-come, first-served, determine the smallest r such that the long-run probability that a book is immediately available to an arriving customer is at least 0.8. (*Hint:* Calculate the long-run probability that at least one book is on the shelf.)

(b) Suppose a book requester who finds no volumes available leaves immediately (does not queue). Show that the number of books in (on the shelf) can be described by a birth-and-death process $N(t)$ with

$$\lambda = (r-j)\mu \qquad j = 0, 1, 2, \ldots, r-1,$$
$$= 0 \qquad\qquad j \geq r,$$
$$\mu_j = \lambda \qquad\qquad j = 0, 1, 2, \ldots, r,$$
$$= 0 \qquad\qquad \text{otherwise.}$$

(*Hint:* If $N(t) = j$, then $N(t + h) = j + 1$ if a book is returned. Since $(r-j)$ books are out, the probability of a return is $(r-j)\mu h$. The probability that $N(t+h) = j - 1$ is the probability of a request, λh.)

(c) For the model of (b), calculate the probability that an arriving customer is able to get a book immediately.

11. The research department of a large company produces ideas for new products at the Poisson rate λ per year. Each new idea is passed to a development division, which must draw up plans for manufacture, iron out difficulties, set up a manufacturing plant, and so on. The time for conversion from idea to marketable product is assumed to be an exponential random variable with mean μ^{-1}. Ideas are dealt with in the order of their appearance, and so occasionally several ideas are waiting to "go commercial." Since competition is also working in the same area, it has been estimated that if an idea has not gone through the development stage (including any wait necessary for other previous ideas to pass through that stage) within time d, then the probability that another company markets the product idea first is $1 - e^{-kd}$.

(a) Calculate the (nonconditional) probability that our company markets a new idea first. (*Hint:* Compute the expectation of $1 - e^{-kd}$ by use of the density function of long-run total delay D in a single-server queue.)

(b) When the company markets a new product first, it realizes a net gain G_1, whereas otherwise (competition markets first) the net gain is G_2 $(G_2 < G_1)$. Supposing that development rate, μ, is fixed, show that the expected net profit rate is

$$\pi(\lambda) = G_1 \lambda \left(\frac{\mu - \lambda}{\mu - \lambda + k} \right) + G_2 \lambda \left(\frac{k}{\mu - \lambda + k} \right)$$

and that the optimal value of λ is

$$\lambda^* = \mu + k - \sqrt{(1 - G_2/G_1)k(\mu + k)}.$$

(*Hint:* Use (10.3.34) and conditional probability.)

12. Consider Example 10.3.4.

(a) Find the numerical value of the probability that the stock will be sold at its peak, given that $\lambda = 1$, $\mu = 1.5$. Compare to $\lambda = 1$, $\mu = 3$.

(b) Suppose that if approval to sell is given before the stock reaches its peak, the sale is made at the peak, whereas if the approval is not obtained until after the peak, sale is made immediately. Compute the expected amount received for the stock.

13. An investment advisor believes that the price of the common stock of a corporation will advance at the rate $\$d$ per day. The current price is p_0. Because of delays in obtaining approval for the transaction, the advisor anticipates that if he immediately recommends buying (say, 100 shares), a random delay time, D, will elapse before the transaction is complete. His actual purchase price will then be $p_0 + dD$.

(a) If the distribution function of D is given by the density $f_D(x)$, express the probability that his actual purchase price is at least twice the current price.

(b) If D has the density of the delay at a single-server system with arrival rate λ and service rate μ, namely

$$f_D(x) = e^{-(\mu-\lambda)x}(\mu-\lambda) \qquad x \geq 0, \qquad (\mu > \lambda)$$
$$= 0 \qquad\qquad x < 0,$$

obtain the expected price paid for the stock.

14. A freeway is accessed by way of several entrance ramps; the situation at one of these appears as below:

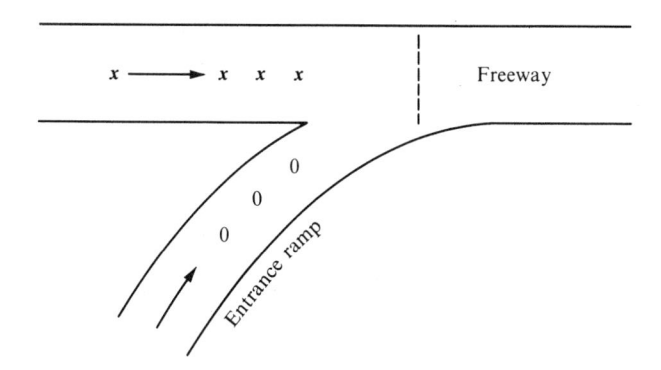

Here the x's represent vehicles (cars, trucks, buses) on the main road, and the 0's represent side-road vehicles attempting to merge. Assume that a sideroad car will enter only if he is at the head of the line on the entrance ramp and that there is a gap of at least L time units (L is called the *critical gap*) before the appearance of the next main-road vehicle at the merge point, identified by the dotted line on the diagram above. Assume that main-road cars are arriving at the merge point in accordance with a Poisson process of rate λ.

(a) Imagine that you are driving a side-road car and that your car has just moved into position at the head of the line on the entrance ramp. What is the probability that you can enter the freeway immediately? (*Hint:* Compute the probability that no main-road vehicle will appear within time L.)

(b) Let T equal a time gap between two consecutive main-road vehicles. Find the probability that at least n main-road vehicles pass before you are able to enter the freeway. (*Hint:* Let $T_1, T_2, T_3, \ldots$ denote gaps between, respectively, the moment you move to head of line and the first main-road arrival, the moment between first main-road arrival and the second, and so on. $\{T_i\}$ are independently and exponentially distributed. The probability that you merge after at least n is the probability of the event $(T_1 < L) \cap (T_2 < L) \cap \cdots \cap (T_n < L)$.)

(c) Find the expected number of main-road cars that pass before freeway merger is possible.

(d) Suppose there are two types of drivers that may appear at the entrance ramp: fast and slow. Fast drivers appear with probability p and slow with probability q; $p + q = 1$. Successive drivers of cars at the merge point are, independently, fast or slow. Fast drivers have critical gap L_f, and slow drivers have critical gap L_s. Compute the expected number of main-road cars that pass an arbitrary waiting side-road car. (*Hint:* Compute the expectation above, given that the car (driver) is either fast or slow, and remove the condition.) Explain why it would be incorrect to simply find the expected critical gap (equal to $pL_f + qL_s$) and substitute into the result of (c).

15. A machine is able to produce a saleable product at a certain rate, but occasionally a processing failure occurs and the product produced thereafter is worthless until the failure is rectified. Detection of the failure is accomplished by an occasional inspection of the machine's output. If the machine is operative at t, suppose it fails in $(t, t+h)$ with probability essentially λh. Suppose, too, that inspection occurs in a Poisson manner, with rate μ. Assume that rectification of the machine failure requires a negligible time. All time units are in hours.

(a) Let the status of the machine be 0 (operative) and 1 (inoperative). Show that the long-run probabilities p_0 and p_1 of these two states satisfy

$$\lambda p_0 = \mu p_1$$

and thus that

$$p_1 = \frac{\lambda}{\lambda + \mu}.$$

(b) Suppose the machine produces a product worth $100 per unit, that it does so at a rate of 50 units per hour, and that $\lambda^{-1} = 10$. Furthermore, let the cost of maintaining the inspection rate μ be 40μ ($ per hour). Set up an expression for the total long-run expected cost rate, where total cost is the sum of maintenance cost and inspection cost. Select the value of μ that minimizes this cost rate.

(c) Suppose that in addition to the inspection cost we must consider the repair cost, which is $5000 per repair. Select the optimal inspection rate, μ.

(d) If the repair time following discovery of a failure is of exponentially distributed duration with mean m, it is necessary to distinguish three states: 0 (operative), 1 (inoperative; failure not yet discovered), 2 (repair in progress). Argue that the long-run probabilities p_0, p_1, and p_2 satisfy the balance equations

$$\lambda p_0 = \frac{1}{m} p_2,$$

$$\mu p_1 = \lambda p_0,$$

$$\frac{1}{m} p_2 = \mu p_1.$$

From these it follows that since $p_0 + p_1 + p_2 = 1$,

$$p_0 = \frac{1/\lambda}{1/\lambda + 1/\mu + m}.$$

Now recalculate the answers to (a), (b), and (c).

10.4 SIMPLE WAITING-LINE MODELS— A SUMMARY

In the previous sections, the elements of various waiting-line or queuing situations have been detailed. Illustrations of model derivations, using the balance-equation approach, have also been given. In this section results for a number of simple model types are summarized. Explicit formulas will be given for the following quantities.

(i) The *number of customers in the system* in the long run. That is, letting $N(t)$ denote the number of customers waiting and being served at a time t after the process starts, then we are concerned with

$$\lim_{t \to \infty} P\{N(t) = j\} = p_j \qquad (j = 0, 1, 2, \ldots),$$

where the latter exists. It can be shown that p_j is equivalent to the long-run fraction of time that there are j customers in the system.

(ii) The *queue*, or *waiting line length*—that is, the number of customers awaiting (not receiving) service. If $Q(t)$ denotes queue length, then $Q(t)$ is computable from $N(t)$. For example, suppose $N(10) = 3$ in a single-server queuing system. Obviously, one customer is receiving service, and $Q(10) = 2$.

(iii) The *waiting time*, denoted by $W(t)$, *of a customer entering the system* at time t. $W(t)$ is the time that elapses from the moment the customer enters the system and joins the queue (if any) until his service time commences. In order to determine $W(t)$, a knowledge of $N(t)$ and the scheduling rules or priorities involved is necessary.

(iv) The *delay*, $D(t)$, *of a customer who enters the system* at time t. $D(t)$ is the sum of the waiting time and the service time of the arriving customer.

A. The Poisson-Arrival, Single-Server, Exponential-Service-Time System

A concrete example of such a system is furnished by one repairman (the server) who repairs machines that fail. Failures (arrivals) are considered to be Poisson, joining a waiting line if the repairman is busy. In order to see how the line develops, let us suppose that on a given day the first arrivals occur at times (measured in minutes from 8:00 A.M.)

$$15, 27, 33, 49$$

and that the corresponding service times for the customers arriving at these times are

$$14, 10, 8, 11.$$

Then the number of customers in the system varies as follows:

$$N(t) = \begin{cases} 0 & 0 \le t < 15 \\ 1 & 15 \le t < 27 \\ 2 & 27 \le t < 29 \\ 1 & 29 \le t < 33 \\ 2 & 33 \le t < 39 \\ 1 & 39 \le t < 47 \\ 0 & 47 \le t < 49 \\ 1 & 49 \le t \ldots \end{cases}$$

According to our assumption, the times between successive arrivals—that is, the *interarrival times*

$$15, 12, 6, 16$$

—are samples from an exponential distribution (see Theorem 10.2.1), as are the service times. Thus by drawing appropriate random numbers and combining them, the evolution of a queuing process may be *simulated*. More will be said about this technique later.

The following results may be obtained. They hold in the long run—that is, as the time, t, since the process start becomes large (as $t \to \infty$).

In what follows, λ represents the arrival rate of customers to the service system, and μ represents the service rate. Both are in units of customers per unit time.

1. The probability that there are exactly n $(n = 0, 1, 2, \ldots)$ customers in the system is

(10.4.1) $$P\{N = n\} = (1 - \rho)\rho^n \quad \text{if } \rho = \frac{\lambda}{\mu} < 1.$$

Thus the probability that the server is idle (there is no customer present to be served) is $1 - \rho$.

2. The expected number of customers in the system is

(10.4.2) $$E[N] = \frac{\rho}{1 - \rho}.$$

3. The expected queue length (number of customers awaiting service) is

(10.4.3) $$E[Q] = \frac{\rho^2}{1 - \rho}.$$

4. The expected waiting time for a newly arrived customer is, when service is "first-come, first-served,"

(10.4.4) $$E[W] = E[N] \cdot \frac{1}{\mu} = \frac{\rho}{1 - \rho} \frac{1}{\mu}.$$

5. The expected total delay for a newly arrived customer (waiting time plus service time) is

(10.4.5) $$E[D] = \frac{1}{1 - \rho} \frac{1}{\mu}.$$

The parameter $\rho = \lambda/\mu$ is called the *utilization factor* or *traffic intensity parameter*. The results above are valid only if $\rho < 1$; if $\rho \geq 1$, the queue length and waiting times will tend to grow indefinitely.

EXAMPLE 10.4.1. The arrival rate of failed machines is $\lambda = 1/12$ (machines per minute). The repair rate is $\mu = 1/8$ (machines per minute)—that is, the expected time to repair a single machine is eight minutes. Then

$$\rho = \frac{1/12}{1/8} = \frac{2}{3}.$$

According to (10.4.3) and (10.4.4),

$$E[N] = \frac{2/3}{1 - 2/3} = 2 \text{ (machines)};$$

$$E[W] = 16 \text{ (minutes)}.$$

Suppose now that the failure rate of machines increases by 20%—that is, that $\lambda = 1/10$. Then

$$\rho = \frac{1/10}{1/8} = \frac{4}{5},$$

and

$$E[N] = 4$$

while

$$E[W] = 32.$$

Notice that a 20% increase in arrival rate has *doubled* the expected number of machines waiting and the expected waiting time for an arriving customer. The effect of small changes in the traffic intensity parameter, ρ, is pronounced when ρ is close to unity. Thus if a service system is characterized by long waiting lines and times, rather modest increases in the service rate bring about dramatic reductions in waiting times. As our numerical example indicates, the opposite tendency is also present: if arrival rates are modestly increased, waiting times may increase many times over.

EXAMPLE 10.4.2. Again consider the repair situation above. Management has learned of the availability of a new piece of test equipment that will increase the repair rate to $\mu = 1/6$. The cost of operating this equipment is $C_M = 10$ ($ per minute). The cost incurred in lost production when a machine is out of service is $C_D = 5$ ($ per minute). Should the new test equipment be purchased?
 In order to decide whether or not the test equipment is worth the expense, we will compare expected costs. Let D represent the delay experienced by a failed machine (the sum of waiting time and actual repair time). Expected total delay for a failed machine is, *without* the equipment, given by (10.4.5):

$$E[D] = \frac{1}{1 - \rho} \cdot \frac{1}{\mu}.$$

Since the machine failure rate is λ (measured, for example, in failures per hour), the expected number of minutes of delay accumulated per unit time is equal to machine failure rate (arrival rate) times the expected delay, $E[D]$, experienced by a failed machine:

$$\lambda E[D] = \lambda \left(\frac{1}{1 - \rho} \cdot \frac{1}{\mu} \right) = \frac{\rho}{1 - \rho};$$

consequently the delay cost rate is

$$C_D \lambda E[D] = \frac{\rho}{1 - \rho} C_D.$$

Expected total cost rate *with* the machine is the sum of delay cost rate and machine cost:

$$\frac{\rho'}{1 - \rho'} C_D + C_M,$$

where ρ' denotes the traffic intensity parameter computed on the basis of the faster, machine-aided repair rate μ. Thus we decide to adopt the machine if

$$\frac{\rho'}{1 - \rho'} C_D + C_M < \frac{\rho}{1 - \rho} C_D$$

or, equivalently, if

(10.4.6)
$$\frac{C_M}{C_D} < \frac{\rho}{1 - \rho} - \frac{\rho'}{1 - \rho'}.$$

If, as was assumed first, $\lambda = 1/12$, $\mu = 1/8$, and $\mu' = 1/6$, then, since

$$\frac{C_M}{C_D} = 2$$

and

$$\frac{\rho}{1 - \rho} - \frac{\rho'}{1 - \rho'} = 2 - 1 = 1,$$

the machine does not justify its cost and should *not* be adopted. If, however, the failure rate is increased to $\lambda = 1/10$, then

$$\frac{\rho}{1 - \rho} - \frac{\rho'}{1 - \rho'} = 4 - 1.5 = 2.5,$$

and the machine should be adopted.

B.   The Poisson-Arrival, Parallel-Server, Exponential-Service-Time System

An obvious way of increasing service capacity is to employ several parallel servers. Figure 10.2.3 illustrates the configuration. If a servers are used ($a \geq 1$) and $\lambda < a\mu$, then it may be shown that, in the long run, the following formulas describe various aspects of the waiting-line process.

1. The probability that there are exactly n customers in the system is

$$P\{N = n\} = p_0 \frac{(\lambda/\mu)^n}{n!} \qquad \text{for } n = 0, 1, 2, \ldots, a,$$

(10.4.7)
$$= p_0 \frac{(\lambda/\mu)^n}{a! \, a^{n-a}} \qquad n = a + 1, a + 2, \ldots,$$

where

(10.4.8)
$$p_0 = \left[\sum_{n=0}^{a} \frac{(\lambda/\mu)^n}{n!} + \left(\frac{\lambda}{\mu}\right)^a \frac{1}{a!} \left(\frac{\lambda/\mu a}{1 - (\lambda/\mu a)}\right) \right]^{-1}.$$

p_0 is the probability that all servers are idle.

2. The expected number of customers in the system is

(10.4.9)
$$E[N] = \frac{\lambda}{\mu} + p_0 \left(\frac{\lambda}{\mu}\right)^a \frac{1}{a!} \frac{\lambda/\mu a}{[1 - (\lambda/\mu a)]^2}.$$

3. The expected queue length (number of customers awaiting service) is

(10.4.10)
$$E[Q] = p_0 \frac{1}{a!} \left(\frac{\lambda}{\mu}\right)^a \frac{\lambda/\mu a}{[1 - (\lambda/\mu a)]^2}.$$

4. The expected waiting time is, in case service is "first-come, first-served,"

$$(10.4.11) \qquad E[W] = \frac{E[Q]}{\lambda}.$$

5. The expected customer delay (waiting plus service time) is

$$(10.4.12) \qquad E[D] = E[W] + \frac{1}{\mu}.$$

The use of the results above may be illustrated in terms of our repair example.

EXAMPLE 10.4.3. The acquisition of a large government contract has necessitated a doubling of the number of (failure-prone) machines to be serviced. This means that the overall failure rate is now $\lambda = 1/6$, and a single repairman with repair rate $\mu = 1/8$ would soon be hopelessly swamped. Even the acquisition of the test equipment of Example 10.4.2 would not suffice to keep the machine waiting line under control, and so the addition of a repairman is indicated. We next examine the properties of the two-server system, using these formulas.

The probability that there are exactly n customers in the system when $a = 2$ can be expressed as

$$P\{N = n\} = p_0 \frac{(\lambda/\mu)^n}{n!} \qquad \text{if } n = 0, 1, 2,$$

$$(10.4.13)$$

$$= p_0 \frac{1}{2!} \frac{(\lambda/\mu)^n}{2^{n-2}} \qquad \text{if } n = 3, 4, 5, \dots .$$

You can now show that (10.4.13) is equivalent to

$$P\{N = n\} = p_0 \qquad \text{if } n = 0,$$

$$(10.4.14)$$

$$= 2p_0 \left(\frac{\lambda}{2\mu}\right)^n \qquad \text{if } n = 1, 2, 3, \dots .$$

If we substitute into (10.4.8), we find that

$$(10.4.15) \qquad p_0 = \frac{1 - \rho}{1 + \rho} \qquad \text{if } \rho = \frac{\lambda}{2\mu} < 1.$$

This is the long-run probability that the two repairmen are simultaneously idle. If $\lambda = 1/6$ and $\mu = 1/8$ (minutes^{-1}), then

$$\rho = \frac{1/6}{2(1/8)} = \frac{2}{3},$$

and, for the two-server system,

$$p_0 = \frac{1 - (2/3)}{1 + (2/3)} = \frac{1}{5}.$$

In order to compute the expected waiting time for a machine, we first find the expected number of machines queued for repair. Using expression (10.4.10), we have

$$(10.4.16) \qquad E[Q] = p_0 \frac{1}{2} \left(\frac{\lambda}{\mu}\right)^2 \frac{\lambda/2\mu}{[1 - (\lambda/2\mu)]^2} = 2p_0 \frac{\rho^3}{(1 - \rho)^2} = \frac{2\rho^3}{1 - \rho^2}.$$

For the parameter values of Example 10.4.3,

$$E[Q] = 2 \frac{(2/3)^3}{1 - (2/3)^2} = \frac{16}{15}.$$

Therefore, from (10.4.11),

$$E[W] = \frac{16}{15} \frac{1}{1/6} = \frac{32}{5} = 6\frac{2}{5} \text{ minutes.}$$

The total expected delay incurred by an arrival is

$$E[D] = E[W] + \frac{1}{\mu},$$

$$= 6\frac{2}{5} + 8 = 14\frac{2}{5} \text{ minutes.}$$

It is interesting to contrast the expected waiting time for the two-repairman system with the expected waiting time obtained if, under otherwise the same circumstances, it were possible to double the service rate for the single-server system of Example 10.4.3 in response to the doubled arrival rate. In this case

$$\rho = \frac{1/6}{1/4} = \frac{2}{3},$$

as before. The expected waiting time may be found by use of (10.4.4):

$$E[W] = \frac{2/3}{1 - (2/3)} \cdot 4 = 8 \text{ minutes.}$$

Thus the wait for service tends to be shorter if two servers are installed. On the other hand, the expected total delay in the present case is

$$E[D] = 8 + 4 = 12 \text{ minutes,}$$

which is smaller than the corresponding delay in the two-server case. It can also be shown that the probability that an arriving customer experiences no wait is greater in the present two-server system than in the single-server system. If total delay is the relevant criterion in a problem, as will often be the case, then the previous example shows that the analyst should not stop with the estimation of the waiting-time distribution alone.

C. The Poisson-Arrival, Multiple-Server, Exponential-Service-Time System with Limited Capacity

In various practical situations there are physical constraints on the length of a waiting line. For example, in banks, barber shops, and doctor's offices, the waiting room size is limited. Likewise, in factories and job shops, where space is at a premium, it is not possible to allow work in process to build up indefinitely between production stations or machines. When the waiting line (or work-in-process inventory, as in the latter example) is at its limiting size, further additions to the line are prohibited. Customers arriving during such "blocked" periods may either go elsewhere or wait externally. If the "blocking queue" is in the middle of a sequence of series operations (see Figure 10.2.4), then those operations coming before it may be forced to a stop until the block is worked out and room once again appears for a queue. It should be mentioned that, while the foregoing discussion has dealt with *physical* restrictions upon the length of a waiting line, *psychological* limitations may also operate: if the line becomes too long, certain arriving customers will balk at joining it. Much the same type of mathematical model applies in either case.

The model of part B above placed no limits on the length of the waiting line. In general, if the probability of exceeding the limits is small, where the probability of doing so may be calculated from (10.4.1), there is no need to worry about them. However, if utilization of the system is high—that is, $\rho = \lambda/a\mu$ is close to, or above, unity—or if waiting capacity is severely limited, alterations must be made in the models of B.

Suppose that c $(c \geq 1)$ is the maximum allowable number of customers permitted in the system. That is, the number waiting plus the number being served cannot exceed c. Let $c > a$, a being the number of servers, since otherwise some servers would always be idle. Then it may be shown that the probability that there are exactly n customers in the system is

$$P\{N = n\} = p_0 \frac{(\lambda/\mu)^n}{n!} \qquad n = 0, 1, 2, \ldots, a,$$

(10.4.17)
$$= p_0 \frac{(\lambda/\mu)^n}{a! \, a^{n-a}} \qquad n = a + 1, a + 2, \ldots, c,$$

where

(10.4.18)
$$P_0 = \left[\sum_{n=0}^{a} \frac{(\lambda/\mu)^n}{n!} + \left(\frac{\lambda}{\mu} \right)^a \frac{1}{a!} \left\{ \frac{(\lambda/a\mu) - (\lambda/a\mu)^{c-a+1}}{1 - (\lambda/a\mu)} \right\} \right]^{-1}$$

is the long-run probability that all servers are simultaneously idle. Expression (10.4.17) holds regardless of the value of ρ, since the possibility of infinitely growing queues is eliminated. Now using the probability distribution (10.4.17), it is possible to provide the same kind of general formulas for various system parameters that were given before. It turns out that these general formulas are complicated, and thus somewhat uninformative. The *numerical* values for expectations of number in the system and queue, as well as the length of waiting time, are obtainable from (10.4.17). We shall only provide explicit algebraic formulas for two special, but important, cases.

I. *The Single-Server System with Limited Waiting Space**

The following results may be shown to hold by putting $a = 1$ in (10.4.17).

1. The probability that, in the long run, there are exactly n customers in the system is

(10.4.19)
$$P\{N = n\} = \frac{1 - \rho}{1 - \rho^{c+1}} \rho^n \qquad n = 0, 1, 2, \ldots, c,$$

where $\rho = \lambda/\mu$. This expression is valid for any value of ρ—not just for $\rho < 1$ as in A. However, when $\rho = 1$, the expression (10.4.19) takes the form 0/0; evaluation

---

* You should compare this model to a similar discrete Markov-chain model in the chapter on Markov chains.

by L'Hospital's rule shows that all states are equally likely: $P\{N = n\} = (c + 1)^{-1}$. Later formulas must be modified accordingly.

2. The expected number of customers in the system is

$$(10.4.20) \qquad E[N] = \frac{\rho}{1 - \rho} \left[\frac{1 - c\rho^c(1 - \rho) - \rho^c}{1 - \rho^{c+1}} \right].$$

3. The expected waiting time is

$$(10.4.21) \qquad E[W] = \frac{\rho}{1 - \rho} \cdot \frac{1}{\mu} \left[\frac{1 - c\rho^{c-1}(1 - \rho) - \rho^c}{1 - \rho^{c+1}} \right] + \frac{1 - \rho}{1 - \rho^{c+1}} \rho^c w,$$

where w represents the wait experienced at another facility by a customer who arrives when there is no waiting space left.

4. The expected delay is

$$(10.4.22) \qquad E[D] = \left[\frac{1}{1 - \rho} - \frac{\rho^c}{1 - \rho^{c-1}} \right] \frac{1}{\mu} + \frac{1 - \rho}{1 - \rho^{c+1}} \rho^c d,$$

where d represents the delay at the facility of second choice.

EXAMPLE 10.4.4. The clients of a particular consultant arrive at his office according to a Poisson process and await service in a waiting room. The latter contains $c - 1$ chairs. If a prospective client arrives to find the chairs all taken, he selects an alternative consultant and never returns. Suppose the consultant's average charge per customer is \$100, that the arrival rate, λ, is 1.5 customers per hour, the service rate, μ, is 1 customer per hour, and that at present there are three chairs in the waiting room. At what rate, in \$ per hour, is the consultant losing prospective business?

From (10.4.19), the long-run probability that all chairs in the waiting room are filled (and one customer is talking to the consultant) is

$$P\{N = 4\} = \frac{1 - 1.5}{1 - (1.5)^5} (1.5)^4 = 0.38.$$

Since customers arrive at rate $\lambda = 1.5$ customers per hour, the expected number per hour that encounter a full house is $(1.5) \times (.38)$, or 0.57, and hence the consultant is losing approximately \$57 per hour.

II. The Parallel-Server System without Waiting Space

If $c = a$ in (10.4.17), then any customer who arrives to find all servers busy is lost.

1. The probability that there are exactly n customers in the system is

$$(10.4.23) \qquad P\{N = n\} = p_0 \frac{\rho^n}{n!} \qquad n = 0, 1, 2, \ldots, c,$$

and

$$(10.4.24) \qquad p_0 = \left[\sum_{n=0}^{c} \frac{\rho^n}{n!} \right]^{-1},$$

where $\rho = \lambda/\mu$.

2. The expected number of customers in the system is

$$(10.4.25) \qquad E[N] = \sum_{n=0}^{c} n \frac{\rho^n}{n!} = \rho \sum_{n=0}^{c-1} \frac{\rho^n}{n!}.$$

3. The expected delay for an arriving customer is

$$(10.4.26) \qquad E[D] = \sum_{n=0}^{c-1} p_0 \frac{\rho^n}{n!} \frac{1}{\mu} + p_0 \frac{\rho^c}{c!} d,$$

where d is the delay experienced by a customer who encounters all servers busy and must turn elsewhere.

EXAMPLE 10.4.5. A particular company has positions for three salesmen. Applicants for these jobs appear (in a Poisson manner) at a rate of two per year; if all jobs are filled, they look elsewhere. Those who hold the jobs do so for an exponentially distributed time that averages one year. What is the probability that all jobs are filled? Since

$$\rho = \frac{2}{1} = 2,$$

$$p_0 = \left[1 + \frac{\rho}{1!} + \frac{\rho^2}{2!} + \frac{\rho^3}{3!} \right]^{-1},$$

$$= \left[1 + \frac{2}{1!} + \frac{2^2}{2!} + \frac{2^3}{3!} \right]^{-1} = \frac{3}{19};$$

this is the probability that all three salesmen's jobs are open. The probability that all are filled is

$$P\{N = 3\} = p_0 \frac{\rho^3}{3!},$$

$$= \left(\frac{3}{19} \right) \frac{2^3}{3!} = \frac{4}{19}.$$

The model above may also be used to discuss a simple, but rather important, *inventory problem*. We illustrate this interpretation in the following example.

EXAMPLE 10.4.6. The airplanes in a large fleet occasionally require major and lengthy engine overhaul. Such overhaul is conducted at a certain repair depot. Assume that the arrival rate at the depot of aircraft requiring an engine overhaul is λ. Since overhaul is a lengthy procedure, the depot keeps on hand some spare engines. The idea is that if an airplane requiring engine overhaul arrives, a spare may be immediately installed so the airplane may resume flight operations while the overhaul is being conducted on the original engine. All engines are regarded as interchangeable between airplanes. The problem is to determine the number, s, of spare engines to be stocked at the repair depot.

Let us assume that each overhaul requires an independently and exponentially distributed time duration with mean μ^{-1}. Each engine is worked on independently, so there is no queuing for repair facilities (this is probably a questionable assumption).

Let $N(t)$ denote the number of engines undergoing overhaul at time t. Notice that if $N(t) = 0$, then all s spares are available for installation, if $N(t) = 1$, the one engine is on repair but $s - 1$ are available, and so on. If, on the other hand, $N(t) \geq s$, then no spares are available and, in addition, $N(t) - s$ airplanes are grounded for engine overhaul. Thus the expression (10.4.23) tells us that with probability

$$(10.4.27) \qquad P\{N < s\} = \sum_{n=0}^{s-1} p_0 \frac{\rho^n}{n!},$$

fewer than s engines are on overhaul at the time of a request; hence this is the probability that an immediate replacement is possible. If $N \geq s$, then an arriving aircraft must wait; the probability of this event is

$$(10.4.28) \qquad P\{N \geq s\} = \sum_{n=s}^{\infty} p_0 \frac{\rho^n}{n!}.$$

The expected number of engines in excess of s on overhaul is the expected number of aircraft grounded while awaiting engines and is

$$(10.4.29) \qquad E[\text{grounded aircraft}] = \sum_{n=s}^{\infty} (n - s) p_0 \frac{\rho^n}{n!}.$$

Finally, since no limit has been placed on the number of engines undergoing overhaul, $c = \infty$, and thus

$$p_0 = \left[1 + \frac{\rho}{1!} + \frac{\rho^2}{2!} + \cdots \right]^{-1} = e^{-\rho}.$$

Referring to (10.4.23), we see that the long-run probability that n engines are simultaneously undergoing overhaul is

$$(10.4.30) \qquad P\{N = n\} = e^{-\rho} \frac{\rho^n}{n!} \qquad n = 0, 1, 2, \ldots;$$

the number undergoing overhaul has the *Poisson distribution*. Supposing that $s = 0$, the expected number undergoing overhaul is ρ; if $s = 1$ the expected number undergoing overhaul is

$$E[\text{grounded aircraft} \mid s = 1] = \sum_{n=1}^{\infty} (n - 1) e^{-\rho} \frac{\rho^n}{n!}.$$

$$(10.4.31) \qquad = \sum_{n=1}^{\infty} n e^{-\rho} \frac{\rho^n}{n!} - \sum_{n=1}^{\infty} e^{-\rho} \frac{\rho^n}{n!},$$

$$= \rho - [1 - e^{-\rho}].$$

Since $0 < 1 - e^{-\rho} \leq \rho$, the expected number of grounded aircraft is reduced, as is to be expected. Additional spares will of course improve the availability of engines.

D. The Poisson-Arrival, Series-Server, Exponential-Service-Time System

Many production processes require a sequence of activities to be performed in sequence. Figure 10.2.4 shows the flow of customers through servers for this arrangement. If arrivals at the system are Poisson, with rate λ, if the service times are independent and the service time at Server i $(i = 1, 2, \ldots, a)$ has rate μ_i, and if there is unlimited waiting space between individual servers, then in the long run the following formulas describe the status of the process.

    1. The joint probability that there are exactly n_1 customers at Server 1, n_2 at Server 2, $\ldots$, n_a at Server a is

(10.4.32) $\qquad P\{N_1 = n_1, N_2 = n_2, \ldots, N_a = n_a\} = (1 - \rho_1)\rho_1{}^{n_1}(1 - \rho_2)\rho_2{}^{n_2} \cdots$
$$(1 - \rho_a)\rho_a{}^{n_a}$$

where $\rho_i = (\lambda/\mu_i) < 1$ $(i = 1, 2, \ldots a)$.*

    2. The expected number of customers in the system is

(10.4.33) $\qquad E[N_1 + N_2 + \cdots + N_a] = \dfrac{\rho_1}{1 - \rho_1} + \dfrac{\rho_2}{1 - \rho_2} + \cdots + \dfrac{\rho_a}{1 - \rho_a}.$

    3. Assuming a "first-come, first-served" discipline, the expected waiting time accumulated by a customer passing through the entire system is the sum of his expected waiting times at each stage:

(10.4.34) $\qquad E[W_1 + W_2 + \cdots + W_a] = \dfrac{\rho_1}{1 - \rho_1}\dfrac{1}{\mu_1} + \dfrac{\rho_2}{1 - \rho_2}\dfrac{1}{\mu_2} + \cdots + \dfrac{\rho_a}{1 - \rho_a}\dfrac{1}{\mu_a}.$

    4. The expected total delay of a customer passing through the entire system is the sum of the delays at each stage:

(10.4.35) $\qquad E[D_1 + D_2 + \cdots + D_a] = \dfrac{1}{1 - \rho_1}\dfrac{1}{\mu_1} + \dfrac{1}{1 - \rho_2}\dfrac{1}{\mu_2} + \cdots + \dfrac{1}{1 - \rho_a}\dfrac{1}{\mu_a}.$

    EXAMPLE 10.4.7. A continuous production process involves three stages: assembly, adjustment, and inspection. The service times at each stage may be taken to be independently and exponentially distributed random variables with the following rates:

Stage

Rate (hours^{-1})	1: Assembly	2: Adjustment	3: Inspection
μ	1.0	1.5	1.8

Now if an indefinitely large backlog of units (customers) exists, the first stage may be thought of as having an infinite queue. Consequently the assembly server is constantly busy, and so, because his service or processing times are independent and exponential, the output from the assembly stage is a Poisson process with rate μ_1 (see Theorem 10.2.1). Thus

$$\rho_2 = \frac{\mu_1}{\mu_2} = \frac{1}{1.5} = \frac{2}{3} \qquad \rho_3 = \frac{1}{1.8} = \frac{5}{9}.$$

---

    * It may be shown that, in the long run, $N_1, N_2, \ldots, N_a$ are independently and geometrically distributed, as stated here. To see that arrivals at the second stage occur at rate λ, note that the Server 1 is busy with probability λ/μ_1; if busy, a departure occurs with probability $\mu_1\,dt$. Hence the probability of a departure is $(\lambda/\mu_1)(\mu_1\,dt) = \lambda\,dt =$ probability of arrival at Server 2.

The entire time required to produce a single unit is the expected assembly time plus the delay experienced by a unit in passing subsequently through the adjustment and inspection stages. From (10.4.35), the delay time turns out to be

$$E[D_2 + D_3] = \frac{1}{1 - \rho_2} \cdot \frac{1}{\mu_2} + \frac{1}{1 - \rho_3} \cdot \frac{1}{\mu_3},$$

$$= \frac{1}{1 - \frac{2}{3}} \cdot \frac{1}{1.5} + \frac{1}{1 - \frac{5}{9}} \cdot \frac{1}{1.8},$$

$$= 2 + 1.25 = 3.25 \text{ (hours)}.$$

Adding in the expected assembly time, we find that the expected total production time at the three stages is 4.25 hours. It is also of interest to compute the expected work-in-process inventory—that is, the expected number of partially finished units at stages 2 and 3. From (10.4.33), we have

$$E[N_2 + N_3] = \frac{\rho_2}{1 - \rho_2} + \frac{\rho_3}{1 - \rho_3},$$

$$= 2 + 1.25 = 3.25 \text{ (units)}.$$

Of course the work-in-process inventory represents an investment which, if so desired, may be reduced by preventing the formation of queues between stages. This means that, if at the moment unit n is ready to leave the assembly stage, the preceding unit, unit $n - 1$, still occupies the adjustment stage, unit n is *blocked* and cannot move. Thus assembly is halted until unit $n - 1$ leaves the adjustment stage. It is clear that if blocking can occur, the system production rate goes down; this is the price that is paid for the reduction of work-in-process inventory. We do not here consider models that permit blocking, although such situations frequently arise in practice because of space limitations.

EXERCISES 10.4

1. Use formulas (10.4.9) and (10.4.12) to show that the expected delay in a Poisson-arrival, parallel-server system may be expressed as follows

$$E[D] = E[N]\frac{1}{\lambda}.$$

2. For the single-server system of part A,
   (a) find the probability that a newly arrived customer encounters a queue of more than n customers in length. In other words, find $P\{Q > n\}$.
   (b) use the result of (a) above to draw a graph of the probability that the queue is longer than four as a function of the traffic intensity ρ; take $\rho = 0.2, 0.4, 0.6, 0.8, 0.9, 0.95$.
   (c) show that
   [Expected delay][Probability server is idle] = [Expected service time].

3. Refer to Example 10.4.3. Suppose the reason for doubling the number of machines, and hence the overall arrival or failure rate, is the addition of an entire new factory. One alternative is the establishment of a central two-repairman *pool* into which all requests come; this is the approach of Example 10.4.3. Another is to assign one repairman to each separate factory.

(a) Compare the expected delay experienced when a repair pool is used to that when each factory has its own repairman.

(b) Explain the difference you have found in part (a) in layman's language.

(c) What practical considerations that are not included in our model should be considered before deciding to establish a central pool?

4. Refer to the case of the management consultant's office capacity of Example 10.4.4.

(a) At what rate in \$ per hour will the consultant increase gross profits if he increases the number of chairs in his waiting room from 3 to (i) 4? (ii) 6? (iii) 8?

(b) The consultant requires about one hour of "idle" time per eight-hour day to carry out his correspondence. How many chairs should he put in his office if he wishes to satisfy this requirement as closely as possible? How many prospective clients are turned away per day?

(c) What is the expected waiting time for a client who is able to find a seat in the office if there are three chairs? If there are four chairs?

5. Demonstrate the equivalence of (10.4.13) and (10.4.14).

6. Referring to the setup of Example 10.4.3, show mathematically, for all values of traffic intensity less than unity, that the expected waiting time in a two-server system is less than the expected waiting time in a single-server system with twice the service rate.

10.5* DIFFERENTIAL EQUATIONS FOR POISSON AND BIRTH-AND-DEATH MODELS

The Poisson arrival process and related birth-and-death models were discussed in the previous section. In this section we shall consider certain differential equations associated with these stochastic processes. Actual solution of these differential equations will be carried out only in some very simple special cases. Nevertheless, useful information and understanding are available from them, and they provide another way of deriving the balance equations that we used in the preceding section.

We begin by a discussion of the Poisson process, properties of which were summarized in Theorem 10.2.1. Let us see how the Poisson distribution may actually be derived from Definition 10.2.1. Paraphrasing the latter, we assume that (i) the probability of no arrival in $(t, t + h)$ is $1 - \lambda h + o(h)$, whereas (ii) the probability of exactly one arrival in $(t, t + h)$ is $\lambda h + o(h)$, and (iii) the probability of more than one is $o(h)$. Recall that $o(h)$ is a quantity that is negligible compared to h as h becomes small. The probability of any one of the events above is independent of events occurring at earlier times; that is, the Poisson process has the Markov property.

Let us compute the probability that exactly n arrivals ($n = 0, 1, 2, \ldots$) occur in the time interval $(0, t + h)$, where h is positive and small. Denote this probability by $P_n(t + h)$. Now split the interval above into the two parts, $(0, t)$ and $(t, t + h)$, and consider the manner in which a total of n arrivals can take place in $(0, t + h)$. First, if $n = 0$—that is, no arrivals occur in $(0, t + h)$—we see that there is (i) no arrival in $(0, t)$ and (ii) no arrival in $(t, t + h)$. By independence, then,

(10.5.1) $$P_0(t + h) = P_0(t)[1 - \lambda h] + o(h).$$

Now subtract $P_0(t)$ from both sides and divide by h:

(10.5.2) $$\frac{P_0(t + h) - P_0(t)}{h} = -\lambda P_0(t) + \frac{o(h)}{h}.$$

Now let h tend to zero. The right-hand side tends to $-\lambda P_0(t)$, since $o(h)$ is negligible compared to h and hence the ratio vanishes. The left-hand side has a limit, and the latter is the *derivative* of $P_0(t)$. Thus we obtain the differential equation

$$(10.5.3) \qquad \frac{dP_0}{dt} = -\lambda P_0(t),$$

which is easily solved to give

$$(10.5.4) \qquad P_0(t) = e^{-\lambda t},$$

provided that initially there are no arrivals present ($t = 0$).

Next, if $n \geq 1$, a total of n arrivals can occur if any of the following mutually exclusive events take place: in $(0, t + h)$ (i) n arrivals occur in $(0, t)$ and none occur in $(t, t + h)$ or (ii) $(n - 1)$ arrivals occur in $(0, t)$ and one occurs in $(t, t + h)$ or (iii) for $2 \leq j \leq n$, $n - j$ arrivals occur in $(0, t)$ and j arrivals occur in $(t, t + h)$. The probabilities associated with these events are, respectively,

    (i) $P_n(t)[1 - \lambda h + o(h)]$ by (10.2.1);
    (ii) $P_{n-1}(t)[\lambda h + o(h)]$ by (10.2.2);
    (iii) $P_{n-j}(t)[o(h)] = o(h)$ by (10.2.3).

Since these events are mutually exclusive, we add their probabilities to obtain

$$P_n(t + h) = P_n(t)[1 - \lambda h + o(h)] + P_{n-1}(t)[\lambda h + o(h)] + o(h),$$
$$= P_n(t)[1 - \lambda h] + P_{n-1}(t)\lambda h + o(h).$$

If now $P_n(t)$ is subtracted from both sides and the result is divided by h, there results

$$\frac{P_n(t + h) - P_n(t)}{h} = -\lambda P_n(t) + \lambda P_{n-1}(t) + \frac{o(h)}{h}.$$

Let h tend to zero; the result is the differential equation

$$(10.5.5) \qquad \frac{dP_n}{dt} = -\lambda P_n(t) + \lambda P_{n-1}(t) \qquad n = 1, 2, 3, \dots.$$

One may verify by direct substitution that the Poisson distribution (10.2.4) actually satisfies this equation. A direct derivation is recursive: substitute the expression for $P_0(t)$ into the equation above with $n = 1$ to obtain

$$(10.5.6) \qquad \frac{dP_1}{dt} = -\lambda P_1(t) + \lambda e^{-\lambda t}.$$

Now rewrite this as*

$$\frac{d}{dt}[P_1(t)e^{\lambda t}]e^{-\lambda t} = \lambda e^{-\lambda t},$$

$$\frac{d}{dt}[P_1(t)e^{\lambda t}] = \lambda.$$

---

* We use throughout the "integrating factor" method for solving differential equations of the form

$$\frac{dy}{dx} + a(x)y = b(x);$$

Now integrate and use the fact that $P_1(0) = 0$:

$$\int_0^t \frac{d}{dt}[P_1(t)e^{\lambda t}]\,dt = \int_0^t \lambda\,dt$$

or

$$P_1(t)e^{\lambda t} = \lambda t,$$

so

(10.5.7)
$$P_1(t) = (\lambda t)e^{-\lambda t}.$$

An induction argument completes the derivation.

Observe that this derivation can be carried out even if the arrival rate is a function of t, denoted by $\lambda(t)$.

Equations analogous to (10.5.5), but allowing for jumps both up and down, may be derived in a similar manner. Suppose we wish to find the probability that the system is in state j at time $t + h$. That is, we seek

(10.5.8)
$$P\{N(t + h) = j\,|\,N(0) = i\} = P_{ij}(t + h).$$

Now either (i) the system was in state j at time t and no change (jump) occurred in the time interval $(t, t + h)$ or (ii) the system was in state $j - 1$ at t and an arrival appeared in $(t, t + h)$ or (iii) the system was in state $j + 1$ at t and a departure took place in $(t, t + h)$. All other events have negligible probability. Adding the probabilities of these mutually exclusive events, we obtain

(10.5.9)
$$P_{ij}(t + h) = P_{ij}(t)[1 - (\lambda_j + \mu_j)h + o(h)] + P_{i,j-1}(t)[\lambda_{j-1}h + o(h)]$$
$$+ P_{i,j+1}(t)[\mu_{j+1}h + o(h)].$$

Now if $P_{ij}(t)$ is subtracted from both sides, the result is divided by h, and h is allowed to become small, the differential equation

(10.5.10)
$$\frac{dP_{ij}(t)}{dt} = -(\lambda_j + \mu_j)P_{ij}(t) + \lambda_{j-1}P_{i,j-1}(t) + \mu_{j+1}P_{i,j+1}(t)$$

---

namely, since

$$\frac{d}{dx}\left[e^{\int_0^x a(z)\,dz}\right] = a(x)e^{\int_0^x a(x)\,dz},$$

we have, by rules for differentiating products, that

$$e^{\int_0^x a(z)\,dz}\left[\frac{dy}{dx} + a(x)y\right] = \frac{d}{dx}\left[ye^{\int_0^x a(z)\,dz}\right],$$

so we integrate:

$$y(x)e^{\int_0^x a(z)\,dz} = \int b(x)e^{\int_0^x a(z)\,dz}\,dx + \text{constant}$$

or

$$y(x) = y(0)e^{-\int_0^x a(z)\,dz} + e^{-\int_0^x a(z)\,dz}\int_0^x b(u)e^{\int_0^u a(z)\,dz}\,du.$$

results. Clearly we wish to make $\mu_0 = 0$, since no service may be completed when there are no customers present. Under some circumstances, too, there will be a maximum queue size, c. For example, waiting room size may be limited; see part C of Section 10.6. In that case, the chance of an arrival that actually enters the waiting room is zero if the room is full; that is, $\lambda_c = 0$.

Again, a steady-state or long-run solution frequently exists, as was true in the case of regular Markov chains:

$$(10.5.11) \qquad \lim_{t \to \infty} P_{ij}(t) = p_j \qquad j = 0, 1, 2, \dots .$$

If the solution does exist, then it can be found by solving the balance equations obtained by putting the derivative equal to zero in (10.5.10). The balance equations are

$$(10.5.12) \qquad \begin{aligned} \lambda_0 p_0 &= \mu_1 p_1, \\ (\lambda_1 + \mu_1)p_1 &= \lambda_0 p_0 + \mu_2 p_2, \\ (\lambda_2 + \mu_2)p_2 &= \lambda_1 p_1 + \mu_3 p_3, \\ &\cdots, \\ (\lambda_j + \mu_j)p_j &= \lambda_{j-1} p_{j-1} + \mu_{j+1} p_{j+1}. \end{aligned}$$

A solution may be carried out by recursion, starting from the first equation:

$$(10.5.13) \qquad p_1 = \frac{\lambda_0}{\mu_1} p_0;$$

then substitution in the second gives

$$(\lambda_1 + \mu_1)\left(\frac{\lambda_0}{\mu_1}\right)p_0 = \lambda_0 p_0 + \mu_2 p_2,$$

so

$$(10.5.14) \qquad p_2 = \frac{\lambda_0 \lambda_1}{\mu_1 \mu_2} p_0 .$$

It may be seen finally that

$$(10.5.15) \qquad p_j = \frac{\lambda_0 \lambda_1 \cdots \lambda_{j-1}}{\mu_1 \mu_2 \cdots \mu_j} p_0 .$$

Now in order for a steady-state solution $\{p_j, j = 0, 1, 2, \dots\}$ to exist, it is necessary that the p_j's as given by the expression (10.4.15) be normalizable, that is, it is necessary that the following series converge:

$$\sum_{j=0}^{\infty} p_j = p_0 \left[1 + \sum_{j=1}^{\infty} \left(\frac{\lambda_0 \lambda_1 \cdots \lambda_{j-1}}{\mu_1 \mu_2 \cdots \mu_j} \right) \right] < \infty .$$

We can then set

$$(10.5.16) \qquad p_0 = \frac{1}{1 + \displaystyle\sum_{j=1}^{\infty} \left(\frac{\lambda_0 \lambda_1 \cdots \lambda_{j-1}}{\mu_1 \mu_2 \cdots \mu_j} \right)}$$

and the p_j's are positive and sum to unity.

EXAMPLE 10.5.1. *Simple Time-Dependent Model.* The previous work has concentrated on long-run or steady-state behavior of stochastic systems. A preeminent reason is the mathematical intractability of the transient problems. Nevertheless, time dependence and questions of rapidity of approach to stationary conditions are of definite interest in applications. Here one simple, readily solvable problem is introduced.

Suppose, then, that there is a single machine (see the last example) and a single repairman. Let the state variable $N(t)$ be unity if the machine is down or inoperative and two otherwise:

$$(10.5.17) \qquad P_{ij}(t) = P\{N(t) = j \mid N(0) = i\} \qquad i, j = 1, 2.$$

Then (10.5.5) shows that the following differential equation describes the development of the probabilities; here μ represents repair rate and λ represents failure rate:

$$(10.5.18) \qquad \frac{dP_{i1}(t)}{dt} = -\mu_i P_1(t) + \lambda P_{i2}(t) \qquad i = 1, 2,$$

subject to the arbitrary initial conditions

$$(10.5.19) \qquad \lim_{t \to 0} P_{11}(t) = 1 \qquad \lim_{t \to 0} P_{21}(t) = 0,$$

and

$$(10.5.20) \qquad P_{i1}(t) + P_{i2}(t) = 1.$$

Now (10.5.18) is easily solved. First substitute for $P_{i2}(t)$ in (10.5.18) to obtain

$$(10.5.21) \qquad \frac{dP_{i1}(t)}{dt} = -(\lambda + \mu)P_{i1}(t) + \lambda.$$

Rewriting, this becomes

$$(10.5.22) \qquad \frac{dP_{i1}(t)}{dt} + (\lambda + \mu)P_{i1}(t) = \lambda.$$

The standard integrating factor method of elementary differential equations next gives

$$(10.5.23) \qquad \frac{d}{dt}[P_{i1}(t)e^{(\lambda + \mu)t}] = \lambda e^{(\lambda + \mu)t}.$$

Now integrate from 0 to t:

$$(10.5.24) \qquad P_{i1}(t)e^{(\lambda + \mu)t} - P_{i1}(0) = \frac{\lambda}{\lambda + \mu}[e^{(\lambda + \mu)t} - 1]$$

or, finally,

$$(10.5.25) \qquad P_{i1}(t) = P_{i1}(0)e^{-(\lambda + \mu)t} + \frac{\lambda}{\lambda + \mu}[1 - e^{-(\lambda + \mu)t}],$$

$$(10.5.26) \qquad P_{11}(t) = e^{-(\lambda + \mu)t} + \frac{\lambda}{\lambda + \mu}[1 - e^{-(\lambda + \mu)t}],$$

$$(10.5.27) \qquad P_{21}(t) = \frac{\lambda}{\lambda + \mu}[1 - e^{-(\lambda + \mu)t}].$$

Several interesting facts may be deduced from the solutions. First, since the exponential tends to zero as the time, t, becomes large,

$$(10.5.28) \qquad \lim_{t \to \infty} P_{11}(t) = \lim_{t \to \infty} P_{21}(t) = p_1,$$

where p_1 satisfies the stationary or balance equation obtained by setting the derivative equal to zero in (10.5.18):

$$(10.5.29) \qquad \begin{aligned} \mu p_1 &= \lambda p_2, \\ p_1 + p_2 &= 1. \end{aligned}$$

Thus we have a direct verification of the fact, asserted earlier, that under certain circumstances the probabilities $P_{ij}(t)$ tend in the long run to the solution of the balance equations. Notice, too, that the approach to the long-run solution, p_j, is exponentially fast—that is, is governed by $e^{-(\lambda + \mu)t}$. The *rate* of approach depends upon $\lambda + \mu$: the larger the failure and repair rates, the sooner are we able to rely on the long-run probabilities as good approximations to the (usually much more complex) time-dependent values $P_{ij}(t)$.

EXAMPLE 10.5.2. *Balking and Reneging.* Often when people find themselves in circumstances involving delay, they react to minimize or avoid it. For example, a man intending to get a haircut or a minor automobile repair or tune-up will put it off if he finds the number waiting ahead of him too long. We say he *balks*, or refuses to join the line. Another tactic is that of leaving a line after a period spent waiting for service. This is called *reneging*. Everyone has seen members of different lines, for example, at banks or supermarkets, switch lines or *jockey* in an attempt to move through the system more rapidly. All of these phenomena may be modeled, but here we shall illustrate only the manner in which balking and reneging may be described for the simplest Poisson-arrival, single-server, exponential-time system. Note that the tactics described are those of the customers. Servers may also react to increased or decreased backlogs; models for such behavior are similar and will not be considered here.

First, to treat balking, let there be a probability, b_j, that a new arrival actually enters the system (joins the line) if j individuals are present. That is, if the probability of an arrival in $(t, t + h)$ is $\lambda h + o(h)$ and if the number in the system is $N(t) = j$, then the probability of an *actual* increase in $N(t)$ from j to $j + 1$ is $\lambda b_j h + o(h)$. Thus we may use the general expression for the long-run or stationary probabilities (10.5.15) with λb_j and hence

$$(10.5.30) \qquad p_j = p_0 \left(\frac{\lambda}{\mu}\right)^j b_0 b_1 \cdots b_{j-1}.$$

As an illustration, the expression

$$(10.5.31) \qquad b_j = \frac{1}{j + 1}$$

for the probability of entering is reasonable, decreasing as it does with j. Its use in (10.5.30) gives

$$(10.5.32) \qquad p_j = p_0 \left(\frac{\lambda}{\mu}\right)^j \frac{1}{j!}.$$

When normalized (as it can be for all values of $\rho = \lambda/\mu$), this model presents us with the Poisson stationary distribution

$$(10.5.33) \qquad p_j = e^{-\lambda/\mu} \frac{1}{j!} \left(\frac{\lambda}{\mu} \right)^j.$$

If this particular kind of balking occurs, the expected number is

$$(10.5.34) \qquad E[N] = \frac{\lambda}{\mu} = \rho,$$

which increases merely linearly with the arrival rate λ, as contrasted with its dramatically nonlinear behavior when all customers remain.

Next consider reneging. Let there be a probability, essentially $r_j h$, that some customer in the waiting line decides to leave in $(t, t + h)$ before reaching the service facility. That is, if $N(t) = j \geq 1$, the probability that some customer leaves is, in the present system,

$$\mu_j = r_j + \mu \qquad j \geq 1;$$

r_j represents the rate of leaving before service and μ the rate of service completion. Again, using the general expression for the long-run probabilities (10.5.15), we find

$$(10.5.35) \qquad p_j = p_0 \frac{\lambda^j}{(r_1 + \mu)(r_2 + \mu) \cdots (r_j + \mu)}.$$

It should be apparent again that there will always be a long-run distribution if reneging of the type described above occurs. No matter how slowly service proceeds, some customers will eventually leave without service, and the longer the line, the more frequent will be the defections. A natural illustration results by supposing that each waiting customer has a constant probability of αh of reneging or defecting at any instant. Then if j customers are in line, $r_j = j\alpha$, and (10.5.15) becomes

$$(10.5.36) \qquad p_j = p_0 \left(\frac{\lambda}{\mu} \right)^j \frac{1}{\left(1 + \frac{\alpha}{\mu} \right)\left(1 + \frac{2\alpha}{\mu} \right) \cdots \left(1 + \frac{j\alpha}{\mu} \right)}.$$

The examples discussed indicate the sorts of models that can be treated in a direct mathematical manner. If other assumptions must be made—for example, that arrivals occur in non-Poisson fashion—then our simple mathematical methods fail. In these numerous cases, one may resort to the use of computer simulation, a technique to be described in a later chapter.

EXERCISES 10.5

1. Suppose customers arrive at an *infinite-server* queuing system in a Poisson manner, with rate λ. Let $N(t)$ denote the number being served at time t. If μ represents the service rate per server, show that
   (a) the overall service rate is $\mu_j = j\mu$ when $N = j$.
   (b) the long-run distribution of N is Poisson.
   Find the expected number of customers undergoing service in the stationary distribution of (b); that is, express the Poisson parameter in terms of λ and μ.

2. Imagine that a minor disease (a cold) spreads in the following manner. There is a finite population, size m. If j individuals $(1 \leq j \leq m)$ have the disease, then the chance that a new individual is infected in $(t, t + h)$ is essentially

$$\lambda_j h = \lambda j(m - j)h \qquad (j = 0, 1, 2, \ldots, m),$$

and the chance that one of those infected recovers is

$$\mu_j h = j\mu h.$$

(a) Argue that there can be no stationary probability distribution for this process, but that if we admit the possibility of a new infection from the outside so that

$$\lambda_0 = \alpha \qquad (\alpha > 0),$$

then such a distribution will exist.

(b) What is the long-run expected number of individuals having the cold?

(c) During what fraction of the time is the population entirely well? During what fraction of the time is the entire population infected with the disease?

(d) How can the model above be modified to serve as a model for the effect of advertising and word-of-mouth gossip on knowledge of a product? (*Hint:* Write out formulas, but do not expect to obtain a neat closed-form solution.)

3. Let λ represent the rate at which calls for service come to a team of two repairmen. The service times are exponentially distributed with mean μ^{-1}, and they are independent.

(a) If $\lambda = 1.5$ calls per day, and $\mu^{-1} = 0.4$ days, find the probability that both repairmen are idle.

(b) Find the probability that both repairmen are busy.

(c) Compute the expected number of calls awaiting attention from a repairman.

4. In the problem above, suppose calls for service go elsewhere whenever both repairmen are occupied. This means that the number of calls present is either 0, 1, or 2—there is no queue.

(a) Show that the equations (analogous to 10.3.11) have the form

$$0 = -\lambda p_0 + \mu p_1,$$
$$0 = -(\lambda + \mu)p_1 + \lambda p_0 + 2\mu p_2,$$
$$0 = -(\lambda + 2\mu)p_2 + \lambda p_1.$$

(b) Solve the last equation, using the fact that $p_0 + p_1 + p_2 = 1$ (hence one equation is redundant).

10.6* WAITING TIMES

An important measure of the effectiveness of a queuing system is the waiting time experienced by an arriving customer. Here we define the *waiting time* to be the total time that elapses from the moment the customer joins the line (if any) until his service commences. *Total delay* is the sum of the waiting time experienced by the customer and his own service time. These concepts have already been introduced in Section 10.3, along with formulas for the expected waiting time and delay in various simple cases. In this section, the derivation of the probability distributions is described. We actually illustrate the ideas by treating only the simple example of a single-server system. However, once the process is understood, you will be able to carry out further derivations by yourself. As has been true previously, only long-run or steady-state results will be obtained. This means that the waiting time of a customer who arrives some "long" time after the system is put into operation is considered.

EXAMPLE 10.6.1. *Waiting Time and Delay for the Poisson-Arrival, Single-Server, Exponential-Service-Time with "First-Come, First Served" Discipline.* The long-run distribution of N, the number of customers present in the system above, where N assumes values $n = 0, 1, 2, 3, \ldots$, is

$$(10.6.1) \qquad P\{N = n\} = (1 - \rho)\rho^n \qquad \text{if } \rho = \frac{\lambda}{\mu} < 1,$$

as may be shown using the method of the previous section. Thus an arriving customer finds a random (geometrically distributed) number of customers ahead of him, and hence his wait is a random variable. Let W_n be his wait if he finds n customers ahead of him. Clearly $W_0 = 0$. If $n \geq 1$, then his wait is the sum of the remaining service time, S_1', of the customers currently being served plus the sum of the service times of the $n - 1$ customers ahead of him in line. That is,

$$(10.6.2) \qquad W_n = S_1' + S_2 + S_3 + \cdots + S_n.$$

Each service time is an independent sample from the exponential distribution

$$(10.6.3) \qquad P\{S \leq x\} = 1 - e^{-\mu x}.$$

Now it is a fundamental property of the exponential distribution that the *remaining* service time, S_1', also has the distribution (10.6.3). This may be seen intuitively by recalling the memoryless property of the exponential: regardless of how long the incumbent's service time has lasted prior to the appearance of our new customer, the probability of his departure in $(t, t + h)$ is essentially μh, and so the probability that the service lasts a further time x is

$$(1 - \mu h)^{x/h} \to e^{-\mu x}$$

as $h \to 0$; an alternative proof is given in Exercise 1. Thus, *given n, W_n is distributed* like a sum of exponential random variables. The distribution is easily found by recursion. We work with densities for convenience. Let

$$(10.6.4) \qquad f(x) = \frac{d}{dx} P\{S \leq x\} = e^{-\mu x}\mu$$

be the probability density of service time (or remaining service time); let $f_n(x)$ be the probability density of W_n:

$$(10.6.5) \qquad f_n(x) = \frac{d}{dx}\{W_n \leq x\}.$$

Obviously $f_1(x) = f(x)$. Now if $S_1' = y$, then the probability that W_2 is between x and $x + dx$ is

$$\begin{aligned} P\{x < W_2 \leq x + dx \,|\, S_1' = y\} &= P\{x < S_1' + S_2 \leq x + dx \,|\, S_1' = y\}, \\ (10.6.6) &= P\{x - y < S_2 \leq x - y + dx\}, \\ &= e^{-\mu(x-y)}\mu \, dx, \end{aligned}$$

for dx small. Multiplying by the probability that $S_1' = y$ and adding (integrating) over $0 \leq y \leq x$, w have

$$(10.6.7) \qquad \begin{aligned} P\{x < W_2 \leq x + dx\} &= \int_0^x e^{-\mu(x-y)}\mu \, dx e^{-\mu y}\mu \, dy, \\ &= e^{-\mu x}(\mu x)\mu \, dx, \end{aligned}$$

and so the probability density of W_2 is

$$f_2(x) = e^{-\mu x}(\mu x)\mu.$$

Now since

$$W_3 = W_2 + S_3,$$

we see that

$$f_3(x) = \int_0^x f_2(x-y)e^{-\mu y}\mu \, dy,$$

$$= \int_0^x e^{-\mu(x-y)}\mu^2(x-y)e^{-\mu y}\mu \, dy,$$

$$= e^{-\mu x}\int_0^x \mu^2(x-y)\mu \, dy,$$

$$= e^{-\mu x}\frac{(\mu x)^2}{2}\mu.$$

Repetition of this procedure shows that

$$(10.6.8) \qquad\qquad f_4(x) = e^{-\mu x}\frac{(\mu x)^3}{3!}\mu$$

and in general that

$$(10.6.9) \qquad\qquad f_n(x) = e^{-\mu x}\frac{(\mu x)^{n-1}}{(n-1)!}\mu \qquad n = 1, 2, \dots .$$

Thus $f_n(x)$ is a special case of the gamma distribution discussed earlier. It may be shown (see Exercise 2) that

$$(10.6.10) \qquad\qquad E[W_n] = \frac{n}{\mu} \qquad n = 0, 1, 2, \dots,$$

and that

$$(10.6.11) \qquad\qquad \text{Var}[W_n] = \frac{n}{\mu^2}.$$

The density $f_n(x)$ is relevant for a given number, n, of customers ahead of our arriving customer. If W is the unconditional waiting time, then the probability density of W is, when $x > 0$, given by

$$P\{x < W \le x + dx\} = \sum_{n=1}^{\infty} P\{x < W \le x + dx \mid N = n\}P\{N = n\},$$

$$= \sum_{n=1}^{\infty} P\{x < W_n \le x + dx\}P\{N = n\},$$

$$= \sum_{n=1}^{\infty} e^{-\mu x}\frac{(\mu x)^{n-1}}{(n-1)!}\mu \, dx(1-\rho)\rho^n,$$

(10.6.12)
$$= e^{-\mu x}(1 - \rho)\rho\mu \, dx \sum_{n=1}^{\infty} \frac{(\mu x\rho)^{n-1}}{(n-1)!},$$

$$= e^{-\mu x}(1 - \rho)\rho\mu \, dx \sum_{m=0}^{\infty} \frac{(\mu x\rho)^m}{m!},$$

$$= e^{-\mu x}(1 - \rho)\rho\mu e^{\mu x\rho} \, dx,$$

$$= (1 - \rho)\rho\mu e^{-(1-\rho)\mu x} \, dx.$$

That is, the waiting time density is itself exponential. Of course the entire distribution of W is *not* exponential, since there is a nonzero probability $1 - \rho$ that the arriving customer will not have to wait. Hence,

$$P\{W \le x\} = P\{W = 0\} + \int_0^x P\{x < W \le x + dx\},$$

(10.6.13)
$$= 1 - \rho + \rho \int_0^x e^{-(1-\rho)\mu x}(1 - \rho)\mu \, dx,$$

$$= 1 - \rho + \rho[1 - e^{-(1-\rho)\mu x}].$$

Thus it follows that the probability that a customer who arrives when the long-run distribution prevails waits a time longer than x is

(10.6.14)
$$P\{W > x\} = 1 - P\{W \le x\},$$
$$= \rho e^{-(1-\rho)\mu x} \qquad x \ge 0, \rho < 1.$$

The expected waiting time is obtainable from (10.6.13) and is

(10.6.15)
$$E[W] = \int_0^{\infty} x(1 - \rho)\rho e^{-(1-\rho)\mu x}\mu \, dx = \frac{\rho}{1 - \rho} \cdot \frac{1}{\mu},$$

an expression that was given earlier. Finally, the *delay* is

$$D = W + S,$$

where S is the service time of the arriving customer. Thus

(10.6.16)
$$E[D] = \frac{\rho}{1 - \rho} \cdot \frac{1}{\mu} + \frac{1}{\mu} = \frac{1}{1 - \rho} \cdot \frac{1}{\mu}.$$

In Exercise 3, you will be asked to show that the probability density of the delay is given by

(10.6.17)
$$f_D(x) = e^{-(1-\rho)\mu x}(1 - \rho)\mu \qquad \rho < 1.$$

Thus total delay itself has the simple exponential distribution in the present case. It is of interest that this result is *exactly* true for our present simple model but is actually *approximately* true under much less restrictive assumptions. Thus the exponential form

$$P\{W > x\} \sim ke^{-cx}$$

can often be anticipated even when arrivals are not Poisson and service times not exponential, particularly as ρ becomes large. Section 10.9 of this chapter discusses such "heavy-traffic" theory.

EXERCISES 10.6

1. Let S have the exponential distribution given by

$$P\{S > x\} = e^{-\mu x}.$$

Interpreting S as a service time or lifetime, show that if S becomes as long as x, then the probability that it reaches $x + y$ is given by $e^{-\mu y}$. (*Hint:* Evaluate

$$P\{S > x + y \mid S > x\} = \frac{P\{S > x, \, S > x + y\}}{P\{S > x\}}.)$$

2. Use the fact that

$$\int_0^\infty e^z z^n dz = n!$$

to find the mean and variance of W_n for the single-server system. As an alternative derivation, use the fact that W_n is a sum of independent and identical exponential random variables, and recall that expectations and variances of such sums are the sums of the expectations and variances.

3. To derive the probability density of total delay in the single-server system, reason that if n customers are present at arrival time, then

$$D_n = S_1' + S_2 + \cdots + S_n + S_{n+1} = W_n + S_{n+1},$$

where S_{n+1} represents the arriving customer's service time. Thus from (10.6.9), observe that the density of D_n is $f_{n+1}(x)$. Finally, remove the condition on n, guided by (10.6.12).

*4. This problem is devoted to deriving the distribution of waiting time for the two-server, one-line system; compare to the setup of Example 10.3.2 and Figure 10.3.1. It is assumed that as soon as either server becomes free, the customer at the head of the line enters the facility and begins service.

   (a) Show, using the two-server stationary probabilities derived in Section 10.3, that the probability that a new customer need not wait is

   $$P\{W = 0\} = p_0 + p_1 = \frac{1-\rho}{1+\rho}(1 + 2\rho) \qquad \rho = \frac{\lambda}{2\mu} < 1.$$

   Compare this to the probability of not having to wait in a single-server system with service rate 2μ.

   (b) Argue that if $n = 2$ customers are present and hence in service at arrival time, then the waiting time is the minimum of the two remaining service times. Thus

   $$P\{W_2 > x\} = P\{S_1' > x\}P\{S_2 > x\} = e^{-2\mu x}.$$

   Fill in the gaps.

   (c) Argue that if n customers are present at the time of arrival, then the conditional density of the waiting time is

   $$f_n(x) = e^{-2\mu x} \frac{(2\mu x)^{n-2}}{(n-2)!} 2\mu.$$

   (*Hint:* Use (b) and try $n = 3$, recalling the memoryless property of the exponential.)

   (d) Utilize the results of Section 10.3 and (c) to show that

   $$P\{x < W < x + dx\} = 4\left(\frac{1-\rho}{1+\rho}\right)\mu\rho^2 e^{-(1-\rho)2\mu x}\, dx \qquad x > 0.$$

Notice that the waiting time is again exponential. Check the expression above by recomputing the answer to (a).

(e) Use the density function of (d) to compute the expected waiting time.

(f) Compute the probability that the total delay, D, exceeds y.

5. A customer comes to a single-server queue with exponential service times (mean μ^{-1}) at a moment when the long-run distribution applies.

(a) Given that there is at least one customer ahead of him, show that the distribution of N is

$$P\{N = n \mid N \geq 1\} = (1 - \rho)\rho^{n-1} \qquad n = 1, 2, \ldots.$$

(b) Suppose our customer's service time is, conditionally, $S = y$. Show that the probability that his service time is shorter than the remaining service time of the server's occupant, *and* of that of each of the other customers in line, is given by

$$\sum_{n=1}^{\infty} (1 - \rho)\rho^{n-1}[e^{-\mu y}]^n = \frac{(1 - \rho)e^{-\mu y}}{1 - \rho e^{-\mu y}}.$$

Continue with (b) to work (c).

(c) Show that the probability that a random arrival's service time is shorter than the (remaining) service times of all ahead of him in line is

$$\int_0^{\infty} e^{-\mu y}\mu dy \left[\frac{1}{1 - \rho e^{-\mu y}} - 1\right]\left(\frac{1 - \rho}{\rho}\right) = \frac{1 - \rho}{\rho^2}[-\log_e(1 - \rho) - \rho]$$

10.7* TIME DEVELOPMENT OF A BIRTH-AND-DEATH MODEL—FIRST-PASSAGE TIMES AND THE BUSY PERIOD

In the previous sections we have described various models based upon the birth-and-death process, but we have concentrated on their long-run performance. This performance is described by the solutions to the stationary or balance equations —for example, by special cases of (10.3.8). Of course the stationary-equation solutions may not accurately describe the system state a relatively short time after the process starts—that is, before steady-state conditions may be presumed to hold. Equally important, there are many situations for which no stationary probabilities exist; examples are furnished by queuing systems that are overloaded so that arrivals occur faster than departures. In a later chapter we intend to provide a mathematical method for deciding whether the long-run solutions do indeed furnish a good approximation. You should refer also to Example 10.4.1 in order to obtain some insight into the problem. By way of contrast to most of our previous discussion, then, this section is devoted to a characterization of the development of a birth-and-death model in time. Once this is in hand, *simulation* of process development by assembling appropriate random numbers is an easy task. Our understanding of process development leads also to analytical results that supplement the long-run probabilities.

Intuitively, one sees that a birth-and-death-process model evolves in time as follows. Starting at state i—that is, with $N(0) = i$—$N(t)$ remains in the initial state for a random time. It then jumps either to state $i - 1$ or $i + 1$, remains in that state for a further time, jumps again, and so on. We shall say that the process $N(t)$ sojourns in state i whenever $N(t) = i$, and we shall define a *sojourn time* as the random time that elapses from a moment at which $N(t)$ enters state i until it first leaves that state again. That is, suppose that i is entered at t', so $N(t') = i$, but that there is a time interval (t'', t') such that $N(t) \neq i$ for $(t'' < t < t')$. Then, letting s_i denote the sojourn time beginning at i, we see that

(10.7.1) $P\{s_i > z\} = P\{N(t) = i$ for all t such that $t' \leq t \leq t' + z \mid N(t') = i\}.$

To find an expression for this probability, we make use of the transition probabilities of birth-and-death-process evolution, in particular (10.3.2c). Let

(10.7.2) $$Q_i(z) = P\{s_i > z\}.$$

We argue that if a sojourn in any state i has lasted for a time interval at least z in duration, then the probability that it lasts for an additional time period h—that is, a total time $z + h$—is simply

(10.7.3) $$P_{ii}(h) = 1 - (\lambda_i + \mu_i)h + o(h)$$

by (10.3.2c). Hence by our fundamental assumptions

(10.7.4) $$\begin{aligned} Q_i(z + h) &= Q_i(z)P_{ii}(h) + o(h), \\ &= Q_i(z)[1 - (\lambda_i + \mu_i)h] + o(h). \end{aligned}$$

Subtracting $Q_i(z)$ from each side, dividing by h, and allowing $h \to 0$, we are presented with the differential equation

(10.7.5) $$\frac{dQ_i}{dz} = -(\lambda_i + \mu_i)Q_i(z),$$

the solution of which is

(10.7.6) $$Q_i(z) = e^{-(\lambda_i + \mu_i)z}.$$

Thus sojourn times are exponentially distributed with density

(10.7.7) $$q_i(z) = -\frac{dQ_i}{dz} = e^{-(\lambda_i + \mu_i)z}(\lambda_i + \mu_i).$$

By the Markov property, once the process leaves state i for state j ($i + 1$ or $i - 1$), the duration of sojourn in that state is uninfluenced by the duration of s_i and other earlier happenings, and thus successive sojourns are independent.

Supposing that the process has sojourned in i for a time z, then again, from (10.3.2), we see that the probability of a jump from i to $i + 1$, say, is $P_{i, i+1}(h)$. Consequently the joint probability that $N(t)$ sojourns in i for time z and then jumps to $i + 1$ in $(z, z + h)$ is

(10.7.8) $P\{N(t) = i$ for all t such that $t' \leq t \leq t' + z; N(t' + z + h) = i + 1 \mid N(t') = i\}$
$= e^{-(\lambda_i + \mu_i)z}\lambda_i h + o(h).$

If the equation above is divided by h, and $h \to 0$, then after multiplication and division by $\lambda_i + \mu_i$, reference to (10.7.8) shows that

$$\lim_{h \to 0} \frac{1}{h} P\{N(t) = i \text{ for all } t \text{ such that } t' \leq t \leq t' + z, N(t' + z + h) = i + 1 \mid N(t') = i\}$$

(10.7.9) $$= [e^{-(\lambda_i + \mu_i)z}(\lambda_i + \mu_i)]\left[\frac{\lambda_i}{\lambda_i + \mu_i}\right]$$

$$= q_i(z)\frac{\lambda_i}{\lambda_i + \mu_i}.$$

The factor $\lambda_i/(\lambda_i + \mu_i)$ clearly represents the probability that a sojourn in state i terminates by jumping to $i + 1$. Thus we see that the sojourn time, s_i, and direction of transition, whether up or down, are independent.

The characterization of birth-and-death-process sample functions in terms of exponentially distributed in-state sojourns, followed by binomial jumps to neighboring states, may be used to obtain various useful and interesting measures of model performance. These measures supplement the description of queuing-system performance given by the stationary or long-run distributions.

DEFINITION 10.7.1. The *first-passage time* from state i to state j, denoted by T_{ij}, is the random time elapsing from a moment at which the birth-and-death state variable is in state i until the moment thereafter when it reaches j. Examples illustrating the relevance of the first-passage-time random variable are the following. These will be discussed more formally later.

EXAMPLE 10.7.1. A computer center is modeled as a single-serve queue with Poisson job arrivals (arrival rate λ) and exponential service times (service rate μ). Let $N(t)$ denote the number of jobs in the system at time t after day beginning. Supposing that no jobs are present when the center opens in the morning, it is of interest to determine the distribution of the time until a backlog of $N = 10$ jobs is on hand. The later time is, of course, $T_{0,10}$, the first-passage time from state 0 to 10. It can be seen that the expectation of $T_{0,j}$ furnishes us with a measure of the rapidity of queue buildup. The latter will provide a guide concerning the usefulness of the stationary distribution (if one exists) for predicting job waiting times.

EXAMPLE 10.7.2. Suppose in the example above that the job backlog at the computer center is i—for example, $i = 20$—at noon. It is of interest to estimate the time that must elapse until this backlog is reduced to a lower value, perhaps zero. If this relaxation time is too long, supplementary service may perhaps be required or jobs must be turned away. A particular case that is of some interest is the following. Suppose the computer has been idle and becomes busy with the arrival of a job. Then the *busy period* is the time until the computer first becomes idle again; clearly T_{10} is the duration of such a busy period.

EXAMPLE 10.7.3. In a particular communications system, two identical machines are arranged redundantly—that is, in such a manner that if one fails the other may take over its job. When a failure occurs, a repairman is available; if repair is completed before the other machine fails, the system operates without interruption. Suppose that both machines fail randomly (at rate λ) and that repair is of exponentially distributed duration (rate μ). Let the state be denoted by $N(t)$, the number of machines down for repair at time t. Then T_{02}, the first-passage time from $N = 0$ to $N = 2$, is recognized as the time until *system* failure. The expectation $E[T_{02}]$ is a useful measure of the value of redundancy and repair capability.

In order to discuss the example above and other examples, it is convenient to begin with the birth-and-death-process representation of this section. Recall that this representation involves exponential sojourns and binomial jumps. In this connection it will be helpful to review the discussion leading up to (10.7.9). Then use of this representation leads to the following result.

THEOREM 10.7.1. If u_i represents the first-passage time from i to $i + 1$ in a birth-and-death process with rates λ_i and μ_i ($i = 1, 2, \ldots$), then the following recurrence formula may be derived:

(10.7.10)
$$E[u_i] = \frac{1}{\lambda_i}\{1 + \mu_i E[u_{i-1}]\},$$

$$E[u_0] = \frac{1}{\lambda_0}.$$

Then the expected first-passage time from i to j ($j > i$) may be found from

(10.7.11)
$$E[T_{ij}] = \sum_{k=i}^{j-1} E[u_k].$$

Proof: Imagine that the system has just entered state i. It subsequently sojourns in state i for time s_i and then either jumps up to $i + 1$ or down to $i - 1$. If it jumps up, the first-passage time is just the sojourn time s_i. One the other hand, if the first jump is down to $i - 1$, then the process level must pass from $i - 1$ to i, and thereafter from i to $i + 1$, before the first passage is completed. Expressing this in symbols,

(10.7.12)
$$u_i = \begin{cases} s_i & \text{if first jump is up} \\ s_i + u_{i-1} + u_i' & \text{if first jump is down} \end{cases}$$

where u_i' is a random variable having the same unconditional distribution as u_i. Now taking conditional expectations and making use of (10.7.7), we obtain

(10.7.13)
$$E[u_i \,|\, \text{up}] = E[s_i] = \frac{1}{\lambda_i + \mu_i}$$

and

(10.7.14)
$$E[u_i \,|\, \text{down}] = E[s_i] + E[u_{i-1}] + E[u_i'].$$

Now multiply (10.7.13) by the probability that the first jump is up and (10.7.14) by the probability of a down jump to obtain the unconditional expectation

(10.7.15)
$$E[u_i] = E[u_i \,|\, \text{up}]\,\frac{\lambda_i}{\lambda_i + \mu_i} + E[u_i \,|\, \text{down}]\,\frac{\mu_i}{\lambda_i + \mu_i},$$

$$= \frac{1}{\lambda_i + \mu_i} + \frac{\mu_i}{\lambda_i + \mu_i}\{E[u_{i-1}] + E[u_i]\},$$

where we have used the fact that u_i' has the same unconditional distribution, and hence the same expectation, as u_i. But if (10.7.15) is solved for $E[u_i]$, expression (10.7.10) is the result. From $\mu_0 = 0$ follows $E[u_0] = \lambda_0^{-1}$. Then one observes that in order for the process to reach j from $i < j$, it must first reach $i + 1$, then $i + 2, \ldots$ until finally j is attained. The total time to accomplish this is

$$T_{ij} = u_i + u_{i+1} + u_{i+2} + \cdots + u_{j-1},$$

and (10.7.11) is obtained by taking expectations.

The theorem will now be used to discuss the examples.

EXAMPLE 10.7.1 (continued). Since $\lambda_i = \lambda$ and $\mu_i = \mu$, we find that

$$E[u_0] = \frac{1}{\lambda},$$

$$E[u_1] = \frac{1}{\lambda}\{1 + \mu E[u_0]\} = \frac{1}{\lambda}\left\{1 + \frac{\mu}{\lambda}\right\},$$

$$E[u_2] = \frac{1}{\lambda}\{1 + \mu E[u_1]\} = \frac{1}{\lambda}\left\{1 + \frac{\mu}{\lambda} + \left(\frac{\mu}{\lambda}\right)^2\right\},$$

(10.7.16) $\cdots,$

$$E[u_j] = \frac{1}{\lambda}\left\{1 + \frac{\mu}{\lambda} + \left(\frac{\mu}{\lambda}\right)^2 + \cdots + \left(\frac{\mu}{\lambda}\right)^j\right\},$$

$$= \frac{1}{\lambda}\left\{\frac{1 - \left(\frac{\mu}{\lambda}\right)^{j+1}}{1 - \frac{\mu}{\lambda}}\right\},$$

where the last expression follows by summing a geometric series. Then from (10.7.11) comes

$$E[T_{0j}] = \sum_{k=0}^{j-1} E[u_k],$$

$$= \sum_{k=0}^{j-1} \frac{1}{\lambda}\left\{\frac{1 - \left(\frac{\mu}{\lambda}\right)^{k+1}}{1 - \frac{\mu}{\lambda}}\right\},$$

(10.7.17)

$$= \frac{j}{\lambda}\frac{1}{1 - \frac{\mu}{\lambda}} - \frac{\left(\frac{\mu}{\lambda}\right)}{(\mu - \lambda)}\sum_{k=0}^{j-1}\left(\frac{\mu}{\lambda}\right)^k,$$

$$= \frac{j}{\lambda - \mu} - \frac{\frac{\mu}{\lambda}}{\lambda - \mu}\left\{\frac{1 - \left(\frac{\mu}{\lambda}\right)^j}{1 - \frac{\mu}{\lambda}}\right\},$$

again by summing a geometric series. The last is the closed-form expression for the expected time to reach j. If $j = 10$, an expression is obtained for the expected time to reach a backlog of ten jobs from a start with no backlog. In the exercises, you will be asked to contrast the behavior of backlog buildup for two systems, one which is oversaturated $(\lambda > \mu)$, and another which will eventually reach an equilibrium $(\lambda < \mu)$.

EXAMPLE 10.7.3. (continued). Let us study the expected time to system failure for this redundant machine example. Let $N(t) = j$ mean that j machines are in a failed condition at t. Suppose that initially $j = 0$. Then

$$(10.7.18) \qquad E[u_0] = \frac{1}{\lambda_0} = \frac{1}{2\lambda},$$

since two machines have twice the failure rate of a single machine. It then follows that

$$(10.7.19) \qquad E[u_1] = \frac{1}{\lambda_1}\{1 + \mu E[u_0]\} = \frac{1}{\lambda}\left\{1 + \frac{\mu}{2\lambda}\right\},$$

by substituting in the value of $E[u_0]$. Hence the expected time to failure is

$$(10.7.20) \qquad E[T_{02}] = E[u_0] + E[u_1] = \frac{1}{2\lambda} + \frac{1}{\lambda} + \frac{\mu}{2\lambda^2}.$$

If no repairman were available (equivalent to $\mu = 0$), then the last expression is merely $(1/2\lambda) + (1/\lambda)$, which may be considerably smaller than (10.7.20), provided μ is relatively large.

A very similar theorem can be derived for the expected first-passage time *down* from level j to level i $(j > i)$.

THEOREM 10.7.2. If d_i represents the first-passage time from i to $i - 1$ in a birth-and-death process with rates λ_i and μ_i, then

$$(10.7.21) \qquad E[d_i] = \frac{1}{\mu_i}\{1 + \lambda_i E[d_{i+1}]\}.$$

The expected first-passage time from j to i $(j > i)$ is

$$(10.7.22) \qquad E[T_{ji}] = \sum_{k=j}^{i+1} E[d_k].$$

Proof: The proof follows from the previous theorem by reversing λ_i and μ_i and replacing $i - 1$ by $i + 1$.

Notice that in this last theorem no boundary condition akin to

$$E[u_0] = \frac{1}{\lambda_0}$$

has been mentioned. We can initialize easily in one of two situations, and these are now illustrated by examples.

EXAMPLE 10.7.4. Recall the machine-repair problem of Example 10.3.3; see also Example 10.7.3 above. There, at most m machines could be awaiting and undergoing repair simultaneously; imagine that this is the case. Consequently, if $j\,(0 \le j \le m)$ denotes the number of machines awaiting or undergoing repair, then if one repairman is on duty we have

$$(10.7.23) \qquad E[d_m] = \frac{1}{\mu},$$

which provides the boundary condition required. To go further, recall that

$$\lambda_j = \lambda(m - j) \quad \text{and} \quad \mu_j = \mu \qquad \text{if } j > 0.$$

Thus

(10.7.24)

$$E[d_{m-1}] = \frac{1}{\mu} \{1 + \lambda E[d_m]\},$$

$$= \frac{1}{\mu} \left\{1 + \frac{\lambda}{\mu}\right\},$$

and

(10.7.25)

$$E[d_{m-2}] = \frac{1}{\mu} \{1 + 2\lambda E[d_{m-1}]\},$$

$$= \frac{1}{\mu} \left\{1 + \frac{2\lambda}{\mu} \left(1 + \frac{\lambda}{\mu}\right)\right\},$$

and so on.

EXAMPLE 10.7.5. Consider a service station confronted by Poisson arrivals of rate λ and having service rate μ (service times are exponentially distributed). Although there is no upper boundary, we can argue that when queue length is $j > 0$, the probability of transition from $j + 1$ to j is the same as that from j to $j - 1$, which is the same as that from $j - 1$ to $j - 2$, and so on, as long as queue length is positive, since $\lambda_j = \lambda$ and $\mu_j = \mu$ are independent of j. Hence the probability distribution of d_j is the same as that of d_{j+1}, and so, in particular,

(10.7.26)
$$E[d_j] = E[d_{j+1}] = E[d_1].$$

Armed with this, we can now substitute into (10.7.21),

(10.7.27)
$$E[d_1] = \frac{1}{\mu} \{1 + \lambda E[d_1]\},$$

and solve for $E[d_1]$. The result is, if $\lambda/\mu < 1$,

(10.7.28)
$$E[d_1] = \frac{1}{\mu} \frac{1}{1 - \frac{\lambda}{\mu}}.$$

More refined methods show that $E[d_1] = \infty$ if $\lambda/\mu \geq 1$. This seems sensible when one recalls that if $\lambda/\mu \geq 1$, the queuing system becomes unstable: at least intuitively we feel that the queue may never dwindle away to zero, and this is reflected in (10.7.28) if μ approaches λ from below.

Notice that d_1 represents a time during which the service facility is constantly busy, starting from a moment at which one customer arrives and ends an idle period. Hence d_1 is naturally called a *busy period*. If at some initial moment there are $i > 0$ customers present, then d_i is the time until the i falls off to $i - 1$. The expected time to empty the system is

(10.7.29)
$$E[T_{i0}] = \sum_{k=i}^{1} E[d_i] = \frac{i}{\mu\left(1 - \frac{\lambda}{\mu}\right)}.$$

EXERCISES 10.7

1. Two machines fail independently at rate 0.05 (hours^{-1}). One repairman is available with repair rate 1 (hours^{-1}).
   (a) What is the expected time until both machines are down simultaneously, supposing that they are initially both operative?
   (b) What is the long-run probability that both machines are in a failed state?

2. A particular common stock's price fluctuates in accordance with a simple birth-and-death-process model: at time t it changes value with probability $\lambda dt + o(dt)$; when it does so it jumps up a point with probability p and down with probability q ($p + q = 1$). There are believed to be certain natural boundaries between which the price changes; let these be \$1 and \$H. (*Hint:* Observe that $\lambda_i = \lambda p$, $\mu_i = \lambda_q$; use Theorem 10.7.1.)
   (a) Suppose an investor buys the stock at 1 (the low). How long must he wait, on the average, until it reaches H?
   (b) For illustration, put $\lambda = 1$ (days^{-1}), and contrast the situation in which $p = 0.4$ to that in which $p = 0.6$. Let $H = 10$.
   (c) Suppose the investor's rule is to invest \$1 when the stock is at its low, wait until the price reaches H, sell, then wait until the price again reaches the low, reinvest \$H, and so on. Estimate the time required for the investor to make \$10H.

10.8   QUEUES WITH ARBITRARILY DISTRIBUTED SERVICE TIMES

The queuing models previously treated in this chapter all made extensive, if implicit, use of the Markovian properties of, say, Poisson arrivals and exponentially distributed service times. In practice, neither arrivals nor service may enjoy convenient "memoryless" properties, and more complex analysis becomes necessary. In this section we shall very briefly describe certain techniques and results for more complex systems. In the following section, certain simple approximate methods will then be given. No attempt will be made to be exhaustive on this subject; you must consult other books and journal articles in order to discover the status of various problems that may arise in practice.

EXAMPLE 10.8.1. *The Single-Server Queue with Poisson Arrivals and Arbitrarily Distributed Service Times.* If the number of arrivals $A(t)$ at a single-server system in a time interval of length t is Poisson, and if the service times S_1, S_2, ..., S_n, ... of customers 1, 2, ..., n are independently distributed in accordance with the distribution $F(x)$ where F need not be exponential, then the method of balance equations is no longer directly applicable. The reason is that if $N(t)$ denotes the number of customers in the system at t, then $N(t)$ need not have the Markov property. The reason is intuitively clear. Suppose $N(t) = 10$ and service times are constant (all of them equal m, where m might be one hour).

$$F(x) = \begin{cases} 0 & \text{if } x < m \\ 1 & \text{if } x \geq m \end{cases}$$

Now apparently knowledge of the elapsed service time of the customer currently in service has considerable predictive power. Suppose that at time t, service has progressed for one-half hour ($m/2$). There is then no chance of a departure from the system in the next short time interval (say one minute in duration). On the other hand, if service has progressed for $59\frac{1}{2}$ minutes, there is certainty that a service will be completed in the next minute. Contrast this situation with one in which service times are exponential. In that convenient situation, with which we are already familiar, the probability of a service completion is always the same, regardless of the elapsed service time.

Notice that if a service has just been completed, leaving a total of i customers in the system, then it is easy to compute the probability that there will be j customers present when the next service terminates. Let the nth service time, S_n, equal x conditionally. Then the number of arrivals during x is given by the Poisson probability expression:

$$(10.8.1) \qquad P\{A(x) = k\} = e^{-\lambda x}\frac{(\lambda x)^k}{k!} \qquad k = 0, 1, 2, \dots.$$

If we let $A(S_n)$ denote the number of arrivals during the nth service time, then using a conditional probability argument we find that the probability distribution of the number of customers added is

$$r_k = P\{A(S_n) = k\} = \int_0^\infty P\{A(S_n) = k \mid S_n = x\}f_{S_n}(x)\,dx,$$

$$(10.8.2)$$

$$= \int_0^\infty e^{-\lambda x}\frac{(\lambda x)^k}{k!}f_{S_n}(x)\,dx,$$

where $f_{S_n}(x)$ is the probability density (assumed to exist) for the service times. Recalling that i customers were left in the system just following the end of service of customer $n - 1$, then with probability

$$(10.8.3) \qquad r_{j-i+1} = P\{A(S_n) = j - i + 1\},$$

exactly $j - i + 1$ new customers arrived during S_n, leaving a total of j customers present. Moreover it is true that the number of Poisson arrivals occurring during S_n is completely independent of the number occurring during S_{n-1}, of those during $S_{n-2}, \dots$. This is apparent when one recollects that successive service times are independent and that the number of Poisson events in nonoverlapping time intervals is independent. Thus it follows that given the number of customers present at the termination of service time $n - 1$, the probability distribution of the number present at the end of the nth service time is determined. In other words if N_n denotes the number of customers in the system at "time" n, then $\{N_n, n = 0, 1, 2, \dots\}$ is a *Markov chain* over the states $0, 1, 2, \dots$ with transition probability matrix given by

$$(10.8.4) \qquad \begin{bmatrix} r_0 & r_1 & r_2 & r_3 & \cdots \\ r_0 & r_1 & r_2 & r_3 & \cdots \\ 0 & r_0 & r_1 & r_2 & \cdots \\ 0 & 0 & r_0 & r_1 & \cdots \\ & \cdots & \cdots & & \end{bmatrix}.$$

There is no limit to the number of states (size of the queue) and so the present Markov chain has an infinite state space. Nevertheless, it may be demonstrated that a long-run limiting distribution will exist if the traffic intensity parameter

$$(10.8.5) \qquad \rho = \lambda E[S] = \lambda\int_0^\infty x f_{S_n}(x)\,dx < 1.$$

Of course, this is the same condition that we encountered earlier when we dealt with birth-and-death-process models.

Although a conventional Markov-chain analysis of this scheme is possible, we shall content ourselves with a simpler discussion. Notice that we may express the number in the system at the end of the $n + 1$st service time as follows:

$$(10.8.6) \qquad N_{n+1} = \begin{cases} A(S_{n+1}) & \text{if } N_n = 0 \\ N_n + A(S_{n+1}) - 1 & \text{if } N_n > 0 \end{cases}$$

The reason for the first line is that if $N_n = 0$, then the $n + 1$st customer must arrive before he can begin service, and at his departure, he leaves behind the number of arrivals during his (the $n + 1$st) service time. Let us take the expectation of N_{n+1}, using expression (10.8.6):

$$E[N_{n+1}] = E[A(S_{n+1})] + E[\max(N_n - 1, 0)],$$

$$(10.8.7) \qquad = E[A(S_{n+1})] + \sum_{j=1}^{\infty} (j - 1)P\{N_n = j\},$$

$$= E[A(S_{n+1})] + \sum_{j=0}^{\infty} jP\{N_n = j\} - P\{N_n > 0\}$$

or

$$(10.8.8) \qquad E[N_{n+1}] = E[A(S_{n+1})] + E[N_n] - P\{N_n > 0\}.$$

Now if a long-run stationary distribution,

$$(10.8.9) \qquad \lim_{n \to \infty} P\{N_n = j\} = p_j,$$

exists, then it is plausible (and may be proved) that

$$(10.8.10) \qquad \lim_{n \to \infty} E[N_n] = \sum_{j=0}^{\infty} jp_j.$$

Let $n \to \infty$ in (10.8.8) and observe that since $E[N_n]$ and $E[N_{n+1}]$ tend to the same limit, we have

$$\lim_{n \to \infty} P\{N_n > 0\} = 1 - p_0 = E[A(S_{n+1})]$$

$(10.8.11)$ or

$$p_0 = 1 - \lambda E[S] = 1 - \rho.$$

More information is available if we square (10.8.6) and take expectations. We obtain

$$(10.8.12) \quad E[N_{n+1}{}^2] = E[A^2(S_{n+1})] + 2E[A(S_{n+1}) \max(N_n - 1, 0)] + E[\{\max(N_n - 1, 0)\}^2].$$

Notice that the number of arrivals during S_{n+1} is independent of the previous history, which involves arrivals during earlier service times. Consequently we have

$$(10.8.13) \quad E[N_{n+1}{}^2] = E[A^2(S_{n+1})] + 2E[A(S_{n+1})] \sum_{j=1}^{\infty} (j - 1)P\{N_n = j\} + \sum_{j=1}^{\infty} (j - 1)^2 P\{N_n = j\}.$$

Simplifying, we find that

$$(10.8.14) \quad E[N_{n+1}{}^2] = E[A^2(S)] + 2E[A(S)](E[N_n] - P\{N_n > 0\})$$
$$+ E[N_n{}^2] - 2E[N_n] + P\{N_n > 0\}.$$

Again if a long-run distribution exists, the expectations $E[N_{n+1}{}^2]$ and $E[N_n{}^2]$ tend to the same limit, and we find after simplification that, if $\rho < 1$,

$$\lim_{n \to \infty} E[N_n] = E[N] = \frac{\rho + E[A^2(S)] - 2\rho^2}{2(1 - \rho)},$$

$$(10.8.15) \qquad\qquad = \rho + \frac{\lambda^2 E[S^2]}{2(1 - \rho)},$$

$$= \rho + \frac{\rho^2}{2(1 - \rho)} \left\{ 1 + \frac{\text{Var}[S]}{E^2[S]} \right\}.$$

You are guided through the evaluation of $E[A(S)]$ and $E[A^2(S)]$ in terms of the service-time distribution in the exercises. The striking thing about the expression (10.8.15) is that the long-run expected number of customers present depends on the *variance*, $\text{Var}[S]$, of the service-time distribution. The implication is that reducing this variance leads to a smaller average queue size. It should be remarked that a more elaborate discussion shows that (10.8.15) gives also the long-run expectation of $N(t)$, where now t is *any* time and not just a moment immediately following customer departure. That these two expectations should be equal is not at all obvious, and such equality does not hold true for other (for example, some priority service) models.

An interesting generalization of the previous model is one that admits service interruptions. In turn, a special and important kind of interruption involves priority customers.

EXAMPLE 10.8.2. The *Single-Server Queuing System with Service Interruptions*. In this model members of a class of low-priority customers demand service at a single facility with rate λ_2. Acting independently of the low-priority customers is a single important high-priority customer, I, who arrives with rate λ_1, demands service for a time B, departs following service to return again later, and so on. The high-priority customer is granted immediate consideration by the server in the sense that when I appears, his service pre-empts that of any low-priority service in progress. Following the completion of I's service requirements, the service of low-priority items commences once again, continuing as long as other low-priority elements are in queue or until customer I once again makes his demand.

Clearly the appearance of I is equivalent to the random *breakdown* of the servicing facility itself. Thus λ_1 represents the failure rate of the facility, and the I service time, B, is the repair time following breakdown; henceforth B will be called the *repair time*. We assume that successive repair times are mutually independent and identically distributed random variables. Times to failure (the time from last repair termination until next failure) are exponentially distributed with mean $\lambda_1{}^{-1}$ and are independent.

Now imagine that low-priority service n begins at some moment, t. If interruptions occur during the low-priority service time, S_n, service immediately ceases for a random time B; following this period service resumes from the point of interruption, and the process continues until finally the low-priority service terminates and the customer leaves at time

$$(10.8.16) \qquad t + S_n + B_1 + B_2 + \cdots + B_{A_1(S_n)} = t + C_n.$$

Here S_n is the nth service time, B_j is the service (or repair) time of the jth interruption to occur during S_n, and $A_1(S_n)$ denotes the total number of I interruptions (breakdowns) to occur during S_n. C_n denotes the *completion time* for customer n; low-priority customers depart the system at the termination of completion times. Since interruptions occur at exponentially distributed time intervals throughout S_n, it is easy to see from the memoryless property of the exponential distribution that successive completion times are independently and identically distributed. The interruption process described is termed *pre-emptive resume*. Alternatively, one must repeat the entire service after each activity; this situation is called *pre-emptive repeat*. Pre-emptive repeat priorities are not treated here

The expectation of arbitrary completion time may be computed by means of conditional expectations. First hold S and $A_2(S)$ fixed conditionally. Then

$$(10.8.17) \qquad \begin{aligned} E[C \mid S, A_2(S)] &= S + E[B_1 + B_2 + \cdots + B_{A_1}(S)], \\ &= S + A_1(S)E[B]. \end{aligned}$$

Now keep S fixed and remove the condition on $A_2(S)$, the number of arrivals. Because of the assumption of exponential failures, $A_2(S)$ is conditionally Poisson with mean $\lambda_1 S$. Thus

$$(10.8.18) \qquad E[C \mid S] = E_{A_2}\{E[C \mid S, A_2(S)]\} = S + \lambda_1 S E[B].$$

Removal of the condition on S finally shows that

$$(10.8.19) \qquad E[C] = E[S](1 + \lambda_1 E[B]).$$

Higher moments may be computed in a similar fashion.

Let $N_n(2)$ denote the number of low-priority customers present immediately following service completion of the nth such customer. Then

$$(10.8.20) \qquad N_{n+1}(2) = N_n(2) + A_2(C_{n+1}) - 1 \qquad \text{if } N_n(2) \ge 1,$$

where $A_2(C_{n+1})$ is the number of low-priority arrivals during the $n + 1$st completion time. Notice the analogy with (10.8.6) when $N_n(2) \ge 1$. If $N_n(2) = 0$, there is a complication: either (i) customer $n + 1$ arrives during an idle period for the server or (ii) customer $n + 1$ arrives to find the server busy serving the high-priority customer, I. In order to treat this problem it is convenient to make a further assumption.

ASSUMPTION. The repair time, B, has an exponential distribution with mean β^{-1}.

The probability of event (i) is computed by recognizing that when an idle period begins, the server may be occupied several times with customer I before customer $n + 1$ makes application for service. A little reflection shows that the model of

Example 10.4.1 describes the server's status at time t: in that model (and notation), identify $N(t) = 1$ with idleness and $N(T) = 2$ with I service. It then follows that

$$(10.8.21) \quad P\{(i) | \text{customer } n+1 \text{ arrives at } t\} = \frac{\beta}{\lambda_1 + \beta} + \frac{\lambda_1}{\lambda_1 + \beta} e^{-(\lambda_1 + \beta)t}.$$

Since the probability density of arrival time for customer $n + 1$ is independently exponential with parameter λ_2, the unconditional probability is

$$(10.8.22) \quad \begin{aligned} P\{(i)\} &= \frac{\beta}{\lambda_1 + \beta} + \frac{\lambda_1}{\lambda_1 + \beta} \int_0^\infty e^{-(\lambda_1 + \beta)t} e^{-\lambda_2 t} \lambda_2 \, dt, \\ &= \frac{\beta}{\lambda_1 + \beta} + \frac{\lambda_1}{\lambda_1 + \beta} \frac{\lambda_2}{\lambda_1 + \lambda_2 + \beta}. \end{aligned}$$

The probability of event (ii) is obtained by subtracting (10.8.22) from unity.

The expression analogous to (10.8.6) takes the form

$$(10.8.23) \quad N_{n+1}(2) = \begin{cases} A_2(B') + A_2(C_{n+1}) & \text{if } N_n(2) = 0 \\ N_n(2) + A_2(C_{n+1}) - 1 & \text{if } N_n(2) \geq 1 \end{cases}$$

Notice that only the term $A_2(B')$ is new; it represents the number of low-priority arrivals during the remaining repair time of I encountered by customer $n + 1$. Because the exponential is memoryless,

$$(10.8.24) \quad B' \begin{cases} 0 & \text{with probability } P\{(i)\} \\ B & \text{with probability } P\{(ii)\} \end{cases}$$

Also, $A_2(B')$ and $A_2(C_{n+1})$ are independently distributed, as is implied by Theorem 10.2.1.

Now after taking expectations throughout (10.8.23), it is seen that

$$(10.8.25) \quad \begin{aligned} E[N_{n+1}(2)] &= \sum_{j=0}^\infty E[N_{n+1}(2) | N_n(2) = j] P\{N_n = j\}, \\ &= (E[A_2(C_{n+1})] + E[A_2(B')]) P\{N_n = 0\} \\ &\quad + \sum_{j=1}^\infty (j - 1 + E[A_2(C_{n+1})]) P\{N_n = j\}. \end{aligned}$$

Under the condition that a long-run distribution exists, we may equate $E[N_{n+1}(2)]$ and $E[N_n(2)]$ as $n \to \infty$. After simplification, there results the expression

$$(10.8.26) \quad \begin{aligned} p_0 &= \lim_{n \to \infty} P\{N_0(2)\} = \frac{1 - \lambda_2 E[C]}{1 + \lambda_2 E[B']}, \\ &= \frac{1 - \lambda_2 E[S](1 + \lambda_1 \beta^{-1})}{1 + \dfrac{\lambda_1 \lambda_2}{\beta(\lambda_1 + \lambda_2 + \beta)}}. \end{aligned}$$

It is apparent that a necessary condition for a long-run distribution to exist is that $\lambda_2 E[C] < 1$.

Now by squaring both sides of (10.8.23) and taking expectations, it is again possible to find an expression for the long-run expectation $\lim_{n \to \infty} E\{N_n(2)\}$. The expression is, however, quite cumbersome and will be omitted here.

A representative priority queuing problem has been described here, but no attempt has been made to provide details. In spite of the simplicity of the model, complex mathematical expressions frequently arise and considerable numerical exploration will often be necessary in order to evaluate alternative scheduling strategies. In the next section some simple, approximate, procedures are outlined, and in Chapter 12 the technique of computer simulation is described. Approximation and simulation are frequently necessary when complex real systems are under study.

EXERCISES 10.8

1. Compare long-run expected systems occupancy, using (10.8.15), for the following service time distributions.
   (a) S is exponential with unit mean.
   (b) S is constant, so S is always equal to unity.
   (c) S has the distribution of the maximum of two independent, exponentially distributed random variables, each with mean $\frac{2}{3}$. ·

2. Use the argument at the end of Section 10.3 and the remark at the end of Example 10.8.1 to show that the expected total delay for a customer arriving to find the long-run distribution in effect is

$$E[D] = \frac{1}{\lambda} E[N] = E[S] + \frac{\rho}{2(1-\rho)} \left\{1 + \frac{\text{Var}[S]}{E^2[S]}\right\} E[S].$$

From this, show that the expected waiting time of such a customer is

$$E[W] = \frac{\rho}{2(1-\rho)} \left\{1 + \frac{\text{Var}[S]}{E^2[S]}\right\} E[S].$$

Therefore the expected waiting time in a constant-service-time system—that is, $(S \equiv 1)$— is exactly one-half that in an exponential-service-time system with the same arrival rate and expected service time.

3. Suppose the service time, S, has density $f(x)$. Show that
   (a) the expected number of Poisson arrivals during a random S, $E[A(S)]$, has the value $\lambda E[S]$. (*Hint:* Conditionally put $S = x$. Then the conditional expectation of $A(S)$, given $S = x$, is λx. Remove the condition, using f to obtain

$$E[A(S)] = \int_0^\infty \lambda x f(x)\, dx.)$$

   (b) $E[A^2(S)] = E[S^2] + \lambda E[S]$. (*Hint:* Condition on S.) Then

$$E[A^2(S)\,|\,S=x] = \sum_{j=0}^\infty j^2 P\{A=j\} = \sum_{j=0}^\infty j(j-1)e^{-\lambda x}\frac{(\lambda x)^j}{j!} + \sum_{j=0}^\infty je^{-\lambda x}\frac{(\lambda x)^j}{j!}.$$

First,

$$\sum_{j=0}^\infty je^{-\lambda x}\frac{(\lambda x)^j}{j!} = \lambda x$$

(the mean of the Poisson distribution) and second

$$\sum_{j=0}^\infty j(j-1)e^{-\lambda x}\frac{(\lambda x)^j}{j!} = \sum_{j=2}^\infty j(j-1)e^{-\lambda x}\frac{(\lambda x)^j}{j!} = \sum_{j=2}^\infty e^{-\lambda x}\frac{(\lambda x)^j}{(j-2)!}$$

$$= (\lambda x)^2 \sum_{j-2=0}^\infty e^{-\lambda x}\frac{(\lambda x)^{j-2}}{(j-2)!} = (\lambda x)^2,$$

then we obtain

$$E[A^2(S)|S = x] = \lambda^2 x^2 + \lambda x.$$

Now removal of the condition on S gives

$$E[A^2(S)] = \int_0^\infty (\lambda^2 x^2 + \lambda x) f(x)\, dx = \lambda^2 E[S^2] + \lambda E[S].$$

(c) The same approach works when S is replaced by any random time, T. We get $E[A^2(T)] = \lambda^2 E[T^2] + \lambda E[T]$. See in particular $E[(A_2(B') + C)^2]$, required for our priority example.

4. Suppose orders arrive at a job shop at Poisson rate $\lambda = 0.87$, and production (service) times are of constant duration unity. Suppose, however, that the production process is occasionally interrupted, owing to a mechanical failure and subsequent repair. The interruptions occur at periods of time that are exponentially distributed, with $\lambda_1^{-1} = 50$, and last for exponentially distributed periods, of mean 2. Interruptions act pre-emptively.
   (a) Compute the long-run expected number of orders in the system (waiting and being served).
   (b) Suppose production breakdowns may occur only when the server is actively engaged in service. Argue that the number of customers present after the nth service completion is given by

$$N_{n+1} = \begin{cases} A(C_{n+1}) & \text{if } N_n = 0 \\ N_n + A(C_{n+1}) - 1 & \text{if } N_n > 0 \end{cases}$$

   where C_n denotes the nth service time plus all the repair times. Find the long-run mean number of orders in the system.

10.9   APPROXIMATE METHODS FOR QUEUES

The models previously introduced have attempted to represent queuing phenomena in a rather detailed manner—that is in terms of single customers. As the complexity of the situation modeled increased—for example, as we considered non-exponential service times and priority scheduling—the resulting formulas became more and more cumbersome and difficult to understand. When one reflects that the situations we analyzed were *all* rather simple, the need for flexible approximate methods becomes apparent. In this section we shall describe a few such simple approximations. These will necessarily be rather heuristically developed and motivated, and no strenuous attempt will be made to be mathematically rigorous. Our exposition is conducted in terms of several prototype examples.

EXAMPLE 10.9.1. *Deterministic Queuing.* There are many practical situations in which arrivals occur very rapidly—so rapidly as to make short-term statistical variations rather insignificant. Furthermore, the arrival rate changes with time. Consider, for instance, the rush-hour situation at the toll booths at the approaches to one of the tunnels entering Manhattan or to the Bay or Golden Gate bridges to San Francisco. If $A(t)$ denotes the total number of vehicles that have arrived by time t following some initial moment, then a graph of $A(t)$ versus time, t, appears as shown in Figure 10.9.1. If measurements are made at time intervals of 15 minutes or so, then since the total number of cars that have arrived in an hour may well number in the

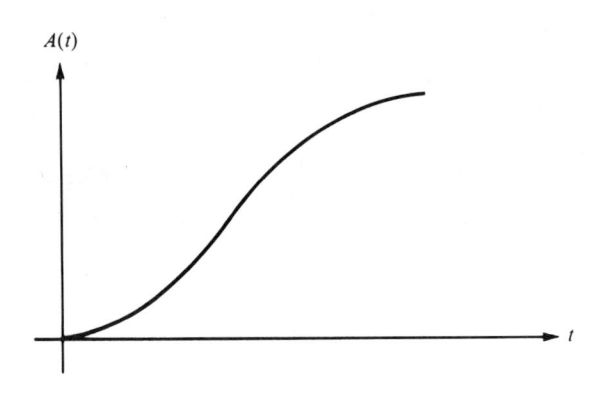

FIGURE 10.9.1

hundreds or even thousands, the graph of $A(t)$ appears essentially continuous. We may think of a *fluid* of vehicles that appears and must be poured through an aperture, where the latter is the toll-gate system. Realistically, the deterministic arrival rate dA/dt thus nearly describes the situation, and this rate may at first be small, reach its peak value, and finally fall off again. We contrast this model to the Poisson arrival models of the previous sections, in which the arrivals occurred quite randomly. In practice, one could estimate $A(t)$ by counting the number of vehicles arriving in adjacent disjoint 15-minute intervals and averaging. Care must, of course, be taken not to average together data from "different" days; for example, Sunday and holiday $A(t)$ curves are certainly quite different from those of normal weekdays, and perhaps weather plays a role as well.

Now to represent service, the cumulative diagram again is of help, and we can disregard minute random fluctuations and represent the total number of departures continuously. Suppose that the maximum output rate, d, is a constant. Then to the degree of approximation adopted here, service is essentially instantaneous and there is no queue so long as $dA/dt < d$. Once dA/dt exceeds d, a queue begins to build up, and a waiting line lasts until the busy period terminates—that is, until accumulated departures, $D(t)$, equal $A(t)$. A picture makes matters clear (see Figure 10.9.2).

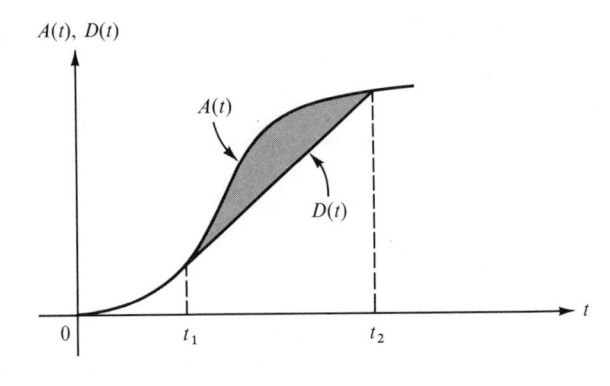

FIGURE 10.9.2

In the region $(0, t_1)$ we have

(10.9.1)
$$d = \frac{dD}{dt} < \frac{dA}{dt},$$

so only rather insignificant queuing due to random fluctuations occurs. The same holds true when $t > t_2$. In between, $A(t) > D(t)$, and at any time t, the number of individuals waiting is

(10.9.2)
$$N(t) = A(t) - D(t).$$

Plainly the total number of customer-hours spent in delay is

(10.9.3)
$$W = \int_{t_1}^{t_2} [A(t) - D(t)] \, dt = \text{shaded area between curves.}$$

The integral above can easily be estimated by counting squares on a graph, using a planimeter, or even by actual integration, provided formulas are at hand. See the Exercises for examples.

The previous example dealt with the rush-hour situation when arriving traffic is exceedingly heavy. In the next model we shall again consider quite heavy traffic, but we will not completely ignore statistical fluctuations in arrivals and departures.

EXAMPLE 10.9.2. *The Saturated Queue and the Normal Distribution.* Let us consider a servicing facility that tends to be quite heavily loaded—that is, one that experiences arrivals at time intervals $A_1, A_2, \ldots, A_n, \ldots$ that are short compared to service times $S_1, S_2, S_3, \ldots, S_n, \ldots$ (here A_n represents the time between the arrival of the $n - 1$st and nth customer, and S_n represents the nth customer's service time). Now it is easy to see that *if*, for example, $A_1 = A_2 = \cdots = A_n = 0$, then the waiting time of customer n, W_n is just the sum of the service times $S_1, S_2, \ldots, S_{n-1}$, *provided* there is no initial waiting customer and provided that service is in arrival order. Furthermore, if the queue is assumed to be usually greater than zero, we have, if $A_i > 0 \, (i = 1, 2, \ldots, n, \ldots)$,

(10.9.4)
$$\begin{aligned}
&W_1 = 0, \\
&W_2 \approx S_1 - A_2, \\
&W_3 \approx S_1 + S_2 - A_2 - A_3 = (S_1 - A_2) + (S_2 - A_3), \\
&\cdots, \\
&W_n \approx (S_1 - A_2) + (S_2 - A_3) + \cdots + (S_{n-1} - A_n), \\
&\cdots.
\end{aligned}$$

The rationale for this expression is as follows. Notice that S_1 would be the waiting time of customer 2 if he arrives just as customer 1 begins service, but if he arrives a time A_2 later, the remaining service time of customer 1 is $S_1 - A_2 \cdots$ provided A_2 is smaller than S_1. Then the waiting time of customer 3 is just that of customer 2, plus S_2, less the time A_3 between the arrival of customer 3 and customer 2. That is, waiting times tend to accumulate. An exact expression for W_n is obtainable in terms of W_{n-1}:

(10.9.5)
$$W_n = \max(W_{n-1} + S_{n-1} - A_n, 0);$$

this is derived in the chapter on simulation, but at this point it is enough to utilize (10.9.4) as an approximation. Now since (10.9.4) represents W_n as a sum of random variables, it is natural to consider an approximation of its distribution by the normal distribution provided the successive terms are independent and of about the same magnitude. Specifically, suppose that $\{A_n\}$ and $\{S_n\}$ are mutually independent sequences of independent random variables. Let δ and σ be certain constants. Then (we drop the approximation signs),

$$\delta n = E[W_n] = E[(S_1 - A_2) + (S_2 - A_3) + \cdots + (S_{n-1} - A_n)],$$

(10.9.6)
$$= E[S_1] - E[A_2] + \cdots + E[S_{n-1}] - E[A_n],$$
$$= n(E[S] - E[A]);$$

likewise

(10.9.7)
$$\sigma^2 n = \mathrm{Var}[W_n] = n(\mathrm{Var}[S] + \mathrm{Var}[A]),$$

and, approximately, as $n \to \infty$,

(10.9.8)
$$P\{W_n \le x\} = \frac{1}{\sqrt{2\pi}\sigma\sqrt{n}} \int_{-\infty}^{(x-\delta n)/\sigma\sqrt{n}} e^{-(1/2)z^2}\,dz.$$

Very plausibly, the expected waiting time tends to grow linearly with n; growth is at rate δ. Obviously, no stationary distribution can exist. It may be shown by more advanced mathematical methods that the approximation above is indeed valid as n becomes large, provided $E[S] > E[A]$.

In our next example, we will show how the normal approximation may, in fact, be used as a basis for finding useful approximations when $E[S] < E[A]$, in which case a stationary distribution will exist.

EXAMPLE 10.9.3. *The Diffusion Equation and Heavy Traffic Theory.* Refer to the normal-distribution approximation to the waiting time, W_n:

(10.9.9)
$$F(x, n) = P\{W_n \le x\} = \frac{1}{\sqrt{2\pi}} \int_{-\infty}^{(x-\delta n)/\sigma\sqrt{n}} e^{-(1/2)z^2}dz.$$

In order to interpolate between integer values of n, replace n by a continuous variable t. Now it may be shown by differentiation with respect to x and to t that F satisfies the *diffusion* or *heat* partial differential equation of mathematical physics:

(10.9.10)
$$\frac{\partial F}{\partial t} = -\delta \frac{\partial F}{\partial x} + \frac{\sigma^2}{2} \frac{\partial^2 F}{\partial x^2}.$$

Next argue by analogy with the theory of Markov chains and queues. If $\delta = E[S] - E[A] < 0$, then the waiting-time process W_n will tend to drift towards zero. Having reached zero, it will be reflected, or will rebound, after the next arrival. Of course, if $E[S]$ is only slightly less than $E[A]$, then most of the time the queue will not be near zero, and hence the boundary will have little influence. A boundary condition must, however, be imposed, and the correct one insists that the relevant solution to (10.9.11), which will be denoted by $G(x, t)$, be such that

(10.9.11)
$$G(x, t) = 0 \qquad \text{if } x < 0.$$

This boundary condition is essential, because if $\delta < 0$, the boundary will surely be reached, and the boundaryless normal-distribution solution to (10.9.10) is of no use. Finally, then, we set the time derivative equal to zero in (10.9.10) in order to discover the long-run distribution, $G(x) = \lim_{t \to \infty} G(x, t)$. Notice the analogy to the balance-equation situation—see (10.4.10)–(10.4.12). The result is the ordinary differential equation

$$(10.9.12) \qquad \frac{\sigma^2}{2} \frac{d^2 G}{dx^2} - \delta \frac{dG}{dx} = 0.$$

The solution to this, obtained by standard methods, is

$$(10.9.13) \qquad \lim_{n \to \infty} P\{W_n \le x\} \approx G(x) = 1 - e^{(2\delta x)/\sigma^2} \qquad x \ge 0,$$
$$= 0 \qquad x < 0,$$

(remember that $\delta < 0$). This implies that the long-run expected waiting time is approximately

$$(10.9.14) \qquad E[W] \approx -\frac{\delta^2}{2\delta} = \frac{1}{2} \frac{\mathrm{Var}[A] + \mathrm{Var}[S]}{E[S] - E[A]},$$
$$= \frac{1}{2} \left(\frac{\mathrm{Var}[A] + \mathrm{Var}[S]}{1 - \rho} \right) E[S], \qquad \rho = \frac{E[S]}{E[A]} < 1,$$

with the approximation improving as $\delta \to 0$ (or as $\rho \to 1$), or, figuratively speaking, when *heavy traffic* conditions prevail. Since the exact solution to the sort of queuing problem addressed in this example is extremely complex, the simple exponential approximation (10.9.13) is quite welcome and useful.

Finally, it may be shown that the time-dependent solution to the diffusion equation with reflecting boundary at zero is given by a relatively simple expression in terms of tabulated functions:

$$(10.9.15)$$

$$1 - G(x, t) = e^{2\delta x/\sigma^2} \frac{1}{\sqrt{2\pi}} \int_{(x+\delta t - w)/\sigma\sqrt{t}}^{\infty} e^{-(1/2)z^2} \, dz + \frac{1}{\sqrt{2\pi}} \int_{(x-\delta t - w)/\sigma\sqrt{t}}^{\infty} e^{-(1/2)z^2} \, dz;$$

the number w represents the waiting time in the system at $t = 0$. In case the system is initially empty, $w = 0$. The solution above is valid for all values of δ, positive or negative. Hence (10.9.15) allows the estimation of the probability of a waiting time in excess of x for the tth arrival.

EXERCISES 10.9

1. A production system begins the day with a backlog of $A(0) = 100$ jobs. Jobs require an average time of one minute in the system; they are carried out in order of arrival with no overlapped operations. New jobs arrive at a rate of one every 1.25 minutes.
   (a) Describe the cumulative arrival and departure curves graphically.
   (b) Find the total time during which a queue exists (the length of the initial busy period).
   (c) What is the total waiting time of a customer involved in the initial queue?

2. Suppose an accident occurs at a point on a freeway, stopping all cars that arrive until its removal. Take $t = 0$ as the accident time. Vehicle arrivals at that point accumulate at rate dA/dt, so the total number of cars stopped by time t after the accident is $A(t)$. Suppose removal requires a time R, and afterwards vehicles leave the accident location at rate $D(t)$.
   (a) Represent the situation graphically.
   (b) Supposing $dA/dt = a$ and $dD/dt = d$ and $a < d$, find the length of time required to clear the accident location. Find the total waiting time experienced by all vehicles involved.
   (c) Suppose removal time, R, is a random variable having a normal distribution with mean m and standard deviation σ ($\sigma \ll m$). Calculate the expected values of the measures of (b).

3. Empirical studies have shown that the accumulated arrivals at a particular toll-gate facility are approximated by the formula

$$A(t) = a\sqrt{t},$$

where t is measured from 7 A.M. The constant a depends on the weather conditions: if the weather is good, $a = 4$, whereas if the weather is bad, $a = 1$. Good weather occurs with probability $p = 0.8$, and bad with probability $q = 0.2$.
   (a) Suppose that if one toll gate is in service, the service rate is one vehicle per unit time. Compute the total waiting time of queuing vehicles on good-weather days and on bad-weather days.
   (b) Compute the mean and variance of the total waiting time, assuming that one toll gate is always used.
   (c) Carry out (b) in the event that two toll gates are open; this means that the toll system will pass two vehicles per unit time.

4. Compare the expected waiting time computed by the expression in Exercise 2, Section 10.8 and that of (10.9.14). Use the service times of Exercise 1, Section 10.8 and $\lambda = 0.7$, 0.8, 0.9, and 0.95.

SUGGESTED READING

Conway, R., Maxwell, W., and Miller, L. *Theory of Scheduling*. Reading, Mass.: Addison-Wesley, 1967.

Cox, D. R., and Smith, W. L. *Queues*. Methuen Monograph. New York: John Wiley, 1961.

Cruon, R. (Ed.) *Queuing Theory (Recent Developments and Applications)*. New York: Elsevier, 1967.

Feller, W. *An Introduction to Probability Theory and Its Applications*, Vols. I and II. New York: John Wiley, 1957 and 1968.

Gaver, D. P. A waiting line with interrupted service, including priorities. *Journal of the Royal Statistical Society* (B), 1962, **25**(1), 73–90.

Gaver, D. P. Diffusion approximations and models for certain congestion problems. *Journal of Applied Probability*, 1968, **5**, 607–623.

Gnedenko, B., and Kovalenko, I. *Introduction to Queuing Theory*. Tr. by D. Louvish. Hartford, Conn.: Daniel Davey and Co., 1969.

Iglehart, D. L. Diffusion approximations in applied probability. In G. Dantzig and A. Veinott (Eds.), *Mathematics of the Decision Sciences, Part 2*. Providence, R.I.: American Mathematical Society, 1968.

Jaiswal, N. *Priority Queues*. New York: Academic Press, 1968.

Lee, A. *Applied Queuing Theory.* New York: St. Martin's Press, 1966.

Morse, P. M. *Queues, Inventories, and Maintenance.* New York: John Wiley, 1958.

Neuts, M. The single server queue with Poisson input and semi-Markov service times. *Journal of Applied Probability,* 1966, **3**, 202–230.

Newell, G. F. Queues with time-dependent arrival rates (I, II, III). *Journal of Applied Probability* , 1968, **5**, 436–451, 579–590, 591–606.

Newell, G. F. *Applications of Queuing Theory.* London: Chapman and Hall, Ltd., 1971.

Prabhu, N. U. *Queues and Inventories.* New York: John Wiley, 1965.

Riordan, J. *Stochastic Service Systems.* New York: John Wiley, 1962.

Saaty, T. *Elements of Queueing Theory, with Applications,* New York: McGraw-Hill, 1961.

Smith, W. L., and Wilkinson, W. (Eds.) *Congestion Theory* (Proceedings of a Symposium). University of North Carolina Monograph Series in Probability and Statistics. Chapel Hill, N.C.: University of North Carolina Press, 1965.

Takacs, L. *Introduction to the Theory of Queues.* New York: Oxford University Press, 1962.

CHAPTER 11

INVENTORY THEORY AND MODELS

11.1 INTRODUCTION

Establishing inventories of raw materials and finished products is common in many manufacturing activities. For example, an inventory of finished goods provides a convenient cushion or buffer, allowing one to order or produce an entire period's supply at once, keeping it in readiness while facilities or managerial effort are employed elsewhere. Of course such a cushion is not established without cost, so the purpose of inventory theory is to consider quantitatively both the advantages and disadvantages of possible inventory-management policies, thus arriving at one that is wise, or even optimal, in particular circumstances.

Although "classical" inventory theory deals with inventories of physical goods, similar management problems arise in other areas and can also be treated mathematically. For example, the problem of acquiring, advancing, and training suitable employees in an organization is an inventory problem of a novel and difficult type. So also is the problem of efficient information handling, storage, and retrieval. The problem of cash-balance management by banks and other financial institutions is an inventory problem that is coming under study from a quantitative, or mathematical, point of view. The problem of optimal control and depletion of natural resources has certain inventory-like characteristics; that is, the proper storage and release of water by systems of dams for the generation of electric power and irrigation may be thought of as an inventory problem. And inventory problems arise also in the military and national defense—these range all the way from small but vital questions concerning the number of spare vacuum tubes or transistors to be carried on a submarine starting on a mission to large issues such as the appropriate size of the nation's stock of nuclear weapons.

Having called attention to many areas in which inventory problems arise, we will now discuss a few prototype models for the more classical situations of storage of physical goods. Emphasis will be placed on situations involving elements of uncertainty or risk to which probability theory is naturally applied. You will recall that several inventory situations were used as illustrations in Chapters 8 and 10.

11.2 AN INTRODUCTORY EXAMPLE—THE ECONOMIC ORDER QUANTITY (EOQ) MODEL

In order to introduce some of the basic notions of inventory theory in a simple way, we begin with the following situation. A manufacturer uses a certain small bolt at yearly rate m. Of course he would not order each bolt required directly from the manufacturer (as he might with an expensive item), so he stocks or inventories a quantity of them. Whenever his supply runs out, he reorders at a certain cost, c_o, called the *ordering cost*, which represents the cost of processing the order or possibly the cost of machine setup if the bolts are manufactured internally. This cost may be expressed in $ per order. It is the cost and inconvenience represented by c_o that militates against ordering each time a bolt is needed. It is easy to see that if orders for Q bolts are placed whenever inventory falls essentially to zero (reasonable if the order delivery time may be assumed negligible), then m/Q orders are placed per year, and the *yearly ordering cost* is $c_o\, m/Q$. Clearly, annual ordering cost is made small if the order quantity, Q, is large. But then a large inventory of bolts will sometimes exist, and consequently a large *carrying cost* will be incurred for the capital tied up in bolts, not to mention the cost of warehousing and storage. Figure 11.2.1 illustrates the inventory variation. The average inventory level is $Q/2$, so if the carrying cost is c_c, expressed in $ per unit in inventory per year, the average annual carrying cost is

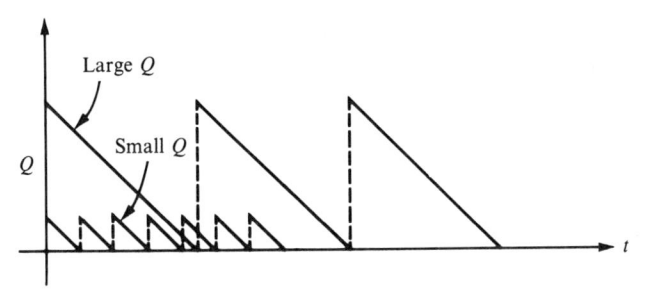

FIGURE 11.2.1.

$c_c Q/2$. The latter cost increases with the order quantity, Q. The sum of the two costs we have considered is the total annual inventory-associated cost,

$$(11.2.1) \qquad C(Q) = c_o \frac{m}{Q} + c_c \frac{Q}{2}.$$

The minimum may be found (assuming that Q may be any positive real number) by differentiation: we obtain

$$\frac{dC(Q)}{dQ} = -c_o \frac{m}{Q^2} + \frac{c_c}{2}.$$

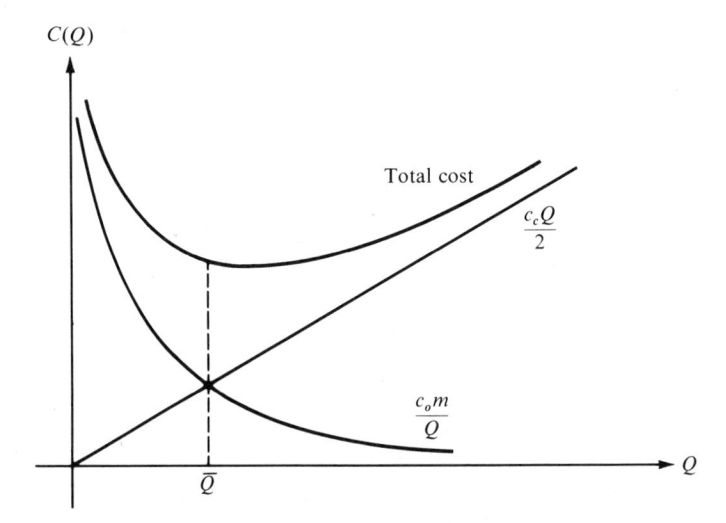

FIGURE 11.2.2. Inventory costs

Equating to zero and solving gives the supplier the optimum order size (economical order quantity, or EOQ),

$$(11.2.2) \qquad \bar{Q} = \sqrt{\frac{2mc_o}{c_c}}.$$

The resulting level of annual cost, by substitution in (11.2.1), is seen to be

$$(11.2.3) \qquad C(\bar{Q}) = \sqrt{2mc_o c_c}.$$

EXAMPLE 11.2.1. The bolts in question cost $0.10 each and are used at a rate of 5,000 per year. The yearly costs assigned are

$$c_o = \$2.00 \quad \text{and} \quad c_c = \$0.02.$$

Frequently, carrying costs are assigned on a percent-of-cost basis; that is, if a 20% figure is used, we would have $c_c = (0.20)(\$0.10) = \$0.02$, as assumed. Now substitution into (11.2.2) gives

$$\bar{Q} = \sqrt{\frac{2(5,000)(2.00)}{0.02}} = 1,000,$$

which is the number of bolts that should be ordered at a time. The total annual cost is

$$C(\bar{Q}) = \sqrt{2(5,000)(0.02)(2.00)} = \$20.$$

The EOQ model is widely used in industry. This is at least in part because of its conceptual and computational simplicity. Another reason is that there is a considerable degree of insensitivity to misestimates of cost or usage rate. We illustrate this effect in Exercise 1. This desirable characteristic extends to more sophisticated models, as will be seen shortly.

One principal deficiency of the simple EOQ model is its failure to account for the natural variability and unpredictability of demand and hence for the possibility of running out of stock. Another is that it fails to allow for the impact of sudden large orders upon clerical or manufacturing facilities of fixed capacity. Such considerations as these must be met by somewhat deeper examination of inventory problems; examples appear in the following section.

EXERCISES 11.2

1. In the problem of Example 11.2.1, suppose that the annual usage of bolts was *estimated* to be 7,500, but was *actually* 5,000.
    (a) Compute the EOQ based on the estimated rate $m_e = 7,500$.
    (b) Compute the resulting actual annual cost.
    (c) Carry out the same computation as in (b) if the estimated annual usage is 2,500.

2. A particular computer center batch processes incoming programs. By this it is meant that when P programs have accumulated, they are put on tape and run. The running time is so short that we consider it to be instantaneous. Assume that the rate of arrival of programs is λ (programs per hour) and that the arrival is regular or uniform throughout the day. That is, the total number of programs that arrive in a time period of duration t is exactly λt. The cost for running a tape of P programs involves both a setup cost, c_s, and a running cost per program, c_r. The total cost of running a batch of size P is thus $c_s + c_r P$, and one is run every P/λ hours. Another cost, that of user waiting, is associated with batch processing. The average or representative customer arrives with his program halfway through a batch accumulation time, so his waiting time is $\frac{1}{2}(P/\lambda)$; since λ customers arrive per hour, the average waiting time incurred per hour is λ times $\frac{1}{2}(P/\lambda)$, or $P/2$. Thus, finally, the total hourly cost of waiting is $c_w(P/2)$, where c_w is the unit cost of waiting.
    (a) Show that the total cost function associated with batch processing is

    $$C(P) = \frac{\lambda}{P}(c_s + c_r P) + c_w \frac{P}{2}.$$

    (b) Find the best batch size, $\bar{P}$.
    (c) Find the total cost if batch size $\bar{P}$ is used.
    (d) Discuss ways in which the model is conceptually approximate. How would you improve the formulation? (*Hint*: What is the effect of assuming that batch processing is instantaneous?)

3. Suppose two locations in a large organization (for example, two job shops) each utilize a particular part. The annual usage rate at each location is m (parts per year), and the ordering costs and carrying costs at each location are the same and equal to C_o (\$) and C_e(\$/year), respectively.

(a) Considering merely the ordering and carrying costs, compare the annual costs of (1) separate inventories at each location and (2) one central inventory used by both locations. (*Hint*: Use (11.2.3).)

(b) Are there advantages to consolidating or centralizing inventories that are not considered in our simple model? Describe some of them.

(c) Are there disadvantages associated with centralized inventories? (*Hint*: Suppose each time a part is required, a workman must walk to the inventory location to obtain it.)

(d) Suppose a workman's time is worth w(\$/year) and that he must walk for a time $L_1 = 15$ minutes if the inventory is centrally located and $L_2 = 5$ minutes if each location has its own inventory. Set up a model to aid in choosing between the two location options. Utilize the numbers of Example 11.2.1

4. Show that the economical order quantity, $\bar{Q}$, is that value of Q that equalizes annual ordering cost and annual carrying cost.

11.3   INVENTORY SYSTEM COMPONENTS

Before passing on to some more elaborate but also realistic and useful inventory models, it seems desirable to say a few words about the components of inventory systems. There is considerable similarity between certain components of such systems and those of the waiting-line systems of the last chapter. In fact, the similarity may be exploited to allow the use or adaptation of certain waiting-line models for inventory analysis; an example has already been furnished by Example 10.6.6. In addition, a characteristic of much inventory theory is an emphasis on the costs and penalties associated with various strategies. Some of these costs have appeared in the last section; we shall shortly elaborate on these and others.

We begin by considering models of the demand for items.

A. Demands

By the term *demand* we shall mean a single expressed customer requirement occurring at a time point. That is, a customer may on a particular occasion demand gasoline, eggs, or automobiles. By *demand size* we mean the magnitude of the demand: ten gallons of gas, one dozen eggs, one car. Thus it becomes convenient to distinguish between the *number* of demands per unit time and the *sizes* of the demands occurring.

The total demand over a time period of length t, $D(t)$, can be written as

$$(11.3.1) \qquad D(t) = S_1 + S_2 + \cdots + S_{N(t)},$$

where S_i is the size of the ith demand and $N(t)$ represents the total number of demands in $(0, t)$. An added feature is that on a given occasion there may be individual demands for several different items, and the demand size for each will differ. Although there is no basic difficulty with generalizing (11.3.1) to account for this "market-basket" situation, we shall talk only about the single-item or commodity case for the present.

Very often, neither the precise number of demands in a time period nor their sizes can be anticipated in advance, so they are characterized as random variables. A frequently useful demand model is one based on the assumption that individual demands occur according to a Poisson process and are of unit size. For discussion of the Poisson process, see Chapter 8. Thus typically the demand for a spare part occurs at, or near, the time of a failure and may (but need not) be for one item. Similarly, the total demand for cars at a warehouse or for taxis at an airport taxi stand is the sum of many individual (perhaps Poisson-like) demand processes. A useful generalization is available by allowing the *number* of demands to be Poisson and the demand *sizes* to be independently and identically distributed random variables in order to represent the fact that successive customers may require quite different quantities of certain items. Under these circumstances we are led to the following definition.

DEFINITION 11.3.1. Suppose the total number of demands over a time period, $N(t)$, is Poisson distributed and the sizes of the individual demands, S_i, $i = 1, 2, \ldots, N(t)$, are independently distributed according to $F(x)$, $x \geq 0$. Then the total demand over a fixed time period $(0, t)$, expressed as in (11.3.1),

$$D(t) = S_1 + S_2 + \cdots + S_{N(t)},$$

has the *compound Poisson distribution*. The random process $\{D(t), t \geq 0\}$ is called the *compound Poisson process* with demand rate λ.

Notice that the compound Poisson process develops in a series of upward jumps, like the Poisson process. However, the jump sizes are now permitted to be of various magnitudes, the latter being governed by the distribution $F(x)$. We state the following theorem concerning the compound Poisson process.

THEOREM 11.3.1. (i) The expected value and variance of the total demand over a period of length t are, respectively,

$$(11.3.2) \qquad E[D(t)] = \lambda t \int_0^\infty x \, dF(x) = \lambda t E[S],$$

$$(11.3.3) \qquad \mathrm{Var}[D(t)] = \lambda t \int_0^\infty x^2 \, dF(x) = \lambda t E[S^2].$$

(ii) As the period length becomes large or, equivalently, as the demand rate, λ, increases (in such a way that $\lambda t \to \infty$), the distribution of $D(t)$ becomes approximately normally distributed:

$$(11.3.4) \qquad \lim_{\lambda t \to \infty} P\{D(t) > \lambda t E[S] + x\sqrt{\lambda t E[S^2]}\} = \frac{1}{\sqrt{2\pi}} \int_x^\infty e^{-(1/2)z^2} \, dz.$$

(iii) The *Laplace transform* of the distribution of $D(t)$ is

$$(11.3.5) \qquad E[e^{-\theta D(t)}] = e^{-\lambda t[1 - \hat{F}(\theta)]},$$

where

$$(11.3.6) \qquad \hat{F}(\theta) = \int_0^\infty e^{-\theta x} \, dF(x)$$

and θ is a real number for which the integral of (11.2.6) converges.

DISCUSSION. (Detailed proofs are omitted.) From the point of view of many applications, the most important parts of the theorem are (i) and (ii). They furnish convenient approximations for use in problems of stocking to meet future demand. As a simple example, we recall the inventory model of Chapter 8. There it was shown that if $F(x)$ represents the distribution of total demand over a time period, then an optimal initial stocking quantity is obtained by stocking $\bar{I}$ items, where

$$(11.3.7) \qquad\qquad F(\bar{I}) = 1 - \frac{c}{p} \qquad (c < p);$$

p is the selling price and c is the unit cost of production. The proof of part (iii) is outlined in Exercise 3. Part (iii) is used as a tool in deriving more complex distributions related to demand and replenishment times. An example appears shortly. The detailed mathematical development may be skipped if desired.

The next example illustrates the application of our procedure for approximating the demand distribution.

EXAMPLE 11.3.1. At a certain large bakery there are on the average 1000 individual demands for bread a day. More precisely, the number of demands for bread on a day, $N(1)$, has the Poisson distribution with mean or expectation 1000. Two-thirds of these demands are for one loaf; one-third are for six loaves; that is, with independent probability $\frac{2}{3}$, a customer requests one loaf of bread, while with probability $\frac{1}{3}$, six are requested. The selling price per loaf is $p = \$0.35$, and the production cost is $c = \$0.10$. In order to determine the optimum number of loaves of bread to be baked in anticipation of daily demand, it is convenient to use the normal distribution approximation of Theorem 11.3.1(ii). First, the expected or mean daily demand is, from (11.3.2),

$$E[D(1)] = \lambda E[S] = (1{,}000)[(\tfrac{2}{3})(1) + (\tfrac{1}{3})(6)],$$

$$(11.3.8) \qquad\qquad = \frac{8{,}000}{3} = 0.67 \times 10^3,$$

and the variance of daily demand is, from (11.3.3),

$$\mathrm{Var}[D(1)] = \lambda E[S^2] = (1{,}000)[(\tfrac{2}{3})(1^2) + (\tfrac{1}{3})(6^2)],$$

$$(11.3.9) \qquad\qquad = \frac{38{,}000}{3} = 12.67 \times 10^3.$$

Next, it is apparent from (11.3.4) that if

$$F(x) = P\{D(t) \le x\},$$

then the normal approximation provides

(11.3.10)

$$F(I) = \frac{1}{\sqrt{2\pi}} \int_{-\infty}^{(I - E[D(t)])/\sqrt{\mathrm{Var}[D(t)]}} e^{-(1/2)z^2}\, dz = \frac{1}{\sqrt{2\pi}} \int_{-\infty}^{(I - 2.67 \times 10^3)/116} e^{-(1/2)z^2}\, dz.$$

Now $\bar{I}$, the optimum production (initial inventory), is found by solving (11.3.7). To carry this out, we use the approximation (11.3.10),

$$(11.3.11) \qquad \frac{1}{\sqrt{2\pi}} \int_{-\infty}^{(I-E[D(t)])/\sqrt{\operatorname{Var}[D(t)]}} e^{-(1/2)z^2} \, dz = 1 - \frac{c}{p} \qquad \left(\frac{c}{p} < 1\right),$$

$$= 1 - \frac{0.10}{0.35} = 0.715,$$

and solve for $\bar{I}$.

To solve, let U_α represent the $\alpha(100)$ percent point for the normal distribution with mean zero and unit variance; that is, U_α satisfies

$$(11.3.12) \qquad \frac{1}{\sqrt{2\pi}} \int_{-\infty}^{U_\alpha} e^{-(1/2)z^2} \, dz = \alpha \qquad (0 < \alpha < 1).$$

Reference to a table of the standard normal distribution shows that if $\alpha = 0.715$ as in (11.3.11), then $U_\alpha = 0.57$. Hence, we see that for the present example the normal approximation gives, for the optimum number of loaves of bread with which to start the day,

$$\bar{I} = E[D(t)] + U_\alpha\sqrt{\operatorname{Var}[D(t)]}, \qquad \alpha = 1 - \frac{c}{p},$$

$$(11.3.13) \qquad = \frac{8,000}{3} + (0.57)\sqrt{\frac{38,000}{3}},$$

$$= 2,667 + 64 = 2,731 \text{ loaves.}$$

Observe that U_α depends only on the cost-profit ratio, c/p, and that if the latter decreases, inventory should be increased. Inventory should also be increased if the variance of demand increases.

We do not mean to imply by our prolonged discussion involving the normal distribution that it is the only distribution of use in inventory studies. Such is far from the case. Recall that we have used the exponential distribution in Chapter 8. It is desirable to bring empirical evidence to bear on the choice of a distribution and also to check for the validity of the choice made. It is also true, however, that the overall cost functions encountered in inventory studies are often very flat, so little is lost by not operating at precisely the right level. Putting this another way, the error made by using a somewhat inappropriate distribution is not likely to be very costly.

It is interesting to note that if the demand rate were doubled, perhaps by consolidating two bakeries of the same size in one central location, the optimum initial inventory would be somewhat *less than* doubled. Let us illustrate this for the present example. If the demand rate is doubled to become $2\lambda = 2,000$, then (11.3.13) gives

$$\bar{I} = \frac{16,000}{3} + (0.57)\sqrt{\frac{76,000}{3}},$$

$$= 5,333 + 91 = 5,424,$$

or 38 loaves less than twice the optimum inventory when demand rate is 1,000. An intuitive explanation for the economy associated with pooling or combining stock in one location is easily furnished. Clearly the stocking of inventory in excess of expected demand (64 loaves when demand rate is 1,000, as in (11.3.13)) is for protection against lost sales caused by unusually large total daily demand. Let us imagine two separate bakeries, each confronted with independent demands averaging 1,000 per day. If each carries the appropriate inventory, as given by (11.3.13), then examination of (11.3.10) and (11.3.11) shows that the chance of a stockout at just one of the two bakeries is 2(0.715)(0.285), or about 0.41. On these occasions bread is left over at one bakery that could have been sold at the other. If the two bakeries were consolidated (actually moved together physically) and the extra stock shared, some of the resulting lost sales could have been avoided. Hence an optimum inventory for the two bakeries acting cooperatively may be made somewhat smaller than the sum of the two optimum inventories when the bakeries are acting independently, as we have just seen to be the case. You should now ask yourself why large companies do not have just one warehouse.

Although consumer demand is usually the largest single source of uncertainty in an inventory problem, it is by no means the only one. Another important factor involving random variation is the procurement or lead time for replenishing a depleted inventory, which we now discuss.

B. Lead (or Procurement, or Replenishment) Time

When demands sufficiently reduce the size of an inventory, it becomes necessary to order replenishment stock so as to be able to meet future demands. The time that elapses from the moment a replenishment order is placed until that order is in stock and ready to satisfy demands is often called the *lead* (or *procurement*, or *replenishment*) *time*. Frequently the lead time exhibits considerable variability, perhaps induced by the work-load variations at a factory, shipping delays, and so on; hence it is naturally treated as a random variable.

The simple EOQ model of the last section may be interpreted as if a lead time or replenishment delay of definite fixed duration were present. Suppose that a fixed known time L is required to furnish an order of any size Q. Then since the demand rate is m, the usage during lead time is $Lm = r$. Hence if an order for Q units is placed when stock falls to level r, we have precisely the situation portrayed in Figure 11.2.1, *provided* $Q > r$. We shall shortly continue with the treatment of the EOQ model, considering the effect of random variations in lead time. But before doing so, an example will be given to show that the distribution of demand during a *random* period (lead time) may actually be more tractable, mathematically speaking, than the corresponding distribution over a fixed period. The actual derivation of our example makes use of the Laplace transform of the compound Poisson distribution given in Theorem 11.3.1(iii). If desired this derivation (see Exercise 5) may be skipped, but the result, given by (11.3.14) below, is noteworthy for its simplicity and because it illustrates the effect of lead-time variability.

EXAMPLE 11.3.2. The demand rate for fuel oil at a certain remote refueling station (an island in the Pacific) is

$$\lambda = 1 \text{ demand per week.}$$

The magnitude of an individual demand is an exponentially distributed random variable with mean

$$\xi = E[S] = 500 \text{ gallons.}$$

Oil is stored in a tank having 1500 gallon capacity. At irregular time intervals a tanker appears to replenish the inventory of fuel oil at the station. The time intervals are long, so the station's policy is to refuel whenever the tanker appears, or, equivalently, to reorder as soon as replenishment has occurred and the tanker departs. Thus the time between two successive tanker appearances is the lead time. We assume that the lead time is an exponentially distributed random variable L, with mean

$$E[L] = v^{-1} = 10 \text{ weeks,}$$

or rate $v = 0.1$ (weeks). Under the assumptions above, it is shown in Exercise 5 that the total demand (in gallons of oil) during a random lead time, which we denote by $D(L)$, has the distribution

(11.3.14)
$$P\{D(L) \le x\} = \begin{cases} 0 & \text{for } x < 0 \\[2mm] \dfrac{v}{v + \lambda} & \text{for } x = 0 \\[3mm] 1 - \dfrac{\lambda}{\lambda + v} e^{-x/[(1 + \lambda/v)\xi]} & \text{for } x > 0 \end{cases}$$

(11.3.15)
$$P\{D(L) > x\} = \frac{\lambda}{\lambda + v} e^{-x/[(1 + \lambda/v)\xi]} \qquad \text{for } x > 0.$$

Since the tank is always full after each visit, the probability of emptiness, or stockout, is, by our previous computations,

$$P\{D(L) > 1500\} = (0.9091)e^{-1500/5500} = 0.69.$$

That is, there is nearly a 70% chance that the tank is empty when replenishment occurs. Apparently, a larger tank or more frequent replenishment visits are required in order to guarantee satisfactory refueling service at the station. This example is investigated further in Exercise 3, where the option of increasing the frequency of tanker visits—that is, reducing the lead time—is considered.

You should not conclude that the setup we have described, in which the entire reorder quantity Q appears simultaneously at the end of a lead time, is the only one possible. This is far from the case. If the item is a relatively inexpensive and fast-moving (frequently demanded) one, then reorders may be furnished from a higher level, or echelon, inventory—for example, a factory warehouse. They may then arrive in a batch as we have postulated. Even then, however, it may be wise to depart from the simple policy described and ship a portion of the quantity Q more rapidly—and expensively—in order to satisfy important needs. Thus the order may arrive throughout, rather than at the end of, the lead time. The phenomenon described above is quite likely to be encountered if the item in inventory is, because of high expense and infrequent usage, not immediately available at a higher level. In that case, the lead time may involve a wait for the production facilities to become available, at the end of which the reordered items become available almost continuously as production proceeds. The appropriate objective is then the coordination of the production rate with demand fluctuations.

Sometimes the inventory serves in a decoupling capacity to absorb the rapid demand fluctuations and allow expensive production rate changes to occur gradually. We shall consider a model of this type later, in Section 11.6.

C. Costs

As has been indicated in the first simple model of the previous section, various costs must be balanced in arriving at an appropriate inventory policy. We shall review these briefly here.

There is, first of all, the cost of actually maintaining a quantity of material in inventory: the *carrying cost*. In the classical commodity-inventory case, this includes warehouse maintenance and rental, insurance on stored items, and possibly the effect of physical deterioration, loss, and obsolescence. Other things being equal, all of these increase with the physical magnitude of the quantity inventoried. It is convenient and fairly accurate to suppose that there is a per-unit cost incurred if a unit of the commodity is carried for a particular period of time; this was assumed in our EOQ model. Of course, exceptions occur—for example, if one warehouse has generally lower storage costs than another and both are being used. Also, obsolescence losses and tax charges tend to occur at definite times. Another somewhat more subtle cost is associated with the capital tied up in inventory. Such capital is unavailable for use in other enterprises and constitutes a penalty. It may be remarked that carrying costs occur in other, perhaps less classical, situations. For example, inventories of people are costly in that salaries must be paid and office space furnished. For another example, the memory facilities of a high-speed computer act very much as a combined factory and factory warehouse, since they contain the program being processed by the actual computer unit. A large main memory capacity allows sizable programs to be executed efficiently, since time consuming swapping of programs in and out between central and peripheral memory is minimized. But large memory units are costly, just as are large warehouses. You will undoubtedly think of other examples illustrating this issue.

A second component of cost in an inventory system is the cost of *ordering* or *procurement* or *replenishment* of the inventory. In our EOQ model we have assumed that such a cost is incurred only at the time each order is placed and that it is fixed. This fixed cost is associated with preparing and communicating the order—for example, for the teletype message to the factory warehouse. It seems likely that ordering cost will also depend on the general level and diversity of activity experienced at the reorder processing facility. If orders for a number of types of commodity tend to arrive in a fluctuating, random manner at a central warehouse, for example, it may be necessary to increase staff (another inventory!) in order to handle these without unduly increasing lead time. This cost is not easily assigned on a per-order basis. Naturally, any special attention given to orders—rush replenishment, expediting, and the like—increases the ordering costs associated with an inventory system. One important component of ordering cost is the *changeover* or *setup* cost that arises when one production facility is used to manufacture several types of commodity. If the facility must be cleaned or retooled in order to handle a new order, a definite time loss and cost results. One feature that has not been mentioned is that of production quality: frequently it is necessary to stabilize the process to obtain satisfactory output each time a change is made. Rejected items must be charged to the setup and hence to the order if a new setup is required. Notice, too, that an ordering or procurement cost occurs when people, rather than commodities, are inventoried: it is the cost of recruitment. A changeover cost or penalty is associated with a computer operation; it is the time penalty involved in swapping program segments back and forth between memory units.

A third major cost category is that of service, or lack thereof. As we have seen, it is usually impossible to guarantee that random demands for commodities may be met directly from inventory. The *stockout* cost resulting when immediate fulfillment of demand is impossible may result in lost sales and lower profits. In our previous examples involving stockouts, we have simply assumed that the stockout cost associated with a lost sale is the lost revenue from the missed transaction, but in other cases it may mean the loss of a customer and all future transactions. If customers are willing to wait—for example, if a "customer" is actually a lower-level inventory in the same company—a *back-ordering cost* may be associated with the wait. Stockout and back-ordering, or failure-to-give-service costs, are associated with other inventory situations. For example, demands in a company for special staff service that are not met internally may require expensive consultants; of course if the demands are infrequent, it may be desirable to meet the needs in just this way. Likewise, slow computer service may require the purchase of new equipment or occasional leasing. Again, such a tactic may be wise.

These, then, are some of the more obvious costs and penalties associated with many inventory operations. In general, a large inventory is costly to maintain, but it tends to decrease ordering and stockout costs, so a balance must be struck. In order to maintain a suitable balance, records must be kept of demand and production behavior. Thus an additional cost is that of the actual *information-handling* and *decision-making* process by which the system is coordinated. We shall not explicitly consider this cost in our models, but its effect may be seen indirectly.

EXERCISES 11.3

1. Derive the expression (11.3.13) from (11.3.11) and (11.3.12).

2. Refer to the problem of Example 11.3.1, and suppose that the probability is 292/297 that a demand is for a single loaf of bread and 5/297 that a demand is for 100 loaves.
   (a) Show that the expected daily demand at a bakery is 8,000/3 loaves, as was true in the Example 11.3.1.
   (b) Find the variance of total daily demand.
   (c) Find the optimum inventory to anticipate a day's demand. Explain the difference between this result and that obtained for the earlier example.
   (d) Suppose two bakeries having the demand characteristics above were combined. Find the optimum inventory. Compare the effect of pooling inventories in the present case with that of the previous example.

3. Refer to the refueling station problem of Example 11.3.2.

   (a) What tank size would be required to assure that the probability of emptiness between successive tanker visits be (i) 0.25; (ii) 0.10?

   (b) Suppose the tank size is I. Show, using (11.3.15), that the probability that stockout does not occur before the next tanker visit on which fuel oil is actually transferred from tanker to station tank is equal to $e^{-I/[(1+\lambda/\nu)\xi]}$. Suppose $I = 1500$ gallons; find the mean lead time, ν^{-1}, such that the probability of emptiness is (i) 0.25; (ii) 0.10. (*Hint*: Sometimes a tanker arrives to find the tank still full because there has been no demand since the last visit.)

*4. The Laplace transform of $D(t)$, where the latter has been interpreted as the total demand during time t, has been given in Theorem 11.3.1 (iii). Show that the following steps lead to the expression (11.3.5).

   (a) Given that there are $N(t) = n$ $(n = 0, 1, 2, \ldots)$ demands during a time interval of length t, the Laplace transform of the sum of the independent demand sizes is

   $$E[e^{-\theta(S_1 + S_2 + \cdots + S_n)}] = \hat{F}(\theta)^n$$

   and

   $$E[e^{-\theta S_1}] = \hat{F}(\theta) = \int_0^\infty e^{-\theta x} \, dF(x).$$

   (*Hint*: By independence, $E[e^{-\theta(S_1 + S_2)}] = E[e^{-\theta S_1}]E[e^{-\theta S_2}]$.)

   (b) Given that $N(t) = n$, then

   $$D(t) = S_1 + S_2 + \cdots + S_n,$$

   so

   $$E[e^{-\theta D(t)} \,|\, N(t) = n] = \hat{F}(\theta)^n.$$

   Therefore, if we remove the condition on $N(t)$, using the Poisson distribution, we obtain

   $$E[e^{-\theta D(t)}] = \sum_{n=0}^\infty E[e^{-\theta D(t)} \,|\, N(t) = n]P\{N(t) = n\},$$

   $$= \sum_{n=0}^\infty \hat{F}(\theta)^n \, e^{-\lambda t} \frac{(\lambda t)^n}{n!},$$

   $$= e^{-\lambda t} \sum_{n=0}^\infty \frac{[\lambda t \hat{F}(\theta)]^n}{n!},$$

   $$= e^{-\lambda t} e^{\lambda t \hat{F}(\theta)},$$

   which is (11.3.5).

*5. In order to derive the distibution of total demand during a random lead time for the refueling-station inventory problem of Example 11.3.2, the following steps may be taken.

   (a) The conditional probability that no demand occurs during a lead time is, *given* $L = t$, $e^{-\lambda t}$. The unconditional probability is thus

   $$\int_0^\infty e^{-\lambda t} e^{-\nu t} \nu \, dt = \frac{\nu}{\nu + \lambda}.$$

   (b) If the magnitudes of demands (numbers of gallons demanded on different occasions) have the exponential distribution, then the Laplace transform, (11.3.6), is

   $$\hat{F}(\theta) = \int_0^\infty e^{-\theta x} e^{-x/\xi} \frac{dx}{\xi} = \frac{1}{1 + \xi\theta}.$$

   (c) Using the result of (b) and (11.3.5), show that the Laplace transform of the total demand during a *fixed* lead time $L = t$ is

   $$E[e^{-\theta D(t)}] = e^{-\lambda t[\xi\theta/(1 + \xi\theta)]}.$$

(d) Using the result of (c), show that the unconditional distribution of demand during an exponentially distributed lead time is

$$E[e^{-\theta D(L)}] = \int_0^\infty E[e^{-\theta D(L)} | L = t] e^{-vt} v\, dt,$$

$$= \int_0^\infty e^{-\lambda t\, [\xi\theta/(1+\xi\theta)]} e^{-vt} v\, dt,$$

$$= \frac{v(1+\xi\theta)}{v+(v+\lambda)\xi\theta}.$$

(e) Verify that the transform above may be put in the form

$$E[e^{-\theta D(L)}] = \frac{v}{v+\lambda} + \frac{\lambda}{v+\lambda} \cdot \frac{1}{1+(1+\lambda/v)\xi\theta}.$$

Since $\dfrac{1}{1+(1+\lambda/v)\xi\theta}$ is the Laplace transform of an exponential distribution with

mean $(1+\lambda/v)\xi$, conclude by the uniqueness property of the transform that (11.3.14) is the required distribution.

11.4   THE EOQ/REORDER-POINT MODEL FOR STOCHASTIC DEMANDS

The simple deterministic (nonrandom) inventory model of Section 11.2 served to introduce some of the fundamental issues in the control of commodity inventories. Realistically speaking, of course, such a simple model ignores a dominant feature of many inventory problems, namely the random variability of demand. Randomly varying demands have been discussed in Section 11.3, part A, and the combined effects of demand and lead-time variations are treated in Section 11.3, part B. Recognition of randomness forces us to face the possibility that inventory stock will run out before the replenishment order arrives; we have met this possibility in several of the previous examples. Our purpose here will be to show how to combine the simple deterministic EOQ analysis with the treatment of the demand-during-lead-time problem. The mathematical treatment presented will be on an approximate or heuristic level. In the next section, a more precise solution to a somewhat simpler problem will be furnished by appealing to the theory of Markov chains. In practice, simple methods similar to those of the present section are frequently used, and are usually entirely adequate.

We begin by summarizing the effect of considering stochastic demands in the EOQ model. The notation used has been introduced earlier.

A. Summary

In order to find the optimal order quantity, $\bar{Q}$, and reorder point, $\bar{r}$,
(a) first find the EOQ,

$$\bar{Q} = \sqrt{2m\frac{c_o}{c_c}};$$

this is the expression (11.2.2); then

(b) solve the equation

(11.4.1)
$$F(r) = \frac{mc_s}{mc_s + \bar{Q}c_c}$$

to find the order point, $\bar{r}$.

In the latter formula, F represents the distribution function of demand over lead time, and c_{so} is the cost of being out of stock by one unit. Recall from Chapter 8 that an expression like (11.4.1) may be solved graphically; Figure 11.4.1 is self-explanatory. In later examples we shall show how to obtain analytical solution to the reorder-point equation.

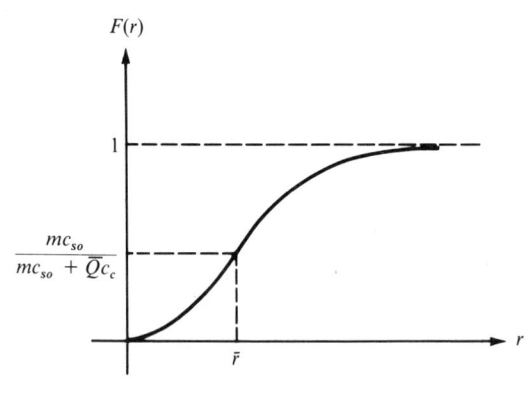

FIGURE 11.4.1

It is emphasized that the $\bar{Q}$ and $\bar{r}$ obtained in steps (a) and (b) are approximate. and that a simple procedure, to be described, may be used to "correct" these initial values.

B. Derivations and Discussion

The derivation of the previous results will be discussed now, and the model will subsequently be illustrated by reconsidering the bolt-stocking problem of Section 11.2, Example 11.2.1, generalized so that demand is stochastic. You may wish to turn immediately to Example 11.4.1 at this point.

Suppose that a reorder point, r, is to be set so that when stock reaches r, an order for Q items is placed. Let $f(x)$ be the probability density function approximating the distribution of demand during lead time:

(11.4.2)
$$P\{D(L) \le y\} = \int_0^y f(x)\, dx = F(y);$$

$F(y)$ denotes the distribution function of demand $D(L)$ during the lead time, L. Then Figure 11.4.2 shows the manner in which the inventory fluctuates.

A glance at the diagram shows that the inventory level immediately after the arrival of the order Q is $Q + r - D(L)$, while the inventory level at the end of the lead

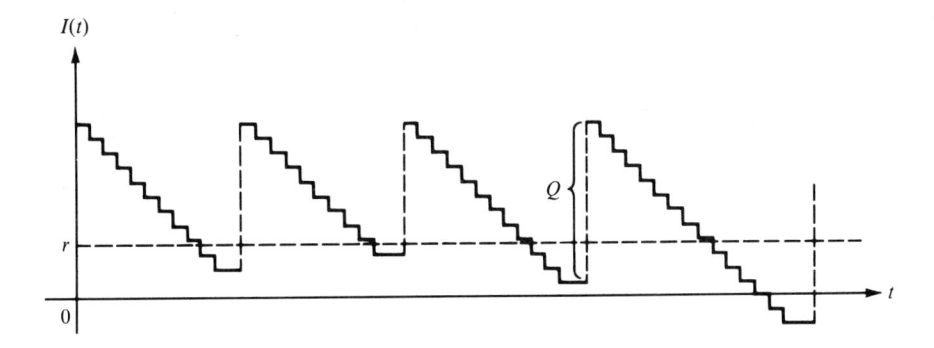

FIGURE 11.4.2

time is $r - D(L)$. Since an inventory carrying charge is made only when inventory is positive, we assess the carrying charge as the average of the expected positive stock levels at the beginning and end of the lead time:

$$(11.4.3) \quad c_c \left[\frac{Q + \int_0^r (r - x)f(x)\, dx + \int_0^r (r - x)f(x)\, dx}{2} \right] = c_c \frac{Q}{2} + c_c \int_0^r (r - x)f(x)\, dx.$$

Thus just *before* a new order arrives, actual inventory stock on hand is $r - D(L)$ if the demand during lead time, $D(L)$, is less than the reorder point, and otherwise is zero. Although demand is stochastic, we can still estimate the average number of orders per year as m/Q, and hence the ordering cost is $c_o m/Q$. Finally, a stockout penalty, c_s, is charged against each unit demanded when an out-of-stock condition prevails— that is, if $D(L) > r$. The expected stockout cost per lead time is

$$(11.4.4) \qquad\qquad c_s \int_r^\infty (x - r)f(x)\, dx,$$

and the yearly stockout cost is then

$$\frac{m}{Q} c_s \int_r^\infty (x - r)f(x)\, dx.$$

Totting up the cost components (11.4.2), (11.4.3), and (11.4.4), we arrive at an expression for expected total annual inventory-associated cost, denoted by $C(Q, r)$:

$$(11.4.5) \quad C(Q, r) = c_c \frac{Q}{2} + c_c \int_0^r (r - x)f(x)\, dx + c_o \frac{m}{Q} + \frac{m}{Q} c_s \int_r^\infty (x - r)f(x)\, dx.$$

Strictly speaking, the expression above is appropriate when "stockout" means sales are lost, not merely back ordered (unsatisfied demands wait). But if stockout penalties are reasonably severe, there will be little difference between the lost-sales and back-ordering cases, since only rarely will stockouts occur in either case. This comment indicates the approach to be taken to finding an approximately optimum choice for Q and r. We first *neglect* the terms containing the integrals in (11.4.5) and find an optimum Q; comparison with (11.2.2) shows that it is simply given by the classical "square-root" formula (11.2.3). Now put the value $\bar{Q}$ into (11.4.5) and differentiate with respect to r to find the best reorder point:

$$\frac{\partial C(\bar{Q}, r)}{\partial r} = \frac{d}{dr}\left[c_c \frac{\bar{Q}}{2} + c_c \int_0^r (r - x)f(x)\,dx + c_o \frac{m}{\bar{Q}} + \frac{m}{\bar{Q}} c_s \int_r^\infty (x - r)f(x)dx\right],$$

$$(11.4.6) \qquad = c_c \int_0^r f(x)\,dx + \frac{m}{\bar{Q}} c_s \int_r^\infty (-1)f(x)\,dx,$$

$$= c_c F(r) - \frac{m}{\bar{Q}} c_s [1 - F(r)].$$

When the last expression is equated to zero, we find the r must satisfy the expression

$$(11.4.7) \qquad F(r) = \frac{mc_{so}}{mc_{so} + \bar{Q}c_c}.$$

If desired, this equation may be solved graphically as shown in Figure 11.2.1.

The values $\bar{Q}$ and $\bar{r}$ obtained as described are approximate. What we really wish is to solve simultaneously the two equations

$$(11.4.8a) \qquad \frac{\partial C(Q, r)}{\partial Q} = c_c \frac{1}{2} - c_o \frac{m}{Q^2} - \frac{m}{Q^2} c_s \int_r^\infty (x - r)f(x)\,dx = 0$$

and

$$(11.4.8b) \qquad \frac{\partial C(Q, r)}{\partial r} = -\frac{m}{Q} c_s + \left[c_c + \frac{m}{Q} c_s\right]F(r) = 0.$$

It is plausible that one can "correct" the first solution—that is, solve the system iteratively. The procedure is as follows: having found $\bar{r}$ by solving (11.4.7), substitute it into (11.4.5). Differentiation with respect to Q then leads to (11.4.8a), with $r = \bar{r} > 0$, and finally to the first corrected order quantity, $\bar{Q}_1$. The latter value is somewhat *larger* than $\bar{Q}$ and thus effectively increases the inventory level slightly to help avoid stockouts. Next, $\bar{Q}_1$ may be used in place of $\bar{Q}$ in (11.4.7); since $\bar{Q}_1$ is larger than $\bar{Q}$, the corrected reorder point, $\bar{r}_1$, is smaller than $\bar{r}$. This process may be repeated until no significant change occurs in the values of Q and r.

EXAMPLE 11.4.1. Let us reconsider the bolt-stocking problem of Example 11.2.1. Recall that

$$c_o = \$2.00, \qquad c_c = \$0.02,$$

and let

$$c_s = \$0.10,$$

the cost of a lost sale. Assume further that lead time is about one week long, with the expected number of bolts demanded during lead time being

$$(11.4.9) \qquad E[D(L)] = \bar{D} = 100,$$

and

$$(11.4.10) \qquad \text{Var}[D(L)] = \sigma^2 = 100.$$

Note that we have already used the square-root formula to find $\bar{Q} = 1000$ bolts. To obtain the first approximation to the reorder point, $\bar{r}$, we must solve (11.4.7); in the present case this is

$$\frac{1}{\sqrt{2\pi}} \int_{-\infty}^{(r-\bar{D})/\sigma} e^{-(1/2)z^2} \, dz = \frac{mc_{so}}{mc_{so} + \bar{Q}c_c},$$

$$= \frac{(5000)(0.10)}{(5000)(0.10) + (1000)(0.02)} = 0.96.$$

If $U_{0.96}$ is the 96th percentile of the unit normal (use normal tables), then

$$U_{0.96} = 1.8,$$

and we have

$$\bar{r} = \bar{D} + U_{0.96} \, \sigma$$
$$= 100 + (1.8)(10) = 118,$$

in round numbers.

We shall not carry out the iterative correction procedure outlined. The necessary steps are outlined in the exercises for the case of a normal distribution of demand during lead time. Instead, we discuss the example above when lead time and demand distribution are such that demand lead time may be assumed to be exponentially distributed.

EXAMPLE 11.4.2. Let us again consider the bolt-stocking problem, keeping all cost and demand parameters the same except that now $D(L)$ will be exponentially distributed with

$$E[D(L)] = \bar{D} = 100$$

and necessarily

$$\text{Var}[D(L)] = \bar{D}^2 = 10,000.$$

Again we have for the first approximation that $\bar{Q} = 1000$, and $\bar{r}$ is the solution of (11.4.7), in this case

$$1 - e^{-r/100} = 0.9615;$$

after doing some arithmetic, the result is

$$\bar{r} = 100 \log_e \frac{1}{0.0385} = 326,$$

approximately. The larger variance of the present example thus considerably increases the reorder point over that found in Example 11.4.1, as is to be expected. It is of interest to compute the reorder point under the assumption that the normal, not the exponential, distribution governs demand during lead time.

We find, following the previous example, that

$$\bar{r} = \bar{D} + U_{0.96} \, \sigma,$$
$$= 100 + (1.75)(100) = 275.$$

Certainly this value for the reorder point differs from that obtained from the exponential—namely, $\bar{r} = 326$. But the important question is: are the costs from following policies implied by $\bar{r} = 326$ and $\bar{r} = 275$ very different? Experience shows that there is often a considerable degree of insensitivity to the precise assumptions made.

EXERCISES 11.4

1. Carry out the solution to Example 11.4.1 when
   (a) $c_s = \$0.25$,
   (b) $c_s = \$0.50$,
   and compare the reorder points in each case. Does $\bar{r}$ increase in proportion to the stock-out cost? Assume the normal distribution for demands during lead time.

2. Repeat the solution of Exercise 1 when demand over lead time is exponentially distributed with the same mean, $\bar{D} = 100$, as above.

3. If the demand-during-lead-time density is assumed normal with mean $\bar{D}$ and variance σ^2, then evaluation of (11.4.8a) requires the following integral:

$$I(r) = \int_r^\infty (x - r)f(x)\, dx = \int_r^\infty (x - r)\,\frac{e^{-(1/2)[(x-\bar{D})/\sigma]^2}}{\sqrt{2\pi\sigma}}\, dx.$$

The integration in terms of tabulated functions may be carried out as indicated below.
(a) Substitute $z = (x - \bar{D})/\sigma$ to obtain

$$I(r) = \int_{(r-\bar{D})/\sigma}^\infty (\bar{D} + \sigma z - r)e^{-(1/2)z^2}\,\frac{dz}{\sqrt{2\pi}}.$$

(b) Next,

$$I(r) = (\bar{D} - r)\left(\frac{1}{\sqrt{2\pi}}\int_{(r-\bar{D})/\sigma}^\infty e^{-(1/2)z^2}\, dz\right) + \frac{\sigma}{\sqrt{2\pi}}\int_{(r-\bar{D})/\sigma}^\infty e^{-(1/2)z^2}\, z\, dz.$$

Observe that the first integral to the right of the equality may be found from a table of the normal distribution.
(c) Substitute $r = \frac{1}{2}z^2$ in the second integral:

$$\int_{(r-\bar{D})/\sigma}^\infty e^{-(1/2)z^2}z\, dz = \int_{(1/2)[(r-\bar{D})/\sigma]^2}^\infty e^{-v}\, dv = e^{-(1/2)[(r-\bar{D})/\sigma]^2}$$

Now the value of $I(r)$ may be determined from a table of the normal distribution and a table of negative exponentials.

4. Evaluate $I(r)$ of Exercise 3 when

$$f(x) = \begin{cases} e^{-x/\bar{D}}\dfrac{1}{\bar{D}} & x \geq 0 \\ 0 & x < 0 \end{cases}$$

(*Hint:* $\int_y^\infty xe^{-x}\, dx = (1 + y)e^{-y}$, as can be shown by integration by parts.)

5. Refer to the problem of Example 11.4.1. Carry out the first iteration to find $\bar{Q}$ and $\bar{r}_1$, as described in the text. Use the result of Exercise 3.

6. Repeat Exercise 5, using the exponential demand distribution. Use the result of Exercise 4.

7. Compare total costs $C(\bar{Q}, \bar{r})$ with $C(\bar{Q}_1, \bar{r}_1)$ for the problem of Example 11.4.1. Use the result of Exercise 3 above.

8. Repeat Exercise 7 when demand is assumed exponential, $\bar{D} = 100$.

9. Suppose demand is actually normal, as in Example 11.4.1. However, suppose $\bar{r}$ is computed on the assumption that demand is exponential with $\bar{D} = 100$. Compare $C[\bar{Q}, \bar{r} \text{ (normal)}] = C(1000, 275)$ and $C[\bar{Q}, \bar{r} \text{ (exponential)}] = C(1000, 326)$.

11.5   A STOCHASTIC INVENTORY MODEL

The developments of the previous sections indicate the manner in which the classical deterministic EOQ model may be extended to account for randomness of demand and lead times. The analysis was mathematically approximate, but wide use of analogous approaches in even more complex problems testifies to its value. Actually, analyses that make fewer blithe approximations may and have been conducted. One such is described in this section.

The situation to be considered here has the following characteristics. A particular item such as a spare part or, perhaps, a particular model of a consumer good such as a refrigerator is stocked at a warehouse. Demand for individual items occurs according to a stationary Poisson process of rate λ (see Chapter 10). When stock of the item reaches a reorder point, a replenishment order is placed with a factory. This order must await its turn at the production facility. The waiting time from the moment the reorder is placed until the item is completely manufactured and returned to the warehouse is a random variable, independent from one reorder occasion to another and having an exponential distribution: if L is a random lead time, then

$$(11.5.1) \qquad \begin{aligned} P\{L < x\} &= 1 - e^{-\mu x} & x \geq 0, \\ &= 0 & x < 0, \end{aligned}$$

where μ^{-1} is the expectation, or mean, of L. Furthermore, it is assumed that the waiting time is mainly caused by the wait in queue at the production facility caused by *other* reorders. Actual production time, once the facility is reached, is negligibly short—so short that the size of the original order may be revised to be current at the moment of production. Note that the provision for revision may require an information transfer at the moment of production as well as that required to place the original order.

Inventory is to be controlled at the warehouse by means of the following *ordering policy*. The maximum number of items stocked at the warehouse is set at M units $(M > 0)$. When stock level (the number of units on hand) falls to level r $(0 < r < M)$, an order for replenishment stock (reorder) is placed. Because reorder sizes may be revised at the last moment, it is assumed that when the replenishment arrives, the warehouse stock level is M.

Choice of M and r is to be made so as to minimize the expected cost rate at the warehouse. Finally, we assume that customers are impatient: if no items are on hand when a demand is made, the disappointed customer takes his business elsewhere and the sale is lost.

In response to the ordering policy and lost-sales assumption, the inventory, or number of units on hand at t, $I(t)$, varies as shown in Figure 11.5.1. You will notice the similarity to Figure 11.4.2. Now, as will shortly become clear, the assumptions of our model assure that $I(t)$ develops as a Markov process in continuous time with

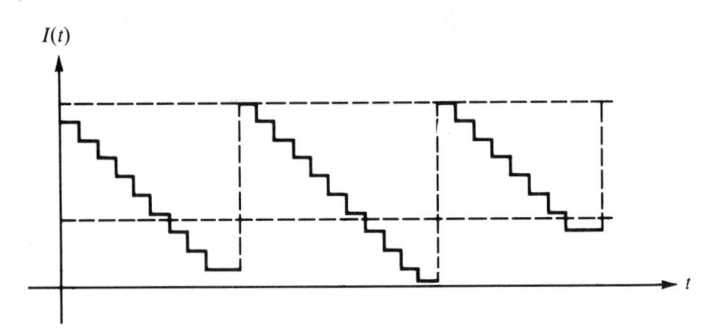

FIGURE 11.5.1

stationary transition probabilities and a finite number $(M + 1)$ of states. Let p_j $(j = 0, 1, 2, \ldots, M)$ be the long-run or stationary probability that the inventory level is at level j:

$$(11.5.2) \qquad \lim_{t \to \infty} P\{I(t) = j\} = p_j.$$

This probability is also the long-run fraction of time that the inventory level is j. We shall set up an overall cost function using the probabilities p_j. After doing so we shall show how these probabilities may be derived, utilizing the demand and waiting-time (lead-time) assumptions. Lastly, we indicate ways to go about selecting the optimal values of M and r. It is interesting that for this model we again find that optimal M is determined by a square-root formula as was true in our first, simple EOQ model.

A. Cost Rates

Consider first the cost associated with being in a zero-stock condition. Suppose the system is in state $j = 0$ at time t. Then a stockout event (a demand with no stock to satisfy it) occurs in time interval $(t, t + dt)$ with probability

$$(11.5.3) \qquad P\{I(t) = 0\}\lambda \, dt.$$

The expected number of such events over a time of length T is obtained by integrating (11.5.3):

$$(11.5.4) \qquad \int_0^T P\{I(t) = 0\}\lambda \, dt = \lambda \int_0^T P\{I(t) = 0\} \, dt.$$

The expected number of stockouts per unit time then results when we divide the expression above by T, and the long-run expected number of stockouts per unit time is approached as T becomes large. But for any j it can be shown that

$$(11.5.5) \qquad \lim_{T \to \infty} \frac{1}{T} \int_0^T P\{I(t) = j\} dt = p_j$$

(the analytically inclined reader should verify this rigorously), so the long-run stockout rate is seen to be λp_0. If the cost of a unit stockout is c_{so}, the long-run cost of stockouts is $c_{so} \lambda p_0$.

When the inventory level reaches the reorder point, r, an order is placed and an ordering cost, c_o, is incurred. The probability that such a reorder event occurs in $(t, t + dt)$ is the probability that $I(t) = r + 1$ *and* a demand takes place in $(t, t + dt)$:

$$(11.5.6) \qquad P\{\text{reorder in } (t, t + dt)\} = P\{I(t) = r + 1\}\lambda \, dt.$$

It then follows by reasoning similar to that used to treat stockouts that the long-run ordering-cost rate is $c_o p_{r+1} \lambda$.

Finally, it is assumed that inventory carrying cost is proportional to the maximum inventory—that is, it equals $c_c M$. When we assemble all of the cost components, we see that the long-run total cost rate is

$$(11.5.7) \qquad C(M, r) = c_{so} \lambda p_0 + c_o \lambda p_{r+1} + c_c M.$$

In order to minimize this expression with respect to M and r, it is necessary to express p_0 and p_{r+1} in terms of these decision parameters, and, of course, in terms of the demand rate λ and the replenishment rate μ.

B. The Inventory Level Stochastic Process

In order to derive the expressions for p_0 and p_{r+1} necessary in the cost function (11.5.7), we will make use of the balance equations introduced in Chapter 10, Section 10.3. Actually, the present process of inventory fluctuation is not a birth-and-death process, yet the balance-equation approach remains applicable. Consider the various states and the manner in which entry into and exit from them take place.

(a) $j = 0$. Entry into state $j = 0$ occurs from state $j = 1$ with rate λ. Exit from this state occurs when an order of size M arrives; this occurs with rate μ. Hence the first balance equation is

$$(11.5.8) \qquad \mu p_0 = \lambda p_1.$$

(b) $j = 1, 2, 3, \ldots, r$. Entry into state j occurs from state $j + 1$ with rate λ. Exit from state j occurs to state $j - 1$ with rate λ *or* to state M (a replenishment order arrives) with rate μ. Equating the rate of transition in with the rate out, we have

$$(11.5.9) \qquad \lambda p_{j+1} = (\lambda + \mu)p_j \qquad \text{for } j = 1, 2, \ldots, r.$$

(c) $j = r + 1, r + 2, \ldots, M - 1$. When the inventory state is above r, there is no replenishment order outstanding. Entry into state j occurs from $j + 1$ with rate λ. The only way of leaving j is again because a demand occurs. Consequently

$$(11.5.10) \qquad \lambda p_{j+1} = \lambda p_j \qquad \text{for } j = r + 1, r + 2, \ldots, M - 1.$$

Finally we require the normalization condition:

$$(11.5.11) \qquad \sum_{j=0}^{M} p_j = 1.$$

Notice that it is not essential to derive the balance equation for $j = M$, since the normalization automatically furnishes it if it is needed.

Now again the balance equations (11.5.8), (11.5.9), and (11.5.10) may be solved recursively. Start with (11.5.8) and proceed to (11.5.9):

$$p_1 = \frac{\mu}{\lambda} p_0,$$

and then

(11.5.12)
$$p_2 = \left(1 + \frac{\mu}{\lambda}\right)p_1 = \left(1 + \frac{\mu}{\lambda}\right)\frac{\mu}{\lambda} p_0.$$

Continuation of this process shows that

(11.5.13)
$$p_j = \left(1 + \frac{\mu}{\lambda}\right)^{j-1}\frac{\mu}{\lambda} p_0 \qquad (j = 1, 2, \ldots, r+1).$$

For $j = r+1, r+2, \ldots, M-1$, one can see from (11.5.10) that

(11.5.14)
$$p_j = p_{j+1} = p_{r+1}$$

(11.5.15)
$$p_j = \left(1 + \frac{\mu}{\lambda}\right)^{r}\frac{\mu}{\lambda} p_0 \qquad (j = r+2, r+3, \ldots, M).$$

In order to determine p_0, bring in the normalization condition (11.5.11):

(11.5.16)
$$1 = \sum_{j=0}^{M} p_j = p_0\left[1 + \frac{\mu}{\lambda} + \left(1 + \frac{\mu}{\lambda}\right)\frac{\mu}{\lambda} \cdots \left(1 + \frac{\mu}{\lambda}\right)^{r}\frac{\mu}{\lambda} + (M - r - 1)\left(1 + \frac{\mu}{\lambda}\right)^{r}\frac{\mu}{\lambda}\right],$$

$$= p_0\left(1 + \frac{\mu}{\lambda}\right)^{r}\left[1 + (M - r)\frac{\mu}{\lambda}\right],$$

and thus

(11.5.17)
$$p_0 = \frac{1}{\left(1 + \frac{\mu}{\lambda}\right)^{r}\left[1 + (M - r)\frac{\mu}{\lambda}\right]},$$

so the long-run distribution of inventory level induced by the assumed ordering rule is at hand. Examination of (11.5.13) shows that the probability that inventory is at any level j below the order point increases rapidly (exponentially) with j and that the probability, p_0, of being in a zero-stock position is thus comparatively small. Interestingly enough, the inventory is equally likely to be at any level, j ($j = r+1, r+2, \ldots, M$), given that it is above the reorder point.

Since an expression for p_0 is at hand, the long-run stockout cost rate is, according to (11.5.17),

(11.5.18)
$$c_{so} p_0 \lambda = \frac{c_s \lambda}{\left(1 + \frac{\mu}{\lambda}\right)^{r}\left[1 + (M - r)\frac{\mu}{\lambda}\right]}.$$

To find the reordering cost rate, make use of (11.5.13) to obtain the expression

(11.5.19)
$$c_{o} p_{r+1} \lambda = \frac{c_{o} \mu\left(1 + \frac{\mu}{\lambda}\right)^{r}}{\left(1 + \frac{\mu}{\lambda}\right)^{r}\left[1 + (M - r)\frac{\mu}{\lambda}\right]}.$$

Finally, since the carrying cost rate is proportional to maximum inventory level, M, the total cost rate is, from (11.5.7),

$$(11.5.20) \qquad C(M, r) = \frac{c_{so}\lambda + c_o\mu\left(1 + \frac{\mu}{\lambda}\right)^r}{\left(1 + \frac{\mu}{\lambda}\right)^r\left[1 + (M - r)\frac{\mu}{\lambda}\right]} + c_c M.$$

It is now possible to select the approximate level of M that minimizes the total cost rate, (11.5.20). For fixed r we differentiate with respect to M:

$$(11.5.21) \qquad \frac{\partial C(M, r)}{\partial M} = c_c - \frac{\mu c + \frac{\mu^2}{\lambda}\left(1 + \frac{\mu}{\lambda}\right)^r c_o}{\left(1 + \frac{\mu}{\lambda}\right)^r\left[1 + (M - r)\frac{\mu}{\lambda}\right]^2}.$$

When the expression above is equated to zero, we obtain

$$(11.5.22) \qquad M_{opt} = r + \left[\sqrt{\frac{\lambda^2 c_{so}}{\left(1 + \frac{\mu}{\lambda}\right)^r \mu c_c} + \lambda\frac{c_o}{c_c}} - \frac{\lambda}{\mu}\right].$$

It is interesting that (11.5.22) involves the *square root* in much the same way as does the classical EOQ formula. Next, one can substitute the expression for the optimum maximum inventory, M_{opt}, back into the cost function (11.5.20) and then proceed to find the optimum reorder point. This last step becomes difficult to carry out mathematically, however. In practical circumstances one would probably find it satisfactory to use a numerical search procedure, which can be carried out conveniently on a computer.

The model above provides an example of the manner in which Markov-chain techniques can be employed in inventory system analysis.

EXERCISES 11.5

1. Let $\mu = 1$ and $\lambda = 0.2$.
   (a) Find the value of M_{opt} for each of the following reorder points: $r = 0, 1, 2, 3, 4$. Let $c_{so} = \$50$, $c_o = \$10$, and $c_c = \$1$. Is the optimum reorder point within the given range of r values?
   (b) If the value of demand rate, λ, shifts from 0.2 to 2, find M_{opt} for each of the r values. Do the same exercise if the shift is from 0.2 to 0.05.

2. Suppose the expected replenishment time, μ^{-1}, tends to zero (μ tends to infinity). Show mathematically that
   (a) the cost function tends to

   $$C(M, r) = Mc_c + \frac{\lambda c_o}{M};$$

   (b) $r_{opt} = 0$ and $M_{opt} = \sqrt{\frac{\lambda c_o}{c_c}}$.

   (c) Explain the difference between the square-root formula of (b) above and the classical EOQ expression (11.5.2).

3. Consider the variation of our inventory model in which each reorder quantity is of *fixed* size Q.
   (a) Letting $r = 1$ and $Q = 2$, set up the balance equations.
   (b) Put $\mu = 1$ and $\lambda = 0.2$ in the result of (a), and find the long-run total cost rate.
   (c) Compare the long-run cost (b) to the result of assuming that $r = 1$, $M = 2$ in the model of the text. Explain any difference observed. What difference would you expect?

11.6   A PRODUCTION-SMOOTHING INVENTORY MODEL

The control rules introduced and evaluated in other sections have been most appropriate for the problems of controlling inventory at such stocking points as field warehouses or, perhaps, individual retail establishments. For the retail establishment, infrequent order placement is desirable in that it reduces the ordering-cost component of total cost. However, when orders are placed, they tend to be large, and it follows also that orders received at a factory warehouse fluctuate widely, inducing a considerable load variation on the production facility.* In this section, we consider the problems that arise when production costs, as well as inventory-associated costs, are considered. The simple rule to be introduced simultaneously controls production and inventory costs.

Let us suppose that a factory or other production facility is responsible for manufacturing a certain item. Demand for the item may be thought of as the accumulated reorders placed by field warehouses. The total demand is felt at a factory warehouse, which is replenished by a factory. It is the production-inventory coordination problem at the factory level with which we shall concern ourselves here. Consequently let X_n denote demand (for example, at factory warehouse) during week n (any other time period would do as well). Now if the year begins with an inventory of B items, and if there is no replenishment, then after the first week the stock level will be $B - X_1$, after the second, $B - X_1 - X_2$; it is plain to see that stock will sooner or later run out. In that event we shall assume that indefinite back ordering is possible. In other words, negative inventories are permitted: if the total demand up to a given moment has exceeded the total production, a backlog exists. It is assumed that the backlog can eventually be made up when replenishment occurs and that no demand is ever lost. This assumption is reasonable when the demands cannot be filled elsewhere, as is likely to be the case when the field warehouses of one company place their replenishment orders with a subdivision of the same company. As has been said before, the total demand is the sum of the field warehouse replenishment orders received by the factory during the week in question.

Now we will give the factory warehouse replenishment or production rule. We shall assume that production level must be established for week n before the actual demand for that week is known. If P_n denotes the number of items produced during week n, then it will almost never be possible to match P_n to X_n (demand during week n)

---

* Frequent, extensive changes in production rates tend to introduce costs associated with hiring, firing, and training personnel. See earlier chapters for a discussion of production smoothing by linear programming.

in advance if X_n fluctuates unpredictably. As we shall see, production cost considerations may make such a policy undesirable even if it were possible.

RULE 1. *Unsmoothed Production Rule.* Always produce the demand of the *previous* week; that is,

$$(11.6.1) \qquad P_{n+1} = X_n \qquad (n = 1, 2, 3, \ldots).$$

Rule 1 forces production to keep up with demand as well as possible under the circumstances. It is instructive to draw up a table showing the effect of adopting this procedure. Note that we are examining our process at the end of the week, after the demand for that week is known and the production of that week has been completed.

TABLE 11.6.1

Week	Demand	Inventory Level	Production
1	X_1	$B + X_0 - X_1$	X_0
2	X_2	$B + X_0 - X_2$	X_1
3	X_3	$B + X_0 - X_3$	X_2
4	X_4	$B + X_0 - X_4$	X_3

From Rule 1, we see that at the end of week 1, the inventory level is the initial level, B, plus production for week 1, X_0 (an estimate), minus the demand for that week. During the second week, production is scheduled to make up the deficit caused by the demand of week 1, and hence $P_2 = X_1$. Just before the P_2 becomes available, the actual deficit is $B - X_1 - X_2 + X_0$, but at the end of week 2, that week's production becomes available, leaving the inventory level at $B - X_2$; so the process continues.

The difficulty with the simple Rule 1 resides in its *overresponsiveness* to demand variations, bringing about rapid and expensive production fluctuations. If a plant is forced one week to produce 300 items and the next to produce 1300, it is not difficult to see that problems arise. One of these is related to the handling of personnel: wide fluctuations in production levels may require large-scale hiring and firing activities or, at the very least, considerable and unforeseeable needs for overtime. Such changes are usually costly. Another problem made more difficult by rapid and excessive production fluctuation is that of stocking sufficient raw materials. The variation in demand for raw materials, occasioned by an attempt to produce to meet weekly finished-item demand, means that raw-material inventories must be maintained at a relatively high level to avoid stockout and production interruptions.

An alternative to the rule described above is Rule 2.

RULE 2. *Super-Smoothed Production Rule.* Always produce the mean of the demand for the nth week.

$$(11.6.2) \qquad P_{n+1} = E[X_n];$$

if all weeks have the same mean demand, as we shall assume for simplicity, then

$$(11.6.3) \qquad P_{n+1} = E[X_n] = m,$$

and we shall always produce the same amount. In Exercise 1, you will be asked to construct a table to show the weekly history of production and inventory levels. Apparently the difficulties with changes in production level referred to before no longer occur, since the production is always constant (for the present simple demand model). However, as can easily be seen, the fluctuations of demand have been entirely transferred to the inventory of finished items. Suppose, for example, that demands are independently distributed with variance σ^2. Then, after n weeks have elapsed, it can be shown that if one follows Rule 2, the variance of the inventory level is

$$(11.6.4) \qquad \text{Var}[I_n \mid Super\text{-}Smooth] = n\sigma^2,$$

while that of Rule 1 is only one-nth as great,

$$(11.6.5) \qquad \text{Var}[I_n \mid Unsmoothed] = \sigma^2.$$

Since a high variance in the finished-items inventory level means considerable variation in storage cost and service, we have eliminated difficulty in one area (production) at the expense of another (inventory).

Although both of the rules described have faults, it is possible to effect a useful compromise between them. The compromise rule tends to smooth production, thus reducing expensive employment costs. However, it does not pass all of the demand fluctuations on to result in uncontrolled and growing inventory fluctuations. Moreover, the procedure to be described is easily understood and put into practice.

RULE 3. *Exponentially Smoothed Production Rule.* Let the production for a given week be a linear combination of the actual demand and the production level of the previous week:

$$(11.6.6) \qquad P_{n+1} = \alpha X_n + (1 - \alpha)P_n;$$

here, α is called the smoothing constant. Notice that if $\alpha = 1$, then the production rule (11.6.6) becomes Rule 1, whereas if $\alpha = 0$, it becomes Rule 2. In practice one can select the smoothing constant α to compromise between Rules 1 and 2 in order to obtain satisfactory overall cost performance. The smoothing constant, α, and the base stock level, B, are thus *decision variables* that may be adjusted to minimize costs associated with the combined production-inventory control process.

In order to build up an understanding of the exponentially smoothed production rule, let us consider Table 11.6.2. Entries in the inventory-level column of the table refer to the status at the end of a week, after the demand for the week is known and after the week's production is completed.

TABLE 11.6.2

Week	Demand	Inventory Level	Production
1	X_1	$I_1 = B - X_1 + P_1$	P_1
2	X_2	$I_2 = I_1 - X_2 + P_2$	$P_2 = \alpha X_1 + (1 - \alpha)P_1$
		$\quad = B - X_2 - (1 - \alpha)X_1 + P_1[1 - (1 - \alpha)]$	
3	X_3	$I_3 = I_2 - X_3 + P_3$	$P_3 = \alpha X_2 + (1 - \alpha)P_2$
		$\quad = B - X_3 - (1 - \alpha)^2 X_2 - (1 - \alpha)^2 X_1$	$\quad = \alpha X_2 + \alpha(1 - \alpha)X_1$
		$\quad\quad + P_1[1 + (1 - \alpha) + (1 - \alpha)^2]$	$\quad\quad + (1 - \alpha)^2 P_1$
		...	...

One can see that for week n we have for the inventory level,

$$(11.6.7) \quad I_n = B - \{X_n + (1 - \alpha)X_{n-1} + (1 - \alpha)^2 X_{n-2} + \cdots + (1 - \alpha)^{n-1}X_1\}$$

$$+ P_1 \left\{ \frac{1 - (1 - \alpha)^n}{\alpha} \right\},$$

and for the production level

$(11.6.8)$

$$P_n = \alpha\{X_{n-1} + (1 - \alpha)X_{n-2} + (1 - \alpha)^2 X_{n-3} + \cdots + (1 - \alpha)^{n-2}X_1\} + (1 - \alpha)^{n-1}P_1.$$

A glance at the expression for P_n reveals the smoothing action of our rule when $0 < \alpha < 1$. Rather than producing to meet the latest demand, Rule 3 brings about the production of a weighted combination of past demands. However, the weighting of the most recent demand is the most pronounced. The weight on demands that occurred j units in the past is proportional to $(1 - \alpha)^j$; the latter diminishes at exponential rate with j, which accounts for the name of the rule. Finally, we notice that Rule 3 has an adaptive feature: if demand size begins to increase or decrease, perhaps due to a change in business level, the production level has a tendency to follow the changes. Of course, Rule 1 does so as well, but is likely to over-react to short-term fluctuations, which can better be absorbed by changing the inventory level.

Before going on to mathematical examination of Rule 3, you may wish to observe its performance against a specific demand pattern. Exercise 2 provides an opportunity to look at several such problems.

We shall study the behavior of Rule 3 under the simple assumption that successive demands arise independently from a normal distribution with mean m and standard deviation σ. Under these assumptions, the following facts may be established.

(a) The inventory level at week n is normally distributed with mean or expected value

$$(11.6.9) \qquad E[I_n] = B - (m - P_1)\frac{1 - (1 - \alpha)^n}{\alpha}$$

and variance

$$(11.6.10) \qquad \text{Var}[I_n] = \sigma^2 \left\{ \frac{1 - (1 - \alpha)^{2n}}{\alpha(2 - \alpha)} \right\}.$$

(b) In the long run, that is, as $n \to \infty$, the mean inventory level tends to

$$(11.6.11) \qquad m_I = E[I] = B,$$

if $P_1 = m$,* and the variance to

$$(11.6.12) \qquad \sigma_I^2 = \text{Var}[I] = \frac{\sigma^2}{\alpha(2 - \alpha)}.$$

(c) The production level of week n is normally distributed with mean

$$(11.6.13) \qquad E[P_n] = m - (m - P_1)(1 - \alpha)^{n-1}$$

---

* If an error is made so that $P_1 \neq m$, then $m_I = B - (m - P_1)/\alpha$.

and variance

(11.6.14) $$\text{Var}[P_n] = \sigma^2 \alpha \left\{ \frac{1 - (1 - \alpha)^{2n-2}}{2 - \alpha} \right\}.$$

(d) In the long run the mean production level tends to

(11.6.15) $$m_P = E[P] = m$$

and the variance to

(11.6.16) $$\sigma_P^2 = \text{Var}[P] = \frac{\sigma^2 \alpha}{2 - \alpha}.$$

(e) A measure of the amount of production-level change between two successive periods is

(11.6.17) $$K = E[(P_n - P_{n-1})^2].$$

In the long run, it can be shown that $E[P_n - P_{n-1}] = 0$, so

(11.6.18) $$K = \text{Var}[P_n - P_{n-1}] = 2 \frac{\sigma^2 \alpha^2}{2 - \alpha}.$$

The last expression allows us to understand the effect of choosing a value of the smoothing constant, α. From (11.6.12) it is clear that the variance of the inventory level, σ_I^2, increases as α is made small, and so it follows that the probability of a back-order situation existing also increases. To compensate for this effect, however, σ_P^2, the variance in production level, and K, the measure of production change, both diminish. If $m \neq P_1$, these statements must be modified.

EXAMPLE 11.6.1. Suppose $m = 1000$ (items per week), $\sigma = 100$, and the smoothing constant $\alpha = \frac{1}{3}$. We shall contrast Rule 3 with the behavior of the un-smoothed Rule 1. The production rule is

(11.6.19) $$P_{n+1} = \frac{1}{3} X_n + \frac{2}{3} P_n.$$

From our formulas we find that

$$\sigma_I^2 = \frac{\sigma^2}{\alpha(2 - \alpha)} = (10,000)\left(\frac{9}{5}\right) = 18,000,$$

so the standard deviation of inventory variation is

$$\sigma_I = 134,$$

while the variance of production is

$$\sigma_P^2 = \sigma^2 \frac{\alpha}{2 - \alpha} = (10,000)\left(\frac{1}{5}\right) = 2,000,$$

giving the approximate production standard deviation

$$\sigma_P = 45$$

and the value of the production-change measure

$$K = 2\frac{\sigma^2\alpha^2}{2-\alpha} = 2(10{,}000)\left(\frac{1}{15}\right) = 1{,}333.$$

Notice that if production had been conducted in accordance with the unsmoothed Rule 1, the standard deviation of production level would have been more than twice as great. In order to compensate for the increase in production smoothness, however, the standard deviation of inventory level has been nearly doubled. This of course means that in order to keep the back-order probabilities equivalent, a higher inventory level must be maintained if Rule 3 is utilized rather than Rule 1.

If desired, the expressions above may be employed to evaluate the total expected cost associated with a particular production-inventory policy. In conformity with the notation of earlier sections, c_c denotes the carrying cost. Let c_B represent the cost associated with the existence of a back-order situation; that is, a cost of c_B is incurred for each period at the end of which $I < 0$. Lastly, let k be the unit cost associated with the measure of production-level difference, $\sqrt{K}$, given in (11.6.17). You will observe that

$$(11.6.20) \qquad \sqrt{K} = \{E[(P_n - P_{n-1})^2]\}^{1/2}$$

has the dimensions of the rate of change of production level, $P_n - P_{n-1}$; hence if there is a cost of k dollars for each unit of such a measure of change in production, an assessment of the cost due to production change will be taken to be $k\sqrt{K}$. The total average cost associated with our inventory policy will be expressed as

$$(11.6.21) \qquad C(B, \alpha) = c_c B + c_B \int_{-\infty}^{0} \frac{e^{-(1/2)[(z-m_I)/\sigma_I]^2}}{\sqrt{2\pi}} \frac{dz}{\sigma_I} + k\sqrt{K},$$

where the dependence on the smoothing parameter α occurs in the expressions for σ_1 and K.

To optimize $C(B, \alpha)$, first let α be fixed and, using the usual rules, differentiate with respect to B:

$$(11.6.22) \qquad \frac{\partial C}{\partial B} = c_c - \frac{c_B}{\sqrt{2\pi}\,\sigma_I} e^{-(1/2)(B/\sigma_I)^2}.$$

A necessary condition that a minimum occur for given B is that the derivative be zero; since $e^{-t} \leq 1$ for $t \geq 0$, it follows that (i) the derivative is always positive, and hence the optimum inventory level $B_{\text{opt}} = 0$ if

$$(11.6.23) \qquad \frac{c_c}{c_B} > \frac{1}{\sqrt{2\pi}\,\sigma_I};$$

otherwise (ii) the optimum inventory level is

$$(11.6.24) \qquad B_{\text{opt}} = \sigma_I \sqrt{2\log\left(\frac{c_B}{\sqrt{2\pi}\,c_c\,\sigma_I}\right)}.$$

EXAMPLE 11.6.2. We use the numbers of the previous example to compute the optimum inventory. Let $c_c = \$0.10$ and $c_{BO} = \$1000$ (management considers it very serious to be out of stock). Then substitution, using (11.6.24), yields

$$(11.6.25) \qquad B_{\mathrm{opt}} = 212 \sqrt{2 \log \left(\frac{1000}{2.50 \times 0.1 \times 134} \right)} = 350.$$

The probability of being out of stock is computed as follows:

$$\int_{-\infty}^{0} \frac{1}{\sqrt{2\pi}} e^{-(1/2)[(z-m_1)/\sigma_I]^2} \frac{dz}{\sigma_I} = \int_{-\infty}^{-m_1/\sigma_1} \frac{e^{-(1/2)v^2}}{\sqrt{2\pi}} dv = \int_{-\infty}^{-2.62} \frac{e^{-(1/2)v^2}}{\sqrt{2\pi}} dv,$$

$$= 0.0044$$

The next step is to substitute the value of B_{opt} obtained back into the cost function (11.6.21) and then minimize the latter by choice of α. We shall not carry out this step analytically, but rather we suggest that it be done by a numerical-search procedure. For example, it would probably be sufficient in practice to evaluate $C(B_{\mathrm{opt}}, \alpha)$ for values of α in steps of 0.1 from 0 to 0.9 and pick the smallest cost. Notice that for purposes of computation, it is convenient to write the cost function as

$$(11.6.26) \qquad C(B_{\mathrm{opt}}, \alpha) = c_c B_{\mathrm{opt}} + c_{BO} \int_{-\infty}^{-B_{\mathrm{opt}}/\sigma_1} \frac{e^{-(1/2)v^2}}{\sqrt{2\pi}} dv + k \sqrt{K},$$

The integral term may then be determined from a standard table of unit normal probabilities. Finally, a word of caution is necessary: the expression for the mean carrying cost, $c_c B$, is really only an approximation. Since inventory level is normally distributed with mean B, and since negative inventories (back orders) are allowed, the true carrying cost should be proportional only to the expected *positive* inventory, as follows:

$$(11.6.27a) \qquad \text{Carrying cost} = c_c \int_{0}^{\infty} z \frac{e^{-(1/2)[(z-m_1)/\sigma_I]^2}}{\sqrt{2\pi}\sigma_I} dz,$$

$$(11.6.27b) \qquad = c_c \int_{-m_1/\sigma_1}^{\infty} (m_1 + v\sigma_I) \frac{e^{-(1/2)v^2}}{\sqrt{2\pi}} dv.$$

But

$$(11.6.27c) \qquad c_c \int_{-\infty}^{\infty} (m_1 + v\sigma_I) \frac{e^{-(1/2)v^2}}{\sqrt{2\pi}} dv = c_c B.$$

As a consequence, our B_{opt}, as determined from (11.6.25), is *too small*. This will not matter if the stockout penalty, c_B, is much larger than the carrying cost, c_c, as was true in Example 11.6.2. If the latter is not the case, then a modification must be made in the cost function by using (11.6.27b). Unfortunately, a simple formula for B_{opt} no longer results. An approximately optimum solution can of course be found by numerical methods.

EXERCISES 11.6

1. Construct a table analogous to Table 11.6.1 showing the evolution of inventory when rule 2 is in use.

2. The demands for ten consecutive weeks are as follows:

Week	Demand, X
1	872
2	1193
3	934
4	968
5	1005
6	890
7	1109
8	992
9	1038
10	1116

   (a) Taking $B = 100$ and applying Rule 1, develop an example of Table 11.6.2. How many times is the factory warehouse out of stock? What is the maximum production-level change between two consecutive weeks? Let $X_0 = 1000$.

   (b) Again, for $B = 100$, apply Rule 3 with $\alpha = \frac{1}{2}$ to construct an example of Table 11.6.2. Answer the questions of (a) above.

   (c) Carry out the calculations of (b) for $\alpha = \frac{9}{10}$.

3. (a) Derive expressions (11.6.7) and (11.6.8) for the inventory and production levels at the end of the nth week.

   (b) Derive expression (11.6.9) by taking expectations through (11.6.7). (*Hint*: Recall that if X and Y are two random variables, not necessarily independent, then $E[aX + bY] = aE[Y] + bE[Y]$, a and b being constants.)

   (c) Derive expression (11.6.10). (*Hint*: If X and Y are independent random variables, then $\mathrm{Var}[aX + bY] = a^2\mathrm{Var}[X] + b^2\mathrm{Var}[Y]$.)

   (d) Use the fact that the sum of two independent, normally distributed random variables has the normal distribution to show that I_n and P_n are normally distributed.

   (e) Derive the expressions (11.6.11) through (11.6.18), using (11.6.7) and (11.6.8).

SUGGESTED READING

Arrow, K., Karlin, S., and Scarf, H. *Studies in the Mathematical Theory of Inventory and Production.* Stanford, Calif.: Stanford University Press, 1958.

Hadley, G., and Whitin, T. *Analysis of Inventory Systems.* Englewood Cliffs, N.J.: Prentice-Hall, 1963.

Holt, C., Modigliani, F., Muth, J., and Simon, H. *Planning Production, Inventories, and Work Force.* Englewood Cliffs, N.J.: Prentice-Hall, 1960.

Iglehart, D. Capital accumulation and production for the firm: Optimal dynamic policies. *Management Science*, 1965, **12**(3), 193–205.

Magee, J. F. *Production Planning and Inventory Controls.* New York: McGraw-Hill, 1958.

Vienott, A. The status of mathematical inventory theory. *Management Science*, 1966, **12**(11), 745–777.

Veinott, A. On the optimality of (s, S) inventory policies: New conditions and a new proof. In G. Dantzig and A. Veinott (Eds.), *Mathematics of the Decision Sciences, Part 2.* Providence, R. I.: American Mathematics Society, 1968.

Wagner, H. *Principles of Operations Research.* Englewood Cliffs, N.J.: Prentice-Hall, 1969.

CHAPTER 12

SIMULATION

12.1 INTRODUCTION

In previous chapters we have described mathematical models for a variety of problems. We have also illustrated the way in which useful conclusions and decision procedures may be derived from these models. These derivations involved manipulation and simplification of the models mathematically—that is, by means of algebra and the calculus—plus the eventual use of some form of computation. The computation ranged from a simple formula substitution in queuing theory to the use of the simplex algorithm of linear programming. Often such calculations are conveniently made on a digital computer, and some examples have been given of this process and its results.

Under many realistic circumstances it is difficult or practically impossible to follow to a solution the route described above. For such cases, a mathematical model may be set up to relate various random and nonrandom system variables; however, the variables may be difficult to manipulate mathematically. For example, the task of calculating analytically the expected waiting time of an order initiated at a large job shop or of a computation requested at a computer center is effectively impossible. One alternative is to build a physical model of the system under study and experiment with it. Of course, this *physical simulation* is likely to be prohibitively time consuming and expensive. Another approach is to simulate the proposed system by first setting up an appropriate *mathematical* model that relates the component quantities and then *experiment* with the mathematical model. The experiment proceeds by drawing samples from appropriate distributions—for example, of the total demands during a lead or replenishment time in an inventory situation—and then calculating costs, and so on, given the use of specified ordering rules. Having observed the manner in which a system may behave over a time period under such simulated conditions, the system may be altered in an attempt at improvement or optimization. In a nutshell, then, simulation is experimental mathematics. Artificial system histories are constructed and averaged in order to obtain estimates of system performances and suggestions for improvement. This is not to say that more orthodox mathematical methods are completely discarded in simulation studies. Frequently, a knowledge of the solution to a simplified model of the system is of considerable use for checking the (usually complex) simulation computer program and perhaps for improving efficiency by increasing the precision of desired estimates. More will be said about this sort of thing in later sections. We shall begin by illustrating the concept of simulation with a simple example.

12.2 SIMULATING SIMPLE RANDOM PROCESSES

In order to simulate the behavior of a system of interrelated components, it is first necessary to describe (model, or imitate the characteristics of) those components. Let us consider the following simple situation.

EXAMPLE 12.2.1. A (supersimplified) job shop consists of one all-purpose machine tool and its operator. For the moment, assume that at the start of every working day a backlog of J jobs exists and that no more will appear on the scene until these are completed. They must be carried out one at a time. The machine's working rate is known, so if the jobs are actually on hand and are known to have manufacturing durations $D_1, D_2, \ldots, D_J$, then there is no trouble in computing the time that the machine will be continually busy: it is $D_1 + D_2 + \cdots + D_J$. There is also no difficulty in arranging the order of the jobs so as to minimize the number of job hours waited—the "shortest-job-first" rule will do the trick. See the exercises in Section 10.2.

However, suppose we wish to estimate the behavior of the shop as it varies from day to day—for example, if the daily backlog, J, varies randomly as do job durations. Considerations that stem from different scheduling rules, individual job-due-date requirements, and possible machine breakdowns or operator errors further complicate the problem of deciding whether the machine is adequate to handle the load. In order to attack such complex problems, it is often useful to proceed by simulation. Specifically, the steps are as follows.

(a) Analyze historical data, or data from similar operations, in order to describe the probability distribution of J and the job durations. For illustration here, we will *assume* that the distributions of J and of D_j ($j = 1, 2, \ldots, J$) are known and fixed. In reality one must live with estimates and with the possibility of weekly or seasonally changing distributions. In other words, our initial model may require later refinement. The model-construction and data-analysis phase of a study is naturally very important, whether the analysis is to be conducted by simulation or by a mathematical technique (or a mixture of methods). However, we do not attempt to elaborate on this aspect.

(b) Generate a possible or synthetic shop load for a day—that is, determine a possible value of J and of job durations $D_1, D_2, \ldots, D_J$. The actual value, say $J^{(1)} = 3$ jobs on day 1, will be called a *realization*; $J^{(1)}, J^{(2)}, \ldots$, and so on must be chosen with probabilities appropriate to anticipated future system behavior. J and D_j ($j = 1, 2, \ldots, J$) are the probabilistic components referred to earlier.

(c) Use the results of (b) to calculate quantities of interest under a given scheduling rule; for example, the delivery time of job k, the duration of which is D_k, or the total job-hours waited.

(d) Repeat steps (b) and (c) until the estimates obtained are statistically stable enough for the purpose intended. We will show later how to measure the degree of stability achieved by computing the variance and standard deviation of the estimate of the quantity sought.

In this section we shall focus on step (b) above. We shall suppose that in Example 12.2.1 the distribution of J is specified,

$$(12.2.1) \qquad\qquad P\{J = j\} = P_j,$$

and is the following:

j	P_j
0	0.3
1	0.4
2	0.2
3	0.1

(12.2.2)

Similarly, the distribution of the job durations is given. For the moment we denote this distribution by $F(x)$; it may well turn out that it is given empirically in the form of a step function, as shown in Figure 12.2.1, or perhaps in the form of a smoothed version

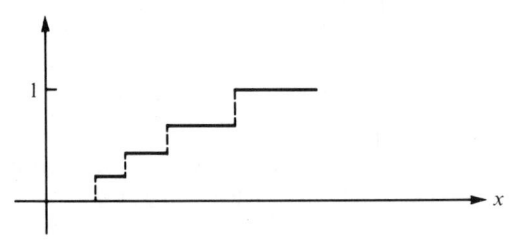

FIGURE 12.2.1

of such a step function. Smoothing can be accomplished by replacing the steps by ramps joining the discontinuity points. As will be seen, however, there is often convenience attached to utilizing specific distributions, such as the gamma, normal, or Poisson. Finally, in what follows immediately we will be assuming that J and the various job durations are *statistically independent*, so individual realization of job numbers and their durations may be obtained without reference to each other. The introduction of dependence is discussed at a later stage.

We will now show how to obtain realizations from the distribution of (12.2.1) or, specifically, (12.2.2). As a basic input to this step, we require a *random-number generator* or *table*. Without going into much detail, such a generator, usually a subroutine or program available at a computer center, furnishes a sequence of "random" digits taking the values 0, 1, 2, ..., 9—that is, a sequence of numbers that take on with approximately equal frequency any of the given values in no particular pattern. Numbers in the sequence are intended to imitate statistically a sequence of independent realizations of a discrete uniform random variable. If groups of, say, five or ten such numbers are formed with a preceding decimal, then the result can be taken as the realization of a uniformly distributed random variable over [0, 1] accurate to five or ten decimals. Denote such a variable by R. Consequently a random-number generator produces numbers expressed, say, to five-decimal accuracy that are samples from the rectangular or uniform density

$$(12.2.3) \qquad h(x) = \begin{cases} 1 & \text{for } 0 \le x \le 1 \\ 0 & \text{otherwise} \end{cases}$$

These numbers tend to behave statistically like a sequence of independent samples from such a distribution.

In fact, the numbers are generated by a perfectly well-determined arithmetic process and are therefore termed *pseudorandom*. Starting from a given number, or "seed," they are computed sequentially, which is a convenience since a given sequence may be regenerated and need not be stored. However, we shall act as if the numbers that come from a random-number generator are indeed a sequence of independent realizations of a uniformly distributed random variable.

A segment of a typical page in a table of random numbers—the output of a random-number generator—might appear as in Figure 12.2.2. Use of such entries will be illustrated next.

54	13	05	46	31	—
95	27	22	17	39	—
22	39	44	74	80	—
69	95	21	30	11	—

FIGURE 12.2.2

EXAMPLE 12.2.2. We wish to draw a realization of J, the number of jobs backlogged at our simple job shop for the first week, using the distribution of (12.2.2). Proceed as follows: assign the digits

$$\begin{aligned} 0, 1, 2 \quad &\text{to the event } J = 0, \\ 3, 4, 5, 6 \quad &\text{to the event } J = 1, \\ 7, 8 \quad &\text{to the event } J = 2, \\ 9 \quad &\text{to the event } J = 3. \end{aligned}$$

Now select a one-digit random number from the table segment in Figure 12.2.2. By construction of the table, or the random-number generator, each digit in the table is equally probable. That is, the digits 0, 1, 2, ..., 9 occur with approximately equal frequency, or each with probability 0.1. Therefore, the probabilities associated with the various J values by (12.2.2) are as desired. Using the entries across the top line of the table fragment, we obtain the first five daily job backlogs as shown below.

$$\text{Jobs:} \quad J^{(1)} = 1 \quad J^{(2)} = 1 \quad J^{(3)} = 0 \quad J^{(4)} = 1 \quad J^{(5)} = 0$$

$$\text{Random Numbers:} \quad 5 \qquad 4 \qquad 1 \qquad 3 \qquad 0$$

Using the second line of Figure 12.2.2, the corresponding result is (perhaps for the following week):

$$\text{Jobs:} \quad J^{(6)} = 3 \quad J^{(7)} = 1 \quad J^{(8)} = 0 \quad J^{(9)} = 2 \quad J^{(10)} = 0$$

$$\text{Random Numbers:} \quad 9 \qquad 5 \qquad 2 \qquad 7 \qquad 2$$

In Exercise 1, you will be asked to compute the mean and variance of the distribution (12.2.2) and also that of the sample obtained above. The effect of small-sample randomness is plainly visible in that the mean of the first two weeks' numbers of jobs does not equal the mean of the parent distribution. This illustrates the need for taking a number of samples in order to maintain a sufficiently low error of estimate.

The method just described is useful for drawing samples from any discrete distribution. Another related procedure will now be described. This is called the method of the *probability integral transformation*. Its effect is again to transform a uniform random number into a random number with prescribed distribution.

THEOREM 12.2.1. Suppose R is uniformly distributed over $[0, 1]$—that is, has density (12.2.3). Then if $F(x)$ is a distribution function, the random variable

$$(12.2.4) \qquad\qquad X = F^{-1}(R)$$

has distribution $F(x)$. Here $F^{-1}(\cdot)$ represents the inverse function corresponding to F: if the image of each x under F is y so that $y = F(x)$, then F^{-1} supplies the corresponding image, x, of y and $x = F^{-1}(y)$. In terms of calculations, to find X given R, one must solve the equation $F(X) = R$; this may be represented graphically as shown in Figure 12.2.3.

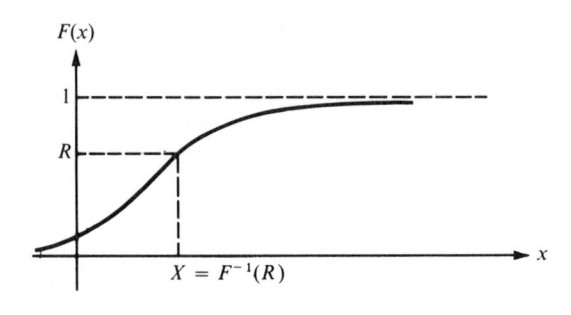

FIGURE 12.2.3

Proof: Since R is uniformly distributed,

$$(12.2.5) \qquad\qquad P\{R \le y\} = y \qquad (0 \le y \le 1).$$

Now for any x there is a unique y such that $F(x) = y$ (see Figure 12.2.3). Thus

(12.2.6) $$P\{R \leq F(x)\} = F(x),$$

and hence, if we solve backwards,

(12.2.7) $$P\{F^{-1}(R) \leq x\} = F(x).$$

Thus $F^{-1}(R) = X$ has the distribution $F(x)$, as claimed.

Although the figure above illustrates the situation when F is continuous and increasing—that is, possesses a positive density function, the same method works when the distribution is discrete.

EXAMPLE 12.2.3. The annual income of individuals in a certain area has the distribution

(12.2.8) $$F(x) = \begin{cases} 0 & \text{for } x < 0 \\ 1 - \dfrac{1}{1 + x^2} & \text{for } x > 0 \end{cases}$$

Here income is in thousands of dollars. It is desired to draw a sample of an individual annual income, X, from the distribution above. According to the theorem it is only necessary to solve

(12.2.9) $$R = F(X) = 1 - \frac{1}{1 + X^2},$$

where R is a uniformly distributed (pseudo) random number. The result is

(12.2.10) $$X_1 = \sqrt{\frac{R}{1 - R}}.$$

You should notice that if R represents a uniformly distributed random number in the range $[0, 1]$, then so does $1 - R$. Consequently, one could just as well generate an annual income X_2 from R by computing

(12.2.11) $$X_2 = \sqrt{\frac{1 - R}{R}}.$$

Of course one should be warned *not* to use the *same* number R to generate both (12.2.10) and (12.2.11) *if* the X values desired are to be *independent*. Sometimes, as will be pointed out later, the deliberate incorporation of dependence in a simulation is a wise move.

EXAMPLE 12.2.4. Refer to the manufacturing durations of Example 12.2.1, and let the jth duration D_j be exponentially distributed with expected value $m > 0$. That is,

(12.2.12) $$P\{D > t\} = 1 - F_D(t) = e^{-t/m} \qquad \text{for } t \geq 0.$$

In order to obtain a sample duration, we may solve

$$(12.2.13) \qquad\qquad R = F_D(D) = 1 - e^{-D/m}.$$

The result is

$$(12.2.14) \qquad\qquad D = -m \log_e(1 - R).$$

Again it is convenient to substitute R for $1 - R$, thus eliminating the need for a subtraction from unity.

The difficulty with the method just described is that of computing the inverse —that is, actually solving for X the equation $R = F(X)$. In certain cases, as illustrated above, this may be carried out easily using standard subroutines (square root, logarithm) available at a computer center, but for others the computation becomes more onerous and alternatives are worth exploring. We shall describe a few of these here. The first may be called the *method of composition*.

EXAMPLE 12.2.5. The time, T, until the first failure of a computing machine has the gamma density

$$(12.2.15) \qquad\qquad f_k(t) = e^{-tk/m} \frac{(tk/m)^{k-1}}{(k-1)!} \frac{k}{m},$$

where k is a positive integer. Then

$$(12.2.16) \qquad\qquad E[T] = m \quad \text{and} \quad \text{Var}[T] = \frac{m^2}{k};$$

T may be represented as follows

$$(12.2.17) \qquad\qquad T = T_1 + T_2 + \cdots + T_k,$$

where $T_1, T_2, \ldots, T_k$ are independently and exponentially distributed, each having mean

$$(12.2.18) \qquad\qquad E[T_j] = \frac{m}{k}.$$

Consequently, to generate T, one first generates k uniform random numbers $R_1, R_2, \ldots, R_k$, then finds

$$(12.2.19) \qquad\qquad T_j = -\frac{m}{k} \log(R_j) \qquad j = 1, 2, \ldots, k,$$

and finally

$$T = -\frac{m}{k} \log R_1 - \frac{m}{k} \log R_2 - \cdots - \frac{m}{k} \log R_k,$$

$$(12.2.20) \qquad\qquad = -\frac{m}{k} [\log R_1 + \log R_2 + \cdots + \log R_k],$$

$$= -\frac{m}{k} \log(R_1 R_2 R_3 \cdots R_k),$$

where the last form is computationally desirable since the logarithm need be taken only once.

The example above yields an exact result: T is precisely distributed in the gamma form under our assumptions. The following example introduces a frequently useful approximation, again by means of composition.

EXAMPLE 12.2.6. Suppose one believes that weekly price changes of a certain security are normally distributed with mean m and variance σ^2. It is desired to simulate a sequence of weekly prices, and for this the price changes y_n for weeks $n = 1, 2, \ldots,$ are required. In Chapter 7, reference was made to the central-limit theorem of probability, whereby the distribution of a *sum* of independently and identically distributed random variables is approximately normal, the approximation improving as the number summed increases. Let us therefore consider the variable

$$(12.2.21) \qquad Z = R_1 + R_2 + \cdots + R_K,$$

where $R_1, R_2, \ldots, R_K$ are independently and uniformly distributed over $[0, 1]$. Then it is possible to show that

$$(12.2.22) \qquad E[Z] = \frac{1}{2} K \quad \text{and} \quad \mathrm{Var}[Z] = \frac{K}{12}.$$

According to the central-limit theorem, the variable

$$(12.2.23) \qquad V = \frac{Z - \frac{1}{2}K}{\sqrt{K/12}}$$

is, for large K, approximately normally distributed with mean zero and unit variance:

$$(12.2.24) \qquad E[V] = 0, \qquad \mathrm{Var}[V] = 1.$$

In order to generate a realization of Y_n, it is only necessary to *first* add up K random numbers, subtract $\frac{1}{2}K$ from the sum, and finally divide by $\sqrt{K/12}$ in order to obtain a normal random number and *second* multiply by σ (standard deviation) and add m:

$$(12.2.25) \qquad Y_n = \sigma V + m,$$

which is easily seen to be (approximately) normal with desired mean and variance.

In order to simplify computations, $K = 12$ is a popular choice. One should note that the "approximate normal numbers" so obtained are, unlike true normal numbers, restricted in range, since the sum (12.2.21) is always confined to the interval $[0, \pm K]$. Thus if we are attempting to study matters that depend on extreme values of Y_n, the method of generation given above is likely to be untrustworthy and should be replaced.

Another method that produces more exact results but that is somewhat more difficult to program is that of Box and Muller. Let R_1 and R_2 be independent and uniform random variables over $[0, 1]$. Then

$$X = (-2 \log_e R_1)^{1/2} \cos 2\pi R_2$$

and

$$Y = (-2 \log_e R_1)^{1/2} \sin 2\pi R_2$$

are independently normal random variables having mean zero and variance one.

Still another interesting and useful procedure for generating realizations of random numbers from a distribution is worth describing here. It is the so-called *rejection method*. Its basis is given in the following theorem.

THEOREM 12.2.2. Suppose it is desired to obtain a random sample X from the distribution having density $f(x)$, where (for convenience) $0 \le x \le 1$ and $f(x) \le \bar{f}, \bar{f}$ being finite. One may proceed as follows:

(a) Select two independent random numbers R_1 and R_2, where R_1 and R_2 are both uniformly distributed over $[0, 1]$.

(b) Compute $cf(R_1)$ and compare R_2 to it. Here c is best taken as the reciprocal of the maximum value of f: $c = (\bar{f})^{-1}$. If $R_2 \le cf(R_1)$, take $X = R_1$ and begin again with a new pair of random numbers R_1' and R_2'. If $R_2 > cf(R_1)$, reject the pair and begin again with a new pair.

Notice that not all of the pairs of numbers R_1 and R_2 will produce a realization X, so this method may seem inefficient. There are, however, ways of improving its efficiency; see the references. The procedure may be validated as follows.

Proof: The sample (R_1, R_2) is accepted if $R_2 \le cf(R_1)$. The sample is accepted *and* $R_1 (= X) \le x$ if

(12.2.26) $$R_1 \le x \quad \text{and} \quad R_2 \le cf(R_1).$$

Thus

(12.2.27) $$P\{X \le x\} = P\{R_1 \le x \,|\, \text{Acceptance}\} = \frac{P\{(R_1 \le x) \cap (R_2 \le cf(R_1))\}}{P\{R_2 \le cf(R_1)\}}.$$

Then, letting R_1 take on mutually exclusive values between zero and x,

(12.2.28) $$P\{X \le x\} = \frac{\int_0^x cf(y)\, dy}{\int_0^1 cf(y)\, dy} = \int_0^x f(y)\, dy,$$

which demonstrates that X has the desired distribution with density f.

EXAMPLE 12.2.7. A certain project's completion time, X, is believed to have the beta density over the interval $[A, B]$:

(12.2.29) $$f(x) = 12\left(\frac{x-A}{B-A}\right)^2 \left(1 - \frac{x-A}{B-A}\right)\frac{1}{B-A} \quad A \le x \le B,$$
$$= 0 \quad \text{elsewhere}$$

First, it is convenient to reduce the range of the random variable to $[0, 1]$ by considering the density of the new variable Y:

(12.2.30) $$f_Y(y) = 12y^2\,(1-y).$$

Then, after finding a realization of Y, we convert it to X as follows:

(12.2.31) $$X = A + (B - A)Y.$$

Differentiation shows that the maximum value of $f_Y(y)$ occurs at $y = 2/3$, and

$$(12.2.32) \qquad f_Y\left(\frac{2}{3}\right) = (12)\left(\frac{2}{3}\right)^2\left(\frac{1}{3}\right) = \frac{16}{9}.$$

Theorem 12.2.2 tells us to proceed as follows: select R_1 uniformly distributed over $[0, 1]$, and select a corresponding R_2. Multiply f_Y by $9/16$:

$$cf_Y(y) = \frac{9}{16} f_Y(y).$$

R_2 is now utilized as described in the theorem: if

$$R_2 \leq \left(\frac{9}{16}\right)[12R_1{}^2(1 - R_1)],$$

accept R_1 and set it equal to Y; otherwise reject the pair and begin again.
Figure 12.2.4 illustrates the procedure described.

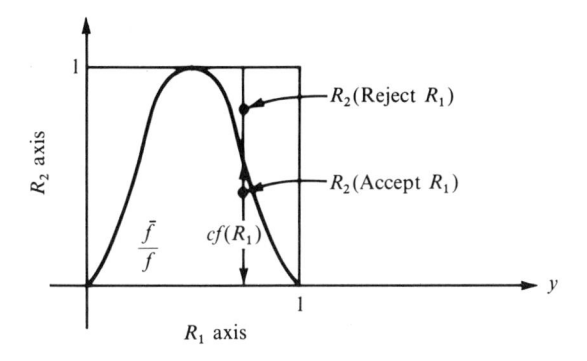

FIGURE 12.2.4

Other methods for generating random samples from specific distributions are available; see the exercises. We conclude this section by showing how to simulate some simple and useful random processes.

EXAMPLE 12.2.8. Consider a consumer who utilizes one of k products (for example, brands of coffee), his affiliation at time n (week or day n) being represented by a Markov chain. That is, $X_n = j$ means that on week n he is utilizing product j (j is one of the numbers $1, 2, 3, \ldots, k$), and the sequence of values $\{X_n\}$ is a Markov chain with a one-step transition matrix having the elements

$$p_{ij} = P\{X_n = j \mid X_{n-1} = i\}.$$

We ask for a realization of such a chain—that is, a sequence that constitutes a random sample from a Markov chain with the given one-step transition probabilities. The realization may be constructed as follows. Having started at i ($X_0 = i$), we may be guided by Example 12.2.2 to obtain a sample realization for X_1:

$$P\{X_1 = j \mid X_0 = i\} = p_{ij}.$$

j	p_{ij}
1	p_{i1}
2	p_{i2}
$\vdots$	$\vdots$
k	p_{ik}

Specifically, if, for example, $k = 4$, and then we have the following sample realization.

j	p_{ij}
1	0.1
2	0.5
3	0.3
4	0.1

Then one would generate a one-digit random number between 0 and 9; if 0 resulted, make $X_1 = 1$; if any of the numbers 1, 2, 3, 4, 5 resulted, make $X_1 = 2$; if one of the numbers 6, 7, 8 resulted, make $X_1 = 3$; if 9 occurred, make $X_1 = 4$. Suppose then that the random number 7 occurred, meaning that $X_1 = 3$. We then realize X_2 in exactly the same way as was done above, using the distribution given by $p_{3,j}$. So the process will continue for as many steps as are required.

EXERCISES 12.2

1. Show how to simulate the outcomes when a fair six-sided die is tossed. You have available a table of random numbers or a random-number generator.

2. Simulate the outcomes of 100 throws of a pair of dice.
   (a) Using Exercise 1, estimate by simulation the probability that a pair of sixes is thrown before a pair of ones. (*Hint:* How many times did two sixes turn up in 100 trials? How does the result compare with a calculation?)
   (b) Suppose one die is "loaded"; that is, the probability of a one is 0.5 and the other faces are equally likely. Repeat the estimate of part (a).

3. An airplane's flight time from San Francisco to New York depends on wind conditions, and these vary from hour to hour. Suppose that the plane's velocity during the first hour after takeoff is uniformly distributed between 550 and 650 miles per hour.
   (a) Show how to simulate to obtain a realization of the plane's distance from San Francisco at the end of the first hour.
   (b) Take the distance from San Francisco to New York to be 3000 miles. Assume that the wind conditions change independently and hourly and, consequently, that at the end of each hour the velocity for the next hour is selected from the uniform distribution described above. Use simulation to estimate the expected flight time and the probability that the flight time takes no more than 4 hours and 45 minutes. Start by simulating 100 flights.

4. Consider the job-scheduling problem of Examples 12.2.1 and 12.2.2. Suppose job durations are independently sampled from the exponential distribution (12.2.12).

(a) Suppose that four jobs are initially present. Estimate the expected time to complete their service. Can you do this problem analytically?

(b) Suppose the durations of the four jobs are D_1, D_2, D_3, and D_4 (D_i is measured in hours). If they are served in arrival order (D_1 first, then D_2, and so on), then show that the total job-hours of delay is $W = 4D_1 + 3D_2 + 2D_3 + D_4$. Calculate analytically (derive a formula for) $E[W]$ and $\text{Var}[W]$. (*Hint:* If three jobs wait for an hour, then three job-hours are accumulated.)

(c) Suppose the jobs are served in order of increasing duration: first $D_{(1)}$, then $D_{(2)}$, and so on, where $D_{(1)}$ represents the smallest among D_1, D_2, D_3, D_4. Show that the total of the job-hours of delay is

$$W' = 4D_{(1)} + 3D_{(2)} + 2D_{(3)} + D_{(4)}.$$

Can you analytically find the expectation of W'? Use the memoryless property of the exponential. Then simulate to estimate $E[W']$ and $\text{Var}[W']$.

5. Continue with the setup of Exercise 3.

(a) Simulate W': draw 20 sets of four-job duration; then find the total delay in each case and average. Call the estimate W_{20}'.

(b) Estimate the variance of $E[W_{20}']$ as follows. First estimate the variance of W':

$$\widehat{\text{Var}}[W_{20}'] = s_{W'}{}^2 = \frac{1}{19} \sum_{i=1}^{20} \{W'(i) - \overline{W_{29}'}\}^2,$$

where $W'(i)$ is the delay of the ith of the 20 sets. (If the number of independent realizations averaged is n, then an *unbiased* estimate of the variance of W' is

$$\widehat{\text{Var}}[W_{20}'] = \frac{1}{n-1} \sum_{i=1}^{n} \{W'(i) - \overline{W_{20}'}\}^2.)$$

(The term *unbiased* means that the expectation of the estimate equals the parameter being estimated). Next, divide by 20: since

$$\text{Var}[\overline{W_{20}'}] = \text{Var}\left[\frac{W'(1) + W'(2) + \cdots + W'(20)}{20} \right],$$

$$= \frac{1}{20} \text{Var}[W],$$

we estimate by means of

$$\widehat{\text{Var}}[\overline{W_{20}'}] = \frac{s_{W'}{}^2}{20}.$$

12.3   ON SIMULATING A SINGLE-SERVER QUEUE

In Chapter 10 we outlined a number of simple queuing models and showed how long-run and first-passage-time information can be obtained for them. In addition, certain simple approximation procedures were discussed very briefly.

In spite of the existence of these mathematical methods, there is quite often a need for other practical tools with which to study waiting-line or queuing situations and, for that matter, other probabilistic problems. Several specific reasons are as follows: (i) arrivals need not be Poisson or even nearly Poisson, nor, if Poisson, need they be stationary (the arrival rate may depend on the time of day); (ii) service times may not be exponentially distributed nor independent; (iii) we may be interested in time-dependent (transient) behavior—that is, in the waiting times experienced by the first few customers to arrive during a day. Simulation is often invoked to deal with these and other much more complex questions. In this section we indicate by example how this may be done. In the following section we illustrate several highly useful Monte Carlo methods—so-called *variance-reduction techniques*—for improving the efficiency of a simulation. Throughout this section our example will be the *single-server system*, with arbitrary service-time distribution and arbitrarily distributed times between consecutive arrivals. You should realize that the single-server situation is only a convenient illustration. Actually, the practical application of simulation techniques is frequently made to complex systems of queues.

THEOREM 12.3.1. Let S_n denote the service time of the nth customer to arrive at a single server, and let A_n denote the time between the arrivals of the $n-1$st and nth customers. W_n is the waiting time of the nth customer. As usual, this means the time until the nth customer begins service, measured from the moment at which he joins the waiting line (if any). Then the following recursion holds:

$$(12.3.1) \quad \begin{aligned} W_n &= W_{n-1} - A_n + S_{n-1} && \text{if } W_{n-1} + S_{n-1} \geq A_n, \\ &= 0 && \text{otherwise.} \end{aligned}$$

In an alternative notation,

$$(12.3.2) \quad \begin{aligned} W_n &= (W_{n-1} - A_n + S_{n-1})^+ \\ &= \max(W_{n-1} - A_n + S_{n-1}, 0). \end{aligned}$$

Proof: Let t_n be the arrival time of the nth customer, $n = 1, 2, 3, \ldots$. Then the time at which the $n-1$st customer leaves the system is $t_{n-1} + W_{n-1} + S_{n-1}$, since he leaves after he has arrived, waited, and completed service. Since the arrival time of customer n is $t_n = t_{n-1} + A_n$, his waiting time is

$$(12.3.3) \quad W_n = (t_{n-1} + W_{n-1} + S_{n-1}) - t_n,$$

provided the right-hand side is positive, and is zero otherwise. That is,

$$(12.3.4) \quad \begin{aligned} W_n &= (t_{n-1} + W_{n-1} + S_{n-1}) - (t_{n-1} + A_n) \\ &= W_{n-1} + S_{n-1} - A_n && \text{if } W_{n-1} + S_{n-1} - A_n \geq 0, \end{aligned}$$

and is zero otherwise. Thus (12.3.1) and (12.3.2) are verified.

It may be remarked that no probability assumptions need be made about the distribution of A_n and S_n at this stage. For instance, simulation allows us to consider correlated service or arrival times, if desired. Such is definitely *not* the case if a purely mathematical approach is taken.

Notice that if we define the nth step size as

$$(12.3.5) \quad \Delta_n = S_{n-1} - A_n,$$

where Δ_n can be negative as well as positive, then

$$(12.3.6) \quad W_n = (W_{n-1} + \Delta_n)^+$$

is a *random walk*, with nth step size Δ_n, and constrained by a reflecting boundary at zero.

The next example illustrates the manner in which a simple queue may be simulated.

EXAMPLE 12.3.1. Suppose that in a single-server queue

(a) $F(x)$ is the distribution function of the inter-arrival times, $\{A_n\}$.

(b) $G(y)$ is the distribution function of the service times, $\{S_n\}$.

We are assuming here that F and G do not depend on n. Actually, it is little more difficult to include dependence on n, if this is indicated. For example, the service times of jobs that appear early in a day may differ from those coming in later. We shall also assume, for illustration only and not because it is technically essential, that the interarrival times are mutually independent; the same will be true of the service times. We then utilize the methods of the previous section to construct a sequence of inter-arrival times (samples from F)

$$A_1^{(1)}, A_2^{(1)}, A_3^{(1)}, A_4^{(1)}, \ldots$$

and service times (samples from G)

$$S_1^{(1)}, S_2^{(1)}, S_3^{(1)}, S_4^{(1)}, \ldots .$$

Here the superscript represents the first realization. Then, starting from zero and assuming that initially there are no customers present,

$$w^{(1)} = 0, \, w_2^{(1)} = (S_1^{(1)} - A_2^{(1)})^+, \, w_3^{(1)} = (w_2^{(1)} + S_2^{(1)} - A_3^{(1)})^+, \ldots .$$

In order to estimate, say, the expected waiting time of customer 4, we must repeat the procedure above, obtaining new sequences of interarrival times and service times, and from these the waiting times, of the fourth customer on k different realizations:

$$w_4^{(1)}, w_4^{(2)}, w_4^{(3)}, \ldots, w_4^{(k)}.$$

These can then be averaged to obtain an estimate of $E[W_4]$, the expected waiting time of customer 4. Denoting the estimate by a circumflex (hat), we have

(12.3.7)
$$\hat{E}[W_4] = \frac{w_4^{(1)} + w_4^{(2)} + \cdots + w_4^{(k)}}{k}$$

One will often be interested in the manner in which waiting time changes with time, or with the number of the customer. If, in the problem above, $E[A] > E[S]$ or, equivalently, the traffic-intensity parameter

(12.3.8)
$$\rho = \frac{E[A]}{E[S]} < 1,$$

then we expect that the dependence of $E[W_n]$ on n will appear as in Figure 12.3.1, provided the system starts with no customers present. Examination of Figure 12.3.1 helps to remind us of the need for simulation. As was shown in the chapter on queuing theory, it is sometimes possible to calculate, by simply substituting into a formula, the long-run value of expected waiting time (the mean of the stationary distribution). This serves as an approximation to the expected waiting time of a customer who arrives a "long time" after the process begins. But what is a "long time"? Intuitively, we feel that $E[W_\infty]$ better approximates the expected waiting time of the 100th customer than

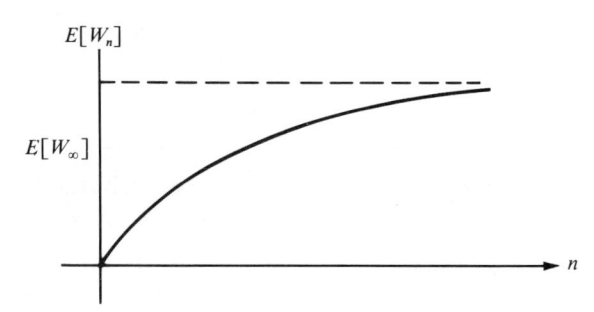

FIGURE 12.3.1. Expected waiting time of the nth customer

that of the 4th, but to obtain a quantitative assessment, one must either solve very complex equations or simulate. Usually simulation is the more readily available tool. There exist simulation languages, such as SIMSCRIP and GPSS, for the digital computer that ease the writing of computer programs for simulating quite complex queuing systems. You are referred to specialized texts on simulation for a thorough discussion of simulation languages. The remainder of this chapter will be devoted to methods for improving the efficiency of simulations and to further examples to which the simulation technique may usefully be applied.

Concerning efficiency, it is important to keep in mind the fact that the estimate (12.3.7) of $E[W_4]$ is itself a realization of, or sample from, a random variable, namely the average

$$\hat{E}[W_4] = \frac{W_4^{(1)} + W_4^{(2)} + \cdots + W_4^{(k)}}{k}.$$

If we independently repeat the k-realization simulation, we do not expect to obtain the same numerical value for $\hat{E}[W_4]$ again. If the successive realizations are conducted by using independent samples from the $\{A_n\}$ and $\{S_n\}$ distributions, then $W_n^{(1)}$, $W_n^{(2)}$, ..., $W_n^{(k)}$ are statistically independent, and all have the same distribution as W_n. Therefore, if we imagine averaging over a very large number of k-realization estimates, which is equivalent to taking the expectation, we find

(12.3.9)
$$E\{\hat{E}[W_n]\} = \frac{E[W_n^{(1)}] + E[W_n^{(2)}] + \cdots + E[W_n^{(k)}]}{k}$$

$$= \frac{kE[W_n]}{k} = E[W_n],$$

and so our estimate is unbiased, or correct on the average.

Next, we are interested in a measure of the likely deviation of our estimate from its expected value; the variance of the estimate provides this measure. Since our individual realizations are independent, we have

(12.3.10)
$$\text{Var}\{\hat{E}[W_n]\} = \frac{\text{Var}[W_n^{(1)}] + \text{Var}[W_n^{(2)}] + \cdots + \text{Var}[W_n^{(k)}]}{k^2},$$

$$= \frac{k\,\text{Var}[W_n]}{k^2} = \frac{\text{Var}[W_n]}{k}.$$

It follows that as k increases, the variance decreases, and hence our estimate approaches the true value. Thus an obvious way to increase the precision of the estimate is simply to increase the number of realizations. Yet it is easy to see that this procedure is costly in computing effort, particularly when a complex system, for example, one involving many servers, is under study. We shall shortly provide some ideas for improving this situation.

EXAMPLE 12.3.2. To illustrate the variability of the simulation results as well as that of the actual waiting times, we shall analytically find the distribution of W_n, for $n = 2$, in a simple system.

We suppose that $\{A_n\}$ is a sequence of independent random variables with common exponential distribution

(12.3.11)
$$\begin{aligned} F(x) &= 1 - e^{-\lambda x} & x &\geq 0, \\ &= 0 & x &< 0. \end{aligned}$$

Likewise, $\{S_n\}$ is a sequence of independently and exponentially distributed random variables:

(12.3.12)
$$\begin{aligned} G(y) &= 1 - e^{-\mu y} & y &\geq 0, \\ &= 0 & y &< 0. \end{aligned}$$

Now let us consider (12.3.1). First, $W_1 = 0$. Then

$$\begin{aligned} P\{W_2 = 0\} &= P\{\max(0 - A_2 + S_1, 0) = 0\}, \\ &= P\{A_2 > S_1\}, \end{aligned}$$

(12.3.13)
$$= \int_0^\infty P\{A_2 > y \mid S_1 = y\} e^{-\mu y} \mu \, dy,$$

$$= \int_0^\infty e^{-\lambda y} e^{-\mu y} \mu \, dy = \frac{\mu}{\lambda + \mu}.$$

Then, for $z > 0$,

$$\begin{aligned} P\{W_2 > z\} &= P\{0 - A_2 + S_1 > z\}, \\ &= P\{S_1 > z + A_2\}, \end{aligned}$$

(12.3.14)
$$= \int_0^\infty P\{S_1 > z + x \mid A_2 = x\} e^{-\lambda x} \lambda \, dx,$$

(12.3.15)
$$= \int_0^\infty e^{-\mu(z+x)} e^{-\lambda x} \lambda \, dx = e^{-\mu z} \frac{\lambda}{\lambda + \mu}.$$

It turns out that with probability $\mu/(\lambda + \mu)$ customer 2 does not wait, whereas with complementary probability $\lambda/(\lambda + \mu)$ he waits, and, given that he waits, his conditional probability density is exponential: $e^{-\mu z} \mu$. This is the same as the service-time density. Then

(12.3.16)
$$E[W_2] = \frac{\lambda}{\lambda + \mu} \left(\frac{1}{\mu} \right).$$

and

$$(12.3.17) \qquad \text{Var}[W_2] = E[W_2{}^2] - E^2[W_2] = \frac{2}{\mu^2} \frac{\lambda}{\lambda + \mu} - \frac{1}{\mu^2} \left(\frac{\lambda}{\lambda + \mu} \right)^2.$$

Specifically, suppose $\lambda = 0.9$ and $\mu = 1$. Then

$$(12.3.18) \qquad E[W_2] = \frac{0.9}{0.9 + 1} = 0.474, \qquad \text{Var}[W_2] = 0.723,$$

and the standard deviation of W_2 is 0.85.

Although the very simple problem above can be entirely solved by mathematical analysis, it is quite apparent that the difficulties of doing so increase rapidly with n; even to find $E[W_3]$ and $E[W_4]$ is very tedious. We are thus led to carry out a simulation. Suppose that we obtain k *independent* realizations in order to estimate $E[W_2]$. For this we need merely obtain the random numbers that are realizations of service and interarrival times:

$$(12.3.19) \qquad S_1{}^{(1)}, S_1{}^{(2)}, \ldots, S_1{}^{(k)}$$

and

$$(12.3.20) \qquad A_2{}^{(1)}, A_2{}^{(2)}, \ldots, A_2{}^{(k)}.$$

Then substitute $S_1{}^{(j)}$ and $A_2{}^{(j)}$ into (12.3.1) in order to obtain the jth realized value of W_2, namely $W_2{}^{(j)}$, and average:

$$(12.3.21) \qquad E[\hat{W}_2] = \frac{W_2{}^{(1)} + W_2{}^{(2)} + \cdots + W_2{}^{(k)}}{k}.$$

Now by construction,

$$(12.3.22) \qquad E\{E[\hat{W}_2]\} = E[W_2]$$

and

$$(12.3.23)$$
$$\text{Var}\{E[\hat{W}_2]\} = \frac{\text{Var}[W_2{}^{(1)}] + \cdots + \text{Var}[W_2{}^{(k)}]}{k^2},$$
$$= \frac{\text{Var}[W_2]}{k}.$$

Let us again use the specific parameters that led to (12.3.18) in order to determine k so that the standard deviation of our estimate of $E[W_2]$ is (arbitrarily) no more than 10% of $E[W_2]$. To satisfy this requirement, we need

$$\frac{0.85}{\sqrt{k}} = (0.1)(0.474),$$

approximately; solving, we find that k must be at least 324. The indications are that quite a few realizations must be carried out in order to pin down the desired expected value accurately.

EXAMPLE 12.3.3. In order to illustrate our point further, let us consider a simple random walk *without* the annoying boundary of (12.3.1)—that is, the condition that $W_n \geq 0$. Such a structure approximately represents a waiting-time problem when we start with a large initial backlog: say, $W_0 = 50$. Then for at least the first few customers there is very little chance that the boundary will intervene, and so, in effect,

$$(12.3.24) \qquad W_n = W_{n-1} - A_n + S_{n-1} = W_{n-1} + \Delta_n.$$

To make matters a little simpler, we imagine that a customer (the zeroth) arrives initially so that

$$W_1 = W_0 + S_0 - A_1,$$
$$W_2 = W_1 + S_1 - A_2 = W_0 + (S_0 - A_1) + (S_1 - A_2),$$
$$\cdots .$$

Then, referring to (12.3.5),

$$\Delta_n = S_{n-1} - A_n.$$

In principle, the distribution of W_n can now be calculated by finding the distribution of the sum of the Δ_n's,

$$(12.3.25) \qquad W_n = W_0 + \Delta_1 + \Delta_2 + \cdots + \Delta_n,$$

and the latter is naturally approximated by the normal distribution as n increases. We easily find that

$$E(W_n) = W_0 + \sum_{i=1}^{n} E[\Delta_i] = W_0 + \sum_{i=1}^{n-1} E[S_{i-1}] - \sum_{i=1}^{n} E[A_i],$$

$$(12.3.26) \qquad \approx W_0 + n\left[\frac{1}{\mu} - \frac{1}{\lambda}\right],$$

if we use the exponential distributions (12.3.11) and (12.3.12). Likewise, we can show that

$$(12.3.27) \qquad \text{Var}[W_n] \approx n\left[\frac{1}{\mu^2} + \frac{1}{\lambda^2}\right].$$

If we use the specific parameters $\lambda = 0.9$ and $\mu = 1$ and put $n = 100$, then, approximately,

$$(12.3.28) \qquad E[W_{10}] = 50 + 100\left[1 - \frac{1}{0.9}\right] = 39$$

and

$$(12.3.29) \qquad \text{Var}[W_{10}] = 100\left[1 + \frac{1}{(0.9)^2}\right] = 224.$$

Again let us ask for the number of *independent* realizations to average in order to determine $E[W_{10}]$ so that the standard deviation of our estimate is not more than 10% of the true value. We need

$$(12.3.30) \qquad (0.1)(39) = \sqrt{\frac{224}{k}},$$

from which k should be at least 15. It might be noted that the relatively large mean value accounts for the rather small number of independent observations required to satisfy our accuracy criterion in this case.

The point of the last two examples was to show that an expected waiting time can be estimated by simulation *but* that a large number of *independent* realizations may be required to do so. In Section 12.4 we show how certain Monte Carlo tricks can be used to improve the efficiency of such simulations.

12.3(A) TIMING CONSIDERATIONS IN SIMULATION

The single-server queuing example exhibited one way in which the time dimension may enter a simulation problem. In that example, significant events—the arrivals of customers—marked the passage of time. Such a simulation might be said to employ *event-paced timing* or to be a simulation that proceeds by *variable time increments*. Absolute clock time is in the background, since the emphasis is on the waiting time of the nth customer, no matter when he arrives. Very little extra information would have to be recorded to keep track of the elapsed time, since the nth customer arrives at time $A_1 + A_2 + \cdots + A_n$, the sum of the interarrival times.

An uncritical look at the usual queuing models of Chapter 10 leads one to adopt *fixed-increment timing* for a simulation. For this, the time is split up into disjoint intervals of length h: $[0, h)$, $[h, 2h)$, $[2h, 3h)$, ..., $[(n-1)h, nh)$, ... If we are dealing with a birth-and-death model with arrival rate λ and departure rate μ and if we are interested in the system state at $t = nh$, we can express N_n, the number in the system at "time" n, as follows:

$$N_n = N_{n-1} + \begin{cases} 1 & \text{with probability} \quad \lambda h \\ 0 & \text{with probability} \quad 1 - (\lambda - \mu)h \\ -1 & \text{with probability} \quad \mu h \end{cases}$$

except when $N_n = 0$, in which case there is no jump to -1. Given an initial condition, the simulation is straightforward but also inefficient. If h is small, as must be the case if λh is to approximate the correct probability of an up-jump during h, then most of the time spent in the simulation involves *no change* in N. Suppose that $(\lambda + \mu)h = 0.1$, a reasonable choice to make so that the arrival of two or more customers during one time increment, h, can be neglected for many practical purposes. Then for every actual *change* in N (a jump up or down), about ten time increments will go by without change. Since for each of these increments a random number must be drawn, the sampling procedure is uneconomical. It would in this case be far more economical to use variable time increments—that is, draw a random number to represent the time between changes and then draw another to represent the extent of the change. In the case above, the time between changes is exponentially distributed with mean $(\lambda + \mu)^{-1}$ and with probability of an up-jump of $\lambda/(\lambda + \mu)$ and of a down-jump of $\mu/(\lambda + \mu)$. Of course, if the birth-and-death process has time-dependent parameters, $\lambda = \lambda(t)$ and $\mu = \mu(t)$, then the fixed-time-increment procedure may be simpler to program. If one approximates $\lambda(t)$ by a step function so that $\lambda(t) = \lambda_i$, for $t_{i-1} \le t < t_i$, say, then event-paced timing is again possible; one must only keep track of the time interval in which the latest arrival has occurred and use the appropriate λ value.

A different way to use fixed-increment timing is suggested by the discussion of approximations in Section 10.9 of Chapter 10.

EXAMPLE 12.3(A).1. Imagine that during evening rush hour an accident occurs on a freeway near a large city. Almost immediately a queue of many cars begins to develop behind the congestion point at the accident scene. Surveillance of the queue could well be conducted at fixed (say, 15-minute) time intervals, during which changes would occur because of vehicles arriving at the tail of the traffic jam and others departing—somewhat more slowly, at least initially, from the head, or accident scene. Suppose for the moment that exactly $c = 30$ cars depart from the accident scene during each 15-minute period and that the number of cars, $Z(t)$, joining the end of the line is Poisson with mean $m(t)$, where t is measured from the beginning of the jam (accident time). The time dependence of $m(t)$ reflects the fact that the number of cars on the freeway varies throughout the rush hour. Then, to a good approximation, the number of cars in the jam at "time" t is

$$J(t) = J(t - 1) + Z(t) - c,$$

provided $J(t)$ and $J(t - 1) > 0$; the jam ends for the smallest $t = t^*$ such that $J(t^* - 1) > 0$ but $J(t^*) \leq 0$. Note that we neglect the possibility that the jam ends in the middle of a 15-minute period.

The suitability of such a model under heavy utilization conditions seems clear. Of course the Poisson assumption is only illustrative. It may be quite adequate to let $Z(t)$ have a normal distribution with time-dependent mean and variance. Certainly a simulation model conducted in the manner outlined will be a great deal easier to work with than will be one based on the assumption that arrivals are specified by their interarrival times. It is the distribution of the *number* arriving or passing a point in a fixed time interval that traffic engineers will actually measure.

Many other models may be structured in a similar fashion. Illustrative examples are given in the exercises, and these should suggest others.

EXERCISES 12.3

1. Find the distribution of the waiting time of the second and third customers to arrive at a single-server system when interarrival times are each one unit ($A_n - 1$) and S_n is exponential with rate $\mu = 0.9$. Also find
   (a) $E[W_2]$ and $Var[W_2]$.
   (b) Suppose the problem above is done by simulation. How many independent realizations are required in order that the standard deviation of your estimate be 10% of its expected value?

2. Refer to the simple job shop model of Example 12.2.1. Suppose $J = 3$ and the durations of these three jobs are independently distributed according to the exponential density having mean m (hours).
   (a) Show that the expectation of the total number of job-hours spent in shop (waiting plus processing, or service, time) is $6m$ if the jobs are taken in arrival, or first-come, first-served, order. (*Hint:* Three jobs wait until the first is done, then two, and so on.)
   (b) Find the variance of the number of job-hours waited.
   (c) Suppose the answer to (a) was found by simulation. If $m = 1$, how many independent realizations would be required in order that the standard deviation of the estimate equal 0.25 hour? Discuss the problem when the job-duration distribution is uniformly distributed and when it is arbitrary.

3. Referring to Exercise 2, suppose that the job durations are always known before processing begins. The shortest-processing-time-first rule is followed—that is, the job with shortest duration is first completed, then the next, and so on.
   (a) By simulation, estimate the expected total waiting time (in job-hours) for the three jobs. Take $m = 1$.
   (b) Estimate the variance of your estimate of the total expected waiting time.
   *(c) Compute the answer to (a) analytically. (*Hint:* Compute the distribution of the smallest value and so on of a sample of size three from an exponential distribution.)

4. An airplane lands and reaches the gate at $t = 0$. There are N passengers aboard. Suppose that the time for the first debarking passenger to reach the taxi stand has the exponential distribution with mean $E[A_1] = 1/N$, that the interarrival time between first and second is exponential with mean $E[A_2] = 1/(N-1)$, and, in general, that the interarrival time between $n - 1$st and nth is exponential with mean $E[A_n] = 1/(N-n+1)$ $(n = 1, 2, \ldots, N-1)$. Upon reaching the taxi stand, passengers join a single-server queue, and the service time to load a cab and depart—S_n for the nth arrival—has a uniform distribution over the range 0 to 5 (minutes). Successive service times are independently distributed.
   (a) If $N = 100$, simulate in order to estimate the expected value of the *maximum* taxi waiting time encountered by an arriving customer.
   (b) Estimate the expected time required for all passengers to receive a taxi and depart.
   (c) Estimate the expected number of passenger-minutes spent waiting for taxicabs.

5. Repeat the simulation of the previous problem, but let $N = 200$. Do the measures (a), (b), and (c) double?

6. Consider the baggage-handling and claim problem associated with the aircraft landing. Assume that passengers reach the baggage claim area according to the arrival process of Exercise 4. Suppose that baggage reaches the claim area according to the following random process. A random time, T, elapses following airplane landing. Thereafter, at regular time intervals of duration d, suitcases are deposited in the claim area. Suppose each passenger has one suitcase and that suitcases appear in the claim area in completely random order. Let T be exponentially distributed with mean 15 (minutes) and $d = 0.20$ (minutes).
   (a) Estimate by simulation the expected total delay experienced by customers in the claim area. Assume that once a passenger's suitcase has appeared and he is present, it is immediately removed.
   (b) Estimate the expectation and variance of the *maximum* time required by a passenger to receive his suitcase.
   (c) Suppose the expected time, $E[T]$, can be shortened to 7.5 minutes. Estimate the improvement in the measures (a) and (b).

7. It is often possible to give reasonable approximate solutions to problems by simple methods. If need be, these solutions can be refined or improved by simulation. Consider Exercise 4 in the following light.
   (a) Let $n(t)$ be the number of passengers who have arrived at the taxi stand by time t. Treat $n(t)$ as a continuous (differentiable) and deterministic function of t. Then the rate of passenger arrival at time t is, according to the assumptions above, approximately

   $$\frac{dn(t)}{dt} = N - n(t).$$

   Solve this differential equation to show that

   $$n(t) = N(1 - e^{-t}).$$

   (b) Assume that the output (taxi-acquisition) rate is approximately $1/E[S_n] = (2.5)^{-1}$ minutes as long as there are passengers waiting.

(c) The number, $Q(t)$, of passengers waiting at t is approximately the number arriving minus those who have left:

$$Q(t) = N(1 - e^{-t}) - \alpha t \qquad \alpha = \frac{1}{E[S_n]}.$$

There is no waiting at $t = 0$, and none after the emptying time $t_e > 0$ such that $Q(t_e) = 0$. The equation above, $Q(t) = 0$, must be solved graphically or numerically.

(d) Maximum queue size occurs at the time $t = t_m$ such that $\dfrac{dQ}{dt} = 0$. That is,

$$t_m = \log_e \frac{N}{\alpha}.$$

This provides an approximate answer to (a) of Exercise 4.

(e) How would you use the representation of $Q(t)$ given in (c) to approximate (b) and (c) of Exercise 4? Why is such an approximation valuable?

8. A particular machine is in one of three states during day n (assume the machine is new on day 0): available = state 1, undergoing preventive maintenance = state 2, down for repair = state 3. It changes state in accordance with the Markov chain having one-step transition matrix shown.

		State j, Day $n+1$		
		1	2	3
State i, Day n	1	$0.5 + 0.2\left(\dfrac{n}{n+5}\right)$	0.1	$0.4 - 0.2\left(\dfrac{n}{n+5}\right)$
	2	0.8	0.2	0.0
	3	$0.6\left(\dfrac{n}{n+7}\right)n$	0	$1 - 0.6\left(\dfrac{n}{n+7}\right)$

(a) Simulate the first 25 days of the machine's history, and tabulate the number of days on which it is in each state. Start with $S_1 = 1$, where S_n ($n = 1, 2, 3, \ldots$) represents the state variable on day n.

(b) Repeat the simulation 100 times, and calculate the fraction of the time the machine is down for repair (unavailable) during the first 25 days. Would you expect this number to increase or decrease during the second 25 days?

(c) Suppose the machine has been in operation for 100 days. How can you *approximate* the probability that the machine is available on day n ($n > 100$) by analytical methods? (*Hint:* Notice that although the Markov transition probabilities depend on n, they tend to become constant as n increases. Apply results from stationary Markov chains.) How would you check your results by simulation?

(d) Give a reason for allowing the transition probabilities to change with time as they do.

9. A factory smokestack that is located in a city emits smoke at a height of 100 feet above a completely flat plane. Suppose there is a prevailing wind from west to east and that city population is uniformly distributed from the smokestack base running in an easterly direction for ten miles, with five houses per linear mile within the city limits. The city ends after ten miles; house and population density abruptly drop to zero. Assume that the number of smoke particles emitted per one-minute time period is 10^6; treat each one minute's worth of smoke as a "smoke packet" that random walks according to the following rules.

(a) If a packet starts from smokestack tip at time 0, then its vertical height above the plane is $Z(0) = 100$ feet, and its horizontal displacement in an easterly direction is $X(0) = 0$ (the smokestack location is the origin).

(b) Suppose weather conditions are such that if t is measured in one-minute increments,

$$Z(t) = Z(t - 1) + Y(t),$$

where $\{Y(t)\}$ is a sequence of independent random variables having a normal distribution with

$$E[Y(t)] = -0.5 \text{ feet},$$
$$\text{Var}[Y(t)] = 1 \text{ (foot)}^2.$$

The smoke packet hits the ground surface (possibly a house) when, for the first time, $Z(t) \leq 20$ (feet).

(c) The smoke packet moves in the easterly direction at a rate of four miles per hour.

Simulate the process above to answer the following questions.

(d) Estimate the probability that a smoke packet will come to earth ($Z = 0$) within the city limits. For this part of the study disregard the presence of houses.

(e) Estimate the probability that a smoke packet will hit a house. (*Suggestion:* Assume the linear dimension of a house in the direction of smoke travel is 50 feet so that a packet must fall on a linear set of the following kind:

$$\{x \mid x_i \leq x < x_i + 50; \quad i = 1, 2, \ldots 50\}.$$

Try arranging the houses regularly; that is, $x_i = 1050i$ feet. Then compare the answer to the answer one gets if it is assumed that the probability that a smoke packet will hit a house is just the fraction of presented area given by house roofs:
$$\frac{5 \times 10 \times 50}{10 \times 5280}.)$$

(f) Criticize the model and extend it. That is, let the horizontal wind velocity change randomly, introduce a temperature inversion (modeled by a reflecting barrier at, say, 1000 feet), and so on.

12.4   MONTE CARLO METHODS—VARIANCE REDUCTION

The previous section describes the simulation of a simple queuing process. The discussion shows that the averaging of several independent realizations creates an estimate that is "near" the quantity being estimated. However, it is also clear that in order to obtain precise estimates, it is necessary to create and average many such realizations. We now suggest methods for dealing with this situation and for improving the efficiency of simulation experiments.

First it seems worthwhile to list two simple principles.

1. *Never simulate if you can calculate the answers mathematically.* If the problem at hand can be solved by known mathematical methods (for example, by applying queuing theory in particular or probability theory in general), then simulation is unnecessary and introduces sampling variability that may otherwise be avoided. If the problem is *partially* solvable analytically, it is often profitable to do that part separately, sampling only when absolutely necessary. As we shall see, use of approxi-

mate analytical solutions—solutions to similar, perhaps oversimplified, but mathematically tractable problems—are often of considerable use in conjunction with simulation when dealing with a complex situation.

2. *Perform comparative simulations when possible.* Often simulations are carried out to compare two systems having different parameters, distributions, scheduling rules, and so on. Let us say that we are considering the expected waiting time of customer n in two systems. Denote the waiting time in system i by $W_n(i)$, $i = 1, 2$. Then the difference is

$$(12.4.1) \qquad \delta = E[W_n(1)] - E[W_n(2)],$$

and an estimate is formed by simulating k realizations of each process and forming and subtracting the sample means:

$$(12.4.2) \qquad \hat{\delta} = \overline{W}_n(1) - \overline{W}_n(2).$$

Now if both sets of k realizations are independently created—that is, by using different sequences of random numbers—then $\overline{W}_n(1)$ and $\overline{W}_n(2)$ are independent, and

$$\mathrm{Var}[\hat{\delta}] = \mathrm{Var}[\overline{W}_n(1)] + \mathrm{Var}[\overline{W}_n(2)],$$

$$(12.4.3) \qquad = \frac{1}{k}\{\mathrm{Var}[W_n(1)] + \mathrm{Var}[W_n(2)]\}.$$

Suppose, on the other hand, that when a random number, R_j, is used to create a realization of the jth $(j = 1, 2, \ldots, n - 1)$ service time in system 1,

$$(12.4.4) \qquad S_j(1) = G_1^{-1}(R_j),$$

and *the same random number* is used to create the jth service time in system 2,

$$(12.4.5) \qquad S_j(2) = G_2^{-1}(R_j).$$

Suppose this is done for each j (each service time) and also for each interarrival time. It is clear that the pairs of realizations thus created will be similar and that if such paired realizations are averaged, then $\overline{W}_{in}(1)$ and $\overline{W}_n(2)$ will tend to be positively related or correlated. Thus, when such a comparative technique is used,

$$\mathrm{Var}[\hat{\delta}] = \mathrm{Var}[\overline{W}_n(1)] + \mathrm{Var}[\overline{W}_n(2)] - 2\,\mathrm{Cov}[\overline{W}_n(1),\,\overline{W}_n(2)],$$

$$(12.4.6) \qquad = \frac{1}{k}\{\mathrm{Var}[W_n(1)] + \mathrm{Var}[W_n(2)] - 2\,\mathrm{Cov}[W_n(1),\,W_n(2)]\},$$

and, because of the positive covariance, it is apparent that (12.4.6) will be smaller than (12.4.3). While the inexorable $1/k$ law of variance reduction still holds, comparative simulation almost always greatly reduces the coefficient of $1/k$ and hence the variance of the estimate of difference.

We shall now describe several other methods for improving simulation efficiency. All of these, in one way or another, capitalize on the advantage of reusing basic random numbers, as described. In order to render the discussion somewhat more general, the following formulation seems useful.

We are concerned with a system and a particular response variable, W, which is influenced by several other variables, $X, Y, \ldots$; we denote these collectively by $\underline{X}$. For example, W might be the waiting time of an aircraft at an airport; then $\underline{X}$ represents the interarrival times of the planes appearing previously on that day (or portion thereof), their runway occupancy times, and so on. The modeling process involves relating W to $\underline{X}$; the $\underline{X}$ variables are often taken to be random variables. We then investigate the distribution of W in terms of that of $\underline{X}$, and we are interested in figures of merit such as the expected value of W, the probability that W will exceed some value, and so on. That is, we seek to find characteristics of the probability distribution of

$$(12.4.7) \qquad W = f(\underline{X}),$$

where f is presumed known but is usually a complicated function. We now outline briefly some procedures for studying the distribution of W or certain of its characteristics such as its mean, $E[W]$. The first procedure is familiar from our previous examples.

A. Straightforward Sampling

In order to obtain a sample value of W, we first obtain a sample value of $\underline{X}$ and then compute W by means of (12.4.7). More specifically, $\underline{X} = (X, Y, \ldots)$ may be found by first selecting a vector of pseudorandom numbers and then converting these to realizations, or samples, of $X, Y, \ldots$, utilizing the probability integral transformation or an equivalent—that is, by solving

$$(12.4.8) \qquad X = F_X^{-1}(R).$$

$F_X(\cdot)$ is the distribution function of X and R represents a random number uniformly distributed over $(0, 1)$. A set of k independent realizations of W, denoted by $\{W^{(j)}; j = 1, 2, \ldots, k\}$, may then be averaged to obtain an unbiased estimate of $E[W]$:

$$(12.4.9) \qquad \hat{E}[W] = \frac{1}{k} \sum_{j=1}^{k} W^{(j)},$$

having variance

$$(12.4.10) \qquad \operatorname{Var}\{\hat{E}[W]\} = \frac{1}{k} \operatorname{Var}[W].$$

B. Antithetic Variables

Frequently, the response W is consistently positively or negatively associated with one or more of the input variables, say X. That is, if interarrival times in a queue realization are larger than normal, the waiting times will be smaller than normal, and so on. Suppose then that the random number R creates a realization X and that X is large; then $1 - R$ will tend to create a corresponding realization X' that is small. At a small programming cost one can generate *antithetic* realizations $W^{(j)}$ and $W'^{(j)}$, in turn the result of $\underline{R}$ and $1 - \underline{R}$. The antithetic realizations are then averaged to obtain the final estimate. Permutations of the random numbers among the components of $\underline{X}$ to obtain further antithetic realizations *may* also be profitable, but not invariably.

EXAMPLE 12.4.1. Consider the unrestricted random-walk queuing model of Example 12.3.3. Starting with large initial wait, W_0, we have

$$(12.4.11) \qquad W_n = W_{n-1} + S_{n-1} - A_n = W_{n-1} + \Delta_n,$$

where

$$W_1 = W_0 + S_0 - A_1 = W_0 + \Delta_1,$$

(12.4.12) $$W_2 = W_0 + S_0 - A_1 + S_1 - A_2 = W_0 + \Delta_1 + \Delta_2,$$

$$\cdots$$

Let $S_i(1)$ and $A_i(1)$ denote, respectively, the service time of the ith customer and the interarrival time between customers $i - 1$ and i in realization 1, and let $S_i(2)$ and $A_i(2)$ denote the corresponding random variables in realization 2. These will be referred to as *comparison realizations*, or *antithetic pairs*. We will generate realizations of $S_i(1)$, $A_i(1)$ and $S_i(2)$, $A_i(2)$ as follows:

(12.4.13) $$S_i(1) = G^{-1}(R_i), \qquad A_i(1) = F^{-1}(R_{i'});$$

(12.4.14) $$S_i(2) = G^{-1}(1 - R_i), \qquad A_i(2) = F^{-1}(1 - R_{i'}).$$

Here R_i and R_i' are independent and uniformly distributed; one can obtain realizations by simply assigning the pseudorandom number generated by computer, or obtained from a table, alternately to generate service and interarrival times. Notice that if R_i is, by chance, large, then $S_i(1)$ will tend to be large. However, $1 - R_i$ will then tend to be small, and a small value for $S_i(2)$ will result. Hence $S_i(1)$ and $S_i(2)$ tend to be negatively correlated, or *antithetic*. If, for example, $S_i(1)$ and $S_i(2)$ are antithetic versions of exponentially distributed random variables with unit mean, then it may be shown that

$$\text{Cov}[S_i(1), S_i(2)] = 1 - \frac{\pi^2}{6} \approx -0.64.$$

From the antithetically generated service and arrival times we can generate antithetic pairs or comparison realizations leading to W_n and W_n'. Intuitively, W_n and W_n' are seen to be negatively correlated. Next W_n and W_n' are averaged and the process may then be repeated k times; the final estimate becomes

(12.4.15) $$\hat{E}[W_n]_A = \left[\frac{W_n(1) + W_n'(1)}{2} + \frac{W_n(2) + W_n'(2)}{2} + \cdots + \frac{W_n(k) + W_n'(k)}{2}\right]\frac{1}{k},$$

$$= \frac{\overline{W}_n + \overline{W}_n'}{2}.$$

Now

(12.4.16) $$\text{Var}\{\hat{E}[W_n]_A\} = \frac{1}{2k}\{\text{Var}[W_n] + \text{Cov}[W_n, W_n']\},$$

and because of the negative correlation artificially introduced, the variance here is typically smaller than the variance obtained by running $2k$ independent realizations.

C. Stratification

The stratification method in a sense extends the antithetic idea. Again, in brief, we can segment the unit interval over which R ranges into, say, three equal parts:

$$r_1 = \left(0, \frac{1}{3}\right), \qquad r_2 = \left(\frac{1}{3}, \frac{2}{3}\right), \qquad r_3 = \left(\frac{2}{3}, 1\right).$$

We then select a subrange, r_i, at random, using one random number. Within r_i, a value for $R(1)$ is selected in accordance with a random number uniform over $(0, \frac{1}{3})$; here $R(1)$ denotes the random number that generates $X(1)$, a variable associated with realization 1. To obtain $S(2)$, the corresponding variable for realization 2, it is necessary to add $\frac{1}{3}$ to $R(1)$, thereby obtaining $R(2)$—a subtraction of unity will possibly be required to locate $R(2)$ in the range $(0, 1)$. From $R(2)$ we create $X(2)$. Another addition of $\frac{1}{3}$ to $R(2)$, together with a subtraction of unity if necessary, generates $R(3)$ and hence $X(3)$ for realization 3. Note that this stratification procedure may be carried out for each variable in $\underline{X}$ and that, in the case above, two independent random numbers generate three parallel realizations. Actually, six realizations can be generated by the procedure above, provided the second uniform random number, over $(0, \frac{1}{3})$, is treated antithetically inside that interval.

It can be seen that stratification tends to force an equal distribution of X across companion realizations and hence a systematic correlation of the corresponding values $W^{(j)}(1)$, $W^{(j)}(2)$, and $W^{(j)}(3)$. The average,

$$(12.4.17) \quad \hat{E}[W]_s = \frac{1}{k} \sum_{j=1}^{k} \left[\frac{W^{(j)}(1) + W^{(j)}(2) + W^{(j)}(3)}{3} \right] = \frac{\overline{W}(1) + \overline{W}(2) + \overline{W}(3)}{3},$$

thus tends to have a variance smaller than that obtained from $3k$ independent realizations.

The techniques just described are useful for reducing the sampling variability of simulations, but they fail to employ extra information that may exist concerning the approximate behavior of a system. Next to be described are several procedures that involve the simultaneous use of simulation with approximate models and concomitant information.

D. Control Variates

A classical and useful estimating procedure that involves the use of an approximate model operates as follows. We desire to estimate $E[W]$, where W is related to $\underline{X}$ by (12.4.7). We are able to *calculate* (analytically or numerically) the expectation of W^* relatively easily; W^* is the variable of a model approximating that giving W. We might have either

$$(12.4.18) \qquad\qquad W^* = f^*(\underline{X})$$

or

$$W^* = f(\underline{X}^*)$$

or even

$$(12.4.19) \qquad\qquad W^* = f^*(X^*);$$

an asterisk will generally be used to denote an approximation.

We then simulate both W and W^*, utilizing the same sequence of random numbers, $\underline{R}$. That is, comparing (12.4.18) and (12.4.7), the values of $\underline{X}$ are identical across realizations to as great a degree as possible. This implies that W and W^* will be positively correlated. We now estimate $E[W]$ as follows:

$$\hat{E}[W]_C = E[W^*] + \frac{1}{k}\sum_{j=1}^{k} W^{(j)} - \frac{1}{k}\sum_{j=1}^{k} W^{*(j)},$$

(12.4.20)

$$= E[W^*] + \overline{W} - \overline{W^*}.$$

If expectations are taken it is seen that

(12.4.21) $$E\{\hat{E}[W]_C\} = E[W^*] + E[\overline{W}] - E[W^*] = E[W],$$

and so the estimate is unbiased. Owing to the built-in correlation between W and W^*, we have

(12.4.22) $$\mathrm{Var}\{\hat{E}[W]\} = \frac{1}{k}\{\mathrm{Var}[W] + \mathrm{Var}[W^*] - 2\,\mathrm{Cov}[W, W^*]\}.$$

Consequently, if the quantity in brackets on the right-hand side is smaller than $\mathrm{Var}[W]$, then an improvement has been achieved over straightforward simulation. This is equivalent to requiring that the control variable, W^*, exhibit the property

(12.4.23) $$\frac{\mathrm{Cov}[W, W^*]}{\mathrm{Var}[W^*]} > \frac{1}{2}.$$

It will, of course, not always be easy to see that (12.4.23) is satisfied in advance. However, if the results of several realizations are available, one can simply compare the empirically determined variances of a straightforward and a control variate estimate to assess the contribution of the latter.

E. Control and Regression

The form of (12.4.20) suggests another possibility for improving precision, namely that of a correction of the form

(12.4.24) $$\hat{E}[W]_{C,R} = \overline{W} + \beta(\overline{W^*} - E[W^*]),$$

where β is selected to minimize the variance of the estimate $E[W]_{C,R}$. Since

(12.4.25) $$\mathrm{Var}\{\hat{E}[W]_{C,R}\} = \mathrm{Var}[\overline{W}] + 2\beta\,\mathrm{Cov}[\overline{W}, \overline{W^*}] + \beta^2\,\mathrm{Var}[\overline{W^*}],$$

simple differentiation and straightforward simplification yield for the optimum β the value

(12.4.26) $$\beta_0 = \frac{-\mathrm{Cov}[W, W^*]}{\mathrm{Var}[W^*]} = -\mathrm{correlation}\,[W, W^*]\left(\frac{\mathrm{Var}[W]}{\mathrm{Var}[W^*]}\right).$$

If this value of β is utilized, the resulting optimal *regression-adjusted* estimate has variance

$$\mathrm{Var}\{\hat{E}[W]_{C,R}\} = \frac{1}{k}\left\{\mathrm{Var}[W] - \frac{\mathrm{Cov}^2[W, W^*]}{\mathrm{Var}[W^*]}\right\},$$

(12.4.27)

$$= \frac{1}{k}\mathrm{Var}[W]\{1 - (\mathrm{correlation}[W, W^*])^2\}.$$

Notice that the variance of this estimate is always at least as small as $\text{Var}[\overline{W}]$ and hence will, in theory, always be an improvement over simple estimates; ordinary control variates need not have this property (see (12.4.23)). On a practical note, we remark that the required covariance will not be known and hence must be estimated from data. Since the control variable model has been chosen for its analytical tractability, $\text{Var}[W^*]$ is sometimes known. We are led to the use of the estimated optimal β,

$$(12.4.28) \qquad \hat{\beta}_0 = -\frac{\frac{1}{k}\sum_{j=1}^{k}(W^{(j)} - \overline{W})(W^{*(j)} - E[W^*]}{\text{Var}[W^*]},$$

and it is now clear that the realistic estimate is

$$(12.4.29) \qquad \hat{E}[W]_{c,R} = \overline{W} + \hat{\beta}_0(\overline{W^*} - E[W^*]),$$

which may no longer be unbiased, although the bias typically decreases as the sample size, k, increases. There is, of course, no need to restrict attention to linear corrections; estimates of the form

$$(12.4.30) \qquad \hat{E}[W]_r = \overline{W} + \alpha + \beta_1(\overline{W^*} - E[W^*]) + \beta_2(W^* - E[W^*])^2$$

may also be worth investigation.

F. Concomitant Variables

Suppose that realizations of the random variables $\underline{X}$ are used to create realizations of W, where the response on the jth realization is

$$(12.4.31) \qquad W^{(j)} = f(\underline{X}^{(j)}).$$

Quite commonly, $W^{(j)}$ and $X_i^{(j)}$ are monotonically related, and we can put

$$(12.4.32) \qquad \text{Cov}[W^{(j)}, X_i^{(j)}] = c_i,$$

where c_i is either positive or negative. Furthermore, we actually *know* $E[X_i^{(j)}] = E[X_i]$, since $\underline{X}$ is a given specified input. Since sampling only k times will naturally mean that the realized X values deviate from their means, a linear correction to the simple average suggests itself:

$$(12.4.33) \qquad E[W]_c = \overline{W} + \sum_{i=1}^{I} \gamma_i(\overline{X}_i - E[X_i]).$$

The weights γ_i ($i = 1, 2, \ldots, I$) can be estimated in terms of the covariance of W and X_i, and the resulting estimate is unbiased and consistent (tends in probability to $E[W]$) asymptotically as k, the sample size, increases. There is no restriction to a linear correction.

EXAMPLE 12.4.2. The methods just described are well illustrated by consideration of a very simple queueing problem. Recall that the waiting time, W_n, of the nth arrival to a single-server facility may be written as

$$(12.4.34) \qquad W_n = \max[W_{n-1} - A_n + S_{n-1}, 0].$$

where A_n is the interarrival period elapsing between the $n - 1$st and the nth addition to the queue (or entrance to the server) and S_n is the service time of the nth customer. When $E[A] < E[S]$, the queue tends to grow, and little analytical information is available. Intuition suggests that in this case, the annoying boundary necessitating the "max" in (12.4.34) is eventually of no importance, and the distribution of W_n approaches that of $W_n{}^*$, where

$$(12.4.35) \qquad W_n{}^* = W_{n-1}^* - A_n + S_{n-1}$$

as n becomes large. Apparently $W_n{}^*$ is approximately normally distributed (if A_n and S_n have finite variances), and so we feel that W_n is also approximately normal as n increases. We shall display the effects of applying various of the variance-reduction methods described to estimate $E[W_n]$ for selected values of n. In particular we focus on the control and concomitant-variables approaches. For a control variable, it is quite natural to select the simple boundaryless random walk $W_n{}^*$ when $E[A] < E[S]$. For a concomitant variable, it is tempting to select

$$(12.4.36) \qquad \sum_{i=1}^{n} A_i \quad \text{and also} \quad \sum_{l=1}^{n} S_l,$$

since, intuitively speaking, an increase in the former is associated with a small W_n, while an increase in the latter induces an increase in W_n. Also, $E[A_n] = nE[A]$ and $E[S_{n-1}] = (n - 1)E[S]$.

Numerical examples for the following cases will now be presented. In each of these, service times are taken to be exponentially distributed with mean μ^{-1}:

$$(12.4.37) \qquad \begin{aligned} P\{S_n \le x\} &= 1 - e^{-\mu x} & x \ge 0, \\ &= 0 & x < 0. \end{aligned}$$

The interarrival times are taken to be either constant (regular arrivals) or exponentially distributed; in each case the mean is unity.

The tables illustrate the value of some of the proposed estimating procedures. The service system selected for study is quite simple: customers arrive (regularly in Table 12.4.1, in Poisson fashion in Table 12.4.2) at a single server where their service

TABLE 12.4.1. Estimated wait of nth customer (regular arrivals, exponential service at single server, based on 25 realizations)

$E[A_n] = 1, \mu^{-1} = E[S_n] = 1.111$

			n: 5	10	25	50	100	150	200
Straightforward:	(1)	Mean	1.19	1.87	4.51	7.85	11.43	17.04	23.60
	(2)	Variance	.124	.128	.605	1.356	2.758	6.795	10.678
Antithetic:	(3)	Mean	1.35	2.51	5.11	8.67	14.50	19.68	24.88
	(4)	Variance	.054	.141	.256	.367	.622	1.370	1.770
Random Walk:	(5)	Mean	.44	.99	2.67	5.44	11.00	16.55	22.11
Control:	(6)	Mean	1.48	2.91	5.92	9.86	16.01	22.12	28.00
$(\beta = 1)$	(7)	Variance	.039	.102	.373	.763	.963	1.296	1.427
Straightforward	(8)	Mean	1.42	2.27	5.49	9.48	14.62	22.50	29.08
and Concomitant:	(9)	Variance	.019	.042	.144	.366	.446	1.715	3.864
Antithetic and	(10)	Mean	1.38	2.10	5.16	8.78	15.01	21.72	27.46
Concomitant:	(11)	Variance	.014	.106	.165	.093	.093	.671	1.350
Control:	(12)	Mean	1.39	2.43	5.33	9.03	14.54	20.94	27.13
$(\beta \text{ estimated})$	(13)	Variance	.016	.034	.126	.198	.445	.733	.832

TABLE 12.4.2. Estimated expected wait of nth customer (Poisson arrivals, exponential service at single server, based on 25 realizations)

$E[A_n] = 1, \mu^{-1} = E[S_n] = 1.111$

			n: 5	10	25	50	100	150	200
Straightforward:	(1)	Mean	2.15	2.77	6.92	11.93	19.84	25.65	29.28
	(2)	Variance	.225	.295	1.119	1.832	2.692	6.596	11.446
Antithetic:	(3)	Mean	1.95	3.33	6.62	11.22	17.30	24.33	29.55
	(4)	Variance	.062	.107	.271	.558	1.079	1.964	3.239
Random Walk (W_n*):	(5)	Mean	.44	.99	2.67	5.44	11.00	16.55	22.11
Control:	(6)	Mean	1.63	3.05	6.13	9.81	15.70	21.55	27.23
$(\beta = 1)$	(7)	Variance	.125	.225	.477	1.026	1.278	1.396	1.393
Straightforward	(8)	Mean	1.69	2.86	6.04	10.79	17.93	22.46	27.64
and Concomitant:	(9)	Variance	.148	.087	.162	.443	1.201	1.565	2.307
Antithetic and	(10)	Mean	1.73	3.22	6.15	10.83	17.61	24.09	29.57
Concomitant:	(11)	Variance	.025	.054	.074	.216	.368	1.016	.974
Control:	(12)	Mean	1.84	2.92	6.41	10.65	17.03	22.38	27.41
(β *estimated*)	(13)	Variance	.051	.78	.196	.397	.866	1.040	1.297

times are exponential with mean 10/9. Even so, the transient response of such a system is not easily characterized mathematically, and so simulation suggests itself.

Rows (1) and (2) of the tables show the results obtained if 25 independent realizations are averaged to obtain $\overline{W}_n$ as an estimate of $E[W_n]$. Then, using the same random numbers, we simulated the process again antithetically and averaged to obtain the antithetic estimate $\overline{W}_n(a)$. Comparison of the variances in rows (2) and (4) indicates that the antithetic device produces an improvement even after the labor of simulating a total of 50 realizations is taken into account. The improvement is smaller for Table 12.4.2 than for Table 12.4.1, probably because of the added variability contributed by the random arrivals.

Next the simple control variable device is applied; see rows (6) and (7). The control is the boundary-free random walk.

According to the variances computed, this control estimate seems to perform somewhat better than the antithetic estimate for large n (customer numbers) and less well for intermediate n, although the small differences observed may be due to sampling errors. Certainly one is led to explore further the comparative values of "antithetic" and "control" as inherent process variability builds up: control seems better than antithetic in Table 12.4.2 than in Table 12.4.1. A combination of antithetic with control might be profitable.

Rows (8) and (9) display the effect of adjusting a straightforward estimate (see row (1)) in accordance with the concomitant variable that equals the sum of the first n service times in Table 12.4.1; Table 12.4.2 considers both service and arrival times as concomitant variables. The latter device behaves in a manner comparable to antithetics and to control. Rows (10) and (11) exhibit the results of applying concomitant variables to the components of the antithetic estimate of (3) and (4). This adjusted estimate seems to be more effective than the others for the present problems. Rows (12) and (13) indicate the value of a regression-adjusted control procedure; one should compare the variances of (7) with those of (13).

Finally, it goes without saying that the techniques suggested and illustrated above will be useful when simulating other systems. Another application is explored in the following section, and the problems suggest still others.

EXERCISES 12.4

1. Refer to Exercise 2 of the previous section. Simulate to estimate the answer to part(a), first by using 30 independent realizations and second by averaging 15 realization averages with their 15 antithetic versions. Compare the (estimated) variance of your estimates.

2. Use antithetic-variable techniques to repeat Exercise 3 of the previous section.

3. Consider the airplane-landing, taxi-stand problem of Exercise 4 of the previous section. Observe that the simulated realizations leading to (a), (b), and (c) are each negatively related to the total time required for all arrivals to occur, and hence that time should be a useful concomitant variable.
    (a) Show that the expected time for all arrivals to occur is

    $$E[A_1 + A_2 + \cdots + A_N] = \frac{1}{N} + \frac{1}{N-1} + \cdots + \frac{1}{2} + 1.$$

    (b) Use the result of (a) to improve the efficiency (lower the variance of) simulation-generated answers to the problem.
    (c) Can consideration of the service times be used to improve estimates? How?

4. Let S_t denote the sales in week t of a certain product. The development of S_t is modeled as follows:

    $$S_{t+1} = aS_t + U_t + b,$$

    where $\{U_t\}$ is a sequence of independent random variables with the *logistic* distribution

    $$F(x) = \frac{e^x}{1 + e^x} \qquad -\infty < x < \infty.$$

    (a) Suppose $a = 0.7$ and $b = 4$; generate ten weeks of sales data. Start with $S_1 = 4$.
    (b) Use the results of (a) to estimate the average sales during the first ten weeks, given that $S_1 = 4$.
    (c) Compare the results of (b) to what occurs when $b = 0.1$.
    (d) Can $\sum_{t=1}^{9} U_t$ be used as a concomitant variable? Does its use improve the estimate of $E[S_1 + S_2 + \cdots + S_{10}]$?
    (e) Try antithetic estimates. How does one draw an antithetic realization from the logistic distribution?

5. Each month an insurance company collects premiums of \$100,000. The total amount of the claims on the ith month, X_i, is approximately log-normally distributed: That is, $\log X_i = Y_i$ is normally distributed with mean m and variance σ^2.
    (a) Use the fact that for log-normal X and real s,

    $$E[X^s] = e^{ms + (1/2)s^2\sigma^2}$$

    to show that

    $$E[X] = e^{m + (1/2)\sigma^2}$$
    $$\mathrm{Var}[X] = e^{2m + \sigma^2}[e^{\sigma^2} - 1].$$

    If $E[X] = \$95,000$ and $\mathrm{Var}[X] = 2(E[X])^2$, determine m and σ^2.
    (b) Show that in order to simulate a realization of one month's claims, one first finds

    $$Y = m + \sigma Z,$$

    where Z is normal with mean zero and unit variance. Then $X = e^Y$ is a realization of a log-normal variable.

(c) Suppose the company starts out with $300,000. Simulate to estimate the probability that the company runs out of capital (is ruined) before three years (36 months) elapse. Let U_n be the company's fortune after n months; then

$$U_n = U_{n-1} + 100,000 - X_n,$$

X_n being the claims during month n. Ruin occurs if $U_n \leq 0$.

(d) How would you use antithetic variables in this problem? (*Hint:* Changing the sign of Z in part (b) generates an antithetic Y.)

12.5 NETWORK SIMULATION

Many complex projects may be viewed as collections of individual tasks that must be performed in a specified precedence order. The representation of such projects by networks or graphs has been described at an earlier stage in this book. Frequently the precise durations of the various tasks in the network are unknown and may be thought of as random variables having a probability distribution. This implies that the entire project duration is a random variable. Our task is to obtain information about the project-duration probabilities in terms of the component task-duration distributions. Such information may be used to decide when to begin an entire project (for example, break ground for a new building), the objective being to assure completion before a due date with specified probability. Alternative formulations that assign costs to lateness and earliness are also of interest.

EXAMPLE 12.5.1. A building project involves first a ground-breaking task, then preliminary construction, which can only begin after the ground breaking. Following this, final construction and plumbing and wiring occur simultaneously. The project graph (Program Evaluation and Review Technique—PERT chart), or network, appears in Figure 12.5.1.

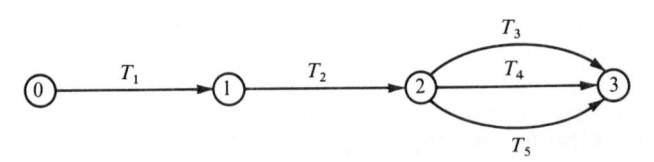

FIGURE 12.5.1

Node 0 represents project start, node 1 represents completion of ground breaking, with T_1 being the time to complete that task. Node 2 denotes the termination of the preliminary construction phase; T_2 is the duration of this task. When node 3 is reached, the building project is complete. Following completion of tasks leading to node 2, the three tasks, final construction (time T_3), plumbing (time T_4), and wiring (time T_5), proceed independently and concurrently. Project completion time in this case may be expressed as

(12.5.1) $$C = T_1 + T_2 + \max(T_3, T_4, T_5).$$

Having the distribution functions of T_1 through T_5, one may in principle find that of C. Recall that sums of independently distributed random variables have a distribution that is the convolution of the component distributions:

$$P\{T_1 + T_2 \le x\} = F_{T_1} * F_{T_2}(x),$$

(12.5.2)
$$= \int_0^x F_{T_1}(x - y)f_{T_2}(y)\, dy,$$

where f_{T_2} is the density function of T_2. Also, the distribution of the maximum of three independently distributed random variables has the product form

(12.5.3) $$G(x) = P\{\max(T_3, T_4, T_5) \le x\} = F_{T_3}(x)F_{T_4}(x)F_{T_5}(x).$$

For the present example, then, we can express the distribution function of C as

(12.5.4) $$P\{C \le x\} = F_{T_1} * F_{T_2} * G(x).$$

Analysis of more complex and realistic networks will involve even more extensive combinations of the convolution and multiplicative operations. For a great many distributions of task durations, and for projects having many jobs, it will be very tedious to compute the exact distribution of C analytically—that is, in terms of neat formulas. Thus the simulation of network completion times suggests itself as an approach for estimating the distribution of C.

Simulation of a network is basically the same process as that of simulating a queue. The straightforward approach is to obtain realizations of each task duration and combine to form a realization of project completion time. The process is then repeated n times, and the distribution of C is estimated, for example, by means of

(12.5.5) $$\hat{P}\{C \le x\} = \frac{\text{number of realized } C \text{ values} \le x}{n}.$$

If the expected completion time is to be estimated, the average of n independent realized completion times suggests itself: if $C^{(i)}$ is the ith simulated completion time,

(12.5.6) $$E[C] = \frac{1}{n} \sum_{i=1}^{n} C^{(i)} = \bar{C}.$$

Since the estimate $\bar{C}$ suffers from possible imprecision because of the expense of creating many network realizations, application of the variance-reduction methods of the last section is suggested.

EXAMPLE 12.5.2. To illustrate the manner in which the *antithetic-variables* method may be used, consider the very simple series network below.

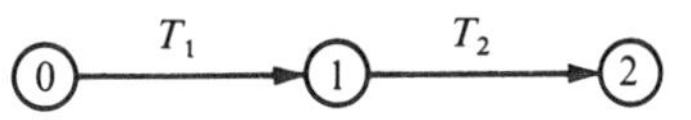

FIGURE 12.5.2

Here,

(12.5.7) $$C = T_1 + T_2.$$

To obtain one realization of C, denoted by $C^{(1)}$, obtain a realization of T_1 and another of T_2, perhaps by

(12.5.8)
$$T_1^{(1)} = F_{T_1}^{-1}(R_1),$$
$$T_2^{(1)} = F_{T_2}^{-1}(R_2),$$

where R_1 and R_2 are independent random numbers. Then

(12.5.9)
$$C^{(1)} = T_1^{(1)} + T_2^{(1)}.$$

Now an antithetic realization may be formed by creating

(12.5.10)
$$T_1^{(1)'} = F_{T_1}^{-1}(1 - R_1),$$
$$T_2^{(1)'} = F_{T_2}^{-1}(1 - R_2),$$

and

(12.5.11)
$$C^{(1)'} = T_1^{(1)'} + T_2^{(1)'}.$$

The antithetic estimate is then the average

(12.5.12)
$$C_A^{(1)} = \frac{C^{(1)} + C^{(1)'}}{2};$$

n such realizations may be obtained and averaged to estimate $E[C]$. Typically the variance of the resulting estimate is smaller than the variance of the estimate obtained by use of $2n$ independent realizations. The following example illustrates the gain for one situation.

EXAMPLE 12.5.2 (continued). Suppose that T_1 and T_2 are both exponentially distributed with unit mean and the antithetic procedure is applied. It is stated in the last section that antithetic exponentials have the covariance

(12.5.13)
$$\text{Cov}[T, T'] = 1 - \frac{\pi^2}{6} = -0.64.$$

This fact allows the variance of $\bar{C}$ to be computed exactly.

$$\text{Var}[C_A^{(1)}] = \text{Var}\left[\frac{C^{(1)} + C^{(1)'}}{2}\right],$$

(12.5.14)
$$= \frac{1}{4} \text{Var}[T_1^{(1)} + T_2^{(1)} + T_1^{(1)'} + T_2^{(1)'}],$$

$$= \frac{1}{4}\{\text{Var}[T_1^{(1)} + T_1^{(1)'}] + \text{Var}[T_2^{(1)} + T_2^{(1)'}]\},$$

since T_1 and T_2 are independent. Now

$$\text{Var}[T_1^{(1)} + T_1^{(1)'}] = \text{Var}[T_1^{(1)}] + \text{Var}[T_1^{(1)'}] + 2\,\text{Cov}[T_1^{(1)}, T_1^{(1)'}],$$

(12.5.15)
$$= 2 + 2\left(1 - \frac{\pi^2}{6}\right) = 2(0.36) = 0.72,$$

so

(12.5.16)
$$\text{Var}[C_A^{(1)}] = \frac{1}{4}\{2 \times 0.72\} = 0.36,$$

and if n such antithetic estimates are averaged,

$$(12.5.17) \qquad \text{Var}[\bar{C}_A] = \frac{0.36}{n}.$$

If, on the other hand, $2n$ straightforward estimates were averaged, the variance would be

$$(12.5.18) \qquad \text{Var}[\bar{C}] = \frac{1}{n};$$

thus the variance has been reduced by about one-third.

It should now be clear that the other methods of variance reduction described earlier, alone or in combination, are worth considering when networks are to be simulated.

EXAMPLE 12.5.3. The network depicted in Figure 12.5.3 is of more realistic size and complexity. A mathematical analysis is difficult, in particular because of the presence of the "crossing" link of duration T_{10}. If all task times have the same

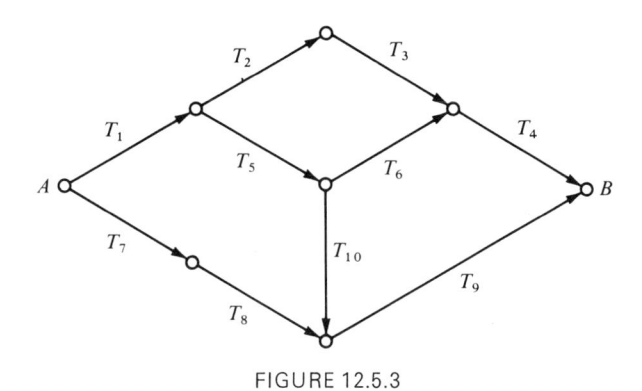

FIGURE 12.5.3

mean, which is assumed here, the partial network of Figure 12.5.4 is suggested as a means for constructing a *control* variable. Let $T_{AB}^{(C)}$ denote the completion time of the latter network. It is assumed that all task times are independently and exponentially distributed with the same mean:

$$(12.5.19) \qquad E[T_1] = E[T_2] = \cdots = E[T_{10}] = 10.$$

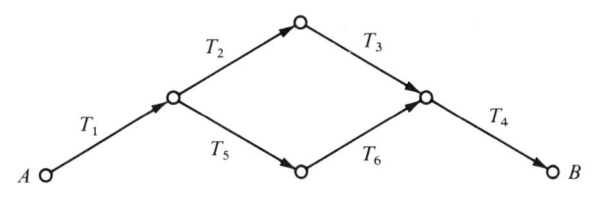

FIGURE 12.5.4

It may then be shown by mathematical analysis that

$$(12.5.20) \qquad E[T_{AB}^{(C)}] = 47.5 \qquad \mathrm{Var}[T_{AB}^{(C)}] = 418.8.$$

The steps are omitted here, but the point is that it is a great deal easier to obtain (12.5.20) analytically than it would be to carry out a comparable calculation for T_{AB}, the completion time for the full network.

The expectation of completion time for the full network was estimated by means of simulation. Figure 12.5.5 summarizes the results characteristic of $N = 50$

	Straight	Control	Control-Regression	Antithetic	Antithetic-Control
$E[T_{AB}]$	54.7	54.9	54.7	54.9	54.6
Variance of Estimate (estimated)	7.9	5.3	4.1	3.5	1.2

FIGURE 12.5.5

experiments. The last column represents a combination of antithetic and control methods. To construct the estimate, individual realizations of T_{AB} and $T_{AB}^{(C)}$ and their antithetic twins, T_{AB}' and $T_{AB}^{(C)'}$, are constructed. Then T_{AB} and T_{AB}' are averaged to give t_{AB}; $t_{AB}^{(C)}$ is similarly obtained as the average of $T_{AB}^{(C)}$ and $T_{AB}^{(C)'}$. Finally, the control estimate is

$$E[T_{AB}]_{A,C} = t_{\overline{AB}}(t_{AB}^{(C)} - E[T_{AB}^{(C)}]).$$

Many such combinations are possible. Their effectiveness for particular problems must usually be assessed by computation of the sample variance of the estimates, since exact analytical expressions are nearly always unattainable. Remember that the variance of the Monte Carlo estimates suggested here and in the last section is *not* equal to the variance of the completion time itself. Efficient estimation of $\mathrm{Var}[T_{AB}]$ from the data arising from an antithetic simulation poses problems that will not be considered here.

EXERCISES 12.5

1. A project graph appears as follows:

T_1 and T_2 are independently distributed, each having the uniform density

$$f_{T_i}(x) = \begin{cases} 0 & \text{for } x < 5 \\ 0.1 & \text{for } 5 \le x \le 15 \\ 0 & \text{for } x > 15 \end{cases}$$

(a) Calculate

$$E[C] = E[T_1] + E[T_i],$$
$$\mathrm{Var}[C] = \mathrm{Var}[T_1] + \mathrm{Var}[T_2].$$

(b) Show that if R denotes a uniform random number over $[0, 1]$, then T_i, $i = 1, 2$, may be realized as

$$T_i = 5 + 10R.$$

(c) Estimate $E[C]$ by straightforward sampling. Use a sample size (number of independent realizations of C) equal to 20. Use as the estimate of T_1 the mean of the outcomes of the sample realizations (alternatively, average the largest and smallest outcomes alone and compare to the more conventional estimate).

(d) Obtain the variance of the estimate of (b), first by making use of the sample variance and second by using the exact variance calculated in (a).

2. Continue with the example of Exercise 1.

   (a) Carry out ten straightforward simulations of C and their antithetic twins. Average to obtain an estimate of $E[C]$. Compare to the analytical result obtained in part (a) of Exercise 1.

   (b) Form an estimate of the probability that $C \leq 12.5$, using the straightforward sampling procedure of Exercise 1 and the antithetic realizations of (a) above. Use (12.5.5) to form the estimate. (*Comment:* It would be interesting for an entire class to obtain estimates of the probability above and then compare results.)

3. Write a computer program to simulate the completion time of the network of Figure 12.5.3. Do the same for the control network of Figure 12.5.4. Show that the completion time of the latter may be expressed as

$$T_{AB}^{(C)} = T_1 + \max(T_2 + T_3, T_5 + T_6) + T_4.$$

What is the corresponding expression for the completion time of Figure 12.5.3?

4. The following strategy for scheduling jobs is called "round robin." It is sometimes used in processing computer programs. Imagine that four jobs await service. A job is given a *quantum*, q, of processing effort; that is, it is processed during a time interval $t, t \leq q$. If the time to complete the job is less than q, then the job completes after t and three jobs remain. The processor immediately moves on to the next job. If the time to complete exceeds q, then after q elapses, processing moves on to the next job. When each of these has received at most one quantum of attention, the processor returns to the original job and the procedure repeats.

   (a) Suppose four jobs are initially present with durations X_1, X_2, X_3, X_4. X_i is uniformly distributed over the range zero to ten (minutes). Let $q = 2.5$, and estimate the expected number of job-minutes spent waiting.

   (b) Carry out the problem above when job durations are exponentially distributed having mean five.

   (c) It is realistic to assign an *overhead* time, d, to account for the delay in changing the processing activity from one job to another when a quantum time is completed. Given $d = 0.5$ minute, study the variation of expected total job-minutes of delay with variations in q by plotting a graph of estimated expected job-minutes waiting time versus q. Start with q values 0.25, 0.5, 0.75, 1.0, 2.0, 3.0. Fill in others where needed.

   (d) Carry out (c) analytically under the assumption that job times are exponentially distributed as in (b). (*Hint:* Exploit exponential memorylessness.)

5. Cars arrive at a toll gate according to a Poisson process with rate $\lambda = 20$ per hour. This means that the times between successive arrivals are exponentially distributed and have expected length three minutes. Let A_i denote the (exponentially distributed) time between arrival $i - 1$ and i. Let $N(t)$ denote the total number of cars that have arrived in a time of duration t; for example, $N(10)$ is the number of cars arriving between 8 : 00 and 8 : 10 A.M.

   (a) Construct ten realizations of $N(10)$, using the fact that $N(t) = k$ if and only if $A_1 + A_2 + \cdots + A_k < t < A_1 + A_2 + \cdots + A_k + A_{k+1}$ (the kth arrival must occur before t and the $k + 1$st after t).

   (b) Using (a), estimate

$$(1) \ P\{N(10) = 0\}, \qquad (2) \ P\{N(10) = 3\}, \qquad (3) \ E[N(10)].$$

6. A simple machine is either operative (up) or undergoing repair (down). Let U_i denote the duration of the ith up duration, and let D_i be the ith down duration. In other words, the system is up at time t, having been up at time 0, if

(i) $U_1 > t$

or

(ii) $U_1 + D_1 < t < U_1 + D_1 + U_2$

or

(iii) $U_1 + D_1 + U_2 + D_2 < t < U_1 + D_1 + U_2 + D_2 + U_3$

....

Furthermore, let the distribution of up and down times be given by

$$P\{U_1 > x\} = e^{-x}$$

and

$$P\{D_i > y\} = e^{-2y},$$

and let the state variable be

$$N(t) = \begin{cases} 1 \text{ if the machine is up} \\ 0 \text{ if the machine is down} \end{cases}$$

(a) Construct 10 realizations of $N(t)$ for $0 \le t \le 15$, using the initial condition $N(0) = 1$.
(b) Estimate

$$P\{N(15)\} = 0.$$

(c) Describe how you would use the results of (a) to estimate the probability that the system is up at $t = 15$ *and* has not been down for more than a consecutive time period (down duration) longer than 0.5 for $0 \le t \le 15$. (*Hint:* Consider the fraction of realizations having the property that $N(15) = 1$ and that have no down periods greater than 0.5.)

SUGGESTED READING

Abelson, R. P. Simulation of social behavior. In G. Lindsey and E. Aronson (Eds.), *The Handbook of Social Psychology.* Vol. II. (2nd ed.) Reading, Mass.: Addison-Wesley, 1968.

Burt, J. M., and Garman, M. B. Conditional Monte Carlo: A simulation technique for stochastic network analysis. Working Paper No. 157, Western Management Science Institute, University of California, Los Angeles, February 1970.

Conway, R. W. Some tactical problems in digital simulation. *Management Science*, 1963, **10**(1), 47–61.

Fishman, G. S., and Kiviat, P. J. The analysis of simulation generated time series. *Management Science*, 1967, **13**(7), 525–557.

Fishman, G. S. Estimating sample size in computing simulation experiments. *Management Science*, 1971, **18**(1), 21–38.

Gaver, D. P. Statistical methods for improving simulation efficiency. *Proceedings of the Third Annual Conference on Applications of Simulation*, Los Angeles, December 1968.

Halton, J. A retrospective and prospective study of the Monte Carlo method. *SIAM Review*, 1970, **12**(1), 1–63.

Hammersley, J., and Handscomb, D. C. *Monte Carlo Methods.* New York: John Wiley, 1964.

Hillier, F. S., and Lieberman, G. J. *Introduction to Operations Research.* San Francisco: Holden-Day, 1967.

Maier, R. C., Newell, W. T., and Pazer, H. L. *Simulations in Business and Economics.* Englewood Cliffs, N.J.: Prentice-Hall, 1969.

Naylor, T. H., Balintfy, J. L., Burdick, D. S., and Chu, K. *Computer Simulation Techniques.* New York: John Wiley, 1966.

Naylor, T. H. (Ed.) *The Design of Computer Simulation Experiments.* Durham, N.C.: Duke University Press, 1969.

Page, E. S. Computers and congestion problems. In W. L. Smith and W. E. Wilkinson (Eds.), Proceedings of the Symposium on Congestion Theory. Chapel Hill, N.C.: University of North Carolina Press, 1964.

Page, E. S. On Monte Carlo methods in congestion problems: II. Simulation of queuing systems. *Operations Research*, 1965, **13**, 300–305.

Pasquill, F. *Atmospheric Diffusion.* Amsterdam: Van Nostrand, 1962.

Proceedings on Simulation in Business and Public Health. First Annual Conference of American Statistical Assn. (New York Area Chapter) and Public Health Assn. of New York City, 1966.

Shreider, Y. A. *Method of Statistical Testing (Monte Carlo Method).* New York: Elsevier, 1964.

Siegel, A. (Ed.) *Proceedings of the Symposium on Computer Simulation as Related to Manpower and Personnel Planning.* Washington, D.C.: Naval Personnel Research and Development Lab., 1971.

Stern, A. C. (Ed.) *Air Pollution.* Vols. I and II. New York: Academic Press, 1962.

Tocher, K. D. *The Art of Simulation.* London: English Universities Press, 1963.

Wagner, H. M. *Principles of Operations Research.* Englewood Cliffs, N.J.: Prentice-Hall, 1969.

CHAPTER 13

PROGRAMMING AND PROBABILITY APPLICATIONS

13.1   MATRIX GAME THEORY

In the first part of this book we considered deterministic optimization problems that were stated in the following form: optimize a function $f(x_1, \ldots, x_n)$ of n variables, perhaps subject to constraints. In order to apply the solution to such a problem, we had to have an application in which the person or organization modeled had control of *all* the n variables.

In the later parts of the book we also studied problems in which some of the variables were not controlled but varied randomly subject to known probability distributions. In such cases, we saw that we could "integrate out" such variables and reduce such an optimization problem to one of the first kind.

Game theory considers situations in which there are two or more players, each one of which controls some but not all of the variables of a given function or functions. In addition there may be "chance" players whose actions vary according to known distributions and can be dealt with as in the previous paragraph. In a game-theory situation, the concept of optimization does not make sense because, in order to achieve an optimum, one must have complete control of all variables. We shall see that instead of optimization principles, other concepts such as minimax principles must be sought.

Matrix game theory is a special branch of game theory in which it is assumed that there are exactly two players whose interests are diametrically opposed in the sense that what one player wins, the other player loses. In game-theory parlance, such games are called *two-person zero-sum games*. It can be shown, although we will not do so here, that every such game can be represented as a matrix game.

In order to define a matrix game, we assume there are two players, R and C. Player R controls the rows of the matrix and player C controls the columns. Suppose the matrix is m by n with entries a_{ij} as in Figure 13.1.1. If player R chooses row i and

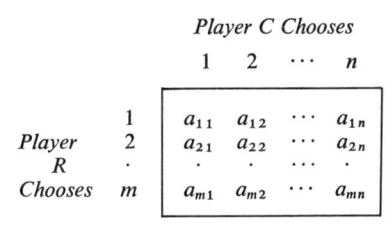

FIGURE 13.1.1

player C chooses row j, then the payoff from player C to player R is the amount a_{ij}. In case a_{ij} is positive, this represents a payment of C to R. And if a_{ij} is negative, this represents a payment of R to C.

The choices $1, 2, \ldots, m$ are called *pure strategies* for R; similarly, the choices $1, 2, \ldots, n$ are called *pure strategies* for player C. An example will make this clear.

EXAMPLE 13.1.1. There are two cities located in a predominantly rural area with no other nearby cities. About 70% of the urban population live near city 1 and the remaining 30% live near city 2. The cities are ten miles apart, as in Figure 13.1.2.

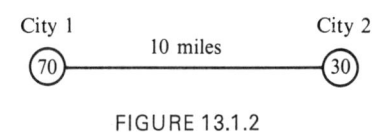

FIGURE 13.1.2

Two competing department stores, one large and one small, have decided to locate in the area. They estimate that if both are located in the same city or at the same distance from a city, the larger will get 60% of the business of that city; if the large store is closer to a city than the small store, it will get 80% of that city's business; and if the small store is closer to a city than the large store, the large store will still get 40% of that city's business.

Assuming that the stores have no other competitors in the immediate area, we can set up the payoff matrix for the various possible locations of the stores as in Figure 13.1.3, where the payoffs in the matrix represent the total percentage of business that the large store gets for a given configuration of locations of the two stores. The main diagonal entries of the matrix are easy to calculate since they correspond to both stores locating in the same city, and hence in each case, the big store will get 60% of

Small Store Location

		City 1	City 2
Big Store	*City 1*	60	68
Location	*City 2*	52	60

FIGURE 13.1.3

all business. If the big store locates in city 1 and the small store locates in city 2, then the big store gets 80% of the big city's business plus 40% of city 2's business, which gives a total of $0.8(70) + 0.4(30) = 56 + 12 = 68$. Similarly, if the big store locates in city 2 and the small store locates in city 1, the big store gets 0.8 of city 2's business and 0.4 of city 1's business for a total of $0.8(30) + 0.4(70) = 24 + 28 = 52$.

The question now is, where shall each store locate? If the big store could optimize, it would locate in city 1 and have the small store locate in city 2. But the big store can't control where the small store locates. All the big store can do is to observe that it is always better for him to locate in city 1 than in city 2, *regardless of what the small store does*: the big store always gets 8% more business by locating in city 1 rather than in city 2. Hence the big store's optimal strategy is to locate in city 1.

Now let us consider where the small store should locate. Note from Figure 13.1.3 that the small store gets all the business that the big store does not get. Hence the small store is trying to minimize the big store's outcome. Observe that if the small store locates in city 1, then *regardless of what the big store does*, it will have 8% more business (since the big store will have 8% less business) than if it located in city 2. Hence the small store's optimal strategy is also to locate in city 1.

Thus if both stores follow their optimal strategies, they will both locate in city 1, the larger, and the big store will get 60% of the business from both cities while the small store gets the remaining 40%.

The game in Figure 13.1.3 is an example of what is called a *strictly determined game* since it has a solution in pure strategies. The entry, 60, in the upper left-hand corner is the minimum entry in the first row and the maximum entry in the first column, and it is called a saddle-value entry of the matrix. The value of the game is the saddle value 60.

These concepts can be generalized to larger games.

DEFINITION 13.1.1. An entry a_{ij} of the $m \times n$ matrix game A is said to be a *saddle-value entry* of the game if it is equal to the minimum entry in the ith row and the maximum entry in the jth column. Matrix game A is *strictly determined* if and only if it has one or more saddle values. All saddle values are equal (see Exercise 2), and the value of the game is equal to the saddle value. Optimal strategies for the two players are:

For player R: Choose a *row* that contains a saddle-value entry.

For player C: Choose a *column* that contains a saddle-value entry.

The game is said to be *fair* if it has zero value.

EXAMPLE 13.1.2. Let us give another example of a strictly determined game by considering an extension of the previous example to a three-city location problem.

Suppose the three cities with their relative populations and distances are as in Figure 13.1.4. The rules for capture of business are as in the previous example. The

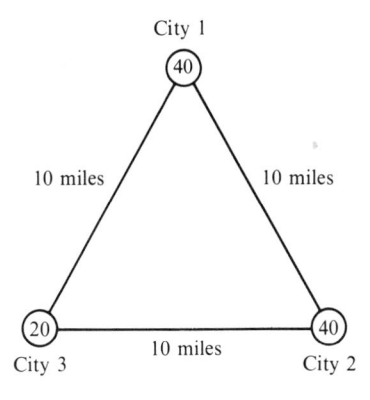

City 1

10 miles   10 miles

20   10 miles   40
City 3   City 2

FIGURE 13.1.4

calculation of the payoff matrix is as before and is given in Figure 13.1.5. In this case, notice that each of the entries of 60 in the upper left-hand 2×2 matrix is a saddle

		Small Store Location		
		City 1	City 2	City 3
Big Store	City 1	60	60	64
Location	City 2	60	60	64
	City 3	56	56	60

FIGURE 13.1.5

value since each is equal to the minimum entry in its row and also equal to the maximum entry in its column. Therefore the value of the game is 60 and the optimal strategies for each store are to locate in either city 1 or city 2.

You may wonder whether every matrix game has a saddle-value entry. A little experimentation with even 2×2 matrices will show that many matrices do not (see Exercise 3). The next example illustrates a game without a saddle value.

EXAMPLE 13.1.3. Peter and Paul are playing the following penny game. Paul holds either one or two pennies in his hand and Peter tries to guess the number. If he guesses correctly, he gets the pennies; otherwise he must give the number of pennies he guessed to Paul. The payoff matrix is shown in Figure 13.1.6. It gives the

		Paul Holds	
		1 Penny	2 Pennies
Peter	1 Penny	1	−1
Guesses	2 Pennies	−2	2

FIGURE 13.1.6

amounts Peter gets. Paul gets the negatives of these amounts. A quick examination of the matrix shows that there are no saddle-value entries.

How shall the players play a game that doesn't have saddle-value entries? It is clear that it is dangerous for Peter to always guess the same number, say one, because if he does, Paul will always hold two pennies in his hand and Peter will always lose. Similarly, it is dangerous for Paul always to hold the same number of pennies in his hand, since Peter will quickly learn what that number is and always win. The same arguments hold for either player playing according to some definite pattern such as alternating from one choice to the other each time. Even fairly complicated patterns of play will eventually be learned. Thus each player should select between his choices according to a patternless or random scheme. In other words each player should put a probability distribution on his pure-strategy choices. Such a probability distribution is called a mixed strategy.

DEFINITION 13.1.2. Let A be the payoff matrix of an $m \times n$ matrix game. A *mixed strategy* for the row player is an m-component row vector w satisfying

(13.1.1) $w \geq 0$ and $wf = 1$,

where f is a column vector of m ones. Similarly, a *mixed strategy* for the column player is an n-component column vector x satisfying

(13.1.2) $x \geq 0$ and $ex = 1$,

where e is a row vector of n ones.

Notice that a mixed strategy w puts a probability distribution on the rows of A while a mixed strategy x puts a probability distribution on the columns of A.

EXAMPLE 13.1.3 (continued). Suppose Peter uses the mixed strategy $w = [\frac{2}{3}, \frac{1}{3}]$ and Paul uses the mixed strategy $x = \begin{bmatrix} \frac{1}{2} \\ \frac{1}{2} \end{bmatrix}$. We see that

$$wA = [\tfrac{2}{3}, \tfrac{1}{3}] \begin{bmatrix} 1 & -1 \\ -2 & 2 \end{bmatrix} = [0, \ 0],$$

so Paul's expectation is zero regardless of which alternative he chooses. In other words if Peter uses this strategy he can guarantee that his expected winnings are 0 regardless of what Paul does. Similarly, we compute

$$Ax = \begin{bmatrix} 1 & -1 \\ -2 & 2 \end{bmatrix} \begin{bmatrix} \frac{1}{2} \\ \frac{1}{2} \end{bmatrix} = \begin{bmatrix} 0 \\ 0 \end{bmatrix},$$

so if Paul uses this strategy, he can guarantee that his expected losses are 0 regardless of what Peter does.

You may wonder how each player could actually implement his mixed strategy. This can be done in practice by flipping coins, spinning pointers, selecting a random number from a table, and so on.

We will call the pair of mixed strategies described above optimal for the game and we will say that the value of the game is 0, because these strategies have the property that each player, by his own actions alone, can assure himself of achieving at least the value of the game. We shall adopt a similar definition for arbitrary matrix games as follows.

DEFINITION 13.1.3. Mixed strategies w and x are optimal for the matrix game A, and v is its value if these quantities satisfy

$$(13.1.3) \qquad\qquad wA \geq ve,$$

$$(13.1.4) \qquad\qquad Ax \leq vf,$$

where e and f are as in Definition 13.1.2.

EXAMPLE 13.1.1 (continued). For the matrix game in Figure 13.1.3, the strategies

$$w = [1,\ 0] \quad \text{and} \quad x = \begin{bmatrix} 1 \\ 0 \end{bmatrix} \quad \text{and} \quad v = 60$$

are optimal because

$$wA = [1,\ 0]\begin{bmatrix} 60 & 68 \\ 52 & 60 \end{bmatrix} = [60,\ 68] \geq 60[1,\ 1] = ve$$

and also

$$Ax = \begin{bmatrix} 60 & 68 \\ 52 & 60 \end{bmatrix}\begin{bmatrix} 1 \\ 0 \end{bmatrix} = \begin{bmatrix} 60 \\ 52 \end{bmatrix} \leq 60\begin{bmatrix} 1 \\ 1 \end{bmatrix} = vf,$$

which satisfies the definition.

EXAMPLE 13.1.2 (continued). You should verify that optimal strategies for the matrix game of Figure 13.1.5 are

$$w^{(1)} = [1,\ 0,\ 0], \qquad w^{(2)} = [0,\ 1,\ 0],$$

and

$$x^{(1)} = \begin{bmatrix} 1 \\ 0 \\ 0 \end{bmatrix} \quad \text{and} \quad x^{(2)} = \begin{bmatrix} 0 \\ 1 \\ 0 \end{bmatrix}.$$

You should also check that convex combinations of optimal strategies are also optimal. For instance,

$$w = \frac{1}{4} w^{(1)} + \frac{3}{4} w^{(2)} = [\tfrac{1}{4},\ \tfrac{3}{4},\ 0]$$

and

$$x = \frac{1}{3} x^{(1)} + \frac{2}{3} x^{(2)} = \begin{bmatrix} \frac{1}{3} \\ \frac{2}{3} \\ 0 \end{bmatrix}$$

are easily shown to be optimal.

The calculations we did in Example 13.1.3 show that the strategies found there are optimal by the definition above.

In Exercise 4, formulas are derived for finding the optimal mixed strategies for any 2×2 matrix game.

In order to show that matrix games need not be square, let us work a rectangular example.

EXAMPLE 13.1.4. Peter and Paul now play the following pennies game. Paul holds from one to four pennies in his hand; Peter guesses "even" or "odd." If he guesses correctly he gets the number of pennies that Paul holds; if not, he must pay that number of pennies to Paul. The payoff matrix is easily seen to be that shown in Figure 13.1.7. How can we solve this 2×4 game that does not contain any saddle-

		Paul Holds			
		1 Penny	2 Pennies	3 Pennies	4 Pennies
Peter	Even	−1	2	−3	4
Guesses	Odd	1	−2	3	−4

FIGURE 13.1.7

value entries? One way is to take all 2×2 submatrices and find the corresponding mixed strategies from the formulas given in Exercise 10. If we do that, we find that Peter has a unique optimal strategy, namely $w = [\frac{1}{2}, \frac{1}{2}]$. However, Paul has many optimal strategies. The four that are obtained by looking at submatrices are:

$$x^{(1)} = \begin{bmatrix} \frac{2}{3} \\ \frac{1}{3} \\ 0 \\ 0 \end{bmatrix}, \quad x^{(2)} = \begin{bmatrix} 0 \\ \frac{3}{5} \\ \frac{2}{5} \\ 0 \end{bmatrix}, \quad x^{(3)} = \begin{bmatrix} 0 \\ 0 \\ \frac{4}{7} \\ \frac{3}{7} \end{bmatrix}, \quad x^{(4)} = \begin{bmatrix} \frac{4}{5} \\ 0 \\ 0 \\ \frac{1}{5} \end{bmatrix}.$$

And, of course, any convex combination of these is also optimal, as can be seen directly or else from the theorem shortly to be proved.

The inequality expressions in (13.1.1)–(13.1.4) might make you think that perhaps there is a connection between game theory and linear programming, and indeed this is the case as the following theorem and its proof indicate.

THEOREM 13.1.1. (a) For any $m \times n$ matrix game A there exists a value v and optimal strategies w and x satisfying conditions (13.1.1)–(13.1.4).

(b) The set of optimal strategies for each player is a bounded polyhedral convex set.

Proof: (a) Since the row player gets the matrix entries, he wants to make v large or, equivalently, make $-v$ small. Hence, using conditions (13.1.1) and (13.1.3), we can define the following minimizing linear programming problem:

$$\text{Min} \ -y$$

Subject to:

$$(13.1.5) \quad \begin{aligned} wA - ye &\geq 0 \\ w(-f) &= -1 \\ w &\geq 0 \end{aligned}$$

Notice that the unconstrained variable y is (temporarily) taking the place of the value variable v. Also, for reasons that will become clear, the equality constraint $wf = 1$ was multiplied through by -1, which does not affect it. Now suppose we define the dual problem to (13.1.5), using the components of x as dual variables corresponding to the constraints $wA - ye \geq 0$ and a dual variable z corresponding to the constraint $w(-f) = -1$. Using the rules for constructing dual problems, we have:

$$\text{Max} \ -z$$

Subject to:

$$(13.1.6) \quad \begin{aligned} Ax - zf &\leq 0 \\ -ex &= -1 \\ x &\geq 0 \end{aligned}$$

where z is also an unconstrained variable. Notice that the constraints $Ax - zf \leq 0$, $-ex = -1$, and $x \geq 0$ correspond to (13.1.2) and (13.1.4). (The reason that the equality constraints $wf = 1$ and $ex = 1$ were multiplied through by -1 was so that the first problem, which has $\geq$ constraints, would end up a minimizing problem and the second, with $\leq$ constraints, would be maximizing.)

The only thing wrong with the formulation so far is the fact that we have two variables, y and z, each of which plays the role of the value v in its respective problem. However, we will show that both problems have a solution, which is $y = z = v$.

To prove that (13.1.5) has a solution is easy: let w be any probability vector (that is, one that satisfies $w \geq 0$ and $wf = 1$); then choose the unconstrained variable y to be very negative—so negative that $wA - ye \geq 0$ is satisfied. In the same way, if x is any probability vector, then choosing z to be very large and positive assures that $Ax - zf \leq 0$ is satisfied.

Since both the primal and dual problems have feasible solutions, it follows that they both have optimum solutions and the duality theorem says that at the optimum the values of their objective functions are equal—that is, $-y = -z$. Hence we can choose $v = y = z$ at the optimum, and we see that the constraints of (13.1.5) and (13.1.6) are exactly those found in (13.1.1)–(13.1.4), proving that the optimum w, x, and v solve the matrix game A.

(b) The fact that the sets of optimal mixed strategies is a polyhedral convex set follows from the same theorem for linear programming problems in general. The fact that they are bounded follows from the fact that they are probability vectors.

Actually we proved more than Theorem 13.1.1 in the course of the proof above since we provided an equivalent linear programming problem whose solutions were the same as solutions to the matrix game A. The simplex method can be used to solve the linear programming problem and therefore the matrix game. The bordered rectangle for the linear programming problem is given in Figure 13.1.8.

	x_1	x_2	$\cdots$	x_n	y	
w_1	a_{11}	a_{12}	$\cdots$	a_{1n}	-1	≤ 0
w_2	a_{21}	a_{22}	$\cdots$	a_{2n}	-1	≤ 0
.	.	.	$\cdots$	.	.	.
w_m	a_{m1}	a_{m2}	$\cdots$	a_{mn}	-1	≤ 0
y	-1	-1	$\cdots$	-1	0	$=-1$
	≥ 0	≥ 0	$\cdots$	≥ 0	$=-1$	

FIGURE 13.1.8

EXAMPLE 13.1.3 (continued). Set up the initial tableau for the game of Figure 13.1.6. Following the rules above and representing each equality constraint as a pair of inequalities, we obtain the tableau shown in Figure 13.1.9. In the tableau the

x_1	x_2	z	$-z$	s_1	s_2	s_3	s_4	
1	-1	-1	1	1	0	0	0	0
-2	2	-1	1	0	1	0	0	0
-1	-1	0	0	0	0	1	0	-1
1	1	0	0	0	0	0	1	1
0	0	1	-1	0	0	0	0	0

FIGURE 13.1.9

variables s_1, s_2, s_3, and s_4 are the slack variables. Notice that the b vector is not nonnegative, so some kind of a Phase I/Phase II procedure or its equivalent is necessary to start off the computation; thus we will not do it here.

Linear programming is a very effective tool for solving matrix games; however, this need not be discussed further since it would simply repeat results given in earlier chapters.

EXAMPLE 13.1.5. Let us discuss a final, somewhat larger example. Peter and Paul each choose a number between 1 and 5, the sum is computed, and Peter gets even sums while Paul gets odd sums. The payoff matrix is given in Figure 13.1.10.

Paul Chooses

		1	2	3	4	5	
	1	2	-3	4	-5	6	
	2	-3	4	-5	6	-7	
Peter Chooses	3	4	-5	6	-7	8	$=A$
	4	-5	6	-7	8	-9	
	5	6	-7	8	-9	10	

FIGURE 13.1.10

In the matrix there are 12 positive entries that sum to 86 and 12 negative entries that sum to -72. Hence it is not clear whether or not the game is fair. However, it turns out that the value is zero so the game is fair. Because the game is symmetric and $v = 0$, optimal strategies for the row and column players are the same. Two such optimal strategies for Peter are

$$w^{(1)} = [\tfrac{1}{4}, \tfrac{1}{2}, \tfrac{1}{4}, 0, 0],$$
$$w^{(2)} = [\tfrac{1}{8}, 0, 0, \tfrac{1}{2}, \tfrac{3}{8}],$$

as you can easily check.

EXERCISES 13.1

1. Show that the following games are strictly determined and find their values and optimal strategies.

(a)
10	1	8	1
3	1	4	1
-1	0	12	1

(b)
3	5
1	12

(c)
3	5
1	-12

(d)
-1	2	0	-1
-7	9	10	0
-1	2	5	-1

2. Suppose a matrix game A is strictly determined with a saddle-value entry at a_{11} and a_{33}.
   (a) Show that $a_{11} = a_{33}$.
   (b) Show that $a_{13} = a_{31} = a_{11}$.
   (c) Prove, in general, that all saddle values are equal.

3. For the 2×2 matrix game,

a	b
c	d

   show that it is *not* strictly determined if and only if a and d are either both bigger than or both smaller than b and c. (This condition is called *separation of diagonals*.)

4. If the 2×2 game

a	b
c	d

   is not strictly determined, show that the following formulas give the optimal strategies and value for the game:

$$w_1 = \frac{d-c}{a+d-b-c} \qquad w_2 = \frac{a-b}{a+d-b-c}$$

$$x_1 = \frac{d-b}{a+d-b-c} \qquad x_2 = \frac{a-c}{a+d-b-c}$$

$$v = \frac{ad-bc}{a+d-b-c}$$

5. Use the formulas of Exercise 4 to solve the following games:

(a)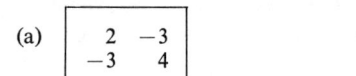

(b)

(c)

6. Paul offers to play the following game with Peter: "You take a red ace and a black deuce and I'll take a red deuce and a black trey; we will simultaneously show one of the cards; if the colors don't match, you pay me, and if the colors match, I'll pay you; moreover if you play the red ace, we will exchange the difference of the numbers on the cards; but if you play the black deuce, we will exchange the sum of the numbers. Since you will pay me either \$2 or \$4 if you lose and I will pay you either \$1 or \$5 if I lose, the game is obviously fair." Show that this game is not fair and that Paul will win, on the average, 25¢ each time it is played. Find the optimal strategies.

*7. A square matrix game is said to be *symmetric* if $a_{ij} = a_{ji}$, for $i, j = 1, \ldots, n$. Show that if the value of a symmetric game is zero, and any optimal strategy for the row player is also optimal for the column player, then $w^o A = 0$ and $A(w^o)' = 0$.

8. Rework Example 13.1.2 with the following diagram indicating distances between and populations of the three cities:

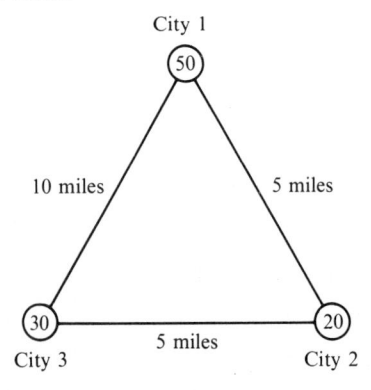

9. (a) Show that the 2×4 matrix game in Example 13.1.4 has six 2×2 subgames.
(b) Solve each of the subgames found in (a) and determine which of these solutions give solutions to the original game. Verify that the four optimal strategies mentioned in the example can be found this way.

10. Show that the two optimal strategies mentioned in Example 13.1.5 actually solve the game described there.

11. A matrix game A is said to be *skew-symmetric* if $a_{ij} = -a_{ji}$, for $i, j = 1, \ldots, n$.
(a) Show that if w is a probability vector such that $wA \geq v$ and x is the transpose of w, then $Ax \leq v$.
(b) Use (a) to show that the value of a skew-symmetric matrix game is always zero.
(c) Show that optimal strategies for the row and column players are transposes.

*12. Theorem 13.1.1 states that every matrix game has a solution. This is the so-called minimax theorem of the theory of games. The following steps show why the name "minimax theorem" is appropriate. Let w^o, x^o, and v be optimal mixed strategies and value for the matrix game A.
(a) Show that $w^o A x^o = v$.

(b) Show that $v = \min_j (w^oA)_j$, where $(w^oA)_j$ is the jth column of w^oA.

(c) Show that $v = \min_j \max_w (wA)_j$, where $(wA)_j$ is the jth column of wA.

(d) Show that $v = \min_x \max_w wAx$.

(e) By a similar series of steps, show that $v = \max_w \min_x wAx$.

(f) Use steps (a)–(e) to prove the *minimax theorem*: for any matrix A there exist probability vectors w^o and x^o such that

$$\max_w \min_x wAx = w^oAx^o = \min_x \max_w wAx.$$

*13. Use the theorem of the alternative to show that if w^o, x^o, and v are the optimal strate-gies and value of the matrix game A, then:

(a) If $(w^oA)_j > v$, then $x_j{}^o = 0$, where $(w^oA)_j$ is the jth column of w^oA.

(b) If $(Ax^o)_i < v$, then $w_i{}^o = 0$, where $(Ax^o)_i$ is the ith row of Ax^o.

13.2 CHANCE-CONSTRAINED PROGRAMMING

In the earlier parts of this book we have not considered the problem of obtaining the exact values of the coefficients of a linear programming problem. In actual practice this may be a difficult task, sometimes even impossible. Some coefficients are easy to determine because they reflect a physical situation such as a pipeline constraint. But other coefficients may, in fact, be random variables. For instance, demand for a product or the output of an agricultural plot may vary in a random way. There have been several different approaches to the problem of incorporating random variables as coefficients of a linear programming problem, and in each case very difficult technical problems have been encountered. We shall treat one special case here, namely the chance-constrained programming model of Charnes and Cooper. In Section 13.5 we shall treat another approach—linear programming with recourse. Still others may be found in the literature cited at the end of the chapter.

In order to construct an example of chance-constrained programming we will find it necessary to invert a probability distribution. Therefore we digress to discuss an example before we go on to define chance-constrained programming.

EXAMPLE 13.2.1. It is easy to see that the function

$$(13.2.1) \qquad F(x) = \begin{cases} 0 & \text{for } x < d - l \\ \dfrac{1}{2}\sqrt[3]{(x - d)/l} + \dfrac{1}{2} & \text{for } d - l \le x \le d + l \\ 1 & \text{for } d + l < x \end{cases}$$

is a symmetric distribution with mean d. It is pictured in Figure 13.2.1. We have chosen an algebraic distribution function in order to be able to carry out the inversion explicitly. The curve in the figure is the graph of the equation $y = F(x)$. Suppose now we have a specific value of y, where $0 \le y \le 1$. What argument x is such that $y = F(x)$? By definition of the inverse function, the answer is $x = F^{-1}(y)$; that is, the value of the inverse function F^{-1} at y is that argument x such that $F(x) = y$. This is illustrated in Figure 13.2.1. Suppose now we regard y as the independent variable and x as the

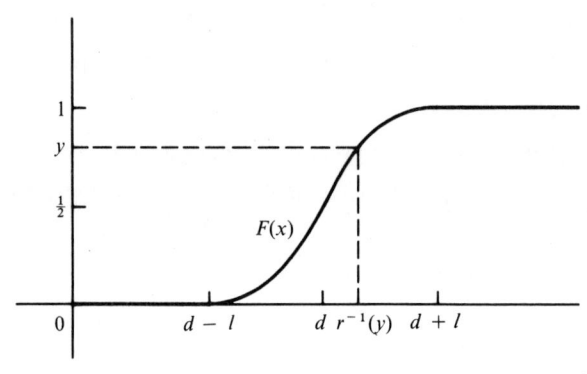

FIGURE 13.2.1

dependent variable and plot the graph of $x = F^{-1}(y)$ for $0 \leq y \leq 1$. First we solve equation (13.2.1) for x in terms of y, obtaining

$$(13.2.2) \qquad x = F^{-1}(y) = d + l(2y - 1)^3 \qquad \text{for } 0 \leq y \leq 1.$$

The graph of $F^{-1}(y)$ is shown in Figure 13.2.2. Notice that it is just the graph of $y = F(x)$ reflected through the 45° line.

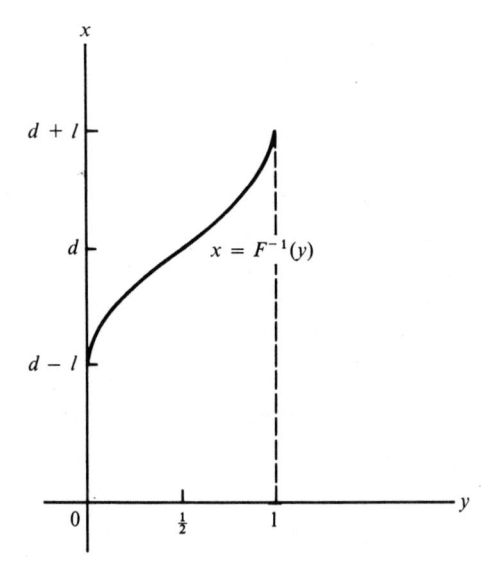

FIGURE 13.2.2

In principle, any probability distribution can be similarly inverted. Of course, it is not always possible to find an algebraic expression such as (13.2.2) for the inverse function, but it is always possible to compute a table of the inverse function that will serve the same purpose.

In order to state a chance-constrained programming problem, let us start with an ordinary linear programming problem in minimizing form:

$$\text{Min } wb = \sum_{i=1}^{m} w_i b_i$$

(13.2.3)   Subject to:

$$\sum_{i=1}^{m} w_i a_{ij} \geq c_j$$

where we have included the nonnegativity constraints in the A matrix. We have written the problem in summation form because we want to look at individual constraints. Suppose now that the a_{ij}'s and b_i's are known fixed numbers but that the right-hand sides, the c_j's, are random variables with known independent probability distributions $F_j(z)$. In other words,

(13.2.4) $$P[c_j \leq z] = F_j(z).$$

Note that the constraints in (13.2.3) are meaningless because it is in general impossible to choose the w_i's so that they are satisfied for all possible outcomes of the random variables c_j. However, we can replace the constraints by

(13.2.5) $$P\left[\sum_{i=1}^{m} w_i a_{ij} \geq c_j\right] \geq \alpha_j,$$

where $0 < \alpha_j \leq 1$ is a number that measures the "probability of achieving the jth constraint." We can also define

(13.2.6) $$\rho_j = 1 - \alpha_j,$$

which is the "probability or risk of not achieving the jth constraint." It must be emphasized that when we replace the constraint of (13.2.3) by (13.2.5) we have given up the requirement that all constraints must always be satisfied. Sometimes they are satisfied, sometimes not, depending on the actual realization of the random variable c_j.

Thus we derive from (13.2.3) the following *chance-constrained programming problem*:

$$\text{Min } \sum_{i=1}^{m} w_i b_i$$

(13.2.7)   Subject to:

$$P\left[\sum_{i=1}^{m} w_i a_{ij} \geq c_j\right] \geq \alpha_j$$

Now how do we solve this problem? The techniques of ordinary linear programming simply cannot handle chance constraints. However, if we rewrite (13.2.5) and use (13.2.4), we see that (13.2.5) becomes

(13.2.8) $$P\left[c_j \leq \sum_{i=1}^{m} w_i a_{ij}\right] = F_j\left(\sum_{i=1}^{m} w_i a_{ij}\right) \geq \alpha_j.$$

Now we use the fact mentioned earlier that a probability distribution function $F_j(z)$ can be inverted, and we rewrite (13.2.8) as

(13.2.9) $$\sum_{i=1}^{m} w_i a_{ij} \geq F^{-1}(\alpha_j)$$

and note that this is an ordinary inequality constraint of the type we are very familiar with. Constraint (13.2.9) is called the *deterministic equivalent* for the probabilistic constraint (13.2.5). Notice that the derivation above can be carried through in every case in which the F_j's are independent distributions.

We can now replace the chance-constrained programming problem of (13.2.7) by its *deterministic equivalent*, the ordinary linear programming problem below.

$$\text{Min} \sum_{i=1}^{m} w_i b_i$$

(13.2.10)   Subject to:

$$\sum_{i=1}^{m} w_i a_{ij} \geq F^{-1}(\alpha_j)$$

This problem can be solved by ordinary techniques.

EXAMPLE 13.2.2. Let us apply the techniques above to the critical-path example of Section 5.1. In Example 5.1.1, we had a six-job project in which each job had known completion times. Suppose, as often is the case, that the times for the individual jobs are not known exactly but that only a probability distribution for each is known. Specifically, we shall assume that for each job in the project, we know a crash time, $d - l$, and a pessimistic time, $d + l$, and that the actual job times are distributed between these two times according to the probability distribution (13.2.1). The actual data are shown in Figure 13.2.3, and the project graph is shown again in Figure 13.2.4.

Job	Crash Time	Pessimistic Time	d	l	$F_j(z)$
T_1	9	29	19	10	$(\frac{1}{2})\sqrt[3]{(z-19)/10}$
T_2	8	18	13	5	$(\frac{1}{2})\sqrt[3]{(z-13)/5}$
T_3	1	3	2	1	$(\frac{1}{2})\sqrt[3]{(z-2)/1}$
T_4	19	31	25	6	$(\frac{1}{2})\sqrt[3]{(z-25)/6}$
T_5	21	53	37	16	$(\frac{1}{2})\sqrt[3]{(z-37)/16}$
T_6	7	27	17	10	$(\frac{1}{2})\sqrt[3]{(z-17)/10}$

FIGURE 13.2.3

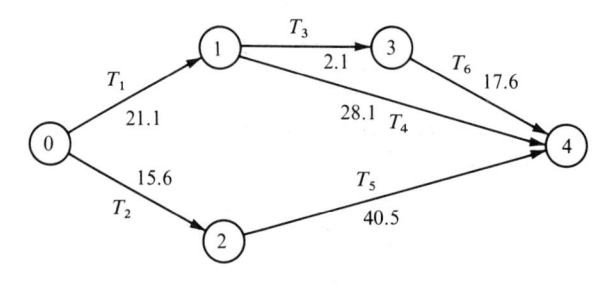

FIGURE 13.2.4

Now let us state the problem given in (5.1.2) as a chance constrained programming problem with given achievement levels. We set $w_0 = 0$ and have the following problem.

$$\text{Min } w_4$$

Subject to:

(13.2.11)

$$
\begin{aligned}
P[\; w_1 \qquad\qquad\qquad &\geq T_1] \geq 0.8 \\
P[\qquad + w_2 \qquad\qquad &\geq T_2] \geq 0.9 \\
P[-w_1 \qquad + w_3 \qquad &\geq T_3] \geq 0.7 \\
P[-w_1 \qquad\qquad + w_4 &\geq T_4] \geq 0.9 \\
P[\qquad - w_2 \qquad + w_4 &\geq T_5] \geq 0.8 \\
P[\qquad\qquad - w_3 + w_4 &\geq T_6] \geq 0.7
\end{aligned}
$$

Notice that we have six chance constraints with distributions as given in Figure 13.2.3. Now we use formula (13.2.2) to invert each of the distributions as shown in Figure 13.2.5. These calculations are very easy to do if one uses the fact that $(0.4)^3 = 0.064$, $(0.6)^3 = 0.216$, $(0.8)^3 = 0.512$.

Job	d	l	$F^{-1}(z)$	α_j	$F_j^{-1}(\alpha_j)$
T_1	19	10	$19 + 10(2y - 1)^3$	0.8	21.1
T_2	13	5	$13 + 5(2y - 1)^3$	0.9	15.6
T_3	2	1	$2 + (2y - 1)^3$	0.7	2.1
T_4	25	6	$25 + 6(2y - 1)^3$	0.9	28.1
T_5	37	16	$37 + 16(2y - 1)^3$	0.8	40.5
T_6	17	10	$17 + 10(2y - 1)^3$	0.7	17.6

FIGURE 13.2.5

We can now state the deterministic equivalent problem to (13.2.11) as follows.

$$\text{Min } w_4$$

Subject to:

(13.2.12)

$$
\begin{aligned}
w_1 \qquad\qquad\qquad &\geq 21.1 \\
w_2 \qquad\qquad &\geq 15.6 \\
-w_1 \qquad + w_3 \qquad &\geq 2.1 \\
-w_1 \qquad\qquad + w_4 &\geq 28.1 \\
- w_2 \qquad + w_4 &\geq 40.5 \\
- w_3 + w_4 &\geq 17.6
\end{aligned}
$$

Note that (13.2.12) is an ordinary critical-path problem. The times are marked on Figure 13.2.4, and it is easy to see that the longest path consists of 0–2, 2–4 and involves only jobs T_2 and T_5. Notice also that because this path is considerably longer than the other two paths, it is possible to set higher levels of achievement for the other jobs. In fact, on each path except the critical path, it is possible to set at least one achievement level equal to 1. This is discussed in Exercise 1.

There are many other variations of the chance-constrained programming model, which include variations on the form of the objective function and more complicated decision rules. Refer to the cited literature for details.

EXERCISES 13.2

1. Redo Example 13.2.2 with the following changes:
   (a) $\alpha_1 = 1$, all other α_j's the same.
   (b) $\alpha_3 = 1$, all other α_j's the same.
   (c) $\alpha_4 = \alpha_6 = 1$, all other α_j's the same.

2. Redo Example 13.2.2 with the distribution functions

$$F_j(z) = \begin{cases} 0 & \text{for } z < d - l \\ \dfrac{1}{2}\,[(x-d)/l]^3 + \dfrac{1}{2} & \text{for } d - l \leq z \leq d + l \\ 1 & \text{for } d + l < z \end{cases}$$

and the achievement levels

$$\alpha_1 = 0.6, \qquad \alpha_2 = 0.7, \qquad \alpha_3 = 0.5, \qquad \alpha_4 = 0.8, \qquad \alpha_5 = 0.7, \qquad \alpha_6 = 0.6.$$

3. Show that the derivative of (13.2.1) does not exist when $x = d$, but that it exists everywhere else.

4. Derive the dual problems for (13.2.3) and for (13.2.10), and give interpretations in each case.

5. Find the deterministic equivalent for the following chance-constrained programming problem in maximizing form:

$$\text{Max} \sum_{j=1}^{n} c_j x_j$$

Subject to:

$$P\left[\sum_{j=1}^{n} a_{ij} x_j \leq b_j\right] \geq \alpha_j$$

Assume that the distributions of the b_j's are given by $F_j(z)$ and that these are independent.

6. Discuss a chance-constrained programming version of the shortest-path problem of Section 5.1 in which the lengths of the paths of the network are random variables with known independent distributions.

7. For the maximal-flow problem of Section 5.1, discuss a chance-constrained-programming version in which the capacities of the arcs are random variables with known independent distributions.

13.3   MARKOV DECISION THEORY

In many situations the effects of making a given decision may not be known exactly but merely probabilistically. For instance, when a new machine is purchased, its length of life may not be known exactly, but a probability distribution of lifetimes may be available. Also, when making an inventory decision, the exact demand that will occur during the next month is unknown, but past demands can be used to make probabilistic predictions. Markov decision theory, developed by R. Howard, provides a framework in which to analyze these situations. As we shall see, Markov decision models can be solved by either dynamic programming or linear programming techniques. We will discuss the various solution approaches here, together with their advantages and disadvantages.

Consider a situation in which a process can be in exactly one of r different states at each time. We label these states $0, 1, \ldots, r - 1$. In each state i there is a set $D(i)$ of possible decisions that can be taken, and if decision d in $D(i)$ is made, there is probability p_{ij}^d of moving from state i to state j, where

$$(13.3.1) \qquad \sum_{j=0}^{r-1} p_{ij}^d = 1.$$

In other words, we must go from state i to some other state on the next move. We also assume that there is a certain cost c_i^d of making decision d when in state i. For instance, the cost might be that of producing a certain number of goods of a given kind. Finally, we assume there is a discount factor α that is used to discount future profits.

EXAMPLE 13.3.1. A certain manufacturing company has a warehouse that can stock up to five units of a given product. It has found that the demand for its product is as follows:

Number:	0	1	2
Probability:	$\dfrac{1}{4}$	$\dfrac{1}{2}$	$\dfrac{1}{4}$

When the company reorders, there is a setup cost of 10 plus a variable cost of 1 per unit. Delivery takes one time period. Company policy dictates that there should always be enough on hand to meet any demand and that when reordering, either 2 or 3 units should be ordered. Finally, there is a storage charge of \$1 per unit per time period on goods in inventory, and $\alpha = 0.8$.

Let us set this up as a Markov decision problem. There are six states, 0, 1, 2, 3, 4, and 5, representing the number of units currently in inventory. When in state i, the manufacturer can decide to produce d units (provided $2 \le d + i \le 5$) at a cost of $c_i^d = 10 + 2d$, where d is 2 or 3. Since the new goods arrive at the end of the time period in question, the probabilities of moving to other states are given by:

$$p_{i, i+d}^d = \frac{1}{4}, \qquad p_{i, i+d-1}^d = \frac{1}{2}, \qquad p_{i, i+d-2}^d = \frac{1}{4}.$$

Figure 13.3.1 gives the possible state-decision pairs, i, d, and the corresponding probabilities of moving to each of the other states j. The most important thing to notice about the table is that *if we make a unique decision for each state i, then we obtain an ordinary Markov chain.* Such a unique decision for each state i is called a *stationary policy,* and we shall consider only solutions involving stationary policies.

		State j					
i	d	0	1	2	3	4	5
0	2	$\frac{1}{4}$	$\frac{1}{2}$	$\frac{1}{4}$	0	0	0
	3	0	$\frac{1}{4}$	$\frac{1}{2}$	$\frac{1}{4}$	0	0
1	2	0	$\frac{1}{4}$	$\frac{1}{2}$	$\frac{1}{4}$	0	0
	3	0	0	$\frac{1}{4}$	$\frac{1}{2}$	$\frac{1}{4}$	0
2	0	$\frac{1}{4}$	$\frac{1}{2}$	$\frac{1}{4}$	0	0	0
	2	0	0	$\frac{1}{4}$	$\frac{1}{2}$	$\frac{1}{4}$	0
	3	0	0	0	$\frac{1}{4}$	$\frac{1}{2}$	$\frac{1}{4}$
3	0	0	$\frac{1}{4}$	$\frac{1}{2}$	$\frac{1}{4}$	0	0
	2	0	0	0	$\frac{1}{4}$	$\frac{1}{2}$	$\frac{1}{4}$
4	0	0	0	$\frac{1}{4}$	$\frac{1}{2}$	$\frac{1}{4}$	0
5	0	0	0	0	$\frac{1}{4}$	$\frac{1}{2}$	$\frac{1}{4}$

FIGURE 13.3.1

Since there are two decisions in states 0, 1, and 3 and three possible decisions in state 2 (and only one decision in each of states 4 and 5), there are, in all, $2 \times 2 \times 2 \times 3 = 24$ possible stationary policies. In Exercise 1, we ask for enumeration of the 24 resulting Markov chains. Although it is not true that each of these Markov chains is regular, it is true that each has a unique fixed vector on the left (see Exercise 2). Hence this fixed vector gives the long-run behavior for each stationary policy.

DEFINITION 13.3.1. Consider a Markov decision process with r states and decision sets $D(i)$ for each state i. By a *stationary policy*, we mean a unique decision $d(i)$ in $D(i)$. By a *regular Markov decision process* we mean one in which each Markov chain corresponding to a stationary policy has a unique fixed vector on the left.

The important thing to notice about a stationary policy is that it does not depend on time. A nonstationary policy makes a unique decision $d(i, t)$ in $D(i)$ for each state i and time t. In other words, a nonstationary policy makes a decision depend on the state i and the time t: the decision made in state i may be different at different times. Given a stationary or nonstationary policy and a discount factor α, it is possible to calculate the expected discounted cost of the policy.

THEOREM 13.3.1. A regular Markov decision process always has an optimal (lowest expected cost) solution that is stationary.

We shall not prove this theorem here; instead refer to the bibliography at the end of the chapter.

In order to further analyze Markov decision processes we make a definition.

DEFINITION 13.3.2. For each state $i = 0, 1, \ldots, r - 1$, we define x_i to be the expected discounted cost of being in state i when the optimal (stationary) policy is used.

THEOREM 13.3.2. The numbers x_i satisfy the following:

(13.3.2)
$$x_i = \operatorname*{Minimize}_{d \text{ in } D(i)} \left\{ c_i^d + \alpha \sum_{j=0}^{r-1} p_{ij}^d x_j \right\}.$$

Proof: Assume we are in state i. For each decision d in $D(i)$, we incur (with certainty) the cost c_i^d plus the expected costs

$$\sum_{j=0}^{r-1} p_{ij}^d x_j$$

on moving to the next state. Discounting the latter by multiplying by α gives the expression in the braces of (13.3.2). Finally, in order for the stationary policy to be optimal, it must select a decision d in $D(i)$ that minimizes these expressions.

Notice that if we knew the optimal stationary policy $d(i)$, then the x_i's would satisfy the following equations:

(13.3.3)
$$x_i - \alpha \sum_{j=0}^{r-1} p_{ij}^{d(i)} x_j = c_i^{d(i)}.$$

The two expressions (13.3.2) and (13.3.3) have given rise to two different methods for solving for the x_i's, namely, the *value-iteration method* and the *policy-iteration method*. Both of these techniques are generally employed in dynamic programming.

The flow diagram for the value-iteration method is shown in Figure 13.3.2. Notice that the computation in the main step of the program only involves finding the minimum of a finite set of numbers, which is very fast. Also, the memory requirements for a computer program for this method are small because the previous values of the x_i's are all that must be remembered. It can be shown that the value-iteration method will converge for regular Markov decision processes, but that in general the convergence is not finite. However, experience has shown that this computational process finds the optimal policy after a relatively few steps, and the rest of the computation is needed only if very accurate estimates of the x_i's are required.

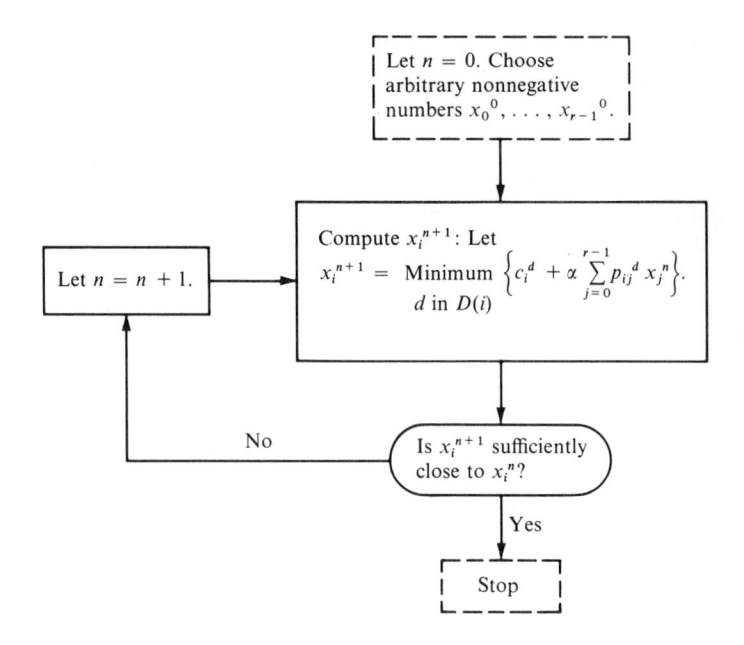

FIGURE 13.3.2. The value-iteration method for Markov decision processes

As we saw in Example 13.3.1, the number of stationary policies is the product of the number of possible decisions at each state. It is not hard to see that for a realistic inventory problem, the number of stationary policies can easily run into the thousands or millions (see Exercise 3). Hence, the value-iteration method is probably the best for very large problems.

The flow diagram for the policy-iteration method for Markov decision process is shown in Figure 13.3.3. Notice that it begins by choosing an arbitrary policy. Then it temporarily assumes that it is optimal so that the corresponding x_i's can be determined by solving (13.3.3). Then the method uses these x_i's to check to see if the current policy is optimal. If it is, it will satisfy (13.3.2). If not, we use (13.3.2) to select the next trial policy.

It can be shown that the policy-iteration method converges in a finite number of steps, and so it would seem that it should be superior to the value-iteration method. However, notice that the amount of computational effort required to go around the loop of Figure 13.3.3 is considerably more than that required for Figure 13.3.2 because, each time, a set of r equations in r unknowns must be solved. This also means that the memory requirements for a computer program are greater, since solving simultaneous equations requires a fairly large working memory.

However, if the number of states (that is, r) is small, the policy-iteration method will easily fit into the memory space of current computers, and the computation time will be very reasonable. Hence the policy-iteration method is preferable for small problems having values of r up to perhaps 1000.

Still another technique that is available for solving Markov decision problems for $r \leq 1000$ is linear programming. This may be a little surprising since equation (13.3.1) looks like a nonlinear problem. However, the following example shows that

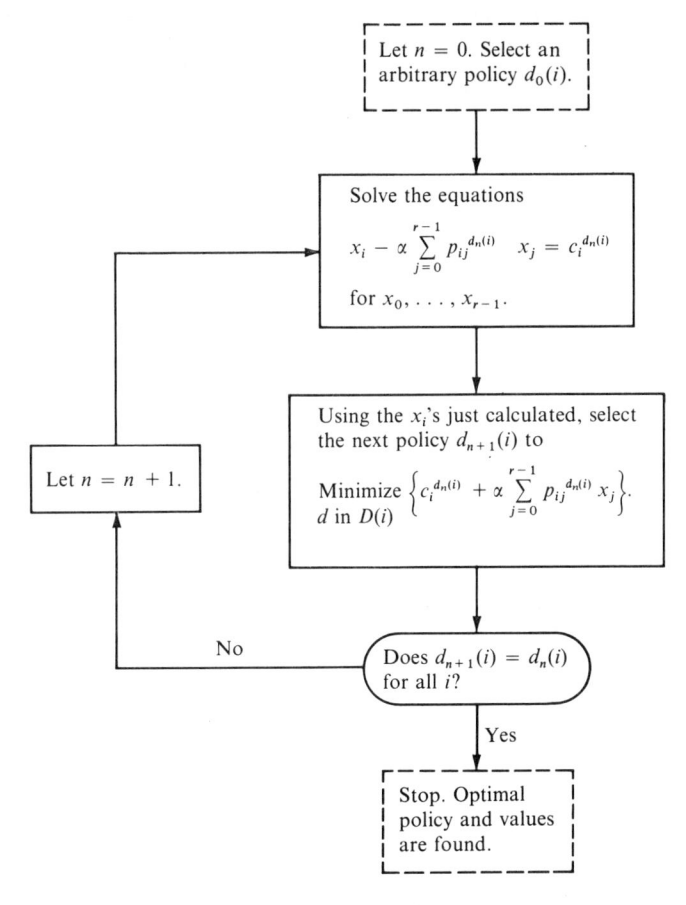

FIGURE 13.3.3. The policy-iteration method for Markov decision processes

the problem of selecting the minimum of a finite set of numbers can be formulated as a linear programming problem.

EXAMPLE 13.3.2. Suppose we have the problem of finding the minimum of the finite set of numbers $\{15, 8, 21, 7\}$. One way of doing this is to solve the following linear programming problem:

$$\text{Max } x$$

Subject to:

$$(13.3.4) \qquad x \le 15$$
$$x \le 8$$
$$x \le 21$$
$$x \le 7$$

This is obvious since the four constraints say that x must be less than each of the numbers in the set and the objective function is to make x as large as possible; hence the optimal solution is to make x exactly equal to the smallest number, which in this case is obviously 7. The dual problem to (13.3.4) is as follows.

$$\text{Min } 15w_1 + 8w_2 + 21w_3 + 7w_4$$

(13.3.5)   Subject to:

$$w_1 + w_2 + w_3 + w_4 = 1$$
$$w_1, w_2, w_3, w_4 \geq 0$$

The solution here is also obvious: set $w_4 = 1$ and $w_1 = w_2 = w_3 = 0$. Notice that here exactly one of the dual variables is positive and the rest are zero.

Although Example 13.3.2 seems very trivial, we are going to use the idea that it represents to solve the minimization equation (13.3.2) by means of linear programming. To do this we note first that (13.3.2) implies that the x_i's must satisfy each of the following inequalities:

(13.3.6) $$x_i - \sum_{j=0}^{r-1} p_{ij}^{\,d}x_j \leq c_i^{\,d} \qquad \text{for all } i \text{ and all } d \text{ in } D(i).$$

This set of inequalities can be rewritten in a slightly different way by defining δ_{ij} to be

(13.3.7) $$\delta_{ij} = 1 \quad \text{if } i = j \quad \text{and} \quad \delta_{ij} = 0 \quad \text{if } i \neq j.$$

Then (13.3.5) is the same as

(13.3.8) $$\sum_{j=0}^{r-1} (\delta_{ij} - \alpha p_{ij}^{\,d})x_j \leq c_i^{\,d} \qquad \text{for all } i \text{ and all } d \text{ in } D(i).$$

One way to choose the x_i's to satisfy (13.3.8) is to make them all zero, but that would not solve (13.3.2). Hence we use the trick employed in Example 13.3.2 above; we choose arbitrary positive numbers $s_0, s_1, \ldots, s_{r-1}$ and define the following linear programming problem.

$$\text{Max } \sum_{j=0}^{r-1} s_j x_j$$

(13.3.9)   Subject to:

$$\sum_{j=0}^{r-1} (\delta_{ij} - \alpha p_{ij}^{\,d})x_j \leq c_i^{\,d} \qquad \text{for all } i \text{ and all } d \text{ in } D(i)$$

As in Example 13.3.2, it is easy to show that a solution to (13.3.9) is a solution to (13.3.2) and vice versa. By the usual rules, the dual to (13.3.9) is given by (13.3.10).

$$\text{Min } \sum_{i=0}^{r-1} \sum_{d \text{ in } D(i)} w_i^{\,d} c_i^{\,d}$$

(13.3.10)   Subject to:

$$\sum_{i=0}^{r-1} \sum_{d \text{ in } D(i)} w_i^{\,d}(\delta_{ij} - \alpha p_{ij}^{\,d}) = s_j \qquad w^d \geq 0$$

In the problem of (13.3.10), $w_i^{\,d}$ is the dual variable corresponding to the constraint in (13.3.9) for state i and decision d in $D(i)$. As in Example 13.3.2, the solution to the dual problem (13.3.10) will have exactly *one* w_i^d positive for d in $D(i)$, and this positive dual variable indicates the correct choice for the optimal policy when the process is in state i. Let us return to the first example to see this.

EXAMPLE 13.3.1 (continued). The bordered matrix for the dual linear programs for the example is given in Figure 13.3.4. In order to explain the numbers, note

	x_0	x_1	x_2	x_3	x_4	x_5	
w_0^2	.8	-.4	-.2	0	0	0	≤ 13
w_0^3	1	-.2	-.4	-.2	0	0	≤ 15
w_1^2	0	.8	-.4	-.2	0	0	≤ 14
w_1^3	0	1	-.2	-.4	-.2	0	≤ 16
w_2^0	-.2	-.4	.8	0	0	0	≤ 1
w_2^2	0	0	.8	-.4	-.2	0	≤ 15
w_2^3	0	0	1	-.2	-.4	-.2	≤ 16
w_3^0	0	-.2	-.4	.8	0	0	≤ 2
w_3^2	0	0	1	-.2	-.4	-.2	≤ 16
w_4^0	0	0	-.2	-.4	.8	0	≤ 3
w_5^0	0	0	0	-.2	-.4	.8	≤ 4
	1	1	1	1	1	1	1

FIGURE 13.3.4

first of all that all of the s_i's have been set equal to 1. Second, the c_i^d numbers are calculated as a combination of production cost plus expected inventory holding cost; for instance, the 13 in the first row consists of the cost 12 of producing two units plus 1 for the holding cost for the mean inventory of 1 unit. The solution to this linear programming problem is given in Figure 13.3.5. Also, the optimal dual solution

State i	Expected Discounted Cost, x_i
0	40.05
1	37.82
2	30.19
3	27.05
4	24.83
5	24.17

FIGURE 13.3.5

produced positive values for the variables w_0^3, w_1^3, w_2^0, w_3^0, w_4^0, and w_5^0 and zero values for the other dual variables. Therefore the optimal stationary policy is to order three units when in states 0 and 1 and to order nothing when in each of the other states. In Exercise 7, you will be asked to set up the problem when the order can be either two, three, or four units.

Intuitively, the solution in Figure 13.3.5 seems quite reasonable since $\alpha = 0.8$ means that we are discounting the future at a rate of 20% per year. In other words, we really don't care about anything after five years in the future. So if we start in state 0, for instance, we can expect to have to reorder only approximately three times during the next five years at a cost of 13 to 15 each time. Hence the expected cost of 40.05 is plausible.

Suppose now we let α approach 1 from below. As the discount factor increases, we take more and more of the future into account, hence the expected discounted cost should rise. This is true, and as α gets close to 1, the expected cost goes to infinity. Hence it is impossible to set $\alpha = 1$ in the linear programs (13.3.9) and (13.3.10).

There is still another technical reason why one can't set $\alpha = 1$ in the problems above. If P is the transition matrix of a regular Markov chain, the matrix $I - \alpha P$ is not singular when $\alpha < 1$ but it is singular when $\alpha = 1$. This is discussed further in Exercise 8.

In order to study the case when $\alpha = 1$, we define a new variable, x, which is to be equal to the average cost incurred in each time period. Then we try to determine *relative values* x_j of being in each of the states $j = 0, \ldots, r - 1$. In order to do this, we solve the following pair of dual programs:

$$\text{Max } x$$

(13.3.11)   Subject to:

$$\sum_{j=0}^{r-1} (\delta_{ij} - p_{ij}^d)x_j + x \leq c_i^d \qquad \text{for all } i \text{ and all } d \text{ in } D(i)$$

and

$$\text{Min} \sum_{i=0}^{r-1} \sum_{d \text{ in } D(i)} w_i^d c_i^d$$

(13.3.12)   Subject to:

$$\sum_{i=0}^{r-1} \sum_{d \text{ in } D(i)} w_i^d(\delta_{ij} - p_{ij}^d) = 0$$

$$\sum_{i=0}^{r-1} \sum_{d \text{ in } D(i)} w_i^d = 1, w_i^d \geq 0$$

EXAMPLE 13.3.1 (continued). Let us solve the example with $\alpha = 1$. The bordered matrix of the dual programs (13.3.11) and (13.3.12) is given in Figure 13.3.6.

	x_0	x_1	x_2	x_3	x_4	x_5	x	
w_0^2	.75	$-.5$	$-.25$	0	0	0	1	≤ 13
w_0^3	1	$-.25$	$-.5$	$-.25$	0	0	1	≤ 15
w_1^2	0	.75	$-.5$	$-.25$	0	0	1	≤ 14
w_1^3	0	1	$-.25$	$-.5$	$-.25$	0	1	≤ 16
w_2^0	$-.25$	$-.5$	.75	0	0	0	1	≤ 1
w_2^2	0	0	.75	$-.5$	$-.25$	0	1	≤ 15
w_2^3	0	0	1	$-.25$	$-.5$	$-.25$	1	≤ 16
w_3^0	0	$-.25$	$-.5$	.75	0	0	1	≤ 2
w_3^2	0	0	0	.75	$-.5$	$-.25$	1	≤ 16
w_4^0	0	0	$-.25$	$-.5$	.75	0	1	≤ 3
w_5^0	0	0	0	$-.25$	$-.5$	.75	1	≤ 4
	0	0	0	0	0	0	1	

FIGURE 13.3.6

Notice that a new column must be created to correspond to the new variable x. Otherwise the entries are easily obtained from Figures 13.3.1 and 13.3.4. The solution to this model gives an average cost of 6.33 and the relative costs given in Figure 13.3.7.

State i	Relative Cost, x_i
0	6.34
1	3.13
2	−2.90
3	−6.66
4	−9.87
5	−11.93

FIGURE 13.3.7

In Exercise 9, you will be asked to explain these relative costs, particularly the negative ones. The optimal solution to the dual problem turns out to give the same policy as that found for $\alpha = 0.8$; that is, order three units when in states 0 and 1 and order nothing in the other states.

EXERCISES 13.3

1. Enumerate the 24 possible Markov chains obtained by different stationary policies.

2. For each of the chains in Exercise 1, verify that there is only one fixed vector on the left.

3. (a) Show that the number of stationary policies is equal to
$$|D(0)| \cdot |D(1)| \cdot \cdots \cdot |D(r-1)|,$$
where $|D(i)|$ is the number of decisions in the set $D(i)$.
   (b) Show that if $r = 20$ and $|D(i)| \geq 2$, for $i = 0, \ldots, r-1$, then there will be more than a million stationary policies.

4. Carry out a few steps of the value-iteration method for the problem in Example 13.3.1. How many iterations does it take to get the optimal policy?

5. Estimate the amount of computation needed to find the optimal policy for Example 13.3.1 by the policy-iteration method, using a computer if you have one.

6. Use a method similar to that in Example 13.3.2 to find the maximum number in the set $\{2, -17, 52, 13\}$ by means of linear programming. State and interpret the dual problem.

7. Set up the problem in Example 13.3.1 if the manufacturer can reorder either 2, 3, or 4 units.

8. (a) Show that the transition matrix
$$\begin{bmatrix} \frac{1}{2} & \frac{1}{2} \\ 1 & 0 \end{bmatrix}$$
is regular.
   (b) Show that if $a < 1$, the matrix
$$Z = \begin{bmatrix} 1 & 0 \\ 0 & 1 \end{bmatrix} - \alpha \begin{bmatrix} \frac{1}{2} & \frac{1}{2} \\ 1 & 0 \end{bmatrix}$$
is nonsingular.
   (c) Show that if $\alpha = 1$, the matrix Z is singular.

*9. (a) Show that if we replace a solution x_j by $x_j + k$, where k is any constant, $x_j + k$ is still a solution to (13.3.11).

(b) Use the result in (a) to show that relative costs can always be changed by adding a constant to all of them.

(c) Use (b) to show that the relative costs in Figure 13.3.7 are reasonable for the problem solved there.

13.4   MULTILOCATION INVENTORY MODELS

In previous chapters we have described a variety of inventory models. However, only one inventory location was considered in each case. Practical considerations often require that inventories be kept at various locations—for example, each of several news stands must be supplied with afternoon papers. Models will now be introduced for such situations.

EXAMPLE 13.4.1. There are S distinct stocking points (news stands, warehouses, ships at sea), and each has its own probability distribution of demand for an item, D_i $(i = 1, 2, \ldots, S)$ over some specified time period:

$$(13.4.1) \qquad P\{D_i \leq x\} = F_i(x) \qquad i = 1, 2, \ldots, S.$$

Let the probability density function of F_i be $f_i(x)$. Assuming that a fixed amount of inventory stock, I, is available, the problem is to allocate an amount, I_i, to each of the S locations so as to minimize the expected number of locations that experience a stockout—that is, insufficient stock to meet demand. If I_i is allocated to location i, the probability of a stockout is

$$(13.4.2) \qquad P\{D_i > I_i\} = 1 - F_i(I_i).$$

Now consider the random variable Z_i.

$$(13.4.3) \qquad Z_i = \begin{cases} 1 & \text{if } D_i > I_i \text{ (stockout)} \\ 0 & \text{if } D_i \leq I_i \text{ (no stockout)} \end{cases}$$

Then

$$(13.4.4) \qquad N = Z_i + Z_2 + \cdots + Z_s$$

represents the number of stockouts among the S locations, and

$$(13.4.5) \qquad E[N] = E[Z_1] + E[Z_2] + \cdots + E[Z_s]$$

is the expected number of stockouts. Furthermore, from (13.4.2) and (13.4.5),

$$(13.4.6) \qquad E[N] = \sum_{i=1}^{s} [1 - F_i(I_i)].$$

The problem is now to minimize $E[N]$ subject to the constraints

$$(13.4.7a) \qquad \sum_{i=1}^{s} I_i \leq I$$

and

$$(13.4.7b) \qquad I_i \geq 0 \qquad i = 1, 2, \ldots, S.$$

You will recognize that this problem involves optimization with inequality constraints and that the Kuhn-Tucker procedure of Section 6.3 is applicable; see Theorem 6.3.2. It is also clear that minimization of

$$E[N] = \sum_{i=1}^{s} [1 - F_i(t_i)] = S - \sum_{i=1}^{s} F_i(I_i)$$

is equivalent to maximizing $\sum_{i=1}^{s} F_i(I_i)$. Thus for convenience we shall translate to maximization of the latter sum. Form the Lagrangian function

$$(13.4.8) \qquad L = \sum_{i=1}^{s} F_i(I_i) - \lambda \left[\sum_{i=1}^{s} I_i - I \right] + \sum_{i=1}^{s} \mu_i I_i,$$

where λ and μ_i are nonnegative. Differentiation leads to

$$(13.4.9) \qquad \frac{\partial L}{\partial I_i} = f_i(I_i) - \lambda + \mu_i,$$

which is condition (a) of Theorem 6.3.2. For condition (b), observe first that $\lambda > 0$, since it is clear that in order to minimize total expected stockouts all available stock must be assigned to locations. In other words, (13.4.7a) is an equality. At location i, one of the following conditions must prevail:

$$\begin{array}{cc} \textit{Condition (a)} & \textit{Condition (b)} \\ \mu_i = 0, I_i > 0, & \mu_i > 0, I_i = 0. \end{array}$$

Thus either I_i satisfies $f_i(I_i) = \lambda > 0$ or $I_i = 0$. Assume that the demand density has a single maximum as in Figure 13.4.1. It follows that the minimum occurs at a point

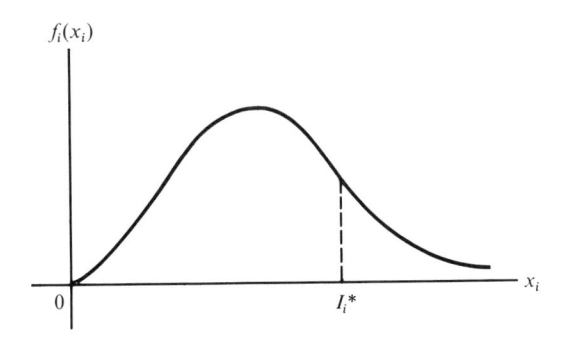

FIGURE 13.4.1

such that the density is sloping downwards ($df_i/dx < 0$)—that is, beyond the *mode* of the distribution. Since such points occur beyond the maximum and hence $P\{D_i \le I_i^*\} > 0.5$ in many cases, the answer is intuitively appealing. Practically speaking, one is assured that at all locations that receive stock, the condition $f_i(I_i) = \lambda > 0$ prevails; otherwise $I_i = 0$. This reduces the number of alternative allocations that must be tested and reveals the qualitative fact that under the problem conditions stated above, some locations should receive no stock. Such *extreme-point solutions* are quite common in practice.

EXAMPLE 13.4.2. Let $S = 2$ and suppose the demand distributions are exponential: for $i = 1, 2$ and $r_i > 0$,

$$(13.4.10) \qquad F_i(x) = \begin{cases} 1 - e^{-r_i x} & x \geq 0 \\ 0 & x < 0 \end{cases}$$

The Kuhn-Tucker conditions state that at the minimum of $E[N]$ (maximum of L), we have one of the following:

$$(13.4.11) \qquad r_1 e^{-r_1 I_1^*} = r_2 e^{-r_2 I_2^*}, \qquad I_1^* + I_2^* = I, \qquad 0 \leq I_1^*, I_2^* \leq I$$

or

$$(13.4.12a) \qquad I_1^* = I, I_2^* = 0$$

or

$$(13.4.12b) \qquad I_1^* = 0, I_2^* = I.$$

In this case it is possible to solve (13.4.11) explicitly. The solution is

$$(13.4.13) \qquad I_1^* = \frac{1}{r_1 + r_2} [r_2 I + \log(r_1/r_2)],$$

provided $0 < I_1^* < I$. Otherwise, $I_1^* = 0$ or I. See Exercise 4.

It is interesting to consider an alternative formulation of the problem described in which profits are introduced.

EXAMPLE 13.4.3. Again there are S stocking points having demand distributions $F_i(x)$. Let us suppose that the price that may be charged for an item varies from location to location (for example, prices are 10% higher west of the Mississippi); p_i is the price at location i. Then the expected profit at location i is

$$p_i \int_0^{I_i} x f_i(x)\, dx + p_i I_i [1 - F_i(I_i)],$$

and the total expected profit is

$$(13.4.14) \qquad E[P] = \sum_{i=1}^{s} \left\{ p_i \int_0^{I_i} x f_i(x)\, dx + p_i I_i [1 - F_i(I_i)] \right\}.$$

Taking account of constraints (13.4.7a and b), we have the Lagrangian

$$(13.4.15) \quad L = \sum_{i=1}^{s} \left\{ p_i \int_0^{I_i} x f_i(x)\, dx + p_i I_i [1 - F_i(I_i)] \right\} - \lambda [I_i - I] + \sum_{i=1}^{s} \mu_i I_i.$$

Partial differentiation then leads to the condition

$$(13.4.16) \qquad \frac{\partial L}{\partial I_i} = p_i [1 - F_i(I_i)] - \lambda + \mu_i.$$

Again it is clear that $\lambda > 0$ and also that the Kuhn-Tucker conditions show that one may or may not stock at location i, depending on whether $\mu_i > 0$ or $\mu_i = 0$. Provided location i is stocked, we find that

$$(13.4.17) \qquad 1 - F_i(I_i) = \frac{\lambda}{p_i}.$$

This expression may be inverted to solve for the actual value of I_i in terms of λ.

EXAMPLE 13.4.4. We repeat the previous example with (13.4.14) as the measure of effectiveness of the stocking policy. For an interior minimum, it must occur that

(13.4.18)
$$p_1 e^{-r_1 I_1*} = p_2 e^{-r^2(I - I_1*)}.$$

Otherwise the Kuhn-Tucker conditions show that extreme-point solutions may result.

EXERCISES 13.4

1. Refer to Example 13.4.1.
   (a) Show that $I_1* = 0$ if $I < (1/r_2) \log(r_2/r_1)$.
   (b) Show that $I_2* = 0$ if $I < (1/r_1) \log(r_1/r_2)$.
   (c) Otherwise there is an interior minimum given by

$$I_1* = \frac{r_1}{r_1 + r_2} I + \frac{1}{r_1 + r_2} \log (r_1/r_2).$$

   (*Hint: E[N]* is a convex function of I_1 when $I_2 = I - I_1$.)

2. Suppose we assign a penalty c_i to a stockout occasion at location i. Describe the optimum allocation of inventory rule.

3. A factory has two warehouses, and each has an exponential demand distribution with parameters $r_1 = 0.01$ and $r_2 = 0.02$, respectively. Suppose the unit price of the item demanded is $10 at each. Show that whatever the amount of stock to be distributed, both warehouses receive some stock. Is this necessarily true if the prices are not equal?

4. Extend Example 13.4.1 to the case of arbitrary $S > 0$.

5. Describe the extreme-point solutions for Example 13.4.3.

6. Extend Example 13.4.3 to the case of arbitrary $S > 0$.

13.5   LINEAR PROGRAMMING WITH RECOURSE

In Section 13.2, we dealt with one attempt to handle uncertainty in the coefficients of a linear programming problem. There we introduced chance constraints. Here we shall deal with another approach to the problem, developed by G. B. Dantzig, called *linear programming with recourse*. Less commonly it is called *linear programming under uncertainty*.

The basic idea of this problem is that it is necessary to make a production decision before the exact demand for the product is known. Then, if too much of the product has been made, a penalty cost is incurred; and if too little product has been made, a corrective action, which also has a penalty cost, can be taken. Our objective is to minimize the expected penalty costs. We first study the problem in the single-variable case.

Let b be the random demand with distribution function $F(b)$ and density function $f(b)$. Let y be the amount produced and let y^+ be underproduction and y^- be overproduction. Then we have the equation:

(13.5.1)
$$y + y^+ - y^- = b.$$

Since we cannot have both over- and underproduction, it follows that

(13.5.2) $$y^+ y^- = 0;$$

that is, either $y^+ = 0$ or $y^- = 0$. From this it follows that

(13.5.3) $$y^+ = \frac{1}{2}[|b - y| + (b - y)]$$

and

(13.5.4) $$y^- = \frac{1}{2}[|y - b| + (y - b)],$$

as you can easily check by trying both cases $y \leq b$ and $y \geq b$.

From the last two equations it follows that in order to get the expected value of y^+ and y^-, we will need to find $E[|y - b|]$. Therefore, we shall first study properties of the function $\varphi(y) = E[|y - b|]$.

LEMMA 13.5.1. The function $\varphi(y)$ is continuously differentiable and takes on its minimum when $y = b^m$, where b^m is the *median* of the distribution $F(b)$.

Proof: We have by definition

(13.5.5) $$\varphi(y) = \int_{-\infty}^{+\infty} |y - b| \, dF(b).$$

Since the integrand is positive for all y, so is $\varphi(y)$. It is obviously large for y very large positive or very negative. Differentiating under the integral sign, we obtain

$$\varphi'(y) = \int_{-\infty}^{y} dF(b) + \int_{y}^{+\infty} -dF(b).$$

From this it is clear that $\varphi'(y)$ equals zero only at the 50% fractile—that is, at the median, b^m, of the distribution $F(b)$; hence $\varphi(y)$ has a minimum at this point.

We shall assume that F has a unique median throughout the rest of the section.

LEMMA 13.5.2.

$$\varphi(y) = C + 2 \int_{y}^{b^m} (b - y) \, dF(b),$$

where C is a constant.

Proof: Assume first that $y \leq b^m$. We can break up the integral

$$\phi(y) = \int_{-\infty}^{y} (y - b) \, dF(b) + \int_{y}^{+\infty} (b - y) \, dF(b),$$

$$= \int_{-\infty}^{b^m} (y - b) \, dF(b) - \int_{y}^{b^m} (y - b) \, dF(b),$$

$$+ \int_{b^m}^{+\infty} (b - y) \, dF(b) + \int_{y}^{b^m} (b - y) \, dF(b).$$

By taking the minus sign into the second integral, it can be shown to be equal to the fourth integral, so these will be combined. Next, breaking up the first and third integrals further, we have:

$$\phi(y) = \int_{-\infty}^{b^m} (b^m - b)\, dF(b) + \int_{-\infty}^{b^m} (y - b^m)\, dF(b)$$

$$+ \int_{b^m}^{\infty} (b - b^m)\, dF(b) + \int_{b^m}^{\infty} (b^m - y)\, dF(b)$$

$$+ 2 \int_{y}^{b^m} (b - y)\, dF(b).$$

We now observe that the second and fourth integrals cancel, since b^m is the median of F. Therefore we have, combining the first and third integrals,

$$(13.5.6) \qquad \varphi(y) = E[|b - b^m|] + 2 \int_{y}^{b^m} (b - y)\, dF(b),$$

from which the lemma follows for $y \le b^m$. The proof for the opposite inequality is similar and is omitted.

LEMMA 13.5.3. The function $\varphi(y)$ is convex for all y.

Proof: From (13.5.6), we have

$$\varphi(y) = C + 2 \int_{y}^{b^m} b\, dF(b) - 2y[F(b^m) - F(y)].$$

Differentiating once, we have

$$\varphi'(y) = -2yf(y) - 2[F(b^m) - F(y)] + 2yf(y),$$
$$= -2[F(b^m) - F(y)].$$

Using the fact that $F(b^m) = 1/2$, we obtain further

$$(13.5.7) \qquad \varphi'(y) = 2F(y) - 1.$$

Differentiating a second time yields

$$\varphi''(y) = 2f(y).$$

Clearly, $f(y) \ge 0$ since it is a density function; hence $\varphi''(y) \ge 0$, and the function $\varphi(y)$ is convex as asserted.

We now want to take into account the over- and underproduction penalties. Suppose they are p^- and p^+. For simplicity we shall assume they are equal—that is, $p^- = p^+ = p$.

LEMMA 13.5.4. If over- and underproduction penalties are equal, then the total penalty is given by

$$(13.5.8) \qquad p[E(y^+) + E(y^-)] = p\varphi(y).$$

Proof: Using the definition of $\varphi(y)$ and (13.5.3) and (13.5.4), we have

$$p[E(y^+) + E(y^-)] = \frac{p}{2}\{E|b - y| + E[|y - b|]\} = p\varphi(y).$$

We shall now show by examples how to apply the theory above to a linear programming problem with random demands.

EXAMPLE 13.5.1. Let us return to the truck-scooter example of Chapter 4, Section 4.2. Suppose we initially ignore the production constraints and consider the problem

$$\text{Max } E[2x_1 + x_2 - py_1^+ - py_1^- - py_2^+ - py_2^-]$$

Subject to:

$$x_1 \quad + y_1^+ - y_1^- \qquad\qquad = b_1$$
$$x_2 \qquad\qquad + y_2^+ - y_2^- = b_2$$
$$x_1, x_2, y_1^+, y_1^-, y_2^+, y_2^- \geq 0$$

where b_1 and b_2 are random variables with, for simplicity, the same distribution function $F(b)$. As it stands, the problem equations define y_1^+, y_1^-, y_2^+, and y_2^- indirectly as random variables. Let us use the the previously given technique to solve for the y's and put them in the objective function, thus obtaining an unconstrained problem. It is

(13.5.9) $$\text{Max } 2x_1 + x_2 - p\varphi(x_1) - p\varphi(x_2) = f(x_1, x_2).$$

We can solve this problem by differentiating f with respect to x_1 and x_2 and setting the results equal to zero. We obtain:

$$\frac{\partial f}{\partial x_1} = 2 - p\varphi'(x_1) = 2 - p[2F(x_1) - 1] = 0,$$

$$\frac{\partial f}{\partial x_1} = 1 - p\varphi'(x_2) = 1 - p[2F(x_2) - 1] = 0.$$

From these two equations we obtain

$$F(x_1) = \frac{1}{p} + \frac{1}{2},$$

$$F(x_2) = \frac{1}{2p} + \frac{1}{2}.$$

We can now easily solve for x_1 and x_2 by inverting the distribution F. We see that in each case the optimal action is to order somewhat more than the median demand. The additional amount is dependent on the profit for each product: the higher the profit for an item, the more we produce. Conversely, the higher the penalties, the less we produce, but we always produce at least as much as the median demand, as long as the profit coefficient is positive.

EXAMPLE 13.5.2. Suppose we add to the previous example the production constraints that we had in Chapter 4. Then the same transformation as that used above yields the following problem:

$$\text{Max } 2x_1 + x_2 - p\varphi(x_1) - p\varphi(x_2)$$

Subject to:

(13.5.10)
$$4x_1 + \ x_2 \le 900$$
$$2x_1 + 3x_2 \le 900$$
$$x_1, x_2 \ge \ \ 0$$

Charnes, Cooper, and Thompson have named this kind of problem a *constrained generalized median problem* (see the reference at the end of the chapter). If the production constraints are not binding, the solution to this problem is the same as in the previous example.

By the same analysis as in the previous example, the problem in (13.5.10) can be shown to be equivalent to the following problem:

$$\text{Max } 2x_1 + x_2$$

Subject to:

$$4x_1 + \ x_2 \le 900$$
$$2x_1 + 3x_2 \le 900$$

(13.5.11)
$$x_1 \qquad \le F^{-1}\!\left(\frac{1}{2} + \frac{1}{2p}[2 + 4\ w_1 + w_2]\right)$$

$$x_2 \le F^{-1}\!\left(\frac{1}{2} + \frac{1}{2p}[1 + 2\ w_1 + 3w_2]\right)$$

$$x_1, x_2 \ge 0$$

where w_1 and w_2 are the dual variables associated with the first two constraints. The last two constraints can be interpreted as deterministic equivalent penalty constraints, somewhat in the spirit of chance-constrained programming. Note that here the risk is determined indirectly through the penalties and dual variables, not by means of risk coefficients.

EXERCISES 13.5

1. Establish (13.5.3) and (13.5.4).

2. Rework Example 13.5.1 when the deterministic part of the objective function is $2x_1 - x_2$. Show that we produce *more* than the median demand of x_1 but *less* than the median demand of x_2.

3. Show that problems (13.5.10) and (13.5.11) are equivalent.

4. Rework Example 13.5.1 when we make zero profits on both trucks and scooters. Show that in this case we always ship the median demand in order to minimize total penalty costs.

5. Rework Example 13.5.1 when the distribution functions for x_1 and x_2 are not identical.

6. Rework Example 13.5.2 when the distribution functions are not identical.

7. Assume you are trying to solve a problem that has random demands and production constraints. Consider the advantages and disadvantages of using a chance-constrained-programming model versus a linear-programming-with-recourse model. Do you think it would be easier to obtain risk coefficients from management or penalty functions?

SUGGESTED READING

Charnes, A., and Cooper, W. W. Chance constrained programming. *Management Science*, 1959, **6**, 73–80.

Charnes, A., and Cooper, W. W. *Management Models and Industrial Applications of Linear Programming*. 2 Vols. New York: John Wiley, 1961.

Dantzig, G. B. Linear programming under uncertainty. *Management Science*, 1956, **2**, 131–144.

Dantzig, G. B. *Linear Programming and Extensions*. Princeton, N.J.: Princeton University Press, 1963.

Howard, R. A. *Dynamic Programming and Markov Processes*. New York: John Wiley, 1960.

Luce, R. D., and Raiffa, H. *Games and Decisions: Introduction and Critical Survey*. New York: John Wiley, 1957.

Von Neuman, J., and Morgenstern, O. *Theory of Games and Economic Behavior*. Princeton, N.J.: Princeton University Press, 1953.

ANSWERS TO SELECTED EXERCISES

EXERCISES 1.1

1.

	Oil City	Harrisburg	Chambersburg	Clearfield	
Philadelphia	22	8	10	16	200
Pittsburgh	6	15	10	7.5	150
Wilkes-Barre	16	8	11	10.5	125
	175	185	50	65	

3. Transshipment is allowed, so shortest path is used:

	3	4	5	
1	50	40	60	60
2	30	45	25	40
	10	50	40	

6. (a) One way of setting up the problem is:

	1	1	2	2	3	3	
Adams	1	100	2	100	3	100	2
Brown	3	3	2	2	1	1	1
Jones	2	2	1	1	3	3	1
Smith	100	1	100	3	100	2	2
	1	1	1	1	1	1	

(b) Change the 2 to 1 in line 1. (c) Change the 2's in line 2 to 1's.

7. (a) We show another way of avoiding duplications:

	1	2	3			
Adams	a	100	100	0	100	1
Adams	100	b	100	0	100	1
Adams	100	100	c	0	100	1
Brown	c	b	a	100	100	1
Jones	b	a	c	100	100	1
Smith	a	100	100	100	100	1
Smith	100	c	100	100	0	1
Smith	100	100	b	100	0	1
	2	2	2	1	1	

(b) In 6(a), replace 2 by 4 and 3 and 3 by 7 in line 3. (c) See (a).

9. (a–c)

	M_1	M_2	M_3	M_4	M_5	M_6	Slack	
A	−11	−10	−10	−6	−10	−9	0	180
B	−16	−16	−9	−12	−11	−10	0	145
C	−11	−17	−11	−9	−5	−13	0	110
	51	42	58	53	49	47	135	

12. Suppose we want to make K the sum of the first k variables in the first row.

0	c_{11}	$\cdots$	c_{1k}	M	$\cdots$	M	K
0	M	$\cdots$	M	$c_{1,k+1}$	$\cdots$	$c_{1,n}$	$a_1 - K$
M	c_{21}	$\cdots$	c_{2k}	$c_{2,k+1}$	$\cdots$	$c_{2,n}$	a_2
$\cdot$	$\cdot$	$\cdots$	$\cdot$	$\cdot$	$\cdots$	$\cdot$	$\cdot$
M	c_{m1}	$\cdots$	c_{mk}	$c_{m,k+1}$	$\cdots$	c_{mn}	a_m
K	b_1	$\cdots$	b_k	b_{k+1}	$\cdots$	b_n	

14. (a)

	B	D	
A	100	175	20
B	0	30	b
C	40	50	10
	$15+b$	15	

Parts (b) and (c) will be worked in later sections.

16. The problem formulation prevents duplications and also prevents Adams and Smith from serving on both committees 1 and 3. The formulations in the answers to Exercises 6 and 7 are preferable, since they do not have this deficiency.

EXERCISES 1.2

1. Minimum entry method: $w_{12} = 185$, $w_{13} = 15$, $w_{21} = 150$, $w_{31} = 25$, $w_{33} = 35$, $w_{34} = 65$, cost 3997.5. Northwest corner: $w_{11} = 175$, $w_{21} = 75$, $w_{22} = 150$, $w_{32} = 10$, $w_{33} = 50$, $w_{34} = 65$, cost = 7562.5. VAM: $w_{12} = 150$, $w_{13} = 50$, $w_{21} = 150$, $w_{31} = 25$, $w_{32} = 35$, $w_{34} = 65$, cost = 3962.5.

3. Minimum entry method: $w_{11} = 10$, $w_{12} = 50$, $w_{21} = 0$, $w_{23} = 40$, cost = 3500. Northwest corner method: $w_{11} = 10$, $w_{12} = 50$, $w_{13} = 0$, $w_{23} = 40$, cost = 3500. VAM method: same as minimum entry method.

8. Minimum entry method: $w_{12} = 1$, $w_{15} = 1$, $w_{16} = 0$, $w_{26} = 1$, $w_{31} = 1$, $w_{34} = 1$, $w_{36} = 0$, $w_{43} = 1$, $w_{44} = 0$, cost = 25. Northwest corner method: $w_{11} = 1$, $w_{12} = 1$, $w_{22} = 0$, $w_{23} = 1$, $w_{24} = 1$, $w_{25} = 0$, $w_{35} = 1$, $w_{36} = 0$, $w_{46} = 1$, cost = 34. VAM method: $w_{12} = 1$, $w_{16} = 1$, $w_{24} = 1$, $w_{26} = 1$, $w_{35} = 1$, $w_{36} = 0$, $w_{41} = 1$, $w_{43} = 0$, $w_{46} = 0$, cost = 31.

9. Minimum entry method: $w_{13} = 58$, $w_{15} = 8$, $w_{17} = 114$, $w_{21} = 51$, $w_{24} = 53$, $w_{25} = 41$, $w_{32} = 42$, $w_{36} = 47$, $w_{37} = 21$, cost = 3888.

15. If a row doesn't have a basis cell then there is an unsatisfied demand or a full warehouse so it can't be feasible.

16. Proof by induction. Result is certainly true for $m + n = 3$. Assume that it is true for $m + n = k$ to prove it is true for $m + n = k + 1$. There has to be at least one line with a unique basis element; cross it out, and we are in the case $m + n = k$ so that by the induction hypothesis there are two cells with power 1. At least one of these must not be connected to the cell in the line crossed out; hence, at least two lines have cells with power 1.

18. Result is true for $m + n = 3$ and $m + n - 2 = 1$. Assume it is true for $m + n = k$. Find a line with 0 or 1 element. If we find a line with 0 elements, we are done. If we find a line with 1 element, we cross it out and use the induction hypothesis.

EXERCISES 1.3

1. $w_{11} = 30$, $w_{13} = 20$, $w_{22} = 60$, $w_{23} = 10$, $w_{31} = 20$, cost $= 550$.

3. (Exercise 1) $w_{12} = 150$, $w_{13} = 50$, $w_{21} = 150$, $w_{31} = 25$, $w_{32} = 35$, $w_{34} = 65$, cost $=$ 3962.5.

5. (Exercise 3) $w_{11} = 10$, $w_{12} = 50$, $w_{13} = 0$, $w_{23} = 40$, cost $= 3500$.

10. (Exercise 8) $w_{15} = 1$, $w_{16} = 1$, $w_{22} = 1$, $w_{24} = 1$, $w_{31} = 1$, $w_{43} = 1$, cost $= 21$.

11. (Exercise 9) $w_{13} = 37$, $w_{15} = 8$, $w_{17} = 135$, $w_{21} = 51$, $w_{24} = 53$, $w_{25} = 41$, $w_{32} = 42$, $w_{33} = 21$, $w_{36} = 47$, profit $= 3909$.

16. (Exercise 14)   Best value is $b = 5$. Then the solution is: $w_{11} = 20$, $w_{22} = 5$, $w_{32} = 10$, cost $= 2650$.

17. Optimal solution is: $w_{12} = 1$, $w_{22} = 0$, $w_{23} = 1$, $w_{25} = 1$, $w_{31} = 1$, $w_{33} = 0$, $w_{34} = 1$, $x_1 = 0$, $x_2 = -1$, $x_3 = -1$, $y_1 = 9$, $y_2 = 8$, $y_3 = 11$, $y_4 = 10$, $y_5 = 7$.

20. $w_{11} = 2$, $w_{12} = 2$, $w_{13} = 1$, $w_{32} = 1$, $w_{35} = 4$, $w_{33} = 2$, $w_{34} = 4$, cost $= 14$. There are two alternate optima.

EXERCISES 1.4

16. (a)   (2, 1), B_1, B_2, B_4.   (b)   (2, 3), B_4, B_2, B_3, B_6, B_5.
    (c)   (3, 2), B_2, B_3, B_6.

18. Every node of a cycle has degree 2 and lies on two different lines. Thus, if there is one element of a cycle in a line, there has to be at least one more. But there couldn't be more than two without having a cell with power 3. Hence, there are zero or two cells of a cycle in each line. If we just count the cells once, say by rows, we find that there are an even number in all in the cycle.

20. Let B and B' be two optimal bases with $B \neq B'$, and assume there are optimal dual solutions $x_i' = x_i$ for all i and $y_j' = y_j$ for all j. Let (e, f) be a cell in $B' - B$; by assumption, such a cell exists. Then $c_{ij} = x_i + y_j = x_i' + y_j'$, which is the definition of dual degeneracy (not given in the text).

EXERCISES 1.5

1. Assume that two of the three children should get an extra job.

15	5	20	0	2
11	15	8	0	2
7	20	12	0	2
1	3	1	1	

Answer is Jane washes dishes twice, Jim washes dishes once and makes beds, and Joe sweeps the floor.

2. $a > 1$.   3. $a > 3$.

4. By scaling, we can assume that the supplies a_i and demands b_j are positive integers. Then, make replicas of row i $(a_i - 1)$ times and make replicas of column j $(b_j - 1)$ times, putting 1's for supplies and demands in the new problem. The solution to the

old problem can easily be obtained from the solution to the new problem by grouping rows and columns together again. This method will always work, but causes the numbers of rows and columns to increase enormously.

6. Figure 1.5.6 has cells (1, 3) and (2, 3) in the basis with $w_{13} = w_{23} = 0$. The correct optimum has (1, 2) instead of (1, 3) in the basis with $w_{12} = 0$. Other shipments are as indicated.

7. The alternate optimum is: $w_{13} = 100$, $w_{21} = 70$, $w_{22} = 110$, $w_{31} = 70$, $w_{33} = 70$.

EXERCISES 1.6

1. Range is 2.

3. Range of y_1 and y_3 is 0. Range of y_2 is 3.

4. (Exercise 1) $x_1 = 0$, $x_2 = -10$, $x_3 = 0$, $y_1 = 16$, $y_2 = 8$, $y_3 = 10$, $y_4 = 10.5$.

6. (Exercise 3) $x_1 = 0$, $x_2 = -20$, $y_1 = 50$, $y_2 = 40$, $y_3 = 45$.

7. (Exercise 4)   All x_i's and y_j's are 0.

12. (Exercise 9) $x_1 = 0$, $x_2 = x_3 = -1$, $y_1 = -15$, $y_2 = -16$, $y_3 = -10$, $y_4 = -11$, $y_5 = -10$, $y_6 = -12$.

17. (Exercise 14)   When $b = 5$ the solutions are: $x_1 = 100$, $x_2 = 0$, $x_3 = 20$, $y_1 = 0$, $y_2 = 30$. Since $x_2 + y_1 = 0$, no further savings by transshipping are possible.

18. For each proposed warehouse location, add a new row with transportation costs and with an assumed warehouse capacity. Solve the problem with each new location, and use the dual variable associated with the warehouse to obtain a marginal evaluation of its worth.

20. The set S must have at least $m + n - 1$ cells, and must contain at least one cell in every line. Consider the following algorithm: If a line contains a unique cell of s, then the amount in that line can be shipped by that cell. Remove that line and repeat. If it is not possible to find such a line, pick any cell in S and ship the maximum amount, adjusting the rims and removing that cell from S. Again, try to find a line with a unique cell, and so on. After a finite number of such steps, a feasible and optimal solution will be found.

EXERCISES 1.7

2. (a) $w_{11} = 22$, $w_{12} = 4$, $w_{13} = 14$, $w_{22} = 30$.
    (b) $w_{11} = 22$, $w_{12} = 18$, $w_{22} = 16$, $w_{23} = 14$.

   (c)   If we assume equal net-sales prices from each warehouse, we see that the solution to (b) maximizes net profit while the solution to (a) does not. Usually the correct objective is profit maximization, not transportation-cost minimization.

7. Now the entries in a given row may be c, $c + f(1)$, $c + f(2)$, ..., $c + f(k)$, ..., where $f(k)$ is the storage charge for k months. For perishable goods, $f(k) = M$ (a large number), when k exceeds the shelf life.

10. Put a \$1 cost on the main diagonal in place of 0. The same solution remains optimal.

12. The cost matrix will no longer be symmetric, and the variables w_{ij} and w_{ji} no longer occur in pairs. The quadratic result (1.4.2) no longer holds. However, an ordinary transportation problem results and can be solved easily.

EXERCISES 2.1

1. (a) $\begin{bmatrix} 5 & 0 \\ 0 & 5 \end{bmatrix}$ (b) $\begin{bmatrix} 4 & 0 \\ 0 & 5 \end{bmatrix}$ (c) $u + v$ is not defined.

   (d) $(20, -27)$ (e) $(-14, -1, -20)$ (f) $A + w$ not defined.

   (g) $(h + 3k, -h - 4k)$ (h) $\begin{bmatrix} h & -k \\ -k & h \end{bmatrix}$

2. (a) $\begin{bmatrix} 3 & 4 \\ 0 & 2 \\ -27 & -20 \end{bmatrix}$ (b) $\begin{bmatrix} 6 & 0 & -6 \\ 8 & -18 & 16 \end{bmatrix}$ (c) Not defined.

   (d) (a, b, c) (e) $\begin{bmatrix} a \\ b \\ c \end{bmatrix}$

5.
$$A + 0 = \begin{bmatrix} a_{11} & \cdots & a_{1n} \\ \vdots & & \vdots \\ a_{m1} & \cdots & a_{mn} \end{bmatrix} + \begin{bmatrix} 0 & \cdots & 0 \\ \vdots & & \vdots \\ 0 & \cdots & 0 \end{bmatrix} = \begin{bmatrix} a_{11} + 0 & \cdots & a_{1n} + 0 \\ \vdots & & \vdots \\ a_{m1} + 0 & \cdots & a_{mn} + 0 \end{bmatrix}$$
$$= \begin{bmatrix} a_{11} & \cdots & a_{1n} \\ \vdots & & \vdots \\ a_{m1} & \cdots & a_{mn} \end{bmatrix} = A$$

7. $\begin{bmatrix} x_1 \\ x_2 \\ x_3 \end{bmatrix} = \begin{bmatrix} 86 \\ 18 \\ 24 \end{bmatrix}$

9. $h(a_{ij} + b_{ij}) = ha_{ij} + hb_{ij}$ (for $i = 1, \ldots, m$; $j = 1, \ldots, n$).

11. Two ways. A2 says that both ways of inserting parentheses give the same result.

14. (a) No. (b) Yes. (c) Probably not. (d) Mean and variance, finding the number of people whose salary is greater than a given amount, or whose age is less than a certain amount, and so on.

17. Let $y_j = \underset{i}{\text{Max }} x_j^{(i)}$ and $z_j = \underset{i}{\text{Min }} x_j^{(i)}$; then $z \leq x \leq y$.

EXERCISES 2.2

1. Suppose O_1 and O_2 satisfy A3. Then using A3 and setting $x = O_2$, we have $O_2 + O_1 = O_1$; and setting $x = O_1$, we have $O_1 + O_2 = O_2$: so $O_1 = O_2$.

2. Suppose $-x$ and $-x'$ are additive inverses of x. Then $x - x' = 0$. Adding $-x$ to both sides, we have $-x = -x + (x - x') = (-x + x) - x' = 0 - x' = -x'$.

4. Consider the set of all polynomials $p(t) = p_0 + p_1 t$ where $p_1 \neq 0$. Consider $0p(t) = 0 + 0t$; it is not of degree exactly 1 so the closure law is violated. Many other axioms are also violated.

6. The set P_3 of all polynomials of degree at most 2 consists of all nonvertical lines and all parabolas with vertical axis in the plane.

7. (a) $\begin{bmatrix} 28 \\ -13 \\ 35 \end{bmatrix}$ (b) $\begin{bmatrix} 7/3 \\ -13/12 \\ 25/12 \end{bmatrix}$ (c) No.

9. Yes.

12. (a) Yes.   (b) No.   (c) Yes.   (d) No.   (e) No.   (f) Yes.
(g) No.

13. (a) Dependent.   (b) Dependent.   (c) Dependent.   (d) Dependent.
(e) Independent.

16. (a) Yes.   (b) No.

(c) $\begin{bmatrix} 1 \\ 2 \\ -2 \end{bmatrix} = \frac{1}{2}\begin{bmatrix} -1 \\ 0 \\ -4 \end{bmatrix} + \frac{1}{2}\begin{bmatrix} 3 \\ 4 \\ 0 \end{bmatrix}$

(d) $\begin{bmatrix} 1 \\ 2 \\ -2 \end{bmatrix} = \begin{bmatrix} 1 \\ 0 \\ -5 \end{bmatrix} + 2\begin{bmatrix} 3 \\ -5 \\ -3 \end{bmatrix} + 3\begin{bmatrix} -2 \\ 4 \\ 3 \end{bmatrix}$

17. (a) If x and y are in V'' then $x + y$ is in $V'' \subset V' \subset V$.
(b) If x is in V'' then kx is in $V'' \subset V' \subset V$; hence by Definition 2.2.3, V'' is a subspace of V.

19. Clearly $V'' \supseteq V'$. If $z = c_1 x^{(1)} + \cdots + c_k x^{(k)}$ then $z \in V'$ so any linear combination of $x^{(1)}, \ldots, x^{(k)}$, and z is also in V' and $V' = V''$. If $V' = V''$ then z is in the span of $x^{(1)}, \ldots, x^{(k)}$ and hence z is a linear combination of these vectors.

EXERCISES 2.3

1. (a) 8.   (b) 0.   (c) 15.   (d) 3.   (e) 0.   (f) 9.   (g) Not defined.

2. (a, b) Sum of components of a vector.   (d) Average of components of x and y.
(e) Sum of components of a linear combination.

3. (a) $\begin{bmatrix} -2 & 3 & 0 \\ 0 & 6 & 2 \\ 4 & 0 & -5 \end{bmatrix}$ (b) Not defined.

(c) $\begin{bmatrix} 1 & -4 \\ 8 & -18 \\ -1 & 11 \end{bmatrix}$ (d) $\begin{bmatrix} 1 \\ -1 \\ 8 \end{bmatrix}$ vector of row sums.

(e) $(2, 9, -3)$, vector of column sums.
(f) Not defined.   (g) Not defined.

(h) $GH = \begin{bmatrix} -1 & 1 \\ 1 & -1 \end{bmatrix}$ $HG = \begin{bmatrix} 0 & 0 \\ -5 & -2 \end{bmatrix}$

(j) $(3, -6)$ vector of column sums.   (k) $\begin{bmatrix} 2 & -5 \\ 0 & 8 \\ 9 & -20 \end{bmatrix}$

5. $\sum_k a_{ik}(hb_{kj}) = h\left(\sum_k a_{ik}b_{kj}\right) = \sum_k (ha_{ik})b_{kj}$.

8.
$$A' = \begin{bmatrix} 1 & 0 & 0 \\ 0 & 0 & 1 \\ 0 & 1 & 0 \end{bmatrix} \qquad B' = \begin{bmatrix} -2 & 4 & 0 \\ 3 & 0 & 6 \\ 0 & -5 & 2 \end{bmatrix} \qquad C' = \begin{bmatrix} 1 & 1 & 1 \\ -1 & -2 & -3 \end{bmatrix}$$

$$D' = \begin{bmatrix} -3 & 6 \\ 2 & -5 \\ -1 & 0 \\ 1 & 1 \end{bmatrix} \qquad G' = \begin{bmatrix} 0 & -5 \\ 1 & -1 \end{bmatrix} \qquad H' = \begin{bmatrix} 0 & -1 \\ 0 & 1 \end{bmatrix}$$

10. Let $C = A + B$; then $c_{ij} = a_{ij} + b_{ij}$.
Let $C' = (A + B)'$; then $c_{ji}' = c_{ij} = a_{ij} + b_{ij}$.
Let $D = A' + B'$; then $d_{ji} = a_{ji} + b_{ji}'$
$$= a_{ij} + b_{ij} = c_{ji}'.$$

12. $O_{k \times m} A_{m \times n}$ has dimension $k \times n$ and all entries 0 so it is $O_{k \times n}$. Similarly $AO_{n \times h} = O_{m \times h}$.

14. If the hth and kth rows of A are equal, then using Definition 2.3.2 it follows that the same two rows of AB are equal.

17. The product $xA = 0$ when $x \neq 0$ indicates a linear dependence among the rows of A. Exercise 15 shows that the same dependence exists among the rows of AB; of course, AB may have more dependence relations among its rows than A does.

19. (a) and (d) are symmetric.

21. (a), (b), and (d) are skew-symmetric.

24. Clearly, $\frac{1}{2}(A + A') + \frac{1}{2}(A - A') = A$; so any square matrix A can be written as the sum of a symmetric and a skew-symmetric matrix.

26. If A is skew-symmetric, $a_{ji} = -a_{ij}$. Let $C = A^2$; $c_{ij} = \sum_k a_{ik} a_{kj} = \sum_k (-a_{jk})(-a_{ik})$
$$= c_{ji}; \text{ so } C \text{ is symmetric.}$$

28. (a)
$$\left[\begin{array}{cc|cc} 5 & 0 & 1 & 0 \\ 1 & 0 & 0 & 1 \\ \hline 0 & 1 & 6 & -7 \\ 1 & 0 & -7 & 6 \end{array}\right]^2 = \left[\begin{array}{cc|cc} 25 & 1 & 11 & -7 \\ 6 & 0 & -6 & 6 \\ \hline -6 & 6 & 85 & 1 \\ 11 & -7 & 1 & 85 \end{array}\right]$$

since $\begin{bmatrix} 5 & 0 \\ 1 & 0 \end{bmatrix}^2 = \begin{bmatrix} 25 & 0 \\ 5 & 0 \end{bmatrix}$, $\begin{bmatrix} 6 & -7 \\ -7 & 6 \end{bmatrix}^2 = \begin{bmatrix} 85 & 0 \\ 0 & 85 \end{bmatrix}$.

$$\begin{bmatrix} 0 & 1 \\ 1 & 0 \end{bmatrix}\begin{bmatrix} 5 & 0 \\ 1 & 0 \end{bmatrix} = \begin{bmatrix} 1 & 0 \\ 5 & 0 \end{bmatrix}, \quad \begin{bmatrix} 6 & -7 \\ -7 & 6 \end{bmatrix}\begin{bmatrix} 0 & 1 \\ 1 & 0 \end{bmatrix} = \begin{bmatrix} -7 & 6 \\ 6 & -7 \end{bmatrix}.$$

EXERCISES 2.4

2. If $y \neq 0$, $Ay = 0$ and A has an inverse A^{-1}, then we can multiply by A^{-1} to get $0 = A^{-1}(Ay) = (A^{-1}A)y = Iy = y$, which contradicts the assumption $y \neq 0$.

4. (a) $xP = (x_2, x_1, x_4, x_3)$ (b) $xQ = (x_4, x_1, x_2, x_3)$
(c) $xR = (x_3, x_1, x_2, x_4)$; x_4 stays fixed, x_1 goes to x_2's spot, x_2 to x_3, and x_3 to x_1.
(d) Since each column of a 4×4 permutation matrix has exactly one 1 and all the rest zero, when x is multiplied into it a single component of x is the result. Since each column has a 1 in a different row, the resulting product merely rearranges the entries of x.

6. (a) If P sends x_i into x_j's spot, then $p_{ij} = 1$ and $p_{ik} = 0$ for all $k \neq j$. But then the transpose P' has $p_{ji}' = 1$ and $p_{jk}' = 0$ for all $k \neq i$; so P' sends x_j into x_i's spot.

   (b) Since P sends x_i into x_j's spot and P' sends x_j into x_i's spot for all $i \neq j$, we have $PP' = P'P = I$ so $P^{-1} = P'$.

8. (a)
$$P(a, 2) = \begin{bmatrix} 1 & \frac{1}{2} & 0 \\ 0 & \frac{1}{2} & 0 \\ 0 & -\frac{5}{2} & 1 \end{bmatrix}$$

   (c)
$$P(b, 4) = \begin{bmatrix} 1 & 0 & 0 & 0 \\ 0 & 1 & 0 & 2 \\ 0 & 0 & 1 & \frac{1}{2} \\ 0 & 0 & 0 & -1 \end{bmatrix}$$

   (e) No, because $b_1 = 0$.

11. Consider the (k, i)th entry of PQ where $k = i$: it is $a_k + a_i\left(\dfrac{-a_k}{a_i}\right) = 0$; when $k = i$, it is just $a_i\left(\dfrac{1}{a_i}\right) = 1$. Hence, the ith column of PQ is the ith unit vector. Since all other columns are unit vectors, $PQ = I$.

12. (c) $A^n = \begin{bmatrix} 1 & 0 \\ n & 1 \end{bmatrix}$, $B^n = \begin{bmatrix} 1 & 0 \\ 0 & 2^n \end{bmatrix}$, $C^n = \begin{bmatrix} 2^n & -2^n \\ -2^n & 2^n \end{bmatrix}$, $O^n = 0$, $I^n = I$

14. The (i, i)th entry of D^n is $(d_{ii})^n$. All other entries are 0.

16. The (i, i)th entry of D^{-1} is $\dfrac{1}{a_{ii}}$. All other entries are 0.

18. If P is a modified permutation matrix and P^{-1} is its inverse, then $p_{ij}^{-1} = 0$, if $p_{ji} = 0$, and $p_{ij}^{-1} = 1/p_{ji}$, if $p_{ji} \neq 0$. In other words, P^{-1} is like the transpose but with nonzero numbers replaced by their reciprocals.

EXERCISES 2.5

1. (a) $x_1 = -8$, $x_2 = 0$, $x_3 = -4$.

   (b) $x_1 = 11 - 18x_3 + 35x_4$, $x_2 = 4 - 6x_3 + 14x_4$.

   (c) No solutions.

2. $x_1 = 5 + 2x_3$, $x_2 = -2 - x_3 - 7x_4$.

5. $x_1 = 1 + 2x_4$, $\quad x_2 = 1 - 4x_4$, $\quad x_3 = 1 - x_4$.
   $x_1 = -1 + 2x_4$, $\quad x_2 = 0 - 4x_4$, $\quad x_3 = 1 - x_4$.
   $x_1 = 0 + 2x_4$, $\quad x_2 = 1 - 4x_4$, $\quad x_3 = -1 - x_4$.

6. (a) $\begin{bmatrix} 3 & 2 \\ 4 & 3 \end{bmatrix}$ (b) $\begin{bmatrix} 0 & 4 & -5 \\ 1 & -18 & 24 \\ 0 & -3 & 4 \end{bmatrix}$

(c) $\begin{bmatrix} \frac{1}{2} & -\frac{1}{2} & \frac{1}{2} \\ -\frac{1}{2} & \frac{1}{2} & \frac{1}{2} \\ \frac{1}{2} & \frac{1}{2} & -\frac{1}{2} \end{bmatrix}$ (d) $\begin{bmatrix} 1 & 2 & \frac{4}{3} \\ 1 & \frac{1}{2} & -\frac{5}{6} \\ 0 & 0 & \frac{1}{3} \end{bmatrix}$

(e) $\begin{bmatrix} \frac{1}{2} & -\frac{1}{2} & \frac{1}{2} & 0 \\ -\frac{1}{2} & \frac{1}{2} & \frac{1}{2} & 0 \\ \frac{1}{2} & \frac{1}{2} & -\frac{1}{2} & 0 \\ 0 & 0 & 0 & 1 \end{bmatrix}$ (f) Inverse does not exist.

(g) Inverse does not exist.

8. $ad - bc \neq 0$.   **9.** $\begin{bmatrix} \dfrac{d}{\Delta} & -\dfrac{b}{\Delta} \\ -\dfrac{c}{\Delta} & \dfrac{a}{\Delta} \end{bmatrix}$ where $\Delta = ad - bc$.

12. (a) $\begin{bmatrix} 1 & 0 & 0 \\ -2 & 1 & 0 \\ 1 & -2 & 1 \end{bmatrix}$ $\begin{bmatrix} 1 & -\frac{1}{2} & -\frac{1}{12} \\ 0 & -\frac{1}{4} & \frac{5}{24} \\ 0 & 0 & \frac{1}{6} \end{bmatrix}$

(b) Pivots can always be chosen on the main diagonal. Start pivoting in the lower right corner for lower triangular matrices and move up the main diagonal. Start pivoting in the upper left corner and move down for the upper triangular case.

13. (a) (3/10, 2/5, 3/10).   (b) (1/4, 1/2, 1/4).   (c) (1/4, 1/2, 1/4).
(d) (28/71, 18/71, 25/71).

16. We started with the tableau $(A \,|\, I)$ and ended with $(P \,|\, B)$. Therefore, $BA = P$.

18. If A is square and $x \neq 0$ exists such that $xA = 0$, and if A^{-1} also exists, we have $0 = (xA)A^{-1} = x(AA^{-1}) = xI = x$, contradicting $x \neq 0$. A similar proof works for y.

19. If A is singular, then there is an $x \neq 0$ such that $xA = 0$. But then $xC = (xA)B = 0$ also so C is singular. Similarly, if B is singular, there is a $y \neq 0$ so that $By = 0$, and then $Cy = A(By) = 0$ so that C is singular. Conversely, if C is singular, there is an $x \neq 0$ such that $xC = (xA)B = 0$; if B is nonsingular, then $xA = 0$ so A is singular; if A is nonsingular, then $y = xA \neq 0$ so $yB = 0$ and B is singular. Hence, C is singular only if either A or B (or both) is singular.

EXERCISES 2.6

1. (h)
$$\begin{bmatrix} x_1 \\ x_2 \\ x_3 \\ x_4 \end{bmatrix} = h \begin{bmatrix} -3 \\ 2 \\ 1 \\ 0 \end{bmatrix} + k \begin{bmatrix} -1 \\ 6 \\ 0 \\ 1 \end{bmatrix}$$

2. (a)
$$\begin{bmatrix} 5 \\ 1 \\ -1 \\ 0 \end{bmatrix} \begin{bmatrix} 0 \\ 0 \\ 2 \\ 1 \end{bmatrix}$$

   (b) Two.

   (c) Two. Because $A = M^{-1}T$, any linear dependence had by the rows of T is shared by the rows of A, and conversely.

3. Using the hint, we note that every time we pivot we create a new basis column vector independent of those created previously. But, to be able to pivot on a new row, the new row must be independent of the rows previously pivoted on. Hence, there must be the same number of linearly independent rows as there are columns of A.

EXERCISES 2.7

1. (a), (b), and (d) are parallel; also, (c) and (e) are parallel.

2. The plane whose equation is $x_1 - 3x_2 + 2x_3 = 9$ is parallel to (a), (b), and (c) and passes through the point. Similarly, $-x_1 + 2x_3 = 1$ is parallel to (c) and (e) and goes through the point.

4.
$$\begin{bmatrix} 1 \\ 4 \\ -11 \end{bmatrix} = \begin{bmatrix} 1 \\ 2 \\ -3 \end{bmatrix} + 2 \begin{bmatrix} 0 \\ 1 \\ -4 \end{bmatrix}$$

6. The first line can be written as
$$\begin{bmatrix} x_1 \\ x_2 \\ x_3 \end{bmatrix} = \begin{bmatrix} 2 \\ 4 \\ 0 \end{bmatrix} + \lambda \begin{bmatrix} 2 \\ 2 \\ 1 \end{bmatrix}.$$

   Since $\begin{bmatrix} 2 \\ 2 \\ 1 \end{bmatrix}$ does not satisfy the equations of the second line, they are not parallel.

7. One answer is $x_1 - 4x_2 + 2x_3 = 6$.

9. If we equate the two equations we have
$$k \begin{bmatrix} 1 \\ 1 \\ 1 \end{bmatrix} - t \begin{bmatrix} -1 \\ 1 \\ -1 \end{bmatrix} = \begin{bmatrix} -1 \\ 1 \\ 2 \end{bmatrix}$$

   and these simultaneous equations do not have a solution.

11. If we consider the equations for the two lines and equate them as in 9 above, then we can either solve for the two parameters or not. In the first case the lines intersect, and in the second they are skew.

12. If they are coincident, they are parallel because they (can) have the same equation, so the condition is necessary. For sufficiency, assume they are parallel and coincident with equations $x = A_0 + A_1 k$, $x = B_0 + B_1 t$. Since they are parallel, $A_1 = r B_1$ for some r. Since they intersect, there are values of k and t (say, $\bar{k}$ and $\bar{t}$) such that $\bar{x} = A_0 + A_1 \bar{k} = B_0 + B_1 \bar{t}$ so that they intersect at point $\bar{x}$. But then $A_0 - B_0 = A_1 \bar{k} - B_1 \bar{t} = B_1(r\bar{k} - \bar{t})$. Hence, the first line can be written $x = A_0 + A_1 k = B_0 + B_1(r\bar{k} - \bar{t}) + B_1 r k - B_0 + B_1(r\bar{k} - \bar{t} + rk)$. If we now set $t = r\bar{k} - \bar{t} + rk$ we see it is the same as the second equation.

14. $-x_1 + 7x_2 + 5x_3 = 2.$

17. Suppose the points are

$$\begin{bmatrix} a_1 \\ b_1 \\ c_1 \end{bmatrix}, \begin{bmatrix} a_2 \\ b_2 \\ c_2 \end{bmatrix}, \begin{bmatrix} a_3 \\ b_3 \\ c_3 \end{bmatrix}.$$

The equation of line through the first two points is

$$\begin{bmatrix} a_1 \\ b_1 \\ c_1 \end{bmatrix} + t \begin{bmatrix} a_1 - a_2 \\ b_1 - b_2 \\ c_1 - c_2 \end{bmatrix}.$$

If the third point lies on this line, then for some t' we have

$$\begin{bmatrix} a_1 \\ b_1 \\ c_1 \end{bmatrix} + t' \begin{bmatrix} a_1 - a_2 \\ b_1 - b_2 \\ c_1 - c_2 \end{bmatrix} = \begin{bmatrix} a_3 \\ b_3 \\ c_3 \end{bmatrix},$$

and we can easily rearrange to show that the third vector is a weighted combination of the first two.

18. They both go through the point $\begin{bmatrix} 15 \\ -4 \\ 3 \end{bmatrix}.$

EXERCISES 2.8

1. $x_1 + x_2 + x_3 = 1.$

2. (a) Yes.   (b) No.
(c) The given line passes through (i) and lines in (ii).   (d) Lies in both planes.
(e) This point is not in either plane.

4. (a), (c), and (d) are collinear.

6. (a) $3x_1 + 4x_2 + 2x_3 = 1.$ (b) $x_1 + x_2 + x_3 = 0.$
(c) $2x_1 + 5x_2 + 8x_3 = 5.$

8. Substituting, we have $AC + pAD = b$. We can solve for p unless $AD = 0$, which is exactly the condition that the line be parallel to the plane.

9. (a) (ii).   (b) (iii) or (ii).   (c) (i).   (d) (ii).   (e) (ii).   (f) (ii).
(g) (iii).   (h) (ii).   (i) (iii).   (j) (iii).

12. Given $x = w_0 B_0 - w_1 B_1 + \cdots + w_k B_k$ with $w_0 + w_1 + \cdots + w_k = 1$, multiply the second equation by B_0 and subtract from the first to eliminate w_0. This gives the stated tableau and also the weighted combination form of the equation.

EXERCISES 3.1

1. Extreme points are $\begin{bmatrix} 0 \\ 0 \end{bmatrix}$, $\begin{bmatrix} 4 \\ 0 \end{bmatrix}$, $\begin{bmatrix} 12/7 \\ 12/7 \end{bmatrix}$.

2. (a)

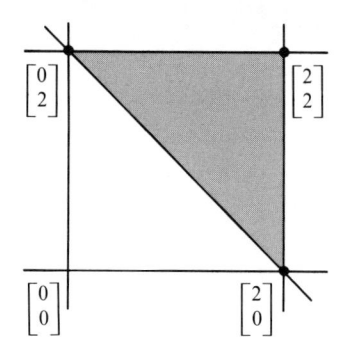

(b)   Set is unbounded. $\begin{bmatrix} 2 \\ 2 \end{bmatrix}$ is an extreme point.

(c)   The convex set is empty.

(d)

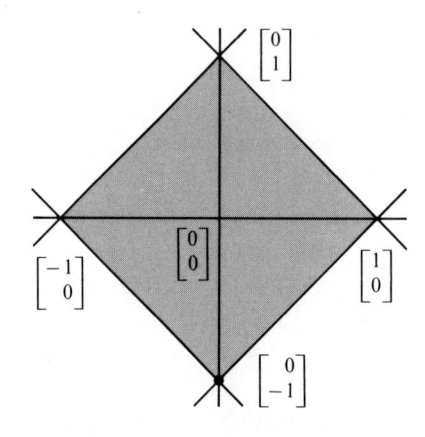

(e)   The convex region is unbounded between the parallel planes $x_1 = 5$ and $x_1 = 3$.

Extreme points are $\begin{bmatrix} 3 \\ 0 \\ 0 \end{bmatrix} \begin{bmatrix} 5 \\ 0 \\ 0 \end{bmatrix}$.

4. (a), (c), (e), and (f) are convex.

6. (a)   We know $A \cap \tilde{A} = \varnothing$; since $A - B \subseteq A$, it follows that $(A - B) \cap \tilde{A} = \varnothing$.

(b)   A new moon is the difference of two circles and is not convex. If we draw the diagonal of a rectangle and remove one of the two resulting triangles we have a convex set (triangle) remaining.

8. No. Let A and B be two disjoint circles.

9. (a) $x \geq 0, y \geq 0, z \geq 0$; all integer $(x, y, z) \geq (0, 0, 0)$.
   (b) $5x + 3y + z \leq 21$; $(4, 0, 1), (3, 2, 0), (3, 1, 3)$, and so on.
   (c) $x \geq 1, y \geq 1, z \geq 1$; $(3, 1, 3), (2, 3, 2), (2, 2, 5), (2, 1, 8)$ $(1, 5, 1), (1, 4, 4), (1, 3, 7)$ $(1, 2, 10), (1, 1, 13)$.
   (d) $x > y$; $(3, 1, 3), (2, 1, 8)$.   (e) $z \leq 4$; $(3, 1, 3)$.
   (f) $5x + 3y + z = 21$; $(3, 1, 3)$.   (g) $x \leq 2$; $\emptyset$.

11. The points are $z = a \begin{bmatrix} 1 \\ 0 \end{bmatrix} + (1 - a) \begin{bmatrix} 0 \\ 0 \end{bmatrix} = \begin{bmatrix} a \\ 1 - a \end{bmatrix}$ and are on the line segment connecting $\begin{bmatrix} 1 \\ 0 \end{bmatrix}$ and $\begin{bmatrix} 0 \\ 1 \end{bmatrix}$.

13. It is a tetrahedron lying in C4.

14. (a) $x \geq 0, y \geq 0, x + y \leq 1$.
   (b) $\begin{bmatrix} x \\ y \end{bmatrix} = \begin{bmatrix} 1/3 \\ 1/3 \end{bmatrix}$. None of the inequalities is tight.
   (c) $\begin{bmatrix} 1/2 \\ 0 \end{bmatrix}$; $y \geq 0$ is tight. $\begin{bmatrix} 0 \\ 1/2 \end{bmatrix}$; $x \geq 0$ is tight.

   $\begin{bmatrix} 1/2 \\ 1/2 \end{bmatrix}$; $x + y < 1$ is tight.
   (d) $\begin{bmatrix} 0 \\ 0 \end{bmatrix}$; $x \geq 0, y \geq 0$ is tight.

   $\begin{bmatrix} 1 \\ 0 \end{bmatrix}$; $y \geq 0, x + y \leq 1$ are tight.

   $\begin{bmatrix} 0 \\ 1 \end{bmatrix}$; $x \geq 0, x + y \leq 1$ are tight.

EXERCISES 3.2

1. If we pivot on 2 in $T^{(0)}$, we get $T^{(3)}$. If we pivot on 5/2 in $T^{(3)}$, we get $T^{(2)}$. If we pivot on 3/5 in $T^{(2)}$, we get $T^{(1)}$. ...

2. (a) $\begin{bmatrix} 0 \\ 0 \end{bmatrix}, \begin{bmatrix} 4 \\ 0 \end{bmatrix}, \begin{bmatrix} 2 \\ 4 \end{bmatrix}, \begin{bmatrix} 0 \\ 6 \end{bmatrix}$.   (b) $\begin{bmatrix} 0 \\ 0 \end{bmatrix}, \begin{bmatrix} 4 \\ 0 \end{bmatrix}, \begin{bmatrix} 144 \\ 248 \end{bmatrix}, \begin{bmatrix} 5 \\ 0 \end{bmatrix}$.

4. If we pivot on the 1 in column 1 of $T^{(0)}$ we get

A_1	A_2	E_1	E_2		
1	2	1	0	4	A_1
0	−5	−3	1	−6	E_2

   which corresponds to the pivot $\begin{bmatrix} 4 \\ 0 \end{bmatrix}$, which does not satisfy the constraint $3x_1 + x_2 \leq 6$.

6. (a, b)

$A_1{}^+$	$A_1{}^-$	A_2	E_1	E_2	E_3		
1	−1	1	1	0	0	6	E_1
2	−2	1	0	1	0	8	E_2
3	−3	2	0	0	1	0	E_3

   (c) $A_1{}^+$ and $A_1{}^-$ are linearly dependent; hence, both can't be in the basis.
   (d) $\begin{bmatrix} 2 \\ 4 \end{bmatrix}, \begin{bmatrix} -12 \\ 18 \end{bmatrix}, \begin{bmatrix} 16 \\ -24 \end{bmatrix}$.

8. Now the extreme points are $\begin{bmatrix} 0 \\ 0 \end{bmatrix}$, $\begin{bmatrix} 20 \\ 80 \end{bmatrix}$, $\begin{bmatrix} 200/3 \\ 100/3 \end{bmatrix}$.

10. If x is any feasible solution with $x \geq 0$ then $a_1 x_1 + \cdots + a_n x_n \leq 0 \leq b$ for any $b \geq 0$. Hence, the constraint is superfluous.

12. (d) The extreme points are $\begin{bmatrix} 0 \\ 0 \end{bmatrix}$, $\begin{bmatrix} 1 \\ 0 \end{bmatrix}$, and $\begin{bmatrix} 3 \\ 2 \end{bmatrix}$. The convex set is unbounded.

EXERCISES 3.3

1. Pivoting on the 2 in the first column of $T^{(0)}$ gives

A_1	A_2	E_1	E_2	E_3		
1	$\frac{1}{2}$	$\frac{1}{2}$	0	0	4	A_1
0	$\frac{1}{2}$	$-\frac{1}{2}$	1	0	2	E_2
0	$\frac{3}{2}$	$\frac{1}{2}$	0	1	8	E_3
0	$-\frac{3}{2}$	$\frac{1}{2}$	0	0	4	

which corresponds to $\begin{bmatrix} 4 \\ 0 \end{bmatrix}$. Pivoting on the second $\frac{1}{2}$ in the A_2 column gives

A_1	A_2	E_1	E_2	E_3		
1	0	1	-1	0	2	A_1
0	1	-1	2	0	4	A_2
0	0	2	-3	1	13/2	E_3
0	0	-1	3	0	10	

which corresponds to $\begin{bmatrix} 2 \\ 4 \end{bmatrix}$. One more pivot brings us to the optimum tableau $T^{(2)}$ in the text.

3. In two pivots the solution is $x = \begin{bmatrix} 4 \\ 0 \end{bmatrix}$, $w = \left(\frac{2}{5}, \frac{1}{5} \right)$.

6. In two pivots we get $x = \begin{bmatrix} 64 \\ 105 \end{bmatrix}$, $w = (411/49,\ 78/7)$.

7. (a)   Min $18x_1 + 12x_2$.

Subject to:

$$20x_1 + 10x_2 \leq 1000$$
$$10x_1 + 15x_2 \leq 400$$
$$20x_1 + 10x_2 \leq 200$$
$$20x_1 \quad\ \leq 150$$
$$x_1 + \tfrac{1}{2}x_2 \leq 5$$
$$2x_1 + x_2 \leq 20$$
$$20x_2 \leq 500$$
$$x_1 \quad\quad \geq 0$$
$$x_2 \geq 0$$

9. $\frac{1}{2} \leq a \leq 3$.

10. Minimizing wc and maximizing $-wc$ are the same. Hence,

$$
\left.\begin{array}{c}
\text{Min } wc \\
\text{Subject to:} \\
wA \geq b \\
w \geq 0
\end{array}\right\} \quad \text{is equivalent to} \quad \left(\begin{array}{c}
\text{Max } -wc \\
\text{Subject to:} \\
-wA \leq -b \\
w \geq \quad 0
\end{array}\right.
$$

and transposing the matrices and vectors and setting $x = w'$ gives the form as stated.

11. $\quad$ Max $-3x_1 - 2x_2$.
    Subject to:
    $$
    \begin{array}{rl}
    -\ x_1 +\ x_2 &\leq -1 \\
    -4x_1 + 2x_2 &\leq -8 \\
    x_1, x_2 &\geq \quad 0
    \end{array}
    $$

EXERCISES 4.1

3. The new point is $(3, 0)$ in Figure 4.1.5.

4. Since $b = 12A_3$, the problem is degenerate. After one pivot, the optimum answer is $x_1 = x_2 = 0$, $x_3 = 12$, value $= 36$, $w_1 = 0$, and $w_2 = 4$.

6. Maximum problem has unbounded solution. Minimum problem is infeasible.

7. $x' = (7, 5, 0, 15)$, value $= 2820$.

8. (a) $x' = (2000, 0, 0)$, value $= 54,000$.
   (b) $x' = (240, 720, 2160)$, value $= 51,840$.
   (c) Gross revenue in (b) is less than or equal to that of (a).

9. $\Delta = (3, 3, 2.5)$, cost $= 172.5$.

EXERCISES 4.2

1. (b) $/T$. Copper.

2. (a) Dividing the pivot row changes dimensions as indicated. Adding multiples of it to other rows does not change their dimensions.
   (c) Since we never pivot in the last row, its dimensions remain unchanged.

3. Subcontract in the plastics shop because the imputed value of additional minutes is $.40, which is greater than the subcontracting cost. Don't subcontract in the assembly shop.

5. Sell zinc and lead but not copper.

7. The resource is available in excess.

9. (a)

$$\text{\$/Ton}$$

		x_1	x_2	x_3	x_4	
	w_{11}	1	0	1	0	3
Tons/Week	w_{12}	1	0	0	1	7
	w_{21}	0	1	1	0	6
	w_{22}	0	1	0	1	4
		25	20	15	30	

$\text{\$/Ton}$

Tons/Week

(b) $w = (15, 10, 0, 20)$, $x' = (3, 0, 0, 4)$, cost $= 195$.

(c)   The simplex dual variables correspond to the special dual solutions discussed in Section 1.6.

EXERCISES 4.3

2.   For the range of b_2, we need $180 - \delta/10 \geq 0$ and $180 + 2\delta/5 \geq 0$, which gives the indicated interval.

4.   From Figure 4.3.3, we have for the range of b_3 that $600 + 4\delta/3 \geq 0$, $3000 - 10\delta/3 \geq 0$, and $2100 - \delta/3 \geq 0$, giving the indicated interval.

EXERCISES 4.4

1.   Write $wA = c$ as $wA \geq c$ and $w(-A) \geq -c$ with vectors of dual variables x^+ and x^-. The new maximizing problem is

$$\text{Max } c(x^+ - x^-)$$

Subject to:

$$A(x^+ - x^-) \leq b$$
$$x^+, x^- \geq 0$$

and the substitution $x = x^+ - x^-$ gives the formulation as in (c).

3.   Min $2w_1 + w_2 - 5w_3$, subject to $w_1 - w_3 \geq 1$, $w_1 + w_2 \geq 1$, $w_2 - w_3 \geq 1$, and w_2, $w_3 \geq 0$; w_1 is unrestricted.

4.   Min $2w_1 + 4w_2$, subject to $w_1 + w_2 \geq 1$, $w_1 + w_2 \geq 2$, $w_1 \leq 0$, and $w_2 \geq 0$. If we increase the 2 on the righthand side, the objective function will decrease at the rate w_1 (which is negative or 0).

5.   Case (a) is in the $A^{(12)}$ area, case (b) is in the $A^{(11)}$ area, and case (c) is in the $A^{(21)}$ area. The $A^{(22)}$ area is the usual case as previously emphasized.

EXERCISES 4.5

1.   (a) $-3x_1 + 5x_2 - x_3 \leq 7$
$2x_1 - 6x_2 - 2x_3 \leq 9$
$x_1 + x_2 + 3x_3 \leq -16$

(b) $-3x_1 + 5x_2 - x_3 \geq 7$
$2x_1 - 6x_2 - 2x_3 \geq 9$
$x_1 + x_2 + 3x_3 \geq -16$

(c)   To get (b), we need merely reverse the signs of (a).

2. (a) $\text{Max}(x_1^+ - x_1^-) - 2(x_2^+ - x_2^-) + 3x_3$

Subject to:

$$-3(x_1^+ - x_1^-) + 5(x_2^+ - x_2^-) - x_3 \le 7$$
$$2(x_1^+ - x_1^-) - 6(x_2^+ - x_2^-) - 2x_3 \le 9$$
$$(x_1^+ - x_1^-) + (x_2^+ - x_2^-) + 3x_3 \le -16$$
$$x_1^+, x_1^-, x_2^+, x_2^-, x_3 \ge 0$$

3. If b has a negative component there is nothing to prove. Hence, assume $b \ge 0$. But then the last added inequality has the negative of the sum of the components of b, and so it is negative.

6. (a) $w_1 - 7w_2 + 6w_3 \ge 5$
$$-9w_1 + 8w_2 - 3w_3 \ge -4$$
$$2w_1 + 3w_2 - 5w_3 \ge -1$$
$$6w_1 - 4w_2 + 2w_3 \ge 0$$

10. $\text{Min } w_1^+ - 2w_2^+ + 3w_3 + w_4$
Subject to:
$$5w_1^+ - 3w_2^+ + 5w_3 - 2w_4 \ge -1$$
$$-7w_1^+ + 2w_2^+ + 4w_3 + 5w_4 \ge 6$$
$$w_1^+, w_2^+, w_3, w_4 \ge 0$$

15. Renumber box 8 to be box 10 and to follow a new box 8, which has the question: Are any of the variables nonpositive? If answer is no, go to box 10. If answer is yes, go to a new box 9 with the instruction: Replace the nonpositive variable by its negative. Then go to box 10.

EXERCISES 4.6

2. The initial tableau is:

x_1	x_2	x_3	y_1	y_2	y_3	y_4	
1	1	0	1	0	0	0	2
0	1	1	0	1	-1	0	1
1	0	1	0	0	0	1	5
-1	-1	-1	M	M	0	0	0

To complete the basis we bring in y_1 and y_2.

1	1	0	1	0	0	0	2	$= y_1$
0	1	1	0	1	-1	0	1	$= y_2$
1	0	1	0	0	0	1	5	$= y_4$
$-1-M$	$-1-2M$	$-1-M$	0	0	M	0	$-3M$	

1	0	-1	1	-1	1	0	1	$= y_1$
0	1	1	0	1	-1	0	1	$= x_2$
1	0	1	0	0	0	1	5	$= y_4$
$-1-M$	0	M	0	$1+2M$	$1+M$	0	$1-M$	

1	0	-1	1	-1	1	0	1	$= x_1$
0	1	1	0	1	-1	0	1	$= x_2$
0	0	2	-1	1	-1	1	4	$= y_4$
0	0	-1	$1+M$	M	0	0	2	

We now have feasibility, since there is no M in the objective function value. Two more pivots bring us to the optimum tableau:

1	1	0	1	0	0	0	2	$= x_2$
1	0	1	0	0	0	1	5	$= x_3$
2	0	0	1	-1	1	1	2	$= y_3$
1	0	0	$M+1$	M	0	1	7	

5. $x' = (0, 4)$, value $= 8$.

7. If x^0 is feasible for (4.6.2) then x^0, $x_{n+1} = 1$ is clearly feasible for (4.6.2), and conversely.

9. (b)

x_1	x_2	x_3	y_1	y_2	y_3		
1	1	$-1/2$	1	0	0	0	$= y_1$
-1	-1	1	0	1	0	0	$= y_2$
0	0	1	0	0	1	1	$= y_3$
-1	-2	$-K$	0	0	0	0	

1/2	1/2	0	1	1/2	0	0	$= y_1$
-1	-1	1	0	1	0	0	$= x_3$
1	1	0	0	-1	1	1	$= y_3$
$-1-K$	$-2-K$	0	0	K	0	0	

1	1	0	2	1	0	0	$= x_2$
0	0	1	2	2	0	0	$= x_3$
0	0	0	-2	-3	1	1	$= y_3$
$1+K$	0	0	$2+K$	$2+2K$	0	0	

Since this problem has an optimal solution with $x_3 = 0$, the original problem has no feasible solutions.

EXERCISES 4.7

2. (a) In the first period, we use the 100 units in inventory and produce 400 for the demand of 500. In period 2, we produce the 600 demanded with regular time. In period 3, we produce 400 with regular time and 400 with overtime for the 600 demand and 200 inventory. Since we used up all the regular time, there is no lower cost production schedule.

    (c) The solution of (a) has very uneven production levels. The solution of (b) uses overtime before regular time in the first period, which is not usual.

3.

Period	1	2	3
Regular	400	400	400
Overtime	0	200	200

This solution is much more satisfactory from a managerial point of view than those in Exercise 2.

5. In a blending problem we mix raw materials to make a product with given characteristics. Usually, we want to make these products as cheaply as possible so the problem is minimizing.

8. $x' = (90,000 \quad 140,000)$, value $= 30,000$.

9. (a) The dual solution is $w = (6.667, 0, 1.111)$ meaning grinder hours are in excess and all the hours on the two other machines are used up.

   (b) The dual solution is $w = (0, 0, 3.33, 0, .1)$ meaning that now both lathes and grinders have excess hours, and if we could sell more B bearings we could get additional profit of 10 cents each.

   (c) From (a) to (b) we increased our production of B bearings, which use twice as much lathe time as A bearings. Hence, we used up all the lathe hours.

11. (a) From row 1, we predict the gross profit in row 2 to be $61{,}400 + .556(1000) = 61{,}956$, which is correct. From row 2 to row 3, our prediction becomes 62,512, which is more than the 61,956 actually realized. This is because the dual solution changes in between.

   (d) In each range, we buy the most valuable machine as evaluated by the dual variables, and from this we can predict the changes in production.

EXERCISES 4.8

3. The interpretation is: if the jth production requirement is oversatisfied, then the corresponding dual value is 0; if the dual value of a requirement is positive, then the production requirement for it is satisfied exactly.

EXERCISES 4.9

1. (a) $b = 5A_3$.
   (b) $x' = (5/3, 5/3, 0)$, $w = (4/3, 4/3)$ and unique.

2. (b) $x' = (4/3, 4/3)$, $w = (0, 1/3, 1/3)$.

3. Under the given assumptions, the vector $x = 0$ is always feasible, and the set of all x vectors is bounded; hence, there is an optimal solution to the maximizing problem.

EXERCISES 5.1

3. (a) 45.

5. If we set $w_0 = 0$ then the values of w_1, w_2, ... are just the numbers marked on the nodes of the graph by the algorithm of Exercise 1.

6. For the primal problem corresponding to a project graph with n jobs and m nodes, we have a variable x_j for each job and a constraint for each node. In the dual problem, we have a variable w_i for each node and a constraint for each job; (4.1.1) and (4.1.2) are specific examples. The coefficient matrix E has a row for each node and a column for each constraint. In each column, there are just two nonzero entries: a $+1$ corresponding to the node at the top of the arrow; and a -1 corresponding to the feather end of the arrow. E is sometimes called the *incidence* matrix.

8. The shortest path problem for the graph of Figure 5.1.1 can be obtained by replacing t_j by $-t_j$ in (5.1.1) and (5.1.2). The algorithm of Exercise 1 will work with this change also. If we set $w_0 = 0$, then all other w_i will be nonpositive. Of course, we must interpret the final answer as being the negative of the length of the shortest path. In general if you want to find the shortest path between two given nodes in a graph, treat one as Start and the other as Finish and carry out the above procedure.

10. (a)   129 days.   (b)   71 days.

11. (a)   Three constraints for the dual problem, one for the primal problem, which is

$$\text{Max}(t_1 + t_3 + t_6)x_1 + (t_1 + t_4)x_2 + (t_2 + t_5)x_3$$

Subject to:

$$x_1 + x_2 + x_3 = 1$$
$$x_i \geq 0$$

(b)   The advantage of the new method is that it has only one constraint, so the problem is a knapsack problem (see Section 5.4) with one variable for each path. If there are only a few paths, the new method is good. However, typically there are thousands of paths in a project graph, so it is not the best method.

13. In the new tableau, the last row and objective function are

0	0	0	0	260	35	10	165	220	80	$\geq K$
0	0	0	-1	0	0	0	0	0	0	

15. (a, b)   If all the data are integers, then increasing the capacity of an arc either leaves the total flow fixed or increases it by 1. Hence, the dual variables must be 0 or 1.

   (c)   Since each w_i is 0 or 1, the optimum value of the dual problem is the sum of the capacities on the arcs for which $w_i = 1$. These form a cut whose capacity is equal to the total flow.

16. (a)   The algorithm of Exercise 1 can't handle constraints connecting jobs, but constraints can easily be added to the linear program.

EXERCISES 5.2

2. $x_1 = x_2 = 0$, $x_3 = 12$, value 48.

4.

x_1	x_2	x_3			
3	4	1	12		$= y_1$
2	3	1	12		$= y_2$
-6	-6	-4	0		$= cx$

x_1	x_2	y_1			
3	4	1	12		$= x_3$
-1	-1	-1	0		$= y_2$
6	10	4	48		$= cx$

5. (a)   Matrix has no inverse.

(c)
$$\begin{bmatrix} 1 & 0 & \frac{1}{2} \\ 0 & 1 & \frac{1}{2} \\ 0 & 0 & -\frac{1}{2} \end{bmatrix} \begin{bmatrix} 1 & 0 & 0 \\ 0 & 1 & 0 \\ 0 & -1 & 1 \end{bmatrix} \begin{bmatrix} 1 & 0 & 0 \\ 0 & 1 & 0 \\ -1 & 0 & 1 \end{bmatrix} = \begin{bmatrix} \frac{1}{2} & -\frac{1}{2} & \frac{1}{2} \\ -\frac{1}{2} & \frac{1}{2} & \frac{1}{2} \\ \frac{1}{2} & \frac{1}{2} & -\frac{1}{2} \end{bmatrix}$$

6. $w_1 = 1$, $w_3 = 3$, value 680.

EXERCISES 5.3

3.

	x_1	x_2	y_1	y_2		
	6	2	3	5	$\leq$	5000
	30	10	6	10	$\leq$	15000
	3	5	0	0	$\leq$	4000
	0	0	4	4	$\leq$	3000
	15	8	10	11		

5. The problem will have $m + \sum_{k=1}^{t} m_k$ rows and $\sum_{k=1}^{t} n_k$ columns.

6. The new proposal creates a new column in the master problem, but the simplex method will not bring that vector into the basis.

EXERCISES 5.4

1. $\delta_1 + 5\delta_2 \leq x \leq 2\delta_1 + 10\delta_2$, $\delta_1 + \delta_2 = 1$, $0 \leq \delta_i \leq 1$, and integer.

3. $x = \delta_1 e^a + \delta_2 e^{-a} + \delta_3 \sin a + \delta_4 \cos a + \delta_5 a^2$
$\delta_1 + \delta_2 + \delta_3 + \delta_4 + \delta_5 = 1$, $0 \leq \delta_i \leq 1$, and integer.

5. $\sum_{k=1}^{n} a_k \delta_k \leq x \leq \sum_{k=1}^{n} b_k \delta_k$, $\sum_{k=1}^{n} \delta_k = 1$, $0 \leq \delta_k \leq 1$, and integer.

6. (a) If $\delta_1 = 1$, $\delta_2 = 0$, the effective constraints are $A^{(1)}x \leq b^{(1)}$; if $\delta_1 = 0$, $\delta_2 = 1$, they are $A^{(2)}x \leq b^{(2)}$. Hence, the result is the union of these two convex sets.

7. We make $\sum \delta_i = 2$, and the truth set is the union of the intersections of pairs of convex sets. Or, $\sum \delta_i = k$, and we have the union of the intersections of k of the convex sets.

10. (a) $x + y > -\delta M$, $2x + y - z \leq (1 - \delta)M$, $-2x - y + z \leq (1 - \delta)M$.
(c) $x + y > -\delta M$, $x - y - 5 \geq -(1 - \delta)M$, $-x + y + 5 \geq -(1 - \delta)M$.

14. Accept 3, 4, 5, value 143.

16. For each good, there are n technological (precedence) constraints plus a nonnegativity constraint; hence, there are $(n + 1)m$ such in all. On each machine we have $\begin{bmatrix} m \\ 2 \end{bmatrix}$ ways of placing one of two goods before the other, hence, $n\begin{bmatrix} m \\ 2 \end{bmatrix}$ either-or constraints, and the same number of integer variables.

18. Optimum tour is 1-3-2-5-4-1, whose distance is 72.

19. $x_{13} = x_{32} = x_{25} = x_{54} = x_{41} = 1$, all other x_{ij}'s $= 0$; $u_1 = 0$, $u_3 = 1$, $u_2 = 2$, $u_5 = 3$, $u_5 = 3$, $u_4 = 4$.

20. $\text{Min} \sum_{i=1}^{n} k_i x_i + \sum_{k=1}^{n} \delta_i b_i$

Subject to:

$$\sum_{i=1}^{n} x_i \geq d$$

$$0 \leq x_i \leq u_i \delta_i$$

$$0 \leq \delta_i \leq 1, \text{ and integer.}$$

23.
$$\text{Min} \sum_{i=1}^{n} (k_i x_i + b_i \delta_i)$$

Subject to:

$$\delta_i u_i \leq x_i \leq \delta_i u_i$$
$$\sum \delta_i = 1$$
$$\delta_i \geq 0, \text{ and } u_0 = 0$$

EXERCISES 5.5

1. (a) -1.   (b) -102.   (c) $2,000,001$.   (d) 0.

2. (a) $\dfrac{9}{11} x_1 + \dfrac{8}{11} x_2 \geq 0$.   (b) $\dfrac{5}{11} x_1 + \dfrac{2}{11} x_2 \geq 0$.

   (c) Let $p = \dfrac{11}{q + 9}$ where $0 \leq q \leq 1$. The fractional cut then is

$$\left[\frac{2q + 7}{11}\right] x_1 + \left[\frac{3q + 5}{11}\right] x_2 = q.$$

3. (a) $2x + 4y \leq 15$.   (b) $2x + 4y \leq 14$.   (c) $2x + 4y \leq 13$.   (d) $2x + 4y \leq 12$
and $2x + 3y \leq 12$.   (e) $2x + 2y \leq 11$.

4. Given $a_1 x_1 + \cdots + a_n x_n \leq b$, we derive $\left[\dfrac{a_1}{p}\right] x_1 + \cdots + \left[\dfrac{a_n}{p}\right] x_n \leq \left[\dfrac{b}{p}\right]$. Since $p > 0$, there
are only a finite number of integer values for each coefficient $\left[\dfrac{a_i}{p}\right]$ or $\left[\dfrac{b}{p}\right]$. Hence, only a
finite number of constraints are possible.

5. Clearly, the fractional parts f_j and f can take on an infinite number of values in (5.5.7).

6. $x_1 = 0$, $x_2 = 1$, $x_3 = 0$, $x_4 = 0$, $x_5 = 1$; value $= 35$.

7. $x_1 = 3$, $x_2 = 3$, $x_3 = 18$.

EXERCISES 5.6

1. (a) Take 1, 4, 5, value 141.   (b) Take 1, 3, 6, value 149.   (c) Take 1, 3, 4,
value 164.

2. (a) Same answer.   (b) Take two of 2, and 1 of 4, value 153.   (c) Take two of 1,
and 1 of 5, value 165.

4. $x_3^1 = 0$, $x_2^1 = 10$, $x_1^1 = 16$, $x_2^2 = 0$, $x_1^2 = 7$, $x_3^2 = 11$, $x = 21$.

7. Set $L = \infty$ in the initial box. Replace the words "upper bound" by "lower bound" in
Fig. 5.6.3; test to see if the current lower bound is greater than the current L.

EXERCISES 6.1

1. (a) Let $f(x) = ax^{2k}$, $f'(x) = 2kax^{2k-1}$, $f'(0) = f(0) = 0$, if $a > 0$. The point $x = 0$ is a
minimum, since, for small ε, $f(+\varepsilon) = a(\varepsilon^k)^2 > 0$ and $f(-\varepsilon) = a(\varepsilon^k)^2 > 0$. The
opposite inequalities hold if $a < 0$.
   (b) Same reasoning.

3. Clearly, $f(0) = |0| = 0$. Let ε be a small positive number; then $f(\varepsilon) = |\varepsilon| > 0, f(-\varepsilon) = |\varepsilon| > 0$, so that 0 is a local minimum.

5. $x = .918$.   **7.** 0.3466.   **8.** 0.7148.

9. For x large in absolute value, say $|x| = 10^{30}$, the highest degree term of a polynomial is dominant. If the degree is odd, $f(M)$, and $f(-M)$ will be of opposite signs for M large enough. Hence, there is no absolute maximum or minimum.

12. (a) In Figs. 6.1.4 and 6.1.5, assume $b_1 - a_1 = 1$; discard an interval of x or $1 - y = x$. In Fig. 6.1.4, to preserve ratios we must have the condition $y/1 = (1 - y)/y$, giving the quadratic $y^2 + y - 1 = 0$.

(b) The positive root of this equation is $y = (\sqrt{5} - 1)/2 = .618034$.

14. $f'(x) = 10x + 11, f''(x) = -10 < 0$, so f is concave.

16. Suppose f and g are concave functions, then

$$(f + g)(tx + (1 - t)y) = f(tx + (1 - t)y) + g(tx + (1 - t)y)$$
$$\leq tf(x) + (1 - t)f(y) + tg(x) + (1 - t)g(y)$$
$$= t(f + g)(x) + (1 - t)(f + g)(y).$$

The concave proof is similar.

19. Let $f(x) = e^{x^2}$; then $f'(x) = 2xe^{x^2}$ and $f''(x) = 2e^{x^2} + 4x^2e^{x^2} = 2e^{x^2}(1 + 2x^2) > 0$ for all x.

22. If f is convex and $f(x) = f(y) = \text{Min } f(x)$ for some pair of points $x < y$, then we have $f(tx + (1 - t)y) = tf(x) + (1 - t)f(y) = f(x)$ for all t in $0 \leq t \leq 1$. If a concave function takes on its maximum at two distant points, then it takes it on at infinitely many points.

EXERCISES 6.2

1. Let $x = \sqrt{4 - y^2}$, so $f(x, y) = f(y) = (\sqrt{4 - y^2} - 1)^2 + y^2$. Finding $f''(x)$ and setting it to 0 gives $y = 0$ from which we find $x = \pm 2$.

3. $(0, 0)$.   **5.** $((1/2)\sqrt{17}, 1/2), ((-1/2)\sqrt{17}, 1/2)$.

7. $(x, y) = (1/4, 1/2), (u, v) = (-13/8, 19/4)$.

EXERCISES 6.3

1. Max is 1.   **3.** (a) 1.   (b) e^{-1}.

5. Min is -1 at $x = -\pi/2$ and $x = 3\pi/2$.

7. The minima are at $x = 0$ and $x = 10$. The maxima are at $x = -10$ and $x = 20/3$.

9. (a) $(0, 5)$, distance $\sqrt{65}$.   (b) $(3, 4)$, distance 5.   (c) distance 0.

11. The constraint $g(x) \geq b$ is equivalent to $-g(x) \leq -b$, which is equivalent to $-g(x) + y^2 + b = 0$. Setting $L = f(x) - \lambda(-g(x) + y^2 + b)$ we get $L_b = -\lambda$. Since increasing b strengthens the constraint, $\lambda \geq 0$.

13. Closest point is $(12\sqrt{5}, 6/\sqrt{5})$.

14. (a) $L = \sum_j c_j x_j + \frac{1}{2} \sum_i \sum_j q_{ij} x_i x_j - \sum_i \lambda_i (\sum_j a_{ij} x_j - b_i) + \sum_j \mu_j x_j$.

(b) Remember, x_j occurs twice in the second term.   (c)   Use rules 1 and 3.

(d) Add the constraint of (b) to the original constraints. Then find a feasible solution to the problem using an arbitrary objective function to make it a linear programming problem.

EXERCISES 6.4

1. For a separable concave function the approximation (6.4.7) will hold but with the constants satisfying $c_{1j} < c_{2j} < \cdots < c_{tj}$. The problem then becomes as in (6.4.9) but with minimization instead of maximization, and reversed inequalities.

2. $x_1 = 3.674$, $x_2 = 2.326$, value $= 47.78$.

3. The function to be minimized is

$$h = 7\sqrt{x_1} + x_2(8 - x_2) - p \left[\frac{1}{x_1 + x_2 - 5/2} + \frac{1}{x_1} + \frac{1}{x_2} \right]$$

EXERCISES 7.1

1. (a) $\{HHH, THH, HTH, TTH, HHT, HTT, THT, TTT\}$.

(b) $\{0, 1, 2, 3\}$, or literally $\{TTT, HTH$ or THH or HHT; and so on$\}$.

(c) $\left\{ H, TH, TTH, \ldots, \underset{(n-1)}{TT}, \ldots, TH, \underset{(n)}{TT}, \ldots, T \right\}$.

2. (a) No heads, two tails before a head, two consecutive heads.

EXERCISES 7.3

5. (a) 3/11.   (b) 5/13.   (c) 3/7.   **6.** (a) 1/2.   (b) 5/11.

EXERCISES 7.4

1. (a) $P\{X \le b\} = P\{X \le a\} + P\{a < X \le b\}$, since the sets $\{X \le a\}$ and $\{a < X \le b\}$ are disjoint, and their union is $\{X \le b\}$. See (7.4.1) (c).

(b) $P\{X > a\} = 1 - P\{X \le a\} = 1 - \int_{-\infty}^{a} f(x)\, dx$.

2. (a) $1 - F_T(100)$.   (b) $F_T(100) - F_T(50)$.   (c) $\dfrac{1 - F_T(100)}{1 - F_T(50)}$.

3. (a) Solve for k: $k \int_0^1 x(1-x)\, dx = 1$, or $k \dfrac{1}{6} = 1$, so $k = 6$.

(b) $P\left\{ X \le \frac{1}{4} \right\} = 6 \left[\dfrac{\left(\frac{1}{4}\right)^2}{2} - \dfrac{\left(\frac{1}{4}\right)^3}{3} \right]$.

EXERCISES 7.5

1. (a) The density must integrate to one:

$$1 = \int_1^\infty Kx^{-6}\,dx = \frac{Kx^{-5}}{-5}\Big|_1^\infty = \frac{K}{5}, \quad \text{or} \quad K = 5.$$

(b) $E[X] = K\int_1^\infty xx^{-6}\,dx = \frac{K}{4} = \frac{5}{4}.$ $E[X^2] = \frac{5}{3},$ $\text{Var}[X] = \frac{5}{3} - \frac{5}{4} = \frac{5}{48}.$

(c) $E[X^2] = \frac{5}{3},$ $E[X^3] = \frac{5}{2}.$

(d) $F_{X^2}(y) = P\{X^2 \le y\} = P\{X \le \sqrt{y}\} = \int_1^{\sqrt{y}} Kx^{-6}\,dx.$

$$f_{X^2}(y) = K(\sqrt{y})^{-6}\frac{1}{2}y^{-1/2} = \frac{5}{2}y^{-7/2}.$$

$$E[X^2] = \int_1^\infty y\frac{5}{2}y^{-7/2}\,dy = \frac{5}{3}.$$

2. (a)
$$F_T(t) = \begin{cases} 0, & -\infty < t < 0.3(\text{hr}) \\ 0.8, & 0.3 \le t < 0.5 \\ 1, & 0.5 \le t \end{cases}$$

(b) 0.34 hrs.   (c) $\text{Var} = 0.0064,$ s.d. $= 0.08.$

3. (a) $E[X] = \frac{1+2+3+4+5+6}{6} = 3.5,$ $\text{Var}[X] = \frac{35}{12}.$

(b) $E[X_1 + \cdots X_n] = nE[X_1] = 3.5n,$ $\text{Var}[X_1 + \cdots X_n] = \frac{35}{12}n.$

5. (b) $x_{\text{med}} = \sqrt[3]{2} - 1.$

EXERCISES 7.6

1. (a) $E[X] = \frac{1+2+3+\cdots N}{N} = \frac{NH}{2}.$ 2. (a) $p^3.$ (b) $p^3 + 2p^2(1-p).$

4. $(1-p)^n.$ It is not likely that each man has precisely the same probability of solving the problem. In any case, the probabilities are unknown.
   (a) $1 - (1-p)^n;$ here $1 - (0.5)^4 = 0.9375.$
   (b) No. If one man had a very high probability, and the others no chance, then the average would be low, and hence the (estimated) chance would be low; yet, a solution would be obtained with at least the high probability referred to.

7. (a) $P\{\text{lose money}\} = P\{S < 10\} = \frac{1}{\sqrt{2\pi}}\int_{-\infty}^{(10-15)/6} e^{-1/2(2)}\,dx = 0.2.$

EXERCISES 7.7

1. (a) $1 - [F(2/5)]^2,$ assuming the plane can fly on one engine.
   (b) expected number of crashes $= (100)[F(2/5)]^2,$ probability of no crash $=$
       $(1 - [F(2/5)]^2)^{100}.$

3. $P\{\max(X_1, X_2, \ldots, X_n) \le t\} = P(X_1 \le t) \cap (X_2 \le t) \ldots \cap (X_n \le t) = P\{X_1 \le t\} \cdot$
    $P\{X_2 \le t\} \ldots P\{X_n \le t\} = G_1(t) \cdot G_2(t) \ldots G_n(t).$ If $G_i(t) = G(t)$, then

$$G_{\max}(t) = [G(t)]^n, \quad g_{\max}(t) = \frac{dG_{\max}}{dt} = nG(t)^{n-1} g(t).$$

10. (a) Obvious: $x^2 + y^2 \le 1$ describes such a disk.
    (b) Area of unit circle is π; so $k = \pi^{-1}$.

    (c) $f_{Y|X}(y; x) = \dfrac{1}{2\sqrt{1-x^2}}$ $-\sqrt{1-x^2} \le y \le \sqrt{1-x^2}$

    $= 0$ otherwise.

    (d) X and Y uncorrelated but dependent.

EXERCISES 7.8

1. (b) Two is carried out under (a). For three,

$$f_Z(z; 3) = \int_0^z e^{-a(z-x)} a(z-x) a e^{-ax} a\, dx = e^{-az} a^3 \frac{z^2}{2}.$$

Now guess that $f_Z(z; n) = e^{-az} \dfrac{a^n z^{n-1}}{(n-1)!}$, and show by induction that

$$f_Z(z; n+1) = f_Z(z; n) * f(z) = \int_0^z e^{-a(z-x)} a^n \frac{(z-x)^{n-1}}{(n-1)!} e^{-ax} a\, dx$$

$$= e^{-az} \frac{a^{n+1}}{n!} z^n.$$

EXERCISES 7.9

1. (a) 1/3.   (b) 2/3.   **2.** (a) 8/26.   (b) 26/51.

3. (a) $P\{H_1|B\} = \dfrac{(2/3)\pi_1}{(2/3)\pi_1 + (1/3)\pi_2}$, $P\{H_1|W\} = \dfrac{(1/3)\pi_1}{(1/3)\pi_1 + (2/3)\pi_2}.$

    (b) $P\{BB|H_1\} = 4.3/6.5$; $P\{BB|H_2\} = 2.1/6.5$; apply Bayes' formula. Same idea for other drawings.

7. (a) $F_{T_x}(t) = \dfrac{\pi_g e^{-gx}(1 - e^{-gt}) = \pi_b e^{-bx}(1 - e^{-bt})}{\pi_g e^{-gx} + \pi_b e^{-bx}}.$

    (b) $f_{T_x}(t) = \dfrac{\pi_g \cdot ge^{-g(t+x)} + \pi_b \cdot be^{-b(t+x)}}{\pi_g e^{-gx} + \pi_b e^{-bx}}.$

    (c) $E[T_x] = \dfrac{\dfrac{1}{g}\pi_g e^{-gx} + \dfrac{1}{g}\pi_b e^{-bx}}{\pi_g e^{-gx} + \pi_b e^{-bx}}.$ Since $b > g$, multiply numerator and denomina-

    tor by e^{gx}. When $x \to \infty$, the fraction $\to g^{-1}$. This stands to reason, for if the machine survives a long time, it must be in the good state; the remaining time in, state is exponential with mean g^{-1}.

    (d) $E[T_x] \to 4$ days.

EXERCISES 7.10

1. $E[e^{-sT}] = \lambda/(\lambda + s)$. The first two derivatives are $(d/ds)E[e^{-sT}] = E[-Te^{-sT}] = -\lambda/(\lambda + s)^2$ and $(d^2/ds^2)E[e^{-sT}] = E[T^2 e^{-sT}] = 2\lambda/(\lambda + s)^2$. Setting $s = 0$: $E[-T] = \lambda/\lambda^2$, so $E[T] = 1/\lambda$. $E[T^2] = 2/\lambda^2$, so $\mathrm{Var}[T] = 2/\lambda^2 - 1/\lambda^2 = 1/\lambda^2$.

2. The Poisson g.f. is $g(z) = e^{-z(1-N)} = E[z^a]$.

$$E[N] = \frac{dg}{dz}\bigg|_{z=1} = -ae^{-a(1-z)}(-1)\bigg|_{z=1} = a$$

$$E[N(N-1)] = \frac{d^2g}{dz^2} = a^2$$

$$\mathrm{Var}[N] = E[N^2] - (E[N])^2 = a^2 + a - a^2 = a.$$

EXERCISES 8.2

1. $1 - e^{-(\bar{I}/1000)} = 1 - (2/7)$, or $\bar{I} = (1000)\ln(7/2) = 1253$, using (8.2.10). And $E[N|\bar{I}] = 1000\{7 - 2[1 + 1.253]\} = \$35$, using (8.2.16).

2. $E[N|I] = \$116$, using (8.2.15). $E[N|\bar{I}] = 100\{5 - 2[1 + \ln(2.5)]\} = \$117$. The exponential demand distribution puts more demands below the mean;   for the cost figures used, it is advisable to stock less than the mean.

3. Since $1 - F_D(\bar{I}) = 1 - \dfrac{c}{p}$, the probability of being out of stock is $1 - F_D(\bar{I}) =$

    $P\{\text{Demand} > \bar{I}\} = 1 - \dfrac{c}{p}$. Thus, the probability of insufficient inventory is $1 - \dfrac{c}{p}$.

    Letting S_n denote the random number of shortages, or stockout periods, observe that S_n has the binomial distribution with mean $E[S_n] = n\left(1 - \dfrac{c}{p}\right)$, and $\mathrm{Var}[S_n] = n\left(1 - \dfrac{c}{p}\right)\dfrac{c}{p}$, since each period is an independent identical trial.

4. Find $\bar{I}$, the optimum inventory. If $80 > \bar{I}$, the limit has no effect: draw a graph of profit versus I.

EXERCISES 8.4

1. (a) $f_p(x|\beta) = \dfrac{(1-x)}{\displaystyle\int_0^1 (1-x)\dfrac{dx}{1}} = 2(1-x) \qquad (0 \le x \le 1)$

    $= 0 \qquad\qquad\qquad\qquad\qquad\qquad \text{otherwise}$

    (b) $P\{\beta \text{ in } 77 | \beta \text{ in } 76\} = \displaystyle\int_0^1 P\{\beta \text{ in } 77 | p = x\} f_p(x|\beta)\, dx$

    $= \displaystyle\int_0^1 x f_p(x|\beta)\, dx = \int_0^1 x\, 2(1-x)\, dx = \dfrac{1}{3}.$

(c)

Method: Work backwards. At D,(77) the optimum yields $\max(8, \frac{1}{3} \cdot 20) = \$8$, so he sells. At D, (76) the comparison is between \$10, and $\frac{1}{2} \cdot 20 + \frac{1}{2} 8 = \$14$. Strategy: wait at D, (76); if β does not buy during 76, sell (for \$8) in 77.

3. (a) Do not launch, since $\frac{5}{3} > \frac{4}{3}$.   (b) $p < \frac{4}{19}$.

4. (a)

		Gain	
		Success	Failure
	Accept	10¢	−20¢
Action	Do not Accept	−5¢	−5¢

(b) $E[\text{Gain}|p, \text{ Accept}] = 10\ p - 20(1-p)$. $E[\text{Gain}|p, \text{ Don't Accept}] = -5$. Take expectation over (random) p values, using prior distribution.

(d) $E[\text{Gain}|\text{Accept}] = 10x \frac{1}{2} - 20x \frac{1}{2} = -5$. $E[\text{Gain}|\text{Don't Accept}] = -5$.

(e) It is a toss-up. What is an argument for accepting the gamble? What is an argument against?

(f) The answers remain the same.

EXERCISES 8.5

1. (a) One opportunity $= \bar{R}_1 = \$25$. Two opportunities $= \bar{R}_2 = \bar{R}_1 + \int_{R_1}^{30} \frac{1}{10}(x - \bar{R}_1)\, dx =$

$25 + 1.25 = \$26.25$. Three opportunities $= \bar{R}_3 = 26.25 + \frac{1}{10}\int_0^{3.75} y\, dy = \$26.95$.

This is the seller's expected gain.

(b) $\text{Prob} = \dfrac{30 - 26.95}{10} = 0.3$.

(c) One opportunity $= \bar{R}_1 = \$30.00$. Two opportunities $= \bar{R}_2 = \$33.75$. Three opportunities $= \bar{R}_3 = \$35.86$. He should pay no more than $\bar{R}_3(c) - \bar{R}_3(a) = 35.86 - 26.95 = \$8.91$.

2. $\bar{R}_m = \bar{R}_{m-1} + \int_{R_{m-1}}^{\infty} (x - \bar{R}_{m-1}) f_m(x)\, dx; \qquad p_m = \bar{R}_{m-1}$.

7. (a) Choose τ to minimize $f(\tau) = \dfrac{\sqrt{\delta\tau}}{1 - e^{-r\tau}}$; that is, solve $\dfrac{df}{d\tau} = 0$, or $e^{r\tau} + 1 = 2\,r\tau$.

This can be done graphically, or by (Newton-Raphson iteration) computer; the answer is $\tau \cong 13 \simeq x$ (optimum size). Notice that the optimum τ doesn't depend on growth rate.

(b) Discounted cost $= \dfrac{\sqrt{13}}{1 - e^{-1.3}} \cong 5$.

EXERCISES 9.1

1. (a)   (c)

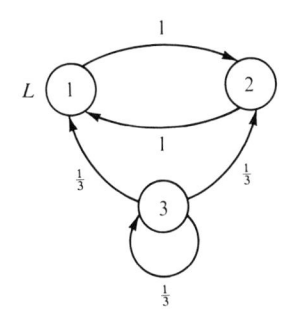
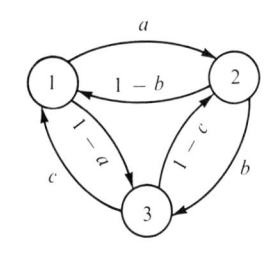

2. (a) $\begin{bmatrix} 0 & 1 & 0 \\ 0 & 0 & 1 \\ 1 & 0 & 0 \end{bmatrix}$ (b) $\begin{bmatrix} 0 & 1/2 & 1/2 \\ 0 & 0 & 1 \\ 0 & 0 & 1 \end{bmatrix}$

3.

$$\begin{array}{c} \\ 0 \\ 1 \\ 2 \end{array} \begin{array}{ccc} 0 & 1 & 2 \\ \begin{bmatrix} 1/2 & 1/2 & 0 \\ 7/12 & 5/12 & 0 \\ 0 & 2/3 & 1/3 \end{bmatrix} \end{array}$$

5.

$$\begin{array}{c} \\ 1 \\ 2 \\ 3 \end{array} \begin{array}{ccc} 1 & 2 & 3 \\ \begin{bmatrix} a & (1-a)/2 & (1-a)/2 \\ (1-b)/2 & b & (1-b)/2 \\ (1-c)/2 & (1-c)/2 & c \end{bmatrix} \end{array}$$

6.

$$\begin{array}{c} \\ 1 \\ 2 \\ 3 \\ 4 \\ 5 \end{array} \begin{array}{ccccc} 1 & 2 & 3 & 4 & 5 \\ \begin{bmatrix} 0 & 1/3 & 1/3 & 1/3 & 0 \\ 1 & 0 & 0 & 0 & 0 \\ 1/2 & 0 & 0 & 0 & 1/2 \\ 1/2 & 0 & 0 & 0 & 1/2 \\ 0 & 0 & 1 & 0 & 0 \end{bmatrix} \end{array}$$

The Markov chain is not regular.

8. Let $q = 1 - a - b$; then the transition matrix is:

	Sell	8	9	10	11	12	13	14
Sell	1	0	0	0	0	0	0	0
8	1	0	0	0	0	0	0	0
9	0	b	q	a	0	0	0	0
10	0	0	b	q	a	0	0	0
11	0	0	0	b	q	a	0	0
12	0	0	0	0	b	q	a	0
13	0	0	0	0	0	b	q	a
14	1	0	0	0	0	0	0	0

11. (a) $x_i \leq M$ for all i, so $x \leq Mf$.
 (b) $pf = f$ and $x \leq f$, so $Px \leq M(Pf) = MP$.
 (c) Since $x_i \leq x_k$ for all i and $p_{kj} \leq 1$, we have

$$(Px)_k = p_{k1}x_1 + \cdots + p_{kj}x_j + \cdots + p_{kn}x_n \leq x_k = M.$$

 (d) $(Px)_i \leq x_k$ for all i by the same proof as (c), hence $Px > x$ is false for every component.
 (e) $x - Px + f \leq 0$ and $K > 0$ implies $Px > x$, a contradiction.

13. (b)

$$
\begin{array}{c}
 \\
A \\
B
\end{array}
\begin{array}{cc}
A & B \\
\left[\begin{array}{cc}
p_A & 1 - p_A \\
1 - p_B & p_B
\end{array}\right]
\end{array}
$$

 (c) $53/200$, $1/8$.
 (d) Not all customers will have the same probabilities, so a number of different chains should be set up for different customer classes.

15.

$$
\begin{array}{c}
AA \\
AB \\
BA \\
BB
\end{array}
\begin{array}{cccc}
AA & AB & BA & B \\
\left[\begin{array}{cccc}
r_{AA} & 1 - r_{AA} & 0 & 0 \\
0 & 0 & r_{AB} & 1 - r_{AB} \\
r_{AB} & 1 - r_{AB} & 0 & 0 \\
0 & 0 & 1 - r_{BB} & r_{BB}
\end{array}\right]
\end{array}
$$

EXERCISES 9.2

1.

$$
N = \begin{bmatrix}
1 & 0 & 0 & 0 \\
0 & 2 & 0 & 1 \\
0 & 1 & 1 & 1 \\
0 & 2 & 0 & 2
\end{bmatrix}, \quad
NR = \begin{bmatrix} 1 \\ 1 \\ 1 \\ 1 \end{bmatrix}, \quad
Nf = \begin{bmatrix} 1 \\ 3 \\ 3 \\ 4 \end{bmatrix}.
$$

2.

$$
N = \begin{bmatrix}
1 & 0 & 0 & 0 & 0 & 0 & 0 \\
5/6 & 10/3 & 8/3 & 2 & 4/3 & 2/3 & 1/6 \\
2/3 & 8/3 & 17/3 & 4 & 8/3 & 4/3 & 1/3 \\
1/2 & 2 & 4 & 6 & 4 & 2 & 1/2 \\
1/3 & 4/3 & 8/3 & 4 & 16/3 & 8/3 & 2/3 \\
1/6 & 2/3 & 4/3 & 2 & 8/3 & 10/3 & 5/6 \\
0 & 0 & 0 & 0 & 0 & 0 & 1
\end{bmatrix}, \quad
NR = \begin{bmatrix} 1 \\ 1 \\ 1 \\ 1 \\ 1 \\ 1 \\ 1 \end{bmatrix}, \quad
Nf = \begin{bmatrix} 1 \\ 11 \\ 17 \\ 19 \\ 17 \\ 11 \\ 1 \end{bmatrix}.
$$

5. Expanding, we have $N_\lambda RF = RF + \lambda QRF + \lambda^2 Q^2 RF + \cdots + \lambda^n Q^n RF + \cdots$, and RF gives the expected return if we terminate at time 0, λQRF gives the expected discounted return if we stop at time 1, and so on. Hence, $N_\lambda RF$ gives the total expected discounted return if we start in each transient state.

7. (a)

	S_H	S_L	H	L
Sell High	1	0	0	0
Sell Low	0	1	0	0
High	1/5	0	2/5	2/5
Low	0	1/2	1/8	3/8

(b)
$$N = \begin{bmatrix} 25/13 & 16/13 \\ 5/13 & 24/13 \end{bmatrix}. \quad NR = \begin{bmatrix} 5/13 & 8/13 \\ 1/13 & 12/13 \end{bmatrix}. \quad Nf = \begin{bmatrix} 41/13 \\ 29/13 \end{bmatrix}.$$

10. (a)

	Sell S.	Sell P.	Skip	Pay
Sell S.	1	0	0	0
Sell P.	0	1	0	0
Skip	2/3	0	0	1/3
Pay	0	1/4	9/16	3/16

(b)
$$N = \begin{bmatrix} 13/10 & 8/15 \\ 9/10 & 8/5 \end{bmatrix}. \quad NR = \begin{bmatrix} 13/15 & 2/15 \\ 3/5 & 2/5 \end{bmatrix}.$$

(c)
$$N_\lambda G = \begin{bmatrix} 1.002 & .034 \\ .057 & 1.021 \end{bmatrix} \begin{bmatrix} 0 \\ 1 \end{bmatrix} = \begin{bmatrix} .034 \\ 1.021 \end{bmatrix}.$$

(d)
$$N_\lambda(G + RF) = \begin{bmatrix} 1.667 \\ 10.031 \end{bmatrix}.$$

13. (a) Use the formula for the sum of a geometric series twice.
(b) $\rho_i = 1 - i/I$. (c) $\rho_i^* = 1 - \rho_i = i/I$.

EXERCISES 9.3

2. $w = (1/6, 1/3, 1/3, 1/6)$.

4. $w = (12/29, 9/29, 8/29)$.

6. There have to be at least two states. For the 2×2 case, the matrix $\begin{bmatrix} .5 & .5 \\ .5 & .5 \end{bmatrix}$ has $d = 1/2$ and is the only such example. For all others, $d < 1/2$.

9. (a) $(2/5, 3/5)$. (b) $(c/(2 - a - d), b/(2 - a - d))$. (c) $(6/13, 4/13, 3/13)$.

11. (a)

	R	N	S
	1/2	1/4	1/4
Nice	1/2	0	1/2
Snow	1/4	1/4	1/2

(b) $P^2 > 0$. (c) $w = (2/5, 1/5, 2/5)$.

13. 6. **14.** 20.

19. $(1.867, 3.2, 1.867)$. These give the mean number of times before the occurrence of each kind of weather.

21. $w = (1/12, 1/6, 1/6, 1/6, 1/6, 1/6, 1/12)$. (a) 1/2. (b) 11.

EXERCISES 9.4

2.

$$N = \begin{array}{c} \\ 0 \\ 2 \\ 2 \\ 3 \\ 4 \\ 5 \\ 6 \\ 7 \end{array} \begin{array}{cccccccc} 0 & 1 & 2 & 3 & 4 & 5 & 6 & 7 \\ \begin{bmatrix} 1 & .91 & .80 & .63 & .55 & .39 & .24 & .12 \\ 0 & 1 & .88 & .70 & .60 & .43 & .27 & .13 \\ 0 & 0 & 1 & .79 & .69 & .49 & .30 & .15 \\ 0 & 0 & 0 & 1 & .87 & .62 & .38 & .18 \\ 0 & 0 & 0 & 0 & 1 & .71 & .44 & .21 \\ 0 & 0 & 0 & 0 & 0 & 1 & .62 & .30 \\ 0 & 0 & 0 & 0 & 0 & 0 & 1 & .48 \\ 0 & 0 & 0 & 0 & 0 & 0 & 0 & 1 \end{bmatrix} \end{array}.$$

3.

$$NR = \begin{array}{c} 0 \\ 1 \\ 2 \\ 3 \\ 4 \\ 5 \\ 6 \\ 7 \end{array} \begin{bmatrix} .46 & .54 \\ .41 & .59 \\ .33 & .67 \\ .15 & .85 \\ .13 & .87 \\ .14 & .86 \\ .19 & .81 \\ .35 & .65 \end{bmatrix}. \qquad Nf = \begin{array}{c} 0 \\ 1 \\ 2 \\ 3 \\ 4 \\ 5 \\ 6 \\ 7 \end{array} \begin{bmatrix} 4.64 \\ 4.00 \\ 3.41 \\ 3.05 \\ 2.36 \\ 1.91 \\ 1.48 \\ 1.00 \end{bmatrix}.$$

EXERCISES 9.5

1. (a–c)

	Send To	Receive From	Class
1	1, 4	1, 2, 4	{1, 4}
2	2, 1, 3, 4	2	{2}
3	3	3, 2	{3}
4	1	4, 1, 2	{1, 4}

   (d)   {1, 4}   {3}

          {2}

2. Ergodic: {1, 4}, {3}. Transient {2}.

4.

$$P^2 = \begin{bmatrix} 1 & 0 & 0 & 0 \\ 0 & 1 & 0 & 0 \\ 0 & 0 & 1 & 0 \\ 1/2 & 0 & 1/2 & 0 \end{bmatrix}, \; P^{2n} = P, \; P^{2n+1} = P^2.$$

5. 12 canonical forms.

6. If the Markov chain is absorbing, it has at least one absorbing state, and from every state it can get an absorbing state. Hence, every nonabsorbing state is transient, and every ergodic state is absorbing. If every ergodic state is absorbing, then there are only transient and absorbing states; hence, the transient states can each get to an absorbing state and the Markov chain is absorbing.

8.

$$\begin{array}{c} 3 \\ 2 \\ 4 \\ 6 \\ 1 \\ 5 \\ 7 \\ 8 \end{array} \begin{array}{cccccccc} 3 & 2 & 4 & 6 & 1 & 5 & 7 & 8 \\ \begin{bmatrix} 1 & 0 & 0 & 0 & 0 & 0 & 0 & 0 \\ 0 & 1/2 & 1/2 & 0 & 0 & 0 & 0 & 0 \\ 0 & 0 & 1/2 & 1/2 & 0 & 0 & 0 & 0 \\ 1/3 & 1/3 & 0 & 1/3 & 0 & 0 & 0 & 0 \\ 0 & 0 & 0 & 0 & 0 & 1/2 & 1/2 & 0 \\ 1/4 & 0 & 0 & 0 & 0 & 1/4 & 0 & 1/2 \\ 0 & 0 & 0 & 0 & 0 & 0 & 0 & 1 \\ 0 & 0 & 0 & 0 & 1 & 0 & 0 & 0 \end{bmatrix} \end{array}$$

EXERCISES 10.2

1. (a) $E[N(2)] = 2 \times 4 = 8 = \text{Var}[N(2)]$; number accumulated between 8:00 and 10:00 = $N(2)$ = number accumulated in 2 hours. $E[N(4)] = 4 \times 4 = 16 = \text{Var}[N(4)]$. $E[N(8)] = 8 \times 4 = 32 = \text{Var}[N(8)]$.

   (b) $P\{N(2) = k\} = P_k(2)$; $P_0(2) = 0.135$, $p_1(2) = 0.271$, $P_2(2) = 0.271$, $p_3(2) = 0.180, \ldots$.

2. (a) $p_n = e^{-a} \dfrac{a^n}{n!} = e^{-a} \dfrac{a^{n-1}}{(n-1)!n} a = p_{n-1} \left(\dfrac{a}{n} \right)$.

   (b) $p_n < p_{n-1} \dfrac{1}{n}$ (if $a < 1$, for $n = 1, 2, \ldots$); $p_n < p_{n-1}$ (if $n \geq 1$).

3. (a) $P\{\text{No failures}\} = e^{-10}$.   (b)   0.8 hour.   (c)   2.4 hours.

   (d) $e^{-10/8} \dfrac{(10/8)^4}{4!}$.

7. (a) $\left| \dfrac{t}{k} \right| = n$ tests can be performed in time t; since they are independent, the probability is $(1 - p)^{[t/k]}$ that $D > t$.

   (b) $(1 - p)^{[t/k]} \cong \left(1 - \dfrac{t\mu}{n} \right)^n \to e^{-\mu t}$.

11. (a) $\displaystyle\sum_{k=26}^{\infty} \dfrac{1}{m+1} \left(\dfrac{m}{1+m} \right)^k = \left(\dfrac{m}{1+m} \right)^{25}$.

   (b) $\displaystyle\sum_{k=0}^{24} k \dfrac{1}{m+1} \left(\dfrac{m}{m+1} \right)^k + 25 \sum_{k=25}^{\infty} \dfrac{1}{m+1} \left(\dfrac{m}{m+1} \right)^k$. This can be summed explicitly.

   Use the formula $\displaystyle\sum_{k=0}^{K-1} k(1 - z)z^k + K \sum_{k=K}^{\infty} (1 - z)z^k = \dfrac{z}{1 - z}(1 - z^k)$.

EXERCISES 10.3

1. $\dfrac{k^2}{k} = k \to 0$ or $h \to 0$. $\dfrac{k^2 f(h)}{k} = h^2 \dfrac{f(h)}{h} \to 0$; since $\dfrac{f(h)}{h} \to 0$, for $f(h)$ is $o(h)$.

2. (b) $E[N] = (1 - \rho) \displaystyle\sum_{j=0}^{\infty} j \rho^j = (1 - \rho) \dfrac{\rho}{(1 - \rho)^2} = \dfrac{\rho}{1 - \rho}$ (from *Hint*).

   (c) $\text{Var}[N] = \dfrac{\rho}{(1 - \rho)^2}$.

3. $\rho = 0.1, E[N] = \dfrac{1}{9}$; $\rho = 0.25, E[N] = \dfrac{1}{3}$; $\rho = 0.50, E[N] = 1$;

   $\rho = 0.75, E[N] = 3$; $\rho = 0.9, E[N] = 9$; $\rho = 0.95, E[N] = 19$. Differentiate $\log E[N]$ to see that $\dfrac{dE[N]}{E[N]} = \left(\dfrac{d\rho}{\rho} \right) \dfrac{1}{1 - \rho}$, thus indicating that a constant percentage change in ρ is amplified more as ρ approaches unity. Or, do a numerical experiment.

4. $\dfrac{E[N \text{ one server}]}{E[N \text{ two servers}]} = \dfrac{\dfrac{\rho}{1-\rho}}{\dfrac{2\rho}{(1+\rho)(1-\rho)}} = \dfrac{1+\rho}{2} \to 1$ as $\rho \to 1$.

As $\rho \to 1$ both servers are nearly always busy; together they act like one server with twice the rate of each.

5. (a) $[\lambda h + o(h)][\mu h + o(h)]^3 = [\lambda h + o(h)][(\mu h)^3 + o(h)] = \lambda \mu h^4 + o(h) = o(h).$

(b) $4p_0 = 2p_1, \ 4p_1 = 4p_2, \ 4p_2 = 6p_3, \ 4p_3 = 6p_4, \ 2p_4 = 6p_5, \ 2p_5 = 6p_6, \ldots.$

(c) $p_j = p_0 \dfrac{\lambda_0 \lambda_1 \cdots \lambda_{j-1}}{\mu_1 \mu_2 \cdots \mu_j}, \ p_1 = p_0 \cdot \dfrac{4}{2}, \ p_2 = p_0 \dfrac{16}{8},$ and so on.

13. (a) $e^{-\lambda L}.$ (b) $(1 - e^{-\lambda L})^n.$ (c) $\sum\limits_{n=0}^{\infty} n e^{-\lambda L}(1 - e^{-\lambda L})^n = e^{\lambda L}.$

(d) The expected number that pass a fast (slow) driver is $e^{\lambda L_f}$; $(e^{\lambda L_s})$ is number that pass a slow driver. Hence, $pe^{\lambda L_f} + qe^{\lambda L_s}$ is the expected number to pass an arbitrary driver; quite different from $e^{\lambda L_f + qL_s}$, which is too small.

EXERCISES 10.4

1. From (10.4.9), $\dfrac{1}{\lambda} E[N] = \dfrac{1}{\mu} + p_0 \left(\dfrac{\lambda}{\mu}\right)^a \dfrac{1}{a!} \dfrac{1}{\mu a\left(1 - \dfrac{\lambda}{\mu a}\right)^2}$

$$= \dfrac{1}{\mu} + \dfrac{E[Q]}{\lambda} = E[D], \text{ from (10.4.11) and (10.4.12)}.$$

2. (a) $P\{Q > n\} = \sum\limits_{j=n+1}^{\infty} (1 - \rho)\rho^j = \rho^{n+1}.$

(b) $P\{Q > 4 | \rho = 0.2\} = 3.2 \times 10^{-4}, \ \ldots, P\{Q > 4 | \rho = 0.9\} = 0.59, \ldots.$

(c) Expected delay $= \dfrac{1}{(1-\rho)\mu}$; Probability server idle $= 1 - \rho$; Expected service time $= \dfrac{1}{\mu}$; multiplication of first two gives last.

3. (a) $\dfrac{E[D | \text{pool}]}{E[D | \text{single}]} = \dfrac{1 + (\lambda/\mu)^2}{1 + (\lambda/\mu)} < 1,$ for $(\lambda/\mu) < 1.$

(b) In a single repairman-per-factory situation, one repairman may sometimes have a backlog while the other is idle.

(c) Travel time to the pool from remote parts of the factory.

EXERCISES 10.5

1. (a) $P\{\text{at least one server out of } j \text{ completes in } dt\} = 1 - (1 - \mu dt)^j = j\mu dt + 0(dt).$

(b) $p_j = p_0 \dfrac{\lambda_j}{(1\mu)(2\mu) \cdots (j\mu)} = p_0 \left(\dfrac{\lambda}{\mu}\right)^j \dfrac{1}{j!} = e^{-\lambda/\mu} \left(\dfrac{\lambda}{\mu}\right)^j \dfrac{1}{j!}$ after normalization.

2. (a) $\lambda_0 = \lambda_0(m - 0) = 0$, meaning that if everyone recovers there is no infection passed on. However, if $\lambda_0 = \alpha > 0$, new infection can always start.

(b) $p_j = p_0 \dfrac{\alpha\lambda(1)(m-1)\lambda(2)(m-2)\cdots\lambda(j-1)(m-j+1)}{(1\mu)(2\mu)\cdots(j\mu)} = p_0 \dfrac{\alpha\lambda^{j-1}(m-1)!}{\mu_j(j)(m-j)!}$

for $1 \leq j \leq m$. Normalize by summing: $p_0 + \sum\limits_{j=1}^{m} p_j = 1$.

(c) Entirely well: p_0; all infected $= p_m$.

EXERCISES 10.6

1. $P\{S > x,\ S > x + y\} = P\{S > x + y\} = e^{-\mu(x+y)}$.

$P\{S > x + y \mid S > x\} = \dfrac{e^{-\mu(x+y)}}{c^{-\mu x}} = e^{-\mu}$.

2. $W_n =$ waiting time, if $n(n > 0)$ customers are ahead. $E[W_n] = E[S_J' + S_2 + \cdots + S_n] =$

$\dfrac{n}{\mu}$; $\mathrm{Var}[W_n] = \mathrm{Var}[S_1' + S_2 + \cdots + S_n] = n\,\mathrm{Var}[S_1] = \dfrac{n}{\mu^2}$; or $E[W_n] = \displaystyle\int_0^{\infty} z e^{-\mu z}$

$\dfrac{(\mu z)^{n-1}}{(n-1)!} \mu\,dz = \dfrac{1}{(n-1)\mu} \displaystyle\int_0^{\infty} e^{-\mu z}(\mu z)^n \mu\,dz = \dfrac{n!}{(n-1)!\mu} = \dfrac{n}{\mu}$.

3. $f_{D_n}(z \mid n) = e^{-\mu z} \dfrac{(\mu z)^n}{n!} \mu$ for $n = 1, 2, \ldots$.

$f_{D_1}(z) = \displaystyle\sum_{n=0}^{\infty}(1-\rho)\rho^n e^{-\mu z} \dfrac{(\mu z)^n}{n!} \mu = e^{-\mu z(1-\rho)}\mu(1-\rho)$.

5. (a) $P\{N = n\} = (1-\rho)\rho^n$, for $n = 0, 2, \ldots$; $P\{N \geq 1\} = \rho$. $P\{N = n \mid N \geq 1\} = \dfrac{(1-\rho)\rho^n}{\rho}$

for $n = 1, 2, \ldots$.

(b) The probability that there are n ahead is given by (a). The probability that each service time $> y$ (thus, our customer's is $<$ all) is $(e^{-\mu y})^n$, conditional on n. Now sum, using (a).

(c) $\displaystyle\int_0^{\infty}\left(\dfrac{1-\rho}{\rho}\right)\left[\dfrac{1}{1-\rho e^{-\mu y}} - 1\right] e^{-\mu y}\mu\,dy = \dfrac{1-\rho}{\rho}[-\log(1-\rho) - 1]$.

EXERCISES 10.7

1. (a) $E[T_{02}] = \dfrac{1}{2\lambda} + \dfrac{1}{\lambda} + \dfrac{\mu}{2\lambda^2} = 230$ hours.   (b) $\dfrac{1}{221} = \dfrac{2\left(\dfrac{\lambda}{\mu}\right)^2}{1 + 2\dfrac{\lambda}{\mu} + 2\left(\dfrac{\lambda}{\mu}\right)^2}$.

2. (a) Use (10.7.17); lower boundary at 1, upper at $H - 1$: $E[T_{0,H-1}] =$

$\dfrac{H-1}{\lambda(p-q)} - \dfrac{\dfrac{q}{p}}{\lambda(p-q)}\left\{ \dfrac{1 - \left(\dfrac{q}{p}\right)^{H-1}}{1 - \dfrac{q}{p}} \right\}$.

(b) $p = 0.4$: $E[T_{0,9}] \simeq 572$. $p = 0.6$: $E[T_{0,9}] \simeq 35$.

(c) A round trip from low to high to low $\simeq 572 + 35 \simeq 600$ days. He makes $\$H - 1$ net on each trip, so he makes nearly $10H$ in 6000 days; another round trip and he is over, but long before the market will have changed!

EXERCISES 10.8

1. (a) $E[N] = \rho + \dfrac{\rho^2}{(1-\rho)}$.   (b) $E[N] = \rho + \dfrac{\rho^2}{2(1-\rho)}$.

Note: reduction of the variance of service time nearly cuts occupancy in half.

(c) $P\{S = \max(X_1, X_2) \le x\} = (1 - e^{3/2x})^2$. $E[S] = 1$, $\text{Var}[S] = \dfrac{5}{9}$; $E[N] = \dfrac{7}{9}\dfrac{\rho^2}{1-\rho}$.

2. $E[D]\dfrac{1}{\lambda}E[N] = \dfrac{1}{\lambda}\left| \rho + \dfrac{\rho^2}{2(1-\rho)}\left\{1 + \dfrac{\text{Var}[S]}{E^2[S]}\right\} \right. = E[S] + E[S]\dfrac{\rho}{2(1-\rho)}\left\{1 + \dfrac{\text{Var}[S]}{E[S]}\right\}$,

since $\rho = \lambda E[S]$. Then $E[D] = E[W] + E[S]$.

4. (b) Breakdowns occur only during service. $E[C] = 1.04$, $\text{Var}[C] = 0.16$. If $\lambda = 0.87$, $\rho \simeq 0.9$, $E[N] = 5.56$. If no interruptions occur ($\lambda_1 = 0$), $\rho = 0.87$, and $E[N] = 3.78$.

EXERCISES 10.9

1. (a) $A(t) = 100 + \dfrac{4}{5}t$; $D(t) = t$, so long as jobs remain.

(b)   Queue exists as long as $A(t) > D(t)$—that is, for 500 minutes.

(c)   If he is the nth customer ($n = 1, 2, \ldots, 100$), he must wait n minutes, using the deterministic approximation.

2. (b)   Time to clear accident $= \dfrac{aR}{d-a}$.

$$\text{Number in line} \equiv Q(t) = \begin{cases} at, & 0 \le t \le R. \\ aR - (d-a)(t-R), & R \le t \le R + \dfrac{aR}{d-a}. \end{cases}$$

$$\text{Total waiting time} = \int_0^{R + aR/d-a} Q(t)\,dt = \int_0^R at\,dt + \int_0^{aR/d-a} [aR - (d-a)z]\,dz.$$

$$= \dfrac{aR^2}{2}\dfrac{d}{d-a}.$$

(c) $E[\text{Time to clear accident}] = \dfrac{am}{d-a}$. $E[\text{Total waiting time}] = (m^2 + \sigma^2)\dfrac{ad}{2(d-a)}$.

3. (a)   Gates tays busy for t_b: $a\sqrt{t_b} = t_b$; that is, $t_b = a^2$. $w_g = \text{Total wait, good day} = \dfrac{1}{6}a^4$,

evaluated at $a = 4$. $= 42.67$. $w_b = \text{Total wait, bad day} = 0.167$.

(b)   Expected wait $= pw_g + qw_b \equiv w$. Variance of wait $= pw_g^2 + qw_b^2 - w^2$.

EXERCISES 11.2

1. (a)   1220.   (b) $20.43.   (c) $Q \simeq 708$. $C \simeq \$21.2$.

2. (a) $\dfrac{\lambda}{P}$ = arrival rate of batches; $C_s + C_r P$ = cost/batch, so cost rate of running batches =

$(C_s + C_r P)\dfrac{\lambda}{P}$; $C_w\dfrac{P}{2}$ = cost rate of waiting. Sum to get answer.

(b) Differentiate in (a): $\bar{P} = \sqrt{\dfrac{2\lambda C_s}{C_w}}$.　　(c) $\lambda C_r + \sqrt{2\lambda C_s C_w}$.

(d) Batches will not arrive at constant rate all day. Costs of waiting will differ between programs.

3. (a) Separate: Total (summed) costs $= 2C(\bar{Q}) = 2\sqrt{2mC_0 C_c}$. Central: Total cost $=$ $C(\bar{Q}) = \sqrt{2(2m)C_0 C_c}$. It costs $\sqrt{2} = 1.41 \ldots$ times as much to separate the inventories as to centralize.

(b) One inventory management and warehouse team (lower administration costs). All orders filled at one location—better control, perhaps.

(c) A large stocking point might be less compact, and hence more in-warehouse stock movements.

4. Annual ordering cost $= \dfrac{mC_0}{\bar{Q}} = \dfrac{mC_0}{\sqrt{\dfrac{2mC_0}{C_c}}} = \sqrt{\dfrac{mC_0 C_c}{2}}$.

Annual carrying cost $= C_c \dfrac{\bar{Q}}{2} = \dfrac{C_c}{2}\sqrt{\dfrac{2mC_0}{C_c}} = \sqrt{\dfrac{mC_0 C_c}{2}}$.

EXERCISES 11.3

1. From (5.3.12), $U_\alpha = \dfrac{\bar{I} - E[D(t)]}{\sqrt{\text{Var}[D(t)]}}$ if $\alpha = 1 - \dfrac{C}{P}$.　　$\bar{I} = E[D(t)] + U_\alpha\sqrt{\text{Var}[D(t)]}$.

2. (a) Expected demand $= \dfrac{(1000)(792)}{297} = \dfrac{8000}{3}$.　　(b) Variance $\simeq 17 \times 10^4$.

(c) $\bar{I} = \dfrac{8000}{3} + 0.57(413) \simeq 2902$.　(d) $\bar{I} = \dfrac{16000}{3} + 0.57\sqrt{2 \times 17 - 10^4} \simeq 5655$.

3. (a) $x_P = \left(1 + \dfrac{\lambda}{\nu}\right)\xi \log\left[\dfrac{\lambda}{P(\lambda + \nu)}\right]$;　　(i) $x_{0.25} \simeq 7100$. (ii) $x_{0.1} \simeq 12{,}150$.

EXERCISES 11.4

1. (a) $\dfrac{mC_{s0} + \bar{Q}C_c}{mC_{s0}} = \dfrac{(5000)(0.25) + (1000)(0.02)}{(5000)(0.25)} \cong 0.984$; $r = 100 + (2.14)(10) \simeq 121$.

(b) $\dfrac{(5000)(0.50)}{(5000)(0.50) + (1000)(0.02)} \simeq 0.993$; $r = 100 + (2.45)(10) \simeq 125$; r is certainly not proportional to stockout cost.

2. $r = \bar{D}\log\left(1 + \dfrac{mC_{s0}}{\bar{Q}C_c}\right)$.　　(a) $r = 100 \log 63.5 = 415$.　　(b) $r = 100 \log 126 = 484$.

4. $\displaystyle\int_r^\infty (x-r)e^{-x/5}\frac{dx}{\bar{D}} = \bar{D}e^{-r/\bar{D}}.$

EXERCISES 11.5

1. (a) $r=0$: $M_{\mathrm{opt}} = 1.8$; $r=1$; $M_{\mathrm{opt}} = 2.33$; $r=2$: $M_{\mathrm{opt}} = 3.24, \dots.$

2. (a) In $\mu \to \infty$ the dominant terms in numerator and denominator of (11.5.20) are like
$$\left(\frac{\mu}{\lambda}\right)^{r+1}.$$ Thus, $C(M, r) = \dfrac{C_0\lambda}{M-r} + C_c M.$ The cost rate is decreased by letting $r=0$.

   (b) Now differentiate, or take limits in (11.5.22) to get the result.

   (c) Carrying cost is proportional to the maximum instead of the average inventory.

3. (a) $\qquad \mu p_0 = \lambda p_1 \qquad\qquad \therefore \qquad p_0 = \dfrac{1}{1 + 2\left(\dfrac{\mu}{\lambda}\right) + 2\left(\dfrac{\mu}{\lambda}\right)^2},$

   $\qquad (\lambda+\mu)p_1 = \lambda p_2 \qquad\qquad p_1 = \dfrac{\mu}{\lambda}p_0,$

   $\qquad \lambda p_2 = \lambda p_0 + \lambda p_3 \qquad\qquad p_2 = \left(1 + \dfrac{\mu}{\lambda}\right)\dfrac{\mu}{\lambda}p_0,$

   $\qquad \lambda p_3 = \lambda p_1 \qquad\qquad p_3 = \left(\dfrac{\mu}{\lambda}\right)^2 p_0.$

   (b) $C(Q,r) = C_{so}\lambda p_0 + C_0 \lambda p_2 + 3C_c$. Substitute from (a) and evaluate. Compare to (11.5.20) with same numbers.

EXERCISES 12.2

1. Simple way: generate a one-digit random number; if it is one of the numbers 1, 2, 3, 4, 5, 6, identify the number with the die face. Otherwise, reject the number (for example, 7) and start again. More complicated: generate a three-digit random number. Die turns up one if number between 1 and 167, die face is two if number between 168 and 334, and so on.

3. (a) $d = 550 + 100r$, where r is a uniform r.n., $0 \le r \le 1$.

   (b) Simulate independently $d_1, d_2, \dots$ as in (a) until $d_1 + d_2 + \cdots + d_n < 3000$, but $d_1 + d_2 + \cdots + d_{n+1} > 3000$. The flight time is then n hours; divide
$$3000 - (d_1 + d_2 + \cdots + d_n)$$
   by $550 + 100r_{n+1}$, the rate during the last leg, to get the remainder in minutes. Average the flight times, and obtain the fraction of flights ≤ 4.75 hours.

4. (a) Simulate 4 job durations, and add. Repeat n times and average. This problem can be done by simply adding the 4 expectations—no simulation.

   (b) 4 jobs wait while D_1 is processed (1, 2, 3, and 4), then 3 jobs wait for D_2, and so on. $W = 4D_1 + 3D_2 + 2D_3 + D_4$. $E[W] = 4E[D_1] + 3E[D_2] + 2E[D_3] + E[D_4] = 10E[D]$ if all have same expectation. $\mathrm{Var}[W] = 16\mathrm{Var}[D_1] + 9\mathrm{Var}[D_2] + 4\mathrm{Var}[D_3] + \mathrm{Var}[D_4]$ if jobs are independent in duration.

   (c) Rearrange jobs: 4 wait for $D_{(1)}$, and so on. $E[W'] = (4)\frac{1}{4}E[D] + (3)\frac{1}{3}E[D] + (2)\frac{1}{2}E[D] + E[D] = 4E[D]$. To simulate, draw a set of 4 job durations, arrange in order, weight by numbers, and add. Repeat $n(=100)$ times and average.

EXERCISES 12.3

1. $P\{W_2 = 0\} = 1 - e^{-\mu}; P\{W_2 \leq x\} = 1 - e^{-\mu(x+1)}.$

(a) $E[W_2] = \int_0^\infty x e^{-\mu} e^{-\mu x} \mu dx = \dfrac{e^{-\mu}}{\mu} \simeq 0.452;$

$\text{Var}[W_2] = \int_0^\infty x^2 e^{-\mu} e^{-\mu x} \mu dx - (E[W_2])^2$

$= e^{-\mu} \dfrac{2}{\mu^2} - \dfrac{e^{-2\mu}}{\mu^2} = 0.85.$

About 400 samples.

2. (b) $\text{Var}[W] = 14\,\text{Var}[D] = \dfrac{14}{m^2}.$ (c) $n = 224$ (exponential); $n = 187$ (uniform).

Note: one must get a preliminary variance estimate.

4. Simulate $W_n = \max(W_{n-1} + S_{n-1} - A_n, 0)$, using $\{A_n\}$ sequence described, $n = 1, 2, \ldots,$ N. Pick out maximum W_n for each realization. Average over k (say, 100) realizations.

(b) Average: $\dfrac{W_1 + W_2 + \cdots W_N}{N} + \dfrac{S_1 + S_2 + \cdots S_N}{N}$. Note: the latter can be done analytically. Repeat for k realizations, and average.

(c) Sum $W_1 + W_2 + \cdots + W_N$. Repeat and average.

5. The measures will not double. See exercise 7.

8. (c) Let $n = \infty$ in matrix and calculate stationary probabilities.

(d) This models the decreased tendency to fail as time goes on and the increased speed of repair (practice effect?).

EXERCISES 12.4

3. (a) Since the time between the $(n-1)$st and nth is $\dfrac{1}{N-n+1}$, the expected time for all is the sum $\dfrac{1}{N} + \dfrac{1}{N-1} + \cdots 1.$

(b) Let $T_N =$ time for all to reach gate. T_N should be negatively correlated maximum waiting time (more spread-out arrivals means less queuing). Use T_N in a concommitant variables sense, fitting the coefficient from data.

4. (d) $\sum U_t$ should be of help.

EXERCISES 12.5

1. (a) $E[C] = 20$, $\text{Var}[C] = \dfrac{200}{12}.$ (b) T_i is uniform over 5 to 15, since R is uniform over $(0, 1)$.   (c) Draw T_i realizations using (b), and add to get C realizations. Average all; compare to largest and smallest computed on estimated variance.

2. (a) $C_i = 5 + 10R_i + 5 + 10R_{i+1}$ $i = 1, 3, \ldots$

$C_i' = 5 + 10(1 - R_i) + 5 + 10(1 - R_{i+1})$

$$\bar{C} = E[\hat{C}] = \frac{1}{r} \sum_i \left(\frac{C_i + C_i}{2} \right)$$

4. (a) If q is small compared to the length of the jobs (not really true in the numerical example), there will be a j such that $(j-1)q \le X_{(1)} \le jq$, $X_{(1)}$ being shortest job duration. Then 4 jobs will be waiting for total job time $rq(j-1)$. In addition, assume that N further quanta (N uniform over 0, 1, 2, 3) are required to reach the shortest job; during this time 4 jobs wait, so add 4 Nq. Finally, add

$$4[X_{(1)} - (j-1)q].$$

Start over with 3.

EXERCISES 13.1

1. (a) $w = (1, 0, 0, 0)$, $x' = (0, 1, 0, 0)$, $v = 1$; there are other solutions.
   (b) $w = (1, 0)$, $x' = (1, 0)$, $v = 3$.   (c) $w = (1, 0)$, $x' = (1, 0)$, $v = 3$.
   (d) $w = (0, 0, 1)$, $x' = (0, 0, 0, 1)$, $v = -1$; there are other solutions.

3. Assume $a > b$. If the game does not have a saddle value, then $a > c$; for c not to be a saddle value, $c > d$; for b not to be a saddle value, $b > d$. A similar proof holds if $a < b$.

5. (a) $w = (7/12, 5/12)$, $x' = (7/12, 5/12)$, $v = -1/12$.
   (b) $w = (1/2, 1/2)$, $x' = (1/2, 1/2)$, $v = 0$.
   (c) $w = (2/5, 3/5)$, $x' = (1/2, 1/2)$, $v = 1/2$.

6.

		Peter	
		Red 1	Black 2
Paul	Red 2	−1	4
	Black 3	2	−5

Optimal strategies are $w = (7/12, 5/12)$, $x' = (3/4, 1/4)$. Value is $v = 1/4$, meaning that Paul wins 25¢ each game on the average.

9. (a) The subgames are:

$$\begin{bmatrix} -1 & 2 \\ 1 & -2 \end{bmatrix} \begin{bmatrix} -1 & -3 \\ 1 & 3 \end{bmatrix} \begin{bmatrix} -1 & 4 \\ 1 & -4 \end{bmatrix} \begin{bmatrix} 2 & -3 \\ -2 & 3 \end{bmatrix} \begin{bmatrix} 2 & 4 \\ -2 & 4 \end{bmatrix} \begin{bmatrix} -3 & 4 \\ 3 & -4 \end{bmatrix}$$

12. (a) Since $w^o A \ge ve$, multiplying by x^o gives $w^o A x^o \ge v$; similarly, since $A x^o \le vf$, multiplying by w^o gives $w^o A x^o \le v$. From these two we have $w^o A x^o = v$.
   (b) Since $(w^o A)_j \ge v$ and $(w^o A)x^o = v$, it follows that $x_j^o > 0$ only if $(w^o A)_j = v$. Hence, $v = \underset{j}{\text{Min}} \, (w^o A)_j$.
   (c) Follows from the fact that w^o solves (13.1.5).
   (f) Follows from the duality theorem.

EXERCISES 13.2

1. (a) Longest path is T_1, T_4, length is 57.1.
   (b) Solution remains unchanged.
   (c) Solution remains unchanged.

4. The dual of (13.2.3) is Max $\sum_j c_j x_j$ subject to $\sum_j a_{ij} x_j \leq b_i$ and $x_j \geq 0$. The dual of (13.2.10) is Max $\sum_j (F^{-1}(\alpha_j)) x_j$ subject to the same constraints. These two are similar except for the coefficients of the objective function. The values of the two may be the same or different.

6. Let A be the incidence matrix E of the project graph and assume that the b_j's are the job times that are random variables. Then (13.2.10) is the deterministic equivalent.

EXERCISES 13.3

3. (a) Since the decisions are independent, the number of ways of making all of them is the product of the numbers of ways of making each one.
   (b) $2^{20} = 1,048,576$.

4. We start the computation:

Step	0	1	2	
x_0	1	15	25.5	
x_1	1	15	18.5	
x_2	1	1	4.5	$\cdots$
x_3	1	1	1	
x_4	1	1	1	
x_5	1	1	1	

EXERCISES 13.4

1. (a) If $I < (1/r_2)\log (r_2/r_1)$, then the numerator of (13.4.15) is negative so that $I_1^* = 0$
   (c) Since $E[N]$ is a convex function, it has a unique minimum that can be found by setting its derivative to 0.

3. If $p_1 = p_2$, then (13.4.20) can always be solved at an interior point. But this is not necessarily true if $p_1 \neq p_2$, since then $\log (p_1/p_2)$ may be either positive or negative.

5. The Kuhn-Tucker conditions are $\mu_i I_i = 0$ so that either $\mu_i = 0$ and I_i is positive (or 0) or $\mu_i > 0$ and $I_i = 0$.

EXERCISES 13.5

2. The equation for x_1 is $F(x_1) = 1/p + 1/2$ just as before, so we order more than the median demand. The equation for x_2 is $F(x_2) = 1/2 - 1/2p$, so we order less than the median demand.

5. The final equations to be solved are $F_1(x_1) = 1/p + 1/2$ and $F_2(x_2) = 1/2p + 1/2$.

7. The question of which method is better depends on the specific application and the relative sophistication of the user.

AUTHOR INDEX

SUBJECT INDEX